Napoleon
A Private View

TREASURES FROM THE BRUNO LEDOUX COLLECTION

FOREWORD BY BERNARD-HENRI LÉVY

INTRODUCTORY TEXTS BY

XAVIER AIOLFI

JACQUES-OLIVIER BOUDON

PIERRE BRANDA

DAVID CHANTERANNE

BERNARD CHEVALLIER

EMMANUELLE PAPOT

LAETITIA DE WITT

ABRAMS | NEW YORK

The objects featured in this book are reproduced here
by kind permission of NJG

Graphic design and artwork: Juste Ciel
artwork finalized with the assistance of Élisabeth Welter
Captions: Bruno Ledoux
Translation from French: Florence Brutton and InPuzzle
Correction and proofreading: InPuzzle

ISBN 978-1-4197-2145-8

Printed and bound in Italy
10 9 8 7 6 5 4 3 2 1

ABRAMS

To my grandfather on my father's side, and my godfather,... who used to read me books illustrated by Job,

To my father... who passed on his passionate interest in history to me,

To my mother, my brother and my sister... who have always supported me,

To Alexia and Olivia... who must never forget that a great collection, like any dream that wants to come to life, takes passion and effort to build,

To Sonia... without whom nothing would have been possible.

To my friends,
To Danielle.

For all of those men who fought for the survival of France and in defense of the universal human right to be born free and to remain free – men from every walk of life, every social class and every nationality, some of them very young but all of them united in courage and inspired by the example of great men in history.

Contents

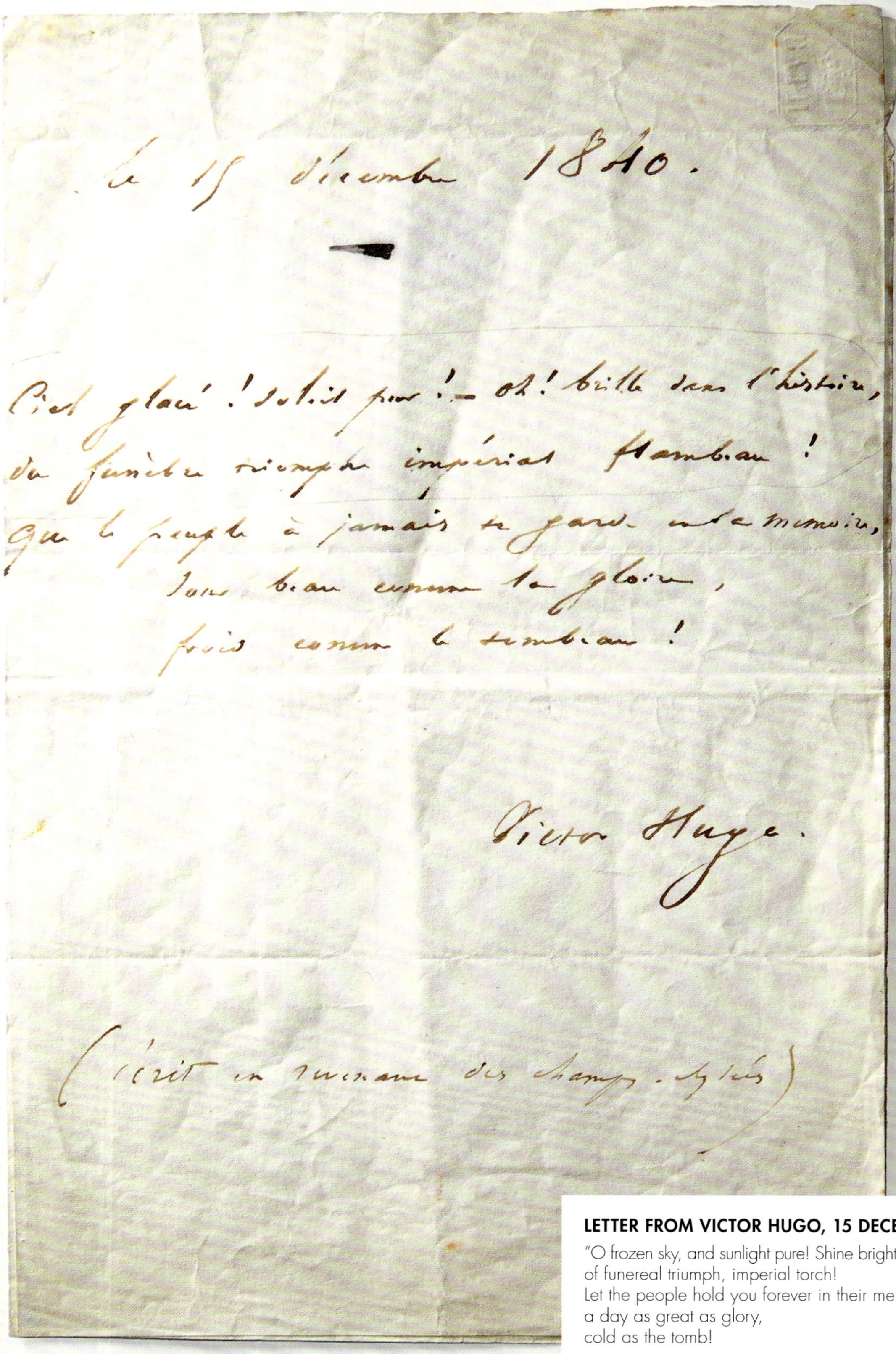

le 15 décembre 1840.

Ciel glacé ! soleil pur ! — oh ! brille dans l'histoire,
du funèbre triomphe impérial flambeau !
Que le peuple à jamais te garde en sa mémoire,
Jour beau comme la gloire,
froid comme le tombeau !

Victor Hugo.

(écrit en revenant des Champs-Élysées)

LETTER FROM VICTOR HUGO, 15 DECEMBER 1840

"O frozen sky, and sunlight pure! Shine bright in the history
of funereal triumph, imperial torch!
Let the people hold you forever in their memory,
a day as great as glory,
cold as the tomb!

(written on returning from the Champs Élysées)"

FROM MONTESQUIOU TO LEDOUX

First, of course, there are the objects.
Napoleon's mailbox.
A pair of ebony and gold pistols dating from the apogee of his glory.
His throne, made by Jacob-Desmalter — the only one in private hands.
His saber, from the gunsmith Le Page.
The Sèvres porcelain that was taken to St Helena.
Josephine's dental kit.
The chemise worn by Louis XVI on the morning he was guillotined.
Some little slippers that had belonged to the King of Rome.
These pieces and the hundreds of others that accompany them are enough to make this collection unique—indeed, with respect to the Revolution and the Empire, it is the largest in the world. But for someone who, like myself, has had the pleasure of discovering the collection with its author, its most interesting aspect lies elsewhere.
It lies in the love story that it tells. Yes, the love story — complete, as is fitting, with the desire, seduction, and possession or inverted possession surrounding each relic. In some cases, the collector gained possession of a long-coveted object; in others the object charmed and conquered him. Is there any great collection that is not secretly inspired by a strain of eroticism?
The fascination of the collection lies, too, in the treatment of chance that it (by the very process of its accrual) employs and reveals. One has to hear Bruno Ledoux tell how he sought and found, or found without seeking, or sought one thing (say, a candelabrum from Napoleon's marriage to Marie-Louise) and found another (such as the kitchen knife used in the attempt to assassinate Napoleon at Schönbrunn Palace)—or how an object, lurking at the intersection of chance and necessity, of a fortuitous or forced encounter, found him. Inanimate objects, have you soul or body? Are you *fatum* or *tuche*? Chance or fate? You are a Möbius strip.
And then there is the philosophy of life for which this collection, like all great collections, is inescapably the metaphor. Robert de Montesquiou, who was one of our very great collectors as well as the model, not only of Proust's Baron de Charlus but also of Huysmans's Jean Des Esseintes (the fictional inventor of the modern collection), said that one collects only if one is simultaneously a lover of singularities and of series, of objects both unique and recurrent, of "rarities" and "Wagnerian "leitmotifs," as Montesquiou says somewhere in his posthumous *Mémoires*. Perhaps this is not unconnected with the quintessentially Proustian place where Montesquiou's collection resides. Regardless, I believe the same is precisely the case with Bruno Ledoux. And why do you collect? Well. To acknowledge the share, in any life, of order and disorder, of what can and cannot be deciphered, of what, in each of us, gives in to the gods and what defies them.
One last word. We know, from Huysmans and Proust, and from Jacques Lacan, that there is no enterprise of this nature that is not accompanied by an insatiable appetite, an endless search, and the obsessional quest for that last object, the eternally absent and invisible beating heart of the collection. It is those absent objects, Objects A, B, and C, as well as the empty spaces that serve as their screens and, literally, as their utopia, that are so blinding in the Ledoux collection. I leave it to the reader to find them.

Bernard-Henri Lévy

The Last Years of the Monarchy, from Versailles to the Temple Prison, Paris

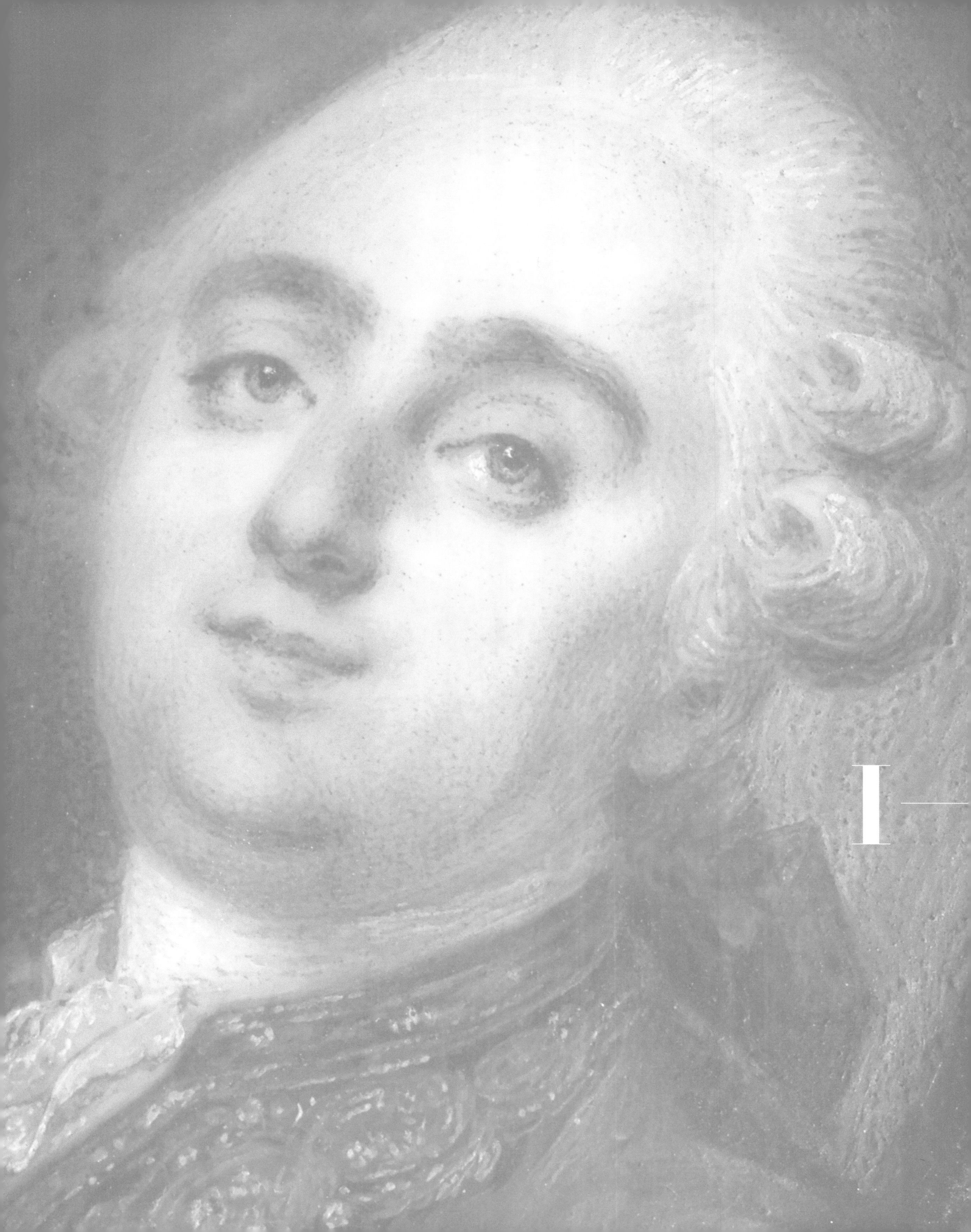

I

The French Revolution, symbolized by the storming of the Bastille on 14 July 1789, gave birth to a new constitutionally based society founded on the rights of man and the citizen. Before long, however, an array of European powers took up arms against France, and the revolutionary movement became radicalized, which in turn led to the fall of the monarchy and the advent of the French Republic. The Reign of Terror took hold, spearheaded by leading revolutionary figures such as Robespierre, Danton and also Hébert. Things calmed down following Robespierre's fall, paving the way for Napoleon Bonaparte to proclaim himself heir to the French Revolution.

Jacques- Olivier Boudon
professor at the Paris-Sorbonne University

THE STORMING OF THE BASTILLE

When the French Revolution broke out in 1789, events in France had reached crisis point. Louis XVI, King of France since 1774, appeared incapable of dealing with the economic crisis caused by France's expenditures in the American Revolutionary War, and even less able to quell the growing rumblings of discontent from every direction. People across the country wanted change, formulating their demands in terms of Enlightenment ideals. The King tried to address matters by summoning the Estates General for its first meeting since 1614. It was an opportunity for French citizens to draw up lists of grievances, called *Cahiers de Doléances*, then elect representatives from the three orders of the realm: the clergy, the nobility and the Third Estate (consisting of the commoners, whose representation had by that time doubled). The opening ceremonies of the Estates General were held in Versailles on 4 and 5 May 1789 amid great disorganization, with the three Estates unable to agree among themselves. Half of the clergy rallied to the Third Estate, whose deputies refused to adjourn until France had been given a new constitution. They then swore the Tennis Court Oath on 20 June, triggering a parliamentary rebellion that saw the Estates General declare itself the National Constituent Assembly on 9 July. As the King pondered his response, the announcement that royal troops had surrounded Paris lit the fuse that ignited the powder keg. Parisian revolutionaries stormed the Bastille — the fortress that had long been a symbol of royal tyranny. In Versailles meanwhile, Louis XVI remained remarkably impassive as those around him prepared to retaliate. He refused to place himself under the protection of army units in the east, as recommended by his brother, the Comte d'Artois. Instead on 15 July 1789 Louis appeared before the National Assembly to announce the withdrawal of troops from the Paris area. The following day he reinstated Necker and the day after that, on 17 July, he returned from Versailles to Paris. There, in the presence of Jean-Sylvain Bailly, Mayor of Paris, and Lafayette, Commander-in-Chief of the National Guard, the King donned the blue-and-red cockade of Paris in recognition of the events of 14 July. But there is considerable ambiguity surrounding Louis' recognition. The King gave way under pressure. He did not join ranks with the revolutionaries of his own accord. The *Vainqueurs* (conquerors) of the Bastille were meanwhile hailed as heroes and the prison was later demolished except for a few pieces that were kept for posterity.

But the flames of revolution were reignited by the Great Fear (in French, *Grande Peur*) that then swept through rural France — a wave of uprisings triggered by social unrest. The National Assembly responded on the night of 4 August by decreeing the abolition of noble privilege. This was followed on 26 August by the Declaration of the Rights of Man and the Citizen, which established the foundations of the new society that was to be created around the ideas of civil equality, liberty and national sovereignty. In other words, Louis XVI was no longer God's representative on earth but the representative of the French people. For safety's sake, a crowd of Parisians escorted the King and the rest of the royal family back to Paris in October 1789. So there was clearly rising tension between the King and the National Assembly from the early days of the Revolution, at a time when major reforms were underway in the areas of administration, justice and religion. The apparent unanimity that prevailed at the *Fête de la Fédération* on 14 July 1790 could not conceal Louis' hostility toward a Revolution that he found abhorrent. Hence his flight from Paris in June 1791 (only to be arrested in Varennes) and his support for war against hostile nations, in the hope that the Austrians and Prussians would restore his Royal Authority. In the event, quite the opposite happened. The first defeats suffered by French forces, badly disorganized by the defection of so many of their officers, so enraged the Parisians that they attacked the Tuileries Palace on 20 June 1792, then again on 10 August. Particularly enraging was the proclamation by the Duke of Brunswick, Commander-in Chief of the allied army, threatening reprisals if anyone so much as laid a finger on the King.

On the night of 10 August, the King and Queen were taken prisoner. The Paris Commune, dominated by the Jacobins, became a driving force of the Revolution while the Legislative Assembly struggled to keep control. It was this climate of uncertainty that fueled the September Massacres: a mass killing of prisoners suspected of being the enemies of the Revolution. Orchestrated by the Paris Commune, the killings were not however confined to the capital but also claimed victims in the provinces. The Princesse de Lamballe was one of the first to fall, followed by other members of the nobility and also the clergy. Shortly afterwards, on 21 September, the newly elected National Convention proclaimed the abolition of the monarchy and the establishment of the republic. This coincided with a military engagement at Valmy that saw France's enemies routed by French troops under the command of General Kellermann – a first, symbolic victory for the young republic that was hailed with cries of 'Vive la Nation'! But this respite proved short-lived. The *Girondins*, still the dominant faction in France's National Convention, had come out against the King the year before and supported the idea of war promoted by their leader Brissot. But their authority was increasingly challenged by the more radical wing of the republican movement, the *Montagnards* ('mountaineers'), so-called because as deputies they sat on the higher benches of the Assembly. While the *Girondins* squabbled among themselves, the *Montagnards* took a united stand in the King's trial, which began in December and ended with a narrow vote in favor of execution. Louis XVI's death on the scaffold reignited European opposition to Revolutionary France. A first coalition was formed that brought together an unlikely alliance of English, Prussian and Austrian forces. France's attempts at mobilization meanwhile, enlisting an additional 300,000 soldiers in February 1793, sparked fierce resistance from some regions, particularly in the west of France. From Brittany to the Vendée, men in their thousands rose up in defense of religion and also the monarchy. France fell into civil war, with vicious fighting on both sides.

THE TERROR

The *Girondins* now faced threats both inside and outside France. They were still in power but visibly undermined by constant hounding from the *Montagnards* and their ringleaders, Danton, Robespierre and Marat. Eventually the *Girondins* were expelled from the Convention altogether, with 29 deputies arrested on the days of 31 May and 2 June 1793. Others fled the city in the hope of stirring up support in the provinces, fomenting opposition and secession in Normandy, Lyon and south-east France. It was now the turn of the *Montagnards* to dominate the Convention and the institutional changes that ensued. The first change was the establishment of the Committee of Public Safety in April 1793, which was joined by Robespierre in July and under his leadership became the political body of the French Revolution. In theory the Committee operated under the oversight of the Convention but in practice it was autonomous, to the point of gaining virtually dictatorial control over France. With hostile armies surrounding the country on all sides, the government was obliged to decree *a levée en masse* — a 'requisition' of all young, able-bodied, unmarried males.

The government then came under pressure from the Parisian popular movement, the *Sans-Culottes*, so-named because its members eschewed the knee breeches worn by the former nobility in favor of the *pantalon* (long trousers). These together with the Phrygian cap and the *carmagnole* (short red jacket) formed the typical *Sans-Culotte* costume — the *carmagnole* as immortalized in the French song that became the *Sans-Culotte* anthem following the storming of the Tuileries. The *Sans-Culottes* with their pikes came to embody the revolutionary spirit — shopkeepers and craftsmen who clamored for more radical action to stave off counter-revolution. Their fears proved well founded on 13 July 1793 when counter-revolution came knocking at the heart of the capital. That day, Charlotte Corday assassinated Jean-Paul Marat at his home in Paris, turning a friend of the people into a martyr for the cause whose remains would be interred in the Pantheon. A few weeks earlier, on 24 June 1793, French deputies had adopted a new Constitution establishing a democratic republic. Known as the *Constitution de l'An 1* (constitution of the Year 1) this had been prefaced by a Declaration of Rights that reflected the principles laid down in 1789 (liberty, civil equality, the right to property) but also included new rights of its own, starting with the right to education. As it turned out, this new Constitution was never actually implemented due to the exceptional measures that followed. Most notably, in September the Committee of Public Safety passed the Law of the Maximum: an attempt to regulate food supplies and wages, to satisfy the Parisian *Sans-Culottes*. Henceforth, the State exercised control over prices and wages in a bid to curb inflation. Then on 10 October, the government declared itself a 'revolutionary government' until such time as peace was restored, which was simply a way of legitimizing dictatorship. But it was in the fight against the enemies of the Revolution that the *Montagnards* really distinguished themselves.

In Paris, the revolutionary tribunal led by notorious public prosecutor Antoine Fouquier-Tinville, became the *Montagnards'* main instrument of struggle — with the nobility and the clergy as their targets of choice. The Law of Suspects, passed on 17 September 1793, stipulated that people could be arrested on the word of informers, and led to the detaining of nearly 500,000 people. The prisons were packed to bursting point, starting with the Conciergerie where Marie-Antoinette rubbed shoulders with Dufriche-Valazé and other *Girondins*. The Temple Tower served as a prison for the royal family. Other national monuments were requisitioned as necessary — the Hôtel de Dreneuc for instance, on the Rue de Provence. A total of 45,000 suspects were executed in Paris and the provinces. The first to lose their heads were the *Girondins*, who were imprisoned in June 1793 then guillotined the following October. Brissot featured among them — but not Dufriche-Valazé, who committed suicide on hearing that he had been sentenced to death. Madame Roland, considered the very soul of the *Girondin* party, was also arrested in the aftermath of the coup of 31 May. She went to the scaffold on 8 November, having spent five months in captivity writing her memoirs. Repression also touched the figureheads of the *Ancien Régime*, starting with

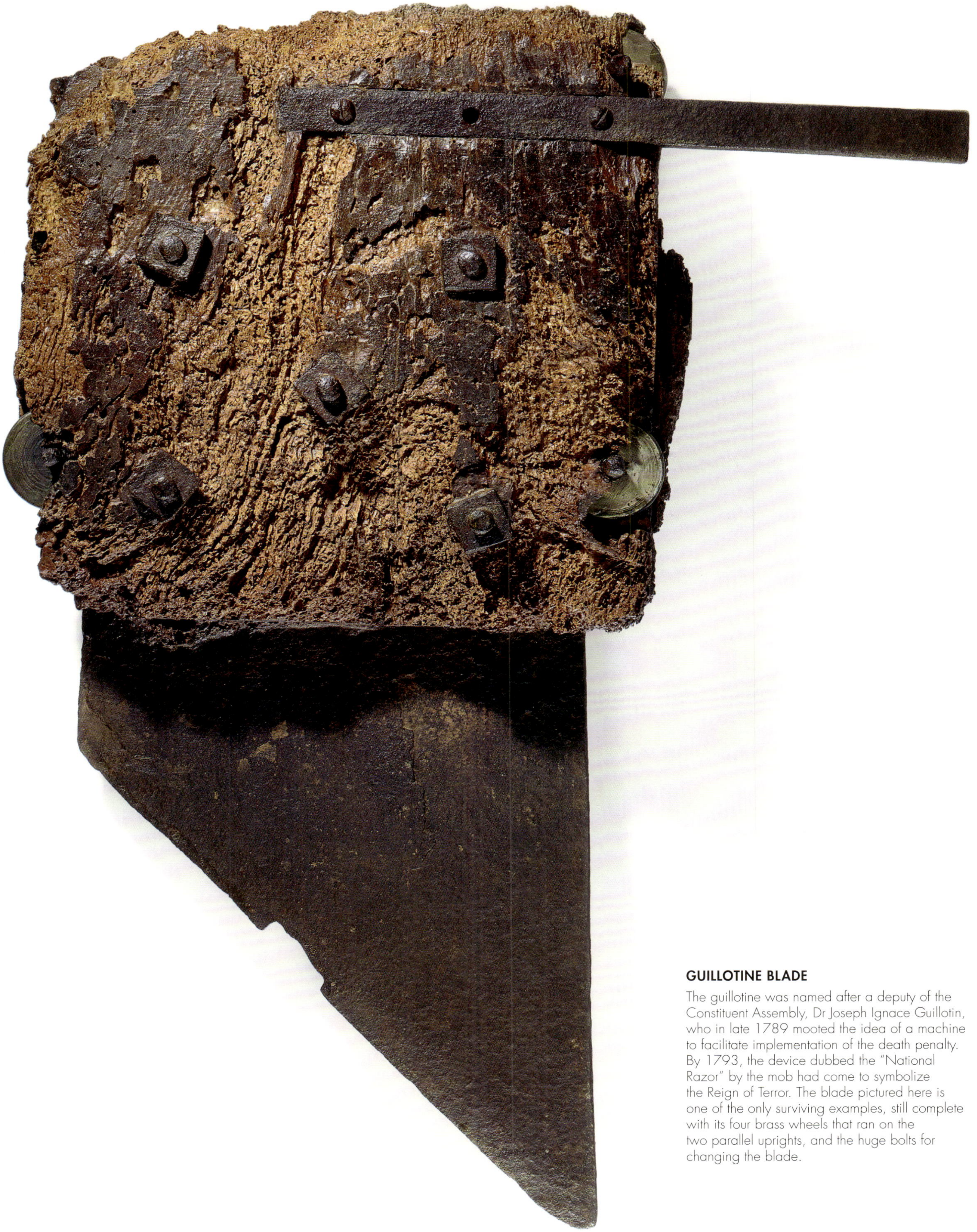

GUILLOTINE BLADE

The guillotine was named after a deputy of the Constituent Assembly, Dr Joseph Ignace Guillotin, who in late 1789 mooted the idea of a machine to facilitate implementation of the death penalty. By 1793, the device dubbed the "National Razor" by the mob had come to symbolize the Reign of Terror. The blade pictured here is one of the only surviving examples, still complete with its four brass wheels that ran on the two parallel uprights, and the huge bolts for changing the blade.

Marie-Antoinette, executed 16 October, followed by the Duke d'Orléans, otherwise known as Philippe Egalité, executed on 6 November. Despite having voted in favor of his brother the King's execution, the Duke was beheaded just the same. The guillotine became the instrument of the Terror par excellence — the two things were inseparable. It became known as *la faucheuse* (the reaper), belying the intentions of its inventor who designed the guillotine as a more humane alternative to beheading with an axe. Its favorite victims were the clergy, a predilection greatly reinforced by the program of de-Christianization waged by the Convention. Targets included the clergy who had taken an oath of loyalty to the Civil Constitution — such as Gobel, Archbishop of Paris, executed in April 1794 despite having renounced his priesthood. From the very beginning of that year, the warring factions within the Assembly were at each other's throats. Robespierre's friends succeeded in eliminating all of Hébert's allies, considered too radical, followed by those of Danton and Camille Desmoulins, considered too moderate. Lives were snuffed out one by one and by June, with trials being conducted without any regard for legal procedure or evidence. Defendants were either acquitted or sentenced to death.

In the provinces, the Convention's "representatives on a mission" were tasked with enforcing government policy and ordering arrests and executions, of which there were many. They displayed particular zeal in hunting down opponents in the west of France: in Brittany, where the war against the *Chouans* intensified; and likewise in the Vendée, whose systematic destruction had been ordered by the Convention on 1 August 1793. The ferocity of the repression in the Vendée is amply illustrated by the operations led by General Thureau (known as the 'Infernal Columns') and the drownings (*noyades*) inflicted on the citizens of Nantes by order of Jean-Baptiste Carrier. There were some 150-200,000 victims. In eastern and northern France, the Convention's *commissaires* also had to exercise political control over military operations. Philippe Lebas, deputy of the Pas-de-Calais, is a prime example. It was his presence alongside General Jourdan that brought victory at Fleurus on 26 June 1794.

This radicalization of the revolutionary dictatorship eventually exasperated the Deputies, particularly since France was now in better shape militarily. Thanks to Carnot's efforts, the enemy's grip on the country had loosened, victory at Fleurus having opened the way for France's entry into Belgium. In the summer of 1794, feeling themselves increasingly threatened, the members of the Convention overwhelmingly agreed to topple Robespierre. He and his friends (Saint-Just, Couthon) were executed on 9 Thermidor Year II (27 July 1794). Lebas, who remained loyal to Robespierre until the end, committed suicide on the following day. The Committee of Public Safety underwent a reshuffle and the prisons were opened. The Thermidorian Convention then came under renewed threat in April 1795, this time from a Jacobin insurrection against the Assembly (with Boissy d'Anglas presiding), which ended with the decapitation of deputy Jean-Bertrand Féraud. But the Prairial Days also provided a useful opportunity to purge the government of Robespierre's last surviving cronies. France was on the threshold of a more moderate regime.

In August 1795 the Deputies adopted a new Constitution that reflected the republican heritage of the Revolution but dissolved the Convention in favor of a separation of powers. Executive power was now in the hands of a five-man Directory; legislative power was divided between two large legislative bodies (the Council of the 500 and the Council of the Ancients). With some seats up for re-election every year, the government lacked any stability. The Convention's parting shot was to add the 'two-thirds decree' to the package, requiring that two-thirds of deputies for the new councils were to be chosen from among the outgoing members of the Convention. This incensed royalists, who had resurfaced following Robespierre's downfall and saw the future elections as their chance to regain power. The result was a royalist uprising in Paris that centered on the west of the city, forcing the Assembly to call out the troops. And it was then that a young general aged just 26 arrived on the scene. His name was Napoleon Bonaparte.

BONAPARTE, SON OF THE REVOLUTION

Bonaparte was certainly not unknown in October 1975, but his military career was at a standstill. It was now three years since the start of the European wars but he himself had seen little combat. His chief military exploit to-date was the retaking of Toulon in December 1793, following its capture by royalist forces in August who then turned it over to the British. His republican zeal thus proved, Napoleon was promoted to the rank of general and had the wind in his sails, until he fell from grace due to his *Montagnard* affiliation when Robespierre was deposed. His refusal thereafter to take command of the Army of the West then left him technically unemployed at the very moment when France was mobilizing for war. But he remained ready for duty and Barras, who the Convention had appointed Commander-in-Chief of the armed forces in Paris, had not forgotten the young gunner who had caught his attention at Toulon. In the event, Napoleon did not disappoint. Ordered by Barras to put down a royalist insurrection in Paris, he famously used grapeshot (*mitraille*) to repulse the royalist mob milling outside the Eglise Saint-Roch (just a stone's throw from the Convention's meeting place). This "whiff of grapeshot"

— as it became known — earned Napoleon the sobriquet of "General Vendémiaire". From that point onward his fortune was made, not least because Barras, elected one of the five Directors, became a leading figure of the Directorial regime. It was around this time that Napoleon met Josephine de Beauharnais — widow of a general in the French Revolutionary Army who was executed in 1794, and Barras' sometime lover. The meeting opened up avenues to greater power, helped by Napoleon winning command of the Army of Italy in March 1796, just a few days after his marriage to Josephine. Over the next 18 months he would distinguish himself on the Italian field of battle, forcing first the Italians then the Austrians to sue for peace. He displayed his talents not only as a military leader but also as a diplomat and potential Head of State, not to mention as a communicator. Napoleon's gift of oratory kept him riding high in popularity despite his departure for Egypt in June 1798.

In his absence, France sank ever deeper into crisis, though curiously not at the expense of consolidating its position in Europe. Following its victories in 1794 and 1795, France annexed large parts of Belgium and the Rhineland in a bid to expand the country to its "natural borders" — or so argued the French. From 1795 onward, the territories were no longer directly annexed but transformed into Sister Republics, with institutions modeled on the French example. France saw itself as exporter of its revolutionary principles abroad. It was committed to putting an end to feudalism and absolute monarchy in Europe, but remained an occupying force just the same, with no qualms about living off the countries it invaded and growing rich at their expense. This included relieving its enemies of their works of art, which were duly packed off to the recently completely Louvre Museum in Paris. By 1798, the so-called "Sister Republics" under French control included the Batavian Republic (The Netherlands), Switzerland and the whole of Italy, itself divided into the Cisalpine (northern) Republic, the Roman Republic and the Parthenopean (Neopolitan) Republic. But this whole edifice was put at risk when the Second Coalition was formed, with Britain and Austria in the driving seat, later reinforced by Russia and the Ottoman Empire, whose entry into the war was a predictable outcome of France's campaign in Egypt. Anglo-Russian forces in Holland and Austro-Russian forces in Italy and Switzerland inflicted heavy defeats on the French, forcing them to withdraw from the greater part of the Italian Peninsula. By the summer of 1799, French borders were once again under threat.

Military crisis then spiraled into political crisis as France's leaders proved incapable of asserting their authority. Elections under the Directory showed that opposition to the regime remained strong, Robespierre's fall having prompted royalists to regroup around a hard core of returning emigrants and nobles who had come out of hiding. Their success in the spring elections of 1797 seriously unsettled republicans, who responded with a coup d'état that successfully purged the assemblies of most of their royalist elements. The Coup of Fructidor, Year V as it became known (September 1797 in the Gregorian calendar) was conducted with the support of Napoleon who dispatched General Augereau to expedite the process.

The "fructidorized" royalists went back into hiding, knowing they could count on support from pockets of resistance in western France, where the *Chouannerie* movement persisted despite the series of peace treaties signed with the government since 1795. General Charette had resumed hostilities in June 1795, at the head of an army composed of Catholic royalists. Captured in March 1796, Charette had then been executed by firing squad on the 29th of the month. Georges Cadoudal on the other hand, leader of the Morbihan *Chouans*, had escaped capture and remained ready for action. In the fall of 1799, with Napoleon just recently returned from Egypt, Cadoudal and his men launched an attack on several towns in Brittany in the hope of inciting a general uprising of royalists across France. This failed to materialize but the royalists remained a threat, reinforced in the last year of the Directory by the increasing influence of the Jacobins. Filled with nostalgia for Robespierre, the Jacobins revived their club and publications and won a major electoral victory in the spring of 1799. The response was not long in coming. Sieyès, now head of the Directory, purged the Government of its Jacobin elements and tried to confine them to the assemblies, plotting a coup d'état that would transform the institutional structures of France and bolster the powers of the Executive. So it was that when Napoleon returned from Egypt in October 1799 he found a country in crisis — which he then painted blacker still so as to justify his intercession. France needed a savior and Napoleon saw himself as that savior. His armies had already redressed the balance militarily and restored peace to France. Napoleon's greatest insight was to position himself as the only officer capable of contributing to Sieyès' long-planned but repeatedly thwarted coup. Having being given command of all the forces in the Paris area, he made inroads into political and financial circles alike, without forgetting to win support from his brothers-in-arms. The result was the Coup of 18 and 19 Brumaire: a bloodless coup d'état that, despite a few hiccups at St Cloud, convinced the Deputies to dissolve the Directory and replace it with a provisional Consulate, headed by Napoleon Bonaparte as the self-appointed strongman of the new regime. This was but the prelude to his nomination as First Consul in December 1799, in which capacity he presented the Constitution to French voters with these words: "The Revolution is over, it has achieved the principles that set it in motion." Heir to the Revolution and the principles of 1789, Napoleon Bonaparte also intended to be the man who would halt the revolutionary process and restore order to the country.

END OF THE FRENCH MONARCHY

The bloody head of King Louis XVI is held up to the crowd on the Place Louis XV, future Place de La Concorde — a symbol of the violent upheavals that shook France in the closing years of the 18th century. Paris resumed its role as capital and the palace of Versailles was abandoned. The luxury of the court was now a distant memory, recalled only in personal effects that stood as moving testaments to the past — a box decorated with a locket of hair or the copper watering can from Marie-Antoinette's much beloved Trianon gardens. The Queen was a prisoner in the Temple Tower when Louis XVI was beheaded on 21 January 1793. She had no illusions about the fate that awaited her but tried to protect her children from the same ordeal, her retinue reduced to those few close friends who were tolerated by her all-powerful jailers. The royal couple's personal effects — soon to become mere relics of the past — were gathered together by the faithful Cléry, the King's valet. He and Marc-Antoine Thierry de Ville d'Avray were among the leading voices to bear witness to a lost age and the sufferings inflicted.

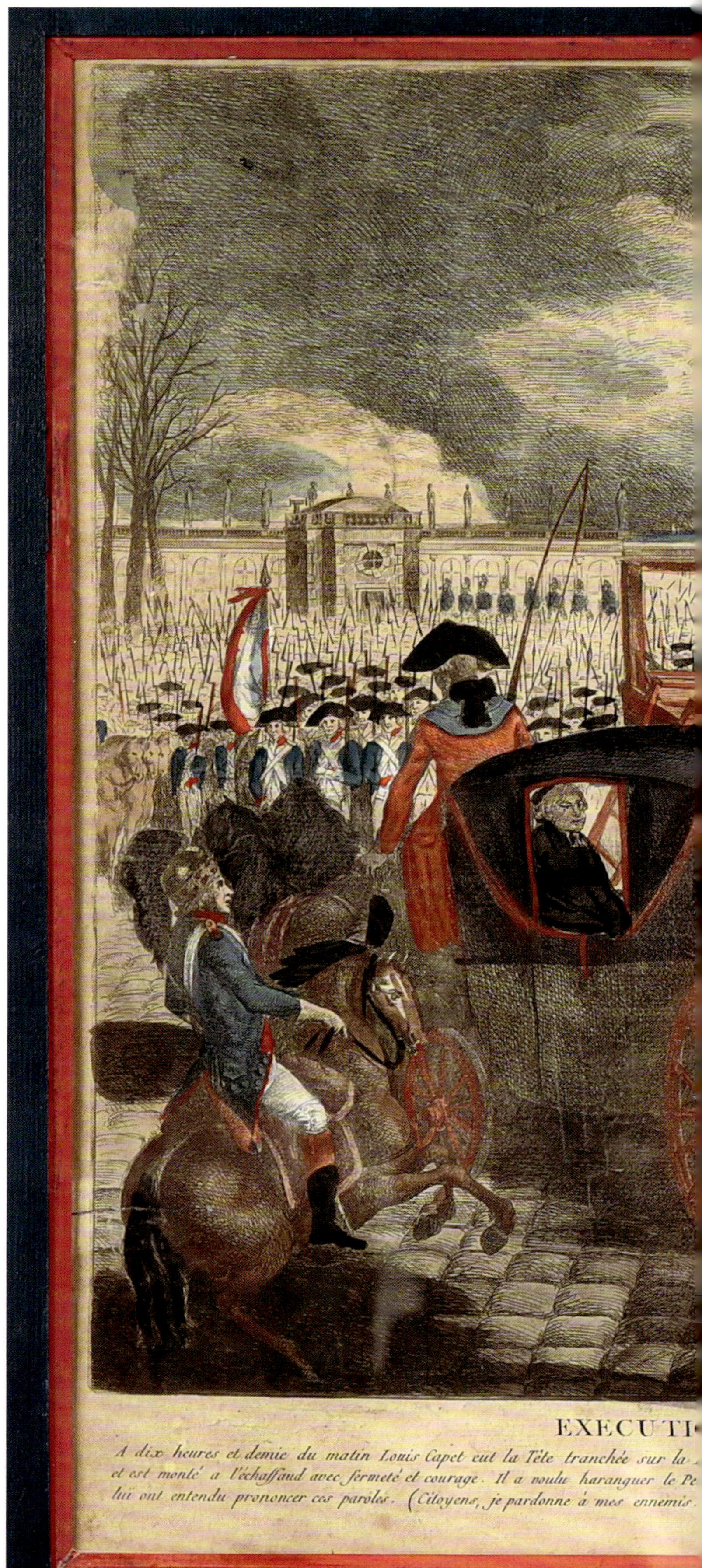

EXECUTION OF LOUIS XVI (LOUIS CAPET), 21 JANUARY 1793, ENGRAVING EMBELLISHED WITH WATERCOLOR

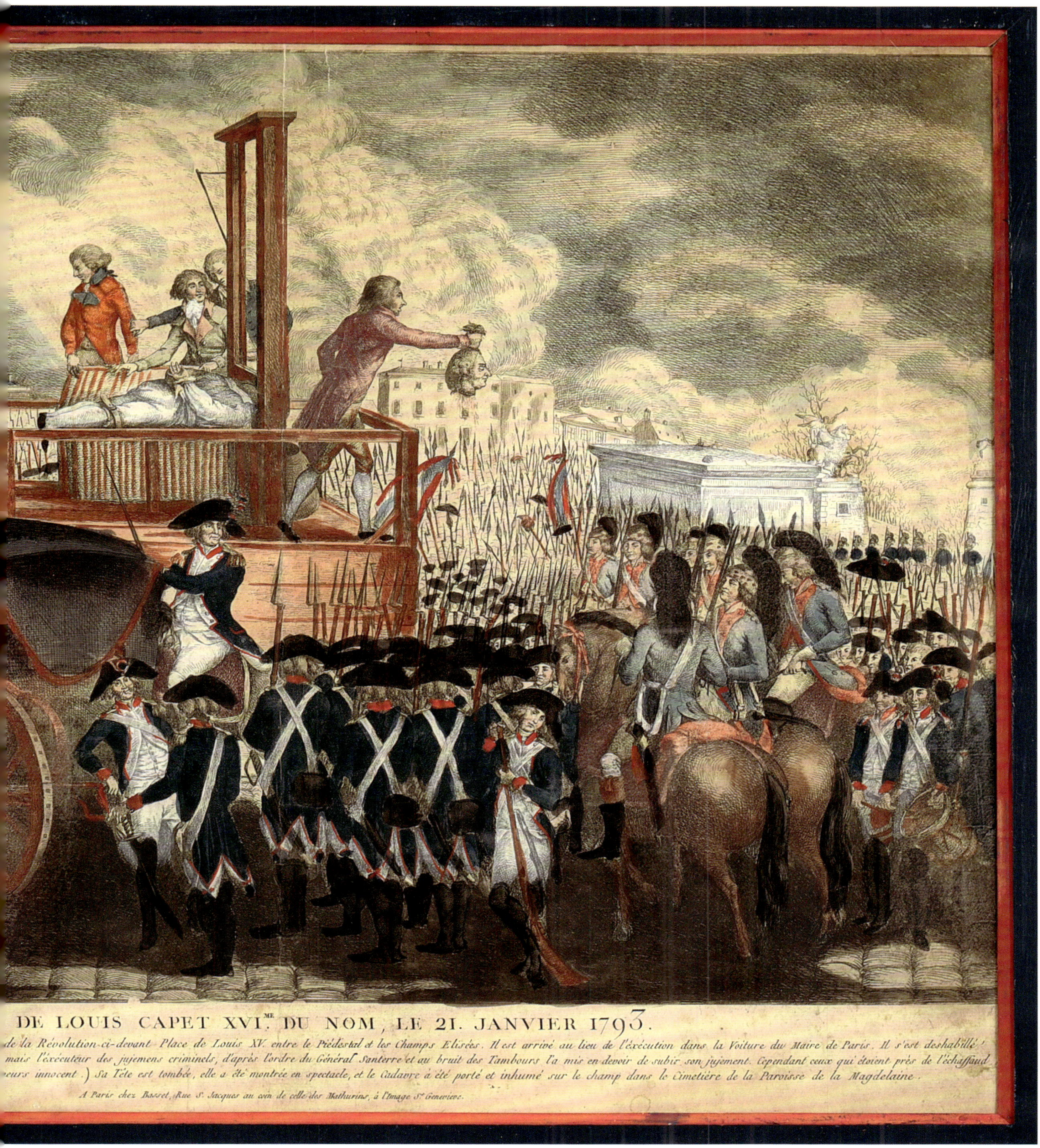
DE LOUIS CAPET XVI.ME DU NOM, LE 21. JANVIER 1793.
de la Révolution-ci-devant Place de Louis XV. entre le Piédestal et les Champs Elisées. Il est arrivé au lieu de l'éxécution dans la Voiture du Maire de Paris. Il s'est deshabillé
mais l'éxécuteur des jujemens criminels, d'après l'ordre du Général Santerre et au bruit des Tambours l'a mis en devoir de subir son jujement. Cependant ceux qui étoient près de l'échaffaud
eurs innocent.) Sa Tête est tombée, elle a été montrée en spectacle, et le Cadavre a été porté et inhumé sur le champ dans le Cimetière de la Paroisse de la Magdelaine.
A Paris chez Basset, Rue S. Jacques au coin de celle des Mathurins, à l'Image S.te Genevieve.

VERSAILLES, THE LAST HOURS: LOUIS XVI AND MARIE-ANTOINETTE

BOX DECORATED WITH THE HAIR OF LOUIS XVI, MARIE-ANTOINETTE AND THE DUCHESS OF ANGOULÊME

Tortoiseshell snuffbox with cover featuring a locket of hair woven from the locks of Louis XVI, Marie-Antoinette and their daughter, Madame Royale, who later became known as the Duchess of Angoulême. A plaque on the underside of the box commemorates their lives.

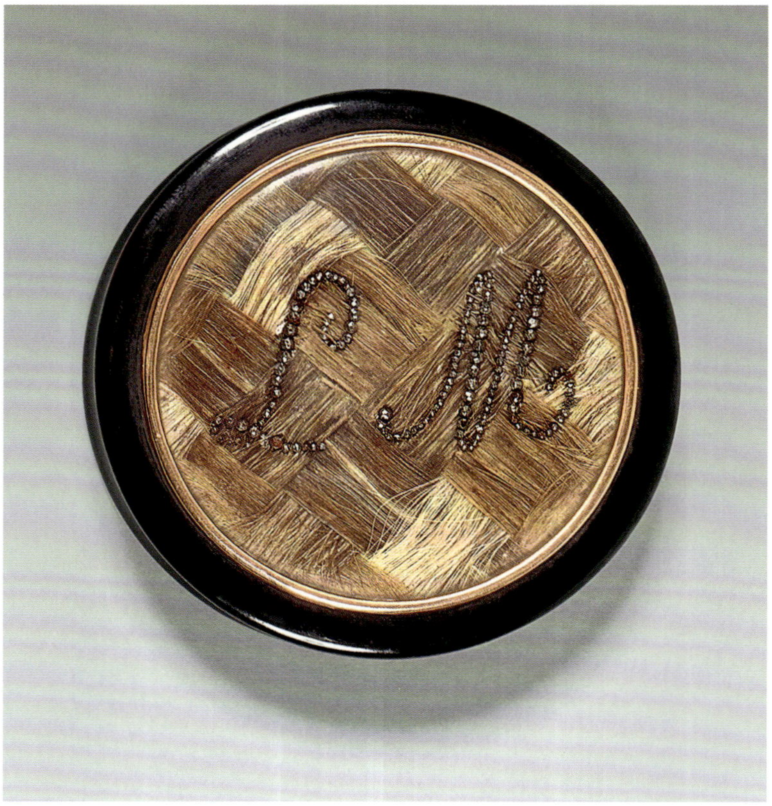

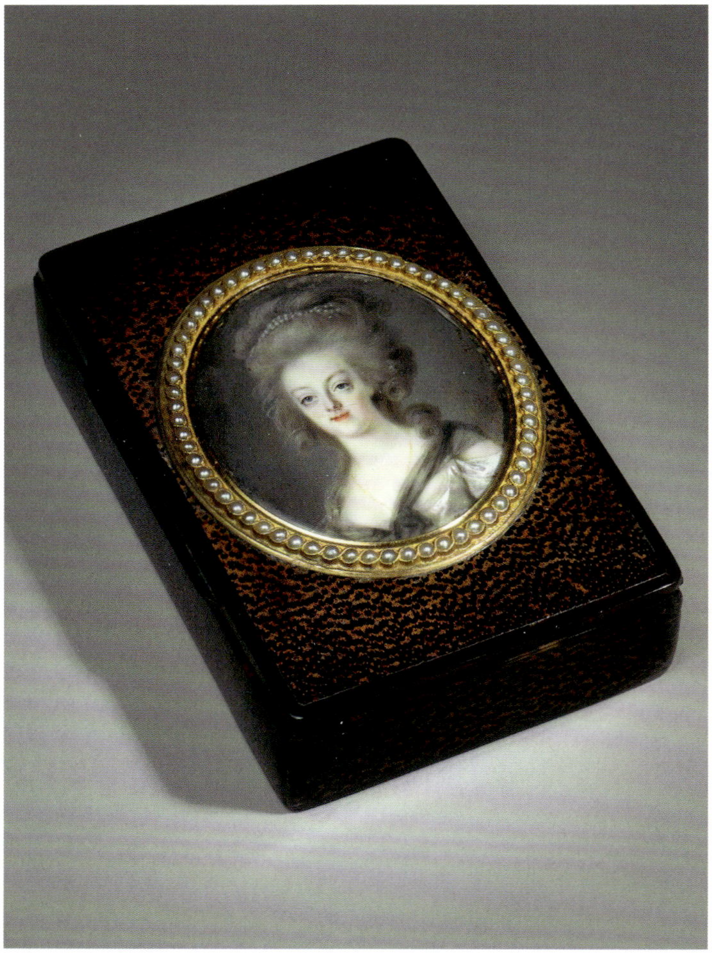

LOUIS-MARIE SICARD, KNOWN AS SICARDI (1743-1825): SNUFFBOX WITH PORTRAIT OF MARIE-ANTOINETTE

Snuffbox from the estate of Marc-Antoine Thierry de Ville d'Avray, the King's valet and Intendant General of the Royal Furniture Repository. Gifted to him by Marie-Antoinette, it depicts her in bust format, wearing a white dress and captured by the brushstrokes of famous French miniaturist Sicardi.

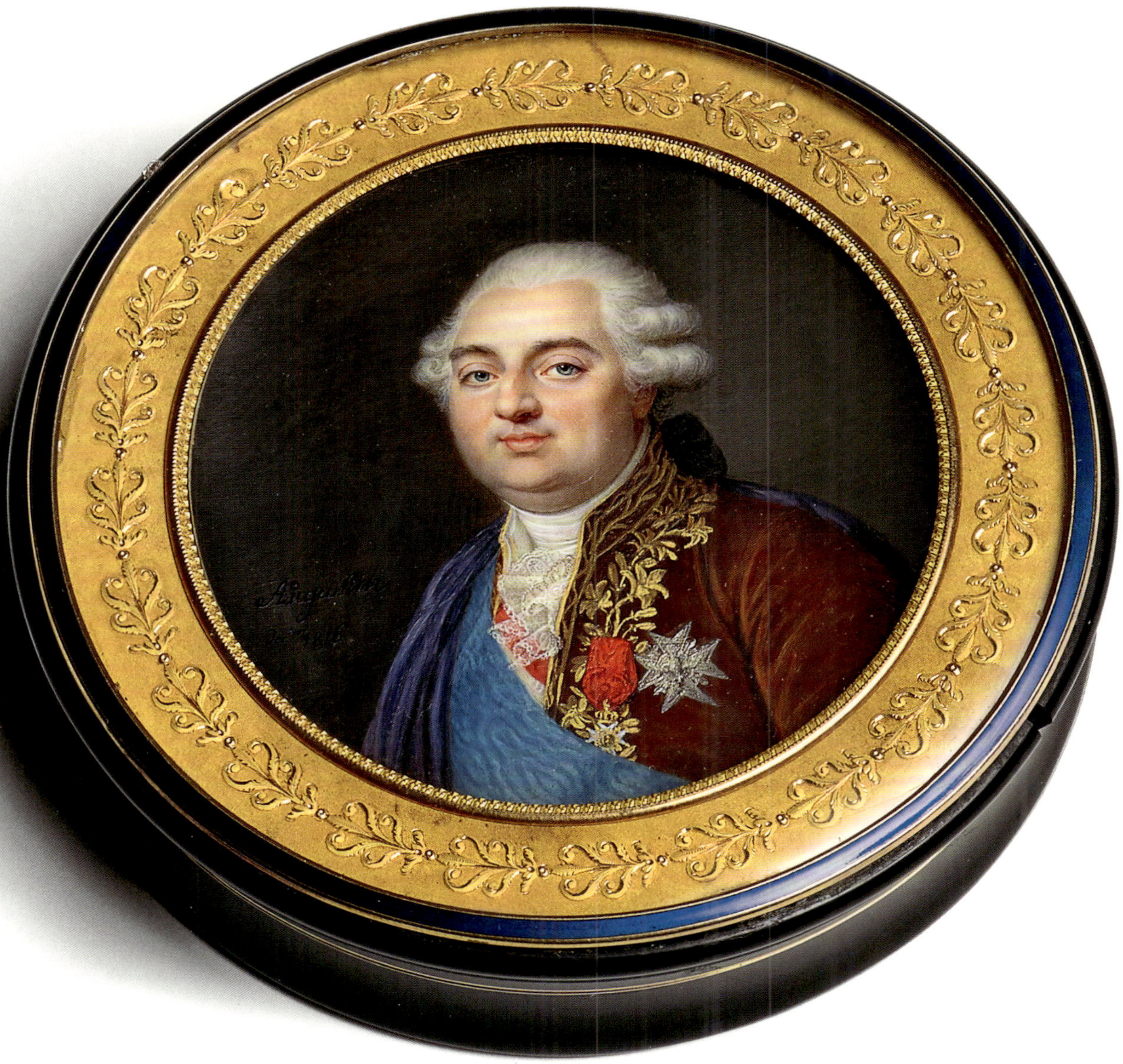

JEAN-BAPTISTE JACQUES AUGUSTIN (1759-1832): SNUFFBOX WITH PORTRAIT OF LOUIS XVI

Tortoiseshell box with gold surround bearing the hallmark of Parisian jewelers Ouizille and Vachette. It features one of the finest posthumous portraits ever painted of the King, dated December 1816 and executed by leading French miniaturist Augustin. The box was a gift from Louis XVII to Raymond, Marquis of Sèze, President of the Court of Cassation, Peer of France, Grand Treasurer of the Order of the Holy Spirit – a token of the King's gratitude for Raymond's defense of Louis XVI at his trial in 1792.

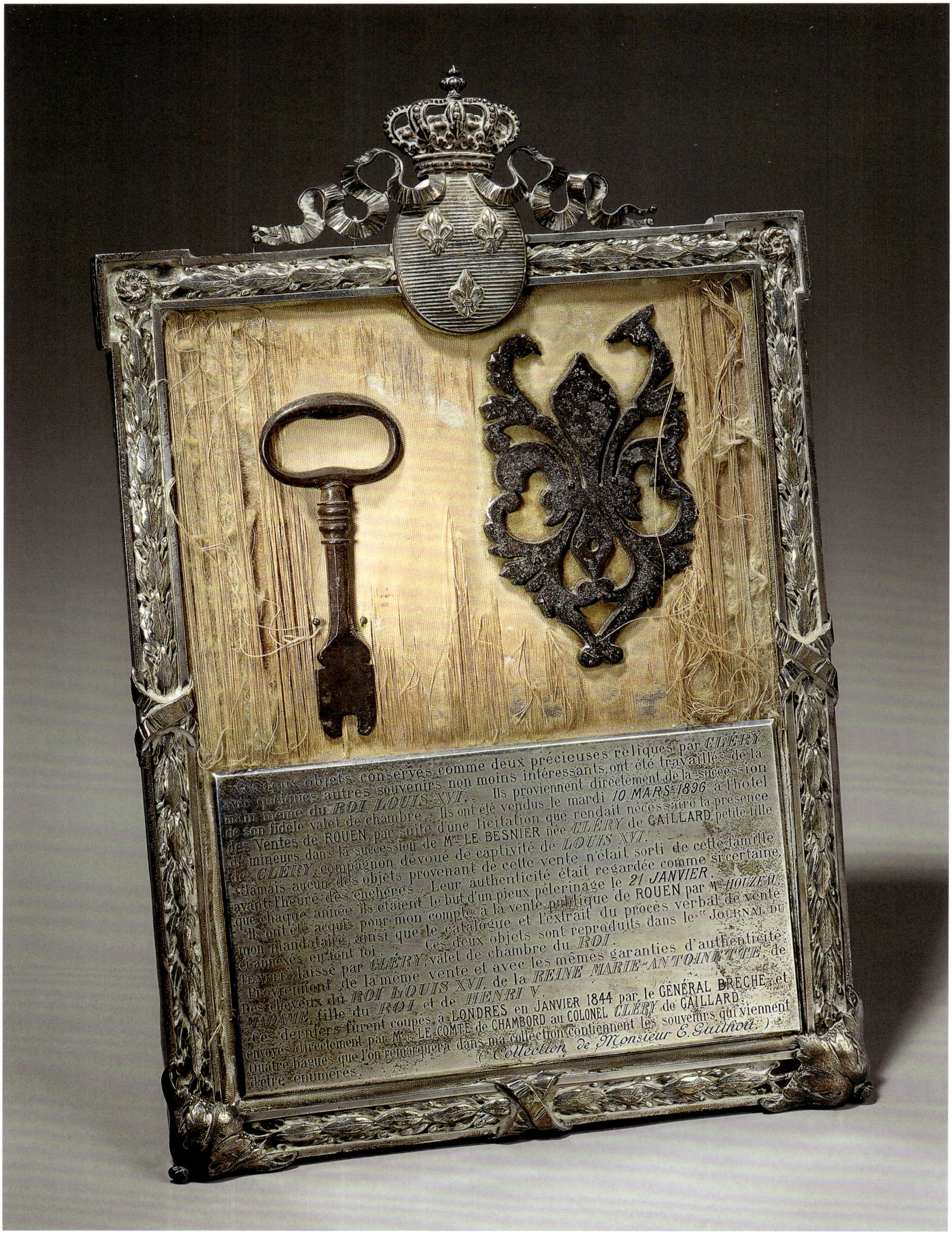
Ces deux objets conservés comme deux précieuses reliques par CLÉRY
avec quelques autres souvenirs non moins intéressants, ont été travaillés de la
main même du ROI LOUIS XVI. Ils proviennent directement de la succession
de son fidèle valet de chambre. Ils ont été vendus le mardi 10 MARS 1896 à l'hotel
des Ventes de ROUEN, par suite d'une licitation que rendait nécessaire la présence
de mineurs dans la succession de Mme LE BESNIER née CLÉRY de GAILLARD, petite fille
de CLÉRY, compagnon dévoué de captivité de LOUIS XVI.
Jamais aucun des objets provenant de cette vente n'était sorti de cette famille
avant l'heure des enchères. Leur authenticité était regardée comme si certaine,
que chaque année ils étaient le but d'un pieux pélerinage le 21 JANVIER.
Ils ont été acquis pour mon compte à la vente publique de ROUEN par Me HOUZEAU,
mon mandataire, ainsi que le catalogue et l'extrait du procès verbal de vente
ci-annexés en font foi. Ces deux objets sont reproduits dans le "JOURNAL DU
TEMPLE" laissé par CLÉRY, valet de chambre du ROI.
Proviennent de la même vente et avec les mêmes garanties d'authenticité.
Des cheveux du ROI LOUIS XVI, de la REINE MARIE-ANTOINETTE, de
MADAME, fille du ROI et de HENRI V.
Ces derniers furent coupés à LONDRES en JANVIER 1844 par le GÉNÉRAL BRECHE, et
envoyés directement par Mgr LE COMTE de CHAMBORD au COLONEL CLÉRY de GAILLARD.
Quatre bagues que l'on remarquera dans ma collection contiennent les souvenirs qui viennent
d'être énumérés.
(Collection de Monsieur E. Guilhou.)

KEY AND LOCK PART HAND-FORGED BY LOUIS XVI

History has it that Louis XVI would amuse himself making locks, an occupation that attested to his fascination with the mechanical arts and science in general. This key and lock part are among the few surviving examples of his handiwork and were preserved by Jean-Baptiste Cléry, the King's valet at the Temple, together with other royal mementoes that were later sold off at a grand sale held in Rouen in 1896.

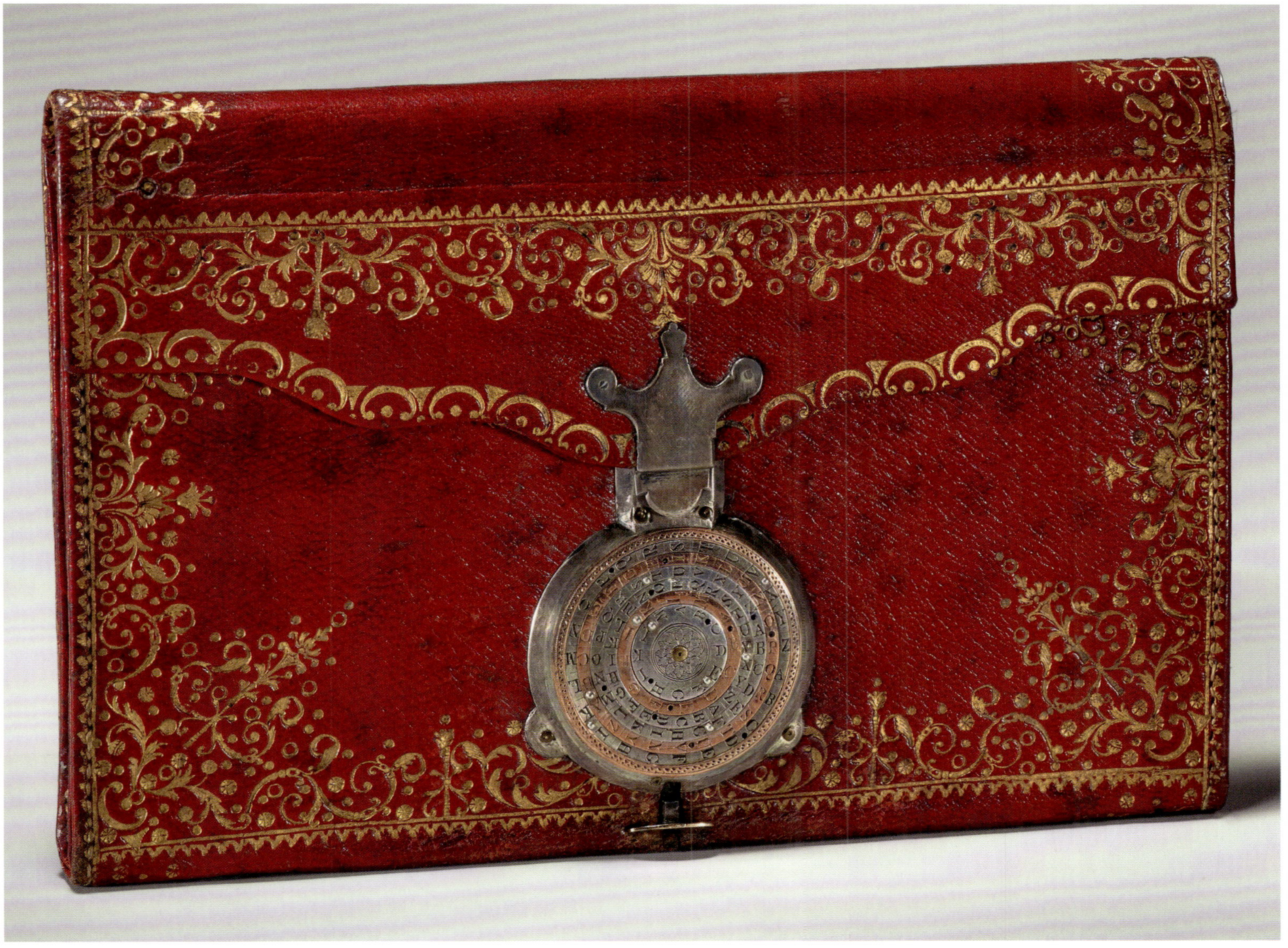

PORTFOLIO WITH SECRET COMBINATION ORIGINALLY BELONGING TO LOUIS XVI

Small red Morocco leather wallet, richly emblazoned with gold *rinceaux* patterns and boasting a most unusual circular lock in white and pink gold. Unique of its kind, the lock features six dials engraved with letters and could only be opened using the secret combination "A Louis" – an ingenious feat of engineering for the times, reflecting the King's appetite for precision instruments. The portfolio was used to transport the letters exchanged between the King and French writer Beaumarchais at the time of the American Revolutionary War, testifying to the bonds forged between the writer-turned-secret agent and his sovereign.

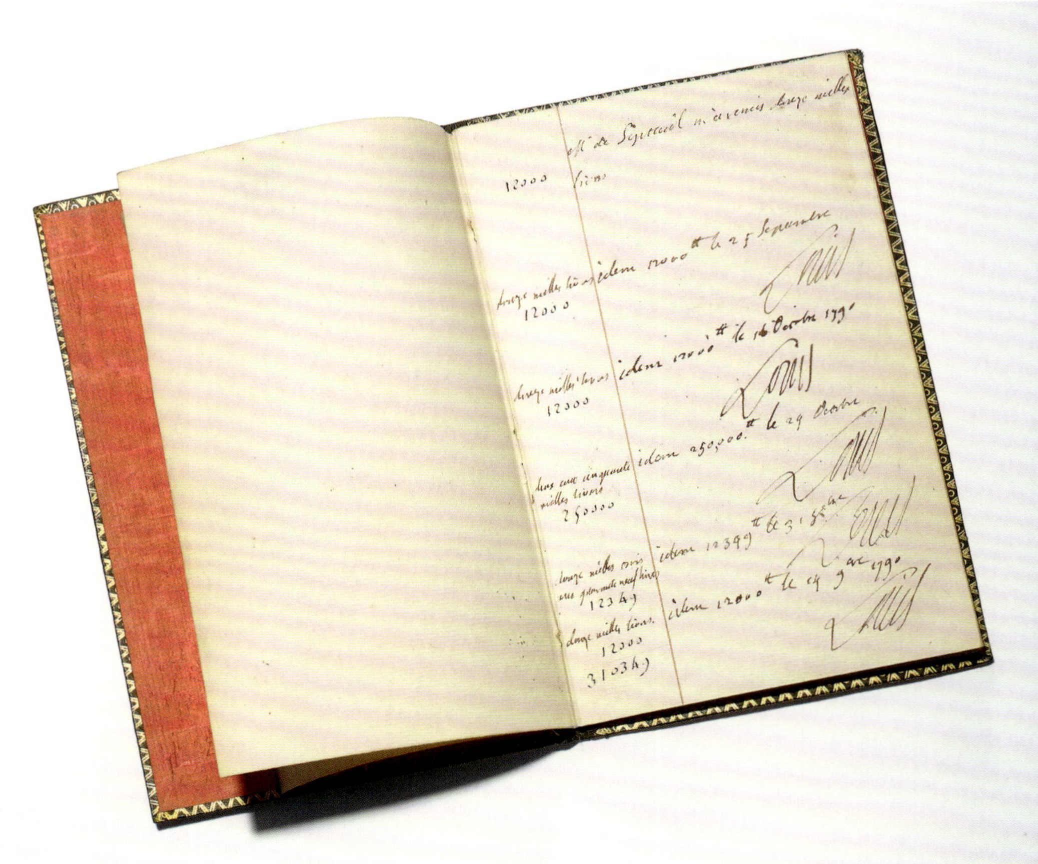

PERSONAL ACCOUNT BOOK OF LOUIS XVI

This small red Morocco leather-bound book was used by Louis XVI to record his personal expenses. Each entry was followed by his signature and the date, making a total of 50 signed entries that come to an end on 5 August 1792. Five days later the King and his family were escorted to the Tuileries Palace before being imprisoned in the Temple Tower.

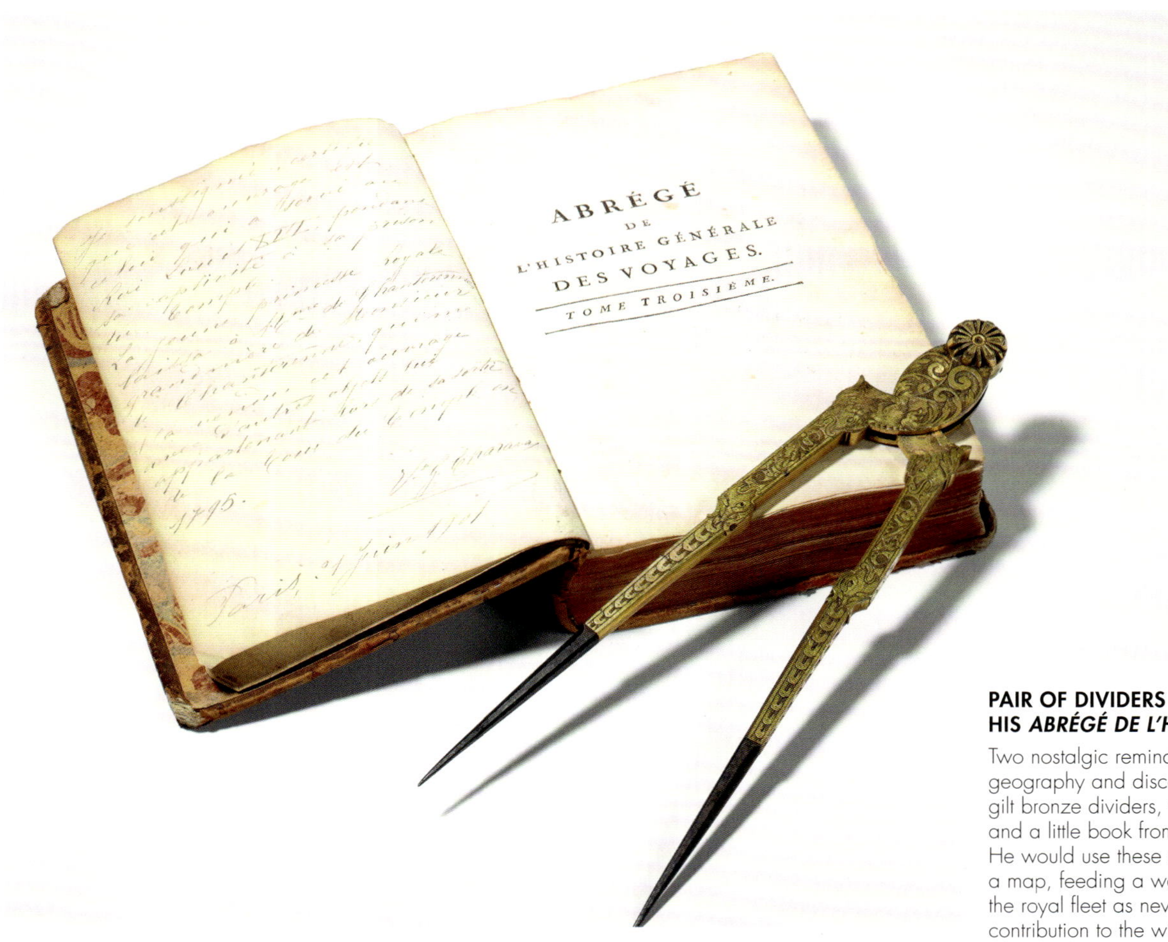

PAIR OF DIVIDERS BELONGING TO LOUIS XVI AND HIS *ABRÉGÉ DE L'HISTOIRE GÉNÉRALE DES VOYAGES*

Two nostalgic reminders of Louis XVI's passion for geography and discovery: a pair of finely engraved gilt bronze dividers, with delicate *rinceaux* decoration; and a little book from his magnificent personal library. He would use these dividers to measure distances on a map, feeding a wanderlust that led him to build up the royal fleet as never before, and make a significant contribution to the winning of American independence.

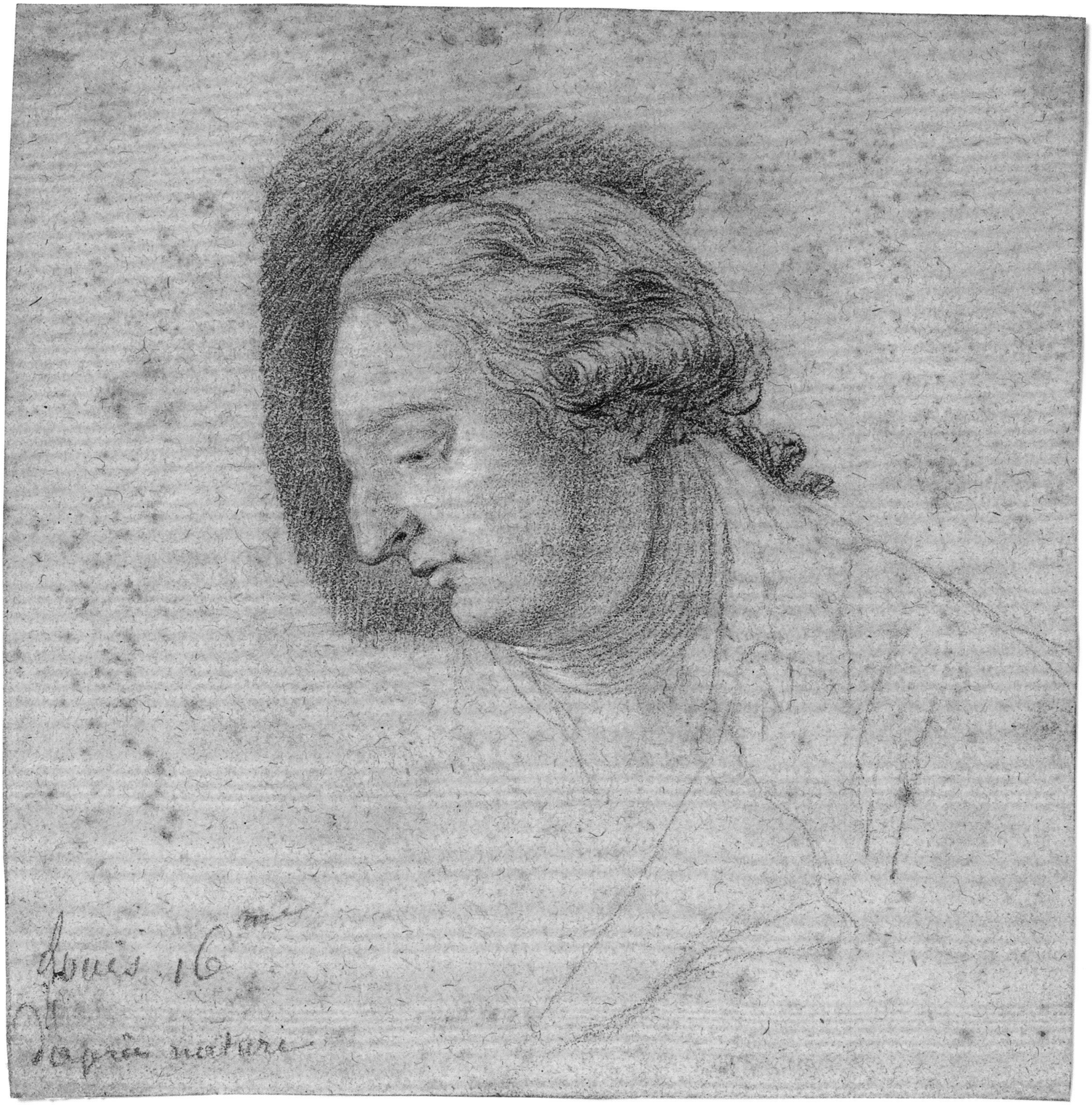

LIFE DRAWING OF LOUIS XVI

This very rare life drawing of Louis XVI captures him at one of his favorite occupations – poring over a document. It shows him half-bent over a table, probably concentrating on a map, quite possibly the map detailing the route of the La Pérouse expedition that was so dear to his heart. An inscription on the back of the drawing names the artist as one Joseph-Louis Leroy, the son of Louis XVI's librarian at Versailles.

PORTFOLIO BEARING THE ARMS OF MARIE-ANTOINETTE, DAUPHINE OF FRANCE

The arms on the cover of this unique and unusually large portfolio leave no doubt as to its original owner. In small-tooled, gilded brown Morocco leather with fleur-de-lis motifs, it consists of several inner flap pockets plus a separate compartment for use as a second portfolio. Now rather heavily restored, it comes from the ducal estate of Crussol d'Uzès and probably once belonged to Anne Emmanuel de Crussol d'Amboise (1726-1794), a Major General and noble deputy at the Estates General of 1789. He was guillotined in Paris on 26 July 1794, preceded on 10 May by his wife Louise Angélique Bersin, and Louis XVI's sister Madame Elisabeth.

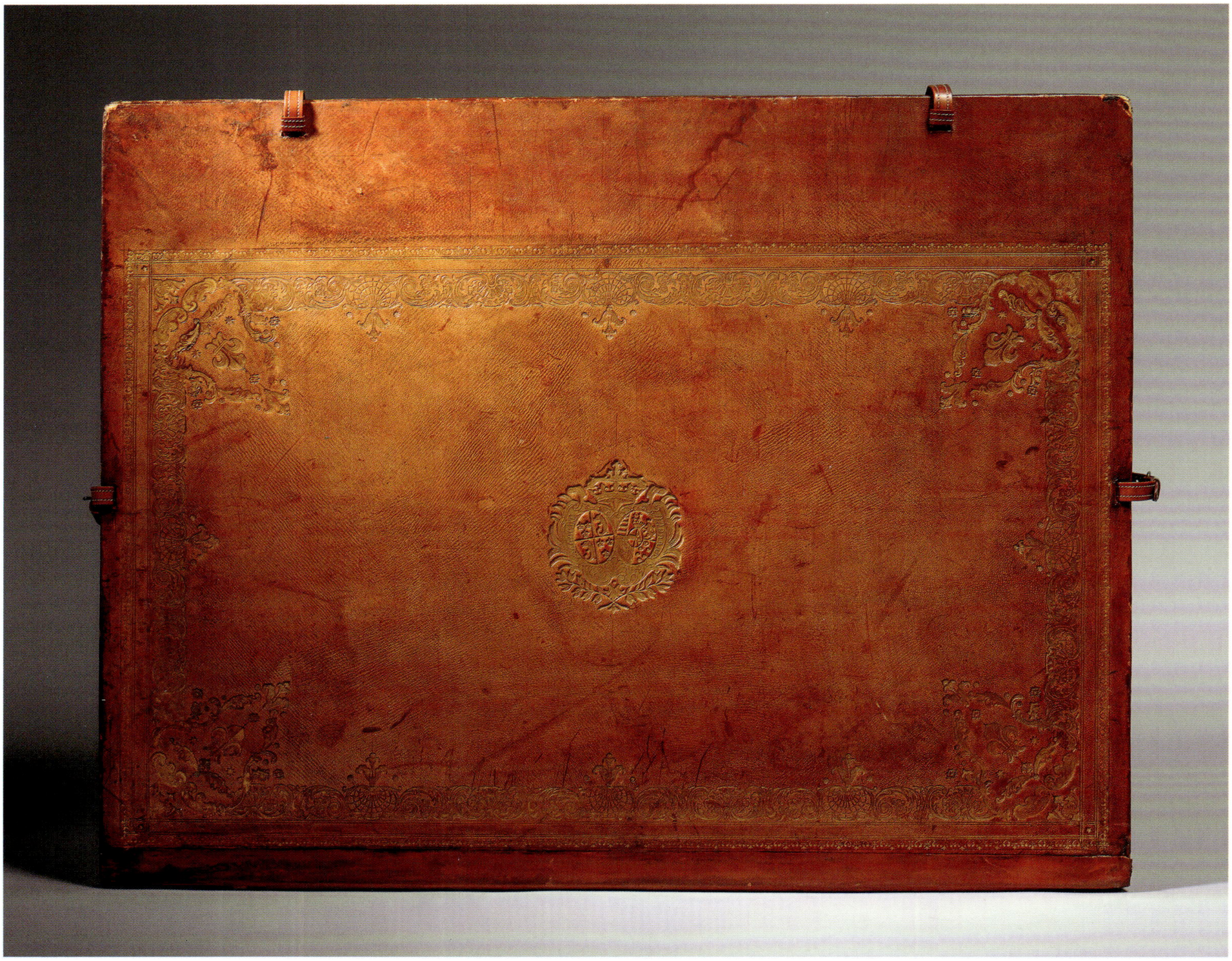

MARIE-ANTOINETTE'S PERSONAL ATLAS, CIRCA 1770-1774

Pictured here is Giovanni Rizzi-Zannoni's *Atlas Moderne ou Collection de Cartes de Toutes les Parties du Globe Terrestre*, published by Lattré et Herissant in 1762. It belonged to Marie-Antoinette when she was Dauphine of France and was specially engraved with her arms in the early years of her marriage to Louis-Auguste, Dauphin of France, crowned King Louis XVI on 10 May 1774. Aged barely 14 when she arrived at court, the future queen was tutored for four years prior to her ascent to the throne. Learning geography would most certainly have formed part of her political education – this atlas, for instance, contains 35 watercolor maps. Volumes bearing her arms as Dauphine of France are extremely rare among the works in her library at the Tuileries Palace (1,371 volumes, inventoried in 1792). Editions like this one, in large folio format, are still more unusual.

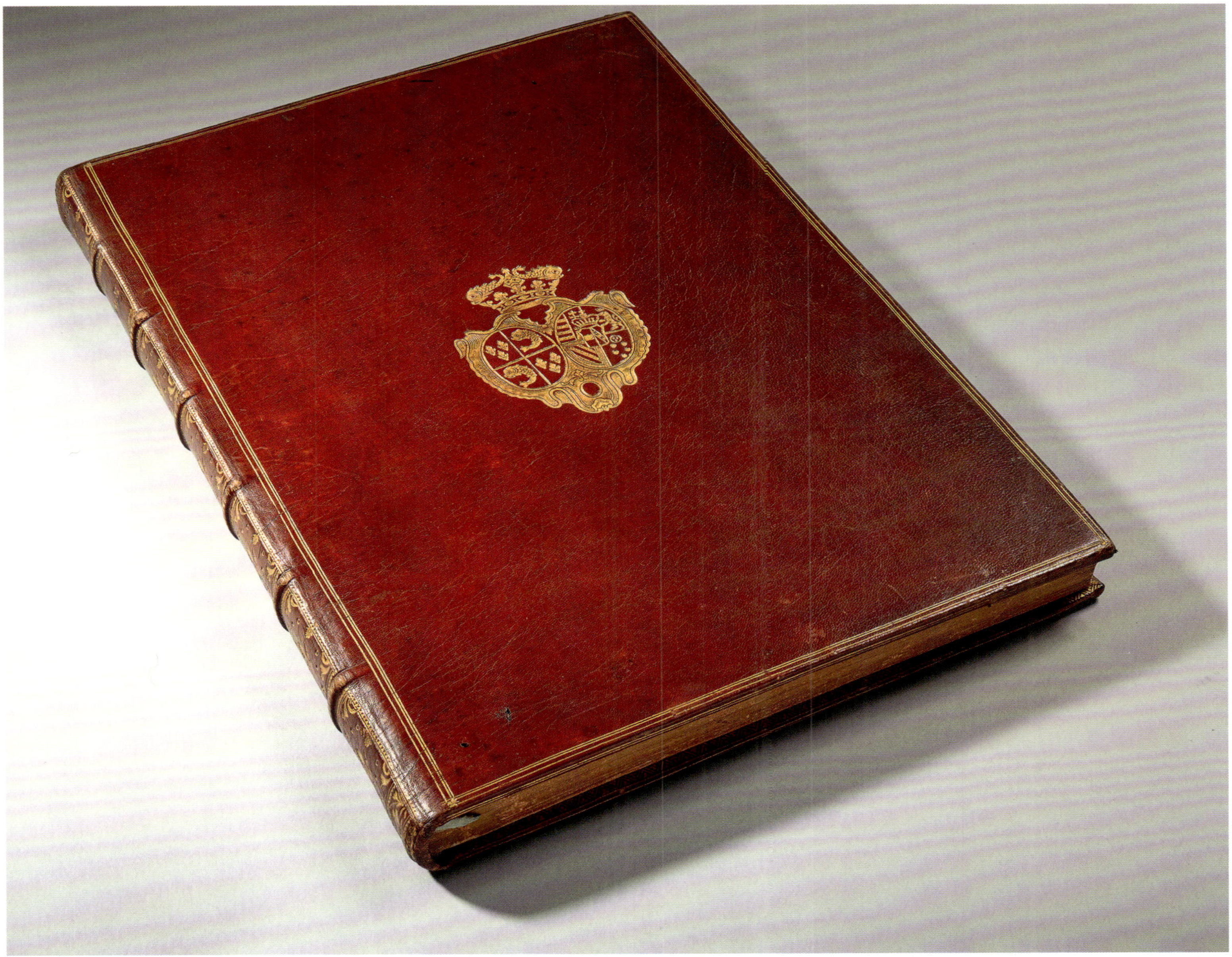

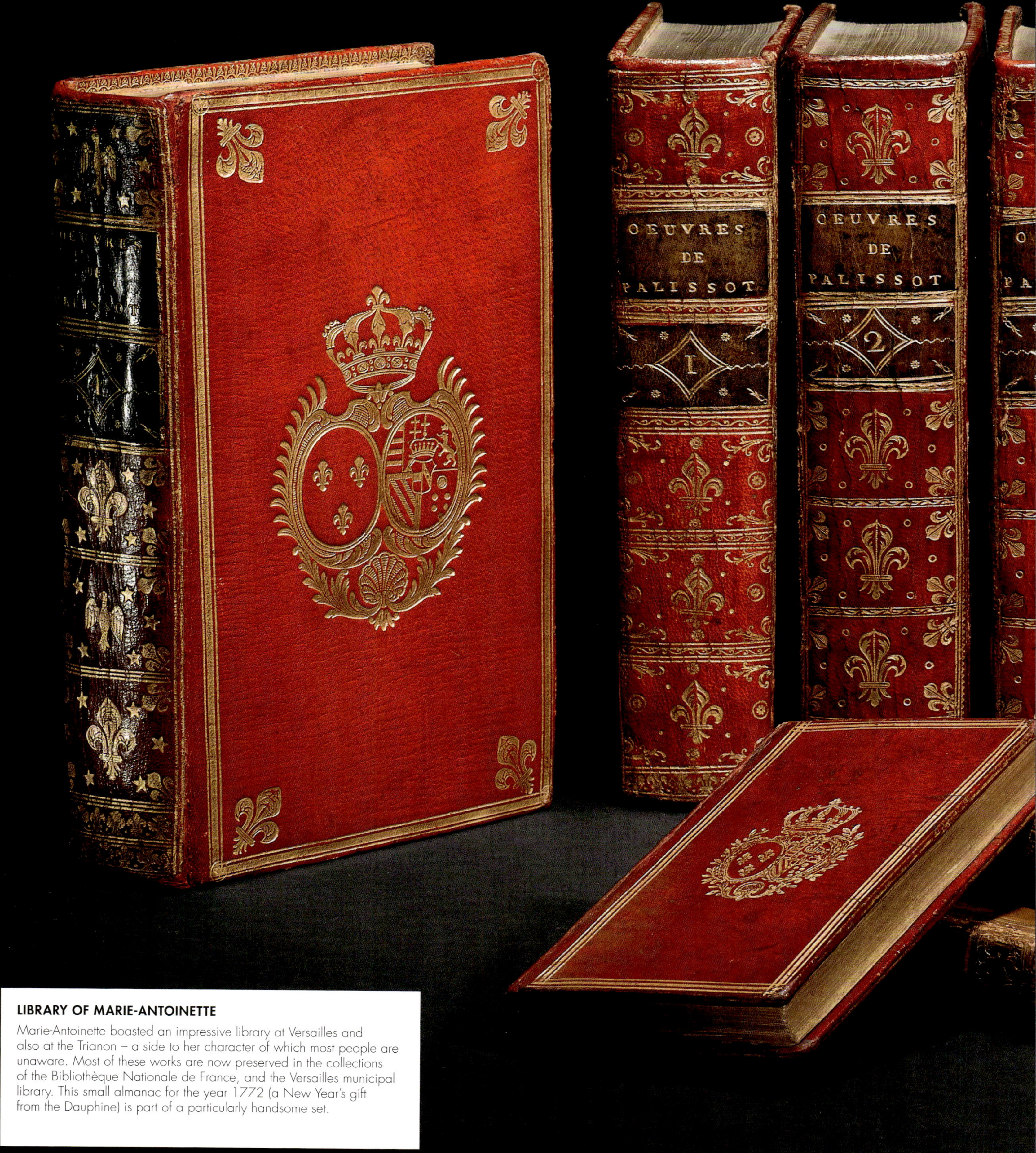

LIBRARY OF MARIE-ANTOINETTE

Marie-Antoinette boasted an impressive library at Versailles and also at the Trianon – a side to her character of which most people are unaware. Most of these works are now preserved in the collections of the Bibliothèque Nationale de France, and the Versailles municipal library. This small almanac for the year 1772 (a New Year's gift from the Dauphine) is part of a particularly handsome set.

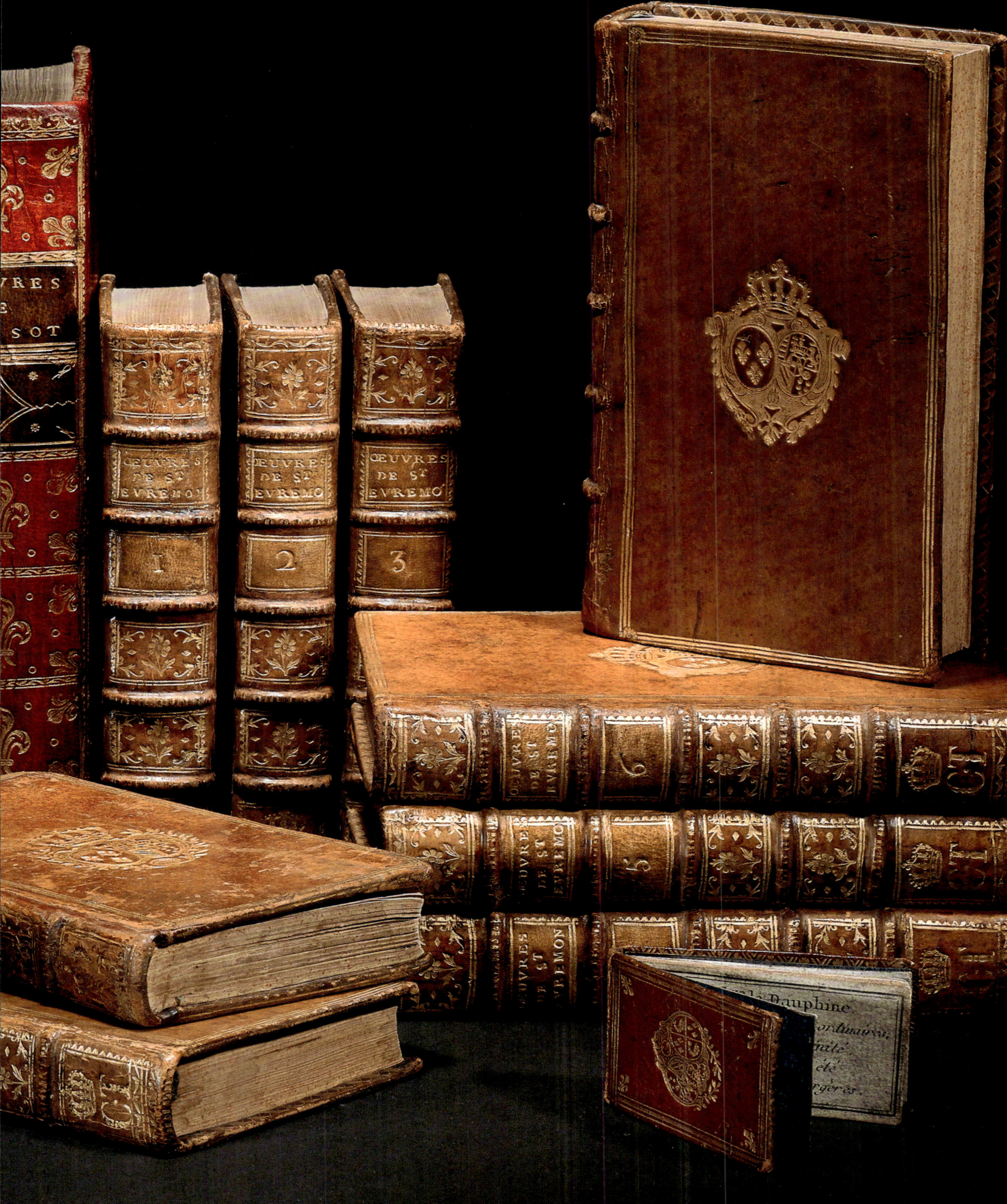
ŒUVRES DE St EVREMO
1
2
3
6
5
Dauphine

COPPER SAUCEPAN FROM THE CHATEAU DE VERSAILLES

This large copper cooking pot, stamped with the place of use and the date 1786, is one of the few everyday objects from the chateau kitchens that have come down to us.

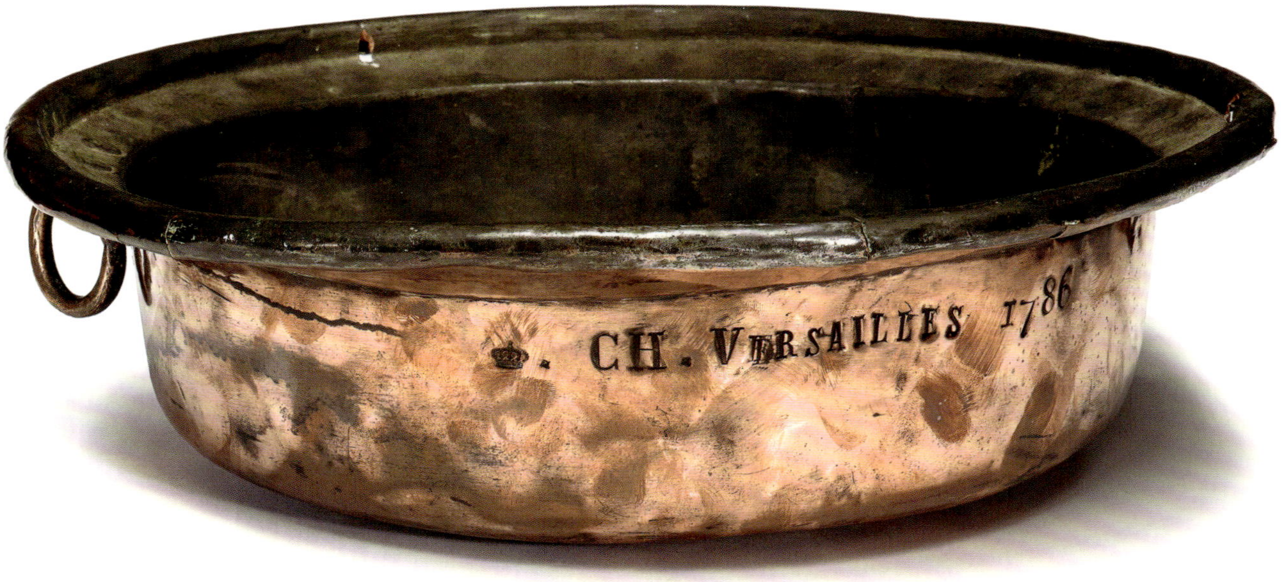

MARIE-ANTOINETTE'S WATERING CAN FROM THE TRIANON PALACE

The copper plaque reads in English as follows: "Watering can originally belonging to Marie-Antoinette, given to the painter Armand Leleux in 1867 by Eudore Soulié curator at the Musée de Versailles." Armand Hubert Leleux (1818-1885), brother of Adolphe Leleux (1812-1891), was a pupil of Jean Auguste Dominique Ingres. Eudore Soulié (1817-1876) was curator at Versailles from 1850 until his death. This watering can is a reminder of how much the sovereign enjoyed the Trianon gardens.

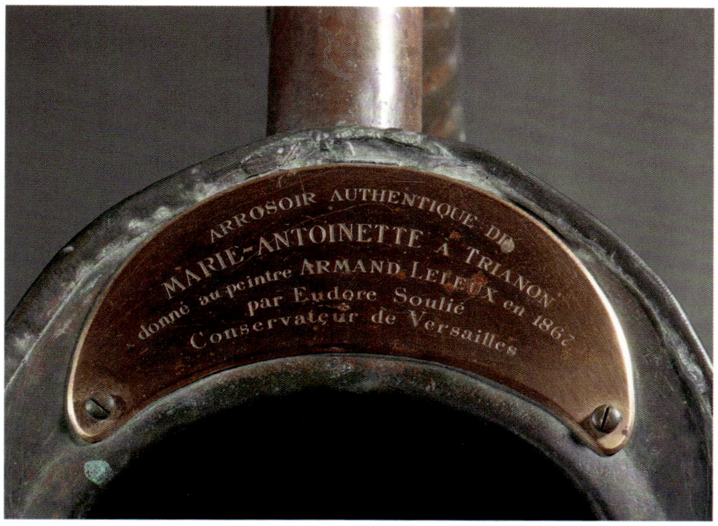

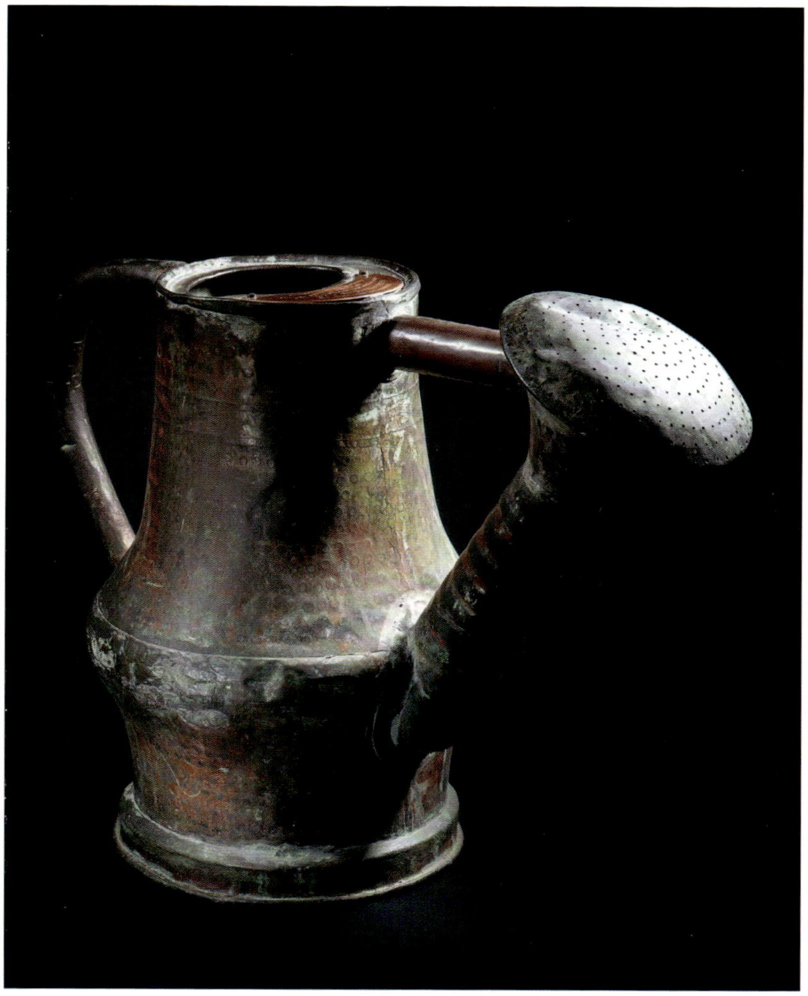

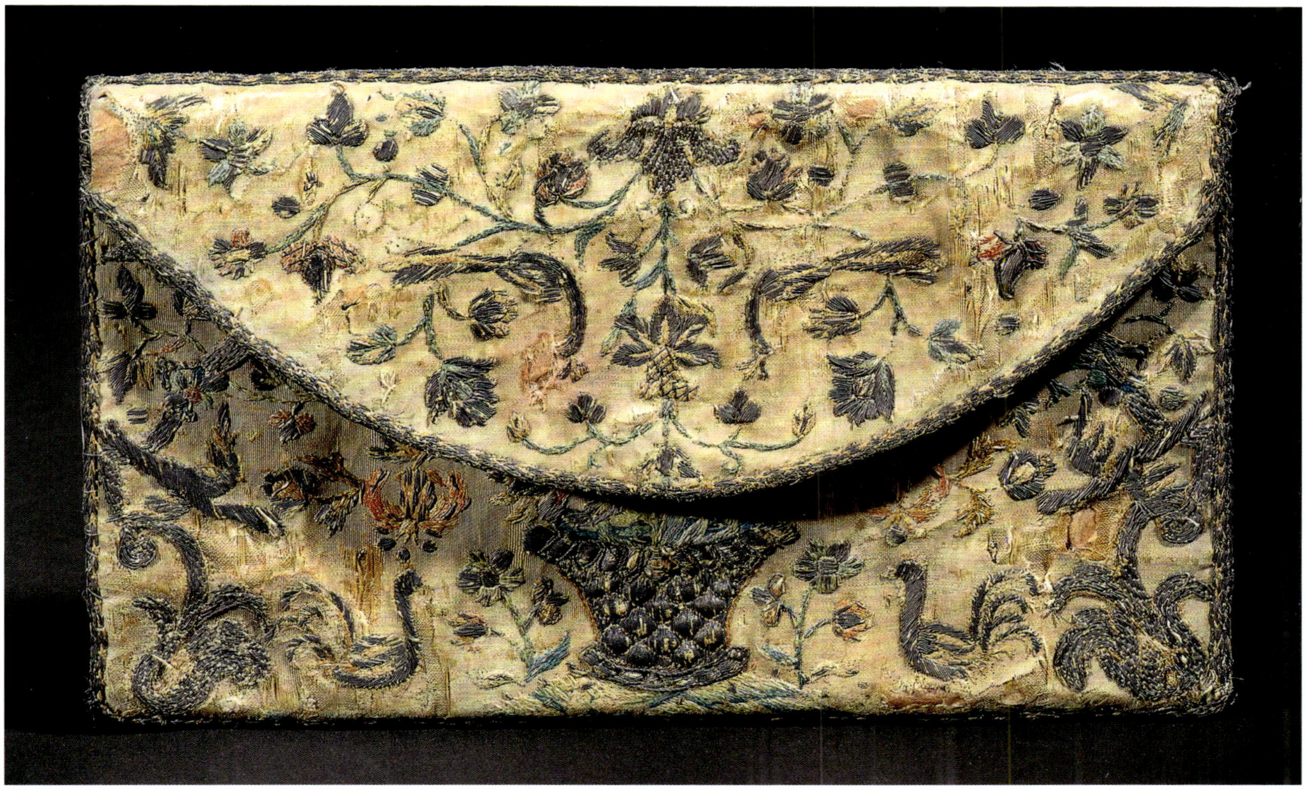

BALL CLUTCH PURSE ATTRIBUTED TO MARIE-ANTOINETTE

Small silk clutch purse, richly embroidered with birds and baskets of flowers, thought to have belonged to the Queen. It comes from the famous Alain Bancel collection of revolutionary paraphernalia (which was sold off in 2003).

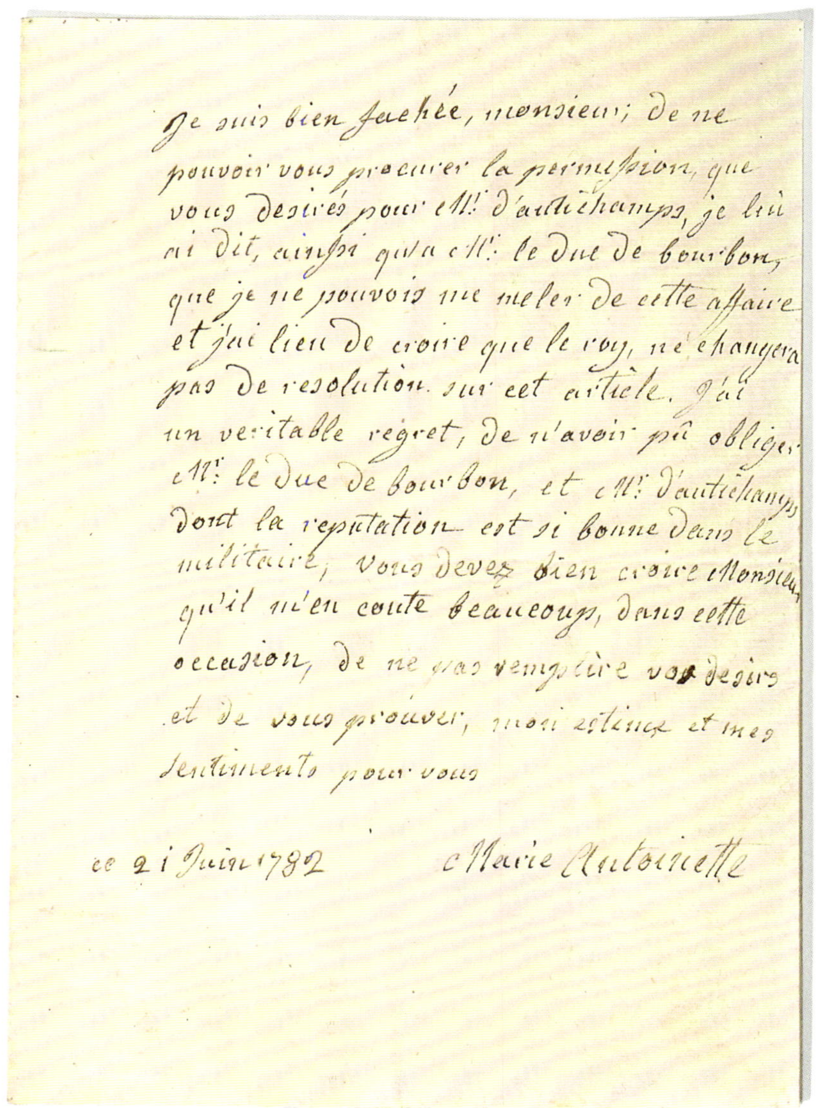

Je suis bien fachée, monsieur; de ne pouvoir vous procurer la permission, que vous desirés pour Mr d'autichamps, je lui ai dit, ainsi qu'a Mr le duc de bourbon, que je ne pouvois me meler de cette affaire et j'ai lieu de croire que le roy, ne changera pas de resolution. sur cet article. j'ai un veritable regret, de n'avoir pû obliger Mr le duc de bourbon, et Mr d'autichamps, dont la reputation est si bonne dans le militaire, vous devez bien croire Monsieur qu'il m'en coute beaucoup, dans cette occasion, de ne pas remplire vos desirs et de vous prouver, mon estime et mes sentiments pour vous

ce 21 Juin 1782 Marie Antoinette

LETTER FROM MARIE-ANTOINETTE

This very rare handwritten letter on plain paper, signed "Marie-Antoinette," was penned in response to a request she received regarding Antoine-Joseph Eulalie de Beaumont, Count of Autichamp (1744-1822), *maréchal de camp* in 1782. It reads in English as follows: "It grieves me greatly Sir to be unable/ to obtain the permission you seek for My Lord d'Autichamps, [but] as I/ told him and My Lord the Duke of Bourbon/ I cannot become mixed up in this affair/and I have reason to believe that the King will not change/ his mind on this issue [...]".

SÈVRES ROYAL MANUFACTORY, JAM POTS FROM MARIE-ANTOINETTE'S SO-CALLED "PERLES ET BARBEAUX" SERVICE

Tray and jam pot set embellished with pearls and cornflowers, dated 1781 and marked with two crowned interlaced L's. It comes from a 295-piece service commissioned for the exclusive use of the Queen from the Sèvres Manufactory in July 1781, delivered on 2 January 1782. Cost: 12,420 *livres*.

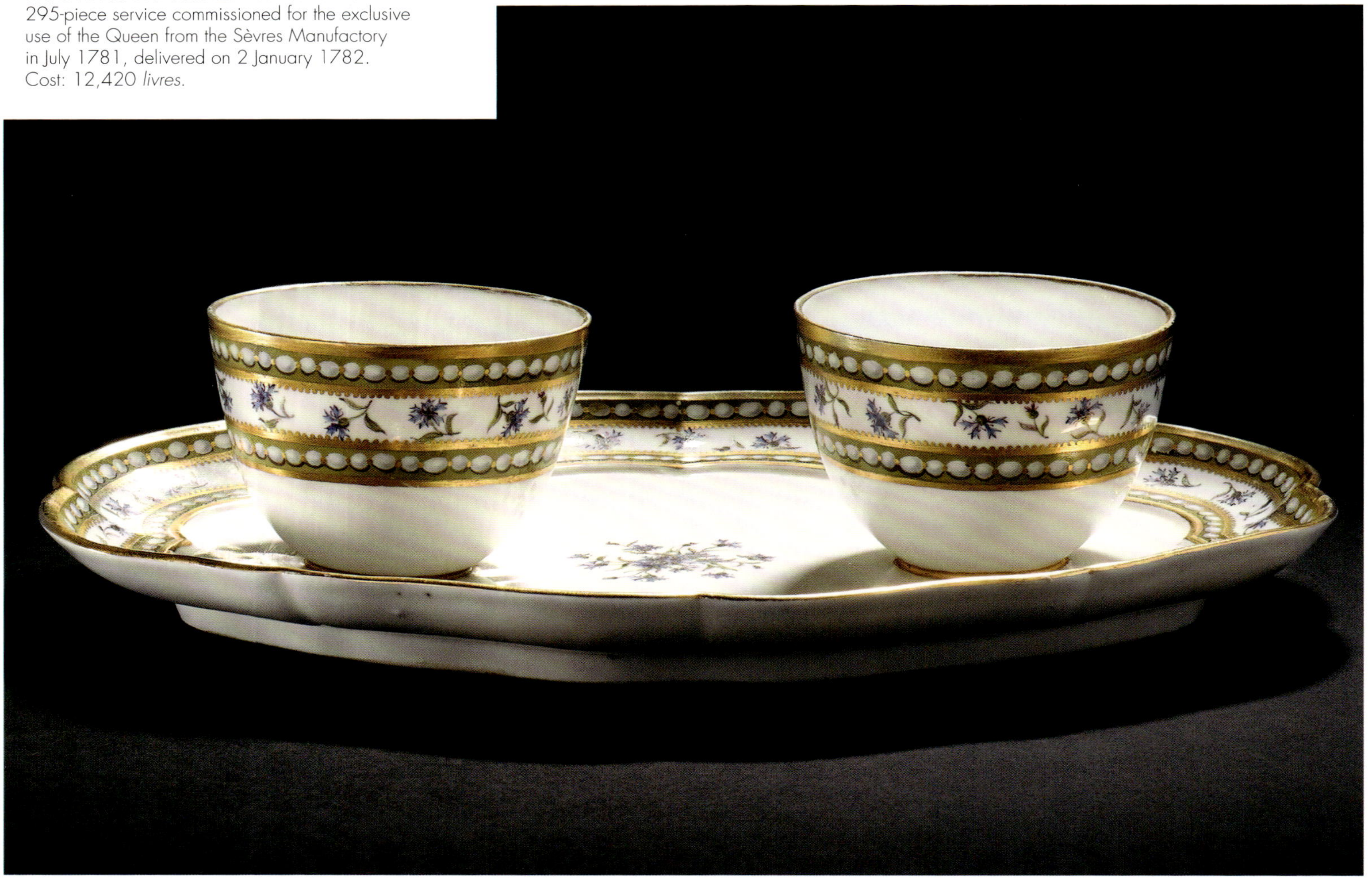

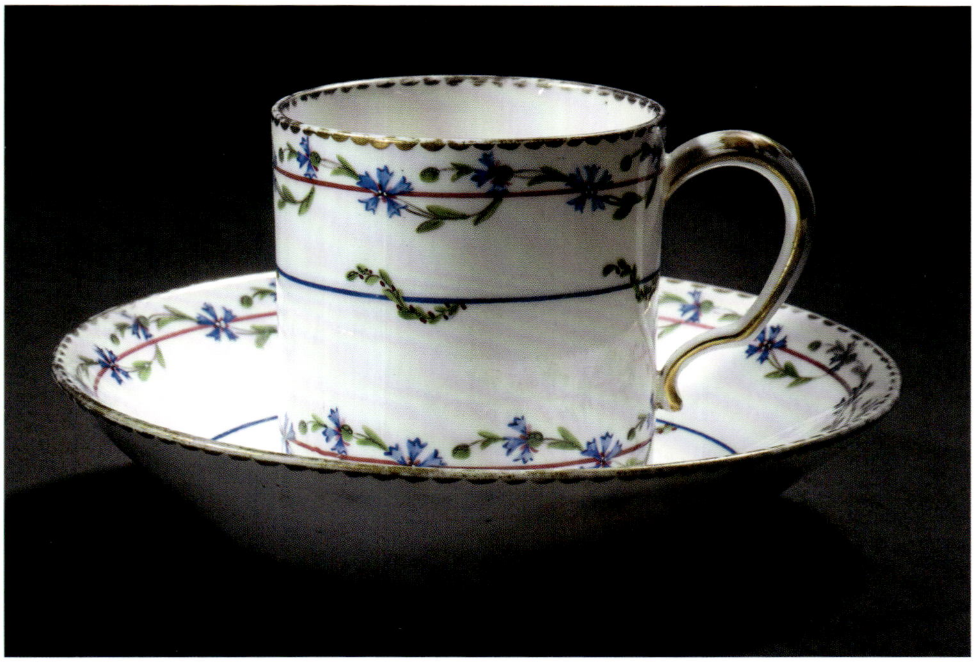

SÈVRES ROYAL MANUFACTORY, *BLEUET* (CORNFLOWER) CUP FROM THE "GOBELET DU ROI" SERVICE

Porcelain service with cornflower motif and pink and blue borders, commissioned in 1782 and delivered to Versailles on 11 May 1783. It was destined for use by the *Officiers du Gobelet* (the King's butlers) responsible for supplying the King's Household with bread, wine and fruit.

FRUIT KNIVES FROM MARIE-ANTOINETTE'S GOLD SERVICE
INVENTAIRE DES SCELLÉS 1791

These fruit knives, hallmarked by Parisian master-goldsmith Henri Clavel and the knife-maker Pierre-François Grangeret, are a superb testament to the refinement of the royal table. On the eve of the Revolution, Marie-Antoinette took almost all of her gold tableware to be melted down at the Royal Mint in order to boost the royal coffers. These two knives, with their ornately carved gold handles, one with gold blade, one with steel blade, are probably the only surviving examples of their type. An inventory taken of the Queen's silver at Versailles on 24 June 1791 lists two knives under entry number 54, "Gold" section, "one with gold blade, one with steel blade" (see pictured list). A copy of that inventory, since acquired by this collection, was countersigned and retained by a certain Bouvier, who was appointed *garde-vaisselle* (yeoman of the scullery) by the *Commissaires Municipaux et* Dépositaire de l'*Argenterie* (municipal commissioners acting as depository for the silver).

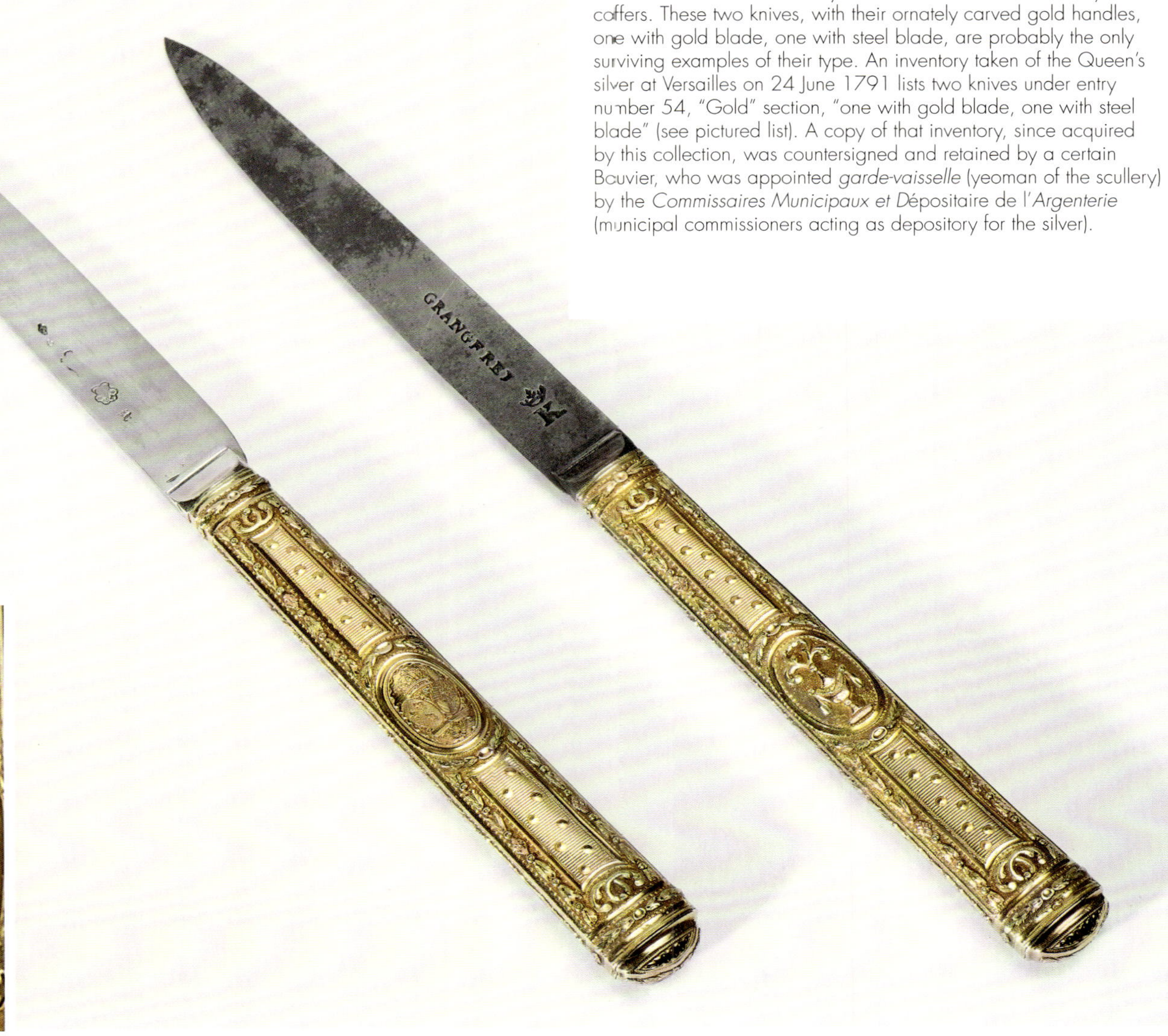

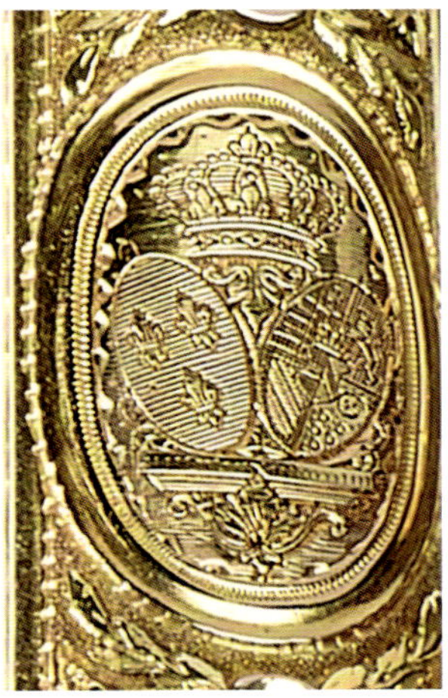

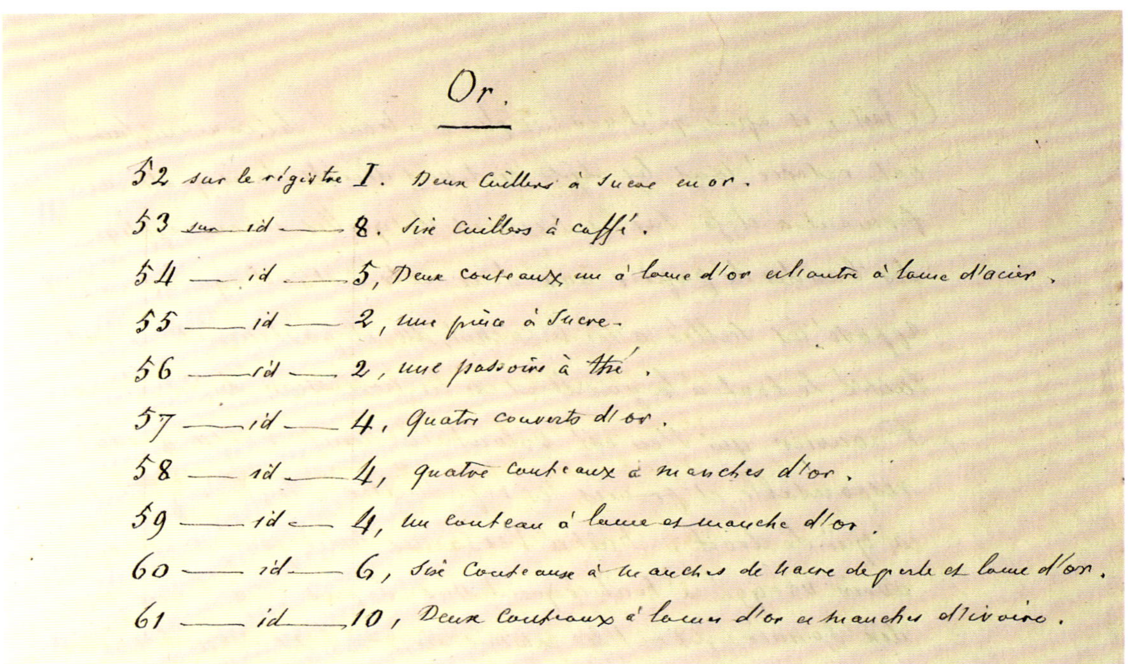

Or.

52 sur le régistre I. Deux Cuillers à sucre en or.
53 sur id 8. Six Cuillers à caffé.
54 — id — 5, Deux couteaux un à lame d'or et l'autre à lame d'acier.
55 — id — 2, une pince à sucre.
56 — id — 2, une passoire à thé.
57 — id — 4, Quatre couverts d'or.
58 — id — 4, quatre couteaux à manches d'or.
59 — id — 4, un couteau à lame et manche d'or.
60 — id — 6, Six Couteaux à manches de nacre de perle et lame d'or.
61 — id — 10, Deux Couteaux à lame d'or et manches d'ivoire.

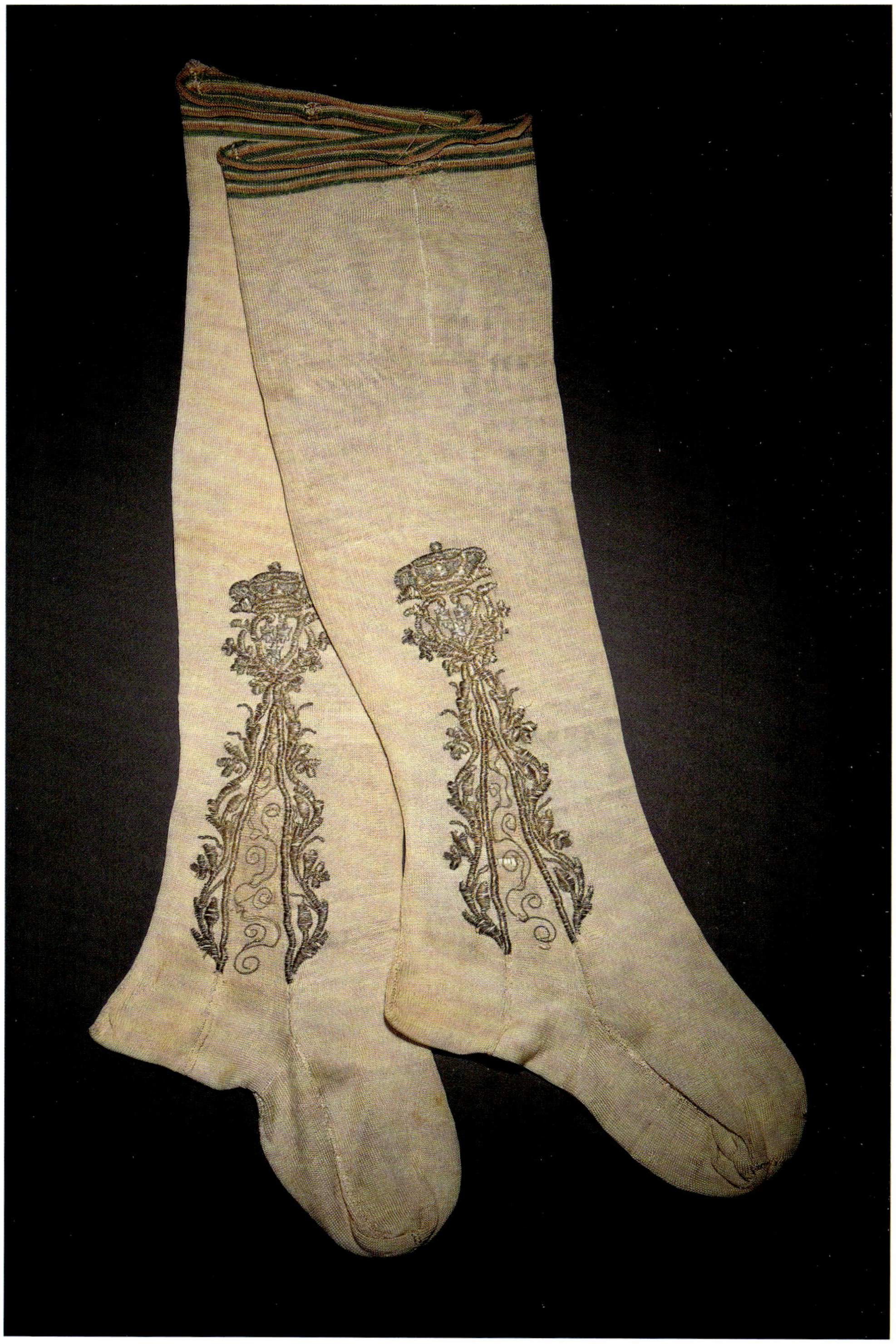

PAIR OF LOUIS XVI'S STOCKINGS

The crowned arms of France on these thigh-high stockings leave no doubt as to their regal provenance. The crest sits atop goldwork and silverwork leaf motifs, embroidered on a cream silk background. Another quite similar pair of Louis XVI's stockings is preserved in the collections of the Musée Carnavalet.

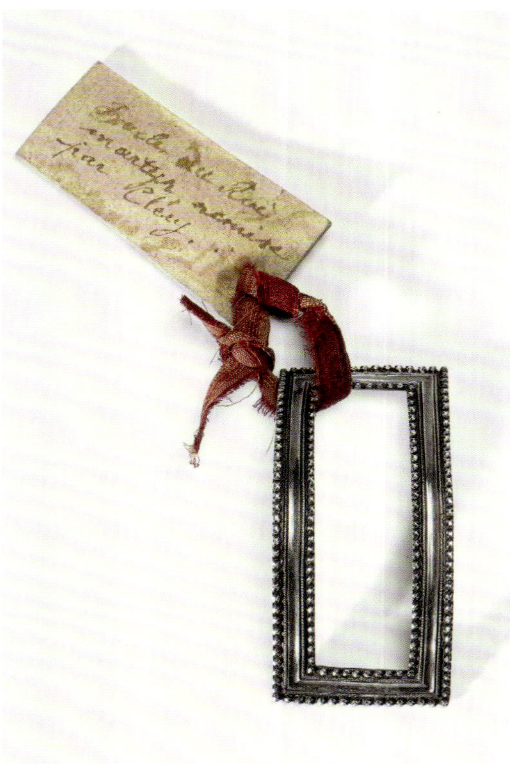

SHOE BUCKLE BELONGING TO LOUIS XVI

This silver buckle bears the hallmark of silversmith François-Noël Devaux (1783-1784), and was passed on to the Duke of Looz-Corswarem (1732-1803) by the loyal Cléry. The Duke had arranged for a memorial mass to be celebrated for Louis XVI a year after his death. This pair was kept by his descendants until it became part of the collection.

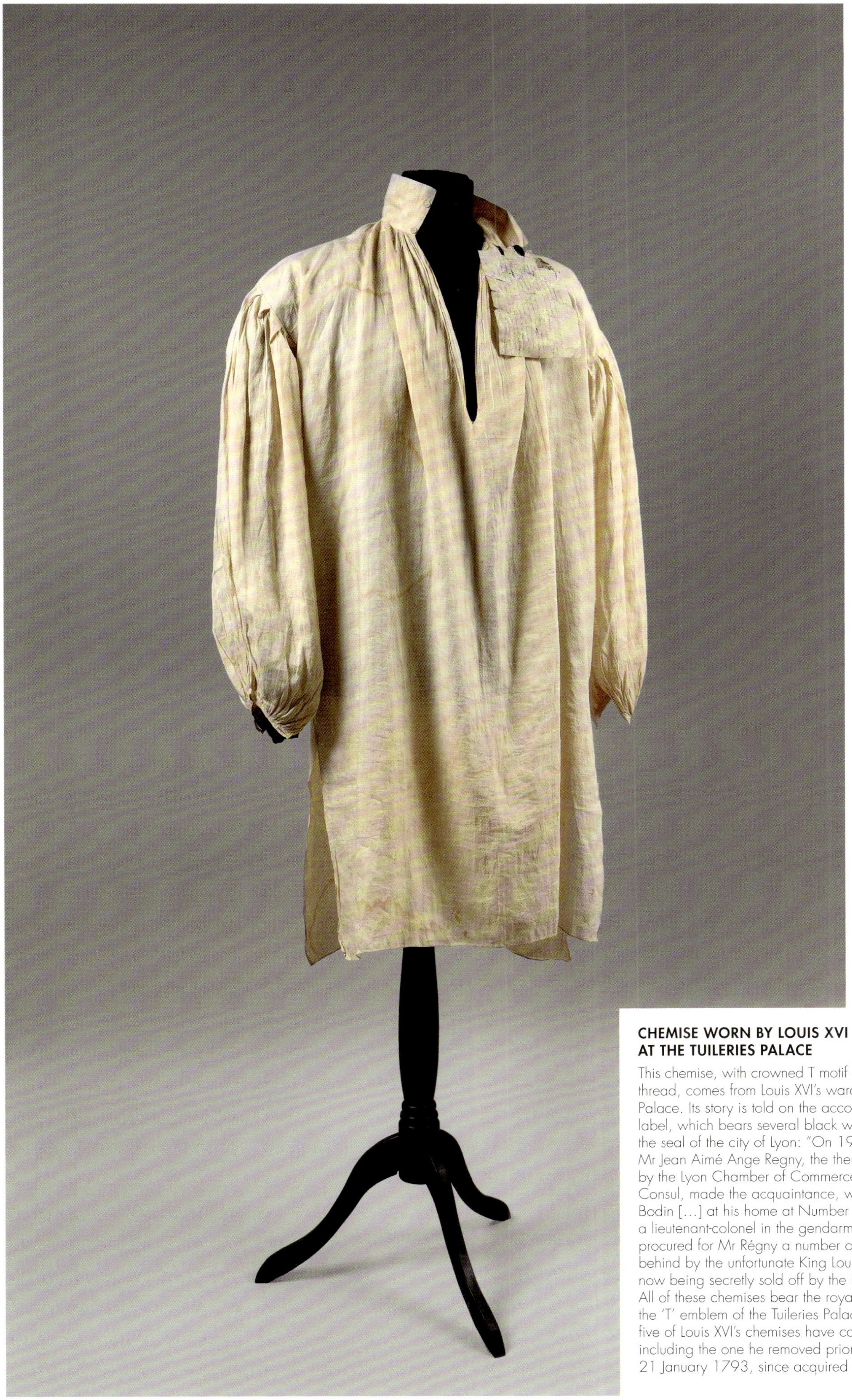

CHEMISE WORN BY LOUIS XVI AT THE TUILERIES PALACE

This chemise, with crowned T motif embroidered with red thread, comes from Louis XVI's wardrobe at the Tuileries Palace. Its story is told on the accompanying parchment label, which bears several black wax seals, including the seal of the city of Lyon: "On 19 October 1801, Mr Jean Aimé Ange Regny, the then deputy appointed by the Lyon Chamber of Commerce to Bonaparte First Consul, made the acquaintance, while visiting Mr ... Bodin [...] at his home at Number 7 Rue du Helder, of a lieutenant-colonel in the gendarmerie [...]. This officer procured for Mr Régny a number of chemises left behind by the unfortunate King Louis XVI, which were now being secretly sold off by the French Government. All of these chemises bear the royal crown and the 'T' emblem of the Tuileries Palace..." Fewer than five of Louis XVI's chemises have come down to us, including the one he removed prior to execution on 21 January 1793, since acquired by this collection.

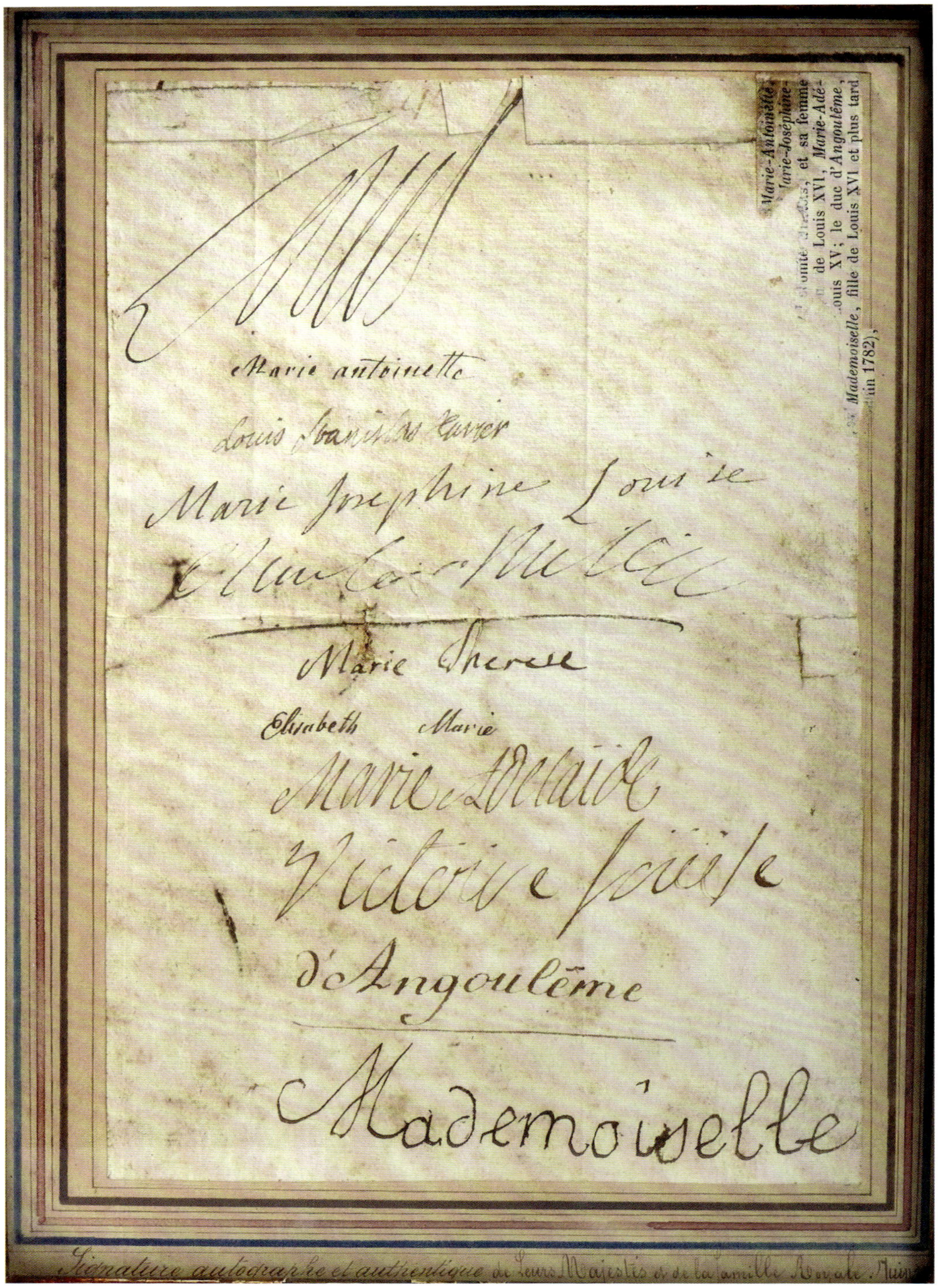

SIGNATURES OF THE MEMBERS OF THE ROYAL FAMILY

It is impossible not to feel deeply moved by this document. One of the most intimate records of the royal family ever captured on paper, it bears the signatures of 10 of its members: Louis XVI, Marie-Antoinette, the Count and Countess of Provence, the Count and Countess of Artois and their son, the Duke of Angoulême and daughter "Mademoiselle," plus, but not pictured here, Louis XVI's sister Madame Elisabeth, and Louis XV's daughters, Madame Adélaïde and Madame Victoire.

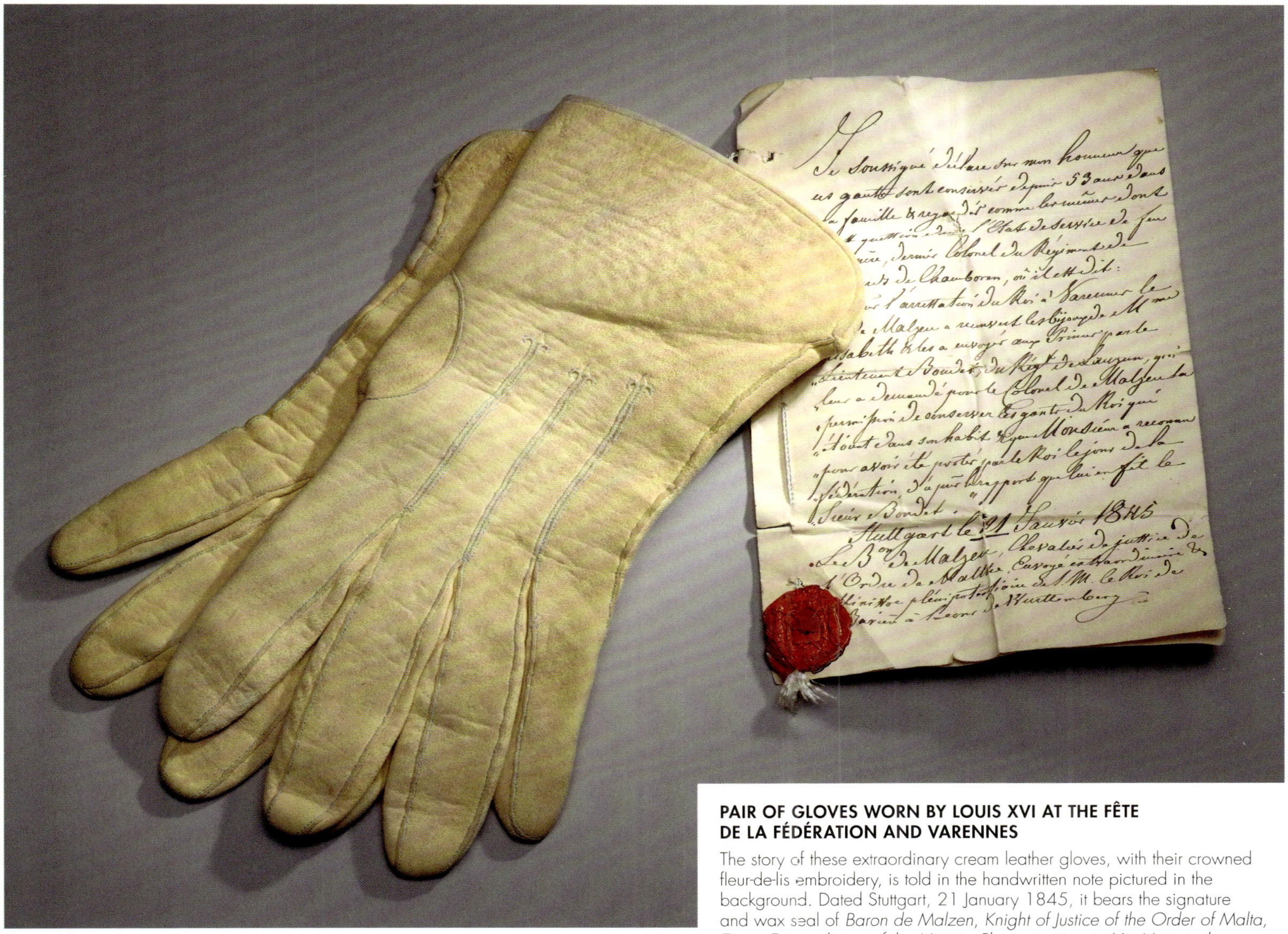

PAIR OF GLOVES WORN BY LOUIS XVI AT THE FÊTE DE LA FÉDÉRATION AND VARENNES

The story of these extraordinary cream leather gloves, with their crowned fleur-de-lis embroidery, is told in the handwritten note pictured in the background. Dated Stuttgart, 21 January 1845, it bears the signature and wax seal of *Baron de Malzen, Knight of Justice of the Order of Malta, Envoy Extraordinary of the Minister Plenipotentiary to His Majesty the King of Bavaria at the Court of Wurttemberg*. The Baron was the son of a former *colonel des hussards* and counter-revolutionary who went over to the enemy following the Varennes incident. Abandoning the King, the Baron's father joined the regiment deployed along the Ardennes, under command of Lieutenant-Colonel Hock. As this note explains, these gloves were "[...] preserved for 53 years by my family, considered to be precisely those described in the statement of service submitted by my late father, the last colonel to lead the Hussars of Chamborant, which states as follows: Following the King's arrest at Varennes, Baron de Malzen recovered the jewels belonging to Mme Elisabeth and sent them to the Princes care of Lieutenant Boudet, Lauzun Regiment, who requested permission on behalf of Colonel Malzen to keep the gloves forming part of the king's attire, which were recognized by 'Monsieur' [the King's elder brother], on the basis of Lieutenant Boudet's report, as having been worn by His Majesty at the Fête de la Federation." The gloves were later gifted in Stuttgart by Baron de Malzen to his fellow officer in the Wurttemberg diplomatic corps, Charles-François-Gabriel-Antoine, known as Viscount de Fontenay (1829-1889), Consul General of France, whose descendants have held onto the precious memento ever since. (F. Feuillet de Conches: *Louis XVI, Marie-Antoinette et Madame Elisabeth, Lettres et Documents Inédits*, Volume II, Paris, Henri Plon).

LA FAYETTE AND CHARETTE: TWO MEN CAUGHT UP IN TURMOIL

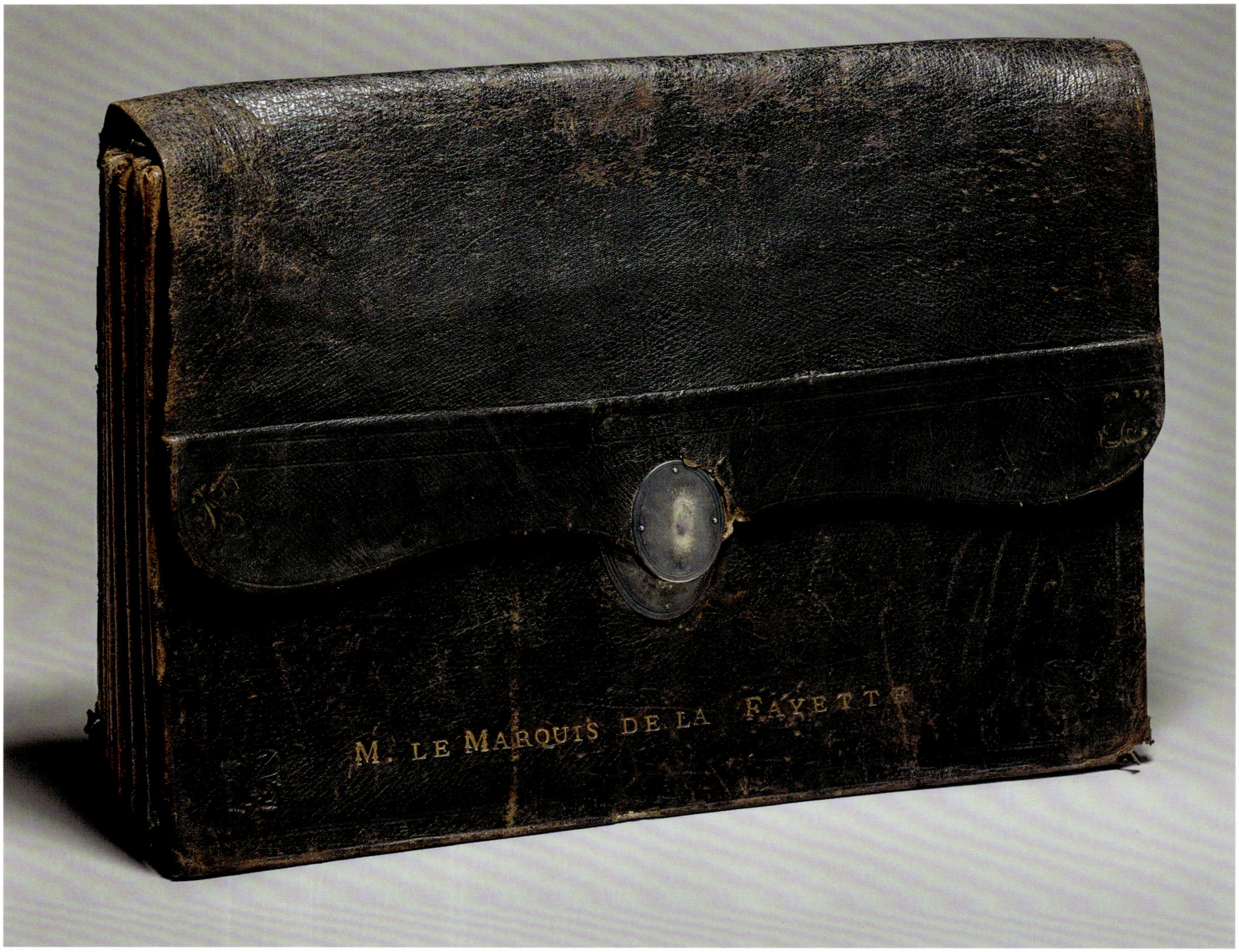

PORTFOLIO BELONGING TO LA FAYETTE

This well-worn black leather portfolio testifies to prolonged daily use, as confirmed by the name on the cover. It belonged to the Marquis de La Fayette, a man whose destiny was closely entwined with the history of France. From Paris to the court of Louis XVI and from the American War of Independence to the Fête de la Fédération, the figure of La Fayette is inseparable from the spirit of liberty.

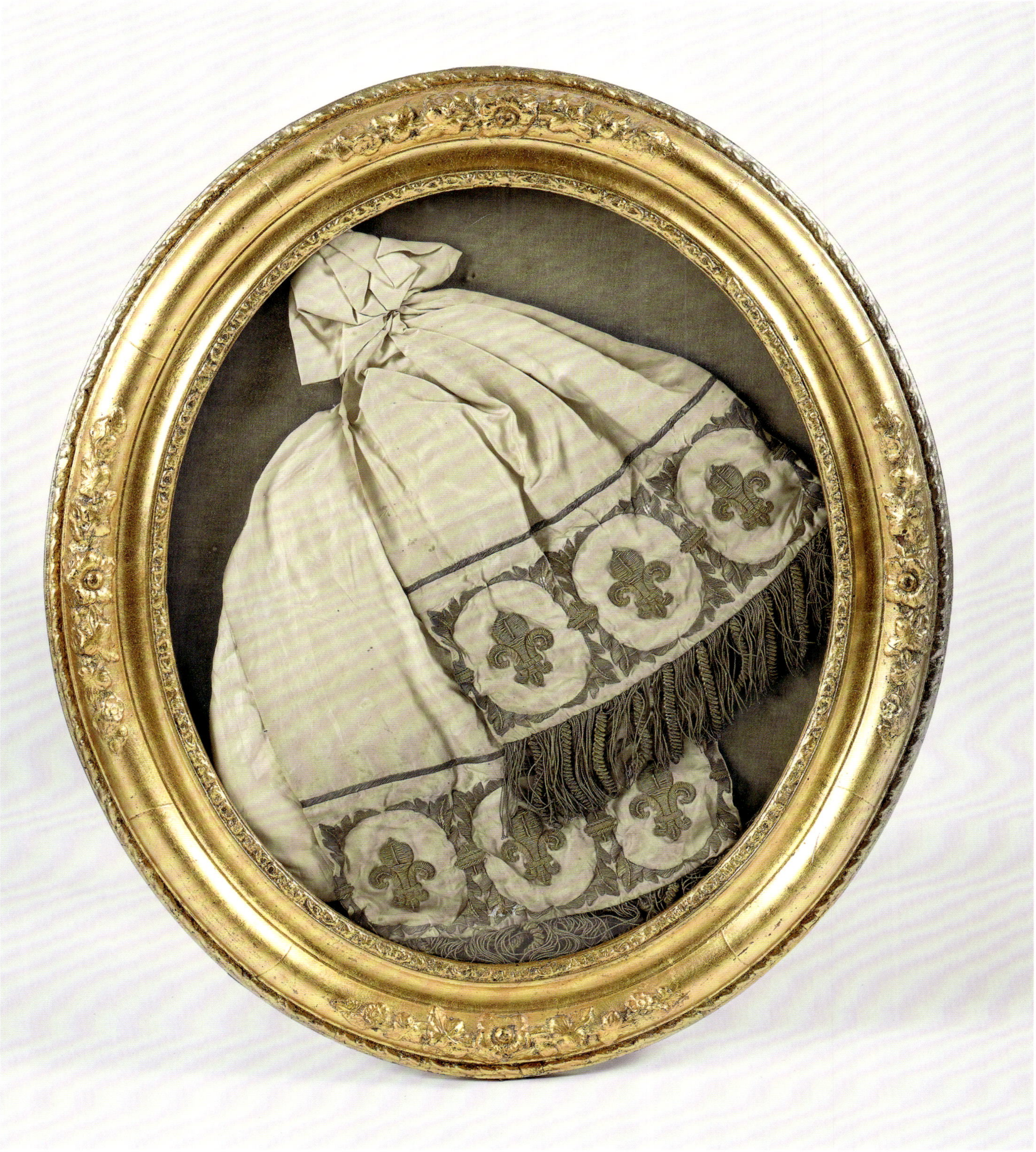

SCARF BELONGING TO GENERAL CHARETTE, LEADER OF THE VENDÉE INSURRECTIONISTS

This cream silk scarf, with fleur-de-lis motifs embroidered with twisted gold thread, encircled the waist of General François Athanase Charette de La Contrie (1763-1796). After joining forces with the Vendée insurrectionists in March 1793, Charette was among the leaders who signed the peace treaty of La Jaunaye in February 1795 before taking up arms once again in June. Appointed leader of the Royalist Catholic army in July, he was captured and shot on 29 March 1796 in Nantes. The scarf has been preserved as a memento by his family ever since, immortalized in a famous portrait executed by Alfred de Chasteigner in 1819.

THE STORMING OF THE BASTILLE

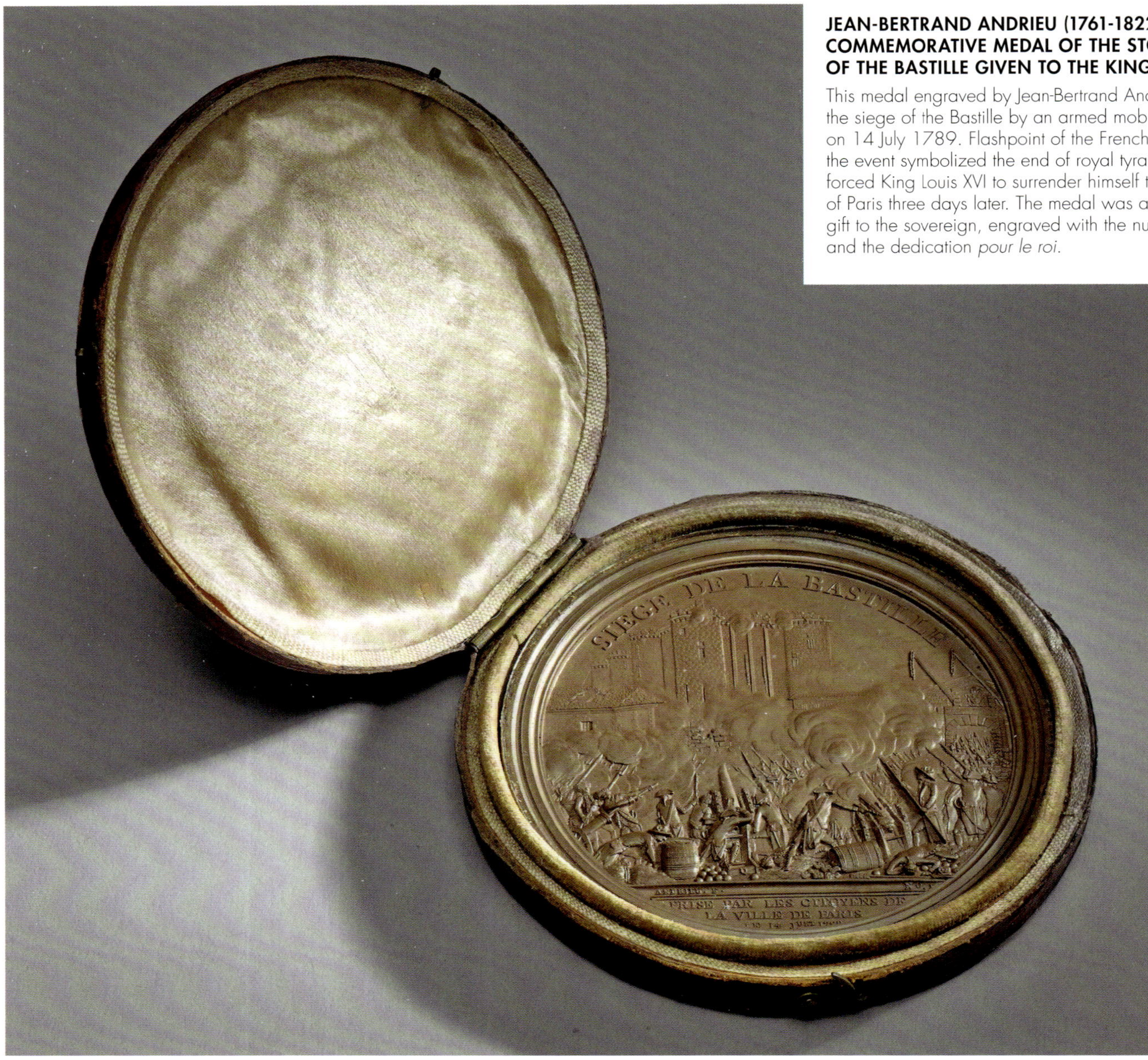

JEAN-BERTRAND ANDRIEU (1761-1822), COMMEMORATIVE MEDAL OF THE STORMING OF THE BASTILLE GIVEN TO THE KING

This medal engraved by Jean-Bertrand Andrieu depicts the siege of the Bastille by an armed mob of Parisians on 14 July 1789. Flashpoint of the French Revolution, the event symbolized the end of royal tyranny and forced King Louis XVI to surrender himself to the people of Paris three days later. The medal was a personal gift to the sovereign, engraved with the number two and the dedication *pour le roi*.

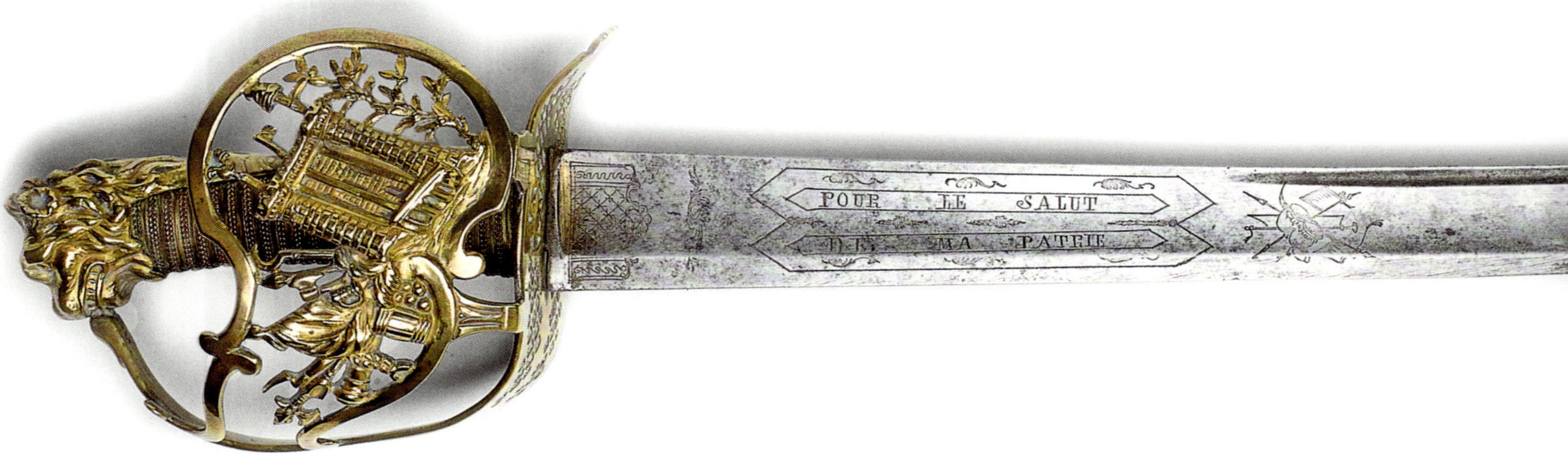

POSTER ANNOUNCING THE DEMOLITION OF THE BASTILLE

Poster dated 29 November 1789 announcing the demolition of the Bastille by the Paris Commune and the granting of the salvage rights to the building contractor Pierre-François Palloy.

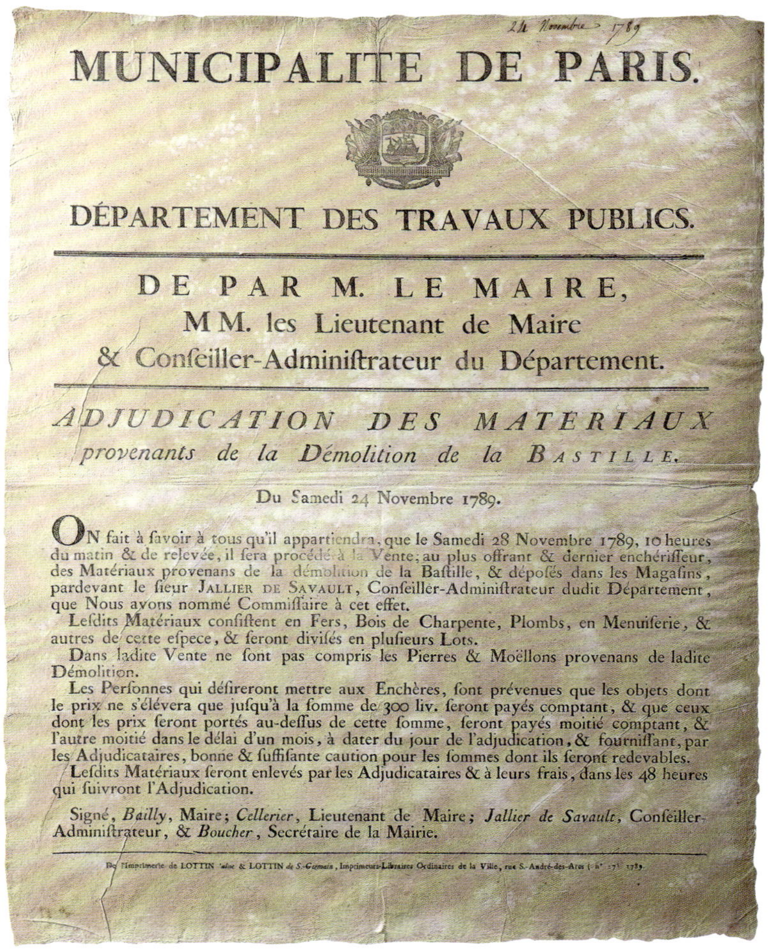

24 Novembre 1789

MUNICIPALITE DE PARIS.

DÉPARTEMENT DES TRAVAUX PUBLICS.

DE PAR M. LE MAIRE,
MM. les Lieutenant de Maire
& Conſeiller-Adminiſtrateur du Département.

ADJUDICATION DES MATERIAUX
provenants de la Démolition de la B A S T I L L E.

Du Samedi 24 Novembre 1789.

ON fait à ſavoir à tous qu'il appartiendra, que le Samedi 28 Novembre 1789, 10 heures du matin & de relevée, il ſera procédé à la Vente, au plus offrant & dernier enchériſſeur, des Matériaux provenans de la démolition de la Baſtille, & dépoſés dans les Magaſins, pardevant le ſieur JALLIER DE SAVAULT, Conſeiller-Adminiſtrateur dudit Département, que Nous avons nommé Commiſſaire à cet effet.

Leſdits Matériaux conſiſtent en Fers, Bois de Charpente, Plombs, en Menuiſerie, & autres de cette eſpece, & ſeront diviſés en pluſieurs Lots.

Dans ladite Vente ne ſont pas compris les Pierres & Moëllons provenans de ladite Démolition.

Les Perſonnes qui déſireront mettre aux Enchères, ſont prévenues que les objets dont le prix ne s'élévera que juſqu'à la ſomme de 300 liv. ſeront payés comptant, & que ceux dont les prix ſeront portés au-deſſus de cette ſomme, ſeront payés moitié comptant, & l'autre moitié dans le délai d'un mois, à dater du jour de l'adjudication, & fourniſſant, par les Adjudicataires, bonne & ſuffiſante caution pour les ſommes dont ils ſeront redevables.

Leſdits Matériaux ſeront enlevés par les Adjudicataires & à leurs frais, dans les 48 heures qui ſuivront l'Adjudication.

Signé, *Bailly*, Maire; *Cellerier*, Lieutenant de Maire; *Jallier de Savault*, Conſeiller-Adminiſtrateur, & *Boucher*, Secrétaire de la Mairie.

De l'Imprimerie de LOTTIN l'aîné & LOTTIN de S.-Germain, Imprimeurs-Libraires Ordinaires de la Ville, rue S.-André-des-Arcs 1789.

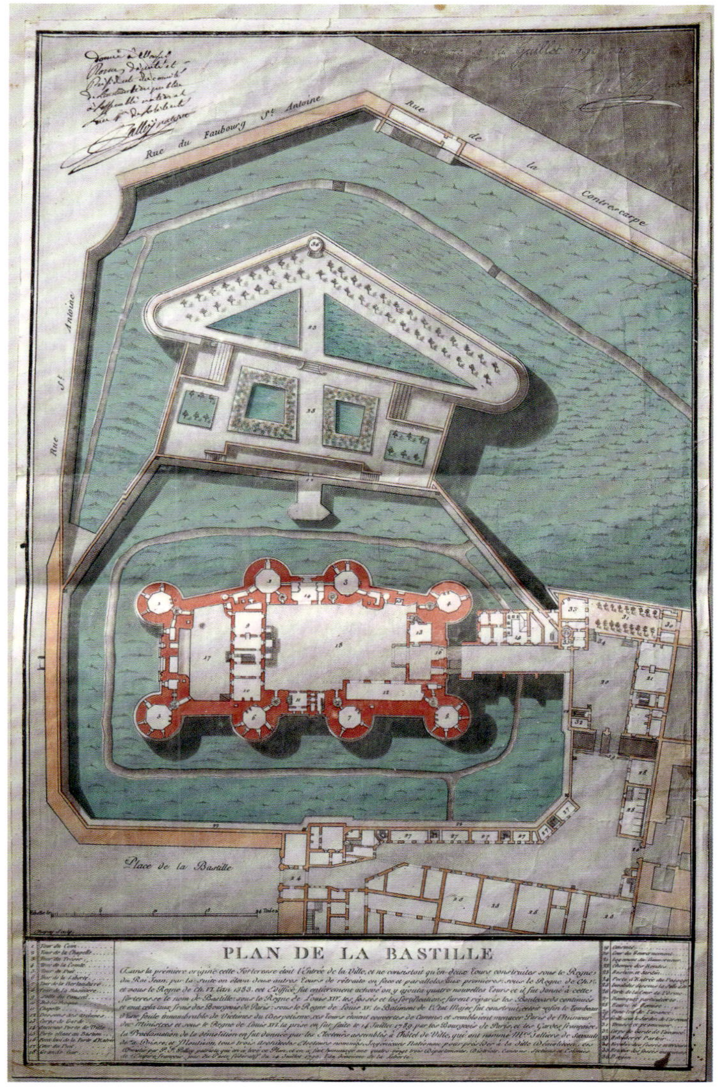

PIERRE-FRANÇOIS PALLOY (1755-1835), WATERCOLOR MAP OF THE BASTILLE GIFTED TO DEPUTY ROMME IN 1792

In the aftermath of the storming of the Bastille, the prison fortress was dismantled. The work was entrusted to a private entrepreneur called Pierre-François Palloy, who employed 800 workmen from 15 July until May 1791. Regarded as one of the shrewdest "businessmen" of his day, Palloy is credited with establishing the Bastille as a site of national memory. He sent miniatures of the Bastille, carved from its dismantled blocks, to the capital cities of each French department and produced medals and maps commemorating the event. The map pictured here is hand-signed and dedicated by *Palloy patriote* to: "Deputy Rom [sic] and the *Assemblé Nation* [sic], Year 4 of Liberty." Charles Gilbert Romme was the architect of the revolutionary calendar, the founder of the Club des Amis de la Lois, the *Montagnard* Deputy for the Puy de Dôme and President of the Committee of Public Instruction.

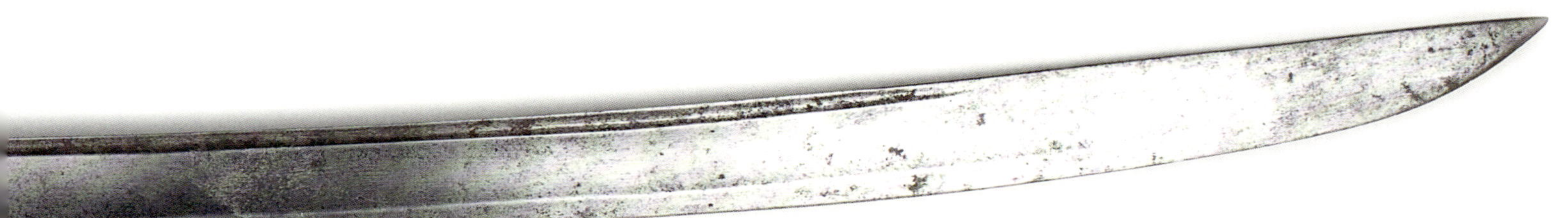

SABER OF THE CONQUERORS OF THE BASTILLE

Bronze and steel sword, of a type known as a Montmorency after the French regiment of the *Ancien Régime* that introduced it, this example was awarded to one of the conquerors of the Bastille (which is represented on the guard) – presumably a member of the bourgeoisie since he subsequently became an officer in the newly formed National Guard. Very few of these sabers have come down to us.

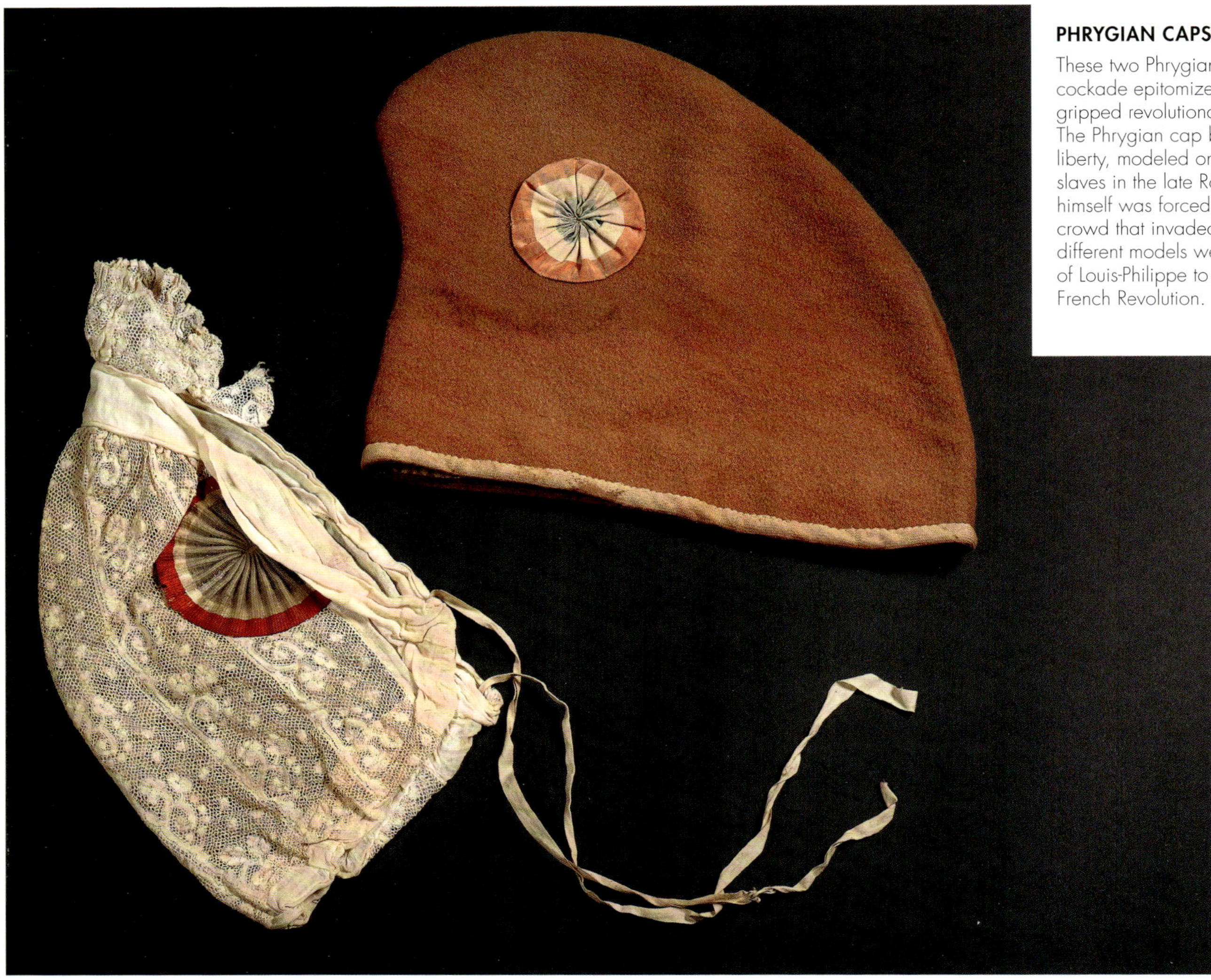

PHRYGIAN CAPS

These two Phrygian caps with tricolor cockade epitomize the new fashions that gripped revolutionary France circa 1792. The Phrygian cap became a symbol of liberty, modeled on the hat worn by former slaves in the late Roman Empire. The King himself was forced to wear one by the crowd that invaded the Tuileries. Many different models were made in the reign of Louis-Philippe to commemorate the French Revolution.

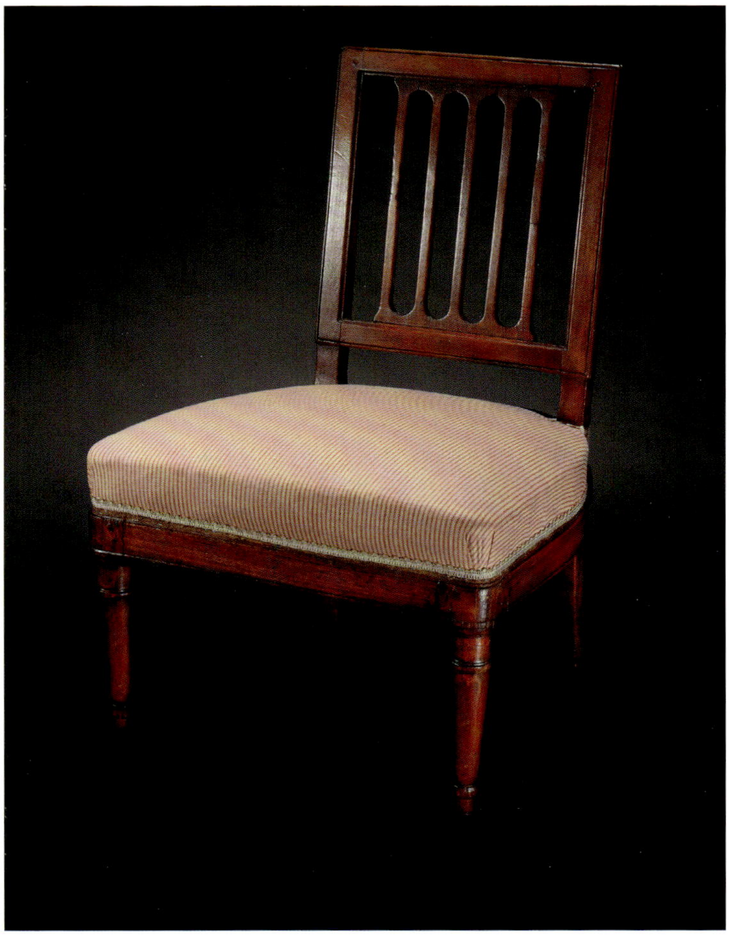

GEORGES JACOB (1739-1814), LOW FIRESIDE CHAIR FROM THE NATIONAL ASSEMBLY (FRENCH REVOLUTION)

This small lathe-back fireside chair (*chauffeuse*), its uprights slimmed down with a rasp, is typical of the work of Georges Jacob. Marked *ASS NAT* and numbered 54, it was part of the furnishings for the National Assembly that came into force in the French Revolution. In the period 1794-1799, Georges Jacob became a regular supplier to the National Convention. An order dated 1794 gives the following details: "Convention: summary minutes of the meeting of the Committee of Inspection, recorded by F Boyer, 16 Ventose Year II: supply of furniture and fittings to the National Convention, supply of furniture and chairs to the committees of Public Health and Public Safety."

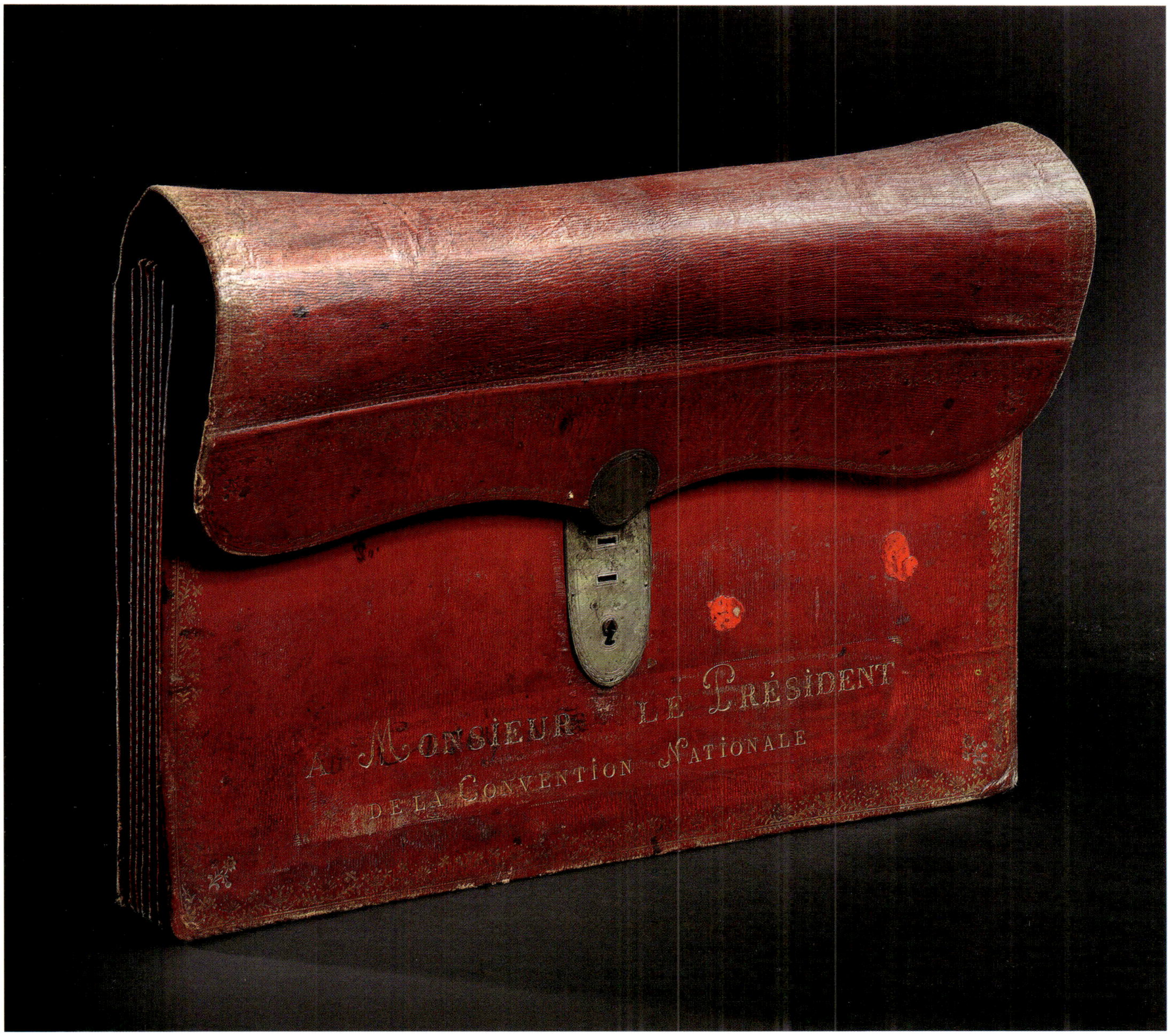

PORTFOLIO OF THE PRESIDENT OF THE NATIONAL CONVENTION

This very rare portfolio in red Morocco leather was designed for the President of the National Convention – the body that governed France from September 1792 until October 1795, following the storming of the Tuileries and the fall of the monarchy. One of its first acts was to establish the First Republic of France.

THE DECLARATION OF THE RIGHTS OF MAN AND THE CITIZEN

ARTICLE I

The purpose of society is for everyone to attain happiness. The Government is established to guarantee people the enjoyment of their natural and imprescriptible rights.

II

These rights are the right to equality, liberty, security, and property.

III

All men are equal by nature and before the law.

IV

The law is the free and solemn expression of the people's will; it is the same for everyone, whether it protects or punishes; it can only order what is right and useful to society; it can only forbid what is harmful to it.

DECLARATION OF THE RIGHTS OF MAN OF 1793

Large painted paper panel by the House of Daguet featuring the Declaration of the Rights of Man, originally intended for public display in places such as in the meeting hall of the Committee of Public Health. The Declaration of the Rights of Man and the Citizen of 1793 served as the preamble to the so-called Constitution of the Year 1 (approved on 24 June 1793 but never implemented). Its 35 articles restated the core principles of 1789 (liberty, civil equality, the right to property) but also added new rights such as the right to public education and the right to resist oppression. Fewer than five examples have come down to us, including one now in the collections of Paris' Musée Carnavalet.

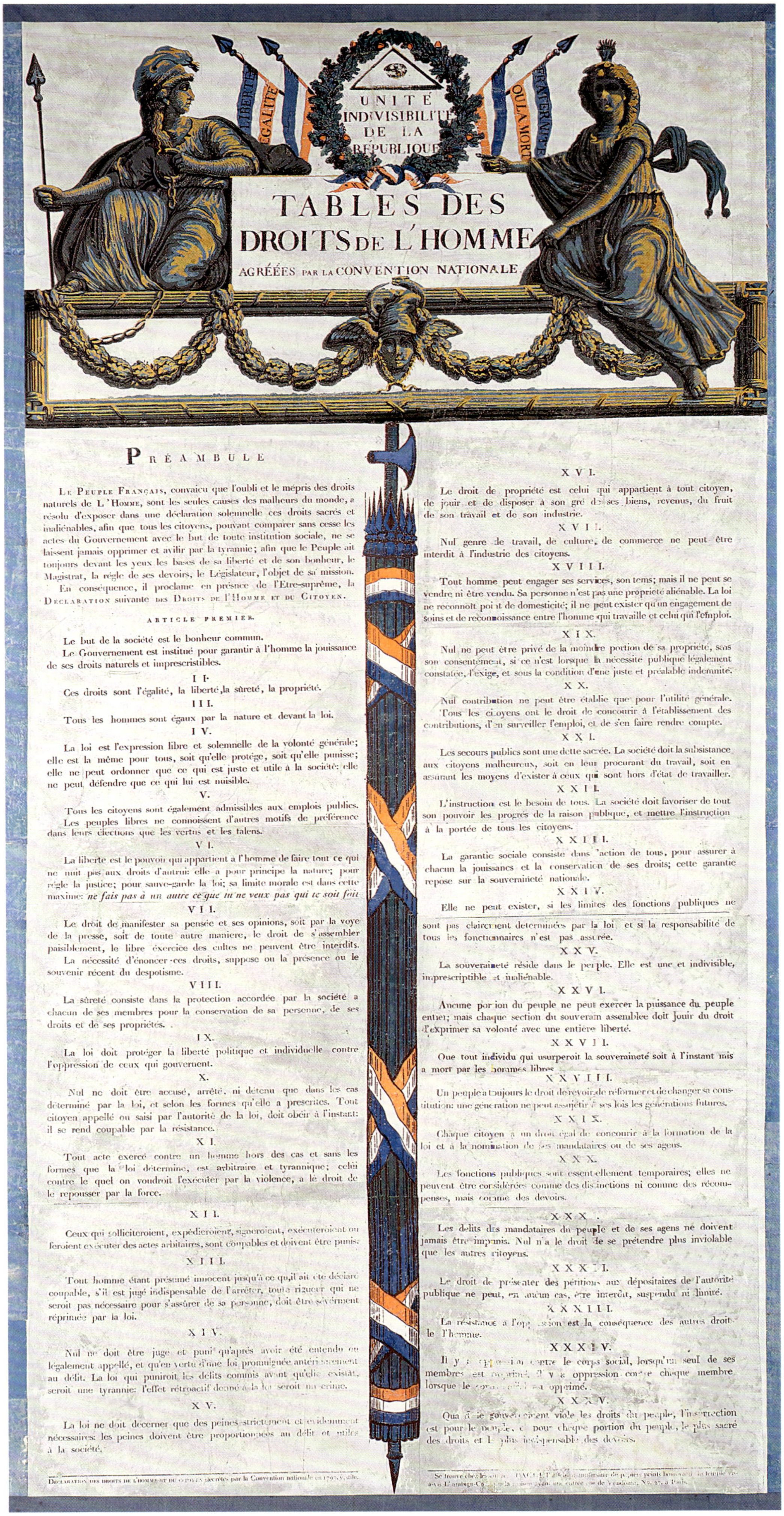

UNITÉ INDIVISIBILITÉ DE LA RÉPUBLIQUE

LIBERTÉ ÉGALITÉ

FRATERNITÉ OU LA MORT

TABLES DES DROITS DE L'HOMME

AGRÉÉES PAR LA CONVENTION NATIONALE

PRÉAMBULE

LE PEUPLE FRANÇAIS, convaincu que l'oubli et le mépris des droits naturels de L'HOMME, sont les seules causes des malheurs du monde, a résolu d'exposer dans une déclaration solemnelle ces droits sacrés et inaliénables, afin que tous les citoyens, pouvant comparer sans cesse les actes du Gouvernement avec le but de toute institution sociale, ne se laissent jamais opprimer et avilir par la tyrannie; afin que le Peuple ait toujours devant les yeux les bases de sa liberté et de son bonheur, le Magistrat, la régle de ses devoirs, le Législateur, l'objet de sa mission.

En conséquence, il proclame en présence de l'Etre-suprême, la DÉCLARATION suivante DES DROITS DE L'HOMME ET DU CITOYEN.

ARTICLE PREMIER.

Le but de la société est le bonheur commun.

Le Gouvernement est institué pour garantir à l'homme la jouissance de ses droits naturels et imprescristibles.

II.

Ces droits sont l'égalité, la liberté, la sûreté, la propriété.

III.

Tous les hommes sont égaux par la nature et devant la loi.

IV.

La loi est l'expression libre et solemnelle de la volonté générale; elle est la même pour tous, soit qu'elle protége, soit qu'elle punisse; elle ne peut ordonner que ce qui est juste et utile à la société: elle ne peut défendre que ce qui lui est nuisible.

V.

Tous les citoyens sont également admissibles aux emplois publics. Les peuples libres ne connoissent d'autres motifs de préférence dans leurs élections que les vertus et les talens.

VI.

La liberté est le pouvoir qui appartient à l'homme de faire tout ce qui ne nuit pas aux droits d'autrui: elle a pour principe la nature; pour régle la justice; pour sauve-garde la loi; sa limite morale est dans cette maxime: *ne fais pas à un autre ce que tu ne veux pas qui te soit fait*

VII.

Le droit de manifester sa pensée et ses opinions, soit par la voye de la presse, soit de toute autre maniere, le droit de s'assembler paisiblement, le libre éxercice des cultes ne peuvent être interdits.

La nécessité d'énoncer ces droits, suppose ou la présence ou le souvenir récent du despotisme.

VIII.

La sûreté consiste dans la protection accordée par la société a chacun de ses membres pour la conservation de sa personne, de ses droits et de ses propriétés.

IX.

La loi doit protéger la liberté politique et individuelle contre l'oppression de ceux qui gouvernent.

X.

Nul ne doit être accusé, arrêté, ni détenu que dans les cas déterminé par la loi, et selon les formes qu'elle a prescrites. Tout citoyen appellé ou saisi par l'autorité de la loi, doit obéir à l'instant: il se rend coupable par la résistance.

XI.

Tout acte exercé contre un homme hors des cas et sans les formes que la loi détermine, est arbitraire et tyrannique; celui contre le quel on voudroit l'exécuter par la violence, a le droit de le repousser par la force.

XII.

Ceux qui solliciteroient, expédieroient, signeroient, exécuteroient ou feroient exécuter des actes arbitaires, sont coupables et doivent être punis.

XIII.

Tout homme étant présumé innocent jusqu'à ce qu'il ait été déclaré coupable, s'il est jugé indispensable de l'arrêter, toute rigueur qui ne seroit pas nécessaire pour s'assûrer de sa personne, doit être sévérment réprimée par la loi.

XIV.

Nul ne doit être jugé et puni qu'après avoir été entendu ou légalement appellé, et qu'en vertu d'une loi promulguée antérieurement au délit. La loi qui puniroit les délits commis avant qu'elle existât, seroit une tyrannie: l'effet rétroactif donné à la loi seroit un crime.

XV.

La loi ne doit décerner que des peines strictement et évidemment nécessaires: les peines doivent être proportionnées au délit et utiles à la société.

XVI.

Le droit de propriété est celui qui appartient à tout citoyen, de jouir et de disposer à son gré de ses biens, revenus, du fruit de son travail et de son industrie.

XVII.

Nul genre de travail, de culture, de commerce ne peut être interdit à l'industrie des citoyens.

XVIII.

Tout homme peut engager ses services, son tems; mais il ne peut se vendre ni être vendu. Sa personne n'est pas une propriété aliénable. La loi ne reconnoît point de domesticité; il ne peut exister qu'un engagement de soins et de reconnoissance entre l'homme qui travaille et celui qui l'emploi.

XIX.

Nul ne peut être privé de la moindre portion de sa propriété, sans son consentement, si ce n'est lorsque la nécessité publique légalement constatée, l'exige, et sous la condition d'une juste et préalable indemnité.

XX.

Nul contribution ne peut être établie que pour l'utilité générale. Tous les citoyens ont le droit de concourir à l'établissement des contributions, d'en surveiller l'emploi, et de s'en faire rendre compte.

XXI.

Les secours publics sont une dette sacrée. La société doit la subsistance aux citoyens malheureux, soit en leur procurant du travail, soit en assurant les moyens d'exister à ceux qui sont hors d'état de travailler.

XXII.

L'instruction est le besoin de tous. La société doit favoriser de tout son pouvoir les progrés de la raison publique, et mettre l'instruction à la portée de tous les citoyens.

XXIII.

La garantie sociale consiste dans l'action de tous, pour assurer à chacun la jouissance et la conservation de ses droits; cette garantie repose sur la souveraineté nationale.

XXIV.

Elle ne peut exister, si les limites des fonctions publiques ne sont pas clairement determinées par la loi et si la responsabilité de tous les fonctionnaires n'est pas assurée.

XXV.

La souveraineté réside dans le peuple. Elle est une et indivisible, imprescriptible et inaliénable.

XXVI.

Aucune portion du peuple ne peut exercer la puissance du peuple entier; mais chaque section du souverain assemblée doit jouir du droit d'exprimer sa volonté avec une entière liberté.

XXVII.

Que tout individu qui usurperoit la souveraineté soit à l'instant mis a mort par les hommes libres

XXVIII.

Un peuple a toujours le droit de revoir, de réformer et de changer sa constitution: une génération ne peut assujétir à ses lois les générations futures.

XXIX.

Chaque citoyen a un droit égal de concourir à la formation de la loi et à la nomination de ses mandataires ou de ses agens.

XXX.

Les fonctions publiques sont essentiellement temporaires; elles ne peuvent être considérées comme des distinctions ni comme des récompenses, mais comme des devoirs.

XXXI.

Les delits des mandataires du peuple et de ses agens ne doivent jamais être impunis. Nul n'a le droit de se prétendre plus inviolable que les autres citoyens.

XXXII.

Le droit de présenter des pétitions aux dépositaires de l'autorité publique ne peut, en aucun cas, être interdit, suspendu ni limité.

XXXIII.

La résistance à l'oppression est la conséquence des autres droits de l'homme.

XXXIV.

Il y a oppression contre le corps social, lorsqu'un seul de ses membres est [illegible], il y a oppression contre chaque membre lorsque le [illegible] est opprimé.

XXXV.

Quand le gouvernement viole les droits du peuple, l'insurrection est pour le peuple, et pour chaque portion du peuple, le plus sacré des droits et le plus indispensable des devoirs.

DÉCLARATION DES DROITS DE L'HOMME ET DU CITOYEN décrétés par la Convention nationale en 1793, v. stile.

Se trouve chez [illegible] papiers peints boulevard du temple vis-à-vis L'ambigu-Co[illegible] la maison ayant une entrée rue de Vendome, No. 27, à Paris.

THE TERROR

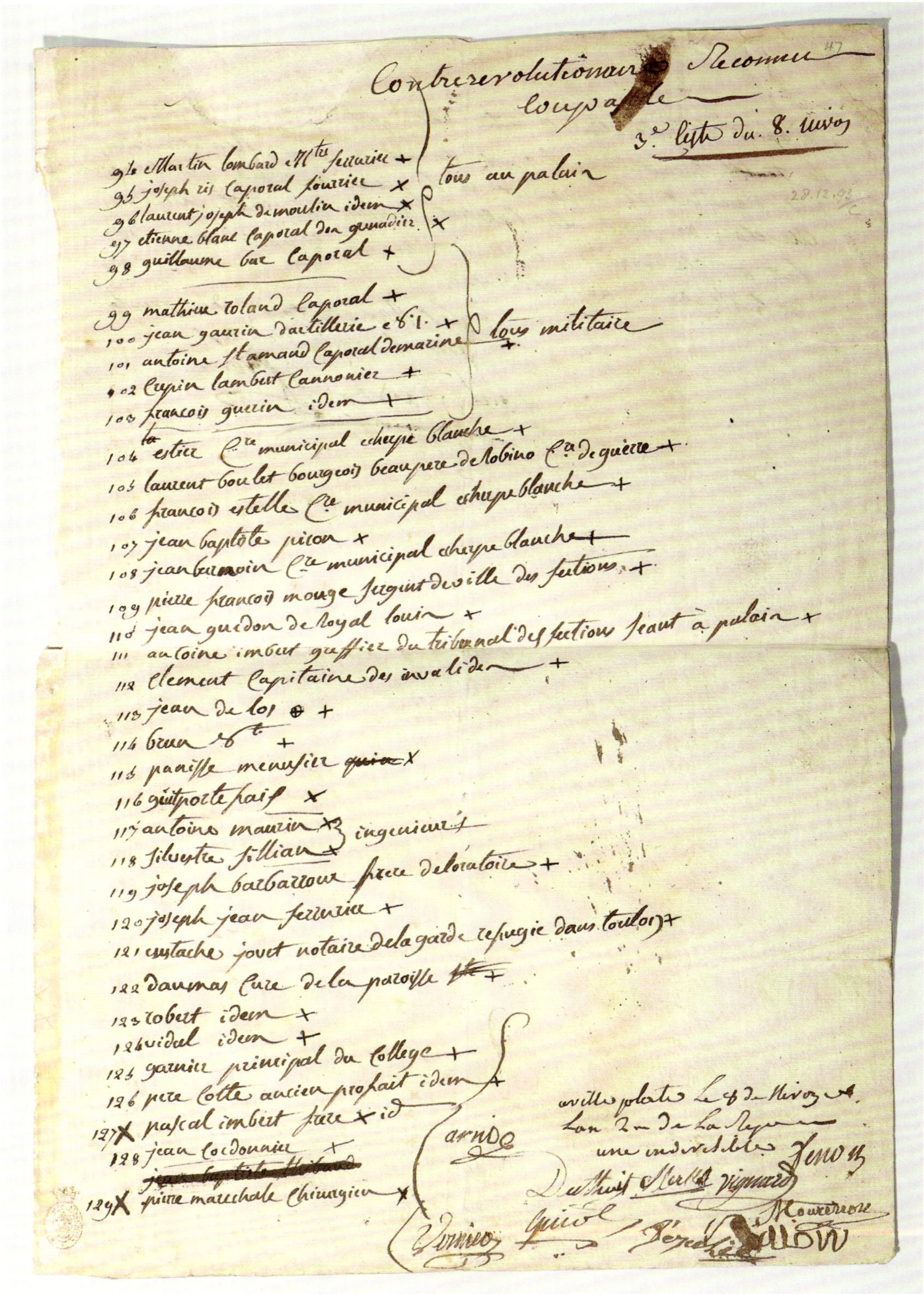

LIST OF PEOPLE SENTENCED TO DEATH SIGNED BY BARRAS AND FRÉRON

This list of "counter-revolutionaries found guilty," dated 8 Nivose Year II (28 December 1793), was drawn up following the French retaking of Toulon from the English in December 1793. Some 700-800 individuals were arrested and executed by firing squad as part of a merciless campaign of repression waged by Louis Stanislas Fréron. Most of those shown here were craftsmen and petty bourgeois, some were soldiers and a few were members of the clergy.

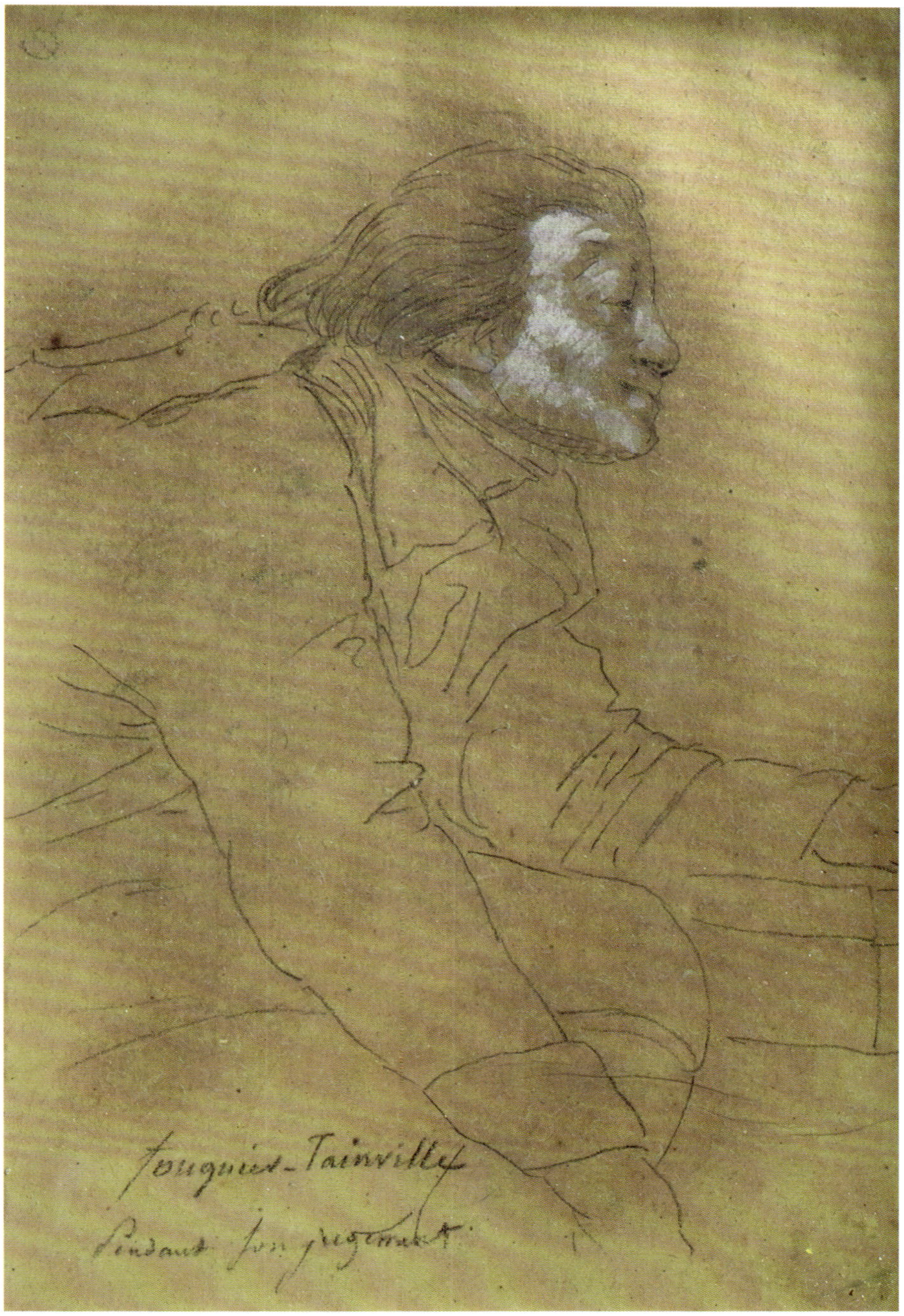

VIVANT DENON, *PORTRAIT OF ANTOINE FOUQUIER-TINVILLE AT HIS TRIAL*

Sketch by Vivant Denon representing Antoine Fouquier-Tinville during his trial. Fouquier-Tinville was the Public Prosecutor (*accusateur public*) of the Revolutionary Tribunal who epitomized the Reign of Terror from March 1793, until he was himself tried by the same tribunal and executed on 7 May 1795.

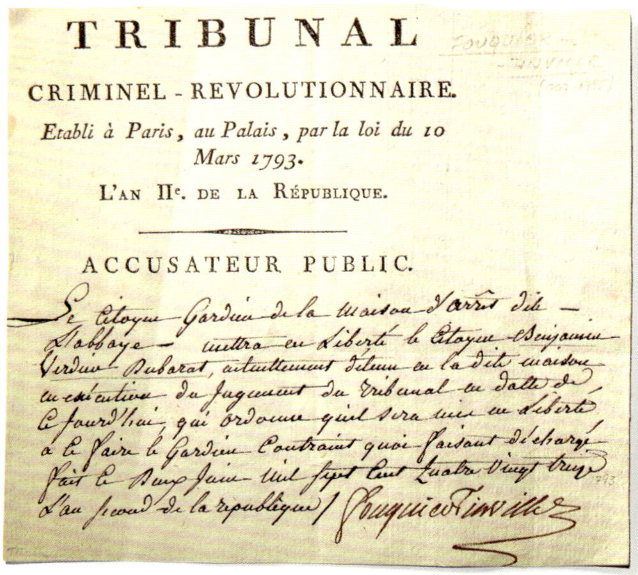

TRIBUNAL

CRIMINEL - REVOLUTIONNAIRE.

Etabli à Paris, au Palais, par la loi du 10 Mars 1793.

L'AN IIe. DE LA RÉPUBLIQUE.

ACCUSATEUR PUBLIC.

Le Citoyen Gardien de la maison d'arrêt dite
l'Abbaye mettra en Liberté le Citoyen Benjamin
Verdier Dubarat, actuellement détenu en la dite maison
en exécution du jugement du Tribunal en datte de
ce jourd'hui, qui ordonne qu'il sera mis en liberté
à ce faire le Gardien contraint quoi faisant déchargé
fait le deux juin mil sept cent quatre vingt treize
l'an second de la république / Fouquier-Tinville

LETTER FROM PUBLIC PROSECUTOR ANTOINE FOUQUIER-TINVILLE (1746-1795)

Letter from the *Accusateur Public*, written on the letterhead of the *Tribunal Criminel Rèvolutionnaire* / Etabli à Paris, au Palais, par la *Loi du 10/ mars 1793/ L'an II, de la République*. Signed Fouquier-Tinville it reads (in English) as follows: "The citizen guard of the prison known as the Abbaye will release citizen Benjamin/ Verdier Dubarat currently detained in the aforesaid prison [...]." The prison of the Abbey of Saint-Germain des Prés was notorious as the site of the September Massacres of 1792 that marked the beginning of the Terror.

VIVANT DENON (1747-1825),
PORTRAIT OF CARRIER DURING HIS TRIAL

Ink and brown wash drawing on paper representing Jean-Baptiste Carrier during his trial. Carrier was the Cantal Deputy sent "on mission" by the Convention to Brittany where he distinguished himself by his ruthless efficiency, most notably the *noyades* (drownings) at Nantes. These were known as "republican marriages" because the victims were preferably a man and a woman who were bound together before being thrown into the water. After the fall of Robespierre, Carrier was himself tried and guillotined in December 1794.

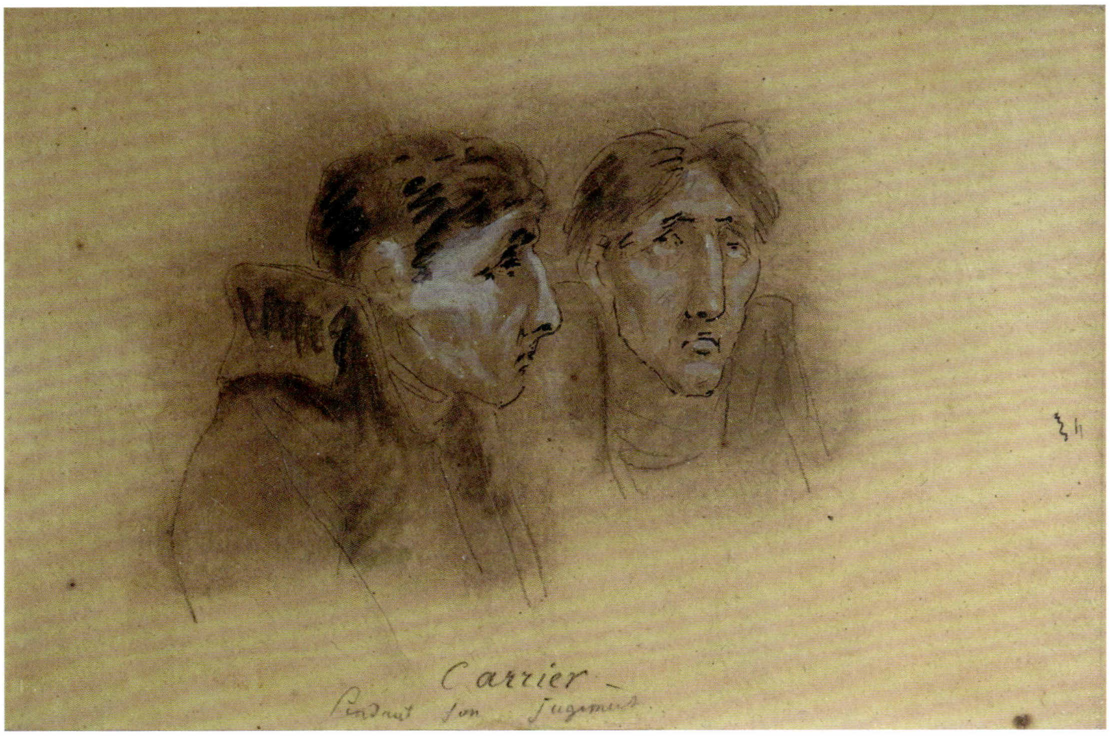

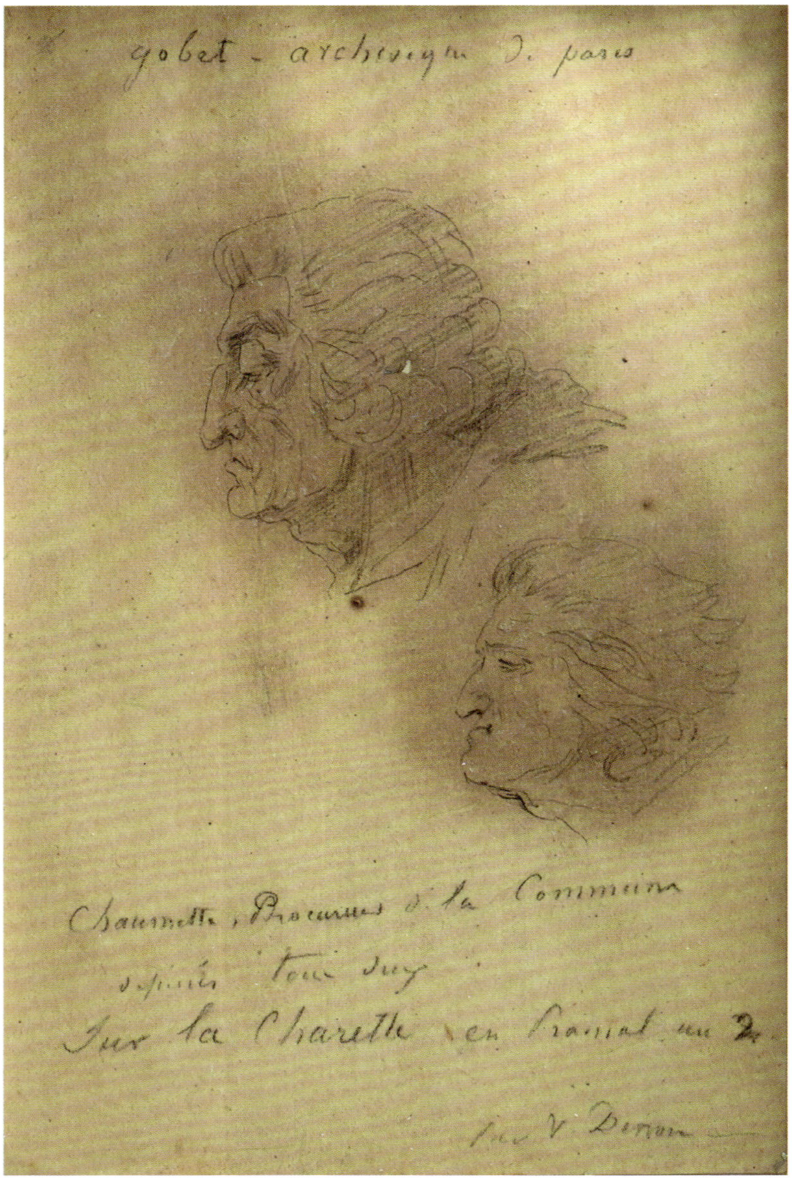

VIVANT DENON (1747-1825),
PORTRAITS OF GOBEL AND CHAUMETTE IN THE TUMBREL

Sketch of Gobel and Chaumette on their way to the guillotine. Jean-Baptiste Gobel was the constitutional bishop of Paris. Pierre-Gaspard Chaumette was procurator-general of the Paris Commune and a member of the Hébertist faction. Both were guillotined on 13 April 1794.

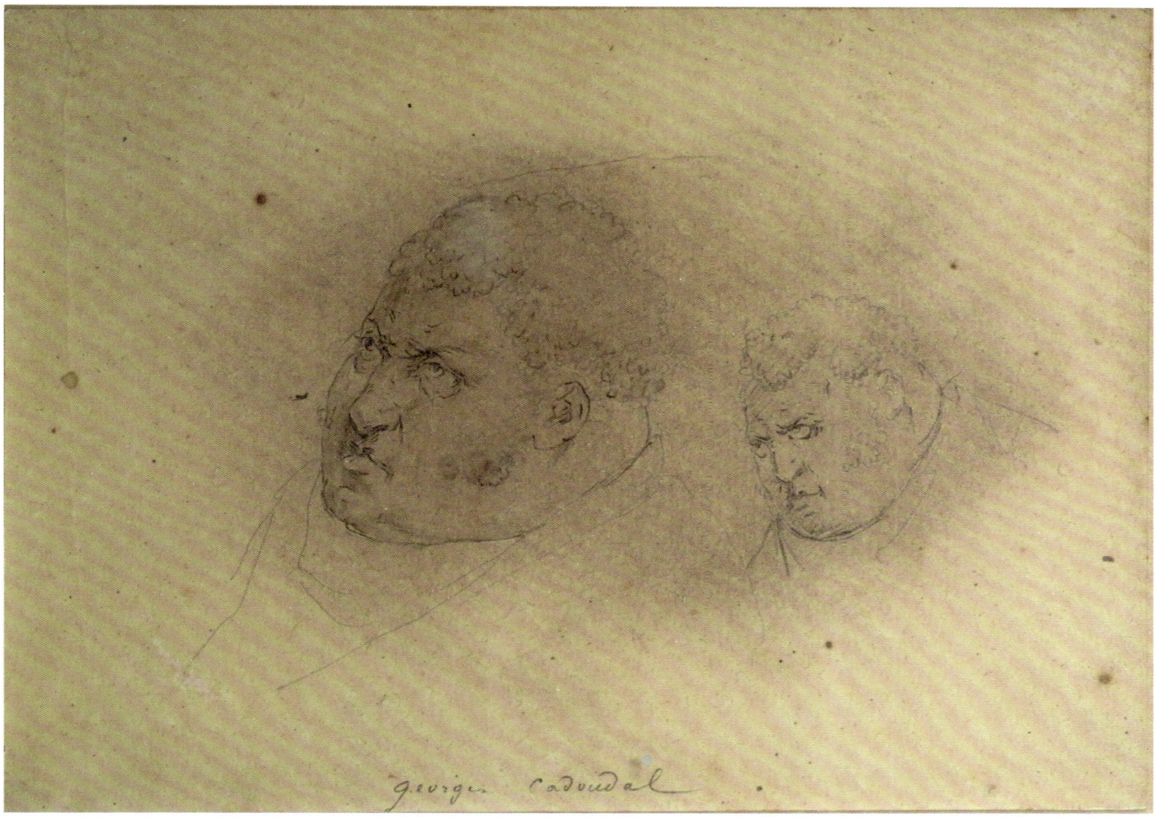

VIVANT DENON (1747-1825),
PORTRAIT OF CADOUDAL

Sketch by Vivant Denon, future director of the Musée Napoléon (now the Louvre Museum), representing Georges Cadoudal. After taking part in the Vendée uprising, Cadoudal became a leader of the Morbihan Chouans and was proclaimed general by his troops. In 1800 he rejected overtures from Bonaparte, whom he continued to conspire against until he was captured and guillotined.

VIVANT DENON (1747-1825), *PORTRAITS OF DANTON AT THE REVOLUTIONARY TRIBUNAL AND HÉBERT IN THE TUMBREL*

A combined portrait by Denon of two men who rivaled Robespierre as *Montagnards*. Pictured right: *Montagnard* extremist Jacques René Hébert, guillotined 24 March 1794. Pictured left: Georges Jacques Danton, representing the more moderate "Indulgent" *Montagnards* faction, executed 5 April 1794.

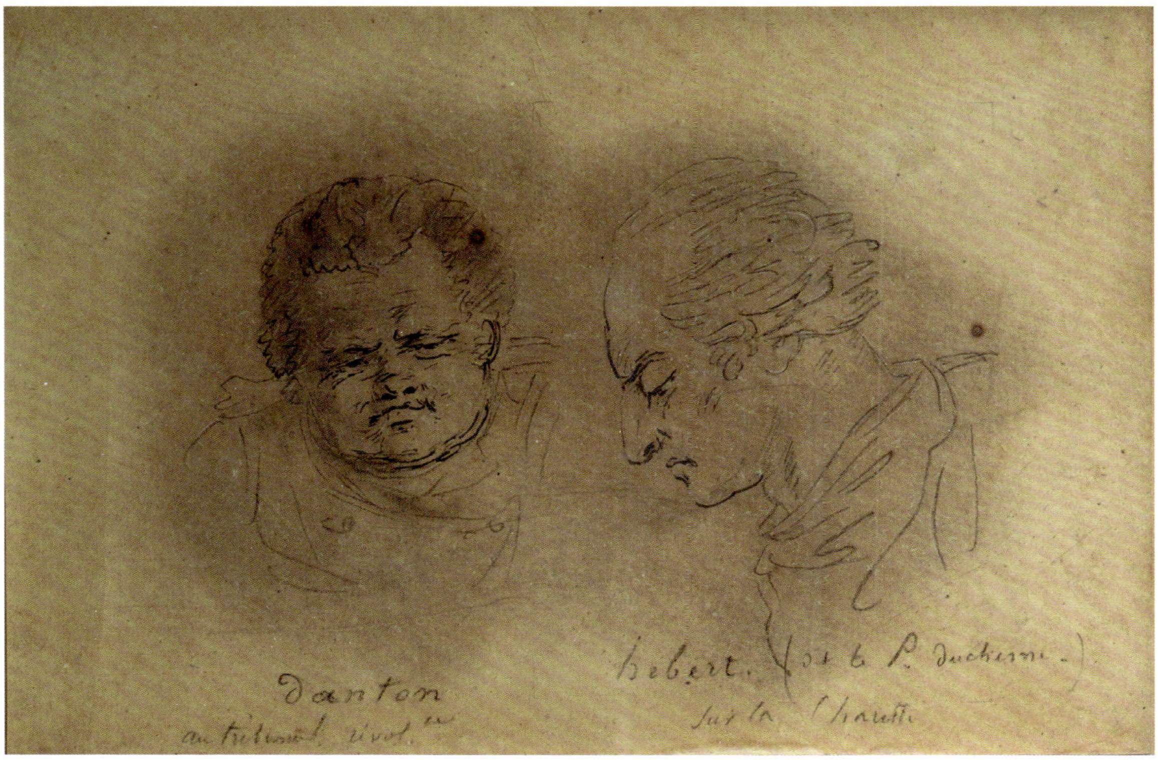

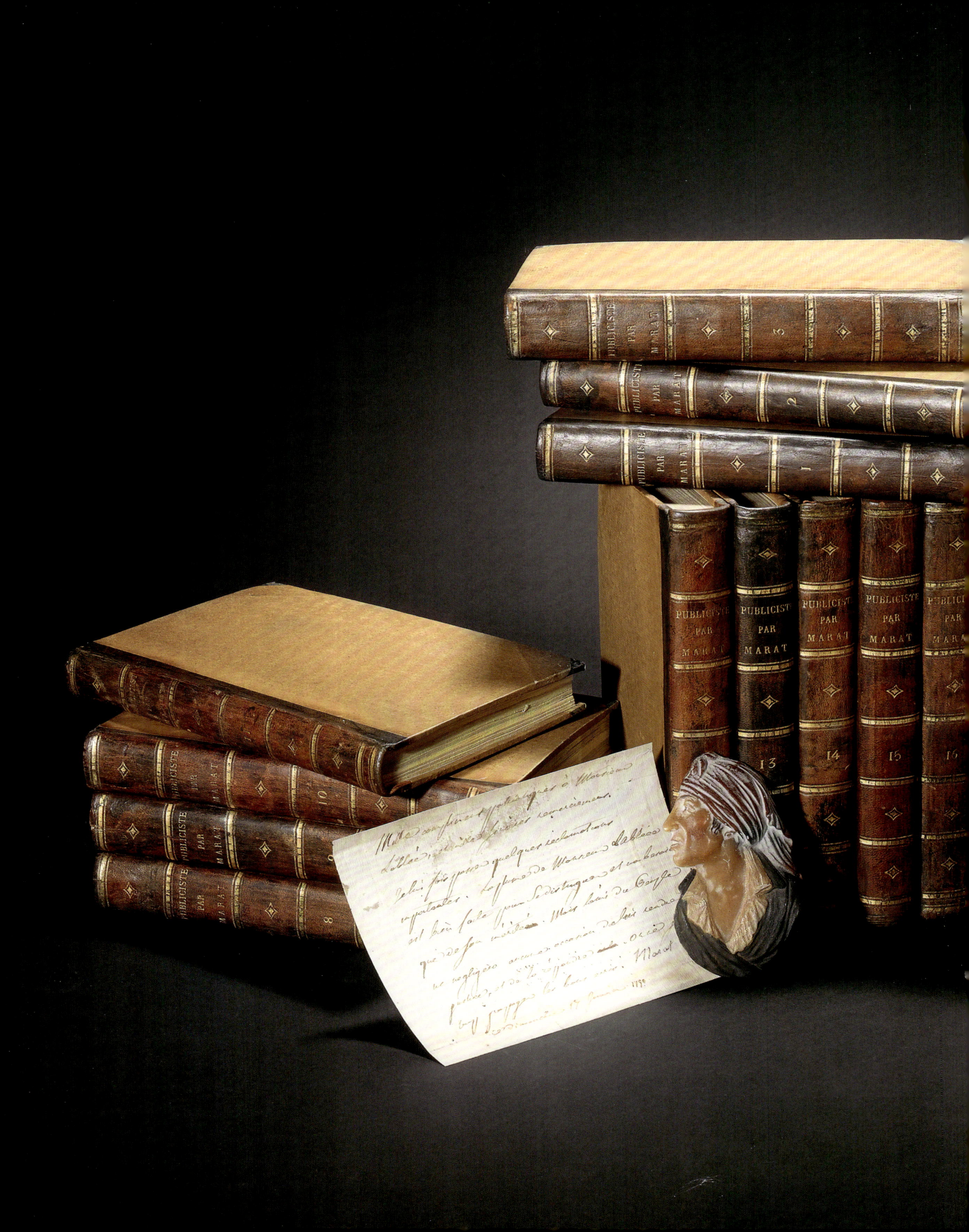
PUBLICISTE PAR MARAT 3
PUBLICISTE PAR MARAT 2
PUBLICISTE PAR MARAT 1
PUBLICISTE PAR MARAT 10
PUBLICISTE PAR MARAT 8
PUBLICISTE PAR MARAT
PUBLICISTE PAR MARAT 13
PUBLICISTE PAR MARAT 14
PUBLICISTE PAR MARAT 15
PUBLICISTE PAR MARAT 16

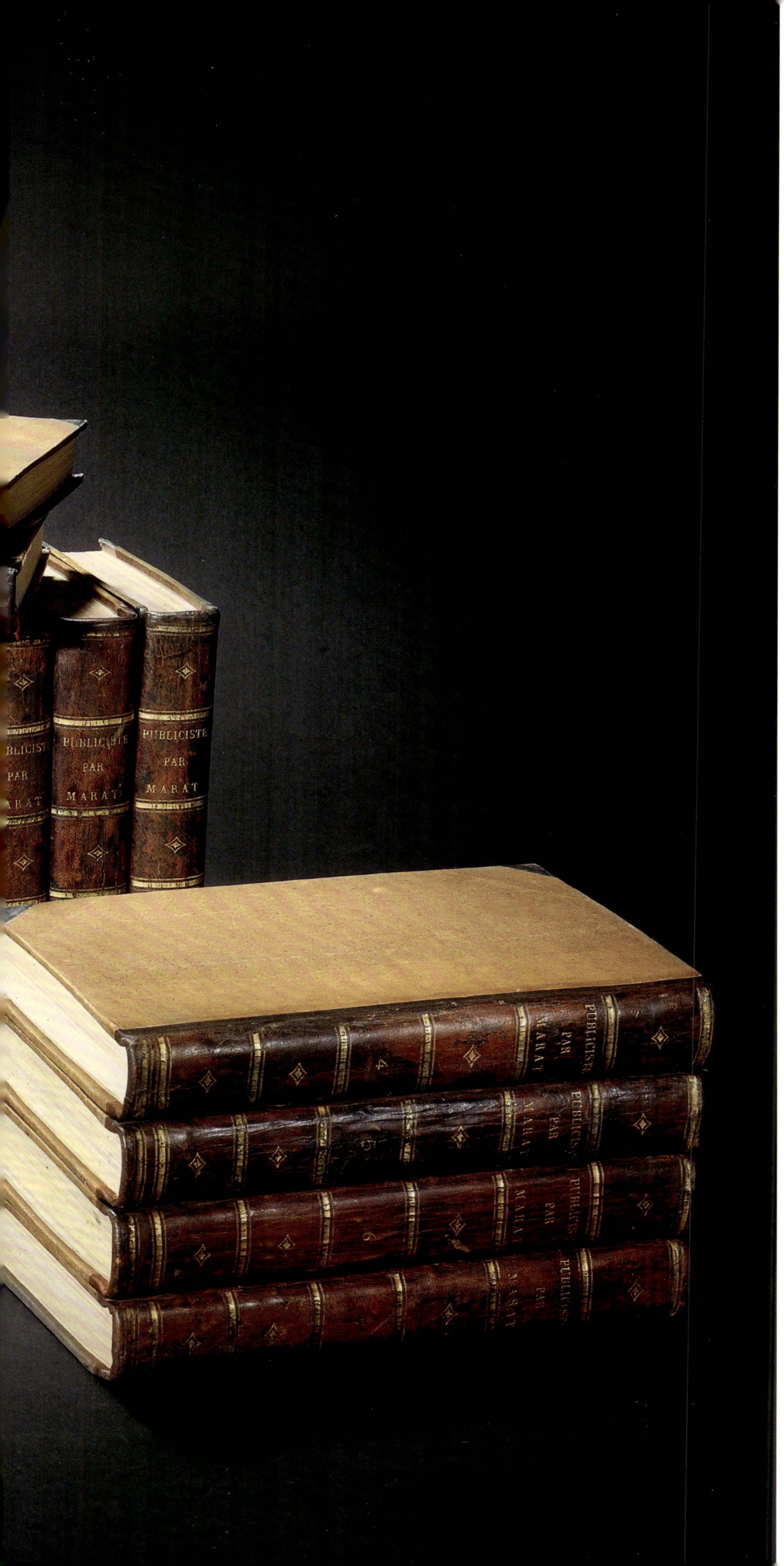

WAX PORTRAIT OF MARAT

Pictured in the foreground is a wax effigy of Jean-Paul Marat (1743-1793) typical of popular culture at the time of the Revolution (cf the other example in Paris' Musée Carnavalet). It shows him in profile, wearing a turban to hide his chronic skin condition. As a *Montagnard* deputy in the National Convention, Marat was a fierce opponent of the Girondins. He was assassinated by Charlotte Corday on 13 July 1793 and became famous after his death as "the people's friend" (*l'Ami du Peuple*) so-named after the newspaper he produced.

MARAT'S NEWSPAPER, *L'AMI DU PEUPLE*

Collected issues of the newspaper founded by Jean-Paul Marat (1745-1793) in September 1789 and published almost without interruption until September 1792. *L'Ami du Peuple* ran from eight to 16 pages, entirely written by Marat who frequently wound up in court for his fiercely outspoken views. After his election to the National Convention, *L'Ami du Peuple* was renamed the *Journal de la République Française* and published until Marat's death. Fewer than five complete sets of Marat's newspaper are known to exist.

LETTRE FROM MARAT TO THE POET JACQUES LABLÉE

Marat sent a letter to the short-lived *Journal des Réclamations* (journal of grievances) founded by Jacques Lablée (1751-1841) in 1790, a poet, lawyer and administrator under the Paris Commune. In the event, Marat's letter was never published. Lablée himself was later imprisoned in the time of the Terror for his *Girondin* sympathies then released after 9 Thermidor. Napoleon's coronation would be commemorated by Lablée in a poem that condemns the Terror.

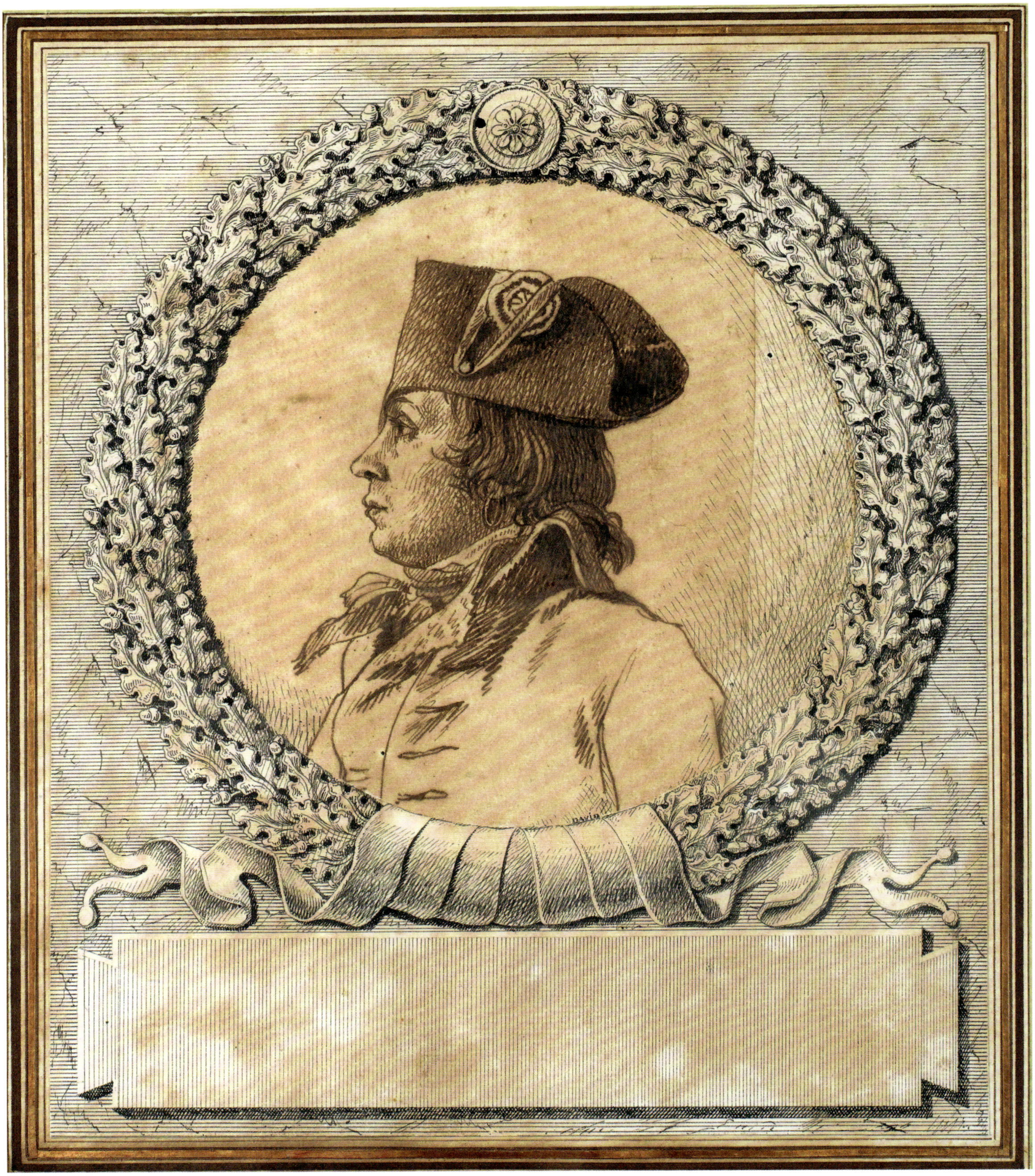

JACQUES-LOUIS DAVID (1748-1825),
PORTRAIT OF MONTAGNARD DEPUTY PHILIPPE LE BAS

This famous drawing in pen and brown ink by the painter David (1748-1825) represents his fellow member in the National Assembly, Philippe François Joseph Le Bas (1765-1794), at a session of the Convention. The deputy for the Pas-de-Calais, Le Bas distinguished himself as a protagonist of the Terror in his native region. He was a close associate of Robespierre, also from the Pas-de-Calais, to whom he remained loyal to the end. Le Bas killed himself on 28 July 1794 to avoid arrest. This drawing is the only known portrait of Le Bas and served as the model for a large bronze medallion by the sculptor and medalist David d'Angers. It comes from the Le Bas family.

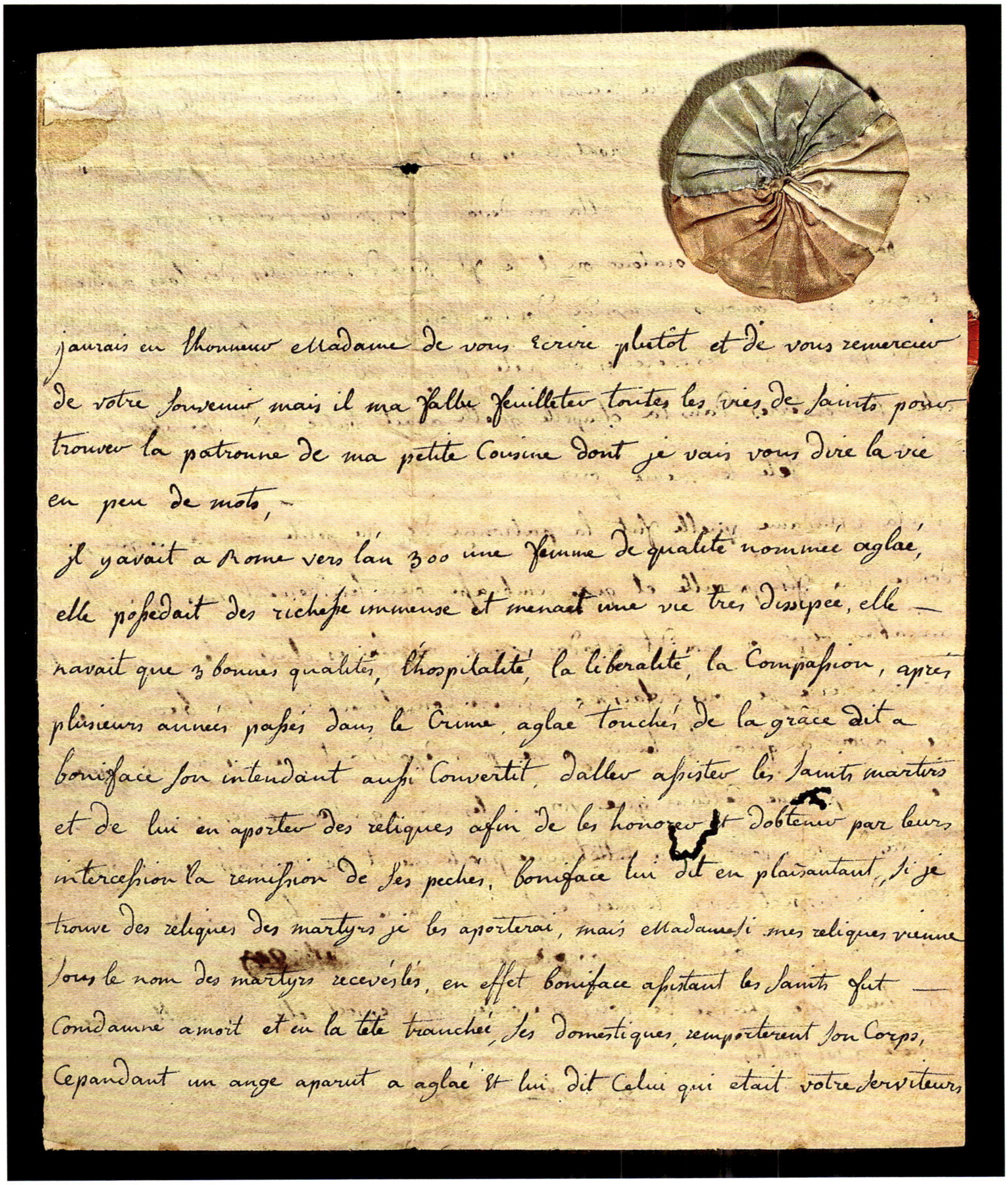

jaurais eu lhonneur Madame de vous Ecrire plutôt et de vous remercier
de votre souvenir, mais il ma fallu feuilleter toutes les vies de saints pour
trouver la patronne de ma petite Cousine dont je vais vous dire la vie
en peu de mots, —
il y avait a Rome vers lan 300 une femme de qualité nommée aglaé,
elle possedait des richesse immense et menait une vie tres dissipée, elle —
navait que 3 bonnes qualités, lhospitalité, la liberalité, la Compassion, apres
plusieurs années passés dans le Crime, aglaé touchée de la grâce dit a
boniface son intendant aussi Convertit, daller assister les saints martirs
et de lui en aporter des reliques afin de les honorer et dobtenir par leurs
intercession la remission de ses pechés, boniface lui dit en plaisantant, si je
trouve des reliques des martyrs je les aporterai, mais Madame si mes reliques vienne
sous le nom des martyrs recevés les, en effet boniface assistant les saints fut —
Condamné a mort et eu la tête tranchée, ses domestiques, remporterent son Corps,
Cependant un ange aparut a aglaé et lui dit Celui qui était votre serviteur,

LETTER BY CHARLOTTE CORDAY WITH COCKADE

Marie-Anne Charlotte de Corday d'Armont (1768-1793) was a young *Girondin* sympathizer from a minor aristocratic family in Normandy and a descendant of Pierre Corneille. Guillotined by order of the revolutionary tribunal on 17 July 1793, Corday became a symbol of counter-revolution, remembered as a woman of extreme piety who showed immense courage throughout her ordeal. Her corpse was interred in the La Madeleine cemetery, the site now marked by a chapel of atonement. Despite her notable place in French history, Charlotte Corday left behind scant evidence of her passing. Virtually all that remains today is this handwritten two-page letter to her cousin, sealed with red wax and signed "Corday" (with cockade also attributed to her); and the famous letter of adieu to her father dated 16 July 1793, now in the Archives Nationales. The tone of this letter, sent from Caen on 24 September 1788, testifies to the strength of Corday's religious beliefs, based on the veneration of saints and martyrs when she was a boarder at the Abbaye aux Dames de Caen. On 9 July 1822 Charlotte's sister gave the letter to a certain Mr Lamouroux.

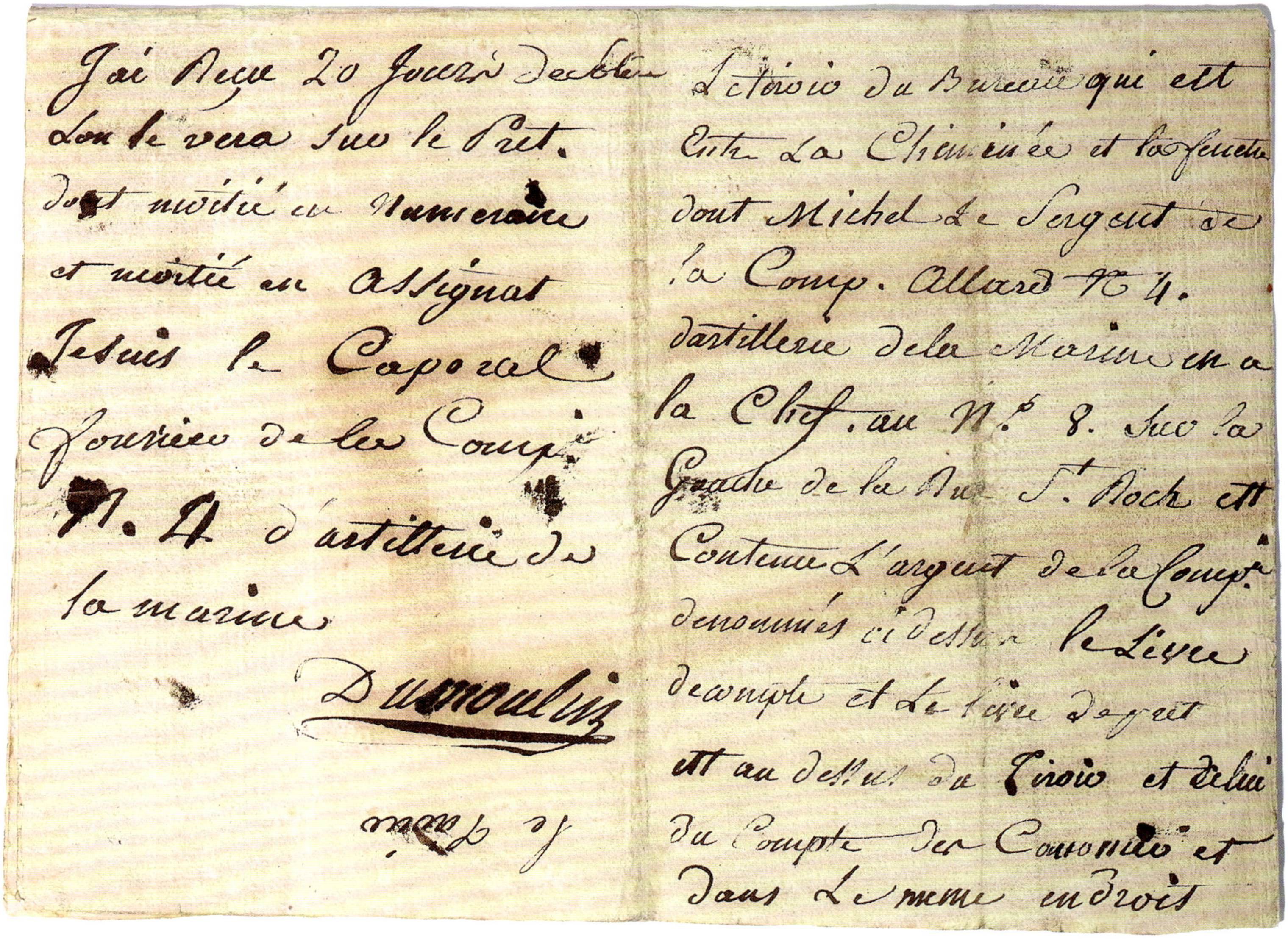

J'ai Reçu 20 Jours de l'Etat
Don le vera sur le Prêt.
dont moitié en Numeraire
et moitié en Assignat
Je suis le Caporal
fourrier de la Comp.e
N. 4 d'artillerie de
la marine

Dumoulin

Le tiroir du Bureau qui est
Entre La Cheminée et la fenêtre
dont Michel Le Sergent de
la Comp. Allard N° 4.
d'artillerie de la Marine en a
la Clef. au N° 8. sur la
Gauche de la Rue St. Roch est
Contenu L'argent de la Comp.e
denommés ci dessus le Livre
de compte et Le Livre de prêt
est au dessus du Tiroir et celui
du Compte des Canonniers et
dans Le meme endroit

STATEMENT FROM CORPORAL DUMOULIN

This handwritten text accompanies the list of guilty counter-revolutionaries (page 44) condemned to death by Barras and Fréron during the siege of Toulon — a city that was taken in 1793 thanks in particular to the young Bonaparte.

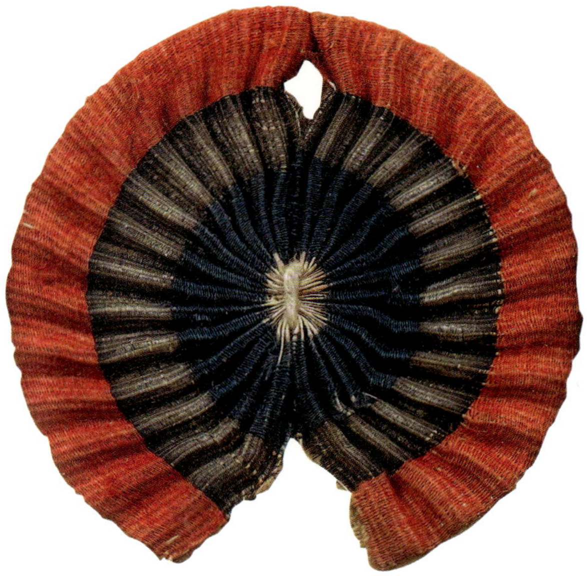

REVOLUTIONARY COCKADE OF *MONTAGNARD* DEPUTY PHILIPPE LE BAS

The tricolor cockade first appeared in 1789 and immediately became a symbol of nationalism and the French Revolution. Philippe Lebas wore his cockade attached to his bicorne hat, as shown in the drawing by the painter David. The cockade comes from the Le Bas family.

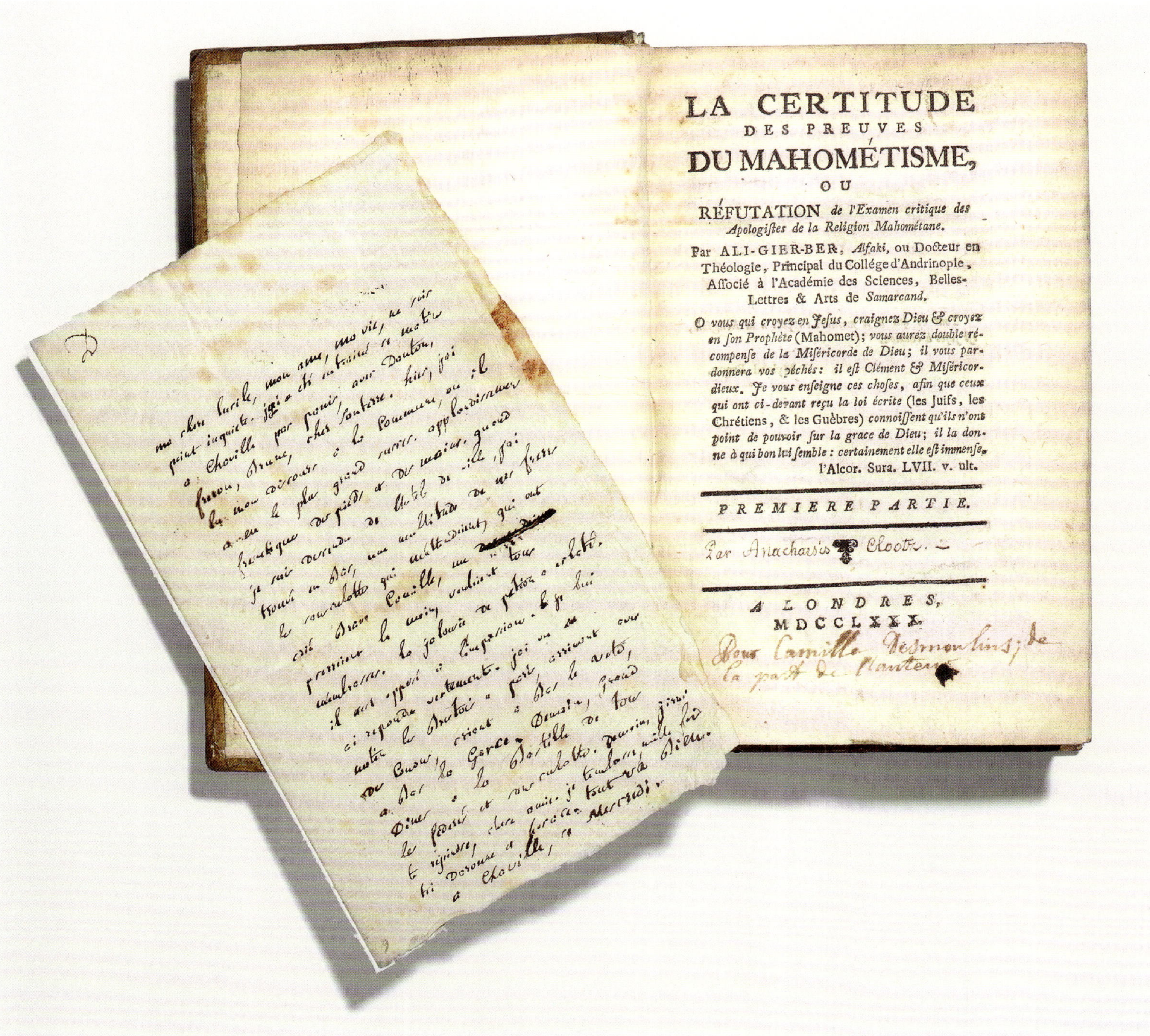

HANDWRITTEN LETTER FROM CAMILLE DESMOULINS

Camille Desmoulins (1760-1794) was a lawyer, journalist, member of the Jacobin club and friend of Danton. He and his wife Lucille (born Laridon-Deplessis) were one of the iconic couples of the French Revolution. Desmoulins wrote this letter to Lucille on 13 July 1792, at a time of crisis brought about by war and the unpopularity of the monarchy. On this particular 13 July, Desmoulins has plans to help reinstate Manuel as procurator-general of the Paris Commune and announces the celebrations to be held the following day commemorating the third anniversary of 14 July 1789.

***LA CERTITUDE DES PREUVES DU MAHOMÉTISME*, BOOK FORMERLY BELONGING TO CAMILLE DESMOULINS**

Anacharsis Cloots was the pseudonym of Jean-Baptiste, Baron de Cloots (1755-1794), a Prussian nobleman and staunch atheist whose commitment to the French Revolution led him to settle in France and become a deputy to the National Convention. Pictured here is the book he published in London in 1780 this copy dedicated to Camille Desmoulins, presenting his arguments for the non-existence of God. The work was widely acclaimed by French revolutionaries.

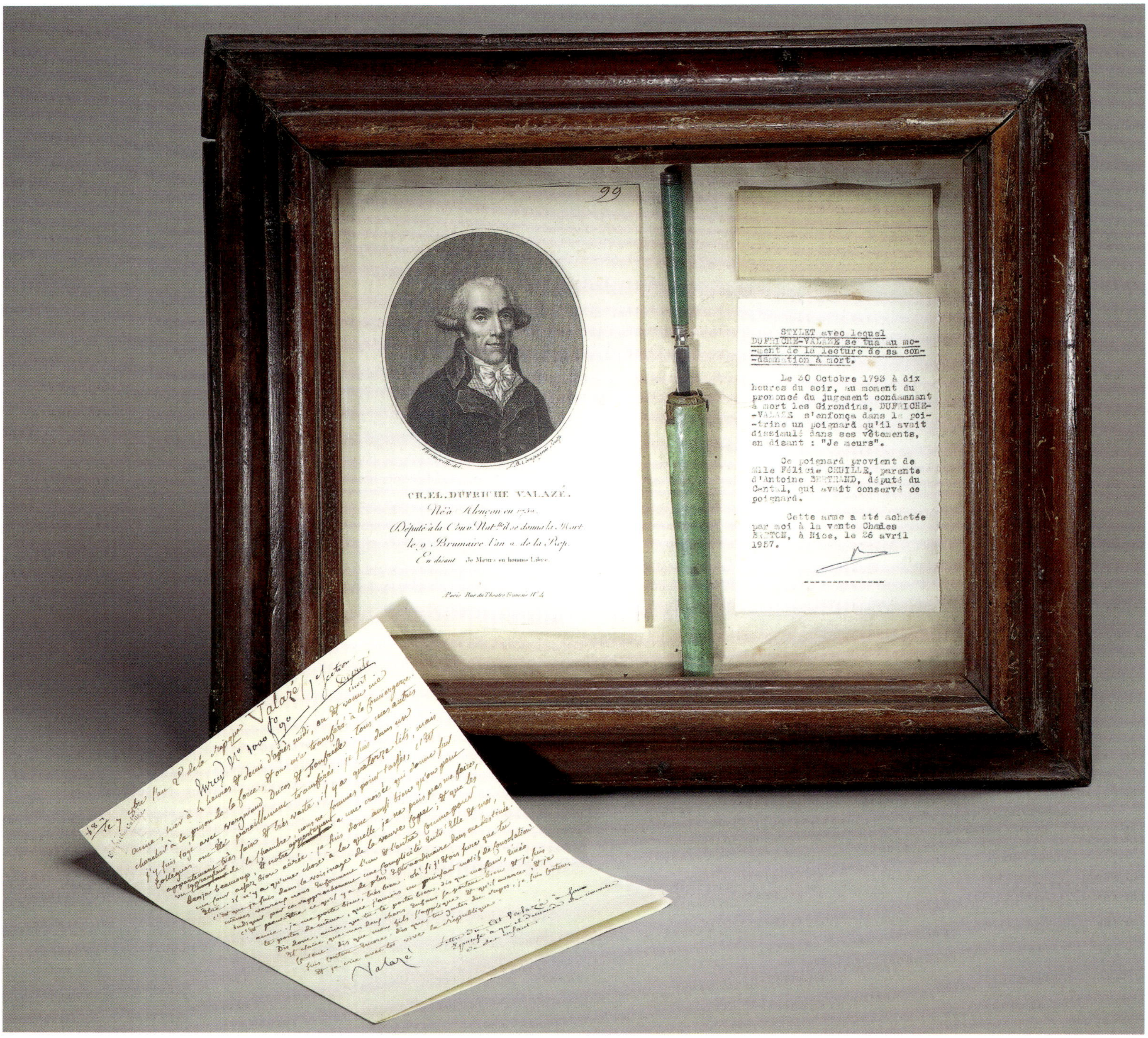

LETTER FROM DUFRICHE-VALAZÉ WITH STILETTO

Handwritten letter by Charles Eléonor Dufriche-Valazé, sent to his wife a few days before his arrest and imprisonment in the Conciergerie. Dufriche-Valazé was among the *Girondin* deputies who were purged from the Convention by the *Montagnards* in the aftermath of 31 May and 2 June 1793, then arrested on 5 October. He stabbed himself to death before the revolutionary tribunal on the day he was sentenced to the guillotine, 30 October 1793, so becoming the first French deputy to commit suicide at a sitting of the Assembly. Pictured in the center of the frame is the stiletto he used to kill himself – a gesture reminiscent of the ancient Romans. It is said that when asked by Brissot why he was trembling, Valazé replied "not trembling, dying."

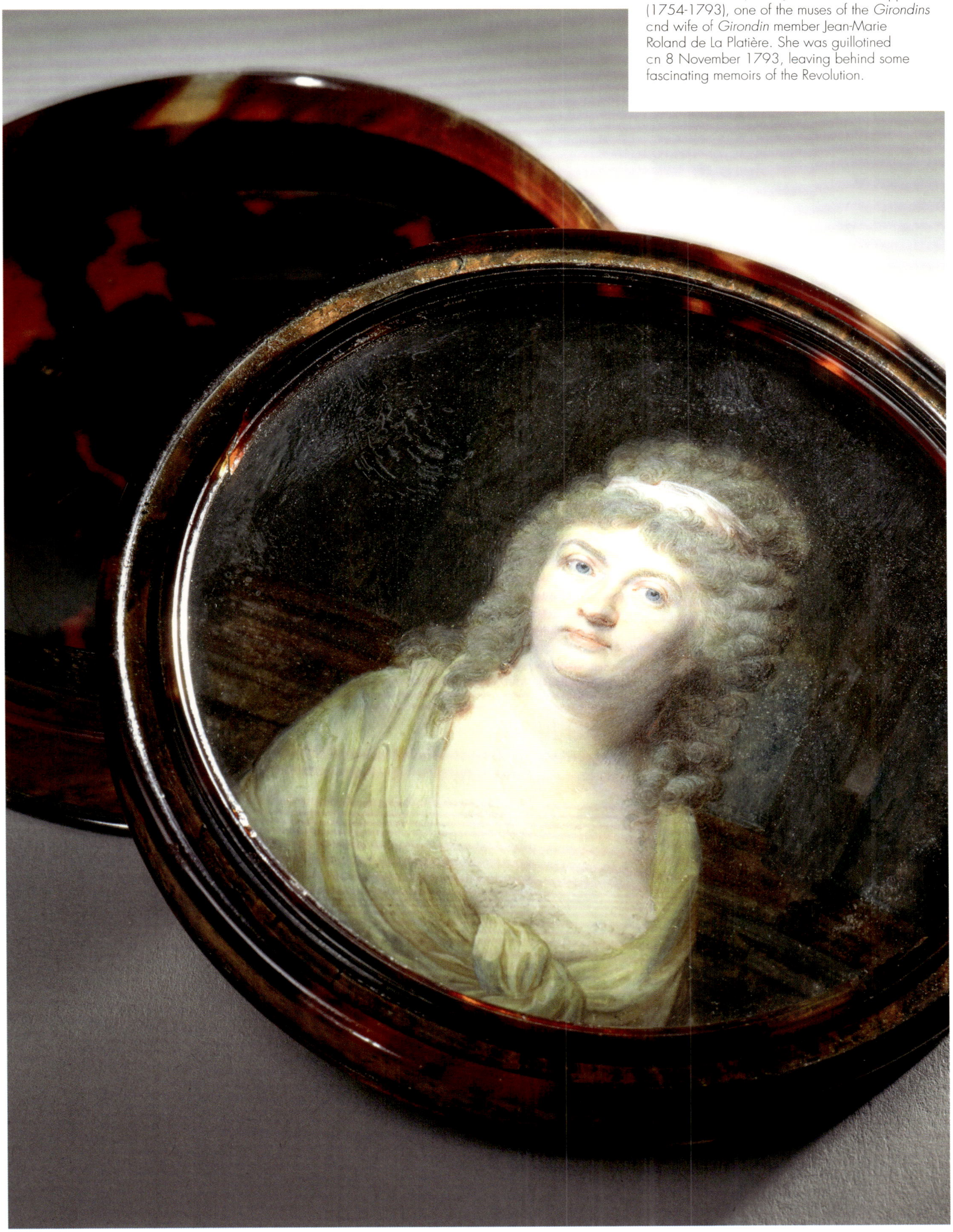

JEAN-BAPTISTE JACQUES AUGUSTIN (1759-1832), *PORTRAIT OF MADAME ROLAND*

Miniature by the painter Augustin representing Madame Roland, born Jeanne-Marie Philippon (1754-1793), one of the muses of the *Girondins* and wife of *Girondin* member Jean-Marie Roland de La Platière. She was guillotined on 8 November 1793, leaving behind some fascinating memoirs of the Revolution.

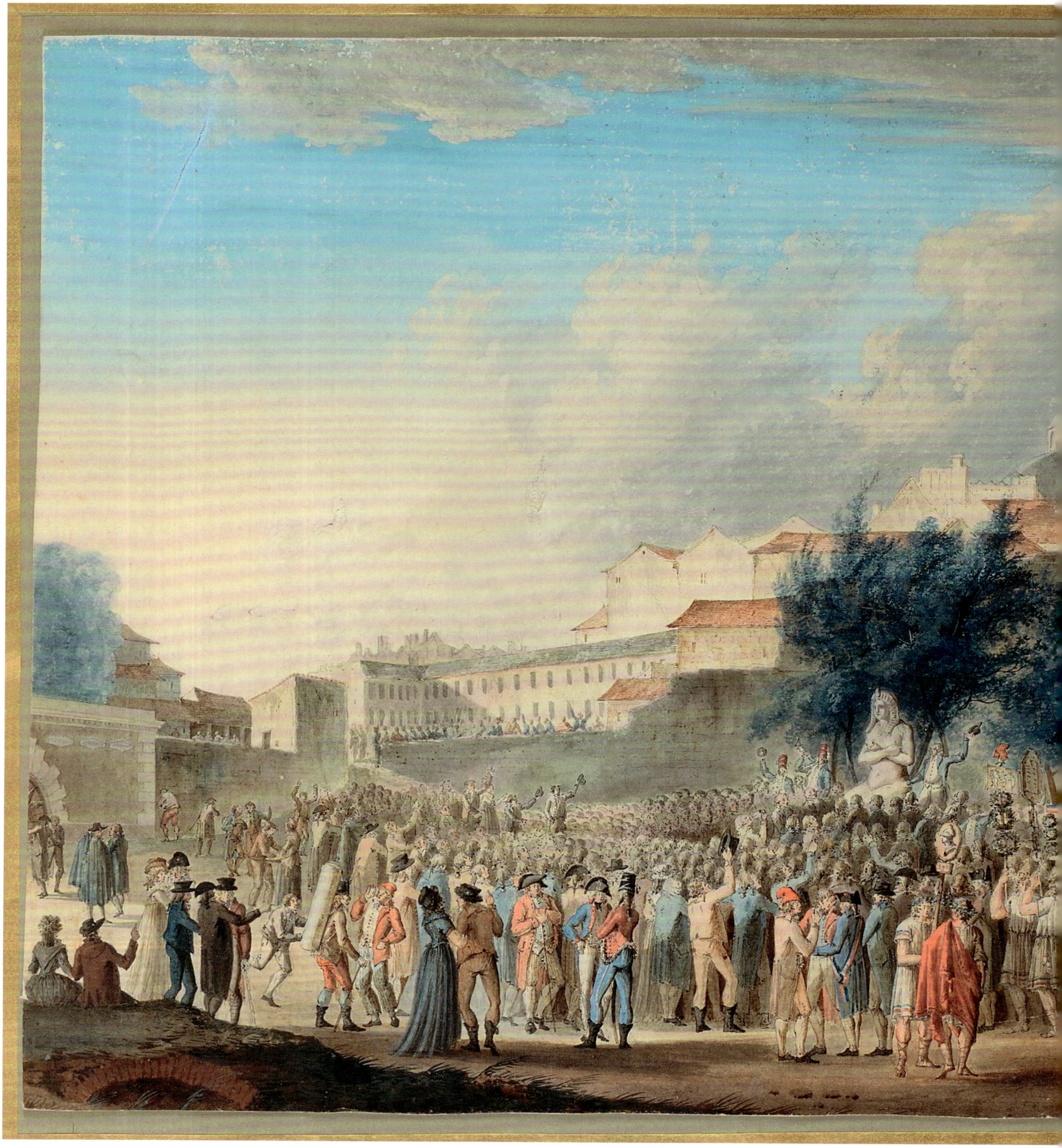

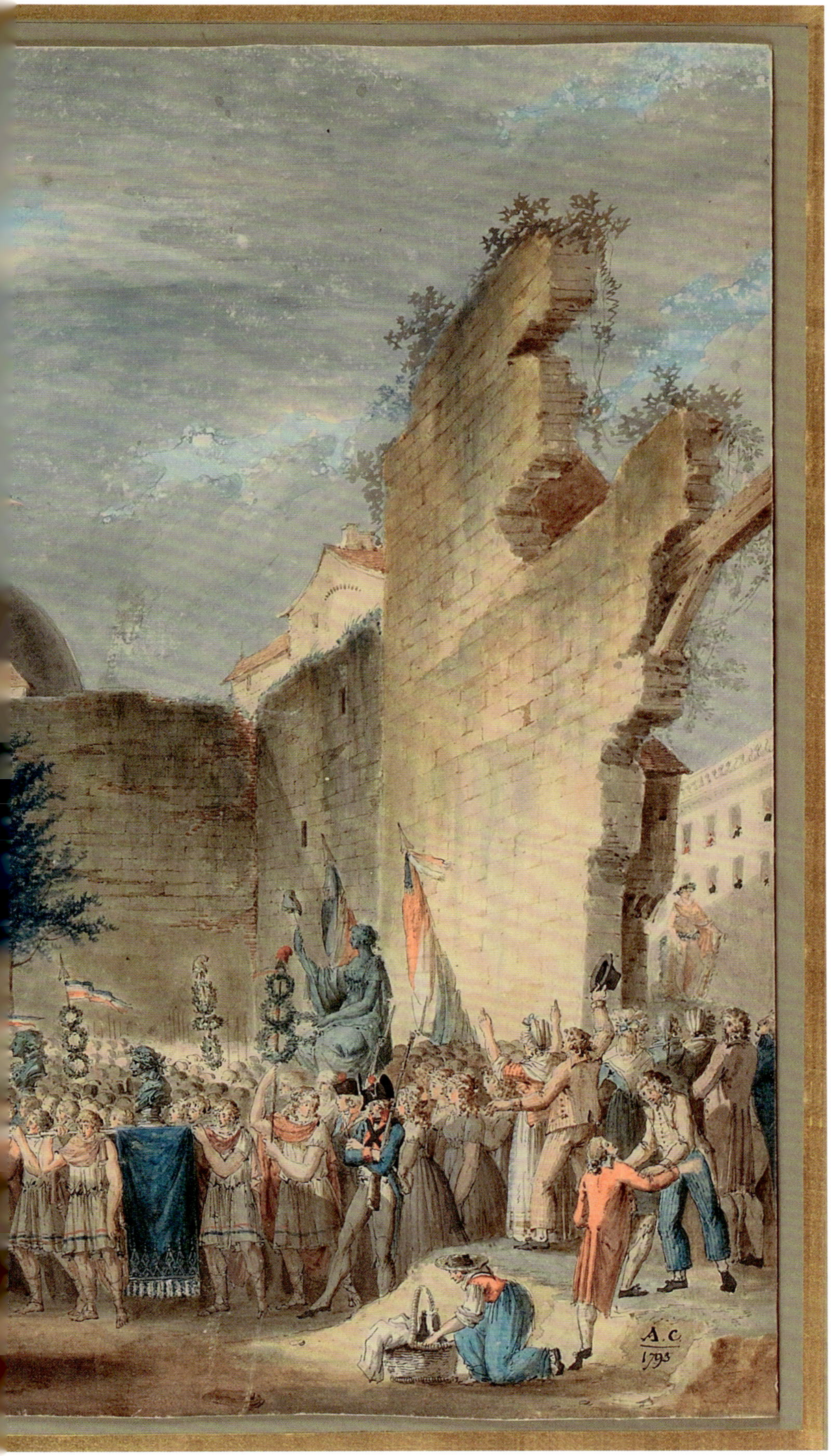

THOMAS-CHARLES NAUDET (1773-1810),
FESTIVAL OF UNITY AND INDIVISIBILITY

The Festival of Unity and Indivisibility of the Nation was held on the former site of the Bastille to celebrate the abolition of noble privilege on 10 August 1792. The festival was organized by the painter Jacques-Louis David and featured the *Fontaine de la Régénération* – a monumental statue modeled after the Egyptian goddess Isis. Elderly visitors were encouraged to drink the rejuvenating waters that sprang from its breasts, symbolizing the rebirth of the French Republic that was declared "one and indivisible" on the same day. The fountain was demolished shortly afterwards. This watercolor painting is very like Naudet's take on that other great festival of the revolutionary epoch, the *Festival of the Supreme Being on the Champs de Mars* (Musée Carnavalet).

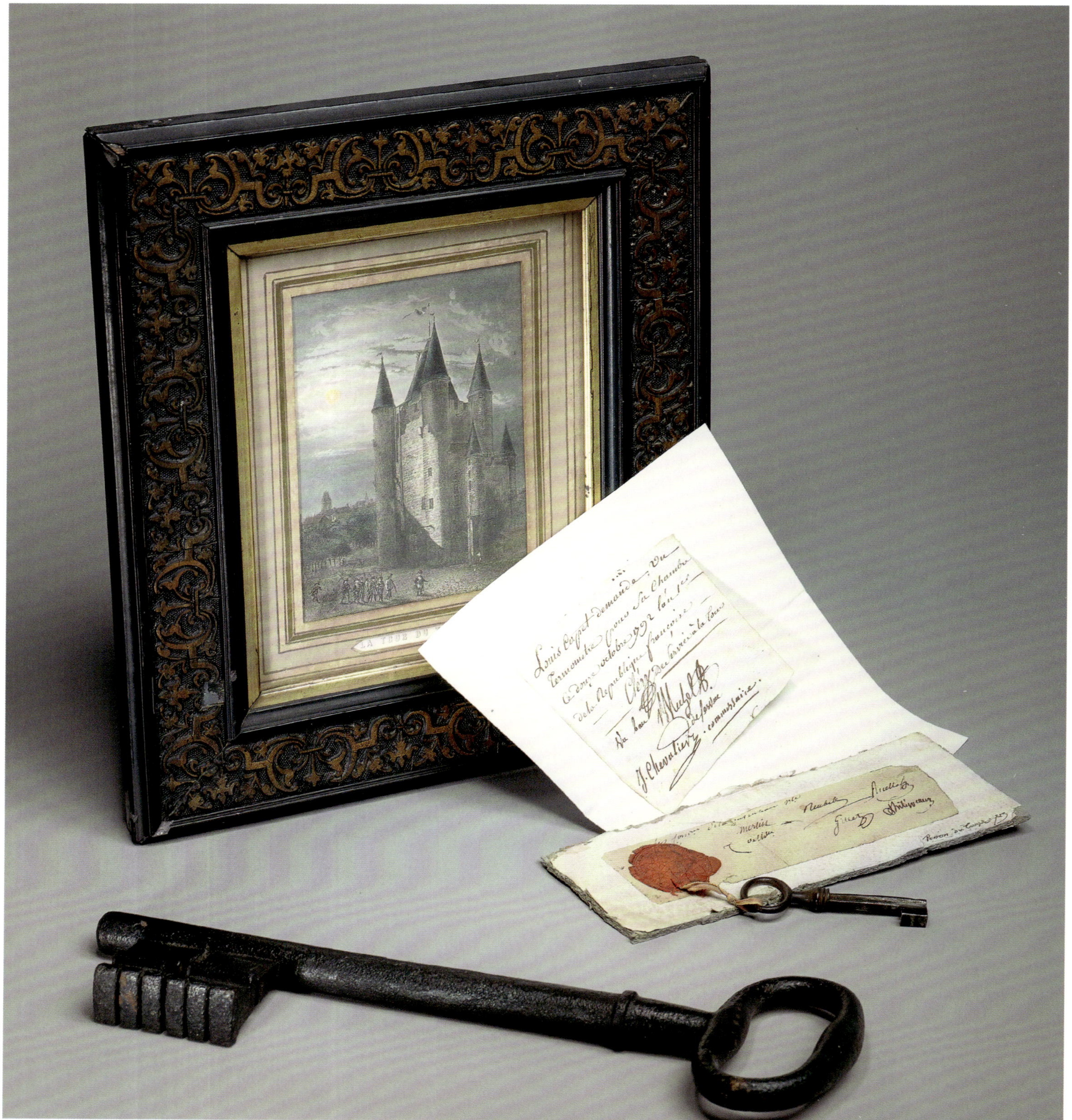

KEYS AND VIEW OF THE TEMPLE PRISON

These two keys are among the last remaining relics of the Temple Tower where the royal family was held captive. The largest key, in wrought iron with a rounded stem, has been exhibited several times. It comes from the Philippe Gille collection, acquired by his police-commissioner grandfather when the tower was demolished. It gives an idea of the size of the building, while the smallest key, used for the Dauphin's cell, is a moving reminder of the boy's captivity. The key is attached to a tricolor ribbon, which is sealed with red wax to a label marked "Commissaires de la Convention Nationale" followed by six signatures including those of Merlin, Gillet and Philippeaux.

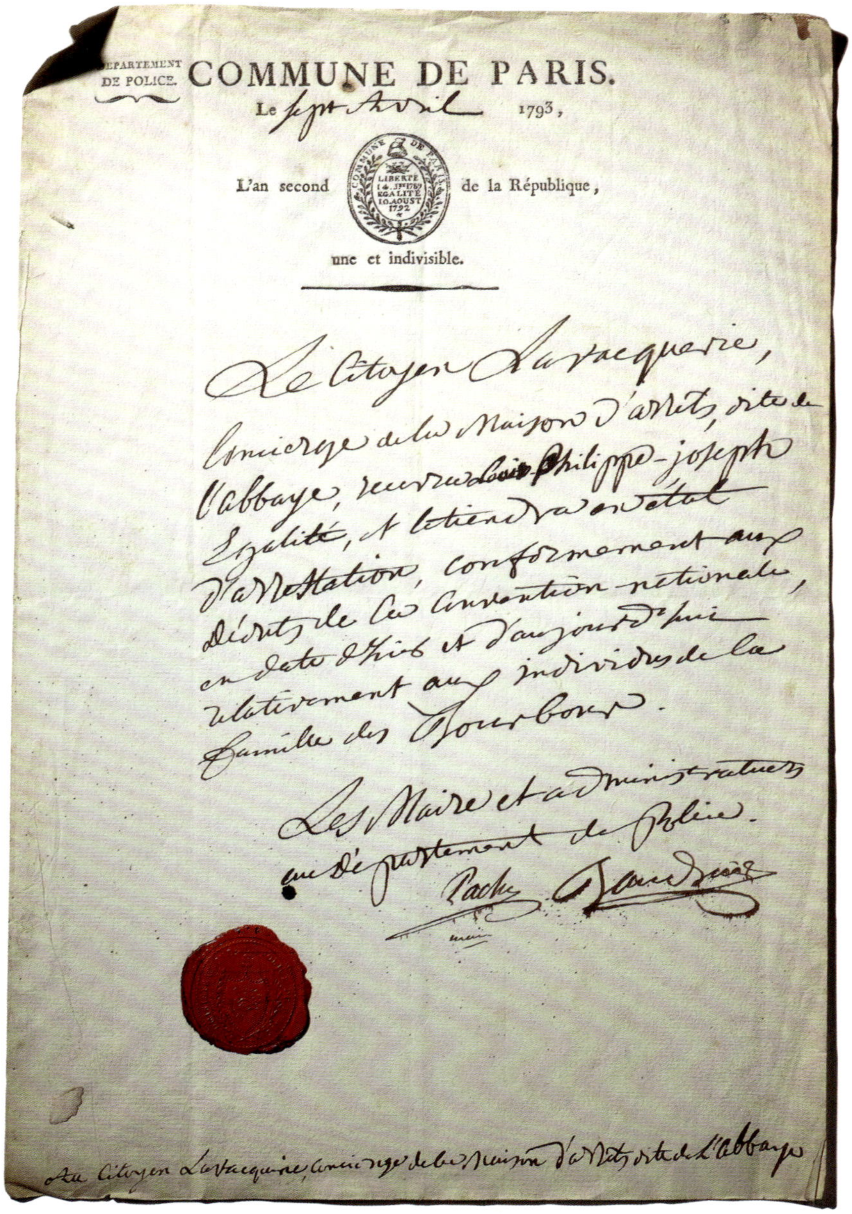

DÉPARTEMENT DE POLICE.

COMMUNE DE PARIS.

Le sept Avril 1793,

L'an second de la République, une et indivisible.

Le Citoyen Lavacquerie, concierge de la Maison d'arrêts, dite de l'Abbaye, recevra Philippe-Joseph Egalité, et le tiendra en état d'arrestation, conformément aux décrets de la Convention nationale, en date d'hier et d'aujourd'hui relativement aux individus de la famille des Bourbons.

Les Maire et administrateurs au département de Police.

Pache

Au Citoyen Lavacquerie, concierge de la Maison d'arrêts dite de l'Abbaye

WARRANT FOR THE ARREST OF PHILIPPE EGALITÉ

Warrant dated 7 April 1793, signed by the pro-*Montagnard* mayor of Paris Jean-Nicolas Paché, for the arrest and incarceration in the Abbaye prison of Philippe Egalité (1747-1793), officially the Duke of Orléans, a cousin of Louis XVI. As a deputy to the Convention, the Duke had voted for the death of the King. But being a member of the royal family, he was arrested all the same and imprisoned. History will remember that he was not there to speak for the King at his trial on 15 January 1793. Philippe Egalité was executed on 6 November 1793.

CHARLES THÉVENIN (1764-1838),
FAÇADE OF THE HÔTEL DE DRENEUC PRISON

Watercolor and gouache painting by Charles Thévenin (1764-1838) representing the façade of the Hôtel de Dreneuc on the Rue de Provence. The building served as a prison in the Terror, then a reception center from 1795 onward for foreign hostages and famous prisoners of war. Inmates were treated with respect and were largely free to come and go as they pleased — among them, Count Louis Philippe de Roffignac and Count von Hatzfeld.

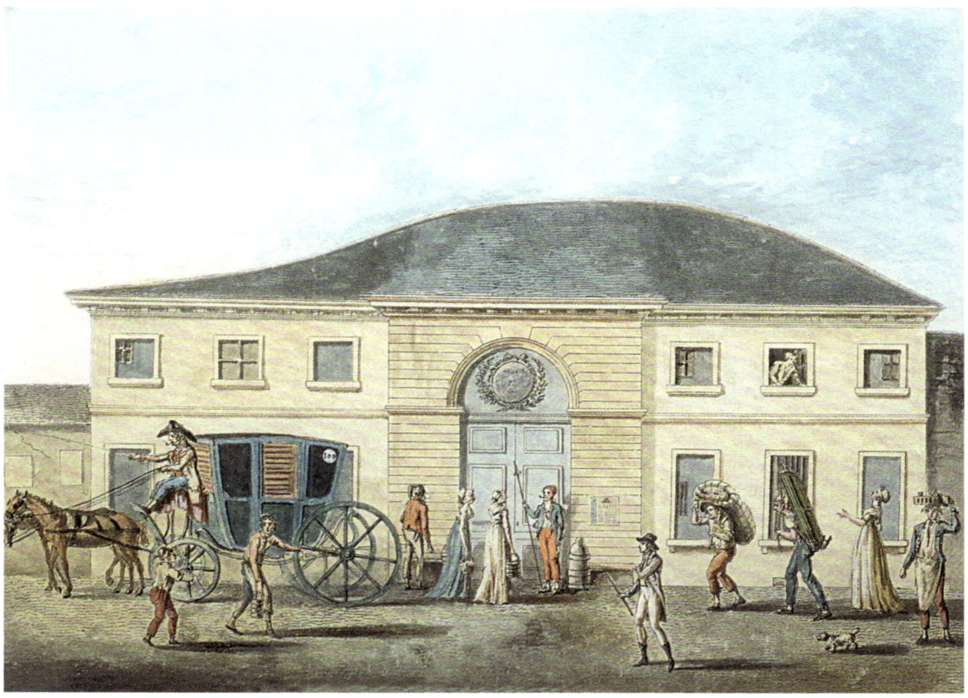

LOUIS XVI IN THE TEMPLE PRISON

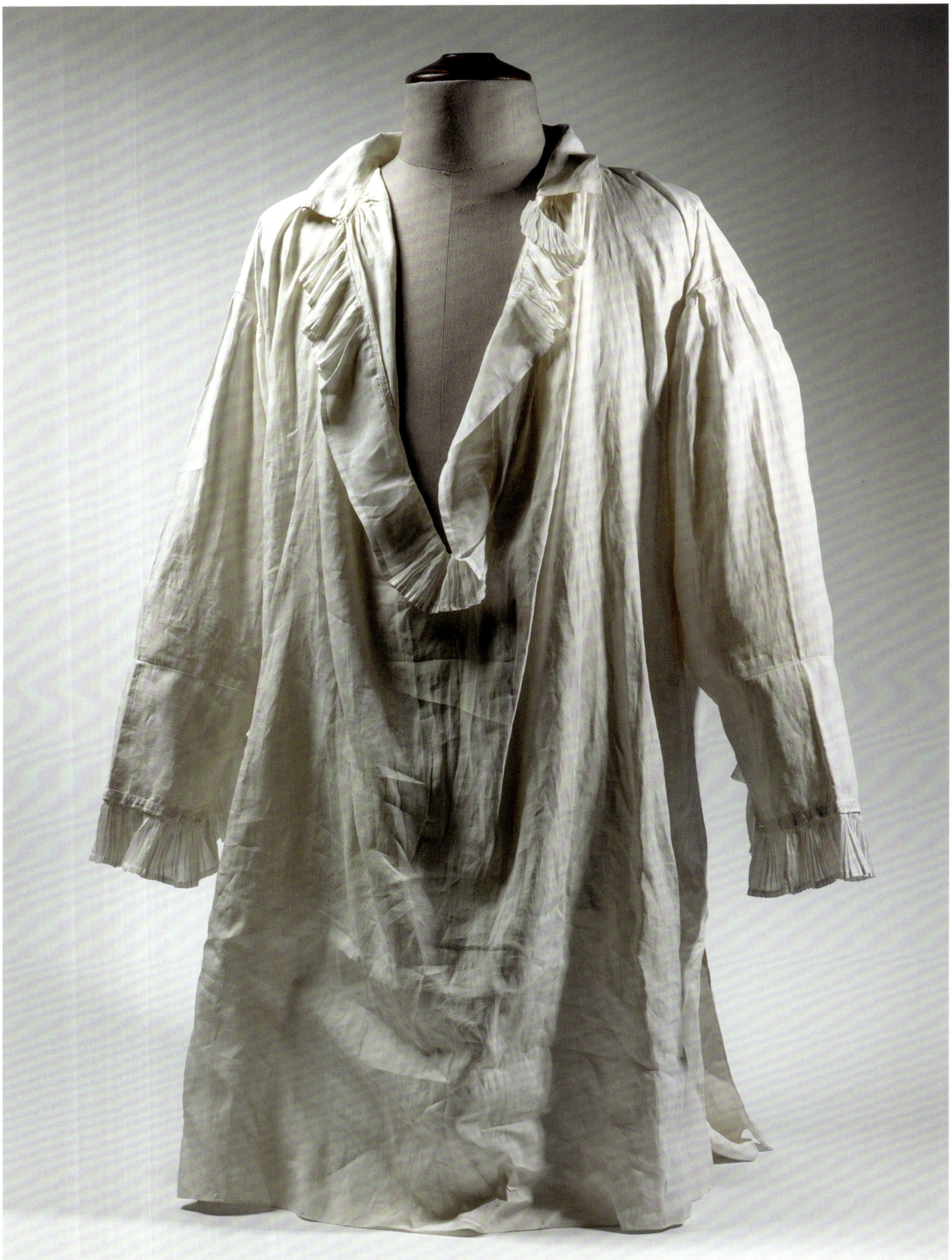

CHEMISE REMOVED BY LOUIS XVI ON THE MORNING OF HIS EXECUTION, 21 JANUARY 1793

Pictured here is the fine muslin chemise with ruffled open collar that was worn by Louis XVI in the Temple, bearing the mark "I.H 19," probably an inventory number, embroidered in red thread. It comes to us from the great-granddaughter of Jean-Baptiste Cléry (Grem de Cléry branch), the King's valet from 26 August 1792 to 21 January 1793. On 13 February 1882 her husband Monsieur Giovanelli gave it to Philippe Gille (1831-1901) who bequeathed it to his son Victor (1884-1964). One of France's most priceless relics, it comes with its original handwritten label, which states (in English) as follows: "worn by the King on the morning of 21 January 1793, before dressing and leaving for the guillotine." It was probably last used on the night of 20-21 January 1793, removed by the King at around 5am in the morning. After washing, he donned a new chemise, followed by a pale brown costume and asked for his confessor, the Abbé Henry Essex Edgeworth de Firmont, who celebrated mass at 6am. Towards 9am, the King and the Abbé boarded a carriage that took them to the Place de la Révolution (now the Place de la Concorde). Louis XVI was beheaded at 10.22am. These are his last words: "I die innocent of all the crimes imputed to me. I pardon the authors of my death and pray God that the blood you are about to spill will never fall upon France ..." His body was immediately transported to the La Madeleine cemetery (now the site of a chapel of atonement) and thrown into a pit, fully dressed, with a covering of quicklime to deter grave robbers. In 1815, following research commissioned by Louis XVIII, the remains of Louis XVI, together with those of Marie-Antoinette, were solemnly exhumed and transferred to the royal basilica of Saint Denis where they rest to this day.

JEAN-FRÉDÉRIC CASENAVE (1770- AFTER 1815), *LOUIS XVI AND HIS CONFESSOR EDGEWORTH AT THE FOOT OF THE GUILLOTINE*

This etching by Jean-Frédéric Casenave shows Louis XVI leaving his confessor at the foot of the guillotine on 21 January 1793. It is modeled on a painting by Charles Benazech (1767-1794), which is now preserved in the collec-ions of Versailles and the Trianon.

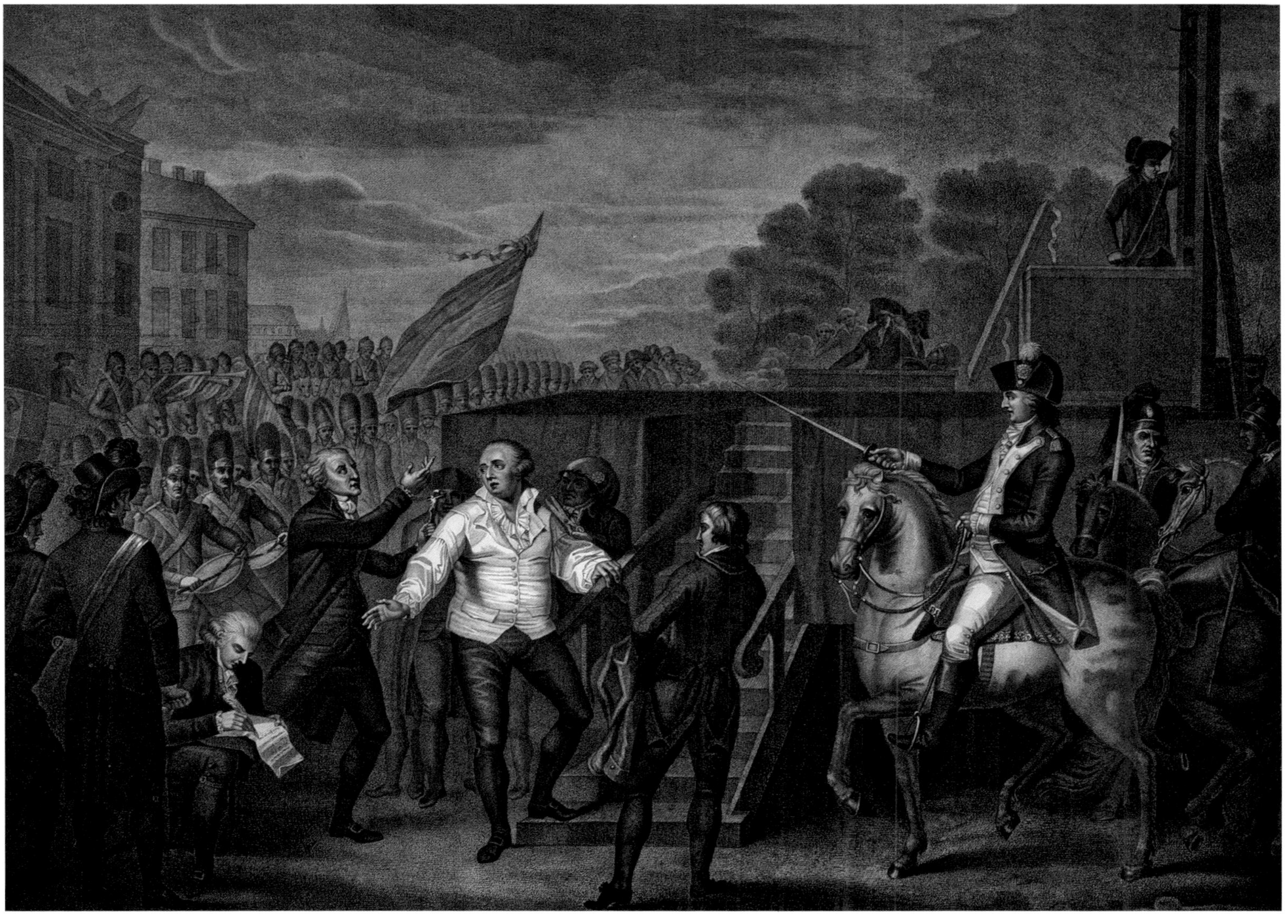

LOUIS XVI'S HEADBAND

This very plain muslin tie headband served to protect the wearer's hair overnight – a poignant reminder of Louis XVI's personal life while in captivity.
The initials *HC* embroidered in red thread are those of the King's ever-faithful valet, Hanet Cléry. On the morning of 21 January 1793, Cléry took away some of the King's personal effects, supposedly for washing, which he then marked with his initials to avoid arousing suspicion. In his *Journal of what took place at the Tower of the Temple (Journal de ce qui s'est passé à la tour du temple)*, written in 1798, he writes that his attendance on the King in the first week at the Tower "was confined to combing his hair in the morning and rolling it up at night …" This headband, together with other belongings such as His Majesty's chemise and the lock decoration and key forged by the King, were left to Cléry's daughter then sold off by his granddaughter at a grand sale of historical memorabilia held in Rouen in 1896. More than a century later, they are finally reunited in the present collection.

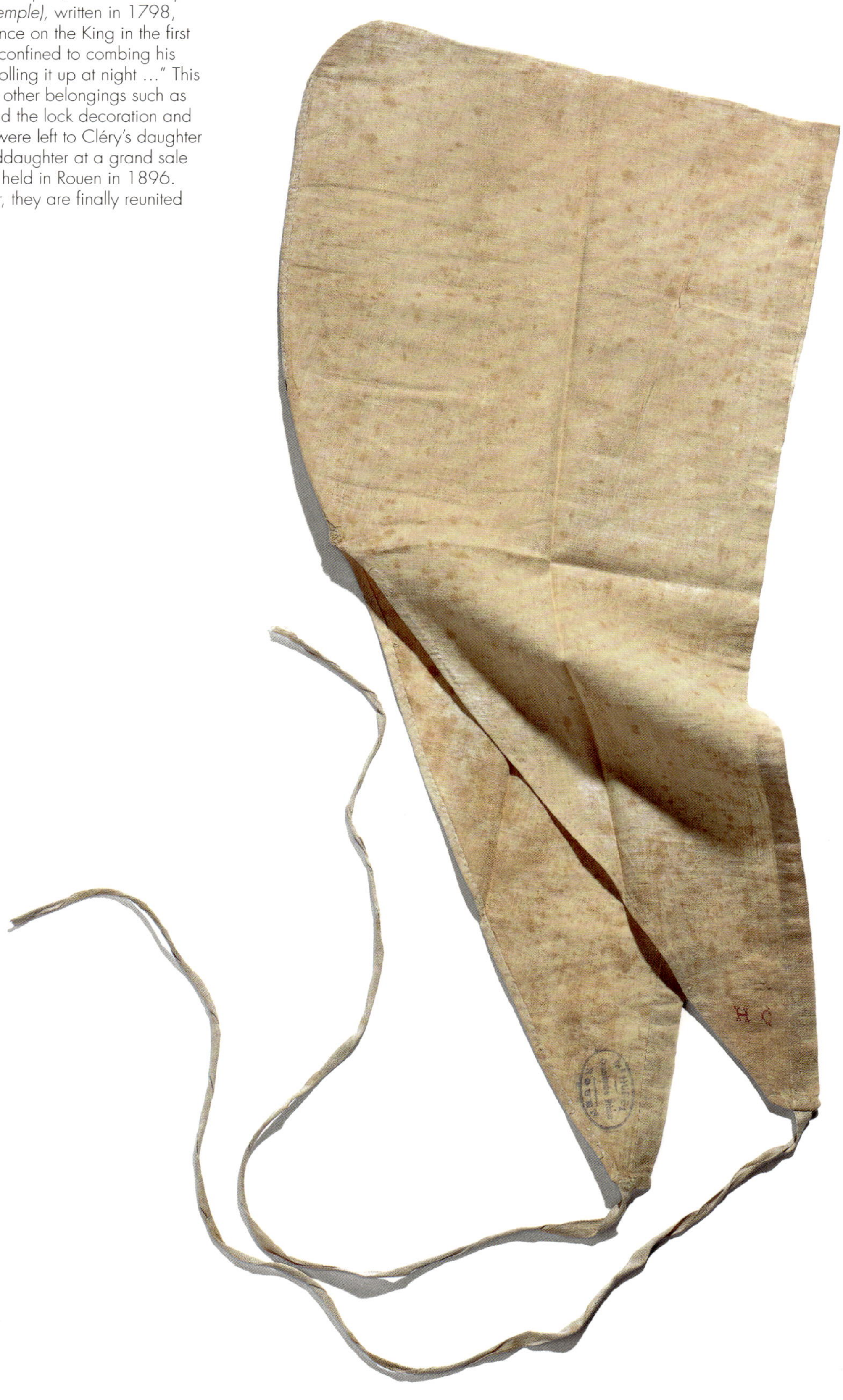

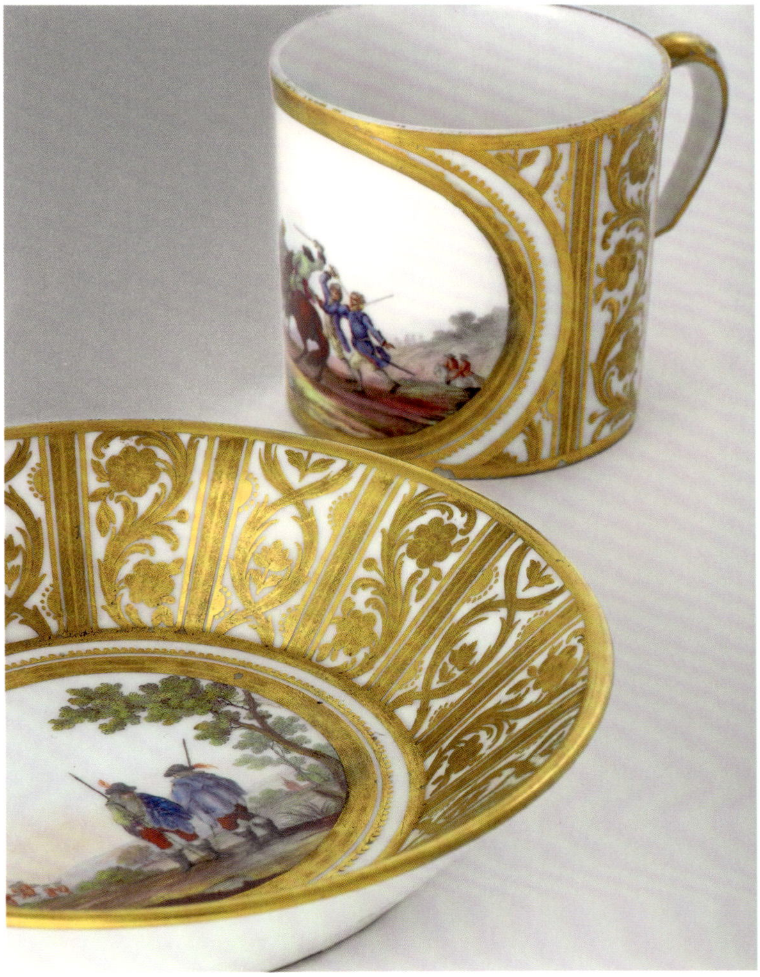

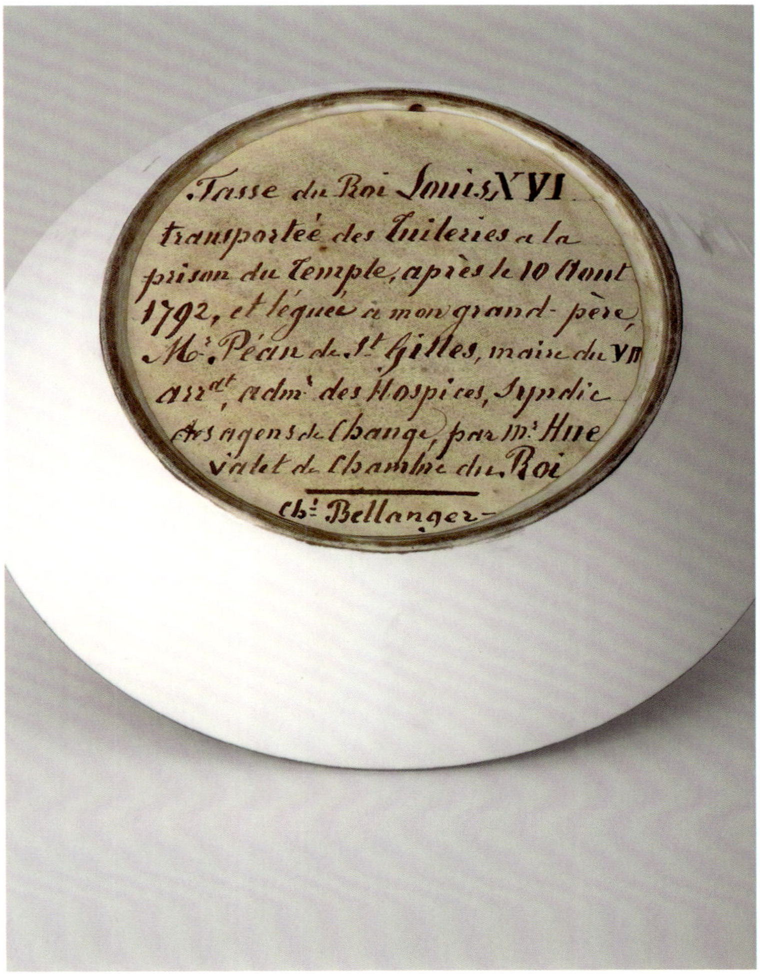

SÈVRES ROYAL MANUFACTORY, CUP USED BY LOUIS XVI AT THE TEMPLE

As attested by an ancient handwritten document, this elegant cup, painted by Philippe Castel, was used by Louis XVI at the Temple then held in safekeeping by his assistant valet François Hüe, who like Cléry followed the royal family into captivity. It subsequently passed into the hands of Louis-Denis Péan de Saint-Gilles, mayor of Paris' 5th Arrondissement from 1808 until 1816. Louis XVI paid tribute to his faithful valets in his will, recommending Hüe's services to his successor and France as a whole. In 1795, Hüe accompanied Marie-Thérèse of France to Austria.

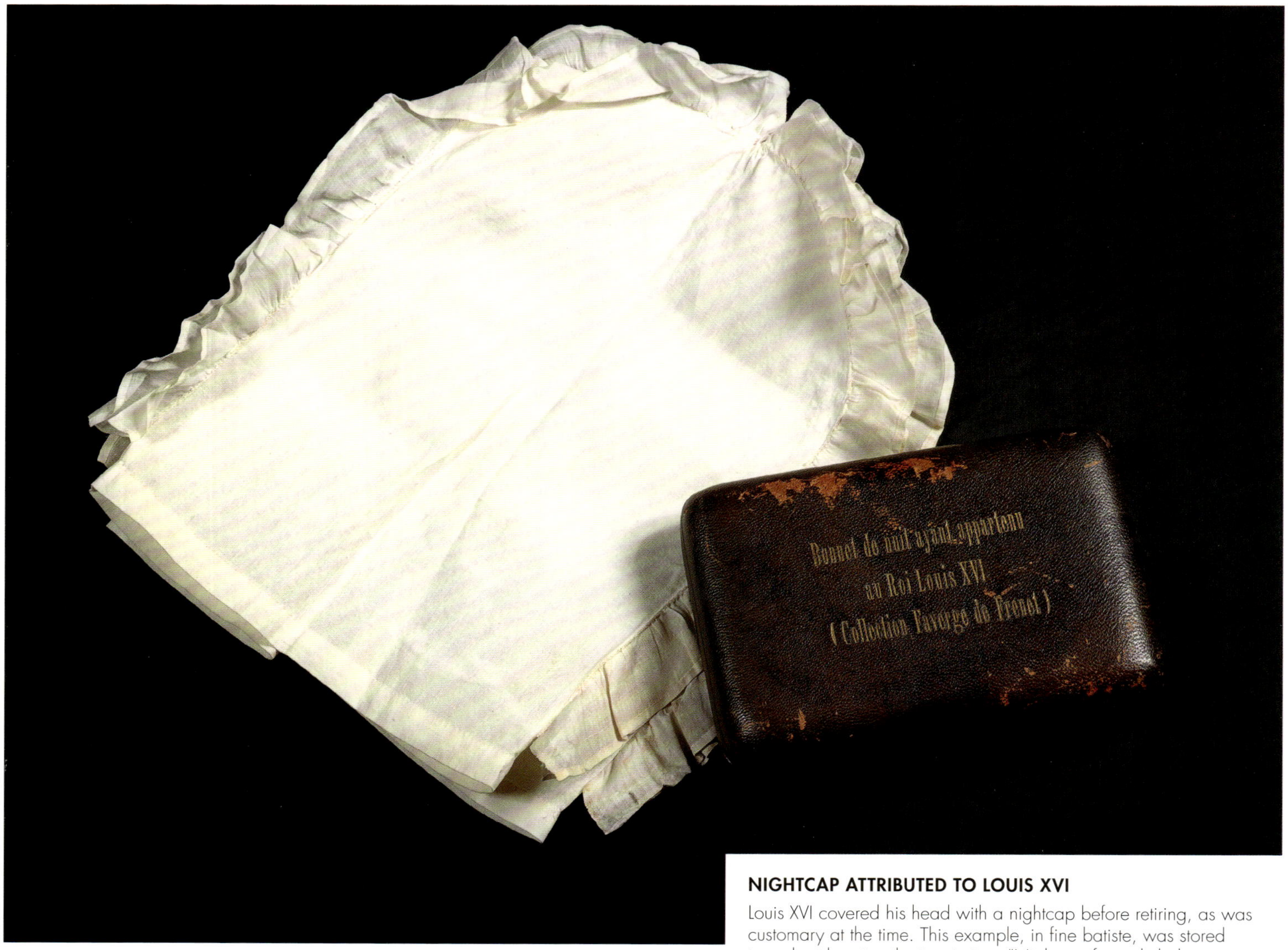

NIGHTCAP ATTRIBUTED TO LOUIS XVI

Louis XVI covered his head with a nightcap before retiring, as was customary at the time. This example, in fine batiste, was stored in a chest bearing the inscription: "Nightcap formerly belonging to Louis XVI *(Faverge de Frenet Collection)*." Despite the absence of any written evidence to that effect, the nightcap's inclusion in the famous collections of Bernard Franck in the late 19th century is proof enough. Reputed to be a real stickler for accuracy, Franck amassed a vast collection of historical objects that set a new benchmark for his fellow collectors.

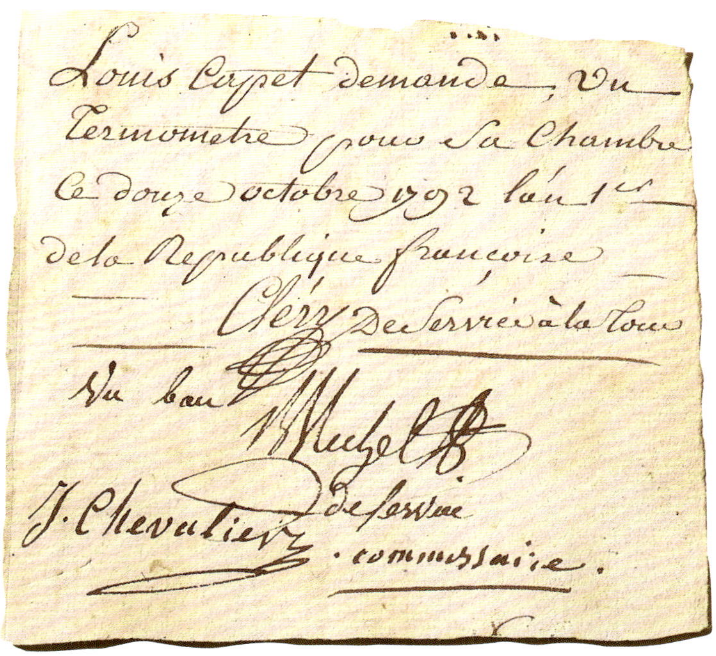
Louis Capet demande, un
Termometre pour sa Chambre
Ce douze octobre 1792 l'an 1er
de la Republique françoise
Cléry De Service à la tour
du ... Michel
J. Chevalier de service
commissaire.

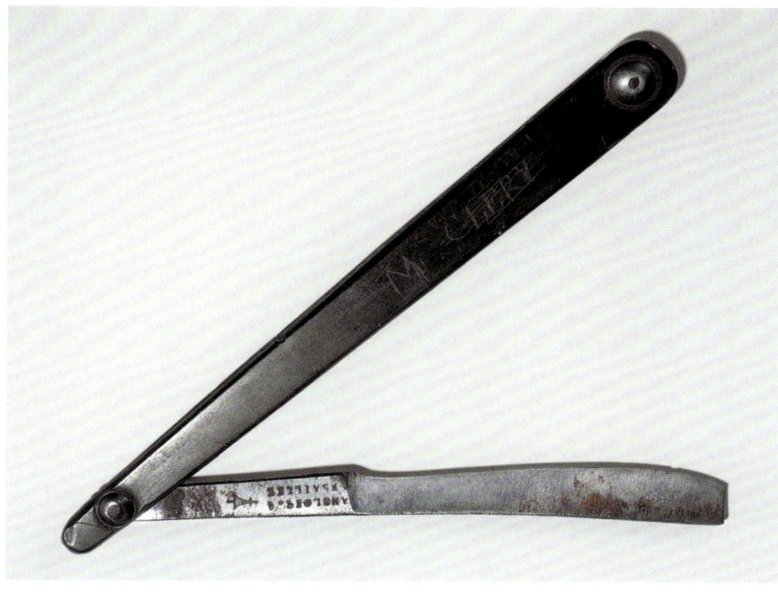

TRICTRAC BOARD AND COUNTERS USED BY THE ROYAL FAMILY AT THE TEMPLE

Board games such as trictrac were among the royal family's only amusements at the Temple. In his *Mémoires* Cléry writes that after dining, "the royal family would gather in the queen's bedroom; their majesties usually played a hand of piquet or a round of trictrac." This was the case on 3 September 1792 – a dark day in French history that saw the head of the Princess de Lamballe impaled on a pike. The Duchess of Angoulême writes in her memoirs that screams were head at 3pm "just as the king and queen had finished eating and were playing trictrac […]." Cléry also describes the occasion when "the noise they were accused of making by jailer Simon came from their game of trictrac, Madame Elisabeth having sought to amuse her niece by teaching her to play." The game pictured here, together with the Dauphin's game of lotto (now preserved in the collections of the Carnavalet Museum, Paris) can be accurately traced back to Jacques Albert Barthélémy (1745 - 1813), Archivist of the Order of Malta at the Temple Tower.

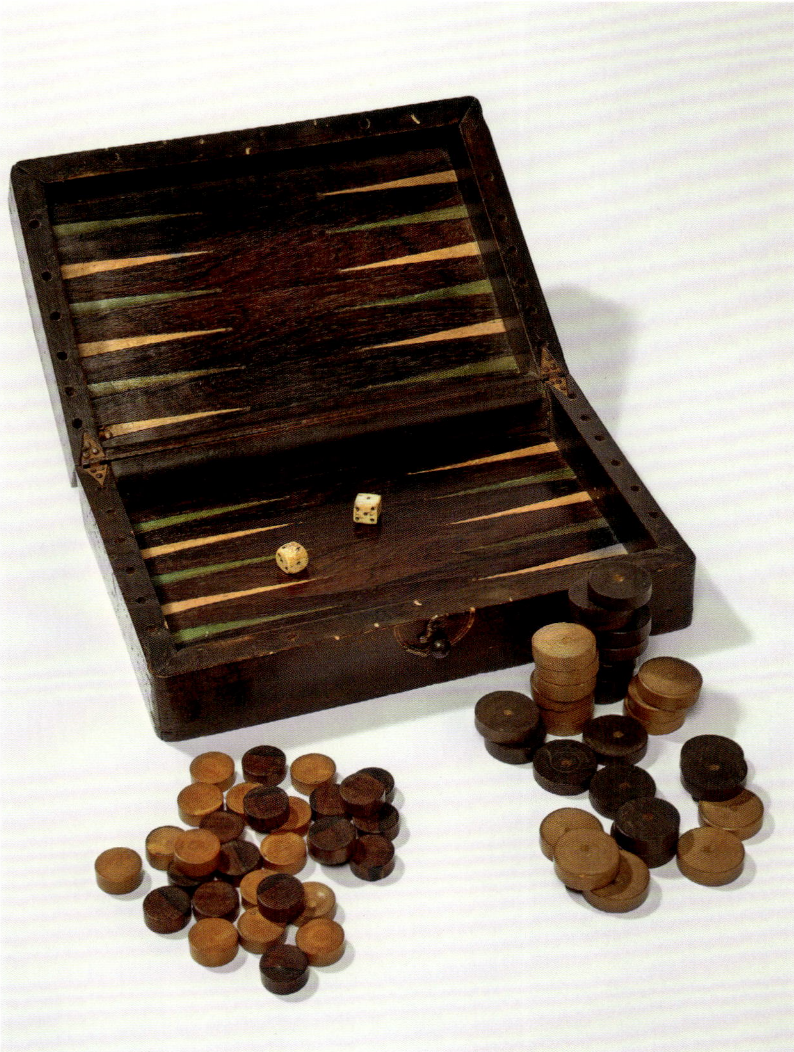

RAZOR AND REQUEST FOR A THERMOMETER FOR LOUIS XVI

This slip of paper, signed by Louis XVI's valet Cléry, testifies to the royal family's straightened circumstances in captivity, not to mention the humiliations inflicted by requests like these, on behalf of a king henceforth known as Louis Capet. Dated 12 October 1792, Year 1 of the French Republic, it says that "Louis Capet" requests a thermometer for his bedroom.
The folding razor pictured here tells the same story. In horn and steel, it is inscribed on one side with the name *M. CLERY* and on the other with the words *N°4 au Temple*. It was among the royal mementoes that were preserved by the Count of Paris then sold off in 2008.

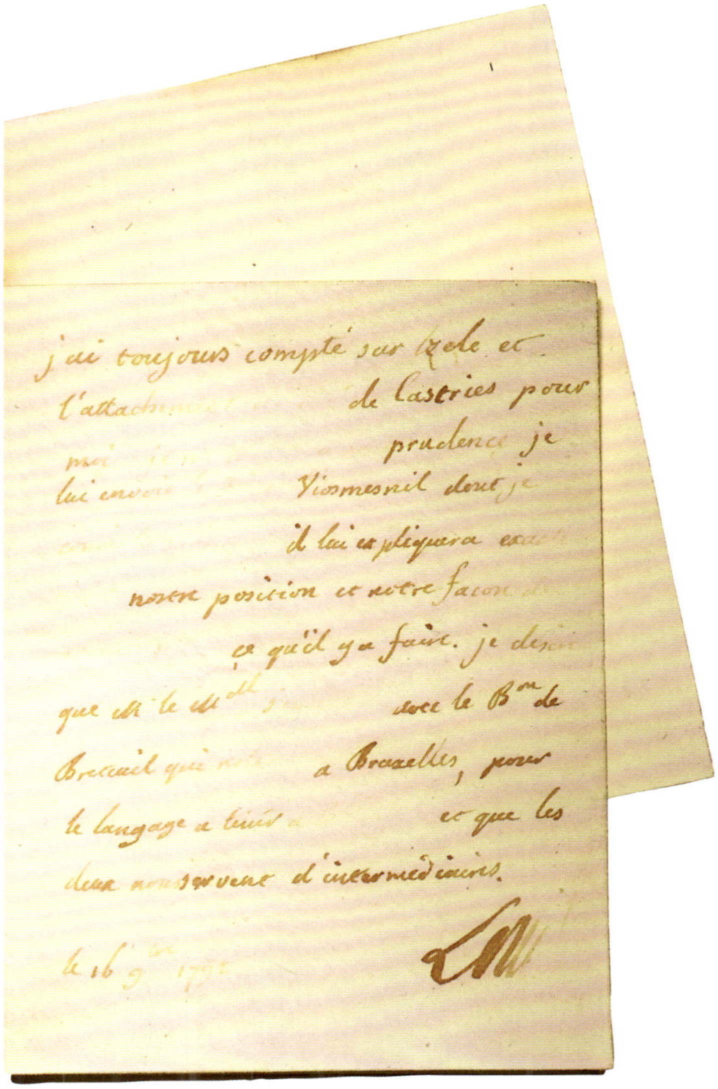

j'ai toujours compté sur le zele et
l'attachm... de Castries pour
... prudence je
lui envoi... Viomesnil dont je
il lui expliquera ex...
notre position et notre façon
ce qu'il y a faire. je desir...
que M. le Mal ... avec le Bon de
Breteuil qui ... a Bruxelles, pour
le langage a tenir ... et que les
deux nous servent d'intermédiaires.

SECRET MESSAGE SENT BY LOUIS XVI TO MARSHAL DE CASTRIES (1727-1801)

Handwritten in sympathetic (invisible) ink based on lemon juice, this extremely rare note from Louis XVI retains the traces of the flames used to reveal the message (the writing turns brown when heated). It testifies to the clandestine exchanges that took place between the King and the French émigrés in Coblenz in the three months before his death, probably facilitated by the Abbé de Firmont. "We have always counted on the unalterable attachment of the Marshal de Castries to our (royal) person. (We entrust ourselves to his) prudence. We are sending him (the good de) Viomesnil who (we know to be of wise counsel). He will inform (Castries) of our position and our view (with regard) to what must be done. We desire that Monsieur le Maréchal and the good de Breteuil, who (remains) in Brussels, should together decide on the appropriate form of address in Coblenz, and that both men should serve as our intermediaries." Noëlle Destremau, a biographer of the King's sister, Madame Elisabeth, writes that the latter succeeded in "communicating with the Abbé de Firmont, who remained in Paris, thanks to the help of Cléry and Turgy. Notes written in invisible ink were tucked around carafe stoppers or slipped into balls of thread or hot-air vents." This note is the sole extant example of a message written in sympathetic ink, and the last known document to have been penned by Louis XVI.

LOUIS XVI'S APPEAL TO THE NATION

This never-published 249-page manuscript presents the final defense of Louis XVI. In mid-December 1792, as the case against him threatened to end in his wrongful execution, King Louis XVI took the advice of his defense lawyer Malesherbes and resolved to draft a *Mémoire* in support of the appeal he would make to the French nation in the likely event that he would be sentenced to death. Within a fortnight he and Malsherbes had prepared a rough draft of the appeal, based on the King's thoughts and recollections. The final version was drawn up by Marc Ferdinand Grouber de Groubentall (1739-1815), a former advocate in the Paris Parlement, who completed the work by around 15 January 1793. On the same day, the Convention (representing judge and prosecutor rolled into one) decreed that its ruling would not be subject to the approval of the people. Louis XVI retaliated the following day by instructing his defense lawyers to inform the Convention that he was launching an appeal to the people. On 17 January the Convention voted in favor of the death penalty, with the right of appeal conclusively denied. On 19 January, Louis XVI put the final touches to his *Appel,* no doubt hoping that his sentence would be commuted. With the agreement of Malesherbes and Groubentall the text was then sent for printing to the J.J. Rainville print works in the Rue de Seine, aiming to send a copy to every household in France. As the pages rolled off the presses, they were proofread and corrected by Groubentall then marked "bon à tirer" (good to print). In the meantime there had been no stay of execution and the Most Christian King had been guillotined. Fearing for his own life, Groubentall cancelled the printing order and quickly destroyed any incriminating documents, including the text of his plea, all except for one copy that was *collationné* (collated), probably by his secretaries, using the set of printers' proofs. This copy was then heavily annotated and reworked in Groubentall's own hand before signing. The first two sheets were amended to include the *Avertissement* initially intended to feature at the top of the version distributed by the King – which in the event was never published. The document was kept hidden by Groubentall who later added the words: "sole proof copy, saved on the day of my arrest 27 March 1793."

A few days before his death, after the restoration of the monarchy in 1815, Groubentall showed the precious document to Louis XVIII, an act for which the Groubentall family was awarded a Civil List pension. His daughter Sophie later offered the manuscript to the rightful heir to the throne of France. Her accompanying letter has survived to this day and reads (in English) as follows:

"Lord, Allow a former Civil List pensioner, daughter of a faithful servant of the Martyr King, to place at your feet the only legacy she was bequeathed by her father, an advocate in the Paris Parlement. Presented here is the manuscript of the *Mémoire* he was commissioned to write by the virtuous Malesherbes but that was doomed never to appear. It therefore belongs not to his daughter but to the heritage of the heir to the virtues and rights of the Martyr King. I have the honor to be, Lord, most respectfully, Your Majesty's most humble, most obedient and most loyal servant and subject. Sophie de Goubentall. Paris, 22 November 1840."

This *Appel* is much more than a simple plea for the defense. Written in the first person, it represents the words of the King and begins with these words "For eighteen years and three months we governed France [...], we were sovereign by right of birth [...]". While Malesherbes and Groubentall were responsible for the research and legal formulation, the ideas expressed are most assuredly those of Louis XVI himself.

The King presents the course of his reign, from his accession to the Throne to his trial. As he reviews all of the events before and during the Revolution, he presents his opinions, justifies his ideas and defends his decisions. In this *Appel* he paints a vast historical fresco that throws light on everything that took place, with the characters seen from different angles and the entire course of the Revolution depicted as a whole and in minute detail. The text is unquestionably the work of Louis XVI, given legal form by Malesherbes and drawn up by Groubentall.

Pictured here is a monument to French history, quite possibly the first major "retrospective" of the Revolution, dictated to his lawyers by the King of France himself.

The set of printer's proofs was also miraculously spared. It reappeared in 1837 and was published in the *Revue Rétrospective, ou Bibliothèque Historique*, Series II, volumes IX-XI. The original document is now housed in the Rare Books Reserve of the Bibliothèque Nationale (*cote* RES-LB41-5145). An article published in the *Quotidienne* of 28 May 1837 retraces the history of the *Appel*:

"This is one of the most important documents, if not the single most important document, ever published by this review. Its history and how it came into our possession deserve to be told. Monsieur de Malesherbes, the King's defense lawyer, finding himself caught up in the fierce debates surrounding the prince's trial, instructed Grouber de Groubentall, an advocate in the Paris Parlement, to draft a memorandum in favor of the accused monarch in the highly likely event that he would be sentenced to death on first hearing and in the largely unfounded hope that the judges would allow the defendant to contest his conviction in an appeal to the people. In a letter to Grouber de Groubentall, bequeathed by the latter to his family, Monsieur de Malesherbes laid out a plan [...] that Groubentall followed to the letter. His *Appel* was delivered to the printer, the pages being proofread by him as the trial was underway. After the fateful sentence was pronounced and the request for an appeal to the people had been rejected, Groubentall, fearing for his own head, quickly destroyed the text of his plea – all except for a single copy [...]. Its whereabouts are unknown – we have asked in vain at the Bibliothèque du Louvre but it has resisted discovery... ."

We wish to thank Roch de Coligny for the research of the present text.

ORIGINAL MANUSCRIPT OF LOUIS XVI'S *APPEL* (DISAPPEARED 1793)

Appel (appeal) of Louis XVI, King of France, to the French people, containing his defenses and grounds put forward in support thereof, pertaining equally to the accusation brought against him by the National Convention, and to the death sentence pronounced by the aforesaid Convention on 17 January 1793. Paris 19 January 1793.

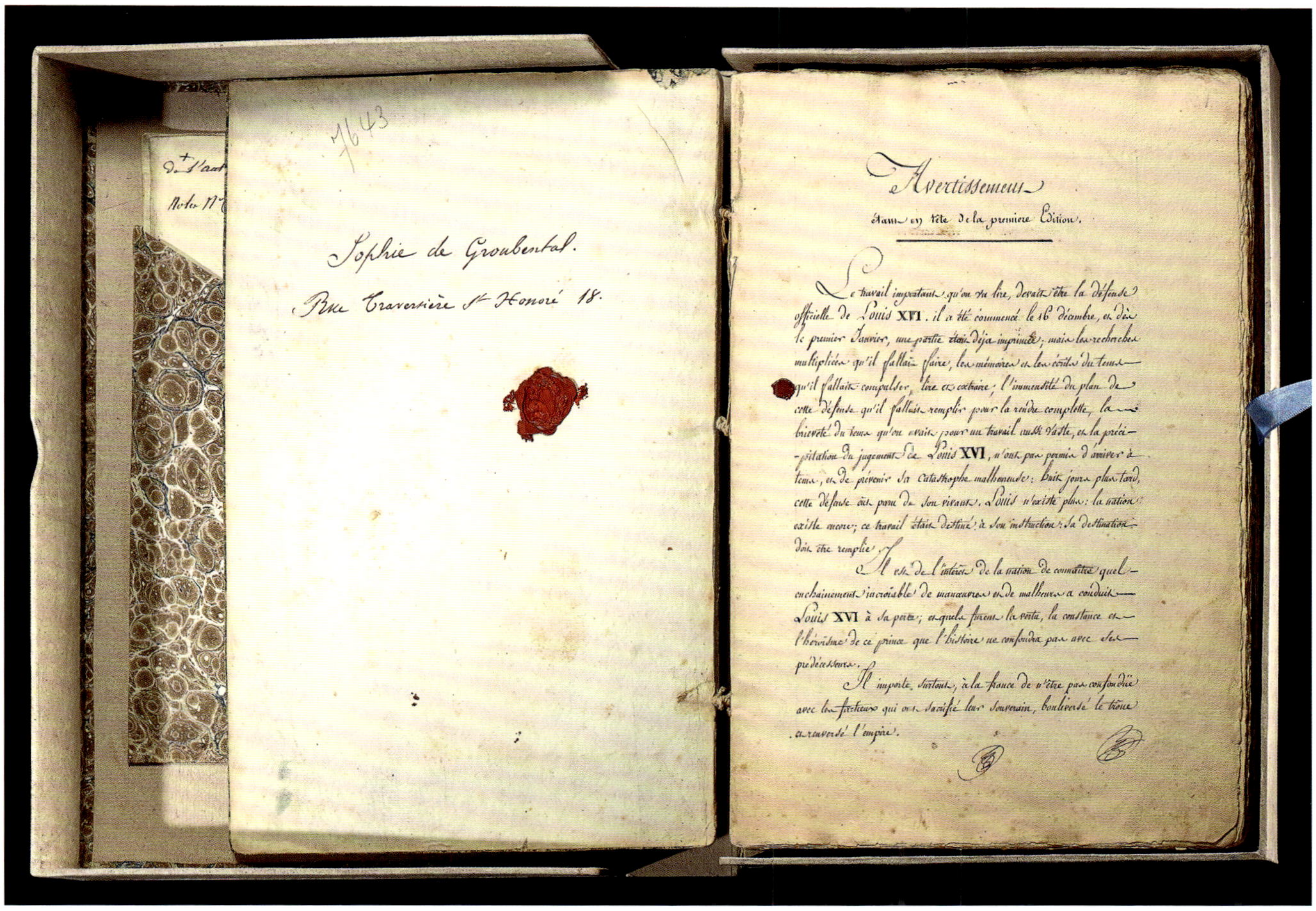

7643

Sophie de Groubentall.
Rue Traversière St Honoré 18.

Avertissement
étant en tête de la première Édition.

Le travail important qu'on va lire, devait être la défense officielle de Louis XVI. il a été commencé le 16 décembre, et dès le premier Janvier, une partie était déjà imprimée; mais les recherches multipliées qu'il fallait faire, les mémoires et les écrits du tems qu'il fallait compulser, lire et extraire, l'immensité du plan de cette défense qu'il fallait remplir pour la rendre complette, la brièveté du tems qu'on avait pour un travail aussi vaste, et la précipitation du jugement de Louis XVI, n'ont pas permis d'arriver à tems, et de prévenir sa catastrophe malheureuse: huit jours plus tard, cette défense eût paru de son vivant. Louis n'existe plus; la nation existe encore; ce travail étant destiné à son instruction, sa destination doit être remplie.

Il est de l'intérêt de la nation de connaître quel enchaînement incroyable de manœuvres et de malheurs a conduit Louis XVI à sa perte; et quelles furent les vertus, la constance et l'héroïsme de ce prince que l'histoire ne confondra pas avec ses prédécesseurs.

Il importe, surtout, à la France de n'être pas confondue avec les factieux qui ont sacrifié leur souverain, bouleversé le trône et renversé l'empire.

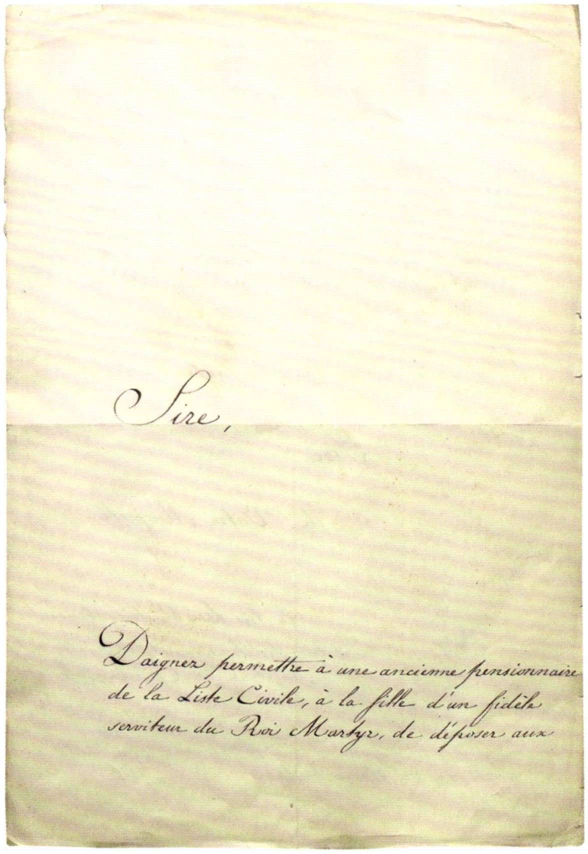

Sire,

Daignez permettre à une ancienne pensionnaire de la Liste Civile, à la fille d'un fidèle serviteur du Roi Martyr, de déposer aux

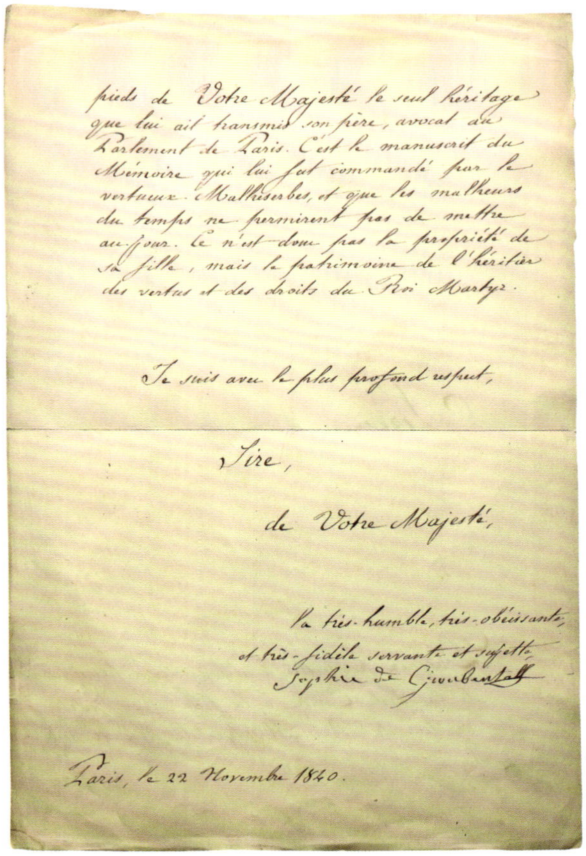

pieds de Votre Majesté le seul héritage que lui ait transmis son père, avocat au Parlement de Paris. C'est le manuscrit du Mémoire qui lui fut commandé par le vertueux Malhesherbes, et que les malheurs du temps ne permirent pas de mettre au jour. Ce n'est donc pas la propriété de sa fille, mais le patrimoine de l'héritier des vertus et des droits du Roi Martyr.

Je suis avec le plus profond respect,

Sire,

de Votre Majesté,

la très-humble, très-obéissante, et très-fidèle servante et sujette,
Sophie de Groubentall

Paris, le 22 Novembre 1840.

MARIE-ANTOINETTE IN THE TEMPLE PRISON

HANDKERCHIEF AND IVORY BOX USED BY MARIE-ANTOINETTE AT THE TEMPLE

This large handkerchief and ivory box bear witness to the Queen's life in the Temple. Marie-Antoinette, like the rest of her family, was allowed few personal effects. An inventory of her belongings, taken on the 26th day of the first month of Year II of the Republic, the day after she was executed, is now stored in the Archives Nationales. It refers to the Queen as Louis Capet's widow and describes the belongings found in her bedroom as follows: "Fifteen fine muslin chemises with lace trimming; one woman's cloak of *raz de Saint-Maur*; two negligees of like fabric […]; four batiste handkerchiefs; […] one towel; […] 24 batiste handkerchiefs; […] one pair of cotton stockings […]." The handkerchief and box were the property of Jean-Baptiste Gomin (1757-1841), one of the two guards of Marie-Antoinette's daughter, Madame Royale. On 29 March 1795, following the departure of the princess, Gomin received permission to retain some of the royal family's personal effects. He later gave them in person to Viscount Alcide de Beauchesne (1800-1873), a Gentleman of the Bedchamber in the reign of Louis XVIII and a head of department at the Archives Nationales. They remained in his family until 2015, together with other belongings that included Louis XVII's waistcoat as featured below.

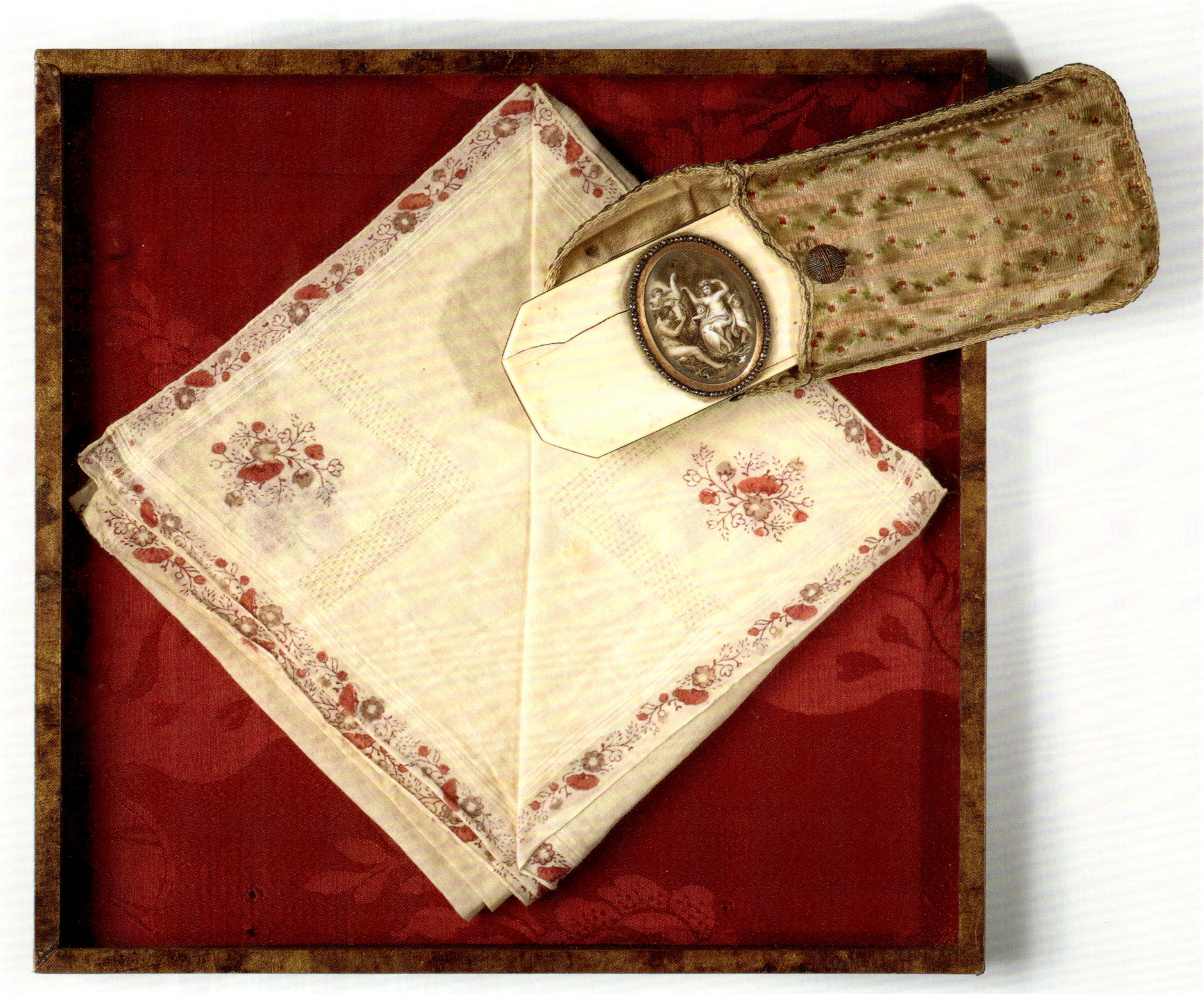

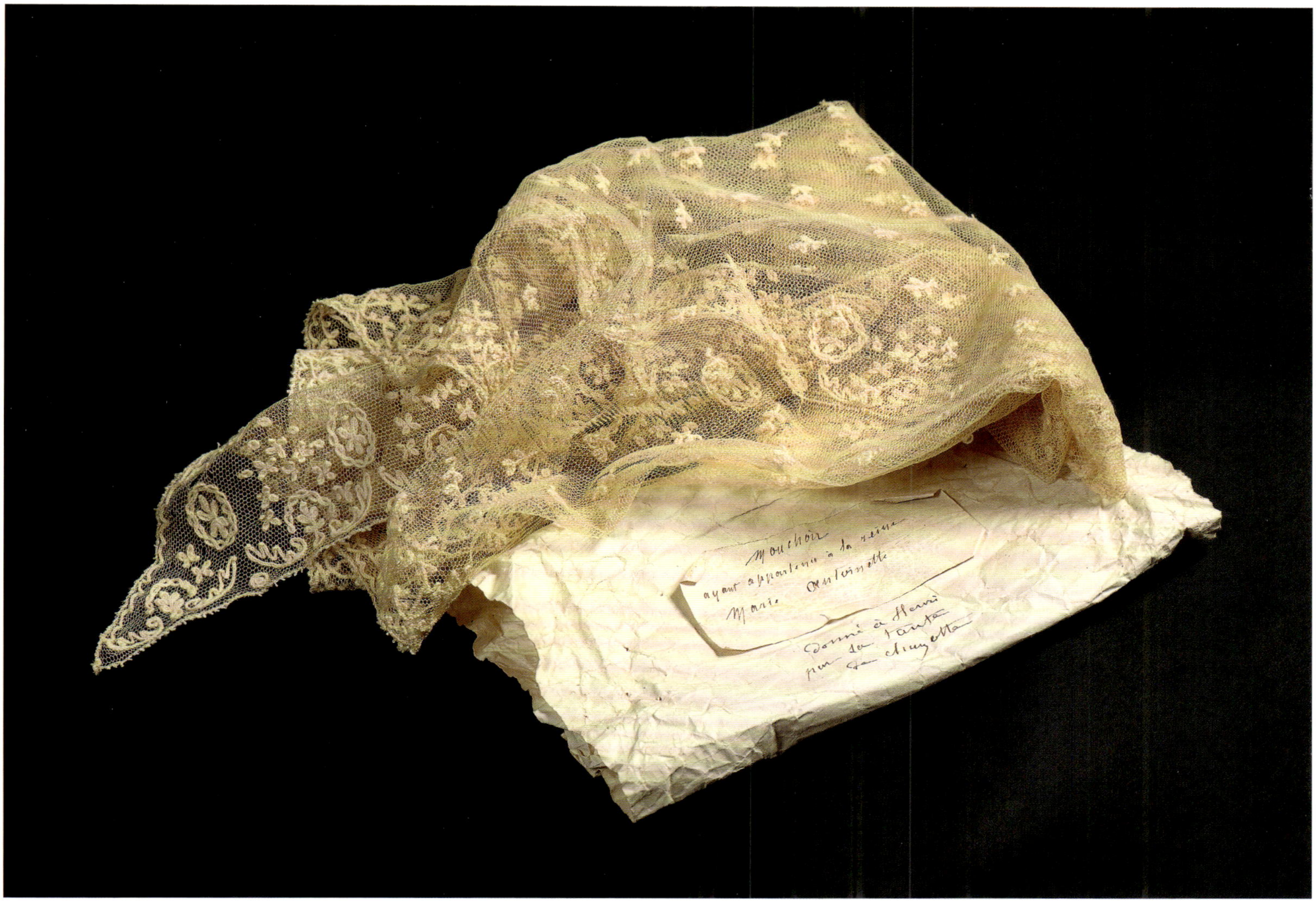

LACE *FICHUS* BELONGING TO MARIE-ANTOINETTE

The collection owns two lace *fichus* that were probably worn by Marie-Antoinette in the English hamlet she had constructed at Le Petit Trianon. Both are of Argentan and Alençon lace embellished with leafy *rinceaux*. This one, complete with original handwritten document retracing its history, was carefully preserved by the estate of Her Highness the Princess Ernest de Ligne, born Diane de Cossé-Brissac (1869-1950). The other, identical except for slight variations in floral decoration, comes from the direct descendants of Alexandre Chappet de Vangel (1765-1838), the officer in charge of protecting the Dauphin and Dauphine. The *fichu* pictured here featured in the *Marie-Antoinette Archiduchesse, Dauphine et Reine* exhibition held at Versailles in 1955, exhibit number 506.

KNITTING NEEDLES USED BY MARIE-ANTOINETTE AT THE TEMPLE

Cléry, who witnessed firsthand how the royal family lived from day to day, writes in his *Mémoires* that their life at the Temple was punctuated by simple activities. The end of the morning, for instance, "was spent sewing, knitting or weaving." This pair of ivory knitting needles was used by Marie-Antoinette at the Temple, fetched for her by jailer Tison's daughter with the permission of the Committee of Public Health. After passing into the hands of Madame Armand Bruat, Governess of the Children of France, the needles were bequeathed to the Bandy de Nalèche family who sold them for a very good price to that inveterate collector of revolutionary memorabilia Alain Bancel, in whose possession they remained until his death in 2003.

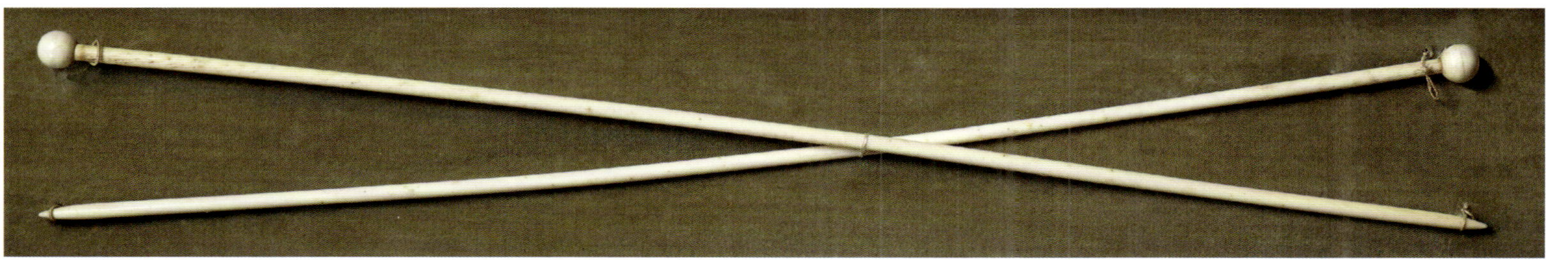

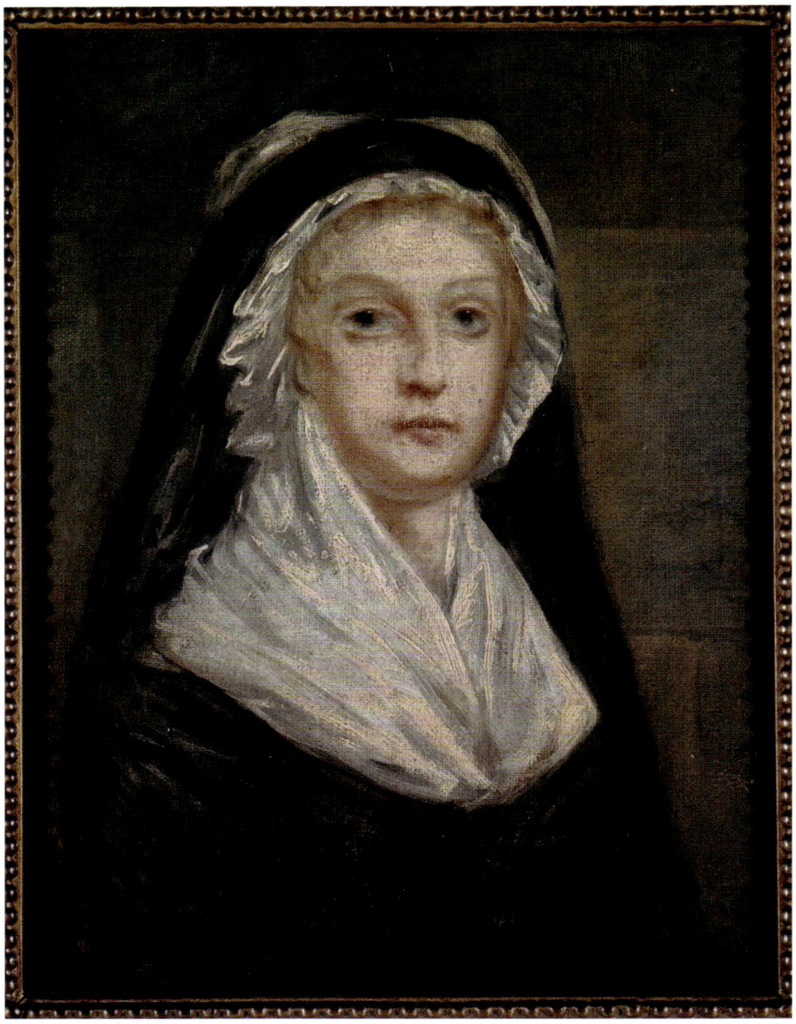

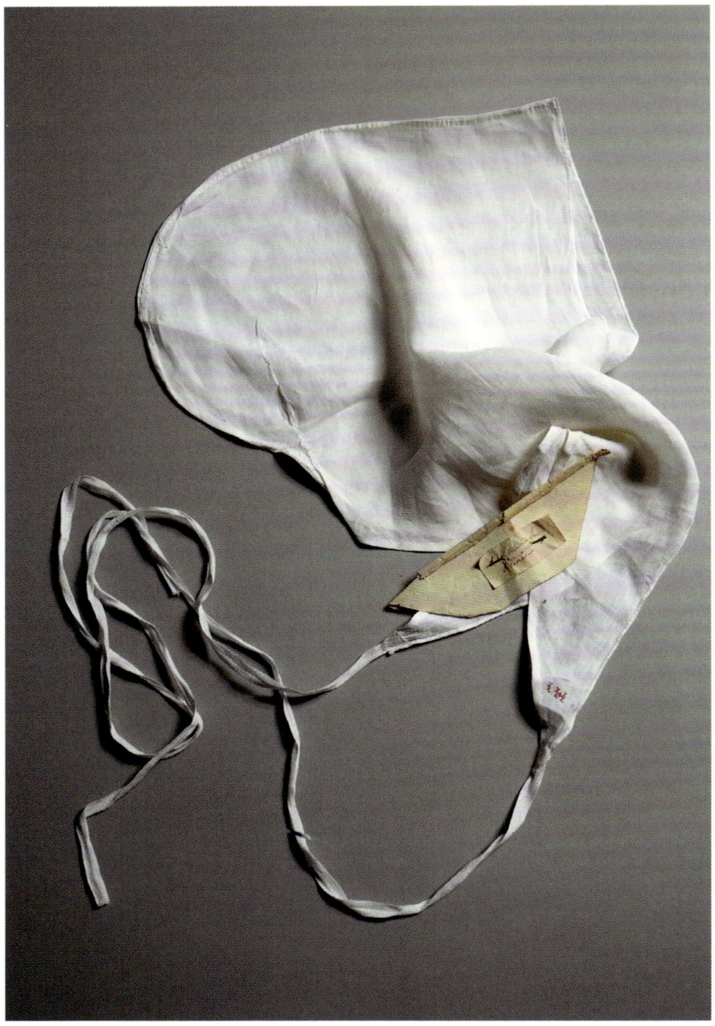

ALEXANDRE KUCHARSKI (1741-1819),
MARIE-ANTOINETTE IN THE TEMPLE PRISON

Coll. Musée Carnavalet

HEADBAND WORN BY QUEEN MARIE-ANTOINETTE AT THE TEMPLE

Fine muslin bonnet worn by the Queen in the Temple prison, with the mark LH (probably an inventory code) embroidered in red thread (cf Louis XVI's chemise, above, bearing the mark LH19). This intimate item of clothing was preserved by the King's valet who left it to his great-granddaughter (Grem de Cléry branch). On 13 February 1882, her husband Monsieur Giovanelli gave it to Philippe Gilles (1831-1901) whose grandfather was police commissionaire at the time of the Revolution. Following the death of his son Victor (1884-1964), the headband was sold on 20 May 1965 to the Hôtel Drouot.

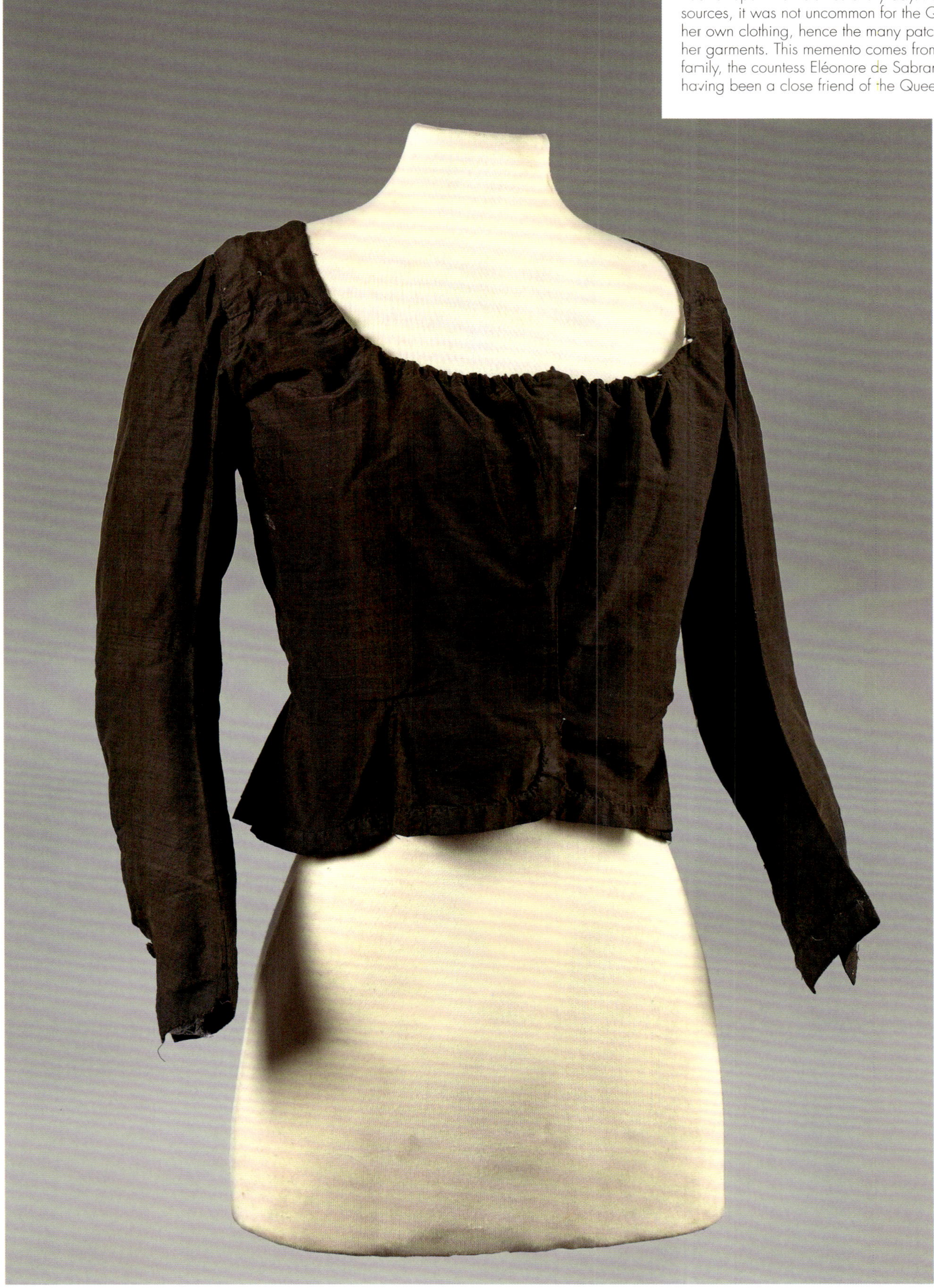

MOURNING BODICE WORN BY QUEEN MARIE-ANTOINETTE AT THE TEMPLE

Following the King's death on 21 January 1793, Marie-Antoinette put in a request for mourning dress. It was granted the very next day, witness this very simple black bodice, so heavily darned that there can be no doubt as to the deprivations endured by the Queen and her children in the Temple Tower. In his journal, Jean-Baptiste Cléry writes that the royal family was so short of garments that the princesses had to repair their clothes every day. According to certain sources, it was not uncommon for the Queen to mend her own clothing, hence the many patches on the inside of her garments. This memento comes from the Sabran-Pontevès family, the countess Eléonore de Sabran (1750-1827) having been a close friend of the Queen.

MARTYRED CHILDREN: FROM VERSAILLES TO THE TEMPLE PRISON

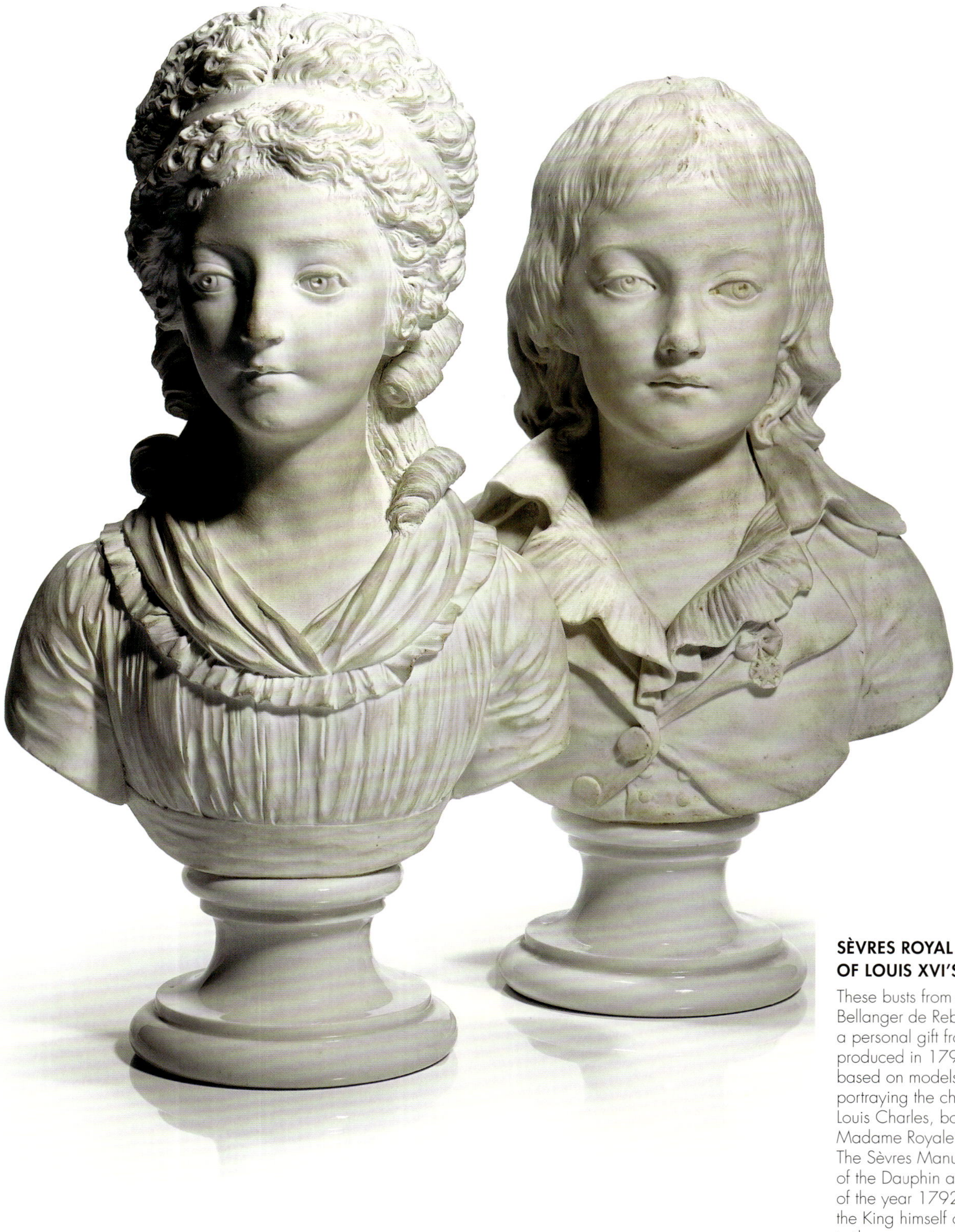

SÈVRES ROYAL MANUFACTORY, BUSTS OF LOUIS XVI'S CHILDREN, C. 1792

These busts from the private collection of the Bellanger de Rebourseaux family were reputedly a personal gift from King Louis XVI. They were produced in 1792 by the Sèvres Manufactory, based on models by Louis-Simon Boizot (1743-1809) portraying the children of France: the Dauphin Louis Charles, born in 1785, and his elder sister Madame Royale, then aged 14.
The Sèvres Manufactory sold a number of busts of the Dauphin and Madame Royale in the first half of the year 1792, among them those bought by the King himself on 9 February that year. As recorded in the accounts, each one sold for 36 *livres*.

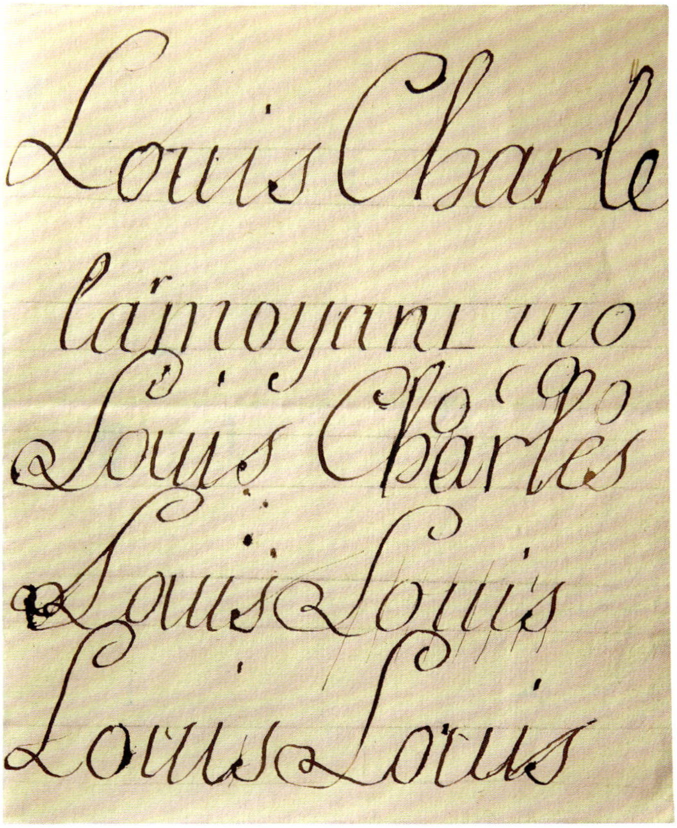

Louis Charle

Louis Charles

Louis Louis

Louis Louis

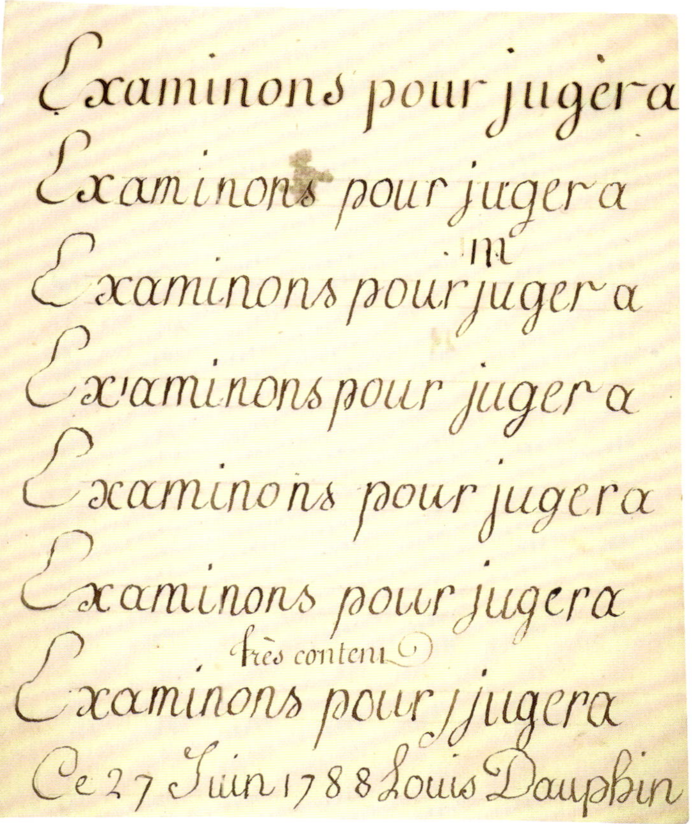

Examinons pour juger a

Examinons pour juger a

Examinons pour juger a

Examinons pour juger a

Examinons pour juger a

Examinons pour juger a

très content

Examinons pour jugera

Ce 27 Juin 1788 Louis Dauphin

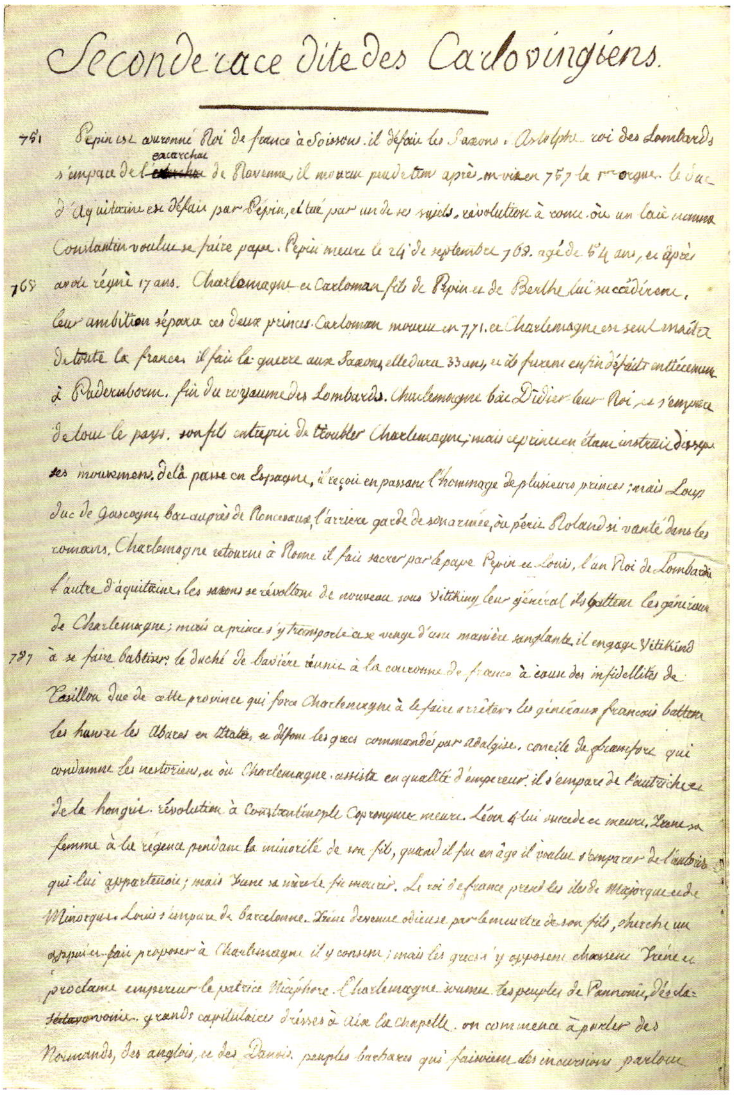

Seconde race dite des Carlovingiens.

751 Pépin est couronné Roi de france à Soissons. il défait les Saxons. Astolphe roi des Lombards s'empare de l'exarchat de Ravenne, il meurt peu de tems après. ... 757 le 1er orgue. le Duc d'Aquitaine est défait par Pépin, et tué par un de ses sujets. révolution à Rome où un laïc nommé Constantin voulut se faire pape. Pépin meurt le 24 de septembre 768. agé de 54 ans, et après avoir régné 17 ans.

768 Charlemagne et Carloman fils de Pépin et de Berthe lui succédèrent. leur ambition sépara ces deux princes. Carloman mourut en 771. et Charlemagne en seul maître de toute la france. il fait la guerre aux Saxons, elle dura 33 ans, et ils furent enfin défaits entièrement à Paderborn. fin du royaume des Lombards. Charlemagne bat Didier leur Roi, et s'empare de tout le pays. son fils entreprit de troubler Charlemagne; mais ce prince étant instruit ... ses mouvemens, delà passe en Espagne, il reçoit en passant l'hommage de plusieurs princes; mais Loup duc de Gascogne bat auprès de Roncevaux l'arrière garde de son armée, où périt Roland si vanté dans les romans. Charlemagne retourne à Rome il fait sacrer par le pape Pépin et Louis, l'un Roi de Lombardie l'autre d'aquitaine. les saxons se révoltent de nouveau sous Vitikind leur général ils battent les généraux de Charlemagne; mais ce prince s'y transporte et se venge d'une manière sanglante. il engage Vitikind

787 à se faire baptiser. le duché de Bavière réuni à la couronne de france à cause des infidélités de Tassillon duc de cette province qui force Charlemagne à le faire arrêter. les généraux françois battent les huns et les Abares en ... et défont les grecs commandés par Adalgise. concile de francfort qui condamne les nestoriens, et où Charlemagne assiste en qualité d'empereur. il s'empare de l'autriche et de la hongrie. révolution à Constantinople Copronyme meurt. Léon 4 lui succède et meurt. Irène sa femme a la régence pendant la minorité de son fils, quand il fut en âge il voulut s'emparer de l'autorité qui lui appartenoit; mais Irène ... Le roi de france prend les isles de Majorque et de Minorque. Louis s'empare de Barcelonne. Irène devenue odieuse par le meurtre de son fils, cherche un appui et fait proposer à Charlemagne il y consent; mais les grecs s'y opposent, chassent Irène et proclament empereur le patrice Nicéphore. Charlemagne soumet les peuples de Pannonie, de la ... grands capitulaires dressés à Aix la Chapelle. on commence à parler des Normands, des anglois, et des Danois. peuples barbares qui faisoient des incursions partout

WRITING EXERCISES OF THE CHILDREN OF FRANCE

Pictured top right, dated 27 June 1788, is an exercise by Louis Joseph Dauphin of France (1781-1789). Beside it, given a *Très content* grade by his writing teacher, is an exercise by his brother Louis Charles (1785-1795), who became Dauphin of France in 1789. Pictured bottom left is a story titled *Seconde Race des Carolingiens*, in the handwriting of Marie-Thérèse Charlotte de France, firstborn child of Louis XVI and Marie-Antoinette. Madame Royale was the only child to survive imprisonment in the Temple. She died in 1851 having assumed her husband's title and become known as the Duchess of Angoulême.

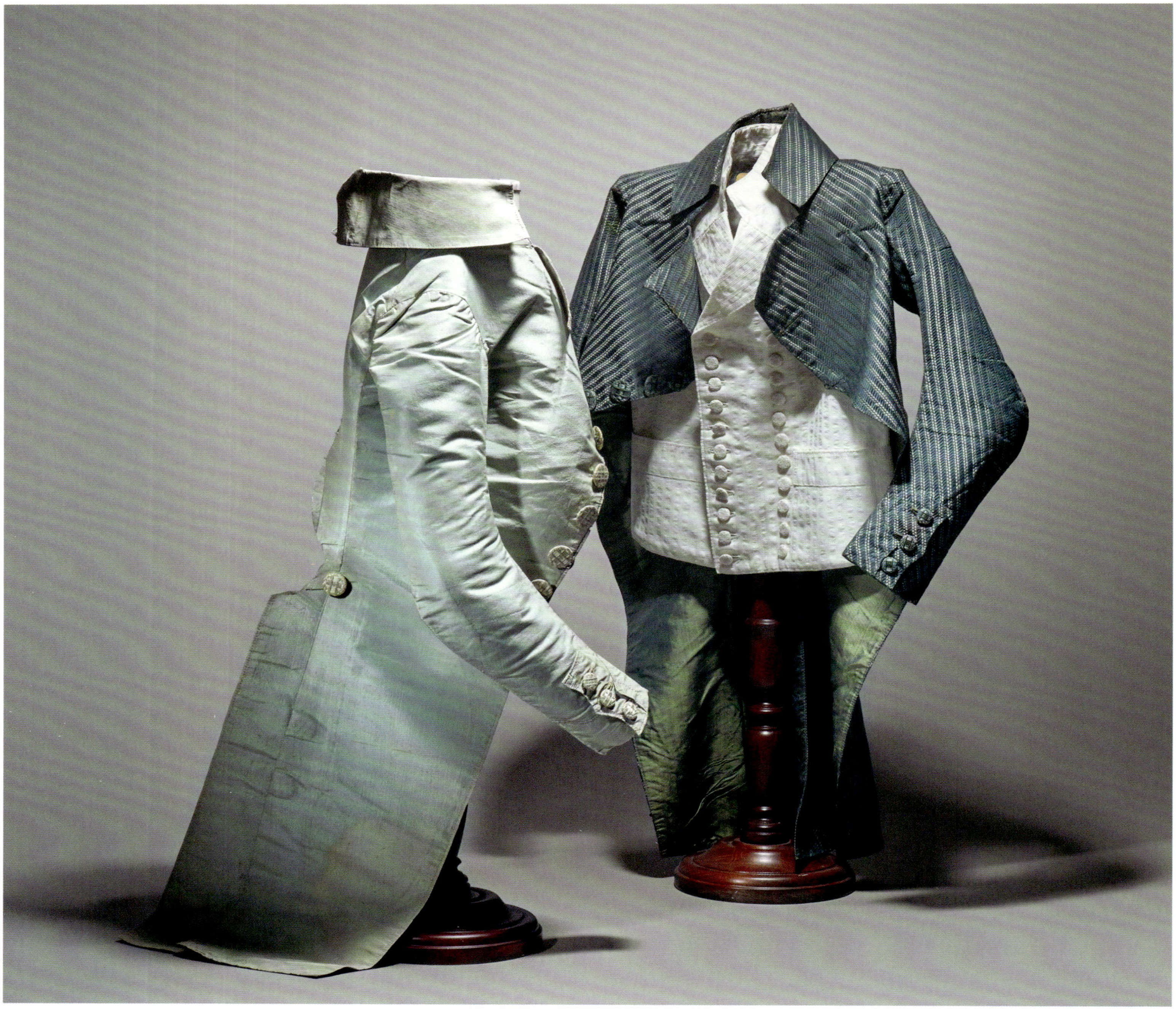

TWO COSTUMES INCLUDING THE SO-CALLED *HABIT BLEU* COSTUME WORN BY LOUIS XVII AT VERSAILLES

The collection owns two of Louis XVII's costumes: a striped green silk costume from Cléry; and the partial remains of a blue silk costume very like the one depicted in the famous portrait by Kucharski. One half was owned by Karl-Wilhelm Naundorff, who was notorious for passing himself off as Louis XVII; the other half was preserved by Louis XVII's sister Marie-Thérèse-Charlotte (1778-1851).

The incredible story of this *habit bleu* goes as follows. On Saturday 17 August 1833 at 9am, Madame de Rambaud, then aged 68, nanny and governess to the Dauphin until 1792, was called in by the advocate Ferdinand Geoffroy to confound the imposter Naundorff. Geoffroy kept a record of their meeting. After questioning the pretender, she said: "Since I was not admitted to the Temple with Mme Touzel, I held onto a small outfit as a reminder of my dear Prince; perhaps you will remember wearing it, and in what circumstances, at the Tuileries?" The *habit bleu* was spread out before the eyes of Naundorff, who exclaimed: "Why yes! I remember it well; it wasn't at the Tuileries but at Versailles, for a party ... and I don't think I have worn it since due to its uncomfortable fit." Overcome by emotion Mme de Rambaud cried out: "Oh my God! Oh my God! It's him! Only my Prince could tell me that." She wrung her hands as the tears came pouring down her face. "Yes! Yes! It was at Versailles and you didn't want to wear it anymore." History will remember that she genuinely believed Naundorff to be the child she had so loved.

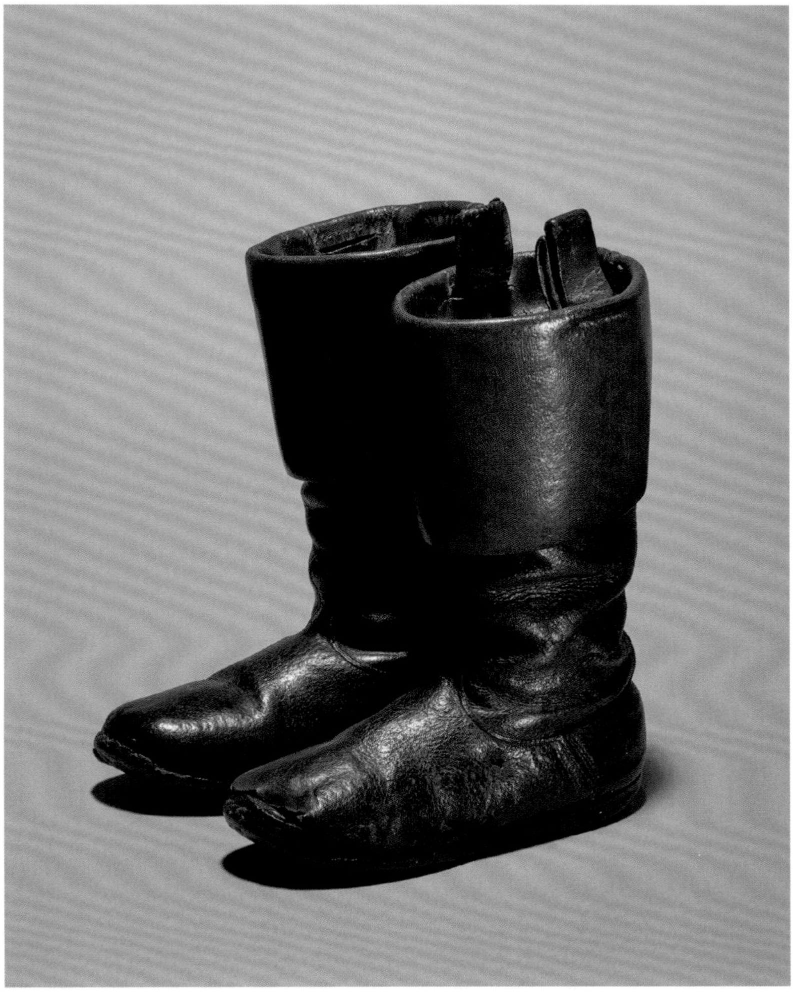

PAIR OF BOOTS WORN BY LOUIS XVII

This small pair of leather riding boots comes accompanied with a handwritten label attesting to its provenance: "At the time of the Terror in 1787 (sic), the Temple jailer Simon sold Sire Peynette, a clothing merchant at the Temple, a small pair of boots belonging to the Dauphin Louis. These were purchased as a memento by my father on one of his three-monthly visits to Paris. Sensing his end was nigh he then gifted them to me while requesting that I keep them in memory of their illustrious owner. Tailleu, 11 Rue Rampon." The boots, now in very bad condition following more than 200 years of damp storage, were exhibited at the Paris "Louis XVII" Exhibition in 1987.

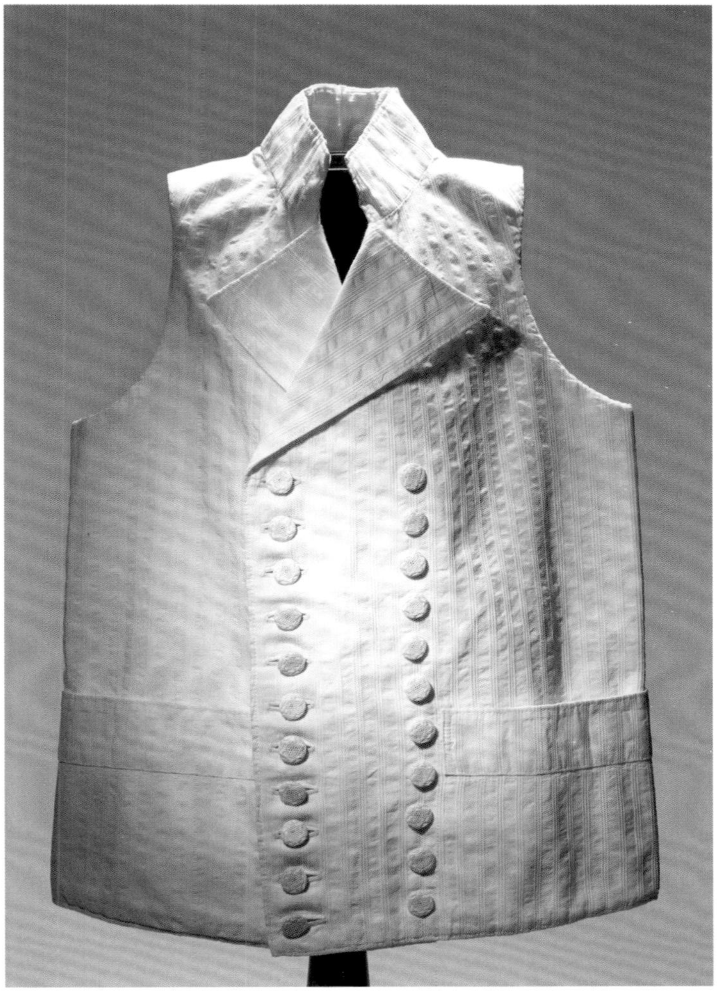

WHITE COTTON WAISTCOAT WORN BY LOUIS XVII IN THE TEMPLE

Pictured here is one of two waistcoats worn by Louis XVII in the Temple. Both are in striped white cotton muslin, with the letter "D" (for Dauphin) embroidered in red thread. In the closing years of the Revolution, François-Etienne Lasne (1758-1841) and Jean-Baptiste Gomin (1757-1841), were granted permission to acquire some of the King's linen and personal effects. Each chose a waistcoat. Lasne later gifted his waistcoat to the parents of Madame Turpin de Crissé, whose descendants kept it until 2003; Gomin gave his waistcoat to Viscount Alcide Hyacinthe de Beauchesne (1804-1873), first biographer of Louis XVII, whose direct descendants kept it until 2005. Both now belong to this collection.

LOUIS XVII AND HIS JAILER

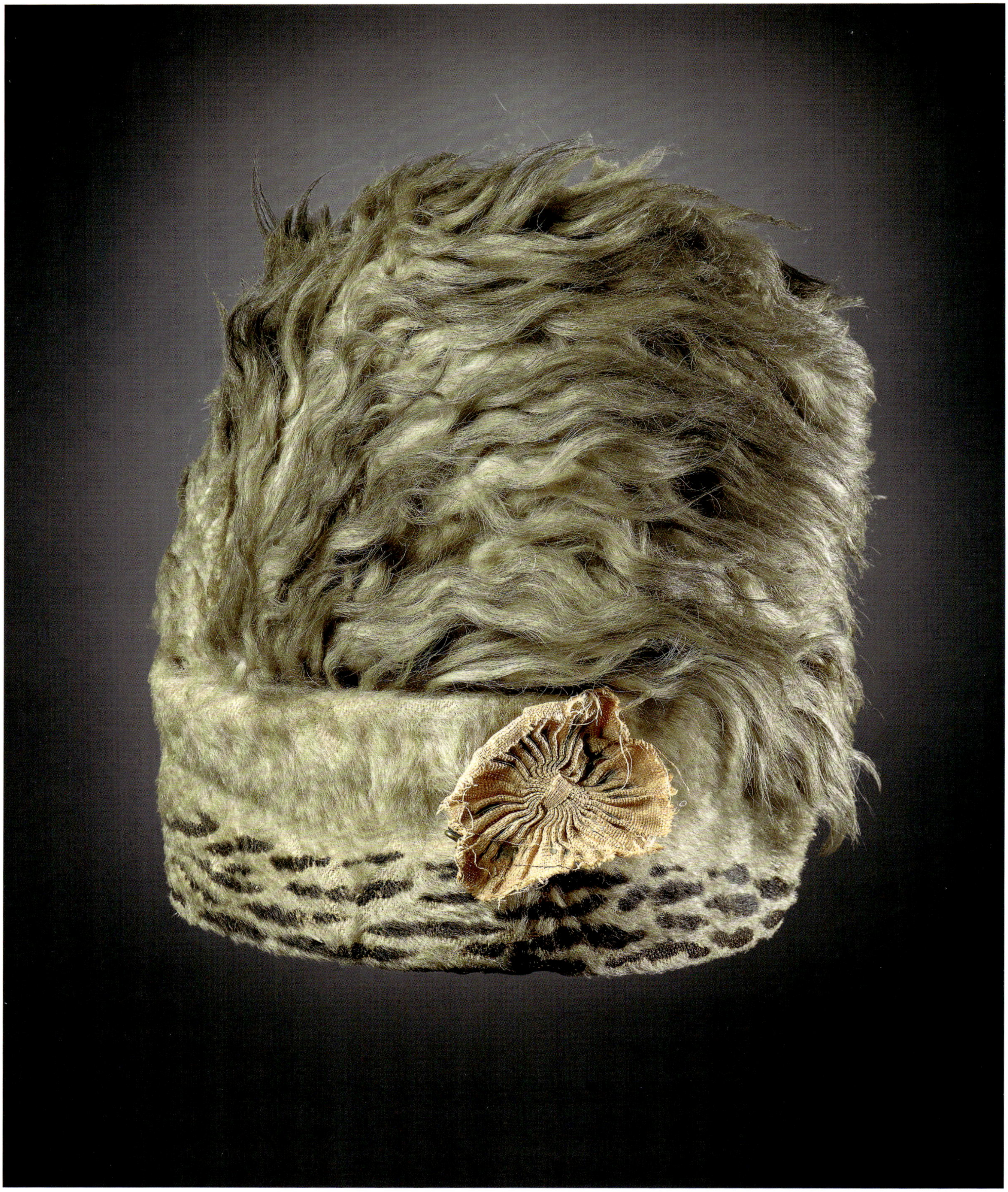

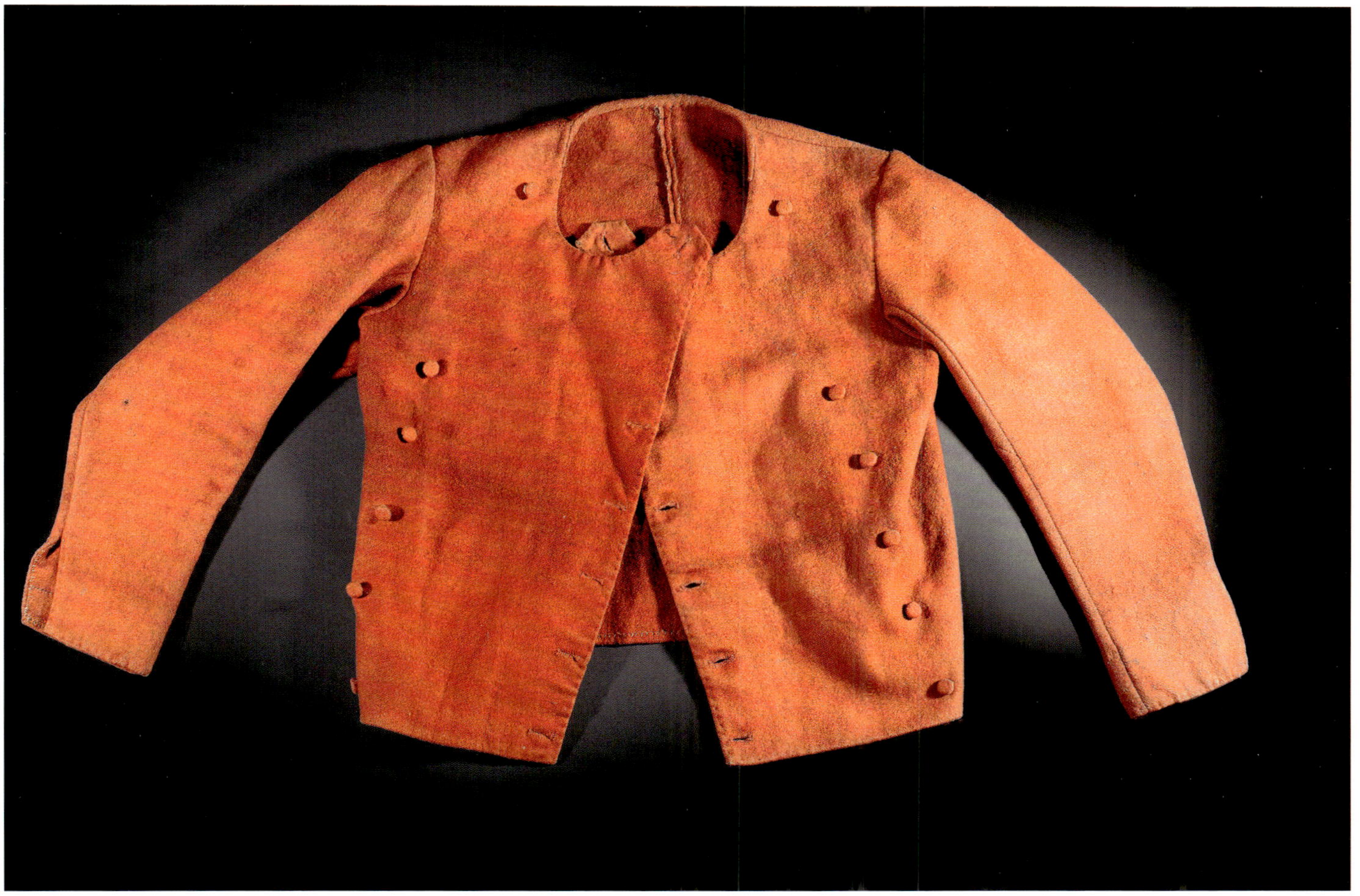

CARMAGNOLE

The *carmagnole* was a short jacket of Piedmontese origin, adopted by the Parisian *sans-culottes* along with the Phrygian cap, pantaloons (long trousers) and pike. It was also the title of a revolutionary song, created after the storming of the Tuileries, which rapidly became the anthem of the *sans-culottes*. Very few *carmagnoles* have come down to us intact. This one comes from the Danton collection. A very similar model is preserved in the Musée de la Mode de la Ville de Paris.

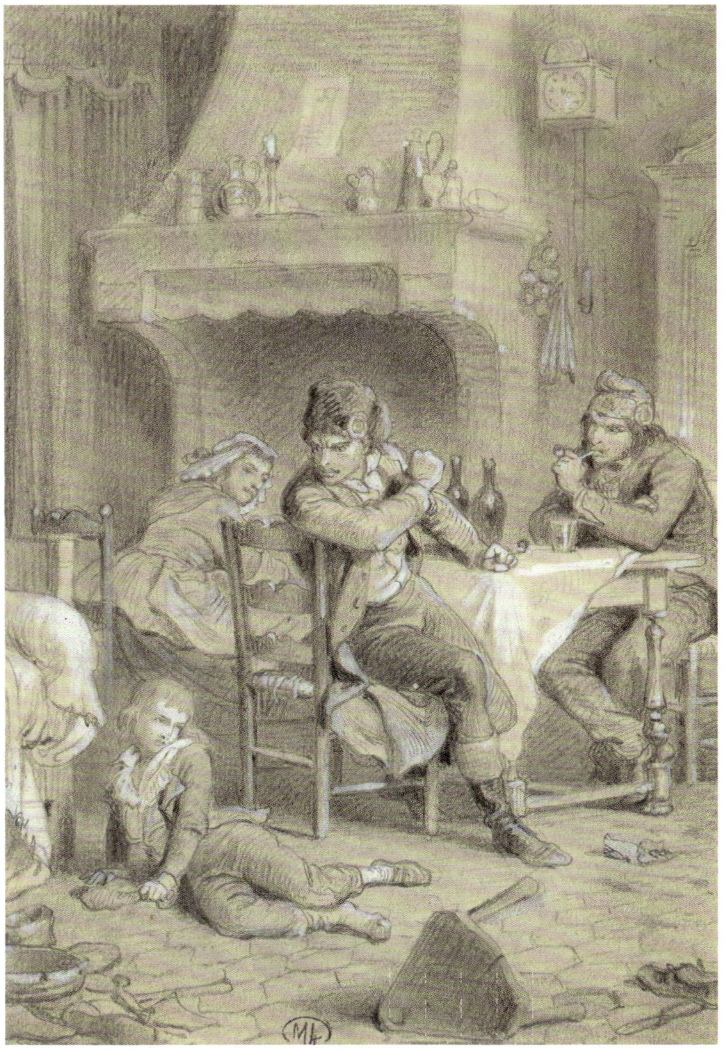

HENRI-FÉLIX EMMANUEL PHILIPPOTEAUX (1815-1884), _THE DAUPHIN OF FRANCE AND THE JAILER SIMON IN THE TEMPLE PRISON_

In this drawing now in the Louvre Museum, Philippoteaux suggests the violence and humiliations inflicted on the Dauphin, future Louis XVII. The jailer Simon is depicted wearing the famous soft woolen cap with revolutionary cockade that has since been acquired by this collection. Louve Museum Collection, Department of Graphic Arts.

WOOLEN HAT WORN BY ANTOINE SIMON, LOUIS XVII'S JAILER IN THE TEMPLE PRISON

Built as part of a fortress by the Knights Templar in the 13th century, the Temple Tower was used as a prison under the Ancien Régime and thus it remained during the French Revolution. Its most notable inmates from 10 August 1792 onward were the members of the royal family. The Committee of Public Health put one Antoine Simon in charge of the King's son – a shoemaker, married without children, who enlisted the help of his wife. Coarse, uneducated and hideous-looking, Simon is remembered as a violent alcoholic in a large woolen hat. Pictured here is a hat from the Danton Collection, still with its original revolutionary cockade.

MEMENTOES

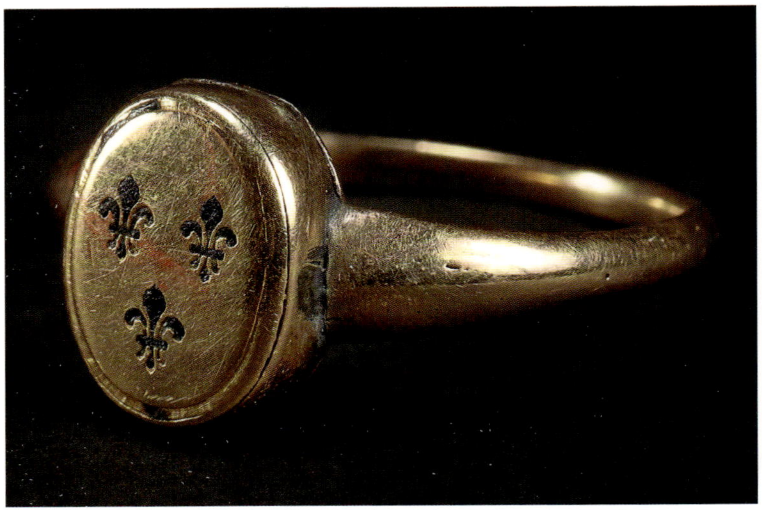

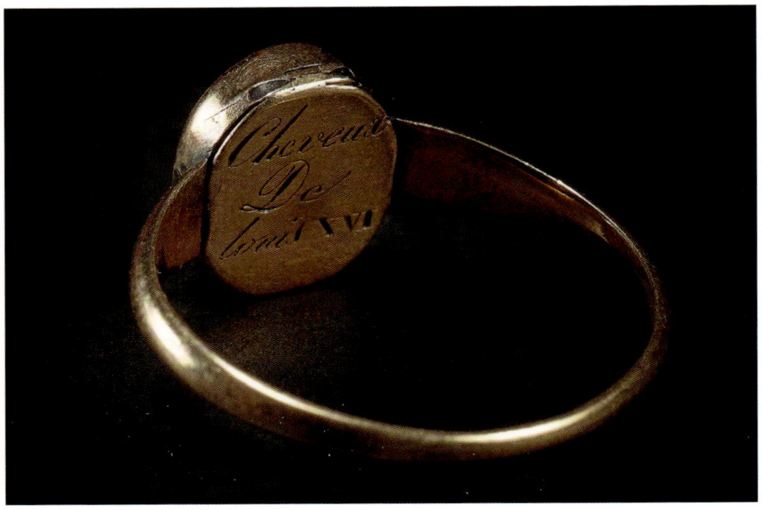

GOLD RING CONTAINING LOUIS XVI'S HAIR

Small, solid gold reliquary ring, embellished with enameled fleur-de-lis and featuring a back-opening bezel that contains Louis XVI's hair. Executioners' perks included the right to sell off their victims' hair. Louis XVI was no exception. The mob rushed to the foot of the guillotine as if to atone for their sins by dipping their hands into the royal blood and buying the locks of hair set aside for the purpose by executioner Samson. This ring came to symbolize the fervor felt by certain royalists and was for many years worn by Alain Bancel, a passionate collector of Ancien Régime and revolutionary paraphernalia, who confirmed that the ring originally belonged to Louis XVII.

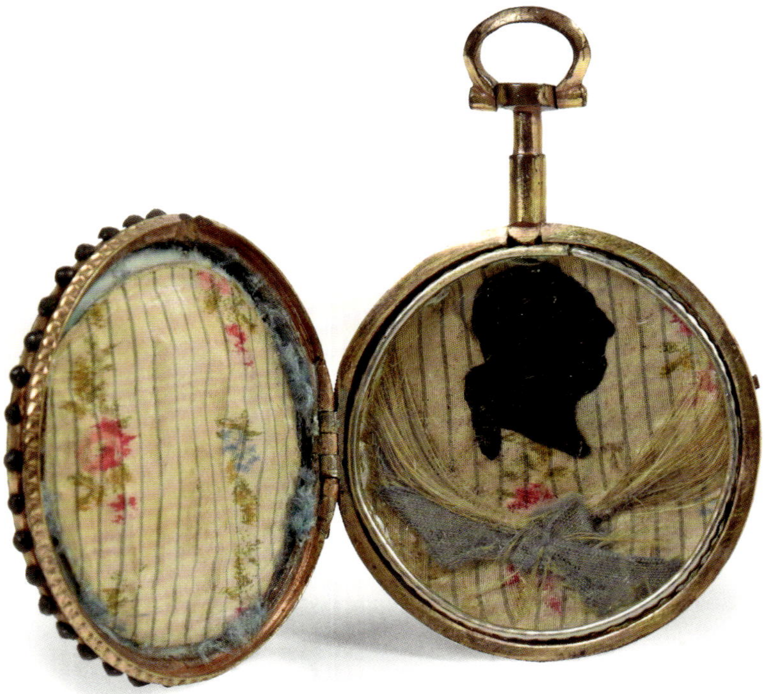

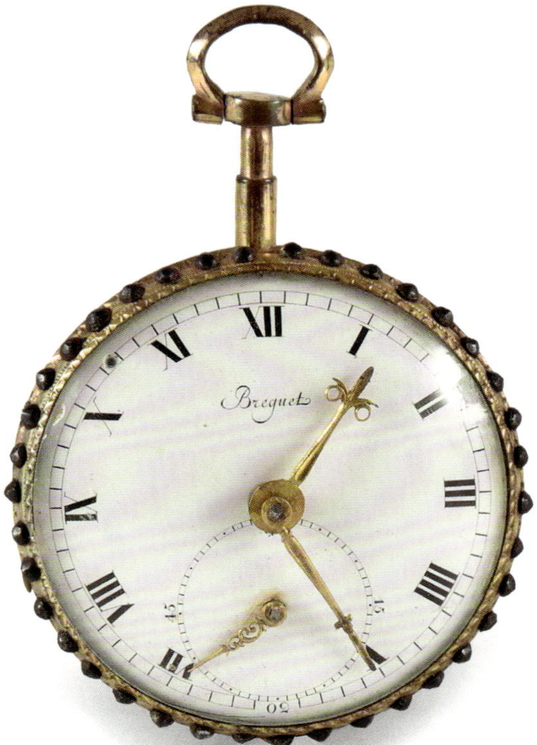

WATCH CONTAINING RELICS OF LOUIS XVI

This Breguet pocket watch, now with its movement removed, was turned into a reliquary under the Restoration. It contains a strand of Louis XVI's hair and a piece of the blue ribbon (*cordon bleu*) of the Order of the Holy Spirit. These are set against a fragment of silk moiré taffeta from a waistcoat worn by Louis XVI, embellished with a cut-out profile of the king facing right.

RELIQUARIES CONTAINING LOCKS OF HAIR OF LOUIS XVI, MARIE-ANTOINETTE AND LOUIS XVII

Pictured here are two picture frames containing strands of hair woven from the locks of Louis XVI, Marie-Antoinette and the Dauphin. Of impeccable provenance, these deeply moving mementoes were lovingly preserved by Thierry de Ville d'Avray, the King's first valet and Intendant General of the Royal Furniture Depository, then by his direct descendants until 2008.

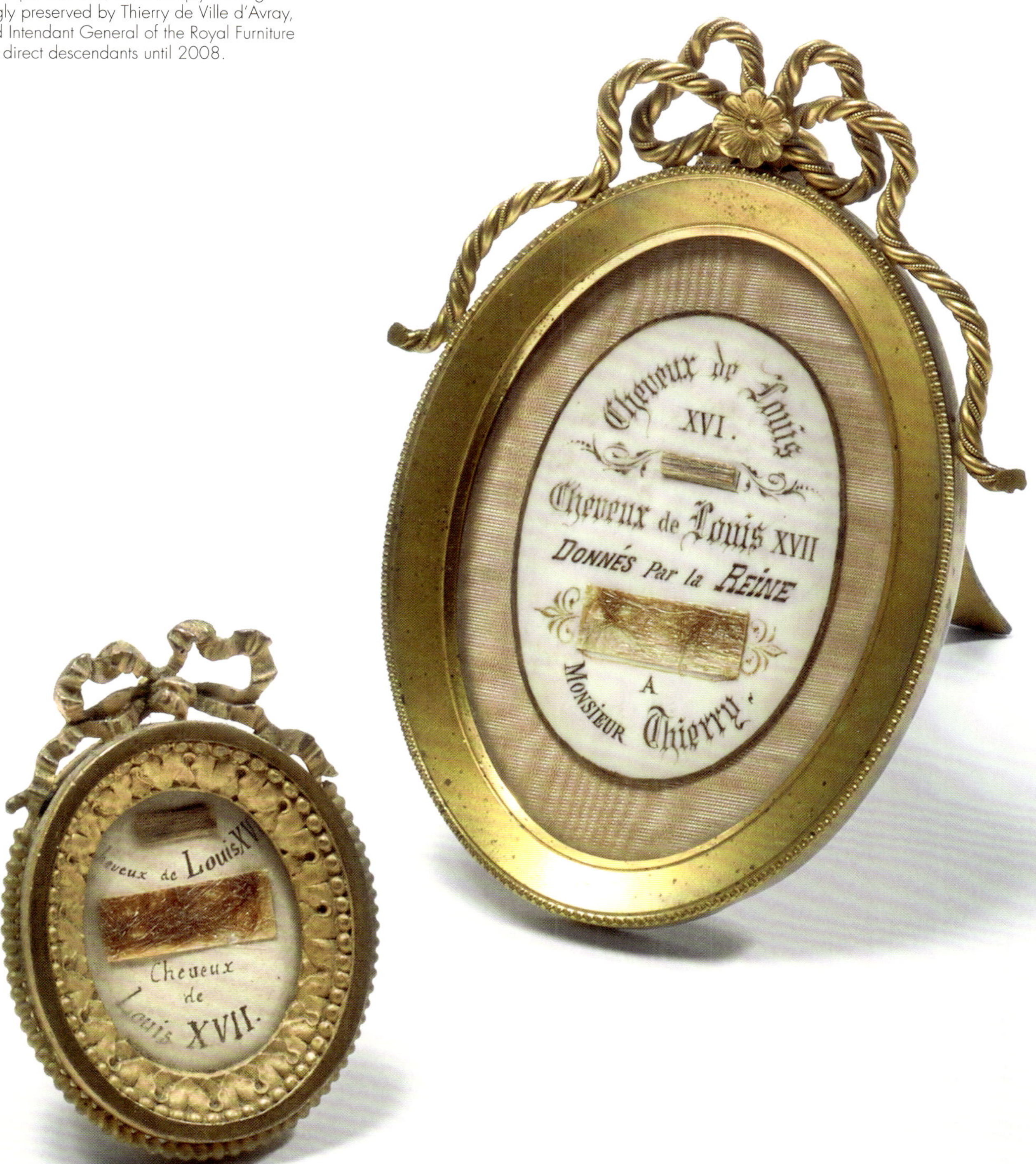

The Ascent to Power

II

For Napoleon Bonaparte, scion of a lesser noble Corsican family, the Revolution marked a fundamental turning point. Despite his family heritage and his years of training at Autun, Brienne and the École Militaire in Paris, he now needed to find a new way forward – become master of his own destiny and take those decisive steps that would lead him to the pinnacle of power.[1]

Emmanuelle Papot
historian

THE EARLY YEARS

Following the break with Paoli, Napoleon and his family left for France in June 1793 and settled in La Valette, near Toulon. His father Carlo having died in Montpellier, Napoleon was now head of the family, designated as the natural successor to the deceased by his great-uncle. The Ledoux Collection includes the amethyst-engraved Heraldic gold ring displaying Carlo Buonaparte's coat-of-arms and monogram (page 92). Napoleon at this point was also the only person capable of providing for his family, having now held various commissions in the French Republican Army. An early portrait by Jean-Baptiste Greuze shows him as a young captain of the artillery, revealing none of the self-assurance and determination seen in portraits executed under the First French Empire. By some stroke of luck, Napoleon's first mission was to report to Avignon to organize gunpowder convoys to the Army of Italy. Suddenly, three years before the victorious campaign that would lead him to Arcole and Rivoli, the conquest of the much-coveted Po Valley looked within his reach. But events in Paris decided otherwise. With the Jacobins and the *Montagnards* increasingly vying for power, and no hope of compromise between federalists and government centrists, the departure for the Alps was postponed.

On 28 July 1793 we find Napoleon returning from a mission that had taken him from Valence to Villeneuve, where he had once again proved his ability to direct artillery fire from the foot of the ramparts. It was on this occasion that he was inspired to write *Le Souper de Beaucaire,* a fictional account of a supper at an inn at Beaucaire. Reading between the lines ones senses a certain political nostalgia for the *Corsitude* movement and *Paolism* (so-named for the great Corsican patriot Pasquale Paoli). But his ambition for military glory prevailed over any aspirations to authorship. A few months earlier, Toulon had fallen into the hands of the British who used the port as a bridgehead for a future royalist reconquest of southern France. Napoleon, then just an unknown French officer, was eventually called in after a series of delays and false starts due to the glaring lacunae in the French High Command's grasp of the local terrain. He received his commission on 16 September, under the orders of General Carteaux, and displayed considerable personal bravery from the outset. Given command of the artillery, Napoleon proved a meticulous tactician, relying on rapid execution supported by continuous crossfire from the fort overlooking the port. But such was the French Chief of Staff's reticence with regard to this young upstart that his first military essays were not immediately crowned with success. All that changed on 16 November with the arrival of General Jacques Dugommier, Carteaux's replacement, who gave Bonaparte a freedom of action that paid dividends one month later. On 17 December, we find him leaving La Seyne to lead a French assault on "Little Gibraltar" and the Fort de l'Eguillette. After repeated attacks, Napoleon had netted dozens of prisoners including most notably, the commander of the allied enemy, General O'Hara, forced to lay down arms. On 22 December, aged just 24, Napoleon was promoted to acting Brigadier General — but this recognition proved to be short-lived. Newly appointed Commander of the Army of Italy, Napoleon rejoined the army camp in Sieg near Nice where he learned that Maximilien Robespierre had been overthrown. As a friend of Robespierre's brother, Napoleon was then imprisoned in Fort-Carré in Antibes. On his release on 20 August 1794, he returned to planning an expedition to Corsica, but this project was eventually abandoned. In Paris, the Directory had forgotten him. He settled in Marseilles and waited for the political furor that gripped France to blow over, meanwhile becoming engaged to the young and docile Désirée Clary (destined for a glittering future as the wife of Jean-Baptiste Bernadotte, future king of Sweden and Norway). He then learned that the War Ministry had entrusted him with a peacemaking mission as brigadier general in command of the infantry in the West, which he declined to accept. Received by General Aubry in Paris, he couched his refusal as follows: "Never. Never shall any French soldier placed under my command shed the blood of our fellow citizens. The Vendée should never have become this field of horror that you have all made of it. I would never sully my sword in this way."[2] After being briefly attached to the Topographical Bureau, stripped of his rank, he was reinstated to direct operations in Turkey. But once again fate intervened: faced with royal agitators in Paris, Barras called on Napoleon to disperse the rebellion.

In Vendémiaire Year III (5 October 1795), on the steps of the Eglise Saint-Roch in Paris, Napoleon fired grapeshot on the men of the Sections, demonstrating a determination and a flair for command in battle that restored peace to the streets of the capital. His efforts were ably seconded by Joachim Murat, who was sent to fetch the cannon from the Sablons military camp.[3]

Napoleon was instantly embraced by the populace and became a hero of the Republic overnight. A pencil portrait by Giuseppe Longhi, dated 1796, perfectly captures his compelling image as France's new savior, unadorned and without artifice (page 93).

Within a week Napoleon had been promoted first to *général de division* then to Commander-in-Chief of the Army of the Interior. He now enjoyed unprecedented prestige, particularly in the eyes of the widow Beauharnais, a muse of the directorial government who accelerated his rise up the military ladder.

The young Corsican and his more experienced paramour were married at the *Mairie* of the 2nd Arrondissement on 9 March 1796. But their honeymoon was cut short because Napoleon had meanwhile been given command of the Army of Italy. He left Paris two days after the wedding and reached Nice in 16 days. Once there, he lost no time reorganizing his troops, having first persuaded generals Masséna, Augereau, Laharpe and Sérurier to adopt Napoleonic tactics. He also addressed his men with impassioned speeches that made them fall on the enemy with a vengeance. "Soldiers," cried Napoleon, "You are poorly fed and almost naked. The government owes you much and can give you nothing. The patience and courage you have shown do you honor but procure you neither worldly goods nor glory. I will lead you into the most fertile plains in the world; there you will find honor, glory, wealth. Soldiers of the Armies of Italy, will you be found wanting in courage?"[4]

The campaign was conducted with swift decisiveness. The young general directed his regiments with martial ardor, ordering them not just to secure victory at Montenotte, Millesimo, Lodi, Castiglione, Bassano, Arcole and Rivoli but also to take the cities themselves. Napoleon neither waited for instructions from Paris nor sought the immediate authority of the Directory. He comported himself like a Head of State in every respect taking all diplomatic matters into his own hands. His prestige elsewhere meanwhile soared, augmented by glowing reports that filled the column inches, prompting prints, engravings and even paintings that celebrated the glory of Napoleon Bonaparte.

In April 1797 Napoleon signed the Preliminaries of Leoben. Six months later, on 7 October 1797, he dictated the terms of the Treaty of Campo-Formio to the plenipotentiaries of Austria.[5] Chief among these terms was the ceding of parts of northern Italy to France and the recognition of French annexation of the left bank of the Rhine. These provisions were then officially ratified at the Congress of Rastatt.

THE EGYPTIAN CAMPAIGN (1798-1801)

Napoleon returned to a hero's welcome in Paris, acclaimed by the crowds and borne aloft in triumph. At the end of December 1797, the *rue Chantereine*, home of the small *hôtel particulier* occupied by Josephine, was rechristened *rue de la Victoire* — a signal honor. But in the eyes of the Directors and other politicians, Napoleon's popularity was becoming an embarrassment. Napoleon was an interloper and it was time to distance him from Paris, never mind that the army and the populace loved him.

After a meeting with the French Foreign Minister Talleyrand, Napoleon the victorious general was charged with a new expedition that indirectly targeted Britain. His objective was to take control of Egypt by putting an end to Ottoman hegemony and cutting off Britain's trade route to India. To succeed in his mission Bonaparte, as a newly elected member of the Institut de France, took the innovative step of taking along a party of 167 French *savants,* among them Monge, Berthollet, Conté and Vivant Denon. His military campaign thus doubled as a scientific expedition, with the specific aim of rediscovering the civilization of the Pharaohs.

This was the basis of the Institut d'Egypte, which was founded on the outskirts of Cairo and modeled on the Institut de France. At its heart was Napoleon's scientific team, whose magnum opus, the *Description de l'Egypte,* would run into several editions and feed the public appetite for all things Egyptian — temples, pyramids, hieroglyphs and also wildlife.[6] The Ledoux collection features several drawings by Napoleon's team of scholars, plus other interesting pieces arising from the expedition (pages 104-107).

The expedition first made a provisioning stop in Malta — an island that had become the "key to the Mediterranean" and which Bonaparte planned to seize — before arriving in Egypt where his soldiers rapidly captured all of the major cities, further convincing the Directory of Napoleon's effectiveness in battle.

From that point onward, Napoleon's ambition knew no bounds. As he would later explain: "I wanted to establish an empire in the East. Great names are only made in the East. I dreamed of Egypt but also of Palestine and Syria. I wanted to be a new Alexander the Great. Going into India meant striking at England at the very heart of her territories. The cradle of religion was a powerful symbol. After Italy and the Arts, it was Jerusalem and St Jean d'Acre that beckoned."[7]

At the Battle of the Pyramids, Napoleon gave his now famous address to the troops: "Soldiers! From the top of these Pyramids, forty centuries are contemplating you." Thus fired with enthusiasm, French forces chased off the Mamluk cavalry, armed wing of Ottoman power, and easily occupied the country. A letter from Bonaparte to Barras, dated 11 October 1798, gives a complete account of the situation in Egypt at the time (page 102).

But Napoleon had himself suffered heavy losses at the Battle of Aboukir Bay: a naval attack led by Admiral Nelson that cost France the larger part of its fleet. Cut off from France, the French now found themselves virtually imprisoned in the very city they had just conquered, Cairo. In order to move swiftly against the combined British and Ottoman forces and become the dominant power in the Middle East, Napoleon dispatched General Desaix

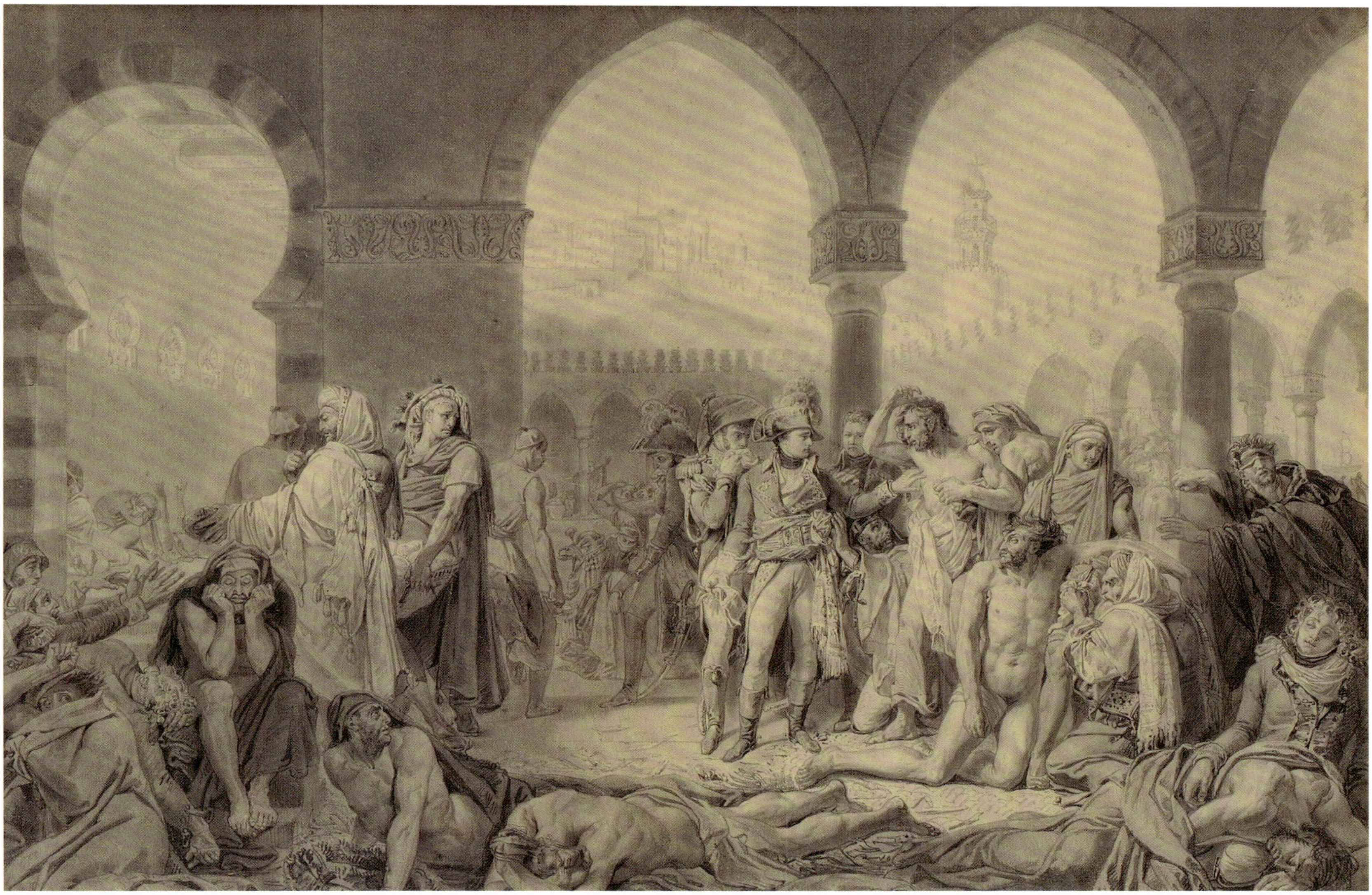

ABRAHAM GIRARDET (1763-1823) AND ANTOINE-JEAN GROS (1771-1835), ATTRIBUTED, *BONAPARTE VISITING THE PLAGUE VICTIMS OF JAFFA*

The Syrian Campaign was intended to crown Napoleon's scientific and military expedition to Egypt. But Jaffa and Acre marked the turning point in his hitherto unstoppable advance, not least because he was rumored to have executed his prisoners on the beach and abandoned his own plague-stricken soldiers to their inevitable fate. This composition by Antoine Gros, commissioned by Josephine in early 1800, was intended to quash such vile rumors and clear the newly appointed First Consul of all suspicion. It was exhibited at the Paris Salon of 1804 to immense critical acclaim.
This drawing of exceptional finesse is based on an etching by Alphonse-Charles Masson, and was executed by Girardet in collaboration with Gros.

to Upper Egypt while he himself led a new expedition to Syria. En route his armies laid siege to Acre but defended by its ramparts, the city resisted capture and Napoleon was forced to retreat. In Jaffa meanwhile the victorious French troops were being decimated by the plague. A rare charcoal sketch by Antoine-Jean Gros shows Bonaparte as a miracle-worker visiting the plague victims of Jaffa (page 85).

On his return to Cairo, Napoleon learned that the Directory was on the verge of catastrophe. The Republican forces sent to pacify the republics beyond the Alps and the Rhine had suffered a series of setbacks. Within France's borders, economic crisis was aggravated by the deplorable image of a rule dogged by accusations of corruption. On the personal front, news filtering from Napoleon's entourage brought rumors of Josephine's infidelity. After having won a second advantage over the Mamluks at the Battle of Aboukir, Bonaparte left General Kleber in charge of his troops and quit Egypt on 23 August 1799 on board his frigate *La Muiron*. He reached France 47 days later having made a brief stop in Ajaccio (the last time he would see the land of his birth), and came ashore regardless of the mandatory quarantine for sailors. On arrival in St Raphaël on 9 October he began a triumphal march on Paris, preceded by press reports and aquatints celebrating his victories in Egypt and Italy and given a hero's welcome everywhere he went. No sooner had he returned, than he was invited to serve as Sieyes' "sword" in a plot to overthrow the Directory.

FIRST CONSUL (1799-1804)

On 18 and 19 Brumaire Year VIII (9 and 10 November 1799), egged on by Talleyrand and the police chief Joseph Fouche, Bonaparte seized power in a two-day coup targeting first Paris then St Cloud. But things had not gone smoothly. Napoleon's intrusion into the assemblies had alienated the deputies and without the support of his brother Lucien and Generals Murat and Lefebvre the coup would have failed. As it was, Napoleon turned this situation to his advantage and was elected provisional Consul with Sieyès and Roger-Ducos, who would soon be replaced by Cambacérès and Lebrun. At the age of thirty, the former Brienne cadet became Head of State.[8] A drawing by Fragonard shows him addressing the Council of Five Hundred on 19 Brumaire in the Orangery (page 116).

Without a minute to spare Napoleon embarked on an ambitious program of reforms and administrative innovations. Before November was out, he had instigated a series of financial, military and political policies, giving priority to the pacification of the Vendée as a vital step toward securing national unity. He had a shrewd idea by then of what was required to achieve "great things": "My policy is to govern men as the majority wish to be governed.[...] That is, I believe, the best way to recognize the sovereignty of the people."[9] Surrounded by former Jacobin ministers and members of the *Ancien Régime* nobility, Bonaparte wisely appointed his brother Lucien, a key player in the Brumaire coup, as interior minister. Another initiative was to give each department its own prefect — government appointed officials with a mandate to implement central government policy at local level. France's constellation of communes was now each led by its own mayor, with the ten most deserving mayors being offered a silk scarf from the First Consul as a reward of merit (page 118).

At the same time, to restore the confidence of manufacturers and French people in general, Napoleon went all out to tackle the economic crisis. This included dismissing any compromised officials and publicly excoriating France's all-powerful banker Gabriel Ouvrard who Napoleon suspected of double-dealing. He also launched a number of initiatives to boost business, patronizing the Society for the Encouragement of Industry and actively promoting exhibitions of French industrial products — trade shows or universal exhibitions before their time you could say.

On 19 February 1800 Napoleon and Josephine moved out of the Petit Luxembourg and moved into the Tuileries Palace, giving the former royal residence a new lease of life. To make his point, a consular court gradually assumed all the privileges of royalty, its ranks being later swelled by the émigrés — nobles, landowners, royalists and priests who had fled the Revolution — who returned to France after nearly a decade in exile.

To distance himself from the capital, the new Head of State paid frequent visits to the Château de Malmaison, which had been acquired by Josephine and undergone extensive refurbishment under the direction of French architects and interior designers Charles Percier and Pierre-François-Léonard Fontaine. This haven of peace served as Napoleon's nerve center and also as a venue for the meeting of the Council of Ministers. Diplomats and councilors were among those invited to visit, bringing their expertise and suggesting new institutions for France.

When time allowed, the Imperial couple also entertained family members at Malmaison, most notably Eugène de Beauharnais, Josephine's son, his sister Hortense and her husband Louis Bonaparte (Napoleon's brother) and sometimes Caroline Bonaparte and her husband Joachim Murat. On such occasions General Bonaparte would seize the opportunity to enjoy his library with its Neo-Pompeian frescoes and furniture by the Jacob brothers. The gardens were another pleasure, with their landscapes evoked by Rousseau and their celebrated roses so lovingly tended by Josephine.[10]

In Paris, the standard of living soared as urban development took hold. Bridges were built (the Pont des Arts for instance) and new roads were laid, the most emblematic of these being the Rue de Rivoli with its Roman-style portico arcades. A long-nourished dream was fulfilled when the Tuileries Palace was joined to the Louvre. The sequential numbering of buildings, two-way traffic and the digging of a sewer network 30km long — all of these were the legacy of Napoleon. So too was the creation of new markets and, particularly dear to the heart of residents, the installation of drinking fountains. The days of insalubrious living conditions would soon be over. The days of celebration had arrived, epitomized by the theaters, Salons and masked balls that increasingly punctuated Parisian cultural life.

There still remained the problem of pacifying the borders. In the spring of 1800 Napoleon launched a new campaign that would take him across the Alps. On 6 May he took command of his army, which was officially led across the Alps by his right-hand man General Berthier, passing through Dijon before attacking the Great St Bernard Pass — an epic scene immortalized in a painting by Jacques-Louis David.

Alas, the Battle of Marengo on 14 June got off to a bad start; it was only when Desaix arrived that victory came into sight for the French. Desaix then lost his life in the battle, on the same day as Kléber was assassinated in Egypt and replaced by Menou. It was without doubt one of the most challenging 24 hours in the first half of 1800. Despite these setbacks, the French win at Marengo allowed Napoleon to secure his position as First Consul. The Bruno Ledoux collection features a circular snuffbox embellished with a silver commemorative medal that was engraved shortly after the victory by Bertrand Andrieu.

His power thus consolidated, Bonaparte returned to Paris to focus on normalizing relations between republican France and her neighbors and partners. On 3 October, France's treaty with the United States was formalized in a ceremony held at the Château de Mortefontaine, the immense property owned by his brother Joseph that had earlier served as the venue for their sister Caroline's marriage to Murat. The following year Austria would sue for peace in the treaty of Lunéville and the year after that the Treaty of Amiens would end hostilities with Great Britain. The culmination of two years of Napoleonic statecraft, the Treaty of Amiens marked the end of lengthy negotiations between the two principal European powers.

But Napoleon's statecraft did not go down well with either former revolutionaries or die-hard royalists and there were repeated attempts on his life. While police chief Fouché kept Bonaparte regularly informed about the plots to assassinate him, the consular couple were very nearly killed on Christmas Eve when a barrel filled with gunpowder (dubbed the "Machine Infernale") exploded in the rue Nicaise as they were going to the opera.

In the eyes of the First Consul, who suddenly understood the fragility of his power, it was time to embark on a new chapter. On 15 July 1801 he signed an agreement with Pope Pius VII (the Concordat of 1801) that re-established the Catholic Church in France, but as part of this agreement he presented another set of laws called the Organic Articles that recognized the right to freedom of worship regardless of religious affiliation. Easter Day 1802 marked the holding of a grand inaugural ceremony in the cathedral of Notre-Dame de Paris, in the presence of numerous prelates. To consolidate his power and in recognition of the return of peace, Bonaparte's authority was extended for a further 10 years.

The pace of reform intensified. The Légion d'Honneur came into being, a new order divided into 16 cohorts (territorial units) and established by Napoleon to reward meritorious civilian or military service to France. He also decided to uphold colonial slavery for the sake of maintaining the status quo in the colonies. Having done all this, he dismissed police chief Fouché, who he suspected of double-dealing, and distanced his brother Lucien, whose calls to reinforce the personal authority of the First Consul amounted to gross insubordination. The move into the chateau of St Cloud came next. The "monarchization" of the regime had begun, albeit hotly disputed by Napoleon.

This was the context for Napoleon's tour of provincial France. Like a king visiting his subjects, the First Consul set off for Normandy with Josephine at his side, returning to Paris to learn, a few weeks later, that his brother-in-law General Leclerc had died in Saint Domingue. The news touched Napoleon profoundly. Shortly afterwards the Act of Mediation was passed, which established a Swiss confederation headed by a *landammann* but under the personal protection of Napoleon. Last but not least, to shore up the French economy, Napoleon inaugurated the Banque de France, established the Franc Germinal as the standard unit of currency and finalized the sale of Louisiana to the United States.

The peace negotiations with England meanwhile dragged on, the main sticking point being the control of Malta, an obligatory port of call for all maritime trade companies. For Bonaparte's next expedition therefore, he marshaled a considerable force at a camp in Boulogne, across the English Channel from Great Britain, and prepared to invade England.

In early 1804, helped by Second Consul Cambacérès (France's de facto Prime Minister) together with Portalis and other seasoned legal experts, Napoleon put the finishing touch to the Consulate's other great undertaking: the drafting of the *Code Civil.* [11]

The Ledoux Collection includes a very pretty gold and enamel snuffbox with a portrait of Cambacérès (page 157).

Napoleon then caught wind of a plot led by *Chouan* leader Georges Cadoudal with the alleged complicity of Generals Pichegru and Moreau. He responded by ordering the immediate arrest of Louis de Bourbon Condé, a *prince du sang* who was suspected

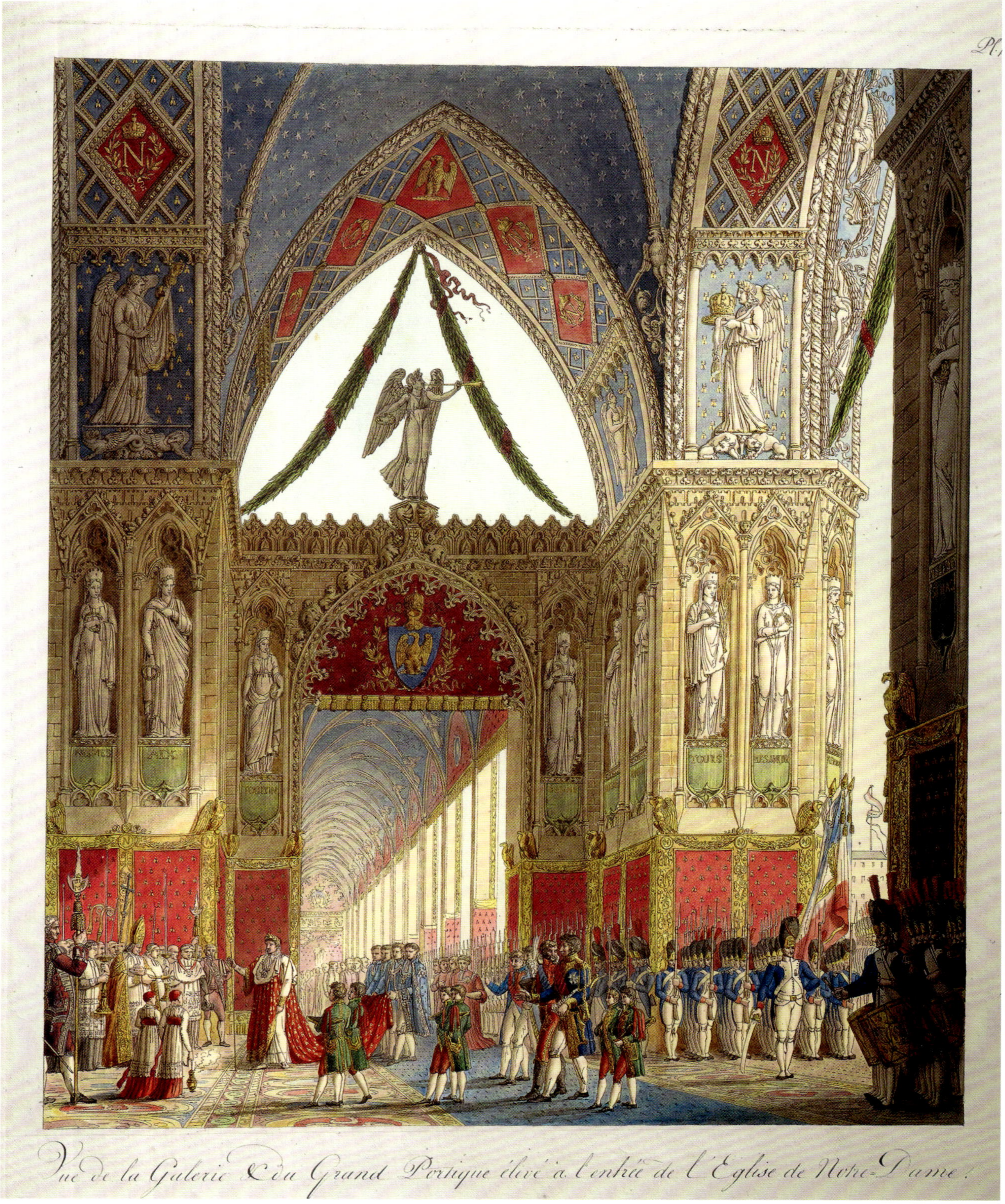

CHARLES PERCIER (1764-1838)
AND PIERRE FONTAINE (1762-1853),
NAPOLEON ENTERING NOTRE DAME

Dressed in his coronation robes, Napoleon stands before the ecclesiastics who are there to greet him at the entrance to the church of Notre Dame. This colorful enhanced engraving is very rich in detail and provides a highly valuable insight into the coronation ceremony. This plate is taken from the *Book of the Coronation*, produced by Pierre François Léonard Fontaine and Jean-Baptiste Isabey.

ANDREA APPIANI (1754-1817) 1817) AND HIS WORKSHOP,
THE EMPEROR NAPOLEON, KING OF ITALY

This very rare signed oil on canvas dated 1805 shows Napoleon in his coronation robes, with the Hand of Justice in his right hand, the necklace of the Grand Master of the Legion of Honor around his neck and a laurel wreath on his head. Appiani opted for a three-quarters portrait of Napoleon, with the focus on the trappings of power, in preference to the full length representations favored by David and Ingres. That same year he was commissioned to execute the official portrait of Napoleon King of Italy and appointed "first painter" to the newly crowned sovereign. The only other known version of this portrait is much smaller with an oblong format, and hangs in the Collegio Trevisio, Casale Monferrato, Italy.

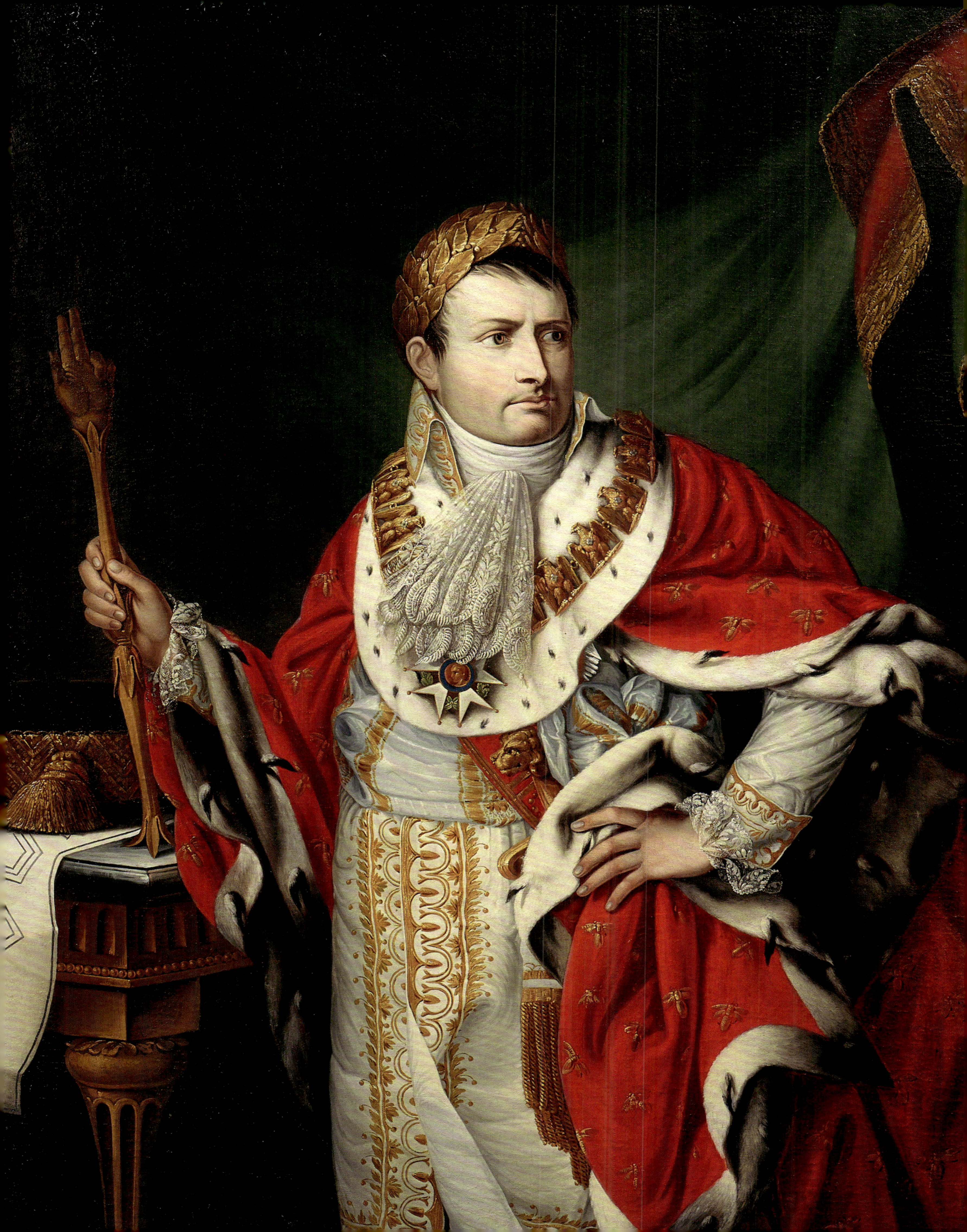

of being the instigator of the plot and brought back from Germany to face execution in the moat of the chateau of Vincennes. As Fouché would subsequently comment after he was reinstated: "The Revolution was the making of Bonaparte." In some ways Napoleon was a committed regicide. In truth it was too late to back-pedal or to recall Louis XVIII from exile as some expected. Having been elected First Consul for life, Napoleon was inexorably destined to become Emperor.

On 18 May 1804 Cambacérès, accompanied by a delegation of senators, repaired to St Cloud to proclaim the elevation to the throne of "Napoleon, Emperor of the French". The following day marked the appointment of 18 "Marshals of the Empire". The sovereign's brothers, Joseph and Louis, were respectively appointed Grand Elector and Constable of France and his sisters were raised to the rank of princesses. Lucien and Jérome, who had married without Napoleon's consent, were meanwhile conspicuous by their absence. Napoleon's mother, "Madame Mère", who had taken their defense, would not be present at the inaugural ceremonies that were planned for the end of the year.

THE CORONATION (1804)

A great admirer of classical culture, Napoleon wished to be thought of as a new Caesar. Negotiations were commenced with Cardinals Caprara and Consalvi with a view to inviting Pope Pius VII to Paris. There still remained the problem of planning the day itself and in particular selecting the venue for such a grand occasion. Having dismissed the idea of Rheims, because it was too intimately associated with the Bourbons, in September the Emperor traveled to Aix-la-Chapelle, before realizing that the pontiff's presence in protestant country would be wholly inappropriate.

In the end, Napoleon decided to hold the ceremony at the cathedral of Notre Dame de Paris, having ruled out Orleans and Lyon and rejected the cathedral of Saint-Louis des Invalides (site of the first distribution of the crosses of the Légion d'Honneur) on the grounds that it was too small. The costumes for the event were designed by the greatest artists of the period (most notably David and Isabey) and made by leading Parisian couturiers. There exist several portraits of Napoleon in coronation robes. François Gérard, whose bust features in the Ledoux Collection, paints a particularly vivid portrait of this exceptional moment in French history (page 125).

The imperial regalia included an ermine-lined mantel that went over the *grand costume*, together with sandals (plus *cothurnes*) and stockings evoking the Carolingian tradition and Roman Antiquity. The Emperor's head would be crowned with a laurel wreath and he would surround himself with the insignia of his power: hand of justice, scepter, orb, imperial rings and chain of the Légion d'Honneur. In homage to Charlemagne and exclusively reserved for the chief dignitaries of the regime, other emblems and objects would be created specially for the occasion.

Josephine, as Napoleon's muse but most of all as his wife and potential bearer of his heir, would take part in the ceremony. Her ceremonial dress would be largely modeled on her husband's and designed to complement the Emperor's own elaborate attire.

The date originally fixed for the ceremony was 18 Brumaire — a date with powerful symbolic associations. Coming exactly five years after the coup d'état, the coronation was in some respects the high point of Napoleonic rule. In the event, the festivities had to be postponed until 2 December due to the sovereign pontiff's late arrival in Paris and the tardiness of the works undertaken around the cathedral.

Some 40,000 guests were sent sealed letters (*lettres closes*) inviting them to attend the ceremony at Notre Dame, which was planned down to the last detail by the imperial and pontifical administrators. On 25 November 1804 Napoleon welcomed Pius VII to Fontainebleau, greeting him at a crossroads known as the Croix de Saint-Hérem. Three days later, the future emperor and the sovereign pontiff made their solemn entrance into Paris.

On the morning of 2 December 1804 the first guests reached the aisles of Notre Dame. The temperature outside was a chilly 37°F. The *vélites* (chasseurs) and the gendarmes then took up their positions and at 9am the papal procession emerged from the Pavillon de Flore (then part of the Tuileries Palace). One hour later the imperial couple also set off from the Tuileries, arriving two hours later at a temporary awning erected behind the cathedral.

Napoleon and Josephine, in their ceremonial costumes complete with crowns and diadems, were then greeted by Cardinal de Belloy, Archbishop of Paris. Members of their respective families and distinguished guests — ministers, cardinals, bishops, deputies, senators, prominent mayors and civilian and military representatives — awaited the arrival of the imperial couple in the nave. It was a moment of great solemnity.

The cathedral was decked out with the imperial colors and decorated with the bees that the future Emperor had chosen as the emblem of his omnipotence. The destruction wrought by the Revolution was meanwhile screened by wood and stucco to designs prepared in haste by architects Percier and Fontaine. Two examples have survived to this day and feature in the Ledoux Collection (pages 124 and 132).

Napoleon and Josephine then took their places facing the choir, seated on small, matching thrones, upholstered in embossed velvet, which had been installed for the occasion. The Pope then proceeded to bless the insignia, and of course consecrate the imperial couple by anointing their heads and foreheads with holy oil.

Then, facing the audience, and breaking with royal tradition by turning his back to the high altar and the clergy, the Emperor took the crown and placed it over his head. A few minutes later, he picked up the Empress' crown from the cushion where it lay and lifted it symbolically over his own head, before placing it very delicately on hers as she knelt before him.[12] The religious ceremony ended with the departure of the Pope. Napoleon at that point was at the far end of the cathedral seated on a great throne looking out over the public. He then pronounced the constitutional oath: "To maintain the integrity of the territory of the Republic, to respect and to cause to be respected the laws of the Corcordat and of freedom of worship, of political and civil liberty, of the irreversibility of the sale of the *biens nationaux*, to raise no taxes except by virtue of the law; to maintain the institution of the Légion d'Honneur; to govern only in view of the interest, the wellbeing and the glory of the French people."[13] Now it only remained to make the details of this great day known to the public. To disseminate the ceremonial proceedings to the widest possible audience, artists Isabey, Percier and Fontaine, supported by the country's most eminent master craftsmen, were commissioned to produce dozens of prints, engravings, medals, tapestries, drawings and paintings.

Jacques Louis David, appointed "First Painter to the Emperor" (a nod to the title bestowed on Le Brun by Louis XIV), was entrusted with the delicate mission of creating four paintings, two of which were eventually completed: *Le Sacre et le Couronnement* (1808) and *La Distribution des Aigles* (1810), representing the grand military parade outside the Ecole Militaire.

Napoleon then devoted a few months to finalizing preparations at the camp in Boulogne, before abandoning the British invasion project altogether. Then he set off to Milan for a second coronation, this time as King of Italy.

This was in early 1805. Napoleon's hegemony over Europe had only just begun. The Battle of Austerlitz, fought at the end of the year on the first anniversary of his coronation in Paris, would take his military prowess to a new level.

Now Napoleon had the whole of Europe at his feet.

1 Vergé-Franceschi, Michel. *Napoléon, une enfance corse*; foreword by Jean Tulard; preface by Charles Napoléon, Paris: Larousse, 2009, p.326.

2 Marquet de Montbreton de Norvins, Jacques. *Histoire de Napoléon*. Paris: Furne et Cie, 1830, p.29.

3 Tulard, Jean. *Napoléon ou le mythe du sauveur*. Paris: Fayard, 1987, p.77. Trans: *Napoleon: the Myth of the Saviour*. London: Weidenfeld & Nicolson, 1984.

4 Thiers, Adolphe. *Histoire de la Révolution française*. Bruxelles: Société Typographique Belge, 1836, volume II, p.277. Trans: *The History of the French Revolution*. London: R. Bentley, 1895.

5 Rouart, Jean-Marie. *Napoléon ou la destinée*. Paris: Gallimard, 2012, p.65.

6 Traunecker, Claude. 'L'Égypte antique de la "Description"' in Henri Laurens (eds) *L'Expédition d'Égypte*. Paris: Armand Colin, 1989, p.368.

7 Tulard, Jean. *Dictionnaire Napoléon*. Paris: Fayard, 1987, p.643.

8 Bainville, Jacques. *Le Dix-huit brumaire et autres écrits sur Napoléon*. Paris: Bernard Giovanangeli, 1998, p.114.

9 Tulard, Jean and Garros, Louis. *Itinéraire de Napoléon au jour le jour*. Paris: Tallandier, 1992, p.216.

10 Chevallier, Bernard. *Joséphine impératrice*. Paris: Le Chêne, 2014, p.133.

11 Imbert, Jean. 'Code civil' in Jean Tulard (eds.), *Dictionnaire Napoléon*. Paris: Fayard, 1989, pp.429-431.

12 Chanteranne, David. *Le Sacre de Napoléon*. Paris: Tallandier, coll. 'Bibliothèque napoléonienne', 2004, p.158.

13 de Ségur, Louis-Philippe. *Procès-verbal de la cérémonie du Sacre et du couronnement de LL. MM. l'Empereur Napoléon et l'Impératrice Joséphine*. Paris: Imprimerie Impériale,Year 13 (1804), p. 58.

THE EARLY YEARS

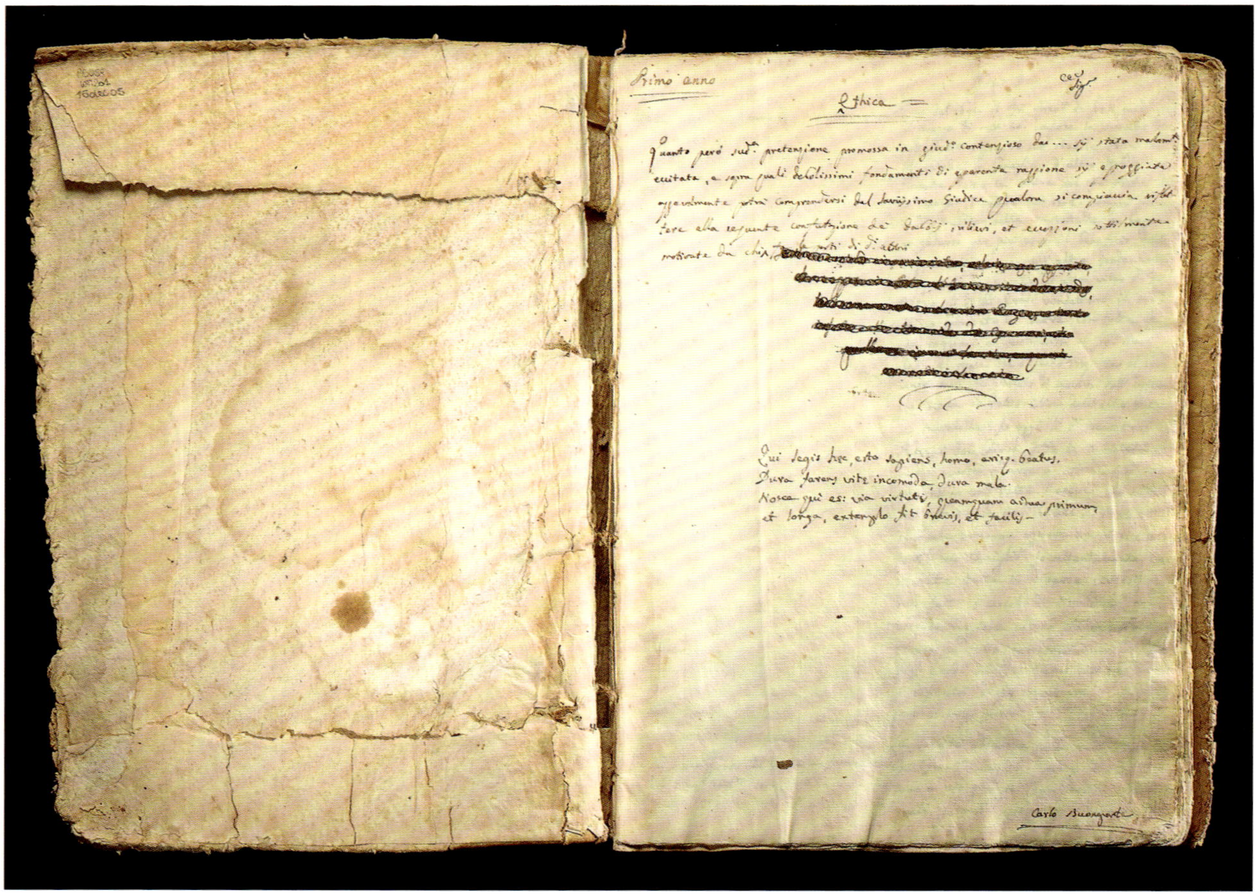

BOOK THAT BELONGED TO CARLO BUONAPARTE, NAPOLEON'S FATHER

This bound ledger is entirely handwritten in Italian, French and Latin. It contains a wealth of archives and papers from Carlo Buonaparte (1746-1785), from his time as an advocate at the Superior Council of Corsica, and provides an interesting insight into his daily work. Documents handwritten by Napoleon's father are extremely rare.

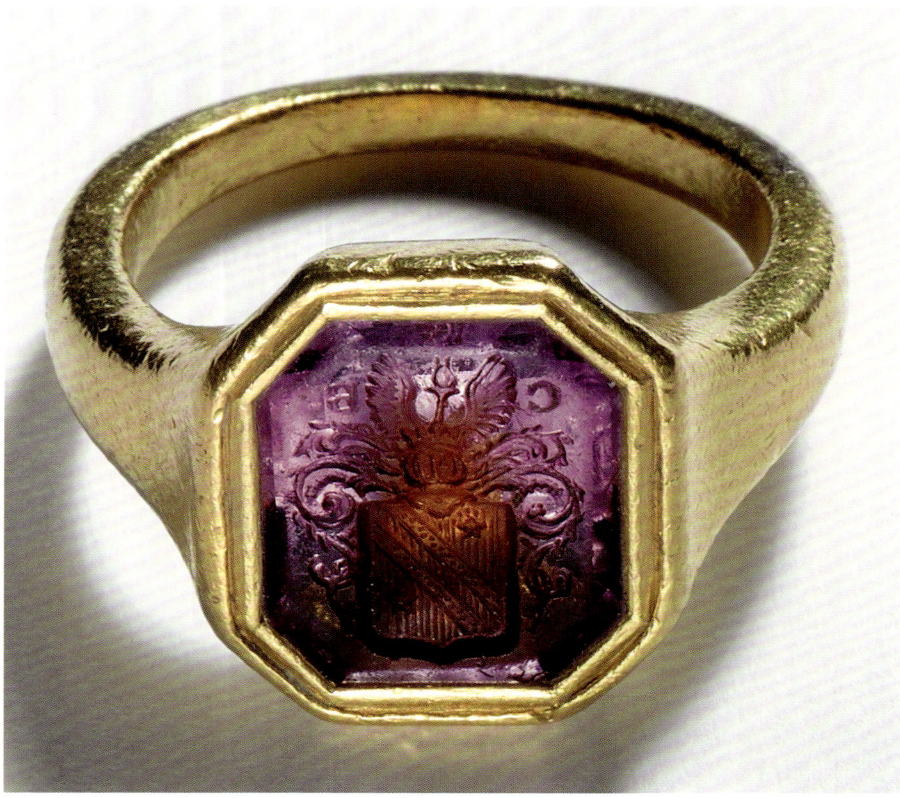

CARLO BUONAPARTE'S SIGNET RING

This superb gold ring, beautifully executed by master Italian craftsmen, features an inlaid amethyst engraved with the family crest and "CB" monogram of Carlo Buonaparte, Napoleon's father. Though born and always resident in Corsica, Carlo became a French citizen when the island was formally annexed to France following the Genoese defeat at the Battle of Ponto Nuovo in 1769. The Buonaparte family was then officially admitted into the noblesse. Appointed secretary of the assembly of the Corsican nobles in 1777, Carlo was received by King Louis XVI at Versailles a year later. Napoleon traveled with him to commence his schooling at Autun. As one of the only known objects bearing the family crest of the Buonapartes, this unique custom signet ring carries enormous symbolic meaning.

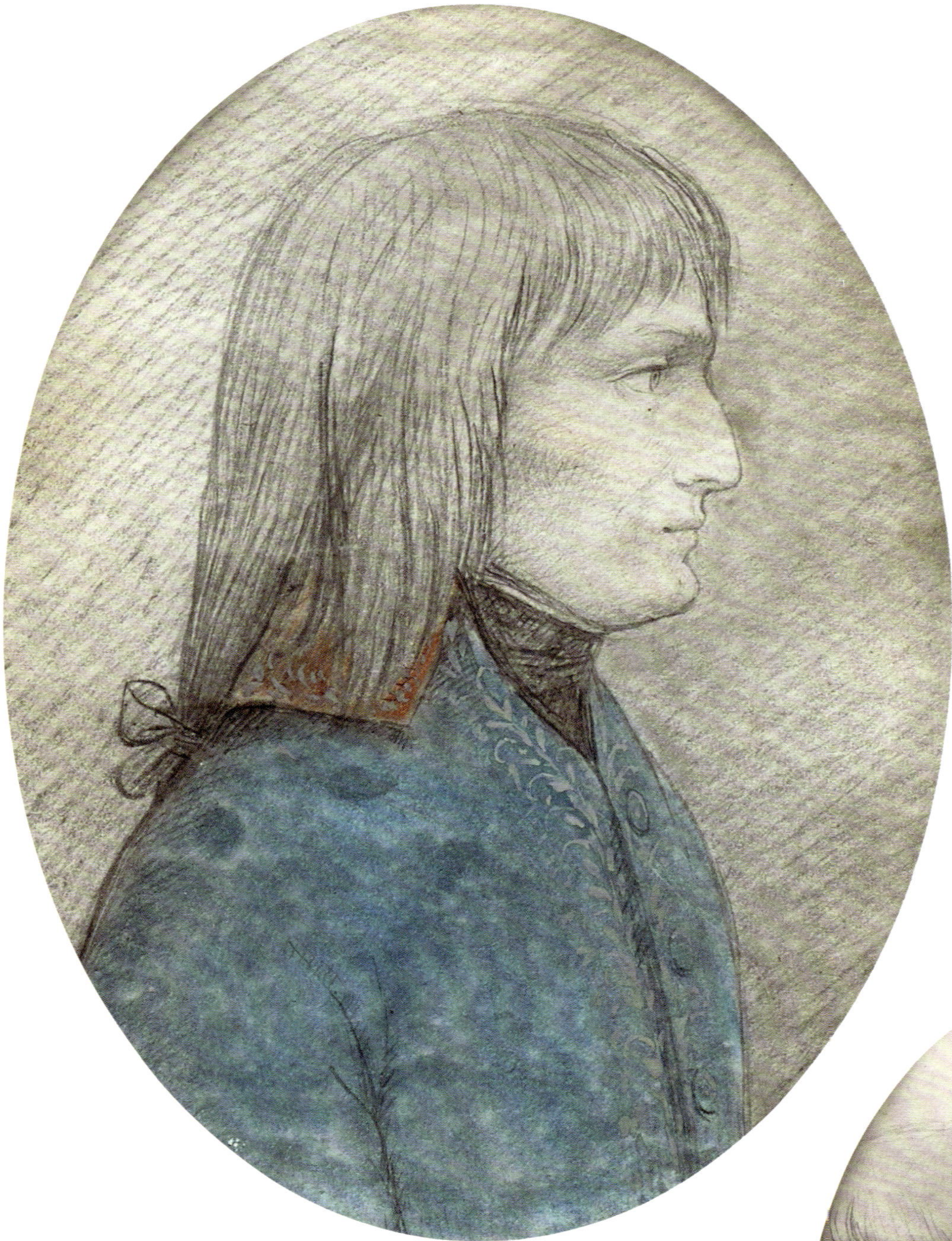

GIUSEPPE LONGHI (1766-1831), FIRST KNOWN PORTRAIT OF BONAPARTE

This bust portrait by the celebrated engraver Giuseppe Longhi is one of the very first certified portraits of Bonaparte, who is shown here with his hair gathered in a pigtail and facing right. Longhi is known to have met Bonaparte in 1796 during the Italian Campaign. Other representations of Napoleon include the later portrait by Antoine Jean Gros (Louvre collection), showing Napoleon in profile turned to the left.

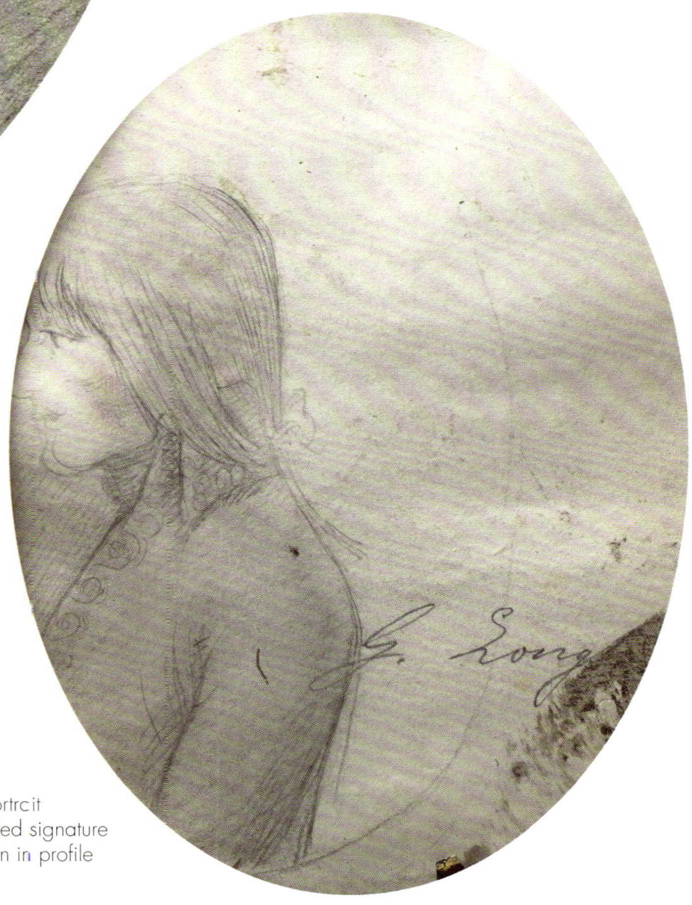

Reverse detail
The reverse of the portrait bears Longhi's penciled signature and shows Napoleon in profile facing left.

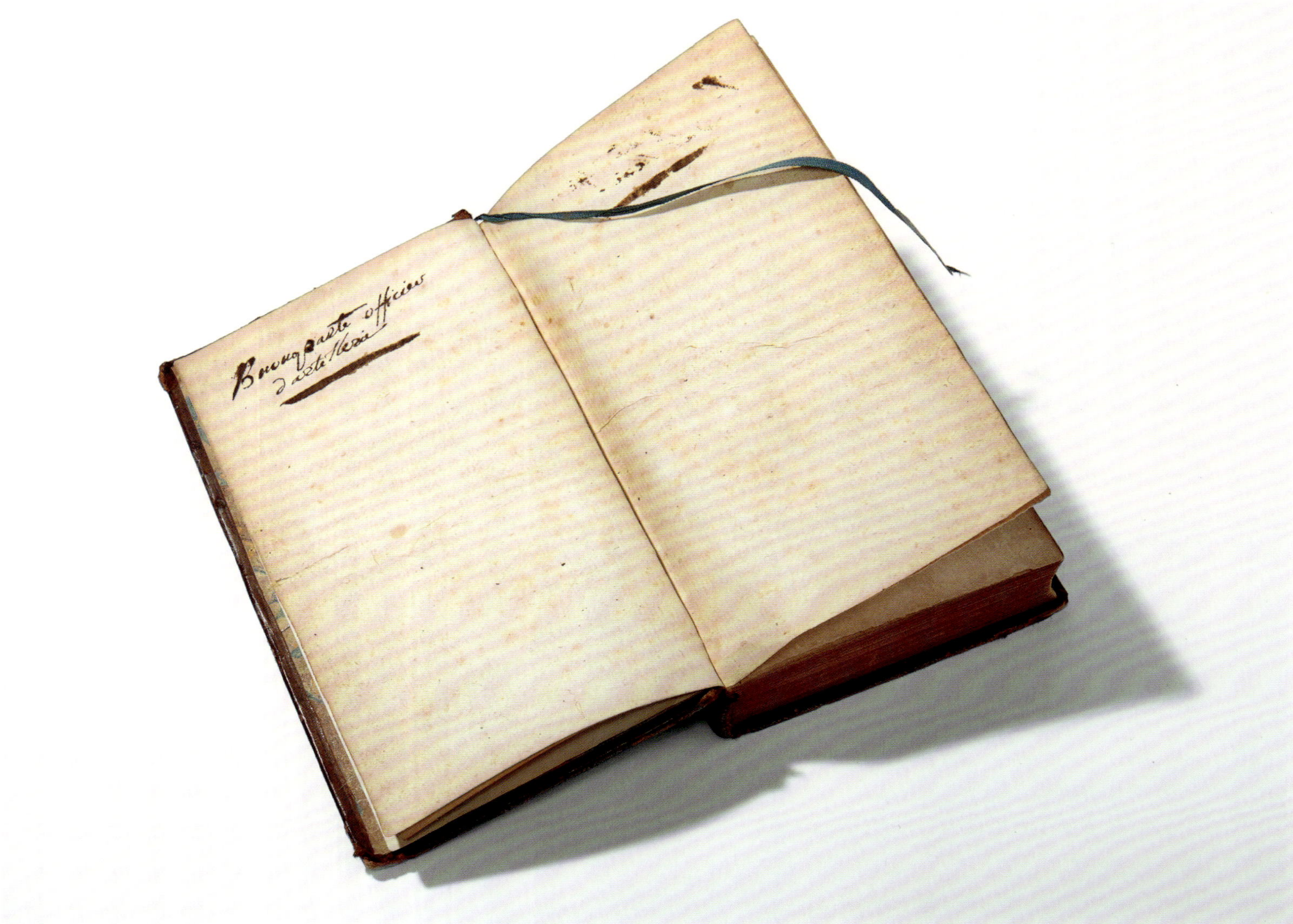

BOOK BELONGING TO BUONAPARTE, ARTILLERY CAPTAIN

This volume of *The Works of Machiavelli* includes a handwritten note in black ink referring to "Buonaparte, artillery captain" which is thought to date from the time when Napoleon was in Corsica, from 1789 to 1793. There is also an inked-in note dating from 1949 which states that: "This book was given to me by the late Baron Alberto Lumbroso, Napoleon historian. It comes from the estate of Mr Minghetti [...]. On the title page, there is the [barely visible] seal of Carlo Buonaparte, Napoleon's father."

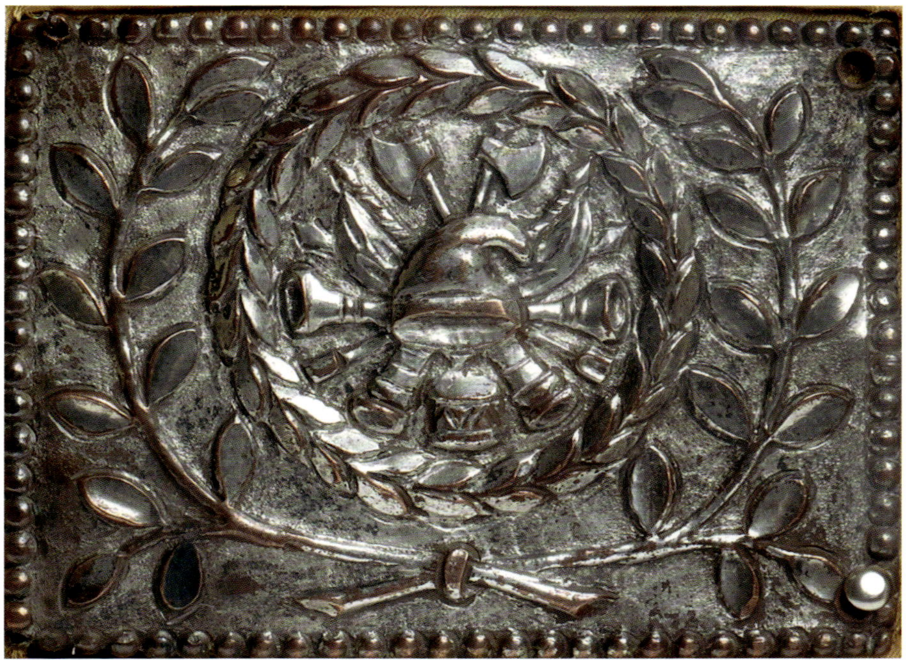

BELT BUCKLE BELONGING TO BONAPARTE AS LIEUTENANT-COLONEL BONAPARTE OF THE CORSICAN NATIONAL GUARD

Metal belt buckle, featuring a Phrygian cap in the center of a palm-leaf framed laurel wreath, worn by Bonaparte in 1792 as a colonel in command of the Corsican National Guard, preserved for posterity by his mother, Maria Letizia Bonaparte. Two years after the Emperor's death, she presented the buckle in homage to Don Pietro Paolo Francesco Carafa, Duke of Traetto. Italian-inspired and handcrafted, the buckle is characteristic of the revolutionary period before regulation uniform.

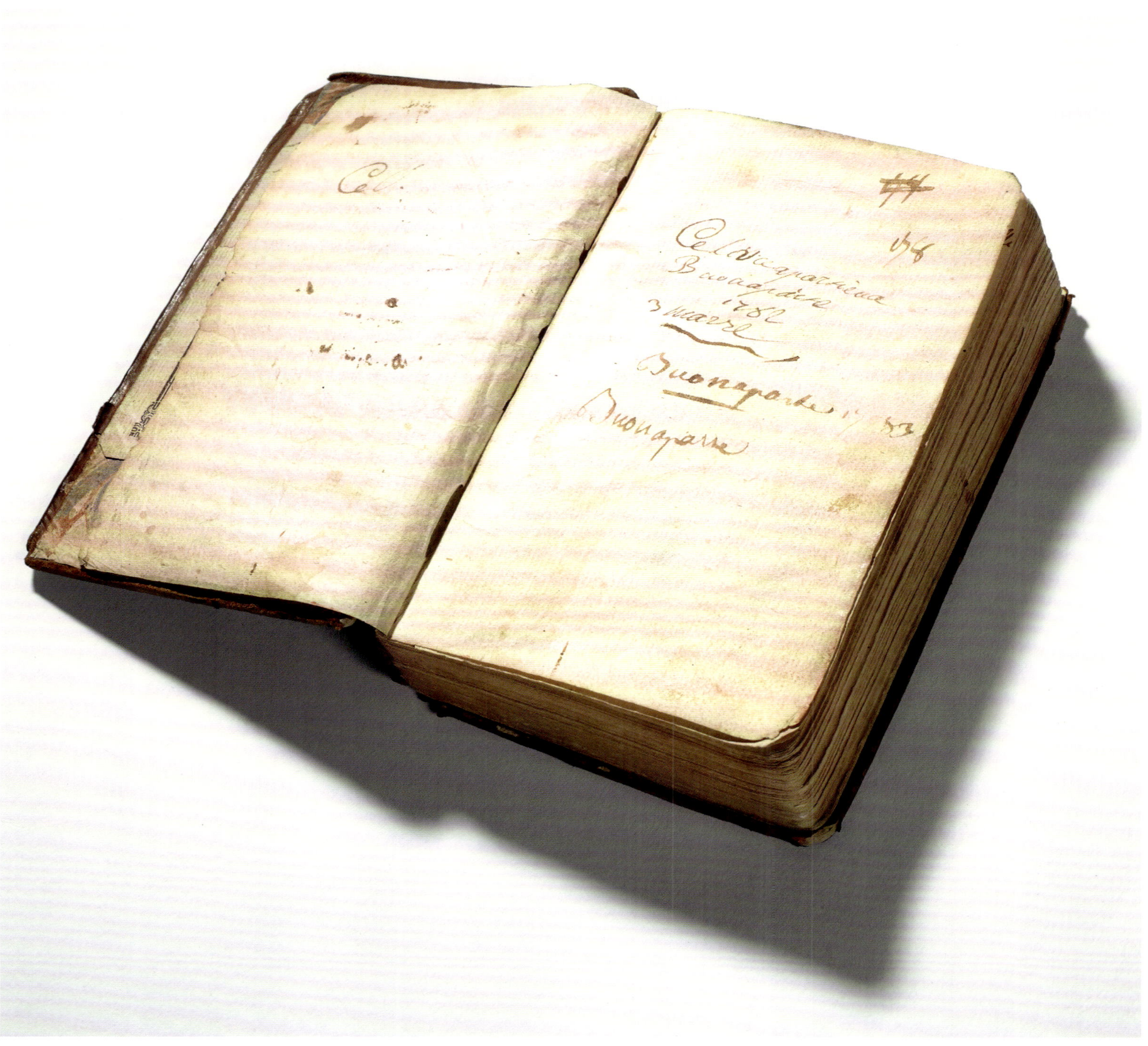

BOOK BELONGING TO BUONAPARTE AT THE BRIENNE MILITARY ACADEMY

Napoleon's education at Brienne military academy from 19 May 1779 to 30 October 1784 improved his rudimentary knowledge of French, which he spoke with a thick Corsican accent that attracted jibes from fellow pupils but spurred him to excel. He threw himself into reading, devouring the classics but also historical works such as this book, *Histoire de Henri le Grand*, published in 1661 by the then archbishop of Paris and provost of the Sorbonne, Hardouin de Perefixe, who was also preceptor to Louis XIV. Flyleaf bears an ex-libris handwritten by the young Napoleon when he was staying in Champagne.

THE 13 VENDÉMIAIRE

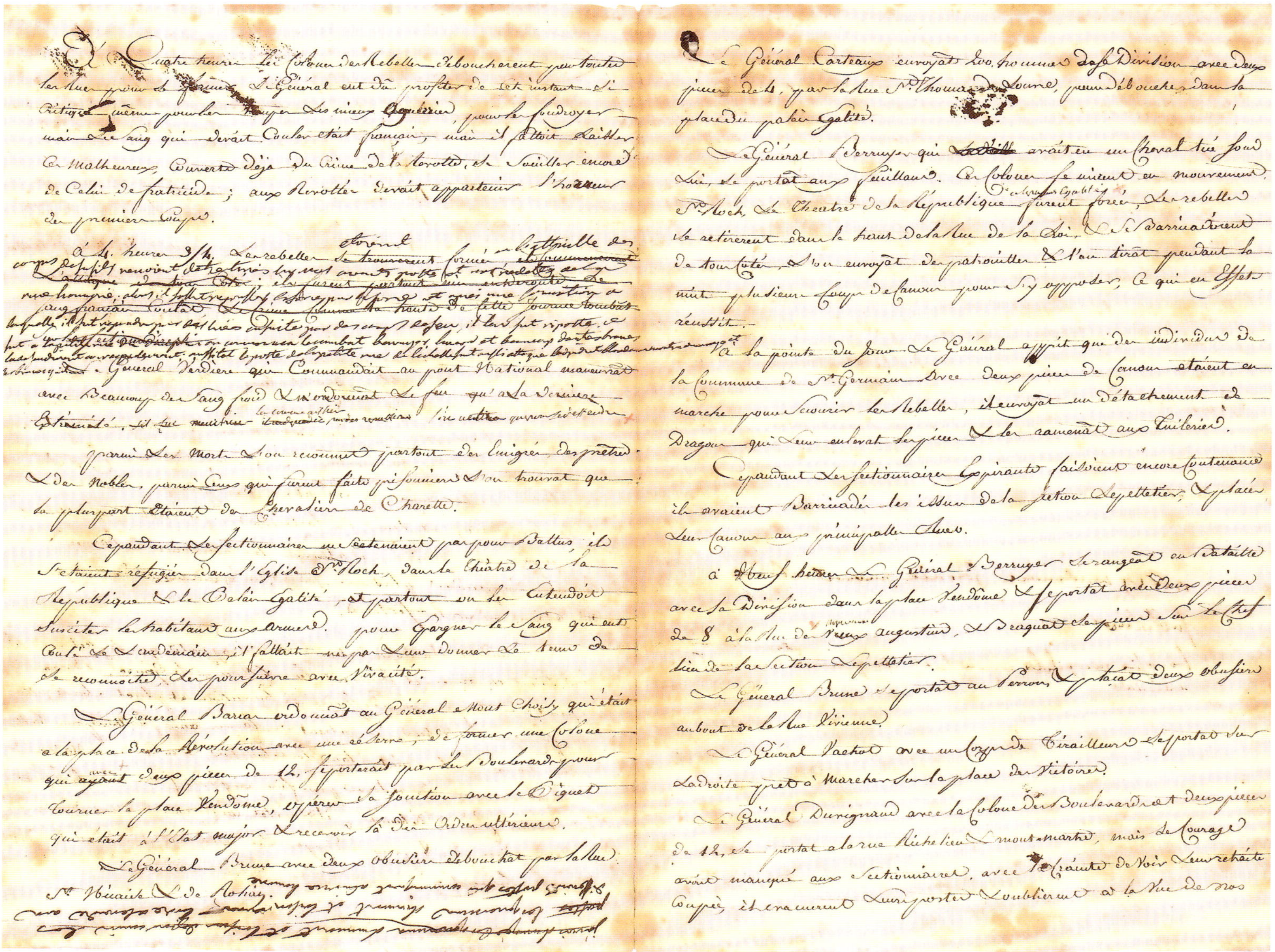
À Quatre heures les Colonnes de Rebelles débouchèrent par toutes les Rues pour se former. Le Général eut dû profiter de cet instant [illegible] même pour les foudroyer mais le sang qui devait couler était français, mais il était laisser ces malheureux couverts déjà du crime de la Révolte, se souiller encore de celui de patricide; aux Révoltés devait appartenir l'honneur des premiers coups.

À 4 heures 3/4 les rebelles [illegible]

[illegible]

Parmi les morts l'on reconnut partout des émigrés, des prêtres & des nobles, parmi ceux qui furent faits prisonniers l'on trouvât que la plupart étaient des Chevaliers de Charette.

Cependant les sectionnaires ne se tenaient pas pour battus, ils s'étaient réfugiés dans l'Église St Roch, dans le théâtre de la République & le Palais Égalité, et partout on les entendait susciter les habitants aux armes. Pour épargner le sang qui eut coulé le 14 vendémiaire il fallait ne pas leur donner le temps de se reconnaître, les poursuivre avec vivacité.

Le Général Barras ordonnat au Général Montchoisy qui était à la place de la Révolution avec une réserve, de former une colonne qui ayant deux pièces de 12, se porterait par le Boulevard pour tourner la place Vendôme, opérer sa jonction avec le piquet qui était à l'état major, & recevoir là des ordres ultérieurs.

Le Général Brune avec deux obusiers débouchât par la Rue St Nicaise & de Rohan [illegible]

Le Général Carteaux envoyat 400 hommes de sa Division avec deux pièces de 4, par la Rue St Thomas du Louvre, pour déboucher dans la place du palais Égalité.

Le Général Berruyer qui [illegible] avait eu un cheval tué sous lui, se portât aux Feuillants. Ces colonnes se mirent en mouvement. St Roch, le Théâtre de la République & le palais Égalité furent forcés, les rebelles se retirèrent dans le haut de la Rue de la Loi & se barricadèrent de tous côtés. L'on envoyât des patrouilles & l'on tirât pendant la nuit plusieurs coups de canon pour s'y opposer, ce qui en effet réussit.

À la pointe du jour le Général appris que des individus de la commune de St Germain avec deux pièces de canon étaient en marche pour secourir les rebelles, il envoyat un détachement de Dragons qui leur enlevat les pièces & les ramenat aux Tuileries.

Cependant les sectionnaires [illegible] faisaient encore contenance, ils avaient barricadé les issues de la section Lepelletier, & placé leurs canons aux principales avenues.

À Neuf heures le Général Berruyer se rangeat en bataille avec sa Division dans la place Vendôme & se portât avec deux pièces de 8 à la Rue des Vieux augustins, & braquât ses pièces sur le chef lieu de la section Lepelletier.

Le Général Brune se portât au Perron & plaçat deux obusiers au bout de la Rue Vivienne.

Le Général Vachot avec un corps de Tirailleurs se portât sur la droite prêt à marcher sur la place des Victoires.

Le Général Duvignaud avec la colonne des Boulevards et deux pièces de 12, se portat à la rue Richelieu & Montmartre, mais le courage avait manqué aux sectionnaires, avec la crainte de voir leur retraite coupée, ils [illegible] leurs postes & oublièrent à la vue de nos [illegible]

HANDWRITTEN ACCOUNT OF THE DAY OF 13 VENDÉMIAIRE, AS TOLD BY BONAPARTE AND BARRAS

This extraordinary previously unpublished manuscript of major historical importance was dictated to Andoche Junot, the young Corsican General's secretary, by Bonaparte and Barras on the evening of the historical day of 5 October 1795 (13 Vendémiaire Year IV on the Republican calendar), to record the day's events. The document, extensively annotated by Bonaparte and Barras, describes how the two main decision-makers experienced the infamous day when the Royalists attempted to overturn the Convention. On behalf of Paul Barras, commander-in-chief of the Interior Army, Bonaparte, then second-in-command, gave the order to open fire on the insurgents on the steps of the church of Saint Roch. Three hundred lives were lost. In the aftermath of the battle, Bonaparte became known as "Général Vendémiaire".

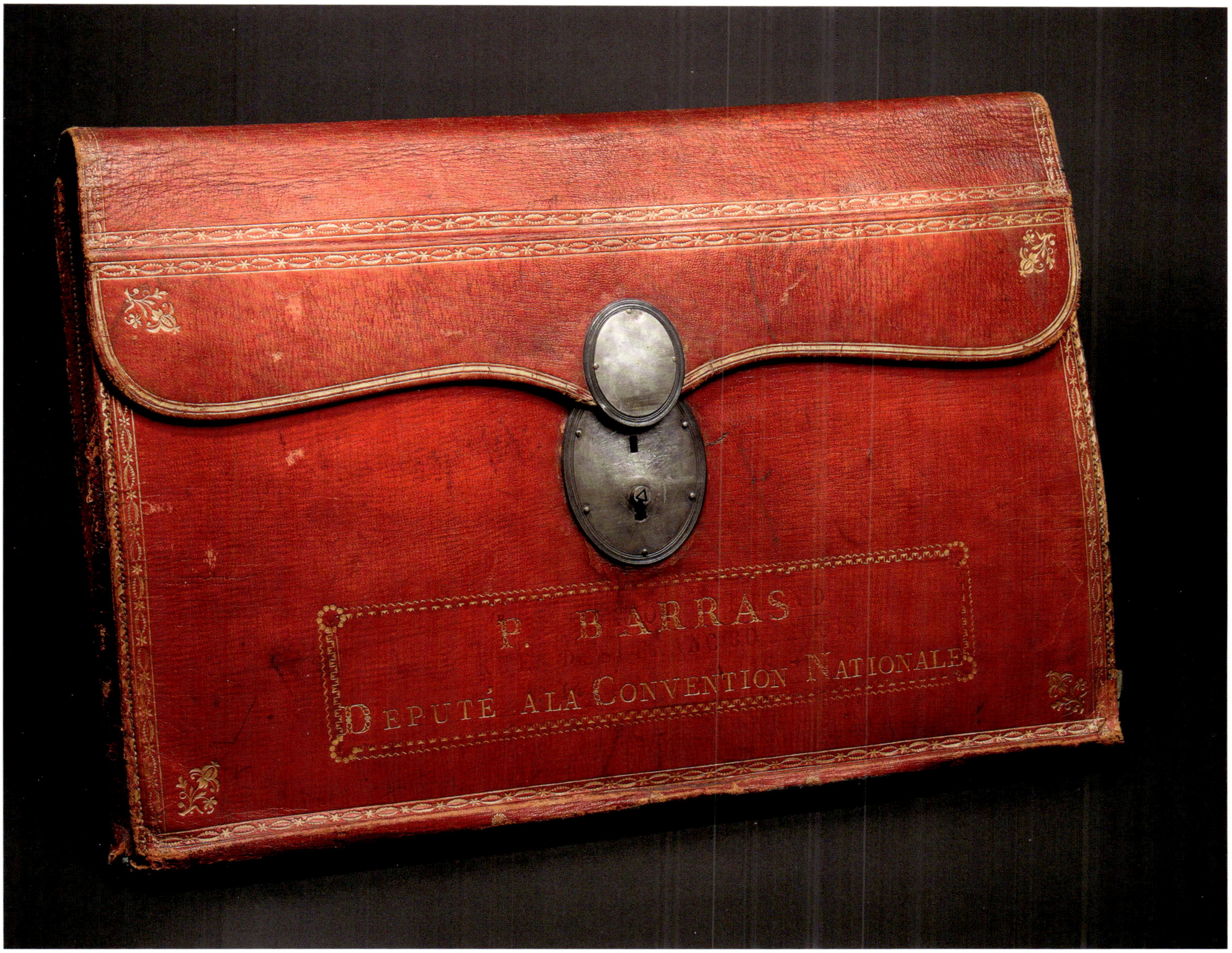

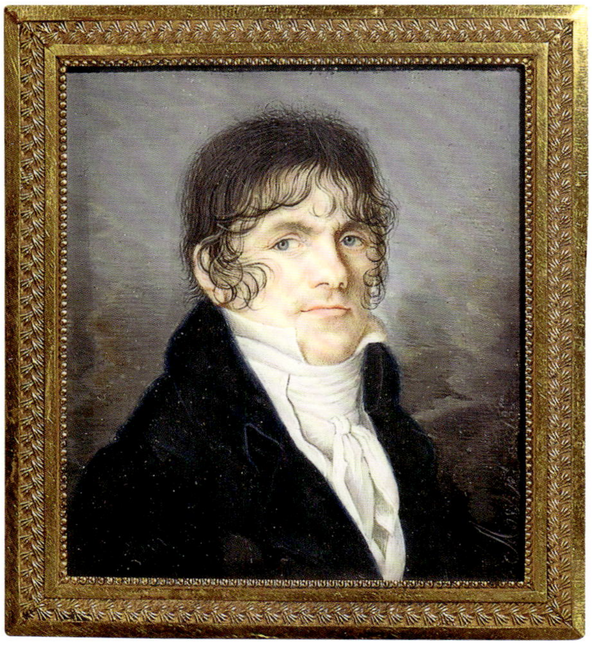

PORTFOLIO AND PORTRAIT OF PAUL BARRAS BY ANTOINE AVY (1776-1814)

Elected a member of the National Convention in 1792, Paul François Jean Nicolas, Viscount of Barras (1755-1829) sat on the same benches as the *Montagnards*. He owned this gold-tooled red Morocco leather portfolio marked: "P. BARRAS DEPUTE A LA CONVENTION NATIONALE". After the siege of Toulon in 1793, he became close to Bonaparte who, by then a brigadier general, went on to join the Army of Italy. Their paths crossed again on 13 Vendémiaire. A key player in the founding of the Directory, of which he became one of the Directors in October 1795, the political, military and sentimental influence of Barras on the young Napoleon's rise to power was decisive. Barras even introduced Napoleon to his former mistress, a certain Josephine, widow of Beauharnais. This historical artifact is of unique value and was exhibited at the 150th anniversary of the French Revolution at Musée Carnavalet in 1939.

THE EGYPTIAN CAMPAIGN (1798-1801)

"Soldiers, remember that from high above these monuments, forty centuries look down upon you": these now famous words were spoken by Napoleon before the Giza pyramids and evoke the young General's ambition as he arrived to conquer Egypt. He spearheaded a military campaign that extended from Alexandria to Cairo and Abukir, commanding his soldiers to victory at the Battle of the Pyramids. On 11 October 1798, four months after landing at Alexandria, he sent Barras, a member of the Directory, an extraordinary handwritten letter, one of only a few known to us, telling him that he received neither mail nor gazette, that he was "keen to hear what you are doing in your Europe" but that he was "in fine form and our situation is rather favorable [...]".

One of the most noteworthy events was the Battle of Abukir in July 1799. The Turkish army had arrived at the port and captured its fort but Bonaparte mounted an assault that routed the Ottomans. History books recount that Murat then took Mustafa Pasha prisoner but in his campaign journal Sergeant Vigo Roussillon claims that he was behind this exploit and proves it with a certificate of honor received from the hands of General Bonaparte. The magnificent flintlock rifle conserved in the collection bears a silver plate on the right-hand side of the weapon, recalling this: "Rifle of Grand Vizier Mustafa Pasha, offered as a reward by General Bonaparte to Sergeant Vigo Roussillon of the 32nd half-brigade on 26 July 1799 at Abukir". News of this important capture was rapidly sent on. Well aware that prolonged absence from Paris would not play in his favor, Bonaparte handed over his powers to Kléber, who became commander-in-chief. Bonaparte set sail on-board the frigate *Muiron* for Paris on 23 August 1799. On 26 August, General Dugua was concerned to hear of his return and criticized his departure, which he thought premature: "all these men who only came because you were leading the expedition, who through their loyalty to you would have sacrificed what they hold dearest for you [...]. Your silence, your departure, has caused them despair [...]".

In Egypt, General Jacques-François de Menou (1750-1810) replaced Jean-Baptiste Kléber, assassinated on 14 June 1800. He obtained the support of Mamluk chieftain Mourad Bey (1750-1801), who offered the new head of the French Army of Egypt the jade-handled dagger shown here (page 103). However, a new era was dawning and Menou capitulated the Eastern lands to the British. He also returned to France, where Bonaparte was now First Consul.

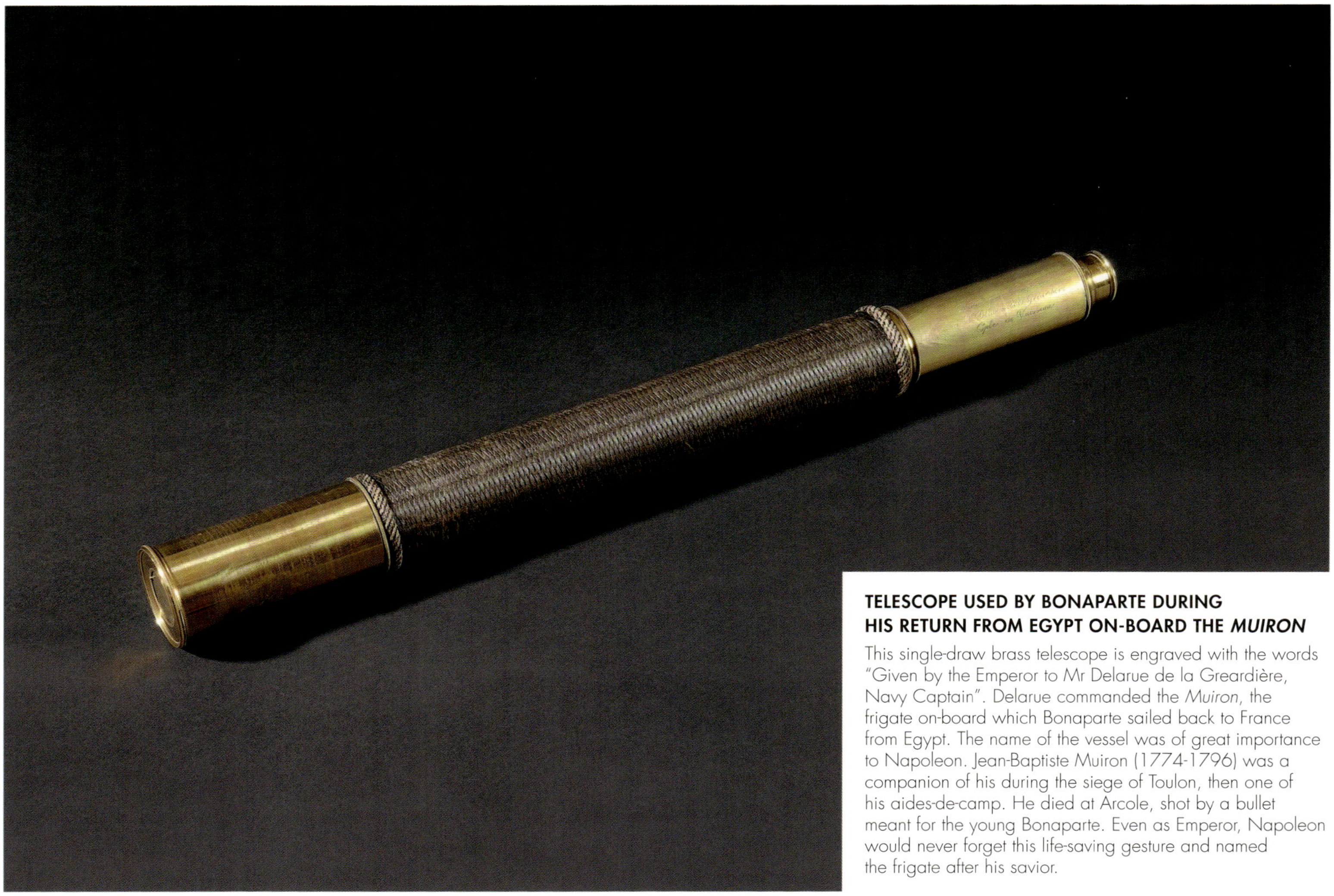

TELESCOPE USED BY BONAPARTE DURING HIS RETURN FROM EGYPT ON-BOARD THE *MUIRON*

This single-draw brass telescope is engraved with the words "Given by the Emperor to Mr Delarue de la Greardière, Navy Captain". Delarue commanded the *Muiron*, the frigate on-board which Bonaparte sailed back to France from Egypt. The name of the vessel was of great importance to Napoleon. Jean-Baptiste Muiron (1774-1796) was a companion of his during the siege of Toulon, then one of his aides-de-camp. He died at Arcole, shot by a bullet meant for the young Bonaparte. Even as Emperor, Napoleon would never forget this life-saving gesture and named the frigate after his savior.

HONORÉ PINEL, *GENERAL BONAPARTE IN EGYPT*

Although forgotten today, painter Honoré Pinel, a pupil of Michel Martin Drolling, exhibited at numerous Salons. He was the son of Philippe Pinel, the doctor known as the 'father of modern psychiatry'. This painting demonstrates how the Egypt campaign remained a source of inspiration for artists throughout the 19th century. Bonaparte appears to erupt from the desert, borne along in a powerful movement by the sand. The work was exhibited under no. 439 at the 1865 Salon.

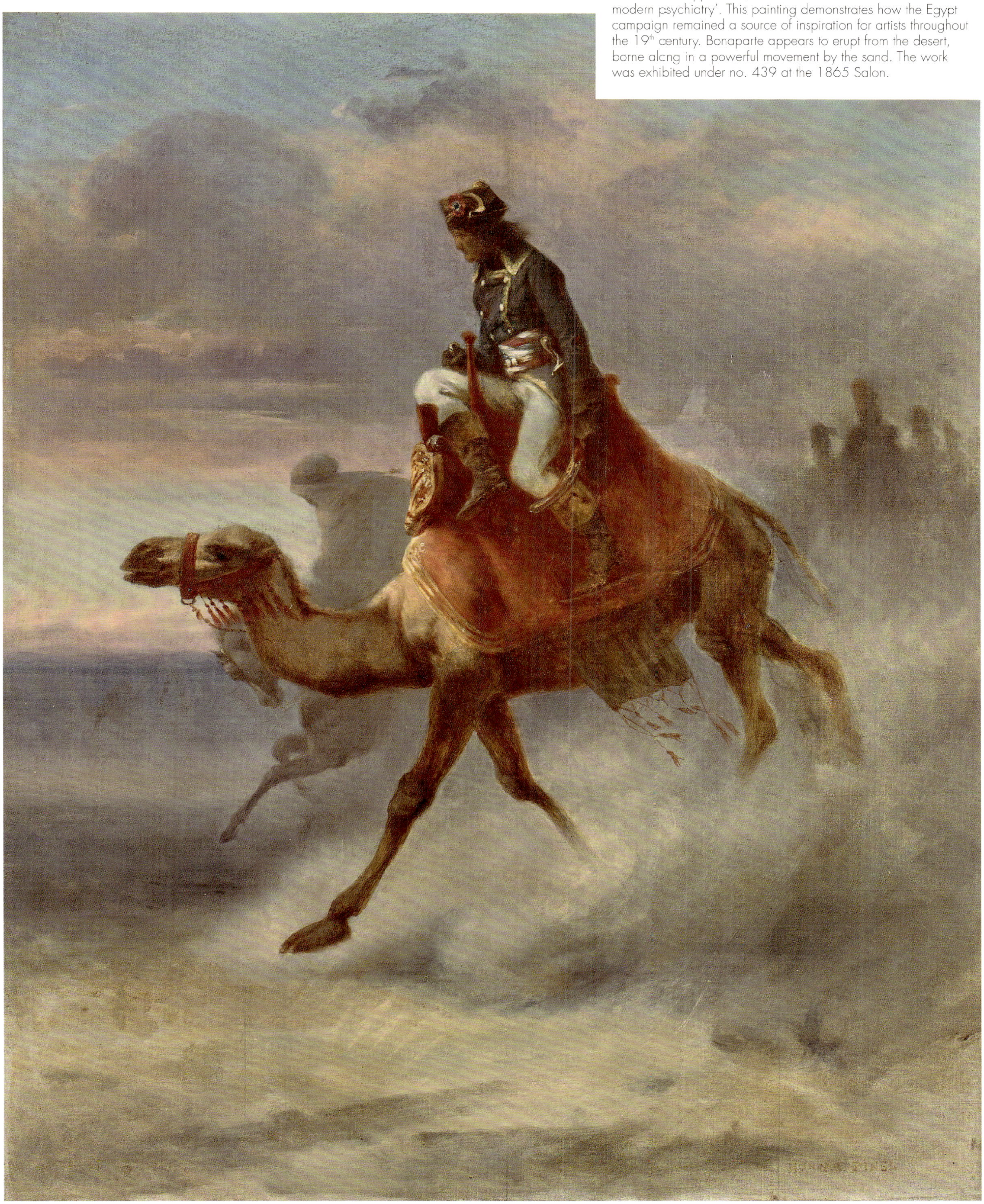

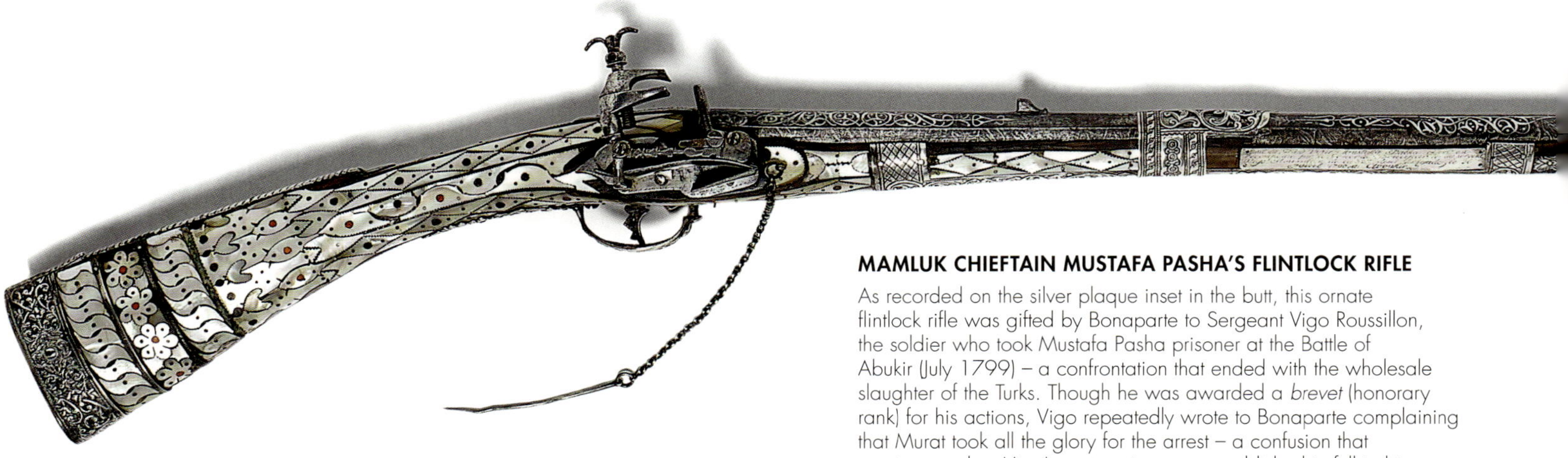

MAMLUK CHIEFTAIN MUSTAFA PASHA'S FLINTLOCK RIFLE

As recorded on the silver plaque inset in the butt, this ornate flintlock rifle was gifted by Bonaparte to Sergeant Vigo Roussillon, the soldier who took Mustafa Pasha prisoner at the Battle of Abukir (July 1799) – a confrontation that ended with the wholesale slaughter of the Turks. Though he was awarded a *brevet* (honorary rank) for his actions, Vigo repeatedly wrote to Bonaparte complaining that Murat took all the glory for the arrest – a confusion that continues today. Vigo's protestations were published in full in his *Journal de Campagne, 1793-1837*.

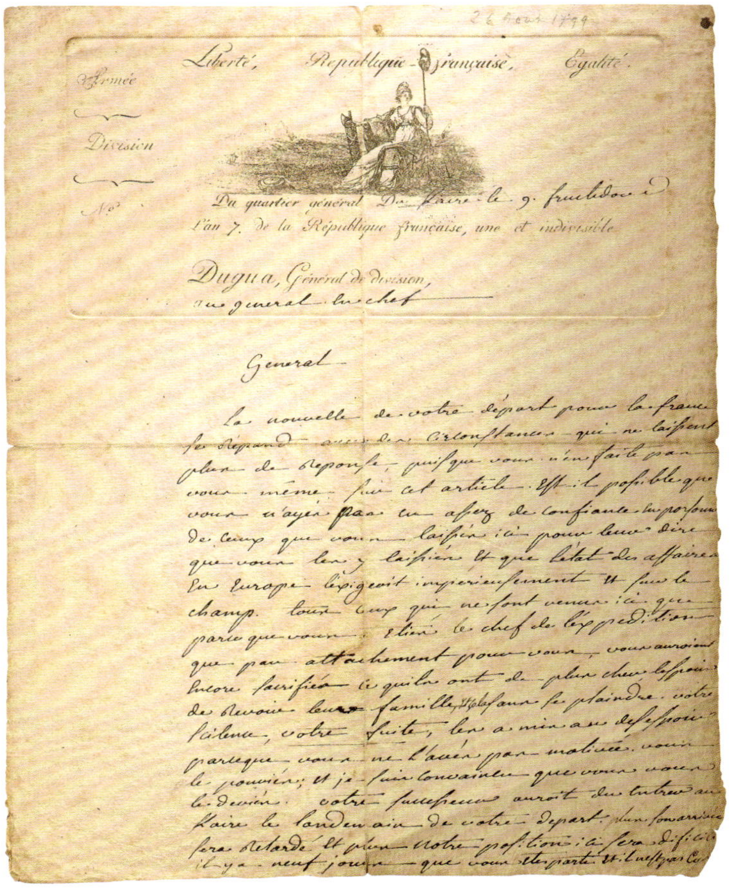

Armée

Division

No.

Liberté, République française, Egalité.

Du quartier général Du Caire le 9 fructidor an 7. de la République française, une et indivisible.

Dugua, Général de division, au general en chef

General

La nouvelle de votre départ pour la france

LETTER DATED 26 AUGUST 1799, FROM DUGUA, GOVERNOR OF CAIRO, TO BONAPARTE, ACCUSING HIM OF ABANDONING THE FRENCH ARMY OF EGYPT TO RETURN TO PARIS

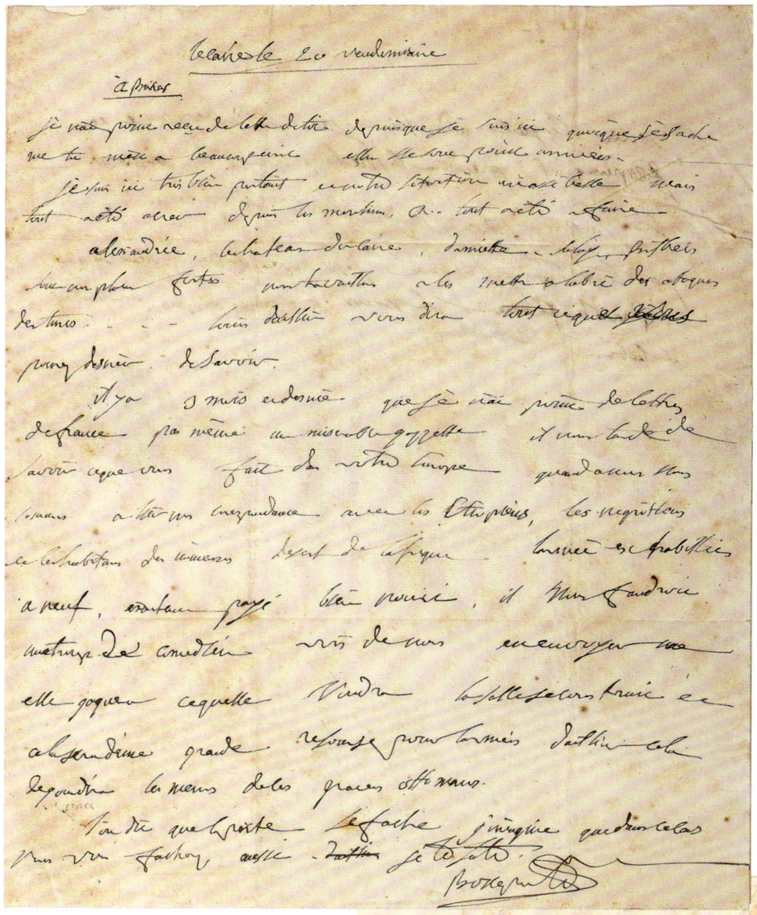

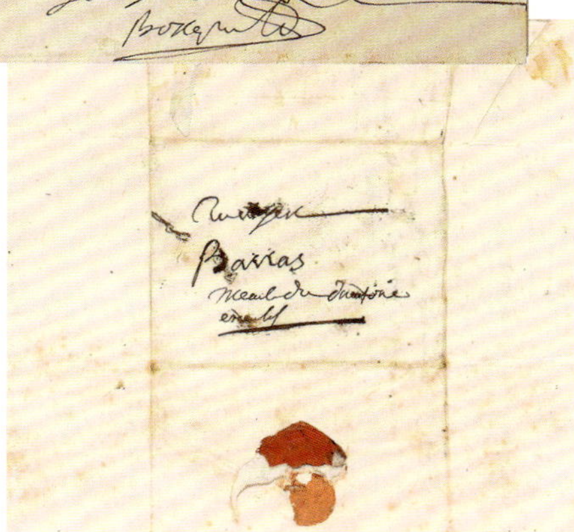

LETTER FROM BONAPARTE TO BARRAS HANDWRITTEN IN CAIRO ON 20 VENDÉMIAIRE YEAR VI (11 OCTOBER 1798) TO UPDATE HIM ON THE SITUATION

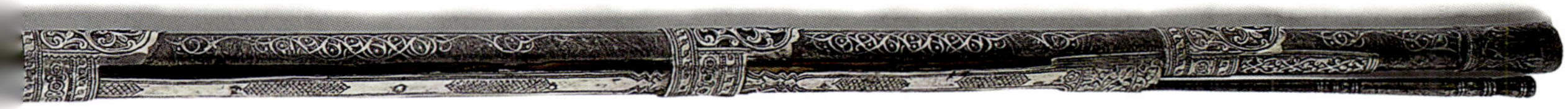

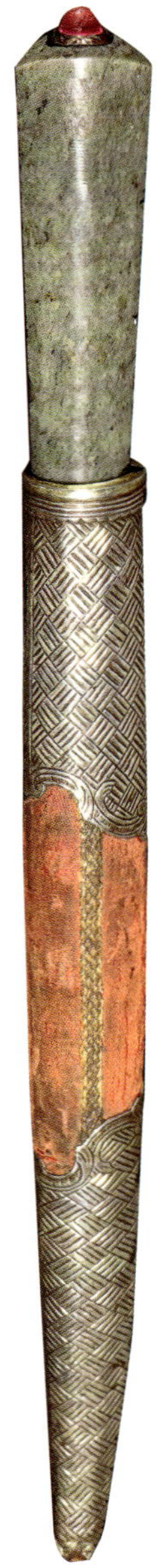

GILDED BRASS DAGGER GIVEN BY MAMLUK CHIEFTAIN MOURAD BEY TO GENERAL MENOU

General Jacques-François de Menou (1750-1810) assumed command of the Army of Egypt following Kléber's assassination on 14 June 1800. He was tasked with evacuating the remaining French forces in Egypt, now on the brink of exhaustion. General Menou converted to Islam, taking the name Abdallah-Jacques, and married a local woman. This gilded brass dagger with jade handle was a gift from his old-enemy-turned-ally, Mamluk chieftain Mourad Bey (1750-1801).

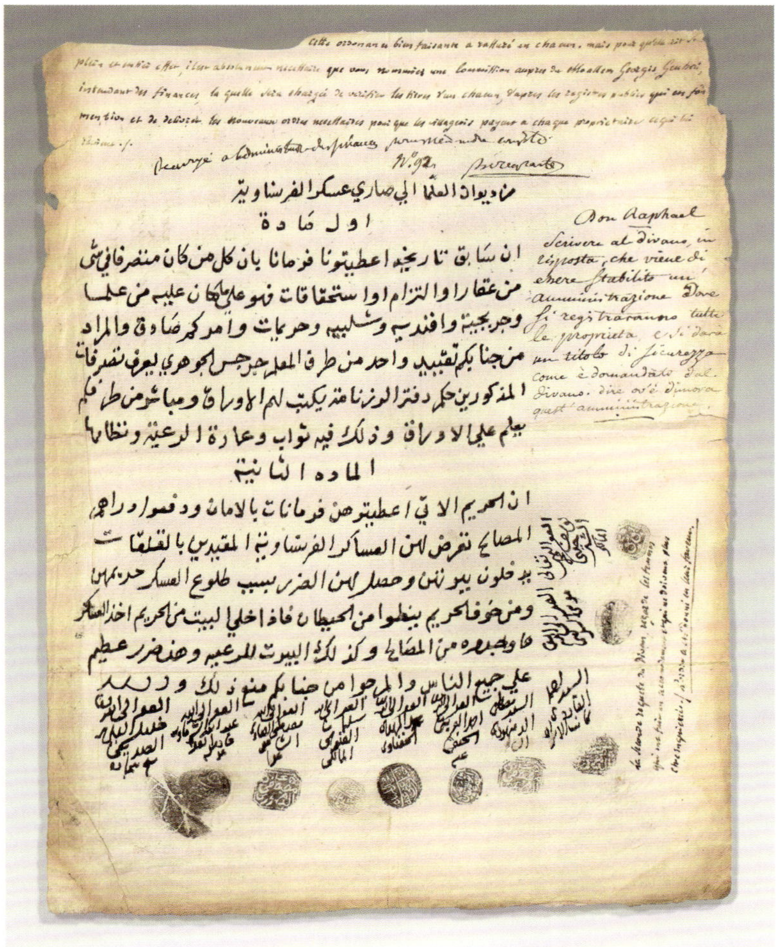

LETTER IN ARABIC, ANNOTATED AND SIGNED BY BONAPARTE, EGYPT, 1798-1799

Including a few handwritten words and his signature "Sent back to the financial authorities for their information", this rare document testifies to the future Emperor's authority during the Egypt campaign. It settles certain questions concerning the life of the Divan.

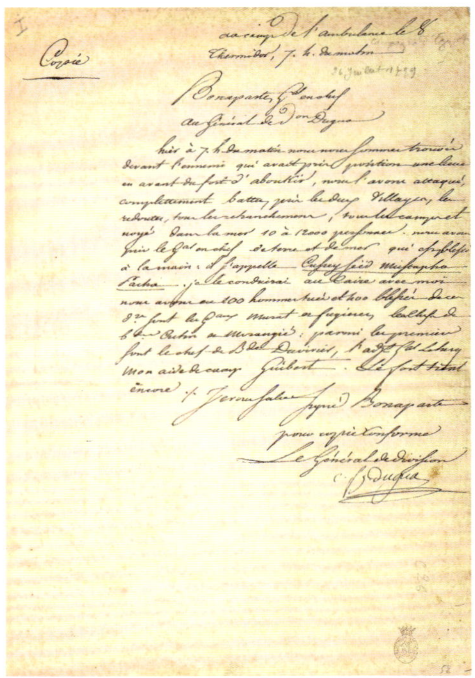

ANNOUNCEMENT OF THE ARREST OF MAMLUK CHIEFTAIN MUSTAFA PASHA AT THE BATTLE OF ABUKIR, 26 JULY 1799

THOMAS-CHARLES NAUDET (1778-1810),
VIEW OF LUXOR DURING THE EGYPT CAMPAIGN

When leaving with his soldiers for Egypt in 1798, Bonaparte was accompanied by 167 scientists charged with recording traces of their discoveries. The artists willingly sketched the views they enjoyed, such as this view of the archaeological site of Luxor with the obelisk in the foreground before the temple ruins. Scientists can be seen taking samples at the site.

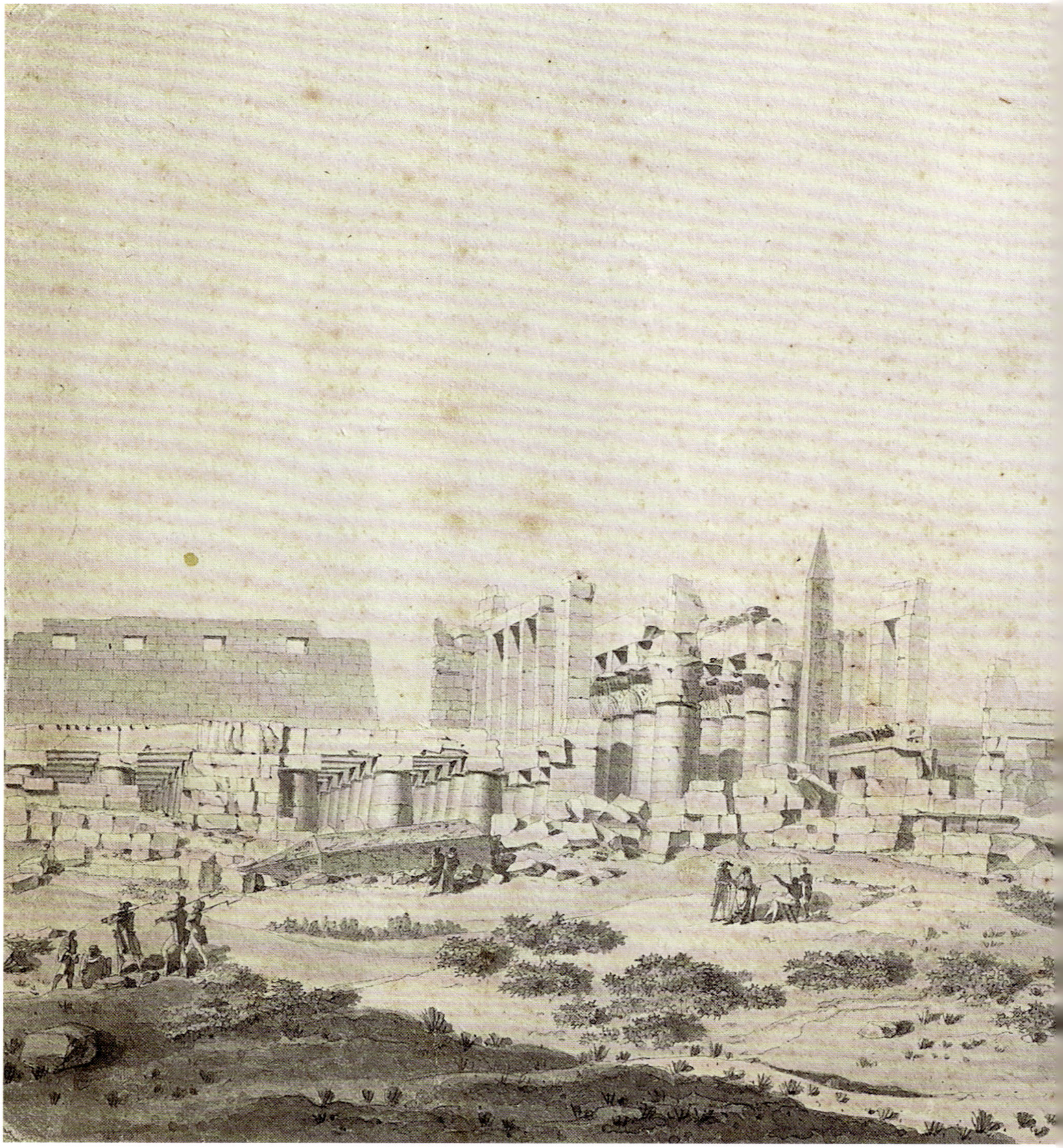

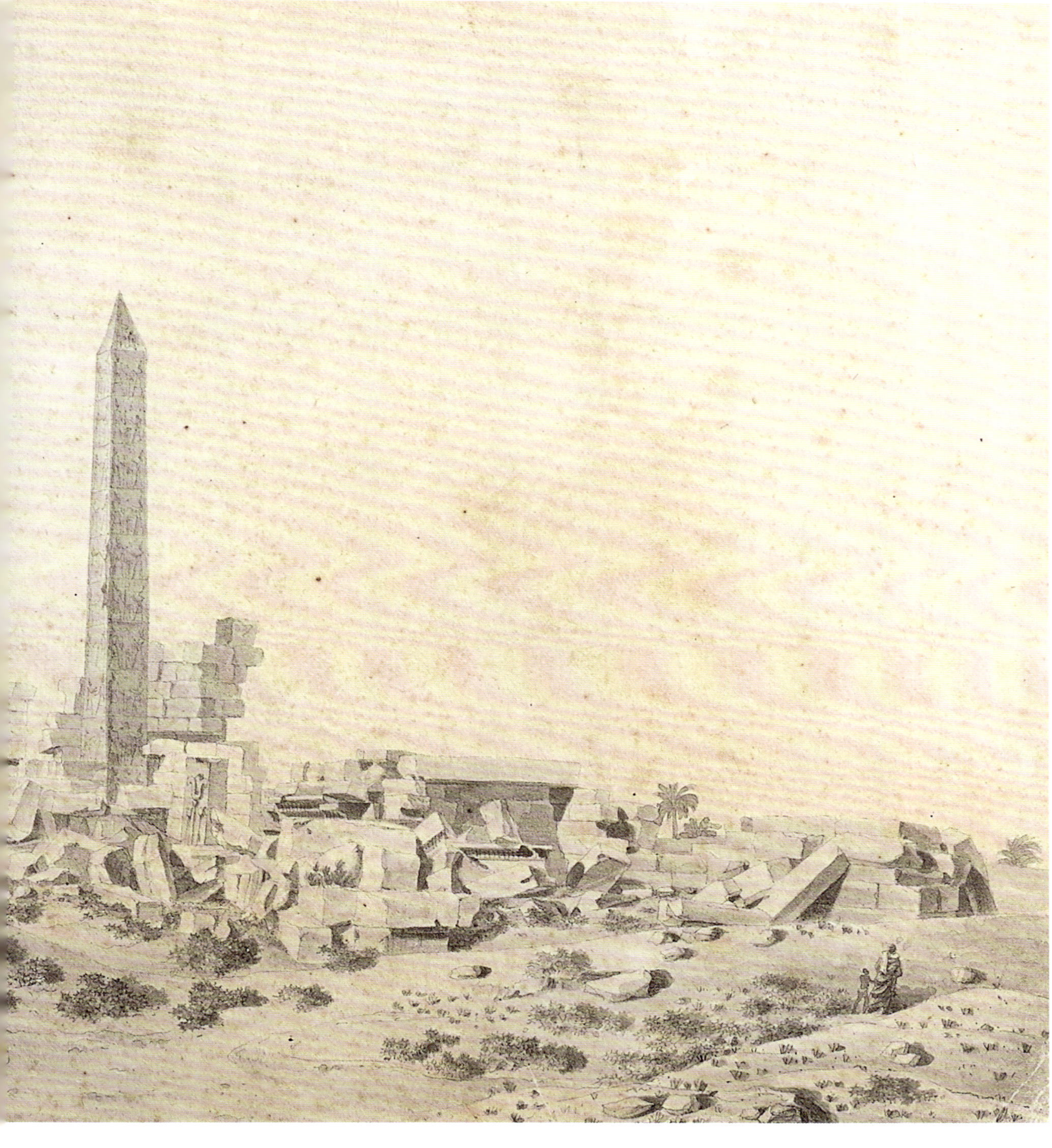

ORIGINAL LAYOUT OF *LA DESCRIPTION DE L'EGYPTE*

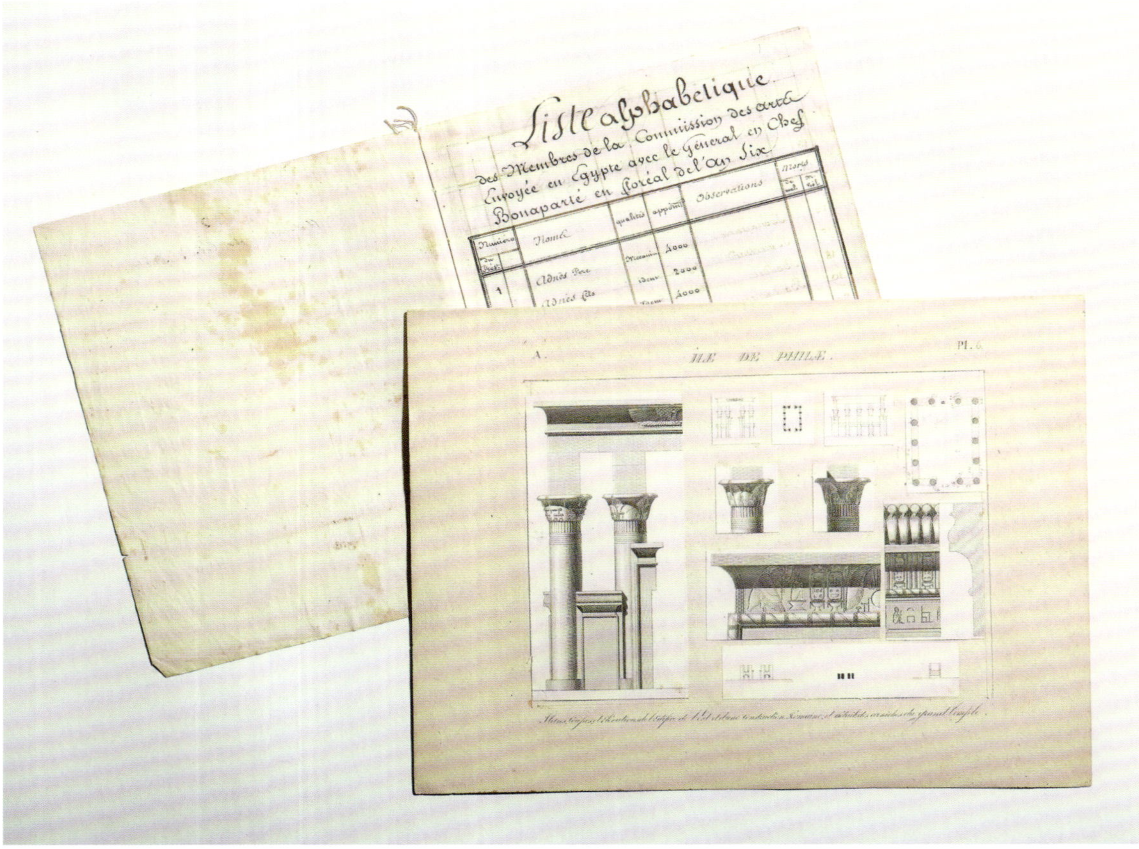

Before embarking on his Egyptian expedition (19 May 1798 – 31 August 1801), Napoleon commissioned a team of *savants* to accompany the French army to Egypt. They included engineers, writers, naturalists and draftsmen, plus two musicians, 22 engravers and a sizeable contingent of other experts charged with documenting and cataloguing the monuments, topography and natural history of Egypt. On 22 November 1799 they decided to compile their findings in a book: *La Description de l'Egypte*. Printing commenced under Napoleon, entrusted to the Imprimerie Impériale, and was completed by the Imprimerie Royale in the reign of Charles X. Consisting of 10 volumes of text and 13 volumes of plates, the book was one of the greatest editorial achievements the world had ever seen, fueling Egyptomania throughout Europe.

This collection owns the only 52 plates still extant. Based on superbly executed watercolor paintings and pencil drawings created in situ, they are all that remain of the book's original layout.

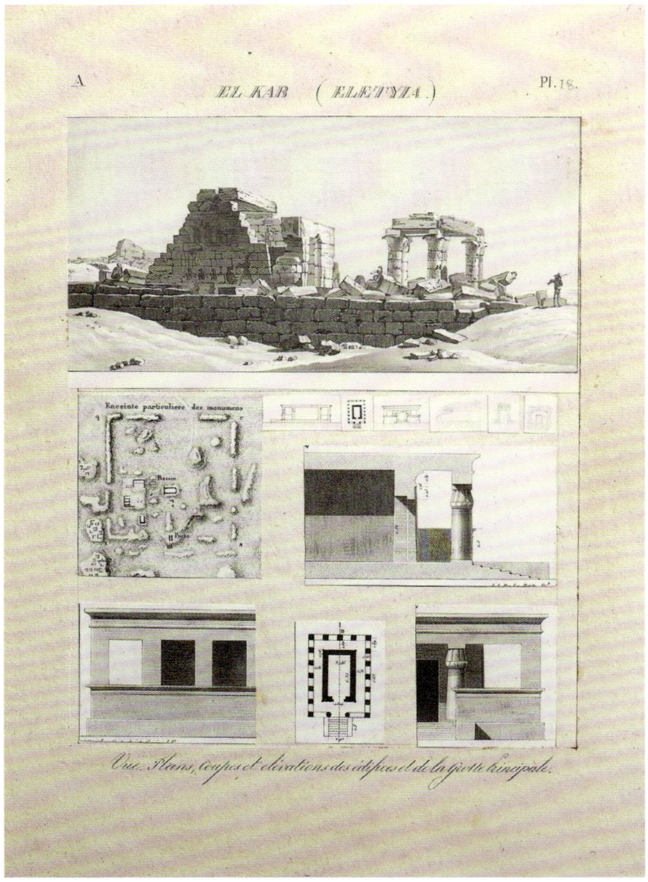

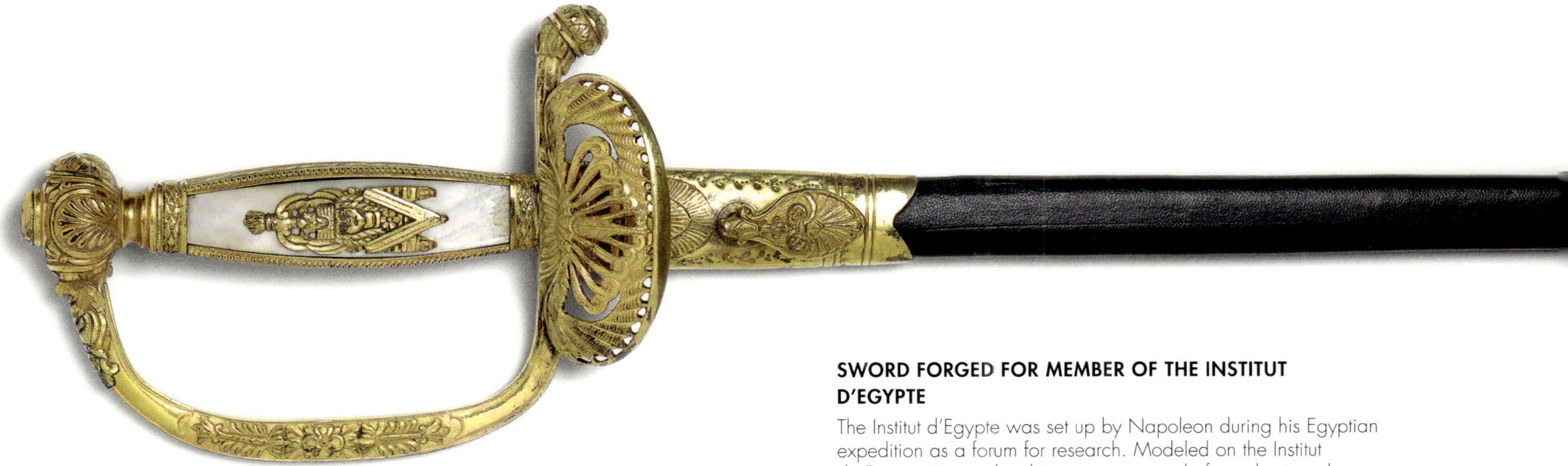

SWORD FORGED FOR MEMBER OF THE INSTITUT D'EGYPTE

The Institut d'Egypte was set up by Napoleon during his Egyptian expedition as a forum for research. Modeled on the Institut de France, its membership was composed of academics who were divided into several sections — mathematics, physics, natural history, political economy, literature and the arts. The first meeting of the Institute took place on 24 August 1798 under the presidency of Gaspard Monge (1746-1818). Pictured here, complete with ornately carved guards and blades, is one outstanding example of the swords that were custom-made for the Institute members.

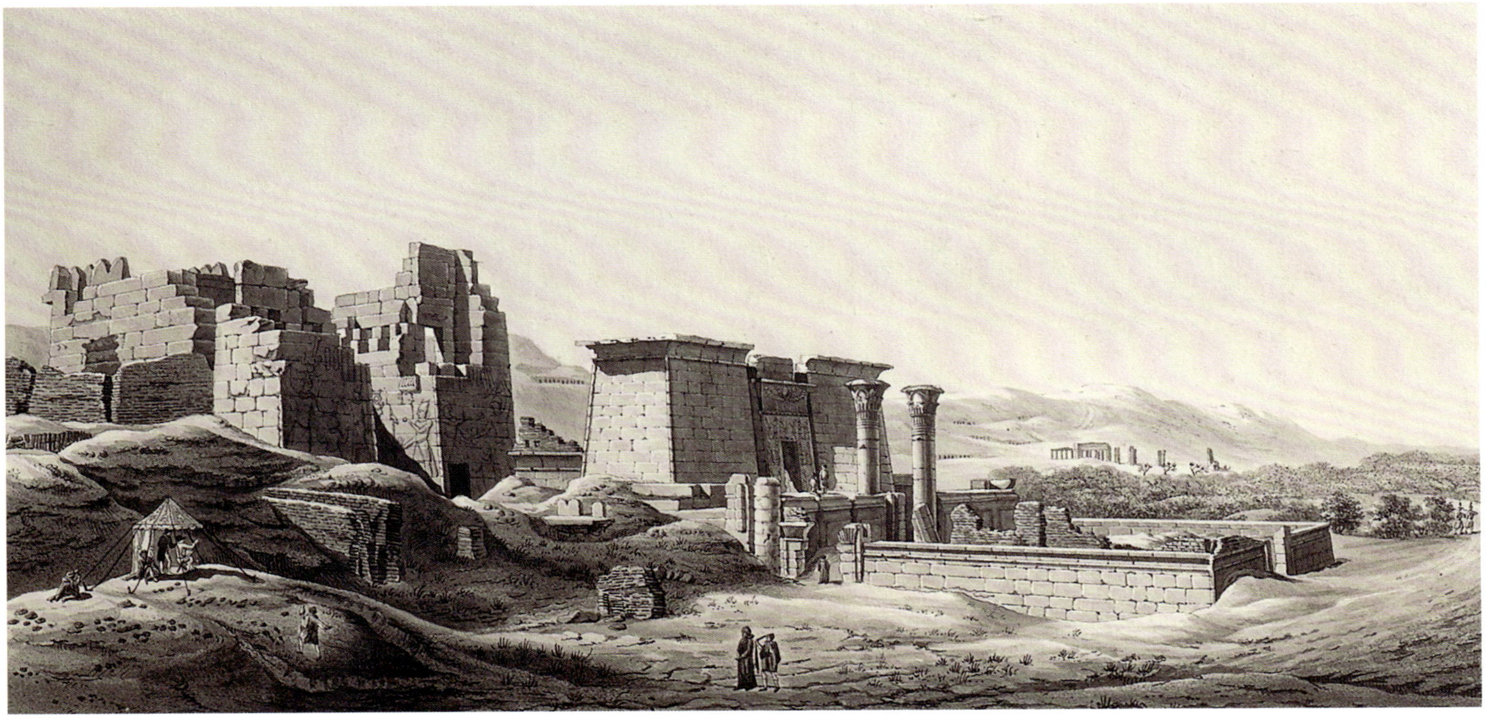

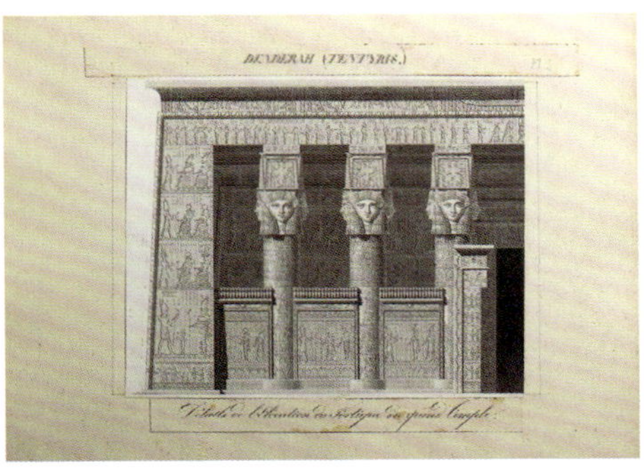

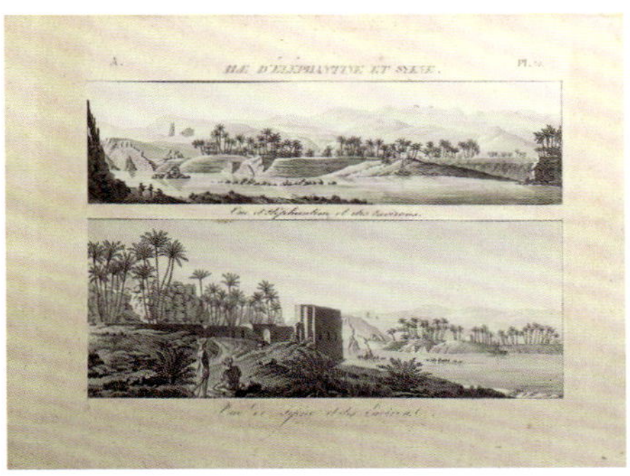

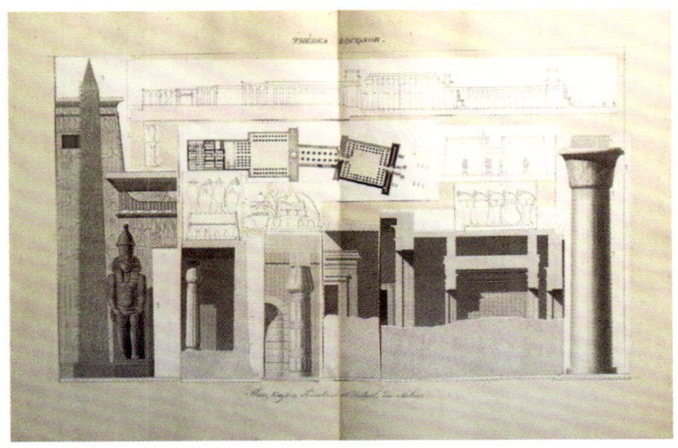

THE SO-CALLED "EGYPTIAN CABARET SET" – MASTERPIECE OF THE SEVRES IMPERIAL PORCELAIN MANUFACTORY

This "cabaret set", commissioned by Napoleon and Marie-Louise in 1813, was a New Year's gift to the Empress' lady-in-waiting, Countess de Luçay, in January 1814. Widely considered to be a masterpiece, the set testifies to the opulent gifts offered by the imperial couple. It is the sixth and certainly the most lavish of the seven cabaret sets they commissioned for others. It is also the only one in private hands and probably the only set still complete with its tray and original presentation box.

Each set is quite different in terms of shape, composition and ornamentation but they are all inspired by Vivant Denon's illustrations for his book, *Travels in Upper and Lower Egypt* (1802) and also the *Description de l'Egypte*. The first cabaret set was for Tsar Alexander I of Russia in 1808 (now in the museum of ceramics in Kuskovo). The second and third sets were for Josephine (the pieces now distributed between the museums of Malmaison, the Fondation Napoléon and the Ledoux Collection). The fourth set, delivered to the Emperor on 31 March 1810, was for the Tuileries (now mainly in the Louvre except for a saucer in the Ledoux collection, page 218). Sets five, six and seven were respectively offered by Marie-Louise to the Duchess of Montebello (Fontainebleau Museum), the Duchess of Bassano (Smithsonian Institute, Washington, and the Ledoux Collection) and Countess de Luçay (Ledoux Collection). Only the Ledoux Collection includes pieces from four of the seven Egyptian cabaret sets.

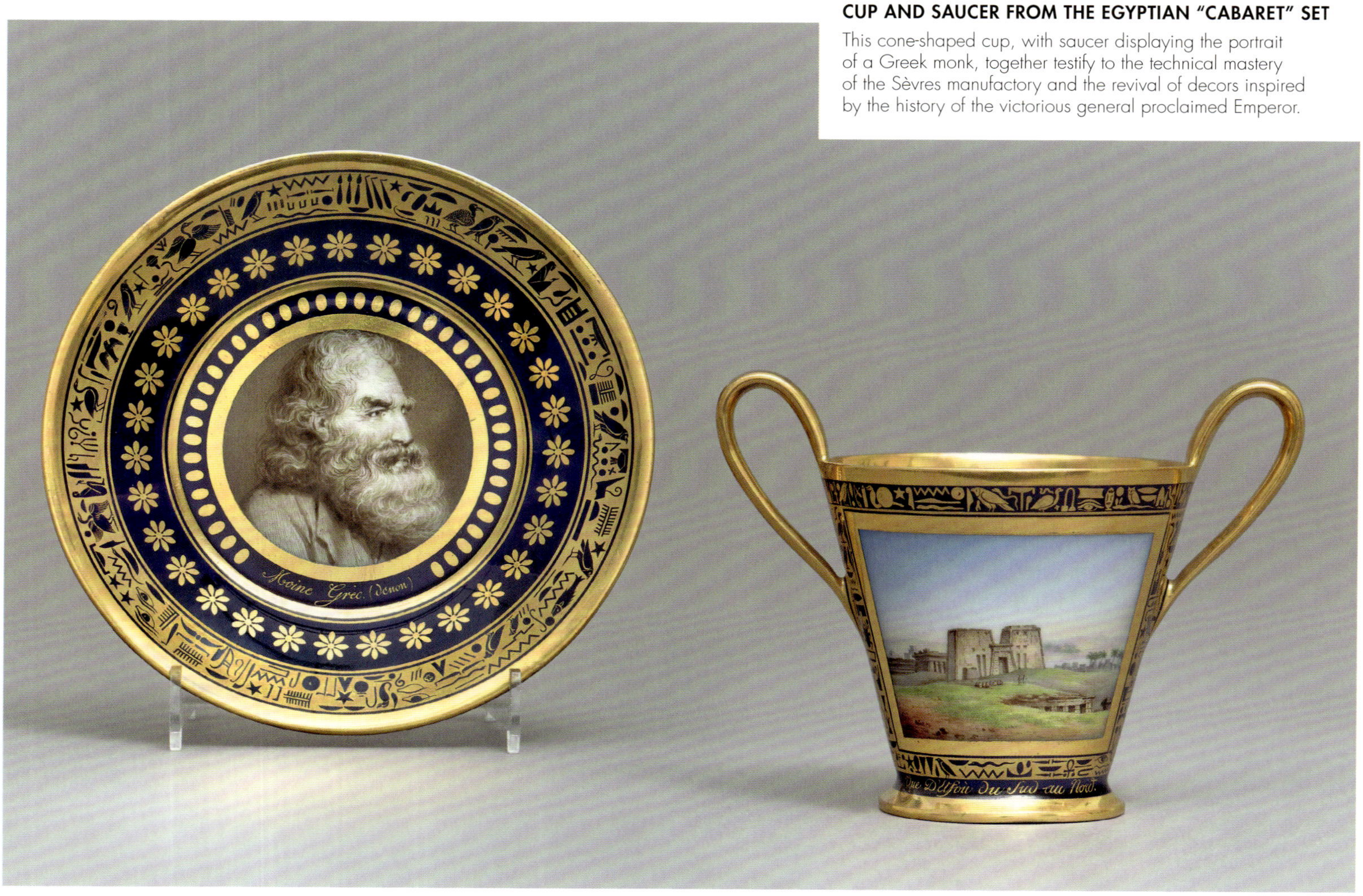

CUP AND SAUCER FROM THE EGYPTIAN "CABARET" SET

This cone-shaped cup, with saucer displaying the portrait of a Greek monk, together testify to the technical mastery of the Sèvres manufactory and the revival of decors inspired by the history of the victorious general proclaimed Emperor.

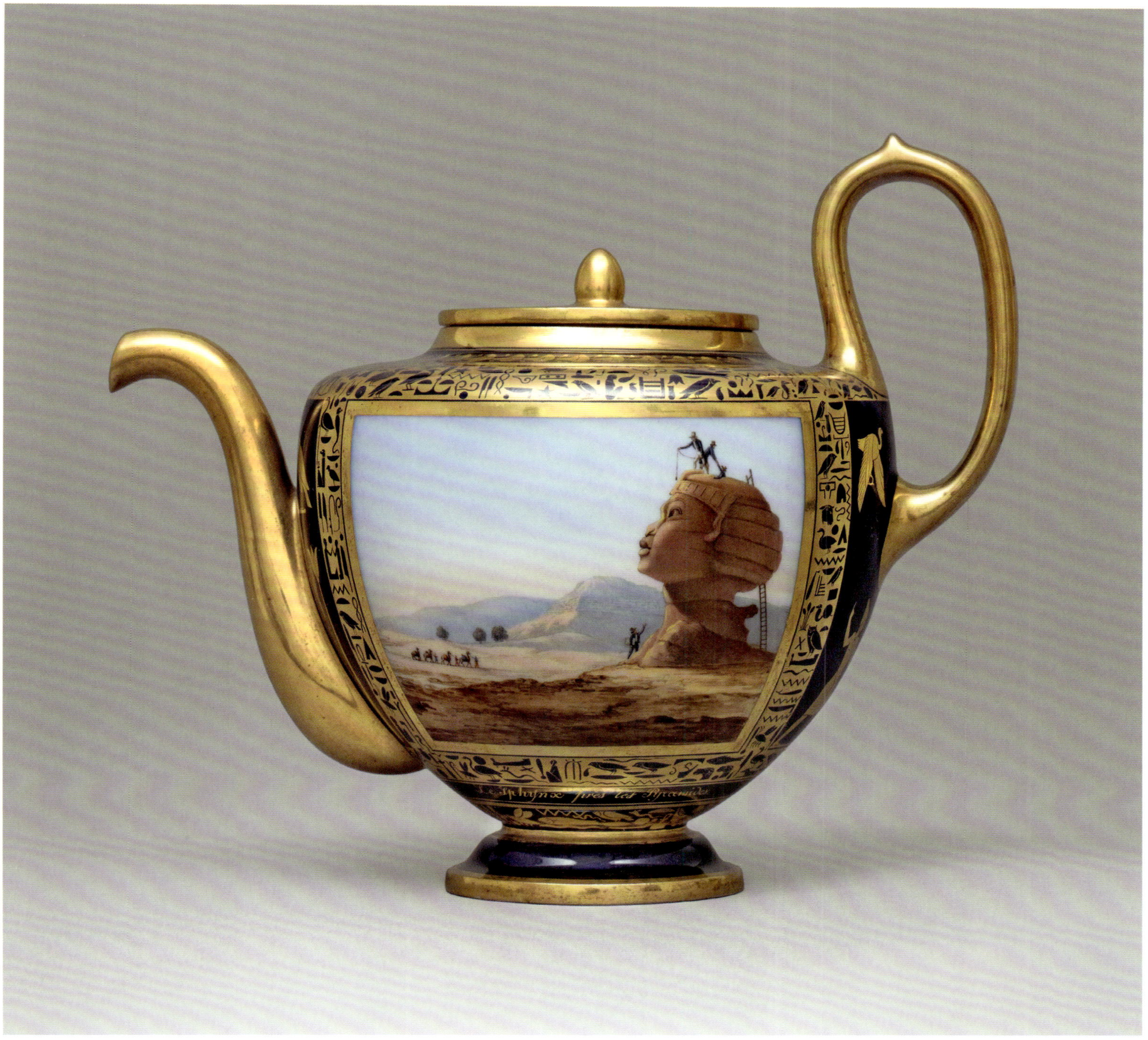

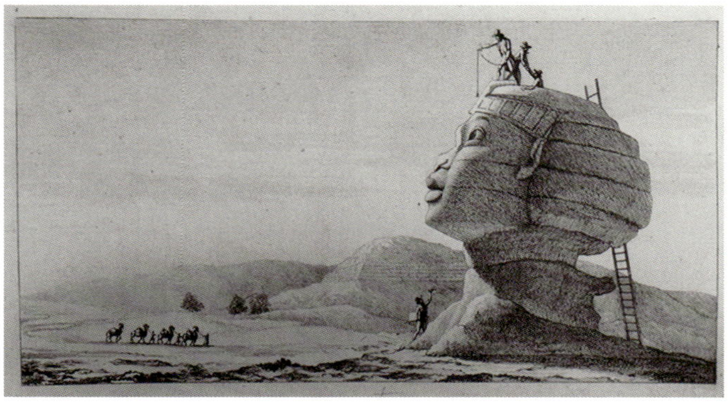

EGYPTIAN CABARET SERVICE TEAPOT

We can see researchers taking their measurements on top of the Giza Sphinx's head. This scene, from a drawing produced on the spot by Vivant Denon, is typical of the iconography illustrating the Egyptian saga. The composition comes from Plate 20b of *Travels in Upper and Lower Egypt.*

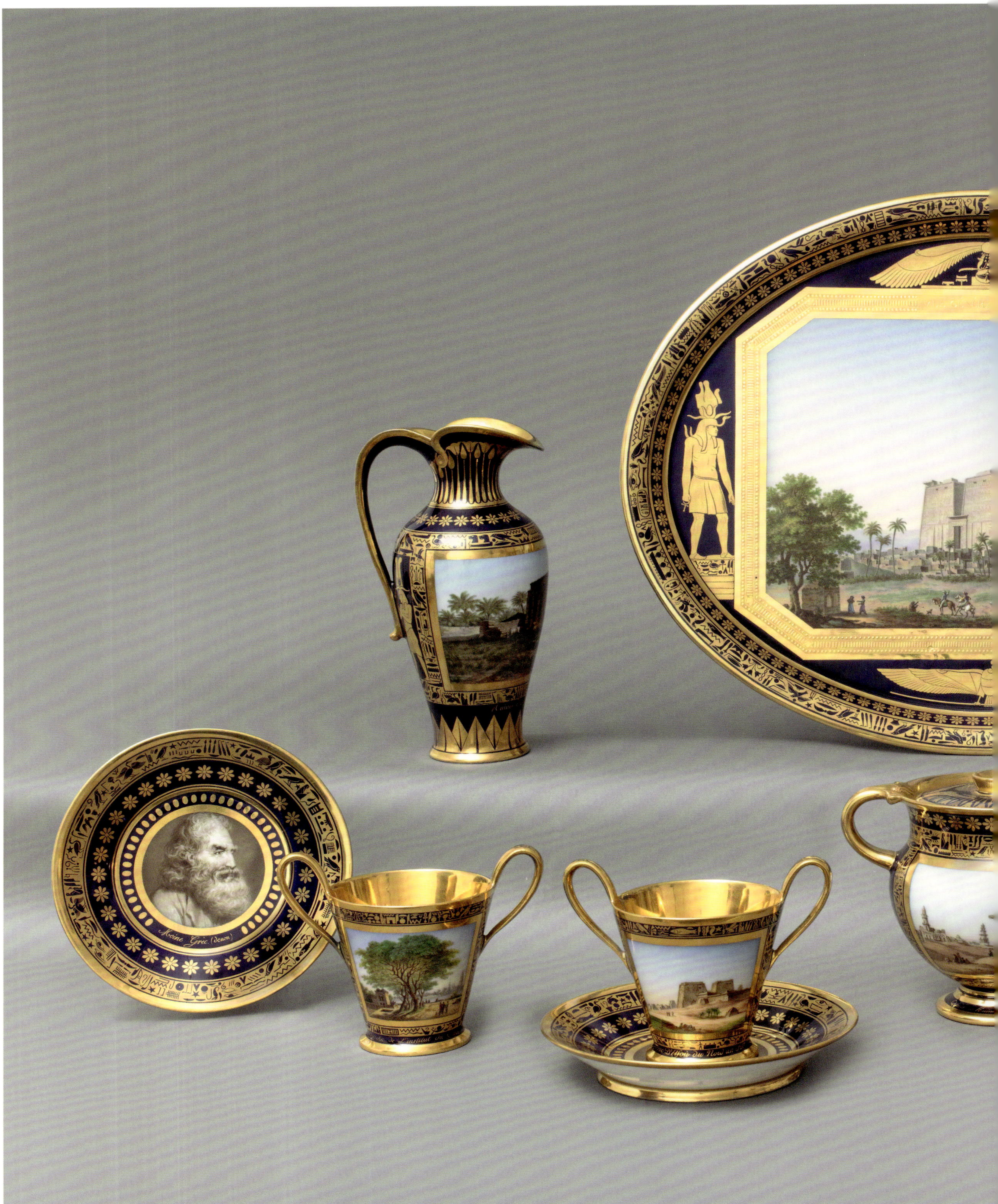

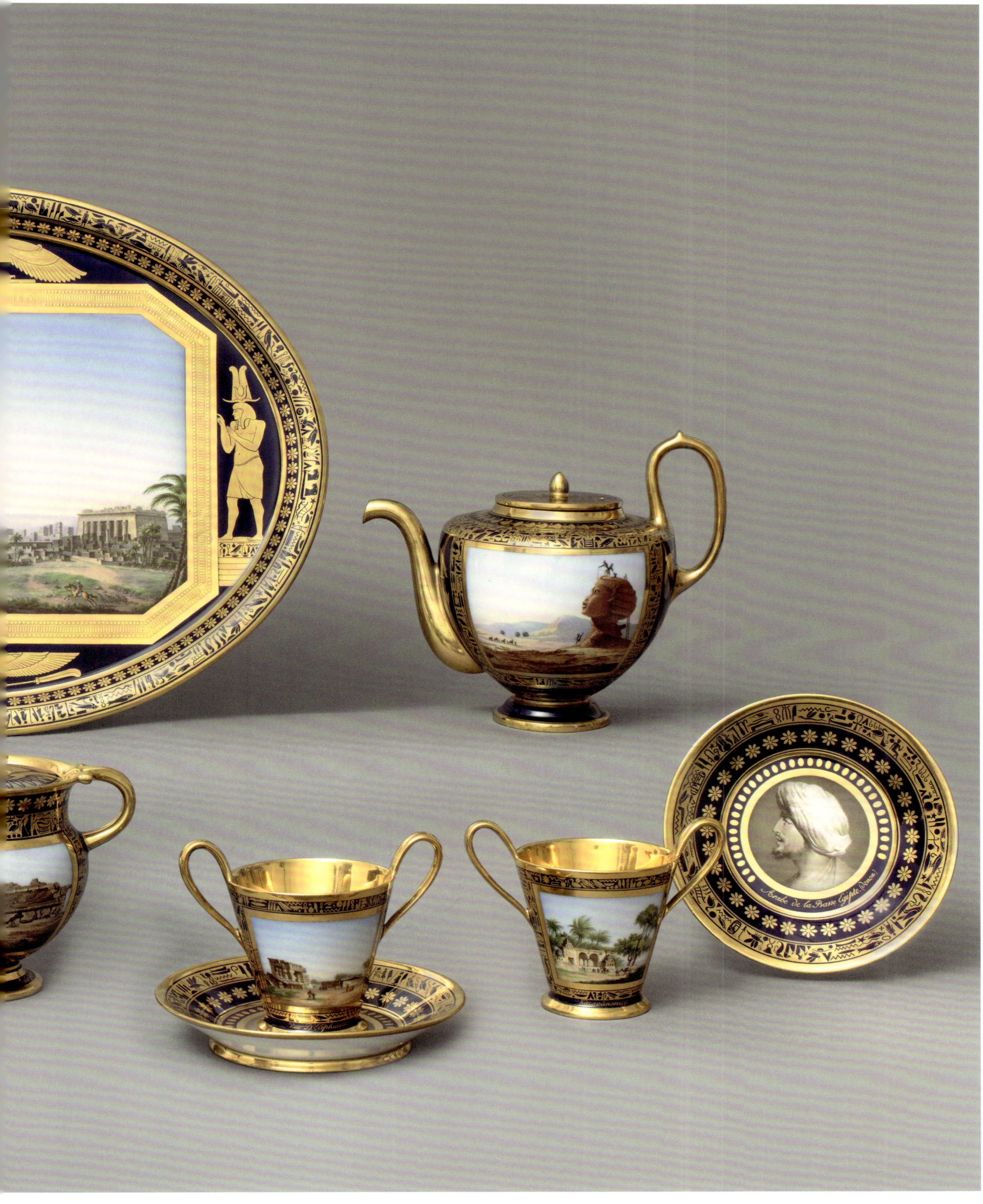
Arabe de la Basse Egipte. (Denon)

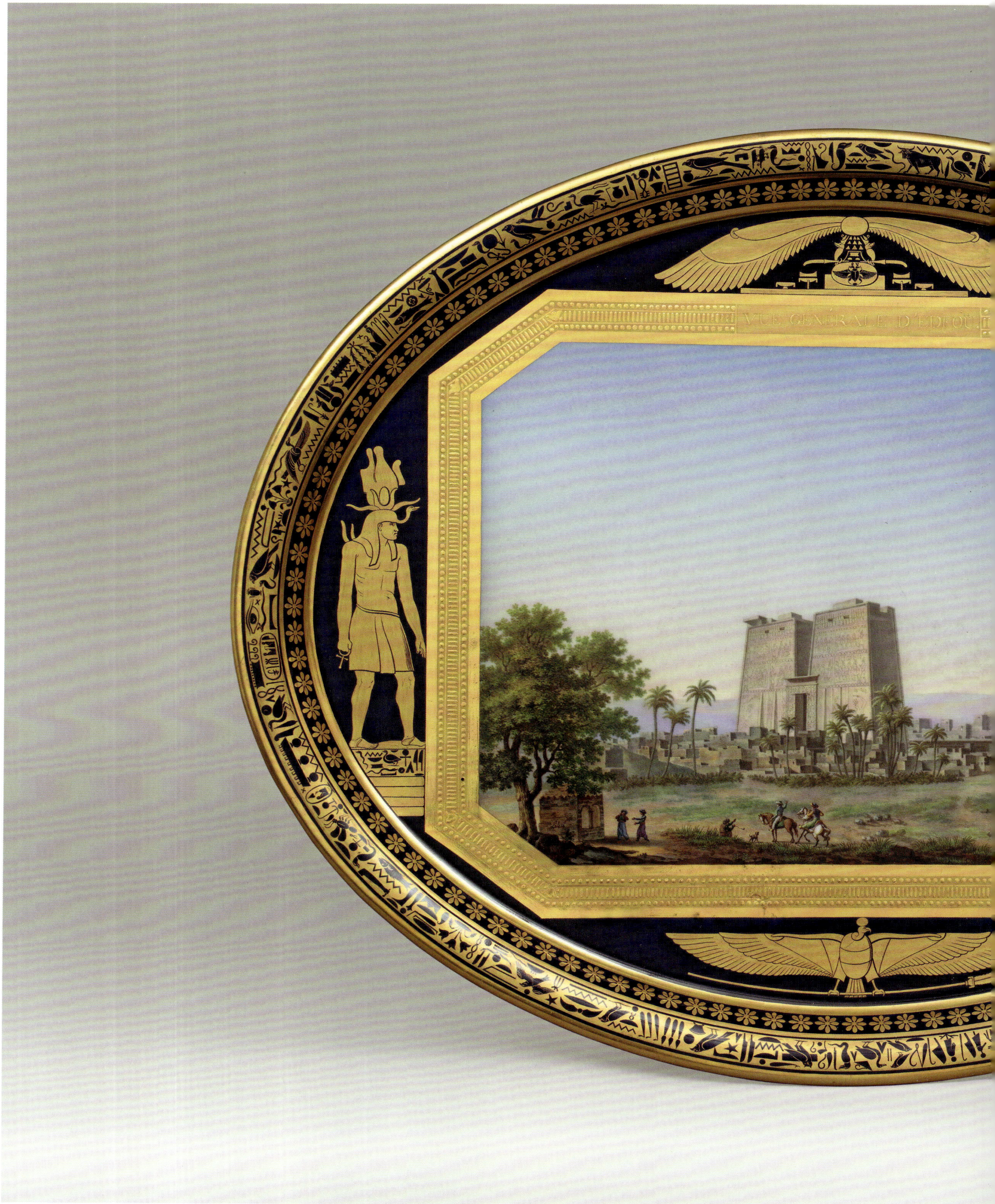
VUE GÉNÉRALE D'EDFOU.

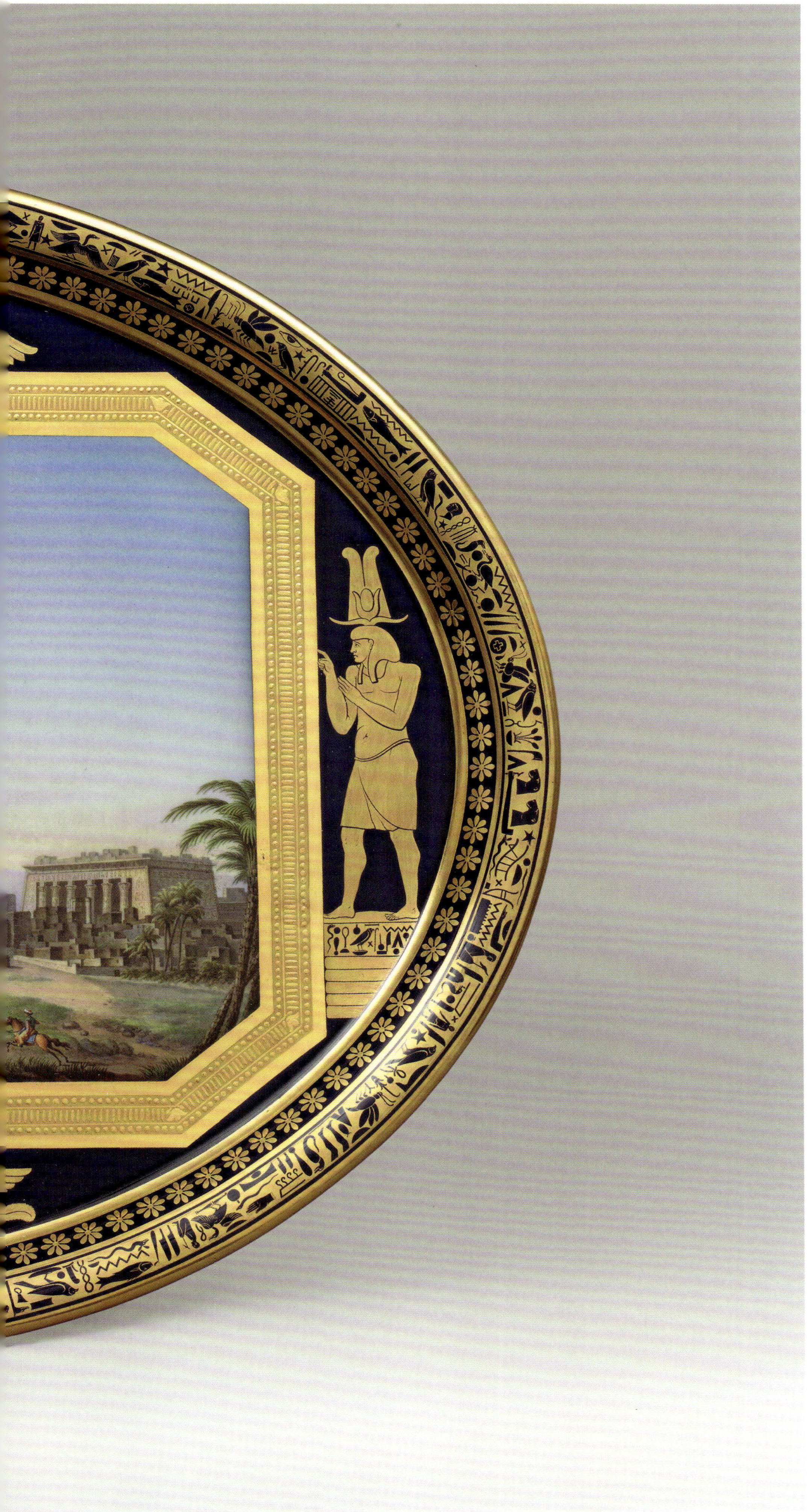

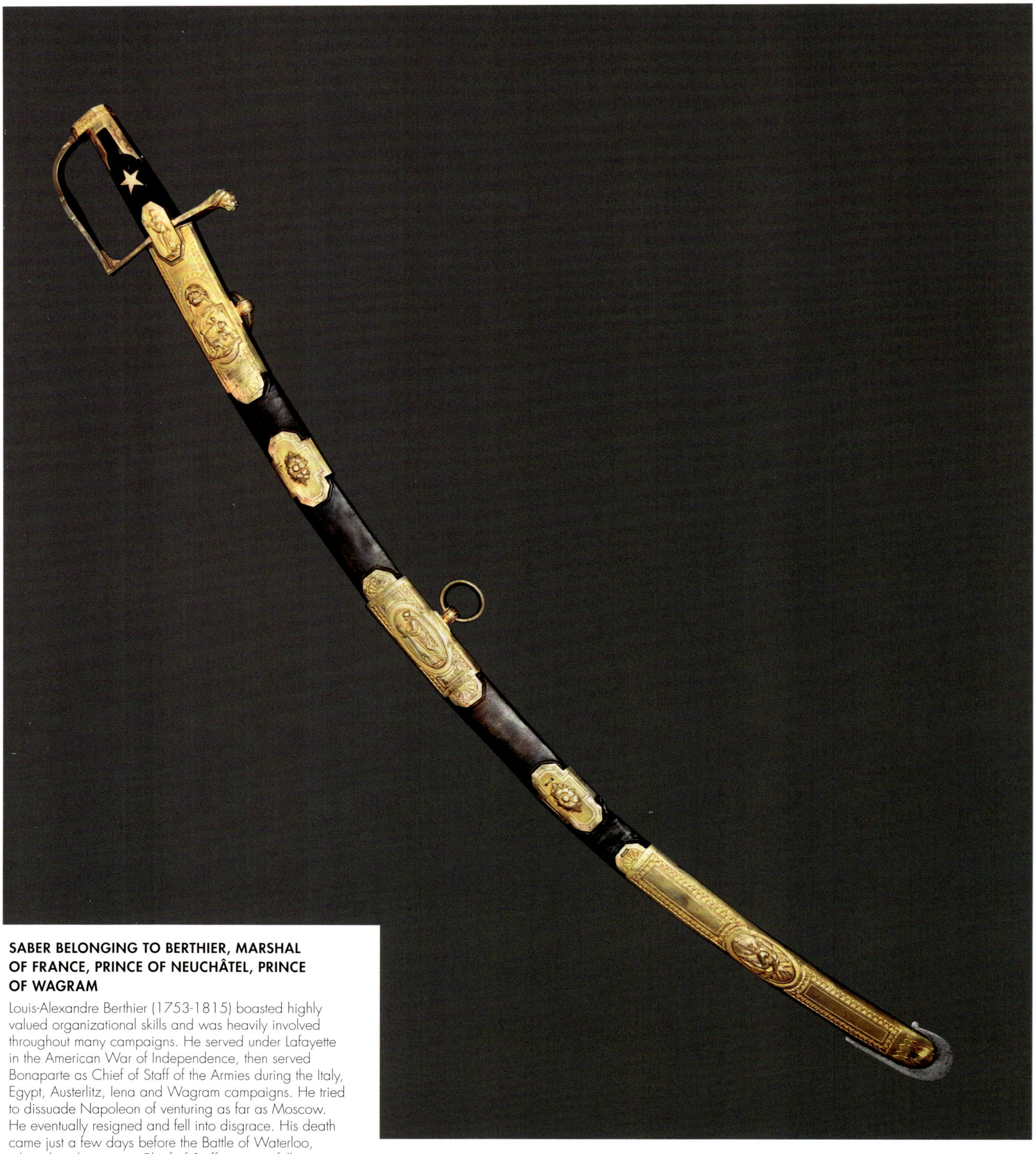

SABER BELONGING TO BERTHIER, MARSHAL OF FRANCE, PRINCE OF NEUCHÂTEL, PRINCE OF WAGRAM

Louis-Alexandre Berthier (1753-1815) boasted highly valued organizational skills and was heavily involved throughout many campaigns. He served under Lafayette in the American War of Independence, then served Bonaparte as Chief of Staff of the Armies during the Italy, Egypt, Austerlitz, Iena and Wagram campaigns. He tried to dissuade Napoleon of venturing as far as Moscow. He eventually resigned and fell into disgrace. His death came just a few days before the Battle of Waterloo, where his absence as Chief of Staff was painfully apparent. As Minister of War under the Consulate, he offered this sword engraved with his initials "A.B", surrounded by a laurel crown, to General Lazare Carnot, who succeeded him on 2 April 1800. The weapon has remained in the family to the present day.

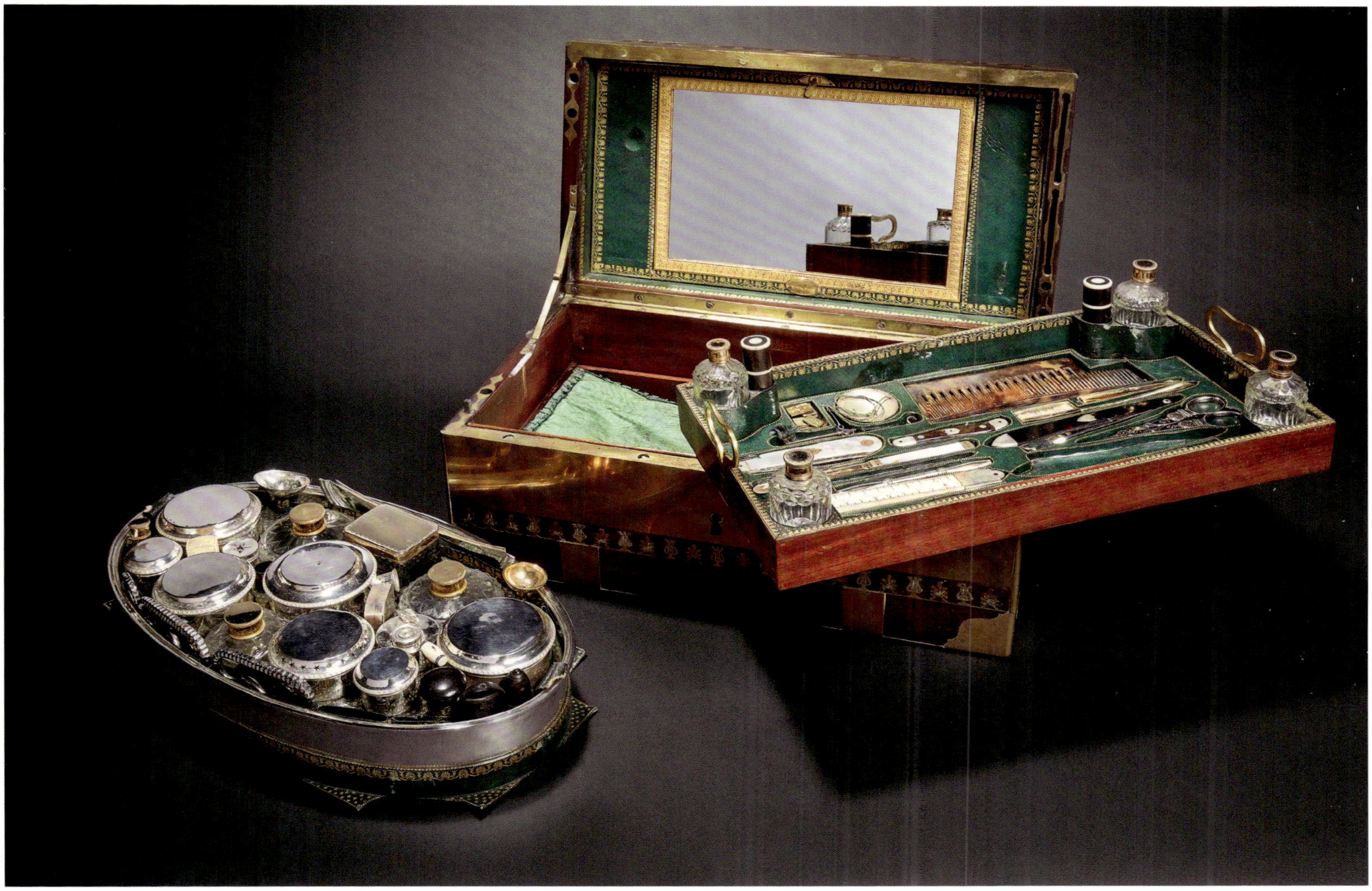

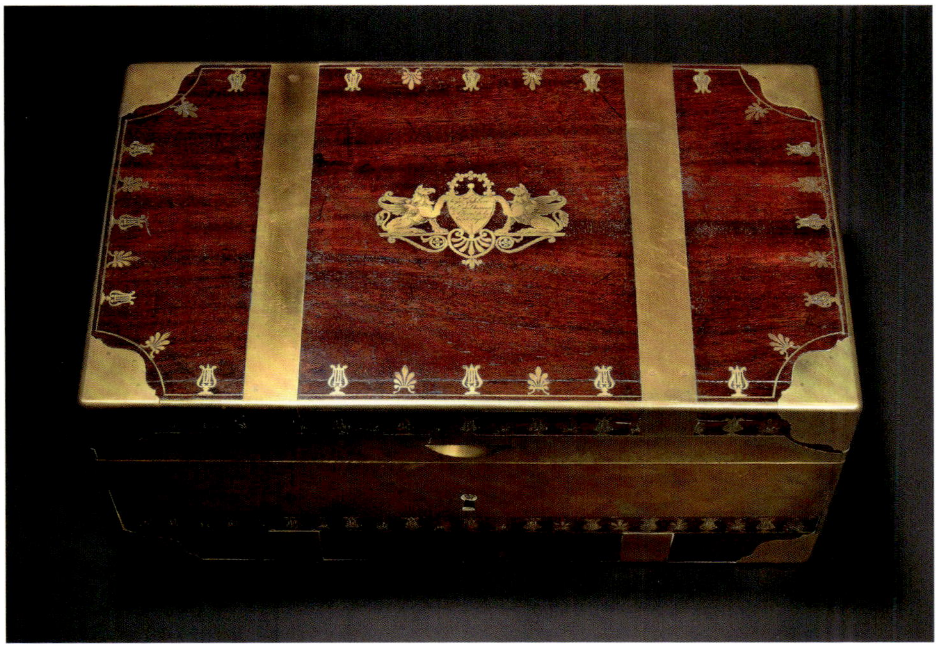

MARTIN-GUILLAUME BIENNAIS (1764-1843), TRAVEL SET BELONGING TO GENERAL LEFEBVRE-DESNOUETTES

Charles Lefebvre-Desnouettes (1773-1822), Major General, Count of the Empire and Grand Ecuyer to the King of Westphalia, fought in numerous battles of the Revolution and the Empire. In 1806, the year that this former aide-de-camp of the First Consul was promoted to the grade of General, he married Marie-Louise-Stéphanie Rollier, daughter of Marie Benielli, the Emperor's cousin. As a wedding gift, the Emperor generously gave them his house on Rue de la Victoire, the house where he had lived as a young general but which had remained uninhabited since. Following family tradition, this superb Biennais travel set, still virtually complete, was apparently given by the Emperor. It has remained in the Lefebvre-Desnouettes family to the present day.

THE FIRST CONSUL

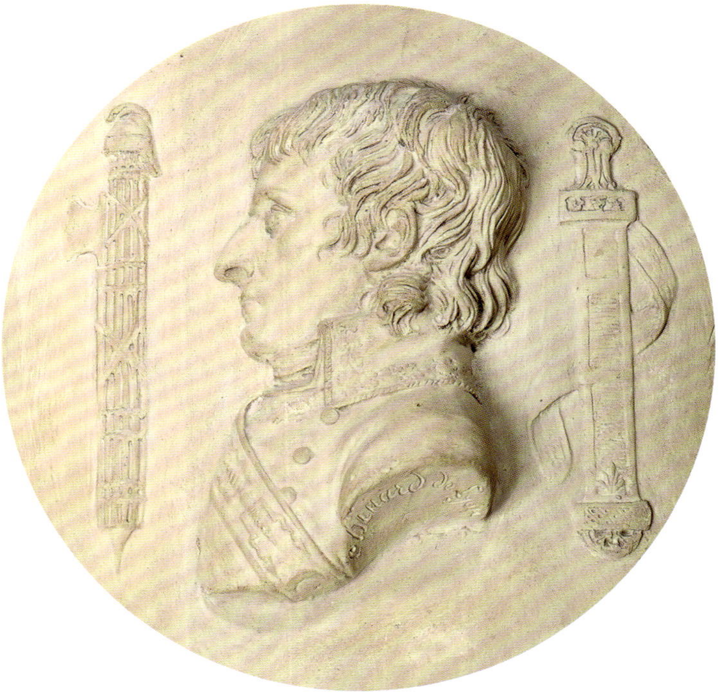

JOSEPH CHINARD (1756-1813), *PROFILE OF NAPOLEON BONAPARTE AS FIRST CONSUL*

Terracotta medallion featuring a bust in profile of Bonaparte as First Consul, flanked on either side by symbols of the French Revolution: on the left, a *fasces lictoriae* (bundle of lictors) crowned by a Phrygian cap; on the right, a Roman sword. The portrait is signed "Chinard de Lyon". The artist Joseph Chinard first laid eyes on Bonaparte in 1799 shortly after his return from Egypt, then again in Lyon the following year. Chinard's terracotta masterpieces propelled him to fame in the late 18th century.

ALEXANDRE-ÉVARISTE FRAGONARD (1780-1850), *THE COUP OF 18 AND 19 BRUMAIRE*

Pencil and brown wash drawing depicting the second day of the Coup d'Etat (19 Brumaire). Napoleon attempts to address the Council of Five Hundred in the Orangery but is shouted down by the deputies and forced to call in the grenadiers. It is only in the evening that the Council of Elders and a few of the deputies set up a provisional government composed of three consuls: Napoleon Bonaparte, Emmanuel Joseph Sieyes and Roger Ducos. This preparatory drawing was the entry presented by Alexandre-Évariste Fragonard (son of Jean-Honoré Fragonard, 1732-1806) to the official painting contest – in the event, François Bouchot was commissioned to execute the work.

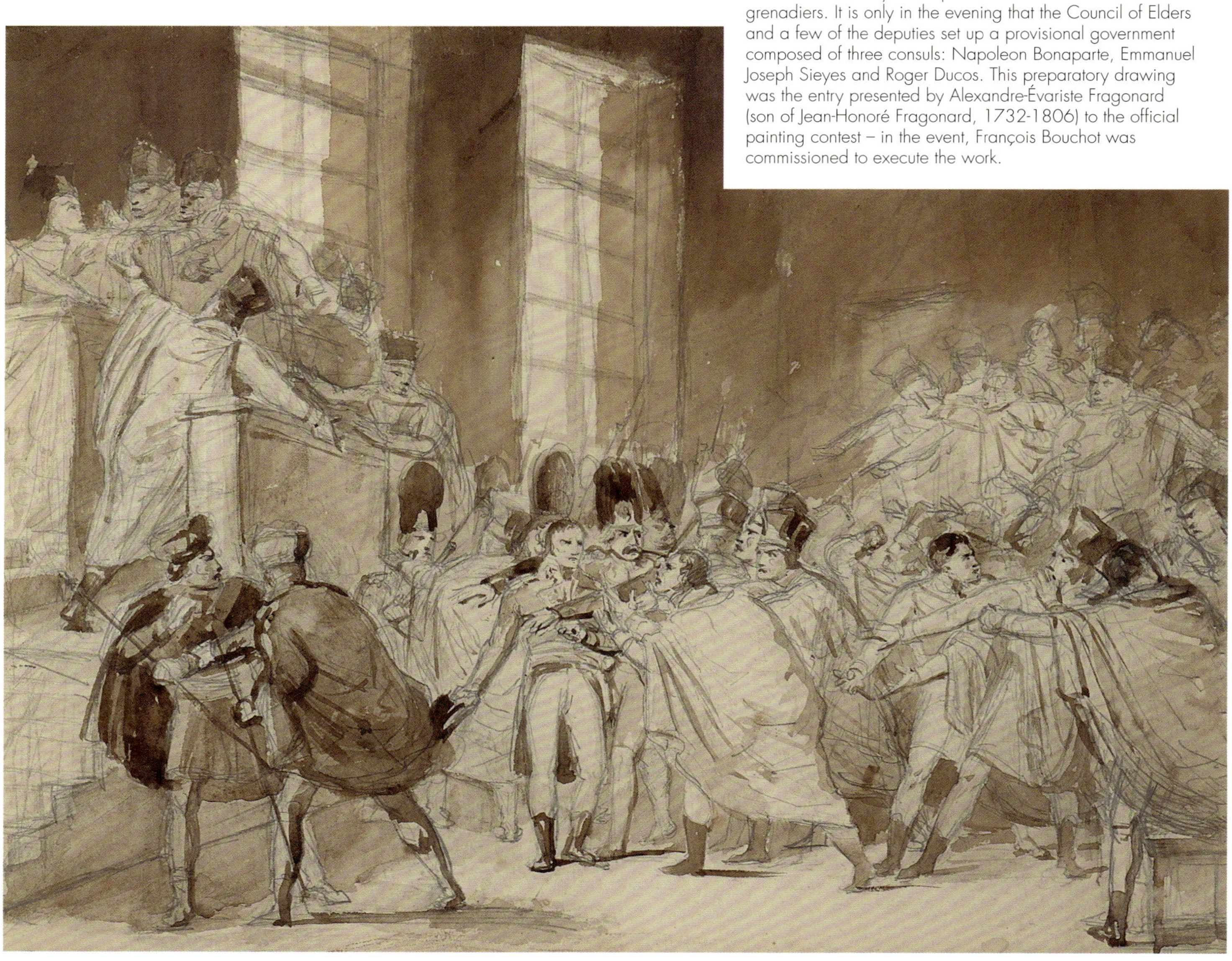

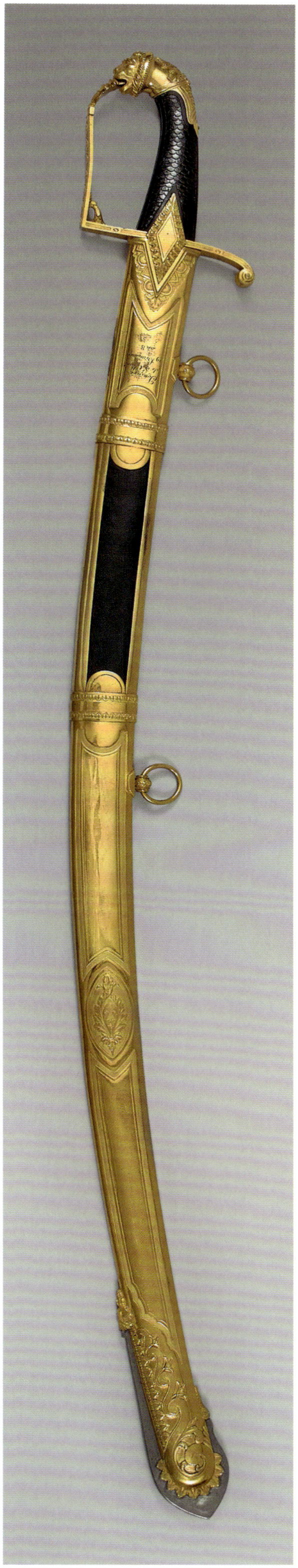

NICOLAS-NOËL BOUTET (1761-1833), BRUMAIRE SABER OFFERED BY BONAPARTE

To thank officers of the 17th military division of Paris who distinguished themselves during the Coup of 18-19 Brumaire, Bonaparte offered each of them a magnificent saber, the model of which was specially made by Nicolas-Noël Boutet, director of the Versailles Manufacture d'Armes. This so-called "Brumaire" saber has an inscription on its pommel: "Journée de Saint-Cloud, 19 Brumaire an VIII" (Day of Saint-Cloud, 19 Brumaire Year VIII). The recipient of this saber is unknown. A few specimens have been listed, including one belonging to General Lefebvre (1755-1820), who accompanied Bonaparte to the Council of Elders and helped drive out deputies from the Council of Five Hundred, or the saber of General Vandamme (1770-1830), conserved at the Musée de l'Armée in Paris.

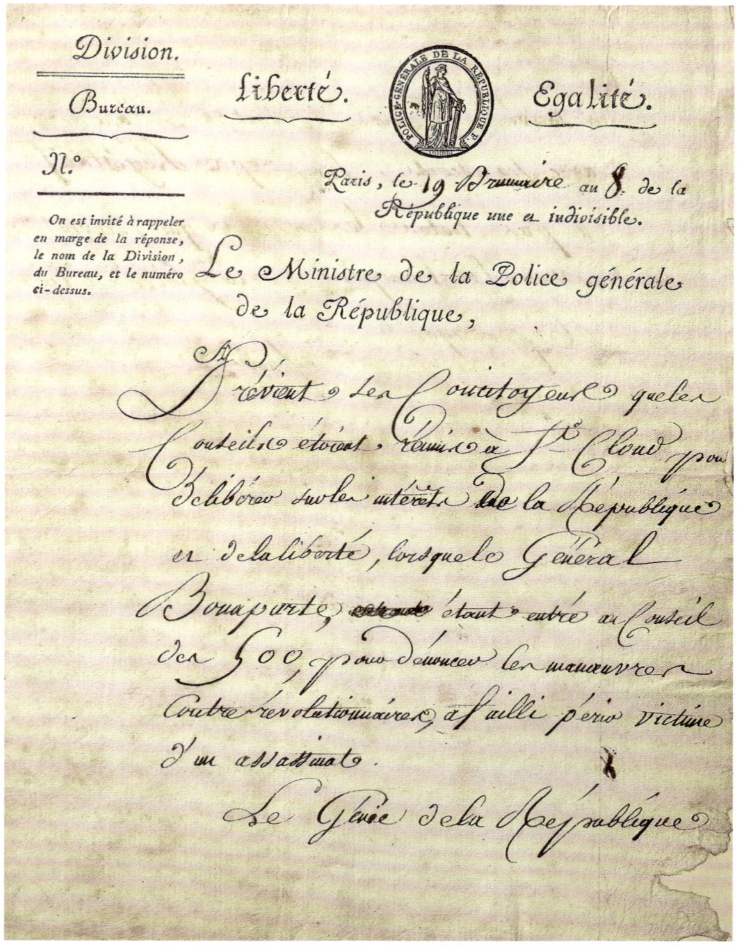

Division.

Bureau.

N.°

Liberté. Egalité.

Paris, le 19 Brumaire an 8. de la République une et indivisible.

On est invité à rappeler en marge de la réponse, le nom de la Division, du Bureau, et le numéro ci-dessus.

Le Ministre de la Police générale de la République,

Prévient les Concitoyens que les Conseils étoient réunis à St Cloud pour délibérer sur les intérêts de la République et de la liberté, lorsque le Général Bonaparte étant entré au Conseil des 500, pour dénoncer les manœuvres contre-révolutionnaires, a failli périr victime d'un assassinat.

Le Génie de la République

HANDWRITTEN LETTER BY FOUCHÉ ANNOUNCING THE COUP OF 18 AND 19 BRUMAIRE

The coup of 18 Brumaire was supported by Joseph Fouché (1759-1820), appointed police chief a few months earlier, who put funds and men at Napoleon's disposal on the evening of Day One. The following day, following the success of 19 Brumaire and Napoleon's seizing of power, Fouché signed a proclamation to be read aloud in Paris theaters.

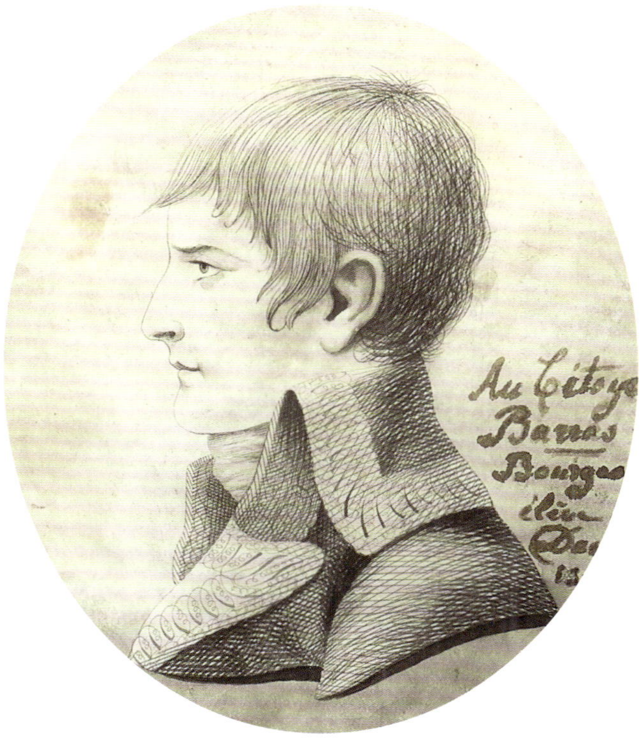

FLORENT FIDÈLE CONSTANT BOURGEOIS (1767-1841), *PORTRAIT OF BONAPARTE*

Bust in profile of the First Consul, signed by Florent Fidèle Constant Bourgeois du Castelet, gifted by the artist to one-time Director and protector of Josephine, Paul Barras. The dedication reads: *Au citoyen Barras, Bourgeois, élève de David 1802* (to citizen Barras, Bourgeois, pupil of David 1802).

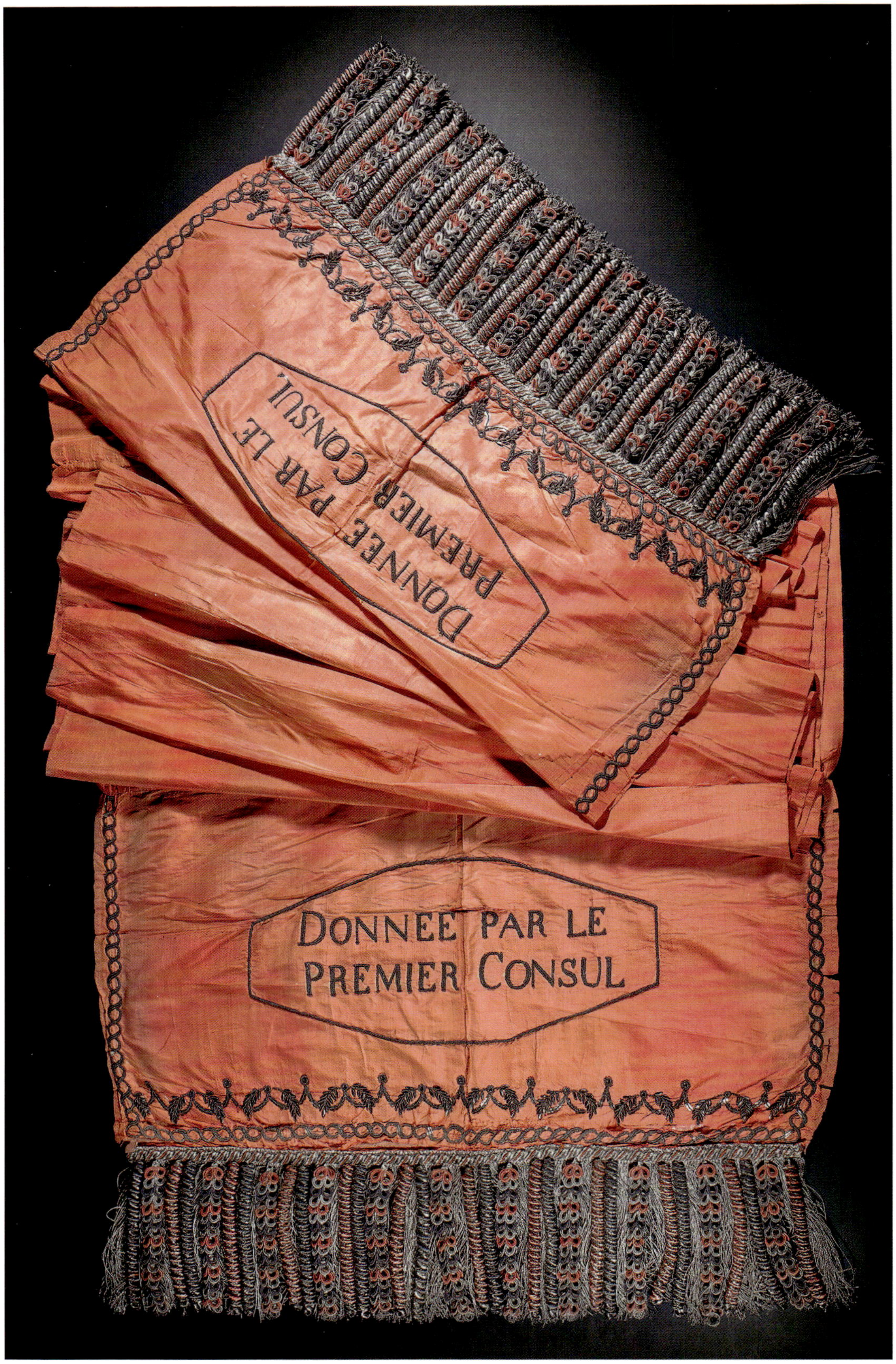

LARGE SILK SCARF AWARDED BY THE FIRST CONSUL TO DESERVING MAYORS

One of 10 scarves awarded to mayors by the First Consul for distinguished service to their towns: Lyon (one for each of the three arrondissements), Rouen, Sedan, Dunkirk, Anvers, Amiens, Granville and Mériel. The list of recipients was sent to Minister Chaptal, on 15 Vendémiaire Year XII (8 October 1803). This scarf is thought to be the only surviving example.

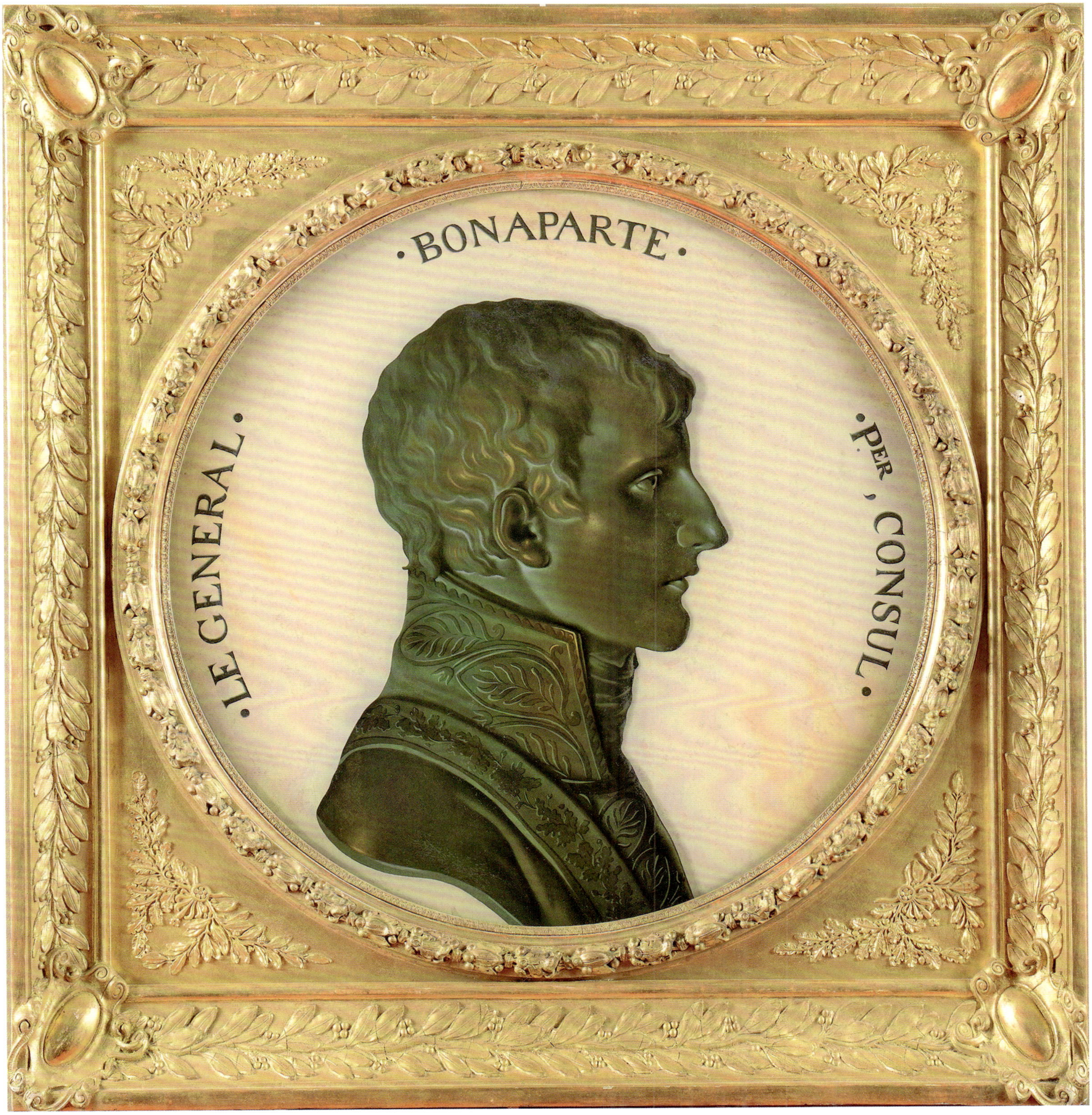

PIAT-JOSEPH SAUVAGE (1744-1818),
PORTRAIT OF THE FIRST CONSUL

General Bonaparte, First Consul, was the subject of an extensive iconography very early on. This sumptuous portrait by Sauvage was produced in a style imitating bas-relief sculptures. The illusion of marble and stone is reminiscent of antique portraits.

MARTIN-GUILLAUME BIENNAIS (1764-1843), SILVER RECTANGULAR BOX AND SPONGE BOX FORMERLY BELONGING TO BONAPARTE

Two silver boxes, originally part of a toiletry *nécessaire* (kit), with engraved lids featuring the monogram "B" in the center of a crest flanked on either side by laurel branches. As indicated by one of the hallmarks, the boxes are the work of goldsmith and purveyor of luxury goods Martin-Guillaume Biennais. Following the Coup of 18 Brumaire, Biennais immediately saw how to win the favor of Napoleon Bonaparte. Tallandier writes that: "On his return from Egypt, General Bonaparte was keen to set up home. But though covered in glory, he had yet to make his fortune and none of the suppliers he contacted were prepared to sell on credit. Biennais was more inclined to believe in the young general's lucky star and fulfilled many of Bonaparte's requirements without worrying about getting paid. When he became emperor, a grateful Napoleon appointed Biennais "First Goldsmith".

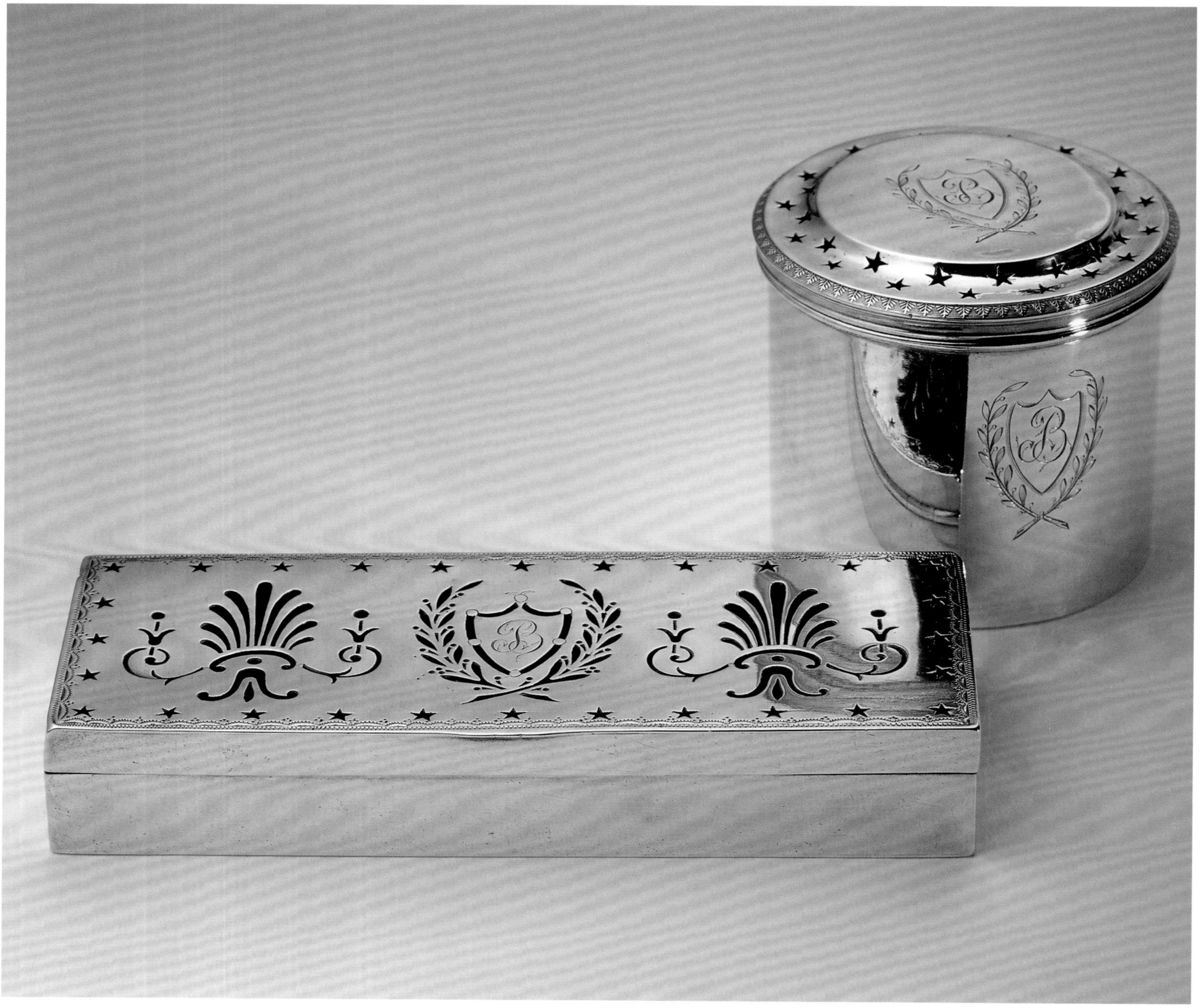

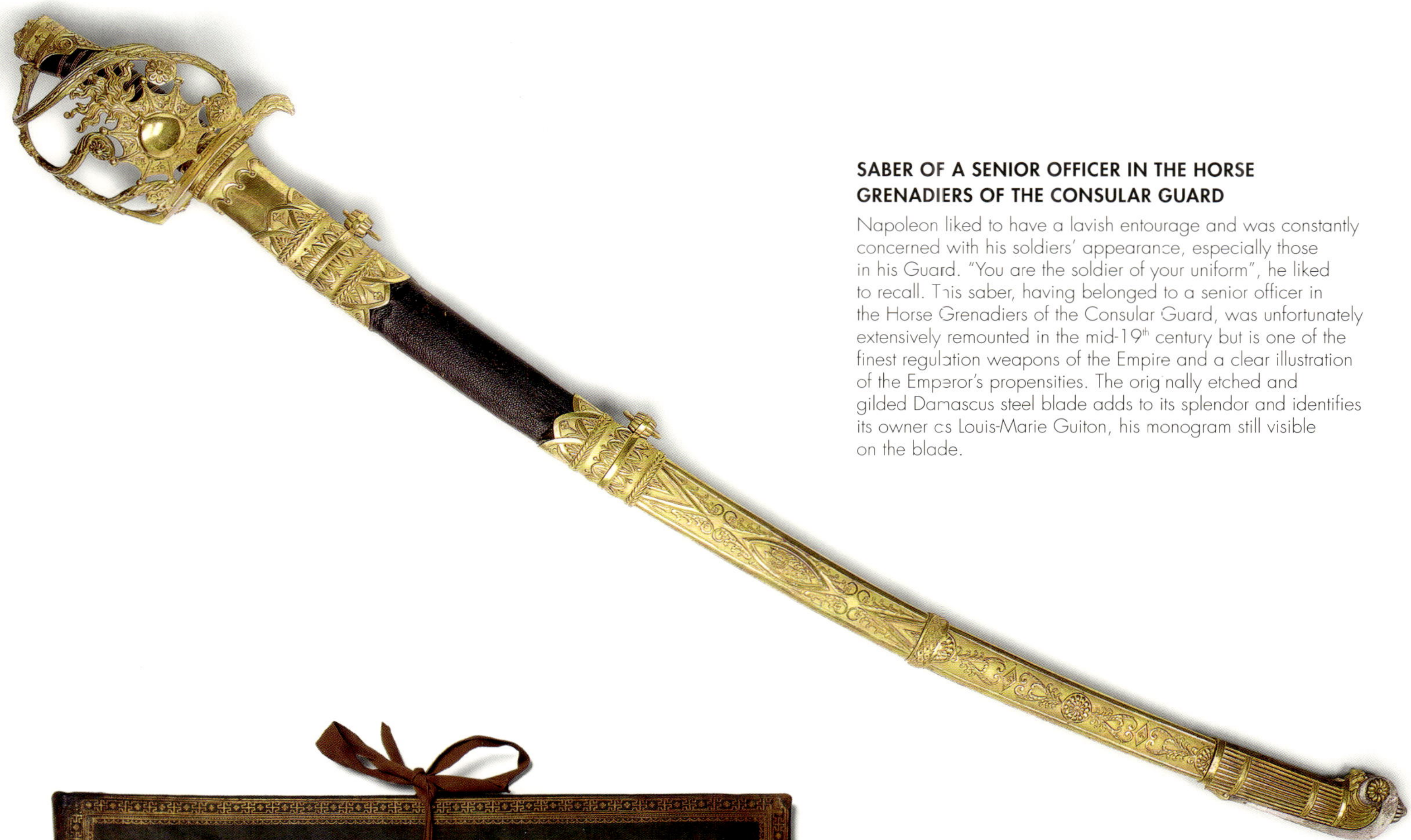

SABER OF A SENIOR OFFICER IN THE HORSE GRENADIERS OF THE CONSULAR GUARD

Napoleon liked to have a lavish entourage and was constantly concerned with his soldiers' appearance, especially those in his Guard. "You are the soldier of your uniform", he liked to recall. This saber, having belonged to a senior officer in the Horse Grenadiers of the Consular Guard, was unfortunately extensively remounted in the mid-19th century but is one of the finest regulation weapons of the Empire and a clear illustration of the Emperor's propensities. The originally etched and gilded Damascus steel blade adds to its splendor and identifies its owner as Louis-Marie Guiton, his monogram still visible on the blade.

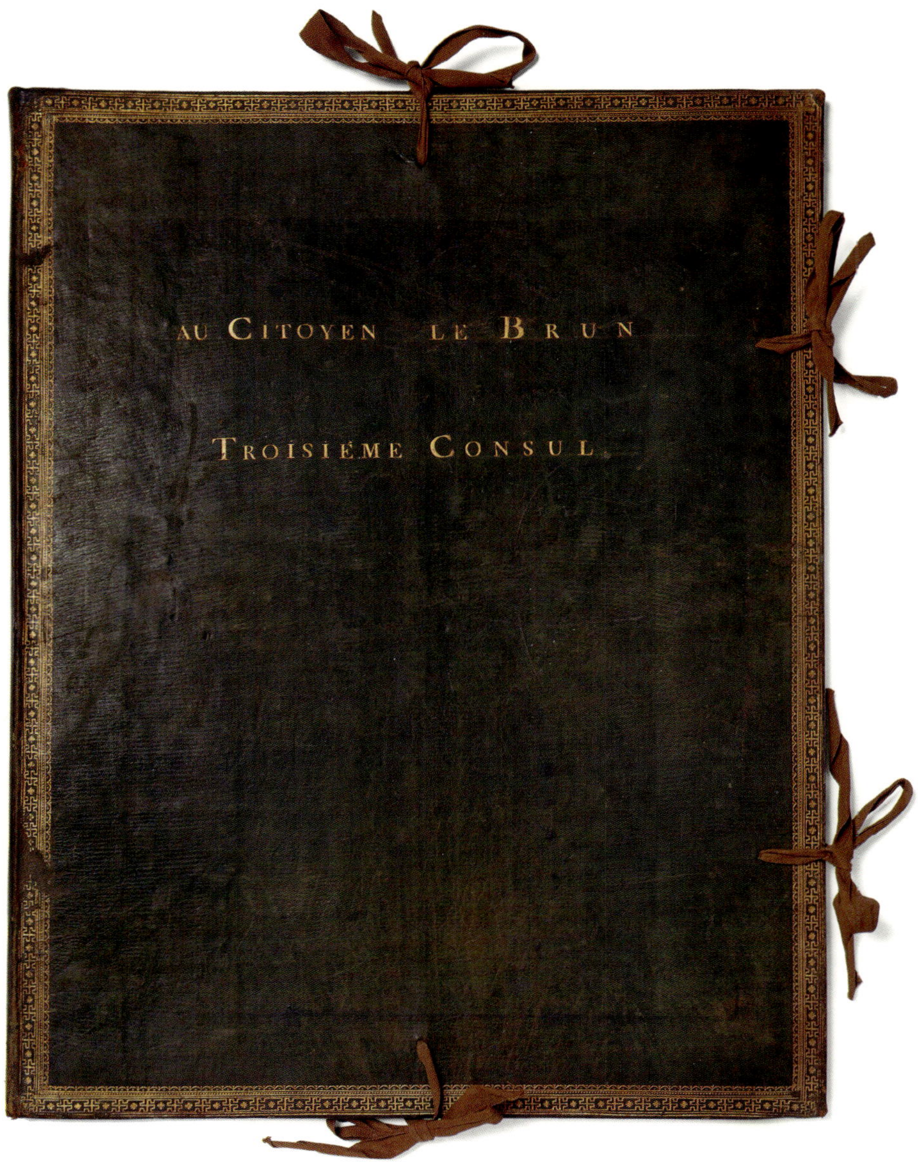

LARGE PORTFOLIO BELONGING TO LE BRUN, THIRD CONSUL OF THE REPUBLIC

This very large portfolio is unique and comes to us from the descendants of Charles-François Le Brun (1739-1824), Third Consul. He worked alongside Bonaparte and de Cambacérès, and was entrusted with financial matters, having previously served René-Charles de Maupéou, Chancellor to Louis XVI in 1768.

THE CORONATION, 1804

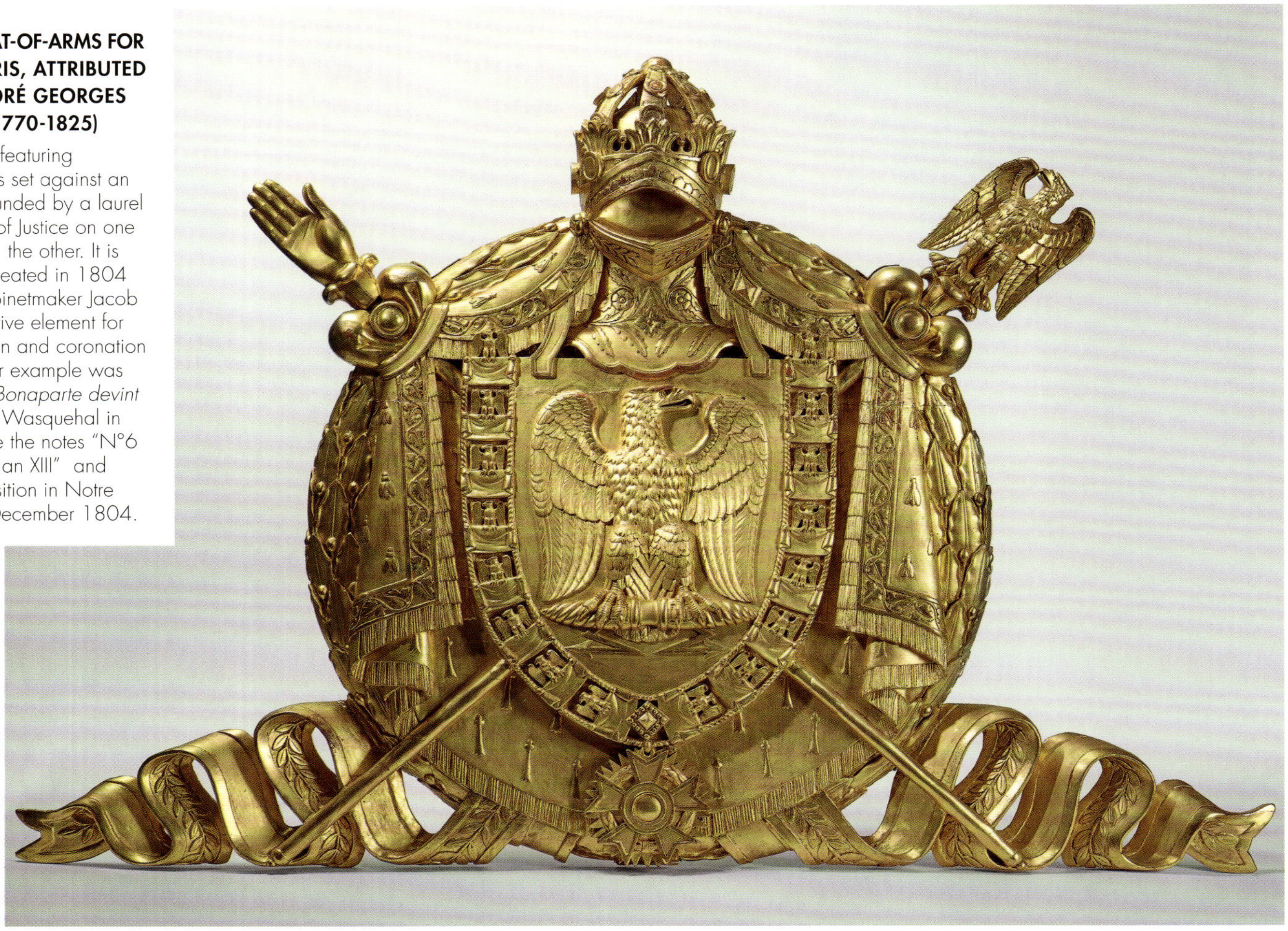

GRAND IMPERIAL COAT-OF-ARMS FOR NOTRE DAME DE PARIS, ATTRIBUTED TO FRANÇOIS HONORÉ GEORGES JACOB DESMALTER (1770-1825)

Ornate wood sculpture featuring the imperial coat-of-arms set against an ermine cloak and surrounded by a laurel wreath, with the Hand of Justice on one side and the Scepter on the other. It is thought to have been created in 1804 by leading Parisian cabinetmaker Jacob Desmalter, as a decorative element for Napoleon's consecration and coronation in Notre Dame. Another example was featured in the *Quand Bonaparte devint Napoléon* exhibition in Wasquehal in 2004. On the back are the notes "N°6 bas côté", "11 frimaire an XIII" and "ND", indicating its position in Notre Dame cathedral on 2 December 1804.

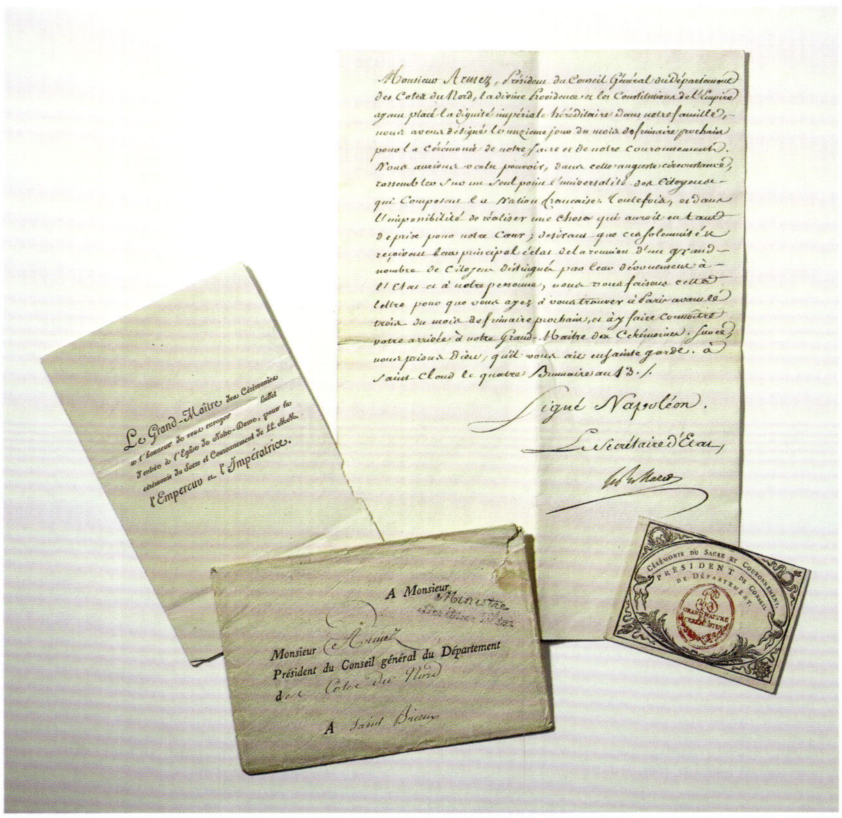

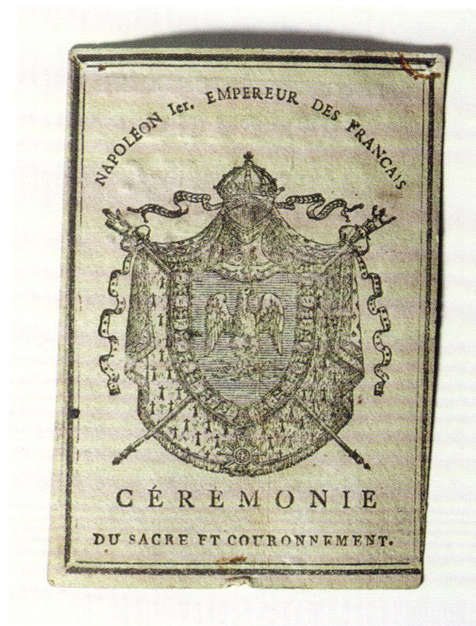

INVITATION TO CONSECRATION AND CORONATION CEREMONY

Attendance at the coronation ceremony was by personal invitation only. This little card opened the door to Nicolas Armez de Pontizac, president of the general council of the Côtes du Nord Department. His seating position is indicated on the back: "left side of throne, 3rd row of the nave, tier number 3."

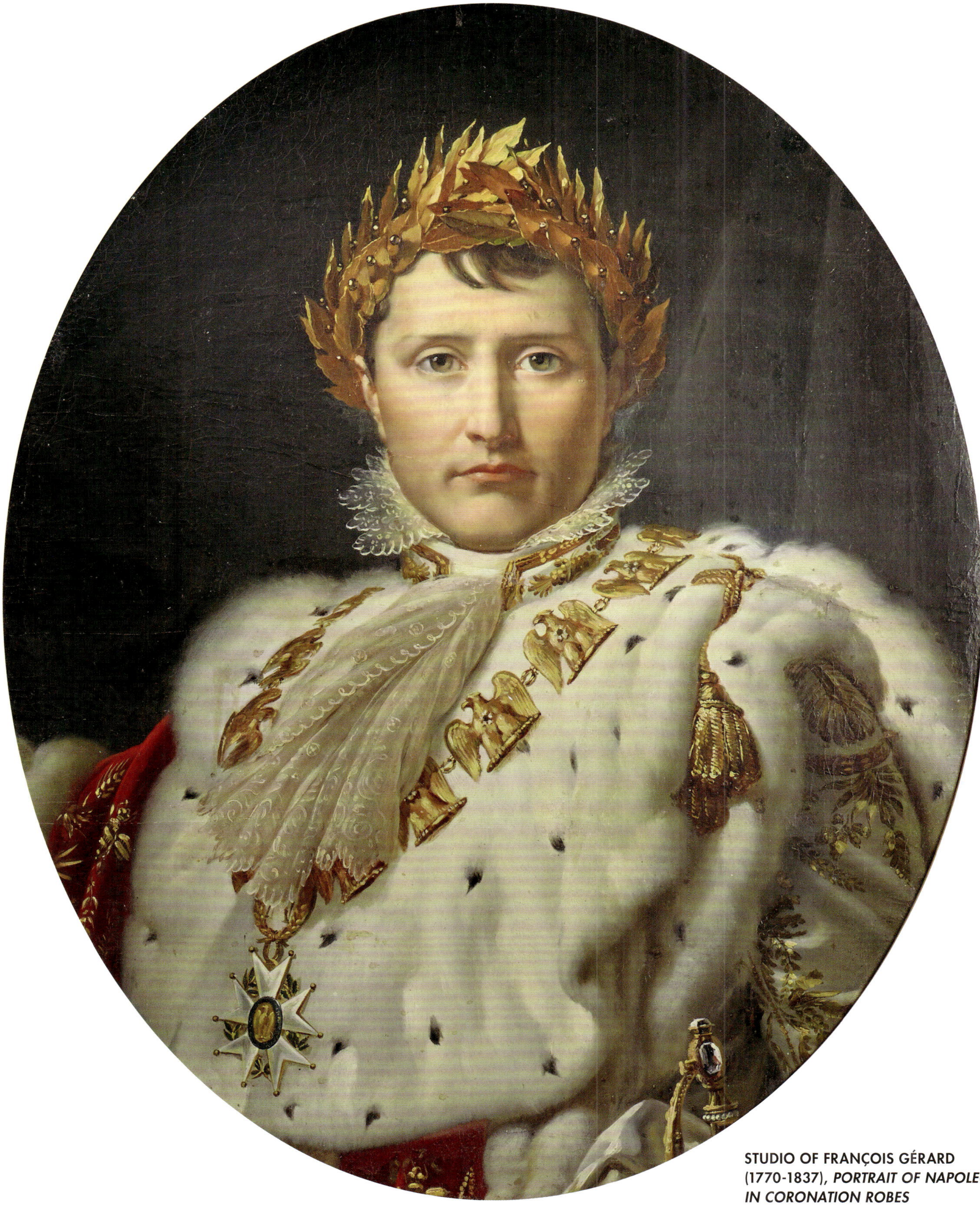

STUDIO OF FRANÇOIS GÉRARD (1770-1837), *PORTRAIT OF NAPOLEON IN CORONATION ROBES*

In 1805 Napoleon commissioned his full-length portrait, dressed in coronation robes. The painting by French artist Gérard was destined for the residence of the then French Foreign Minister, Talleyrand. Pictured here is a bust-length version of that portrait, executed in the artist's studio.

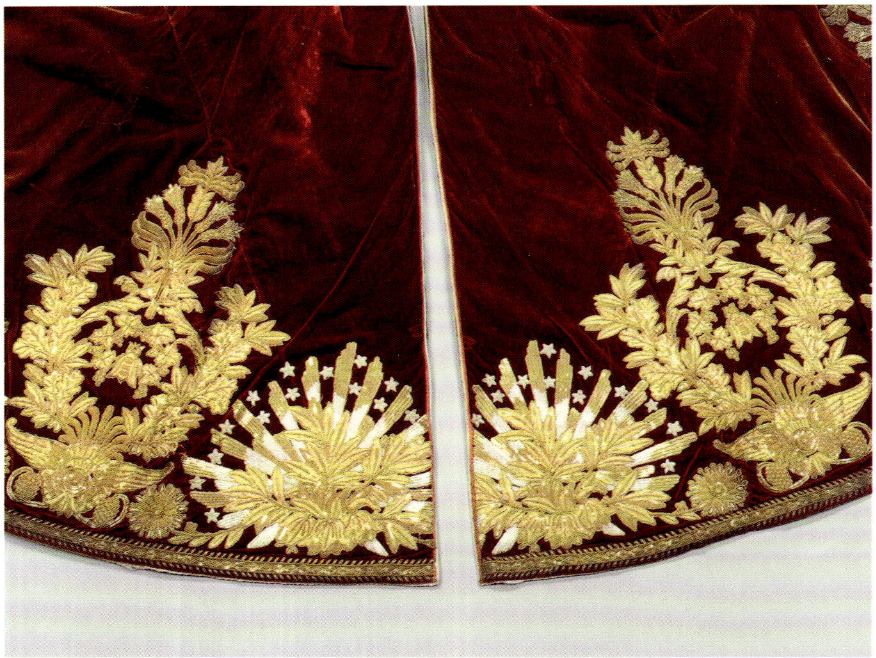

MANTEL WORN BY NAPOLEON AT THE CORONATION

This close-up shows the patterns embroidered in gold thread adorning the mantel worn by the Emperor at his coronation. It matches the piqué pattern kept in the collection.
Château de Fontainebleau museum collection

JEAN-BAPTISTE ISABEY (1767-1855), EMBROIDERY DESIGN FOR THE *PETIT HABILLEMENT* (UNDRESS COSTUME) WORN BY NAPOLEON

Isabey was commissioned to design all of the coronation costumes. Pictured here is one of the embroidery patterns created for the occasion, this one for the hand embroidery on the lower edge of the crimson mantel of the Emperor's undress costume. The bee, chosen symbol of the new sovereign, is just visible here. Executed by the embroiderer Picot, it appears flanked by oak leaves and resting on a winged cartouche that is crowned by palm leaves intermingled with ears of corn.

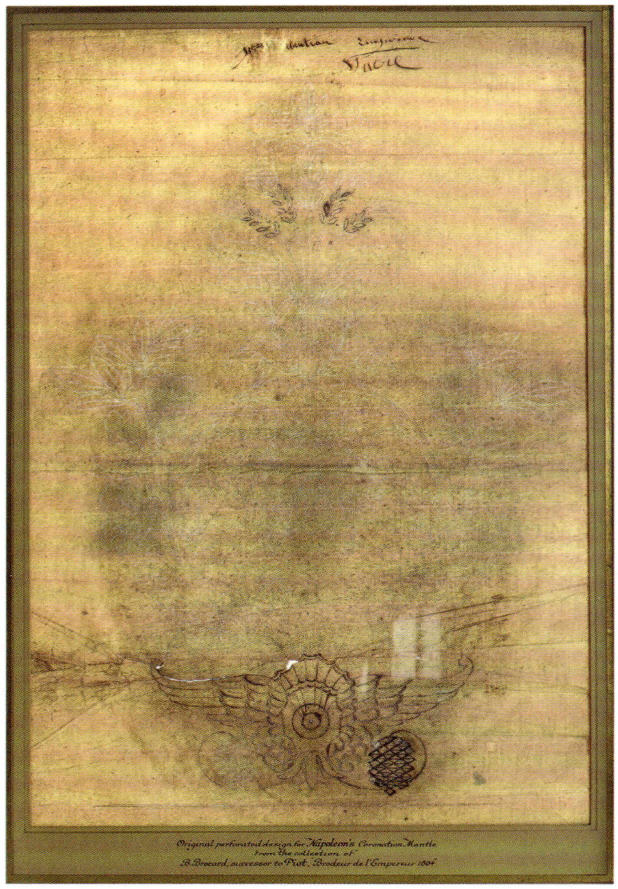

NICOLAS-NOËL BOUTET (1761-1833), CORONATION SWORD OF THE HERALD-AT-ARMS

This very rare gladius-style sword in gilded bronze with garnet velvet sheath is one of four that were commissioned from Versailles master gunsmith Nicolas Boutet for the coronation heralds-at-arms. On the day of the ceremony on 2 December 1804, four heralds-at-arms —Sallengros, Pascal, and Captains Zimmermann and Larcher — were accompanied by the King of Arms, Captain Duverdier. After the oath Duverdier proclaimed: "The thrice glorious and thrice august Emperor Napoleon is crowned and enthroned. Long Live the Emperor." This sword features on Isabey's designs of the costumes of the heralds-at-arms in the *Livre du Sacre* (golden book of the coronation).

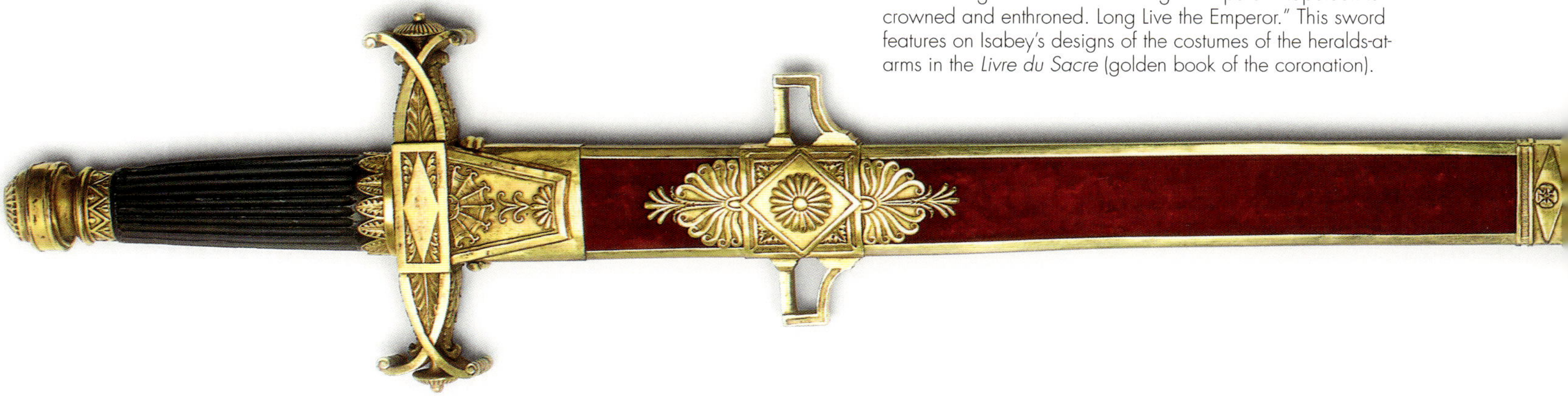

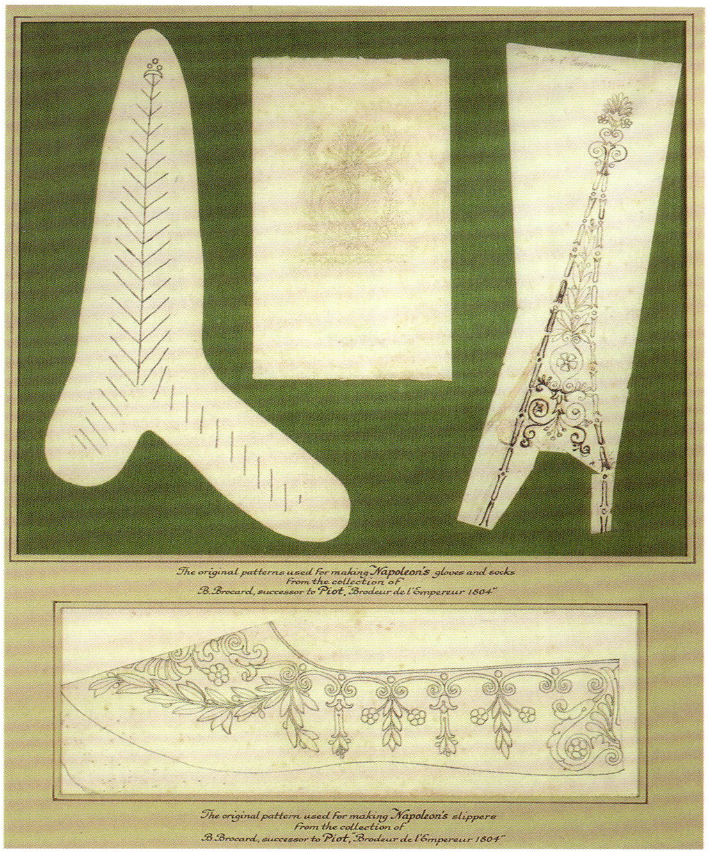

JEAN-BAPTISTE ISABEY (1767-1855), DESIGNS FOR A PAIR OF STOCKINGS AND SLIPPERS FOR THE CORONATION OF NAPOLEON I EMPEROR OF FRANCE

Isabey's designs for the coronation served as models for Parisian craftsmen. The Emperor's white taffeta slippers imitated an antique style known as the *cothurne*, made by master shoemakers Jacques and Berger and embroidered by Augustin Picot with gold thread and sequins to create a symmetrical *rinceau* pattern of leaves, floral motifs and stars. The designs for the stockings feature on the pair of the Emperor's stockings now in the Napoleon museum of the Château de Fontainebleau.

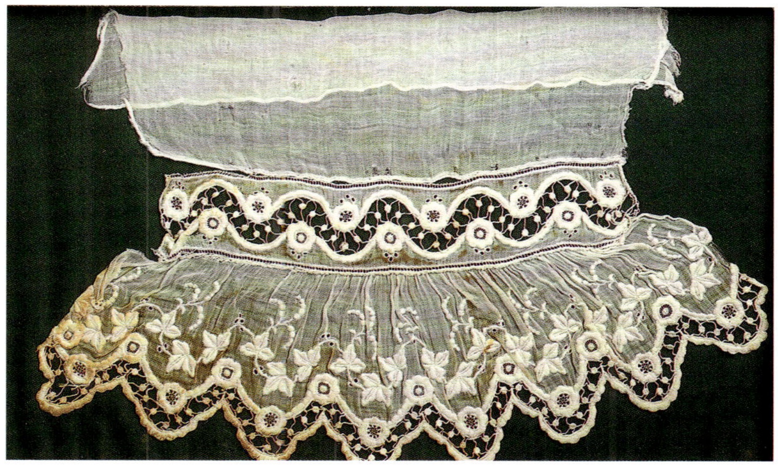

PART OF A LACE COLLAR OF NAPOLEON'S "UNDRESS COSTUME", ATTRIBUTED

This fragment of muslin and wolftooth lace is part of the tie or collar of the so-called "undress costume" worn by Napoleon. The description of the costume indicates that the wolftooth lace collar was made up of several "pieces". The stitch marks on the two sides of this fragment confirm this. The inventory for the ceremony attire lists, under number 27, "Seventeen collar pieces for the costume".

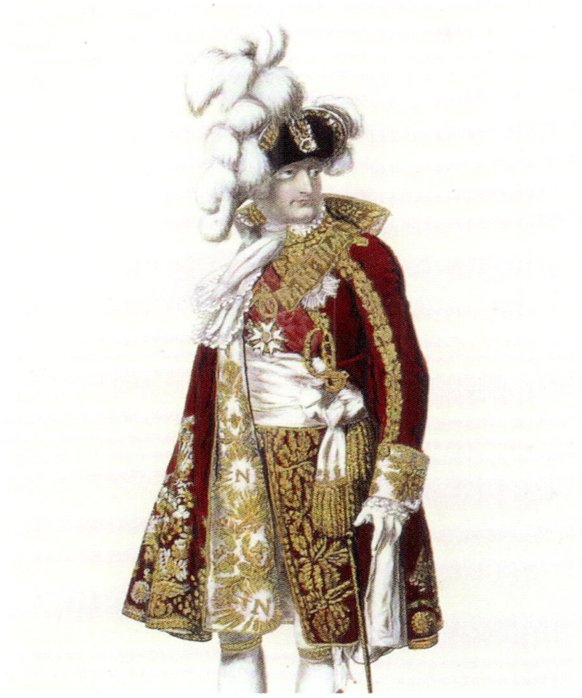

NAPOLEON IN UNDRESS COSTUME

After Jean-Baptiste Isabey, *Livre du Sacre.*

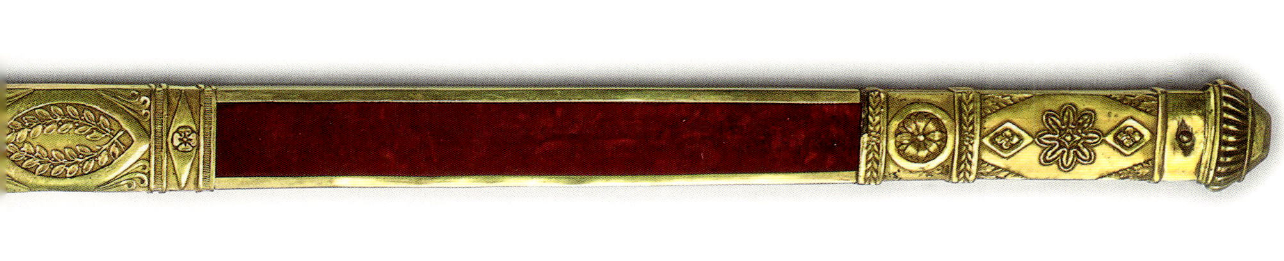

THE *LIVRE DU SACRE*

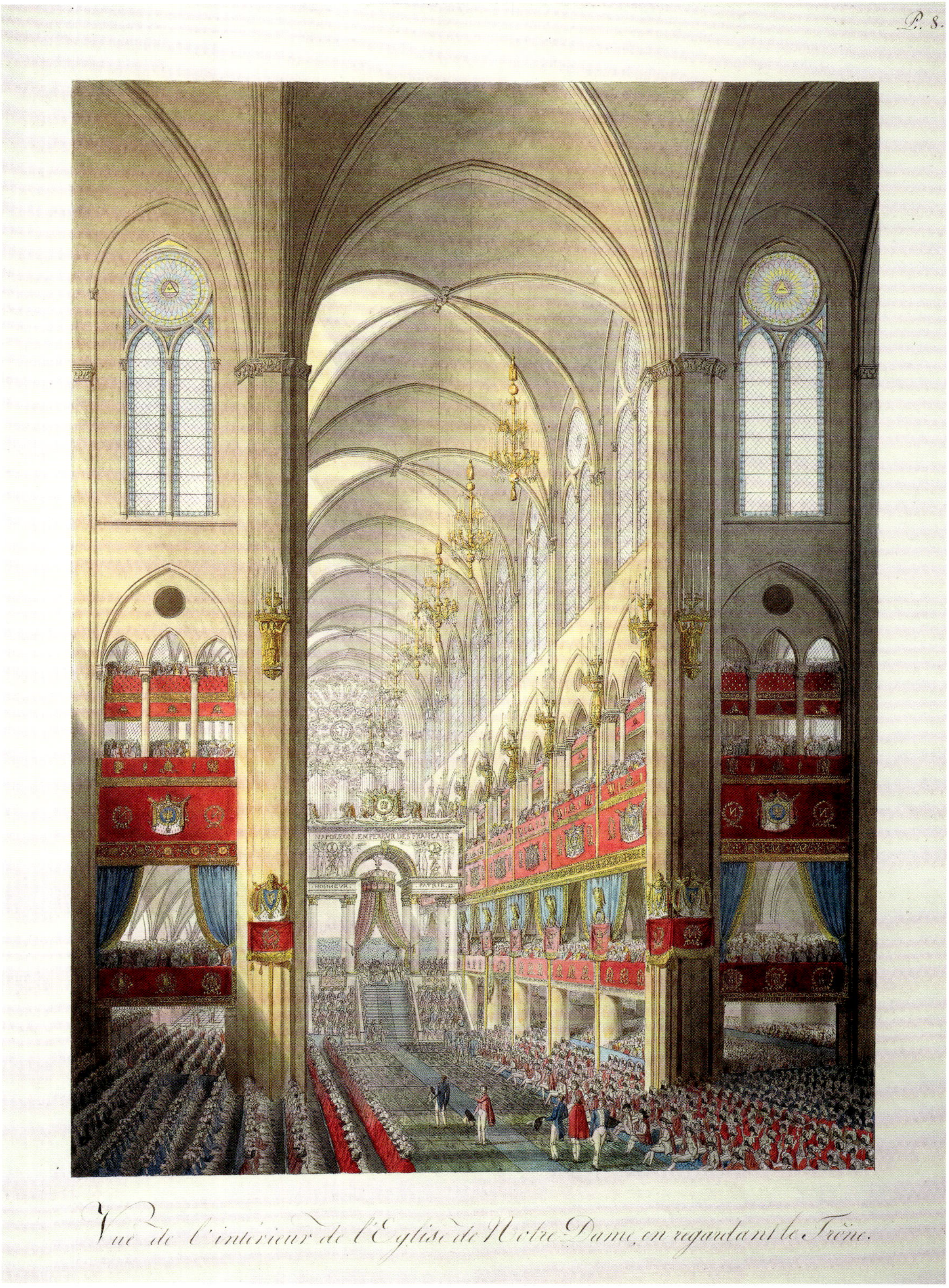

Large-format book published in 1807 by French publishers Leblanc. The full title reads (in English): "Description of the ceremonies and festivities held at the coronation of Their Majesties Napoleon, Emperor of the French and King of Italy, and his august bride Josephine. Compendium of the decorations executed in the church of Notre Dame de Paris and along the Champ de Mars, after the designs of imperial architects Percier and Fontaine and under their supervision." This example belonged to Napoleon's elder brother Joseph Bonaparte, complete with original binding signed "Tessier" and bearing the ex-libris "Morfontaine" (the name of Joseph's property in the Oise department). The work comprised 24 watercolor illustrations plus 12 full-page plates, each plate enhanced with watercolor and a touch of gouache and executed with extraordinary finesse. The first spread displays the title of the book in silver script. The few hand-painted and handwritten editions are thought to be the work of Charles Percier himself and were reserved for the imperial family and European state dignitaries. Fewer than 10 of those editions remain extant.

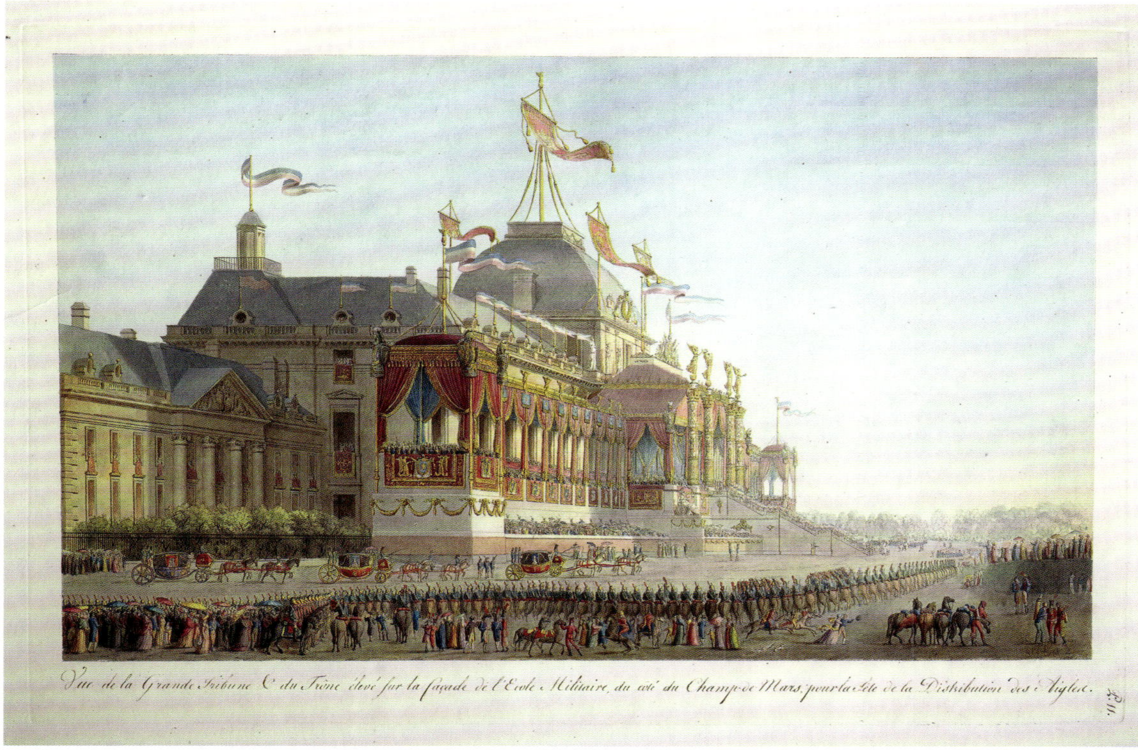

PLATE XI

View of the grandstand and the raised throne on the facade of the École Militaire giving onto the Champ de Mars, for the Distribution of the Eagles celebration.

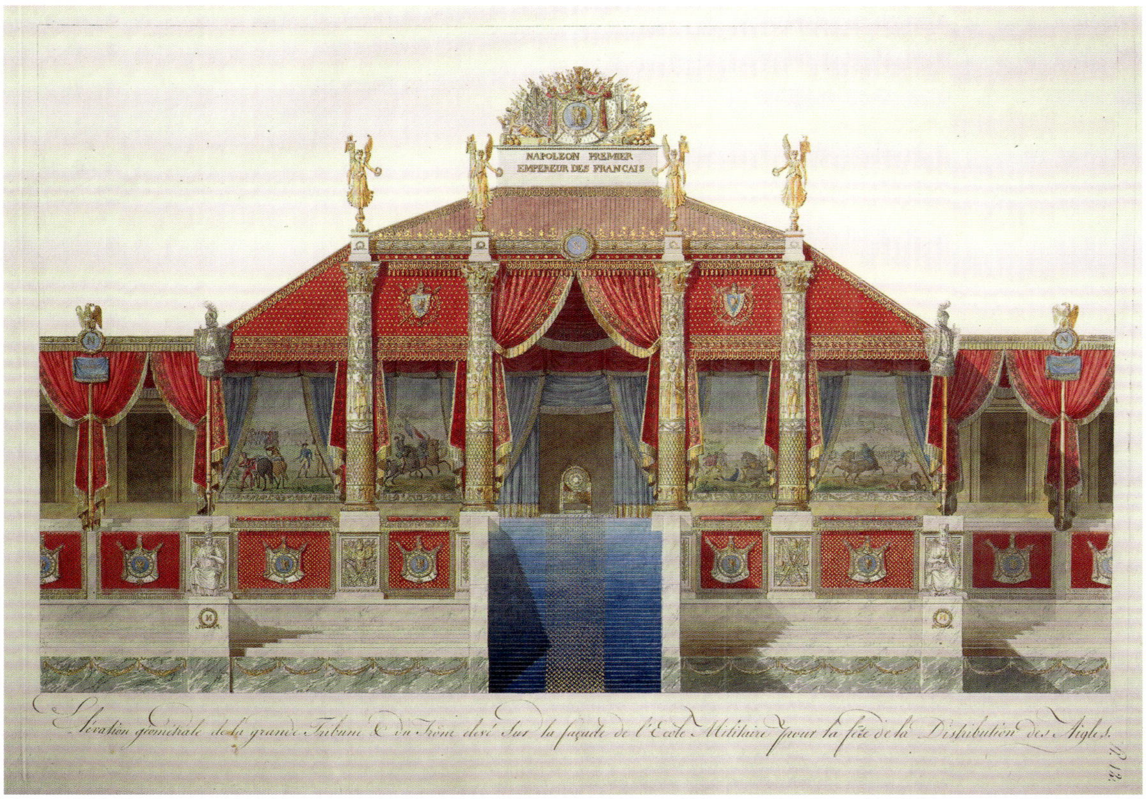

PLATE VIII

View of the interior of the church of Notre Dame looking toward the throne.

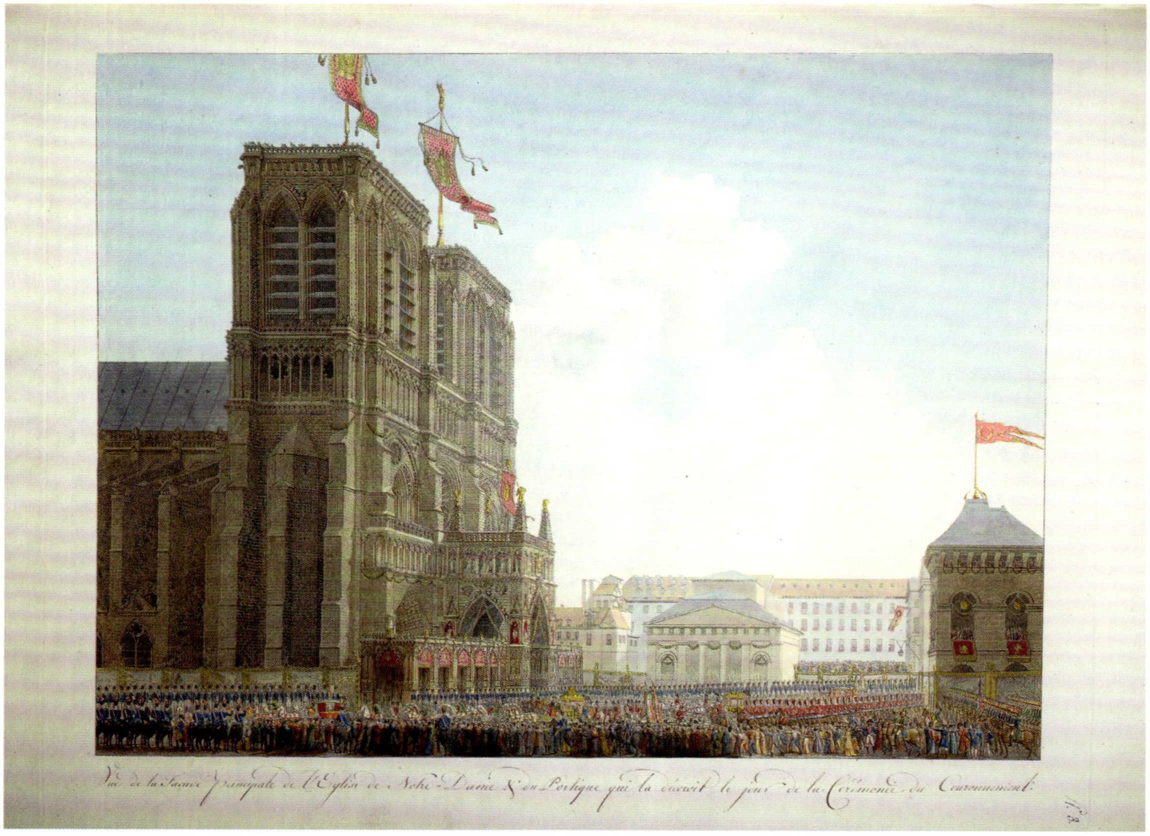

PLATE III

View of the main façade of the church of Notre Dame and the decorative portico erected for the coronation ceremony.

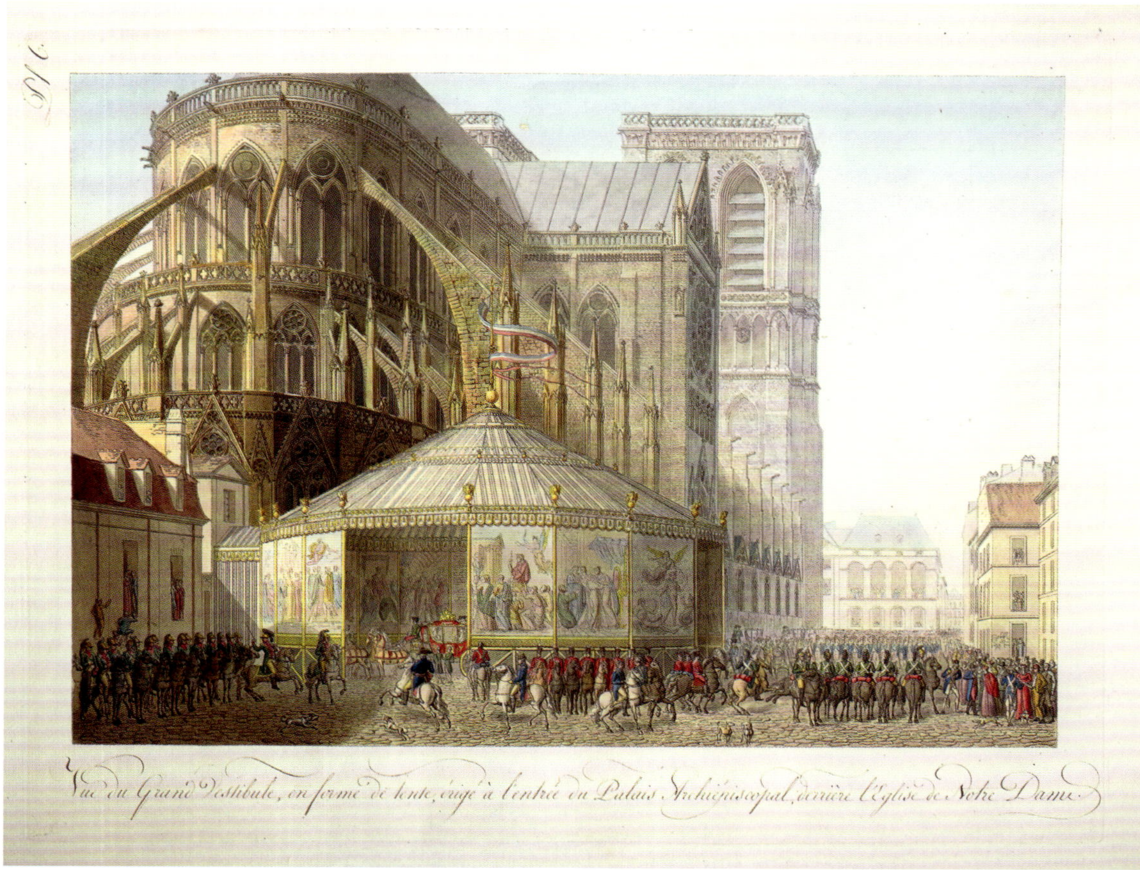

PLATE VI

View of the grand porch, in the shape of a tent, erected at the entrance to the archiepiscopal palace.

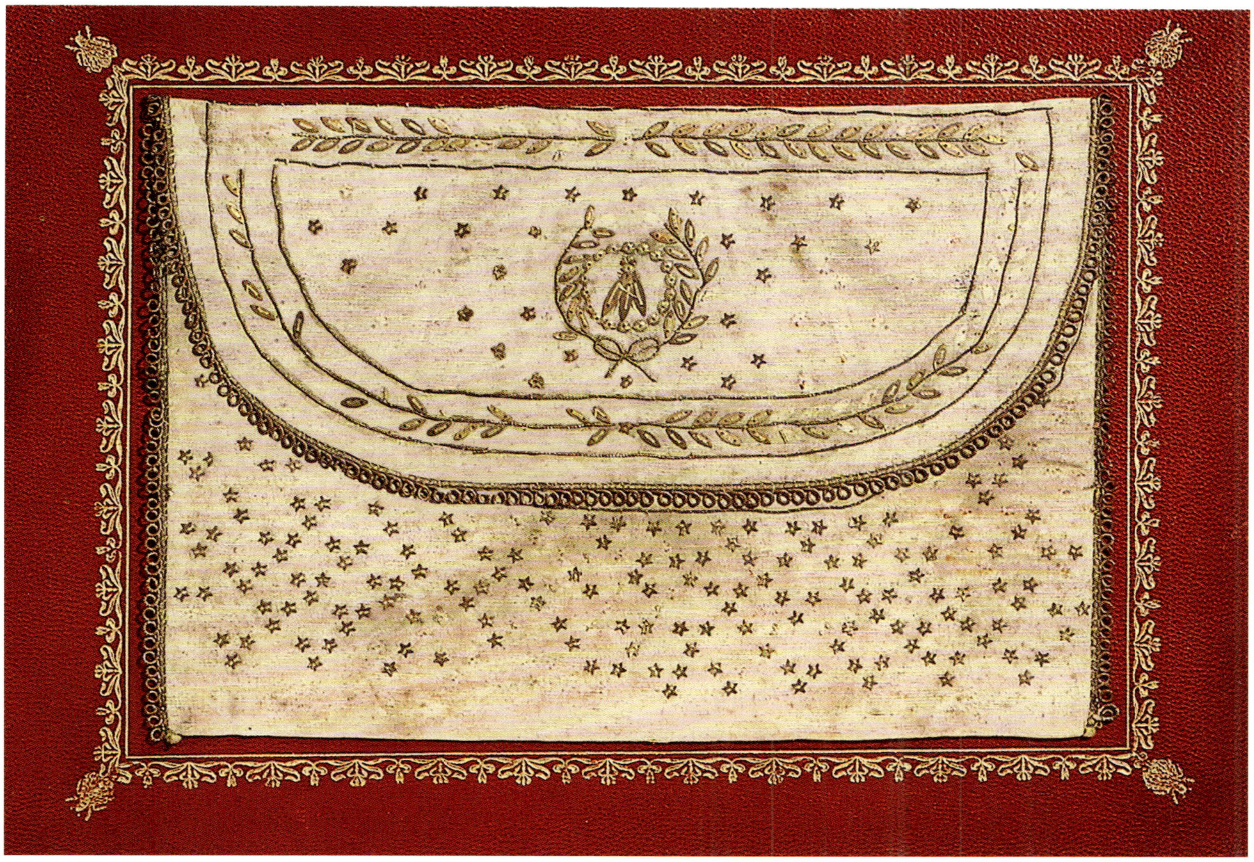

AUGUSTIN-FRANÇOIS-ANDRÉ PICOT (1786-1868), WHITE SATIN PURSE CARRIED ON THE DAY OF THE CORONATION CEREMONY

White satin purse embroidered with gold thread and studded with gold stars, featuring a bee in the center surrounded by a laurel wreath. Made in 1804 for the coronation ceremony by the imperial embroiderer Picot to designs by Isabey. On 18 May 1820, according to a handwritten historical document, this precious memento was given by the now exiled Emperor to General Baron Henri Lenoury (1771-1839) as a mark of his respect. Lenoury's estate was sold off in Louviers in 2002.

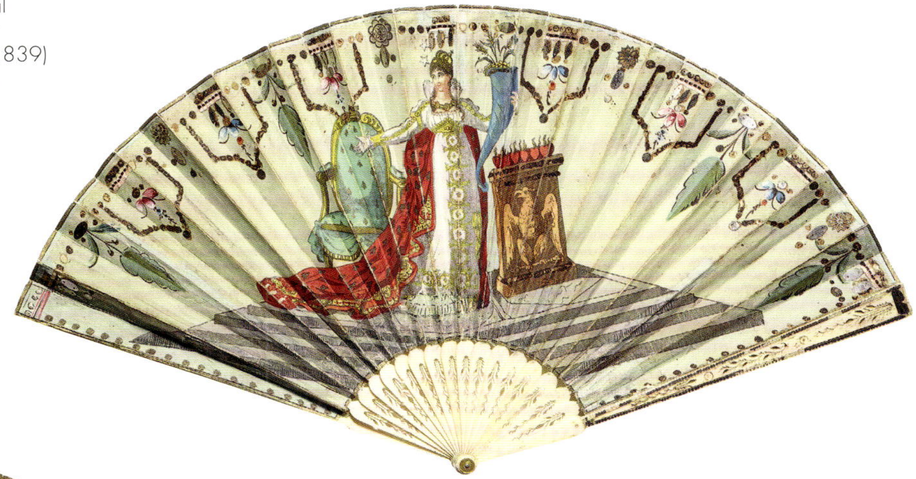

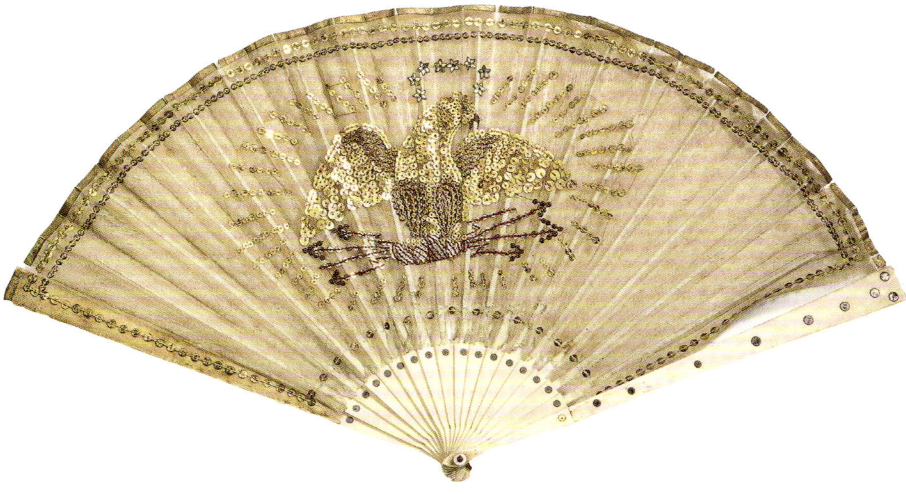

FANS

These two small fans, perfectly matched to the lightweight dresses worn by Josephine and her contemporaries, display telling use of imagery: on the left, a fan featuring a gold sequin-embroidered imperial eagle with spread wings, its head crowned with stars and its talons clutching a thunderbolt; on the right, a fan embossed with a portrait of Josephine in coronation robes, holding a J-shaped horn of plenty that recalls her name. Two very fine and rare reminders of the projection of the imperial image in French society under the First Empire.

PAPAL INSIGNIA ADORNING NOTRE DAME IN PARIS ON THE DAY OF THE CORONATION

Alongside the imperial coat-of-arms, sculpted wooden papal insignia were used to decorate Notre Dame on the day of the coronation. They can be seen in a colored engraving from Depeuille Fils.

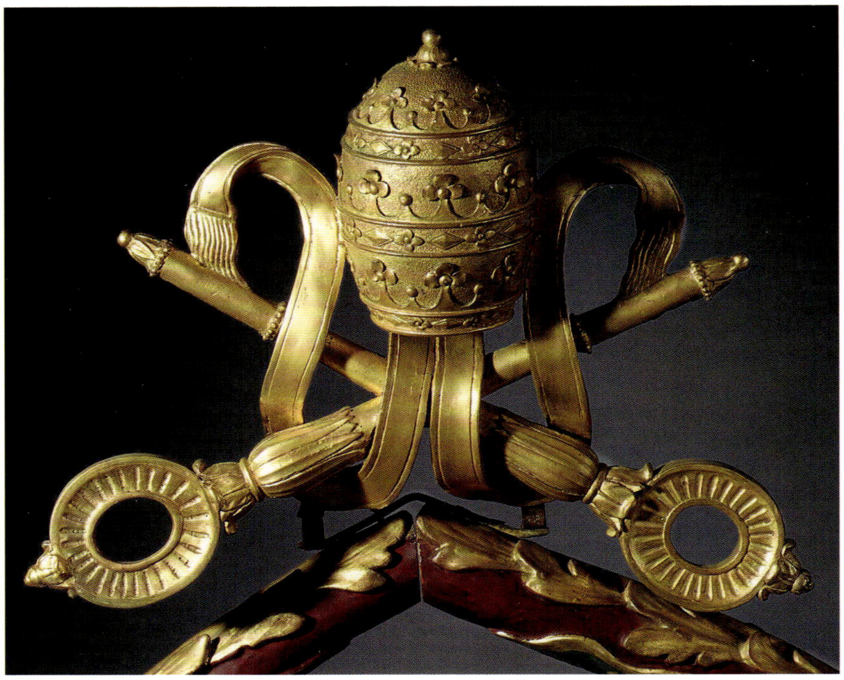

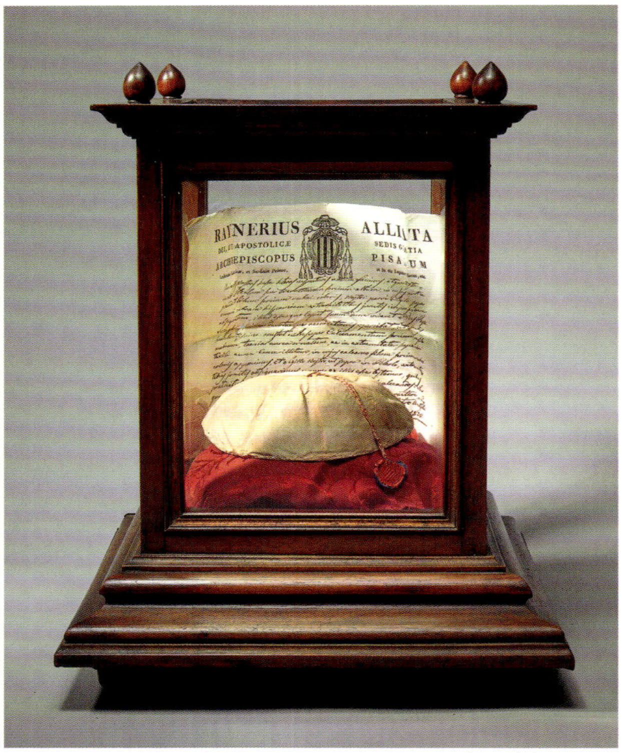

POPE PIUS VII'S SKULLCAP

This Gros de Tours silk skullcap, lined with cream-colored pelt, has been handed down by the descendants of Charles-Maurice de Talleyrand-Périgord (1734-1838), best known as the bold and skilful diplomat and political player of the Directory and Empire. It belonged to Pope Pius VII (1800-1823), as confirmed by the handwritten certificate produced by the archbishop of Pisa in 1832, in Talleyrand's lifetime. History tells us that, in 1802, Pope Pius VII annulled the excommunication of Talleyrand, defrocked as bishop of Autun, so that he could marry a divorcee, Madame Grand. Fontainebleau museum houses another skullcap (F.2476C) that the Pope apparently wore while imprisoned at the Chateau de Fontainebleau between 1812 and 1814. It is of the same origin.

GROGNIER, *BUST OF PIUS VII*

The story of this unusual terracotta bust of Pope Pius VII remains something of a mystery. All we know for sure (from the engraving on the reverse) is that it was given to Baroness de Fontanges in 1805 by the artist Grognier.

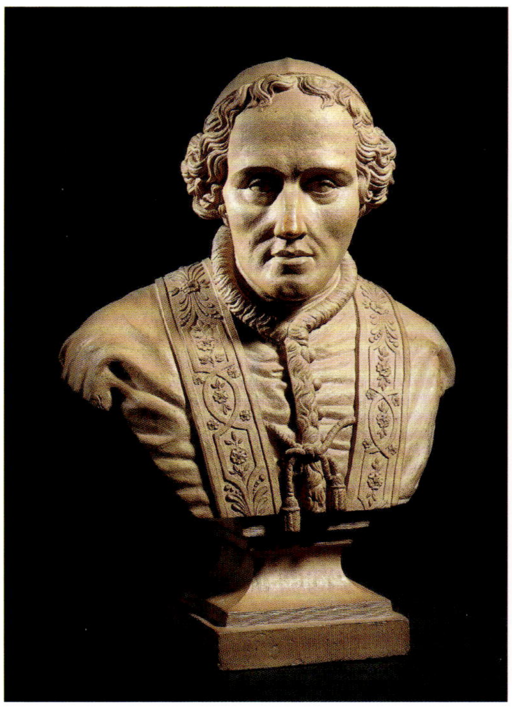

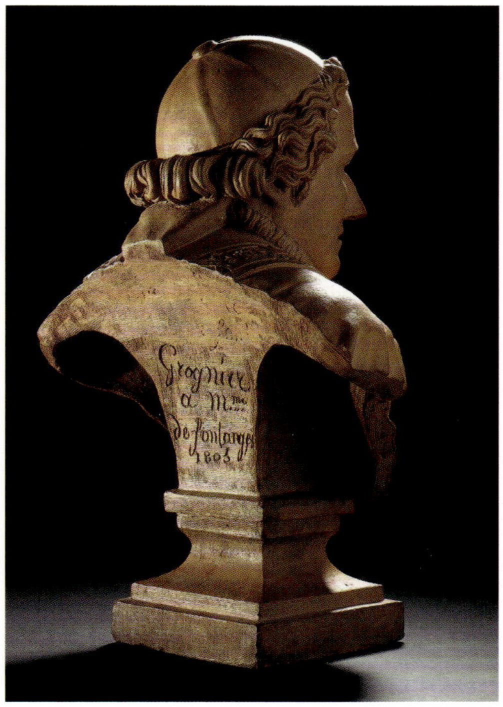

JACQUES-LOUIS DAVID (1748-1825) AND STUDIO, *PORTRAIT OF POPE PIUS VII*

This famous portrait was commissioned by the then director of the Musée Napoléon (now the Louvre), Vivant Denon, to thank the Sovereign pontiff for having attended the Emperor's coronation. It was executed by David in 1805, one of three portraits produced in his studio that included two commissioned by Napoleon (one now in the museum of the Château de Fontainebleau, the other in the Museum of the Châteaux de Versailles and Trianon). The third version, which disappeared in 1879 after accompanying David into exile in Brussels, is listed in the inventory taken after his death in 1826 as having been "merely retouched by Mr David". The Pope never did receive his copy of the portrait.

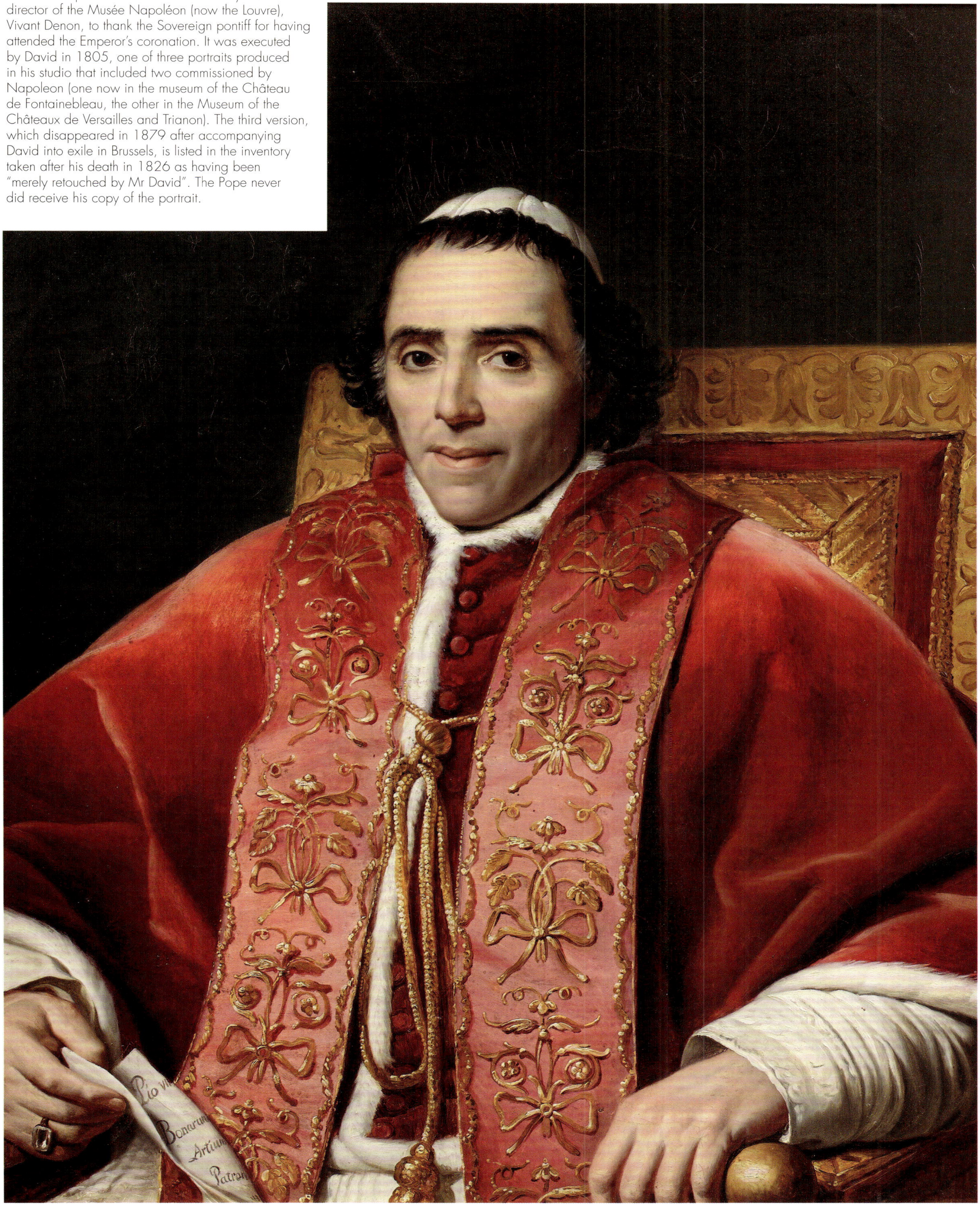

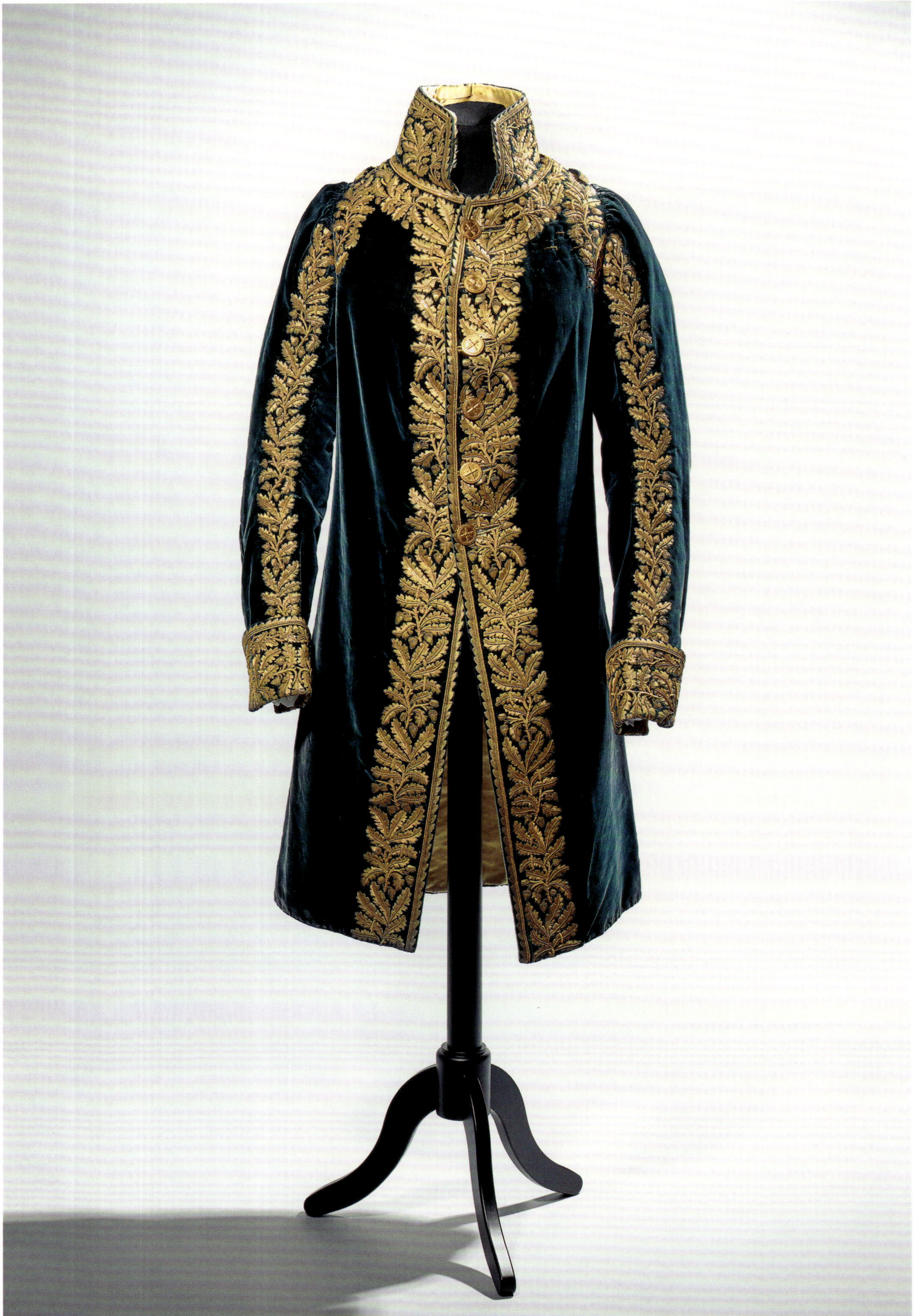

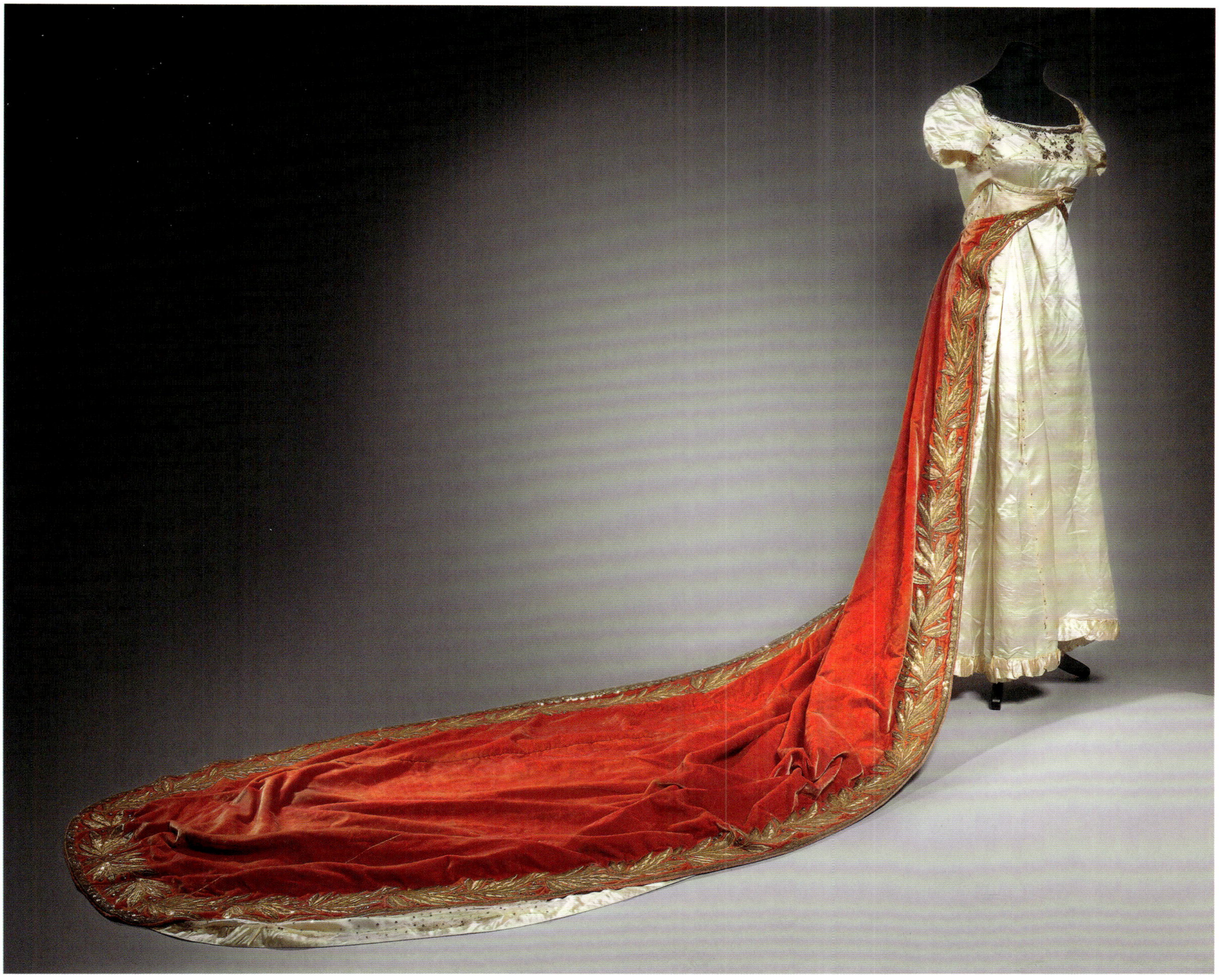

CEREMONIAL COSTUME OF NICOLAS-CHARLES OUDINOT (1767-1847), DUKE OF REGGIO, MARSHAL OF THE EMPIRE

Isabey (1767-1855), a painter and draughtsman for the Emperor's cabinet, ceremonies and external relations, provided the drawings for all the coronation costumes, including this costume designed for the Marshal of the Empire. It is made from blue silk and is richly embroidered with a golden silver-thread oak-tree pattern enhanced with sequins. Nicolas-Charles Oudinot, appointed Marshal of the Empire in 1809, did not take part in the coronation. Following the protocol of the time, he had his costume designed on his appointment to honor his title and to wear at major ceremonies during the Empire then the Restoration. This costume is very rare and no doubt one of very few in private hands. The Musée de l'Armée currently has two similar costumes, one from Marshal Lannes and the other for Marshal Ney. The costume belonging to Marshal Berthier is now part of the collections of the Museum of the Legion of Honor in Paris.

CEREMONIAL DRESS OF ADÈLE D'OSMOND (1781-1866), COUNTESS OF BOIGNE

This very rare ivory satin dress with a long scarlet and gold-embroidered silk-velvet train majestically recalls the splendor of the Emperor's coronation, immortalized by the painter Jacques-Louis David. Napoleon was indeed very keen to restore the resplendence that characterized the *Ancien Régime*. Although she did not take part in the coronation ceremonies, the Countess of Boigne stayed true to that spirit. The great similarity of her gown to that of Countess Bérenger, currently held by the Fondation Napoléon, or that of Amandine-Marie-Georgine de Serent, Princess of Leon, exhibited at the Metropolitan Museum of New York, suggests that it was produced for a major event, possibly the marriage of Napoleon to Marie-Louise.

The Emperor

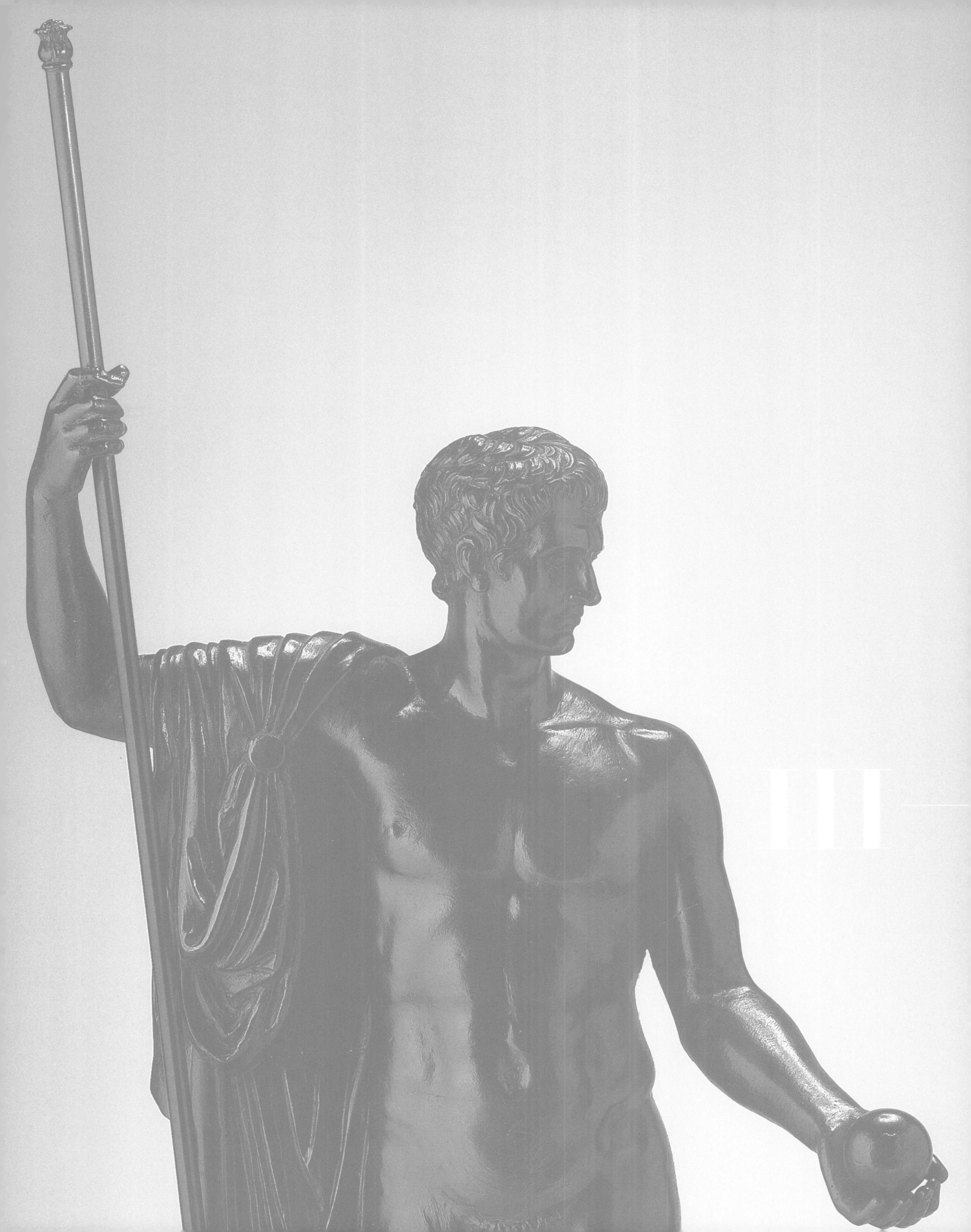

III

"I am but a man after all," sighed Napoleon, marooned on his small island tossed by the wind. So who was he then this "hero en déshabillé" of whom his servant Constant spoke with such affection?[1] *To discover the true face of the sovereign, we have to peek through holes in the tapestries and observe his habits and obsessions, his pleasures and displeasures, the minutiae of his daily life. Only then do the trappings of glory fall away to reveal the intimate portrait of the man beneath. A man of unsettling genius whose daily life in no way diminished his legend.*

Xavier Aiolfi
historian and expert

SMALL PUSS IN BOOTS

To draw closer to the Emperor, let us first examine his appearance. Picturing his facial features is not an easy proposition since none of the portraits can be trusted to show his true likeness. Dubbed "small puss in boots" by Josephine, Napoleon was not actually as short as legend has led us to believe. At 1.69m tall (roughly five and a half feet), he was the average height for his time. All of the known measurements agree to within a few millimeters, including post mortem measurements taken by the doctor on Saint Helena who recorded a height of *5 pieds, 2 pouces, 4 lignes* (equivalent to 1.686m or five feet, 5.5 inches).

Bonaparte was slim at the time of the Revolution but grew fatter with age and fortune. As Emperor, he got shorter and wider and hated it. He had a rather high and prominent forehead, with brown hair thinning around the temples — fine, soft hair, albeit in short supply. He often changed his hairstyle. From the end of the Consulate onward, he is depicted with short neck-length hair. In Italy he had long, free-flowing hair, loosely gathered in a pigtail. When he cut his hair, Napoleon acquired the look that is now part of legend. His soldiers, always quick to notice what their leader did, immediately nicknamed him *Petit Tondu* ("little shaveling"), Napoleon being the only general of the time who eschewed the fashion for thick, flowing locks.

A "piercing gaze that went right through you" is how people described meeting Napoleon's steely blue-gray eyes. Being short-sighted, he sometimes needed opera glasses to see properly and always kept a pair about his person. In his desk he kept a pair of eyeglasses and a pince-nez.

Napoleon had a finely drawn mouth, with evenly proportioned lips that shut tight when he was in a bad mood but opened in a broad smile when he was being charming. His teeth were not particularly straight but very white and in very good condition. Despite his weakness for licorice chews, he took great care of his teeth and boasted a magnificent dental surgeon's kit of his own (page 203).

Napoleon had an aquiline profile with a nose worthy of an ancient Greek bust. An irreproachable nose in every way, so very sensitive that vinegar and Agarwood had to be burnt in the Emperor's bedchamber.

The head under the hat was on the large side, 22 *pouces* (inches) in circumference. It was long rather than wide with slightly flattened temples and very sensitive to touch. His ears were "small and perfectly formed". His neck was short, his shoulders were rounded and his chest was broad and largely hairless. His legs were well turned with shapely thighs. His hands were also very beautiful and always protected by kid gloves or gloves made of reindeer leather, thicker gloves when he went horseback riding (page 147).

Despite habitually biting his nails when impatient or preoccupied, Napoleon took great care of his hands like every other aspect of his appearance.

Napoleon had a strong voice, no doubt a product of army life, but he was incapable of singing in tune. He loved to sing just the same and would often be heard humming or whistling to himself when he was in a good mood, particularly as he got dressed in the morning. Not content merely to murder popular ditties, Napoleon also murdered the French language. He often made mistakes when speaking, such as failing to make the liaison between a consonant and a vowel, or adding the letter 't' to the third person singular or the letter 's' to the first person singular in the future tense. Did he speak with a strong Corsican/Italian accent? History doesn't say. All we know for sure is that he spoke with an Italian-like intonation, placing the stress on the final syllable.

"I AM A CREATURE OF HABIT"

So said Napoleon of himself, and he knew himself well. This same man who was always so fastidious about his person showed a careless disregard for his personal effects. He would regularly wipe his pen on his breeches or shake it above his desk to get the ink flowing, splashing ink over himself in the process. He also liked to wear old uniforms, because he felt more comfortable in them.

Napoleon never slept more than six hours a night, and he rarely wore a watch when he went out despite the collection of timepieces in his wardrobe. One wonders, in fact, whether he had any notion of time at all. He certainly kept very unsociable hours. Time meant nothing to Napoleon. People were expected to attend him at a moment's notice. Talleyrand and others knew to their cost what it was like to be called out by Napoleon in the middle of the night.

It was Talleyrand likewise who upbraided the Emperor for his lack of social graces. His inelegant gait for instance, waddling from side to side with his hands crossed behind his back, or throwing his weight forward as he advanced, hands stuffed into his pockets. He would push people out of the way without even thinking about it, entering a room with all the delicacy of cavalry returning to barracks. Even when wrapped in a domino at a masked ball, Napoleon never went unnoticed,

Then there were his nervous tics, which were quite disconcerting for people unused to his company. When preoccupied, an involuntary movement would agitate his right shoulder, a twitch that caused his mouth to twist from right to left and his arm to extend as he tugged at his sleeve. When in conversation, he would absentmindedly gouge out the arm of his chair with a small knife. These are things that people could hardly fail to notice.

Napoleon lived his life at breakneck speed without ever making a dent in his health. Blessed with nerves of steel, he was built to endure exceptional fatigue. He was hardly ever sick, which was just as well since he had no faith in doctors; and he was curiously unable to hear his own heart beat. He found this anomaly most amusing, particularly since none of his friends could find a pulse in his chest either. He hated medicine but made liberal use of tobacco. Inordinate use, you could say. He would take giant pinches of snuff, sniff it but not breathe it in, then let his snuffbox drop to the floor. At long meetings of the Conseil d'État, he would help himself to the contents of any snuffbox within reach, but was never known to return a snuffbox to its rightful owner.

For all his uncouth ways, Napoleon never forgot that it had been his honor to wear the epaulettes of the King's regiment. He always spoke well of Louis XVI, "that unhappy Prince, so good, so cultured" for whom he felt such affection. Like a natural aristocrat, Napoleon was rough in his affections. He would pull the ears of his favorites, twisting the hapless organ in every direction until the victim cried out in pain. Sometimes he would pinch the "whole of the ear and often both ears at once; and that with a master's hand". His friendly slaps on the back too were delivered with such force that they left people gasping. Mademoiselle Avrillion, first chambermaid to the Empress Josephine, said that the Emperor once pinched her cheek so hard that the mark was still there several days later.[2]

When Napoleon was not watching his language, the old military habits easily returned and with them a barrage of bawdy remarks and colloquial expressions. But he could also come across as tender and thoughtful. Everyone had to have a nickname, even the Empress "ma bonne grosse Louise" (my dear fat Louise) and his manservant Constant, endearingly dubbed "Monsieur Constant, mon fils" (Mr Constant my son), "vilaine bête" (naughty beast) or "grosse bête" (big dummy). Napoleon's physician Corvisart, was meanwhile saddled with the sobriquet of "charlatan".

It was never a good idea to put the Emperor in a bad mood. The least trace of anger would cause his face to contort into a frightening grimace and his voice to sink to a rasp. "His complexion almost seemed to grow paler at will," remarked councilor of state Miot de Melito, who had witnessed several such tantrums. Napoleon was always contrite after his outbursts and quick to seek forgiveness. But he was a stubborn man and quite prepared to do anything to make his point. Threats, entreaties — Napoleon would resort to any means to bring others around to his way of thinking, no matter how long it took. Tender and affectionate at one moment, Napoleon could be extremely petty the next. As he himself once observed, great things brought out the greatness in him but small things revealed his petty side. He delighted in naughty goings-on below stairs and scandalous tittle-tattle. He had an insatiable curiosity to know everything, including what was happening in the servants' quarters.

Patient one moment, impatient the next, cajoling, pedantic, sometimes a gossip, Napoleon lived in a permanent state of tension. When he did manage to withdraw into himself, the outside world ceased to exist. A born autodidact, Napoleon thrived on deliberation and intellectual achievement. He wanted to learn everything and busily accumulated a jumble of information in no particular order. He stopped reading any book he didn't like from the start, throwing it into the fire or out of the carriage window when he was traveling. He applied the same approach to the books that he found other people reading. He would draw closer, take a look at the title, then decide its fate on the basis of what he thought of the author or the genre. He had no qualms about berating the unfortunate reader for their poor taste in literature. Napoleon himself was an avid reader and owned a very fine library — as impressive for its variety of works as for the elegance of some of their bindings (page 196). As Consul, he toyed with the idea of commissioning a new library building with space for 10,000 titles. Wherever he went, his rooms had to be laid out in the same pattern as at the Tuileries Palace. Identical apartments, with furniture of the same style, positioned identically. He only felt at home once his dressing boxes had been opened and his portfolios had been unpacked.

The section of the palace that was reserved for Napoleon comprised two apartments: the State Rooms and Napoleon's private apartment. Napoleon liked to surround himself with staff. "He was a manservant's man," Constant would later comment. From the early days of his ascent to power, he had a taste for being waited upon. As a general, he had three people to assist him and liked to be pampered "in all the luxury that comes with supreme success".

Napoleon's valets were part of his everyday life and he felt no false modesty undressing or bathing in front of them. His body linen was sumptuous. "The uniform makes the man," he used to say, his usual dress being the uniform of a colonel of the Chasseurs à Cheval or the Grenadiers of the Imperial

Guard. As Emperor, he always wore the Grenadier's uniform: coat of royal blue cloth; blue collar without piping; white lapels without piping, cut square; scarlet cuffs without piping; white, three-pointed flaps; scarlet lining without piping, turned back and fastened with hooks and eyes, and decorated with four embroidered gold grenades on white trim; long pockets with scarlet piping; gilt buttons featuring a crowned eagle.
The coat of the colonel of the Chasseurs was green cloth, with pointed lapels and matching cloth lining, and red collar and cuffs (pointed). The facings were decorated with gold embroidered hunting horns and the buttons were Hussar-style marked with a crowned eagle. The epaulettes were quite small and light, with a plain body, narrow border and tassel fringes, attached to the coat by a shoulder strap.
Over (or sometimes under) his waistcoat, Napoleon buckled a sword belt made of plain white buffalo leather (page 166), the same style as those on display in the Bruno Ledoux private museum. This gave simplicity to an otherwise lavish tableau. His sword hung from the belt, and he would only remove it once he had arrived at the Cabinet Office. Napoleon owned four swords: a vermeil sword of French pattern; a sword with a flat blade and an ivory guard; and two swords with gold guards and gold-encrusted tortoiseshell scabbards. Of these, only the last two were in general use. There was also the Austerlitz sword, so-named after the celebrated battle and still worn by Napoleon whenever he could. His collection of handguns was no less impressive, including a magnificent pair of gold-inlaid pistols (page 183). For a man who had created the Order of the Legion of Honor, Napoleon wore surprisingly few of his own medals. He restricted himself to the silver-embroidered Grand Eagle Medallion (page 148) plus two further medals: the Legion of Honor and the Iron Crown. As Emperor he also wore the grand cordon of the Legion of Honor, usually over his waistcoat except on grand state occasions when he sported it over his tunic. Once dressed, with his left hand he would take up the beaver fur hat that had become part of his image, holding it carefully by the corner. With no piping or braiding, the hat's sole decoration was a tricolor cockade held in place by black silk ribbon. It was made by the Emperor's hatter Poupard (page 147).
Having combed his hair, Napoleon was then handed a batiste handkerchief sprinkled with Eau de Cologne. The finishing touches were his snuffbox, eyeglass and a small tortoiseshell box filled with tiny chunks of aniseed-flavored licorice (Napoleon's particular weakness). Amazingly, one of Napoleon's bonbon boxes, a small box patterned with round scales, is now part of the Bruno Ledoux collection complete with its (albeit melted) licorice contents (page 186). Napoleon had a passion for snuffboxes. They were the only items of jewelry he ever allowed himself. He owned a huge variety of designs and liked to offer them as gifts.

CHICKEN AND CHAMBERTIN

Napoleon lunched very early in the day as was the custom at the time. Cooks, skivvies and head waiters had to bide their time until His Majesty declared himself hungry, endlessly replacing the boiling water that kept his lunch warm. The problem was that Napoleon invariably turned up so late that the chicken was burnt to a crisp. The only solution was to prepare several chickens, so there would always be one on the imperial plate. Knowing Napoleon's thriftiness, he might well have been more punctual had he been aware that all this food was going to waste...
There was no dining room as such, the table being laid wherever Napoleon chose to eat. No fancy crockery either. Just chiseled silver flatware bearing the imperial coat-of-arms. The more elaborate silver services, such as the vermeil tableware, were reserved for grand receptions. Napoleon's everyday cutlery was likewise quite plain. The Ledoux Collection includes a wide variety of examples, some testifying to the frugal side of the imperial lifestyle, some to its opulence. For the great state banquets, the everyday silverware flushed vermeil and gold amid the wondrous magnificence of Sèvres porcelain (pages 218-237).
Napoleon was no gourmet. He showed as much disdain for the culinary arts as he did for proper French. He wanted nothing imaginative from his cooks, just the same dishes time and again. In 1810 his everyday menu typically consisted of one *potage* (thick soup), three entrees, two *entremets* (literally the "between-dish" course), two sweets, a cup of coffee and two bread rolls. By the end of the Empire, there were two *potages* on the menu (instead of one) followed by a roast, a single *entremets*, two *hors d'œuvres* (appetizers), four sweets and coffee. Of these, what Napoleon most liked to eat was chicken — chicken Provençal (leaving out the garlic, which didn't agree with him), Italian-style chicken, chicken Marengo, fried chicken, sautéed chicken or roasted chicken.
Besides chicken, Napoleon also liked fried food in general, *vol-au-vents* (filled puff pastry shells), *bouchées à la reine* (chicken and mushrooms encased in flaky puff pastry) and *timbales à la Milanaise* (grilled timbales of pasta Milanese). Pasta was a particular favorite of his, especially Italian-style macaroni sprinkled with Parmesan cheese. His other great love was red mullet, which he insisted on eating at least once every few days. Good quality bread was likewise non-negotiable. Then there were the foods he couldn't stand, starting with lightly cooked red meat. As Napoleon never tired of repeating, red meat had to be cooked until it turned "dark brown" — otherwise it was disgusting. So too were the stringy bits in French beans. "Like eating hairs" he used to say, and though he loved French beans, he avoided them on account of the strings. His policy on beverages was similarly uncompromising:

there was only one wine he could tolerate and that was Chambertin. About as ignorant about wine as he was about food, Napoleon mixed his Chambertin with water and never drank more than a half a bottle per meal. Exile on St Helena would put paid to many of his habits but one thing he could never get used to was the absence of his habitual Chambertin. British "claret" was a very poor substitute.

And what of Napoleon's table manners? In a word: abysmal. He ate at breakneck speed, downing his entire meal in less than 10 minutes. As he himself once famously said at the time of the Consulate: "If you want to dine well, dine with Cambacérès [2nd consul], if you want to dine badly, dine with Lebrun [3rd Consul]; if you want to dine quickly, dine with me." He only ate a fraction of the dishes that were set before him, with no regard for the order of service. He would start with the *entremets,* followed by the *hors-d'œuvre,* then pause to consider the sweets before returning to the roast and finishing up with the soup. This man who was so good at positioning his troops had no sense at all of how flavors work. He gulped down his food without tasting it, cramming huge forkfuls into his mouth and barely pausing to chew, sometimes swallowing it whole as if in a hurry to finish. He would lift the covers off the tureens himself and any dishes that failed to please were promptly removed. His brusque table manners and cursory chewing invariably meant that he spilled food all over himself. It didn't help that he never used a table napkin, no doubt regarding it as pointless. He wiped out dishes and saucepans with pieces of bread and mostly ate with his fingers.

Dinner would always conclude on a sweet note; Napoleon loved *patisseries.* The task of pandering to his pleasure fell to master pastry chef Hubert Lebeau, otherwise known as "the reviver of French patisserie".

TAKE THIS DOWN, MÉNEVAL!

"I recognize that I am the most enslaved of men. My master has no mercy on me, for my master is the nature of things." So explained Napoleon to his wife Josephine. In order to succeed, the Emperor believed in only one thing and that was hard work. He worked his ministers and aides to the bone, and he himself had no limits. "Me, I work all the time and I meditate much," he said. "I work while dining or at the theater and at night I wake up to work." The verb "to work" ruled Napoleon's life so much that he found it hard to delegate to others what he could do himself.

And what better place to work than in the comfort of your own study? Napoleon's study was as small as his empire was vast. It was lit by a single corner window giving onto the garden and instantly identifiable by a magnificent writing desk covered with bronzes. There could be no doubt as to the purpose of the room. Everything about it was conducive to working, with "do not disturb" writ large across the occupant's features. This was the Emperor's room, where nothing could be moved unless he moved it himself. His writing desk featured a sliding roll top that could be closed without disturbing any papers. Napoleon was a real stickler for keeping his papers in order, and woe-betide anyone who forgot it. No one understood filing better than he did. Documents had to be filed in the right order, in matching folders with similar dimensions. The Bruno Ledoux collection features a superb filing cabinet by Biennais of Paris that testifies to Napoleon's "archivist" inclinations (page 189).

Napoleon's den was a place for dictation, not conversation, and it was impossible to take down his every word. His secretary had to content himself with catching characteristic turns of phrase in mid air. That way he got the gist of what was being said without having to interrupt. Napoleon hated having to repeat himself. There was no other choice but to keep up, leaving blanks to be filled in later depending on the recipient and the subject matter. As soon as the Emperor had quit his study, his secretaries would rush to pick up the letters he had thrown on the floor, looking for the missing information. This explains why some of Napoleon's missives lack the imagery that peppered his utterances, devoid of that singular warmth that so enthralled his listeners.

Personally annotated and signed by Napoleon, every document bore his unmistakable mark. His signature was like a flash of lightning in a white sky — a slug of ink, scraped across the page by a nervous hand. It was a command in its own right. An impetuous scrawl, sometimes tinged with a violence that betrayed Bonaparte's underlying anger. Signing aside, Napoleon hated writing. His letters contained words that were barely legible, stuffed full of spelling mistakes and Italianisms. As he himself once said, his thoughts traveled faster than his pen: "I cannot write well because I am caught in two currents, the flow of ideas and the flow of the pen. The ideas go on fastest, and then goodbye to the letters and the lines!" It took a superhuman effort to decipher Napoleon's handwriting — a point made by Councilor of State Thibaudeau who respectfully told the sovereign, on behalf of the entire legislative body, that nobody could understand his handwritten orders. "Don't imagine that I can read them any better myself," retorted Napoleon, tearing up the offending documents. "Far quicker to speak my thoughts out loud. Come and take a seat." And with that, dictation would commence.

Napoleon could cover dozens of different subjects at a single sitting. He used to say that his brain was full of drawers that he could open and close as required. Better still, he could return to a letter that had been pending for several days and continue dictating exactly where he had left off. There were also times, albeit rare, when he would "shut all the drawers" and allow himself a few moments of respite — a few moments to indulge in the pleasures of life, but always to the metaphorical sound of drums, with a slow march playing in the background.

HIS MAJESTY'S PLEASURES

Napoleon sometimes played games. On fine days at La Malmaison, at the time of the Consulate, he would suddenly exclaim "let's play *barres*" and, divesting himself of his coat, race away like a schoolboy let loose in the playground. He also liked games of chance but hated playing for money and when out socializing always gave the gaming tables a wide berth. On the rare occasions that he did deign to play, he was a bad loser and invariably cheated. Impassive in the face of disaster, Napoleon could not stand being bested in a game. He never played chess with Bourienne for instance, knowing him to be the better player. His favorite card game was 421, because it was quick to play. If the card he drew was no good, he would leave it lying on the table waiting to see how the next player fared. In the dreaded event that his opponent beat him, Napoleon would throw down his hand and leave the table in a sulk.

But none of these distractions was equal to a wholesome breath of fresh air at the head of a splendid hunting party. The Emperor did indeed hunt, not so much for pleasure but more to perpetuate a royal tradition — out of dynastic obligation you could say. He loved a good gallop but was no more of a horseman than a marksman. Considered a graceless rider, he was only given horses that were perfectly disciplined. The animals destined to be his mounts underwent a "strict novitiate", conditioned to endure suffering without moving a muscle — and that meant in every possible situation. They also had to be magnificent beasts that would be envied by his courtiers. In the last year of his reign, Napoleon rode nothing but purebred Arabs.

Quite a program for a man who adored the fairer sex and used his charm and power to seduce them. Libidinous and beguiling, Napoleon was driven by frenzied appetites and sudden desires. What other man would return to his tent after battle clamoring for a woman? Napoleon was by and large a boorish lover, quite incapable of waiting. Some put this down to his excessive shyness around women. Whatever the case, he certainly made no concessions to their sensibilities.

But the ogre could also purr like a pussycat with a pretty damsel beside him. "To spend the night between a pretty women and a fine sky [...] seems to me to be happiness on earth," he once wrote to the astronomer Jérôme Lalande.

THE HONORABLE SUB-LIEUTENANT...

Napoleon was a military man to the core. Same habits, same gruffness, same lifestyle, same health. He hated it for instance when a general appeared before him in mufti. "A general out of uniform!" he once exclaimed. "He might as well have come in slippers." It was true to habit that he should personally watch over everything, from weaponry and the cut and color of uniforms right down to the lining of flags (specified in detail in a letter). He never seemed happier than when in the company of the army, bivouacking with his men and admiring their Gallic bravery and stamina. The hardships of a campaign meant nothing to him. Staïki was a case in point: a single room served as the entire army headquarters. It froze so hard that everyone had to huddle together for warmth. "We were so close to each other," wrote Caulaincourt, "that if a needle had fallen it wouldn't have reached the floor." Napoleon was quite prepared to risk his own life, to such an extent that his men sometimes had to protect him from himself. At the battle of Essling for instance, with enemy cannon fire raining down around him, he suddenly heard his guards cry out: "We shall lay down our arms if the Emperor does not go to the rear instantly!" At which Napoleon retired, not daring to alienate the affections of his soldiers.

At other times he was equally quick to draw his sword (or *mettre Flamberge au vent* as the French expression goes). We see him wielding his rapier at the Battle of La Rothière, in France, when he found himself surrounded by Uhlans. At Arcis-sur-Aube, he galloped into the fray that pitted the enemy cavalry against Sébastiani's (he subsequently reminisced that he wanted to die in that battle). Some time later he was nearly unsaddled when he forced his horse to sniff out a shell that exploded on contact. Then there was the fire in Moscow where he narrowly escaped the grips of his old foe *la faucheuse* (the Grim Reaper).

In addition to the dangers of the frontline, Napoleon also faced attempts on his life. On 13 October 1809, a young man called Friedrich Staps came at the Emperor with a knife as he was reviewing the troops outside the palace of Schönbrunn. In the event, Napoleon was miraculously spared and the blade that might have changed the course of history was carefully preserved for posterity (page 190).

But Napoleon didn't always get off so lightly. In Toulon, he received a bayonet wound to his thigh. In Egypt, at the taking of Ramanieh, he sustained serious bruising when he was struck by a horse's hoof. At the Battle of Ratisbon in April 1809, he was hit in the foot by a stray bullet; likewise at the battle of Esling a month later, where a furious General Walther, commander of the Grenadiers à Cheval of the imperial guard, threatened to have Napoleon removed by force unless he withdrew. No stranger to injury, the Emperor fortunately never went anywhere without a field surgeon's kit (page 206).

And where better to conduct a campaign than from the comfort of his own carriage! Napoleon's berlin landaus were as beautifully appointed as his apartments. They were offices on wheels, mobile replicas of his cabinet office complete with drawers, compartments, bookshelves, document holders — nothing was missing. For official visits, he would travel in style in a *berline riche* (a berlin reserved for town). The type of vehicle varied with the journey in question.

For Napoleon's "Hundred Days" he took delivery of a *dormeuse* (sleeper coach): a simple post coach where he could sleep as if in his own bed. It was this vehicle that would be looted by Prussian troops on the nights of 18 and 19 June at Waterloo. The looters seized the occasion to share out the Emperor's belongings, which included medals and a silver box (found under a seat) that they smashed with an axe.

At other times, Napoleon spent the night with local people or, failing that, in his tent. This was invariably erected in haste in the middle of the night: a large, rectangular blue-and-white striped twill campaign tent edged with red wool braid. There were two spaces within the tent: an anteroom and Napoleon's bedchamber, where his aides would assemble his iconic iron cot. The Emperor's last bed is on display at the Musée de l'Armée in Paris. It is the bed in which he died, scene of his very last battle.

1 For original French quotes, see Aiolfi Xavier, *Après tout je ne suis qu'un homme*. Barthélémy, October 2008.

2 Mademoiselle Avrillion, "first chambermaid to the Empress Josephine"; *Mémoires*. Mercure de France, April 2003. These memoirs can be considered apocryphal.

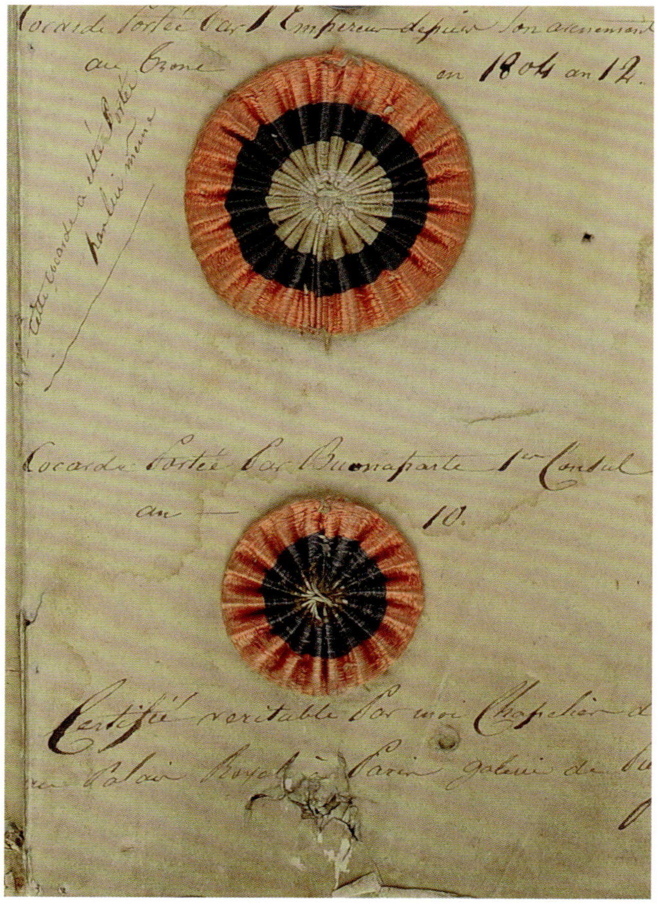

COCKADE FROM THE HAT OF BONAPARTE, FIRST CONSUL, WORN AT THE BATTLE OF MARENGO
COCKADE FROM THE EMPEROR'S HAT, WORN FROM 1804 ONWARDS

These two very rare tricolor cockades were worn successively by the First Consul and the Emperor. What is remarkable and unique is that they come straight from the archives of the Emperor's hatmaker, Poupard, where they have been stored on a piece of card from their era. An indication handwritten by Poupard himself under each of the cockades serves as confirmation: "Cockade worn by Bonaparte 1st Consul, Year 10" and "Cockade worn by the Emperor since his accession to the throne in 1804, Year 12. This cockade was worn by him", then, below the signature, "Certified genuine by myself, hatmaker to the Emperor, resident at Palais Royal in Paris, Galerie de Pierre no.72". Apart from these two, there are no other authentic Napoleon cockades in private hands. Only Poupard supplied the Emperor's personal cockades, which were highly specific and carefully stored by him when replacing the hats. The 1804 cockade, with a diameter of 4.9 cm, is the model most frequently used by Napoleon, red on the outside, then blue, then white in the center. Eleven have been listed but this is the only one that is no longer fitted to a hat. The First Consul's cockade is the only one of its kind. It is smaller, measuring barely 3.5 cm across and has no equivalent, even in the national museums. The oldest hat belonging to Bonaparte, First Consul, is the one worn at Marengo. It is conserved at the Musée de l'Armée in Paris and has lost its cockade.

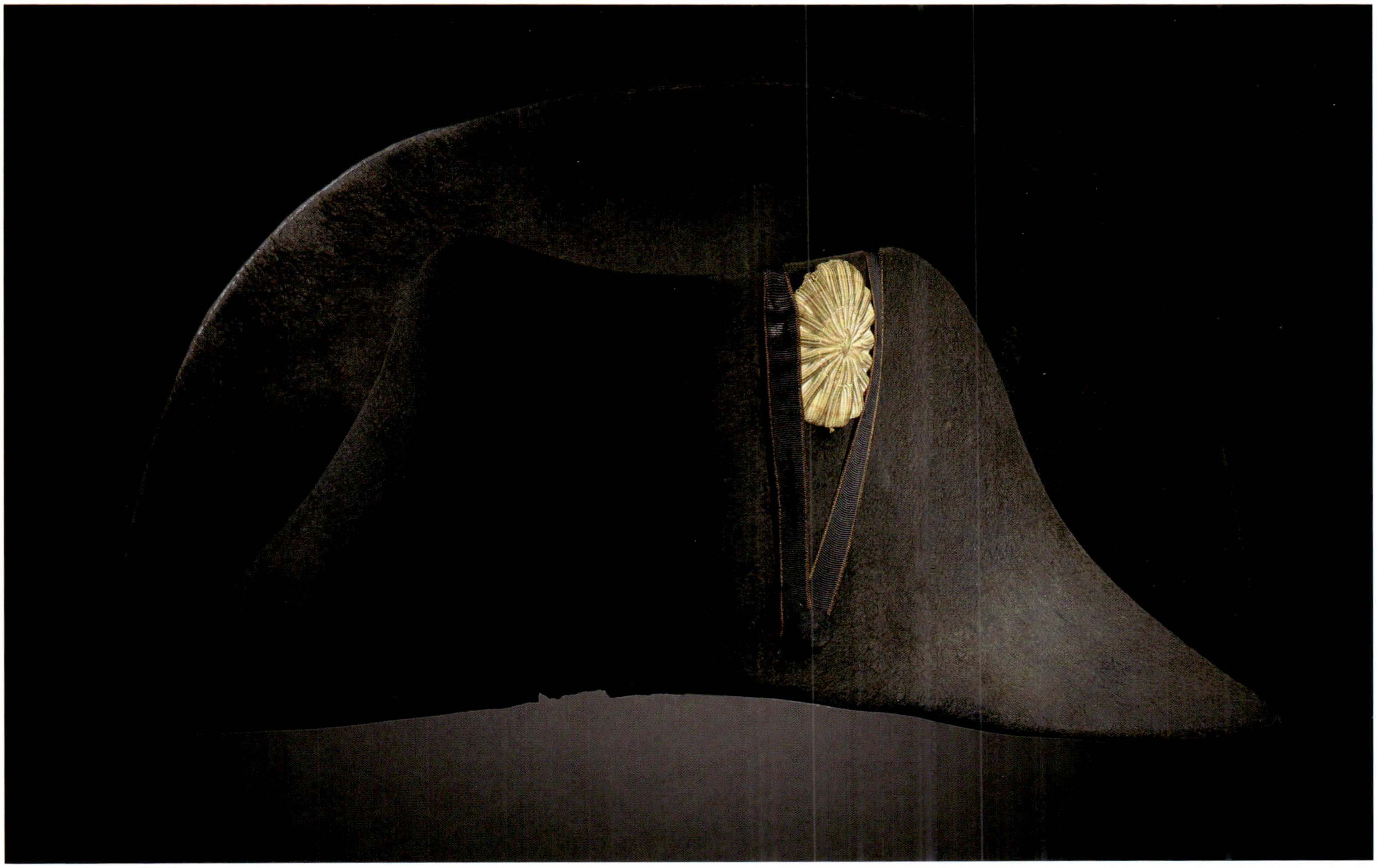

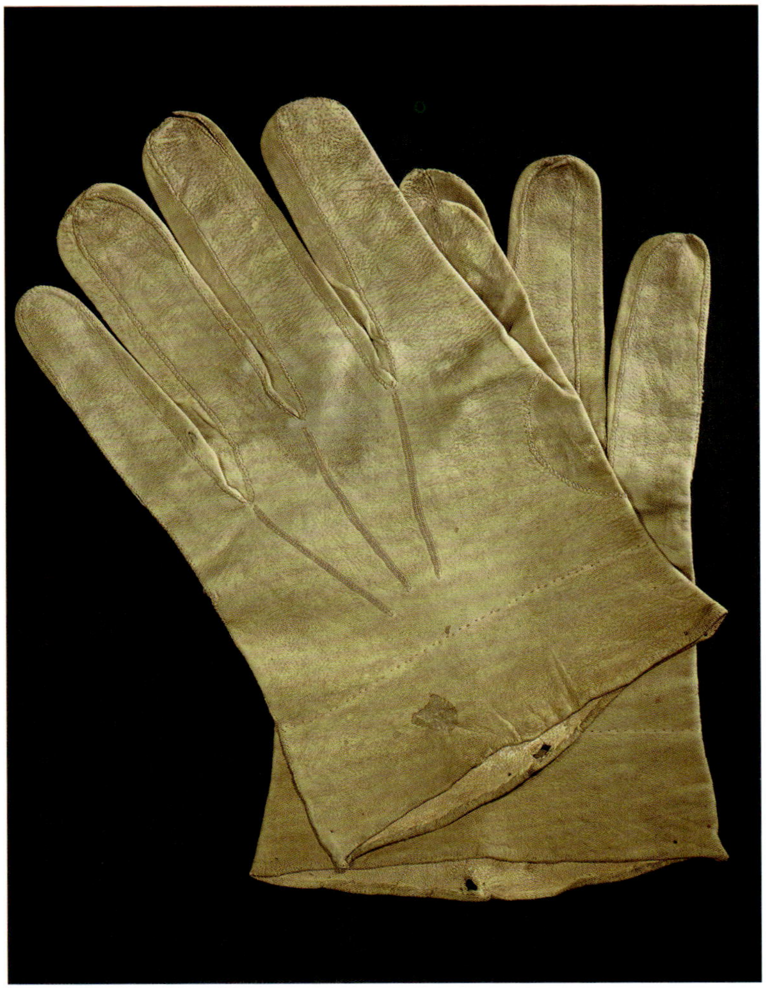

NAPOLEON'S BICORNE HAT, SUMMER 1810

Pictured here is 277 grams of pure history. Napoleon's iconic cocked hat, his so-called *chapeau français*, is a legend incarnate. It came from Palais Royal hatter Poupard, who is believed to have made some 120-170 such hats for the Emperor in his lifetime. Of these only 15 authentic examples survive today. The cockade on this hat is one of the few originals still extant and typical of the two styles worn by the Emperor: non-regulation, small, with the French national colors radiating out from the center, starting with white, then blue, white, red and white again. The dimensions of the hat depended on the season, ranging from 42 to 49 cm long and 20 to 26 cm high. Because the Emperor disliked cold weather, some of his hats had to be much bigger to accommodate a quilted silk lining. This required a corresponding increase in size to ensure an exact fit – up from 56.5 cm to 59 cm. The bicorne hat shown here comes down to us directly from François Berthet, private secretary of the Emperor's brother Jérôme Bonaparte, King of Westphalia, and executor of his estate.
It was exhibited during the "Napoleon and Paris, Dreams of a Capital" exhibition in Ottawa's Museum of Canadian History in 2016, which was held in conjunction with the Musée Carnavalet in Paris.

PAIR OF NAPOLEON'S LEATHER GLOVES

The Emperor had beautiful hands, which he took care to keep that way by protecting them in elegant gloves. Those pictured here, from the private collection of Prince Louis II, are among the only surviving examples and were for many years exhibited in the Napoleon Museum in Monaco.

MILITARY DISTINCTIONS

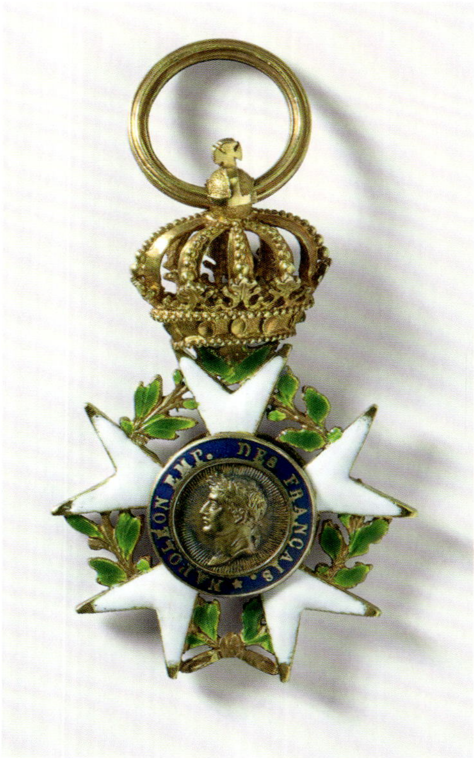

MARTIN GUILLAUME BIENNAIS (1764-1843), HALF-SIZE LEGION OF HONOR BELONGING TO NAPOLEON

Gold enameled Order of the Legion of Honor, Officer's Star, Third Type, Half Size, dated 1808. Part of Bertrand's inheritance, this medal was one of two *petites Légions d'Honneur* that appear in the inventory of effects taken by Marchand, Montholon and Bertrand on 8 May 1821, after Napoleon's death on St Helena. It was found in the mahogany box on the large desk in his study at Longwood, which also contained pencils, pens, rose water and tea from Napoleon's famous *nécessaire des batailles* (battle kit).

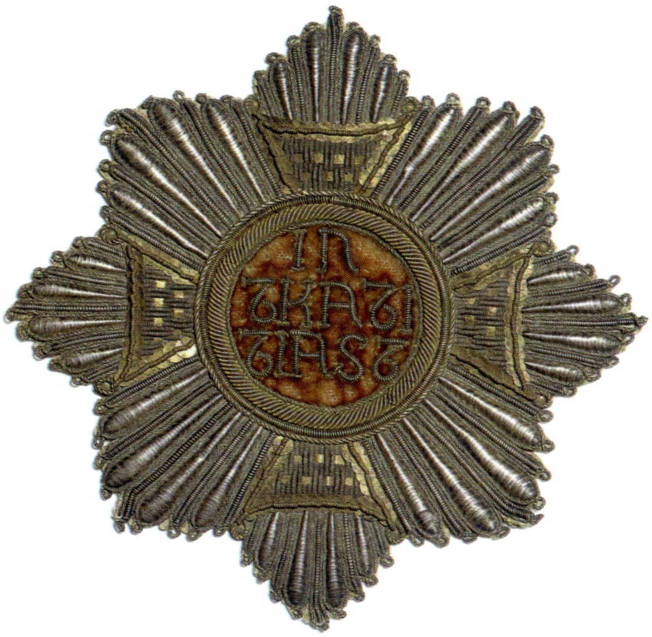

NAPOLEON'S BADGE OF THE BAVARIAN ORDER OF KNIGHTHOOD OF ST HUBERT

Bavaria joined the Empire when the King's daughter married Napoleon's stepson, Eugène de Beauharnais. This badge was discovered when the Emperor's famous Berlin landau was looted at Waterloo and comes from the private collection of Crown Prince Frederick VI of Denmark. Napoleon usually only wore the Legion of Honor and the Iron Cross but as sovereign he was entitled to all foreign decorations, which he was obliged to wear when on an official visit to the country in question. Hence the collection of decorations in his Berlin landau (his second home), most of which are now preserved in national museums.

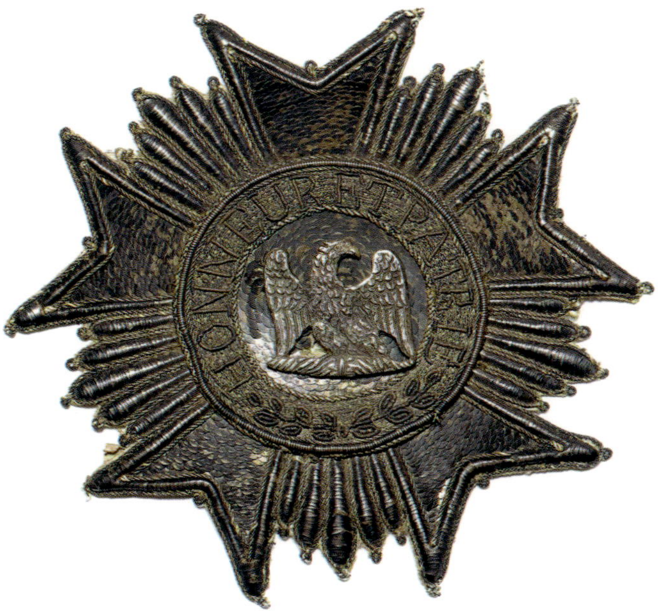

NAPOLEON'S BADGE OF THE GRAND EAGLE OF THE LEGION OF HONOR

As grand master and founder of the Order, the Emperor wore his Grand Aigle badge (now the Grand Croix de la Légion d'Honneur) sewn onto his clothes. A document on the letterhead of Armand Thierry de Ville d'Avray, Lord Steward of the Household of Louis XVIII, describes how the badge was found at the Tuileries after the "Hundred Days" and Waterloo, one of the few personal effects that Napoleon brought with him from Elba. Though inventoried, they were in poor condition and burnt by order of His Majesty with the exception of this badge.

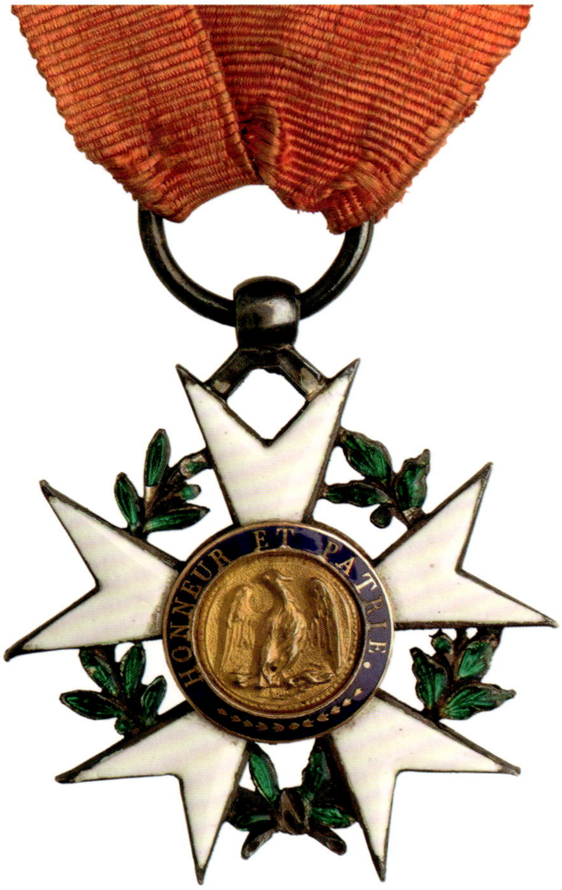

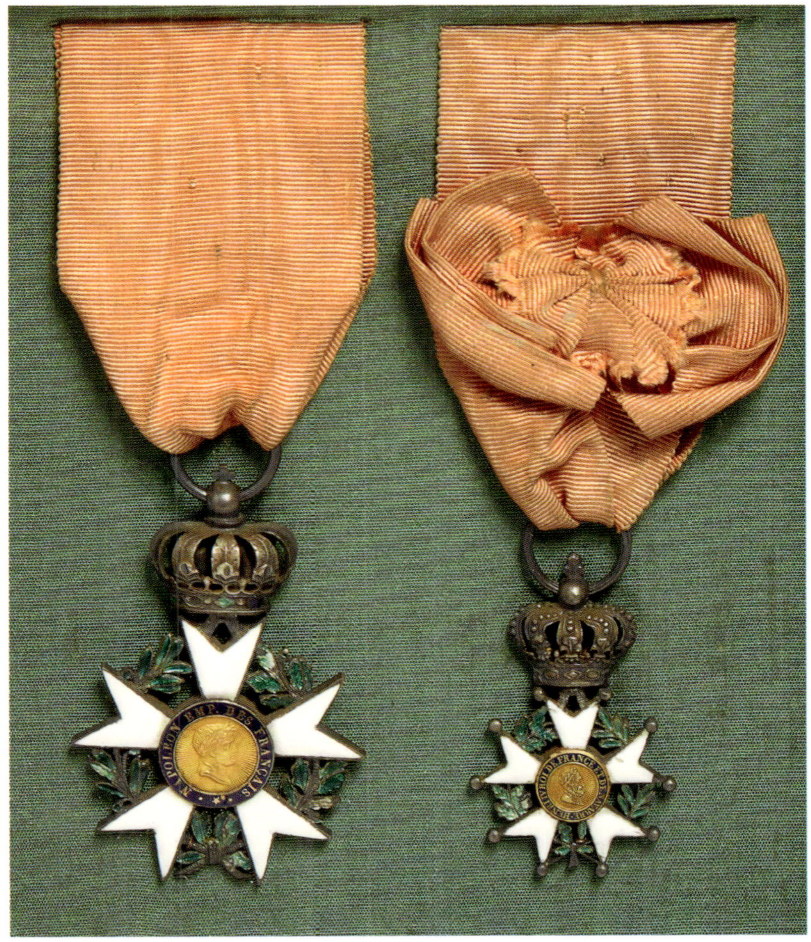

LEGION OF HONOR DECORATION WORN BY NAPOLEON, TAKEN AT WATERLOO

One of the first medal types, matching those from the first ceremonies at Les Invalides and the Boulogne Camp. Made from enameled silver and gold, this small Legion of Honor decoration is the one worn by Napoleon at Waterloo. Removed from the Emperor's "best" uniform, as indicated by the letter dated 17 July 1815 from the Prussian officer named Otto, it was seized by enemy troops at the Vieux Genappe farm as the Napoleonic troops took flight. The same officer picked up other personal objects belonging to the Emperor, including three Biennais silver plates from the campaign service and engraved with the coat-of-arms, and the round tortoiseshell bonbonnière of licorice that Napoleon always kept in his pocket. This unique set of objects went on show at the Museum of the Legion of Honor in Paris in 2012, at an exhibition entitled *La Berline de Napoléon*.

LEGION OF HONOR DECORATION WORN BY NAPOLEON AND GIVEN TO PAINTER GROS, AND ONE BELONGING TO DAVID

Of these two Legion of Honor medals, the smaller one is that of painter Jacques-Louis David and the larger one was Napoleon's. Both were offered to painter Antoine-Jean Gros. They have been framed and are identified in a document written by Gros and attached to the back: "When Monsieur David was appointed Officer in 1808, he gave me this small cross, which he wore regularly, so that I could wear it as I had just been awarded the Legion of Honor by the Emperor that year. I received the larger one from the Emperor himself." It is a well-known story. At the 1808 Salon de Paris, Napoleon decided to play a trick on Gros. The artists to be honored had all been named, apart from Gros, who became very distressed about it. Then the Emperor removed his own Legion of Honor from his chest and offered it to the painter. The story of Gros receiving his decoration from the Emperor himself was recorded by his biographer and pupil, Jean-Baptiste Delestre. David's model, worn by Gros until the Restoration, was altered at that time.

ORDER OF THE THREE GOLDEN FLEECES

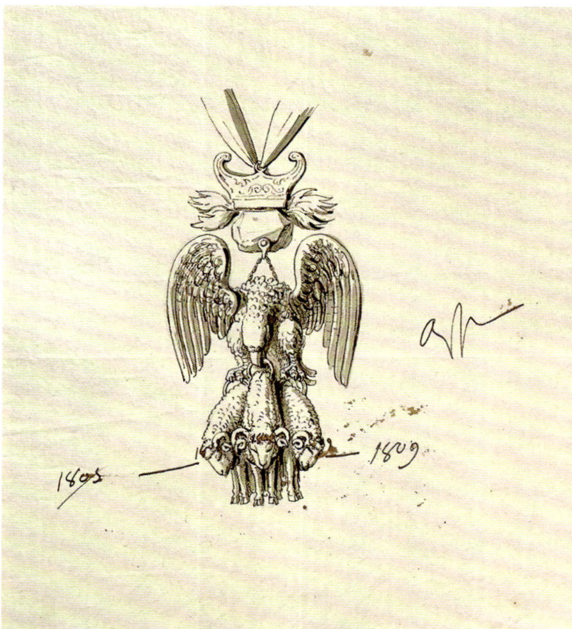

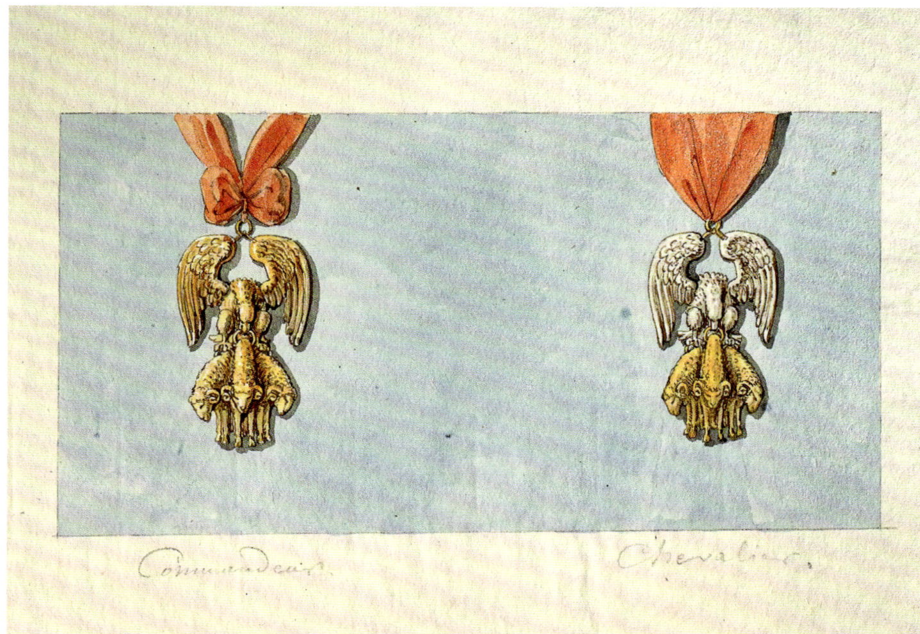

JACQUES-LOUIS DAVID (1748-1825), PREPARATORY DRAWINGS

As these enhanced drawings illustrate, David put forward several variants for this new Order to Napoleon. This first includes the initials of the Emperor, attesting to his desire to follow the project's progress.

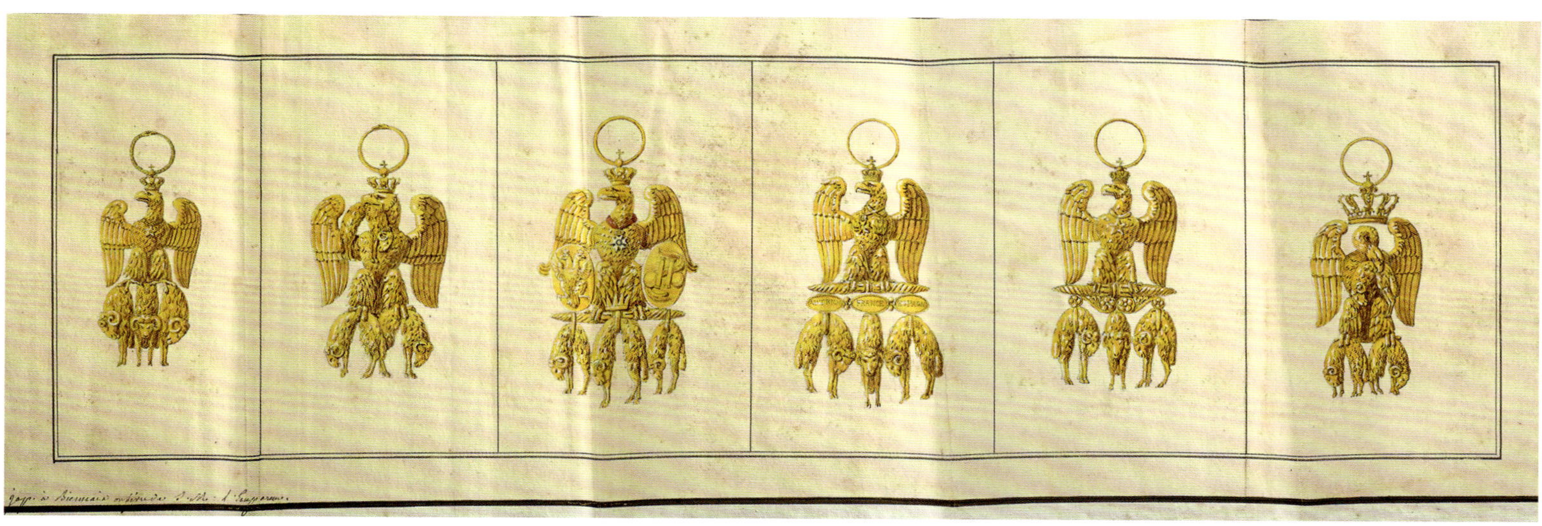

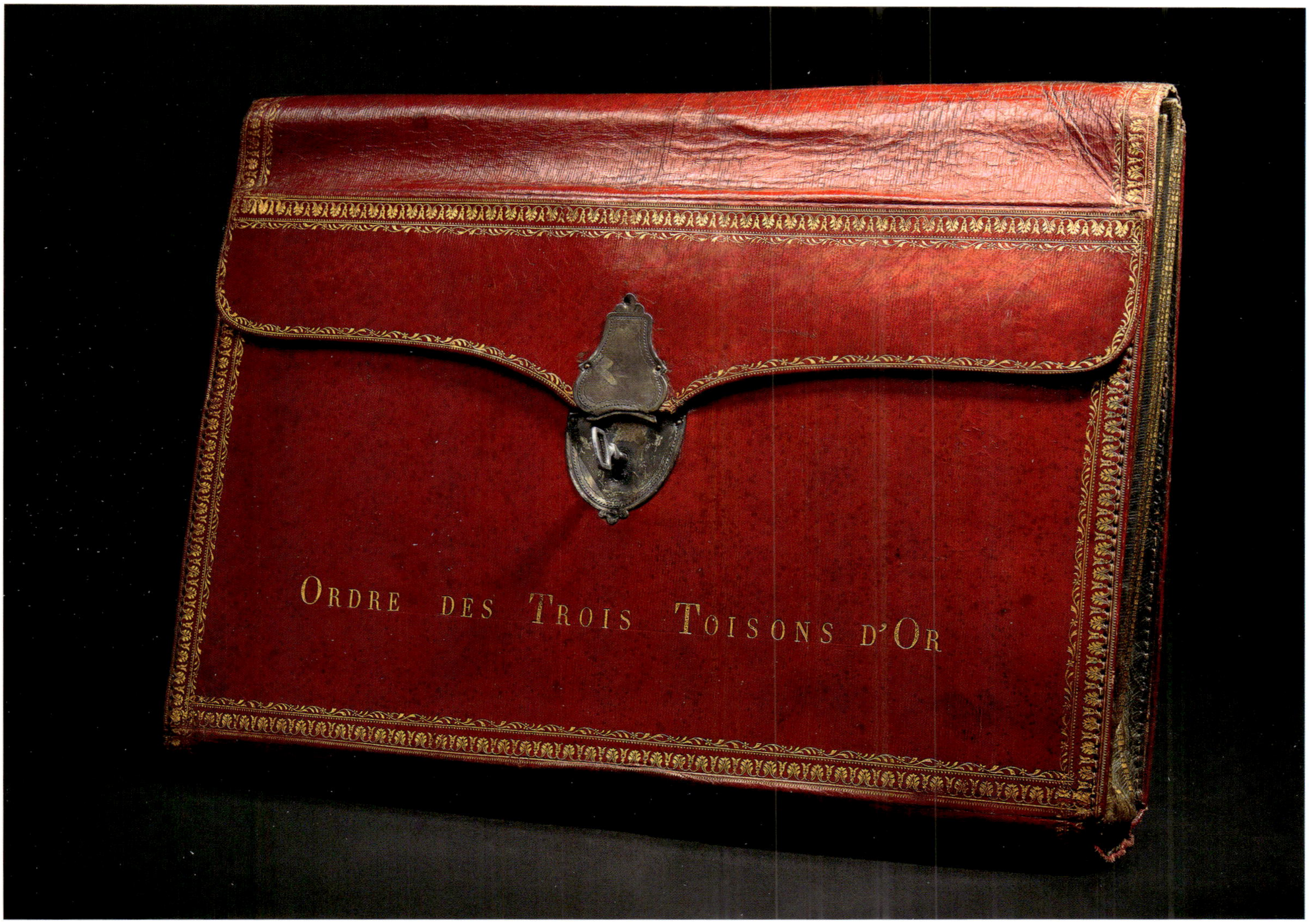

PERSONAL PORTFOLIO OF NAPOLEON, USED FOR THE ORDER OF THE THREE GOLDEN FLEECES AND PREPARATORY DOSSIER

"My eagles have triumphed over the Golden Fleeces of the King of Spain and the Emperors of Germany, so I mean to create for the French Empire an Imperial Order of the Three Golden Fleeces. The sign of this Order shall be my own Eagle with outspread wings, holding in each of its talons one of the ancient Golden Fleeces it has carried off whilst, hanging from its beak, it will proudly display the Fleece I now institute". With these words, Napoleon decided to create a new decoration on 15 August 1809. After crowning his brother Joseph King of Spain on 5 June 1806 and overcoming Austria at Wagram on 6 July 1809, the Emperor was keen to establish an order bringing together the Spanish and Austrian Golden Fleeces and adding a French branch. He referred to the ancient myth of Jason and the Golden Fleece. The golden insignia represents three rams' corpses hanging from a central piece, surmounted by a crowned eagle, its wings outspread, and a blue stone from which orange-colored flares stem on each side.
However, despite the fact that his project was ready from a legal viewpoint, the model for the insignia selected, medalmaker Coudray chosen to produce it, and a list of the first awardees drawn up, Napoleon abandoned his plans; after marrying Marie-Louise, archduchess of Austria, he preferred not to upset his father-in-law, who did not wish to see his own order disappear. In the end the medal was never distributed and the Order was dissolved by Napoleon on 27 September 1813.
Important elements were contained in this red Morocco leather portfolio, including the preparatory drawings requested by Vivant Denon from some major artists of the time, such as David, Biennais and Lejeune, and supplement those conserved at the Museum of the Legion of Honor.

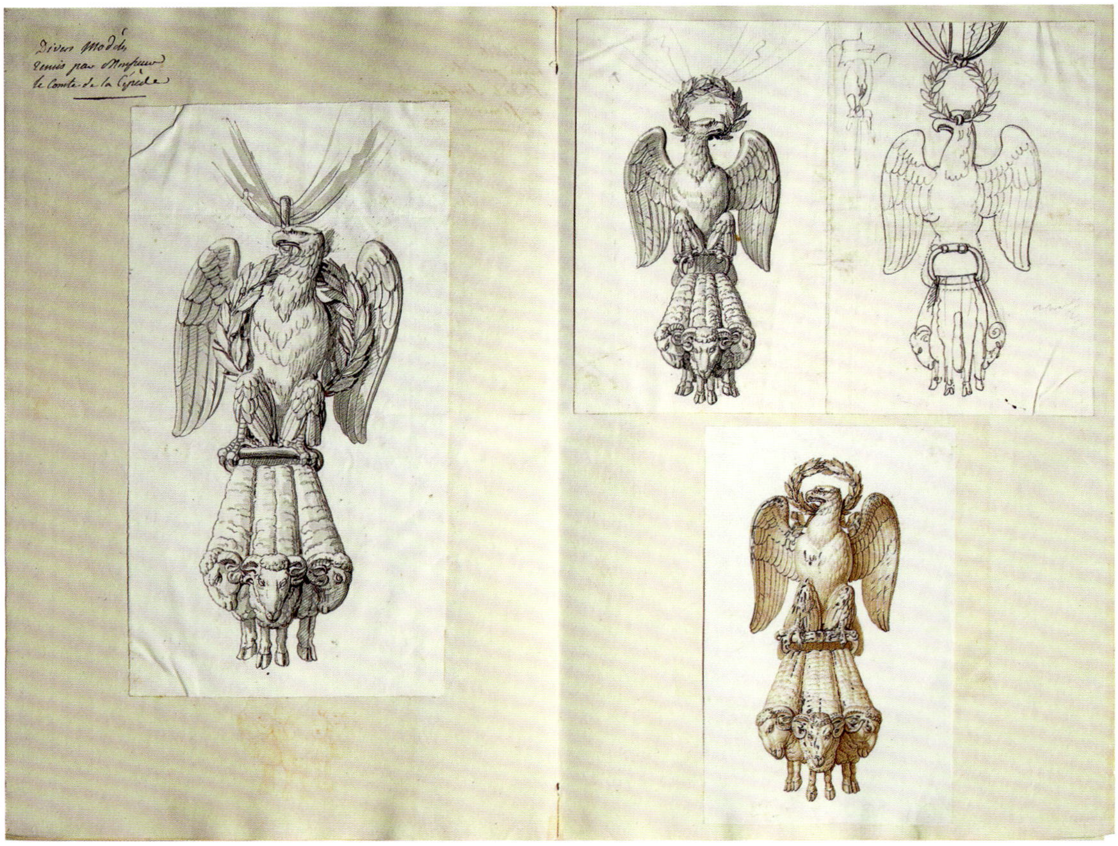

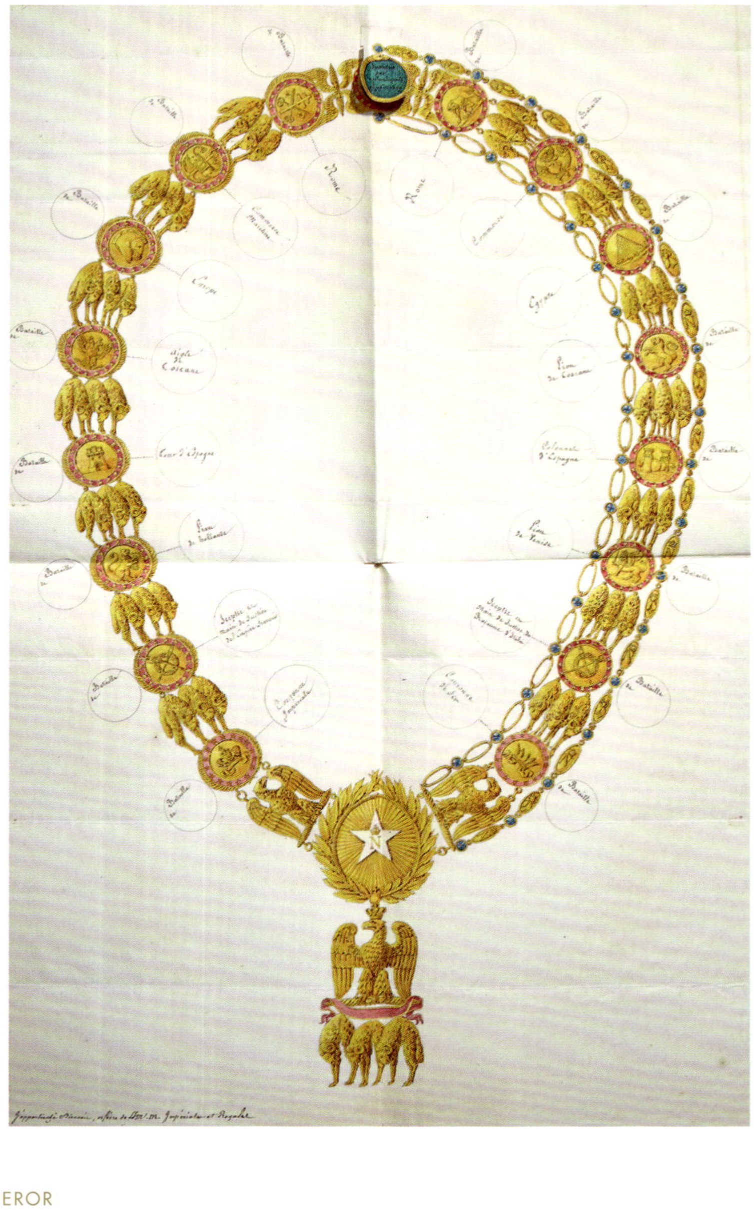

MARTIN-GUILLAUME BIENNAIS (1764-1843), PREPARATORY DRAWING FOR THE COLLAR OF THE ORDER OF THE THREE GOLDEN FLEECES AND OTHER DRAWINGS

The portfolio also contains plates from Biennais, including these versions of the decoration design, plus a proposal for the Collar. The attention given to this project is remarkable, as illustrated by the extraordinary quality of this drawing, enhanced with gold.

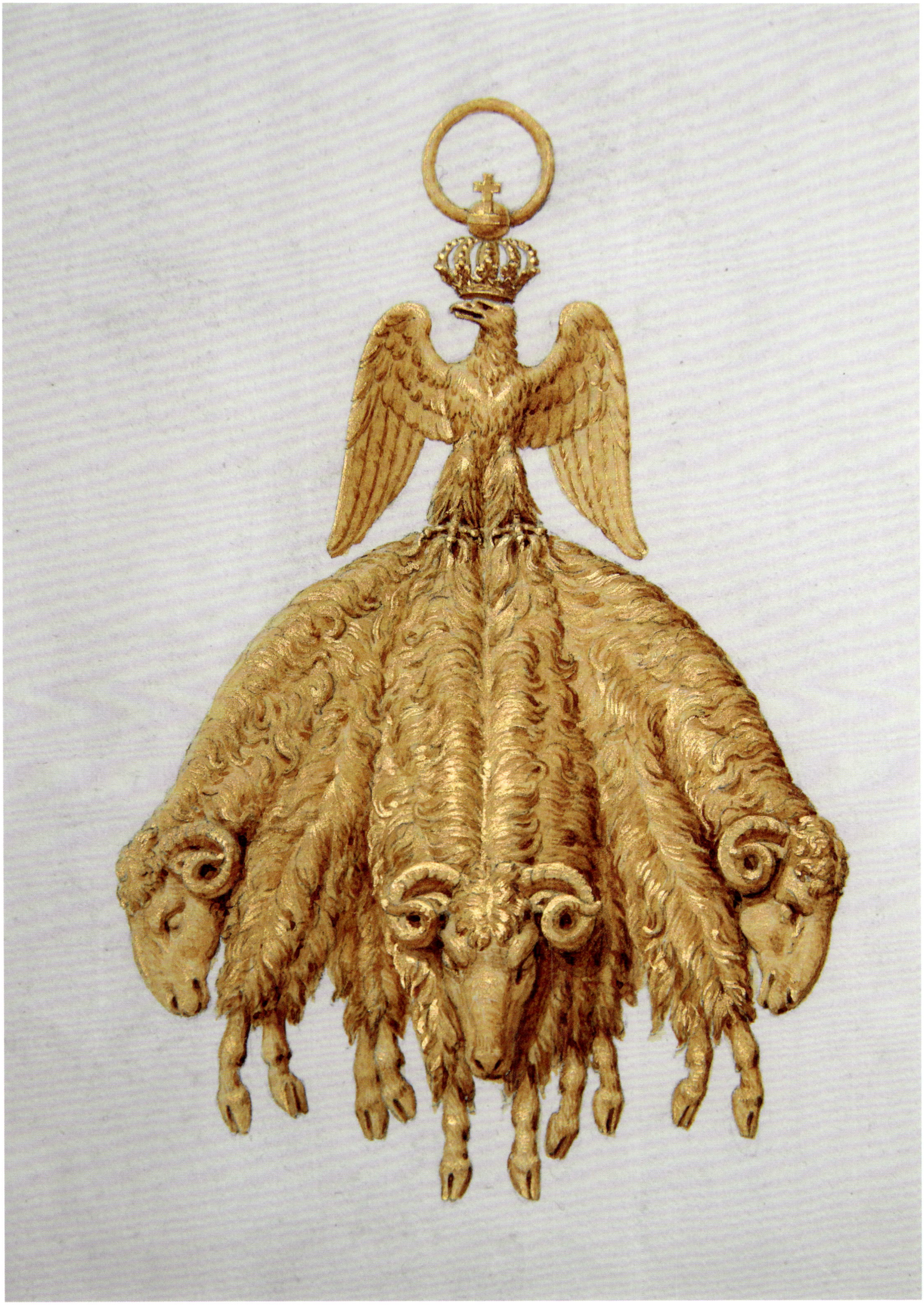

CAMBACÉRÈS

SÈVRES IMPERIAL MANUFACTORY, PLATES FROM THE SERVICE OF ARCHCHANCELLOR CAMBACÉRÈS

This superb set of Sèvres porcelain plates is largely the work of foremost early 19th century artists Swebach, Lebel, Robert and Caron, featuring landscapes, imperial palaces and fables against a purple background. The set was a gift from Napoleon to Archchancellor Cambacérès to celebrate the marriage of Stéphanie de Beauharnais, Josephine's niece, to Charles Frederick, Grand Duke of Baden. Their union on 7 April 1807 sealed an important political alliance for the Emperor. The Duke having joined the Rhine Confederation in 1806, the marriage placed the House of Bonaparte among the great European dynasties.

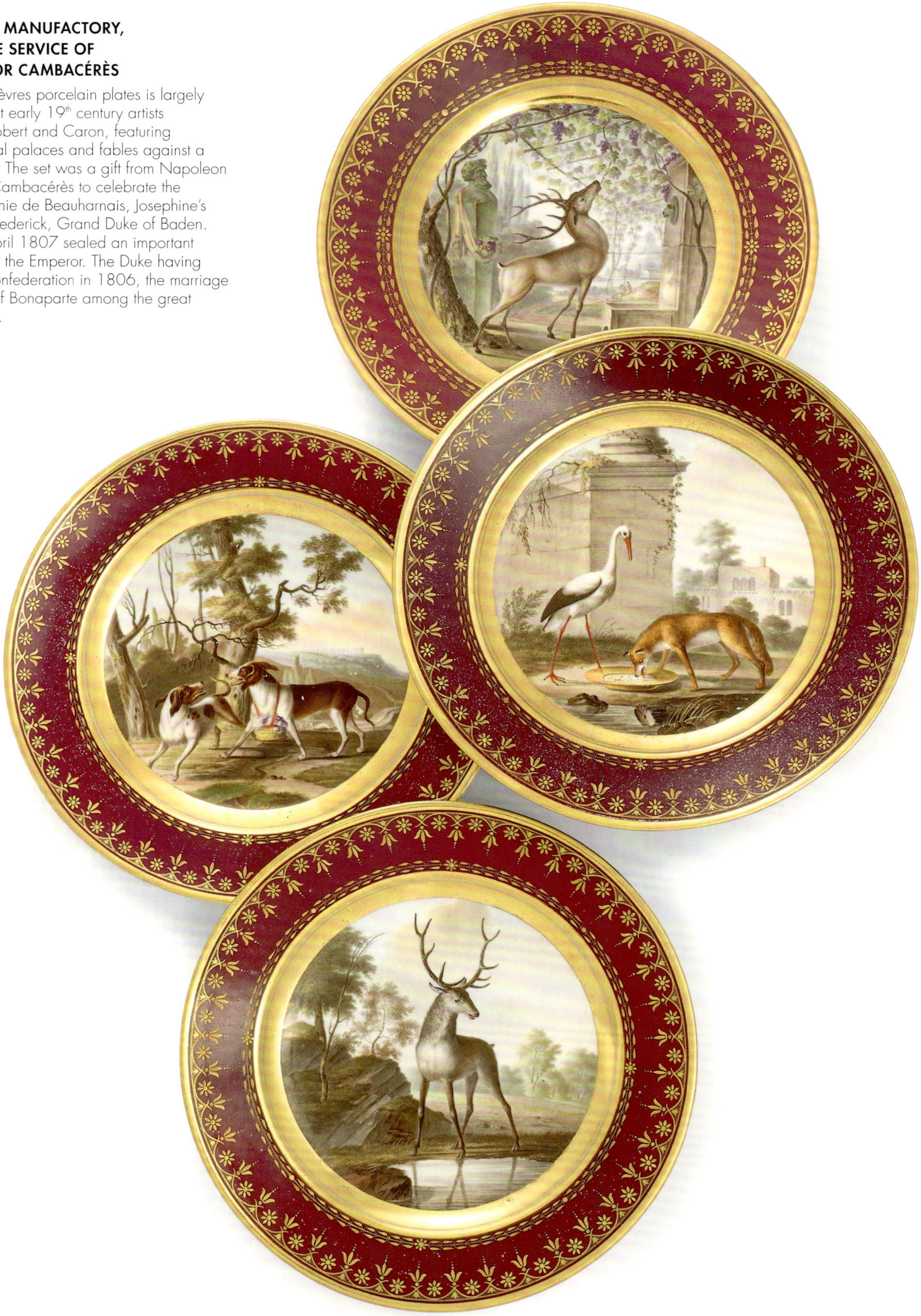

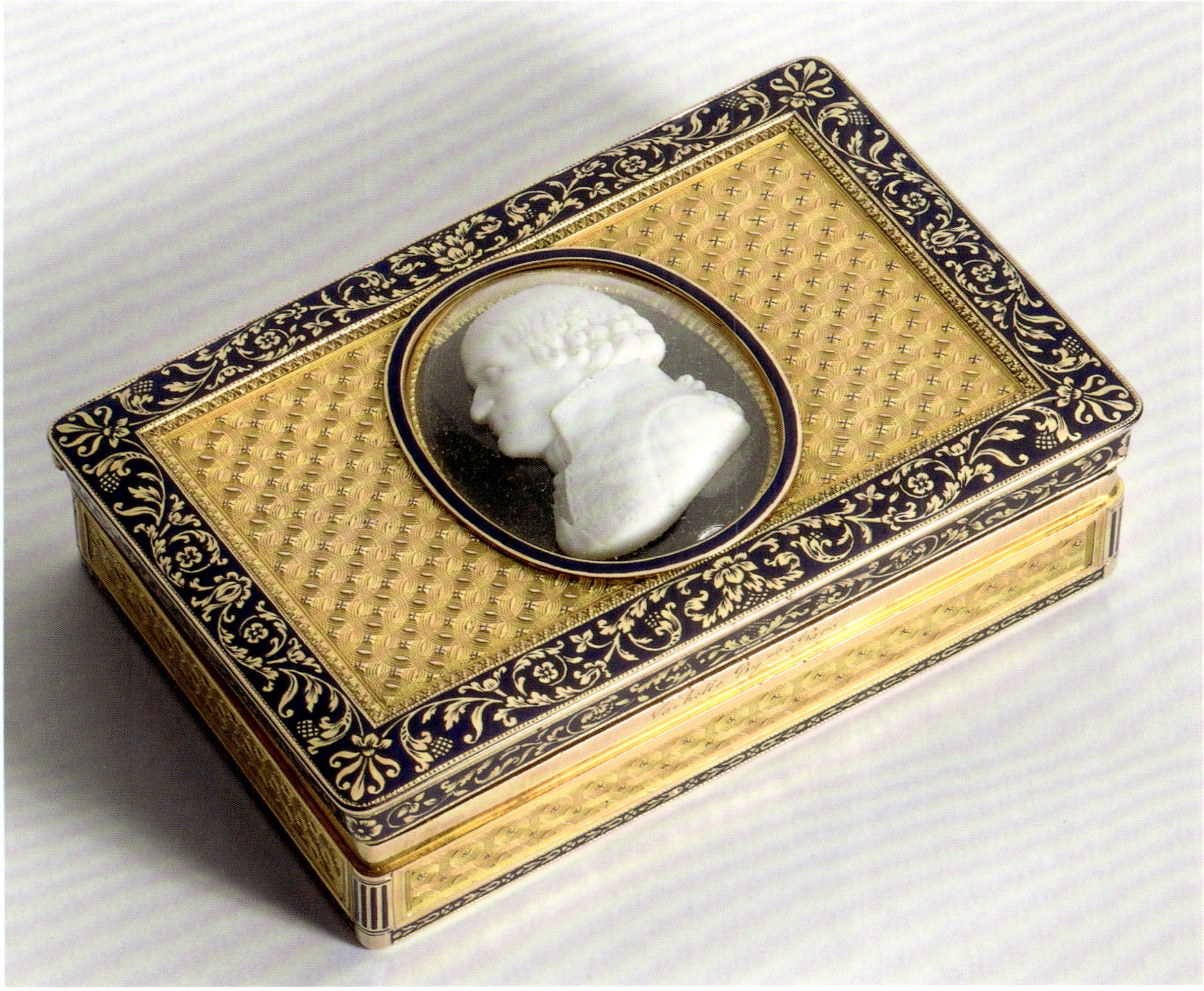

ADRIEN JEAN MAXIMILIEN VACHETTE (1753-1839), SNUFFBOX WITH PORTRAIT OF SECOND CONSUL CAMBACÉRÈS

An agate cameo of the Second Consul by master stone carver Lelievre is the centerpiece for this pretty blue-enameled gold snuffbox by French goldsmith Vachette. Though it was hardstone snuffboxes like this one that really made his reputation, Vachette was also a talented miniature portrait painter skilled in the application of lacquer, green aventurine glass and émail (enamel).

THE FIRST CIVIL CODE (1802)

NAPOLEONIC CODE, ONE OF THE EMPEROR'S PERSONAL COPIES

This volume is the original and only official copy of the Napoleonic Code, later referred to as the Civil Code. Bound with tree marbling, it features the imperial coat-of-arms gold-tooled in the center of the front cover and the smooth back is marked with eagles and a gold star.

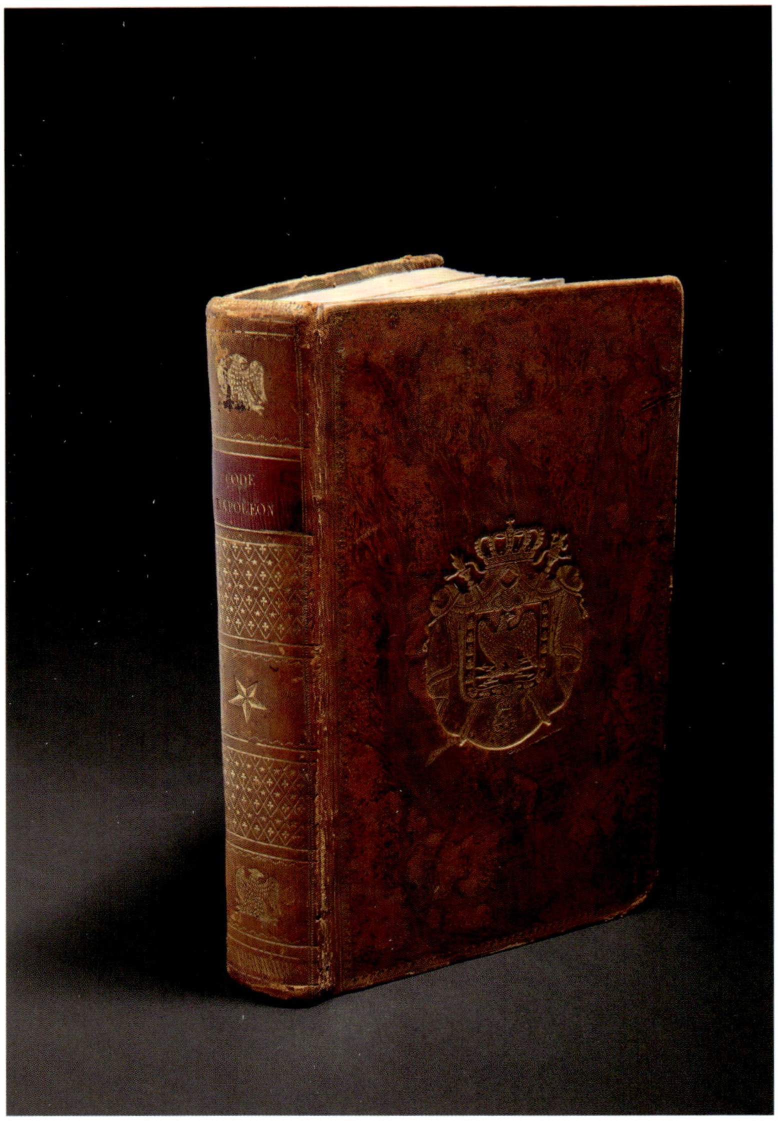

THE VERY FIRST CIVIL CODE, THE ONLY KNOWN COPY DATED 1802

This "Civil Code or Compendium containing the legal texts decreed in Year XI by the National Legislature with the enacting clauses pronounced by the First Consul" printed in "Paris, by Rondonneau, Imprimerie du Dépôt des Lois [printers], Place du Carrousel, Year XI -1802", is the first known copy of the "Civil Code" or "Napoleonic Code". It is dated 1802 (Year XI on the Revolutionary Calendar, between 23 September and 31 December), although the first printed copies of the Code date from 1803 (Year XI, between 1 January and 23 September). There is no other copy bearing this date listed in the public libraries, including the National Library. It also contains handwritten notes in the margins, probably left by one of the drafters to whom this copy no doubt belonged. On 14 August 1800, the First Consul had appointed a commission of four experienced jurists: François Denis Tronchet, Félix Julien Jean Bigot de Préameneu, Jean Etienne Marie Portalis and Jacques de Maleville, to draft the Code, overseen by Jean-Jacques-Régis de Cambacérès. The Civil Code was then voted and promulgated by the First Consul on 21 March 1804 (30 Ventôse Year XII). Civil law was applied in many countries after the Napoleonic Wars. Designed to establish a unified law system by reconciling the Revolution and the Ancien Régime, it owes its success to its simplicity based on four principles: clarity of the law, secularism, individual ownership of property, and employment free from servile obligations. Napoleon had the vision of a great leader. His ambition for political unification and power of the State forced him to unify the law, guaranteeing a minimum degree of civil liberty to citizens, from their birth to the time of their death. At St Helena, he said: "My real glory is not the 40 battles I won – for my defeat at Waterloo will destroy the memory of those victories. What nothing will destroy, what will live forever, is my Civil Code". It is now the most widespread legal framework found across the world, which gives this first 1802 copy – the only one of its kind – unparalleled historical and symbolic significance.

ONLY KNOWN COPY OF THE FIRST PUBLISHED VERSION OF THE MARTINIQUE CIVIL CODE, 1805

This "French Civil Code of Martinique" printed at "Imprimerie de Thounens, père et fils, government printers, Year XIII [1805]", for the Island of Martinique, which contains an array of handwritten annotations in the margins, probably left by Thounens, is valuable in several respects. Firstly, because no other copy is known or listed in the French public libraries, including the National Library and libraries in Martinique. More importantly, however, the 1804 Civil Code, subsequently promulgated in Martinique on 7 November 1805 (16 Brumaire, Year XIV), should not obscure the fact that Bonaparte, probably influenced by Josephine whose family owned large plantations in Martinique, legalized slavery and the slave trade in the decree of 20 May 1802, at the cost of fierce repression in the French West Indies. Marking a break with the Declaration of the Rights of Man and of the Citizen of 1789 and going back on the revolutionary ideals that had abolished slavery in the decree of Pluviôse 1794, this Code for Martinique, which also applied to Guadeloupe and Guyana, may have contained the principles of civil liberty and equality, but only applied to white "French" people, thus excluding slaves after the reinstatement of slavery in 1802. From 1805 to 1848, the date slavery was finally abolished for good, two Codes applied in the French overseas colonies: the Black Code, signed by Louis XIV in 1685, which established the black slave as a person deprived of all legal capacity, and the Civil Code. This very rare, unique document, an important symbol and significant for its remembrance value, reminds us that Bonaparte's reinstatement of slavery in 1802 is quite likely the most inexplicable and unjustifiable decision in Napoleonic history.

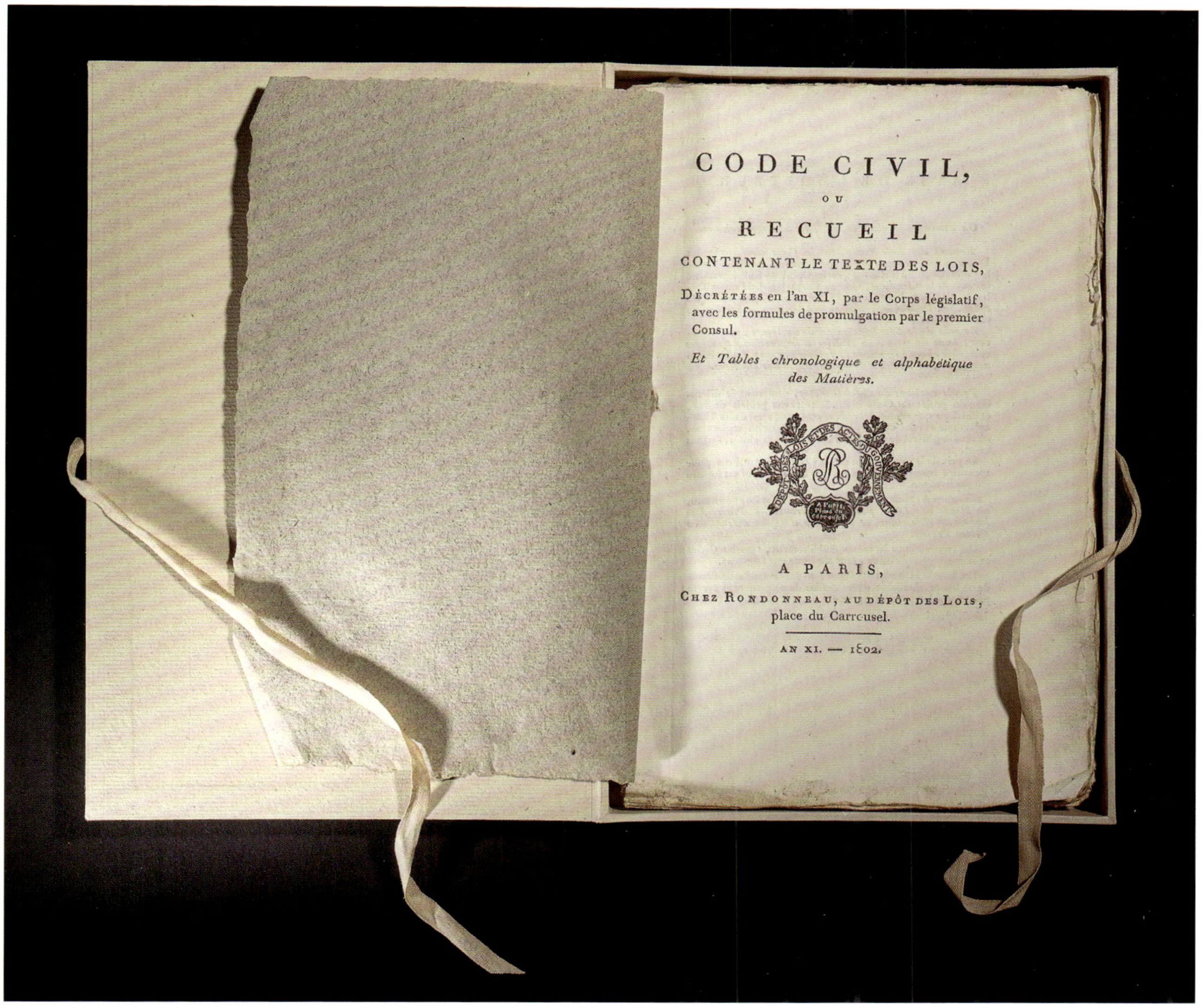
CODE CIVIL,
OU
RECUEIL
CONTENANT LE TEXTE DES LOIS,
Décrétées en l'an XI, par le Corps législatif, avec les formules de promulgation par le premier Consul.
Et Tables chronologique et alphabétique des Matières.
A PARIS,
Chez Rondonneau, au dépôt des Lois, place du Carrousel.
An XI. — 1802.

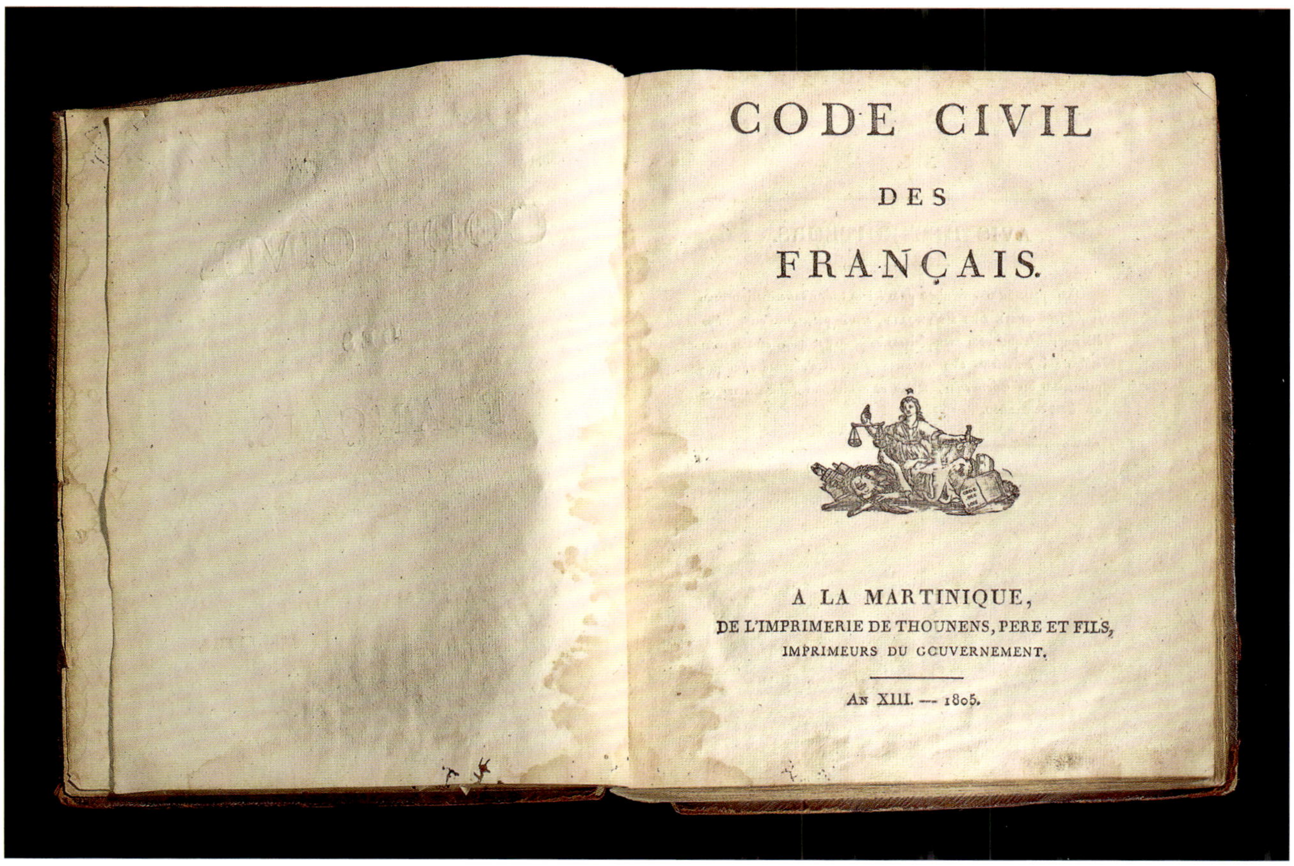
CODE CIVIL
DES
FRANÇAIS.
A LA MARTINIQUE,
DE L'IMPRIMERIE DE THOUNENS, PERE ET FILS,
IMPRIMEURS DU GOUVERNEMENT.
An XIII. — 1805.

BATTLES

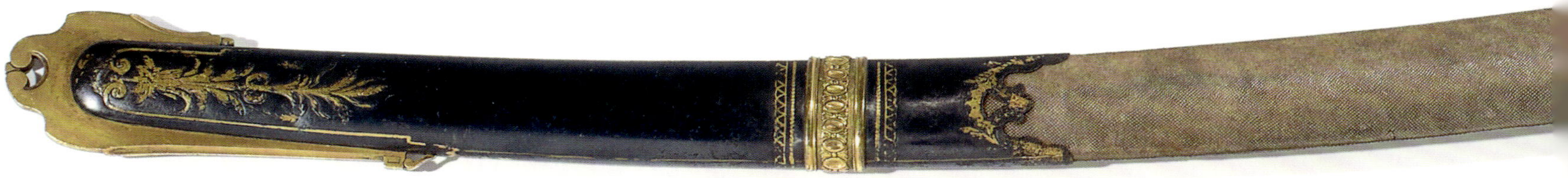

NICOLAS-NOËL BOUTET (1761-1833), DELUXE SABER THAT POSSIBLY BELONGED TO BONAPARTE

This magnificent, very rare deluxe saber comes from the renowned Manufacture d'Armes in Versailles, of which the famous armorer Boutet was appointed "artistic director" in 1792. Its originality and close similarity with the saber of Bonaparte, First Consul, kept at the Musée de l'Armée, suggests they belonged to the same person. However, as the manufacturer's archives have been lost, we cannot be sure today.

LOUIS LAFITTE (1770-1828), *LA PAIX D'AMIENS*, 1802

Large pen and ink drawing by Lafitte depicting the First Consul receiving the signatories of the Treaty of Amiens. The treaty was signed on 25 March 1802 between Britain on the one hand, and France, Spain and the Batavian Republic on the other hand, bringing temporary peace to Europe. Seen behind Bonaparte is a colossal, plinth-mounted, seated statue of the Republic, which holds a terrestrial globe in one hand, supporting the muse Fame, and in the other hand the Sword of Justice.

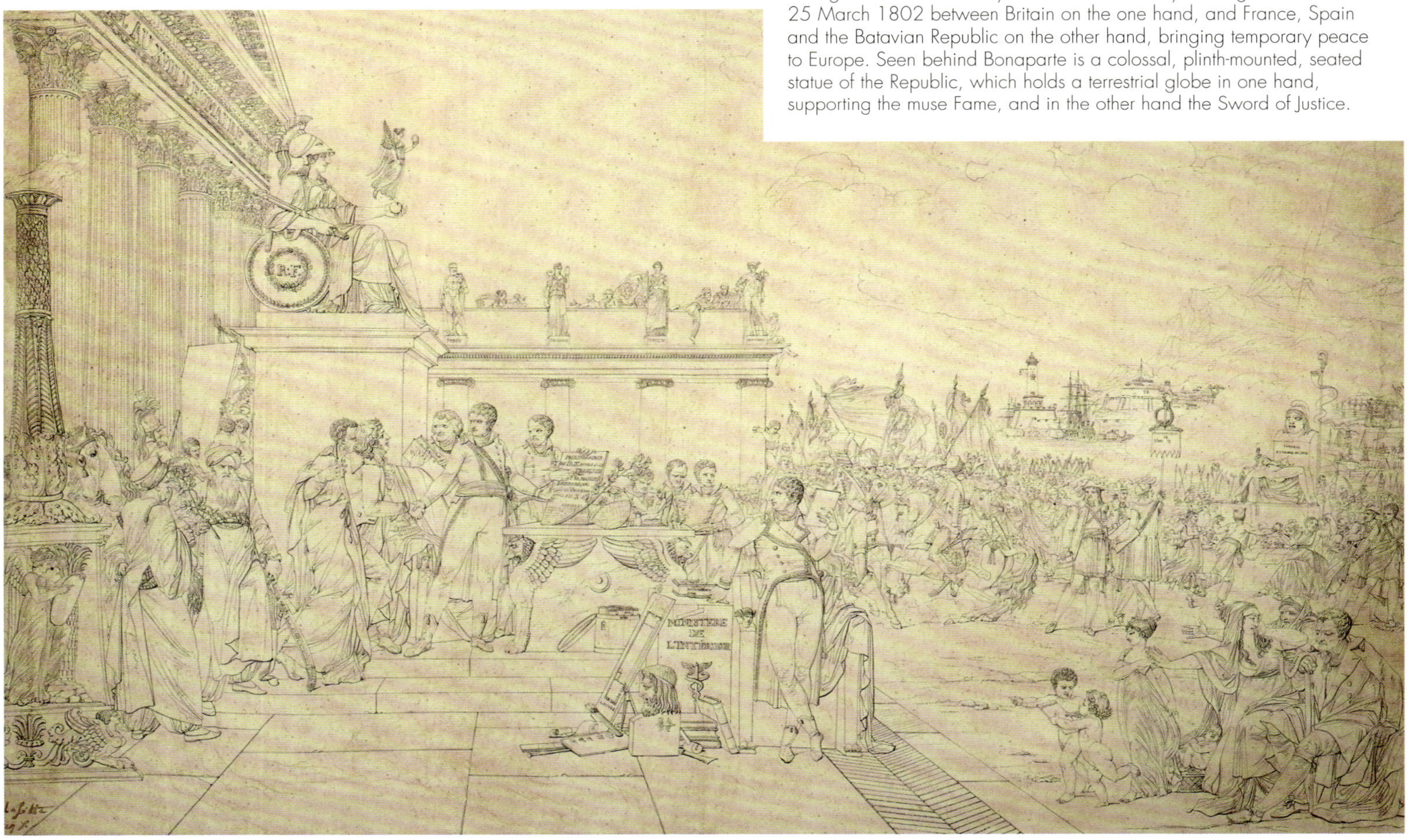

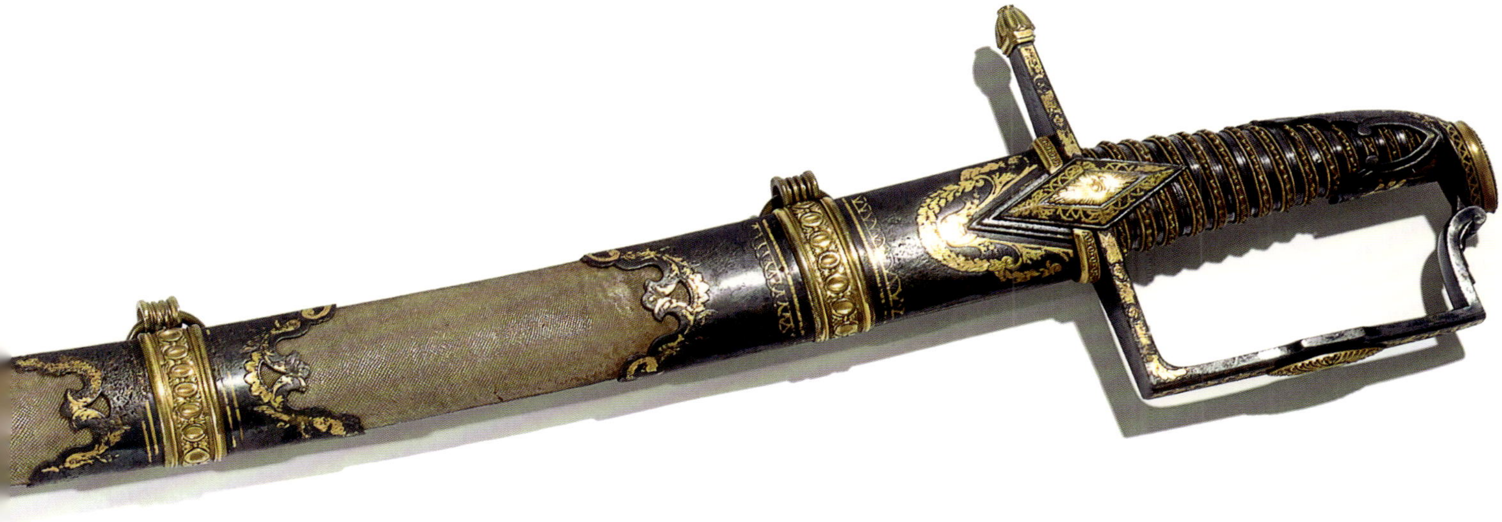

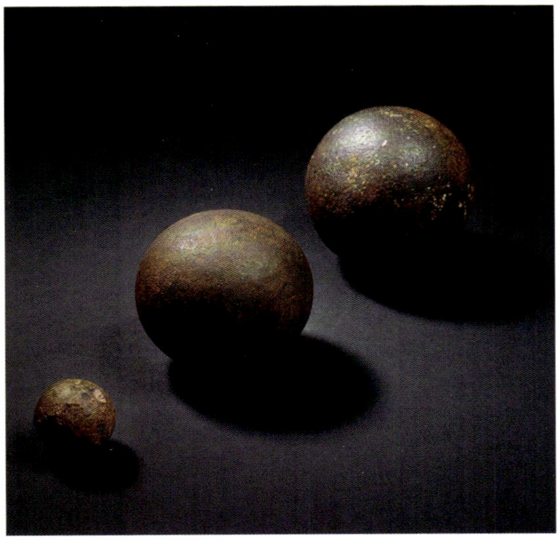

CANNONBALLS FOUND ON THE BATTLEFIELD OF WATERLOO

"Waterloo, dismal plain..." These three words from Victor Hugo's poem *Expiation* capture the tragedy of Napoleon's last battle. Waterloo, that fearful name that sounded the death knell for the glory of France now inspires only sadness – painful memories of a bloody battlefield that still today spews out its relics.

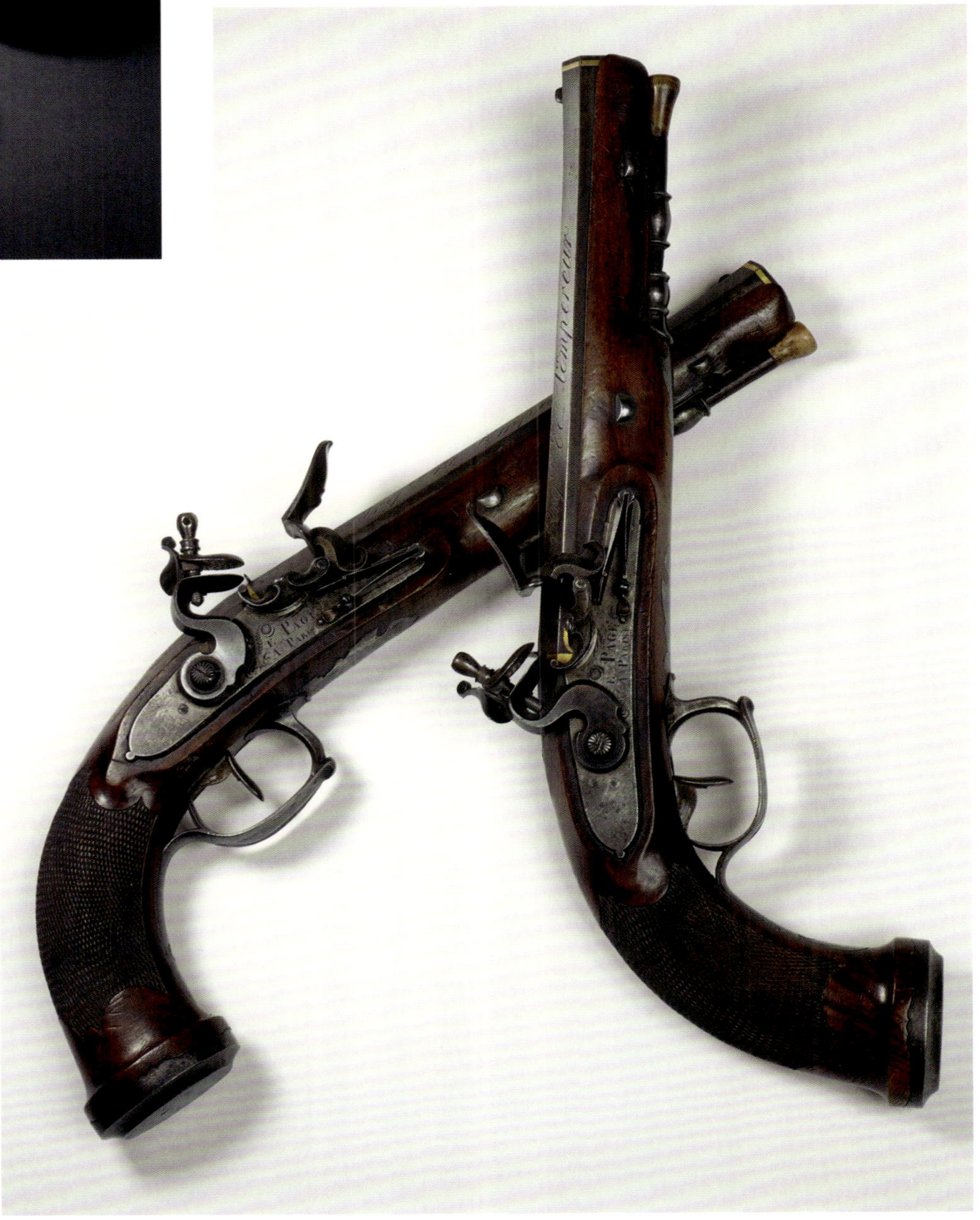

JEAN LE PAGE (1746-1834), PAIR OF PISTOLETS OWNED BY NAPOLEON

Napoleon's Austerlitz sword is famous in history, but his pistols also deserve mention. The pair pictured here were part of a series he commissioned for his personal use, 10 pairs in January 1812 and 13 in February, manufactured by Le Page. Though we know their serial numbers, the pistols themselves have largely been lost to history. These have octagonal, blue-black barrels, gilded muzzle and striker plate, walnut butt and hatched grip. Pistols like these were standard issue following the ruling of 1 Vendémiaire Year XII – but not all of them were specially made by the most famous gunsmith of the period.

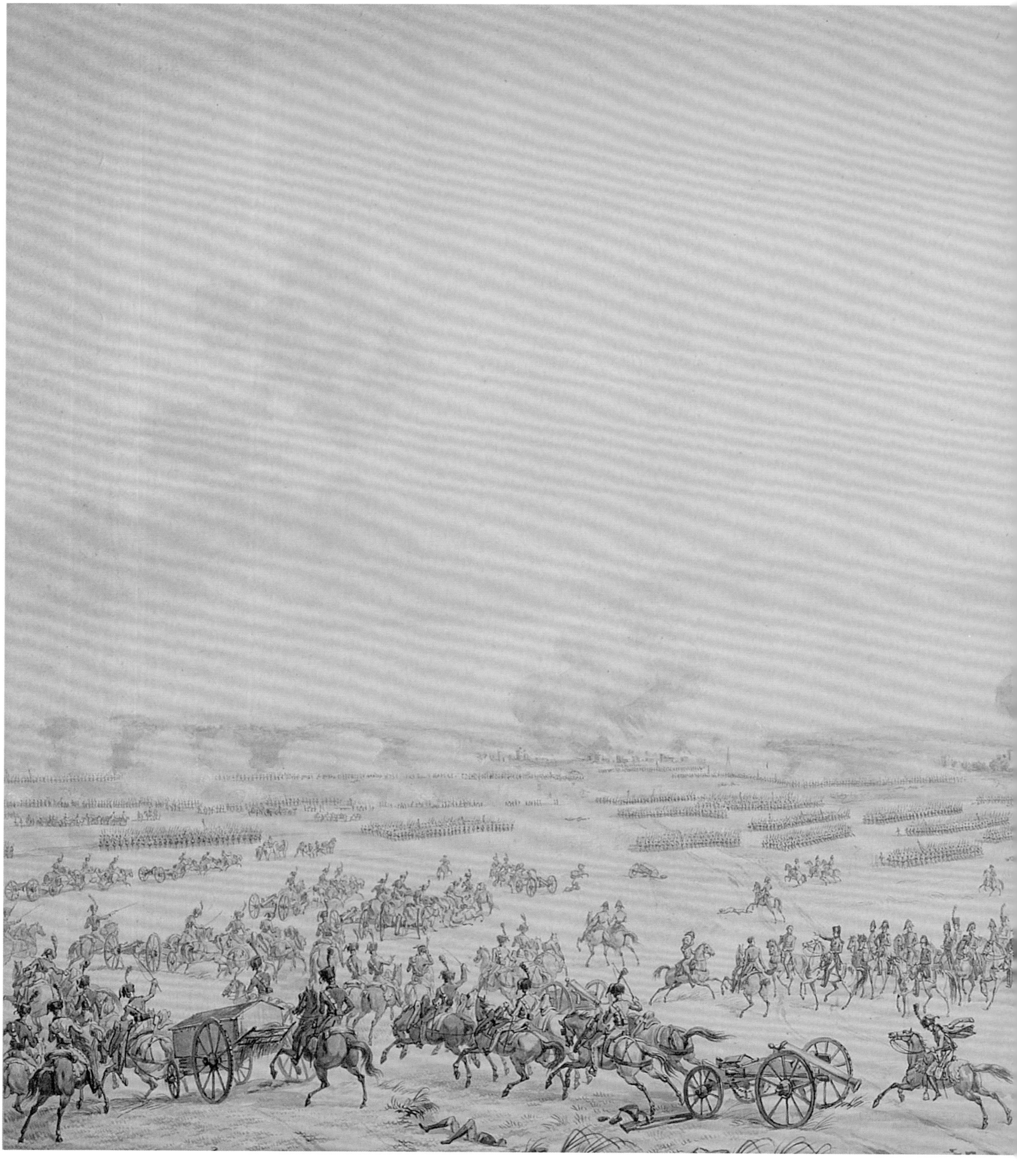

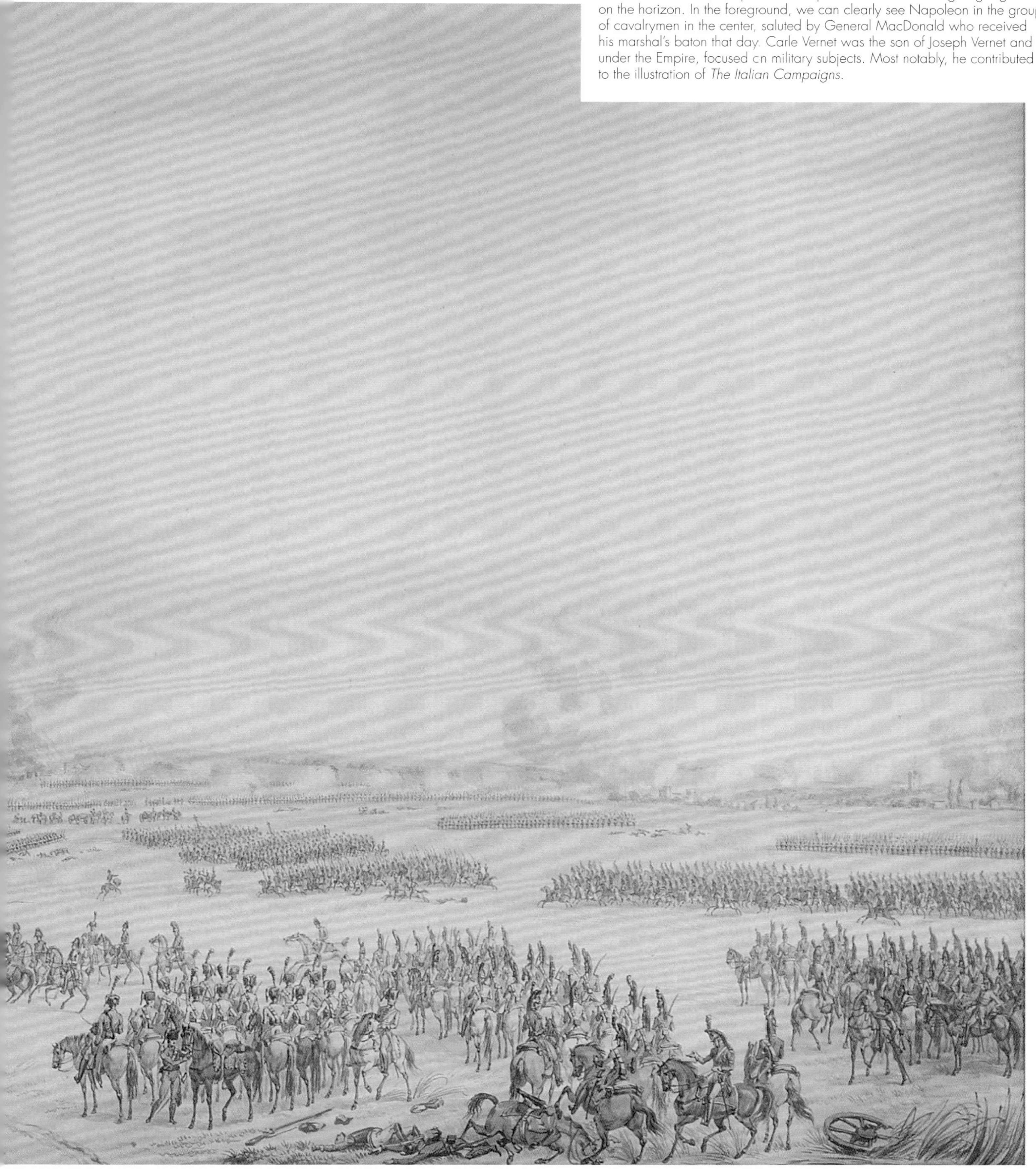

CARLE VERNET (1758-1836), *THE BATTLE OF WAGRAM*, 1809

This vast panorama of the Wagram plain, on the northern bank of the Danube in Austria, shows the Napoleonic troops in order of battle. Fighting rages on the horizon. In the foreground, we can clearly see Napoleon in the group of cavalrymen in the center, saluted by General MacDonald who received his marshal's baton that day. Carle Vernet was the son of Joseph Vernet and under the Empire, focused on military subjects. Most notably, he contributed to the illustration of *The Italian Campaigns*.

MARTIN-GUILLAUME BIENNAIS (1764-1843), ATTRIBUTED, GILDED BRONZE PREPARATORY MODEL OF THE GOLDEN SWORD OF NAPOLEON, KNOWN AS THE AUSTERLITZ SWORD

With its extraordinary chiseled detail, this sword, which can be traced all the way back, was most certainly reconstructed after the Restoration, on the basis of the life-sized gilded bronze preparatory models left by Biennais in his workshop. The gilded parts of the celebrated sword carried by the Emperor at the Battle of Austerlitz were produced under the supervision of the master goldsmith and were completed in several stages: the life-sized wax mock-up and a bronze model were used to ensure the best possible result before chiseling the final piece in gold. Drawings were left in his workshop and are now listed. The Musée de l'Armée in Paris is now home to the specimen that Napoleon referred to as "my sword", the most legendary of weapons having belonged to the Emperor. He took it with him to his final exile on St Helena, then left it to his son. In 1840, it was placed on the casket containing the Emperor's remains when they were returned to France.

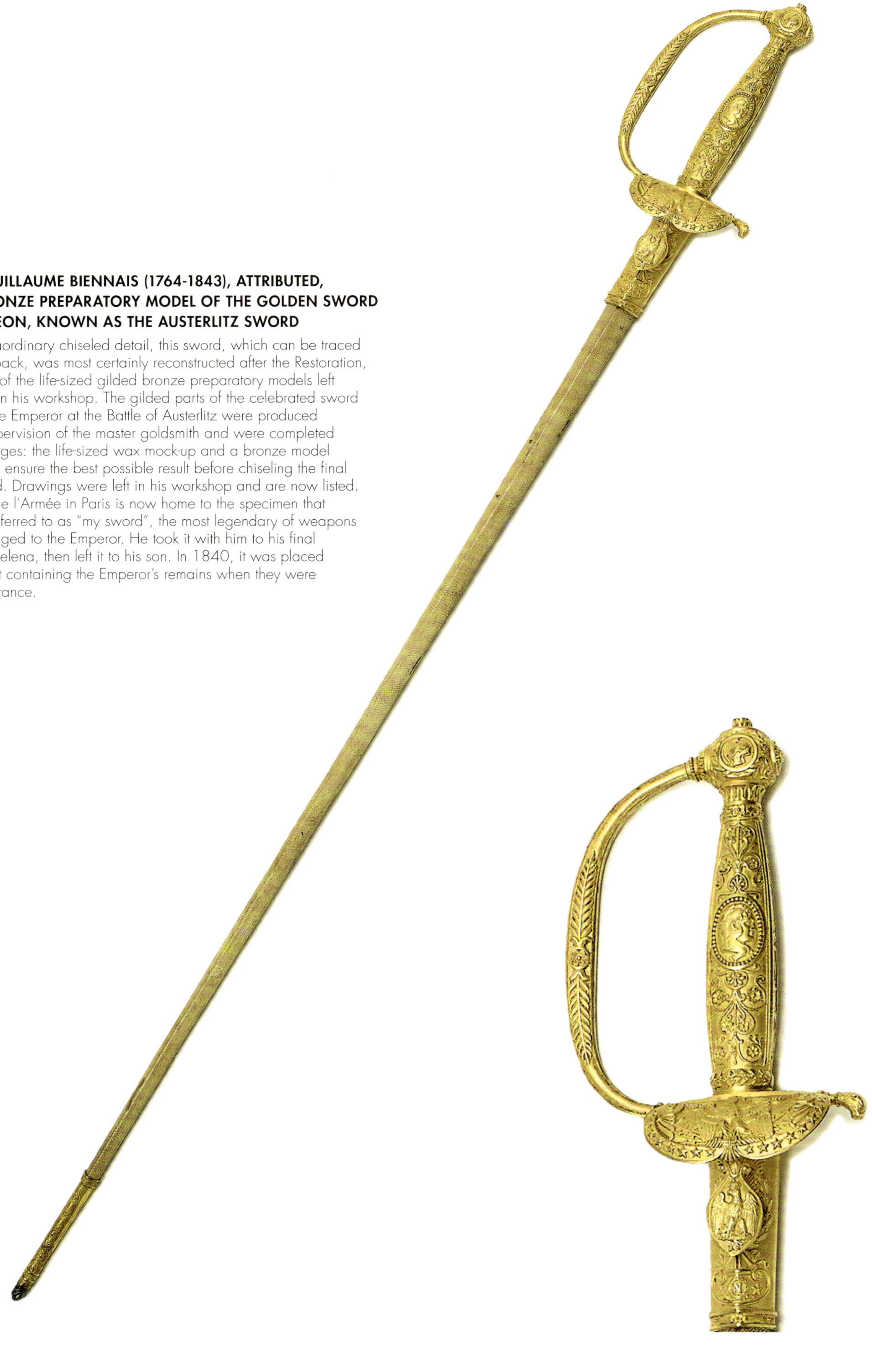

PAUL DELAROCHE (1797-1856) AND HIS WORKSHOP, *NAPOLEON IN HIS STUDY*

Caught while at work, Napoleon is captured standing at his desk, in the half-light. He is wearing the uniform of the Imperial Guard Foot Grenadiers with his Austerlitz sword by his side. Turning his head slightly, he looks right at the onlooker yet appears deep in thought. The stance recalls that of the famous portrait painted by Jacques-Louis David, reinterpreted by Delaroche with greater solemnity. The portrait is the first of a series started by Paul Delaroche in 1838. It was probably commissioned by the dowager countess Lady Sandwich whose daughter, Catherine Caroline, married the illegitimate son of Napoleon, Count Alexandre Colonna-Walewski.

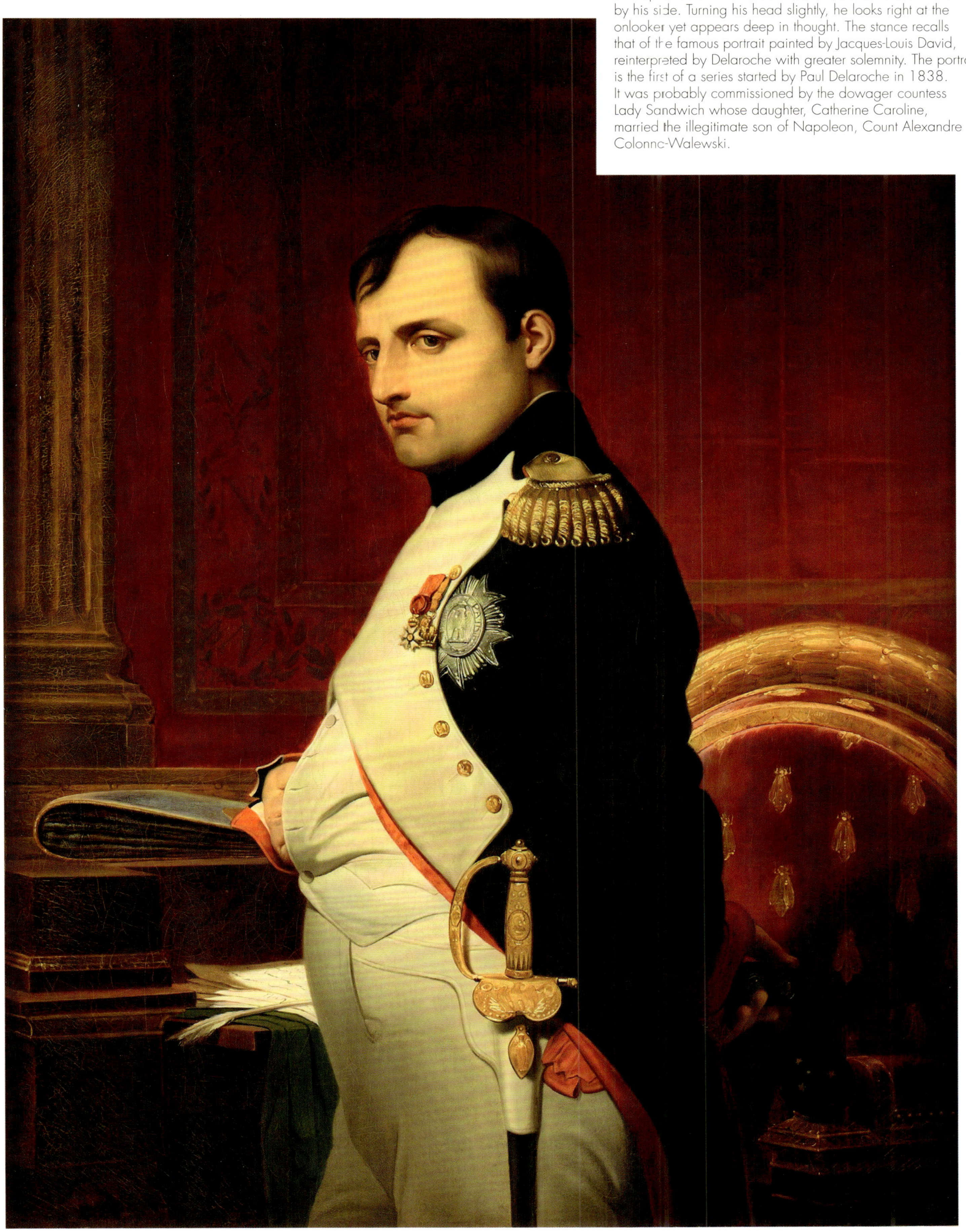

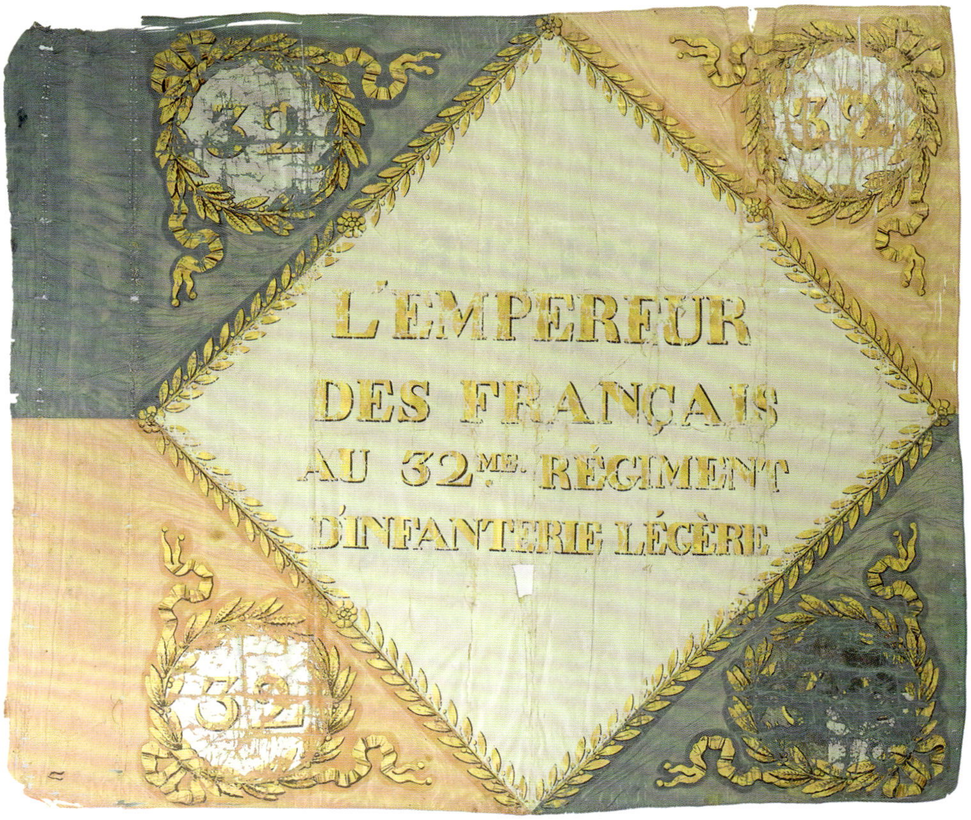

STANDARD OF THE FIRST BATTALION OF THE 32ND LIGHT INFANTRY REGIMENT, 1804 MODEL

Throughout history, an army has always fought under its flag. The presenting of captured standards to a sovereign is a sign of victory, just as the loss of regimental colors brings disgrace on those who have lost them. The flag flies on the frontline, a rallying point for the army it represents. No one understood the importance of flags better than Napoleon, whose attention to their design even extended to their lining. This tricolor silk flag is one of a handful in private ownership, originally the standard of the 32nd Light Infantry Regiment (formed by the foot soldiers of the Grand Duchy of Tuscany).

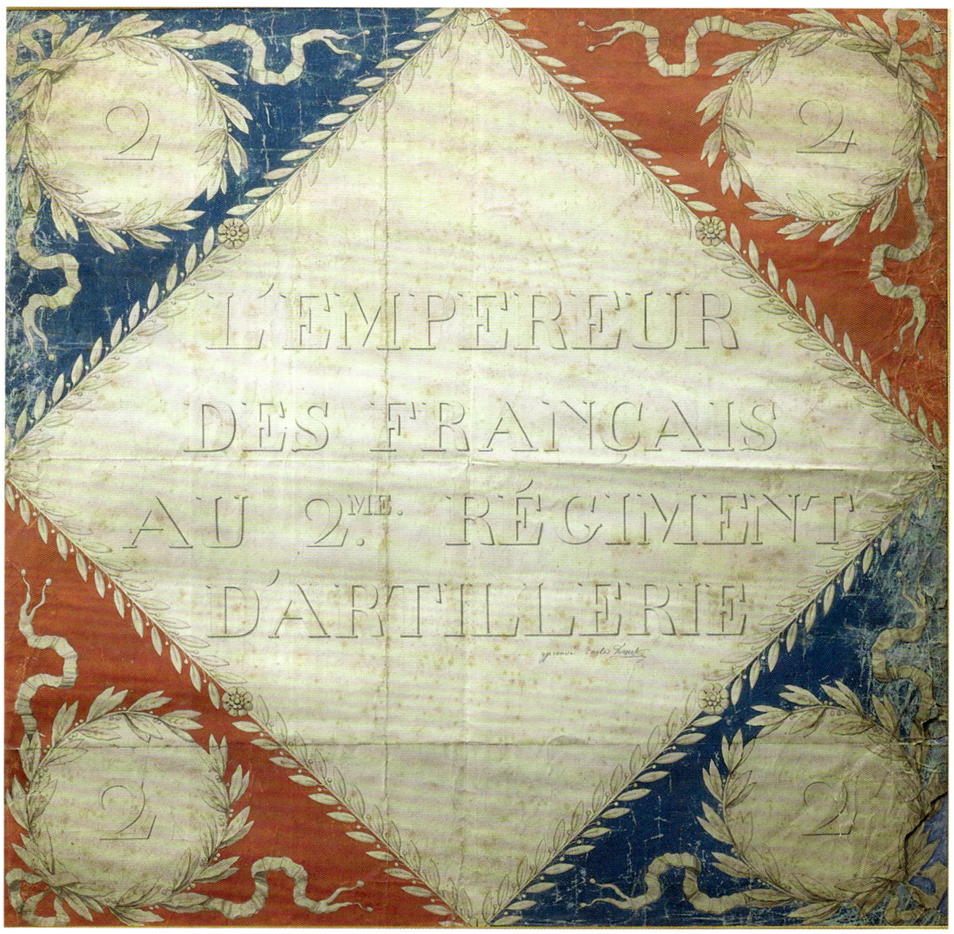

CARLE VERNET (1758-1836), *FLAG DESIGN*

Approved by designer and painter Carle Vernet, as shown by the signature to the bottom of the image, this model of the 1804 version reproduces the iconographic codes of the First Empire. It is a model provided for production at the Picot-Brocard embroidery workshop. The remarkable design was noticed by Frédéric Masson who, in 1910, wrote in volume 55 of *Les Annales politiques et littéraires*: "The books of Picot, for example, indicate that the flags were ordered by Denon on the model of this admirably well conserved 2nd Foot Regiment Flag, which belongs in the interesting collections of Picot's second successor".

PIERRE-CHARLES CIOR (1769 - AP. 1838), *MINIATURE PORTRAIT OF JOACHIM MURAT, KING OF NAPLES AND SICILY*

Murat, unchallenged king of the cavalry and swordsman of repute, led the historic charge at Eylau that pitted 12,000 horsemen against the Russians. As sovereign, he also proved a wise and attentive ruler. Murat was Napoleon's brother-in-law, husband of his sister Caroline, widely considered as a romantic hero who met a tragic end. This miniature masterpiece by Pierre-Charles Cior perfectly captures his brave and dashing demeanor.

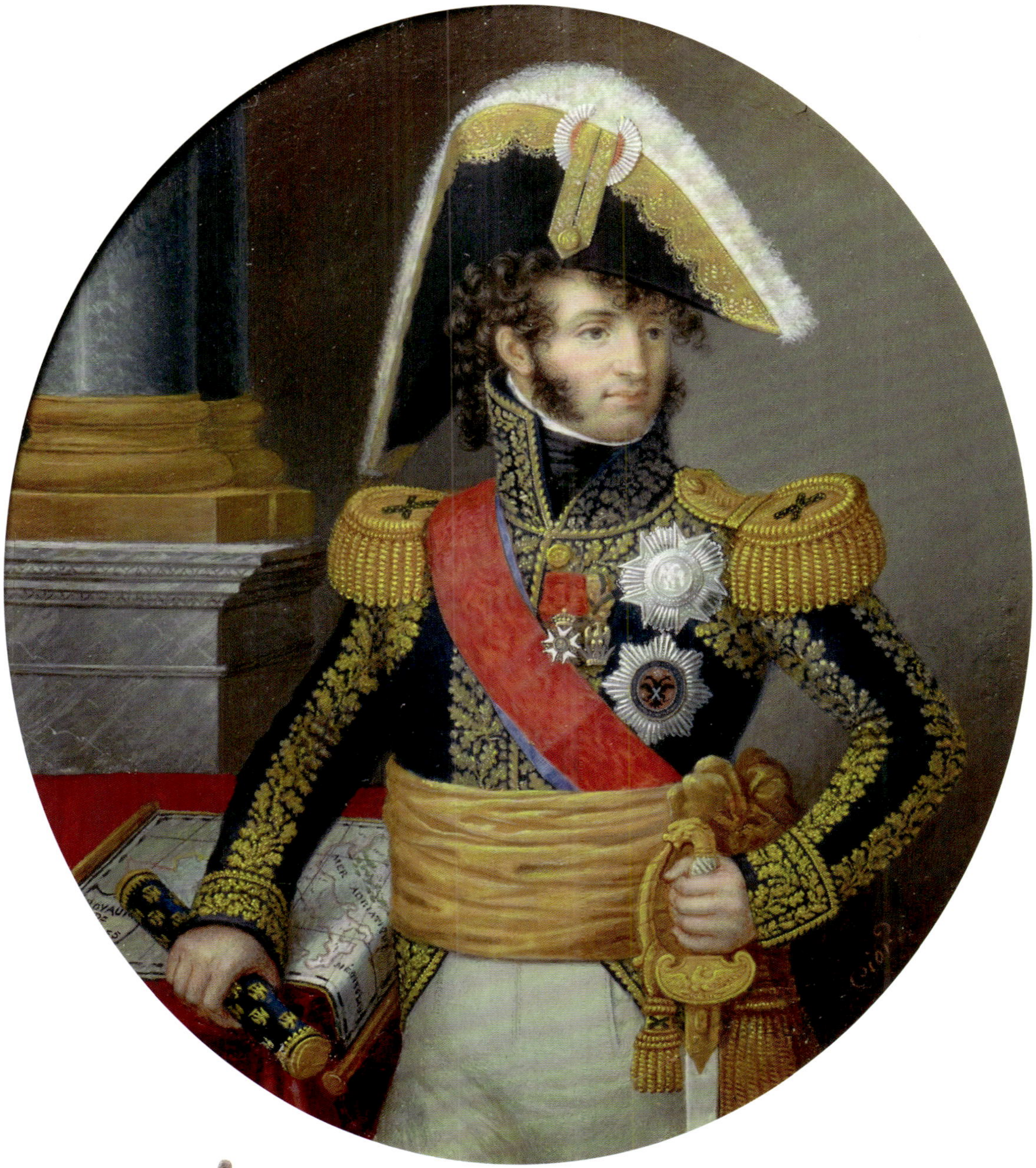

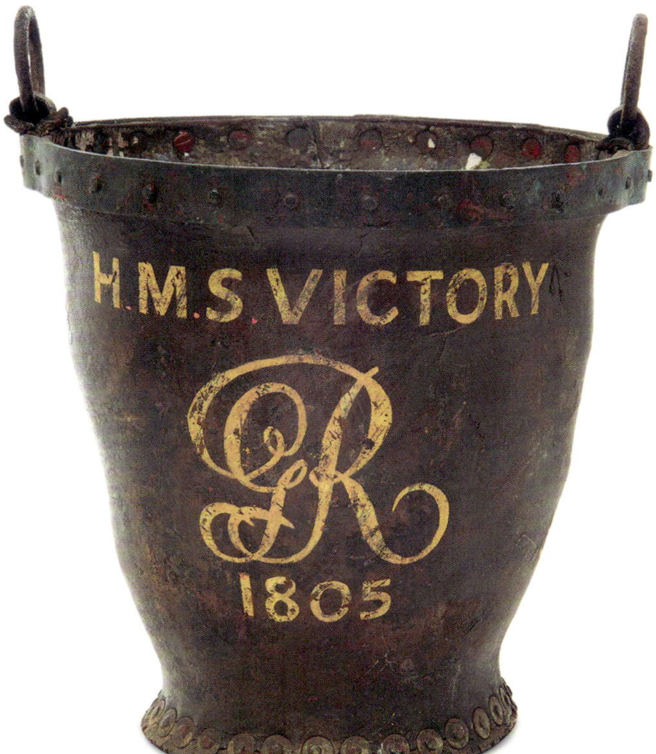

LEATHER BUCKET FROM HMS VICTORY, NELSON'S VESSEL AT THE BATTLE OF TRAFALGAR

As the words on its side show, this leather bucket comes from HMS Victory. The British 104-gun vessel went down in history as the ship of Admiral Horatio Nelson who triumphed over Napoleon at the Battle of Trafalgar in October 1805. As the fleets were about to meet, Nelson sent by flag-code signal what was to become a historical message to encourage his men: "England expects that every man will do his duty". Nelson died on-board HMS Victory at Trafalgar on 21 October 1805, hit by a cannonball from French 74-gun ship, Le Redoutable.

ORIENTAL STYLE SWORD OF PIERRE-CHARLES DE VILLENEUVE

Sword with gilt bronze hilt and strong, oriental-style blade in Damascus steel engraved with the Admiral rank insignia. Used by Villeneuve on the Egyptian Campaign and in the naval battles that followed, including the (best forgotten) French debacle at Trafalgar – a defeat for which Villeneuve was held responsible. Taken prisoner by the British, he fell into disgrace and was exiled to Brittany. He was found dead in 1806 with multiple stab wounds. This precious memento has been preserved by his family ever since.

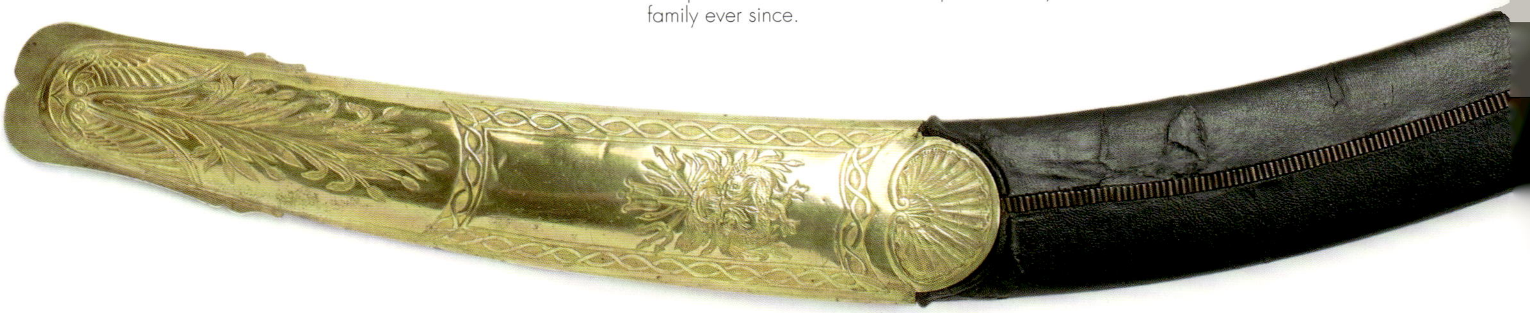

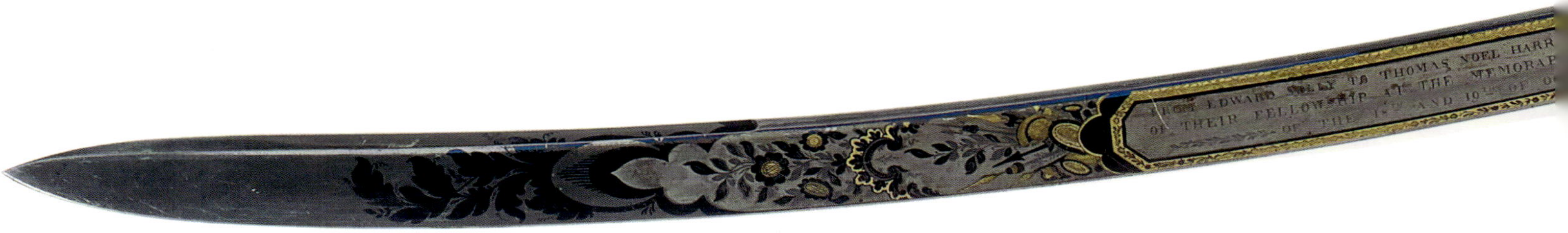

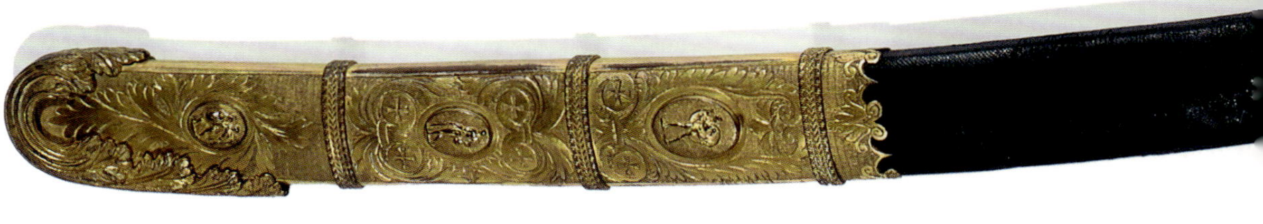

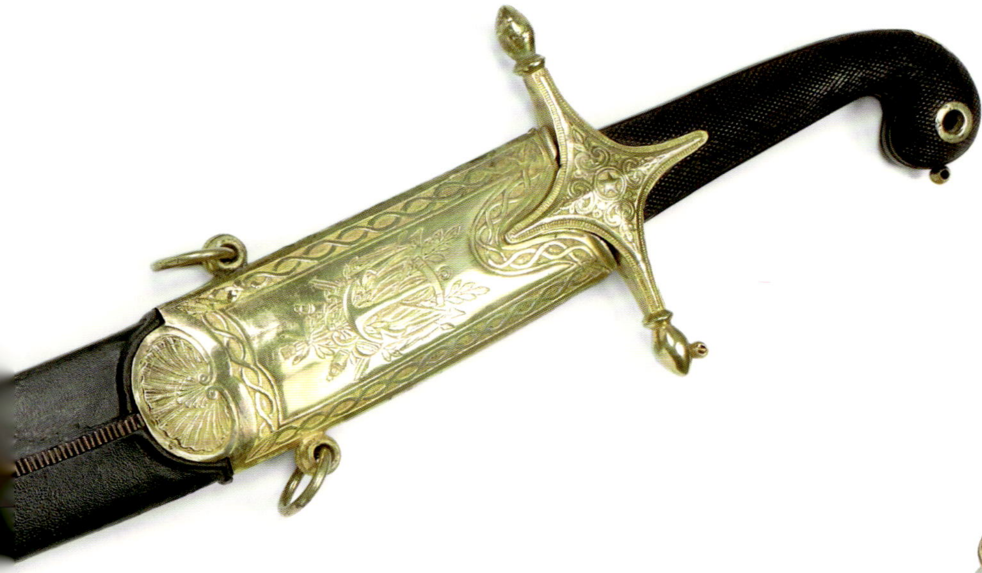

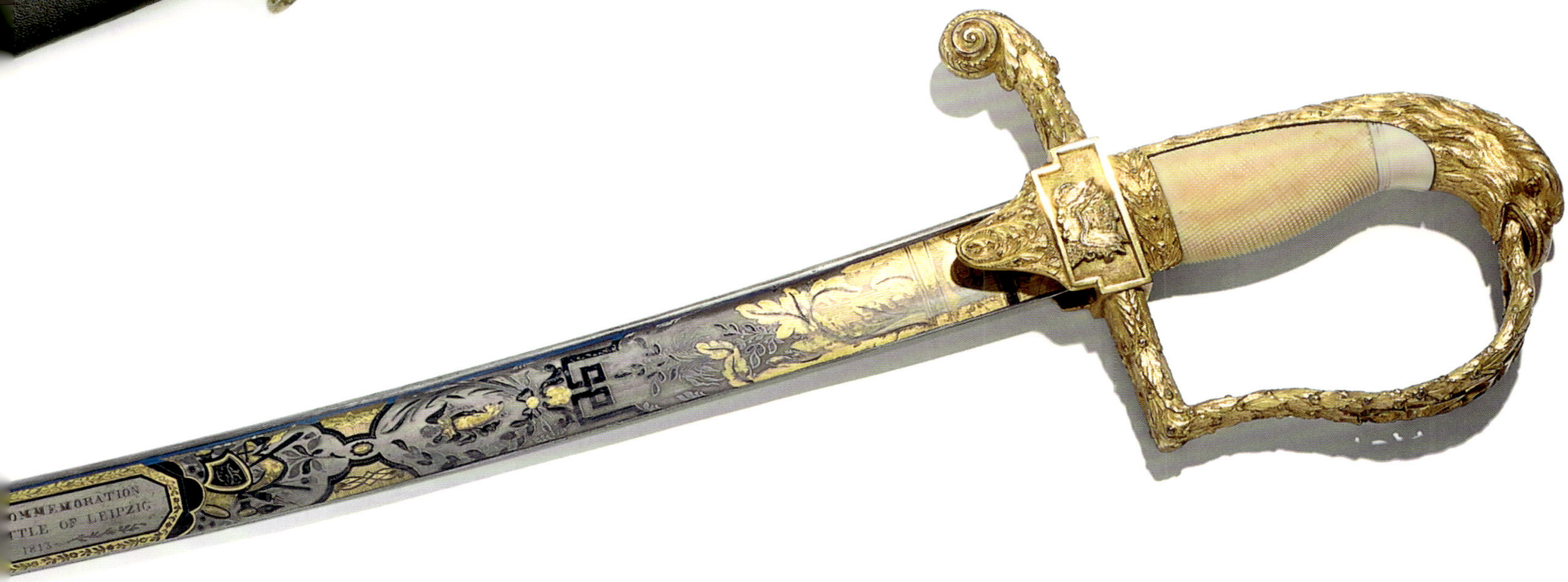

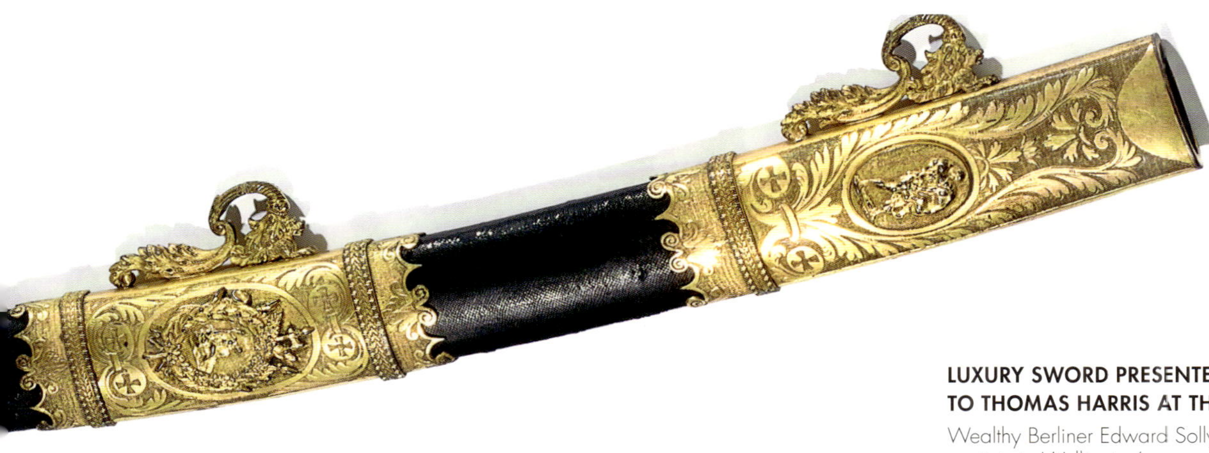

LUXURY SWORD PRESENTED BY EDWARD SOLLY TO THOMAS HARRIS AT THE CLOSE OF THE BATTLE OF LEIPZIG

Wealthy Berliner Edward Solly and Thomas Harris, a young British captain in Wellington's army, crossed French lines to bring news of the allied victory at Leipzig (also known as the Battle of the Nations) to British Foreign Secretary Lord Castlereagh. Pictured here is the ceremonial sword that Solly presented to Harris to mark the success of their mission and to commemorate their new fellowship as brothers-in-arms – a magnificent gift that was a worthy tribute to the triumph of the allies at Leipzig.

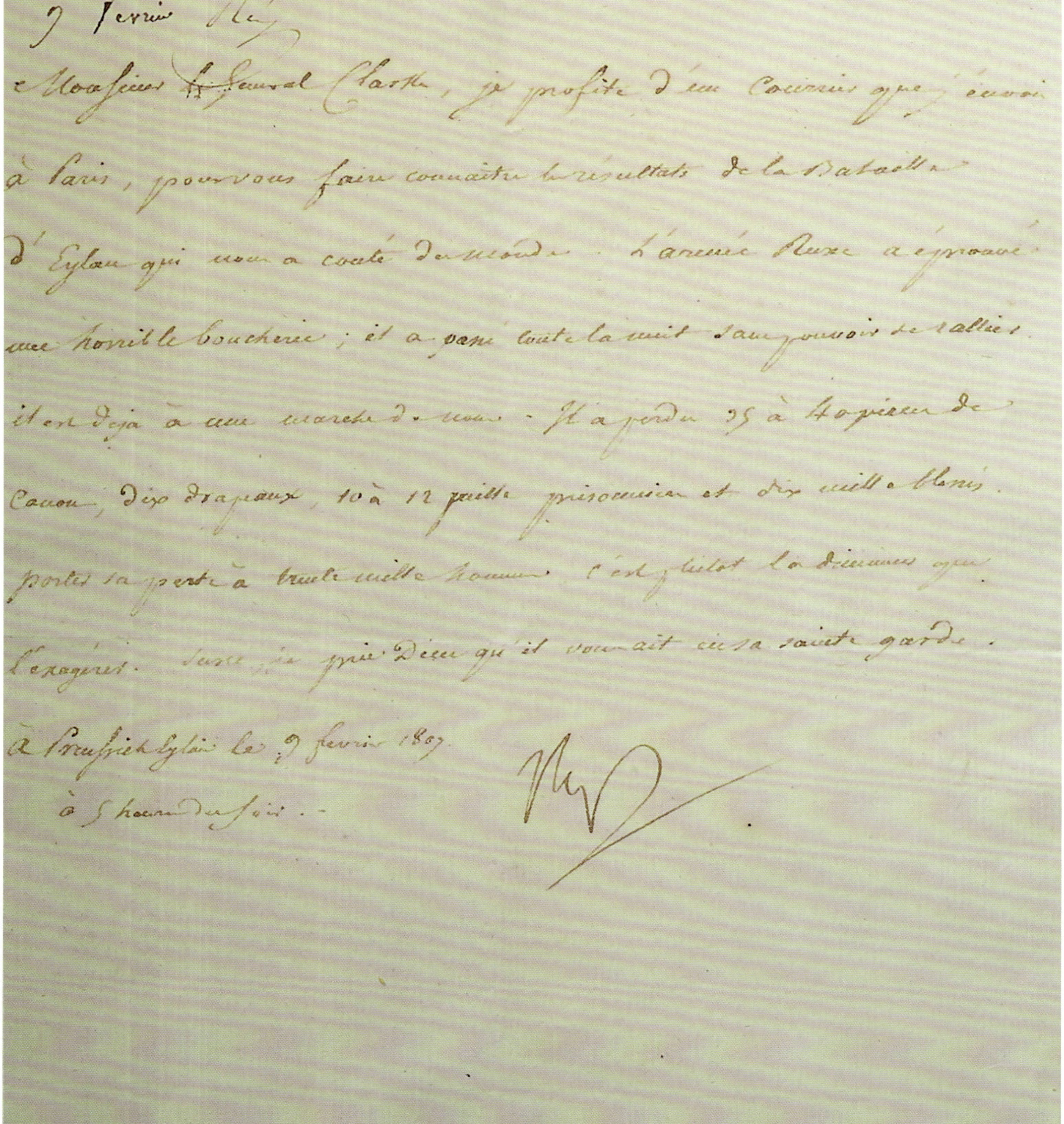
9 février Rép

Monsieur le Général Clarke, je profite d'un courrier que j'envoie à Paris, pour vous faire connaître le résultat de la bataille d'Eylau qui nous a coûté du monde. L'armée russe a éprouvé une horrible boucherie; et a passé toute la nuit sans pouvoir se rallier. Il est déjà à une marche de nous. Il a perdu 35 à 40 pièces de canon, dix drapeaux, 10 à 12 mille prisonniers et dix mille blessés. Je porte sa perte à trente mille hommes. C'est plutôt la diminuer que l'exagérer. Sur ce je prie Dieu qu'il vous ait en sa sainte garde.

À Preussich Eylau le 9 février 1807
à 5 heures du soir.

Np

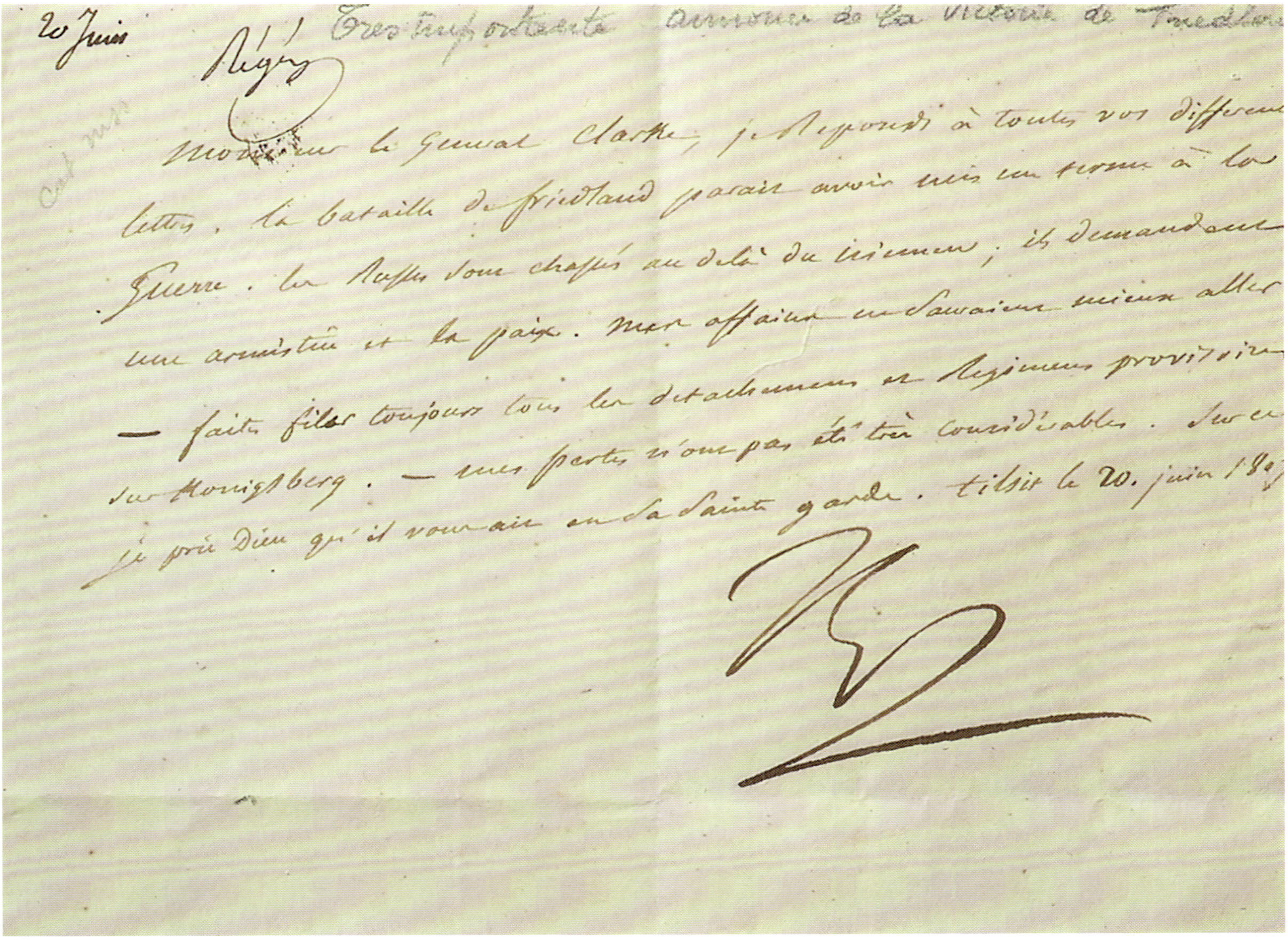
20 Juin — Très importante annonce de la victoire de Friedland

Régny

Monsieur le General Clarke, je reponds à toutes vos differentes lettres. la bataille de friedland parait avoir mis un terme à la Guerre. les Russes sont chassés au delà du niemen; ils demandent une armistice et la paix. mes affaires ne sauraient mieux aller — faites filer toujours tous les detachemens et Regimens provisoires sur Konigsberg. — mes pertes n'ont pas été très considérables. Sur ce je prie Dieu qu'il vous ait en sa sainte garde. tilsit le 20. juin 1807

Napol

LETTER FROM NAPOLEON, DATED 9 FEBRUARY 1807, ANNOUNCING VICTORY AT EYLAU

Napoleon is believed to have signed more than 100,000 letters in his lifetime, some more important than others. The contents of this letter, written to the then Minister of War General Clarke, testify to their dramatic context. Dated 9 February 1807, it was composed on the day following Napoleon's victory at Eylau, penned from northern East Prussia on the banks of the Vistula. "There was a battle yesterday and the victory was ours," writes Napoleon. "But the battlefield was awash with blood." The letter shows a side to Napoleon that is at odds with his reputation as a heartless tyrant. It confirms his shock at what he describes as the "horrible butchery of the Russian troops" – the battlefield strewn with dead and wounded. Contrary to his habit, he remained on the battlefield for a week to supervise the care of the casualties. For all the carnage, the massacre at Eylau would not be conclusive and it would take until June and their defeat at Friedland to force the Russians to sue for peace.

LETTER FROM NAPOLEON ANNOUNCING VICTORY AT FRIEDLAND, 20 JUNE 1807

Friedland marked the start of peace with Russia, heavily defeated by Napoleon. From Tilsit, he sent news of the victory to his War Minister, General Clarke: "The Battle of Friedland appears to have brought the war to an end. The Russians have retreated behind River Neman; they demand an armistice and peace. Things could not be better. Continue to have the detachments and regiments march on Koenigsberg. My losses have not been too heavy," he writes. The letter is signed "Napol". Apart from on official correspondence, the Emperor used no fewer than six different signatures. Depending on how he felt, they ranged from the simple "N" to "Napoleon" spelt out in full, or "Np", "Nap" or "Napol".

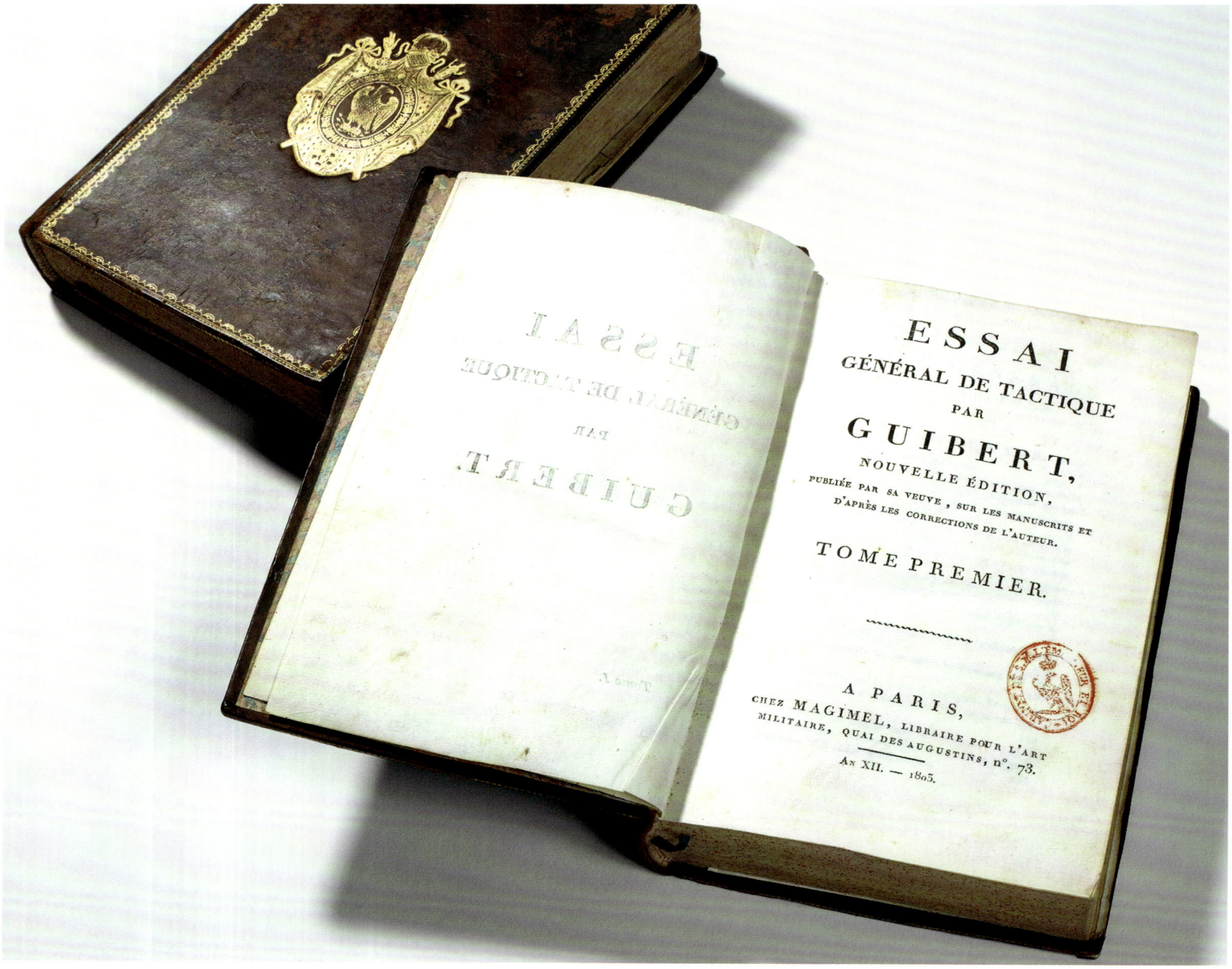

JACQUES-ANTOINE-HYPPOLYTE DE GUIBERT (1743-1790), MILITARY TACTICS BOOK FORMERLY BELONGING TO NAPOLEON

General Guibert's famous two-volume *Essai Général de Tactique* (a general essay on tactics) is probably the most important of all Napoleon's books. It underpinned his approach to strategic thinking and played a fundamental role in the military history of the First Empire. The flyleaf bears the stamp of his personal library.

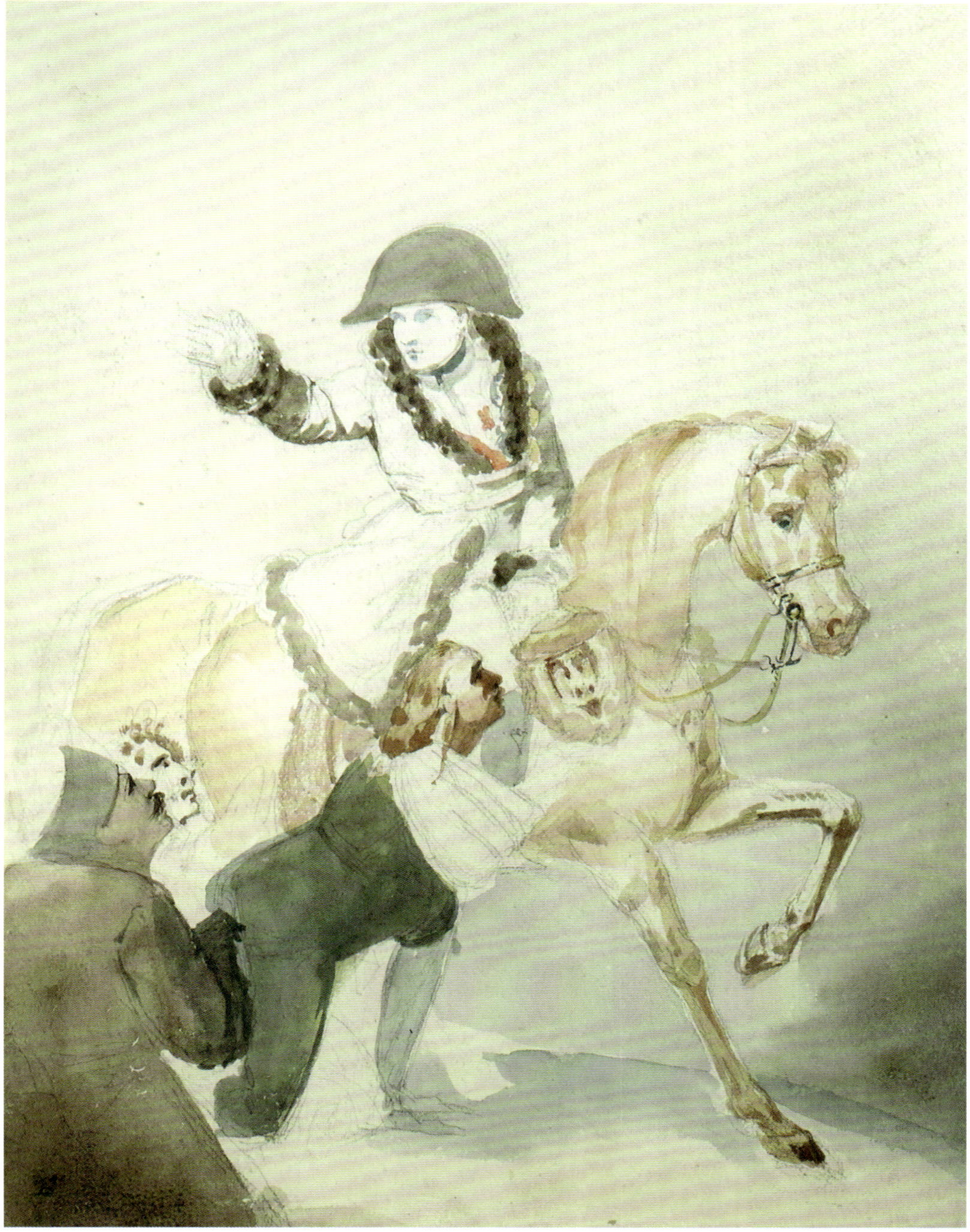

ANTOINE-JEAN GROS (1771-1835),
NAPOLEON VISITING THE BATTLEFIELD AT EYLAU

The Emperor as we like him! On horseback, surrounded by his troops, lifting up his eyes to Heaven, with his right arm outstretched and his palm turned upwards. As if he were blessing the two soldiers at his feet — an impression of solemn majesty reinforced by their kneeling position. Shown here is a preliminary watercolor study for the celebrated painting *Napoléon Visitant le Champ de Bataille d'Eylau,* now held by the Louvre.

NAPOLEON'S IMPERIAL SABER

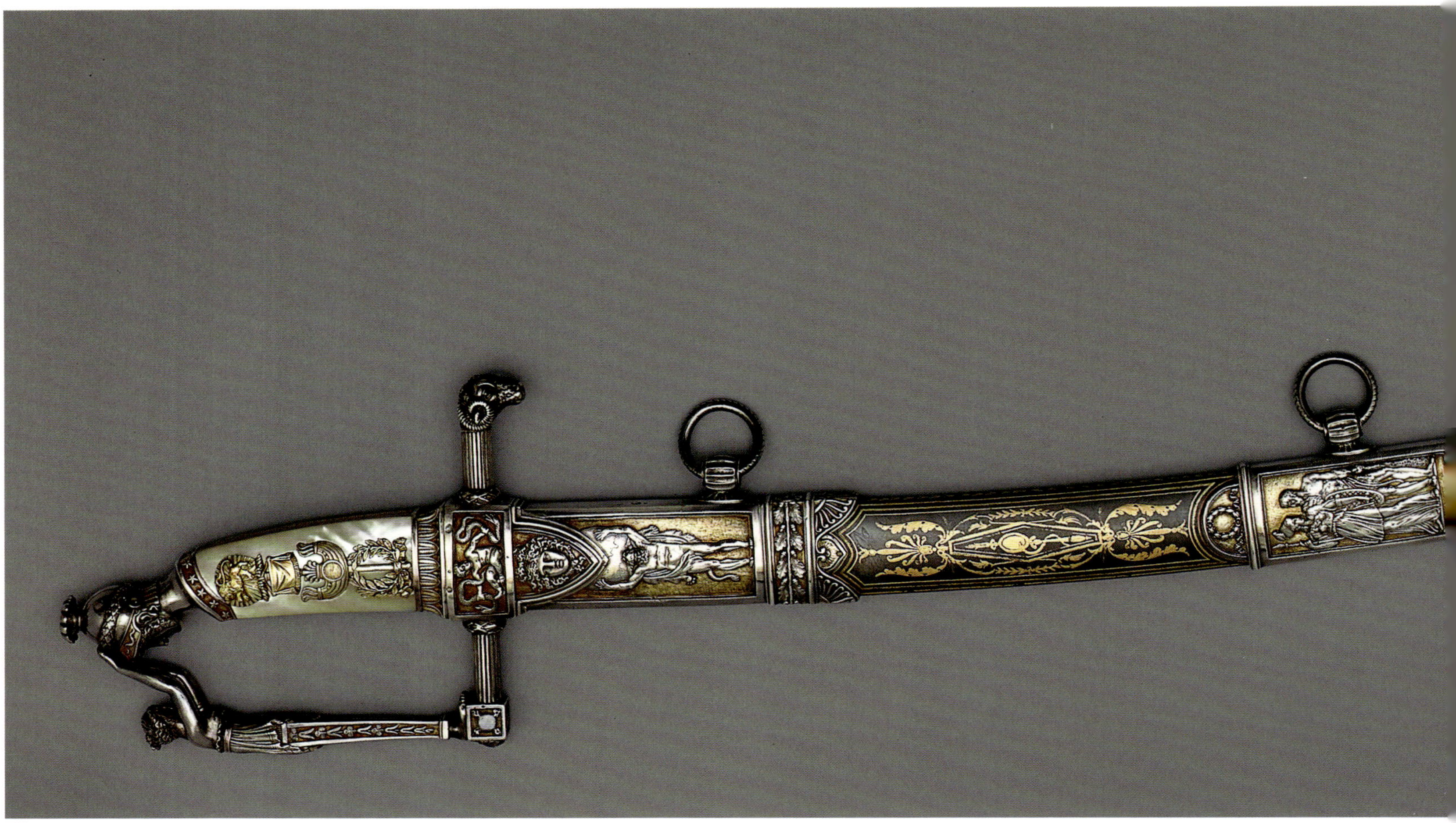

Kept in a private collection since 1970, this saber is the only one known to have belonged to Napoleon the Emperor. Probably the finest ever made, alongside the one by Nicolas-Noël Boutet (1761-1833), and offered by the Directory to Bonaparte after the Italy campaign, it is now conserved at the national museum at the Chateau de Fontainebleau. The thirteen other sabers listed, all in the National Museums, were made for Bonaparte the General or First Consul.

The Emperor's official armorer, Jean Le Page (1746-1834), was commissioned to produce this extraordinary object, the only one of its kind and a sumptuous piece of silverware, enhanced with mother-of-pearl. The beauty and classical motifs of the imperial allegories, chosen under Napoleon's orders, surpass all the other sabers hitherto produced. It was made in two stages.

In 1803, the First Consul decided to order a saber, now kept at the Malmaison national museum, from Le Page. Its curved Klingenthal blade is marked N BONAPARTE FIRST CONSUL. It was delivered on 11 November 1804, not long before the coronation at the church of Notre-Dame in Paris on 2 December. Le Page signed it LE PAGE / ARQUEBUSIER / TO THE EMPEROR.

This magnificent saber took so long to produce because Le Page called on the finest craftsmen of the time, which also justified its considerable cost of 8,000 francs. A detailed description of the saber and its costs appear on a payment reminder drafted by Jean Le Page and sent to the Chief Chamberlain Auguste Augustin-Laurent de Rémusat almost two years after delivery of the saber. The demand was examined by the Emperor whilst in Mainz between 28 September and 1 October 1806. He reduced the amount to 7,000 francs and gave his agreement for payment, which was sent by Rémusat on 15 October 1806. The duplicate sent to Maison de S.M. L'Empereur & Roi, Service du Grand Chambellan, states: "Review of the work done to produce a saber for the Emperor by Lepage, his arquebusier, on 20 Brumaire, Year 13. This weapon in gilded silver and matte vermeil has, over all its surface, allegories representing the Emperor [...]. The blade of this sword is made from Damascus steel from the renowned Klingenthal swordmakers. General Duroc sent it to Sr Lepage to be mounted. The weapon is placed in a yew root box adorned with silver fittings and an inlaid, engraved trim. It is easy to believe that these precious ornaments, produced by the finest artists, were very costly, not to mention the disbursements required for the drawings, the models in wood and in wax and cast iron, and the inevitable changes to a piece where everything must be impeccably made and in perfect harmony. For this saber, which was given to Monsieur de Rémusat, 1st chamberlain of His Highness more than two years ago, Sieur Lepage has settled a sum of eight thousand francs. He hopes that this sum will not seem exorbitant and can give the assurance that his disbursements amount to at least six thousand francs, so he evaluates a job that required great care and a lot of time at only two thousand francs. For the sum of eight thousand francs, cy 8000. Certified true: LE PAGE. The present statement verified and approved for the sum of seven thousand francs. In Mainz on 15 October 1806. The First Chamberlain. REMUSAT".

Between 1806 and 1809, probably just after the settlement, Napoleon, now Emperor, again called on Le Page. He ordered a new, even more sumptuous version of the saber, bearing the symbol of his coronation, the imperial eagle, leaving the consular sword to its fate, probably stored in the costume store of which Rémusat was in charge. It remained as good as new in its original box of rare wood inlaid with silver, in possession of the Rémusat family until 1958 when it was sold to the Malmaison national museum. (inv. MM 58.5.1).

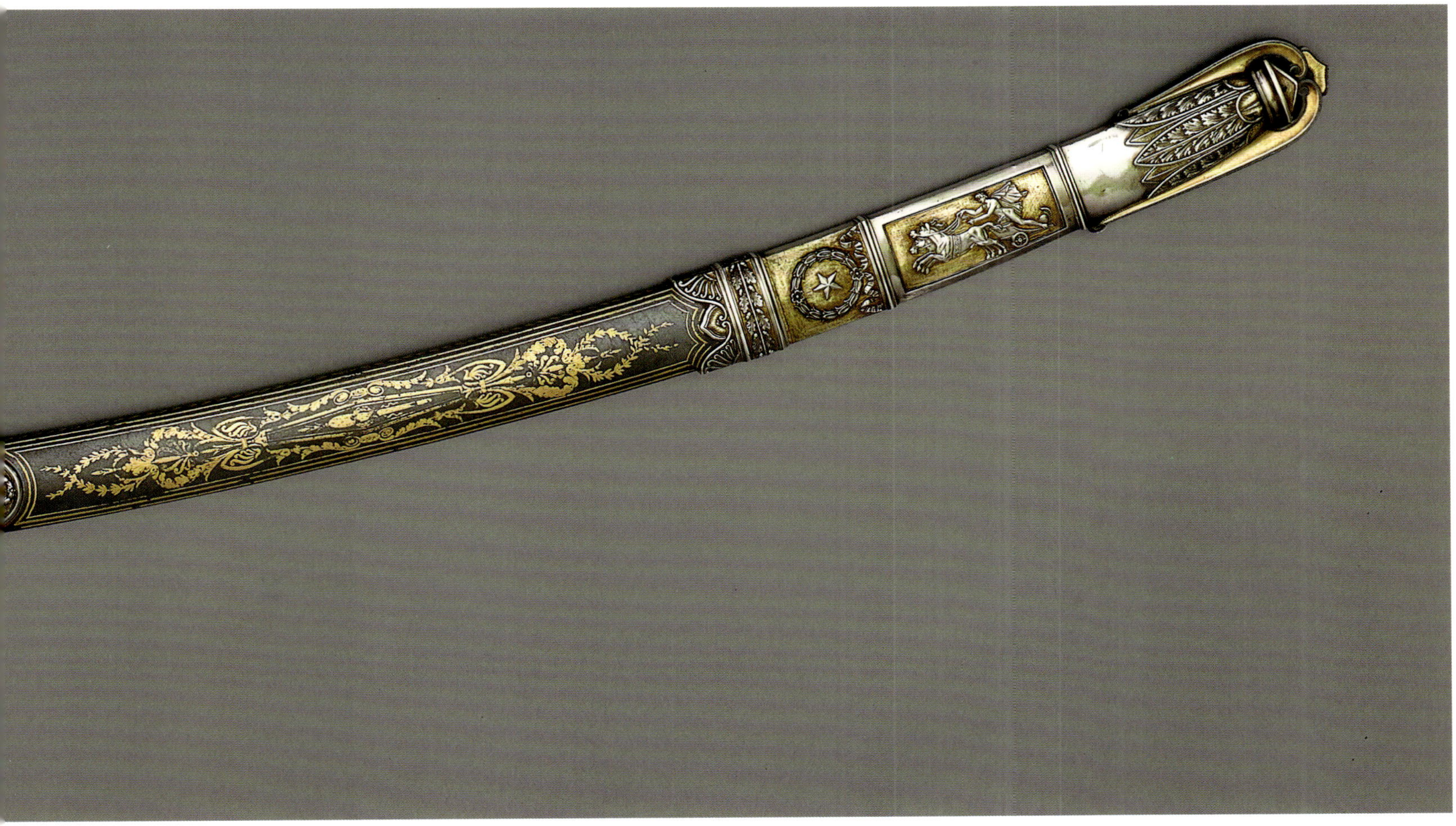

The pre-eminence of the imperial sword, which bears traces of use, is confirmed by Henri Le Page, son of Jean, in a reproduction he made in 1842. With the aim of "assembling and preserving the models" of the legendary sword made by his father, Henri was careful to include imperial elements on the mother-of-pearl hilt, in particular the many stars and the Roman adornments with, in the place of the imperial eagle and the lightning bolts, a cockerel, the republican emblem adopted by Louis Philippe. The consular saber and the imperial saber were the only two blades that Napoleon ordered from Le Page. The prestige of the order and the care the master armorer took in fulfilling them were all the greater for it.

Compared to the consular saber, the most characteristic ornaments of the imperial saber are the mother-of-pearl hilt inlaid with gilded silver Roman imperial motifs, the head of the young hero crowned by Victoria bowing lower and the greater number of stars on his chlamys; the silver trimmings are not entirely gilded, their reliefs are left white and the hollows gilded in contrast. The imperial saber is thus a true masterpiece of the French decorative arts under the Consulate and the First Empire.

The scabbard, in Damascened steel with gold *rinceaux*, is decorated with classical icons on hexagonal shields: a snake and a mirror (Prudence), a shining star (a symbol of happiness), laurels around Hercules' mace (the triumphant force), a lance with a laurel crown (military Victory). It has three carved silver trims, gilded in the hollows. The rainguard is adorned on both sides with Hercules holding up the celestial sphere and, below it, a frieze of oak leaves and Egyptian palm leaves; the hook holding the ring is fluted and fitted with a silver ring engraved with chevrons. The sections meant for the guard wings (the "larmiers" in Le Page's language) are engraved on the front side: "LE PAGE À PARIS" and, on the other side: "ARQ^{ER} DE L'EMPEREUR". The central element is carved on its outer side to show

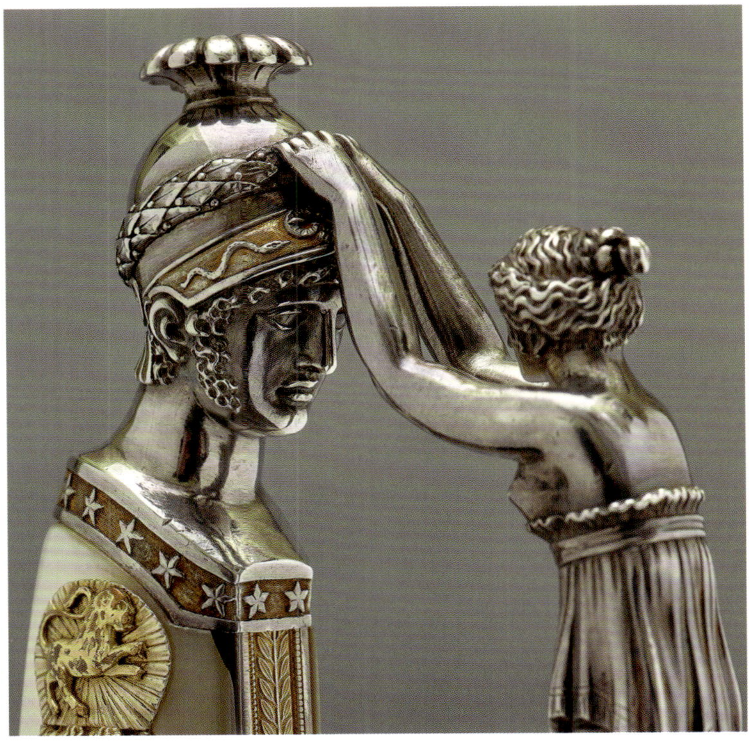

Minerva talking with Hercules and, on the inner side, Time writing History; it also has a hook and a ring identical to those on the rainguard. The large bouterolle is carved from top to bottom with Egyptian palm leaves, an oak leaf frieze, a star in a laurel crown, then an insert showing, on the outer side,

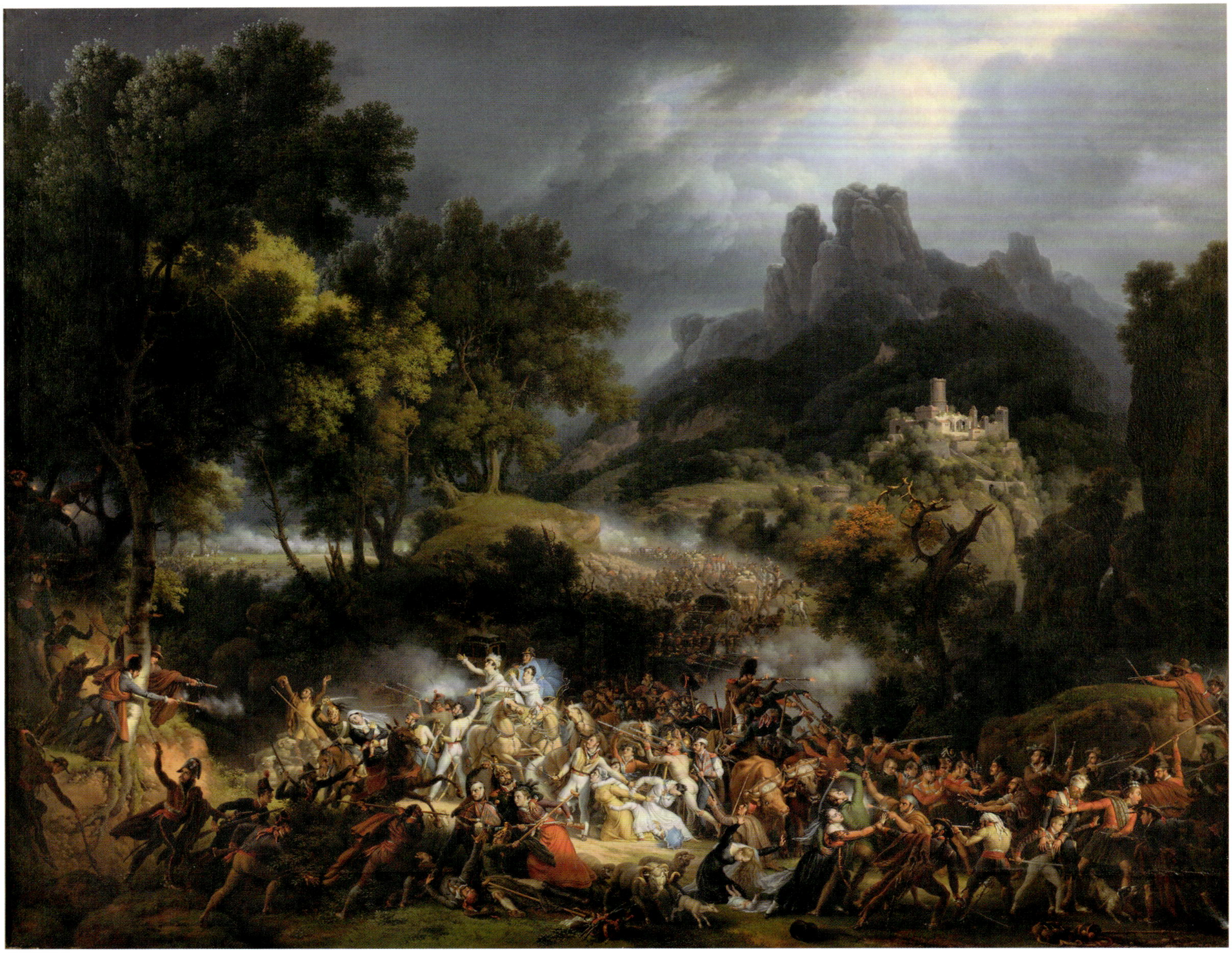

LOUIS-FRANÇOIS LEJEUNE (1775-1848),
ATTACK ON THE CAVALCADE RETURNING THE LADIES OF JOSEPH BONAPARTE'S COURT TO FRANCE

This monumental work is signed by Napoleon's battlefield painter. Here, he has immortalized a tragic moment in Napoleonic history. He depicts the assault on the convoy taking the ladies of the court of King Joseph to France on 25 May 1812.
Collections of the Chateaux de Versailles and Trianon

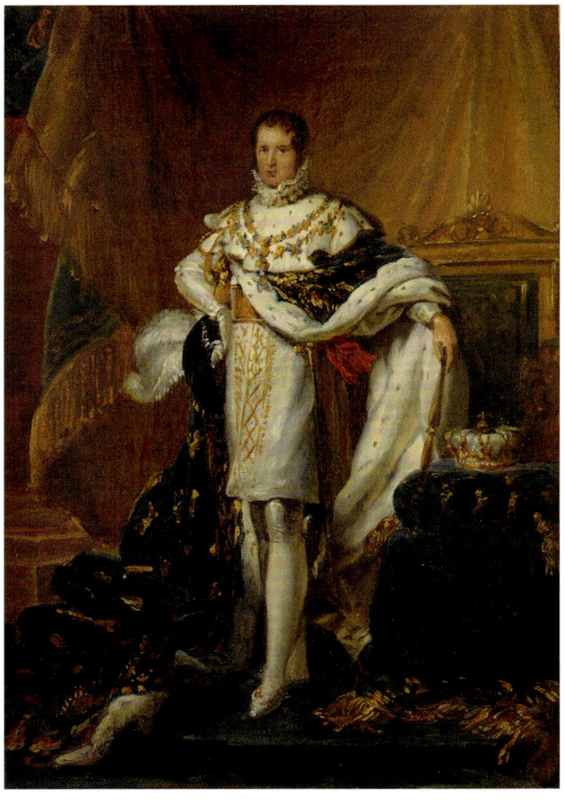

FRANÇOIS GÉRARD (1770-1837),
JOSEPH BONAPARTE

This official portrait of Joseph Bonaparte shows him in coronation robes. Joseph was entrusted with the latest kingdom of the Empire by his brother Napoleon and thus reigned as King of Spain from 1808 to 1813. Very soon, he was faced with internal struggles, then assaults by the Spanish insurgents such as that led by British general, Arthur Wellesley. Forced to flee the capital, he later abandoned his kingdom after the Battle of Vitoria.
Chateau de Fontainebleau museum collection

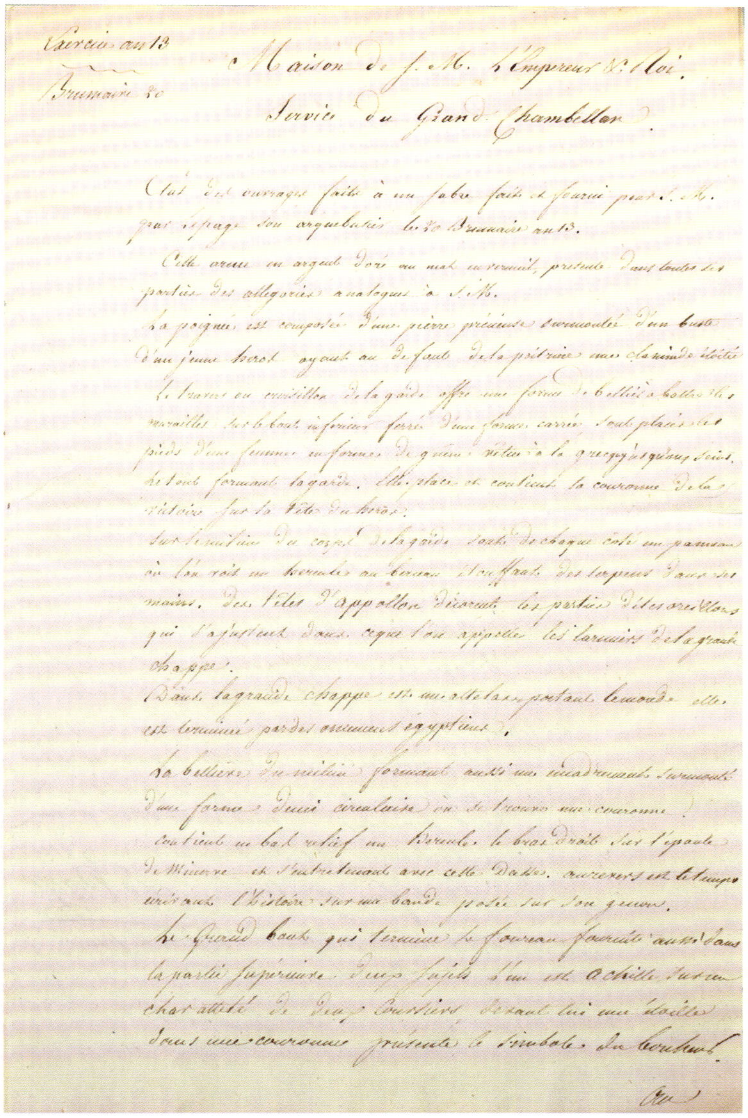

Maison de S. M. l'Empereur & Roi.

Service du Grand Chambellan

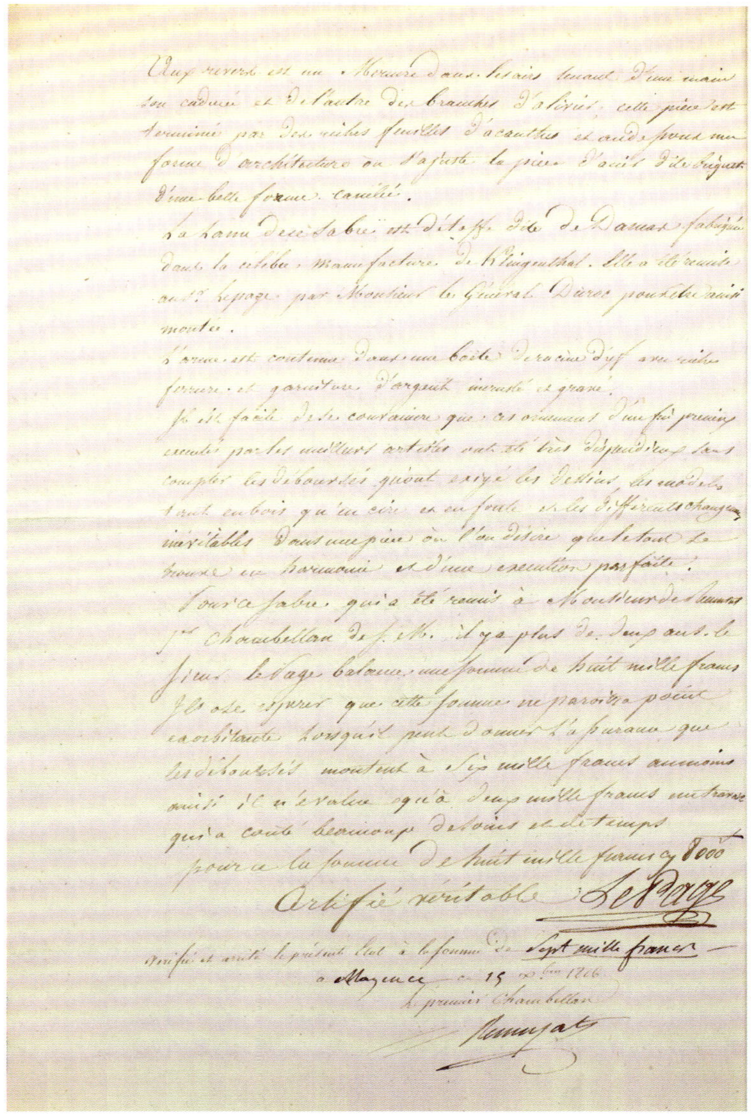

JEAN LE PAGE (1746-1834),
INVOICE FOR NAPOLEON'S SABER

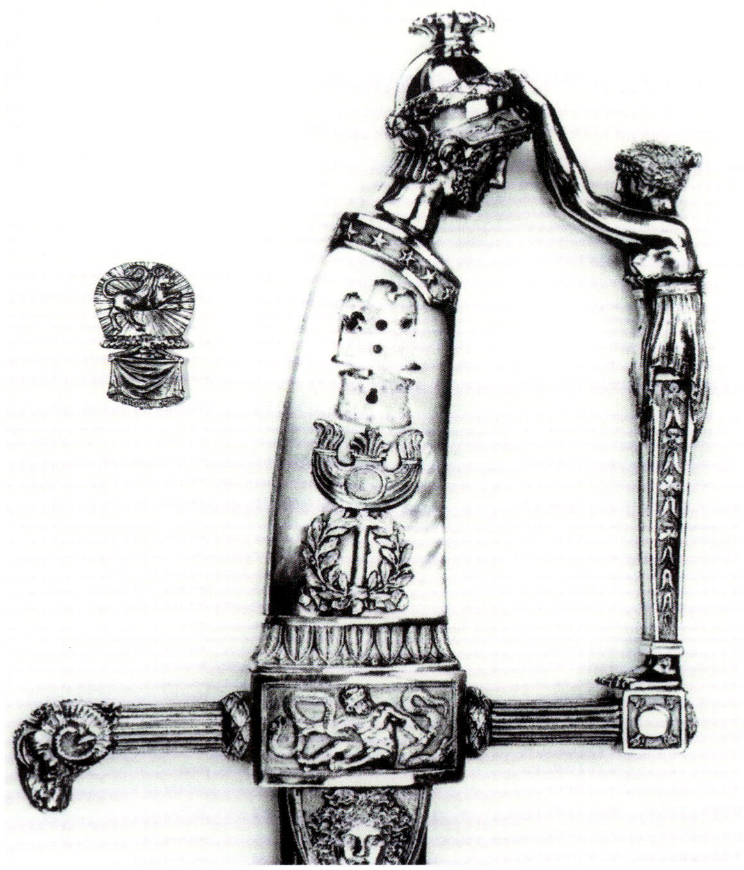

THE HIDDEN IMPERIAL EAGLE

During work to restore the saber, the lion surrounded by radiant glory was removed and revealed the hollow where an imperial eagle was once inlaid in the mother-of-pearl. The original motif had been removed and replaced, confirming the Spaniards' intention to conceal the weapon's prestigious origin.

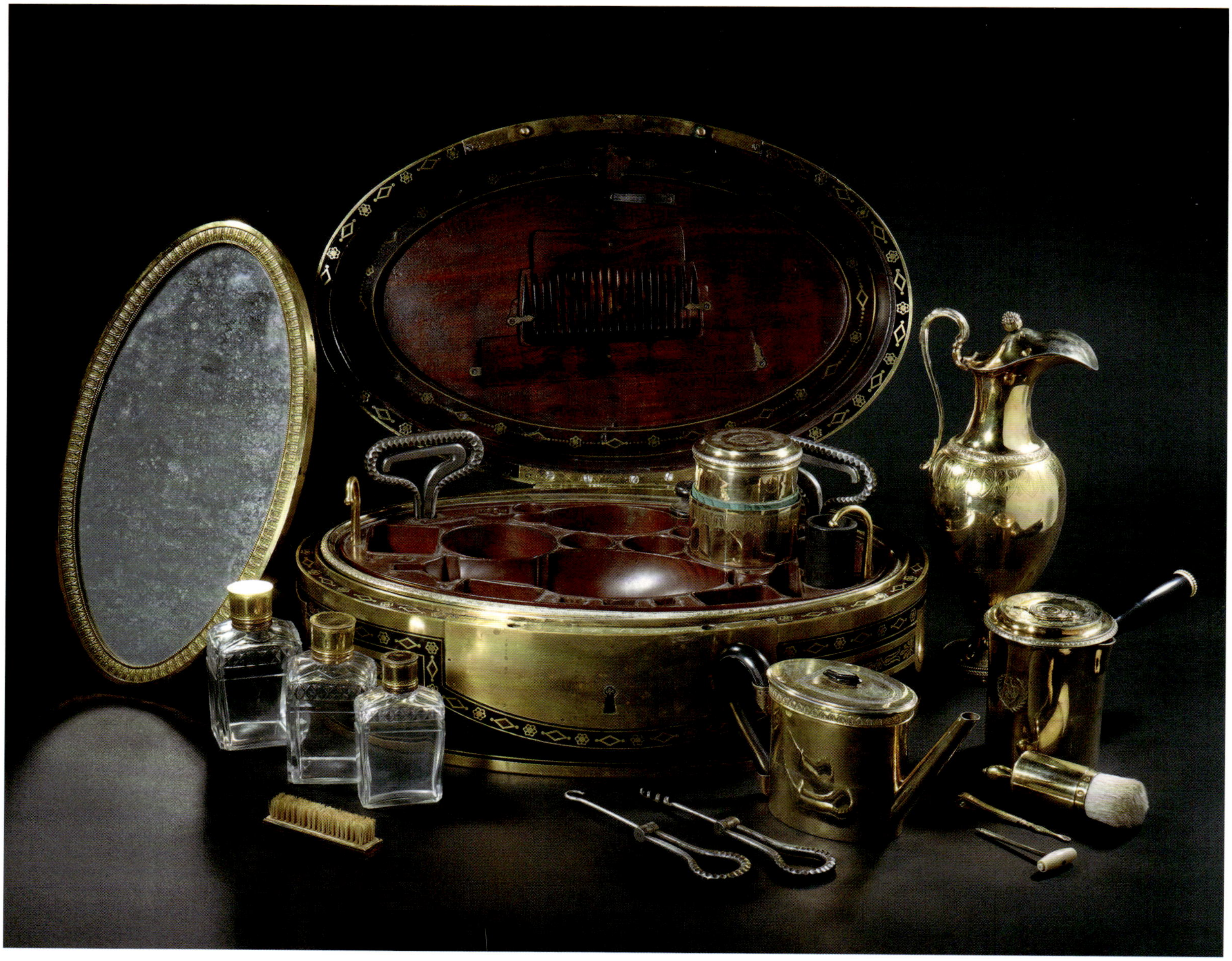

**MARTIN-GUILLAUME BIENNAIS (1764-1843),
VERMEIL TRAVEL SET BELONGING TO GENERAL DROUOT,
THE EMPEROR'S AIDE-DE-CAMP**

This very rare, sumptuous oval travel set made from carved mahogany bears the signature of "Biennais, goldsmith to His Highness the Emperor" and the stamp of Marie-Joseph Gabriel Génu, who produced all the gilded parts. The refinement of the palm-leaf frieze that adorns the different vermeil elements, such as the boxes, cases or bottles necessary for meals or grooming, and their meticulous symmetrical layout, taking up minimum space around the central basin, testify to the artistry of the work of the Emperor's tabletier and goldsmith, Martin-Guillaume Biennais.

This was owned by one of the Empire's best-known generals, Antoine Drouot (1774-1847). Speaking about Drouot, Napoleon said: "There are not to be found in the world two such officers as Murat for the cavalry and Drouot for the artillery". He distinguished himself in virtually all of the Empire's campaigns. He was alongside Napoleon at the time of his abdication at Fontainebleau. The Emperor appointed him governor of the island of Elba. He commanded the Guard at Waterloo. Drouot was nicknamed "the sage of the Grand Army" and would have been made Marshal if he had not been so modest and virtuous. In fact Napoleon, who named him in his will, said that he was: "a man who would live just as satisfied, on his own account, with forty sous a day as he would with the income of a sovereign. He was charitable and religious and his ethics, integrity and simplicity were honored in a century of the most rigid republicanism". We could be right in thinking that this travel set, one of the most extraordinary known, bearing the General's AD initials and too sumptuous for his selfless character, was given to him by the Emperor.

NICOLAS-NOËL BOUTET (1761-1833), PAIR OF CEREMONIAL PISTOLS BELONGING TO NAPOLEON

A magnificent pair of ceremonial pistols, crafted by French master gunsmith Boutet, the butts inlaid with ebony and embossed with gold ornaments featuring mythological deities plus imperial symbols typical of the Emperor's pistols, such as the eagle. They belonged to Ottoman Sultan Selim III (1761-1808), who may have received them from Napoleon himself, as a gift to commemorate the signing of diplomatic agreements. Alternatively, Selim being notorious for his shifting alliances, they may have been given to him by Tsar Alexander I, who in turn received them from Napoleon, the second pair in a presentation set also containing the pistols now in the Musée de la Légion d'Honneur. They were drawn from the private collections of Ottoman Sultan Abdul Hamid II (1842-1918) and are the only examples in private hands.

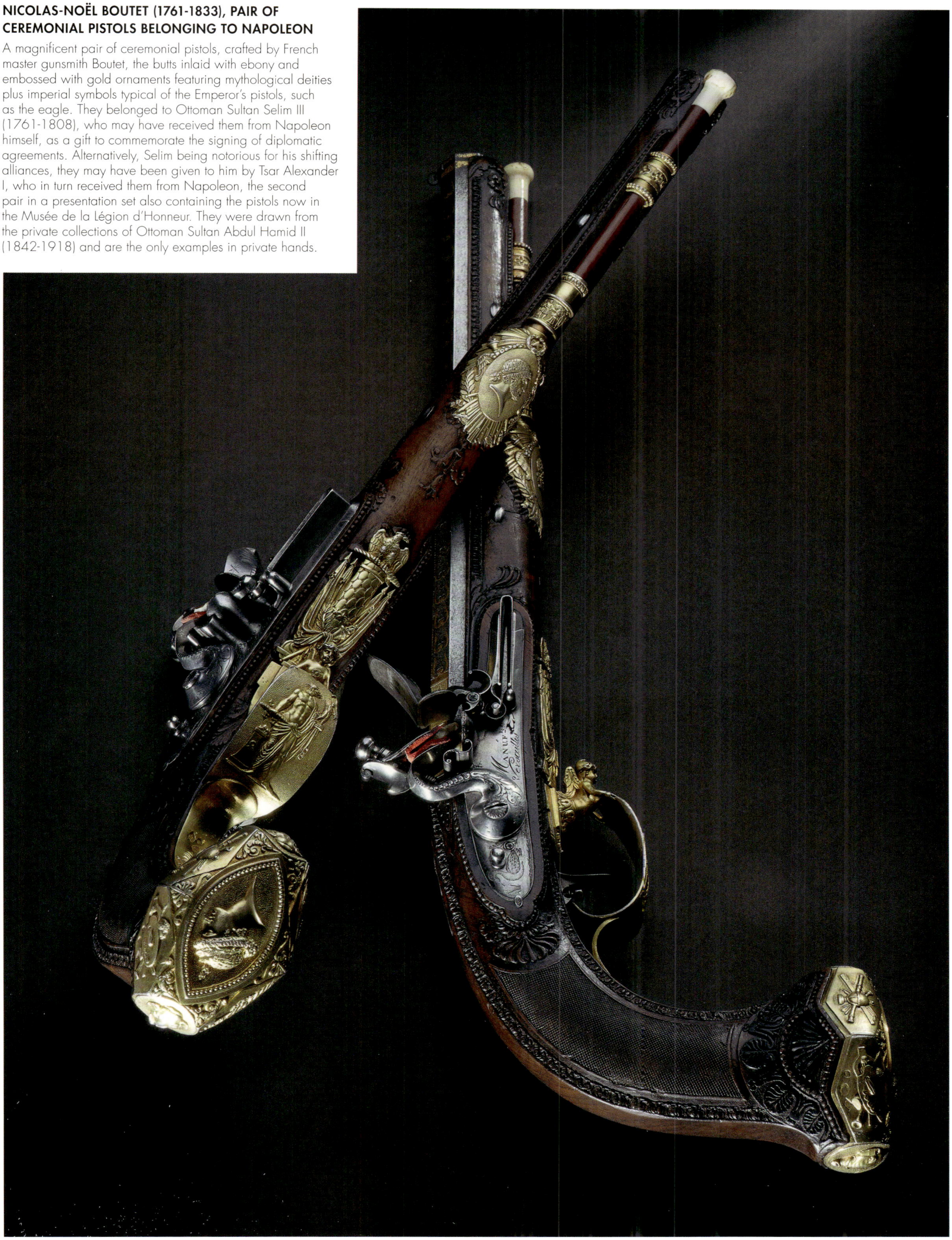

CAMPAIGN LIFE

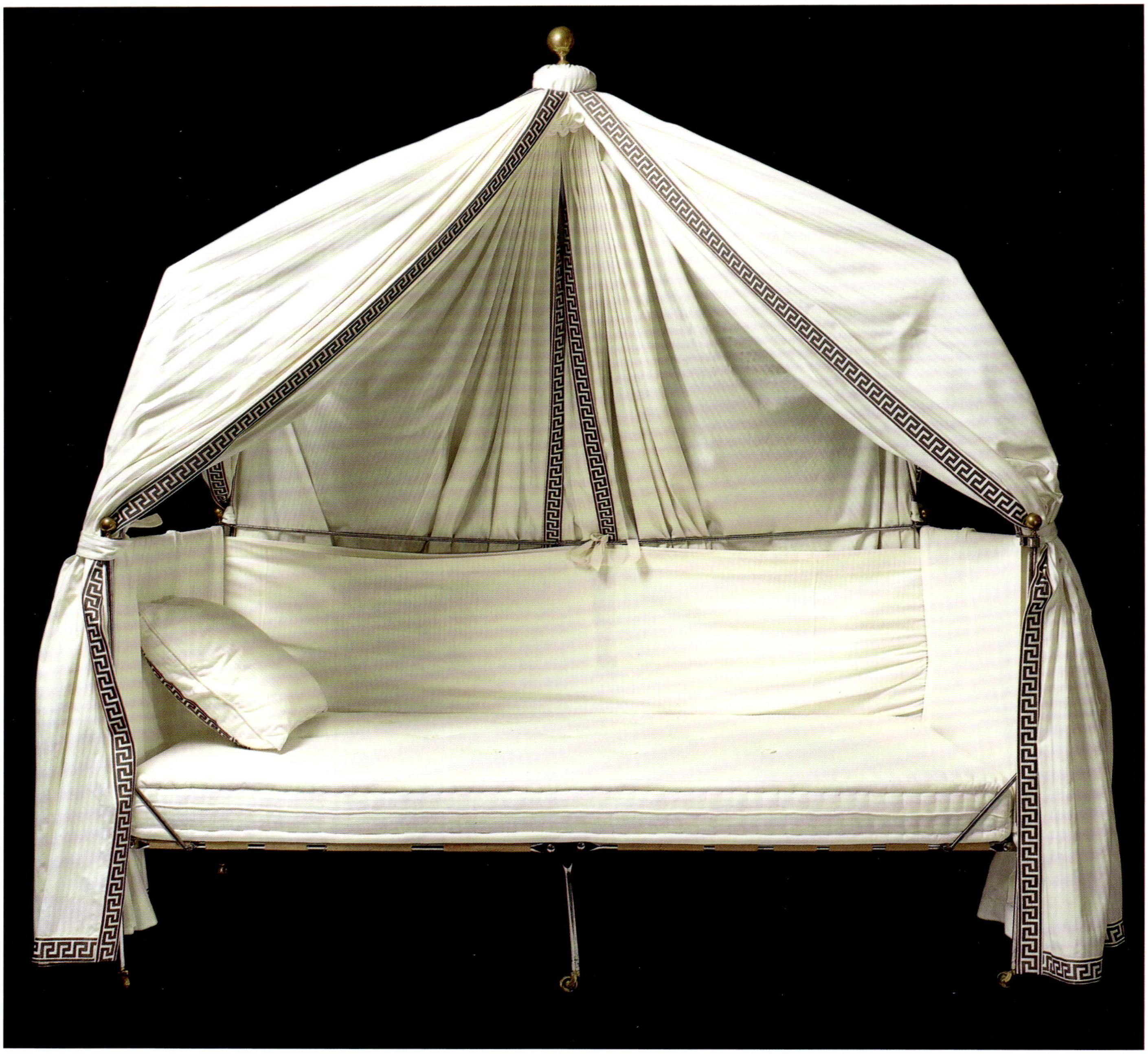

MARIE-JEAN DESOUCHES (1764-1828), NAPOLEON'S IRON BEDS

Locksmith Marie-Jean Desouches invented this polished iron camp bed, with its gilt bronze and ornaments, and which can be folded in two or four. Its clever design meant it could be transported easily and remained perfectly comfortable. Napoleon was impressed and ordered several for his own use.

In his deliveries, Desouches referred to two types of bed, the "small model" and the "large model". It was long believed that the relatively small differences concerned size or shape. However, it turns out that the Emperor's beds, measuring 180–200 cm long, mainly differed in terms of comfort and use. In an invoice dated 1809, Desouches specifies that the "small model" folds in four and is highly portable and "could be transported on the back of a mule" in "a lined leather case" or in a small wooden box. As the beds were used by Napoleon on the battlefield, they had to be easy to carry and take up minimum space in the bivouac.

As Desouches states on his invoice, it comes with an "imperial" or canopy for privacy. None of these requirements applied to the *large model,* no doubt intended for the imperial residences. As he mainly worked at night, Napoleon wanted a camp bed in his study, as it would be faster to prepare than his large state bed. The criteria of mobility, comfort and compactness were less important, which may explain why this model only folds in two, and not four, and why bars can be placed on the back. As it was used in a room, there was no need for a canopy. There were far more of these because they were in constant use, and around a dozen of the *small model,* stamped with the imperial crown and "Desouches" in a circular arc, have become known to us, including this one (above) and Napoleon's model, which Marie-Louise took to Vienna (page 303). The *large model* beds were much rarer. The Ledoux collection owns one with bars, as exhibited at the 1974 Biennial by Napoleon expert Charles Marchal, and a slightly smaller one, probably used by the Empress.

The two beds that Napoleon took to St Helena – his deathbed and the one on which his body was laid out the next day – are regularly the subject of heated debates. The only thing that is certain, if we are to believe General Gourgaud who followed the Emperor to St Helena: "At 10 o'clock, at bedtime, and during the night, the Emperor changes bed three times, going from the large bed to the smaller one, then to the divan"; the two beds taken by Napoleon and used at Longwood were not identical and the difference in comfort was the main point. A *small model* is on show at the Musée de l'Armée in Paris while a *large model,* without its bars, can be seen at Malmaison museum. Before leaving for his final exile, the Emperor no doubt took the precaution of packing his extra beds so he could keep up his routine on this lost island. Drawings made on the spot or produced to match the descriptions provided by his close entourage show the two models, sometimes with bars, adding to the unending debates on the identity of the deathbed.

MARTIN-GUILLAUME BIENNAIS (1764-1843), LARGE TRUNK

When traveling during campaigns, the Emperor's staff had to take along numerous supplies to ensure his comfort. This very rare large linen trunk made from mahogany with brass reinforcements has an interior tray to help organize the various items while traveling. It is signed by the Emperor's tabletier, Martin-Guillaume Biennais.

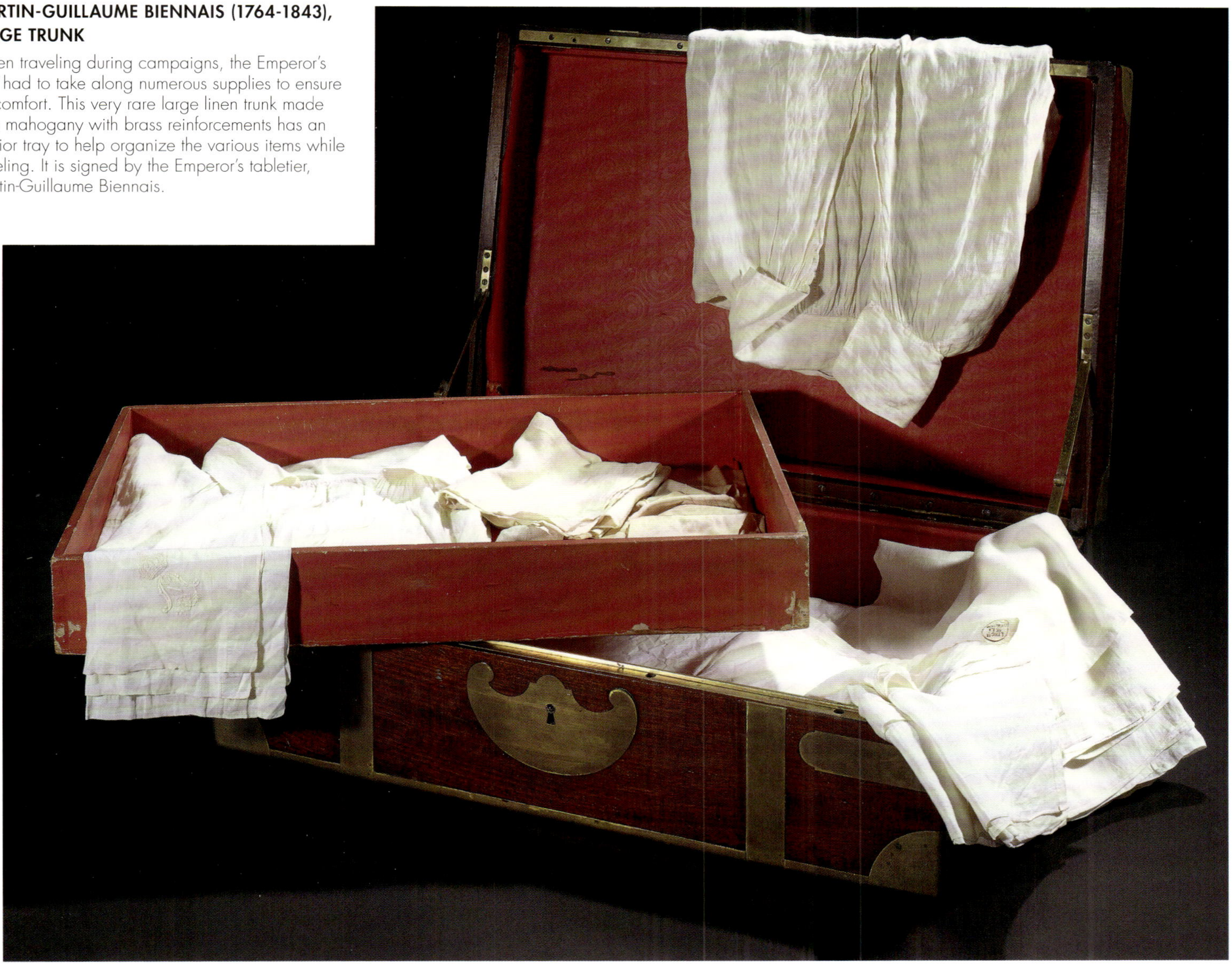

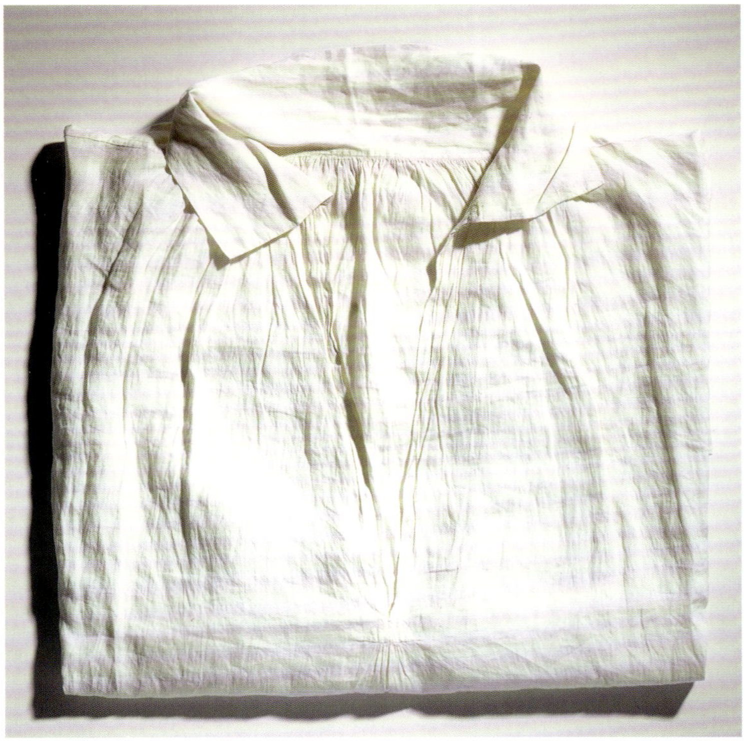

CHEMISES, PAIRS OF STOCKINGS, AND HANDKERCHIEFS BELONGING TO NAPOLEON

These long-sleeve, straight collar batiste chemises, embroidered in red thread with Napoleon's crowned "N" monogram, are one of the last remnants of the vast quantity of personal linen that Napoleon had at his disposal. The purveyors of his linen, the Misses Lolive and de Beuvry, write in their Memoirs that between January and April 1813 they delivered 240 muslin chemises. Forty-seven chemises are recorded in the inventory taken on 8 May 1821 after Napoleon's death, including six that he bequeathed to his son but also 27 that he left to his executors. Three of these are now in the possession of this collection, plus two pairs of stockings and two handkerchiefs.

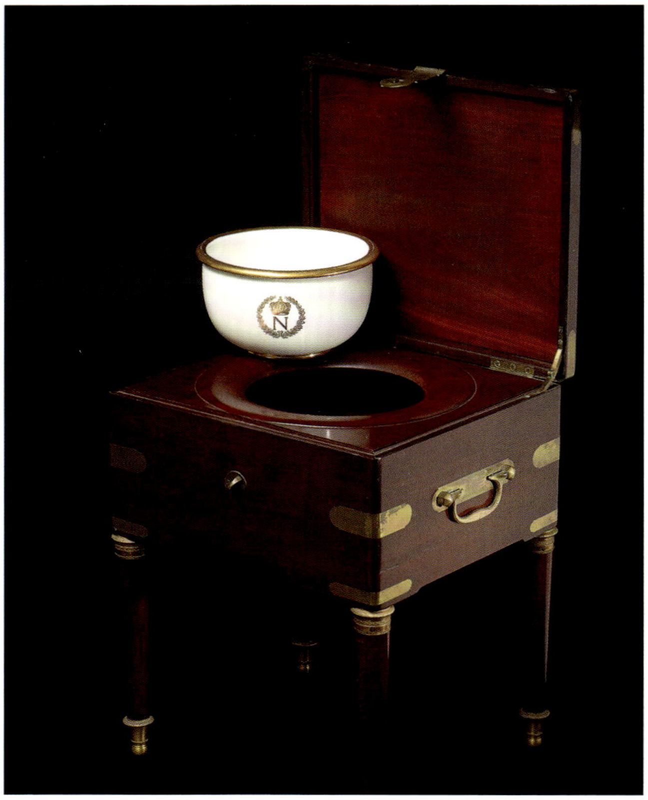

MARTIN-GUILLAUME BIENNAIS (1764-1843), COMMODE

This little mahogany commode with brass ornamentation bears an escutcheon on its lid that has been left blank. It carries the mark of Biennais, and is similar to those that Napoleon would have used while on campaign. The white porcelain chamber pot it comes with bears the Emperor's monogram.

NAPOLEON'S POCKETKNIFE

Napoleon always carried a small, folding pocketknife – the habit of an old soldier perhaps. One thing is certain: he used his pocketknife for all manner of purposes, not least to alleviate the tedium of his Cabinet or Council of State meetings by gouging deep cuts in the precious wood of the arms of his chair – giving furniture repairers much welcome work. This knife, in vermeil and mother-of-pearl with gold ornamentation, was part of General Daumesnil's estate. A very similar model forms part of the collections of the Musée de l'Armée in Paris.

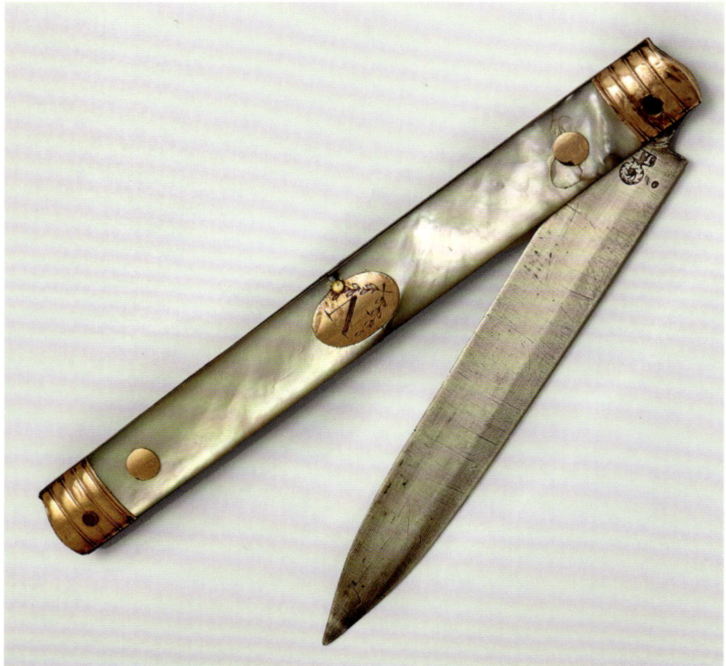

NAPOLEON'S TONGUE-SCRAPER

Napoleon was so meticulous about oral hygiene that in addition to a toothbrush, dental coral and small boxwood toothpicks, he also owned a tongue-scraper. This small, gold and brown tortoiseshell model was used by him on St Helena and is the only example still extant. It comes complete with its original ivory box and was given by Mme Bertrand to Royal Navy officer Captain Hayne after the Emperor's death. The inscription inside the lid reads: "THIS TONGUE SCRAPER BELONGED TO NAPOLEON / AT ST HELENA / AND WAS GIVEN TO Lt R. HAYNE RA / BY MADAME BERTRAND 8TH MAY 1821."

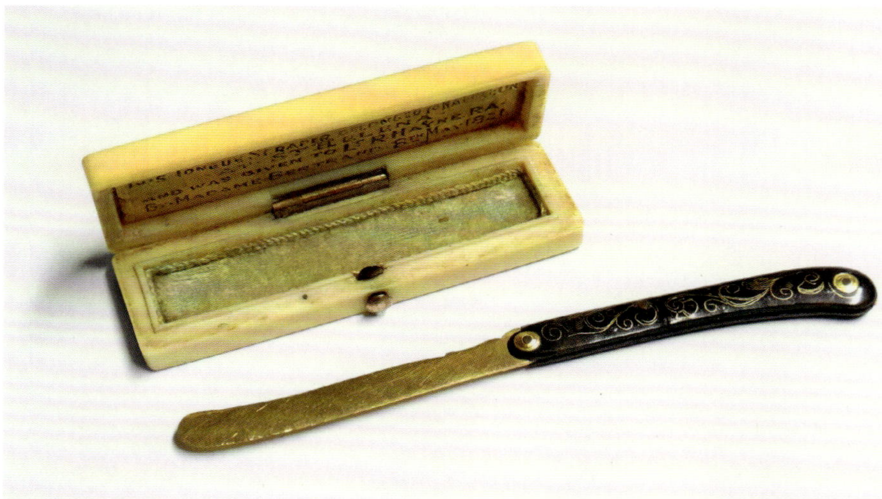

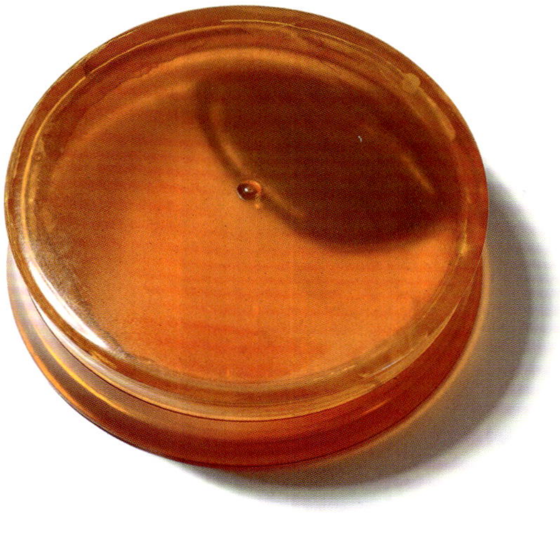

MARTIN-GUILLAUME BIENNAIS (1764-1843), CIRCULAR TORTOISESHELL BONBON BOX BELONGING TO NAPOLEON

Napoleon loved licorice and was never without a small, pale tortoiseshell box full of his favorite bonbons. Pictured here is the only surviving example of just three that were made by celebrated French goldsmith Biennais – a highly personal possession that was stolen by a certain officer Otto at Waterloo, pilfered from Napoleon's famous landau after he fled the battlefield. Astonishingly, it still contains licorice. It was presented in a major exhibition focusing on Napoleon's landau, *La Berline de Napoléon,* staged at the Musée de la Légion d'Honneur in 2012.

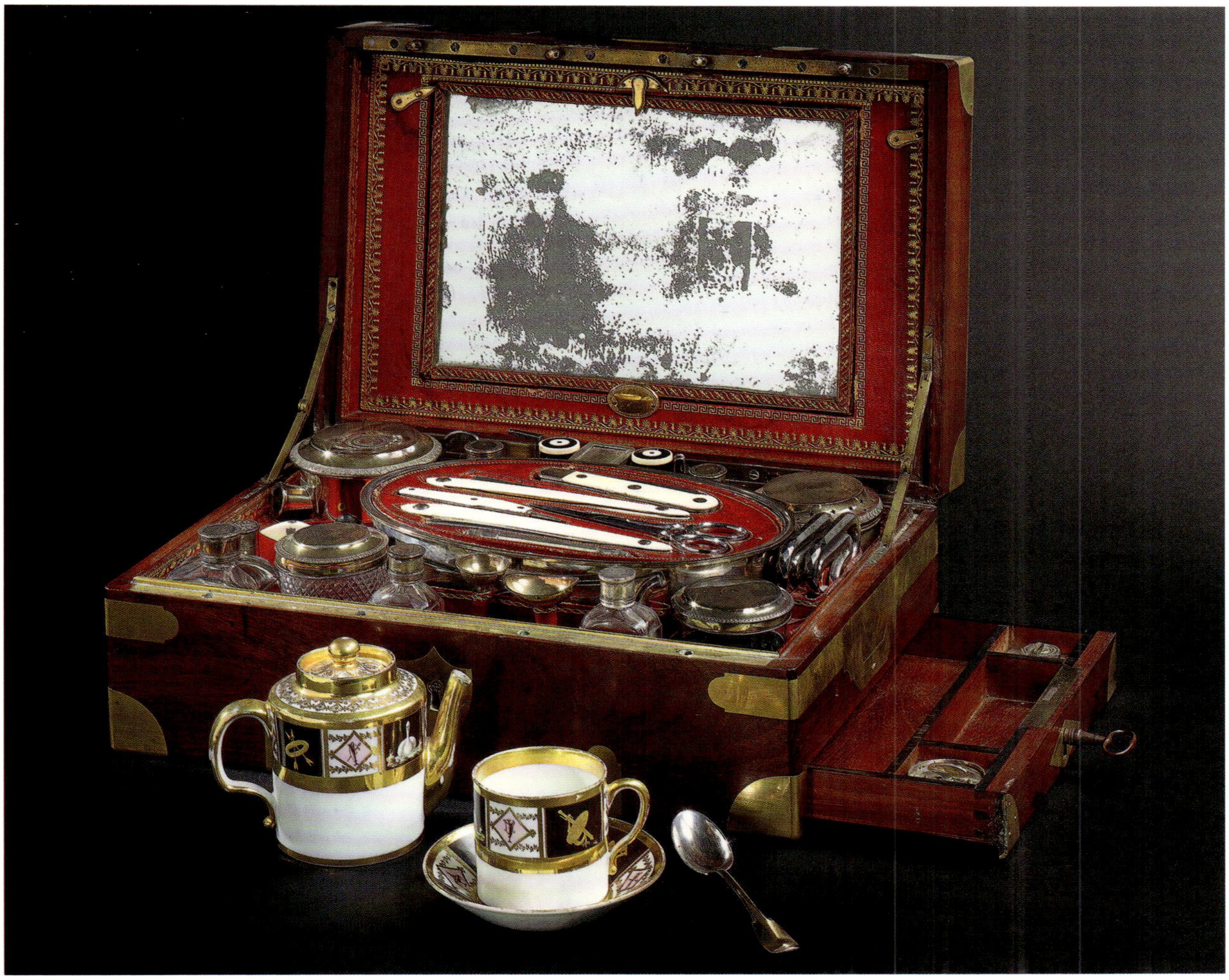

PIERRE-DOMINIQUE MAIRE (1763-1827), TRAVEL SET BELONGING TO DOMINIQUE-JEAN LARREY, CHIEF SURGEON OF THE GRAND ARMY

This set contains many items for use when traveling during campaigns, including razors, a grooming basin and a boot jack. Produced by Pierre-Dominique Maire (1763-1827), Biennais' main competitor, it belonged to Dominique-Jean Larrey (1766-1842), and bears his initials *DL*. This monogram also adorns the precious copy of *Napoleon and his contemporaries* by Auguste de Chambure, which was given to him in 1824 and which was later passed on to the renowned Emile Brouwet collection. Larrey was a baron of the Empire, the best-known medical figure of the First Empire and a pioneer in battlefield medicine. He took part in a multitude of Napoleonic campaigns, from Egypt to Waterloo, where he was injured. His aid and his dedication during the Russian retreat in 1812 were legendary. After spotting him on the battlefield at Waterloo, Wellington allegedly lifted his bicorne and whispered: "I salute the honor of he who passes." But let us leave the last word to the Emperor: "What a brave and worthy man Larrey is! So much care given by him to the Army of Egypt, when crossing the desert and after the siege of Acre, and then in Europe! If the army ever erects a monument to express its gratitude, it should do so in honor of Larrey. [...] It is largely thanks to Larrey that humankind witnessed a revolution in surgery. [...] He is the most virtuous man I have ever met. He leaves me with the memory of a genuinely good man". The collection contains another, smaller travel set having belonged to Larrey, rectangular in shape and known as the "coat rack".

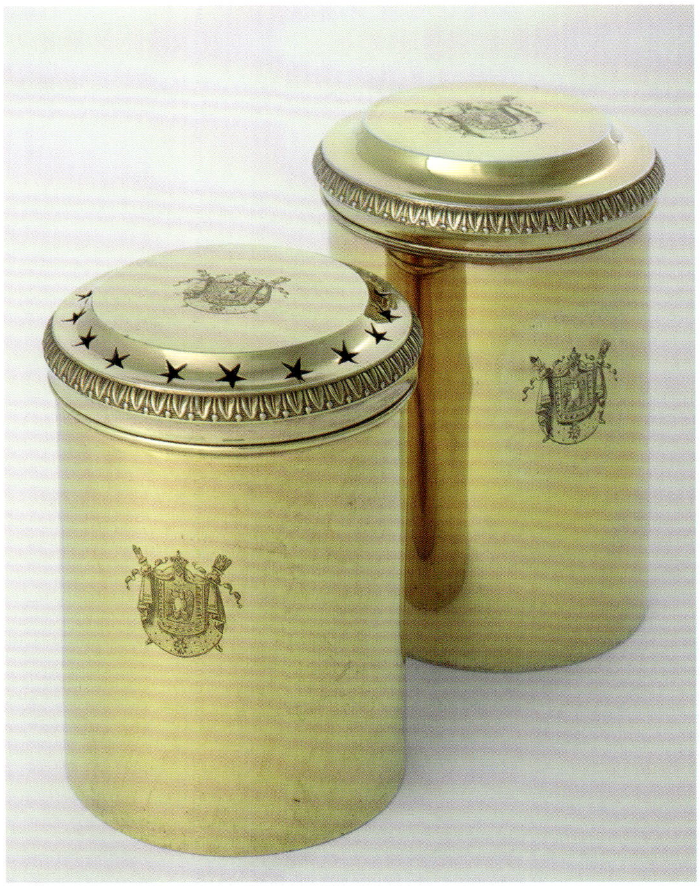

MARTIN-GUILLAUME BIENNAIS (1764-1843), SPONGE BOXES FROM NAPOLEON'S TOILETRY *NÉCESSAIRE*

The Emperor was fastidious about personal hygiene and owned two magnificent, vermeil toiletry sets that were delivered by master goldsmith Biennais in 1806. One is preserved at the Musée Carnavalet. The contents of the other box has almost entirely disappeared – probably stolen when Napoleon's landau was pillaged at Waterloo – apart from a few pieces that are thought to include these two vermeil boxes.
The lids are punctuated with star-shaped holes and the imperial coat-of-arms appears in the center of the lid and also on the outside of the box.

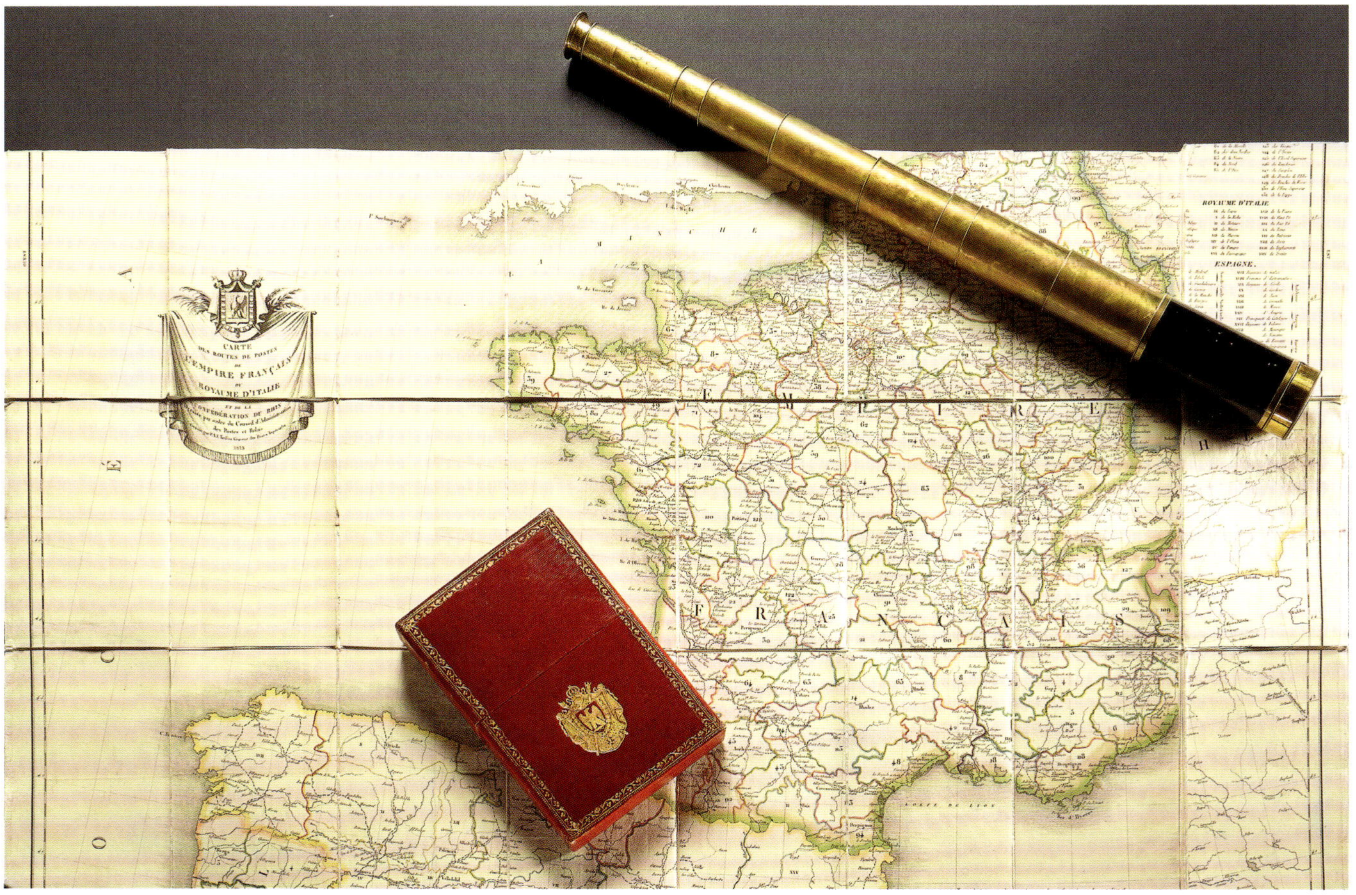

MAP OF GEOGRAPHY UNDER NAPOLEON AND A TELESCOPE

Whether on campaign or at his imperial residences, Napoleon regularly consulted his many maps, which he always kept to hand. In fact, many official portraits depict him with a map placed beside him. They recall not only his conquering ambitions, spelt out in the propaganda, but also his well-known interest in geography. These maps were updated annually and were stored in small red Morocco leather boxes adorned with the imperial coat-of-arms.
On this map a telescope has been placed, like a piece of loot. It was used by British Captain Sandes during the Battle of Salamanca and brought back by Wellington's troops on 22 July 1812, as the engraved inscription indicates. "E.B. Fairfield/Purchased of C. L. Sandes Esq r/3rd – Guards/During the action at Salamanca/July 1812/Harris 47 Holborn London".

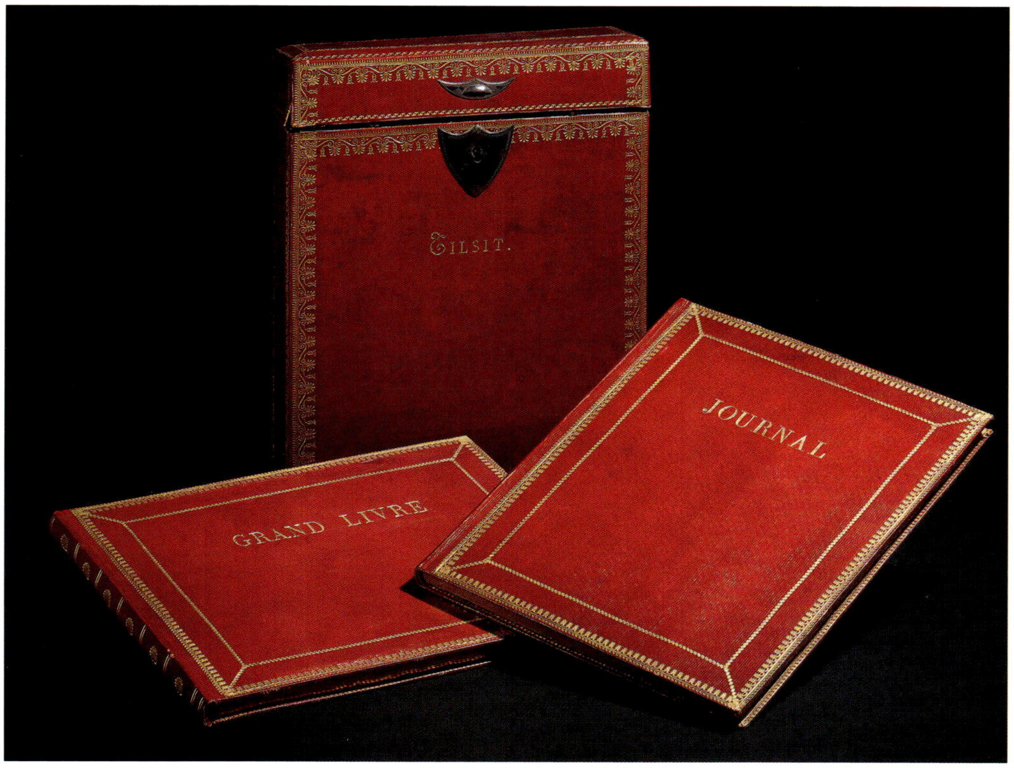

BOX CONTAINING THE TREATIES OF TILSIT

Protecting the "Grand Ledger" and a "Journal", this red Morocco leather case is stamped with the name of "Tilsit" in gold letters. The pages of the two books are completely blank but were probably intended for the report on the negotiations held between Napoleon and Tsar Alexander I on a raft in the middle of the Neman River in the town of Tilsit in July 1807. The treaty sealed the ceasefire in hostilities between France and Russia, the day after French victory in Friedland.

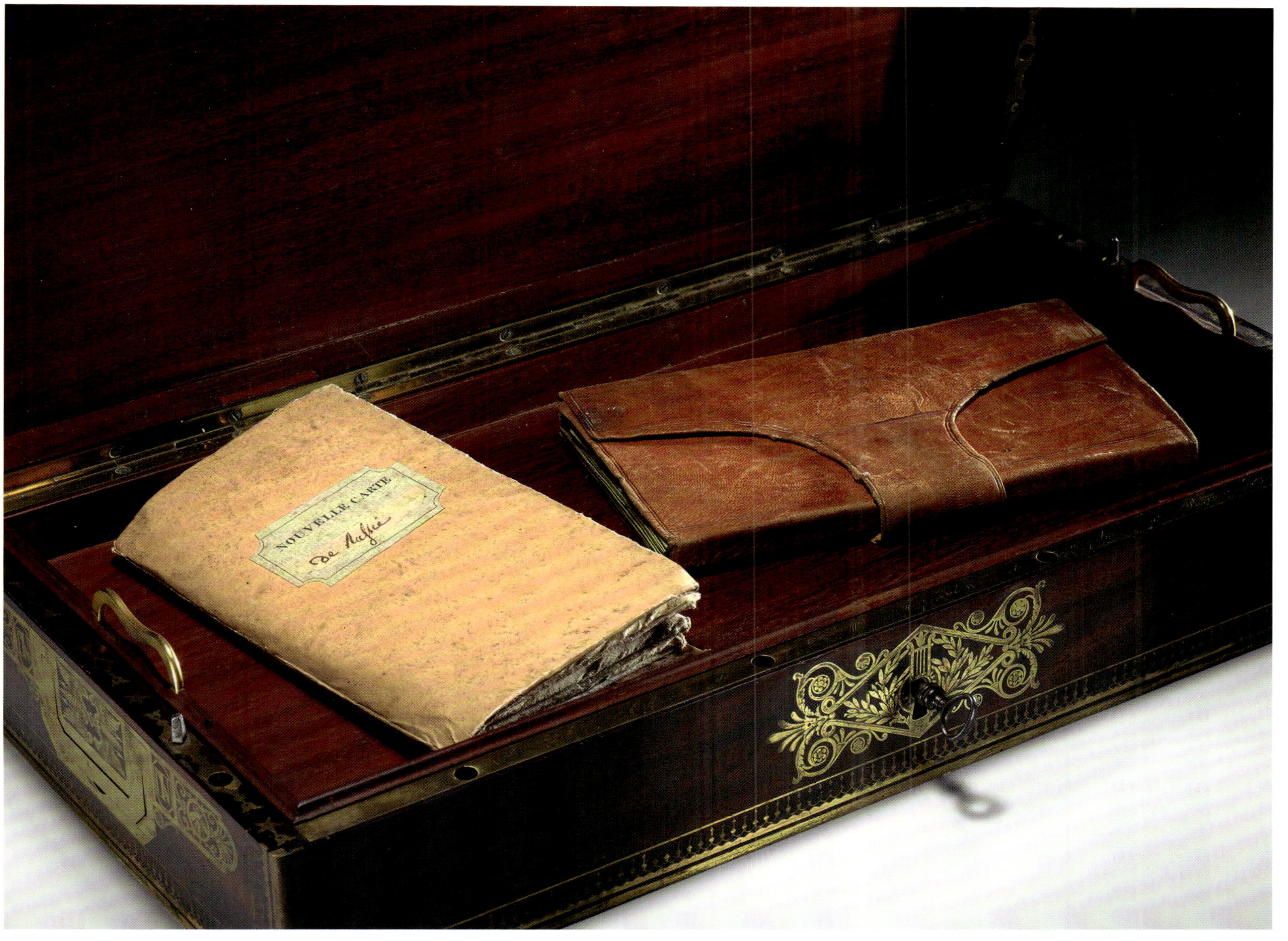

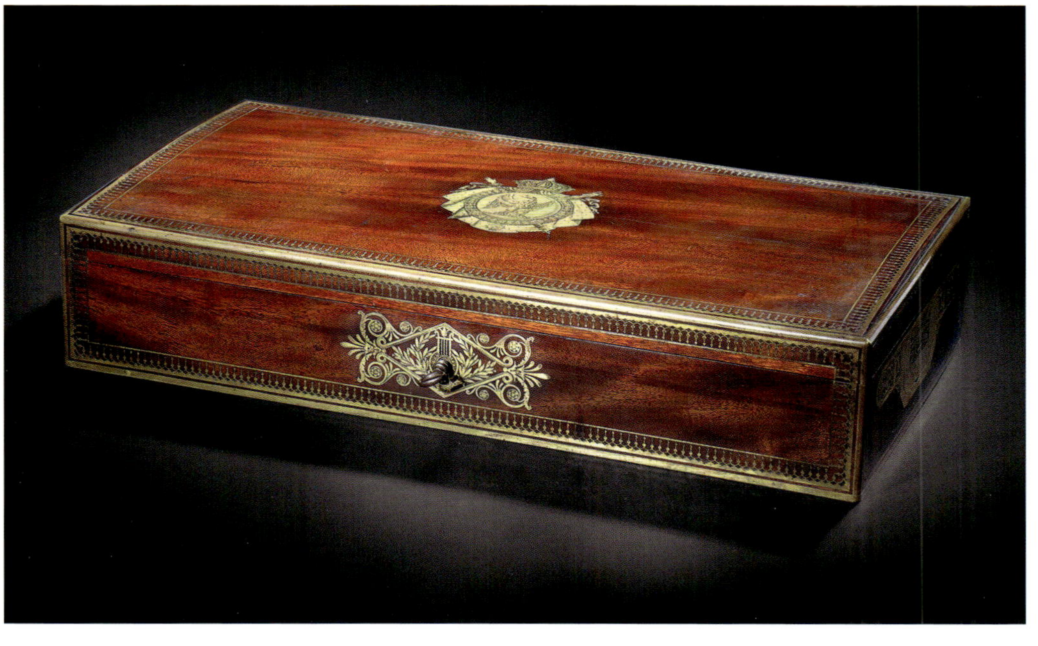

MARTIN-GUILLAUME BIENNAIS (1764-1843), CORRESPONDENCE BOX USED BY NAPOLEON IN RUSSIA

The year 1812 saw the eagle beaten for the first time. As hordes of French soldiers tried to get home across the snowy Russian steppes, Napoleon suddenly abandoned what remained of his army and raced back to France. This large, mahogany dispatch box was left behind, complete with the maps of Russia and wallet shown here. In the end, Napoleon's grand imperial coat-of-arms, for all of its masterful engraving – the "N" positioned at the level of the handles and the ornate winged thunderbolts – was not enough to bring him victory. The most valuable objects, including the soldier's ragged uniforms, were abandoned in a disastrous retreat that still haunts the popular imagination.

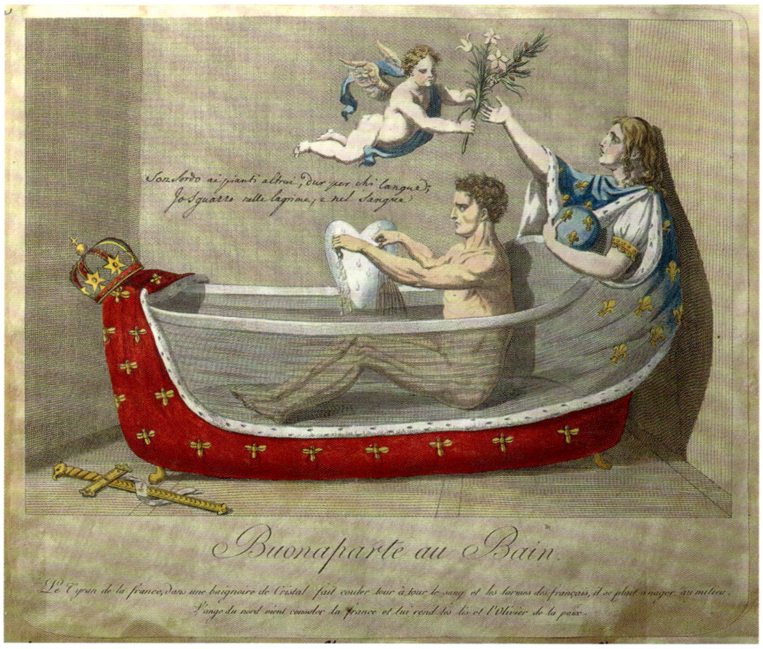
Buonaparte au Bain.
Le Tyran de la france, dans une baignoire de Cristal fait couler tour à tour le sang et les larmes des français, il se plait a nager au milieu.
L'ange du nord vient consoler la france et lui rend les lis et l'Olivier de la paix.

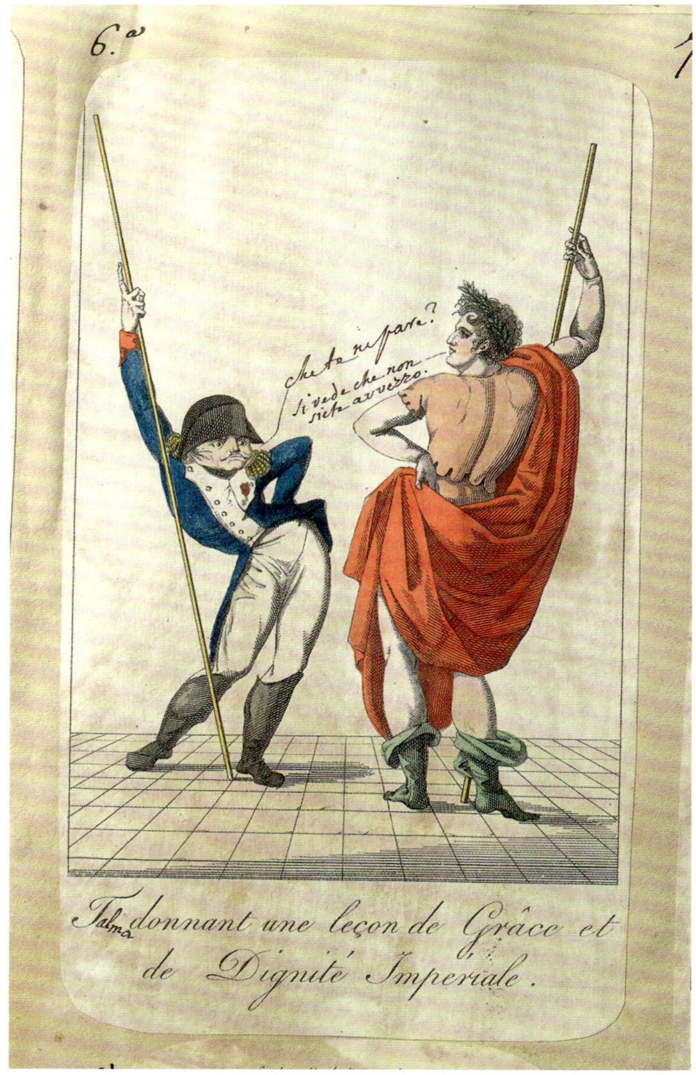
6.a
Talma donnant une leçon de Grâce et de Dignité Imperiale.

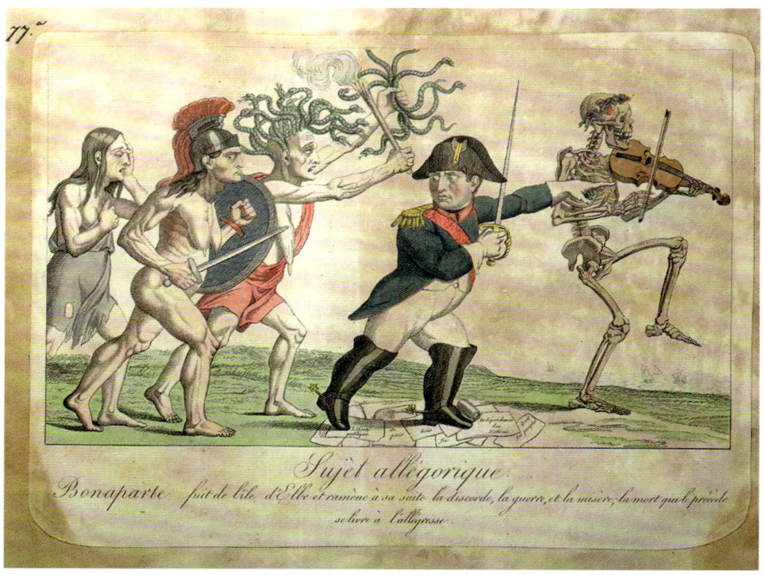
17.a
Sujèt allégorique.
Bonaparte fuit de l'île d'Elbe et ramène à sa suite la discorde, la guerre, et la misère, la mort qui le précède se livre à l'allegresse.

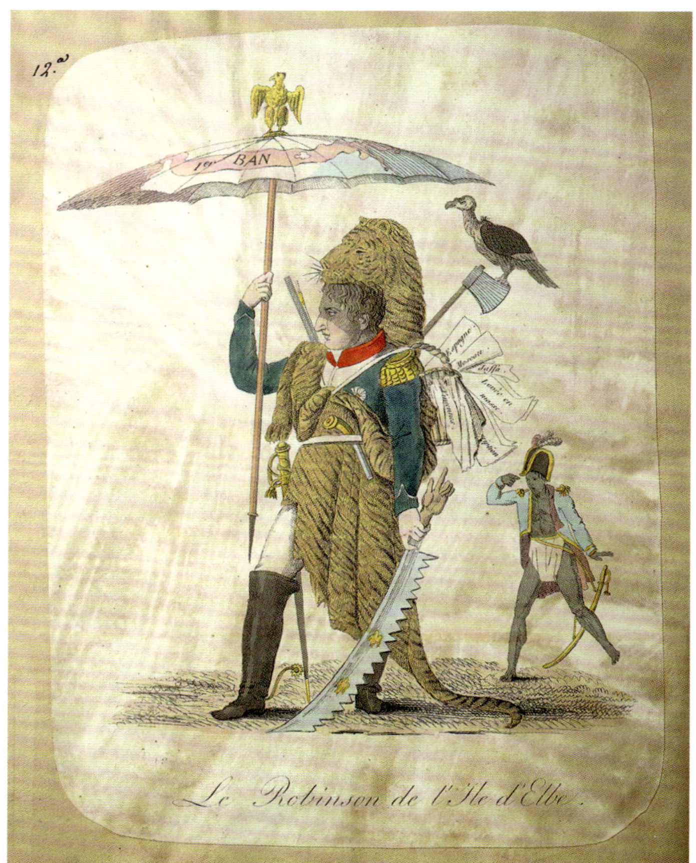
12.a
BAN
Le Robinson de l'Ile d'Elbe.

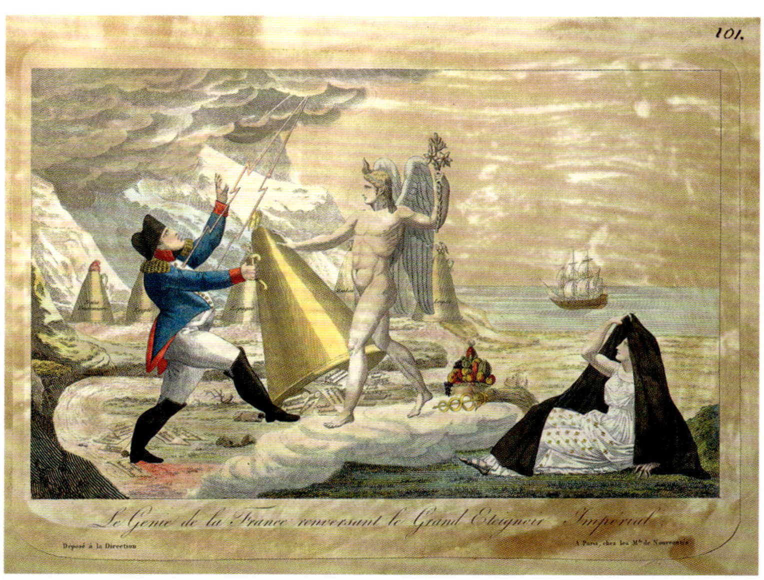
101.
Le Genie de la France renversant le Grand Eteignoir Imperial.
Déposé à la Direction

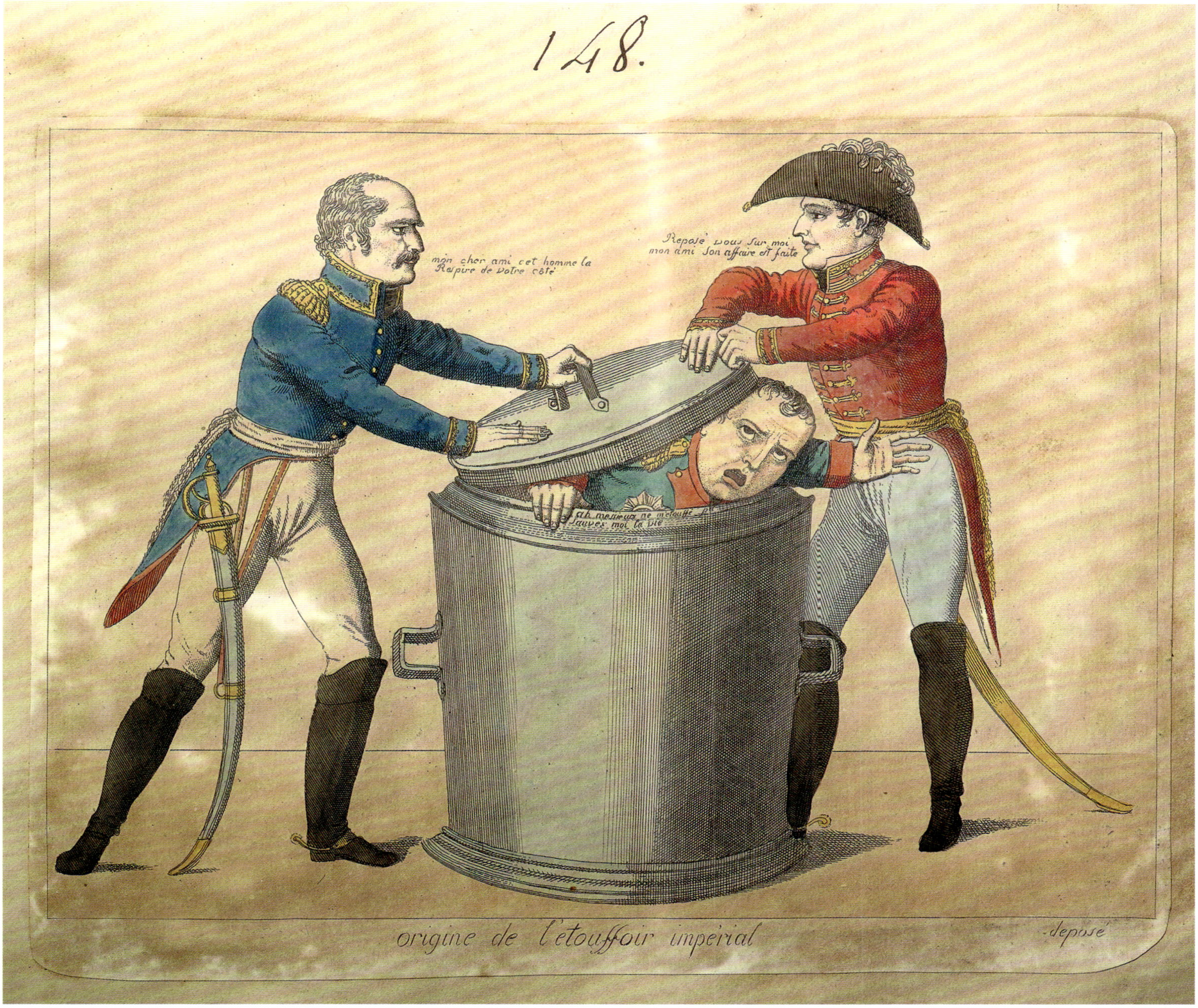

COLLECTION OF CARICATURES OF NAPOLEON BUONAPARTE

Immortalized in countless paintings and illustrations, Napoleon was endlessly lampooned during his reign. This important collection of 164 satirical, not to say daring, hand-colored etchings says a lot about the spirit of the age – not least that people were prepared to take great risks to acquire them. Only available through clandestine channels, very few of them have come down to us intact.

ABDICATION AND ELBA

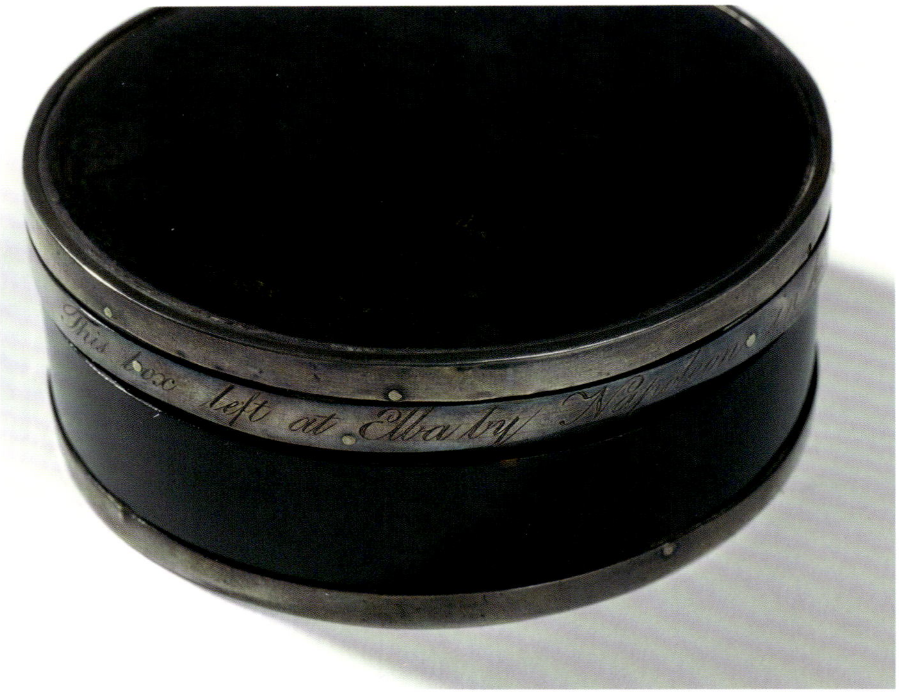

TORTOISESHELL BOX BELONGING TO NAPOLEON, LEFT ON ELBA

Exile to Elba was the first wake-up call before the fall of the Empire. Few objects remain from that ten-month period. This brown tortoiseshell box is a rare souvenir, certified by the inscription that runs around the silver ring on the lid: "This box left at Elba by Napoleon in his flight was given to Revd J.D. Sirr by Mrs Grey". Lord Grey was head of the opposition in the Chamber of Peers. In 1815, he gave an important speech to advise the British government on neutrality when Napoleon returned from Elba.

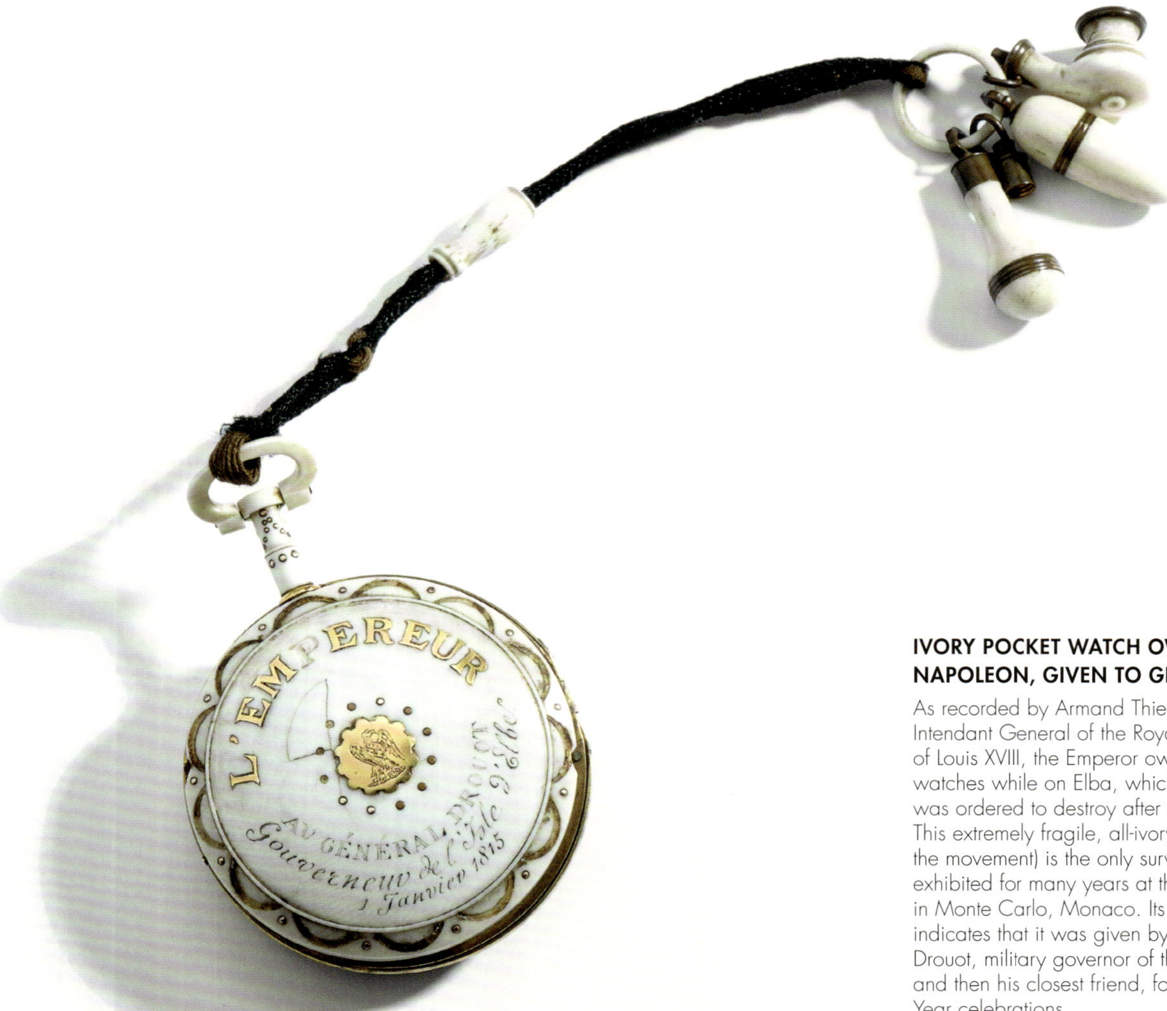

IVORY POCKET WATCH OWNED BY NAPOLEON, GIVEN TO GENERAL DROUOT

As recorded by Armand Thierry de Ville d'Avray, Intendant General of the Royal Furniture Repository of Louis XVIII, the Emperor owned several ivory watches while on Elba, which Ville d'Avray was ordered to destroy after the Restoration. This extremely fragile, all-ivory watch (including the movement) is the only surviving example, exhibited for many years at the Napoleon Museum in Monte Carlo, Monaco. Its gold inscription indicates that it was given by Napoleon to General Drouot, military governor of the island of Elba and then his closest friend, for the 1815 New Year celebrations.

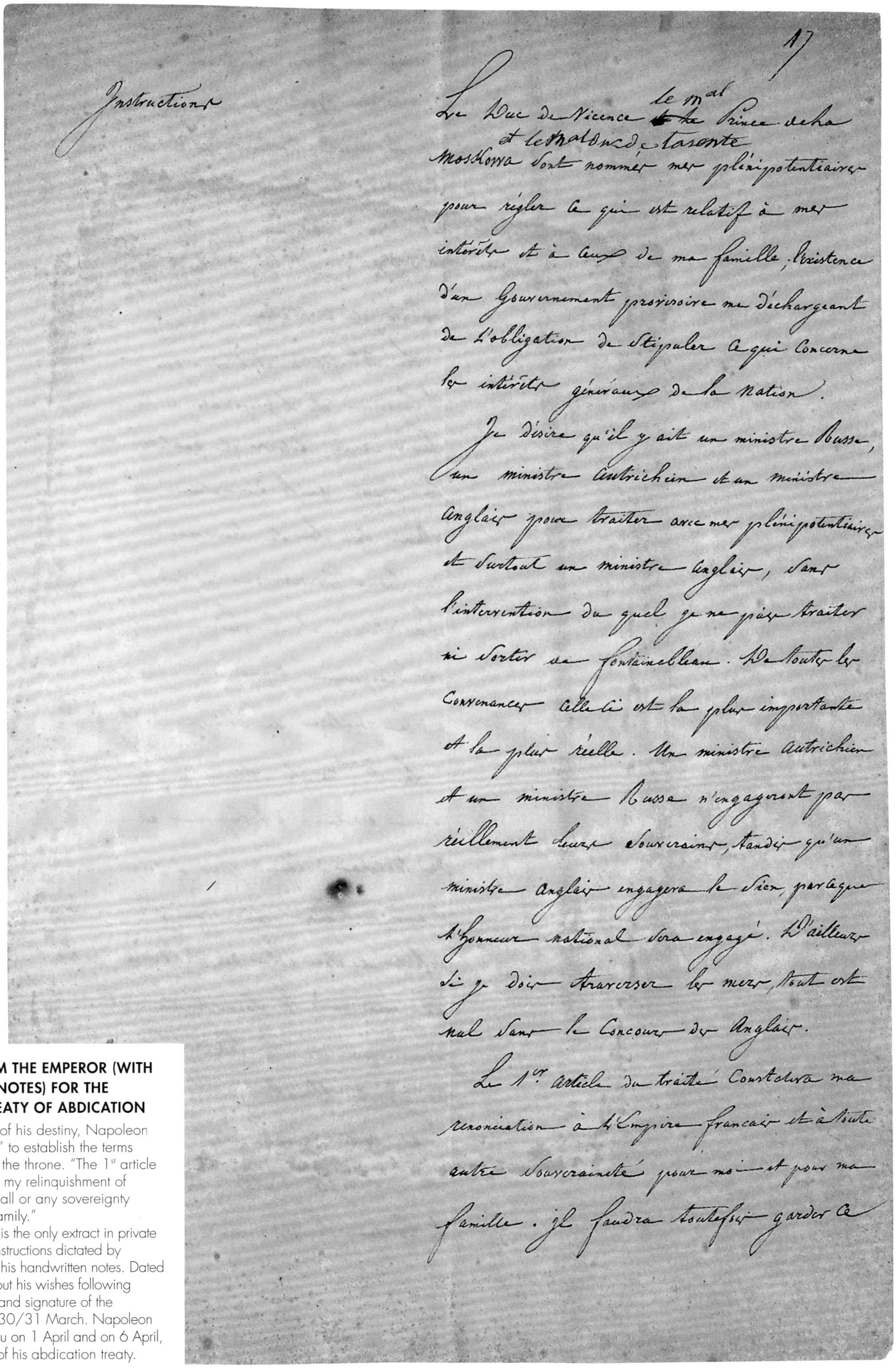
Instructions

17

Le Duc de Vicence le Mal Prince de la Moskowa et le Mal duc de Tarente sont nommés mes plénipotentiaires pour régler ce qui est relatif à mes intérêts et à ceux de ma famille, l'existence d'un Gouvernement provisoire me déchargeant de l'obligation de stipuler ce qui concerne les intérêts généraux de la nation.

Je désire qu'il y ait un ministre Russe, un ministre autrichien et un ministre anglais pour traiter avec mes plénipotentiaires et surtout un ministre anglais, sans l'intervention duquel je ne puis traiter ni sortir de Fontainebleau. De toutes les convenances celle ci est la plus importante et la plus réelle. Un ministre autrichien et un ministre Russe n'engagent pas réellement leurs souverains, tandis qu'un ministre anglais engagera le sien, par lequel l'honneur national sera engagé. D'ailleurs si je dois traverser les mers, tout est nul sans le concours des anglais.

Le 1er article du traité constatera ma renonciation à l'Empire français et à toute autre souveraineté pour moi et pour ma famille. Il faudra toutefois garder ce

INSTRUCTIONS FROM THE EMPEROR (WITH HIS HANDWRITTEN NOTES) FOR THE FONTAINEBLEAU TREATY OF ABDICATION

Keen to remain master of his destiny, Napoleon used these "instructions" to establish the terms of his relinquishment of the throne. "The 1st article of the treaty will record my relinquishment of the French Empire and all or any sovereignty for myself and for my family."
This historical document is the only extract in private hands of the infamous instructions dictated by Napoleon and bearing his handwritten notes. Dated 4 April 1814, they set out his wishes following the capitulation of Paris and signature of the armistice in the night of 30/31 March. Napoleon returned to Fontainebleau on 1 April and on 6 April, signed the final version of his abdication treaty.

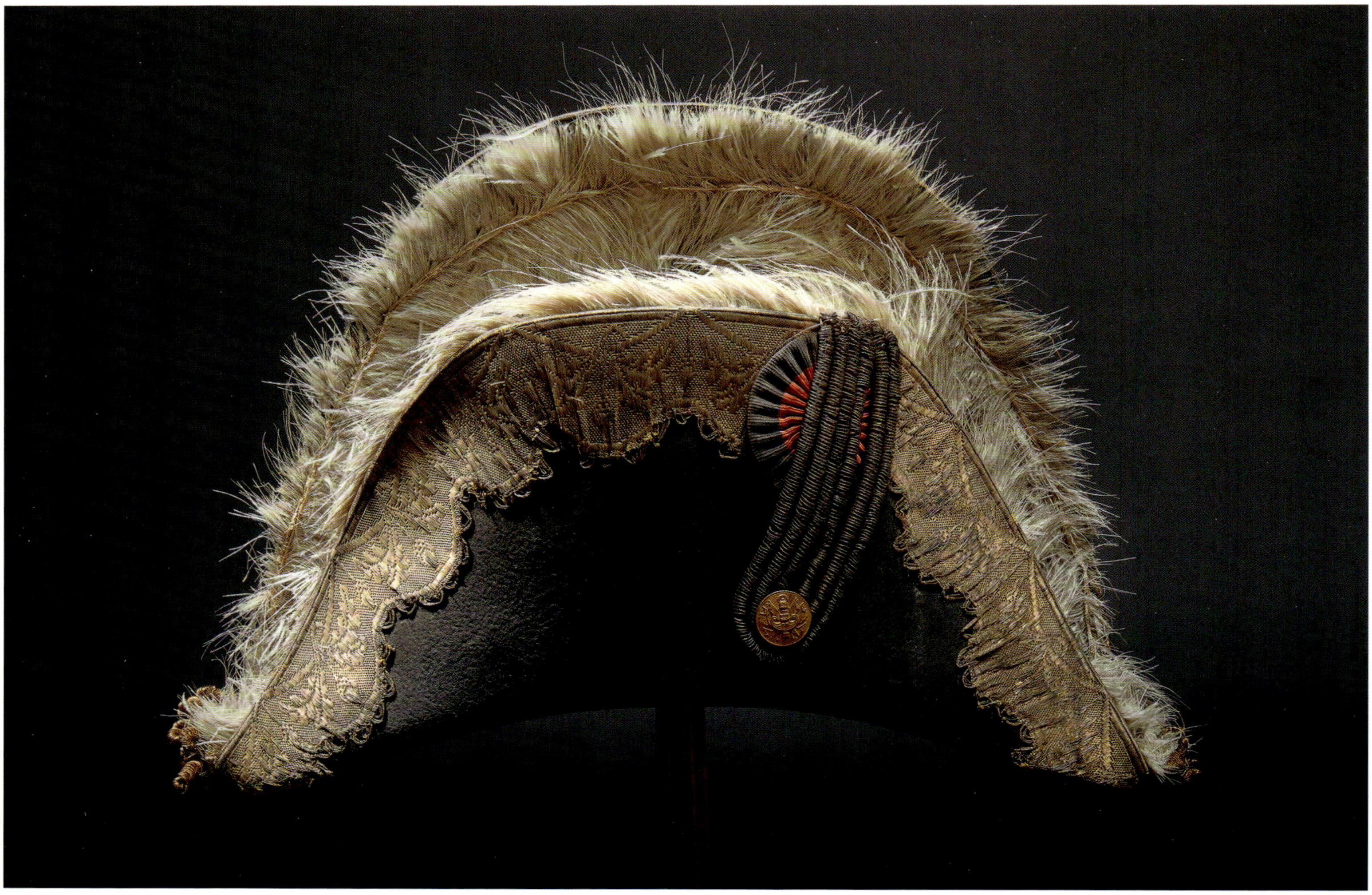

BICORNE HAT OF A MARSHAL OF THE FRENCH EMPIRE OR THE COMMANDER-IN-CHIEF OF AN ARMY CORPS

This black felt hat is probably one of the rarest pieces of regulation headgear from the First Empire. It is decorated with white ostrich feathers, unlike the black feathers that adorn the bicorne hats of generals. It also features a braid held in place by a gold uniform button, whose design varied depending on whether the hat was worn for full dress or in the field. Very few such hats are known to exist today: one that belonged to Jérôme Napoleon is now in the Napoleon Museum at La Pommerie, and the Musée de l'Armée in Paris holds two hats that belonged respectively to Marshal Oudinot and to Lannes.

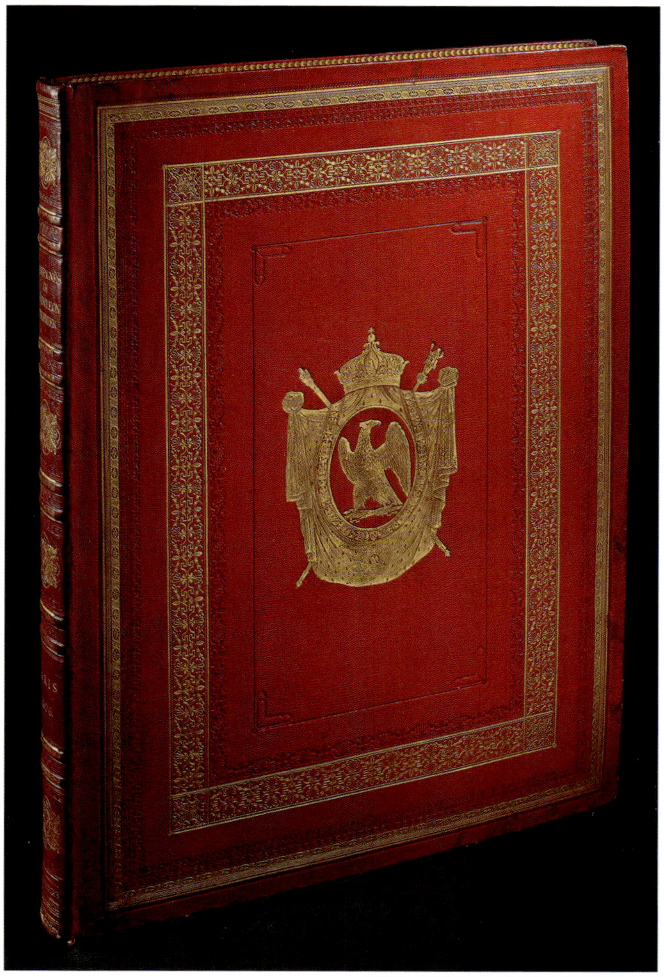

FRANÇOIS BOZÉRIAN (1765-1826), HISTORIC TABLE OF THE ITALIAN CAMPAIGNS

This "Historic Table of the Italian Campaigns from Year IV until the Battle of Marengo [...]" was published in 1806, richly bound in red Morocco leather with the imperial coat-of-arms in gold tooling on the covers. This ornamentation was the work of Bozérian, the celebrated First Empire bookbinder. A sumptuous large-format volume, the work is illustrated with twenty-four engraved plates from original drawings by Carle Vernet.

UNIFORM JACKET BELONGING TO MAJOR GENERAL LAMARQUE (1770-1832)

Very few Major Generals' uniform jackets, in blue serge embroidered with gilded silver thread, have survived intact. Even rarer are those whose provenance we are certain of because they have been kept in the descendants' family. After distinguishing himself in the Revolutionary Wars and at Austerlitz, Jean Maximilien Lamarque served as Joseph Bonaparte's Chief of Staff in Italy. He earned more glory at the Battle of Wagram, where four horses were killed underneath him in the heat of the fighting. He then followed Joseph to Spain with his division, where they won the Battle of Altafulla. Lamarque died of cholera on 1 June 1832. His funeral sparked the anti-monarchist Paris Uprising of 1832, which Victor Hugo used as a backdrop in *Les Misérables*.

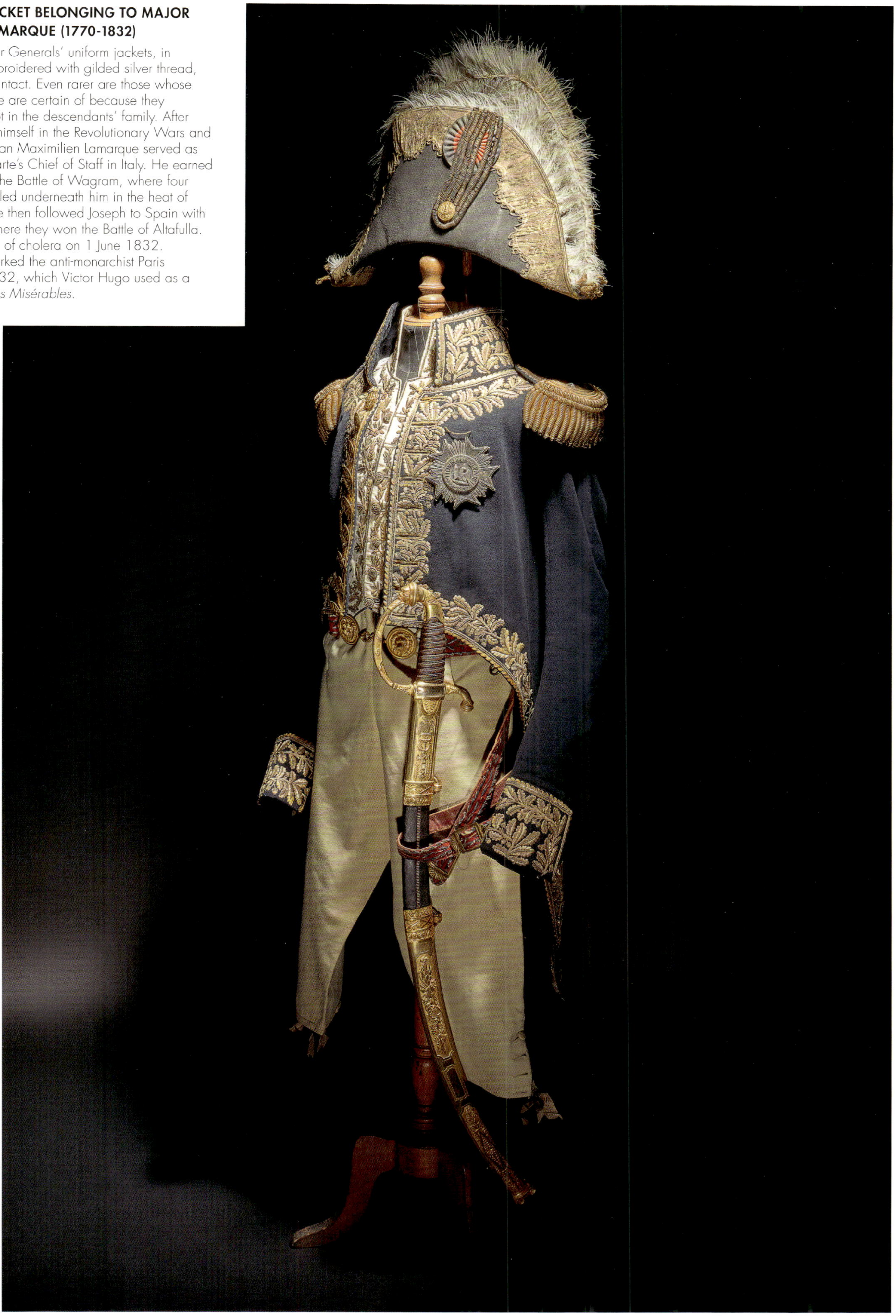

THE "HUNDRED DAYS" AND WATERLOO

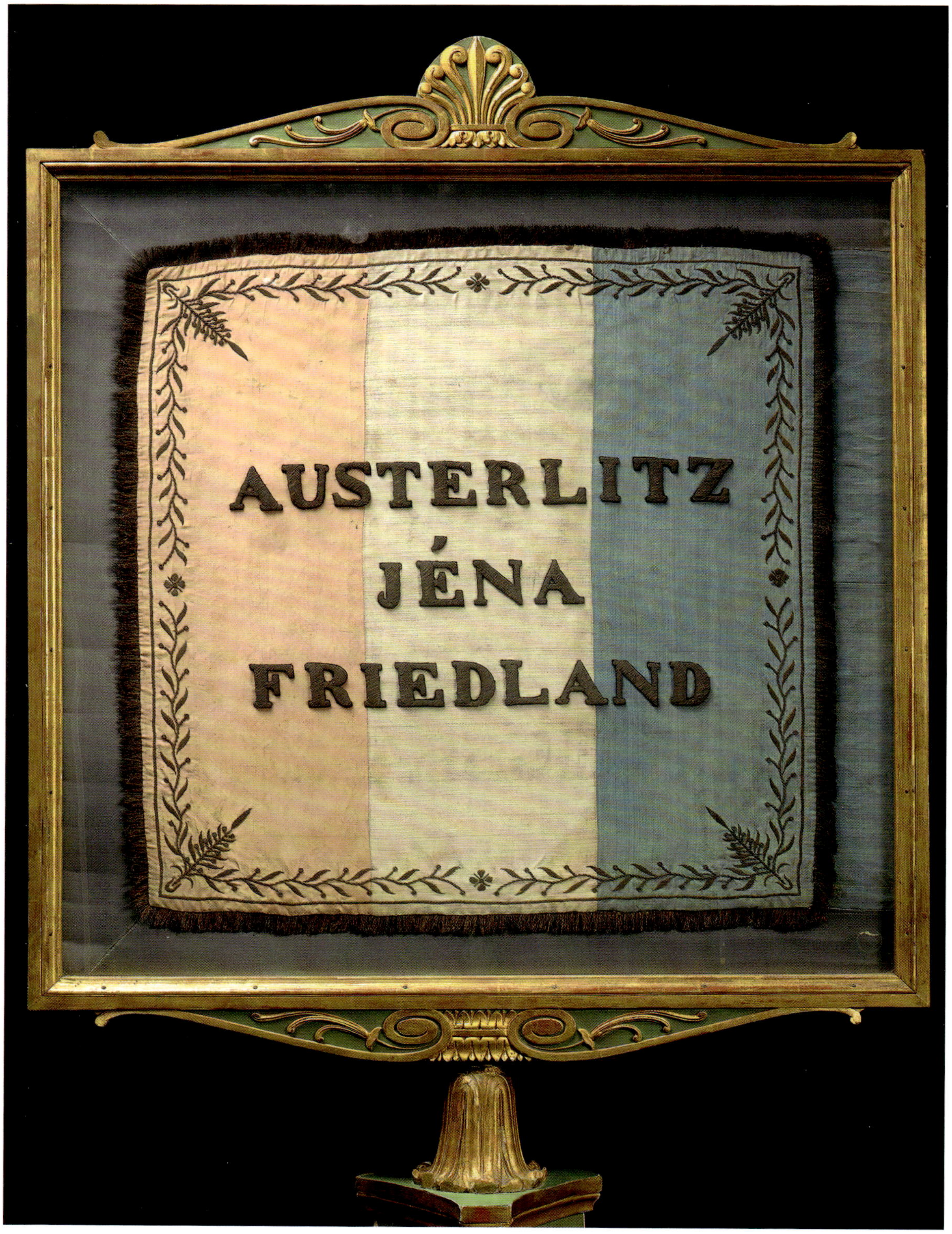

FLAG OF THE 2ND REGIMENT DE HUSSARS, 1815

In tricolor silk embroidered with a frieze of laurel leaves in gold cannetille, this rare flag has the inscription "L'EMPEREUR AU 2ME REGIMENT DE HUSSARDS" on the front, and the name of Napoleon's major victories on the other side "AUSTERLITZ, IENA, FRIEDLAND", battles at which the regiment distinguished itself. The flag was used during the "Hundred Days", in the defense of Belfort in July 1815. With eagles adorning the top of the staff, the flags were the pride of the regiment and a rallying sign for soldiers ready to die for the Emperor and the Nation. This explains why there are very few of them in private hands, as almost all of them are in national museums, most notably the Musée de l'Armée in Paris.

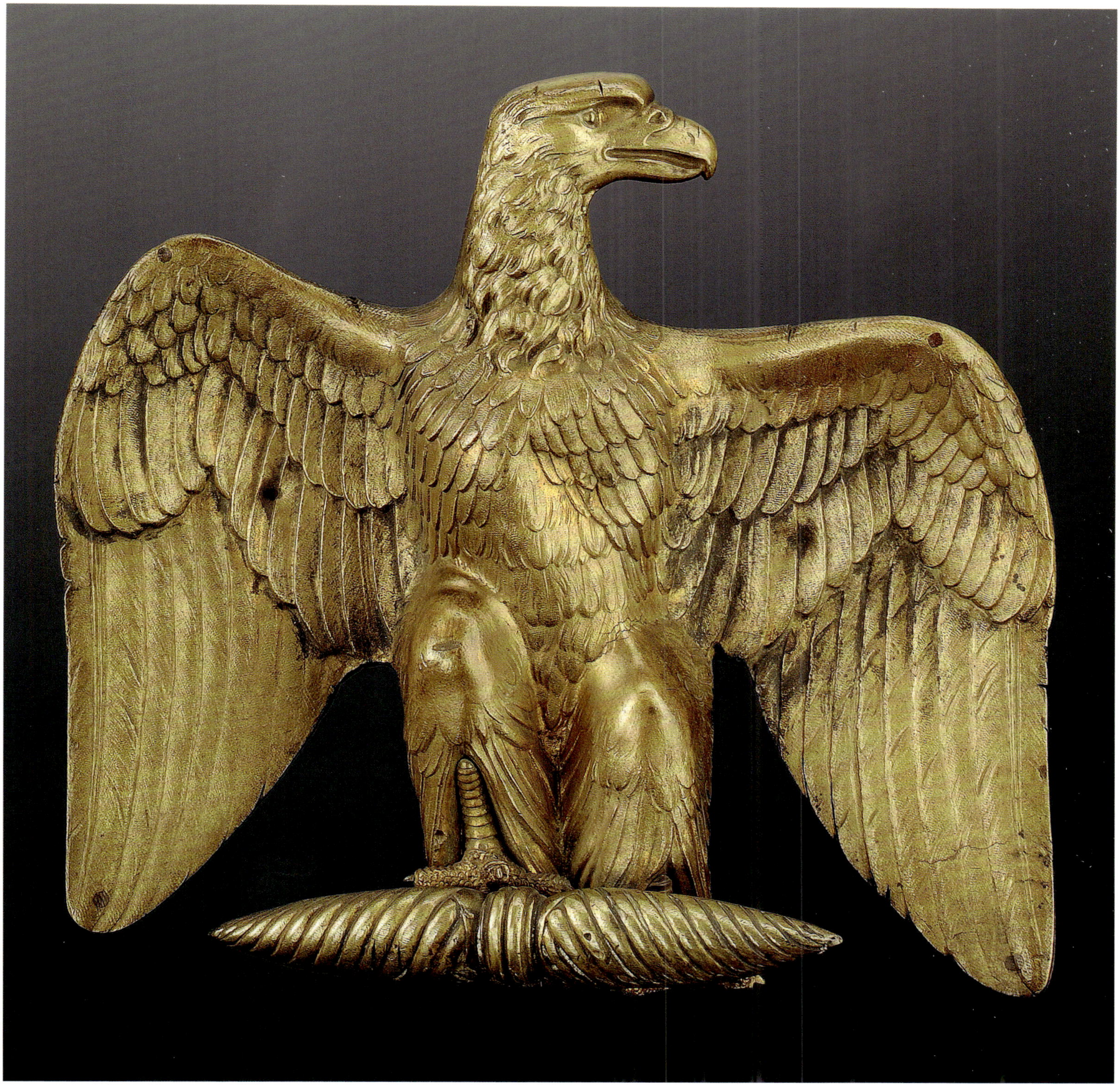

PIERRE-PHILIPPE THOMIRE (1751-1843), "WOUNDED" FLAG EAGLE, 1815

After the proclamation of the Empire on 18 May 1804, Napoleon chose the eagle as the Nation's new emblem. On 27 July, he decided that a gilded bronze eagle, made by the famous bronze-maker Thomire, would be placed on the top of the staff of all new tricolor flags and banners. In all, a total of 1,100 eagles were assigned and the Emperor liked to hand them over personally at the big military parades, saying: "Soldiers, here are your flags! These Eagles will always serve as rallying points for you; they will go wherever your emperor deems their presence necessary to defend his throne and his people. You swear to sacrifice your life to defend them, and to maintain them constantly, through your courage, on the road to victory". They were first distributed at a sumptuous ceremony on the Champs de Mars on 5 December 1804. Immortalized in David's painting, this ceremony remains the most famous of all. At the time of the Restoration, almost all the 1804-model eagles were melted down. When the Emperor returned, he hastily ordered 292 new eagles from Thomire. They were used during the "Hundred Days" but most of them were seized at Waterloo. Of the 76 that remain today, fewer than five are in private hands, including this *wounded* eagle with gashes on its wings and dents on its chest. Those "wounds" only add to its legend.

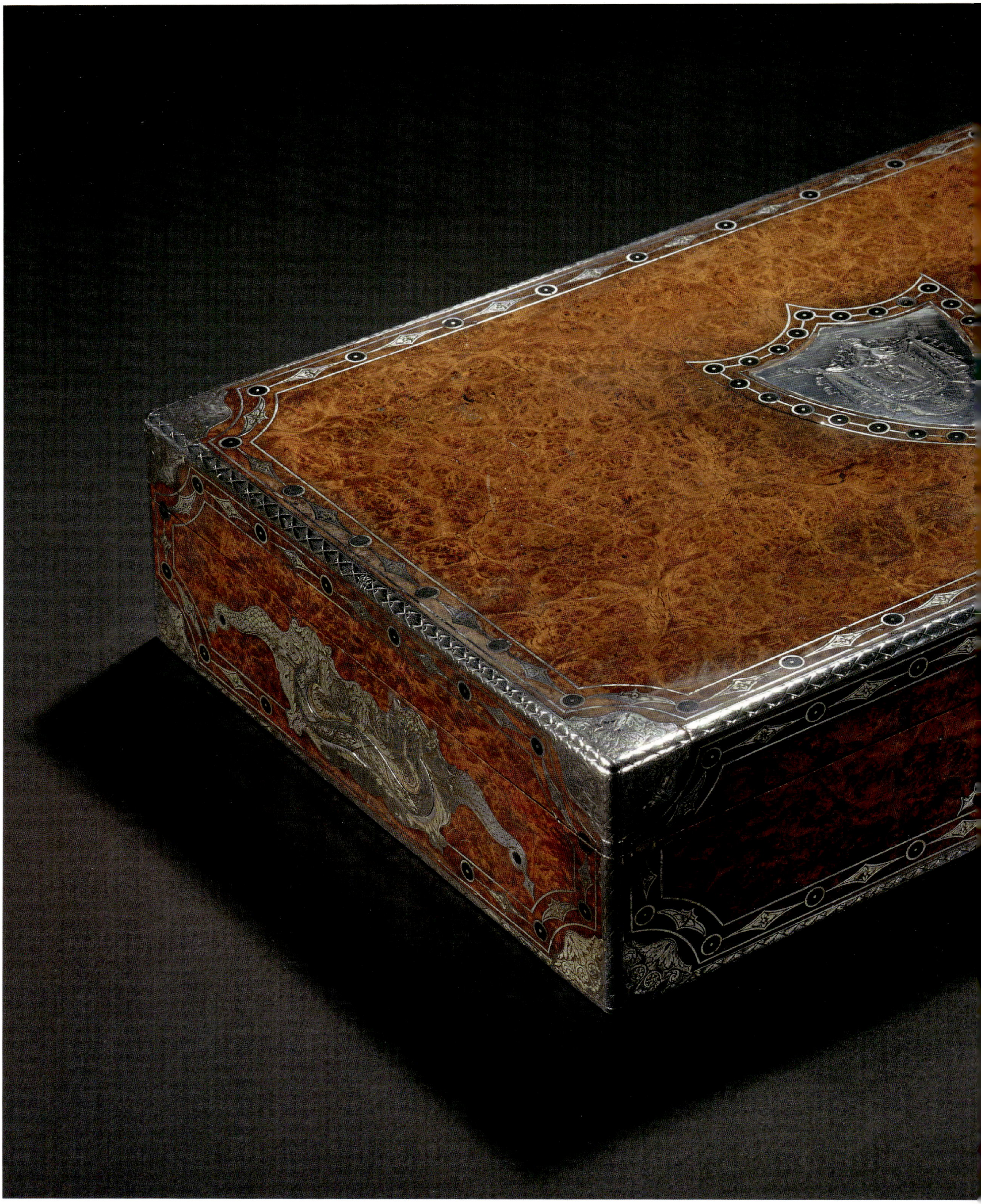

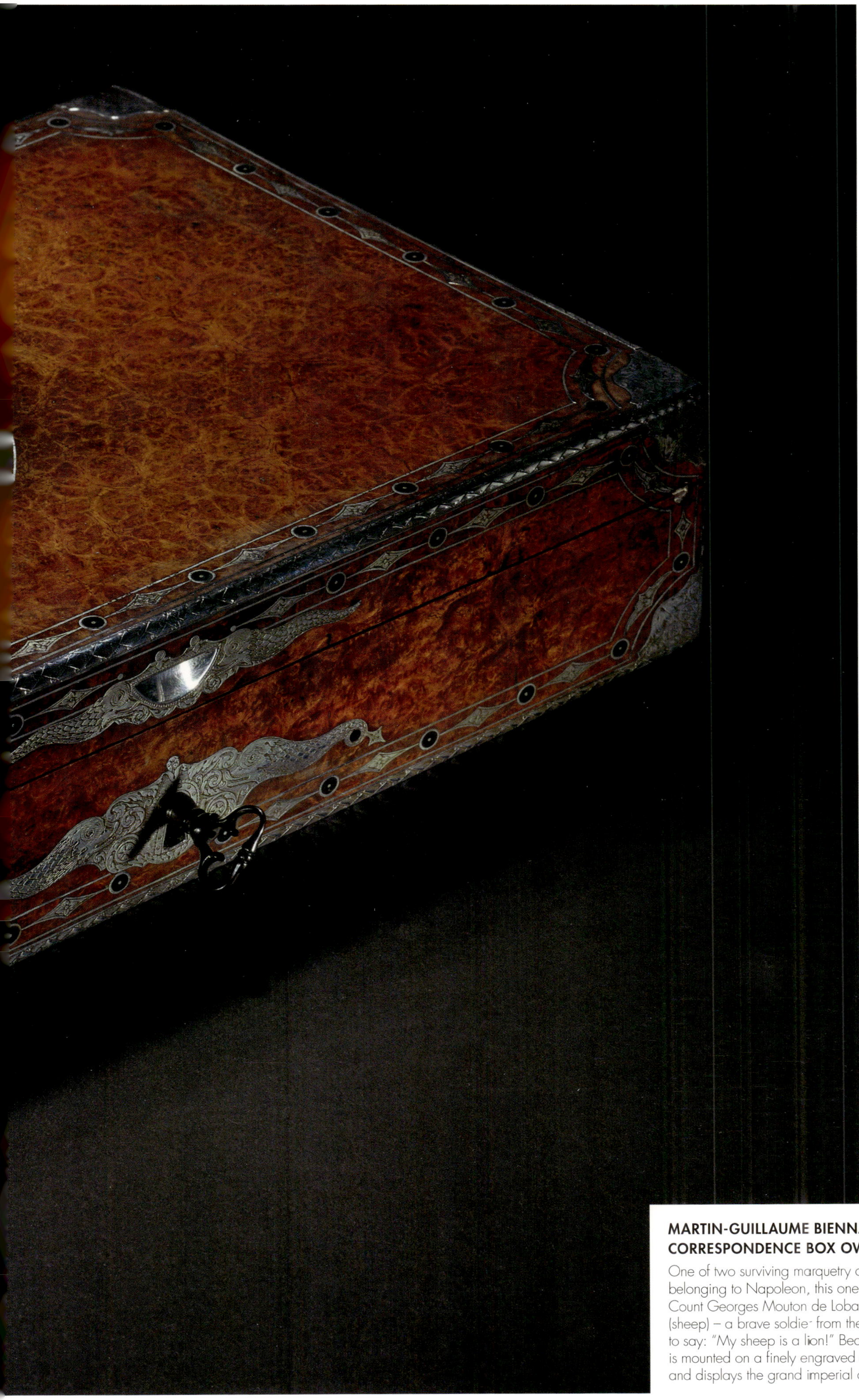

MARTIN-GUILLAUME BIENNAIS (1764-1843), CORRESPONDENCE BOX OWNED BY NAPOLEON

One of two surviving marquetry correspondence boxes once belonging to Napoleon, this one a gift from the Emperor to General-Count Georges Mouton de Lobau, known to his friends as *Mouton* (sheep) – a brave soldier from the Lorraine of whom Napoleon used to say: "My sheep is a lion!" Beautifully crafted by Biennais, the box is mounted on a finely engraved silver frame with decorative inlay and displays the grand imperial coat-of-arms in the center of the lid.

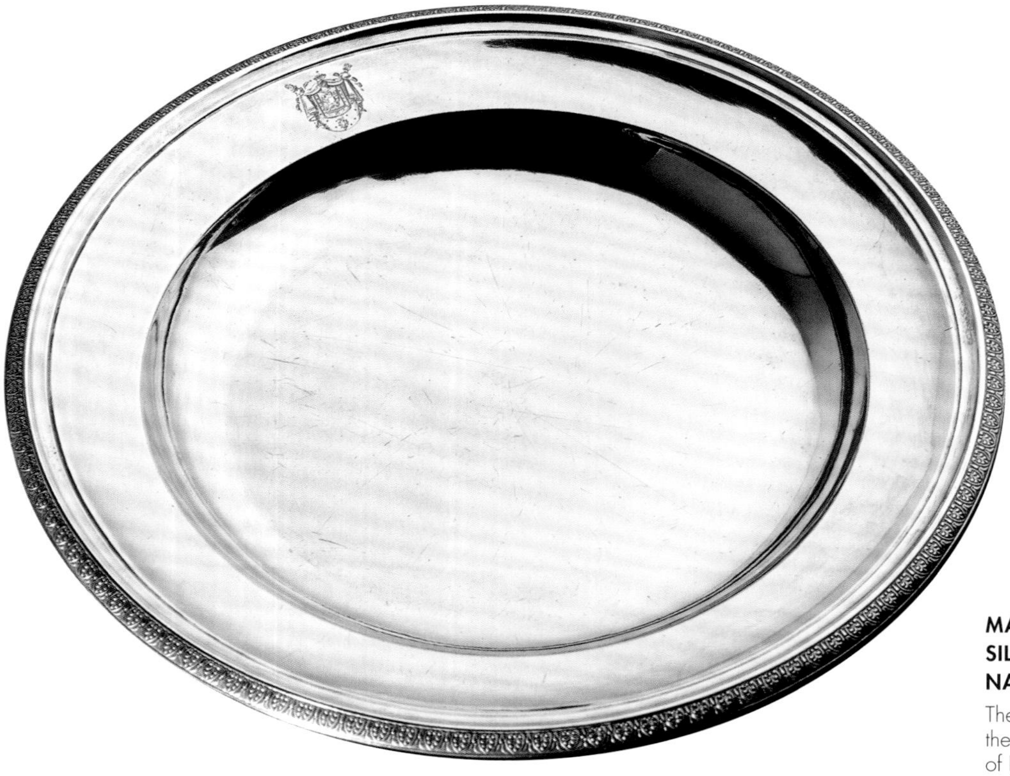

MARTIN-GUILLAUME BIENNAIS (1764-1843), SILVER DISH, PLATES AND CUTLERY FROM NAPOLEON'S "KING OF ITALY" SERVICE

These items of silverware by Biennais, still bearing the grand imperial coat-of-arms of Napoleon King of Italy, are extremely rare since the rest of the dinner service, now in Vienna, was reinscribed with the coat-of-arms of Francis I of Austria. Only three other pieces are known to exist.

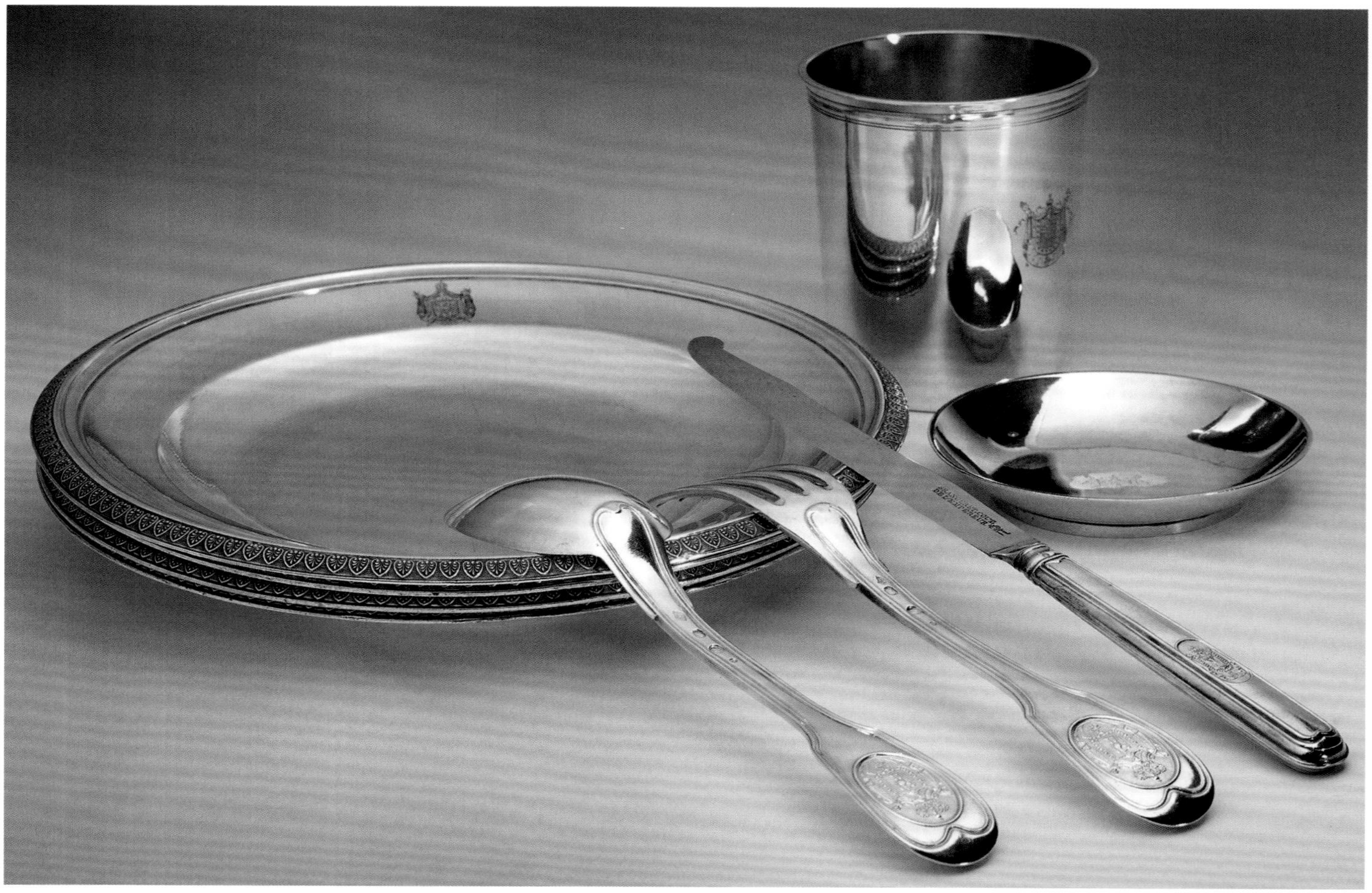

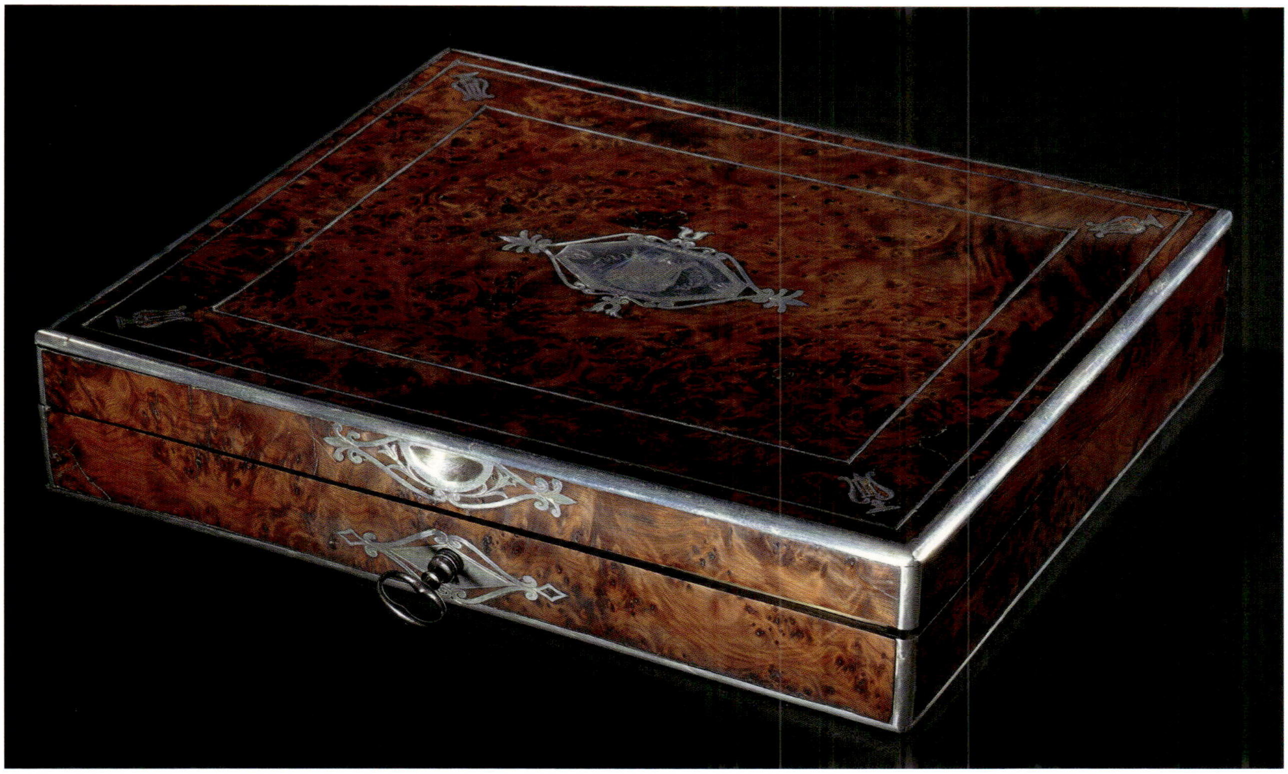

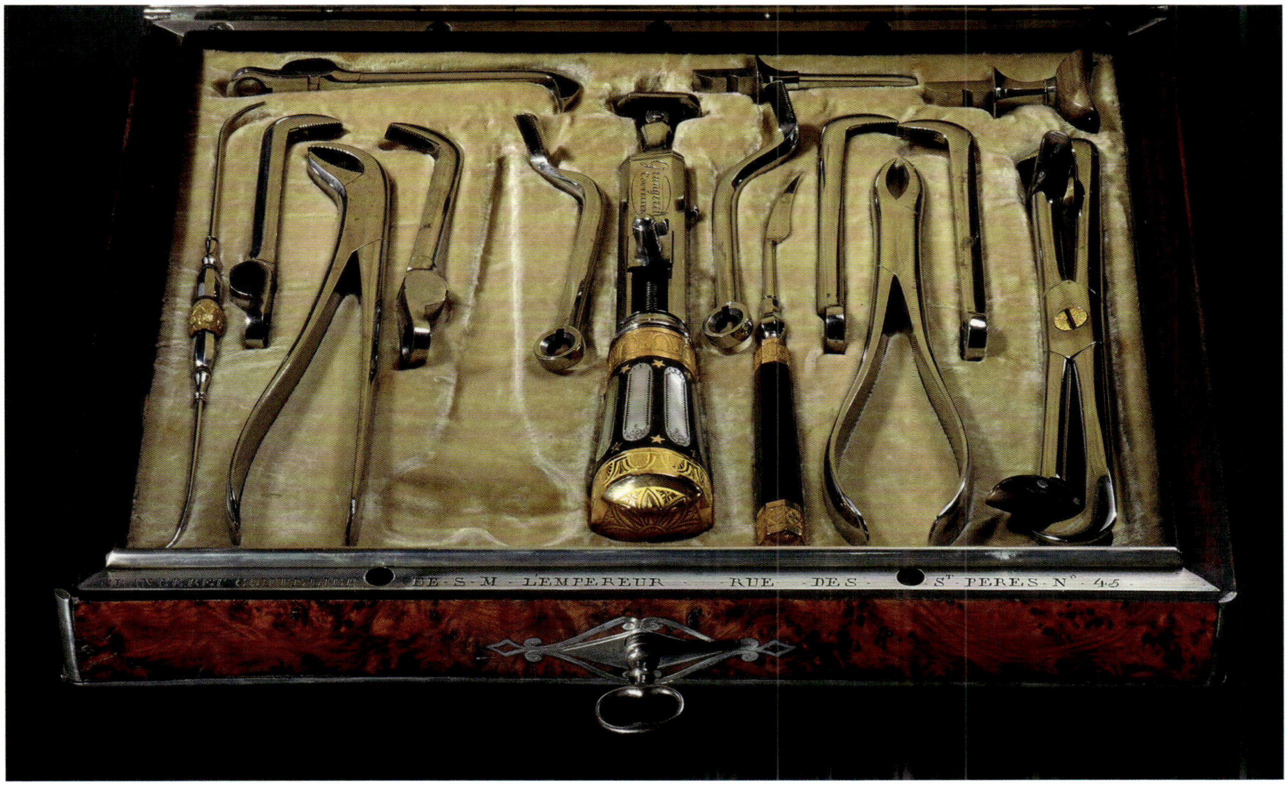

MARTIN-GUILLAUME BIENNAIS (1764-1843), DENTAL *NÉCESSAIRE* BELONGING TO NAPOLEON

This magnificent Thuya burl case with silver trim by Biennais contains dental instruments made by French goldsmith Pierre-François Grangeret. Designed for minor surgical procedures (mainly extractions), the instruments are of chiseled gold, with ebony handles inlaid with gold and mother-of-pearl. Napoleon was meticulous about dental hygiene and commissioned two dental *nécessaires* for use on campaign, each designed under the supervision of his dental surgeon Jean-Joseph Dubois (who quickly switched allegiances from Louis XVI to France's new Emperor). One of them (the will does not specify which of the two) was bequeathed by Napoleon to his son, the King of Rome, the other is held by the Fondation Napoléon.

MARTIN-GUILLAUME BIENNAIS (1764-1843), SILVER PLATE FROM NAPOLEON'S DINNER SERVICE

Silver plates made by Biennais were struck with the grand imperial coat-of-arms on the inner edge. This one has the distinction of bearing the inscription left by the Prussian victor: "A testimony of victory, found in the luggage of the Emperor Napoleon after the Battle of the *Belle Alliance* (the fine alliance) in the environs of Genappe on the night of 18-19 June 1815."

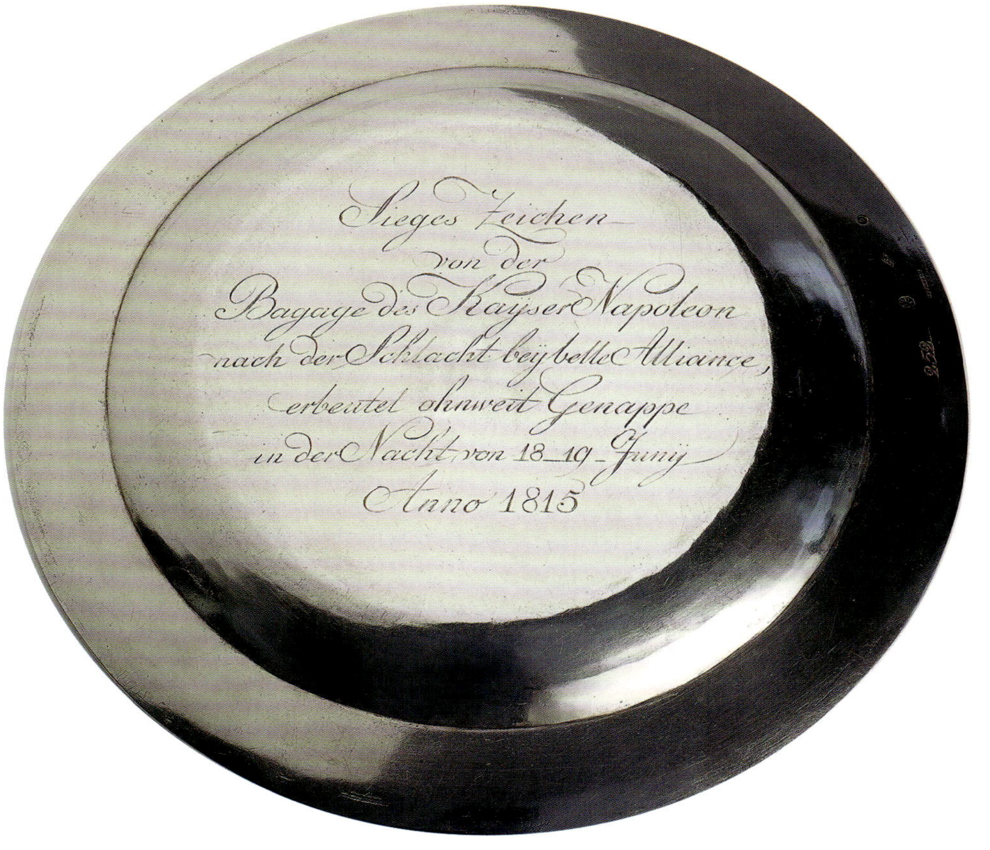

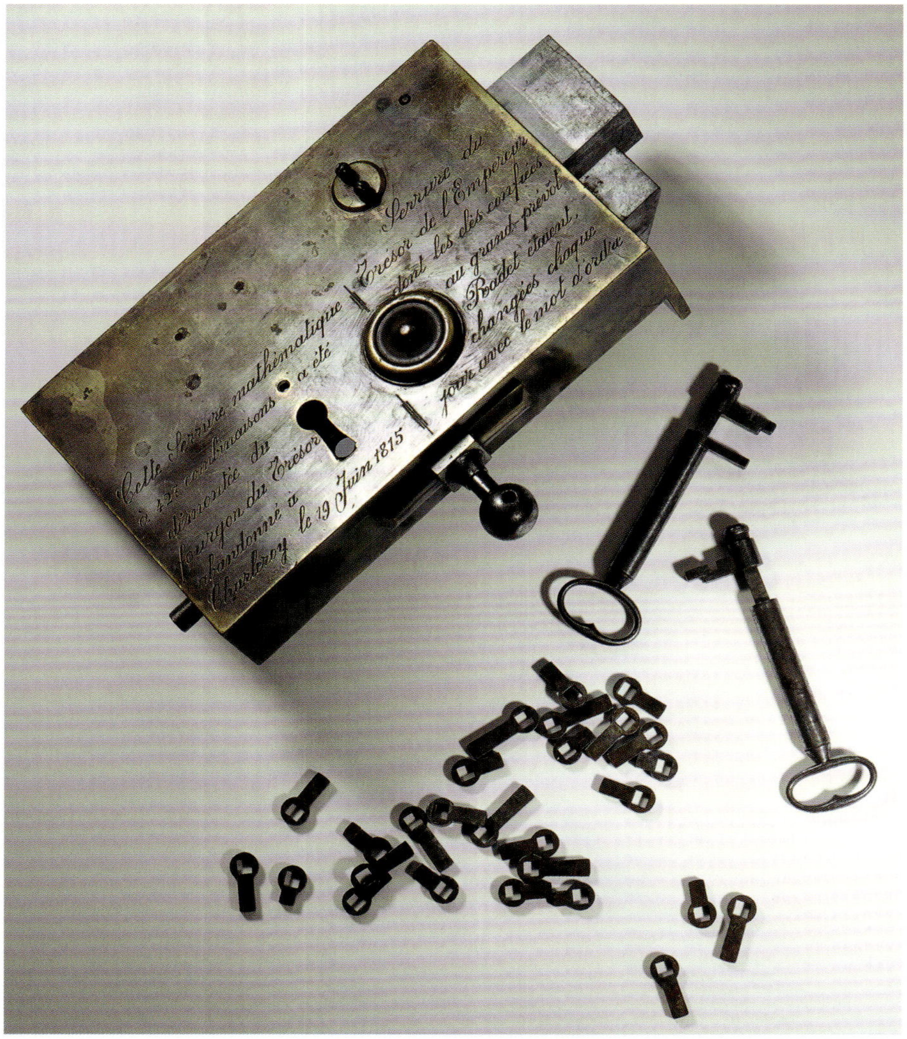

LOCK USED FOR THE WAGON OF THE IMPERIAL TREASURY, SEIZED AT WATERLOO

Because no military campaign is complete without treasure, the Emperor's retinue always included a carriage for the transport of enemy booty. Pictured here is the multipoint locking system used to secure its cargo of coins. The keys were entrusted to General Radet, Grand Provost of the army – who had only to choose from a mere 427 different combinations.

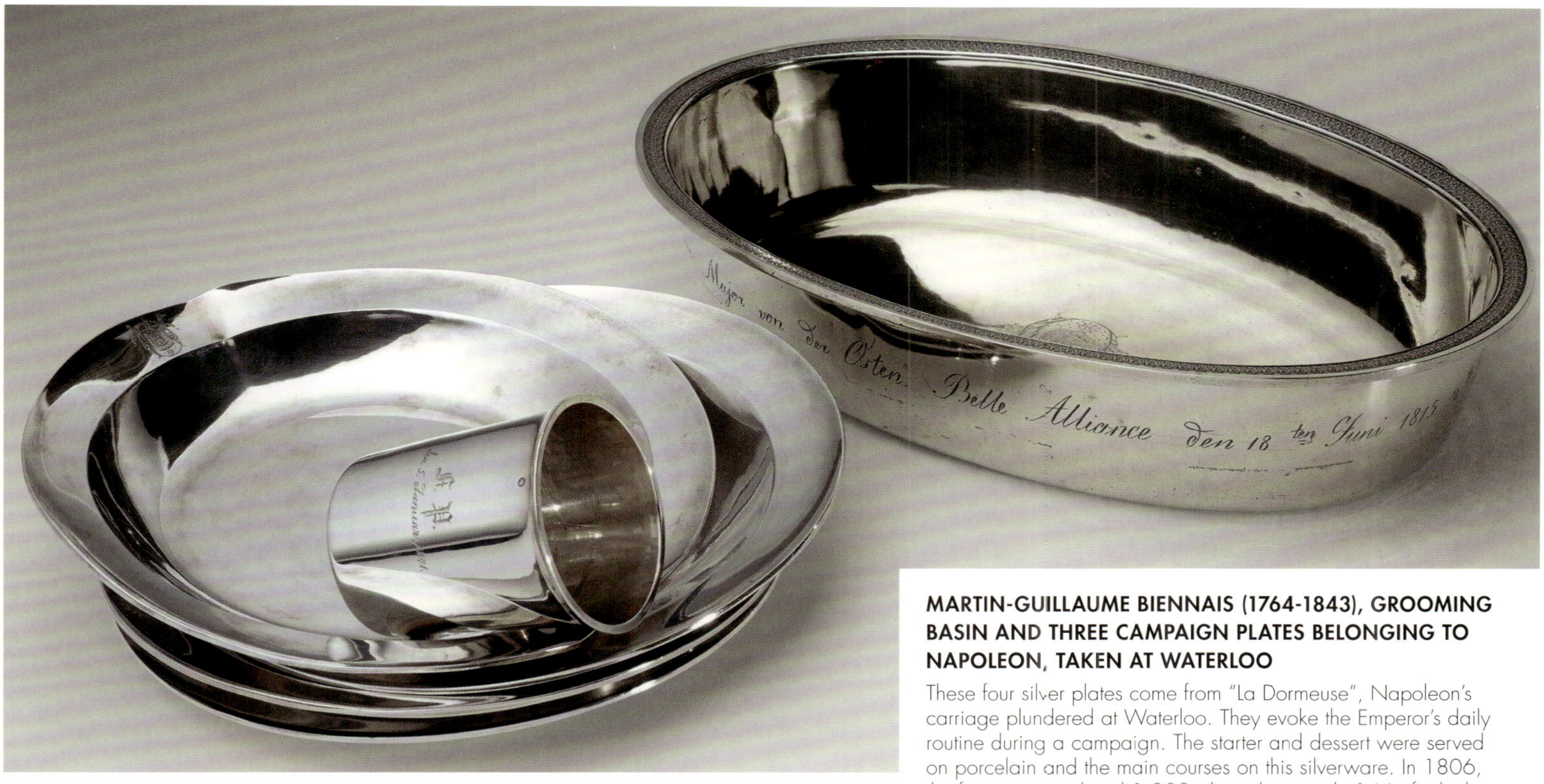

MARTIN-GUILLAUME BIENNAIS (1764-1843), GROOMING BASIN AND THREE CAMPAIGN PLATES BELONGING TO NAPOLEON, TAKEN AT WATERLOO

These four silver plates come from "La Dormeuse", Napoleon's carriage plundered at Waterloo. They evoke the Emperor's daily routine during a campaign. The starter and dessert were served on porcelain and the main courses on this silverware. In 1806, the furniture store listed 1,000 silver plates, only 144 of which were for traveling. The grooming basin bearing the coat-of-arms comes from the Emperor's travel set. Around its edge, it has an engraved inscription describing how it was seized at Waterloo.

BOOT PULLS USED BY NAPOLEON ON ST HELENA

This foldaway pair of boot pulls was a gift from Napoleon's valet, Count Marchand, to Captain William McIlwaine, a British officer aboard the Bellerophon, then the Northumberland, that carried the Emperor to his "small island".

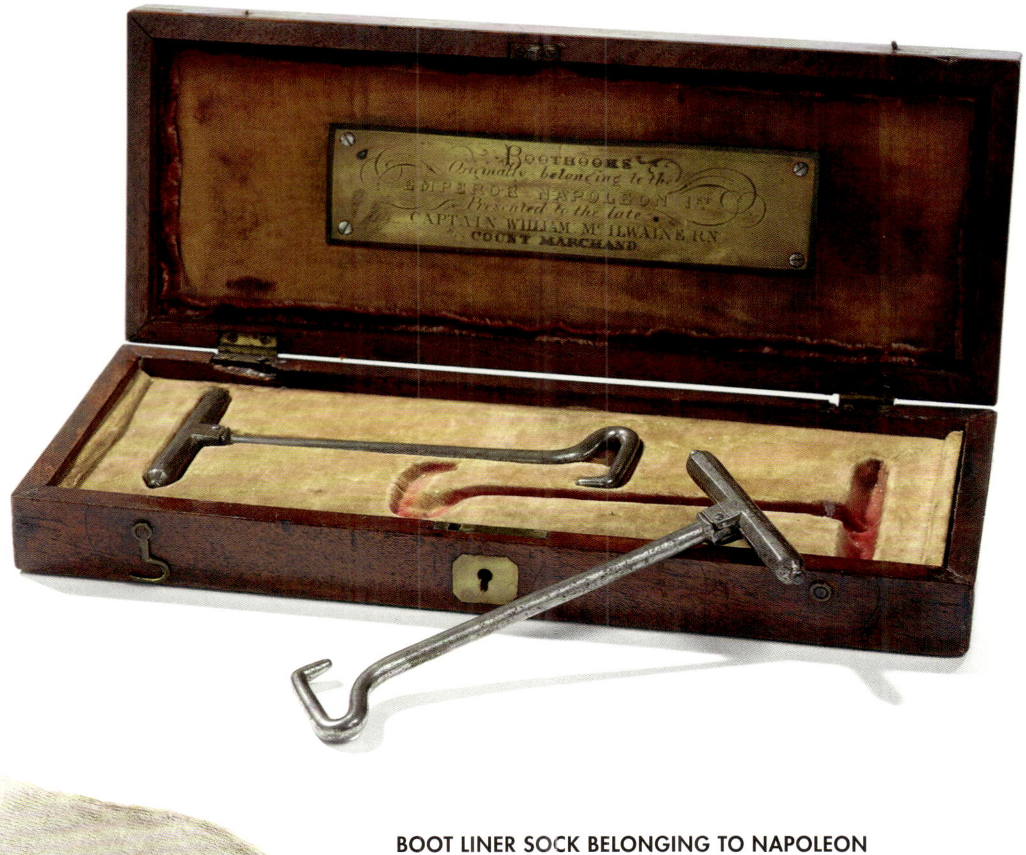

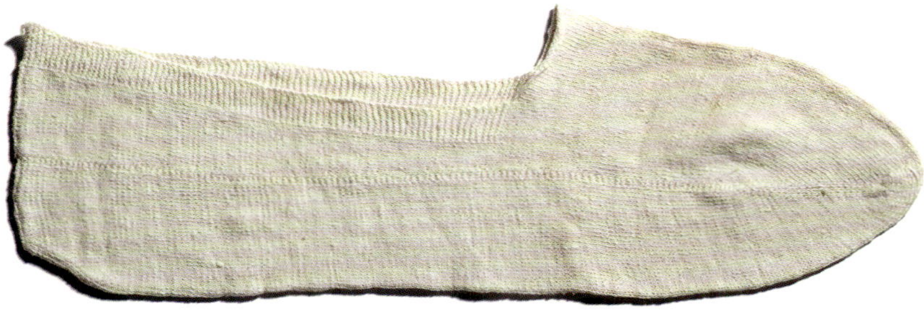

BOOT LINER SOCK BELONGING TO NAPOLEON

One of a pair of cotton liner socks worn by Napoleon over his silk stockings before putting on his boots, part of the estate of General Bertrand who accompanied Napoleon to St Helena. Its companion was for many years exhibited in the Napoleon Museum in Monaco. The Emperor had quite slender feet and patronized an Italian bootmaker to all the Royal Courts of the period.

SMALL SURGICAL KIT TAKEN FROM NAPOLEON'S LANDAU OUTSIDE KRASNOI IN RUSSIA

That the Emperor was not wounded in the retreat from Russia is just as well, since he lost his surgical kit (pictured here) on 15 November 1812 when the Cossacks looted his landau outside Krasnoi. Many years later, it has returned across the Russian Steppes and is once again in our possession. It houses 15 instruments plus thread and fabric, contained in a red Morocco leather case with gold tooling, lined with red velvet and marked with a crowned "N" on either side of the lock.

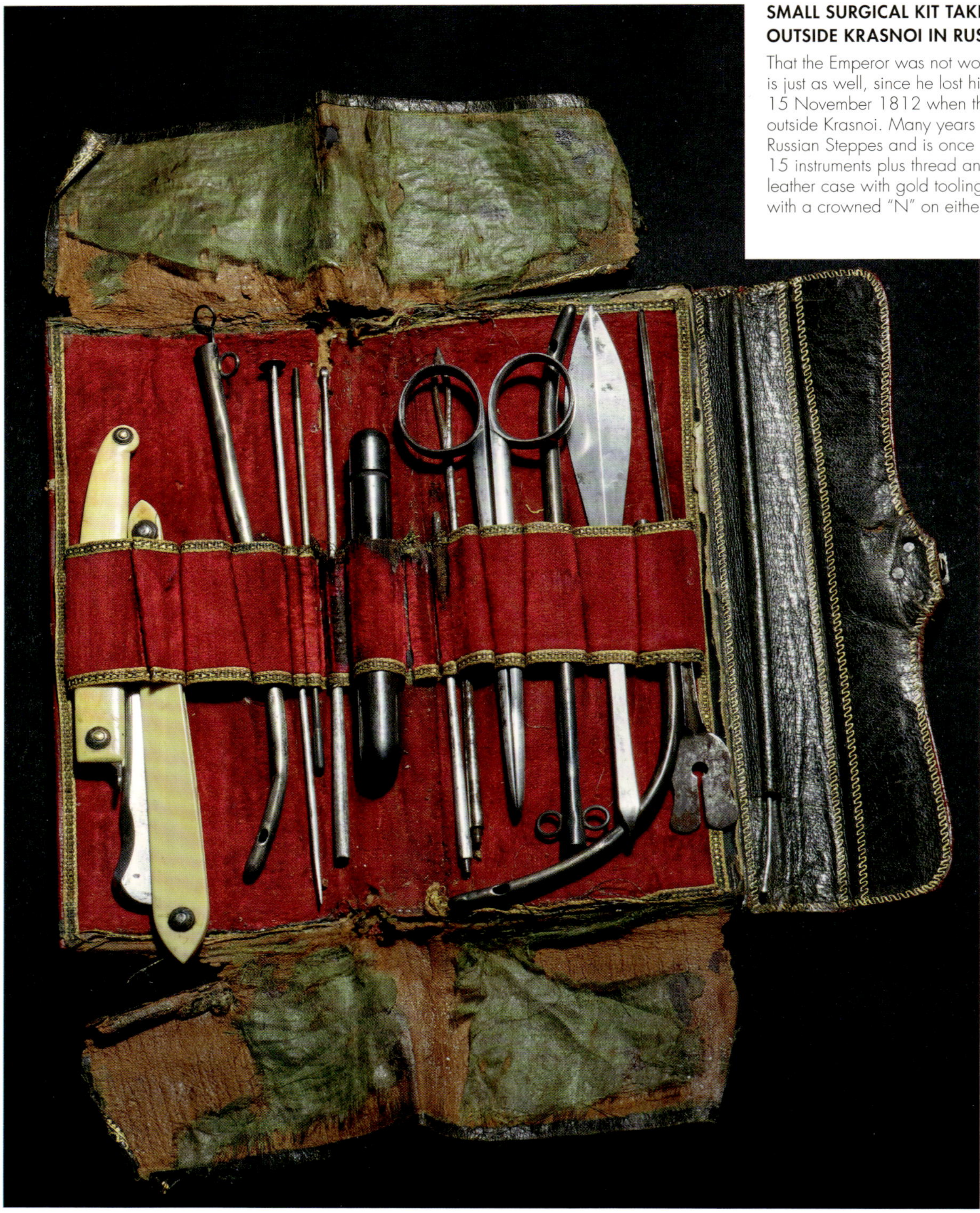

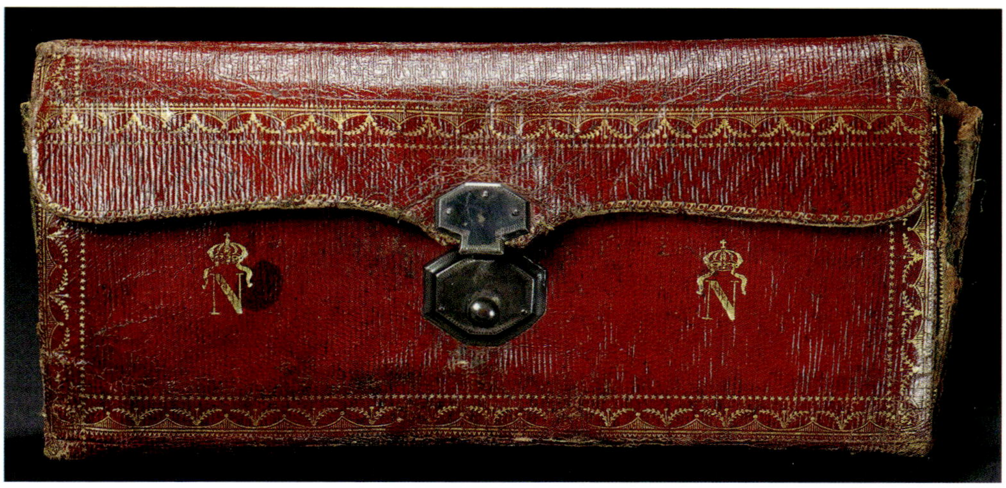

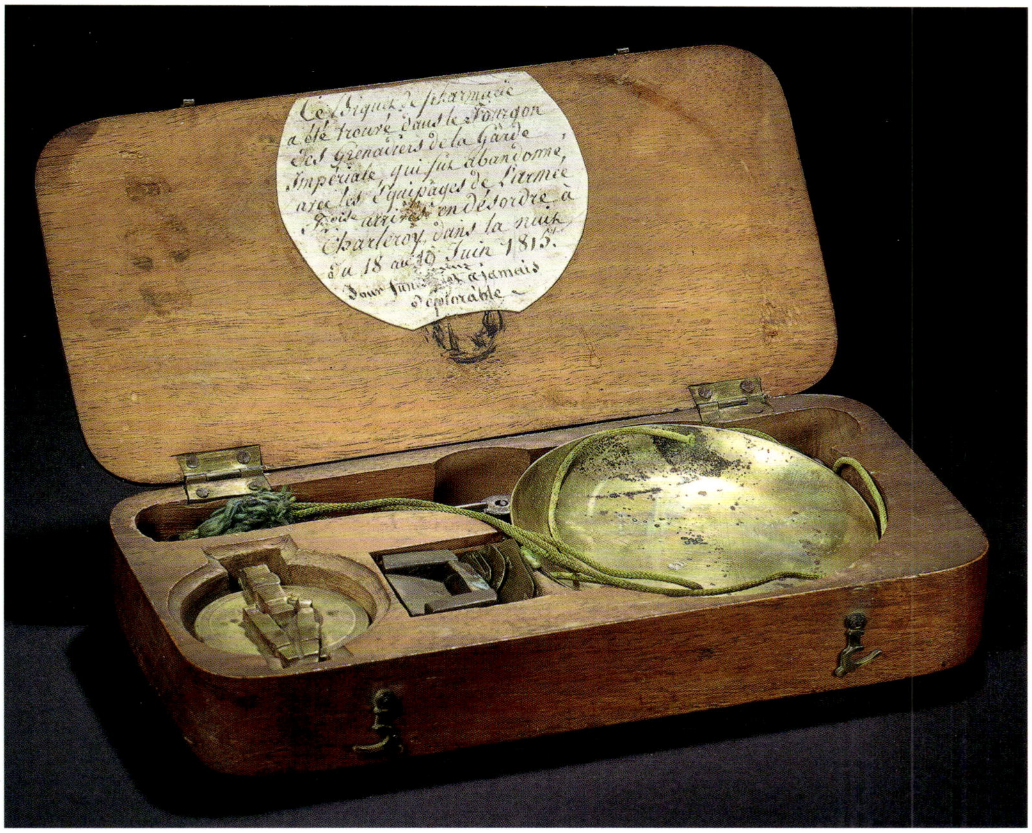

TRAVELING APOTHECARY SCALES FOUND AMONG NAPOLEON'S EFFECTS AT CHARLEROI, IN JUNE 1815

A former captain of the imperial army living in retirement in Charleroi was watching helplessly as French troops suffered their debacle at Waterloo, and just happened to find himself in the Emperor's path when he fled the battlefield. The name of this faithful officer was Hubert Noël and for many years thereafter he collected the objects pillaged from Napoleon's effects, among them this pair of apothecary scales, known as a *biquet* and featuring a lid hallmarked on the outside with a crowned "N" and bearing a red eagle wax seal.

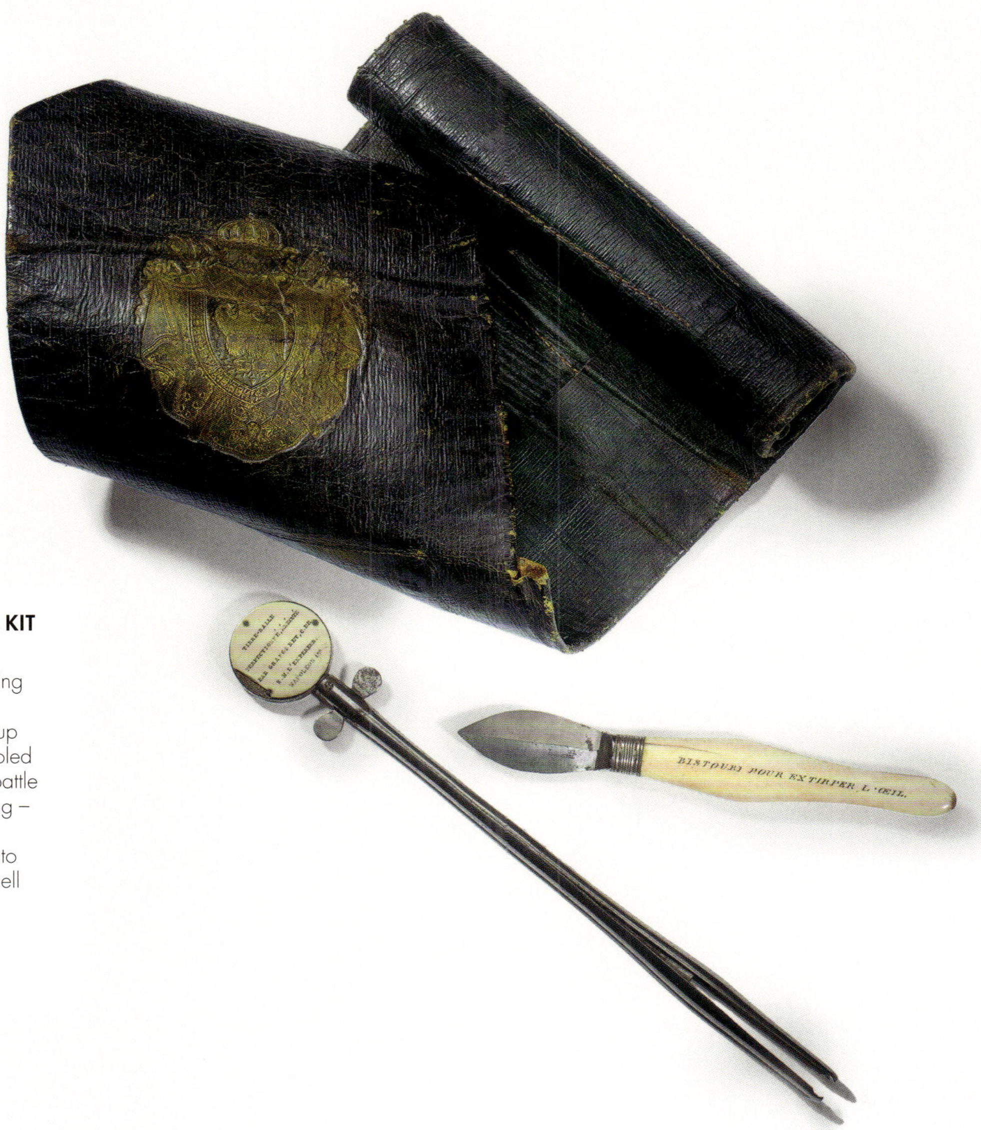

NAPOLEON'S SMALL EMERGENCY SURGICAL KIT

Unlike Biennais' magnificent surgical kits, this small emergency set contains just two instruments, including an ingenious bullet puller designed by Grangeret. They fit neatly inside a green Morocco leather roll-up wallet with the grand imperial coat-of-arms gold-tooled on the outside. Napoleon was often wounded in battle – in Toulon, in Egypt, at Ratisbon and at Aspern-Essling – but his wounds were rarely serious and certainly never enough to prevent him from climbing back into the saddle and returning to the frontline and the smell of gunpowder.

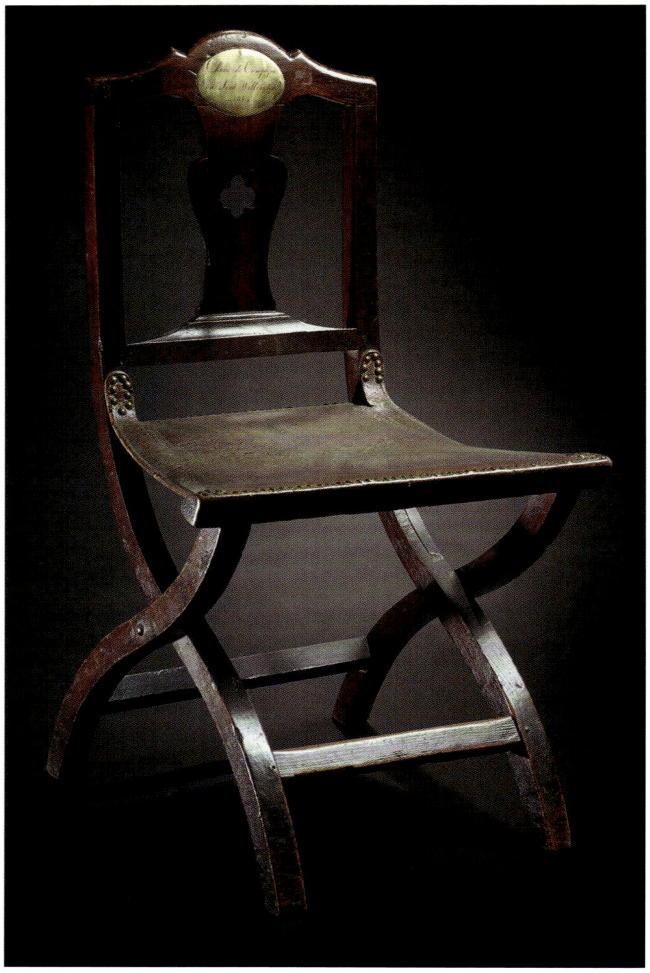

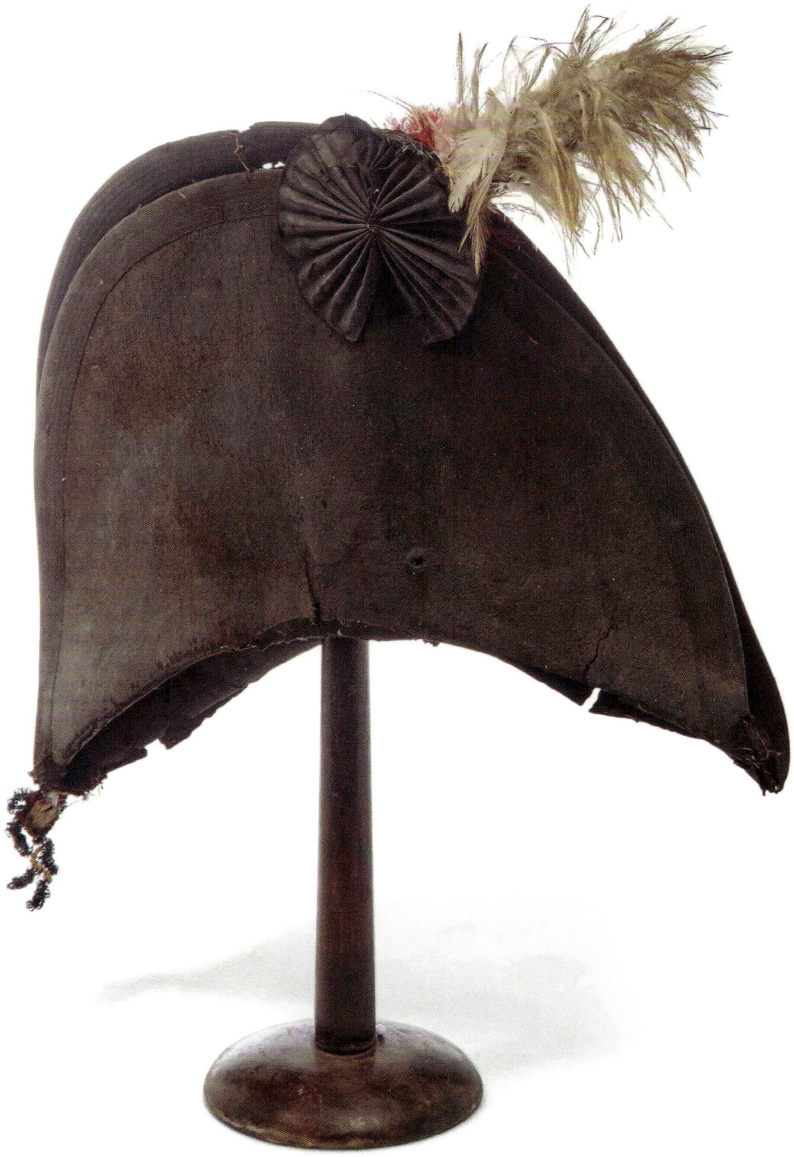

CAMPAIGN CHAIR USED BY THE DUKE OF WELLINGTON AT WATERLOO

The Waterloo of tragic memory reflected here in more sedate terms by the Duke of Wellington's campaign chair – a mahogany-and-leather accessory that played its undoubted part in the battle itself.

WELLINGTON'S HAT

Although the bicorne is less associated with the man than it is with Napoleon, it was a familiar characteristic of the British general, Arthur Wellesley (1769-1852), future Duke of Wellington who would defeat Napoleon at Waterloo. The hat here was given by Wellesley to General Seymons after the triumphant assault on Seringapatam in India in 1799. It has been kept preciously since then by his descendants. It is one of the rare genuine items known and can be fully traced back to its origin. It is also the only one of its kind in France. History can be ironic...

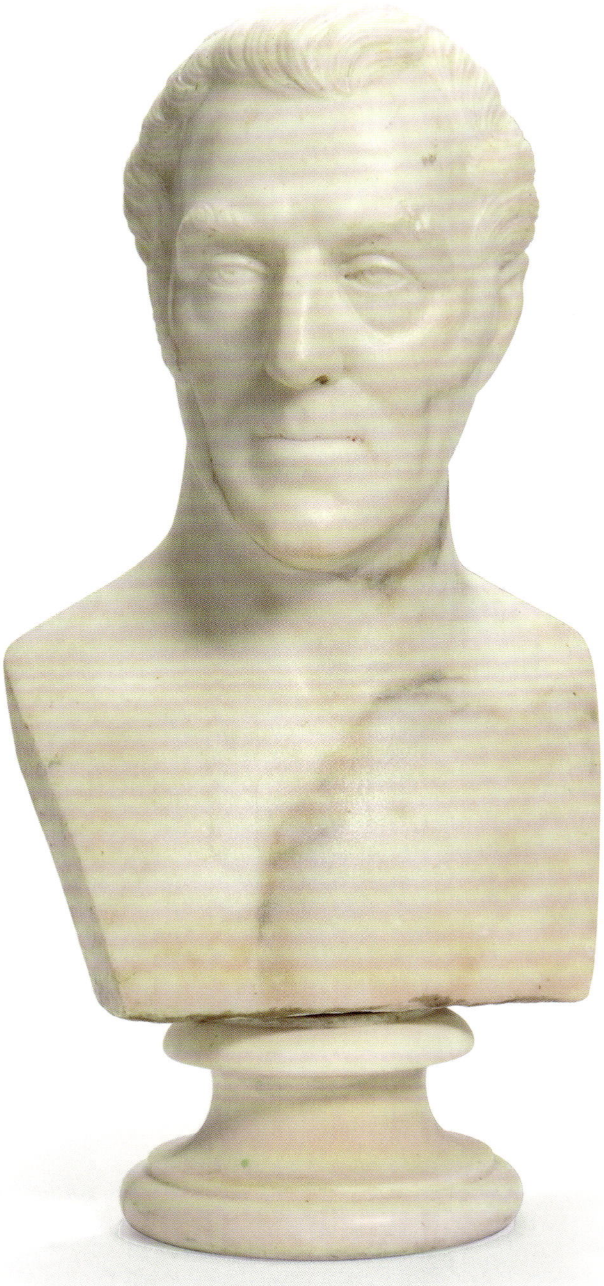

BUST OF WELLINGTON

This marble bust shows the face of Wellington, who successfully fought the Napoleonic armies in Portugal and Spain, then defeated the Emperor at Waterloo with the unexpected arrival of the Prussian armies commanded by Blücher. That battle, which Napoleon had been well on the way to winning, marked the end of the centuries-long war between France and Great Britain. Wellington greatly admired Napoleon's military genius and said that the Emperor's "presence on the battlefield was worth that of 40,000 men". This bust can be compared to that sculpted by Francis Legatt Chantrey (1781-1841), a version of which is kept at the British embassy in Lisbon.

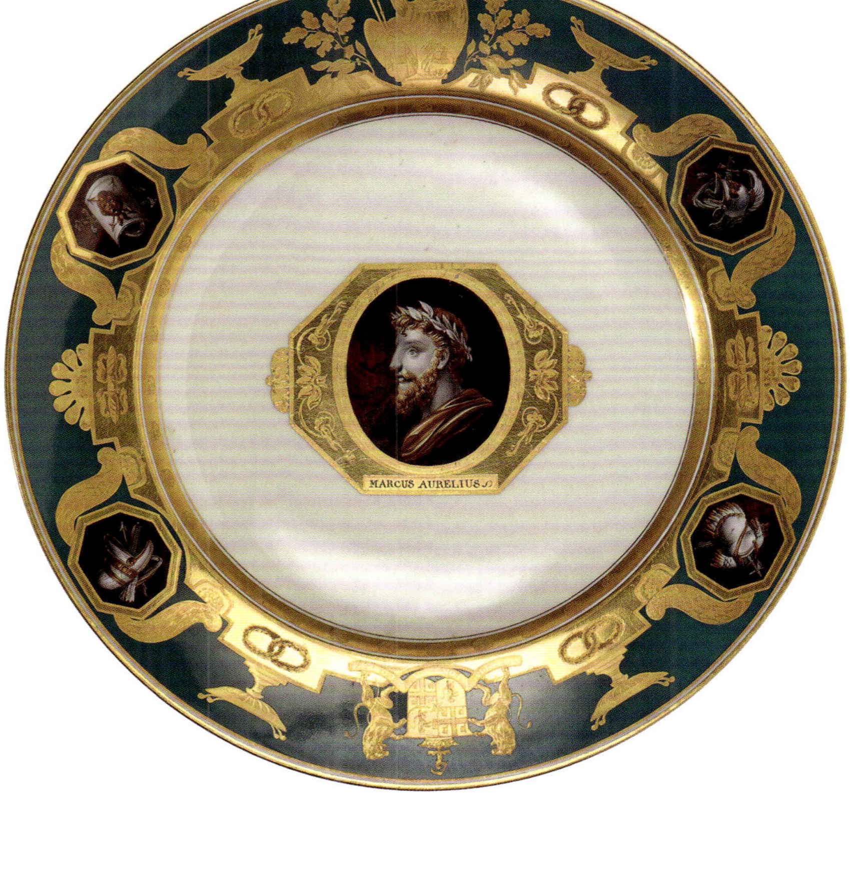

PLATE GIVEN TO WELLINGTON BY THE EMPEROR OF AUSTRIA

Given to Wellington by Francis I, the first Emperor of Austria and father of Marie-Louise, this plate has a portrait of Roman Emperor Marcus Aurelius in its center, painted to imitate a cameo. The green edge is adorned with four warrior trophies, and the coats-of-arms of the Habsburg and Wellington families, surrounded by bowls, laurel crowns and palm leaves. It dates from 1818 and testifies to the relations between Napoleon's conquerors. Some of this service can be found at the Wellington Museum in London.

The Imperial Household

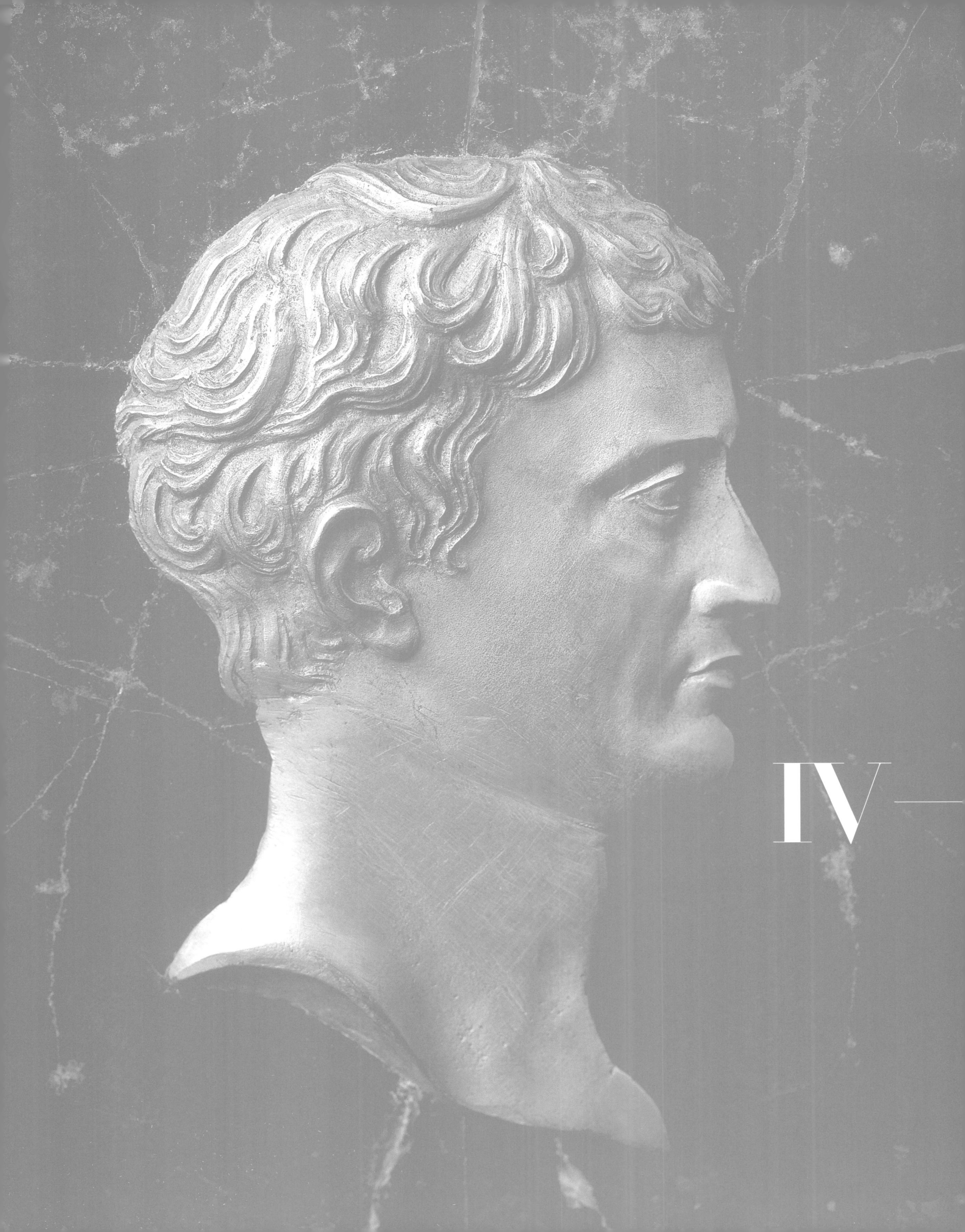

IV

Founded in 1804, the Maison de l'Empereur (Imperial Household) comprised all of the officers and staff in the service of the Emperor. As under the Ancien Régime, it included the Officiers de la Bouche, de la Chambre and Des Ecuries (in English royal tradition, the offices in the gift of the crown, equivalent to Lord Steward, Lord Chamberlain and Master of the Horse) plus domestic staff for menial household duties. In addition to its purely practical role, the Maison was also tasked with overseeing Napoleon's transformation from former Republican general to supreme monarch.
The greatness of His Royal Majesty Napoleon I was at stake.

Pierre Branda
historian, director of collections
at the Fondation Napoléon

NAPOLEON IN MAJESTY

April 1805. Shortly before supper, a messenger was shown into the antechamber of the President of the Conseil d'État, Regnaud de Saint-Jean d'Angély. The messenger bore a note signed by the Emperor's Chamberlain. The note resembled a command and on reading it, Regnaud understood that he had to leave for Fontainebleau where his sovereign awaited him. Some time later, a member of the Tribunate named Carrion-Nizas received the same invitation. The two men dropped everything and, having been provided with horses by the Minister for Posts Lavalette, set off on different routes for the Chateau de Fontainebleau. Carrion was first to be announced – only to be sent away by the Emperor, who was not expecting him, and told to return the following day. Surely some mistake, thought the visitor. Regnaud then arrived in his turn and was announced by Duroc. It was at that point that Napoleon realized the two men had been tricked. It was 1 April and some prankster had thought it clever to pass himself off as a Chamberlain. Paris clutched its sides and fairly rocked with mirth. Not so Napoleon — who ordered Fouché to hold an inquiry. Operating with his usual efficiency, Police Chief Fouché soon flushed out the culprit. We have no idea, alas, who he was or what punishment he received. But one thing is certain: no one tried playing the same trick again.

Did Napoleon have no sense of humor? He was not naturally inclined to levity, certainly, and what he hated most of all was being treated with a lack of respect. The slightest affront to His Majesty the Emperor would be punished. To elevate himself above his subjects, Napoleon chose to isolate himself from others. It was difficult for even his closest friends to gain personal access. Protocol covering palace organization and honorary duties was introduced. For the victorious general of Austerlitz who had his sights set on European dominance, pomp and ceremony were not something he could afford to ignore.

Financed by an annual allowance of several million francs, luxury permeated every aspect of Napoleon's daily life. Furnishings, tableware, stables, carriages, parks and grounds, wardrobe, hunting, chaplaincy and meals — Napoleon spared no expense, but it wasn't purely to maintain appearances. The advent of the First French Empire had enclosed him in a "protective bubble". Henceforth, whether traveling or in residence or in need of a bodyguard, Napoleon no longer relied on the State or the Army for his needs. Instead, his Majesty placed himself exclusively in the care of the Imperial House of France — an institution that existed as an entirely separate entity within the Napoleonic state.

AN OPULENT HOUSEHOLD

Enthusiastic students of the Napoleonic epic will be well familiar with the Emperor's servants: his head valets Constant and Marchand, his secretaries Fain and Méneval, his Mameluks Roustam and Ali, his Grand Marshalls Duroc and Bertrand and his Grand Squire Caulaincourt. Many people believe that Napoleon's servants formed a nucleus of familiars in the service of a modest master. Nothing could be further from the truth. Historical records show that in 1812 the Emperor's Household comprised 3,384 people, including 164 officers, whose combined services represented an annual expenditure of 15 million francs.

Restoring the imperial palaces was especially costly, a task that fell to the household stewards employed in the 40 palaces across the Empire that Napoleon commandeered as his residences. For some of these, the French Revolution had wrought dire consequences — the furnishings sold off, the gardens abandoned and the apartments ransacked. Initial priority was given to making the imperial residences habitable. In Fontainebleau alone, this required the refitting of 54 state apartments, 124 'master' suites for the officers and ladies in waiting and 220 servants' quarters.[1] The next step was to convey the splendor of the Imperial Court — embellish the apartments with decorative features calculated to impress visitors.

In the gardens and grounds likewise, no effort or expense were spared in the pursuit of magnificence. The stewards' achievements were considerable and paved the way for the future restoration of France's palaces, a process that continues to this day. Among the imperial furnishings were certain rare items of furniture dating from the Consulate period. These included two pairs of chairs constructed in the period 1800-1804 and now part of the Ledoux Collection. One pair (page 247) stood in the rooms used by Napoleon's secretary Bourrienne at the Tuileries, before finding their way into the Emperor's private apartments. The other pair (page 243), designed in the Neoclassical style, graced the Grand Cabinet (cabinet room) at the Château de Saint-Cloud.

Within the Emperor's many palaces, six Grands Officiers Civils de la Couronne took precedence over all other imperial dignitaries — a privilege that was merely an extension of palace protocol and in no way alleviated the frequent tedium of their duties.

The Grand Maréchal du Palais (head of the Emperor's military household) was in charge of policing and security, palace maintenance and catering. The Grand Chambellan (English 'Lord Chamberlain') oversaw the Emperor's private chambers and court ceremonies. The Grand Ecuyer (English 'master of the horse') had the superintendence of the sovereign's retinue. The Grand Aumônier (English 'Lord High Almoner') directed the religious affairs of the Household. The Grand-Veneur (English 'Master of the Hunt') commanded the Imperial Hunt; and the Master of Ceremonies was responsible for all ceremonial events and any events in public.

Next in line came an army of *officiers civils*: civil servants who answered directly to the six Grands Officiers, either deputizing for royal administrators or working alongside them in what palace protocol referred to as the *service d'honneur* of the Emperor. This privilege of serving Napoleon was a subject that filled whole chapters in the guide to imperial palace etiquette. One chapter for instance describes the rules to be observed when serving in the state apartments: "Art. 2: when the Emperor or Empress are present in the state apartments or halls of ceremonies, and [they are] in need of some particular thing, the *officier de service* (officer in attendance) in whose remit said item falls shall present it [to their Majesties]."[2] In other words, the Grand Chambellan might occasionally have to wait on the Emperor like a flunky.

It is hard to imagine a more unlikely candidate for this position than the limping French minister Talleyrand (Grand Chambellan from 1804 to 1809). But as once observed by the Countess Potocka, even he would bow to convention when the occasion demanded: "I could not tell you how surprised I was to see him [Talleyrand] advance painfully into the middle of the salon, folded napkin over his forearm and silver platter in hand, and proffer a glass of lemonade to that same monarch who he privately dismissed as a parvenu!"[3]

The *service d'honneur* was particularly important when the imperial couple dined *en grand couvert* — in public, after the manner of the French kings. The Grand Chambellan would stand by with a basin and towel so that the Emperor could wash his hands. The Grand Ecuyer would draw up a chair for His Majesty and the Grand Maréchal would hand him his napkin. The Empress was likewise attended upon by the Premier Préfet (first prefect), Premier Écuyer (first equerry) and Premier Chambellan (first chamberlain). Once blessed by the Grand Aumônier, the meal would proceed under the direction of the prefect on duty. Dishes were brought to the table and served by the Maîtres d'Hôtel (butlers) who then handed the plates to the pageboys for distribution. If the Emperor requested a drink, the Premier Préfet would pour a mixture of wine and water into a glass, which was then proffered by the Grand Maréchal. At the end of the meal, the Grand Chambellan would pour coffee into the Emperor's cup, the Grand Maréchal would take His Majesty's napkin and the Grand Écuyer would draw away his chair. Last of all, the Emperor would be "given the means to wash his hands" by the Grand Chambellan.

Within the state apartments, the throne room was the chamber most on show. It was flanked by some of the most monumental suites within the palace and used for a wide variety of official state functions. Napoleon happily exploited the symbolism of the throne during his reign — an idea that was quite new to the French. The throne as a symbol of power was virtually non-existent under the Ancien Régime. Louis XIV himself used the throne for exceptional audiences on just three occasions, when it was moved to the Grande Galerie at Versailles. The true symbol of royal authority at Versailles was the royal bed, which had epitomized dynastic continuity since medieval times.[4] The throne was by comparison insignificant and, unlike the royal bed, commanded no particular gesture of respect. By placing emphasis on the throne, Napoleon sought to assert his dominance over his contemporaries. No account of his reign can be complete without some reference to the throne — as is plain in the works of David, Ingres and the other great painters of the Empire period. This gives some idea of the importance of the throne in the Ledoux Collection (page 257), which is thought to pre-date the year 1809. The chair features a decorative crown of laurels, with a rounded back typical of the style chosen by Percier and Fontaine to highlight the majesty of Napoleon.

At the palace, the Emperor was attended in turn by a retinue of four officers: chambellans, écuyers, military personnel and palace prefects or adjutants. Every trimester, eight chambellans and four écuyers were appointed for the ordinary service, with 16 chambellans and four écuyers for the extraordinary service. To these 32 officers were added two palace prefects and at least six aides de camp, making a total of 40 serving officers (excluding the Grands Officiers). Within this select gathering, it was no easy task for Napoleon's *premiers chambellans* to explain the new protocol to the regime officials: generals, diplomats, state councilors and senators. It was the responsibility of the *premiers chambellans* to usher guests into Napoleon's presence and to turn away anyone who had no business at the palace. Access to the Emperor's salon (State Cabinet) was governed by palace protocol and depended on rank and the time of day. Napoleon's former brothers-in-arms often found themselves denied entry by his chambellans — an experience that no doubt rankled with some. Henceforth the Emperor's relations with his contemporaries were subject to strict rules of order and decorum, and the chambellans, in their powdered wigs and crimson garb, were an eloquent reminder of the governing power now in place. To make the point doubly clear, a magnificent key that unlocked no door hung from the neck of every chambellan. The key had an oval ring festooned in oak and laurel leaves, with a grand eagle at its center. At the base of the key was a crest bearing Napoleon's monogram (page 238).

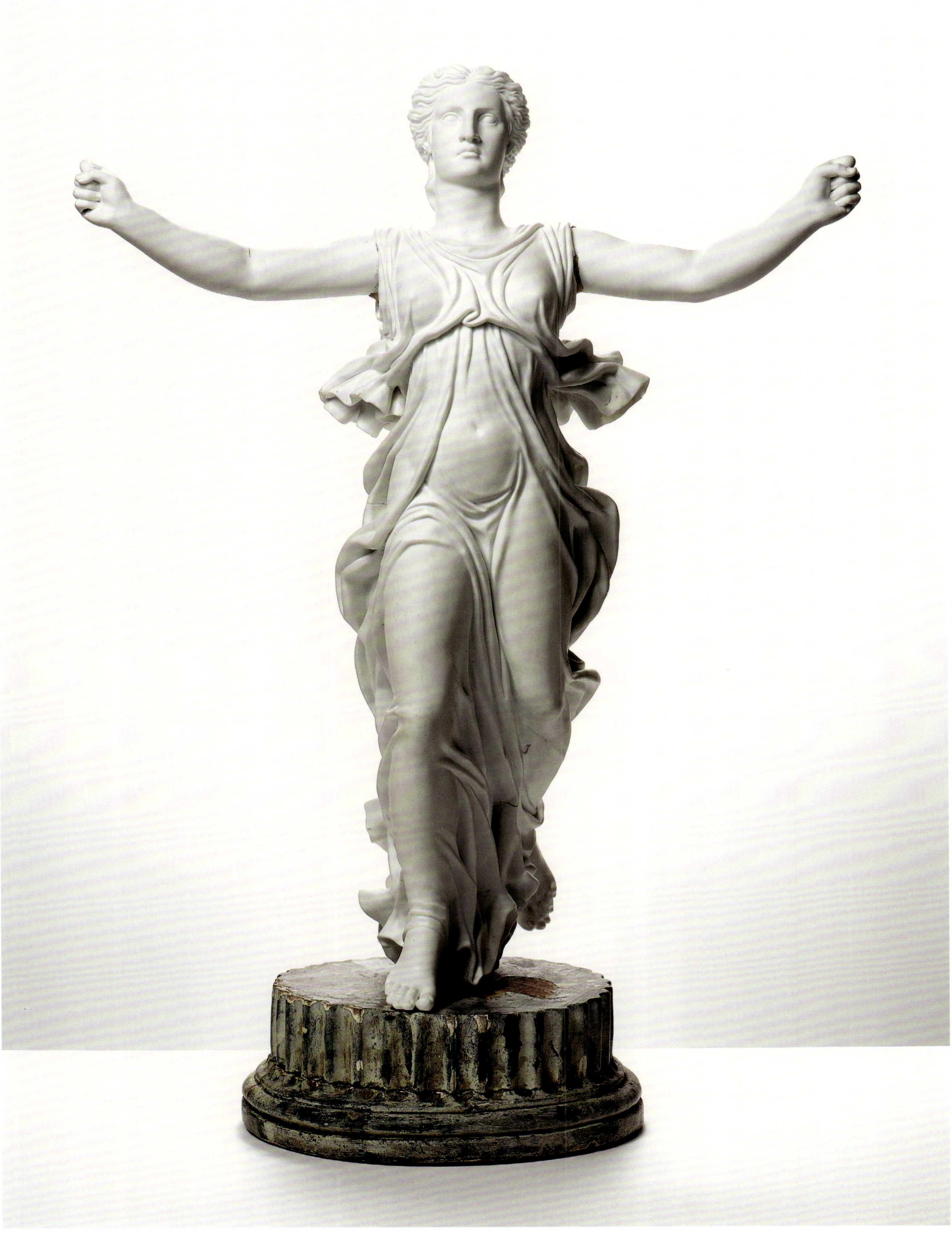

THE EMPEROR'S TABLE

The sovereign's table was abundantly provisioned, even though Napoleon himself spent little time in eating. "Napoleon was as temperate as it was possible for a man to be, [his] breakfast often did not occupy more than eight minutes," wrote the Prefect of the Palace Joseph Bausset-Roquefort in his memoirs[5]. You might expect therefore that the *service de la bouche* would have been kept to a minimum. In fact, the reverse was true. Expenditure on provisioning in the year 1810 amounted to 600,000 francs, rising to one million francs in 1812. This is roughly comparable in magnitude to the annual resources available to the Ministère de la Marine (ministry of the navy) to cover its central administrative costs (warships, ministry and Parisian staff)[6]. Detailed records of food deliveries for the Emperor's Household can be found in the Archives Nationales, and they certainly make impressive reading. The entries for December 1812 (when Napoleon did not return from Russia until the 19th of the month) are as follows: more than three tonnes of meat, half a tonne of charcuterie, several thousand fowl, more than 5,500 eggs, 252 kilos of sugar and half a tonne of butter.

The *service de la bouche* prepared lunch and dinner for the imperial couple, sometimes supper too when Their Majesties were entertaining guests or hosting a ball at court. Napoleon would have lunch at midday, either in his private apartments or in the *salon de service* (where their majesties usually dined). He always ate alone, except between the months of March 1810 and March 1811 when he lunched in the company of Marie-Louise. The Empress' table would normally be set to seat ten, with a typical meal consisting of one potage (thick soup), two relevés (in English, the 'remove'), six entrées, two roasts, six entremets, four hors-d'œuvre (starters), six desserts then coffee and rolls for ten. There would be eight bottles of Beaune wine plus two bottles of finest Burgundy and half a bottle of liqueur. The imperial couple usually shared a table for dinner.[7]

The tableware was as lavish as the dishes. The Household staff included 12 people responsible for the silverware (dishes and domed food covers) and another five who looked after the porcelain and glassware. The silverware included a 746-piece vermeil service, gifted by the Mairie of Paris to commemorate the Emperor's coronation, which alone weighed 600 kilos. By 1806 total silverware comprised more than one thousand items and filled 63 coffers. The Maison also boasted several pieces of silver-gilt by Martin-Guillaume Biennais, most notably a 62-piece tea service and an 82-piece vermeil ordinaire (used for the Court's ordinary silver service). In 1811, following Napoleon's marriage to Marie-Louise of Austria, dozens of additional items of silverware were purchased at a total cost of 688,681 francs. Of this, 482,000 francs was spent on Biennais vermeil for the Service du Grand Maréchal.

The imperial silverware collection was impressive by anyone's standards, already weighing more than a tonne by Year 13.[8] The Bruno Ledoux collection features several items of imperial tableware, most notably silver and vermeil cutlery (page 234-235) displaying Napoleon's coat-of-arms on the handle.

The items of porcelain also ran into hundreds. The Maison was a major client of the Sèvres Porcelain Factory and commissioned tableware designs of exceptional beauty. The Service Particulier de l'Empereur (the Emperor's personal service) and the Egyptian service together count among the finest porcelain ever produced at Sèvres. The Ledoux Collection includes several outstanding examples, most notably the two plates (pages 220-225) from the Emperor's personal service (also known as the Service des Quartiers Généraux or "Headquarters Service"). The plates remain unequaled for their delicacy of execution. Featured on the bottom are exquisitely drawn views of the Simplon Road and the Brandenburg Gate that retain an extraordinary brightness to this day.

The history of the Emperor's personal service is no less fascinating. The service was delivered to Napoleon in 1810 then redesigned by Louis XVIII on his coming to power four years later. The imperial coat-of-arms on the underside of the plate was replaced by the King's monogram (two interlocking L's). Napoleon then used the service again in the period known as the "Hundred Days", and took it with him into subsequent exile on St Helena having pressured Fouché to grant permission. Unfortunately for him, the briefness of his return to the Tuileries in 1815 did not allow time for the removal of the Royal monogram. So it was that throughout his captivity on St Helena, Napoleon was forced to eat off porcelain bearing the Royal Arms of his worst enemy.

Napoleon never renounced his title of Emperor. The title had been granted him by the Senatus-Consultum in Year XII and he expected to be addressed as such — not "General Bonaparte" as his British captors on St Helena were wont to do. A sovereign he had been and a sovereign he would remain until his dying day. Surrounded by the members of his Household, he continued to pursue his destiny even in exile. Just as the Household had been the cornerstone of his tiny kingdom on the island of Elba, so it continued in Napoleon's final place of exile on St Helena — an exile shared by all those who followed him there.

Napoleon's Household at Longwood, the house where he spent most of his captivity, was a small-scale reproduction of the Imperial Household at the Tuileries , complete with a retinue of footmen and officers. The porcelain, silverware and linen also came from the Tuileries, or sometimes other imperial palaces, and should have been inherited by the King of Rome (Napoleon's son). In the event the Austrians saw to it that the boy received nothing, and many of these items have long since disappeared. It is to the great credit of the Ledoux Collection that some survive to the present day. Items such as the last batiste cotton shirts ever worn by the Emperor, his porcelain and his cutlery bring his last days to life before our eyes.

A GAME OF APPEARANCES

For his everyday objects, the Emperor engaged the services of his goldsmith Martin-Guillaume Biennais. Hundreds of items, mainly gold and silverware but also game boxes and toiletry cases, were ordered on his behalf by the Premier Chambellan, Rémusat. Biennais' *mémoires* (nobody said *facture* or invoice in those days) were identifiable by their magnificent letterhead (page 239) but roundly dreaded by the Household accountants who despaired of his astronomical prices. Among his creations were several commode chairs in walnut wood, beautifully upholstered in red morocco, which the Emperor took with him on campaigns.

It is well known that Napoleon wore practically the same thing every day — the uniform of a Colonel of the Chasseurs à Cheval of his Imperial Guard. But perhaps less well known is the sheer cost of his wardrobe, which amounted to 20,000 francs every year, of which 900 francs was spent on each imperial outfit including hat and boots. The Emperor was a valued customer of the tailor Chevalier, who supplied practically all of his clothing requirements: kerseymere jacket and knee-breeches (90 francs), gray redingote in finest Louviers cloth (200 francs), silk or flannel waistcoat (respectively 48 francs and 30 francs), uniform of the Chasseurs à Cheval (210 francs), cordon of the Legion of Honor (3 francs), solid silver, mounted eagle swagger stick (70 francs) and colonel's epaulettes (150 francs).

Napoleon's iconic hat, his so-called *chapeau français*, came from the hatter Poupard and cost 60 francs (cf Poupard mémoire dated 16 March 1807). Made by appointment to the Emperor, it consisted of a black felted beaver fur bicorn with a tricolor cockade held in place by a buttoned silk ribbon trim. Poupard (Poupard & Delaunay from 1811) would make four such hats every year, so ensuring that the Emperor's wardrobe always included a complete set of 12 hats. The remaining items were a muslin cravat (16 francs), supplied by the purveyors of fine linen Misses Lolive and de Beuvry; and riding boots (80 francs) plus silk-lined shoes (15 francs) made by Napoleon's boot and shoemaker, Maître Jacques.

Napoleon was notoriously messy in his habits. His white kerseymere pantaloons and knee breeches never stayed white for very long and his wardrobe had to be regularly replaced. Fastidious about personal hygiene, he changed several times a day, hence the huge quantity of underwear at his disposal. His personal linen, particularly his numerous batiste cotton shirts, were constantly laundered.

This simplicity of appearance served Napoleon well, and delivered a powerful message. Never before had a Head of State devoted such effort to image-building. From the moment he became Emperor, Napoleon engaged virtually every workshop in Paris. Every new campaign, every new ministerial promotion sponsored a flurry of artistic commissions. Napoleon's patronage of the arts was unequaled in the history of France and extended to artists of every description: sculptors, painters, printers, cabinetmakers, ceramicists, weavers, jewelers, goldsmiths and silversmiths. As historian Annie Jourdan points out: "This more than anything reveals Napoleon's true intentions — and obsessions. As First Consul and then as Emperor, his primary and most obvious intention was to surround himself with portraits and busts that exalted his image."[9]

This "obsession with image" reached its climax in the Imperial Palaces where the hero and his exploits were everywhere to be seen. By keeping himself always to the fore, Napoleon aimed to eclipse the memory of the Bourbons in the very places where they had reigned for more than 200 years. It was a bold challenge, and Napoleon's personal commitment to artistic excellence — his insistence on quality over quantity — was clearly central to its success. He was uncompromising in his expectations and kept a close watch on every depiction of himself or his regime. Artworks were grouped together by the Intendant-General of the Imperial Household then submitted for his Majesty's consideration. Napoleon would express his opinion and demand whatever changes he judged necessary. "His Majesty is not satisfied, Sir, with the portrait you have sent me," wrote Grand Marshal Duroc to Intendant-General Daru on 15 September 1807.[10] "His Highness finds the expression on the face too hard and does in any case prefer to be depicted in military uniform."

One month later on 22 October, Daru received a new complaint from the Grand Marshal: "I am returning, Sir, the portrait of His Majesty, as the face lacks sufficient nobility; we conclude that in this as in other works, the painter is striving for a likeness that eludes him and that this leads him to make further mistakes."[11] The paintings in question were not full size portraits but portrait miniatures for snuff boxes (page 250). The works of Daniel Saint for instance, one of whose portrait miniatures features in the Ledoux Collection, were among those scrutinized. From medals to gifts, the use of imperial imagery was supervised down to the smallest detail — the projection of Napoleon Bonaparte as an exceptional figure depended on it. Judging from Napoleon's continuing popularity today, the challenge paid off. The Imperial Household may well have failed to secure his position as Emperor — but it was certainly successful in ensuring that posterity would remember its Master.

1 French National Archives: A.N. O2 164, folio 97.
2 *Étiquette du palais impérial.* Paris, 1806.
3 Potocka, A. *Mémoires de la Comtesse Potocka.* Paris: Plon, 1897, p. 123. Trans: *Memoirs of the Countess Potocka.* London: Grant Richards, 1901.
4 In the absence of the King, the royal bed was guarded by a footman and courtiers had to bow before it.
5 Bausset. *Mémoires anecdotiques sur l'intérieur du Palais.* Paris: Baudouin Frères, 1827, vol. I, p. 3.
6 1,050,767 francs in 1807, source: *Comptes généraux du Trésor public 1807.* Paris: Imprimerie impériale, November 1808.
7 Bibliothèque Nationale. MS, Fr. 6581, folios 17 and 18.
8 French National Archives: A.N., O2 17, folio 122.
9 Jourdan, Annie J. *Napoléon, héros, imperator, mécène.* Paris: Aubier, 1998, p. 313.
10 French National Archives: A.N. O2 6, folio 128.
11 Ibid., folio 155.

THE EMPEROR'S TABLE

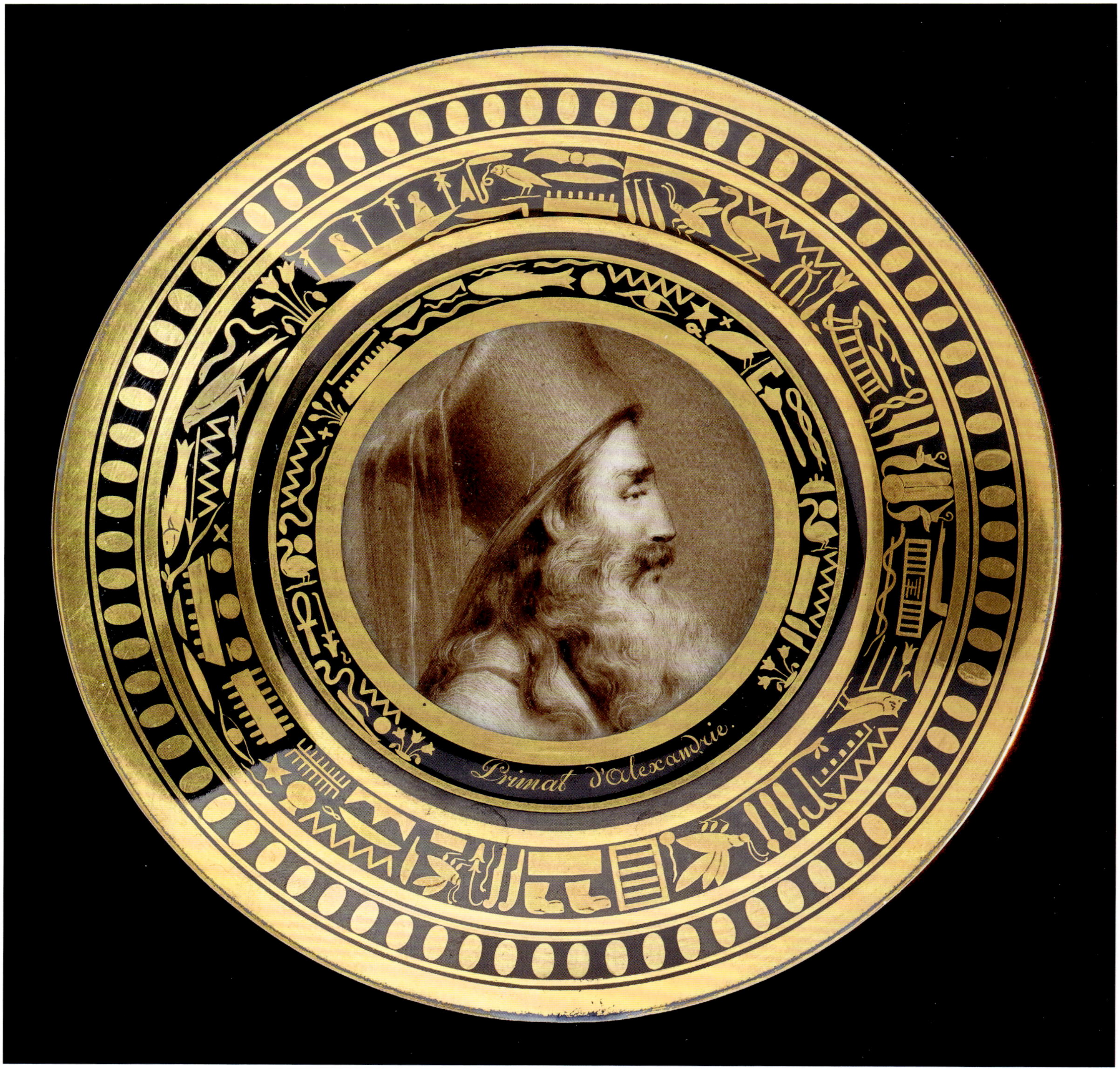

SÈVRES IMPERIAL MANUFACTORY, SAUCER FROM THE EGYPTIAN "CABARET SET" FORMERLY BELONGING TO NAPOLEON

Portrait of the "Primate of Alexandria", one of a series of images sketched from life in Egypt by Vivant Denon for Napoleon's Egyptian "cabaret" set. Commissioned for the occasion of Napoleon's marriage, the set is certainly the most lavish ever produced at Sèvres and was always one of Napoleon's favorites. He took several pieces with him when exiled for the second time in 1815, even though his own monogram had been ground off and replaced with the monogram of Louis XVIII during the "Hundred Days". The set is now on display at the Louvre, with the exception of this saucer and a few other pieces in private hands.

SÈVRES IMPERIAL MANUFACTORY, PLATES FROM NAPOLEON'S SO-CALLED "A VUES DIVERSES" DINNER SERVICE

The Service à Vues Diverses, together with the Service des Quartiers Généraux, ranks among the most valuable tableware ever created for the "Emperor's Private Service". Production commenced under the Empire and was completed under the Restoration. These three plates were produced in the period 1812-1813, featuring: top, a view of the Tuileries gardens dotted with strollers, children and dogs; center, a view of boats on the River Thames, with Greenwich Hospital in the background; bottom, a view by Swebach of "the town of Markranstadt, bordering the plain that was the site of the Battle of Lutzen". The designs recall places of symbolic significance for Europe and topographical views that were familiar to the Emperor. The rims are decorated with a gold frieze on a blue background that is different in each case. Twenty-four plates are now in the museum of the Château de Fontainebleau and only very few pieces of this service are in private hands.

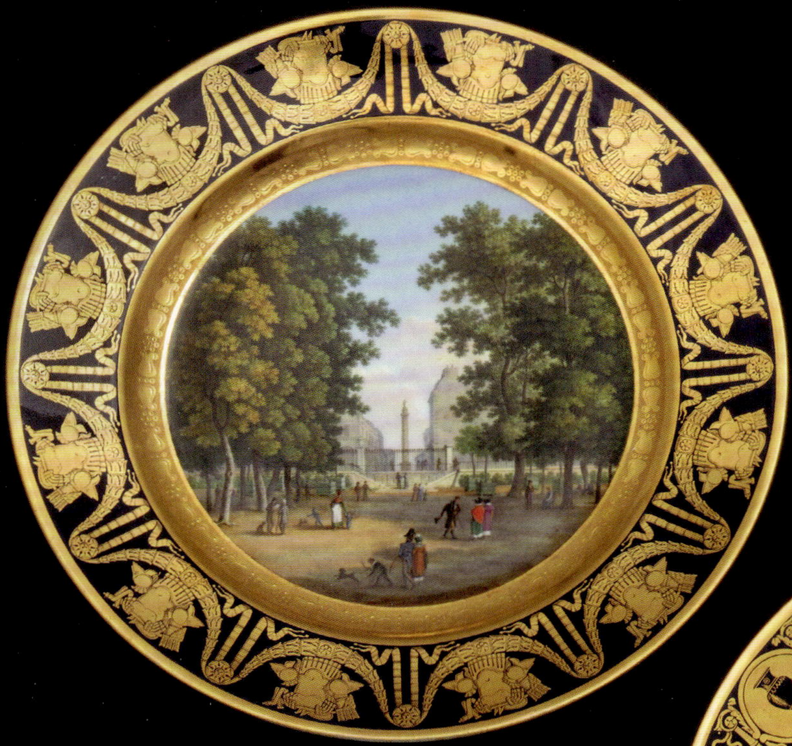

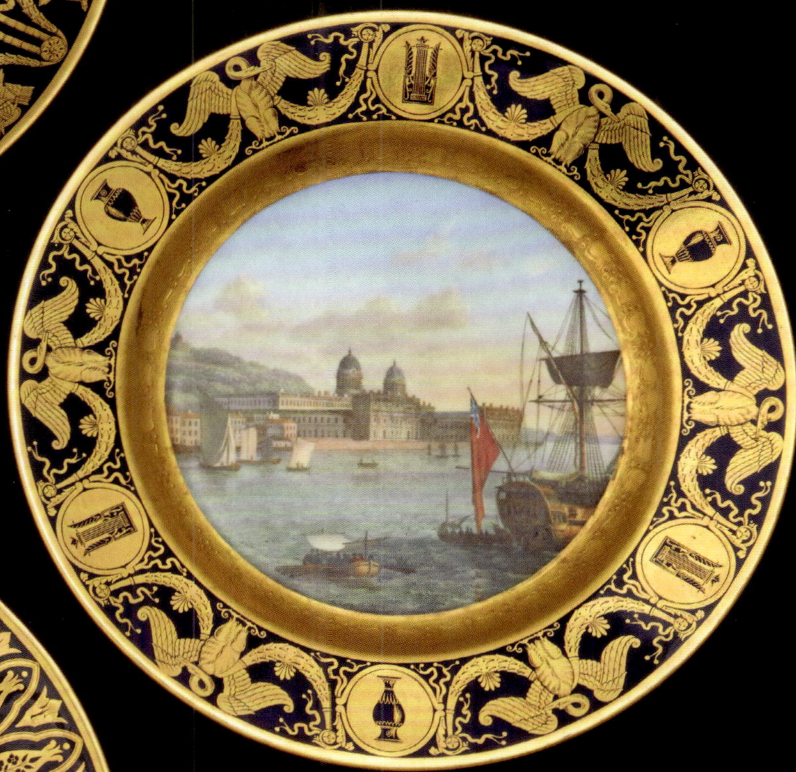

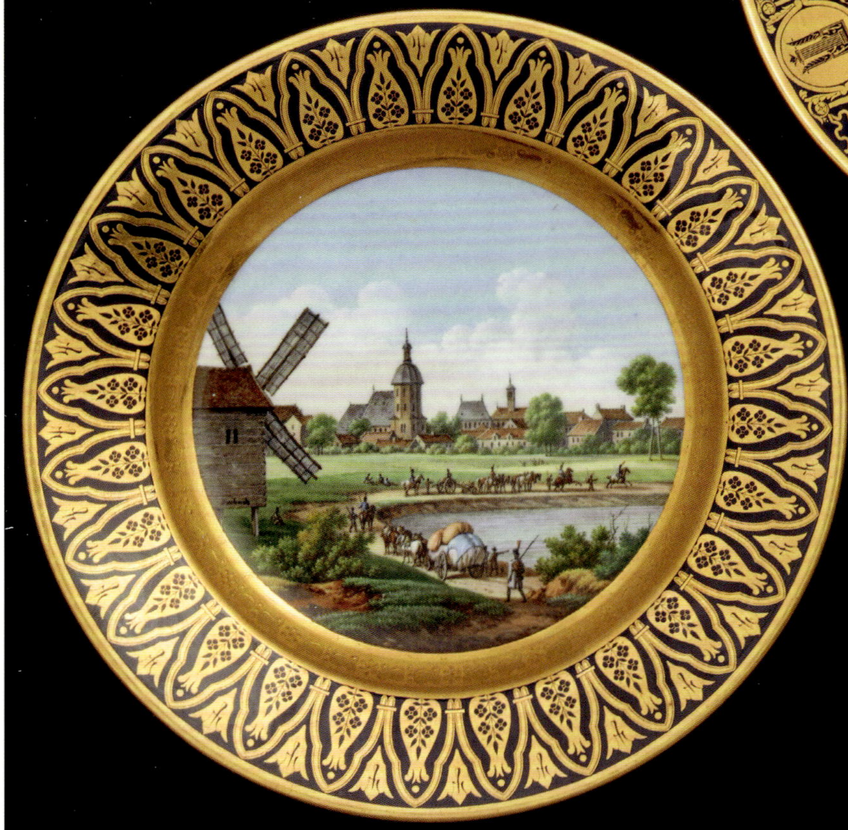

THE EMPEROR'S PERSONAL DINNER SERVICE, KNOWN AS THE "QUARTIERS GÉNÉRAUX"

SÈVRES IMPERIAL MANUFACTORY, SIX PLATES FROM NAPOLEON'S PERSONAL SERVICE

The so-called "Service des Quartiers Généraux" is probably the finest and most unique tableware ever produced at Sèvres. Commissioned by the Emperor for his personal use, it was manufactured in the period 1808-1810 and included a biscuit centerpiece, 24 so-called soup plates d'entrée, 24 so-called plates "à monter" and 72 so-called dessert plates "à décor". Napoleon himself gave precise instructions as to the subjects depicted in the decorations, which are executed with extraordinary finesse. He was particularly insistent that "of these designs, there should be not one battle scene or named individual, but that, on the contrary, the subjects offer only vague allusions that will provoke pleasant memories."

The service was delivered to the Tuileries on 27 March 1810, just in time for Napoleon's marriage to Marie-Louise. It was then used by King Louis XVIII on his coming to power four years later, replacing the imperial insignia and descriptive inscriptions with his own monogram. The service accompanied Napoleon to Longwood where it was wheeled out for ceremonial dinners. In his will, Napoleon expressed the wish to leave 54 plates to his son. In the event the Austrians saw to it that the boy received nothing and the plates were lovingly preserved by the Emperor's loyal entourage until they were eventually sold off. Most of the pieces are now held by national museums, with a few rare exceptions now in private hands. The present collection owns an exceptional set of six plates, including two that form part of a unique triptych depicting the Battle of Lobau and respectively featuring the Emperor's tent, the "Bridge to Lobau Island" and "the Emperor's tents on Lobau Island." The other three plates pictured here respectively represent the Brandenburg Gate, the Simplon Road and, most famous of all, "The frigate La Muiron landing at Ajaccio with Bonaparte in October 1799", for which Napoleon had a particular fondness. Add to these the only known plate from the "à monter" service, and this collection can pride itself on owning a set that is second only to the 23-plate set held by the Château de Fontainebleau and the 19-plate set held by the Fondation Napoléon. The remaining plates are held in the collections of the Museum of Malmaison (three plates), the Royal Museum of Fine Arts of Belgium, Brussels (three plates), the Sèvres Manufactory (two plates) the Chalençon Collections (one plate) and the Louvre (one plate).

There was one plate from his personal service (designed to his own specifications) that was particularly dear to the Emperor's heart: "The frigate La Muiron landing at Ajaccio with Bonaparte in October 1799". It reminded him of his return to France and the beginning of a rise to power that would take him to the very top. But most of all it reminded him of the frigate's namesake, his friend, Jean-Baptiste Muiron who had been killed at the Battle of Arcole taking the bullet that had been destined for Napoleon. In 1807 Bonaparte ordered that the Muiron be kept as a monument "and placed in such a way that it be preserved, if possible, several hundreds of years." Out of all the plates Napoleon took with him to St Helena, it is the only one cited in the memoirs of his companions in exile. According to his valet, Marchand, "all the items [in the service] portrayed views of battlefields or cities. One day, while he was looking at them with Count Montholon, the Emperor lingered over [the plate] showing Ajaccio with the frigate Muiron dropping anchor after arriving from Egypt with General Bonaparte on board. 'Look Montholon [exclaimed Napoleon].' 'That's my home! And I'm sure that's my nursemaid's boat next to the frigate [...]'."

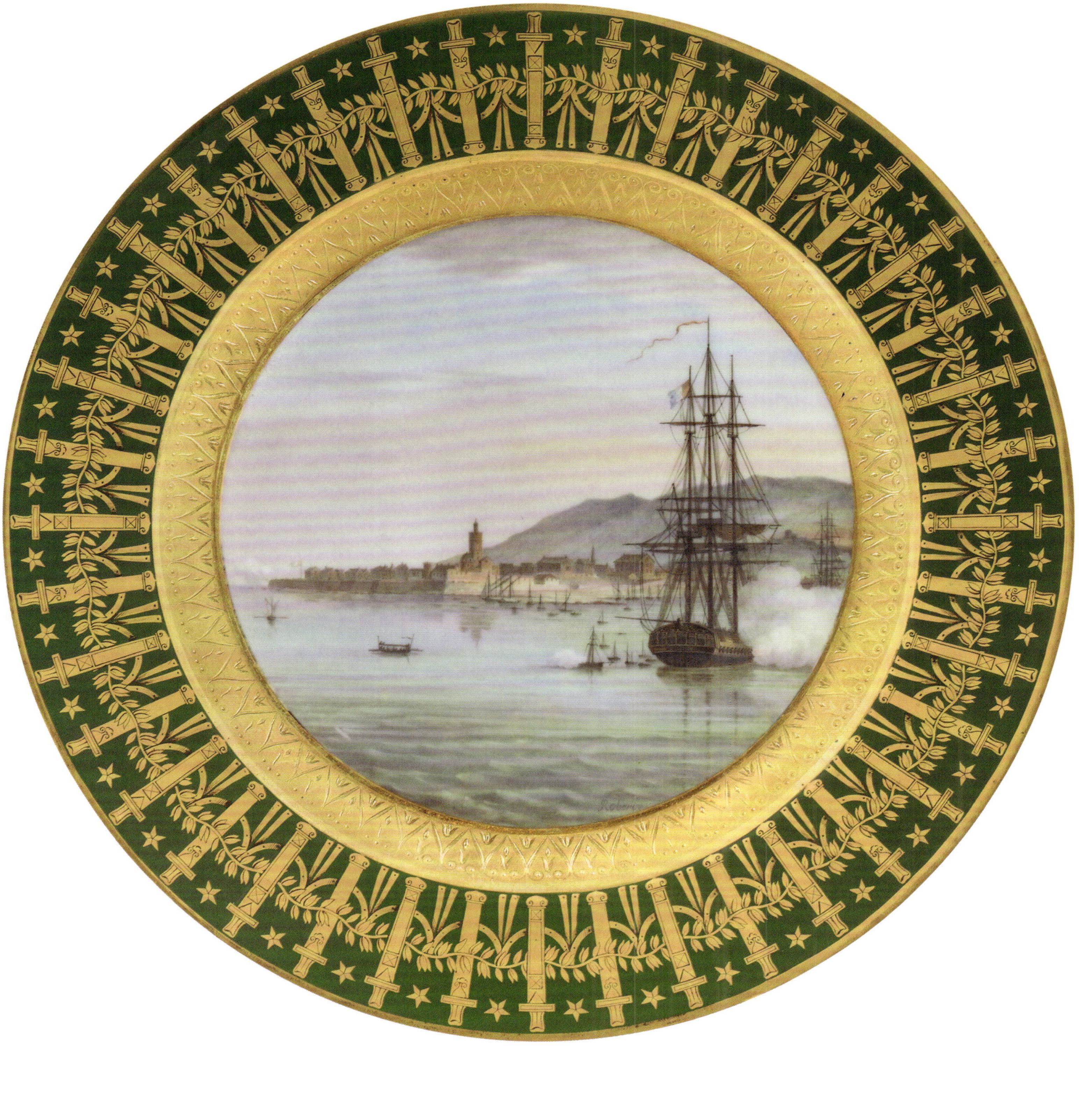

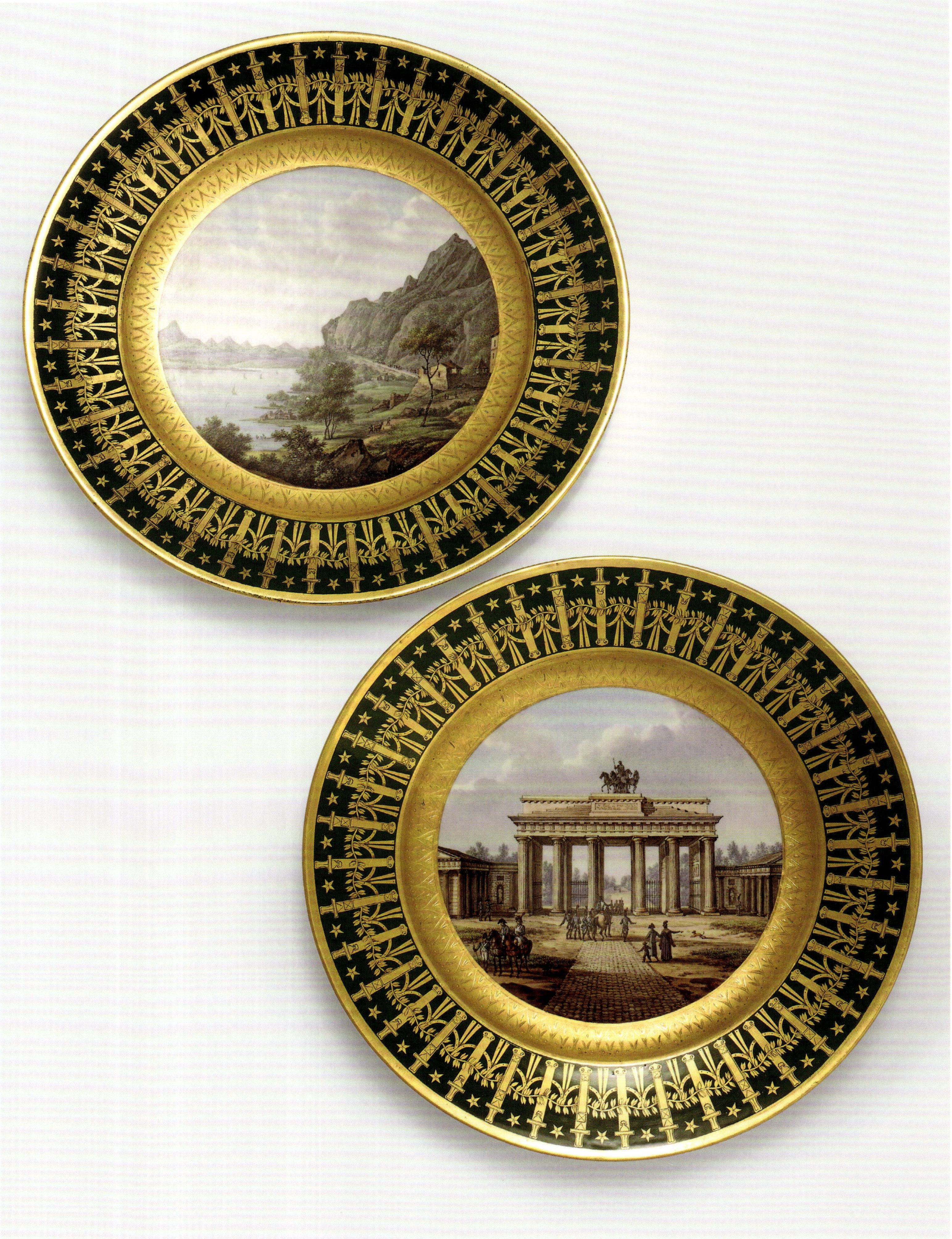

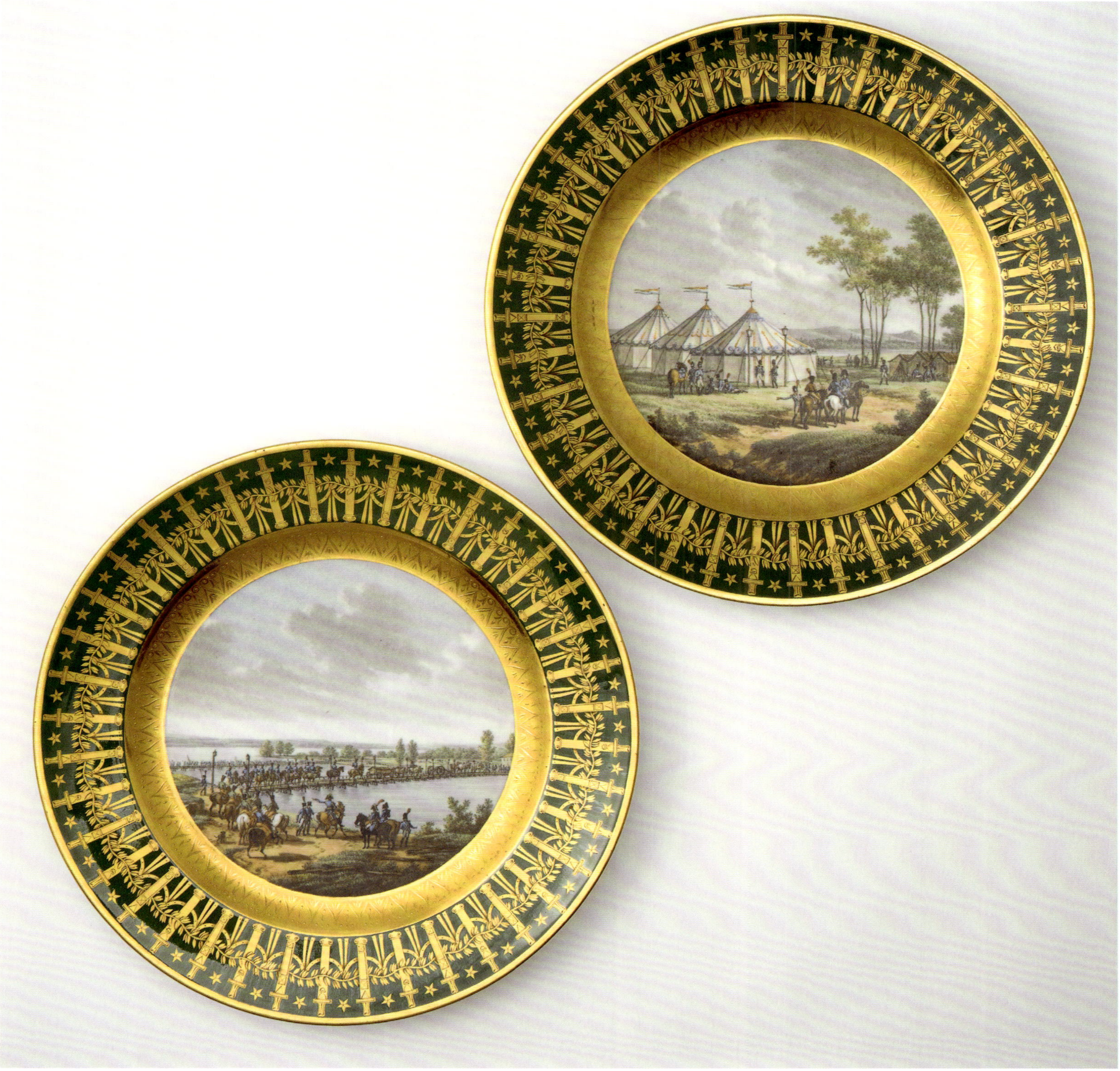

"SIMPLON ROAD"
AND "BRANDENBURG GATE"

"THE EMPEROR'S TENTS ON THE ISLAND OF LOBAU IN THE LOBAU CAMP" AND "COMMUNICATING BRIDGE TO THE ISLAND OF LOBAU"

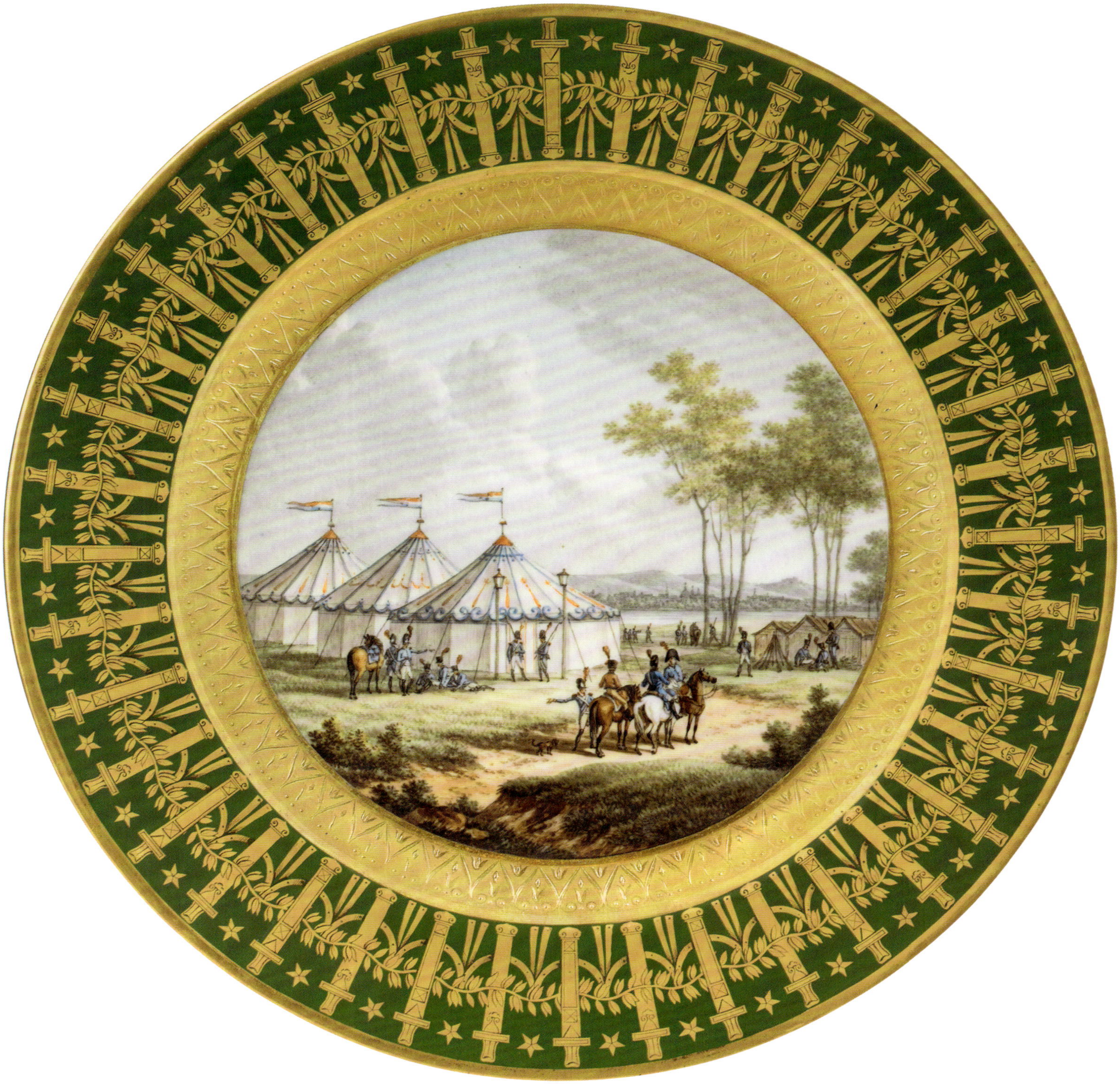

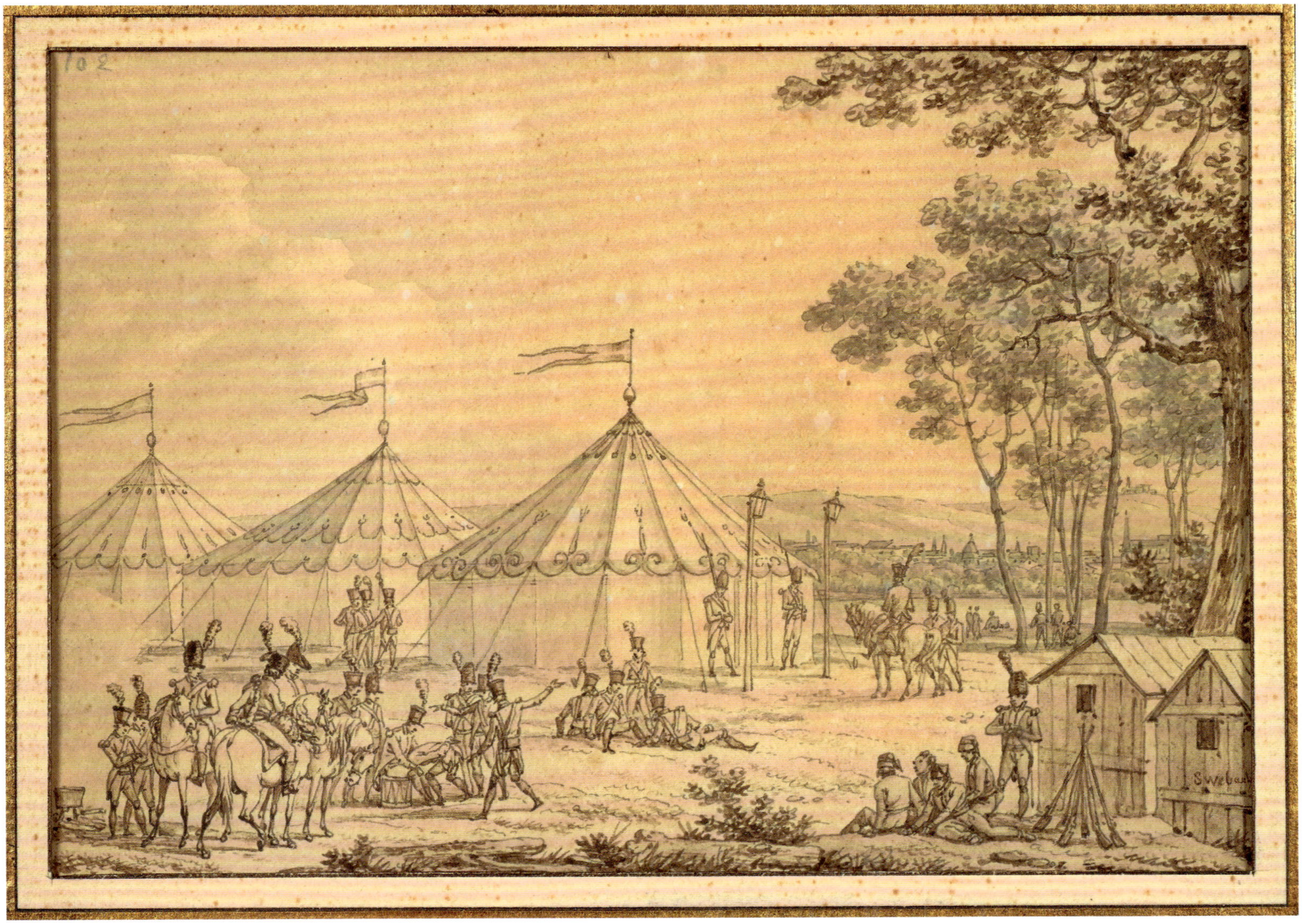

JACQUES FRANÇOIS JOSEPH SWEBACH-DESFONTAINES (1769-1823), DETAIL FROM "THE EMPEROR'S TENTS" PLATE AND DRAWING

This detailed and extremely skilful drawing shows a view of tents and Napoleon's camp set up on the island of Lobau on the Danube from 1-4 July 1809, with a town in the background (probably Aspern). It served as a basis for the decoration on the bottom of one of the plates in the Emperor's personal dinner service produced by the Sèvres manufactory. The artist, Swebach-Desfontaines, was a painter at the manufactory from 1802 to 1813. He slightly altered his composition for Sèvres, shifting the barracks in the foreground of the drawing to the background, and trimming down the groups of soldiers.

SÈVRES IMPERIAL MANUFACTORY, PLATE AND STEM BOWL FROM NAPOLEON'S FONTAINEBLEAU DINNER SERVICE

This stem bowl and plate, one of a pair owned by this collection, were designed for the Emperor's table at Fontainebleau, part of a huge 252-piece dinner service plus "cabaret" set appropriately known as "Fond Rouge, Papillons et Fleurs" (red base, butterflies and flowers). Napoleon took the service with him to Elba in 1814, which explains its subsequent disappearance. All that remain of the service today are a few plates and two stem bowls: the one pictured here plus another held in the collections of the Museum of Château de Fontainebleau.

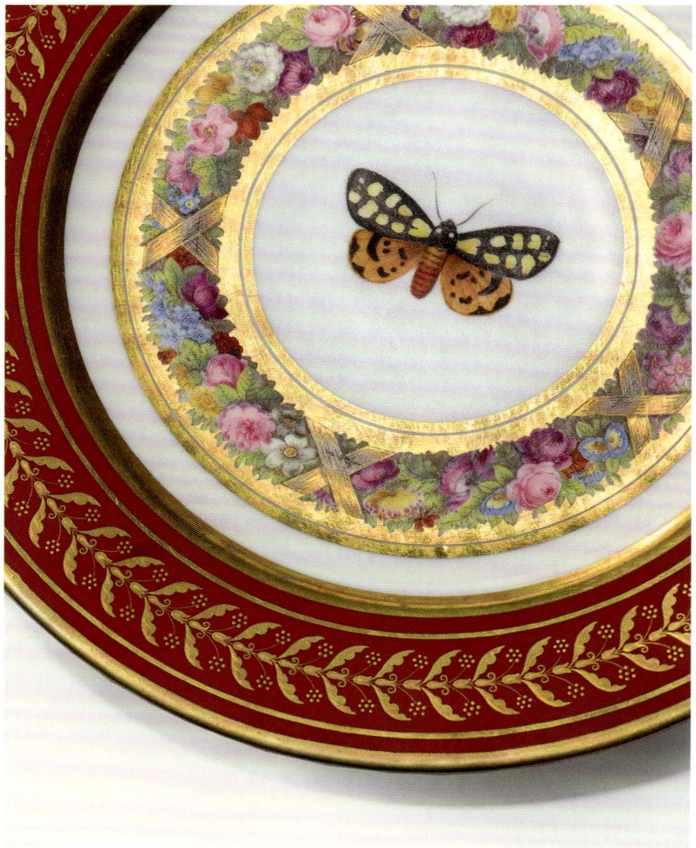

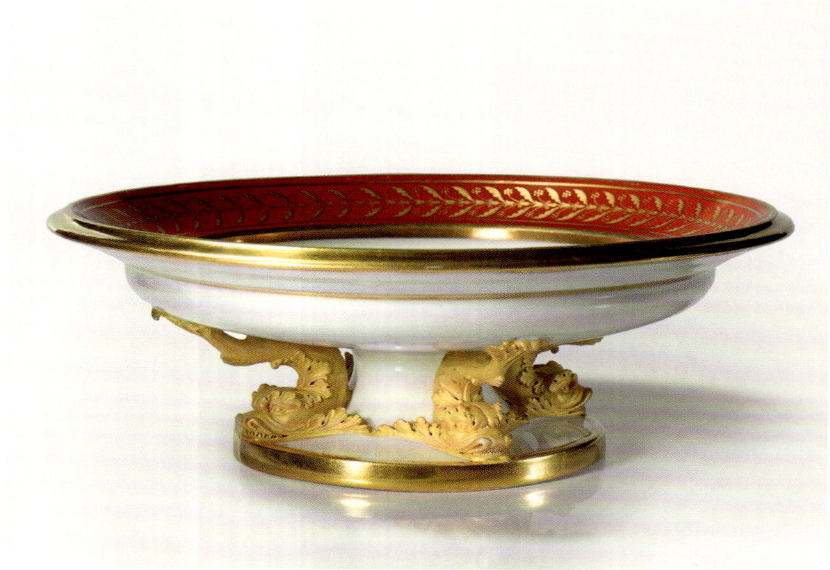

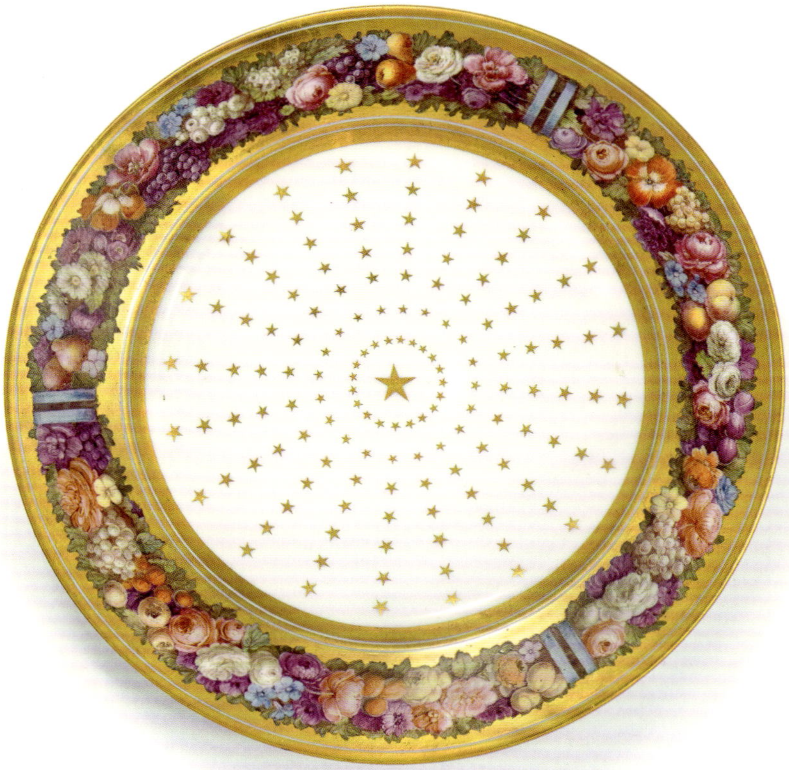

SÈVRES IMPERIAL MANUFACTORY, PLATE WITH GOLD STARS

The pattern of radiating gold stars is set off by an exquisite wreath along the edge that mingles flowers and fruits. The limitations of our current knowledge make us uncertain which residence it was used in. However, its quality illustrates the superb skills of the craftsmen at the Sèvres manufactory.

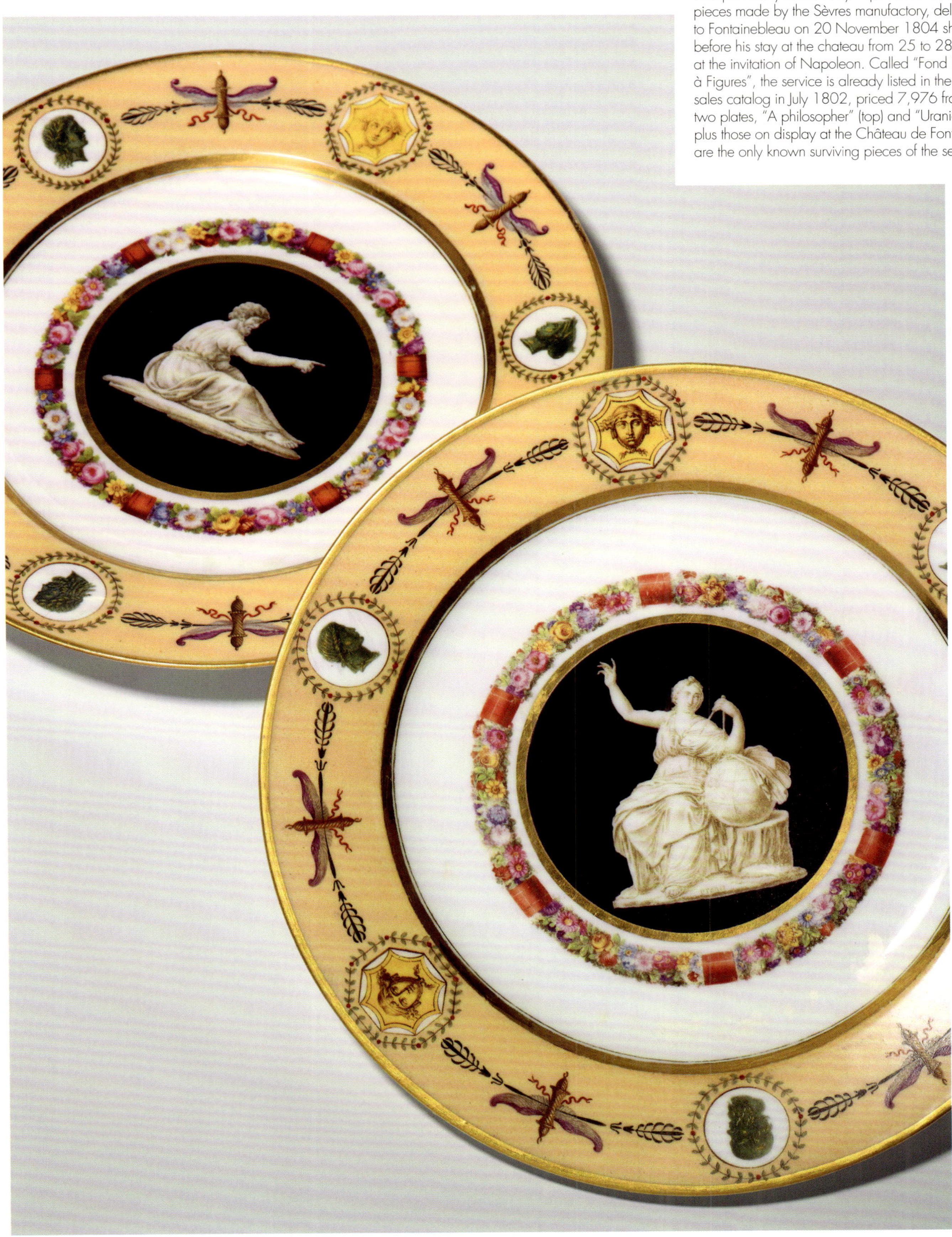

SÈVRES IMPERIAL MANUFACTORY, PLATES INTENDED FOR POPE PIUS VII

Two plates come from a 110-piece dinner service, including most notably one biscuit centerpiece, which was personally selected by Pope Pius VII from several pieces made by the Sèvres manufactory, delivered to Fontainebleau on 20 November 1804 shortly before his stay at the chateau from 25 to 28 November at the invitation of Napoleon. Called "Fond Nankin à Figures", the service is already listed in the Sèvres sales catalog in July 1802, priced 7,976 francs. These two plates, "A philosopher" (top) and "Urania" (bottom), plus those on display at the Château de Fontainebleau are the only known surviving pieces of the service.

THE SO-CALLED "OLYMPIQUE SERVICE"

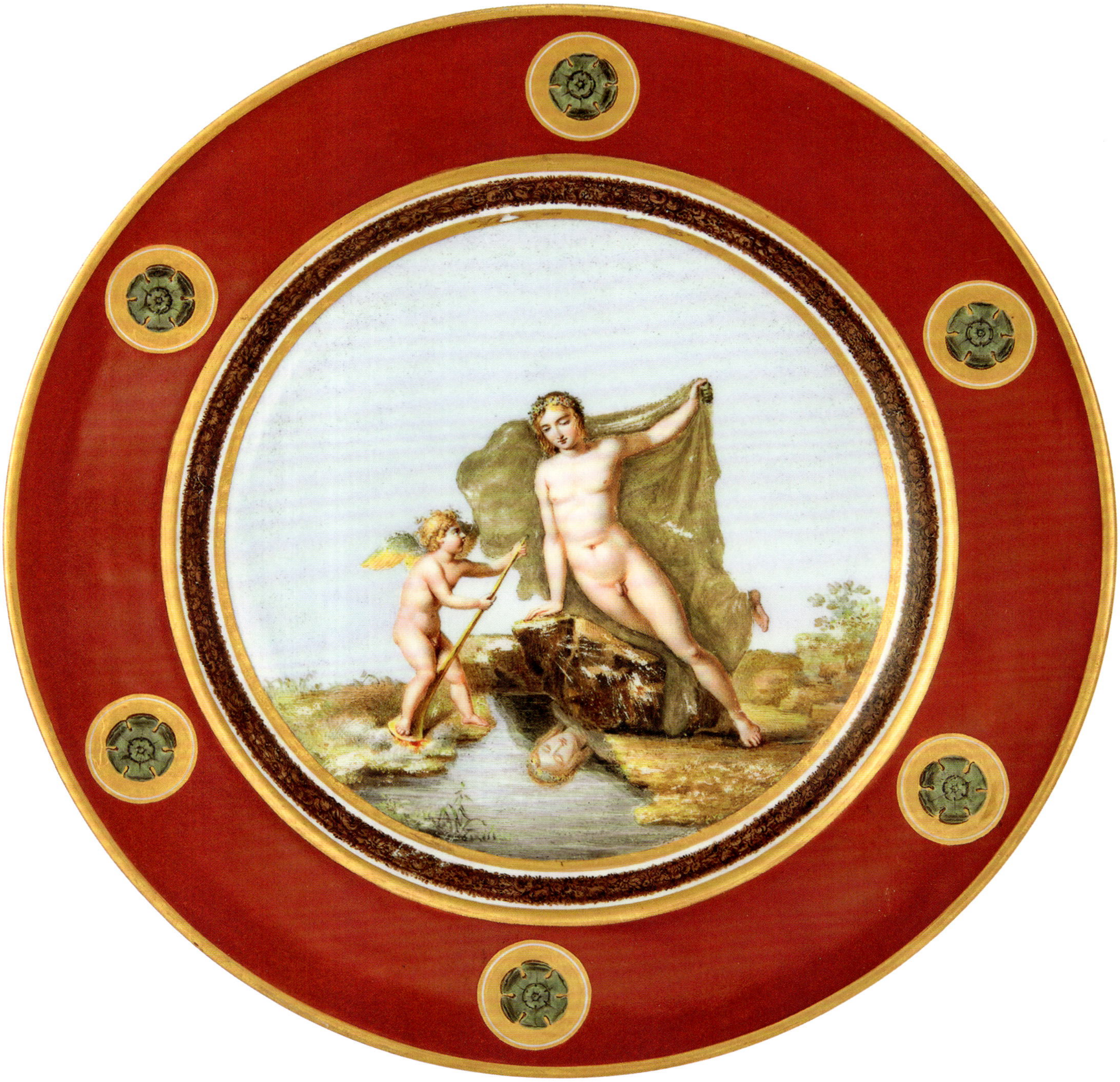

SÈVRES IMPERIAL MANUFACTORY, TWO PLATES, ONE OF WHICH WAS A PRELIMINARY DESIGN FOR NAPOLEON'S SO-CALLED "OLYMPIQUE SERVICE"

The famous Olympique service was delivered to the Tuileries for Napoleon in August 1807, for the wedding of his brother Jérôme, King of Westphalia, to Catharina of Württemberg. In February 1808, Napoleon gave it to Tsar Alexander I to commemorate the Peace Treaty of Tilsit. This is why most of the service can be found in Russia today. It comprises 140 pieces. Its name stems from the subjects depicted in its paintings, which are drawn from Greek mythology. Each design is unique and the final version of every piece has been carefully arrived at through many test runs, as can be seen in one of the two plates shown. The almost complete service is on display in the Armory Chamber at the Kremlin in Moscow. Only a few plates are missing, including the one in the collection.

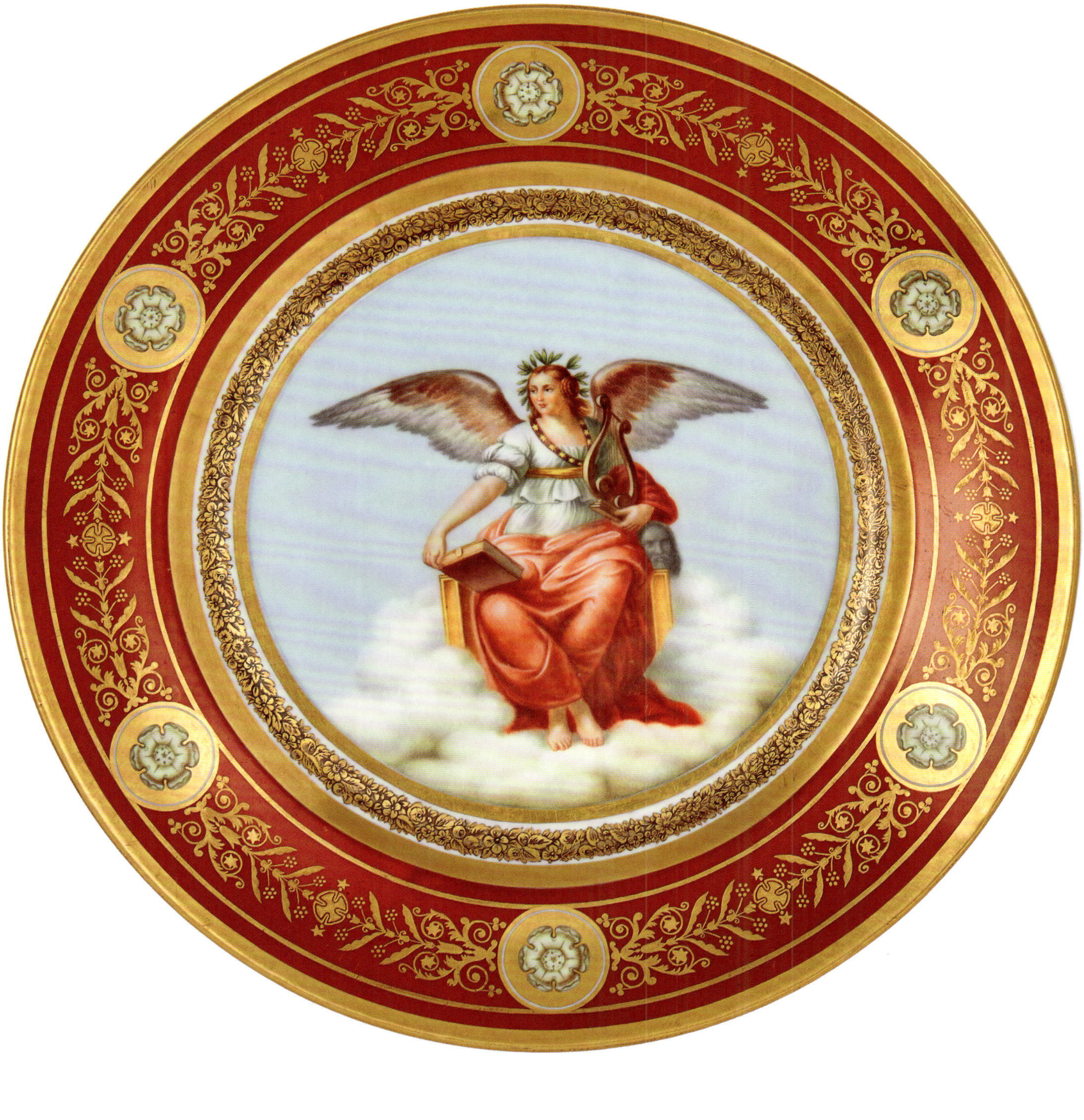

SÈVRES IMPERIAL MANUFACTORY, CANDELABRA AND VICTORY FROM THE SURTOUT DE TABLE FOR THE EMPEROR'S PERSONAL SERVICE

Two magnificent pieces from the surtout de table (table centerpiece) for the Emperor's "Service des Quartiers Généraux", which was delivered to the Tuileries on 27 March 1810 (price: 17,840 francs). The full surtout comprised 27 pieces: one horse-drawn chariot, four candelabras, two tripods, two Medici vases, 16 figures from Antiquity and two Bacchus love seats. Made to designs by Alexandre Brongniart (1770-1847), approved by Napoleon in March 1808, the surtout symbolized the splendor of the imperial court and was used at the grand ceremonial banquet in honor of the marriage of Marie-Louise and Napoleon. Practically all of the pieces are now on display at the Louvre. The Victory figure, driving the central chariot, is probably a replica and comes from the famous Ledoux-Lebard collection.

CHAMPAGNE FLUTE AND CRYSTAL GLASS BELONGING TO NAPOLEON

Probably blown at the Manufacture du Mont-Cenis, official suppliers to the Emperor's House, these two crystal glasses are decorated with just Napoleon's initial under a crown, and a pattern of cut facets. The flute is singular in that it gives a more precise – and very rare – provenance, with the letters "Ton" engraved on its rim. The letters signify Trianon, the residence where this flute was in use.

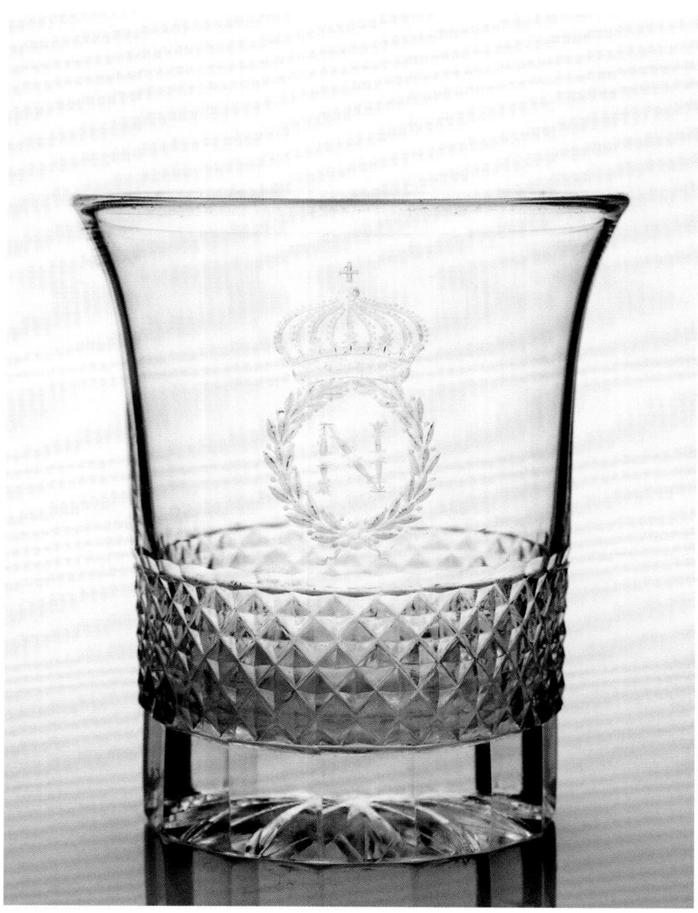

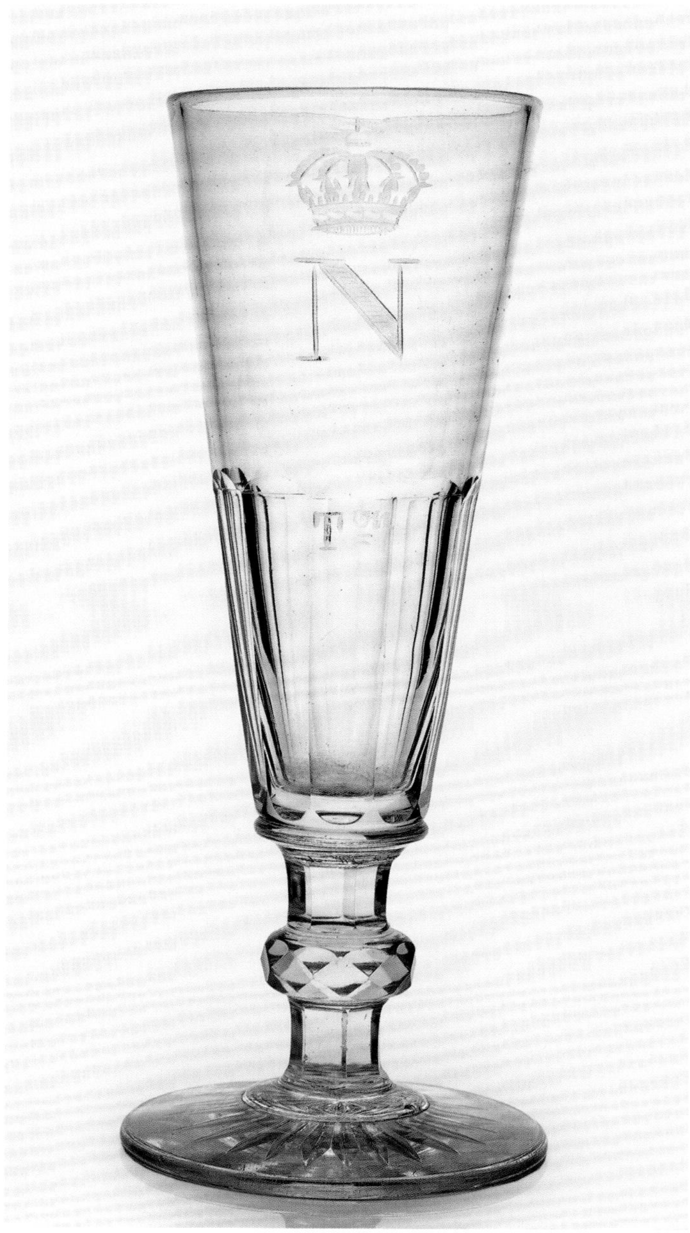

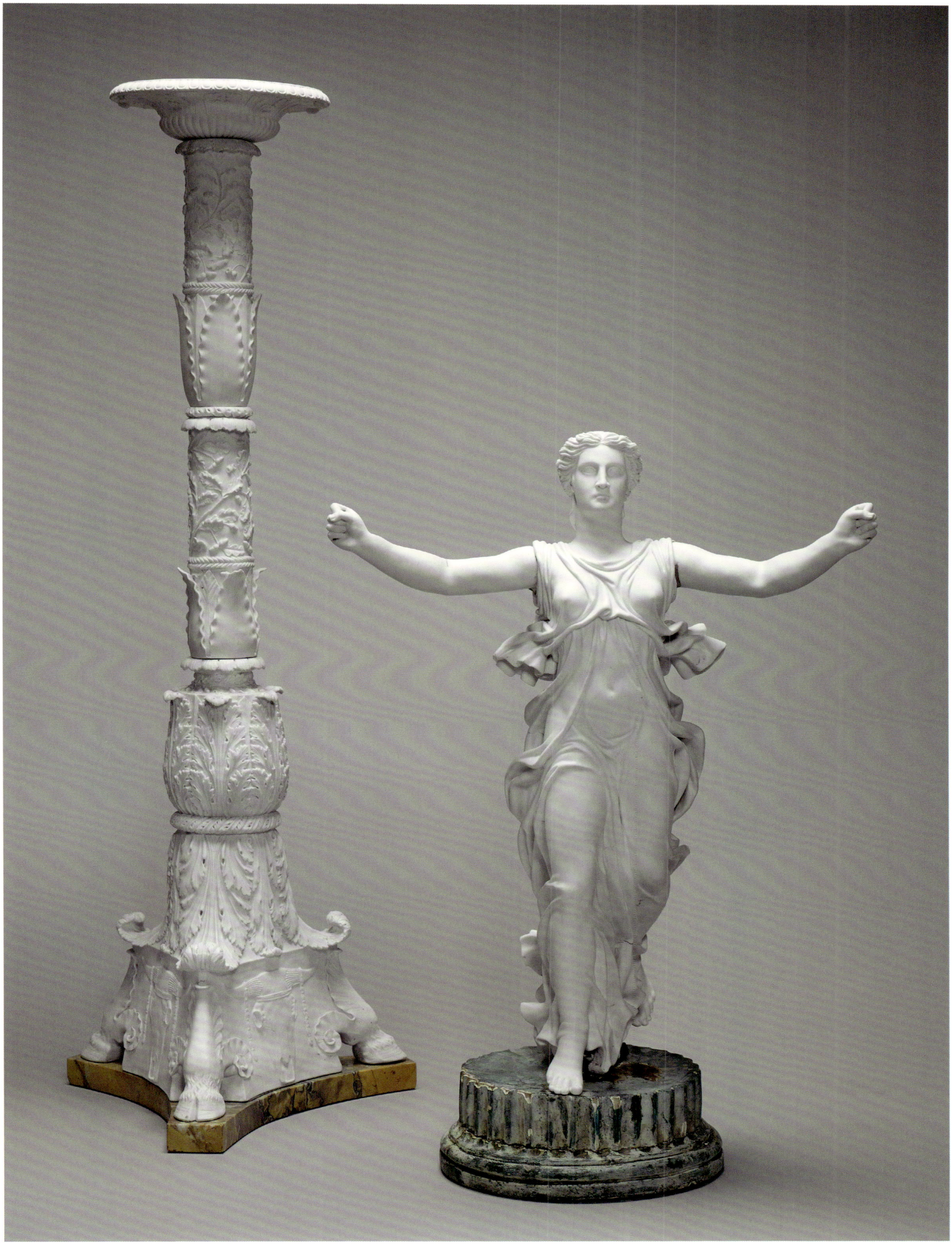

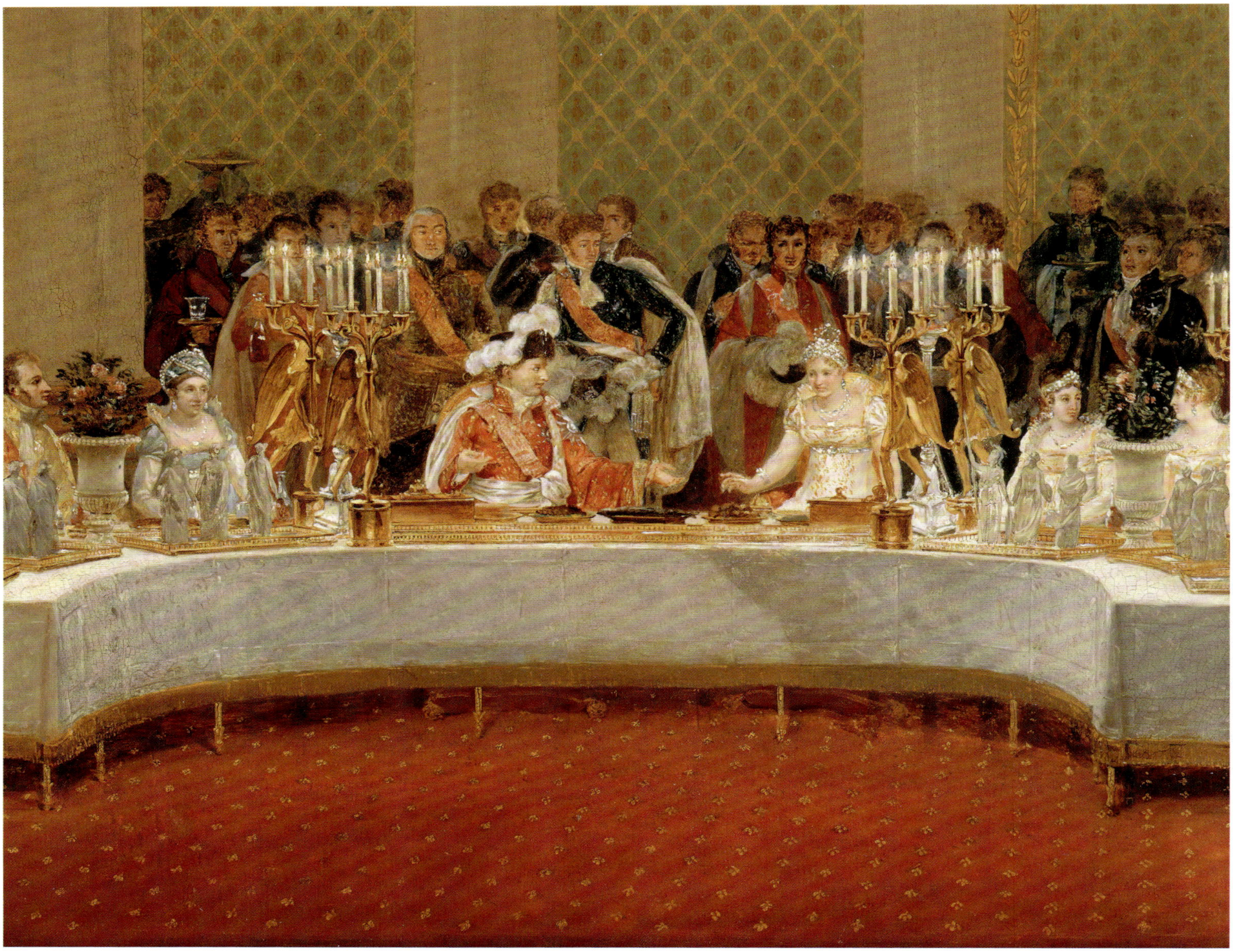

ALEXANDRE BENOÎT JEAN DUFAY (1770-1844),
***WEDDING BANQUET OF NAPOLEON AND MARIE-LOUISE* (DETAIL)**

This famous depiction of the wedding banquet for the Emperor and his young bride provides a precious record. Painted by Alexandre Benoit Jean Dufay (1770-1844) – known as Casanova – it allows us to see the table laid with the various pieces that made up the Emperor's surtout de table, including figures like the Venus Genetrix conserved in the collection.
Château de Fontainebleau collection

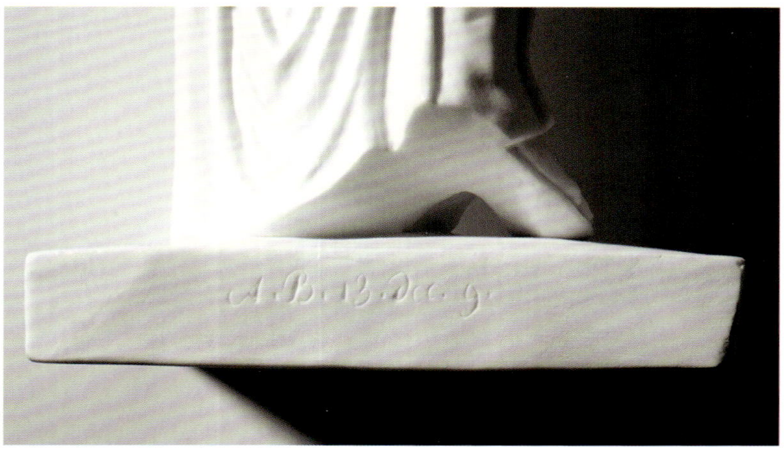

SÈVRES IMPERIAL MANUFACTORY, VENUS GENETRIX FROM THE SURTOUT DE TABLE FOR NAPOLEON'S PERSONAL SERVICE

The surtout de table for Napoleon's personal service was commissioned in 1807 and delivered to the Tuileries on 27 March 1810. It was used for the first time on 2 April to mark Napoleon's marriage to Marie-Louise and comprised 27 pieces: one horse-drawn chariot, four candelabras, two tripods, two Medici vases, 16 figures from Antiquity, including the Victory figure held by this collection, and two Bacchus love seats. The overall design was entrusted to Alexandre Brongniart (1770-1847) and approved by Napoleon in March 1808. All of the pieces were inspired by originals in the Musée Napoleon, the Aphrodite figure being modeled on an original by Diphilus very like the Aphrodite attributed to Callimachus in the Uffizi Gallery, Florence. The exception was Napoleon's chariot, which was the work of French sculptor Antoine Mouton (1765-1835), known as Moutoni.
On the base it has the words "VENUS GENITRIX" cut into it, and further along "L". Underneath is the Empire-era "SEVRES" mark. On the back: "A. B. 13. Dec. 9." (for Alexandre Brongniart, 13 December 1809), confirming his presence at Napoleon and Marie-Louise's wedding table. As far as we know, none of the original sixteen figures of the Emperor's private service that were used for the wedding are known to be in any private or public collection, all the others referred to being subsequent re-editions.

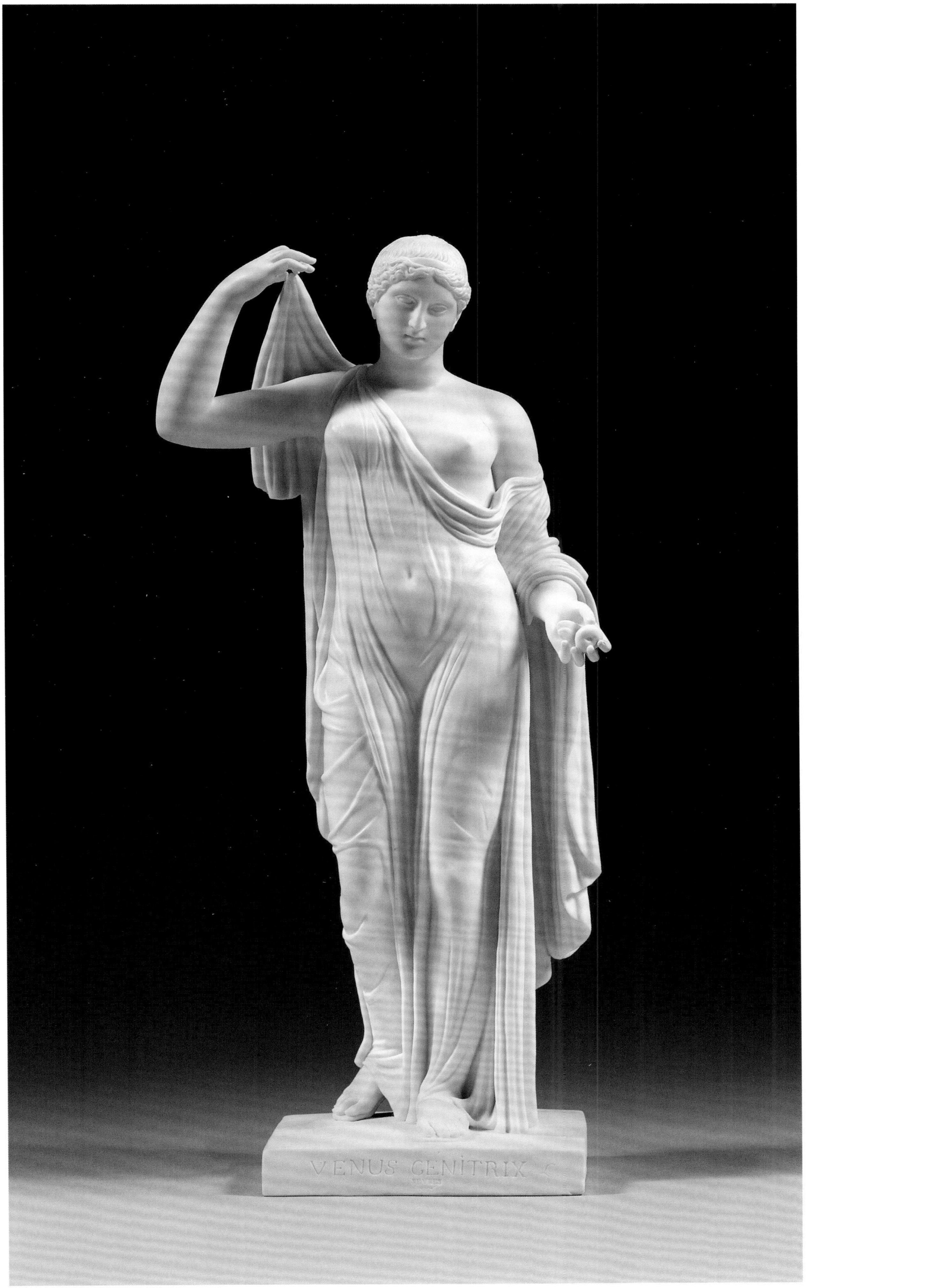
VENUS GENITRIX

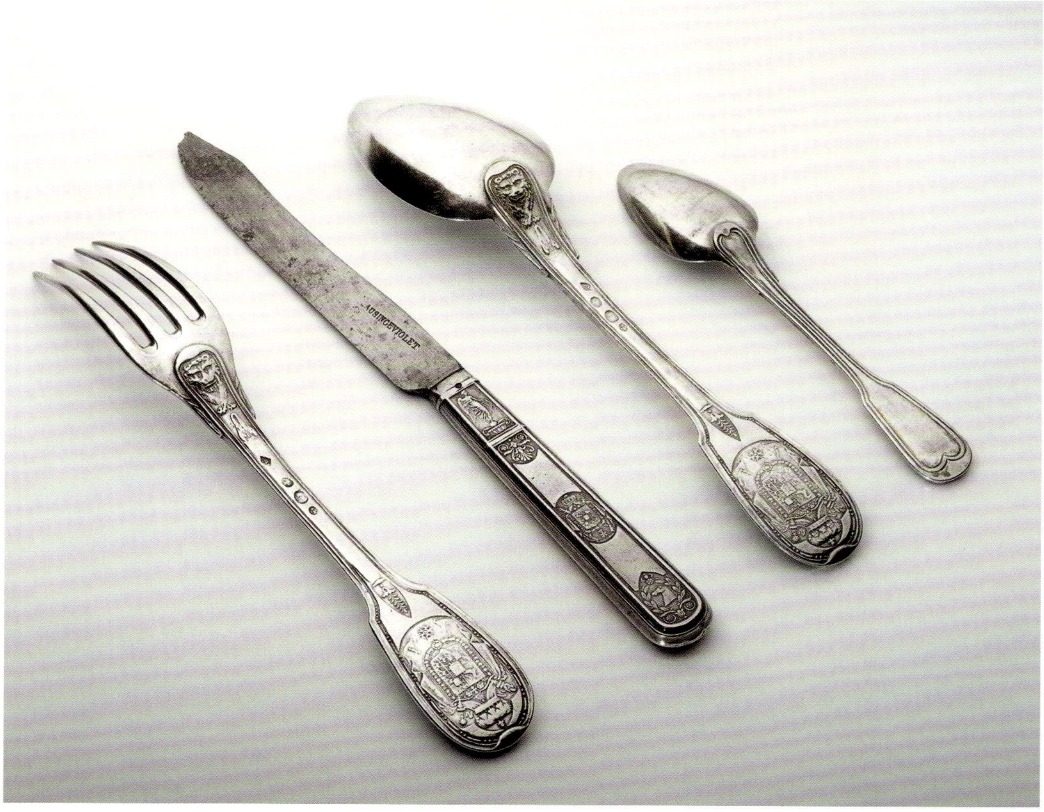

MARTIN-GUILLAUME BIENNAIS (1764-1843), SILVER FLATWARE FROM NAPOLEON'S TABLE SERVICE ON ST HELENA

Fork, spoon and knife in the filet-violon style bearing the coat-of-arms of Napoleon. The mark "Au Singe Violet" is visible on the knife blade, all in upper-case letters. The fork and the spoon are stamped "Biennais" and hallmarked (sterling silver mark, large guarantee mark and the letter "F"). Several pieces of flatware in the same style accompanied Napoleon to St Helena.

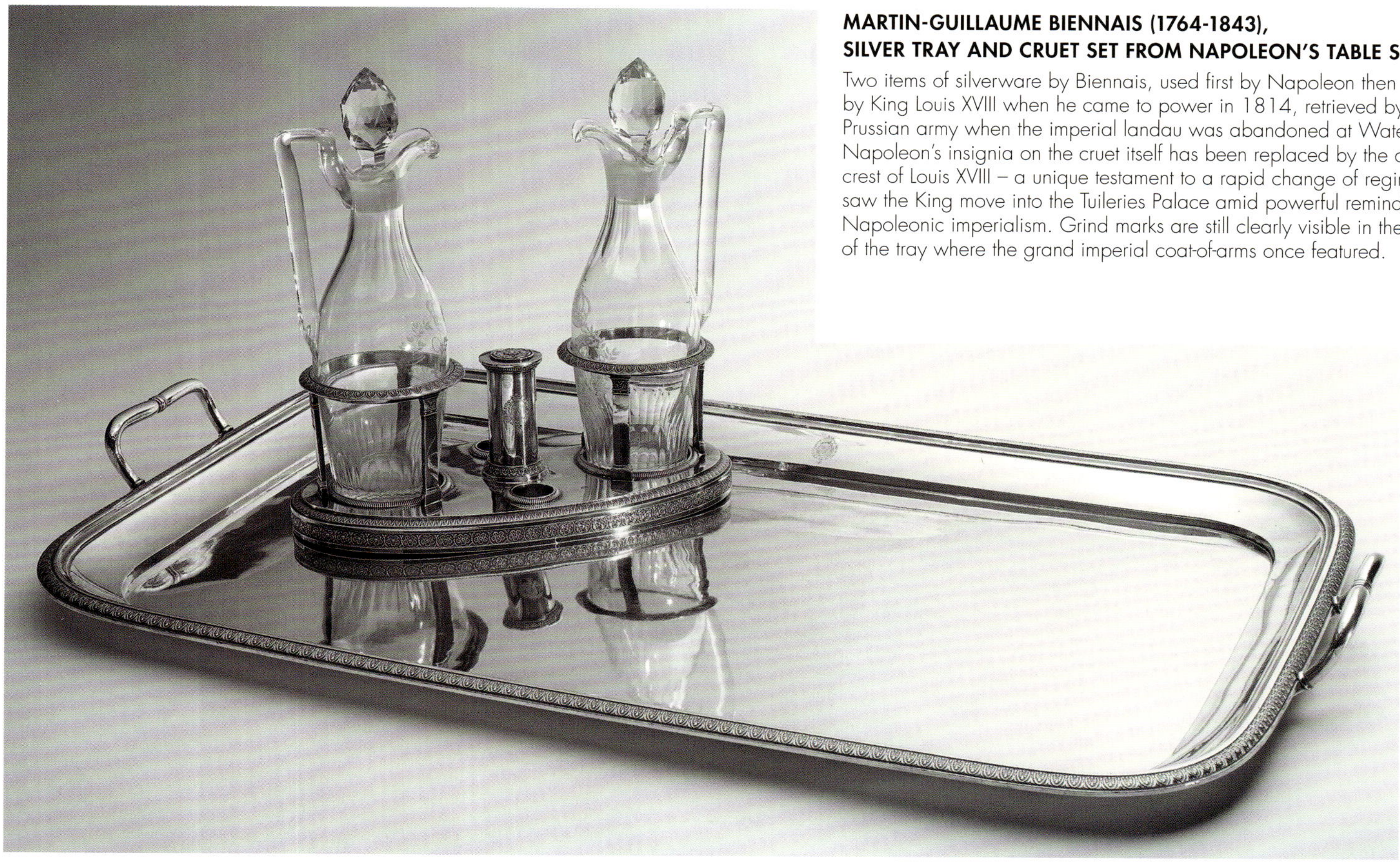

MARTIN-GUILLAUME BIENNAIS (1764-1843), SILVER TRAY AND CRUET SET FROM NAPOLEON'S TABLE SERVICE

Two items of silverware by Biennais, used first by Napoleon then by King Louis XVIII when he came to power in 1814, retrieved by the Prussian army when the imperial landau was abandoned at Waterloo. Napoleon's insignia on the cruet itself has been replaced by the armorial crest of Louis XVIII – a unique testament to a rapid change of regime that saw the King move into the Tuileries Palace amid powerful reminders of Napoleonic imperialism. Grind marks are still clearly visible in the center of the tray where the grand imperial coat-of-arms once featured.

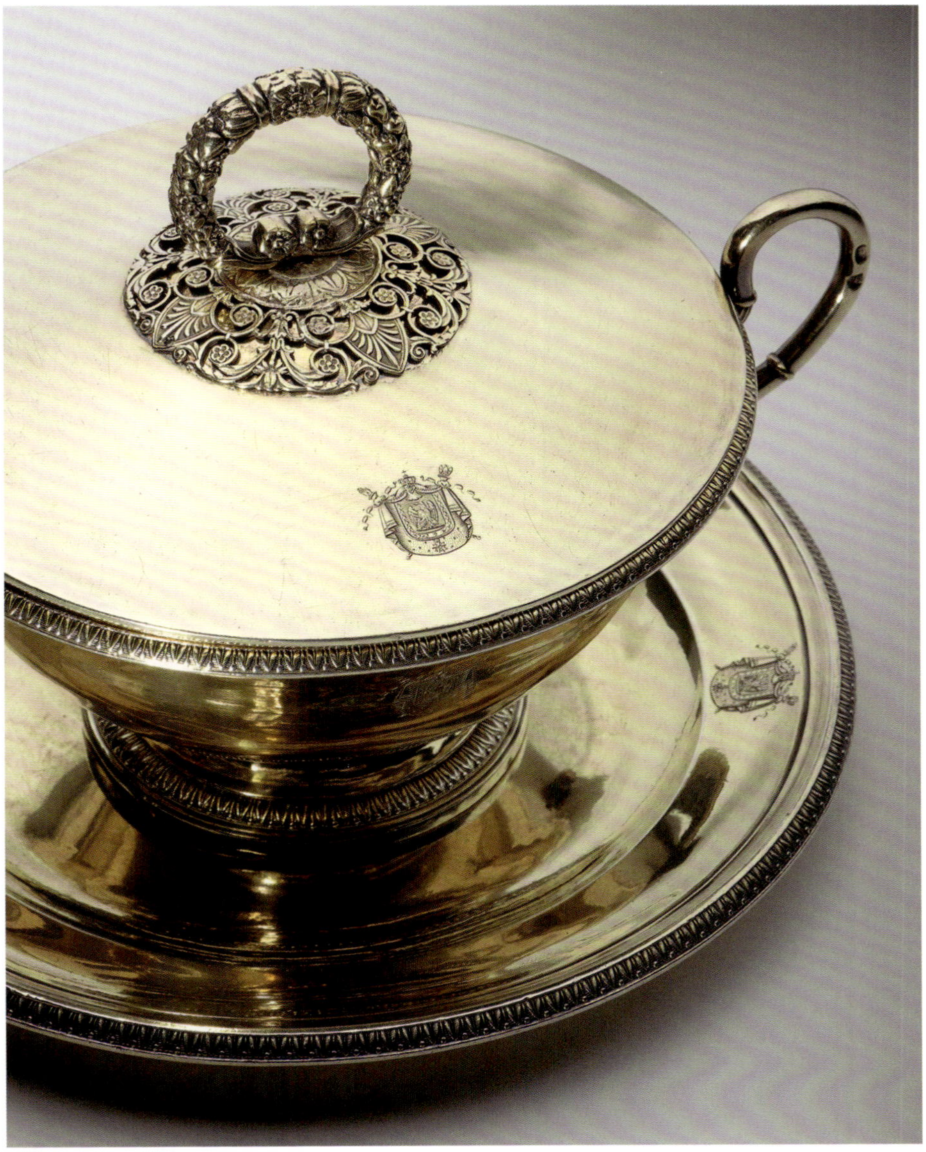

MARTIN-GUILLAUME BIENNAIS (1764-1843), VERMEIL SOUP TUREEN USED BY NAPOLEON AT ST HELENA

This soup tureen on a presentation plate is among the very few vermeil pieces that Napoleon took with him to St Helena. We can therefore be sure that he used it personally. They were passed on to Charles-Tristan de Montholon (1783-1853) who remained loyally by the Emperor's side during his exile on St Helena, until his death on 5 May 1821. In the codicil to his will dated 16 April 1816, Napoleon bequeathed to the three executors of his will, including Montholon: "the silver, jewels, silverware, china, furniture, books, arms, etc., and generally all my belongings on the island of St Helena". In a letter dated 1919, certified by a notary public at Roquefort on 5 February 1920, Montholon's granddaughter, the Marchioness Villeneuve, authenticated the provenance of the vermeil tureen and silverware.

MARTIN-GUILLAUME BIENNAIS (1764-1843), FLATWARE FROM NAPOLEON'S GRAND VERMEIL SERVICE

In addition to the silverware for ordinary service, the Imperial Household also owned a splendid vermeil service by Biennais, which was reserved for state banquets or to honor distinguished guests at the Emperor's table. All of the pieces are stamped with the grand imperial coat-of-arms and exceptional for their delicacy of execution and decoration. The knife is engraved with a horn of plenty and a lion's muzzle. The fork handle features a different decoration, with a horn of plenty and a peacock. The service was destroyed under the Bourbon Restoration, except for a few, very rare pieces that were probably offered as gifts before its destruction.

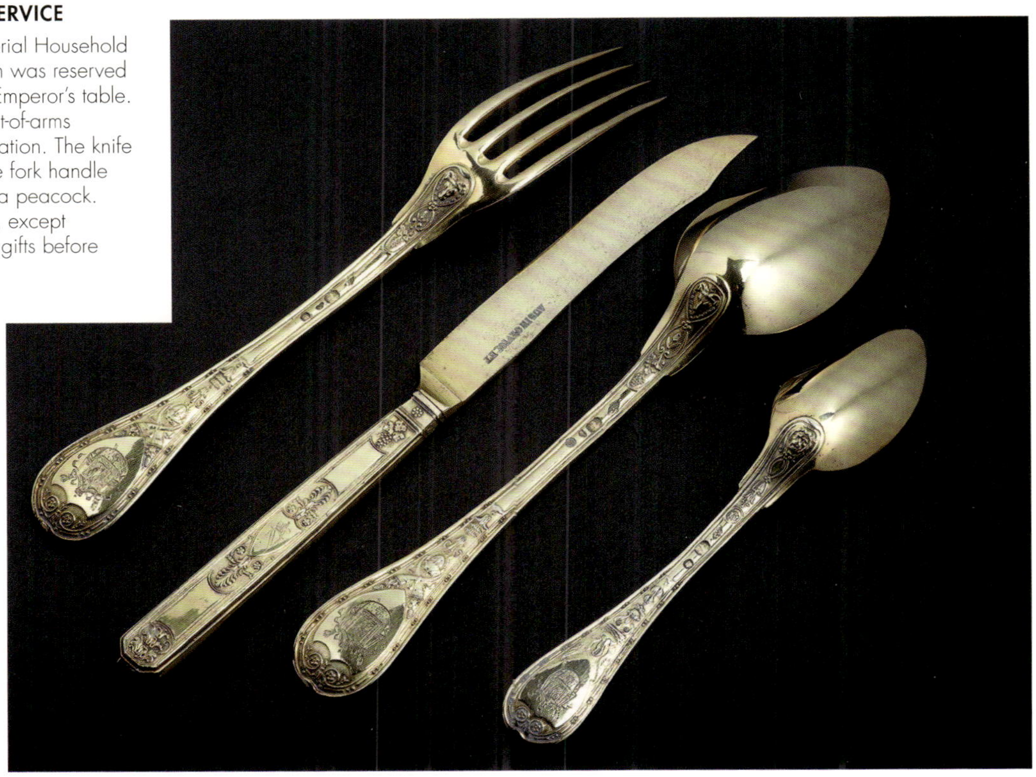

SÈVRES IMPERIAL MANUFACTORY, TWO PLATES "LUCILLA" AND "AUGUSTUS"

Lucilla, Marcus Aurelius's daughter, and Caesar Augustus were the two figures from Antiquity chosen to adorn these plates produced by the Sèvres manufactory. The two cameo portraits are treated in bronze and gold, and set off by a midnight-blue background with a rich multicolored floral and fruit wreath border. These plates are very rare because they were made around 1801-1802 during the French Consulate period, when the manufactory was beginning to get back on its feet after Alexandre Brongniart took over as director.

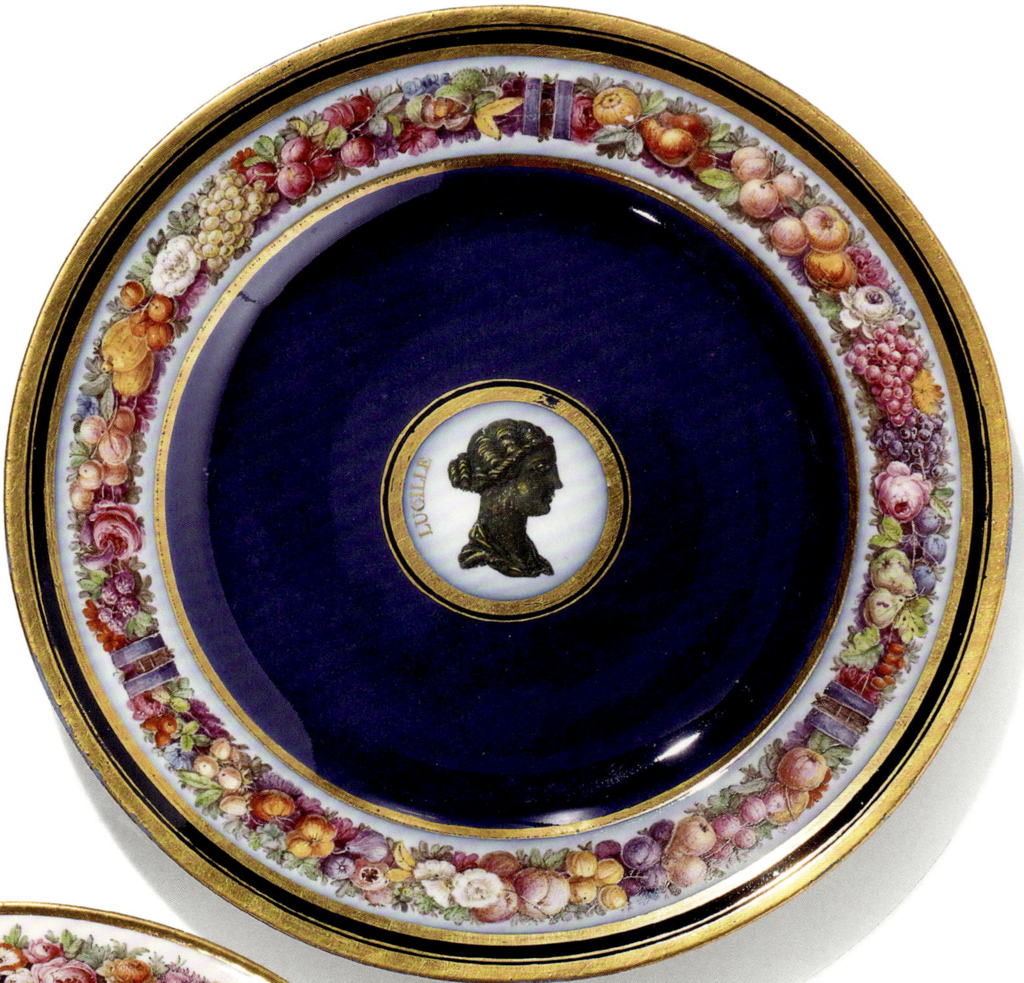

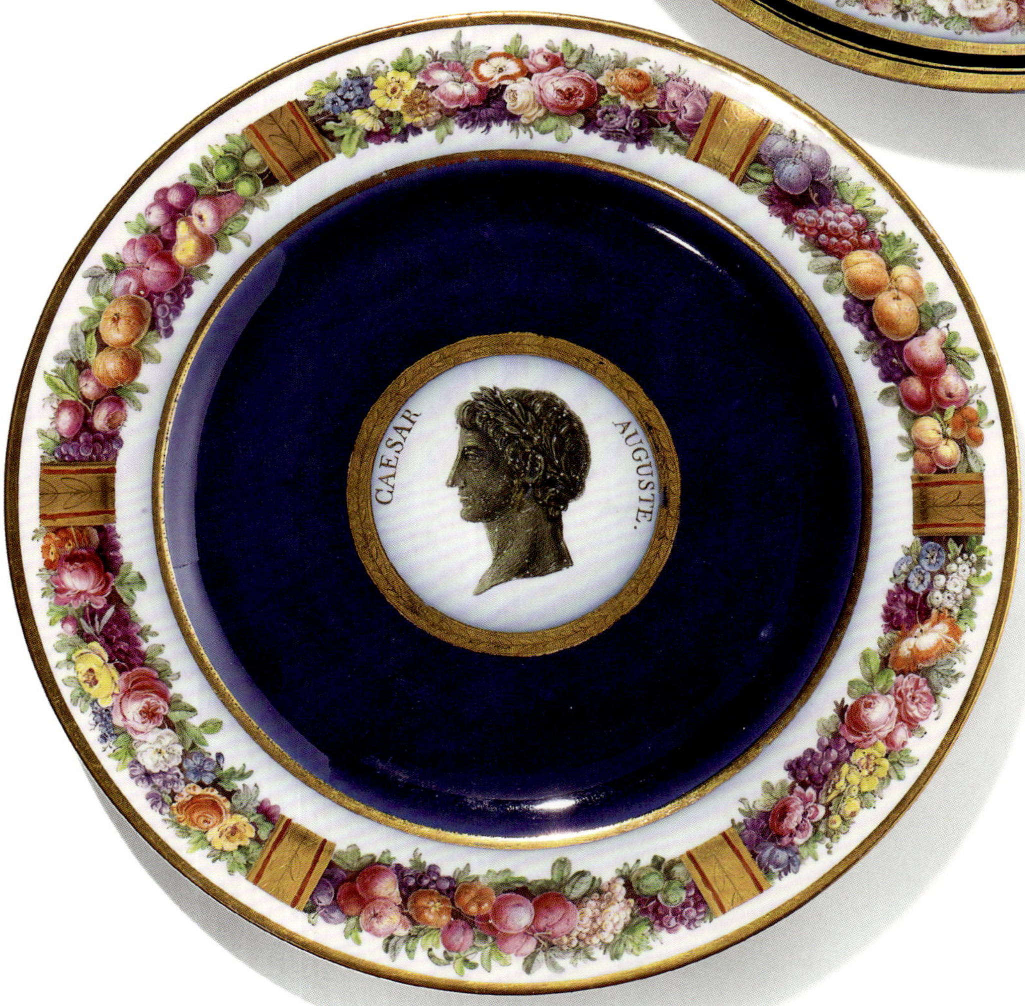

BOTTLE FROM AN OIL AND VINEGAR SET BELONGING TO NAPOLEON

This elegantly crafted bottle is conserved in the collection. It constitutes the oil dispenser with the Emperor's insignia, bearing on its side Napoleon's initial beneath a crown, encircled by laurel branches.

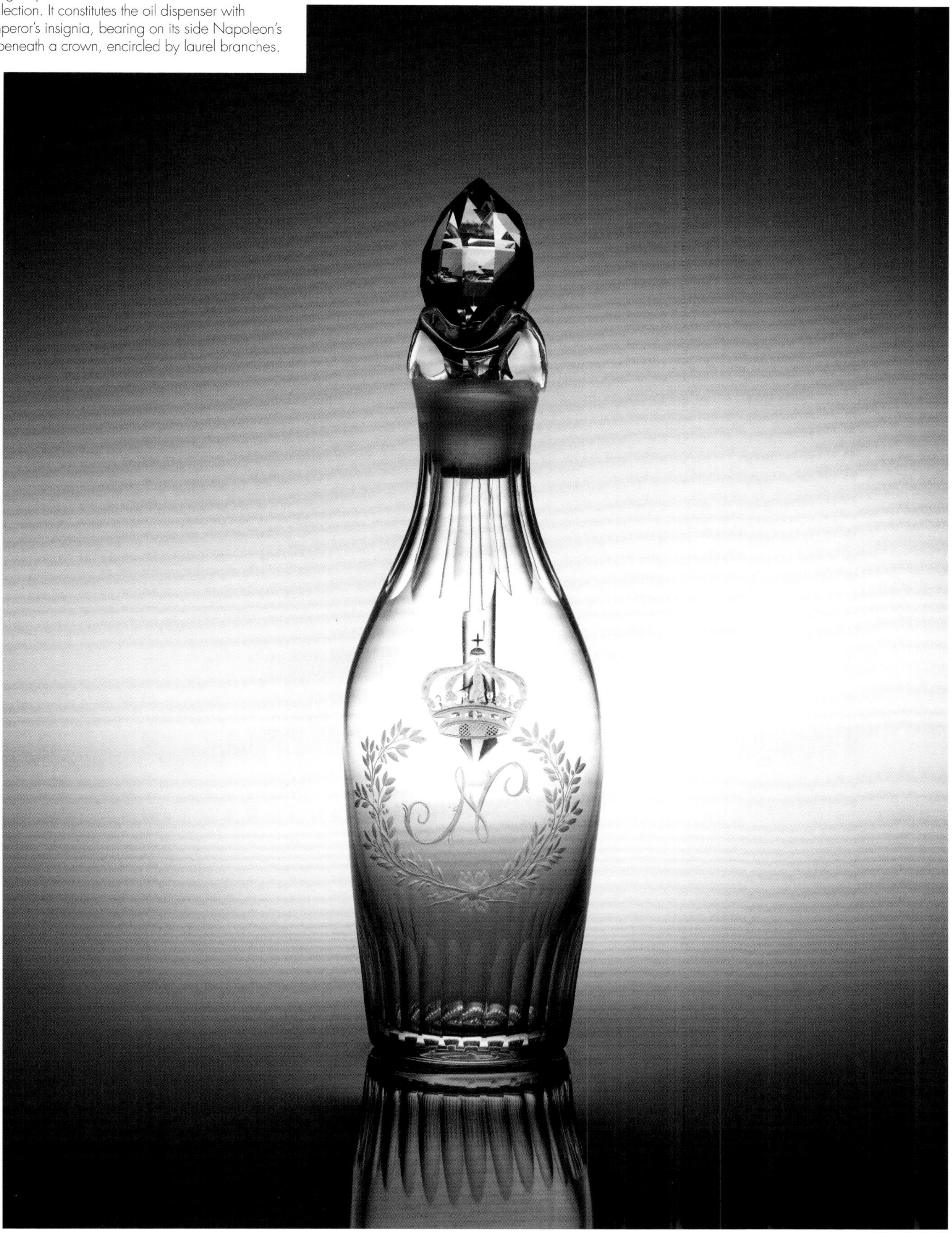

THE EMPEROR'S STEWARDS

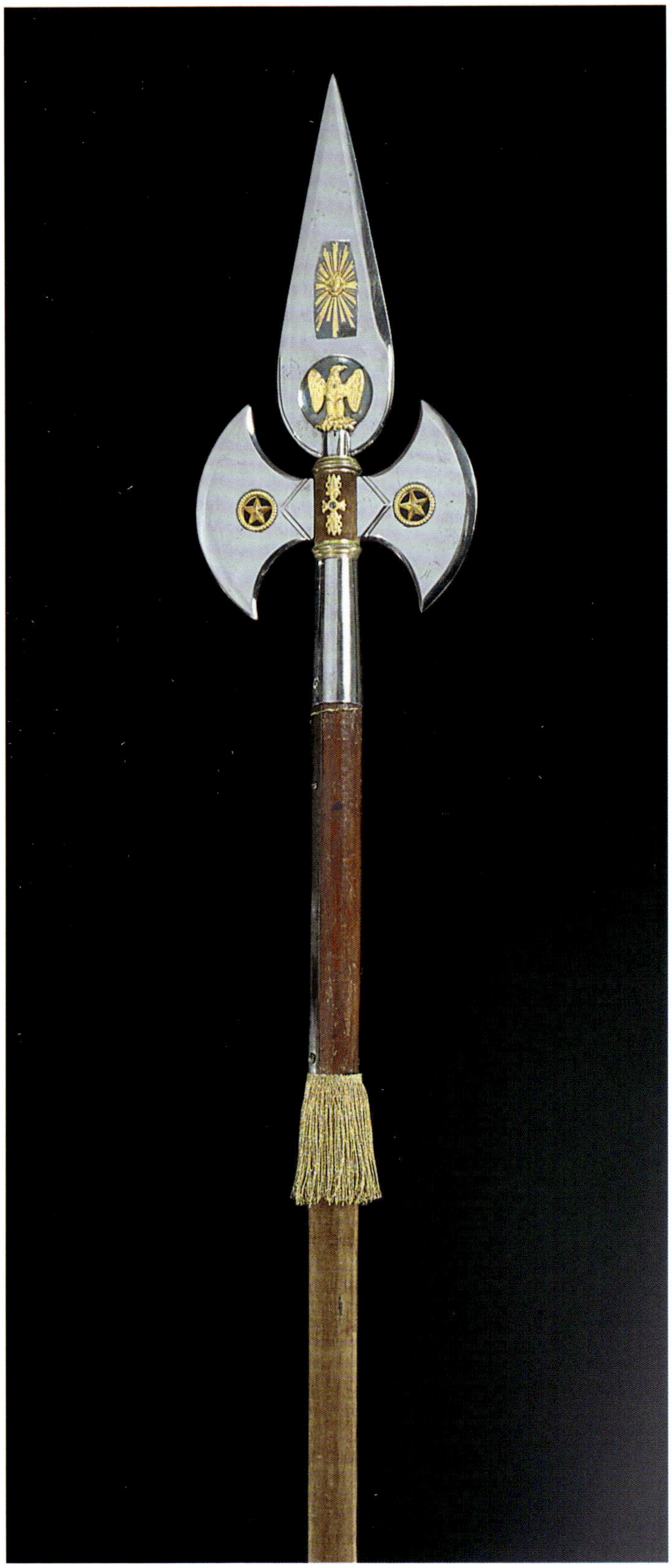

HALBERD OF THE GUARDS OF THE PRIVATE APARTMENTS OF NAPOLEON, KING OF ITALY

This unusual ceremonial halberd was probably used on exceptional occasions only by the guards of the Palace of Milan, as was the custom in Italy. In reality, the Emperor's Italian Household was in the service of Viceroy Eugène de Beauharnais, Josephine's son. This halberd is one of two known examples, the other bearing the crowned "C" monogram of Caroline Murat.

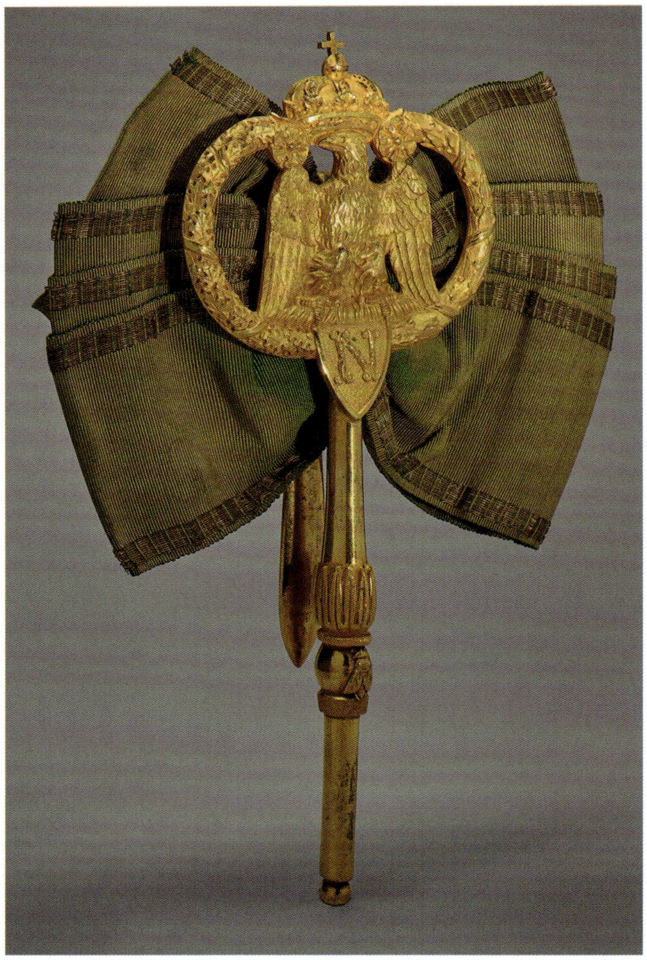

KEY CARRIED BY THE CHAMBELLAN OF THE EMPEROR'S HOUSEHOLD

This large key emblazoned with the imperial monogram was the insignia of office of the chambellan of the Emperor's Household – as many as 65 such keys are known to have been issued by Napoleon. Four chambellans were appointed every trimester. They had sole authority for ushering courtiers and officials into the Emperor's presence, particularly his apartments, and accompanied Napoleon on his travels. This key, still with its green silk ribbon, is one of very few surviving examples.

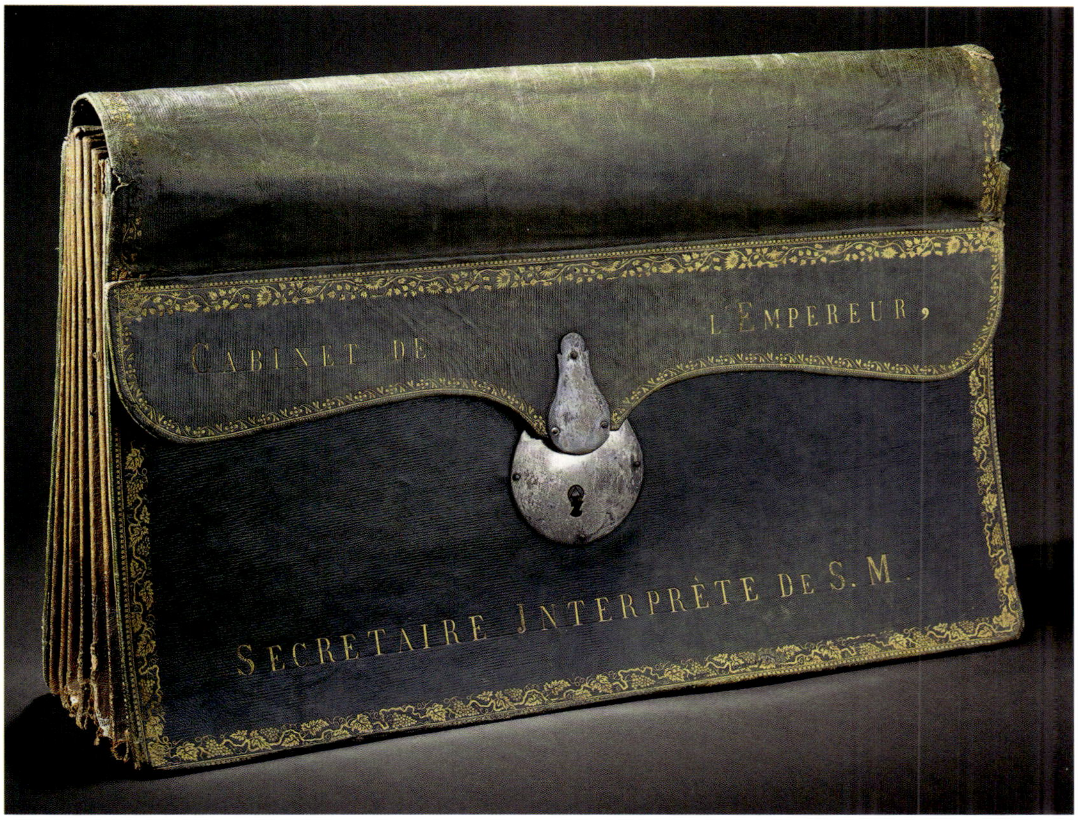

PORTFOLIO OF THE SECRETARY-INTERPRETER OF THE EMPEROR'S CABINET

The Emperor's cabinet was the hub of imperial power and supported Napoleon in his daily work. It comprised some 40-50 members, including secretaries, cartographers, interpreters and guards. The secretary-interpreter was responsible for translating foreign publications – newspapers, dispatches from abroad and official documents – then submitting those translations for Napoleon's attention. This portfolio was used to transport such papers and probably belonged to Baron Elisabeth, Louis, François Lelorgne d'Ideville, auditor to the Council of State, appointed secretary-interpreter on 31 July 1812. More spy than interpreter, the Baron conducted several secret information-gathering missions for the Emperor.

MARTIN-GUILLAUME BIENNAIS' INVOICES

The mémoires (invoices) of French master goldsmith M.G. Biennais, with their magnificent bronze green letterhead and distinctive monkey mark, are now practically as famous as his creations. They stand as testimony to the many prestigious commissions that he executed for the Emperor. This mémoire for instance, dated 31 December 1805, makes particular mention of the grand vermeil nécessaire (kit) engraved with the imperial coat-of-arms. Other items include "six crosses of the Legion of Honor, six diamond-engraved flasks with vermeil stoppers, two vermeil toothbrushes, four vermeil tongue-scrapers, one tortoiseshell comb, one Morocco cushion and one framed easel mirror". The total bill came to 2,343.55 francs. The mémoire is signed and approved by Napoleon's Premier Valet Ambard and his Premier Chambellan, Rémusat.

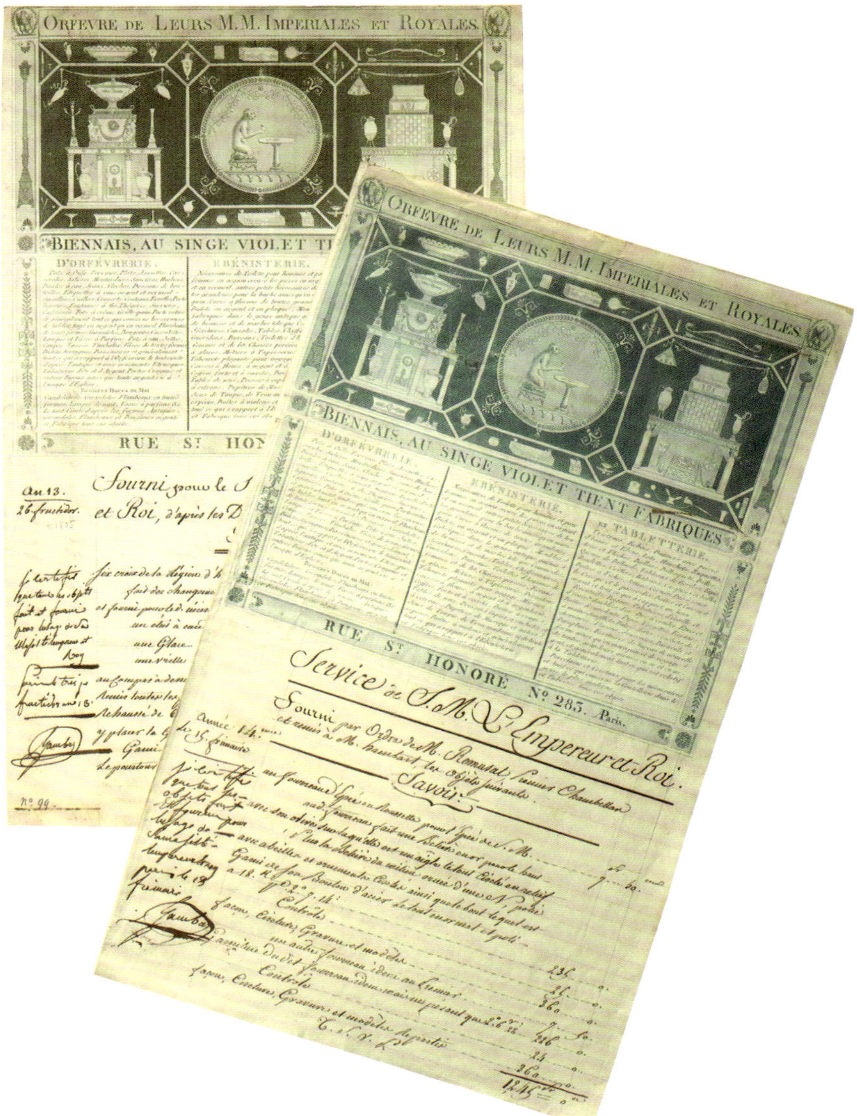

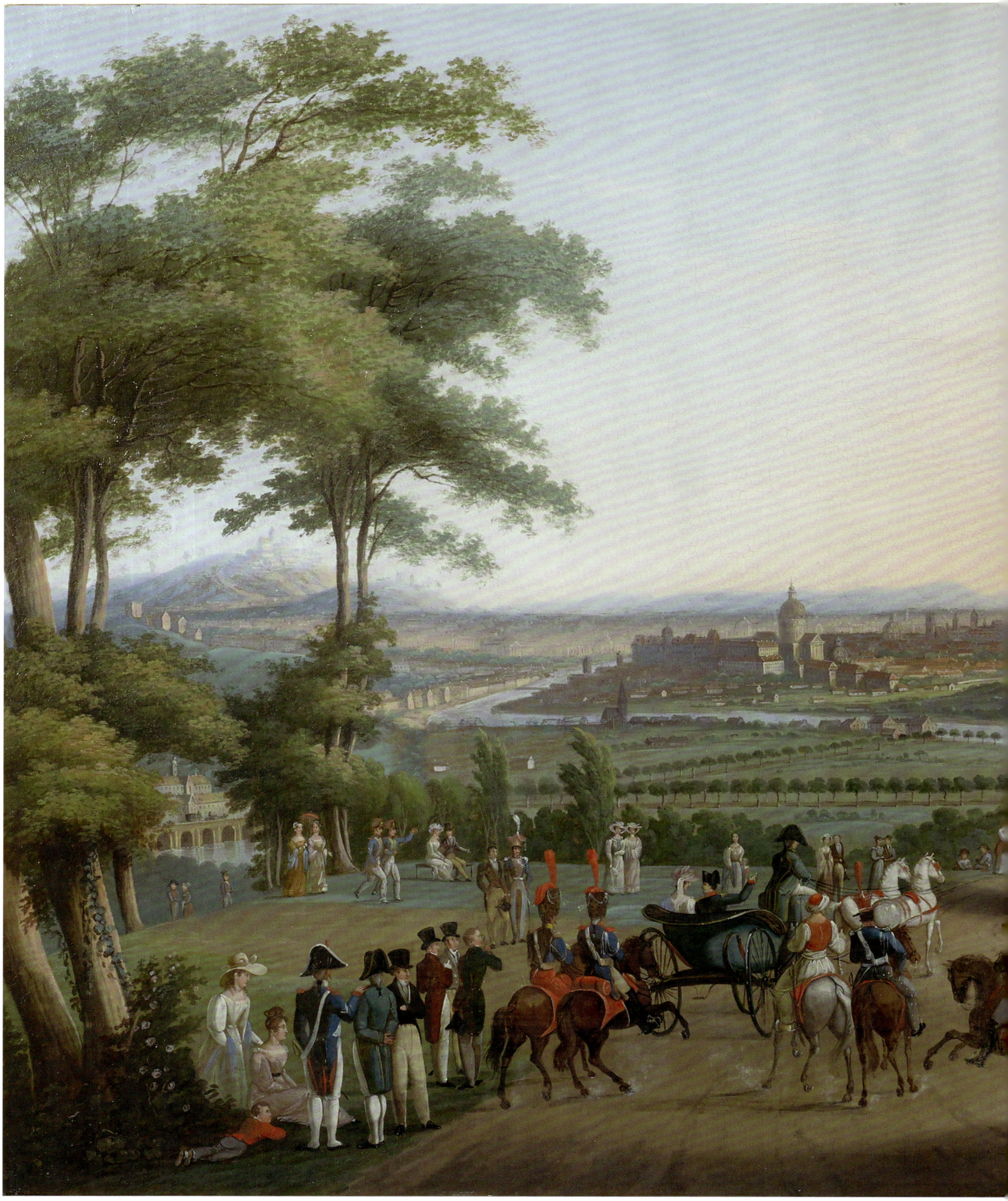

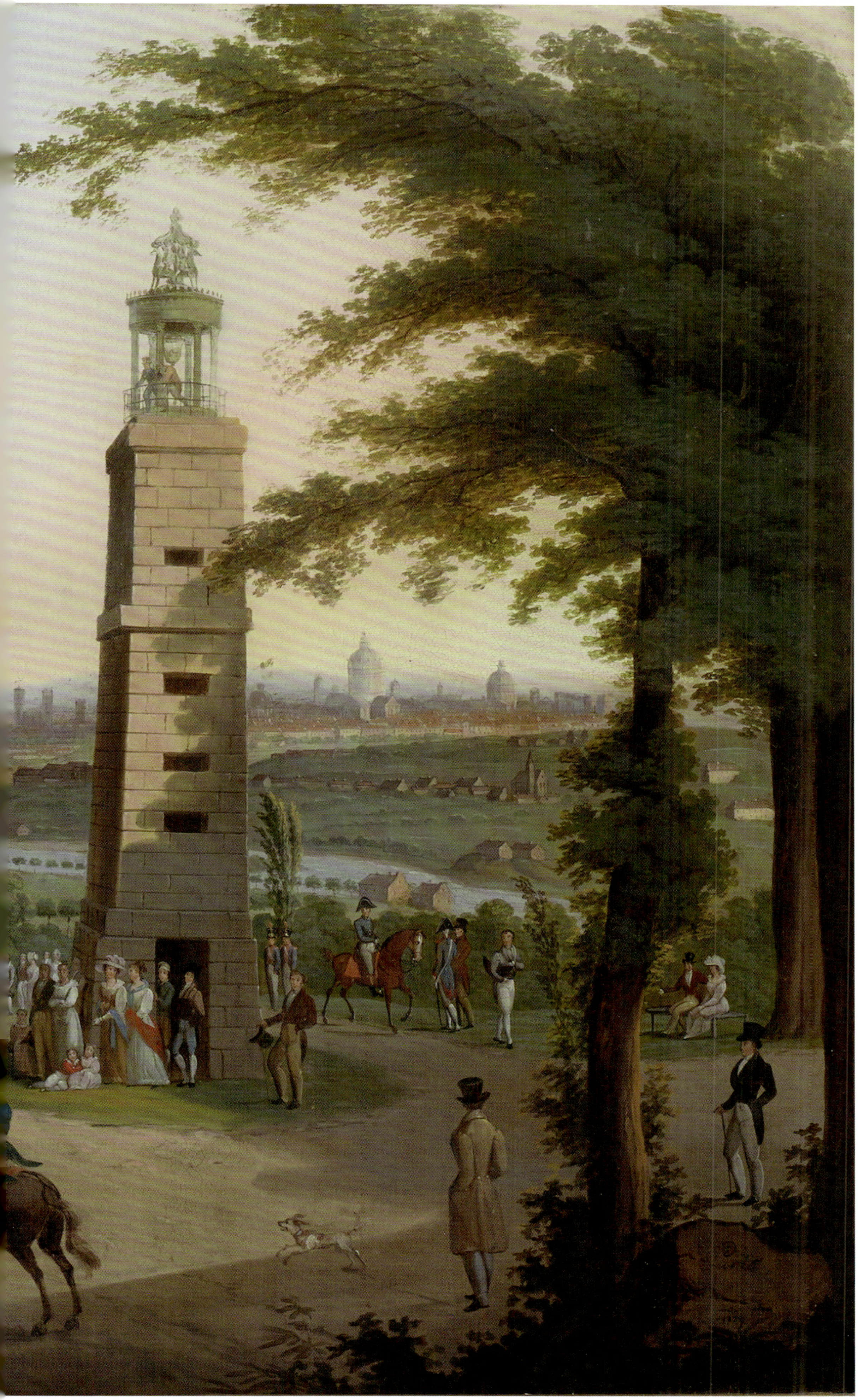

AUSTRIAN SCHOOL, *NAPOLEON ARRIVES BY HORSE-DRAWN CARRIAGE AT THE LANTERN TOWER OF ST CLOUD*

While Napoleon was fond of the Tuileries, he also enjoyed spending time at other residences near the capital, such as the Palace of St Cloud. This painting of the Austrian school depicts the Emperor on a drive in a horse-drawn carriage, near the lantern tower called Demosthenes – a replica of the ancient monument erected in Athens. It would be lit to signal the presence of the Emperor. It was destroyed in 1870 by the Prussians.

THE IMPERIAL RESIDENCES

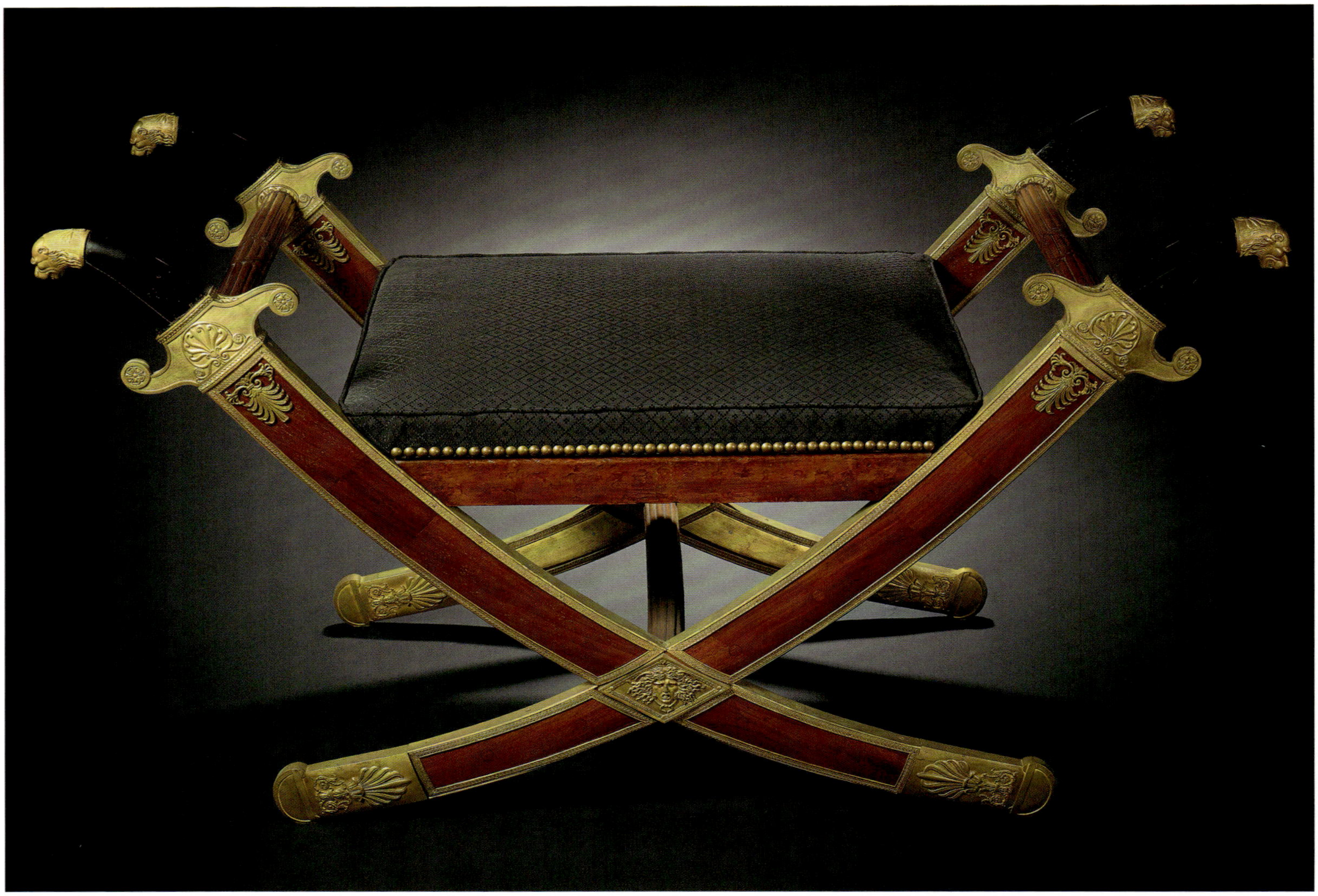

MARTIN-GUILLAUME BIENNAIS (1764-1843), CROSSED SABER STOOL (OR TABOURET DES MARÉCHAUX) DESTINED FOR NAPOLEON'S THRONE ROOM

This extraordinary neoclassical stool by M.G. Biennais was part of the decor of the imperial throne room, featuring a base representing crossed, mahogany sabers of the oriental type with ebony handles. According to imperial protocol, stools like these were for the chief dignitaries of the regime, probably Napoleon's marshals (hence their other name, tabouret des maréchaux), while the chairs and armchairs were reserved for the imperial family and visiting sovereigns. There are only two other known examples, both on display at the Musée du Château de Malmaison.

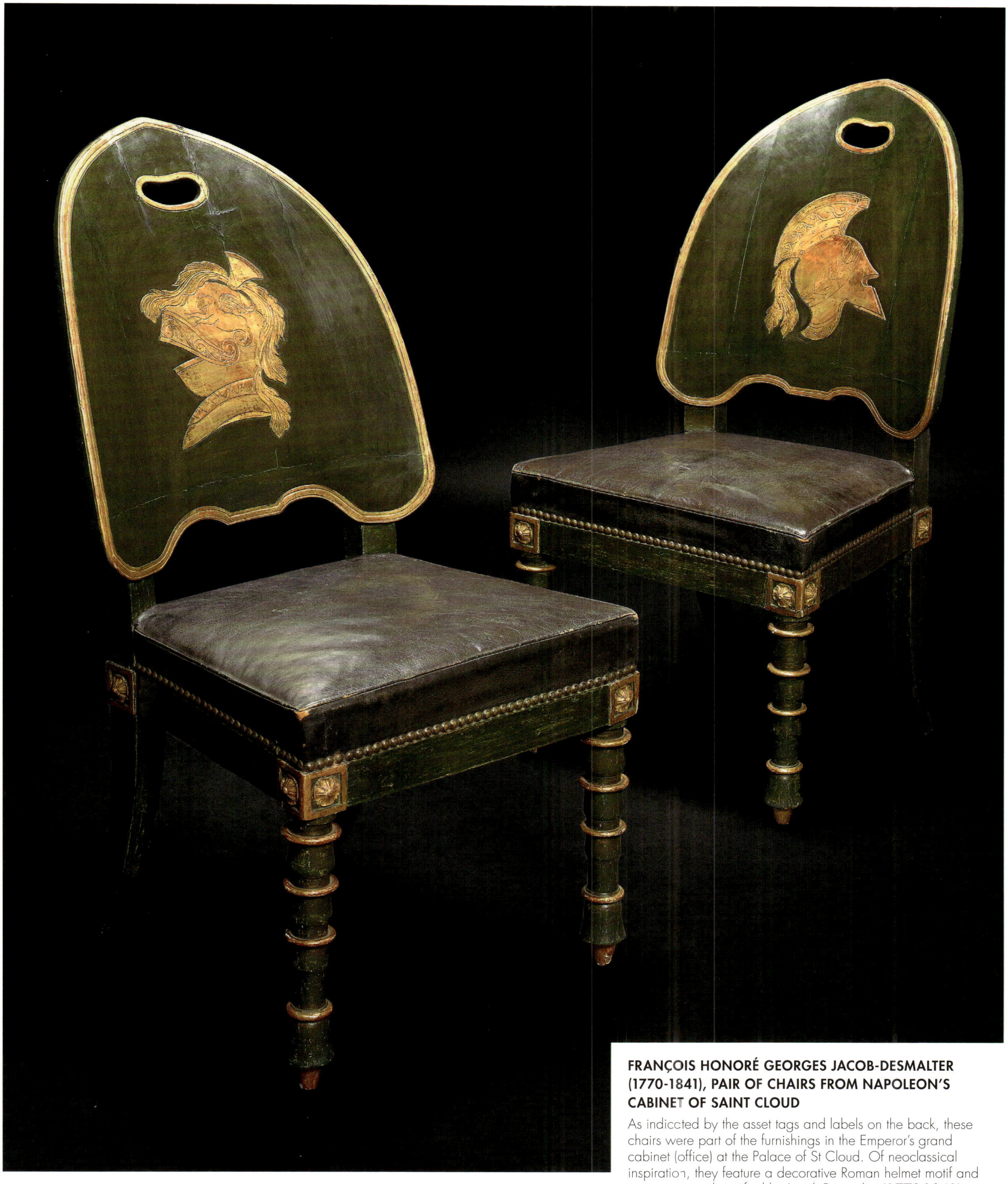

FRANÇOIS HONORÉ GEORGES JACOB-DESMALTER (1770-1841), PAIR OF CHAIRS FROM NAPOLEON'S CABINET OF SAINT CLOUD

As indicated by the asset tags and labels on the back, these chairs were part of the furnishings in the Emperor's grand cabinet (office) at the Palace of St Cloud. Of neoclassical inspiration, they feature a decorative Roman helmet motif and were apparently crafted by Jacob-Desmalter (1770-1841). They were reserved for visitors shown into the Emperor's presence by the chambellan on duty – either ministers or soldiers on official business or persons granted audience by Napoleon. Only five of the original set remain.

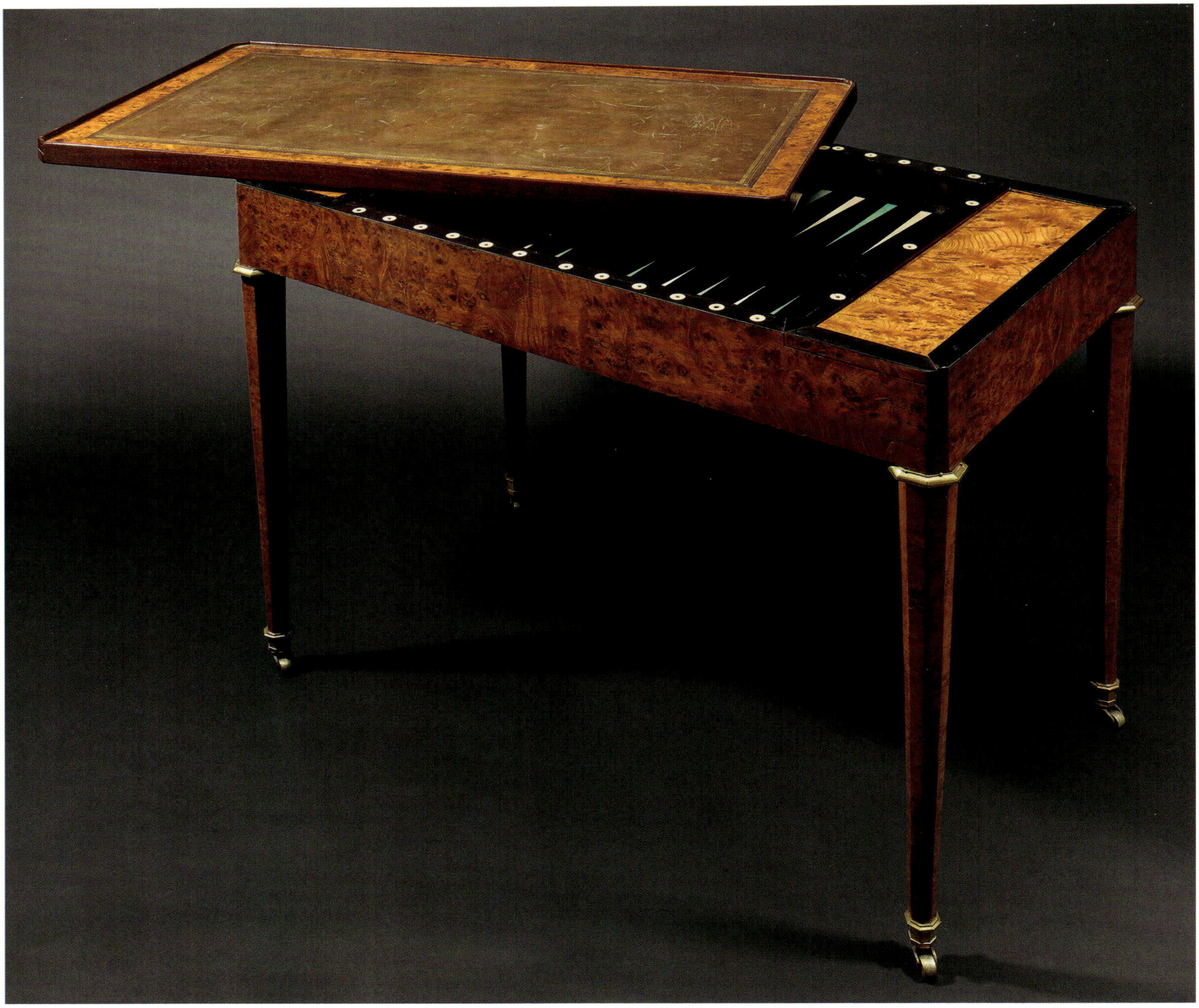

FRANÇOIS HONORÉ GEORGES JACOB-DESMALTER (1770-1841), TRICTRAC TABLE USED BY NAPOLEON AND JOSEPHINE IN THE MUSIC ROOM OF THE CHATEAU ST CLOUD

This game table for playing "trictrac" is veneered in elm burl, mahogany, ebony, and dyed bone. It features a removable tray and stands on a rare base with octagonal tapered legs. It originates from the Château St Cloud that Louis XVI acquired in 1784 for Queen Marie-Antoinette, and which became Napoleon's favorite residence. There were two ivory dice inside, bearing the letters "GR" beneath a crown, the mark of Queen Marie-Antoinette's private furniture store (Grenier des Recollets). Its inventory number (STC 795) indicates that the table was supplied by Jacob-Desmalter in 1811. The furniture store's log book tells us that the table stood in the Music Room, a room that the Emperor had a particular liking for: "Under number 795: A trictrac table in elm, faceted legs with gilt bronze capitals, ferrules and casters; green Morocco-covered top with decorative gilding, ivory ornamentation". Napoleon increasingly favored elm burl for his various imperial palaces from 1806 onwards. At the height of the Continental Blockade, he ended up banning it in order to weaken British trade. The Memoirs of Constant, Head Valet to the Emperor, recount: "She (Madame Bonaparte) liked to stay up late, and at night, when almost all the company had retired to bed, she would play a game of billiards or, more often, trictrac". The Château de Versailles has kept an absolutely identical trictrac table, supplied by Jacob-Desmalter for the Petit Trianon in 1811 ("Le mobilier de Versailles, Chef-d'œuvre du XIXème Siècle", Editions Faton).

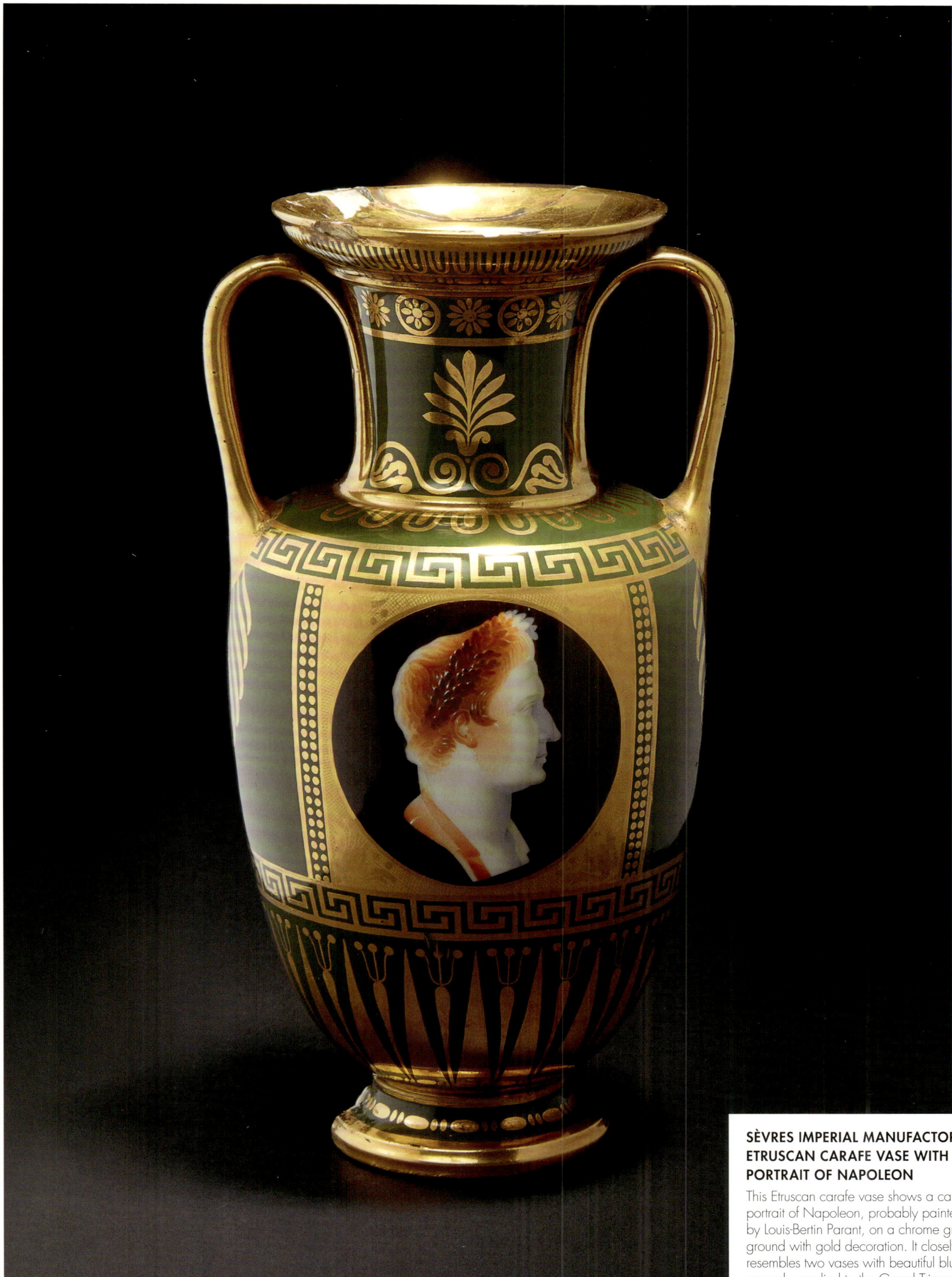

SÈVRES IMPERIAL MANUFACTORY, ETRUSCAN CARAFE VASE WITH PORTRAIT OF NAPOLEON

This Etruscan carafe vase shows a cameo portrait of Napoleon, probably painted by Louis-Bertin Parant, on a chrome green ground with gold decoration. It closely resembles two vases with beautiful blue grounds supplied to the Grand Trianon on 15 December 1809 for the Emperor's bathroom.

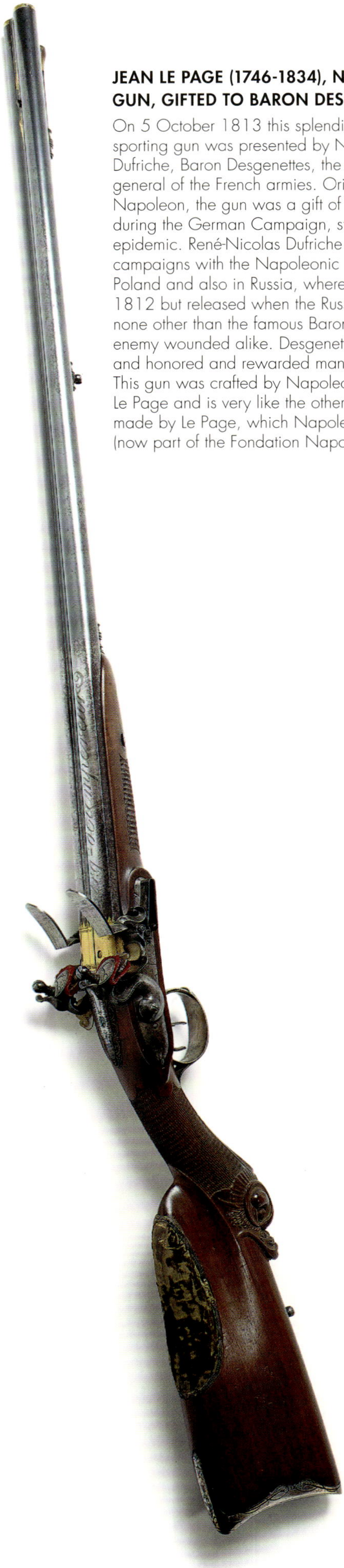

JEAN LE PAGE (1746-1834), NAPOLEON'S SPORTING GUN, GIFTED TO BARON DESGENETTES

On 5 October 1813 this splendid, double-barreled, flintlock sporting gun was presented by Napoleon to René-Nicolas Dufriche, Baron Desgenettes, the distinguished physician-general of the French armies. Originally belonging to Napoleon, the gun was a gift of thanks for the Baron's services during the German Campaign, stamping out the typhus epidemic. René-Nicolas Dufriche Desgenettes served several campaigns with the Napoleonic army, in Italy, Egypt, Austria, Poland and also in Russia, where he was taken prisoner in 1812 but released when the Russians realized that this was none other than the famous Baron who attended French and enemy wounded alike. Desgenettes was universally liked and honored and rewarded many times over by the Emperor. This gun was crafted by Napoleon's Parisian gunsmith Le Page and is very like the other double-barreled sporting gun made by Le Page, which Napoleon gave to Captain Besson (now part of the Fondation Napoléon Collection).

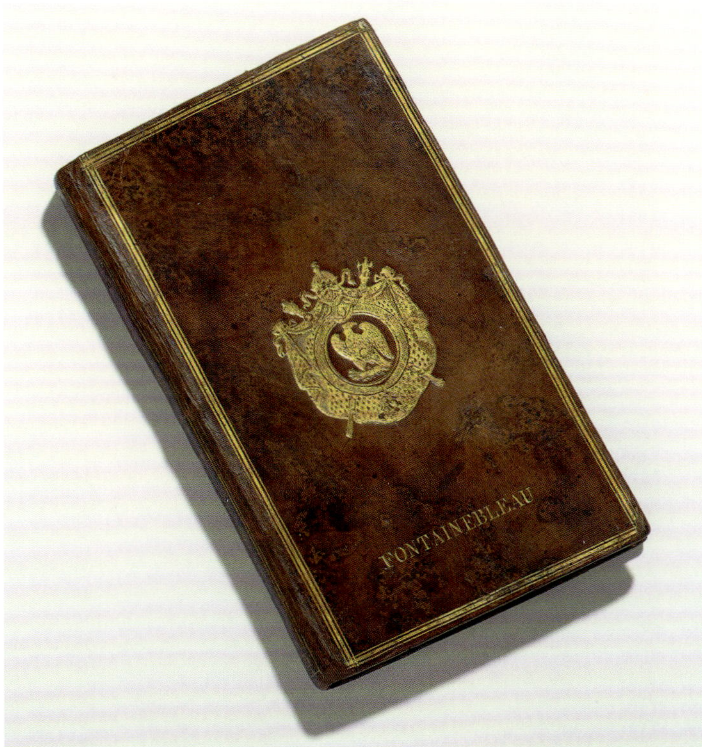

BOOK FROM NAPOLEON'S LIBRARY AT FONTAINEBLEAU

Napoleon was a brilliant autodidact and a voracious reader who attached great importance to his library. Though very hard on his books he insisted they should be arranged with military precision – each book in its rightful place, like his soldiers. His library traveled with him from palace to palace, campaign to campaign and island to island. This book, on *l'ordonnance pour régler le service dans les places* (ordonnance for regulating service by place) comes from his library at the Château de Fontainebleau (as confirmed by the name emblazoned on the cover, under the coat-of-arms). A handwritten note in Italian on the inside indicates that the book remained behind on the island of Elba.

BOOKS FROM NAPOLEON'S LIBRARY AT ST CLOUD

Napoleon's most valuable books come from his library at Château St Cloud, including this book *Juvénal Satires*, published in 1803, comprising a collection of satirical poems written by the Latin author Juvenal in the late 1st and early 2nd centuries. The book is one of the very few still extant due to the château's destruction in 1870 and is particularly unusual for its cover emblazoned with the Bonaparte coat-of-arms and the name "St Cloud".

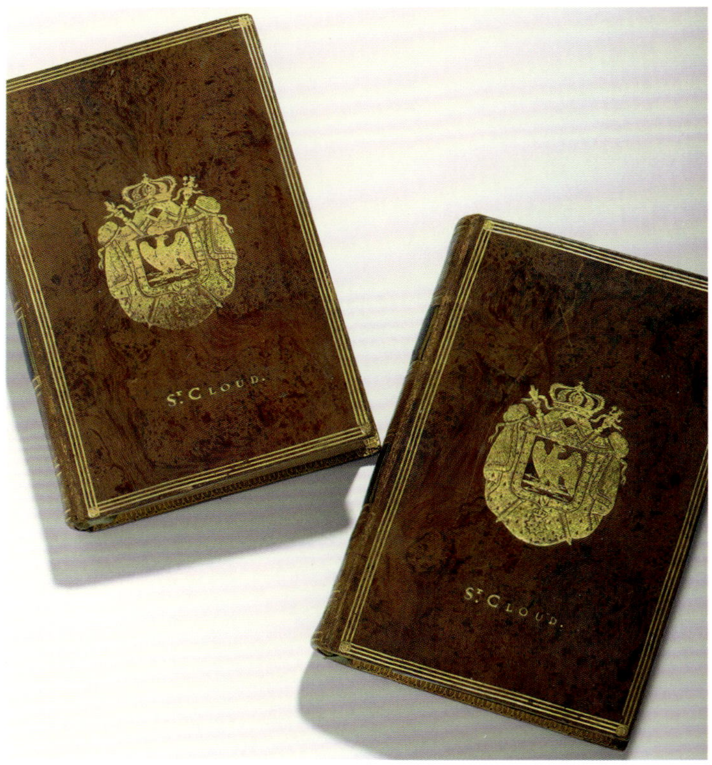

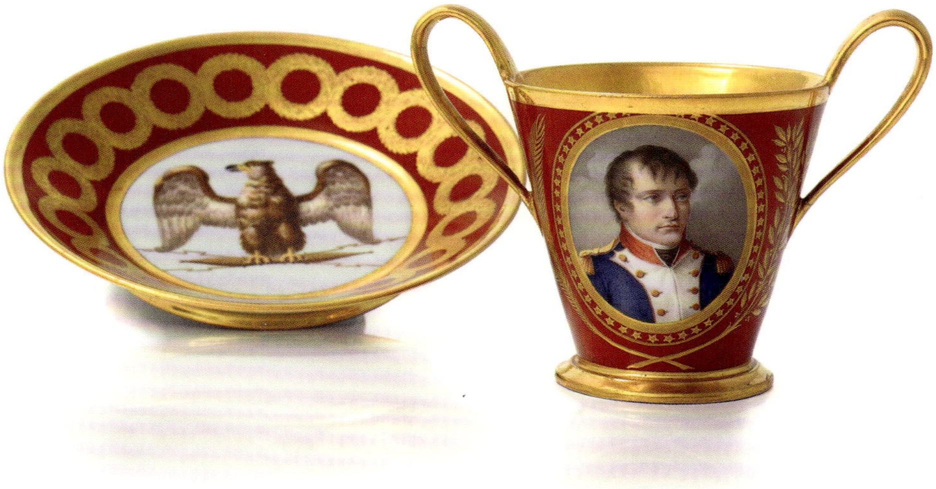

SÈVRES IMPERIAL MANUFACTORY, CUP WITH BONAPARTE'S PORTRAIT

Cone-shaped, twin-handled cup commissioned from the Sèvres Manufactory in 1804. On one side is a bust portrait of the Emperor. On the other side are three entwined wreaths (two of laurel leaves and one of oak leaves), set against a pale blue background within two framed medallions surrounded by fillets, stars, branches of laurel and golden palm leaves. The saucer bears an eagle and thunderbolt at its center, also against a pale blue background, with a decorative gold border of alternating laurel and oak leaves on a red background.

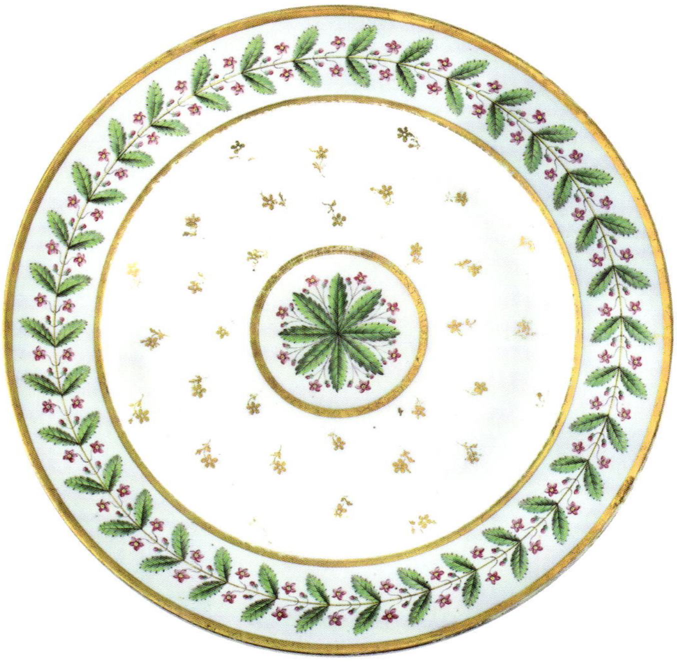

SÈVRES IMPERIAL MANUFACTORY, PLATE BELONGING TO NAPOLEON FOR HIS MARRACQ IMPERIAL PALACE IN BAYONNE

This plate, the only one extant that we know of, belongs to the service comprising 72 flat plates that Napoleon commissioned for his new residence in Bayonne. It is described in the Sèvres manufactory's archives as "Pale blue ground, colored capraire frieze on the base". The Château de Marracq was acquired on 19 May 1808, paid for out of Napoleon's personal treasury. It became an imperial palace and he stayed there with Josephine from 17 April to 20 July 1808. This was where the famous meeting took place in April 1808 which saw the abdication of the Bourbons of Spain in favor of Napoleon, who set his brother Joseph on the Spanish throne. Nowadays only ruins remain of this chateau, which boasted 15 hectares of formal landscaped gardens.

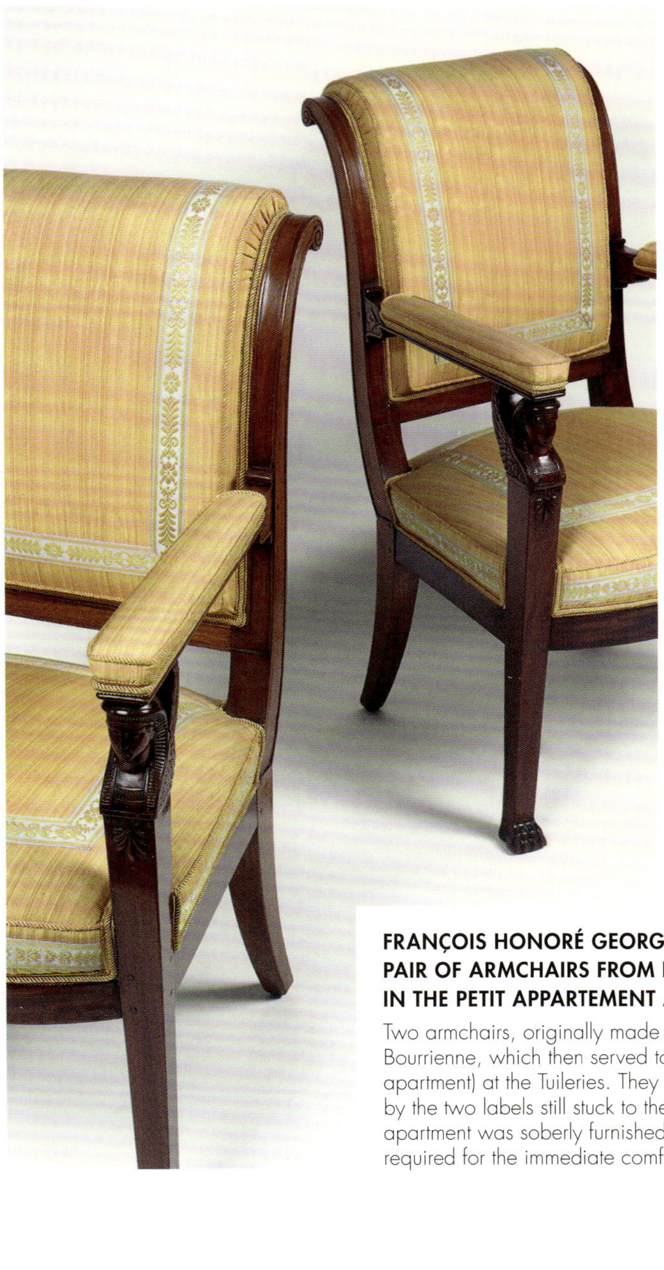

FRANÇOIS HONORÉ GEORGES JACOB-DESMALTER (1770-1841), PAIR OF ARMCHAIRS FROM NAPOLEON'S BEDROOM IN THE PETIT APPARTEMENT AT LES TUILERIES

Two armchairs, originally made by Jacob-Desmalter for Napoleon's First Secretary, Bourrienne, which then served to furnish the Emperor's Petit Appartement (small apartment) at the Tuileries. They stood in Napoleon's bedroom, as indicated by the two labels still stuck to the underside of the seat. The Emperor's inner apartment was soberly furnished – nothing too austere but no more than was required for the immediate comfort of its occupant.

THE IMPERIAL IMAGE

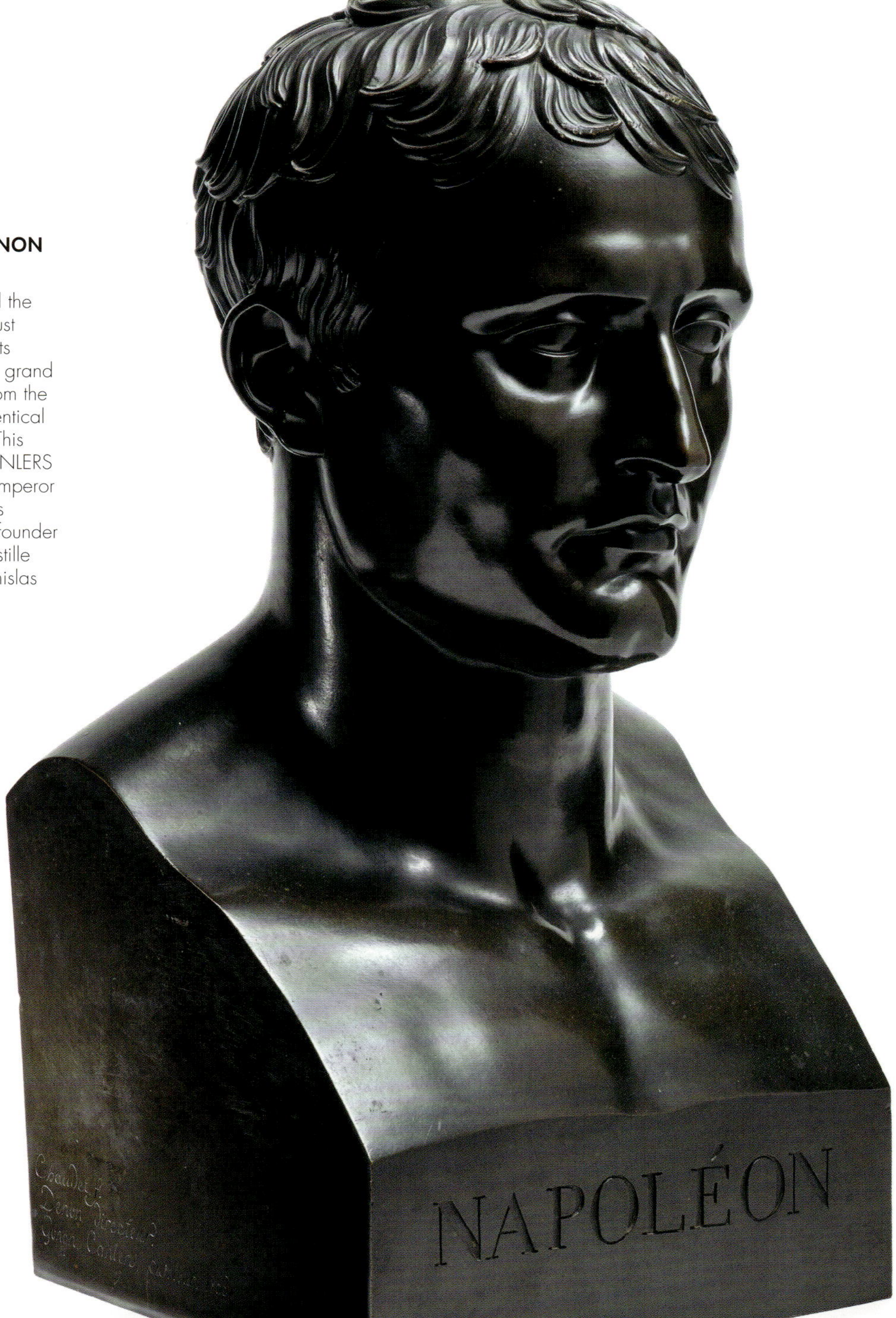

ANTOINE-DENIS CHAUDET (1763-1810) AND VIVANT DENON (1747-1825), LARGE BRONZE BUST OF NAPOLEON

The sculptor Antoine-Denis Chaudet (1763-1810) is considered the foremost official artist of the Napoleonic regime. This bronze bust revisits his famous piece dating from Year XI, one of just 15 busts commissioned by Vivant Denon and exclusively reserved for the grand dignitaries of the Empire. This extremely rare example comes from the famous collections of Baron Yves Jeanpierre. Only two other identical busts are known to exist today, both signed and dated 1808. This bust signed "CHAUDET F. DENON DIRECTEUR. GONON CANLERS CISELEUR. 1806" (see inset) almost certainly belonged to the Emperor and was probably replicated by Chaudet and Denon two years later as gifts for grand dignitaries. Honoré Gonon was an iron founder of repute, appointed to execute the abortive Elephant of the Bastille project. Before 1812 he worked with fellow artist, Charles Stanislas Canlers, an iron founder, chaser and sculptor awarded the Prix de Rome in 1808.

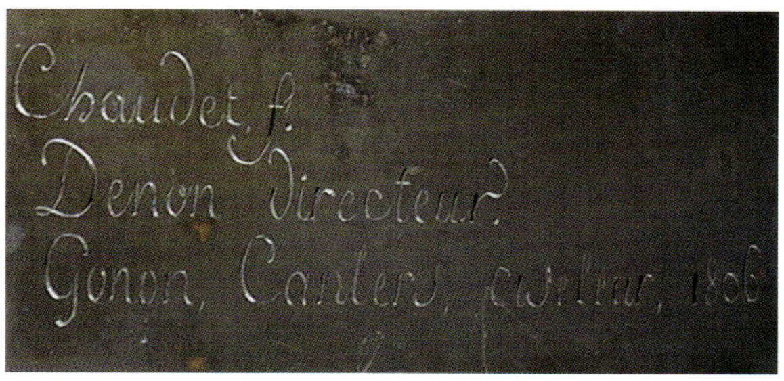

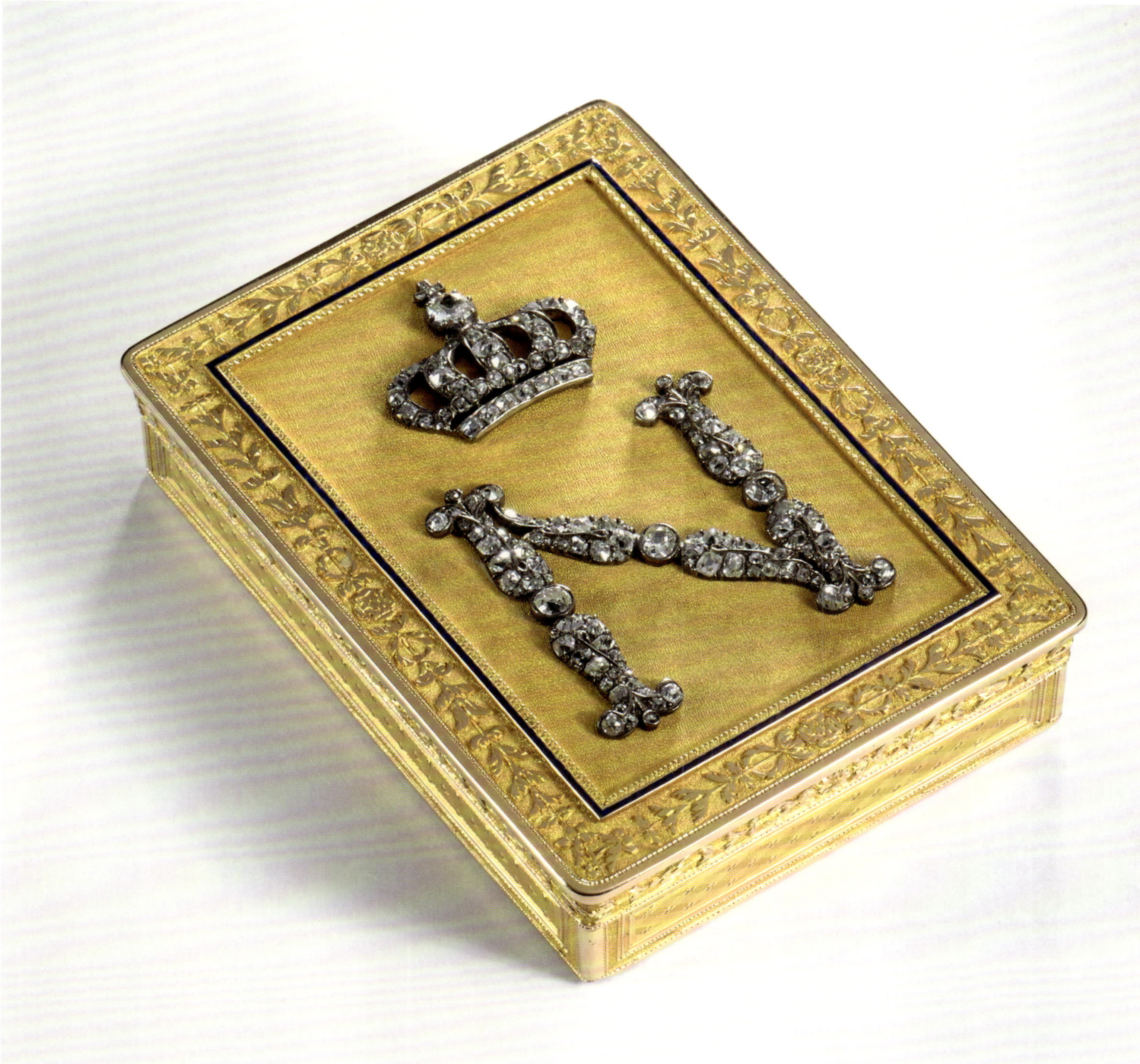

MARIE-ETIENNE NITOT (1750-1809), GOLD AND DIAMOND SNUFFBOX WITH CROWNED MONOGRAM OF NAPOLEON

Chased yellow gold box with leafy guilloche surround and blue enamel fillet, featuring a diamantine, crowned monogram of the Emperor in the center of the lid — an outstanding example of the sumptuous boxes that were offered as gifts by the court of Napoleon, whether to celebrate birthdays, thank a grand dignitary of the Empire or welcome a visiting sovereign. This very rare piece is the work of Marie-Etienne Nitot, founder of present-day House of Chaumet, who worked alongside Marie-Antoinette's jeweler Auber before becoming the official jeweler of the Emperor in 1802. Nitot crafted the crown and the sword for Napoleon's coronation, the latter embellished with the Regent Diamond (the largest diamond in the French crown jewels). He also designed matched sets of jewelry (parures) for the Empresses Josephine and Marie-Louise.

GOLD SNUFFBOX DECORATED WITH A PORTRAIT OF NAPOLEON

This rectangular gold snuffbox is adorned on the lid with an oval miniature on ivory showing Napoleon with his head turned slightly to the right, wearing a Chasseurs de la Garde uniform and the red ribbon of the Legion of Honor. Two medals can be seen on his chest. It is signed by the enamel miniature painter J. Lecourt who was working in France in the early 19th century. There is known to be a portrait of Napoleon signed by this artist and dated 1810 at the National Museum of Schidlof.

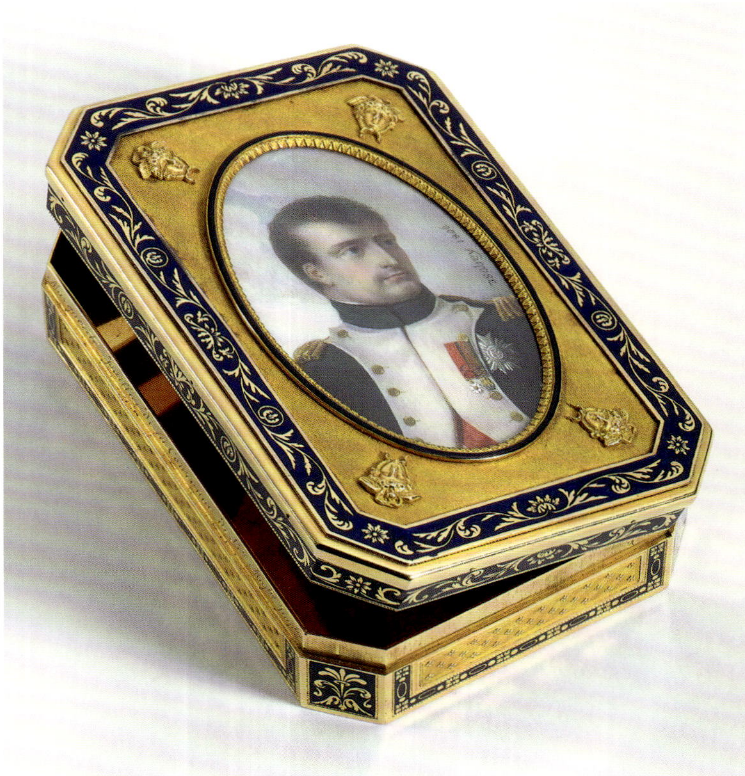

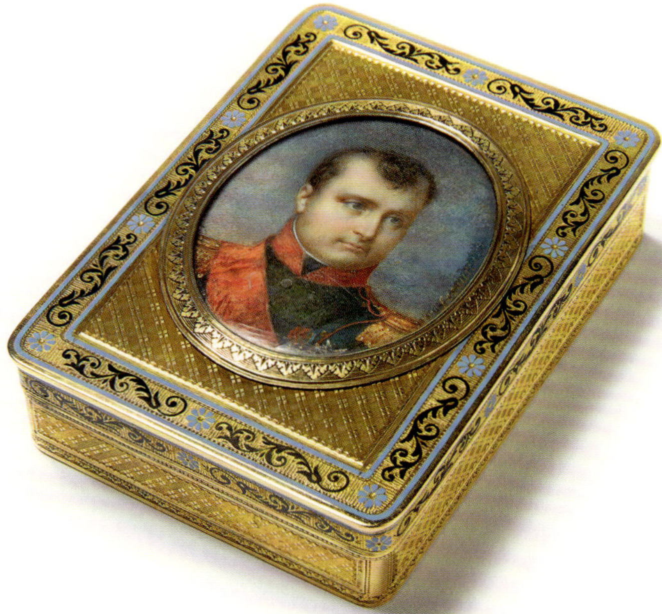

GOLD SNUFFBOX FEATURING PORTRAIT OF NAPOLEON

Gold snuffboxes were the ultimate in diplomatic and courtly gifts and generally reserved for VIPs only. This beautifully made snuffbox, its lid inset with a miniature signed "Isabey", was almost certainly a gift to a person of very high rank. Napoleon is pictured in full dress uniform, which he always much preferred to representations in coronation attire.

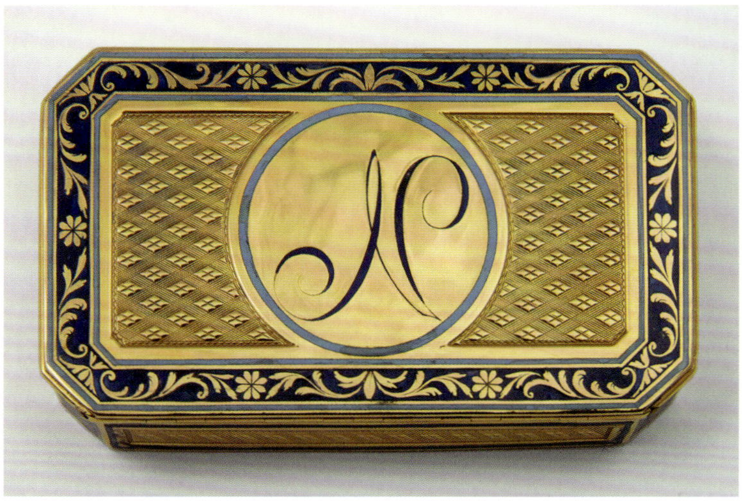

GOLD SNUFFBOX BELONGING TO NAPOLEON, WITH THE INITIAL N

This small rectangular gold snuffbox features a decorative border of flowers and leaves against a blue enamel ground, with Napoleon's initial in blue enamel on a central cartouche. It was crafted by the goldsmith of Napoleon's jeweler, Bernard-Armand Marguerite. A close friend of the Emperor's circle, Marguerite received an imperial commission for one hundred snuffboxes in 1806. Napoleon frequently used this type of snuffbox, which fitted easily into the pocket.

GILT BRONZE PORTRAIT OF NAPOLEON SET IN A SURROUND OF LAPIS LAZULI

Profile portrait of the Emperor, believed to be a gift from his uncle, Cardinal Joseph Fesch, who in 1810 is recorded in the *inventaire des présents* (official list of gifts) as having offered Napoleon "two lapis plaques, profile of the Emperor and the Empress."

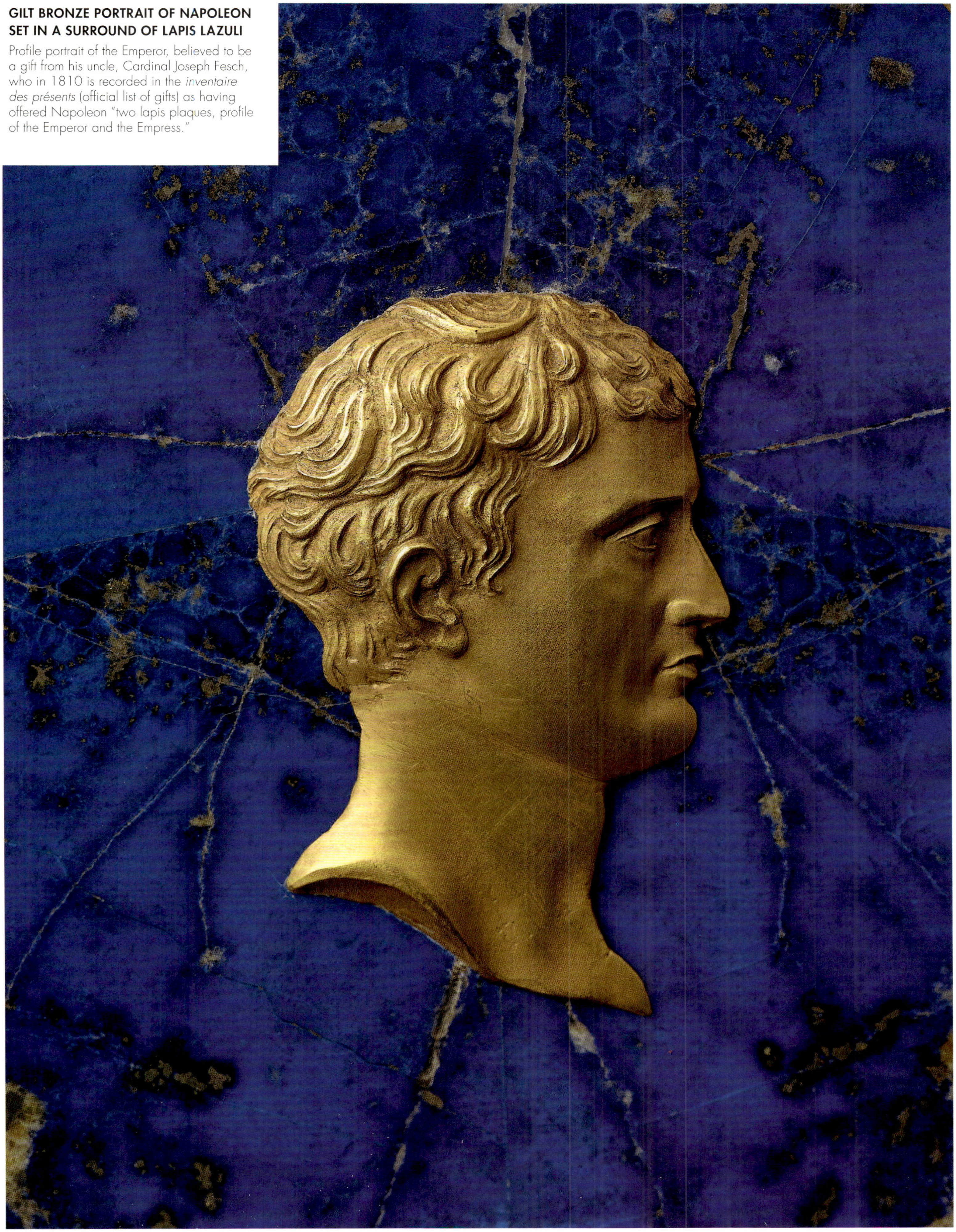

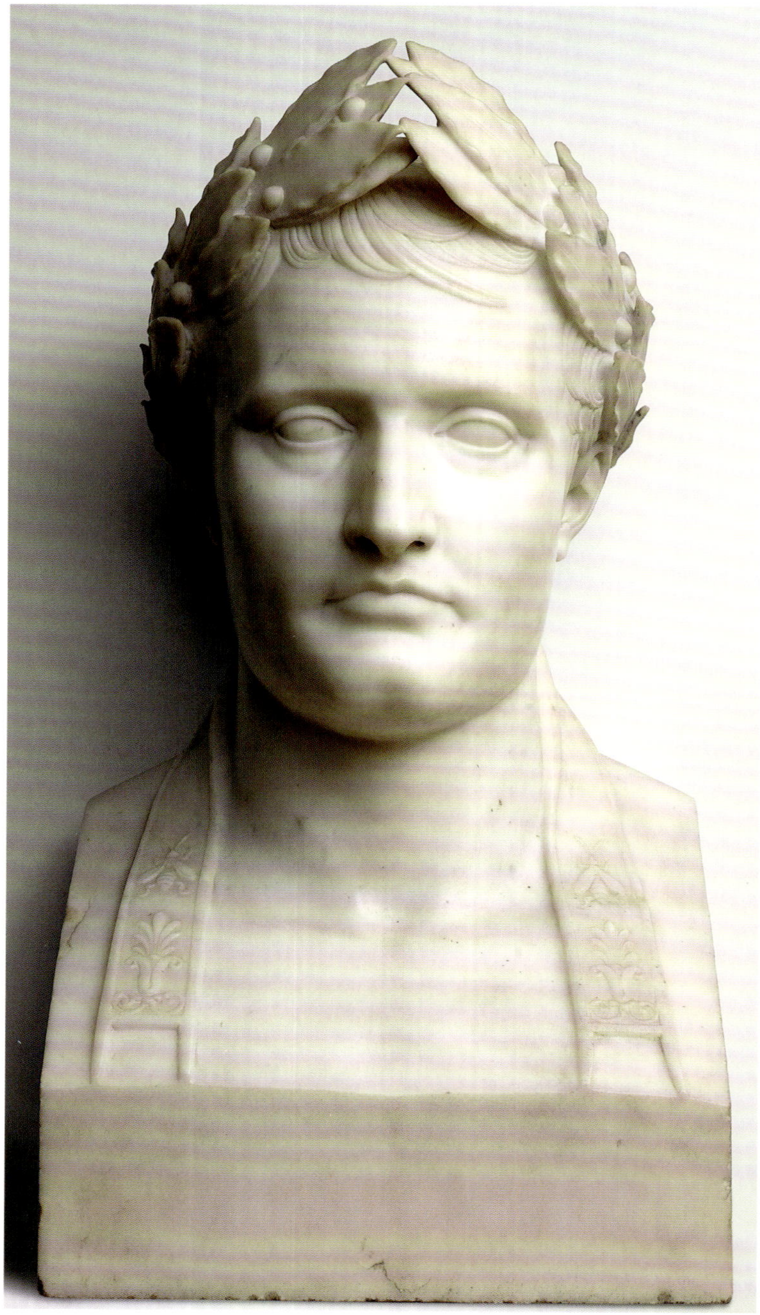

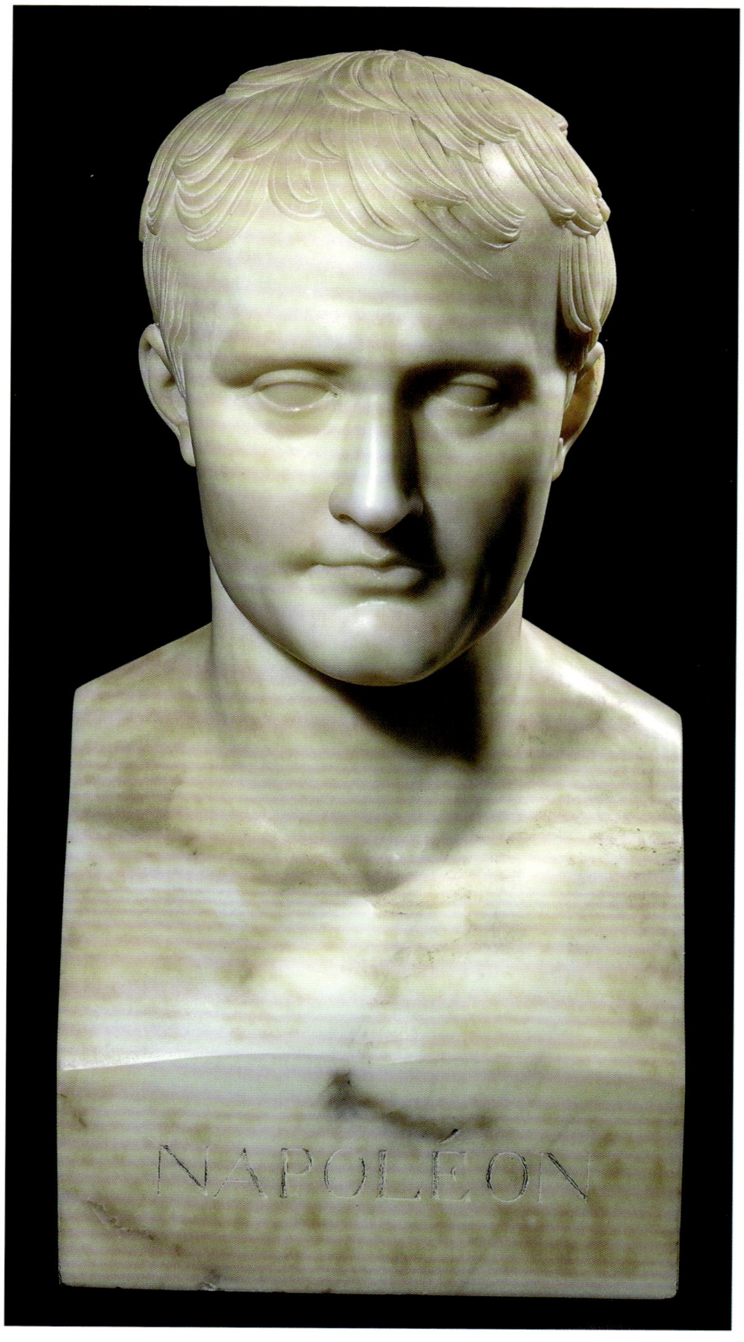

ANTOINE-DENIS CHAUDET (1763-1810), *MARBLE BUSTS OF NAPOLEON WITH LAUREL WREATH CROWN*

In January 1805, Chaudet completed a splendid statue of Napoleon as legislator. The head would later serve as the model for many of the busts of Napoleon that were made under the First French Empire to promote his official image as sovereign. Cast in marble, plaster, bronze and biscuit, they were made by various studios including, from May 1807 onward, the Banca Elisiana, the Carrara workshop established by Napoleon's sister Elisa, which is estimated to have produced around 1,000 busts (some better than others depending on the sculptor). These busts were probably made by Chaudet's studio and are considered particularly fine examples of their type.

ANTONIO CANOVA (1757-1822), AFTER HIS ORIGINAL, *NAPOLEON AS MARS THE PEACEMAKER*

This bronze figure belongs to the very rare series cast in the workshop of Francesco Righetti (1749-1819). It was modeled on a statue by the famous sculptor Antonio Canova. In the guise of Mars the Peacemaker, Napoleon holds a globe in his hand that symbolizes the world. Despite this powerful allegory, Napoleon was unhappy to see himself represented nude. This was the reason the Emperor had not accepted the monumental original, executed in 1806. In 1815 the British government gave it to the Duke of Wellington for display at his London residence Apsley House, where it can still be seen.

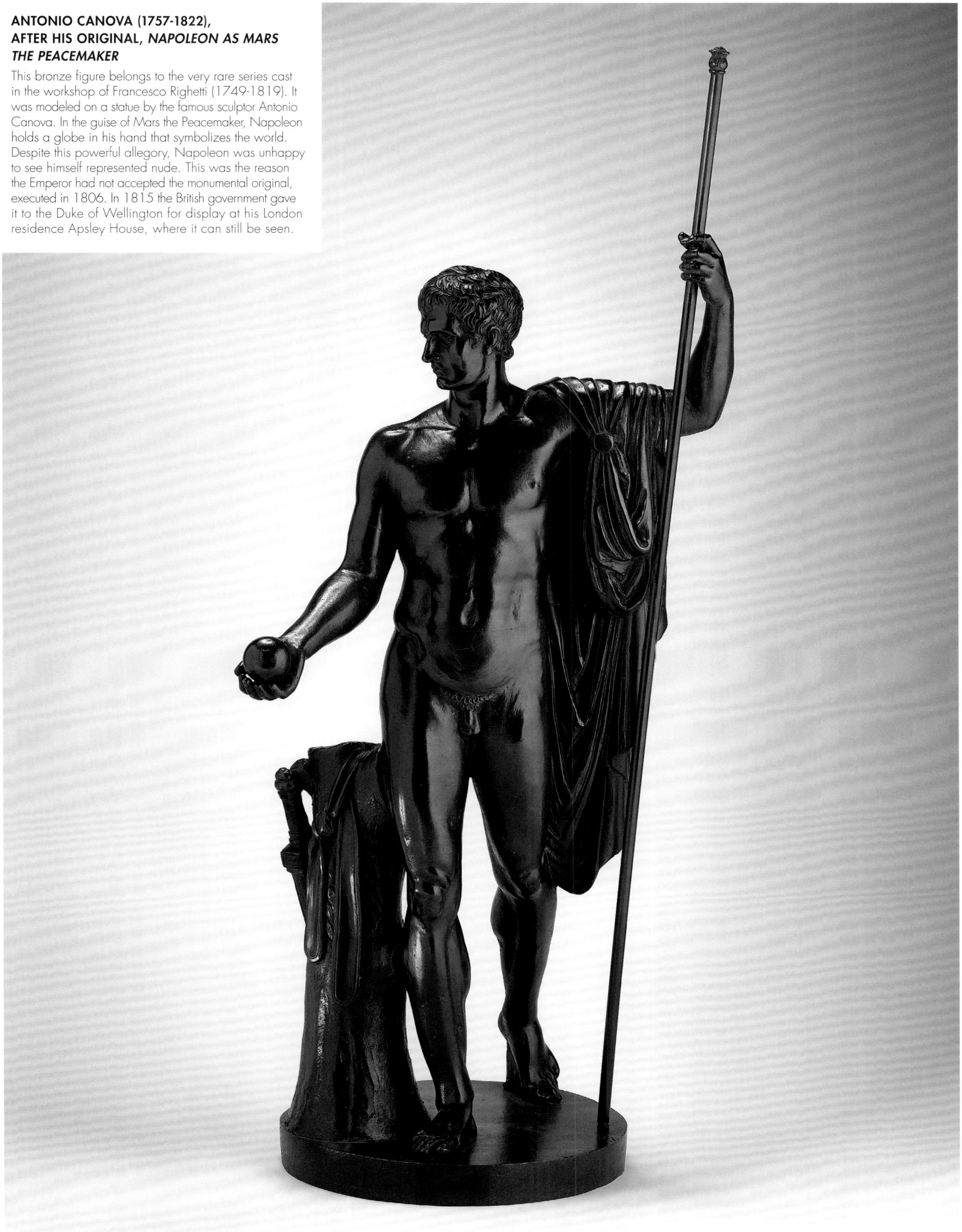

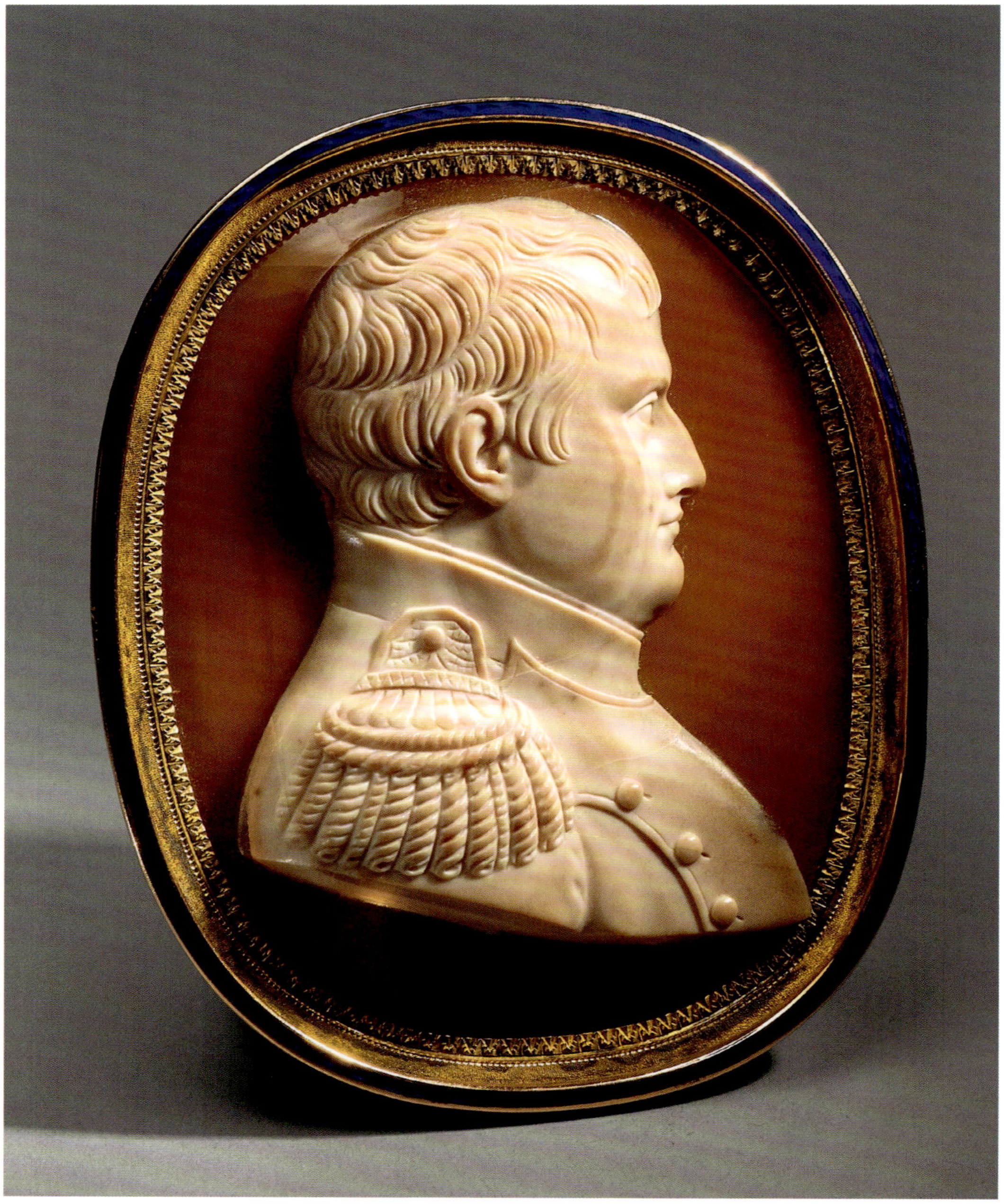

CAMEO IN PROFILE OF NAPOLEON

Napoleon is shown in profile within a vermeil border threaded with blue enamel around the rim, after the bust by Houdon. He wears the uniform of a Colonel of the Foot Grenadiers of the Imperial Guard.

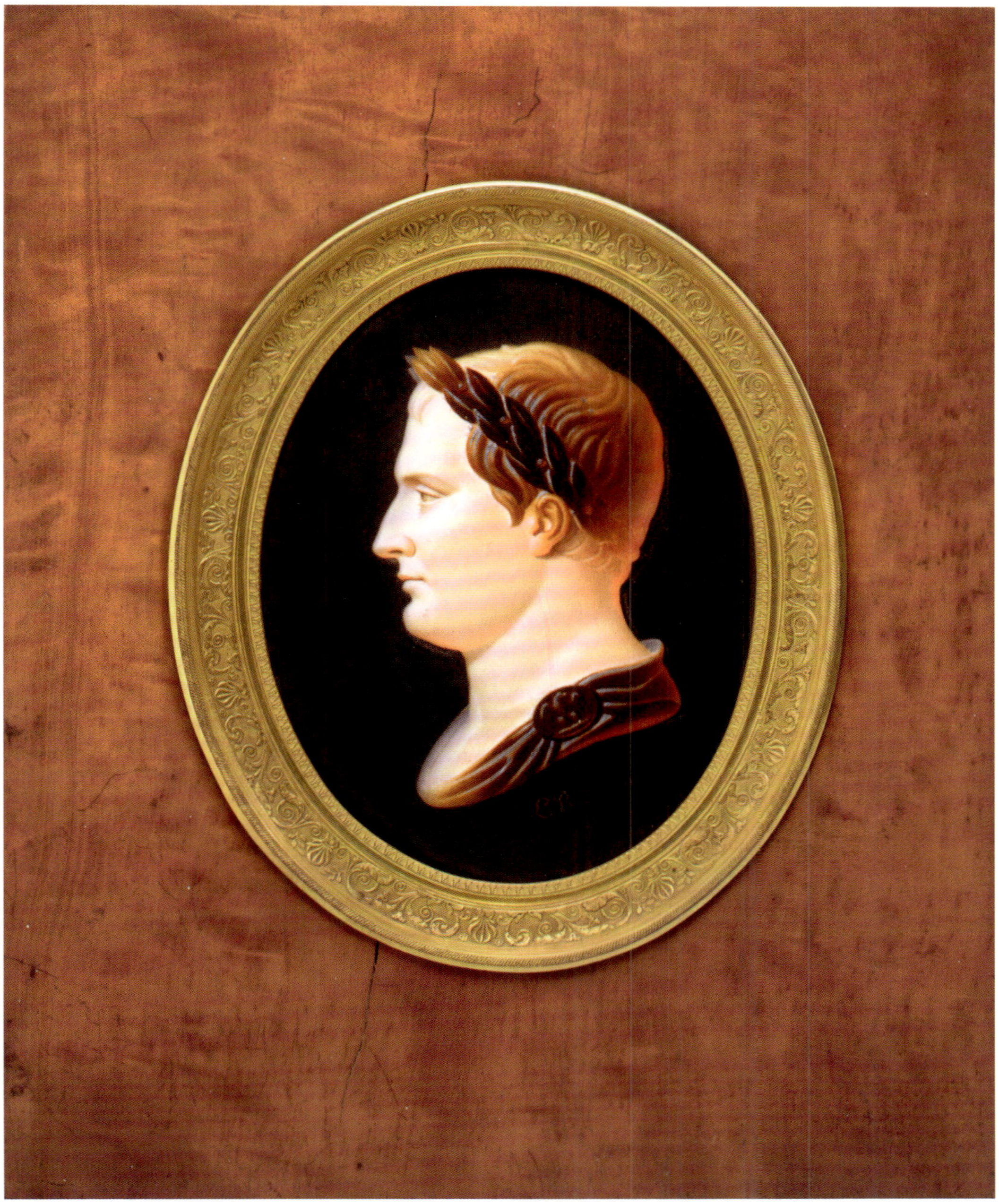

LOUIS-BERTIN PARANT (1761-1851), *PROFILE OF NAPOLEON*

This large miniature on porcelain showing Napoleon depicted in classical style is signed LB Parant. This renowned painter was unrivaled in his technique of replicating the look of cameos.
He is the artist responsible for the very few known portraits of the imperial family, now in the collections of the National Museums. Louis-Bertin Parant only worked for Sèvres as an "extraordinaire", supplying the commissions from his Paris studio. "La Table des Grands Capitaines" is unquestionably his masterpiece, commissioned from the Sèvres manufactory by Napoleon in 1806, and taking him six years to complete.
The same portrait, from Parant, but produced in smaller dimensions for the Berlin KPM manufactory, is also conserved in the collection.

NAPOLEON'S THRONE

This majestic ceremonial armchair is one of Napoleon's five thrones. Each one was a symbol of his imperial policy, used by Napoleon to impose his authority in his five seats of government: the Tuileries Palace, his chief residence as sovereign (throne now in the Louvre); the Palace of St Cloud, his secondary residence (throne now at Fontainebleau); the two legislative assemblies, where the throne stood in the hall of the Corps Législatif (now in the Musée des Arts Décoratifs); the Senate (where his throne remains); and this throne, probably from the Hôtel de Ville de Paris (Paris town hall) as it matches the throne depicted in the famous, official full-length portrait of Napoleon (now at the Musée Carnavalet), which was commissioned by the town hall and executed by Robert Lefebvre in 1809.

Before it was destroyed by fire in 1871, the Paris town hall was the seat of municipal and civic government. Its sumptuous throne room occupied the entire first floor of the main building. The throne itself featured all of the known imperial embellishments (initial N, bee, laurels and thunderbolts) and was probably used for the grand ceremonial reception in honor of the marriage of Napoleon and Marie-Louise on 10 June 1810. It is stamped "JACOB.D./R.MESLEE" on the back and bears an ancient label in black ink that reads "[...] / Trône de L'Empereur / Napoléon Iere (sic)" plus various stencils.

With its lifelike form and ostentatious decoration the throne has a sculptural quality reminiscent of those in the Louvre and Fontainebleau. The back of the chair, richly embroidered with pure gold thread and featuring a grand "N" at its center, is almost identical to its Louvre counterpart. The shape was specifically designed by Percier and Fontaine to exalt the glory of the imperial regime – essential for a ruler who constantly sought to elevate himself above his subjects. Hence the many official portraits of Napoleon that also include a throne. The throne was the embodiment of his imperial power and had to be respected as such.

It was displayed at the *Napoleon and Paris, Dreams of a Capital* exhibition in Ottawa's Museum of Canadian History in 2016, which was held in conjunction with the Musée Carnavalet in Paris.

Size: H. 112.5 cm × W. 66 cm × D. 61 cm; sculpted and gilded wood. Re-upholstered by the Houses of Lesage, Brazet and Declercq, with the approval of the National Museums of France, based on the original model.

We would like to thank monsieur Simon de Monicault, Director of CHRISTIE'S Furniture Department, for the research of the present text.

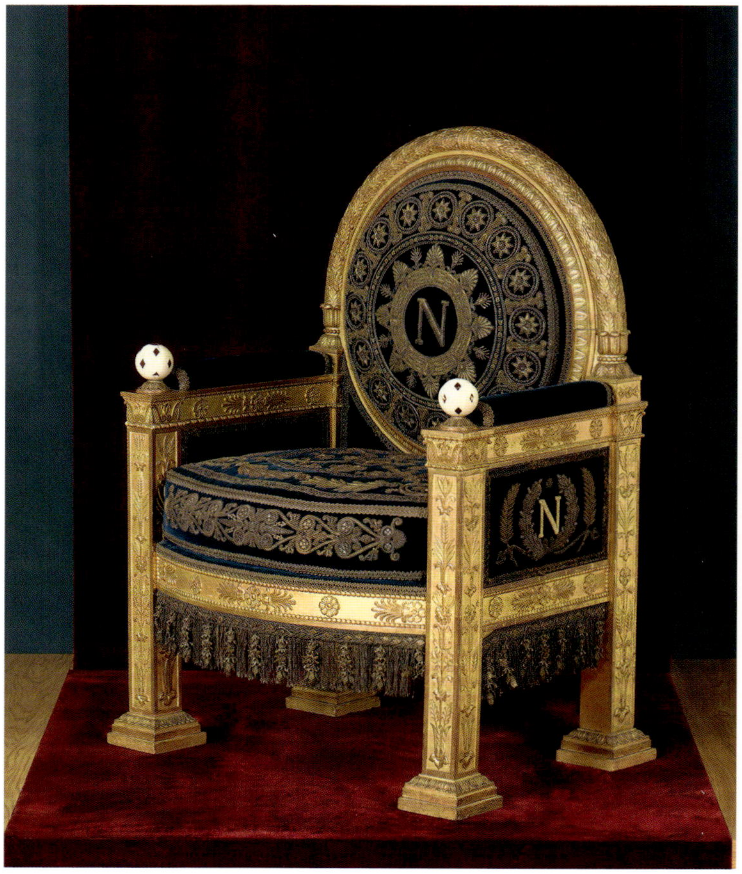

FRANÇOIS HONORÉ GEORGES JACOB-DESMALTER (1770-1841), NAPOLEON'S THRONE CHAIR, 1804

Musée du Louvre collection

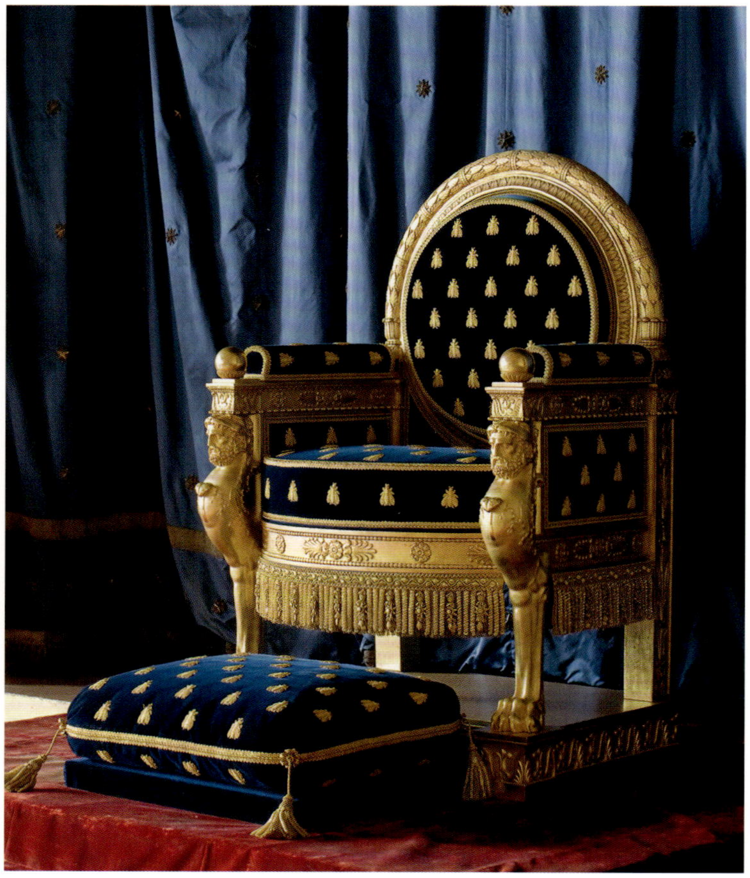

FRANÇOIS HONORÉ GEORGES JACOB-DESMALTER (1770-1841), NAPOLEON'S THRONE CHAIR, 1804

Château de Fontainebleau collection

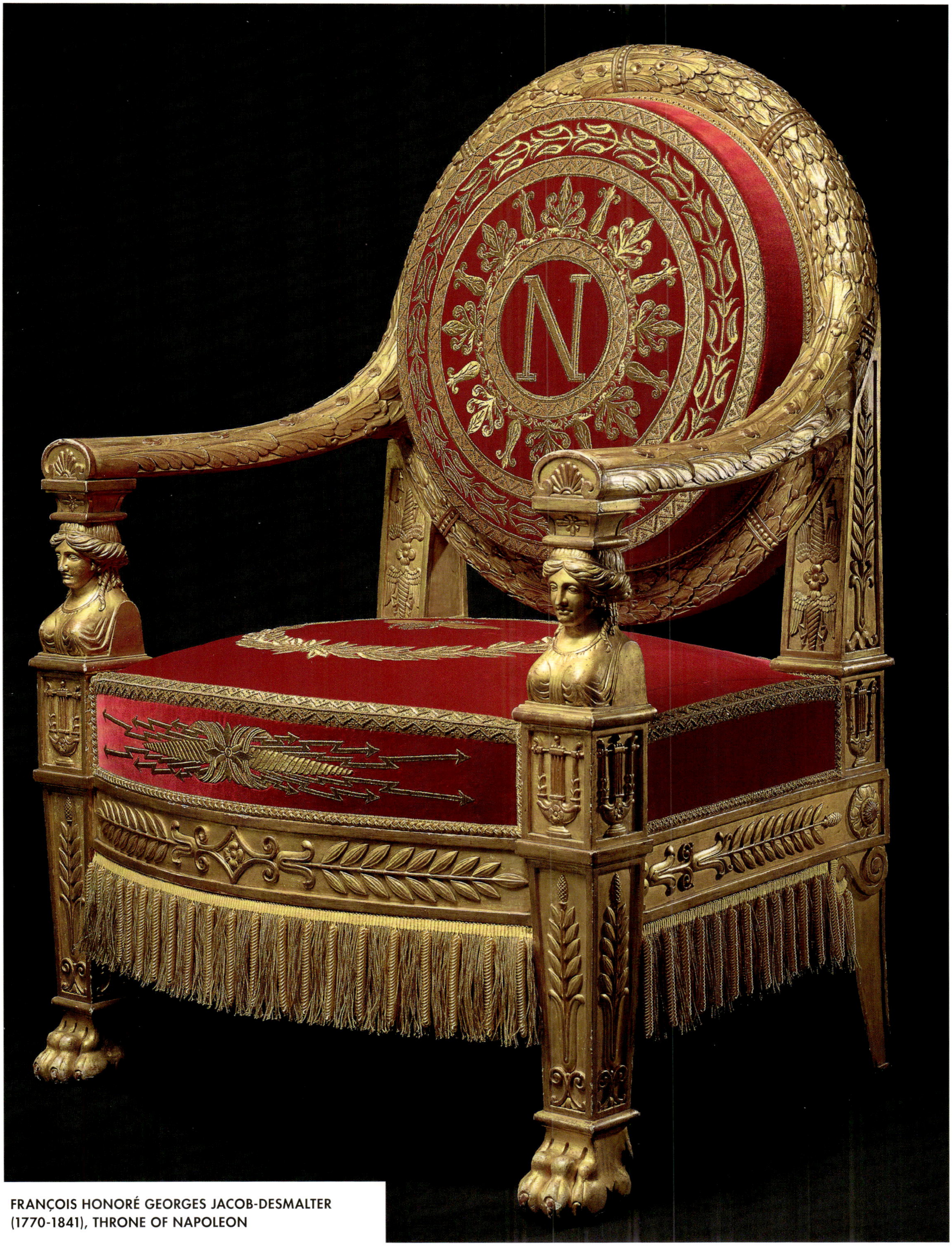

FRANÇOIS HONORÉ GEORGES JACOB-DESMALTER (1770-1841), THRONE OF NAPOLEON

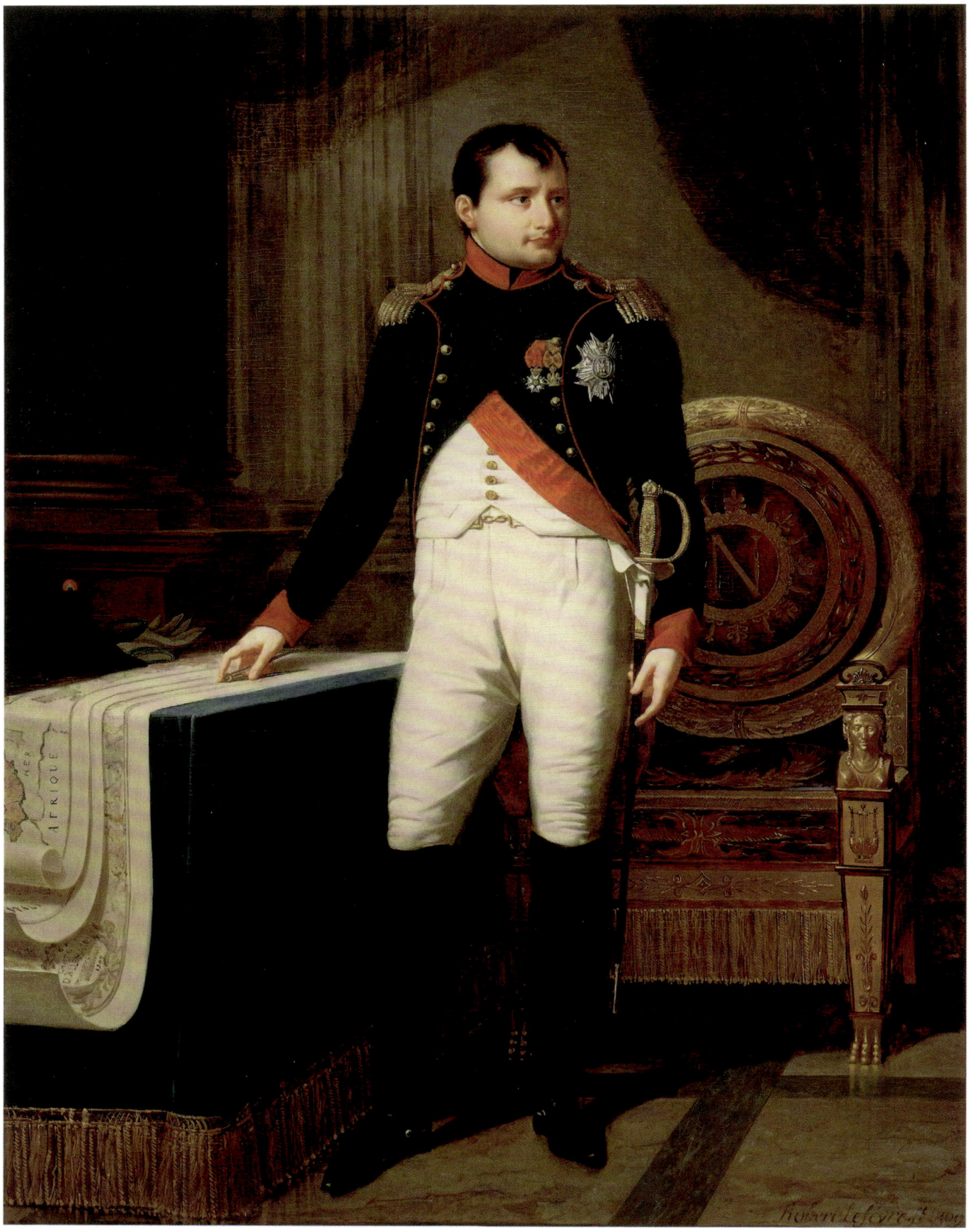

ROBERT LEFÈVRE (1756-1830), *NAPOLEON WEARING THE UNIFORM OF THE CHASSEURS À CHEVAL OF THE IMPERIAL GUARD*

Oil on canvas by Robert Lefèvre, commissioned by the Hôtel de Ville de Paris and delivered in 1809, now in the Musée Carnavalet, Paris. It shows Napoleon standing, consulting maps, wearing his Colonel's uniform of the Chasseur à Cheval of the Imperial Guard. Visible behind him is the throne now held by this collection, the seat embroidered with the imperial bee and the chair back featuring a crowned laurel wreath letter "N."

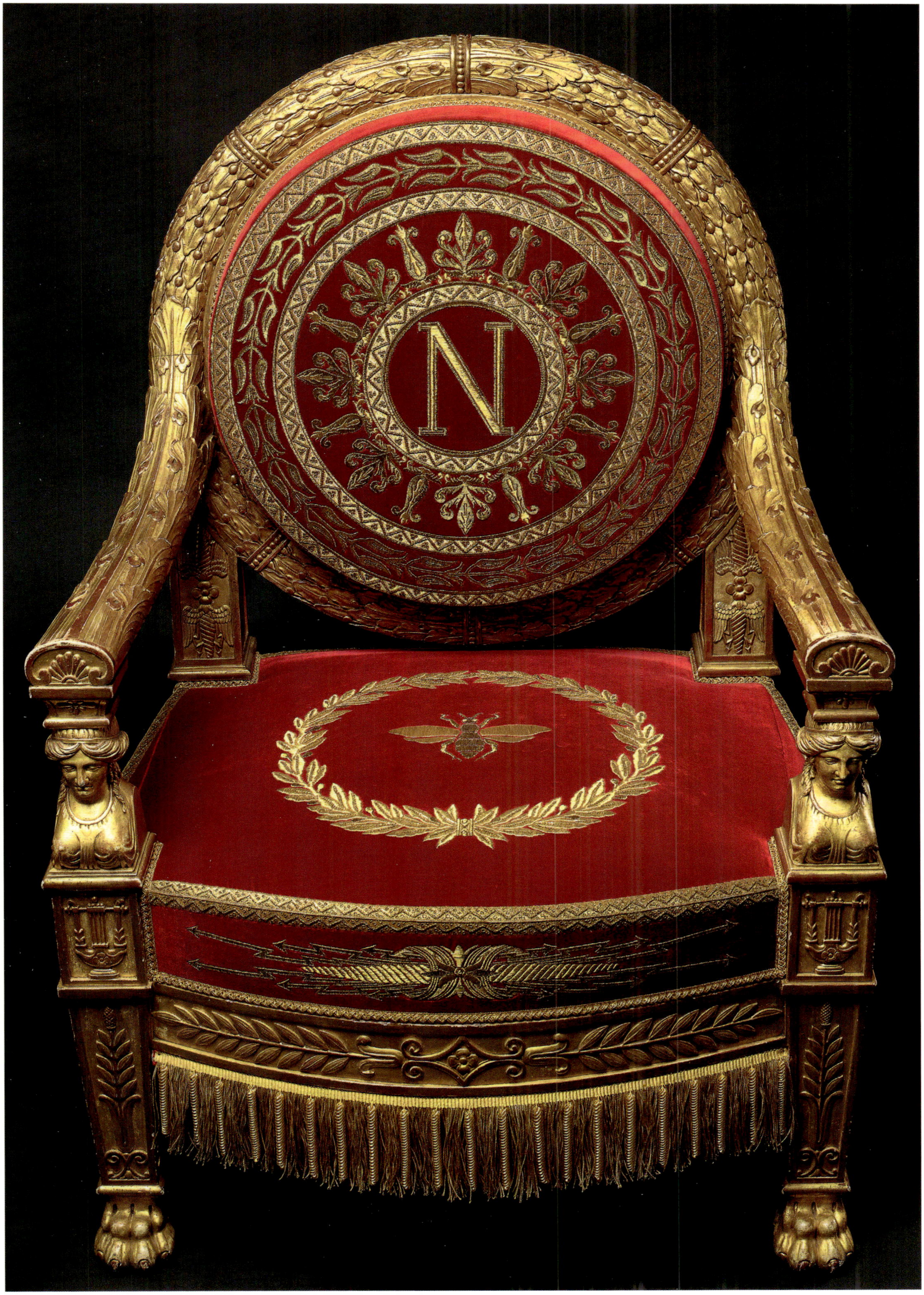

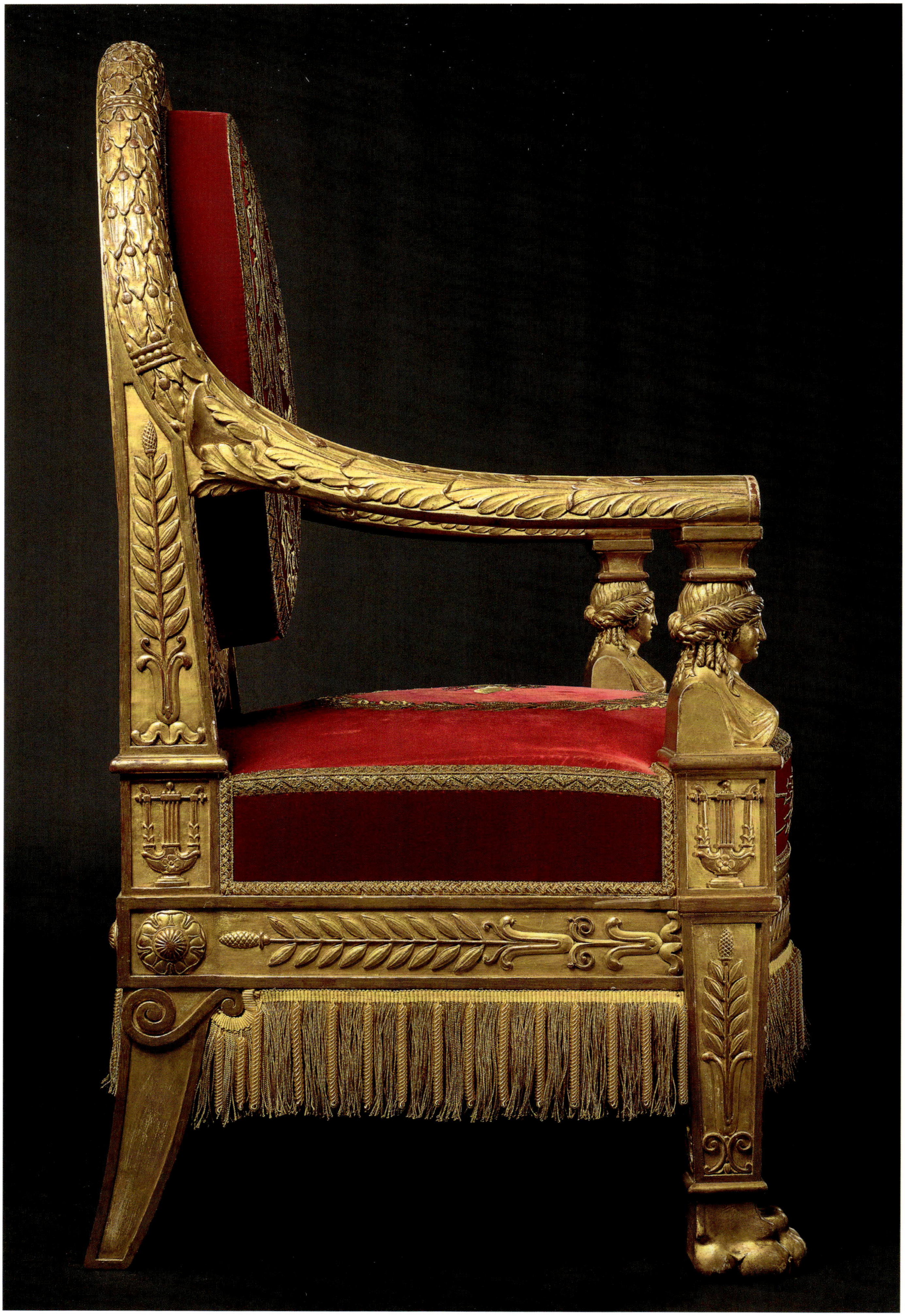

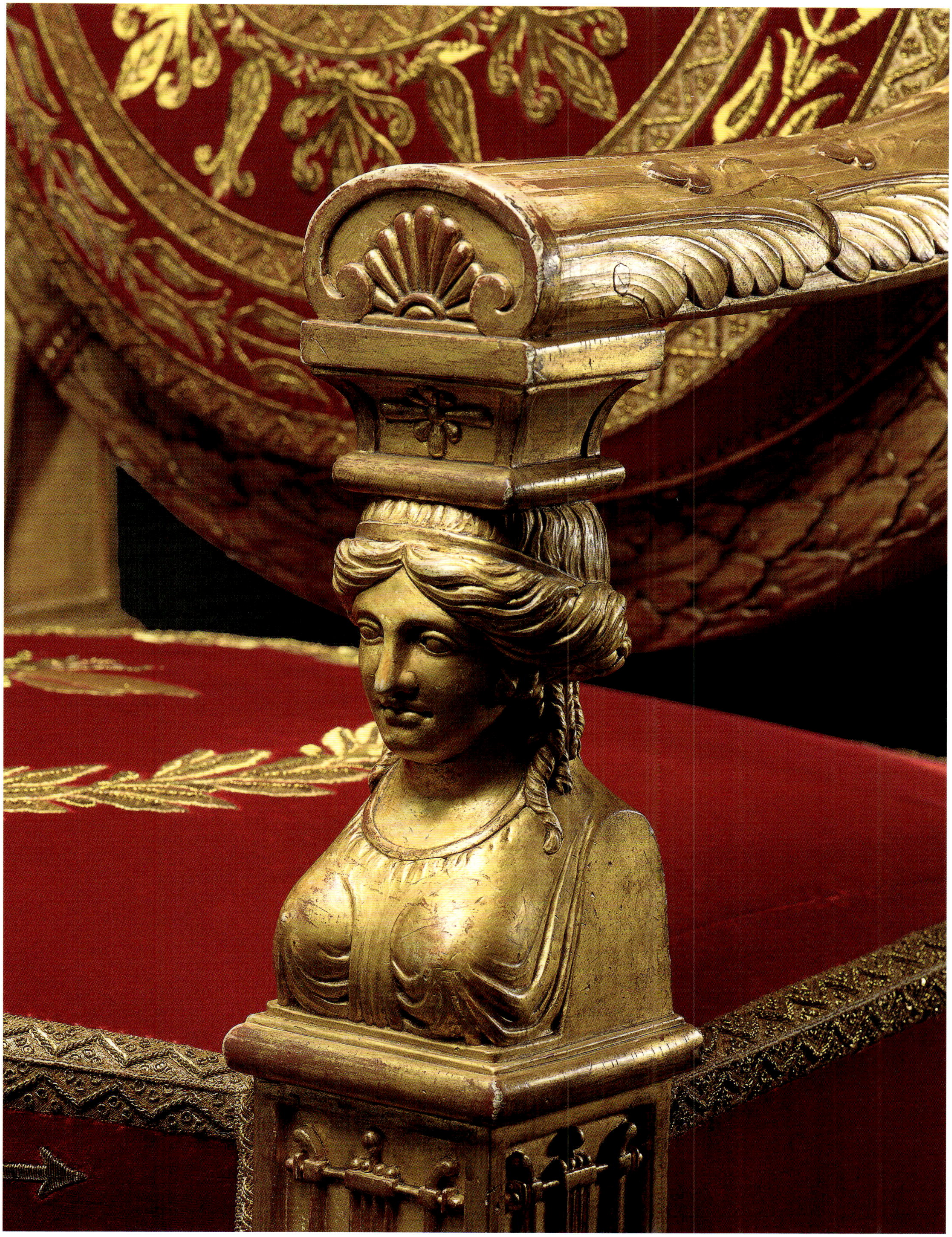

The Empresses and the Imperial Family

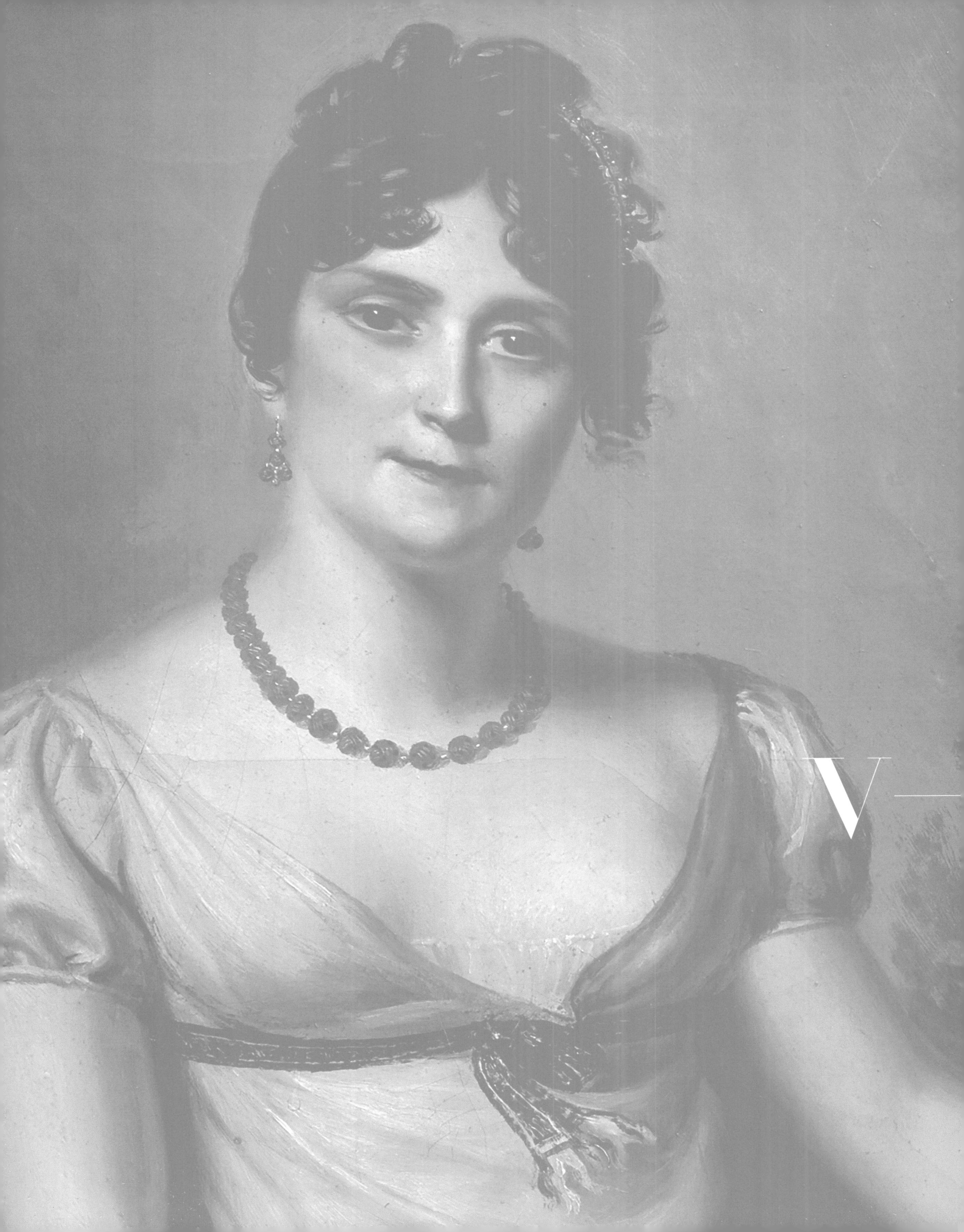

V

Napoleon was married twice, first to Josephine then to Marie-Louise – two Empresses from totally different backgrounds, who each ascended to the Imperial throne and acquired the glorious title of "Her Majesty the Empress and Queen". The title reflected the two crowns worn by their husband as Emperor of the French and King of Italy. With the exception of Lucien Bonaparte who was excluded from the Imperial family, Napoleon's siblings occupied the thrones of France's satellite kingdoms.

Bernard Chevallier
former curator of Malmaison

JOSEPHINE

Marie Joseph Rose de Tascher de la Pagerie was born in Martinique in 1763, the daughter of an old aristocratic family who settled on the island in the early 18th Century. She remained in Martinique until age 16 when she moved to France to marry her aunt's godson, Alexandre, Viscount de Beauharnais. It was an unhappy marriage that ended in separation after just six years but nevertheless produced two children: Eugène, born in 1781, and Hortense, born in 1783.

After returning briefly to Martinique in the period 1788-1790, Rose then lived in France through the troubled days of the French Revolution. Her husband was guillotined in 1794 and she herself only narrowly escaped death after being held prisoner for more than three months in the notorious Les Carmes prison. On her release, she became a muse to the new society that was taking shape under Paul Barras, the powerful and influential force behind the Directory. She first met the young General Bonaparte in the fall of 1795, when she was 32 and he was 26. For Rose their relationship was simply a means to an end — her passport to protection and material security. But for Napoleon it was love at first sight and, as a token of his affection, he renamed her Josephine (the feminine form of her second given name, Joseph). The couple were married in a civil ceremony in March 1796, shortly before Bonaparte went off to lead the Army of Italy in a brilliantly successful campaign that would place him center-stage.

The period 1796-1799 was a difficult time for Josephine. As the wife of the Commander-in-Chief, she spent nearly 18 months travelling through Italy, received with all the honors due to a sovereign wherever she went. News of her (amorous) involvement with Hippolyte Charles and his shady dealings with army contractors then reached the ears of Napoleon, who threatened to divorce her on his return from Egypt. Suitably chastened by the experience, Josephine submitted to her husband's authority and rehearsed for her performance as "First Lady".

It was a position that no woman had ever held before, a role that she and her entourage had to invent in preparation for her accession to the throne. At the beginning of the year 1800 she moved into the Tuileries Palace where she gave audiences. Visitors were admitted into her presence on presentation to the usher of a card bearing the name "Madame Bonaparte". Over the next 14 years her everyday life was minutely regulated, with every waking hour filled by some kind of activity. Her Household as Empress was suitably grand and run on the same lines as the Emperor's. She was the one who mostly decided how the imperial palaces (Compiègne, Fontainebleau, etc.) should be decorated and furnished. She traveled a lot, whether in an official capacity as Napoleon's wife, or in a private capacity when she took the waters. She also took full advantage of her status as sovereign to feed her appetite for the arts. She was an energetic art collector and a devoted patron of artists. Among her protégés were the painters Massot and Garneray, the miniaturists Bouvier, Millet and Saint and the sculptors Houdon and Chinard. She also patronized the Italian composer Spontini, cultivating a taste for drama and music as became her exalted rank. She supported porcelain factories and glassworks (Sèvres and Dihl et Guérhard) and, with virtually unlimited funds at her disposal, gave free rein to her passion for collecting, accumulating antiques and exotica to her heart's delight. As Empress she also had a license to indulge her other two great loves: jewelry (her sumptuous jewelry box was the envy of Europe) and most especially fashion. Josephine was not so much a follower as a creator of fashion, as testified by the superb dress (page 275) and matching slippers (page 285), featured in the Ledoux Collection alongside the invoice from the supplier Lenormand.

Her days were a constant round of activity: reading (taking advantage of the library at Malmaison with its many books bearing Bonaparte's monogram); correspondence (showing interest, as befitted a sovereign, in the lives of the ladies in her entourage, most notably the Duchesse de Frioul); card games (requiring boxes of counters marked with her monogram); needlework; gastronomy; and the many duties incumbent on a public figure. In her private life, Josephine, like her husband, was meticulous about cleanliness and personal hygiene — like Napoleon, she had her own dental kit (page 285). Then there was Malmaison, the couple's charming country house on the outskirts of Paris, reproduced countless times in prints and illustrations. Malmaison was Josephine's refuge, the place where she could devote herself entirely to her passion for natural sciences — zoology, mineralogy and botany, including the planting of a herbarium based on her coat-of-arms.

Sadly for Josephine, she had known since the days of the Consulate that she would never bear the Emperor an heir, and the shadow of divorce dogged her thoughts. She despaired of having a child and attempted to shift the blame for the couple's infertility onto her husband, repeatedly reminding people that, unlike

Napoleon, she had already borne two children by her first marriage (Hortense and Eugène). It was only after his Polish mistress Marie Walewska proved his fertility by bearing him a son, that Napoleon decided to divorce Josephine after 15 years of what had overall been a happy marriage. Their divorce by mutual consent was pronounced at the Tuileries Palace in December 1809. But far from forgetting Josephine, the Emperor made a very handsome settlement on his ex-wife. In addition to maintaining her rank as Empress and keeping the Elysée Palace as her Paris residence, she was given Malmaison and the Chateau Navarre, near Évreux in Normandy, plus an annual income of three million francs for life — enough to provide her with a very comfortable lifestyle.

In the period 1810-1812, Napoleon visited Josephine four times at Malmaison. For propriety's sake, she moved away from Paris on the run-up to his marriage with Marie-Louise and settled in her newly acquired Navarre residence. She stayed there just three times in the years 1810 and 1811, presiding over a small salon that hovered between witty debate and provincial small talk. Her last visit was in April 1814 when she sought refuge in Navarre from the coalition forces that had occupied Paris.

In the summer of 1810, Josephine took the waters at Aix-les-Bains then set off to explore the Alps, a trip that lasted several months and took her across Switzerland and Savoy, exploring all of the places of interest along the way. It was November 1810 by the time she returned to Malmaison and now that she lived there alone, she was free to embrace her newfound vocation as a grandmother. Hortense's children spent the following summer at Malmaison while their mother was away (including her youngest son, "Oui-Oui", who later became the Emperor Napoleon III). Eugène de Beauharnais's three children, on the other hand, had never met their grandmother. As Napoleon's viceroy in Italy, Eugène had been forced to move to Milan, where he remained in the spring of 1812 when his wife found herself pregnant for the fourth time, prompting Josephine to travel to Milan to assist at her daughter-in-law's delivery.

But disaster was in the offing. Napoleon's debacle in Russia affected Josephine deeply, like everything else that touched the Emperor. Henceforth, a pall of gloom descended over Malmaison, where Josephine remained without interruption from October 1812 to March 1814. As the allies drew closer, she went to seek refuge in Navarre but returned to Malmaison within a fortnight, heartened by the news from Paris that Tsar Alexander had requested a meeting. His visit to Malmaison would be the first of many – by the Tsar himself but also by the King of Prussia and the numerous German princes who found themselves in the capital at the time. But the recent events had taken a profound toll on Josephine. For some time now, she had been afflicted with a lassitude and weariness that were affecting her health. On 14 May, she caught a chill while out walking at Saint-Leu but insisted it was nothing and continued to receive her visitors just the same. On 26 May she finally agreed to take to her bed, from which she never rose again. She died three days later, at the age of 51, having spent her final weeks bringing her life to a triumphant conclusion.

Her death could not have been more timely, coming before Napoleon's return from Elba and subsequent "Hundred Days" Campaign. Shortly afterwards, she would have had to choose her allegiances — a decision that would have torn her apart. In the event, she died respected by all, maintaining her rank as Empress and her reputation as a friend of kings.

EUGÈNE AND HORTENSE DE BEAUHARNAIS

Born in 1782, Eugène was the eldest child of Alexandre de Beauharnais and the future Empress Josephine. As a young boy, Eugène was profoundly affected by the French Revolution and his father's execution by guillotine in 1794. When his mother married General Bonaparte, Eugène became his father-in-law's aide-de-camp, and rose to power alongside him. In 1805 he was named a Prince of the Empire and made Napoleon's Viceroy in Italy. The following year, he was officially adopted by Napoleon and married to the daughter of the King of Bavaria. The newlyweds moved immediately to Milan, capital of the newly proclaimed kingdom of Italy, where the visitors who frequented their brilliant court were guaranteed a grand reception. It was this imperative of etiquette that led Eugène to commission a magnificent porcelain service, including matching glasses engraved with his monogram, from the Dihl et Guérhard factory in Paris (page 313).

A natural born soldier, Eugène covered himself in glory in the Russian campaign. He fought to the last to retain the Emperor's hold on Italy, standing by him right up until 1814 when Napoleon was forced to abdicate. This steadfastness won him the respect of the allies and the friendship of Tsar Alexander. After Napoleon was defeated at Waterloo, Eugène fled to his father-in-law's court in Munich and was given the title Duke of Leuchtenberg. He died of an attack of apoplexy in 1824, prematurely worn out by an adventurous but difficult life.

Hortense de Beauharnais, Eugène's sister, was born in 1783 and received an excellent education at the Institution de Mme Campan, which was run by a former chambermaid of Queen Marie-Antoinette. She was then forced into a loveless marriage with Napoleon's brother, Louis Bonaparte, her mother Josephine looking to unite the two families and avoid the specter of divorce. The marriage produced three sons, the youngest of whom would become Napoleon III, Emperor of France.

In 1806, Louis Bonaparte was made King of Holland and settled in The Hague with his wife, which did nothing to improve their relationship. Following Louis' abdication in 1810, the couple separated and Hortense sought comfort in the arms of General de Flahaut. Their illegitimate son, the future Duc de Morney, was born a year later. A woman of refinement, Hortense, like her mother, had a taste for beautiful things. Among her many *objets d'art* was a personally monogrammed music box (page 312) and vegetable dishes (page 312) that she commissioned from Martin-Guillaume Biennais. She had a fondness for the decorative arts and was an accomplished painter, draftswoman and musician. Following the fall of the Empire, she bought the small Swiss chateau of Arenenberg where she lived until her death from cancer in 1837.

MARIE-LOUISE

On 14 December 1809, Josephine having failed to bear Napoleon an heir in 15 years of marriage, the couple were divorced by mutual consent in the *Grand Cabinet* of the Tuileries Palace. The nullification of their spiritual bond was pronounced a month later on 12 January 1810. Immediately afterwards, Napoleon set off in search of a new wife — a "babymaking machine", to use his own inelegant turn of phrase. Having initially thought of Tsar Alexander's sister, he then changed his mind and asked for the hand of Austrian Archduchess Marie-Louise de Habsburg (1791-1847), daughter of Francis I of Austria and a great-niece of Marie Antoinette...

For the sake of political expediency, the young Marie-Louise (aged barely 19 at the time) was accordingly sacrificed to a 41-year-old Corsican who her family saw as the devil incarnate. In March 1810 she married Napoleon by proxy in Vienna and departed for France shortly afterwards. The couple's first meeting was on 28 March 1810 on the outskirts of Napoleon's palace at Compiègne and their marriage was consummated that very night – Napoleon having assured himself that they were already legally married by virtue of the proxy ceremony in Vienna. Their civil wedding took place on 1 April at the palace of Saint-Cloud, followed the next day by their religious wedding, which was celebrated in the Salon Carré of the Louvre palace, a square room that was converted into a chapel for the occasion.

Against all expectations, it started out as a happy marriage. Marie-Louise lost no time in telling her father that Napoleon was a man worth knowing better, and a person she found impossible to resist. Having produced the long-awaited heir — the King of Rome, born on 20 March 1811 — the new Empress afforded her husband the comfort of a conventional relationship that he had never known with Josephine. Napoleon eventually became so taken with Marie-Louise that he departed from his normal behavior, addressing her as "tu" and calling her "Ma bonne Louise", taking her arm as they strolled through the palace gardens and always happy to play with their son. As a naturally unassuming person, Marie-Louise herself was docile and dutiful as a wife but reserved to the point of seeming cold. When they were apart, Napoleon made a point of writing her tender letters in which he called her "Ma bonne Louise", but she would always reply more formally, addressing him simply as "Mon cher ami".

Marie-Louise enjoyed a quiet life in Napoleon's absence, savoring the peace and tranquility of the Tuileries Palace or the Chateau de Saint-Cloud. Fluent in four languages, she spent most of her time reading and boasted a magnificent collection of red, morocco-bound books that were marked with her coat-of-arms. She painted and drew well, skills she learned from Pierre-Paul Prud'hon and Jean-Baptiste Isabey. She also took a genuine interest in the artists themselves, and acquired some of their works. She was an accomplished musician and skilled in the decorative arts, particularly embroidery.

Marie-Louise was portrayed in various media by the greatest artists of the period: in sculpture by Biennais (pages 295), in painting by Gérard and in miniature by Isabey (page 273). She was naturally coquettish and determined to assert herself as Empress, spending sizable amounts of money on clothing and jewelry but always remaining within the limits of her allowance. In addition to her own personal expenses, there was also the not inconsiderable cost of the gift-giving that was expected of an Empress — luxury gifts for her entourage, such as the jewel-studded watches engraved with her monogram that she commissioned from Etienne Nitot (page 302).

Then there were the times when the young woman accompanied her husband on official trips. In the spring of 1810 the imperial couple visited Belgium and Holland (a grand tour that served as their honeymoon). In 1811 we find them in Normandy, then once again in Belgium and Holland. In 1812 Marie-Louise traveled as far as Dresden with Napoleon, where she saw her father for the first time since her marriage. It was when Marie-Louise began to show promise as his representative, effortlessly displaying all the tact required, that Napoleon appointed her regent in his absence. It was now March 1813 and he would henceforth be too preoccupied by his military campaigns to see much of the Empress. But on 24 January 1814, as he said his goodbyes before leaving for the Campaign of France, he never imagined that he would never see his wife or son again.

The night before, Marie-Louise had been made regent for the second time, assisted this time by Joseph Bonaparte as the Emperor's Lieutenant General. On 29 March, with debacle in the offing for French forces, she and the King of Rome were forced to flee the Tuileries under pressure from Joseph. They sought refuge in Blois, which is where Marie-Louise heard the news of the Emperor's abdication.

From that point onward, the young Marie-Louise found herself cast adrift, a helpless victim of events as she struggled to survive amid the wreckage. Alone and abandoned, she met up with her father in

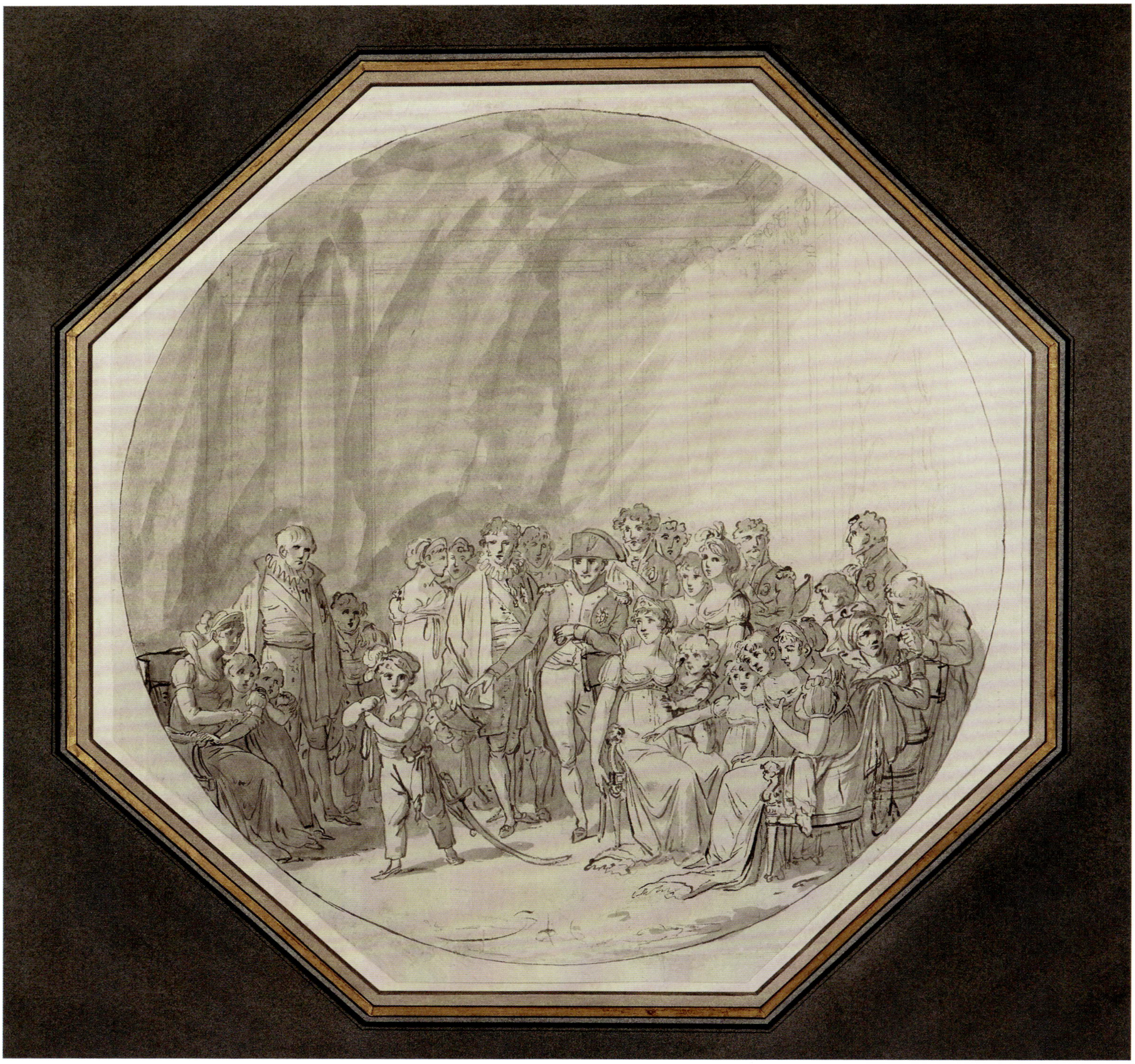

LOUIS-LÉOPOLD BOILLY (1761-1845), *NAPOLEON SURROUNDED BY HIS FAMILY,* 1806

This large drawing in pen and black ink, India ink wash, and pencil, is historically significant for several reasons. Its artist, Boilly, was already famous for his unparalleled depictions of daily life in France between the Revolution and the Empire, and this drawing is the only known picture of Napoleon Bonaparte with the twenty-four members of his family. The people shown around him are: Empress Josephine, Joseph and his wife Julie, their children, Louis and Hortense, their son Napoléon-Louis-Charles, Elisa and her husband Félix Baciocchi, Pauline and her husband Camille Borghèse, Jérôme, Caroline and Joachim Murat, their children, and the Emperor's mother. The intimacy of the composition, the presence of the children, and the simple scene attest to the importance of family ties within the Bonaparte clan. The painter took a few highly symbolic liberties in his work. Over his shoulder, the young Napoléon-Louis-Charles [eldest son of Louis Bonaparte and Hortense de Beauharnais, the King and Queen of Holland] carries his illustrious uncle's saber – the weapon that symbolizes France's offensive. Napoleon is pointing at the child with his forefinger, designating him as heir in the order of succession (the King of Rome would not be born until 1811).

This circular drawing was commissioned by the Emperor in April 1806 to decorate the porcelain centerpiece of a table, and Boilly described it like this: "It shows the young Napoléon pulling the saber of HM the Emperor along behind him. The allegory is a good augur and lets us hope that one day, he may wield it with honor and glory to bring happiness to France. As you can see, it's a subject that can occupy the 24 people and it's perfectly suited to a family painting of this importance". A report from Brongniart dated 8 August 1806 confirms Boilly's commission for "a finished oil painting, of the same size as the one that should be executed on porcelain". The premature death of the Emperor's young protégé Napoléon-Charles on 5 May 1807 put a halt to the project, as Brongniart made clear in a letter to Boilly dated 9 June: "Sir, in the conversation we had together about three weeks ago, we were of the opinion that the subject that had been agreed upon for the painting of the imperial family could no longer be portrayed, following the unfortunate demise of the Royal Prince of Holland, Napoléon-Louis". This very important drawing belonged to Edmond and Jules de Goncourt's collection in 1856. We know, from Brongniart, that the painter undertook two later versions, one of which was kept by Jules Boilly, and another that bore numbers above each figure. Neither is in existence today.

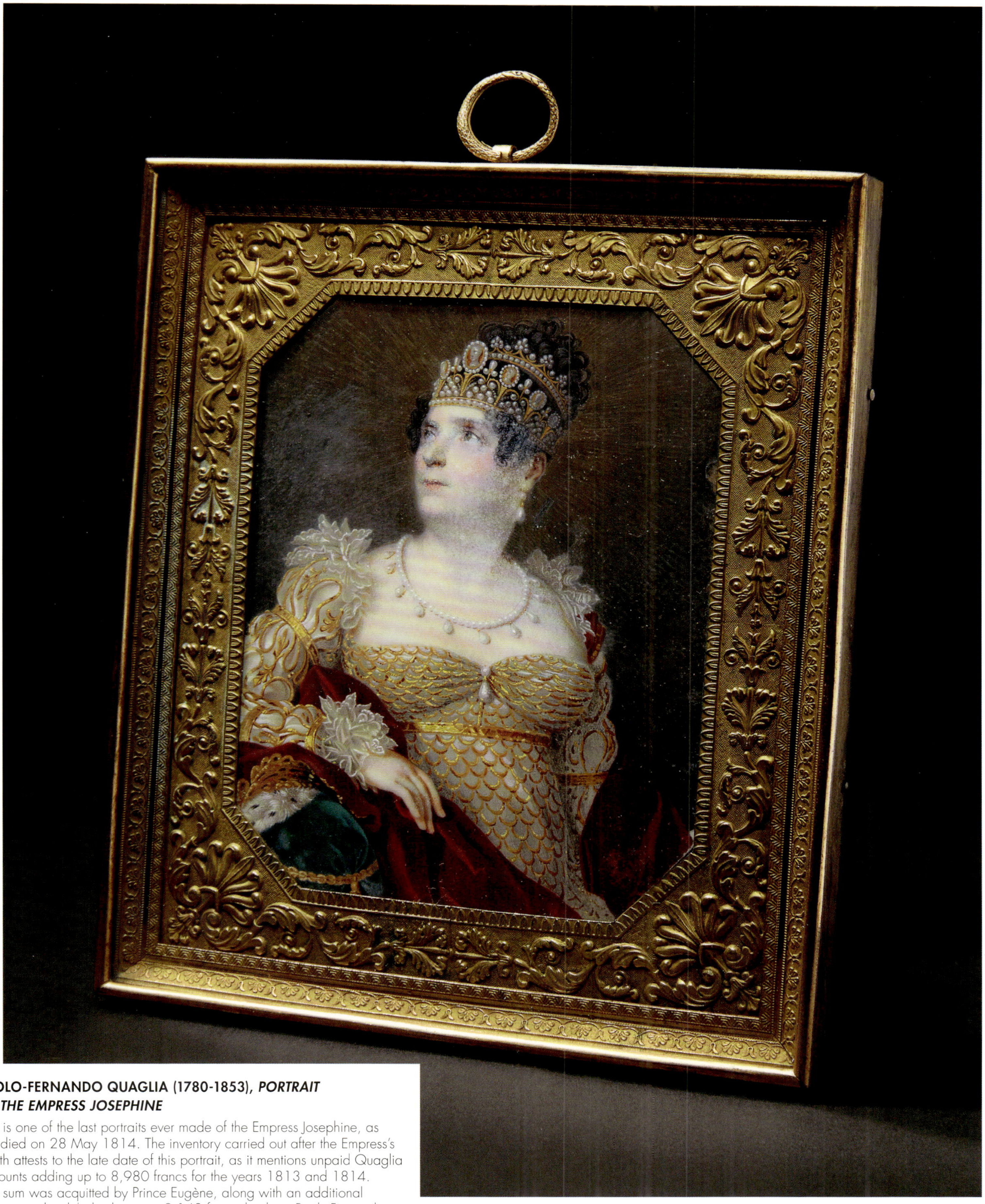

PAOLO-FERNANDO QUAGLIA (1780-1853), *PORTRAIT OF THE EMPRESS JOSEPHINE*

This is one of the last portraits ever made of the Empress Josephine, as she died on 28 May 1814. The inventory carried out after the Empress's death attests to the late date of this portrait, as it mentions unpaid Quaglia accounts adding up to 8,980 francs for the years 1813 and 1814. This sum was acquitted by Prince Eugène, along with an additional sum, since the debt had risen to 9,140 francs by then. Paolo-Fernando Quaglia settled in Paris around 1805 and entered the Empress Josephine's service. As his patron she gave him the opportunity to paint portraits of the imperial family, including Napoleon himself and members of his entourage. This is one of several portraits of the Empress he produced. Another of them is famous for serving as the original for some cups by the Dihl et Guérhard manufactory.

Rambouillet and returned to Austria. From there she continued to write to Napoleon, but her letters would never reach the island of Elba. In the late summer of 1814 she was nevertheless allowed to take the waters at Aix-les-Bains and, by some cunning machination, the dashing General Neipperg was dispatched to escort her. First her advisor then her confidant, the endlessly affable general knew how to make himself indispensable. While out walking one day, Marie-Louise took fright at a clap of thunder and flung herself into his arms... They became lovers shortly afterwards, Marie-Louise meanwhile switching titles from Empress of France to the less elevated condition of Archduchess of Austria.
In 1816, having been granted Parma, Piacenza and Guastalla by the Congress of Vienna, she paid her first official visit to her new duchies, accompanied by Neipperg. The couple had two illegitimate children in Napoleon's lifetime. It was only in August 1821, following the death of the now disgraced Emperor, that they were able to formalize their relationship. Marie-Louise reigned happily over her dominions until her death in 1847. The people of Parma would forever remember their duchess as a wise ruler who encouraged international trade and commissioned great undertakings.

MADAME MÈRE

Letizia Ramolino was born in Ajaccio in 1749 of a noble Tuscan family who settled in Ajaccio at the end of the 15th Century. Aged just 15, she married a young law student called Carlo Maria Buonaparte (1746-1785) who eventually rose to represent the Corsican nobility at the court of Louis XVI. The couple had 13 children, eight of whom survived infancy.
In 1804, apparently unmoved by her son's spectacular ascension to the throne, Letizia declined to attend the coronation, preferring to remain in Rome with her son Lucien who had fallen out with Napoleon. As Emperor, Napoleon gave her the official title "Son Altesse Impériale Madame Mère de l'Empereur" (Her Imperial Highness, Mother of the Emperor). He also made handsome provision for his mother, as for his sisters-in-law, some of which went to pay for decorating and furnishings. In the years following the coronation, she commissioned a magnificent vermeil dining service from Odiot (page 318) and though she was no great reader, the books in her library were marked with her monogram. But she was always careful to set some money aside as a precaution against an uncertain future. When Napoleon was exiled to St Helena, she was refused permission to accompany him as she had done when he was banished to the island of Elba. She retired to her palace in Rome where she died in 1836, having outlived three of her children, Napoleon, Pauline and Élisa, and also her grandson, the Duke of Reichstadt.

JOSEPH BONAPARTE

Joseph Bonaparte, born in Corte in 1768, was the eldest of the Buonaparte children to survive infancy. In 1794 he married Julie Clary, the daughter of a wealthy merchant from Marseilles, then took advantage of Napoleon's ascent to power to carve out a niche for himself as a diplomat.
In 1800 he concluded the Treaty of Mortefontaine between France and the United States, followed by a Treaty of Peace with Austria (1801) and a preliminary peace agreement with England (1802). Joseph was then made a senator and a grand officer of the Legion of Honor by Napoleon, who also gave him the throne of the kingdom of Naples — which Joseph swapped two years later for the Spanish throne (1808). As a patron of the arts, Joseph commissioned a variety of artists, among them the horologist Breguet (page 320).
Forced to leave Madrid after the French defeat, he was made a Lieutenant General by the Emperor in 1814, charged with defending Paris. In the event, he had to abandon his mission and retreated to Switzerland. In the "Hundred Days", he was appointed president of the Council of the Ministers in the Emperor's absence. He then fled to the United States following Napoleon's defeat at Waterloo and established his residence in Point Breeze, near Philadelphia. He died in Florence in 1844.

LUCIEN BONAPARTE

Lucien was the third son of Letizia and Carlo Buonaparte, born in Ajaccio in 1775. He and Napoleon drew closer at the time of the French Revolution, Lucien's outspoken support for the Jacobin movement finding an echo in his elder brother. As Napoleon embarked on his spectacular career, Lucien followed in his wake. In 1799 he was appointed President of the Council of Five Hundred (one of the two assemblies that governed France at the time), a role that made him a crucial figure in the Coup of 18 Brumaire that brought his brother to power as First Consul. Napoleon then made Lucien Minister of the Interior, and later Ambassador to the court of Madrid.
Shortly after Lucien's first wife died, he contravened Napoleon's wishes and married Alexandrine Jacob de Bleschamp in preference to the Queen of Etruria. The two brothers fell out as a result, leaving Lucien no choice but to retire from politics to lands in the Papal States (Rome). While there, he commissioned the artist François-Xavier Fabre to paint his portrait (page 329).
When France annexed the Papal States, Lucien took ship for the United States (1810) but was captured by the British and spent three years under house arrest in England. It was 1815 before he was reconciled with Napoleon, who made Lucien a French prince. He spent his remaining years in Italy and died in Viterbo in 1840.

LOUIS BONAPARTE

Louis Bonaparte was born in Ajaccio in 1778. He was raised by his brother Napoleon and later served as his aide de camp, first in Italy then in Egypt. In 1802 he was married to Josephine's daughter, Hortense, her mother looking to strengthen the ties between her own family and her husband's. The marriage turned out badly and ended with the couple's separation.

In 1804 Louis became Constable of France and in 1806 he was proclaimed King of Holland. Newly empowered as sovereign, Louis sought to break free from Napoleon's authority and supported Dutch interests at the expense of the Continental System (the blockade designed by Napoleon to destroy British trade). In 1810 Holland was annexed to the French Empire and Louis fled to Austria.

He eventually retired from public life altogether and devoted himself entirely to literature. A well-read man, Louis boasted a fine collection of books, among them textbooks on surgery and hydraulics and other scientific works. He settled in Italy after the Fall of Napoleon's Empire and died in Livorno in 1846.

ÉLISA BONAPARTE

Born in Ajaccio in 1777, Élisa was the eldest of the Buonaparte daughters. Following an education at Les Demoiselles de Saint-Cyr (a school for young noble girls), in 1797 she married an under-achieving Corsican officer called Félix Bacciochi (1762-1841). From her earliest years, Élisa was driven by a devouring ambition that soon made up for her lack of good looks. Her efforts bore fruit in 1805 when she was awarded the Principality of Piombino, followed in 1806 by the principality of Lucca, then the Grand Duchy of Tuscany three years later.

She took her role as sovereign very seriously, proving herself a careful and competent ruler, conspicuous for her patronage of the arts and humanities. The goldsmith Martin-Guillaume Biennais was commissioned to cast her image in bronze, as for two other members of the Bonaparte family (page 326); and the sculptor Bartolini made a marble bust of her daughter (page 327). Following the fall of the Empire, Élisa retired to Italy where she died in 1820.

JÉRÔME BONAPARTE

Jérôme was the youngest child of the Buonaparte family, born in Ajaccio in 1784. He was a rather frivolous and thoughtless young man who Napoleon posted to the Mediterranean and the Atlantic. In 1803, while visiting Baltimore, Maryland, he married the young Elizabeth Patterson without his family's consent. By the time they returned to Europe, she was already pregnant with his child.

Under pressure from Napoleon, Jérôme subsequently rejected his wife and child and had the marriage annulled. In 1807 he was made a French prince, married Princess Catherine of Württemberg (daughter of the new King of Württemberg), and was proclaimed King of Westphalia later that year. The couple resided in the capital of Kassel where Jérôme spent more time living the high life than holding together the disparate territories that made up his kingdom. In 1813 he was anyway forced to flee Westphalia and seek refuge in France. Following the Battle of Waterloo where Jérôme fought bravely for his country, he was exiled to Austria then to Rome. He made a comeback in 1849 following the coup d'état staged by his nephew Louis-Napoleon, being appointed Governor of Les Invalides, Marshal of France and president of the Senate. He died in 1860 at the Chateau de Vilgénis, his residence near Paris.

PAULINE BONAPARTE

Born in Ajaccio in 1780, Pauline was just 17 when Napoleon married her off to the distinguished general, Victor-Emmanuel Leclerc. Following his death from yellow fever in 1802 while serving in the ill-fated Saint-Domingue expedition, the Emperor then thrust the easily consolable widow into the arms of Prince Camille Borghèse (1775-1832), the descendant of an illustrious Roman family, who she married in 1803.

By 1806, the newly made princess and Duchess of Guastalla was enjoying a lavish lifestyle apart from her husband with a succession of lovers. Wedded to luxury, she commissioned a vermeil dining service from goldsmiths Biennais and Odiot —some one thousand six hundred pieces engraved with the Borghèse coat-of-arms (page 325) — plus a matching Sèvres porcelain service with a pale blue base (page 324).

In 1814 Pauline joined her beloved elder brother on the island of Elba, then tried in vain to accompany him to St Helena. She retired to Italy thereafter, dying in Florence in 1825.

PIERRE-LOUIS BOUVIER (1765-1836),
PORTRAIT OF JOSEPHINE

In fall 1812, Josephine took advantage of a short stay at Château Prégny-la-Tour, the small residence she acquired near Geneva, to commission various Swiss artists to paint her portrait. Among them was the miniaturist Pierre-Louis Bouvier, who represented her in enamel and ivory and also here, on canvas – his only known painting of Josephine.

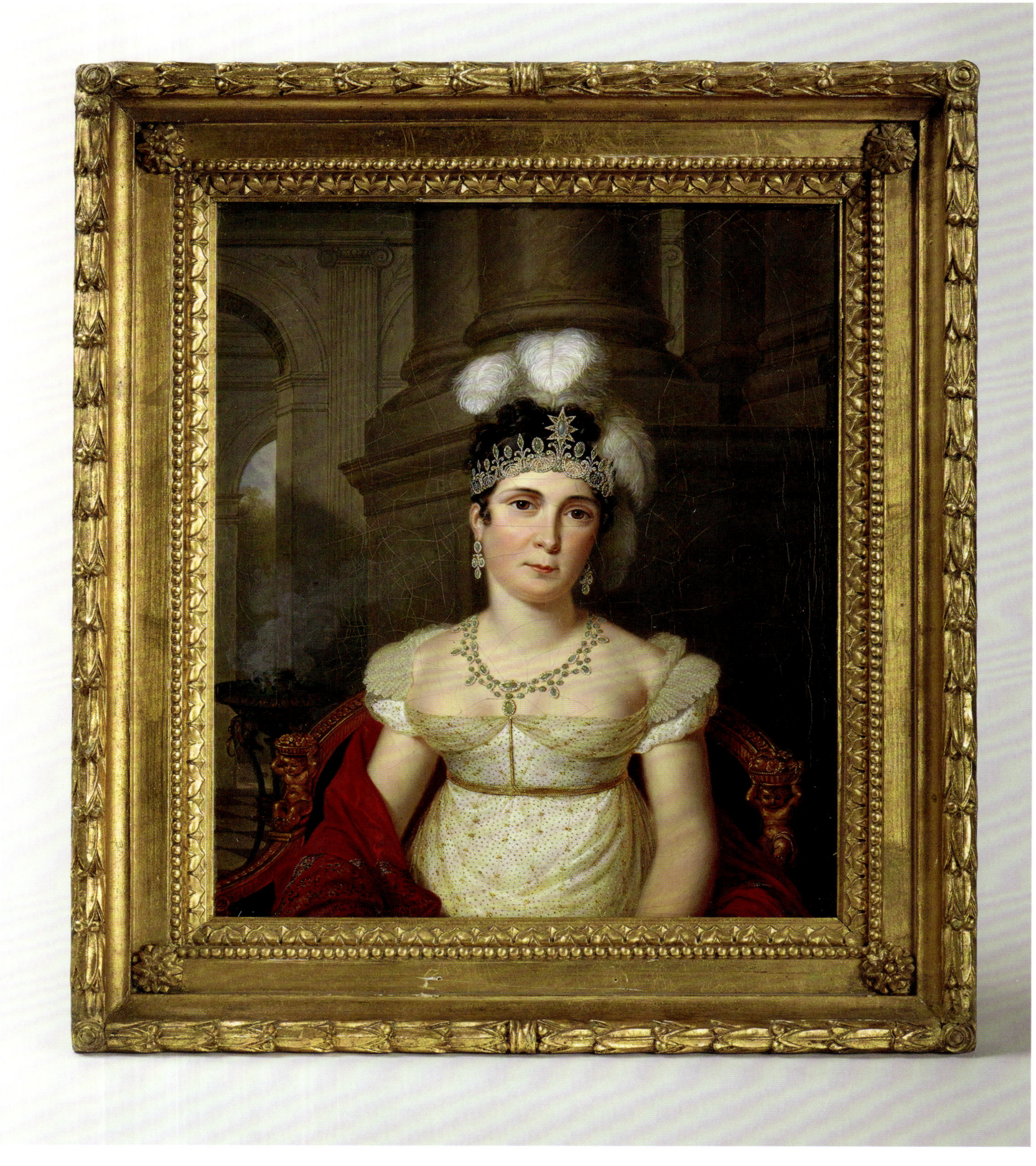

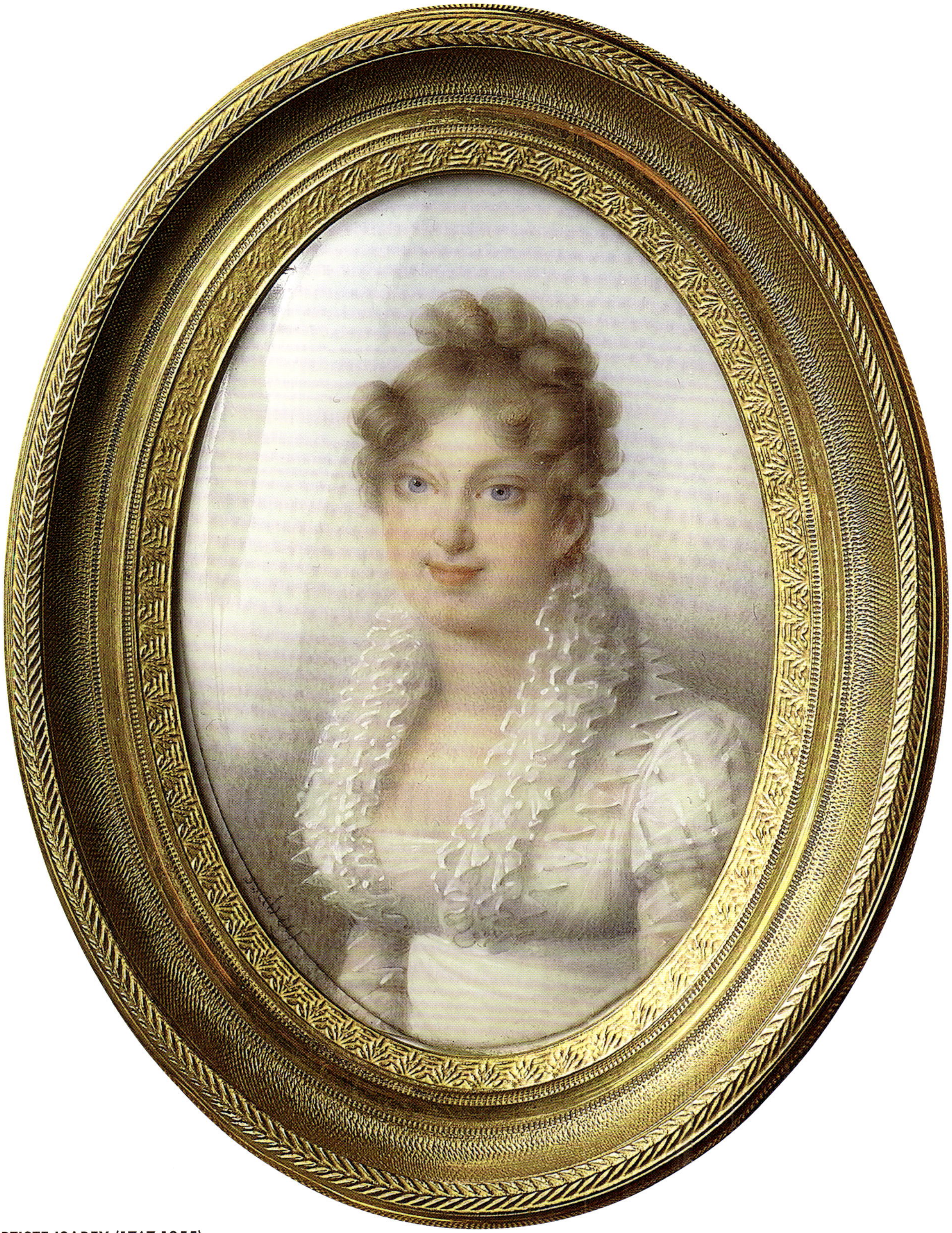

JEAN-BAPTISTE ISABEY (1767-1855),
PORTRAIT OF MARIE-LOUISE

Jean-Baptiste Isabey was drawing master to the new Empress. Shown here is one of several portraits he executed of Marie-Louise, signed by the artist and showing the Empress dressed informally and wearing no jewelry – which suggests that the portrait was destined for someone close to her.

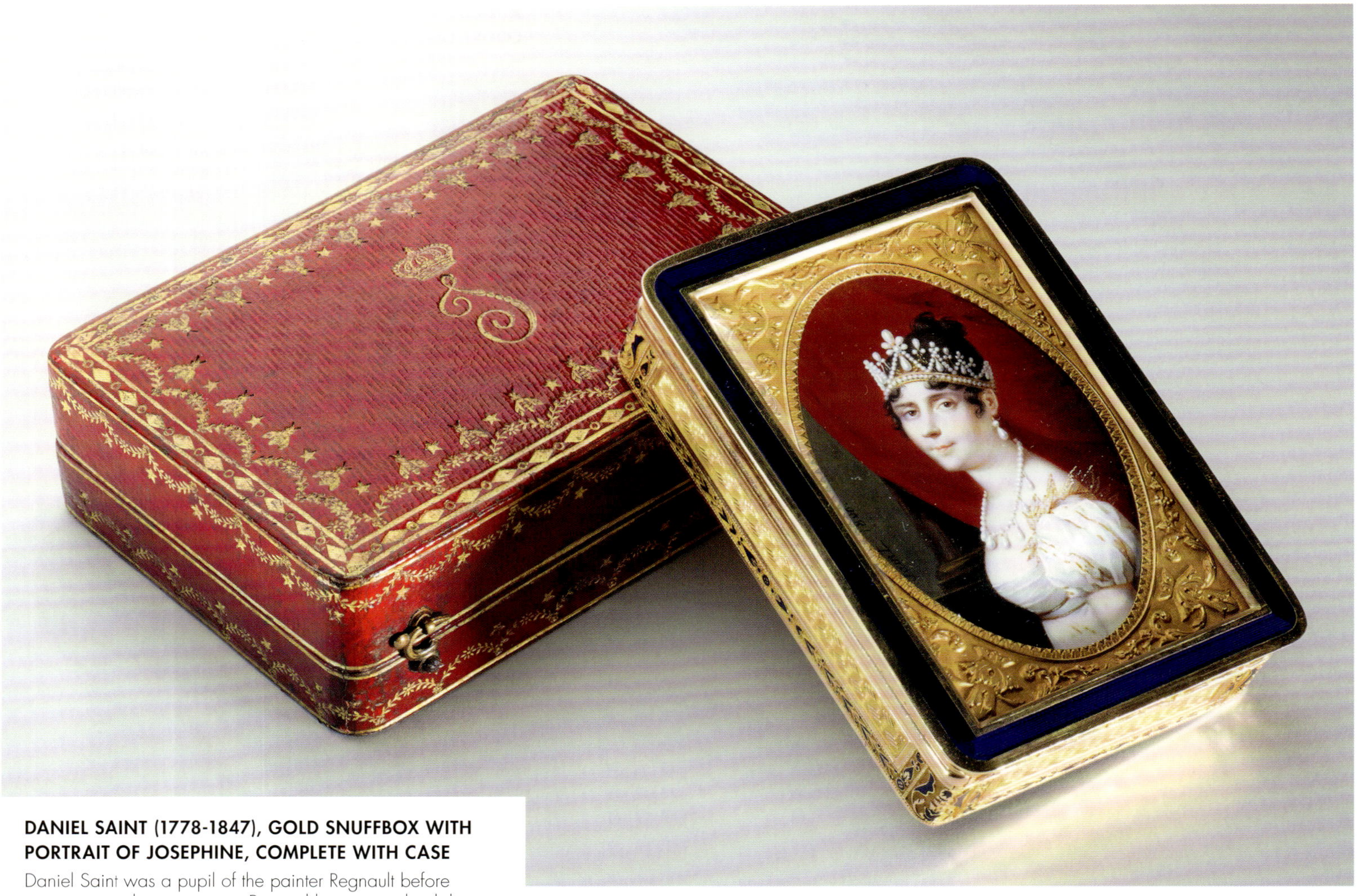

DANIEL SAINT (1778-1847), GOLD SNUFFBOX WITH PORTRAIT OF JOSEPHINE, COMPLETE WITH CASE

Daniel Saint was a pupil of the painter Regnault before turning toward miniature art. Pictured here is a splendid example of his many miniature representations of Josephine: a portrait signed and dated 1808, set in a gold and enamel snuffbox by Paris goldsmith Gabriel-Raoul Morel and bearing the Empress' monogram. Complete with red Morocco leather case.

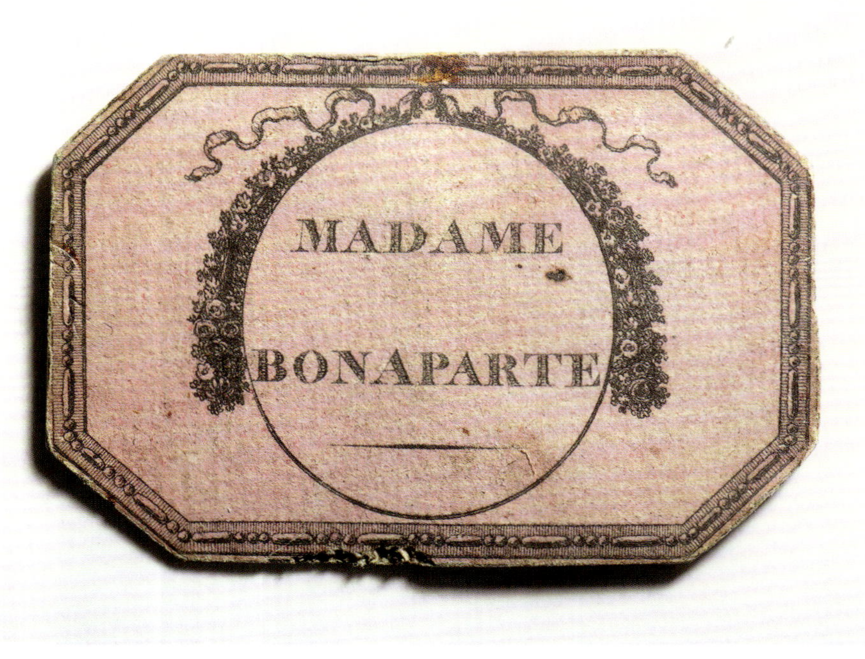

CARD GRANTING AUDIENCE WITH MADAME BONAPARTE

When Josephine moved into the Tuileries as the wife of the First Consul, a new etiquette began to take shape. Four ladies in waiting were appointed to attend her after Napoleon was proclaimed Consul for life in 1802 and admission into her private apartments was henceforth subject to the usher being presented with a card bearing her name.

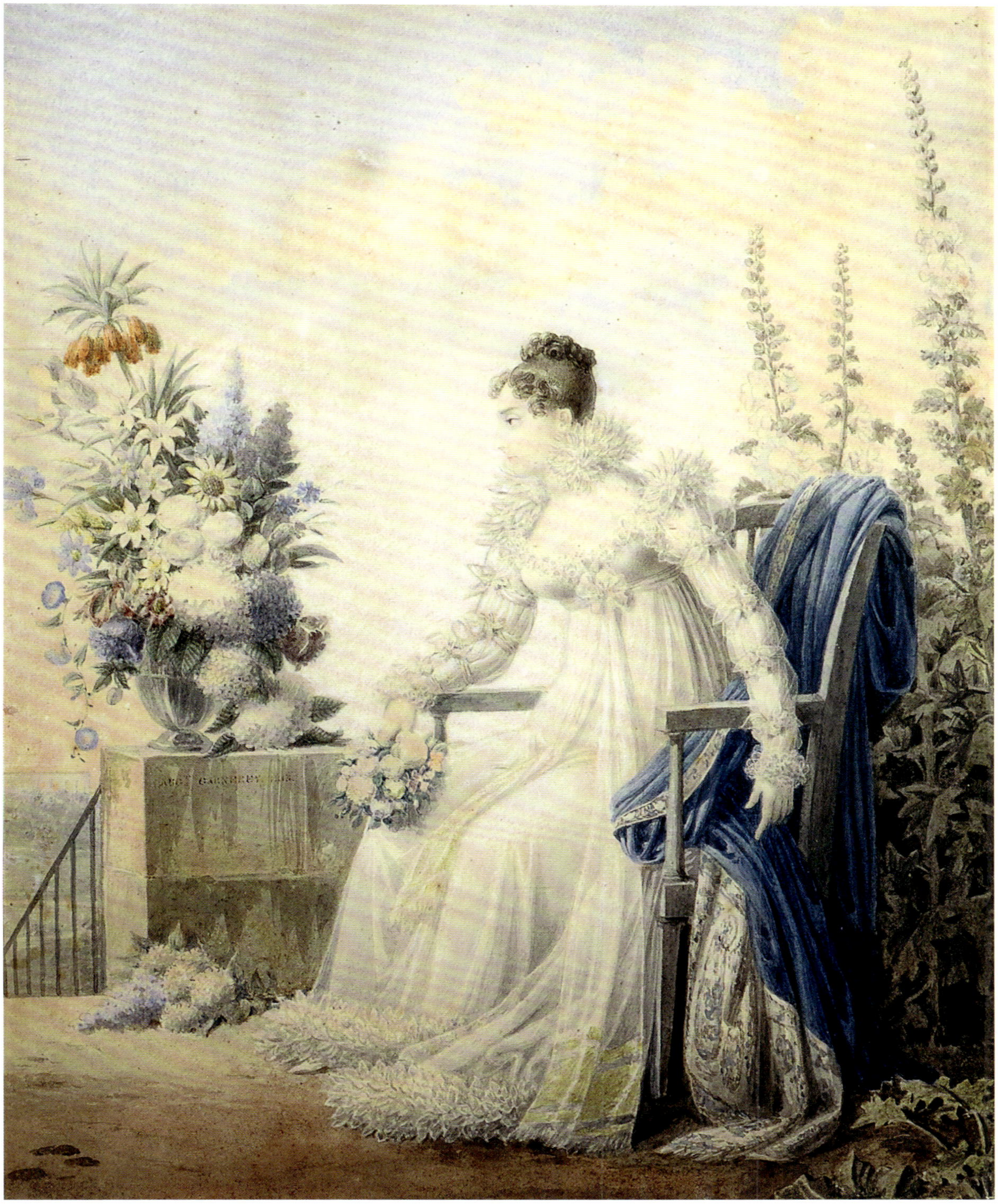

AUGUSTE GARNERAY (1785-1824), *JOSEPHINE*

A very rare watercolor on vellum, signed and dated 1813, similar to another painting signed by the same artist in the same year that shows the Empress with a gothic chateau in the background, seated beside a large vase of flowers. Auguste Garneray painted a series of watercolors of Malmaison for Josephine, which is now on display at the Musée de Malmaison.

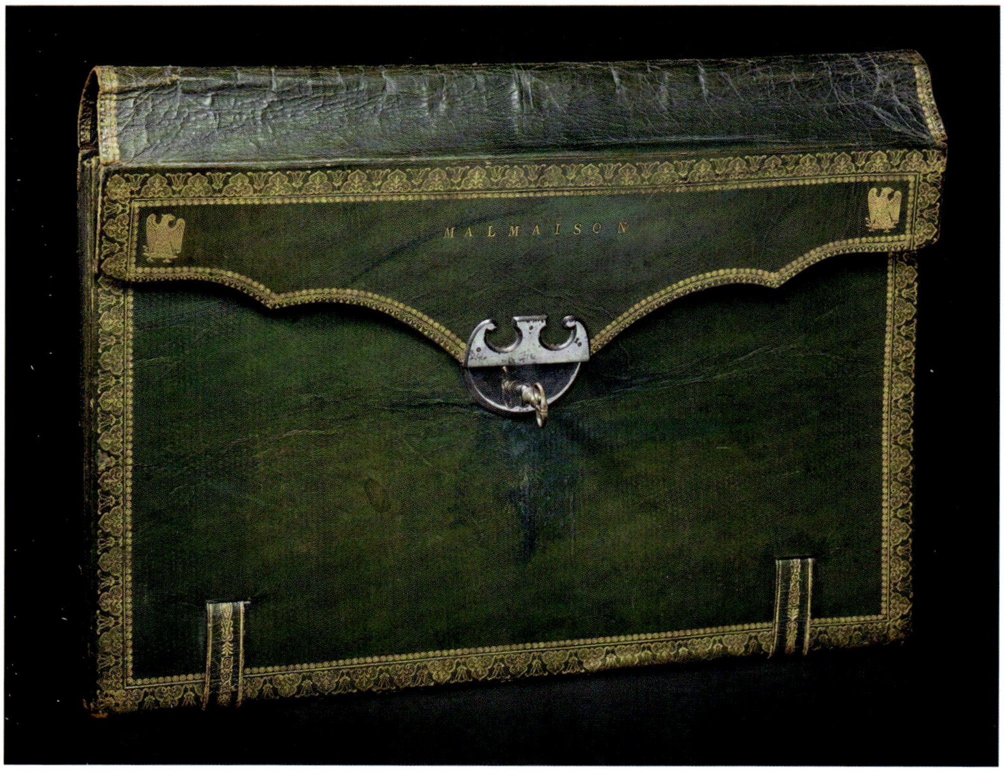

CHÂTEAU DE MALMAISON PORTFOLIO

Portfolio in green Morocco leather, emblazoned "Malmaison" in gold letters, with separate compartments for different documents. Features include a gilded border decoration, an eagle at each corner of the flap and a silver lock, still with original key.

MARTIN-GUILLAUME BIENNAIS (1764-1843), GAMING BOX AND COUNTERS WITH JOSEPHINE'S MONOGRAM

Biennais started out in marquetry and, though appointed First Goldsmith when Napoleon became Emperor, he continued to provide the palace and the Empress Josephine alike with gaming boxes, complete with ivory counters in different colors that were used to keep score in card games.

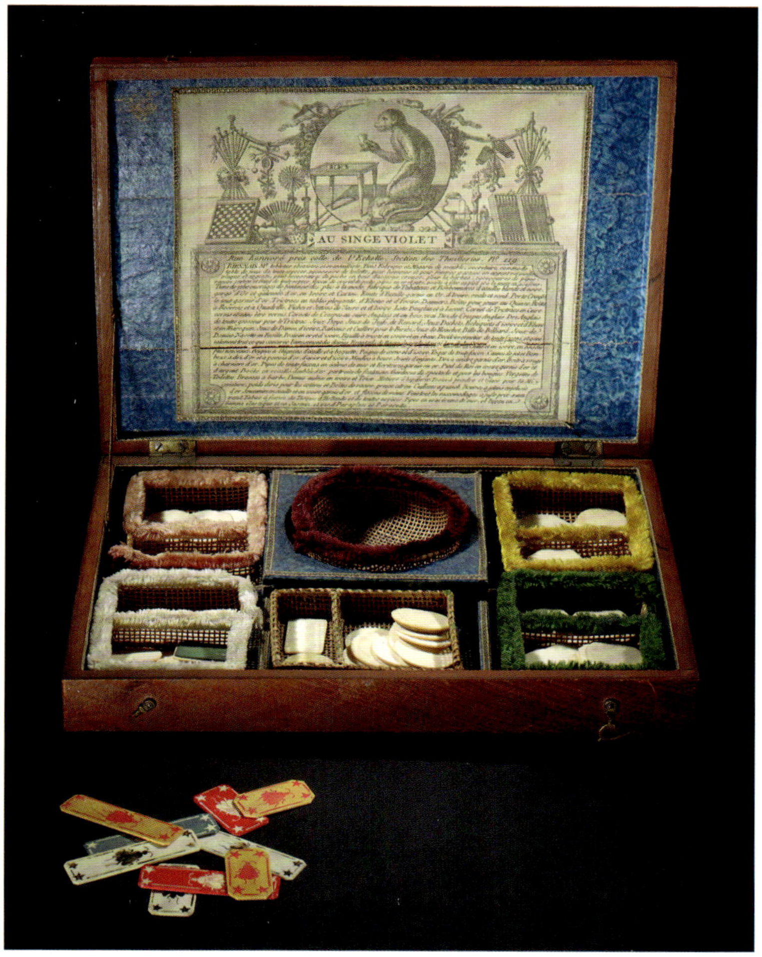

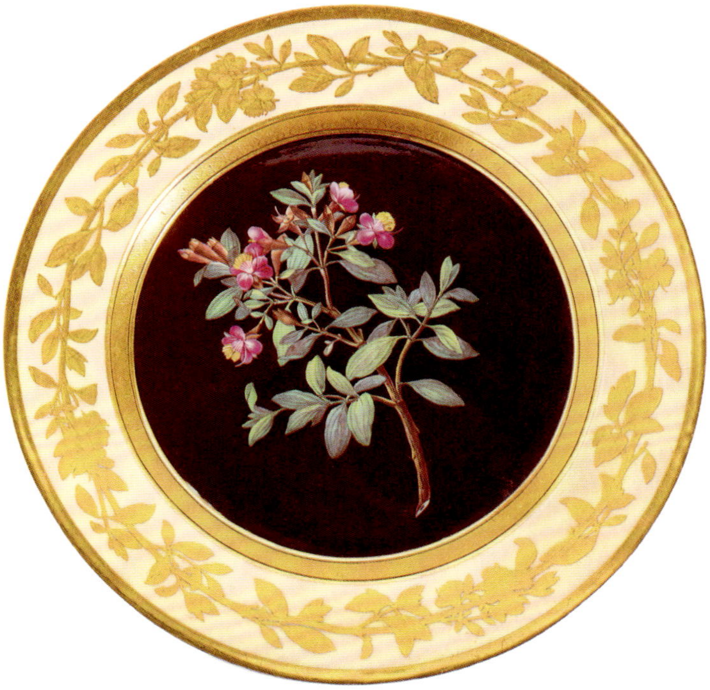

ROYAL PORCELAIN FACTORY, BERLIN, PLATE FROM JOSEPHINE'S BOTANICAL SERVICE

In 1807 the Royal Porcelain Factory in Berlin, knowing Josephine's love of botany, sent her a magnificent dinner service that included 144 plates depicting floral subjects, most of them rigorously copied from the illustrations in the books of Pierre-Joseph Redoute. Featured here on this side plate, against a colored background, is *Rhexia myrtoide* (the name is inscribed on the back). Only very few pieces are still extant.

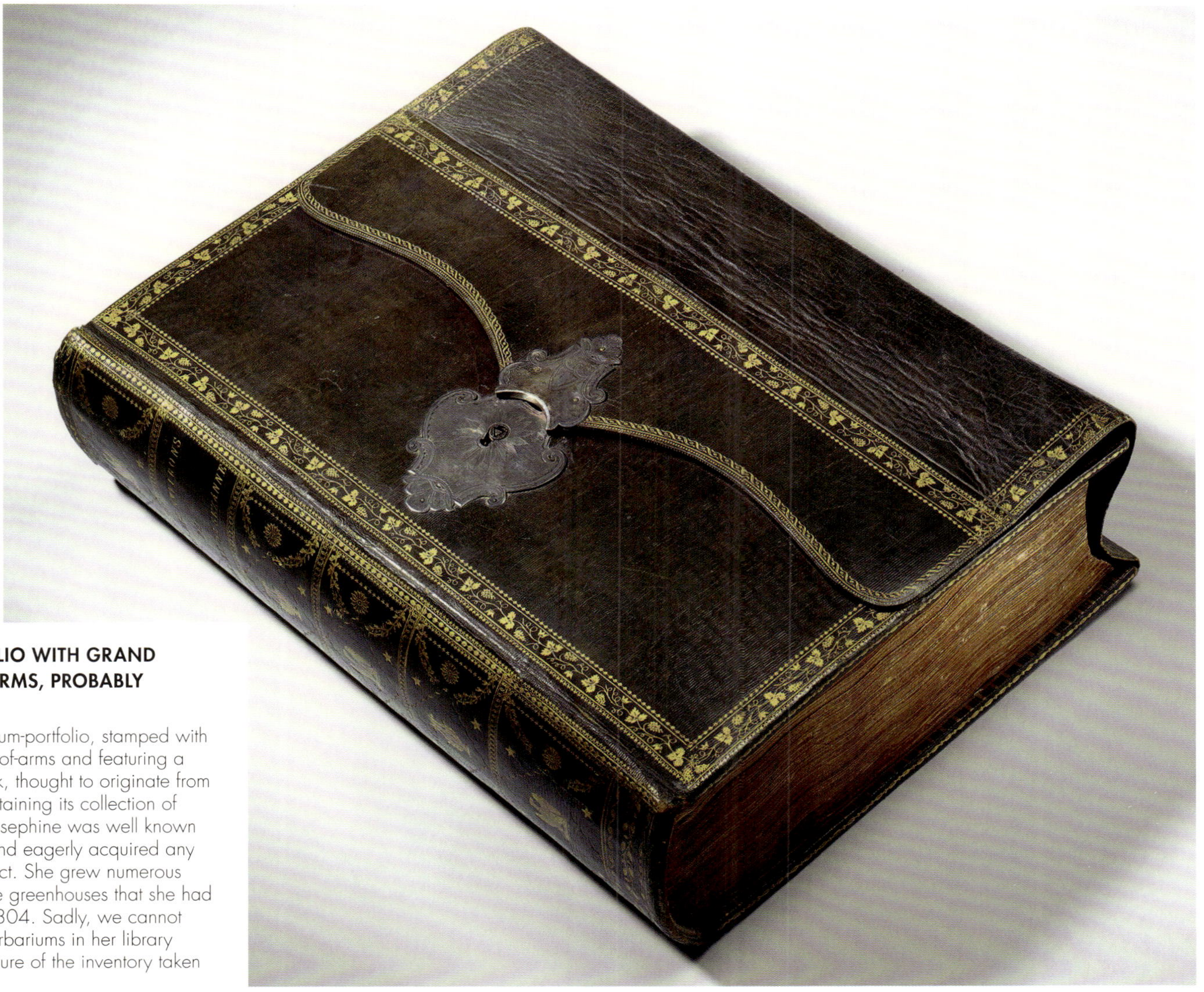

HERBARIUM-PORTFOLIO WITH GRAND IMPERIAL COAT-OF-ARMS, PROBABLY FROM MALMAISON

Morocco-bound herbarium-portfolio, stamped with the grand imperial coat-of-arms and featuring a richly chiseled silver lock, thought to originate from Malmaison and still containing its collection of carefully dried plants. Josephine was well known for her love of botany and eagerly acquired any new books on the subject. She grew numerous flowers and plants in the greenhouses that she had built at Malmaison in 1804. Sadly, we cannot be sure that she kept herbariums in her library due to the imprecise nature of the inventory taken after her death.

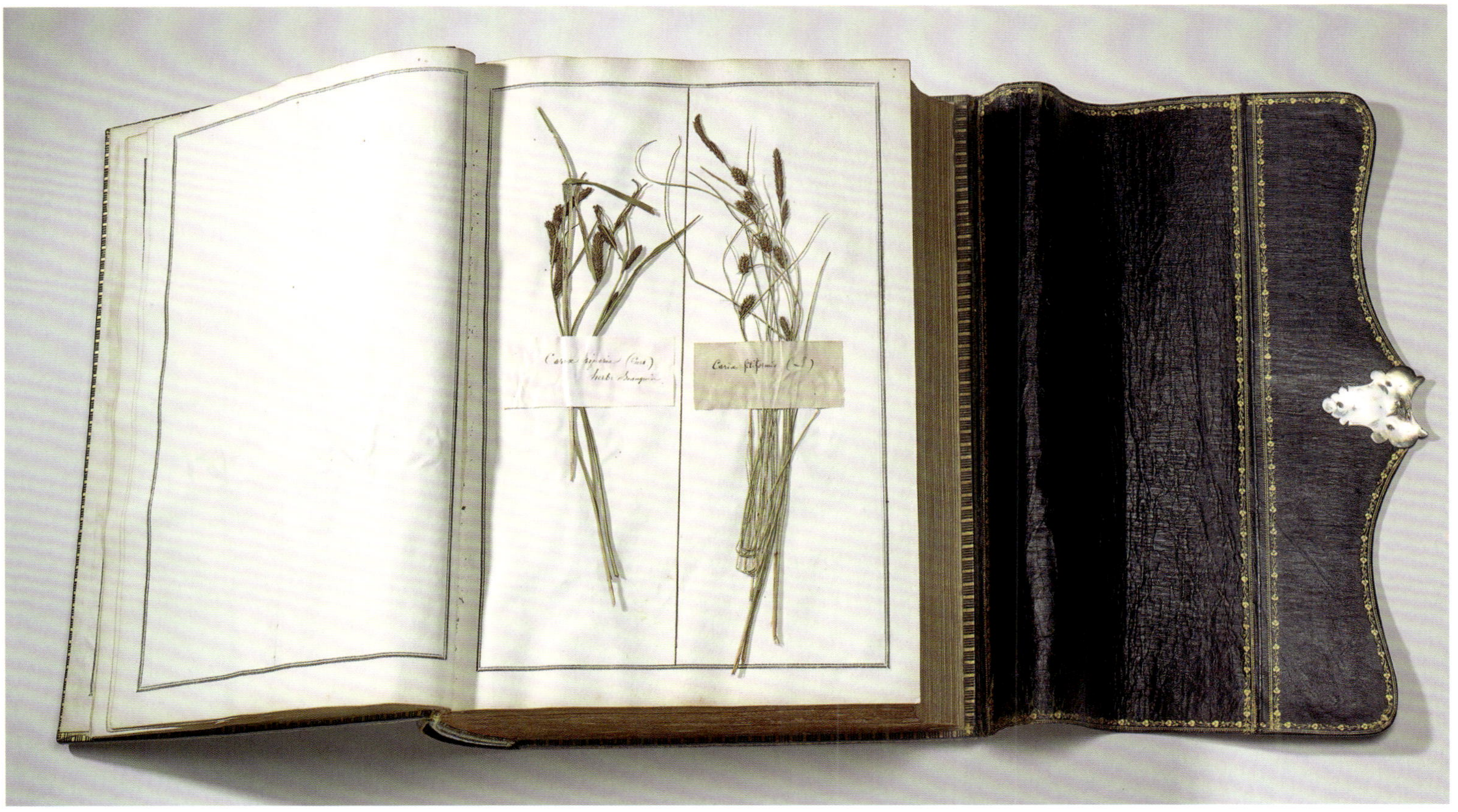

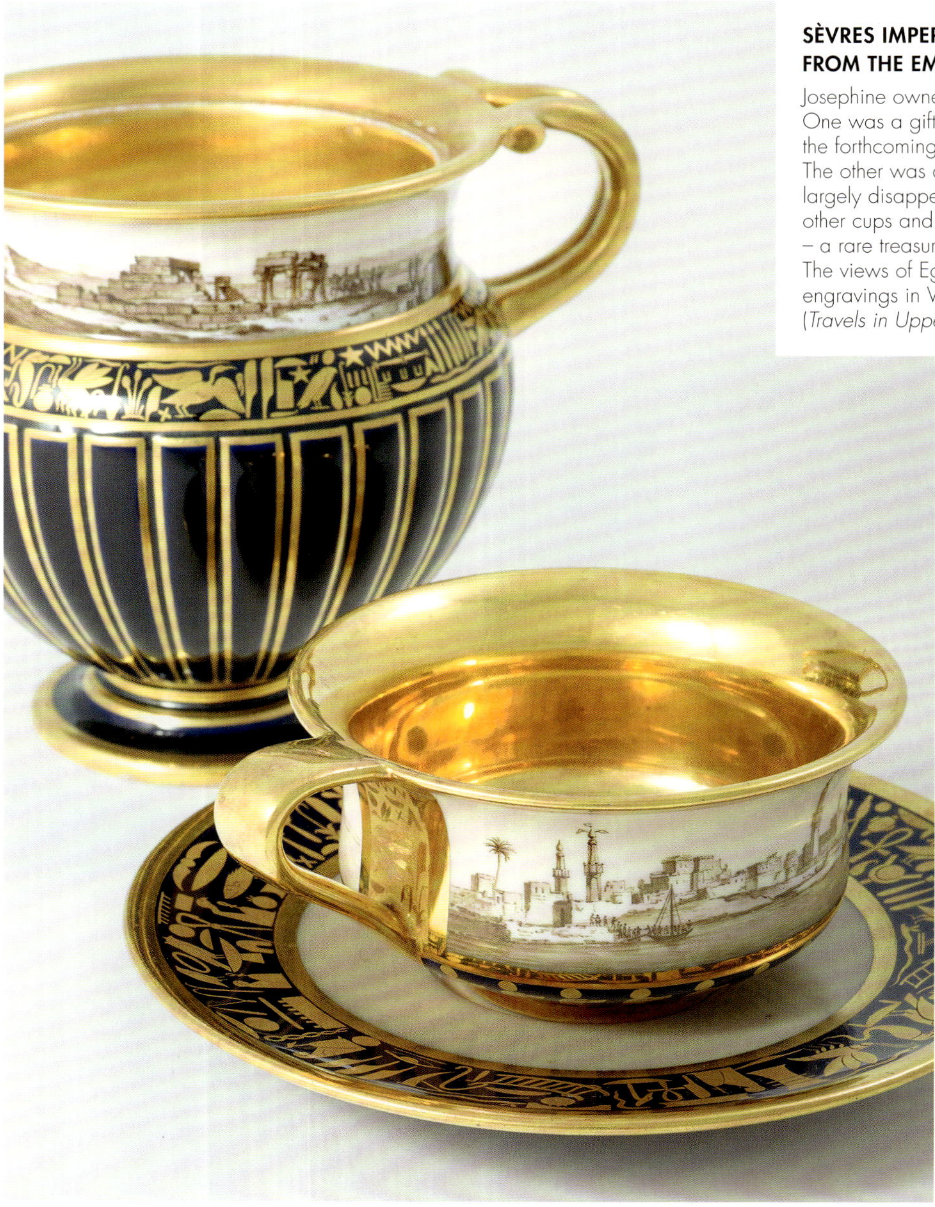

SÈVRES IMPERIAL MANUFACTORY, TEACUP, SAUCER AND SUGAR BOWL FROM THE EMPRESS JOSEPHINE'S EGYPTIAN CABARET SET

Josephine owned two Egyptian "cabaret" sets by the Sèvres Manufactory. One was a gift from the Emperor on 29 December 1808 to celebrate the forthcoming New Year, now part of the Musée de Malmaison collection. The other was delivered on 31 October 1811, after the divorce, and has largely disappeared. This teacup and saucer and matching sugar bowl plus nine other cups and saucers and a teapot now belong to the Fondation Napoléon – a rare treasure, widely considered to be a masterpiece of Sèvres porcelain. The views of Egypt were painted in 1810 by Nicolas-Antoine Lebel after the engravings in Vivant Denon's book, *Voyage dans la Basse et la Haute-Egypte* (*Travels in Upper and Lower Egypt*).

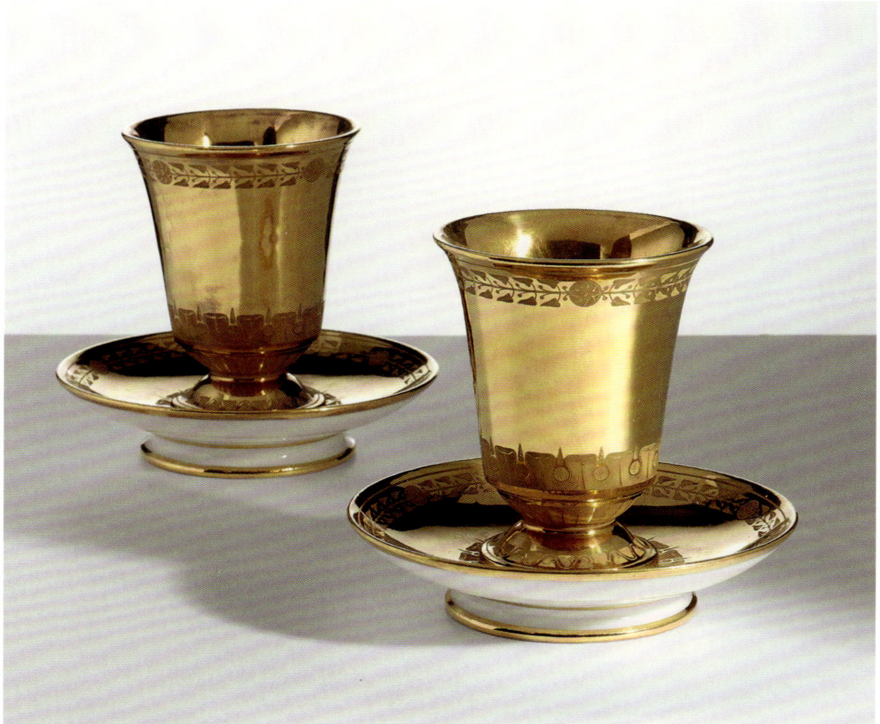

DIHL ET GUÉRHARD PORCELAIN FACTORY, PAIR OF *TASSES À MOUSSE* FROM THE EMPRESS JOSEPHINE'S DINNER SERVICE

In 1813 Dihl et Guérhard made a series of 18 "mousse cups" with saucers, costing 60 francs a piece, to complement the *service riche* (rich dinner service) previously commissioned by the Empress Josephine. The factory specialized in a process called *dorure en plein* (overall gilding) that gave the impression of vermeil.

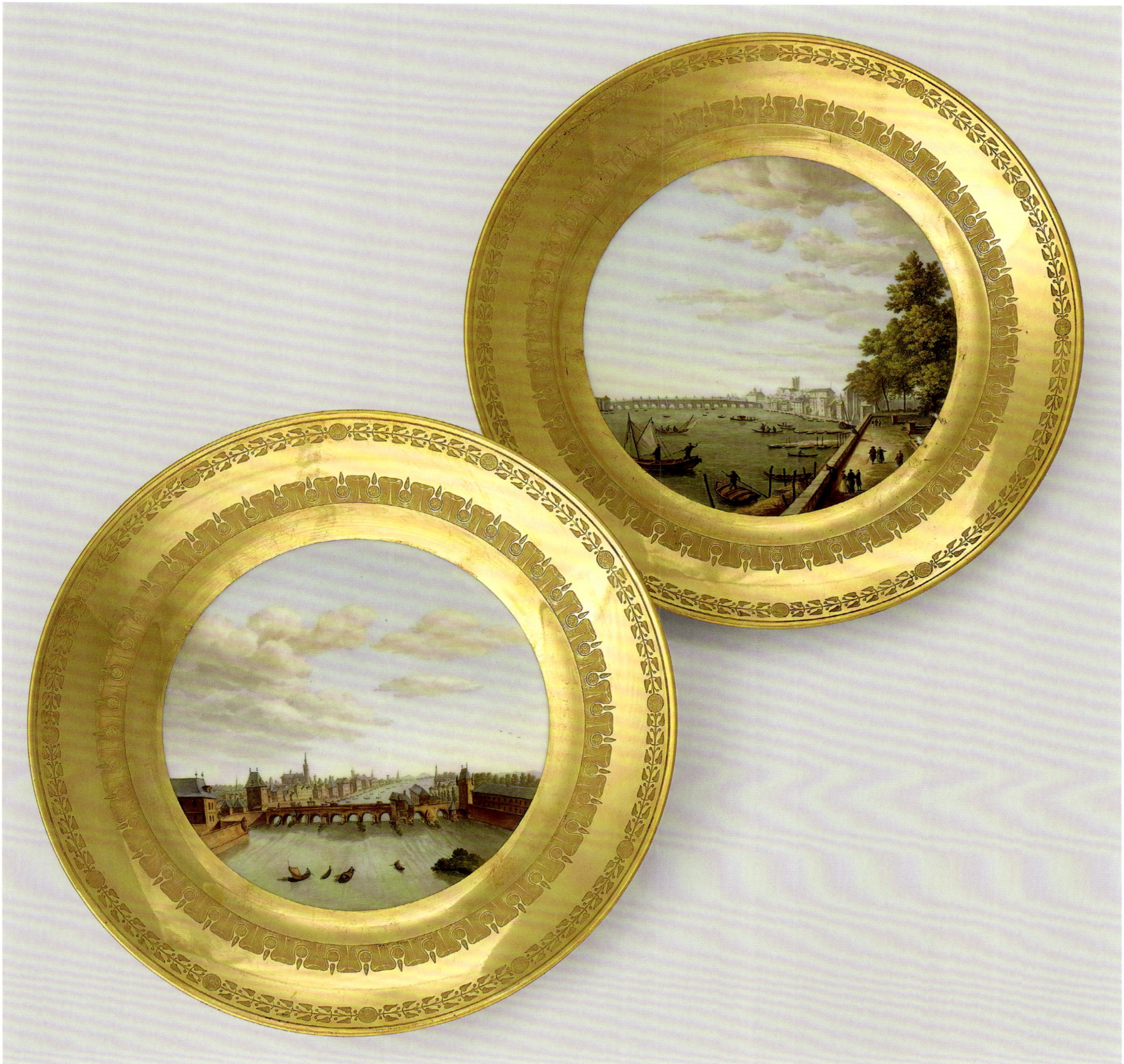

DIHL ET GUÉRHARD PORCELAIN FACTORY, PLATES FROM THE DINNER SERVICE OF THE EMPRESS JOSEPHINE OR THE PRINCE EUGÈNE

After their divorce, Napoleon gave Josephine 30,000 francs to commission a 213-piece porcelain dinner service from the Parisian manufacturer Dihl et Guérhard. The set was delivered somewhere between May and June 1811, further pieces being added in 1812 and 1813, and included 80 pictorial plates (*fonds à tableaux*). Josephine's son Prince Eugène commissioned a similar albeit smaller dinner service comprising 48 pictorial plates. The two sets were amalgamated into one after the Empress' death – hence the confusion over the original owner. Thirty-two pictorial plates are now preserved at the Musée de l'Ermitage, plus another 40 at the Musée de Malmaison.
The two plates pictured here respectively feature a "View of the City of Frankfurt on the Mein" (sic) and a "View of Westminster and the New Bridge to the Northeast of Somerset Gardens, London".

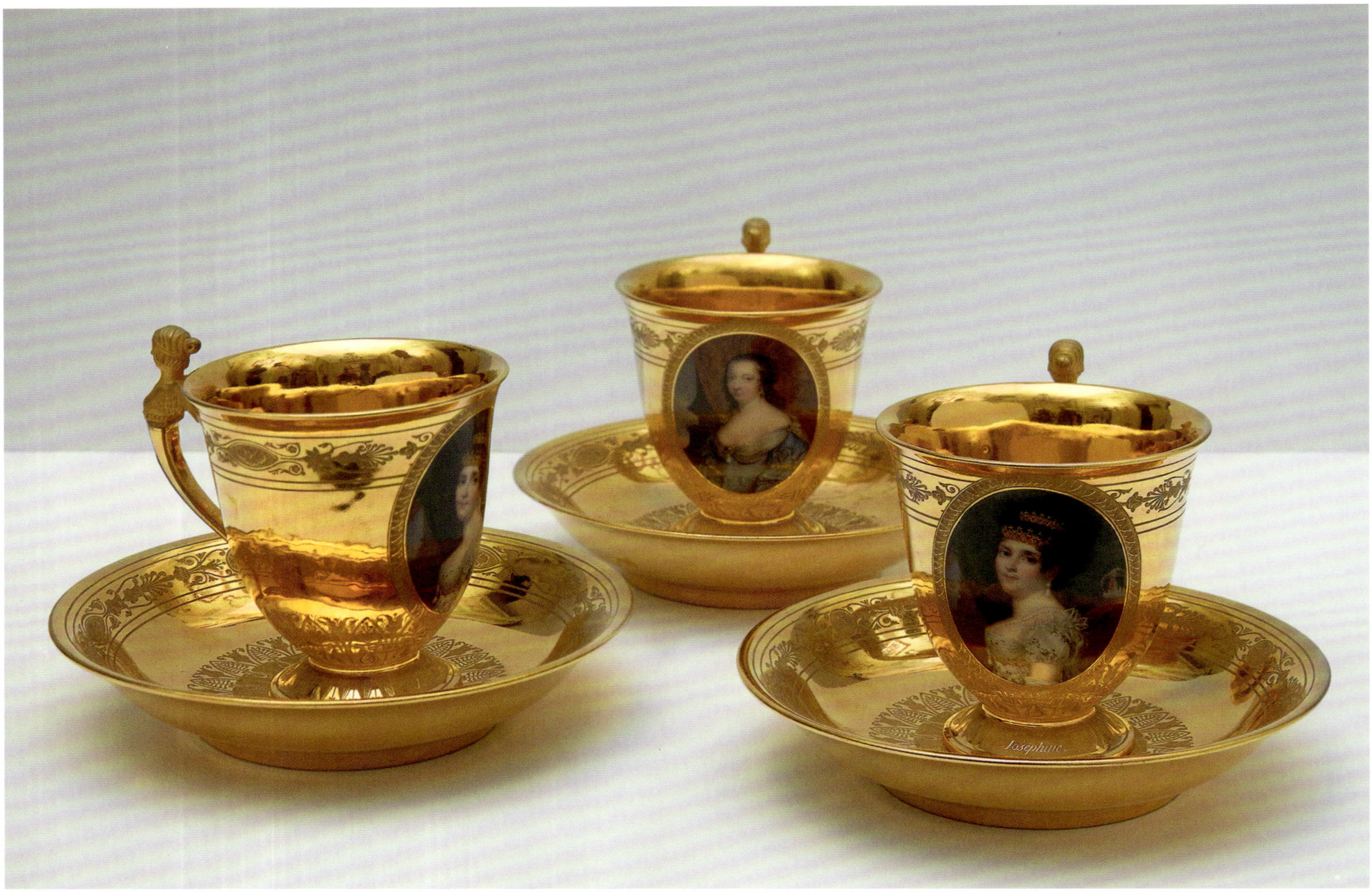

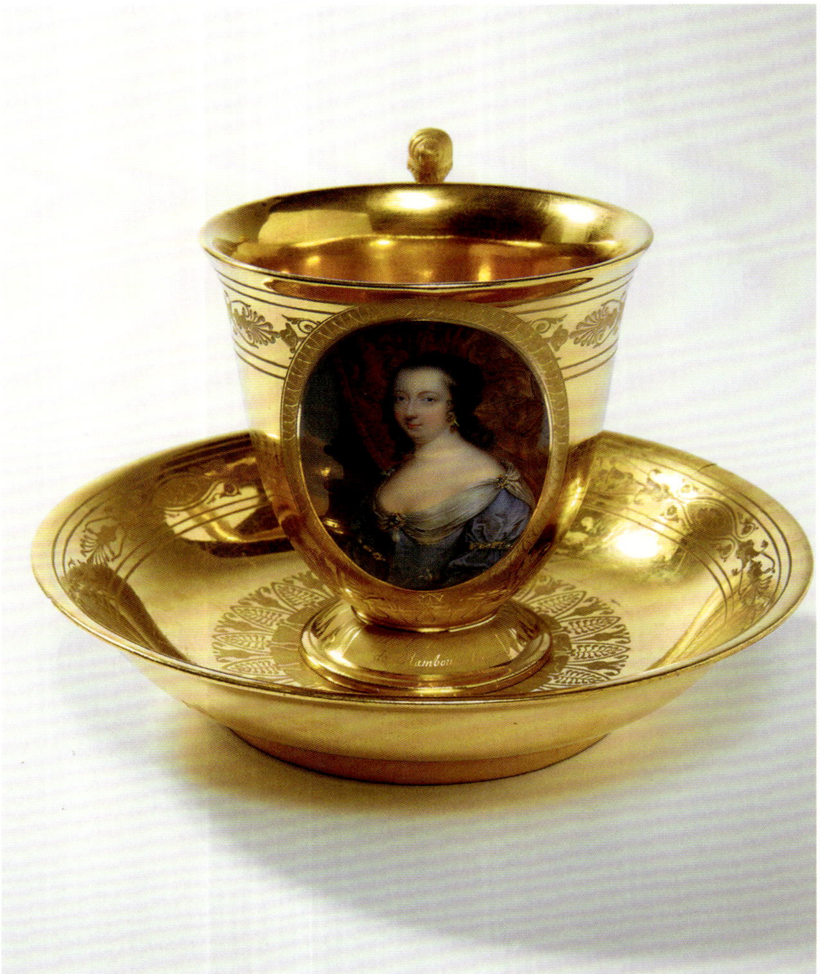

DIHL ET GUÉRHARD PORCELAIN FACTORY, LARGE CUP WITH PORTRAIT OF MADAME DE RAMBOUILLET

This cup belongs to a set commissioned by Empress Josephine from Parisian manufactory Dihl et Guérhard. After their divorce, Napoleon granted credit terms to the Empress, which she used to commission a dinner service from this Parisian manufactory that was in competition with Sèvres. Most of the plates from this dinner service are now preserved at the Hermitage in St Petersburg after having passed out of Josephine's estate. Prince Eugène had a similar dinner service, which had been amalgamated with his mother's.

This cup can be compared to cups with portraits of Madame de Grignan and Marie-Therese of Austria, produced by the Sèvres manufactory and supplied in 1818 for King Louis XVIII's nephew.

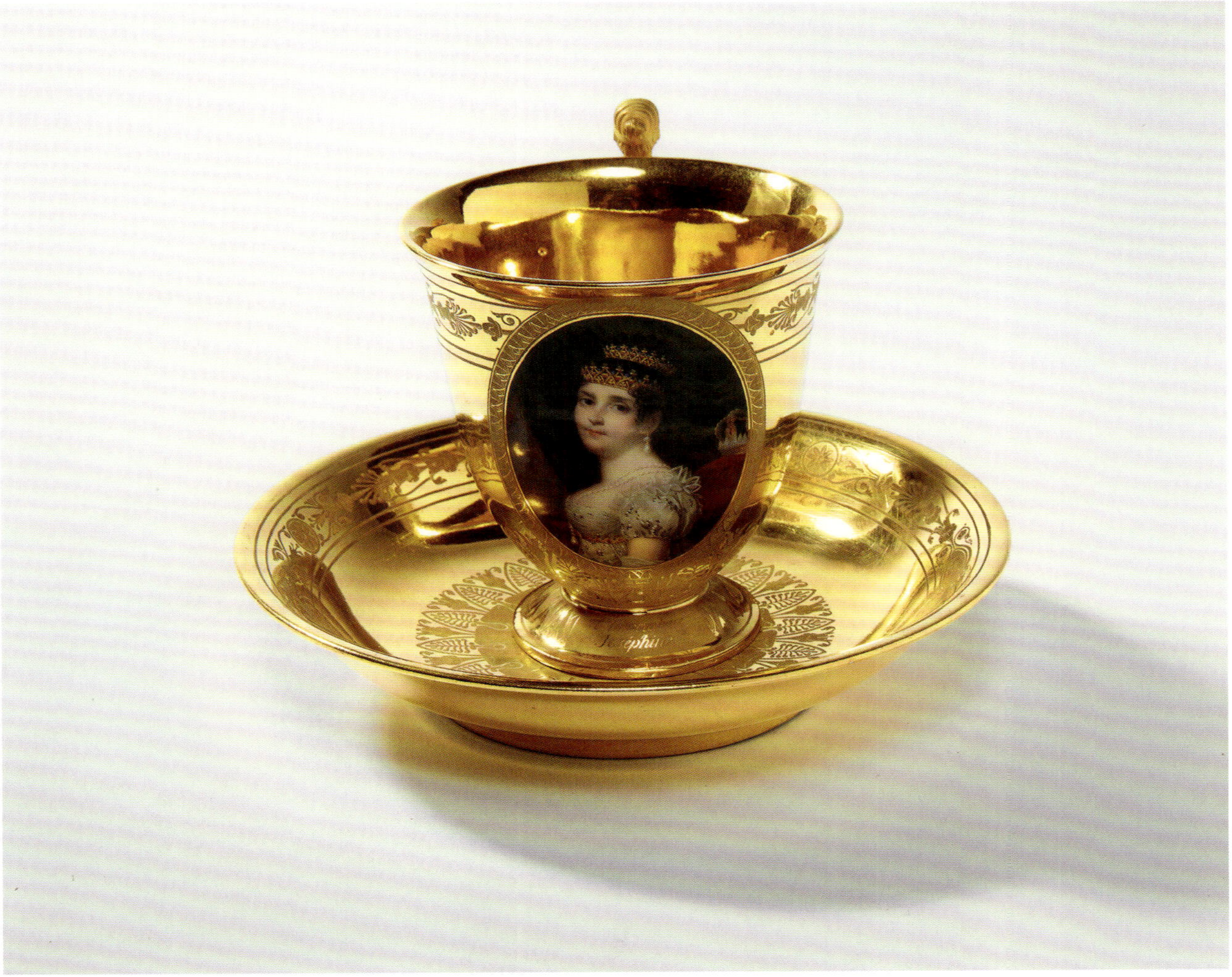

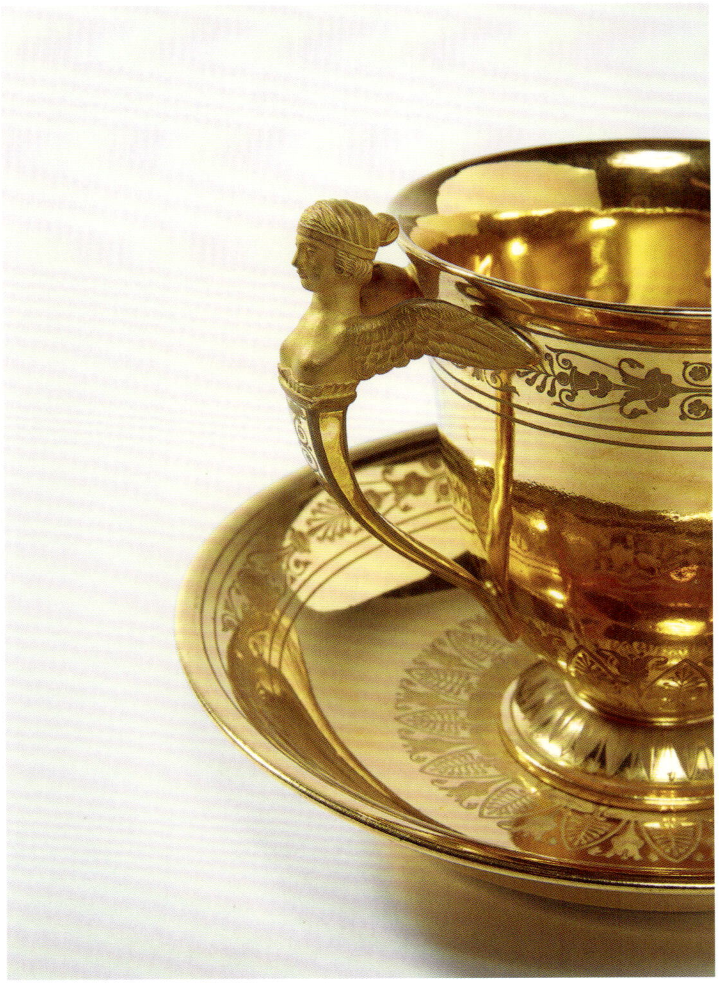

DIHL ET GUÉRHARD PORCELAIN FACTORY, LARGE CUP WITH PORTRAIT OF JOSEPHINE

In her memoirs, Queen Hortense recounted that Napoleon once mentioned how he had no portrait of the Empress. Hortense therefore gave him a cup with a portrait of her mother, after Italian painter Paolo-Ferdinando Quaglia (1780-1853). A perfect illustration of this anecdote, the portrait on this cup is inspired by a miniature executed by Quaglia, which is now held in the Musée Jacquemart-André collections in Paris. The painter settled in Paris around 1805 and entered the Empress Josephine's service. As his patron, she gave him the opportunity to paint portraits of the imperial family, including Napoleon himself. The collection holds two identical cups.

PIERRE-DOMINIQUE MAIRE (1763-1827), WRITING SET IN MOTHER-OF-PEARL AND GOLD, BELONGED TO GENERAL DECAEN, PROBABLY A GIFT FROM JOSEPHINE

This unique and opulent traveling writing set is shaped like an envelope, protected within an outer case. When it opens up, the flap that serves as a writing surface reveals a selection of items including crystal bottles and delicate writing implements, finely crafted in mother-of-pearl and gold. The lock of the travel case bears the manufacturer's mark "Maire fabricant de nécessaires, rue St Honoré n°154". He had probably drafted in the expertise of a craftsman specializing in faceted steel, such as Reynard Schey, a well-known manufacturer located in Rue du Faubourg Saint-Denis who was recognized for high-quality workmanship. This case is considered among the masterpieces of Biennais' chief competitor. It belonged to General Charles Mathieu Isidore Decaen (1769-1832), "Administrateur des Colonies Orientales" from 1803 to 1811, and bears his initials CD on the flap. He is believed to have received it from the Empress herself as a wedding gift. He was close to Josephine and in March 1808 he had brought a female orangutan over from the Indies for his Malmaison residence – the first of its species to reach France alive.

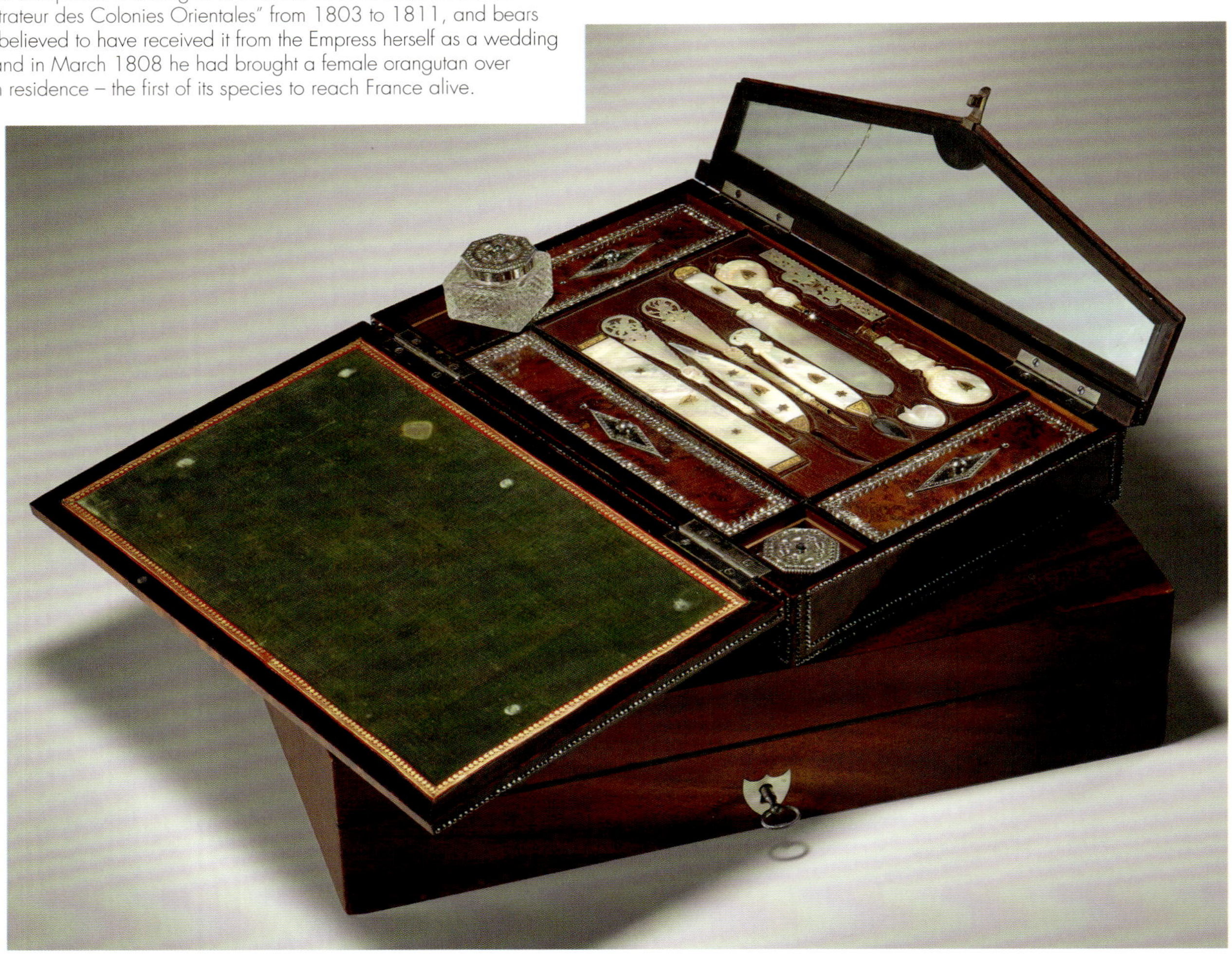

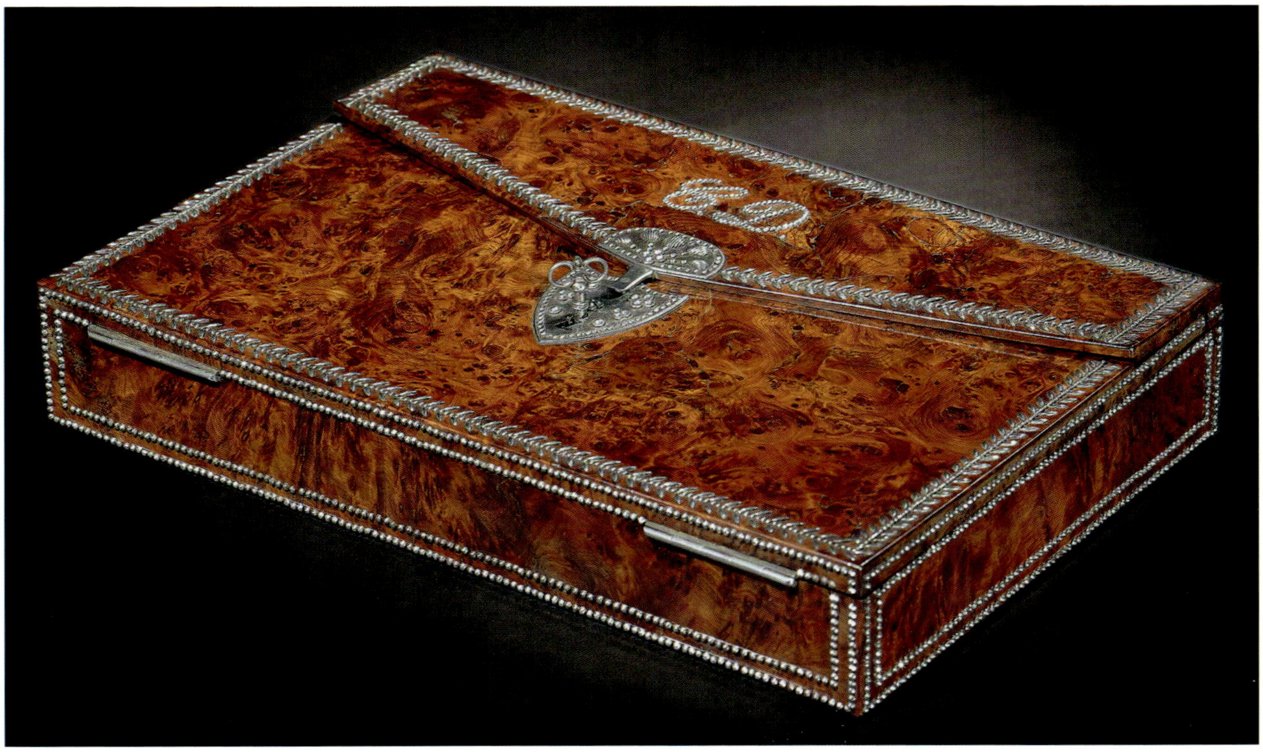

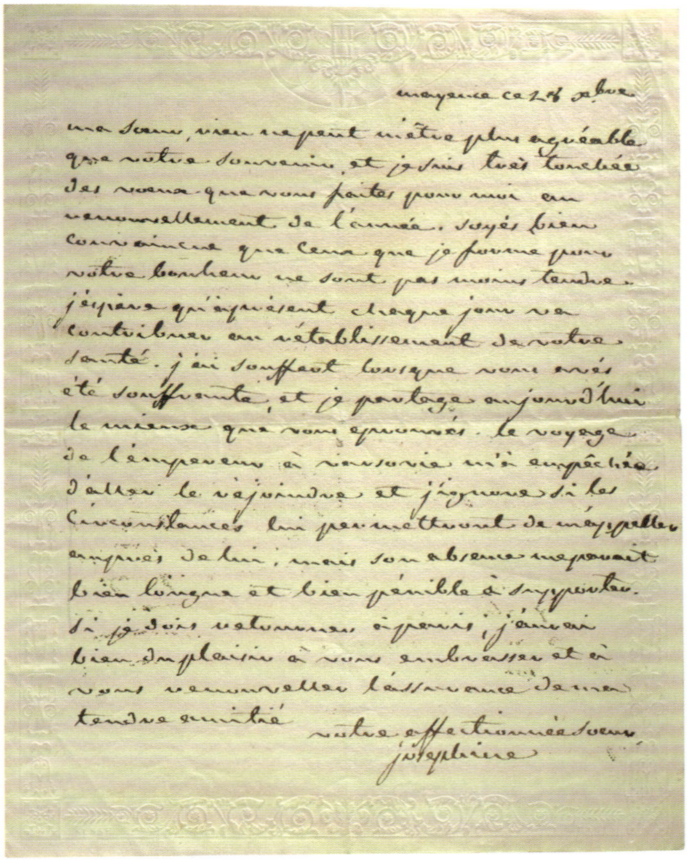

mayence ce 28 xbre

ma sœur, rien ne peut m'être plus agréable que votre souvenir, et je suis très touchée des vœux que vous faites pour moi au renouvellement de l'année. soyés bien convaincue que ceux que je forme pour votre bonheur ne sont pas moins tendres. j'espère qu'aujourd'hui chaque jour va contribuer au rétablissement de votre santé. j'ai souffert lorsque vous avés été souffrante, et je partage aujourd'hui le mieux que vous éprouvés. le voyage de l'empereur à varsovie m'a empêchée d'aller le rejoindre et j'ignore si les circonstances lui permettront de m'appeller auprès de lui; mais son absence me paroit bien longue et bien pénible à supporter. si je dois retourner à paris, j'aurai bien du plaisir à vous embrasser et à vous renouveller l'assurance de ma tendre amitié

votre affectionnée sœur
joséphine

LETTER FROM JOSEPHINE TO PAULINE BONAPARTE

"Sister, nothing could be more pleasant to me than my memories of you…" These words penned by Josephine to Pauline do not give a true picture of the chilly relations that reigned between the Empress and Napoleon's sisters. Although the sisters-in-law corresponded to exchange New Years wishes, an iciness can be read between the lines of apparently affectionate letters like this one dated 28 December 1806.

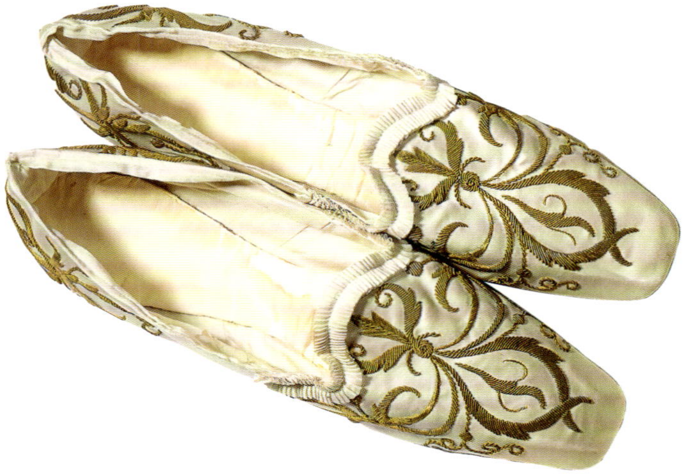

AUGUSTIN-FRANÇOIS-ANDRÉ PICOT (1786-1868), PAIR OF SLIPPERS ATTRIBUTED TO JOSEPHINE OR QUEEN HORTENSE

Hortense had the same shoe size as her mother and inherited her wardrobe when she died, so it's hard to know who owned what. Leather-soled satin slippers like these were extremely fragile, designed to glide over parquet floors and to wear at balls, not at all suitable for outdoor use. Their satin uppers and the opulence of the embroidery suggest illustrious provenance, confirming that they belonged to the imperial family. The boot-maker Cop was one of the principal suppliers of such footwear.

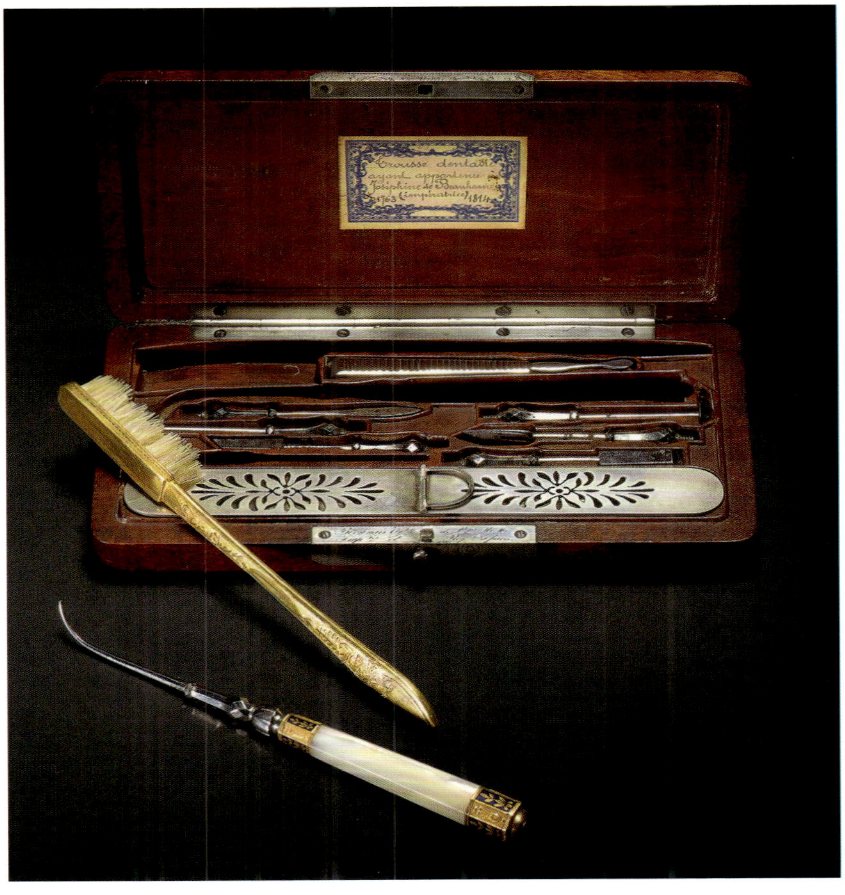

MARTIN-GUILLAUME BIENNAIS (1764-1843), SMALL DENTAL SURGERY *NÉCESSAIRE* BELONGING TO THE EMPRESS JOSEPHINE

Josephine had very bad teeth, probably due to having chewed sugar cane as a child. Like Napoleon she owned a dental *nécessaire* (kit) mainly composed of scaling instruments – such as this one, which to judge by the original label very probably belonged to her. It is apparently one-of-a-kind, packaged in a convenient pocket-size format for an Empress who was meticulous about good oral hygiene. The kit is beautifully made and inscribed "Biennais Orfèvre de L.L. M.M. Imples et Royales à Paris," so postdates Napoleon's coronation as King of Italy in 1805.

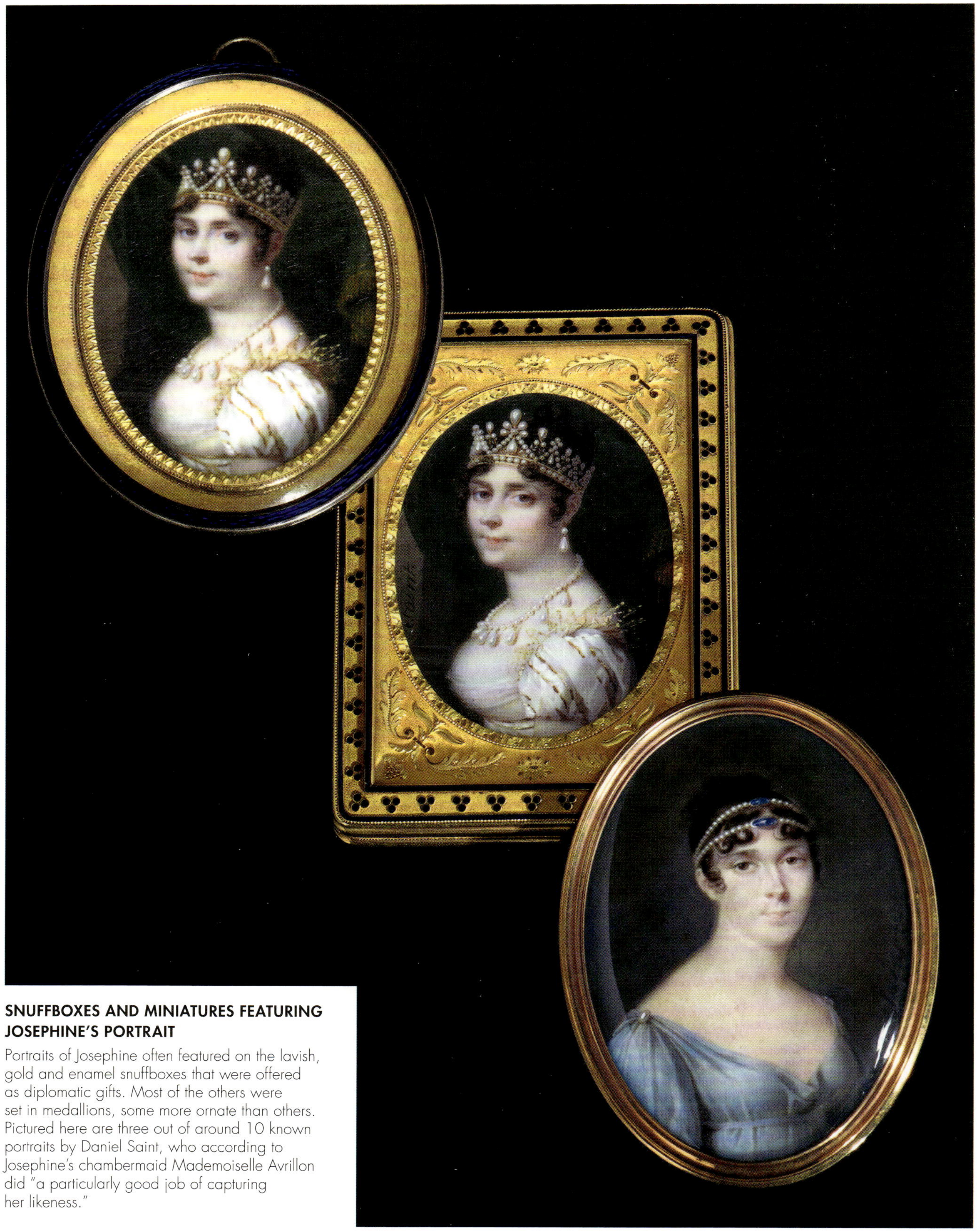

SNUFFBOXES AND MINIATURES FEATURING JOSEPHINE'S PORTRAIT

Portraits of Josephine often featured on the lavish, gold and enamel snuffboxes that were offered as diplomatic gifts. Most of the others were set in medallions, some more ornate than others. Pictured here are three out of around 10 known portraits by Daniel Saint, who according to Josephine's chambermaid Mademoiselle Avrillon did "a particularly good job of capturing her likeness."

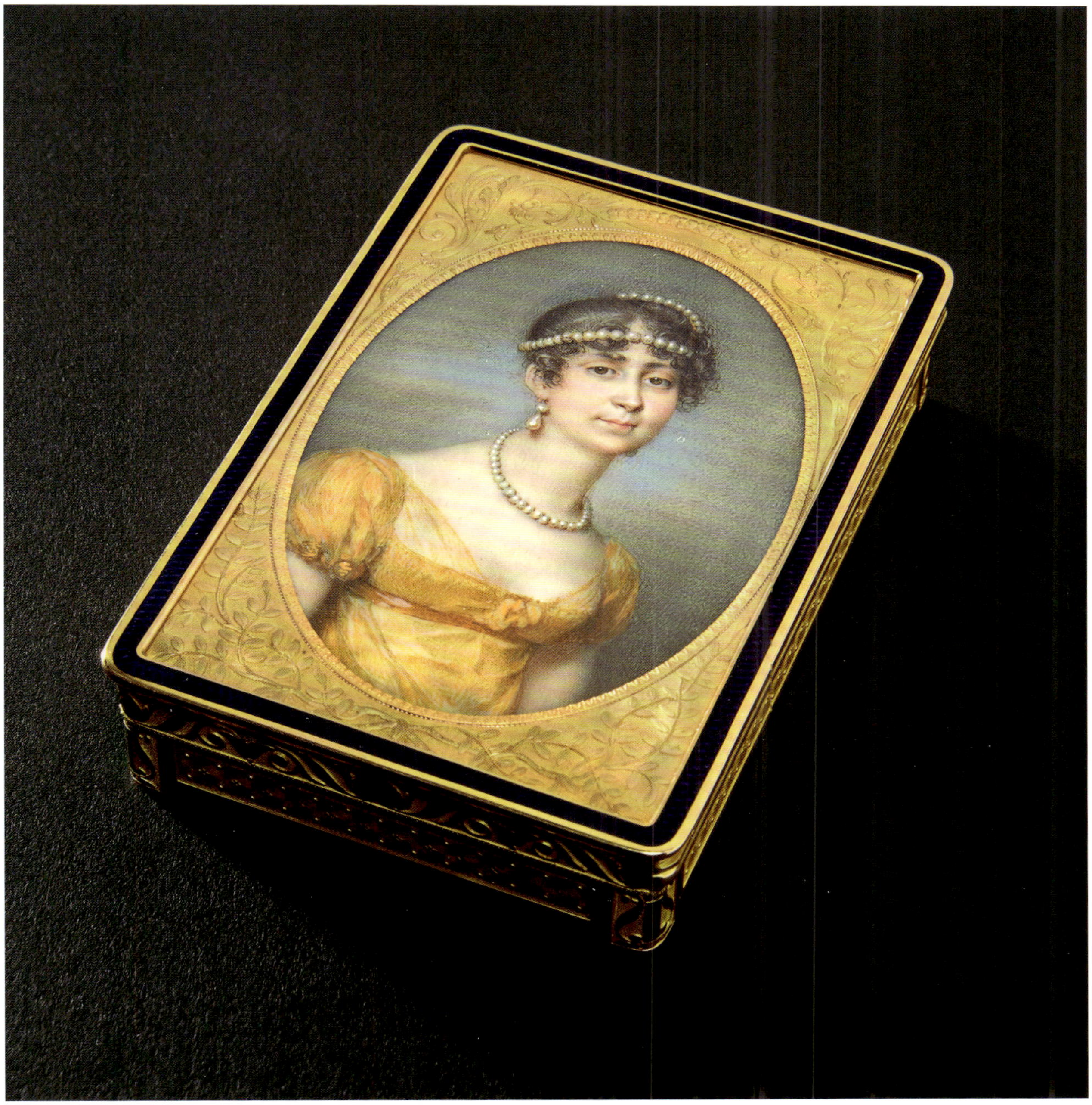

MARIE-ETIENNE NITOT (1750-1809), GOLD SNUFFBOX WITH PORTRAIT OF JOSEPHINE, GIVEN TO THE COMTE DE BÉARN

This stunning gold box with Josephine's portrait illustrates what opulent official gifts the Empress gave. It bears the name of the most talented and sought-after goldsmith in the whole Empire, "Etienne Nitot et fils joailliers bijoutiers de LL MM l'Impératrice, le Roi et la Reine de Westphalie à Paris". Nitot was responsible for crafting Napoleon's Consular Sword set with the magnificent 140-carat "Regent Diamond", the imperial sword, Pope Pius VII's papal tiara, and the wedding jewels of both Empresses Josephine and Marie-Louise. A dedication under the lid tells us about its provenance. "Given by HM Empress Josephine to Mr le Cte de Béarn". The Comte de Béarn (1771-1844) was Chamberlain to Napoleon in 1797, then to Josephine in 1809. He had married Pauline de Galard, the daughter of Madame de Tourzel (1771-1839), Governess to the Children of France who was imprisoned during the Revolution with Madame Royale, Louis XVI's daughter Marie-Thérèse-Charlotte. Snuffboxes by jewelers Nitot – now Chaumet – are exceptionally rare. This one is of even greater historical significance because it bears the only known example of this very realistic and informal portrait of Josephine on its lid. From 2006 to 2008, this box was on loan to the Louvre Museum and exhibited there.

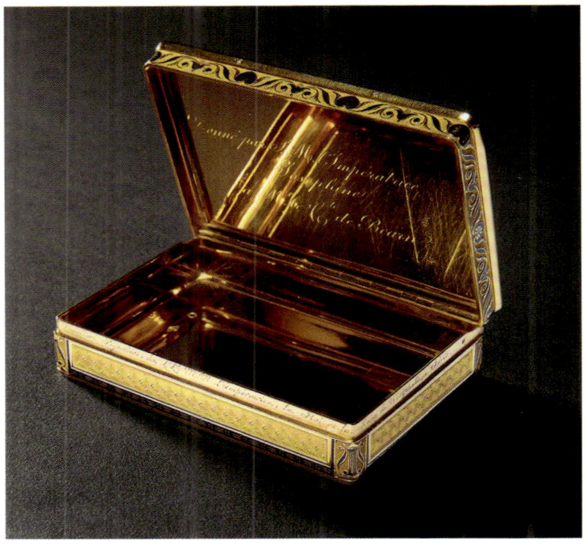

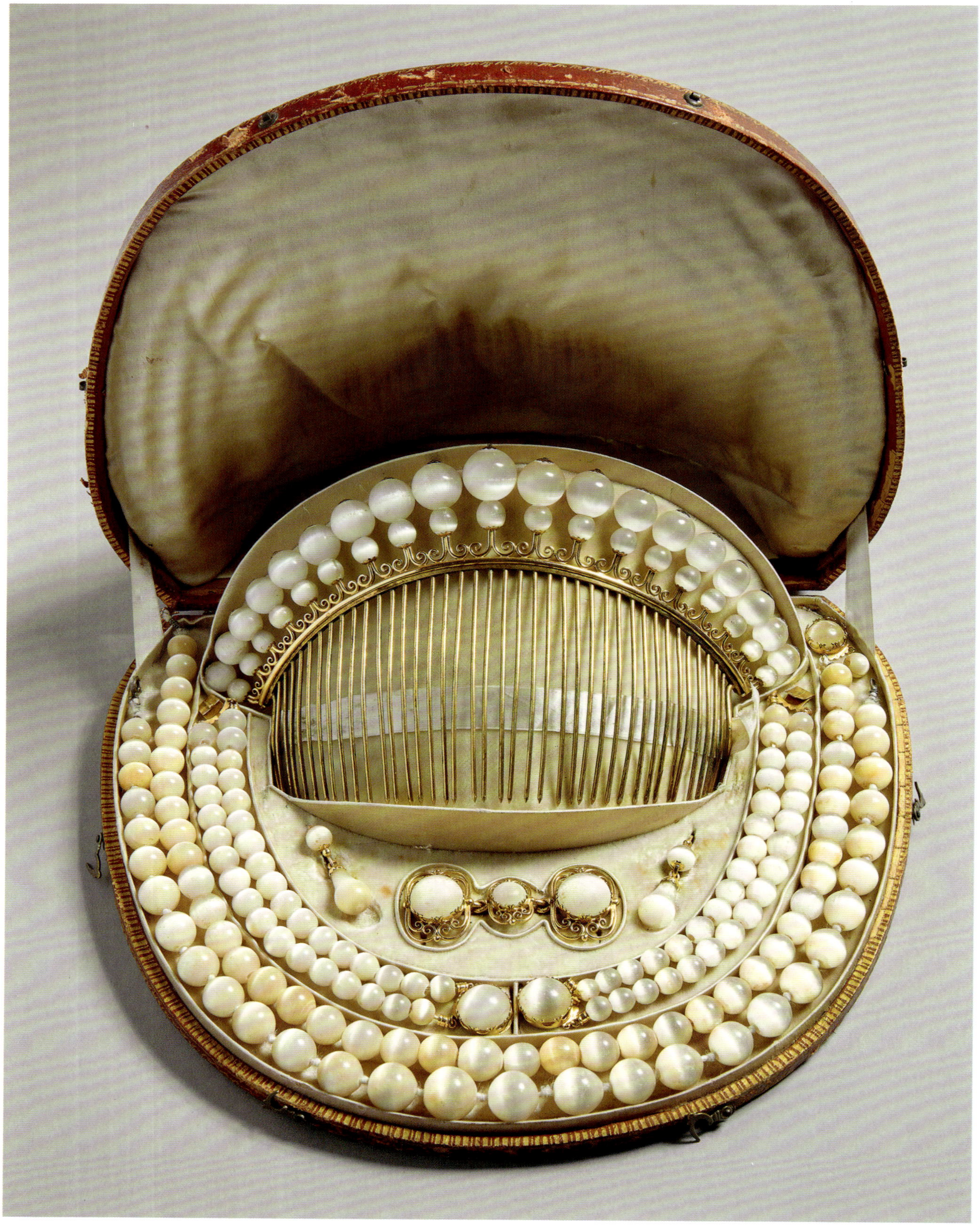

GYPSUM PEARL JEWELRY SET

None of the Empress Josephine's jewelry sets has survived, and very few complete sets from that era still exist. Even the Château de la Malmaison only has empty jewelry cases in its collection, very similar to this one. These cases belonged to Josephine or Hortense and are always individually titled with names like "PARURE DE TURQUOISES" or "PARURE MALACHITES ENTOUREE DE PERLES". The case on display is of red Morocco leather and bears the gold-tooled inscription "PARURE CHATOYANTE". This name refers to the shimmering reflections of gypsum, also known as "plaster stone".
This neoclassical set in gypsum and gold probably dates from the end of the Empire or the beginning of the Restoration, and comprises a diadem, two necklaces, a pair of pendant earrings, a corsage pin, and a pair of two-row bracelets with gypsum clasps. The teeth of the vermeil comb are detachable. Its excellent quality means this set probably belonged to a lady of high status.

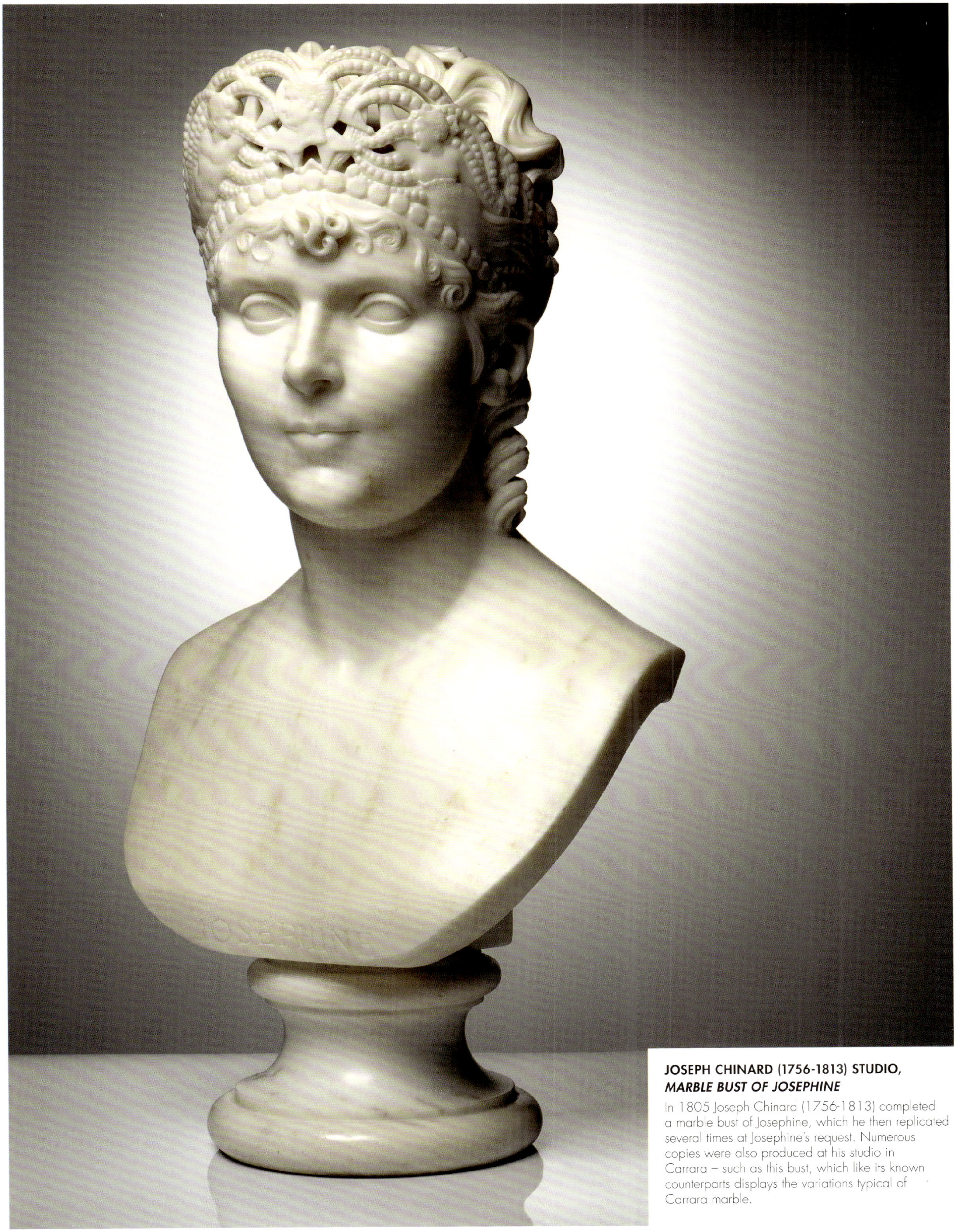

JOSEPH CHINARD (1756-1813) STUDIO,
MARBLE BUST OF JOSEPHINE

In 1805 Joseph Chinard (1756-1813) completed a marble bust of Josephine, which he then replicated several times at Josephine's request. Numerous copies were also produced at his studio in Carrara – such as this bust, which like its known counterparts displays the variations typical of Carrara marble.

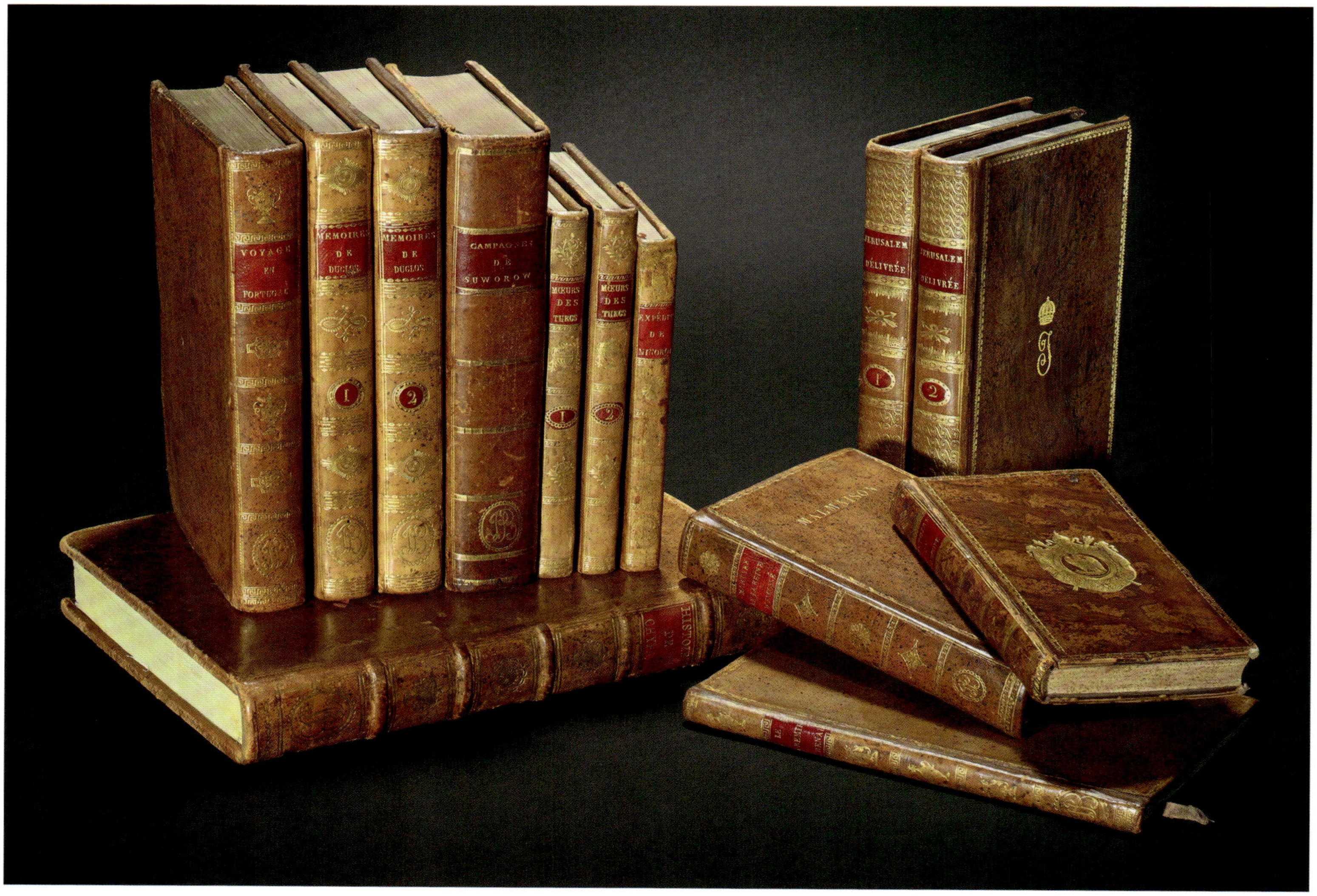

BOOKS FROM THE LIBRARY AT MALMAISON

The library at Malmaison was originally established by Bonaparte and mainly contained books bearing the monogram "BP" on the spine (composed of two superimposed letters for Bonaparte and La Pagerie). This fine collection of books with polished calfskin bindings shows how the library evolved thereafter: while the name "Malmaison" still appears on some of the books, others now display the crowned "J" of the Empress that Josephine added after the divorce.

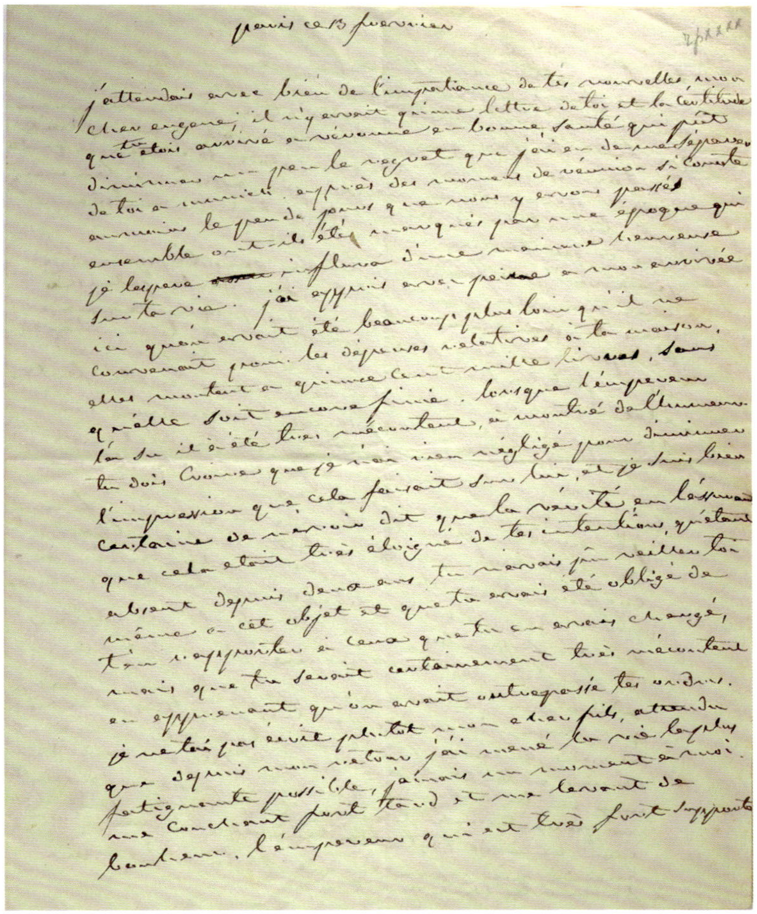 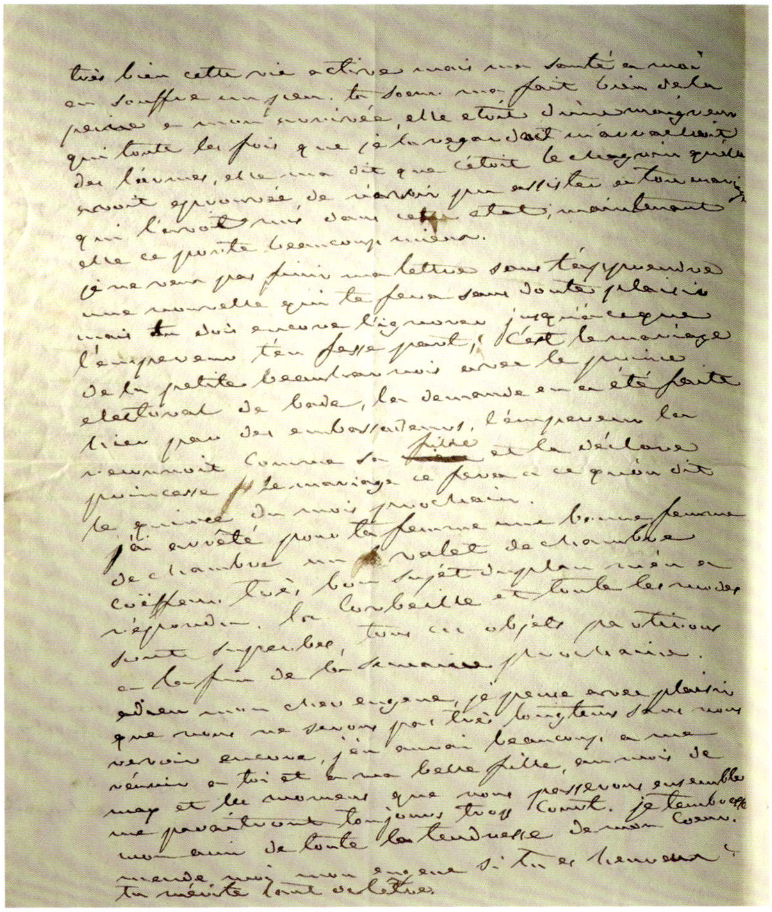

LETTER FROM JOSEPHINE TO HER SON EUGÈNE

Dated February 1806, this letter from Josephine to her son Prince Eugène shows how affectionate their relationship was. The Empress begins her letter "I was waiting to hear from you with great impatience, my dearest Eugène […]". Josephine goes on to reproach her son for his heavy spending on his house, and reports that it has put the Emperor in a bad mood. She also writes about her daughter Hortense and the marriage of Stéphanie de Beauharnais, which had just been announced.

LOUIS-BERTIN PARANT (1768-1751), RECTANGULAR BOX WITH PORTRAIT OF JOSEPHINE

Reproductions of antique cameos were a specialty of French artist Louis-Bertin Parant whose works frequently represented the Empress' profile, featured on small boxes and sword pommels alike.

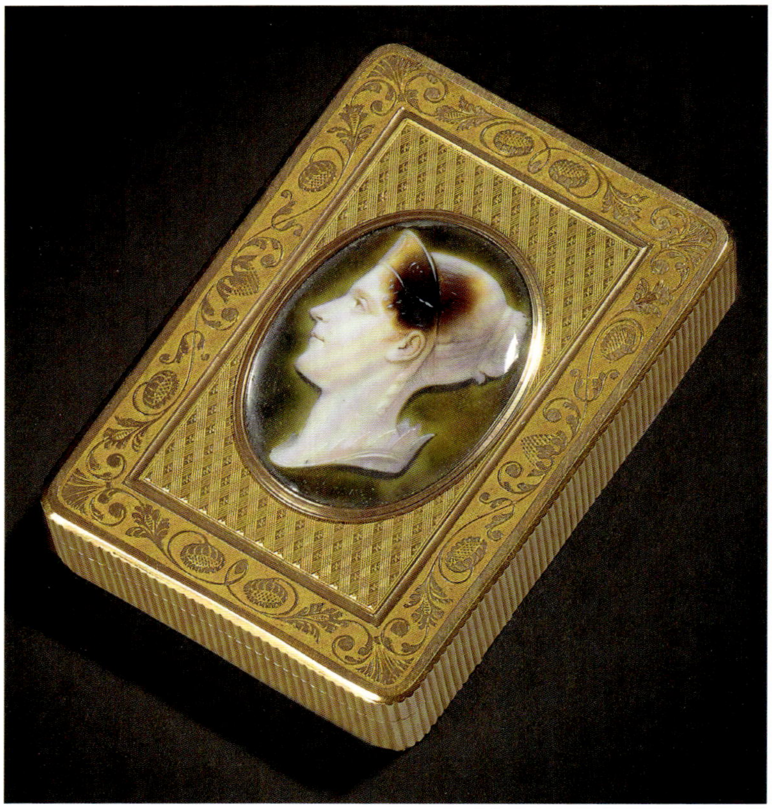

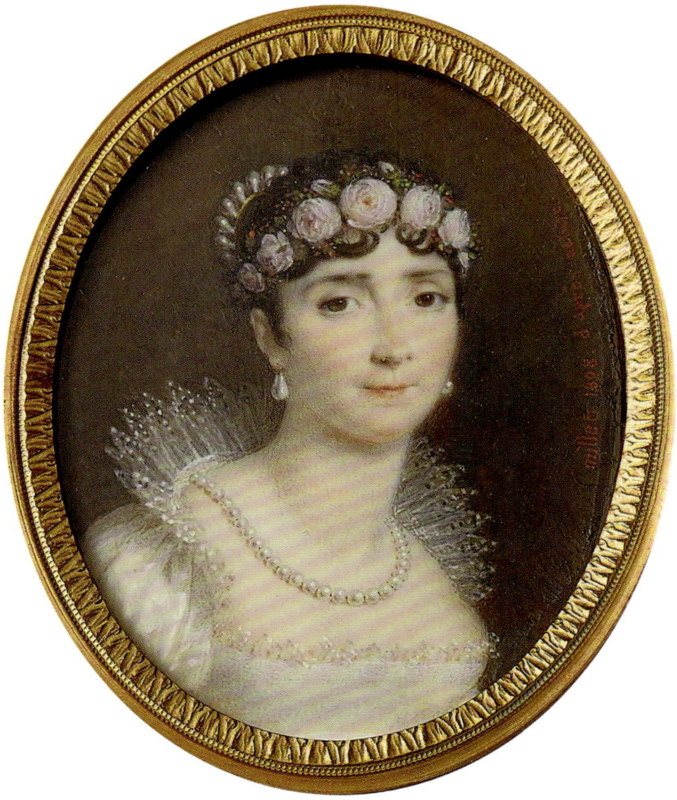

FRÉDÉRIC MILLET (1786-1859), *PORTRAIT OF JOSEPHINE PAINTED FROM LIFE*

Frédéric Millet (1786-1859) was one of the best French miniaturists of his time, and this portrait is certainly one of the finest ever executed of Josephine. It was painted from life in 1808 and though less official than the one by Saint is unique among any of the known representations of the Empress. She is shown wearing hardly any jewelry, her brow encircled by a crown of roses, not the grand diadem of pearls. The portrait's intimate nature and superlative craftsmanship suggest that it was destined for the sovereign.

AUGUSTIN-FRANÇOIS-ANDRÉ PICOT (1786-1868), FRAGMENT OF A GOWN ATTRIBUTED TO THE EMPRESS JOSEPHINE

Josephine's preferred couturier was Louis-Hippolyte Leroy – who knew better than anyone how to keep his prices high. An inventory taken of the Empress' wardrobe in 1809 lists no fewer than 49 grand court costumes and 676 gowns. They included shimmering confections in fine mesh tulle and silver and platinum lame – as illustrated here – that could cost thousands of francs. This large fragment comes from the collections of Marie Brocard, heir to the atelier of Their Majesties' official embroiderer, François-André Picot.

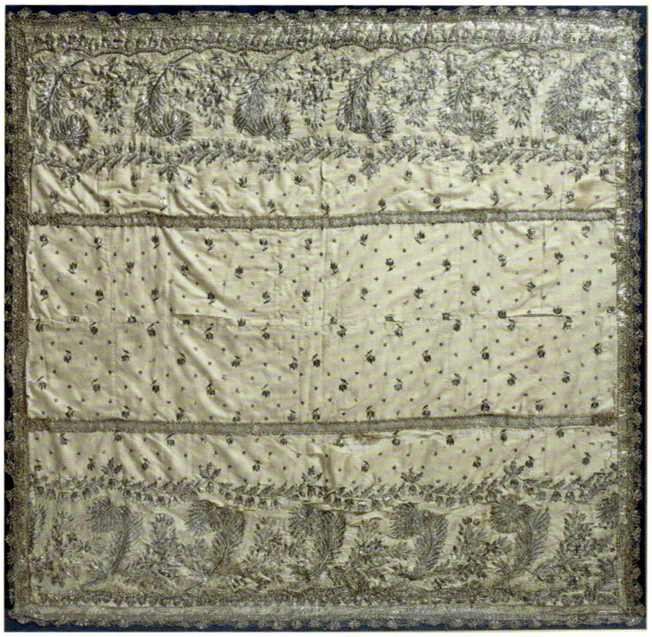

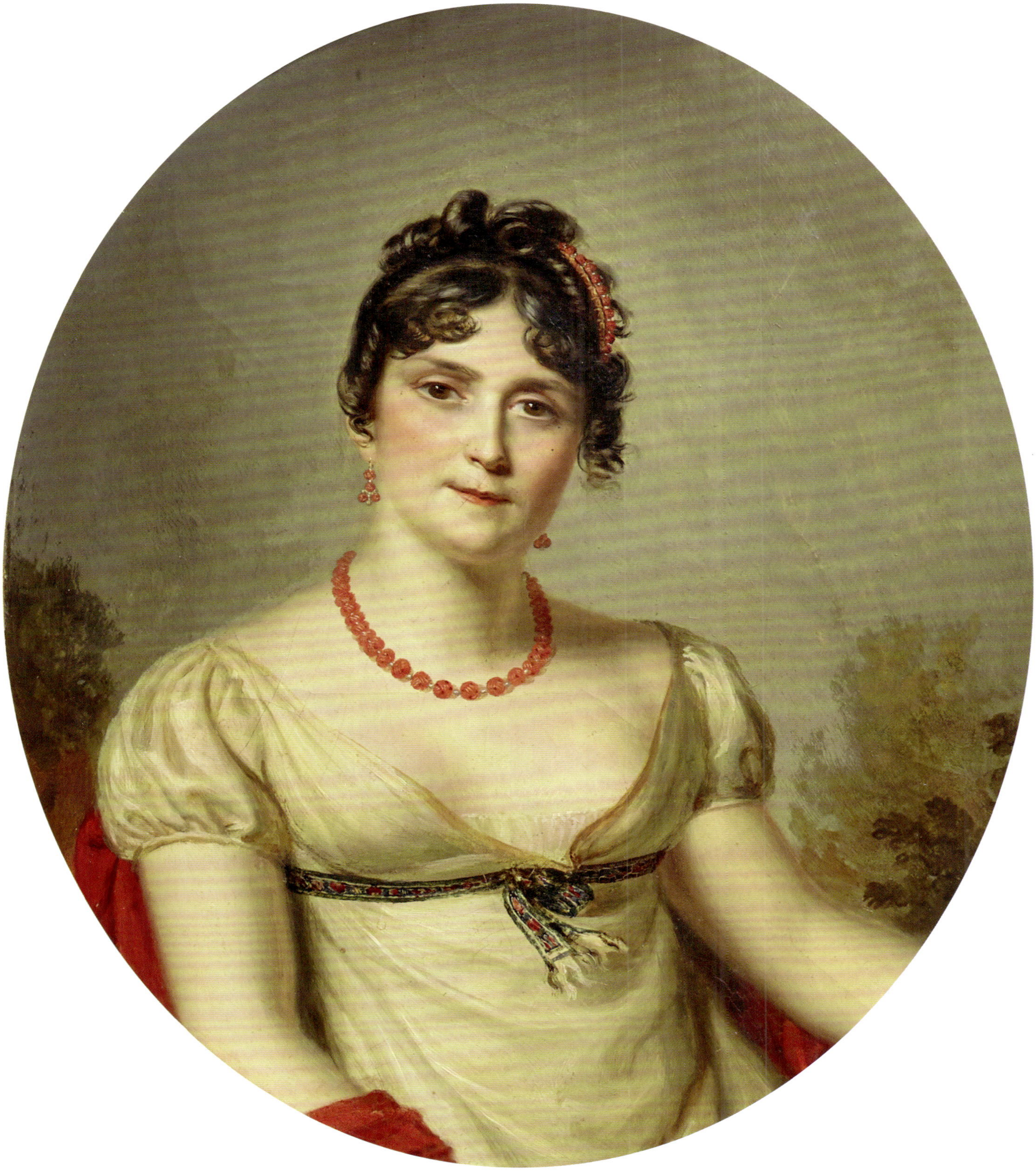

FIRMIN MASSOT (1766-1849), *PORTRAIT OF JOSEPHINE*

In 1812 Swiss portrait artist Firmin Massot was commissioned to paint a full-length portrait of Josephine while she was staying at Pregny. The portrait was executed in collaboration with fellow Swiss artist, the landscape specialist Wolfgang-Adam Töppfer (1766-1847), and so delighted Josephine that she commissioned 25 replicas with identical frames as gifts for family and friends. Four of those paintings have survived, including one at the Musée de Malmaison. The original work is held at the Hermitage Museum in St Petersburg.

MARIE-LOUISE

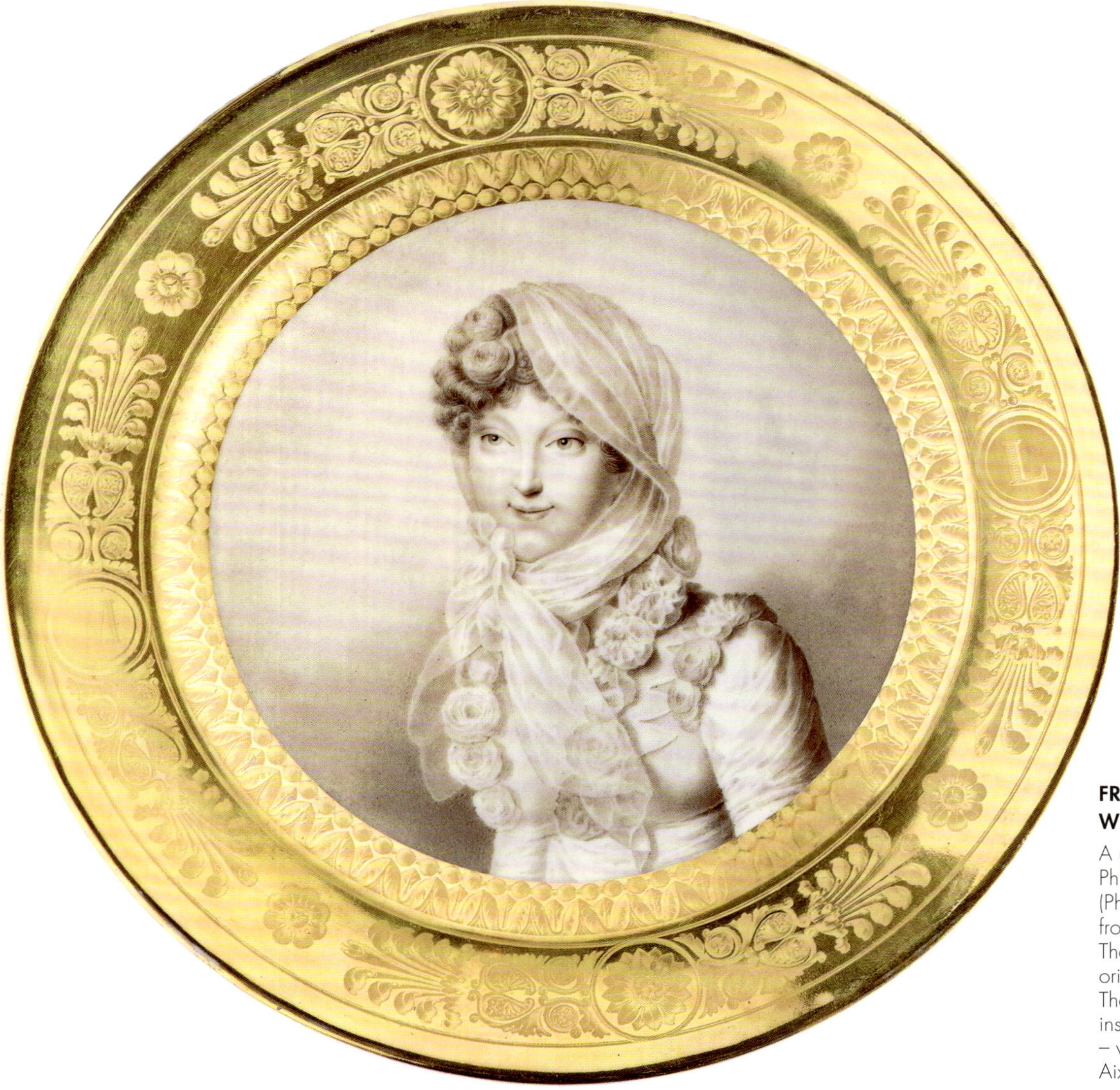

FRANÇOIS-PASCAL PHILIPPINE, PLATE WITH PORTRAIT OF MARIE-LOUISE

A unique porcelain plate by François-Pascal Philippine, known as "Philippine Aîné" (Philippine the Elder), who worked at Sèvres from 1778 to 1791 then 1802 to 1825. The image of Marie-Louise is based on an original by Isabey, framed by the initials "ML". The back of the plate is gold finished and inscribed "Paris le 20 Septembre 1814" – when the Empress was taking the waters at Aix-les-Bains with her future lover Neipperg.

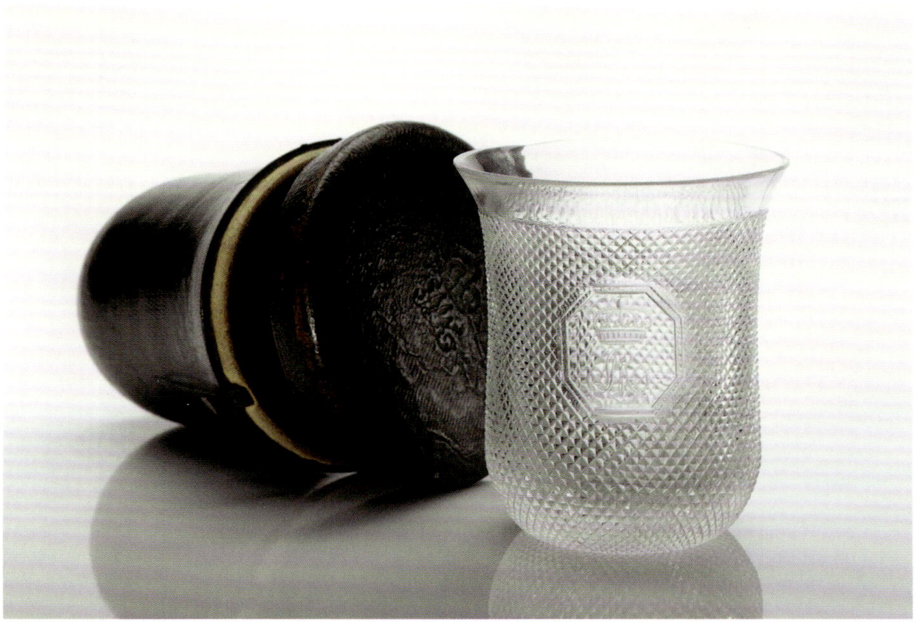

MARIE-LOUISE MONOGRAMMED GOBLET WITH TRAVEL CASE

Cristal goblet with Marie-Louise's monogram and leather travel case still intact, thought to originate from the Mont Cenis crystal works near Creusot – the foremost purveyor of crystal glassware to the imperial court, previously patronized by the Empress Josephine.

MARTIN-GUILLAUME BIENNAIS (1764-1843),
BUST OF EMPRESS MARIE-LOUISE

This small, gilded bronze bust set on a column shows Marie-Louise wearing a diadem, with her hair swept into a chignon. The base bears her initials underneath an imperial crown. It is also engraved with the mark of M-G Biennais "BIENNAIS, ORF[RE] DE LL MM IMP[LES] ET ROY[LES] A PARIS". This piece is one of only two known busts of the Empress executed by the goldsmith. It belongs to the "Napoléonides" series of portraits of members of the imperial family including the Emperor himself, Marie-Louise, Elisa, Pauline, Caroline, Louis, Jérôme, Hortense, Catherine de Wurtemberg and Murat. There were 28 pieces in total, including the wax models and most of the gilded bronze sculptures, which were intended as official gifts for members of the imperial family. The busts of Elisa Bonaparte and Catherine de Wurtemberg also form part of the collection.

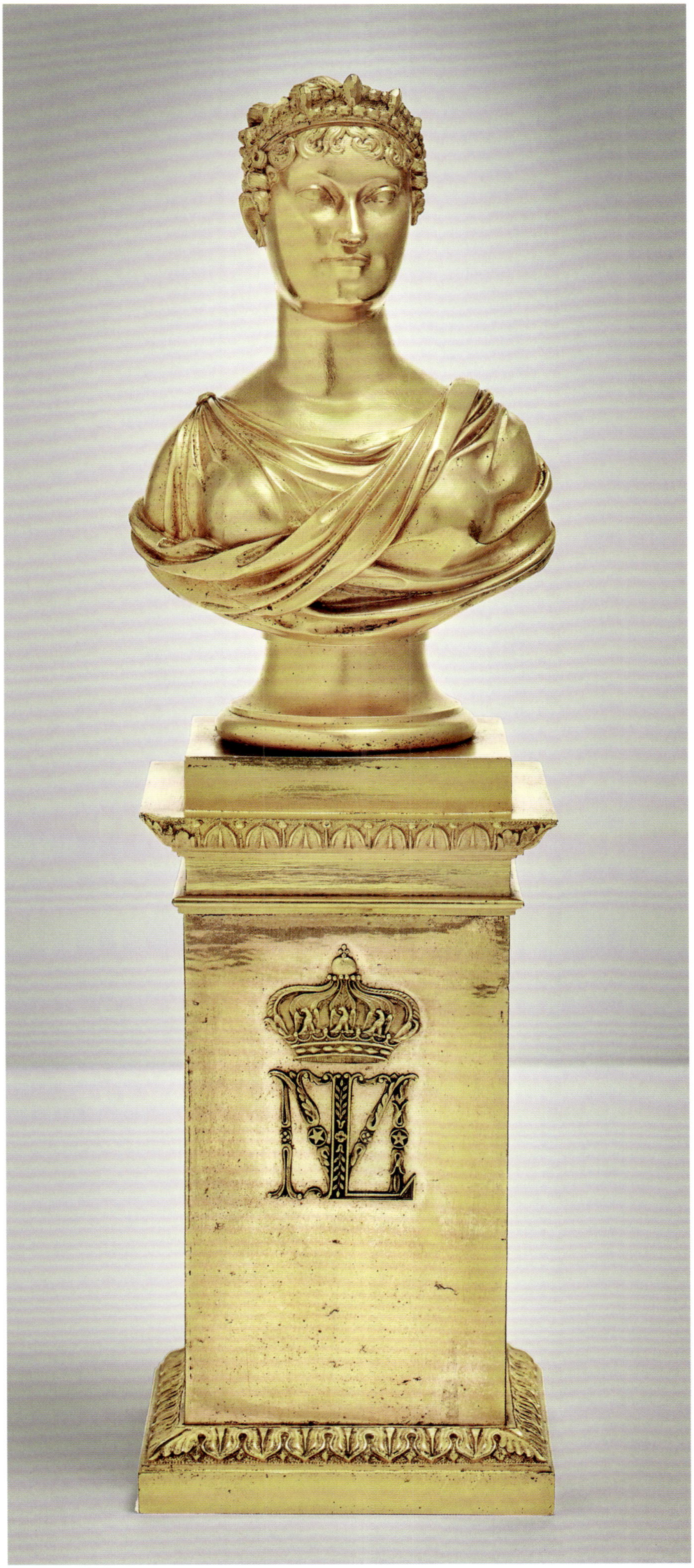

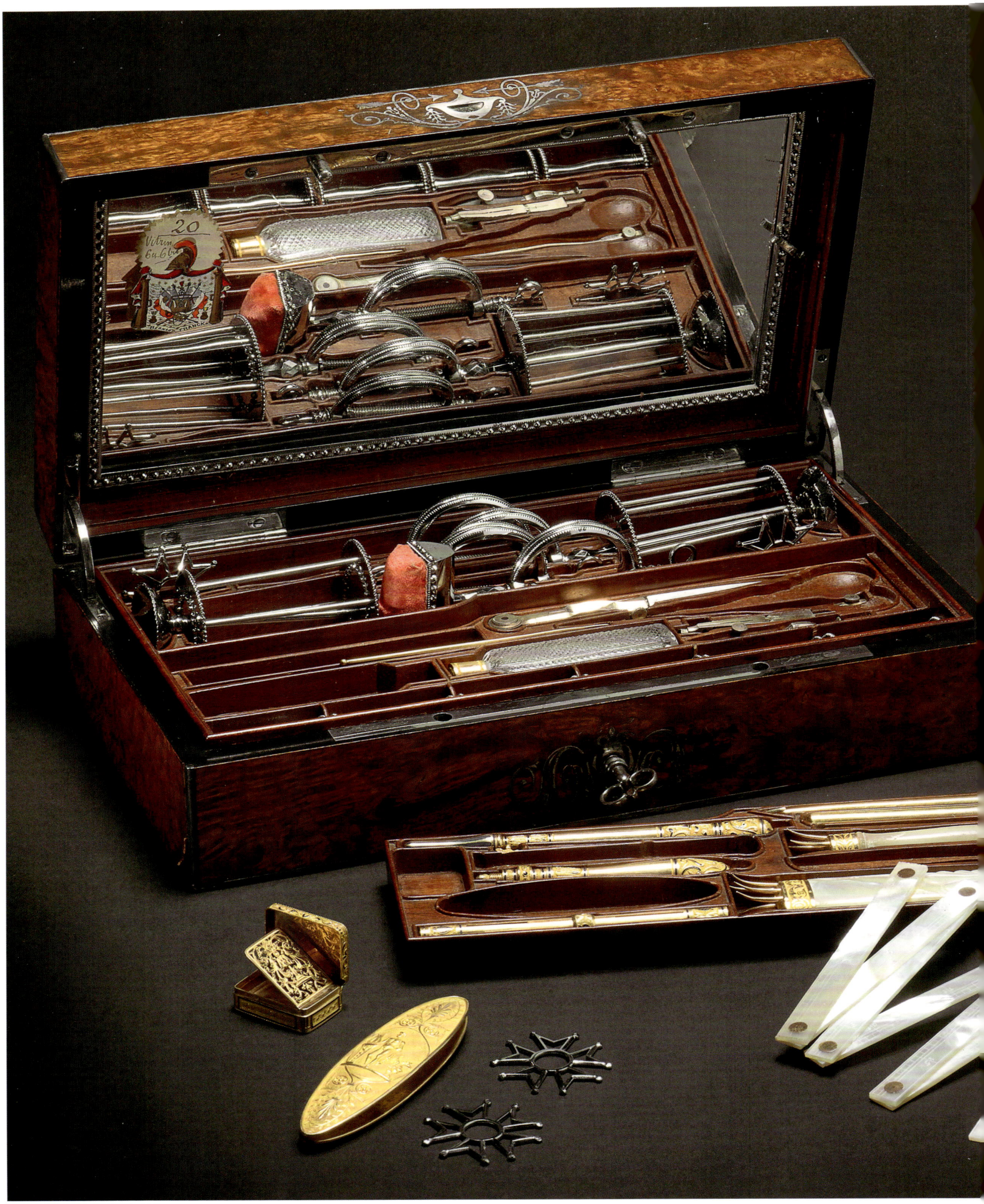

MARTIN-GUILLAUME BIENNAIS (1764-1843), SEWING *NÉCESSAIRE* BELONGING TO MARIE-LOUISE

This sumptuous *nécéssaire* with its 35 needlework accessories in mother-of-pearl, gold, silver, steel and vermeil is said to have belonged to the Empress Marie-Louise, who then gave it to one of her ladies-in-waiting. An illustrious provenance seems particularly likely in view of the bas relief plaque on the lid showing scenes from the Aldobrandini Wedding – a key theme at the celebrations to mark Marie-Louise's marriage to the Emperor.

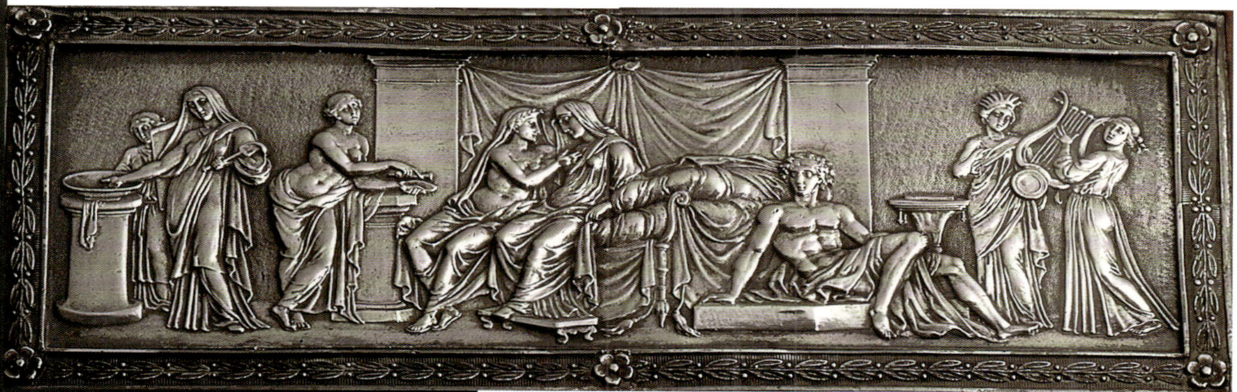

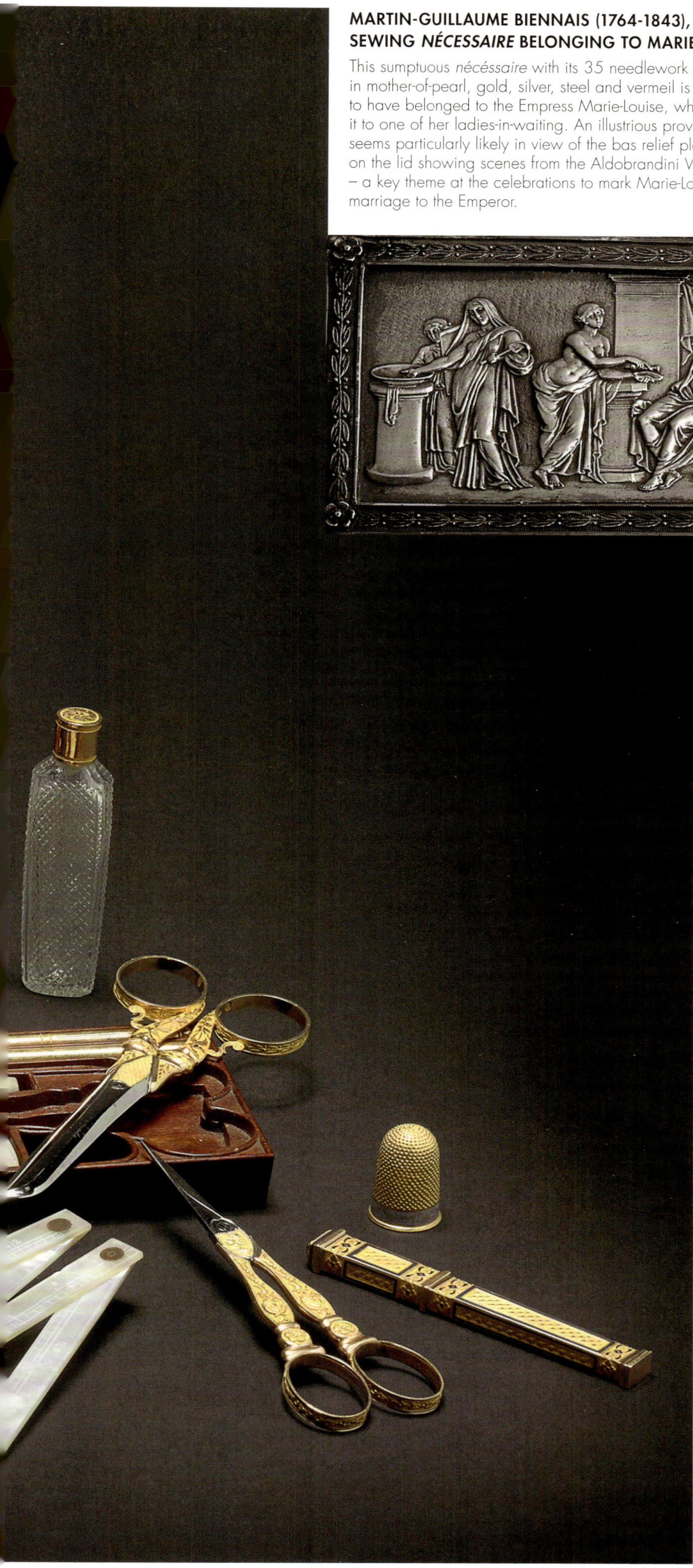

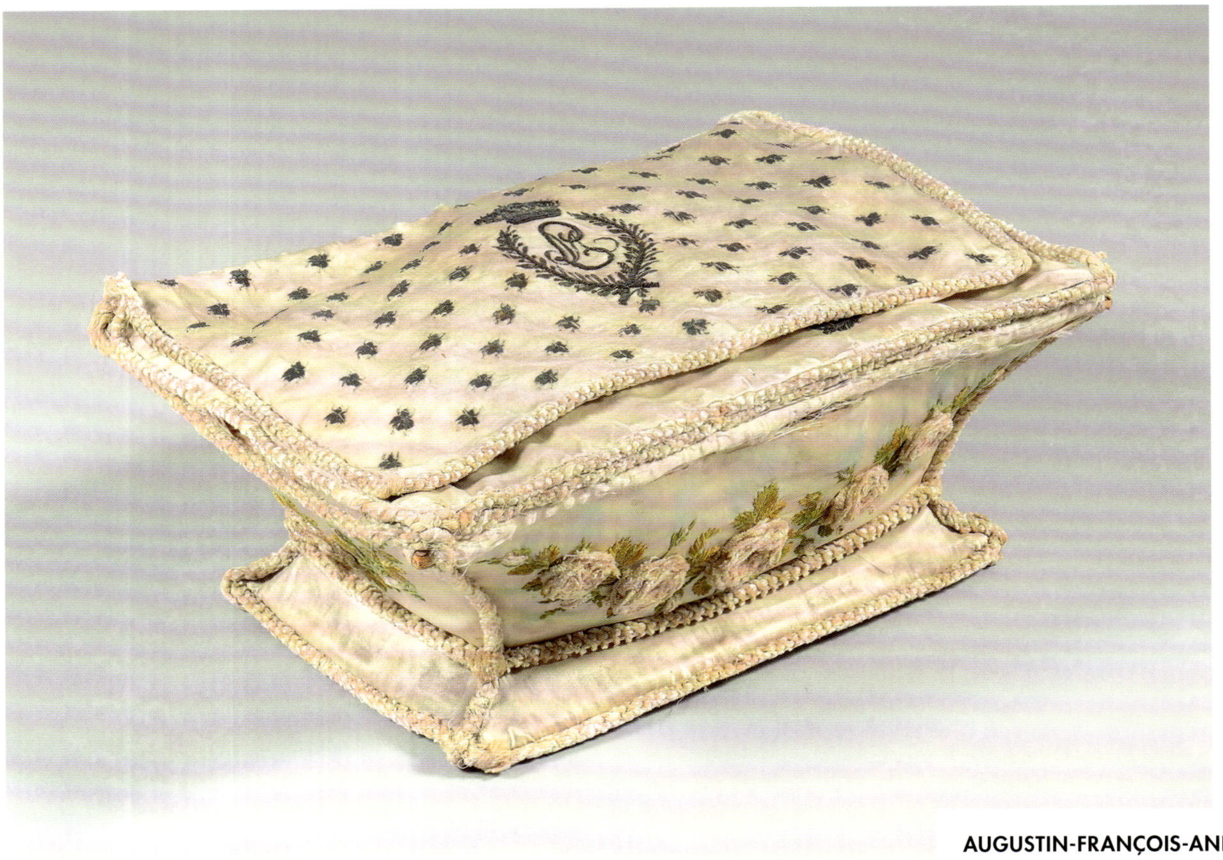

AUGUSTIN-FRANÇOIS-ANDRÉ PICOT (1786-1868), HANDICRAFT BOX BELONGING TO MARIE-LOUISE

This large wicker box covered in cream-colored silk widens out from the base and bears Marie-Louise's initials. It was probably made by Picot. A private object, it shows the refinement of these various baskets that held the intimate belongings serving for the Empress's toilette.

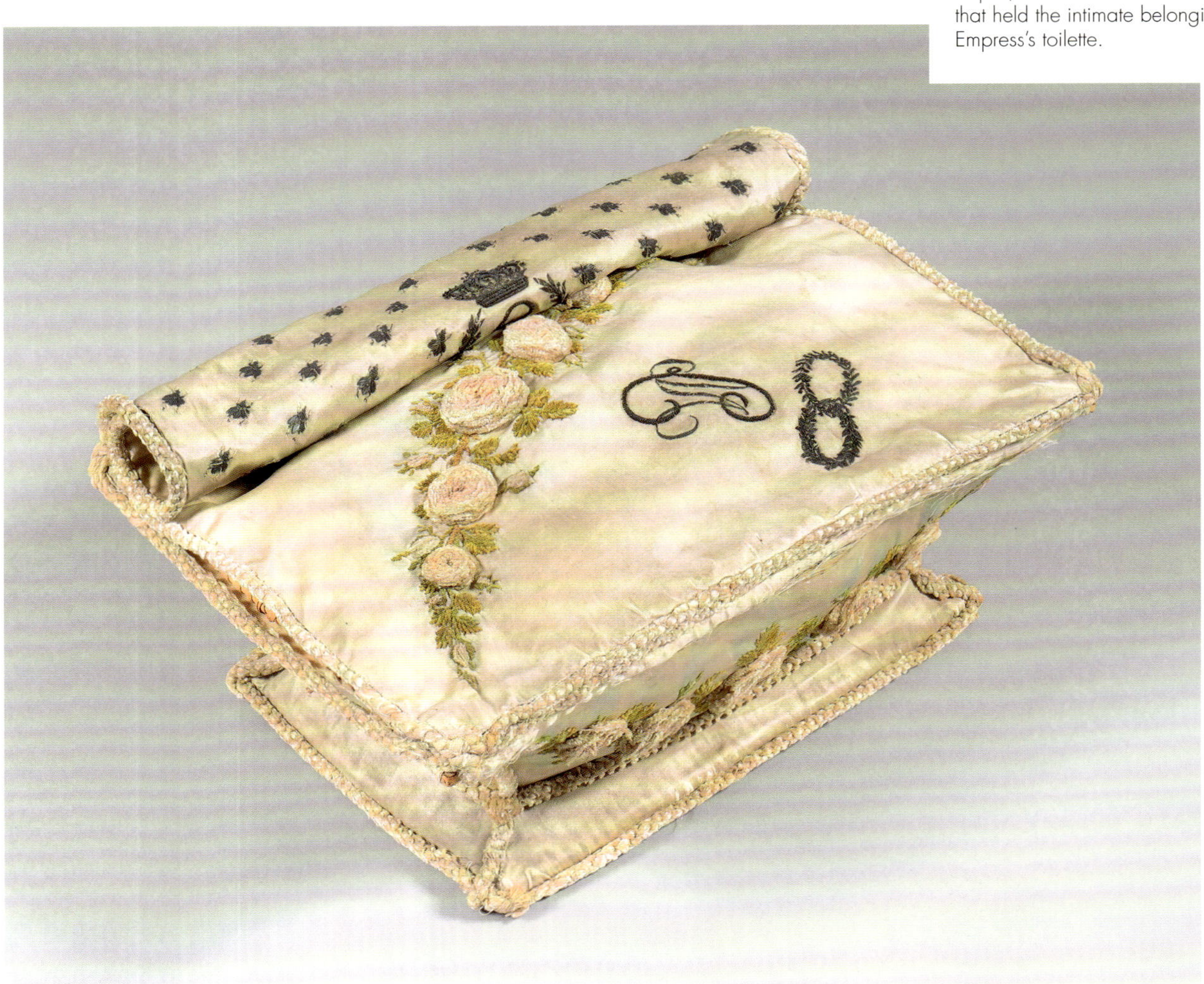

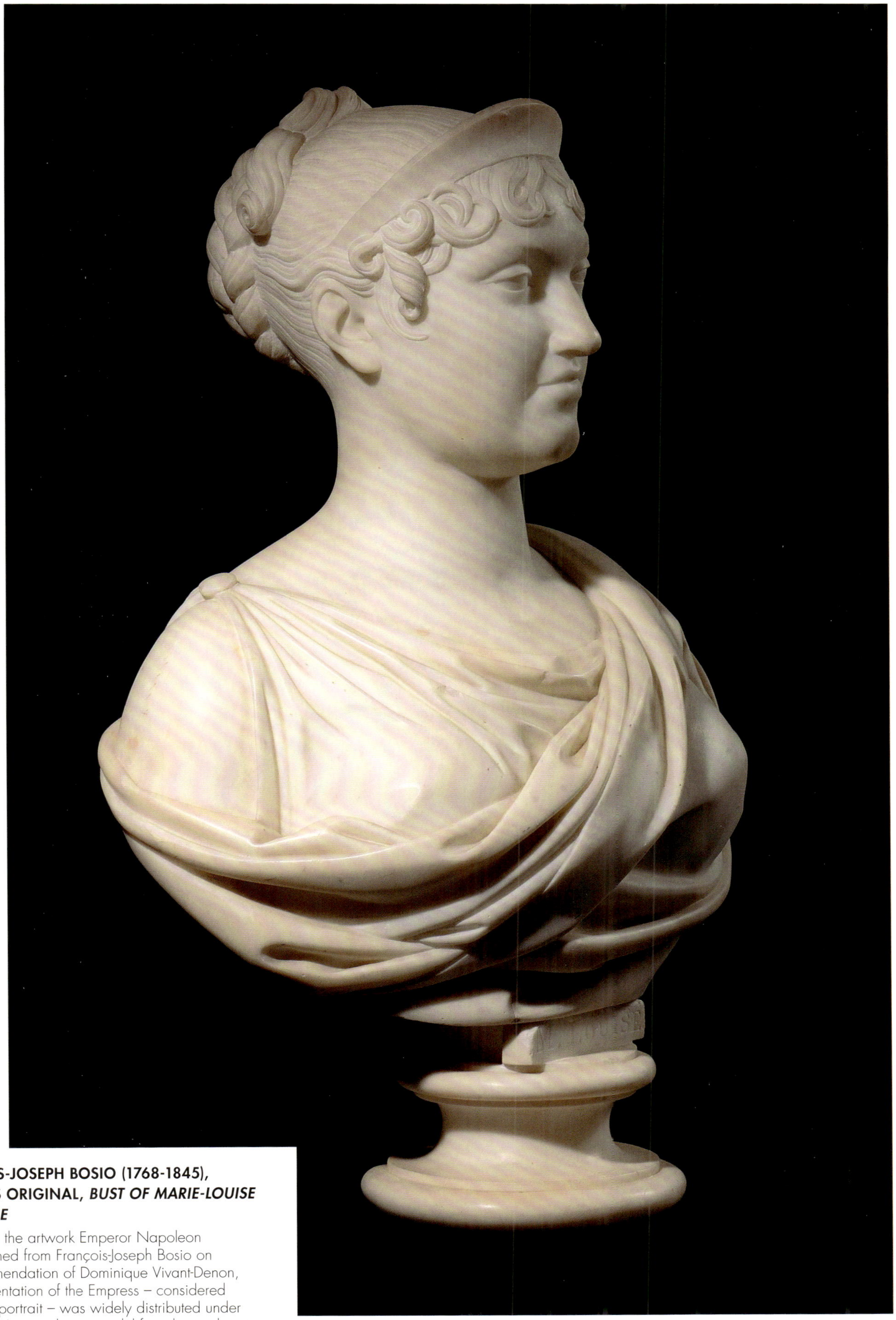

FRANÇOIS-JOSEPH BOSIO (1768-1845), AFTER HIS ORIGINAL, *BUST OF MARIE-LOUISE IN MARBLE*

Inspired by the artwork Emperor Napoleon commissioned from François-Joseph Bosio on the recommendation of Dominique Vivant-Denon, this representation of the Empress – considered an official portrait – was widely distributed under the Empire. It served as a model for other sculptors of the era, such as the Italians Giacomo Spalla and Lorenzo Bartolini.

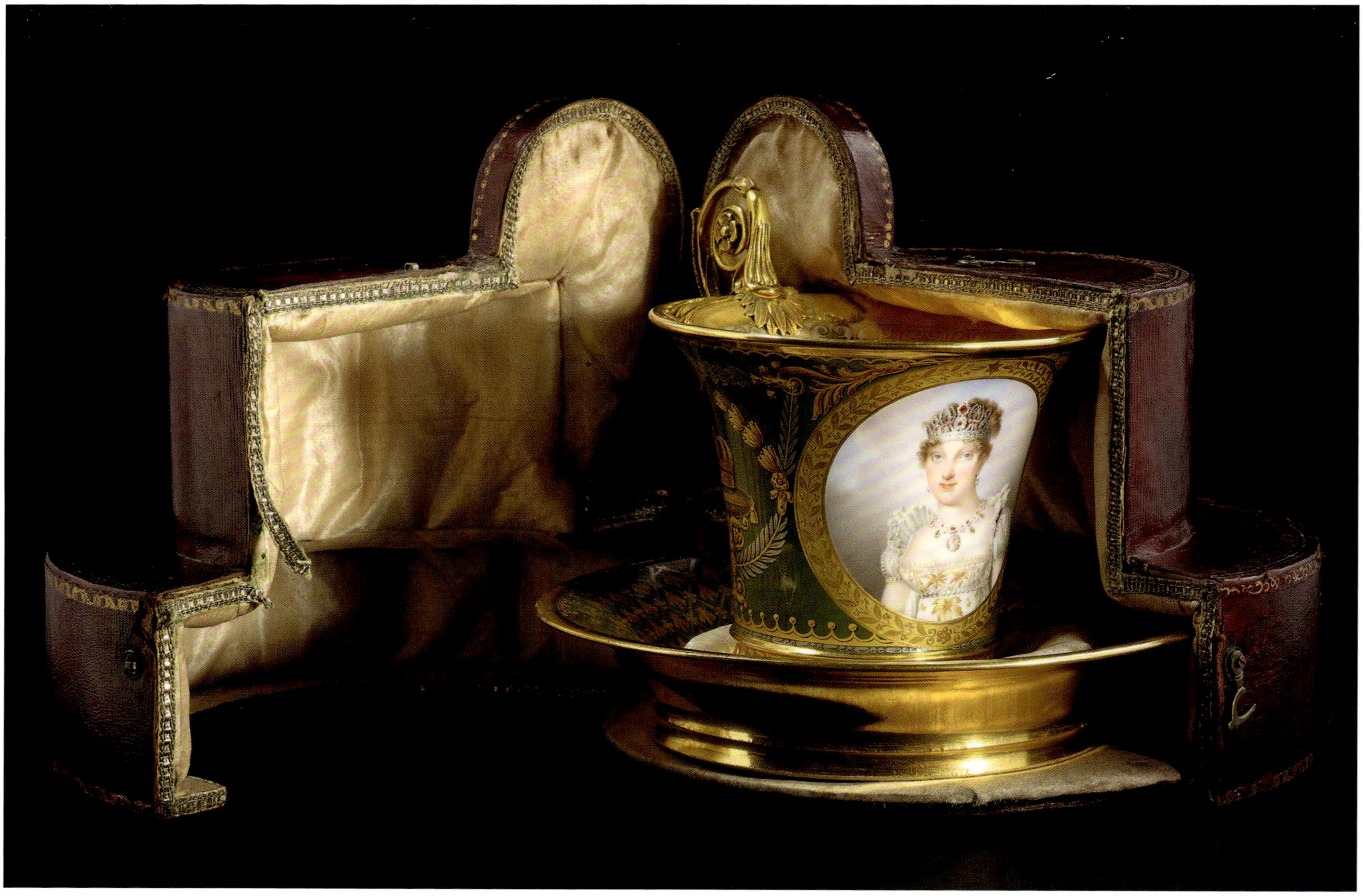

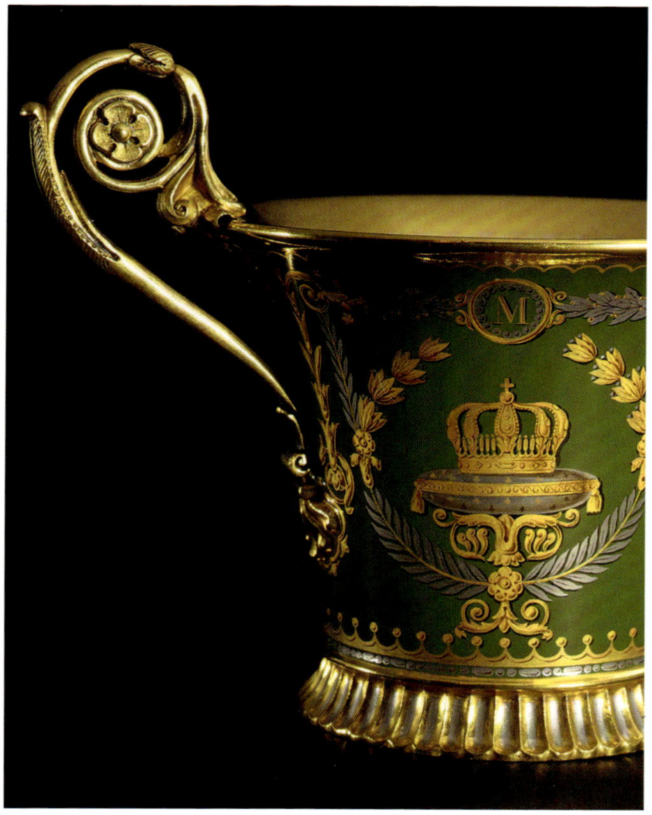

SÈVRES IMPERIAL MANUFACTORY, CUP WITH PORTRAIT OF MARIE-LOUISE, COMPLETE WITH CASE

This sumptuous *tasse jasmin* or "chocolate cup" is one of 14 Empire-period Sèvres porcelain cups bearing Marie-Louise's portrait. It features a vermeil handle and the Empress' portrait, painted in 1812, set against a chrome green background. The cup was intended for the *service des présents* and is still complete with its original Burgundy Morocco leather case.

JEAN-BAPTISTE-CLAUDE ODIOT (1763-1850), LARGE VERMEIL MIRROR

This Odiot-hallmarked vermeil table mirror takes its inspiration from the toiletry accessories (also in vermeil) that were offered by the City of Paris to the Empress Marie-Louise. Its feminine design, themed around the figure of Diana, suggests that it belonged to a member of the imperial family – a superb example of the many prestigious commissions that were entrusted to Odiot as goldsmith to the Court of the Emperor.

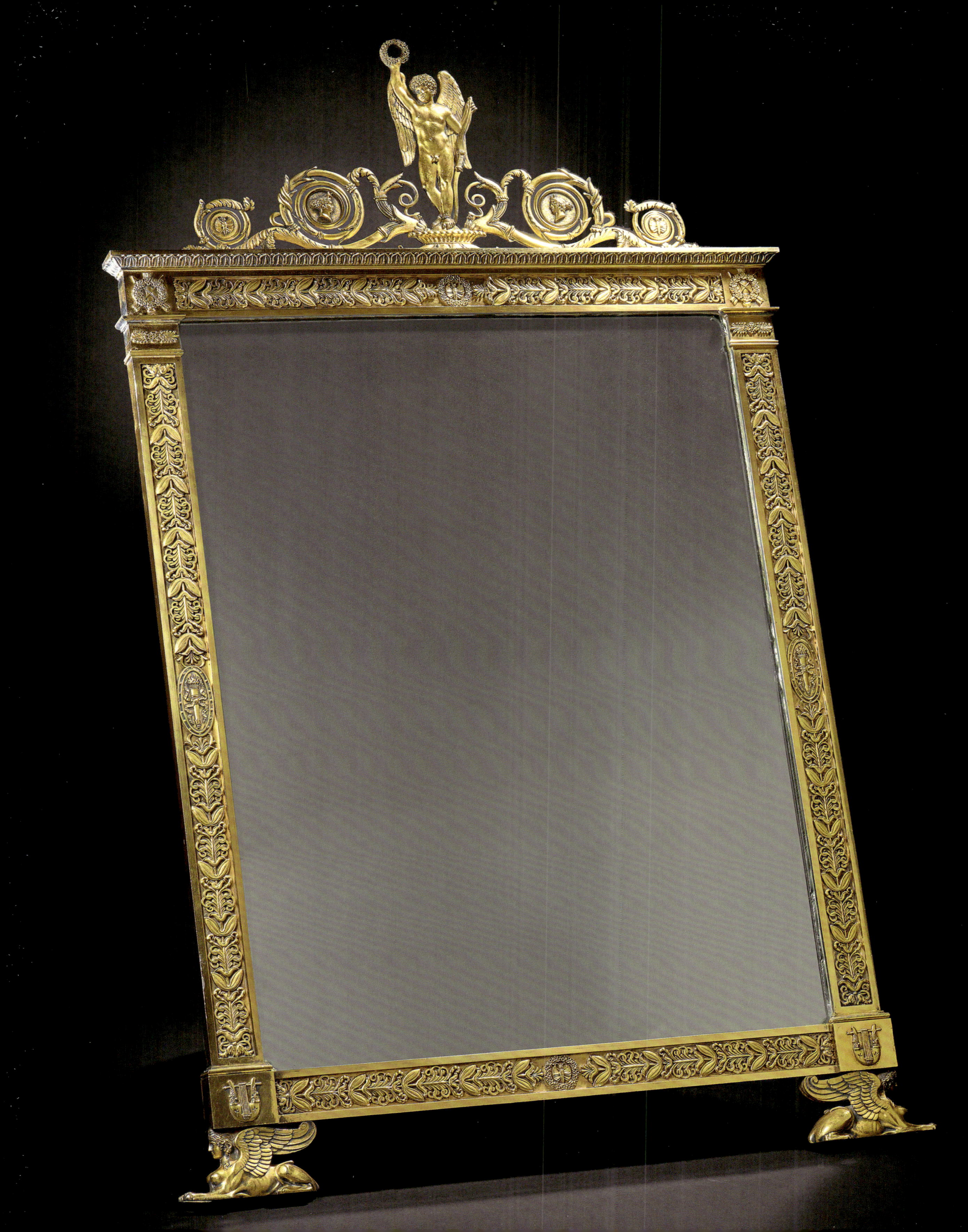

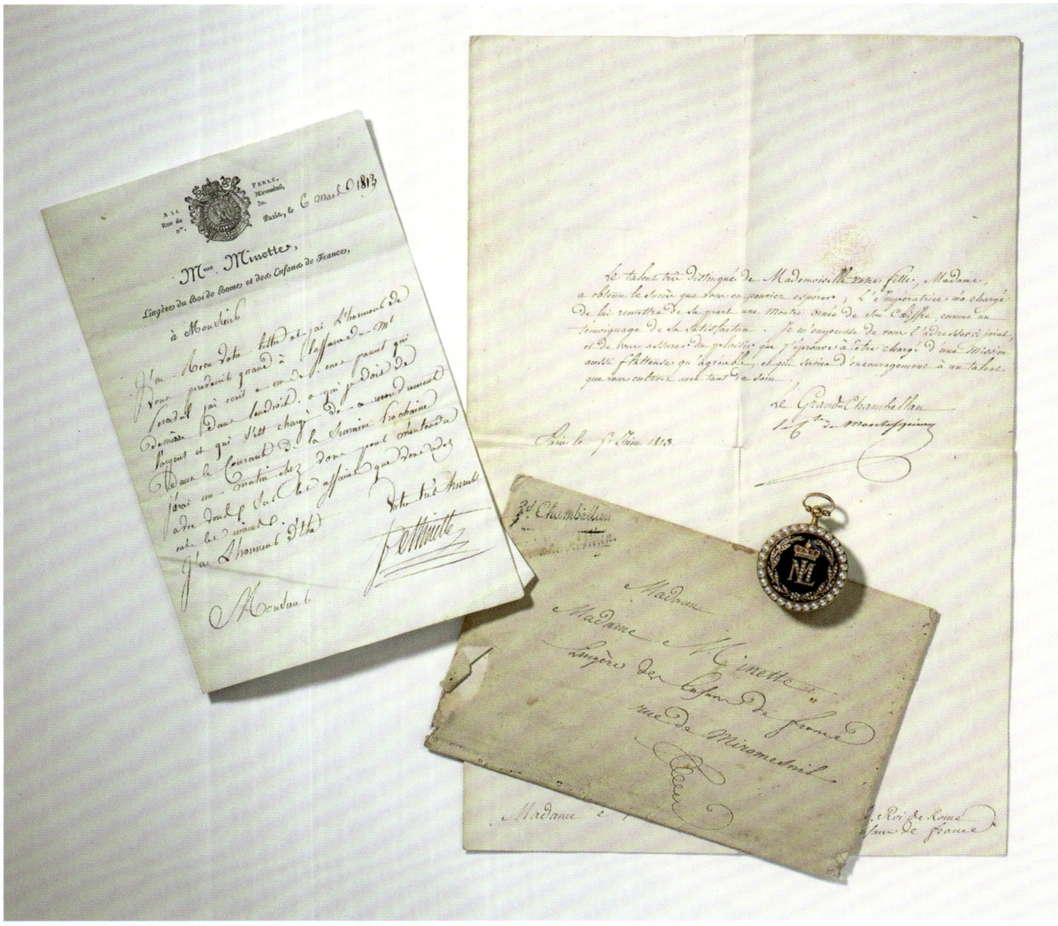

FRANÇOIS-REGNAULT NITOT (1779-1853) AND ABRAHAM BREGUET (1747-1823), MARIE-LOUISE MONOGRAMMED POCKET WATCH

The *service des présents* (imperial gift service) regularly purchased watches with Marie-Louise's monogram from Parisian jeweler François-Regnault Nitot (1779-1853). Most contained movements by famous Swiss horologist Abraham Breguet (1747-1823) – such as this watch, a gift from the Empress to the daughter of Madame Minette, Mistress of the Laundry to the King of Rome, after the young woman sang in her presence. It is one of the few known examples with a well-documented history.

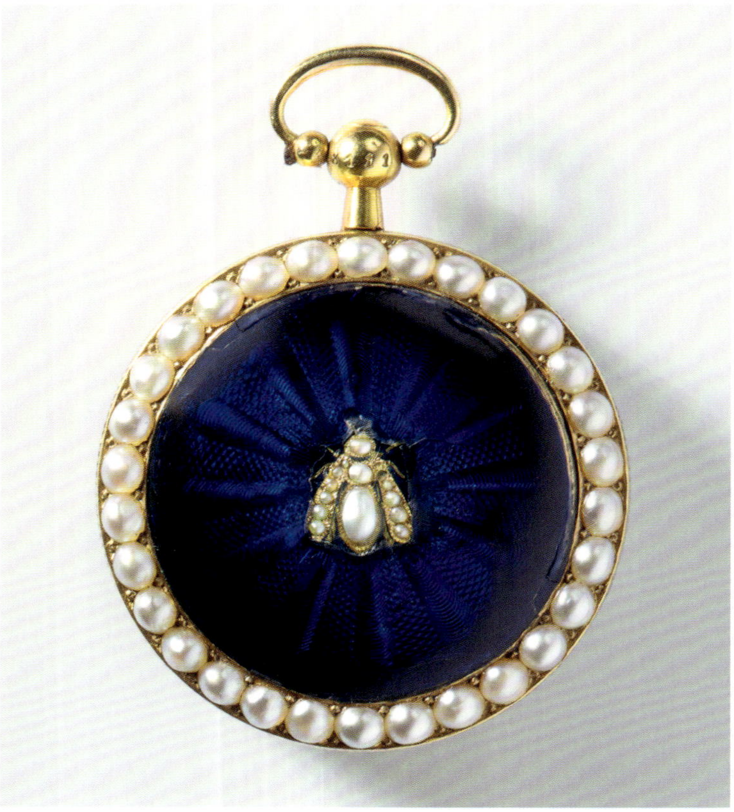

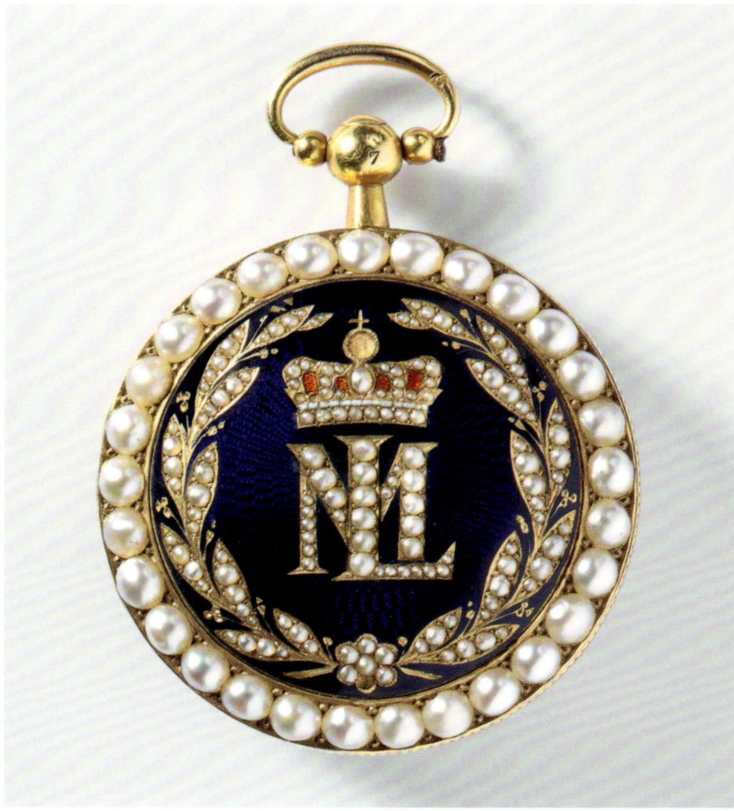

MARIE-JEAN DESOUCHES (1764-1828), NAPOLEON'S IRON BED TAKEN BY MARIE-LOUIS TO VIENNA

In 1803 French locksmith Desouches patented a foldable bed that Bonaparte immediately adopted for his own personal use, followed by members of his entourage. The Empress Marie-Louise took three of the Emperor's iron beds with her when she departed for Vienna after her husband's abdication in 1814. They include the example pictured here, still with its leather carrying case, topped with a gilt bronze crown that was probably added when she became Duchess of Parma. It was said at court that the King of Rome had been born in this bed. It is hallmarked "Desouches", surmounted by the imperial crown, and originates directly from her estate.

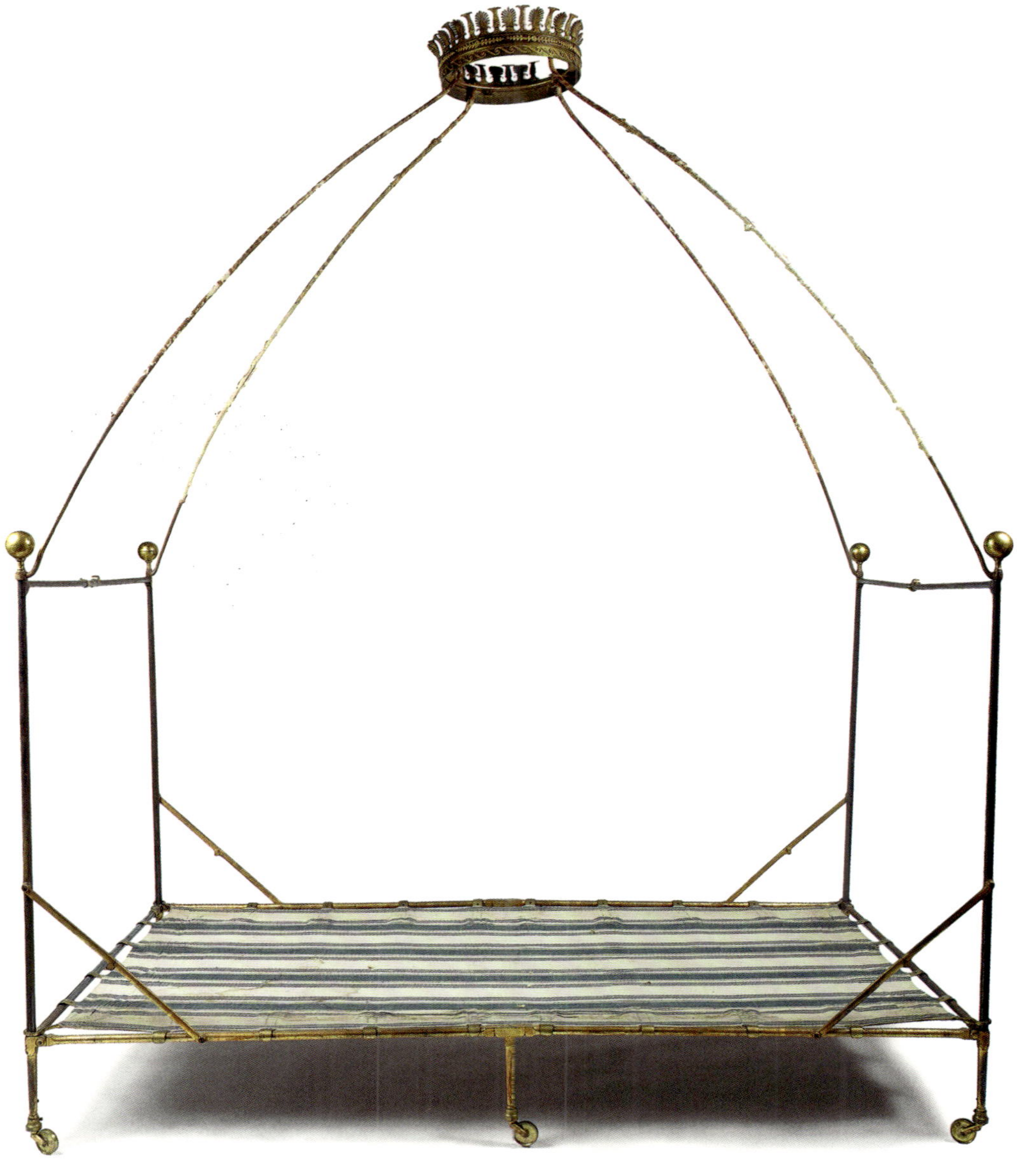

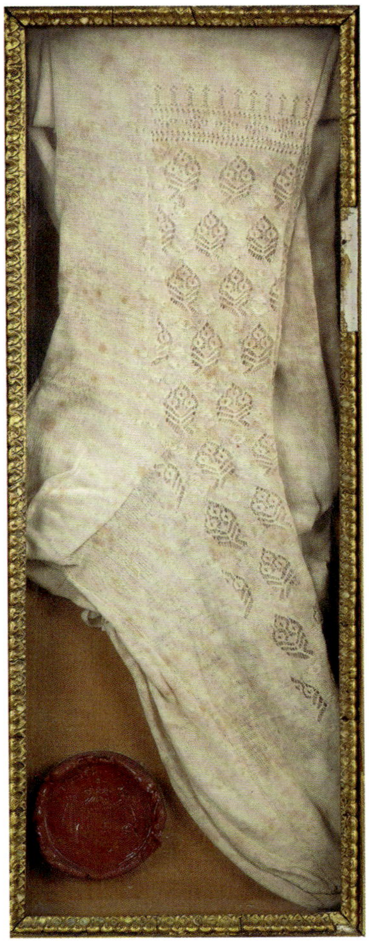

PAIR OF STOCKINGS BELONGING TO MARIE-LOUISE, DUCHESS OF PARMA

After the fall of the Empire, Marie-Louise was given the Italian duchies of Parma, Piacenza and Guastalla, where she ruled until her death in 1847. As Duchess of Parma, she retained her taste for Paris fashion and continued to patronize her former suppliers as Empress, receiving monthly bills for items such as these embroidered stockings.

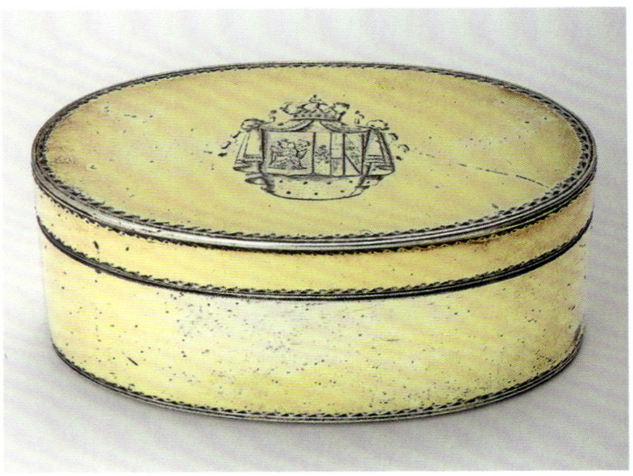

MARTIN-GUILLAUME BIENNAIS (1764-1843), PILLBOX BELONGING TO THE EMPRESS MARIE-LOUISE

This oval vermeil box is one of the very few pieces signed by the goldsmith Martin-Guillaume Biennais that bear the grand coat-of-arms of Marie-Louise. It may be a pillbox, but it could equally well be part of the scattered contents of one of the Empress' *nécessaires*, made to contain toiletry products (soap, almond paste or opiates).

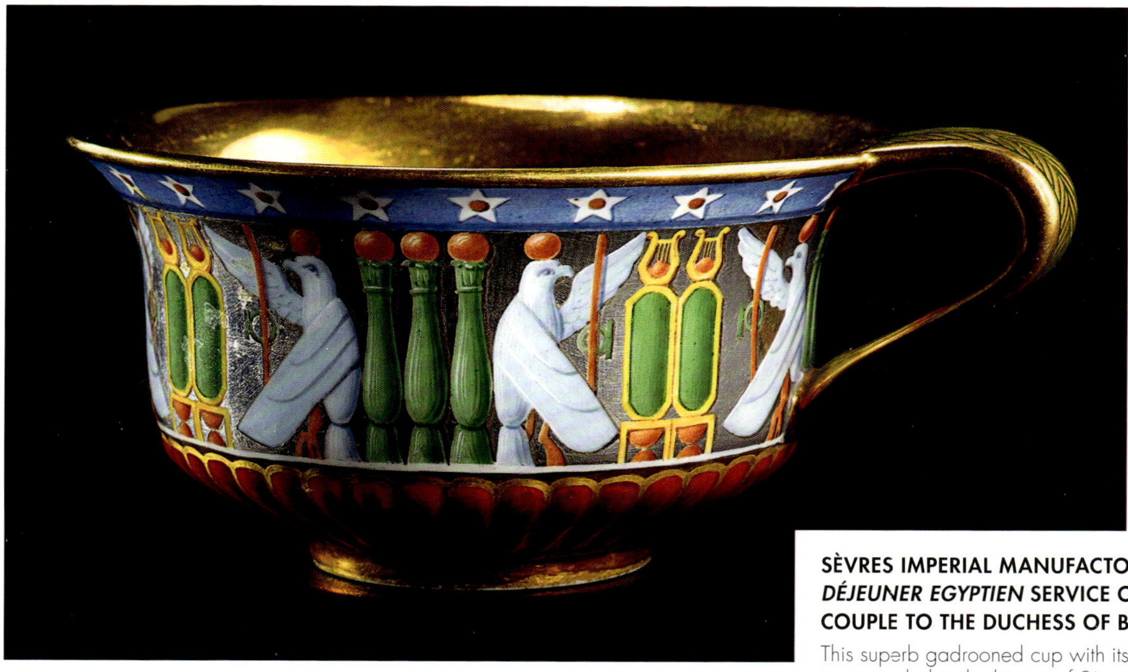

SÈVRES IMPERIAL MANUFACTORY, CUP FROM THE *DÉJEUNER EGYPTIEN* SERVICE OFFERED BY THE IMPERIAL COUPLE TO THE DUCHESS OF BASSANO

This superb gadrooned cup with its brightly colored Egyptian motif is unequaled in the history of Sèvres porcelain and counts among the rarest pieces ever produced at the manufactory. It comes from the sixth of seven Egyptian "cabaret" services produced at Sèvres in the period 1808-1814, the only known surviving piece of a series that originally included four grand molded dishes in every set. The sixth set was made in 1813 and presented to the Duchess of Bassano, née Marie-Madeleine Lejéas (1780-1827), wife of Maret, Duke of Bassano, on New Year's Day 1814.

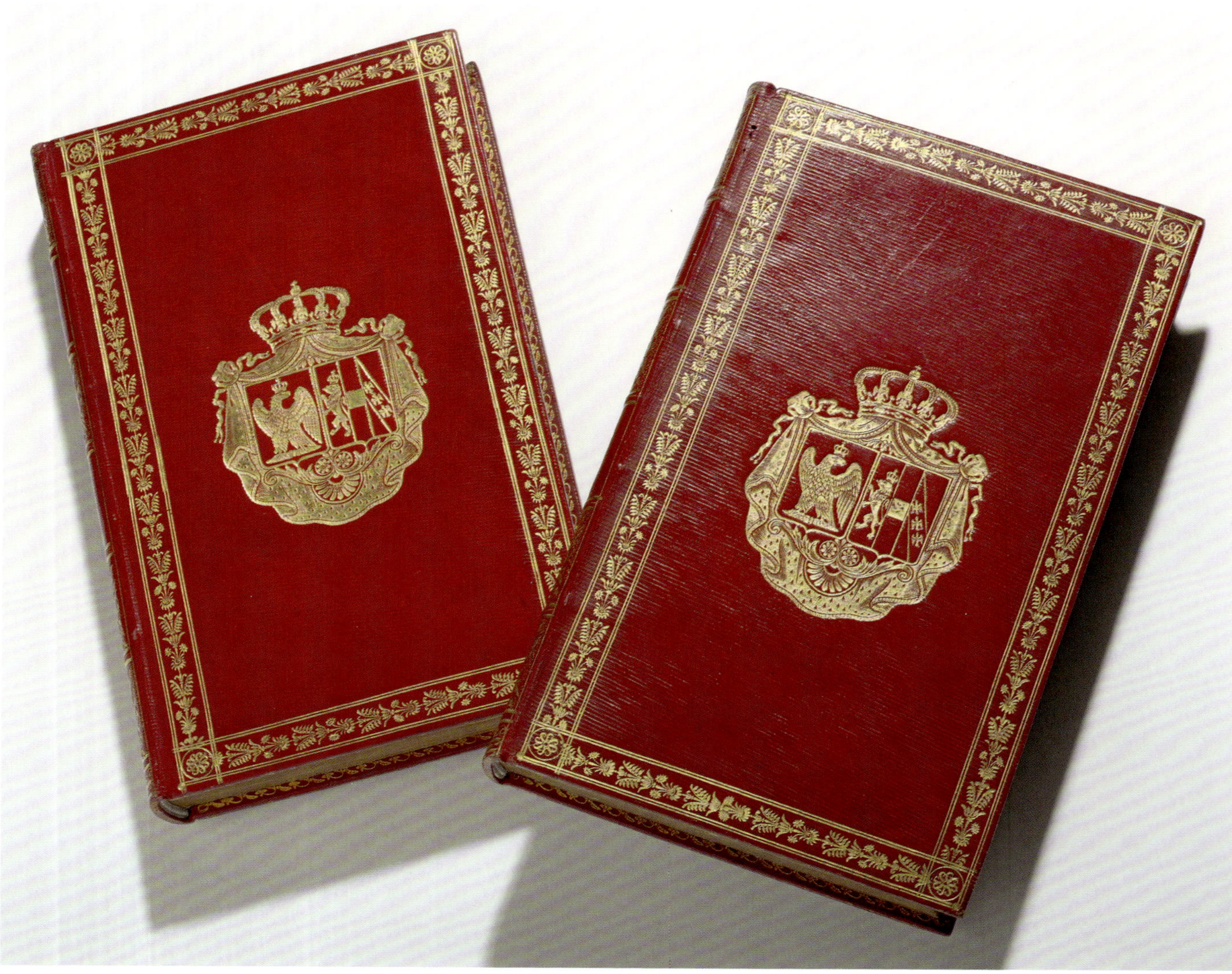

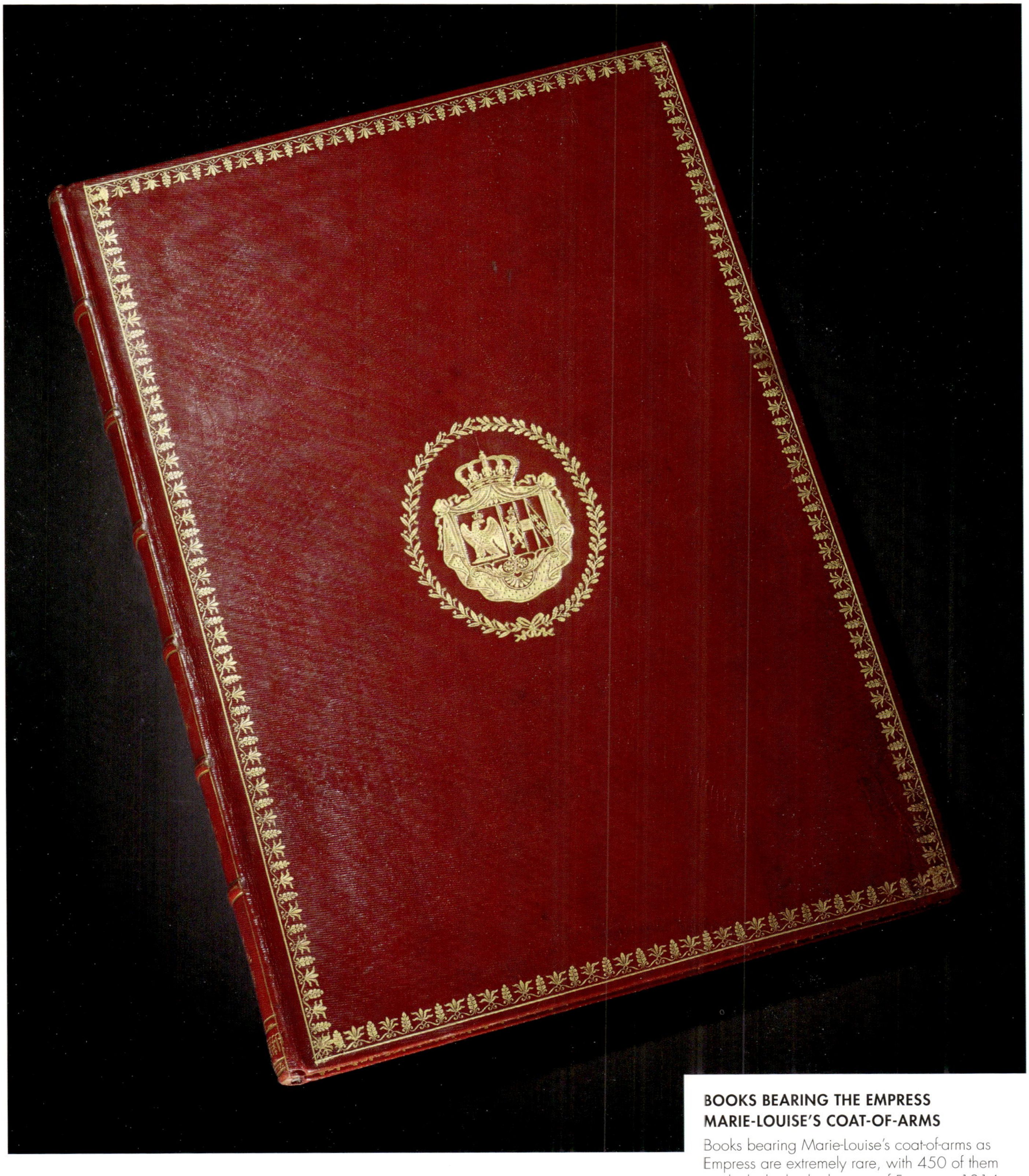

BOOKS BEARING THE EMPRESS MARIE-LOUISE'S COAT-OF-ARMS

Books bearing Marie-Louise's coat-of-arms as Empress are extremely rare, with 450 of them – which she had taken out of France in 1814 – having been donated to the Musée de Malmaison in 1933. Most are in red Morocco leather and their covers bear two escutcheons side by side, the French Empire's heraldic arms on the left and those of Habsburg-Lorraine on the right. Above: a folio of *Paul and Virginie* by Bernardin de Saint Pierre, one of Napoleon's favorite authors.

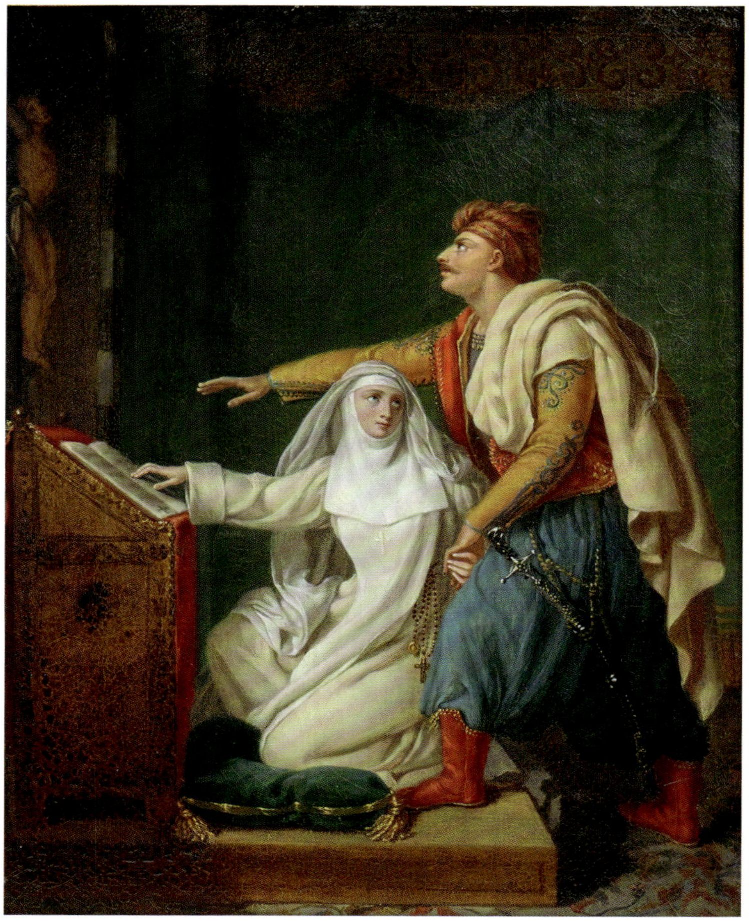

EUGÉNIE SERVIÈRES (1786-1832), *LA CHRÉTIENNE MATHILDE*

La Chrétienne Mathilde marked the highpoint of the career of Eugénie Servières, one of 11 paintings presented at the 1812 Salon that Napoleon acquired for Marie-Louise and had added to his Civil List. The story behind it comes from a Crusade Romance by Mme Cottin, which was such a success that it immediately inspired an engraving by Marie-Pauline Soyer. Servières' painting sold for 2,000 francs (compared to just 800 francs for the Vernet) – a testament to a now-forgotten artist who spoke to the Empress' imagination with his sentimental portrayal of troubadour-style love.

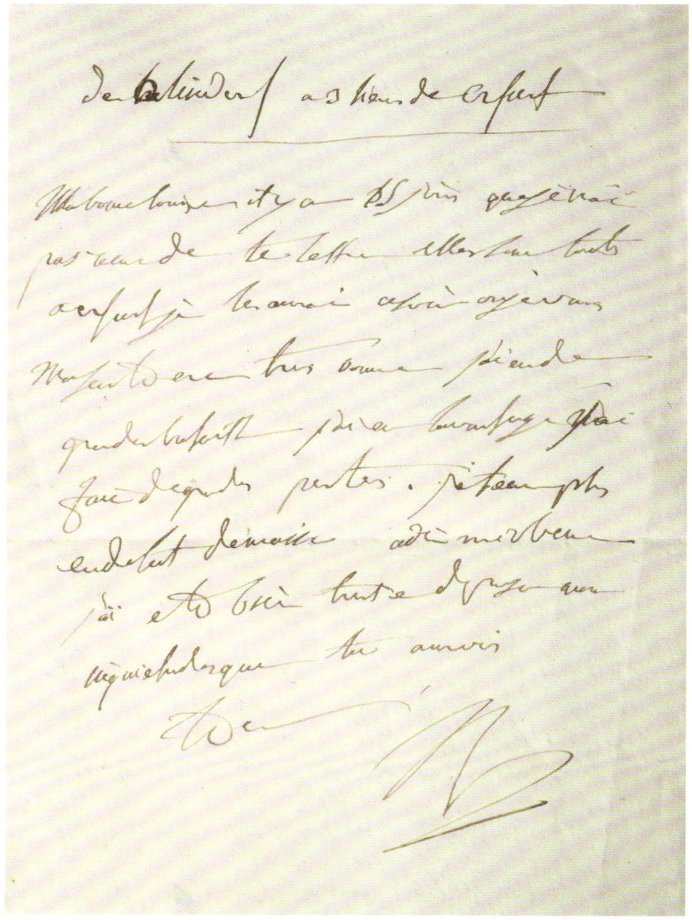

HANDWRITTEN LETTER FROM NAPOLEON TO MARIE-LOUISE

Almost all of Napoleon's letters to Marie-Louise are now in the public domain, with the exception of a few in private hands, such as this veiled account of Napoleon's recent battles, composed following the French defeat at Leipzig. On the night of 22 October 1813 Napoleon spent a few hours in the village of Ollendorf on his way back to Paris, choosing his words carefully to avoid alarming his wife.

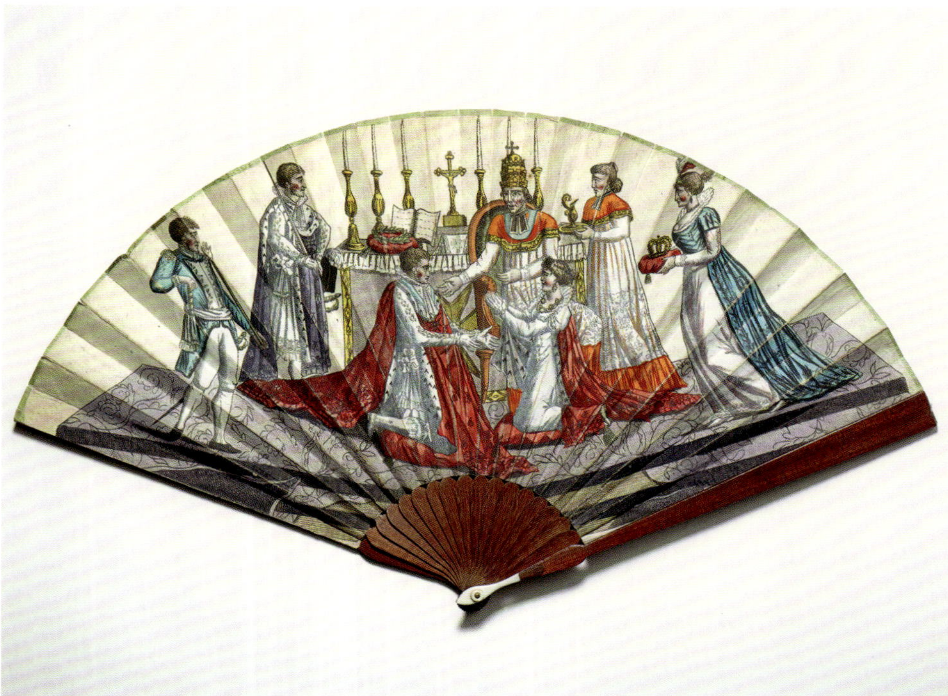

FAN, THE MARRIAGE OF NAPOLEON AND MARIE-LOUISE

Few fans associated with the history of Napoleon and the imperial court have survived. This one, in engraved paper heightened with color, offers one of the few depictions of the Emperor's marriage to Marie-Louise. At the same time, it shows us how widely the imperial image was disseminated through society.

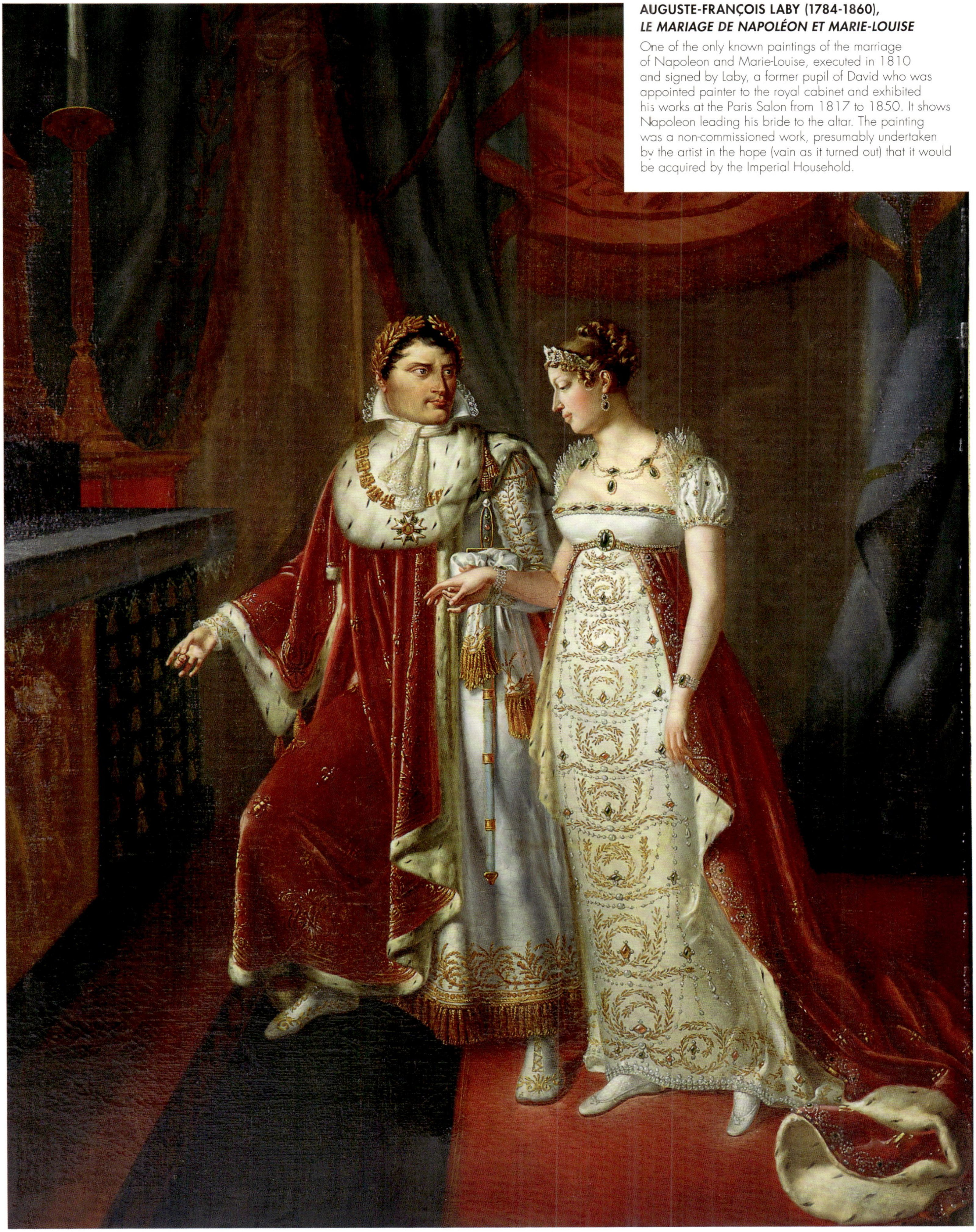

AUGUSTE-FRANÇOIS LABY (1784-1860),
LE MARIAGE DE NAPOLÉON ET MARIE-LOUISE

One of the only known paintings of the marriage of Napoleon and Marie-Louise, executed in 1810 and signed by Laby, a former pupil of David who was appointed painter to the royal cabinet and exhibited his works at the Paris Salon from 1817 to 1850. It shows Napoleon leading his bride to the altar. The painting was a non-commissioned work, presumably undertaken by the artist in the hope (vain as it turned out) that it would be acquired by the Imperial Household.

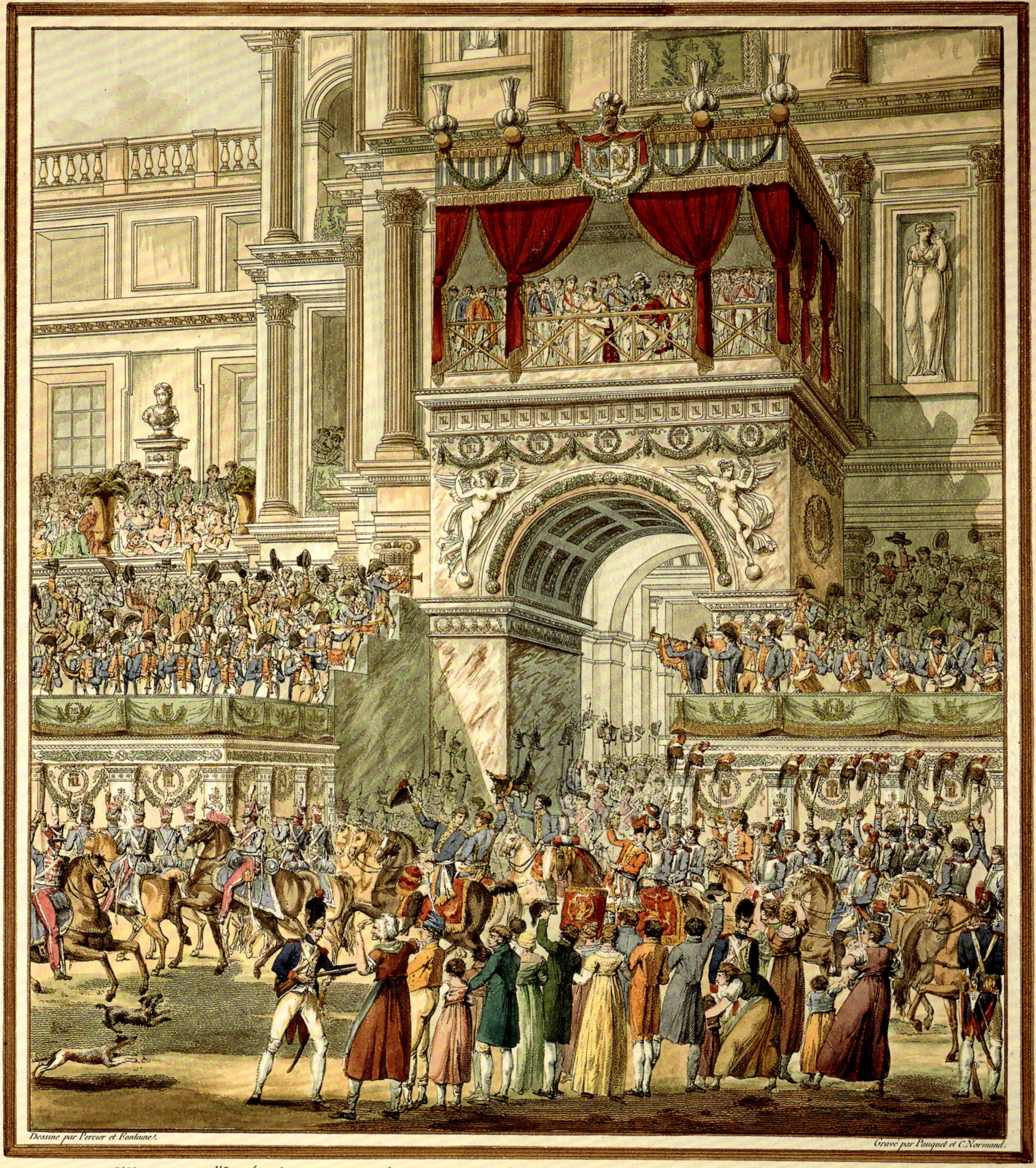

L'Empereur et l'Impératrice recevant sur le Grand Balcon des Tuileries les Hommages des Troupes qui défilent devant elles, le jour de la Cérémonie de leur Mariage.

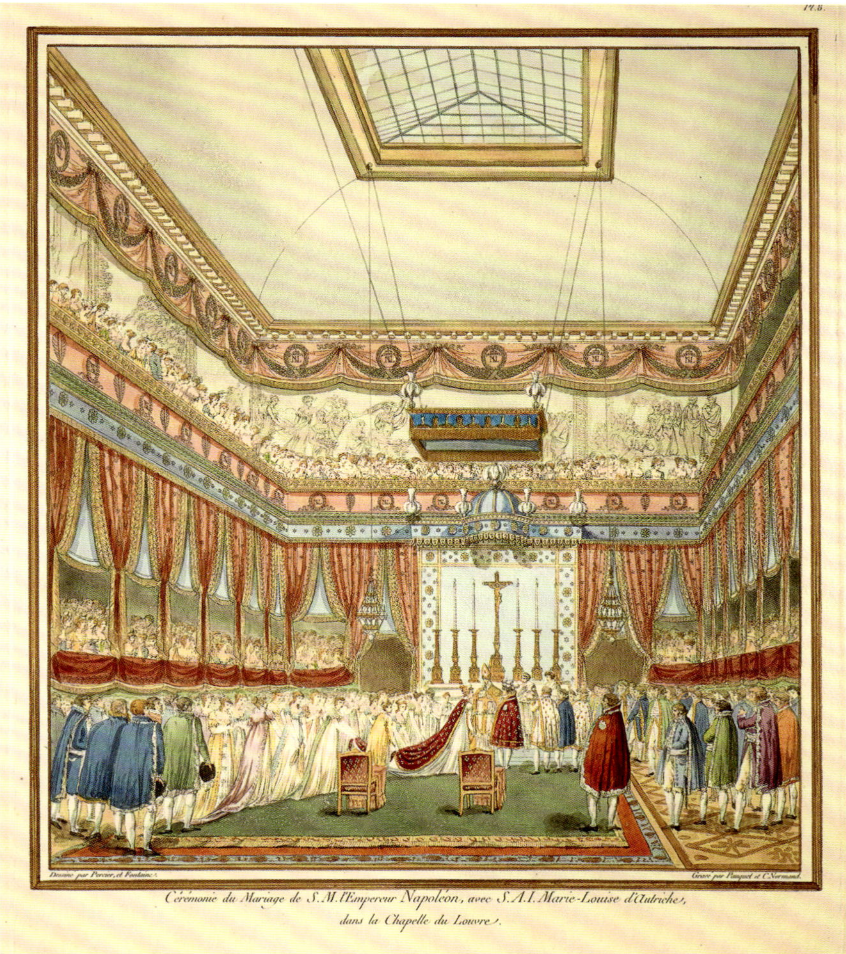

DESCRIPTION OF THE CEREMONIES AND FESTIVITIES HELD TO CELEBRATE THE WEDDING OF HM EMPEROR NAPOLEON AND HIH ARCHDUCHESS MARIE-LOUISE OF AUSTRIA, PARIS, DIDOT THE ELDER 1810.

Following the marriage of Napoleon and the Austrian Emperor's daughter, Percier and Fontaine were entrusted with producing an account of the ceremonies. The text is illustrated with thirteen plates that recount the event chronologically: the civil marriage at St Cloud, the bridal couple's arrival in Paris, then at the Tuileries, alighting from their carriage, crossing the Louvre's Grande Galerie, the ceremony in the Louvre Chapel, the acclamation of the troops, the banquet, fireworks in Place de la Concorde, and the Army Corps's congratulations. The exceedingly rare watercolored copies of this publication, bound by Tessier, were exclusively reserved for the imperial family and the highest French and foreign dignitaries. This one belonged to Marshal Jourdan (1762-1833), the victor at the Battle of Fleurus on 26 June 1794.

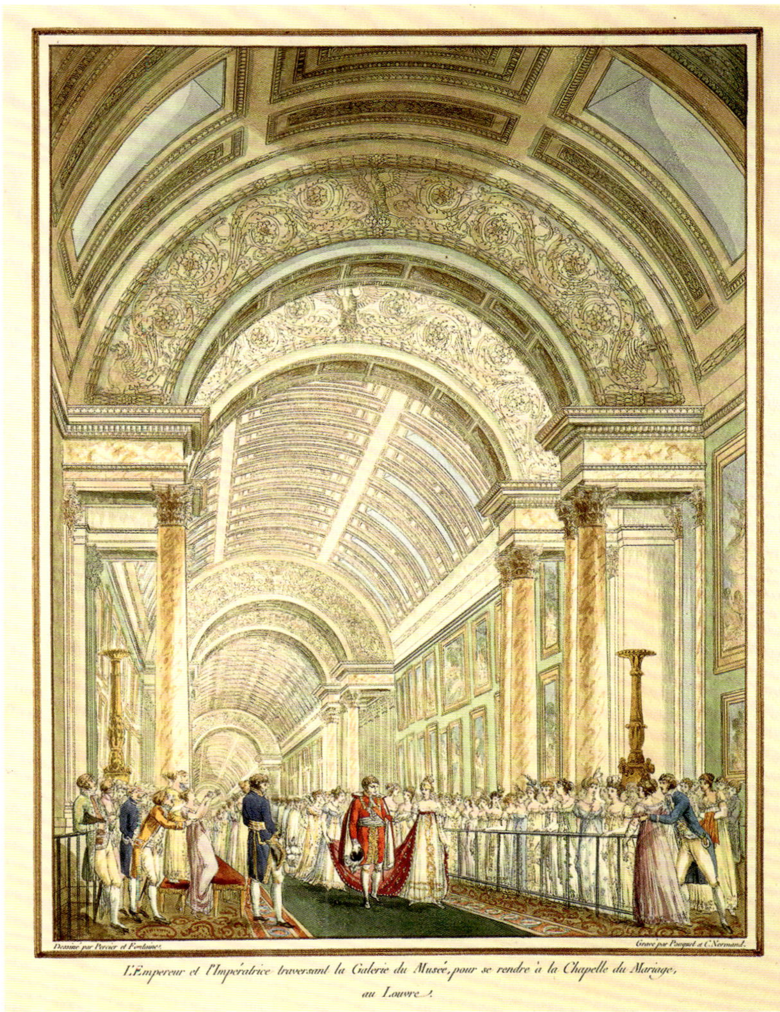

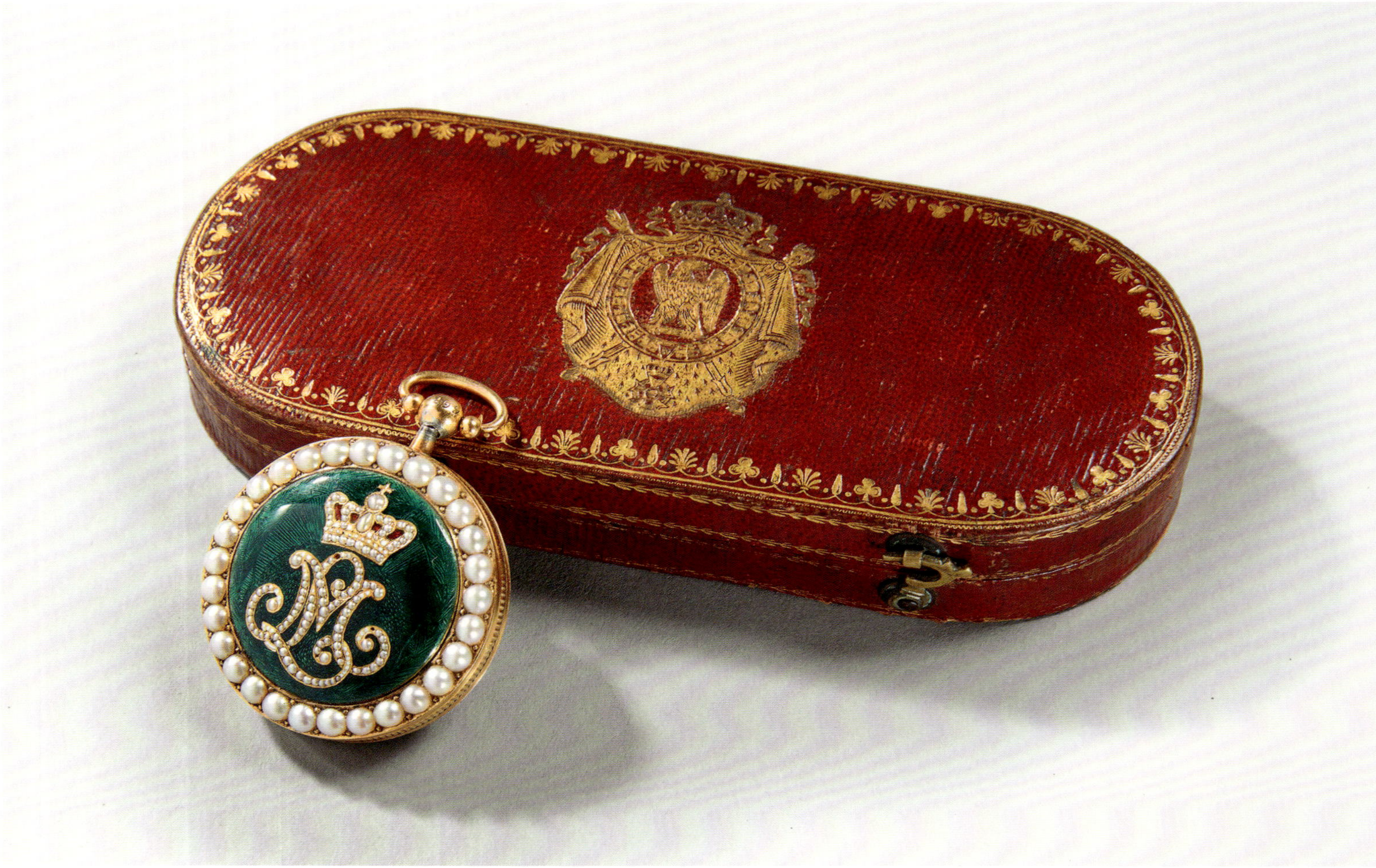

FRANÇOIS-REGNAULT NITOT (1779-1853) AND ABRAHAM BREGUET (1747-1823), WATCH WITH MARIE-LOUISE'S MONOGRAM

This pocket watch in gold, green enamel and pearls bears the number 47 and has been preciously preserved in its original red Morocco leather gold-tooled case bearing the imperial arms. It was made by Nitot and presented to the French Consul to Turin as a token of her gratitude. The Empress's Household records list several commissions for similar pieces, notably in 1811 where they indicate: "Twenty-six assorted small pocket watches in enameled gold, with superb surrounds, initials, and emblems, each accompanied by a chain and key".

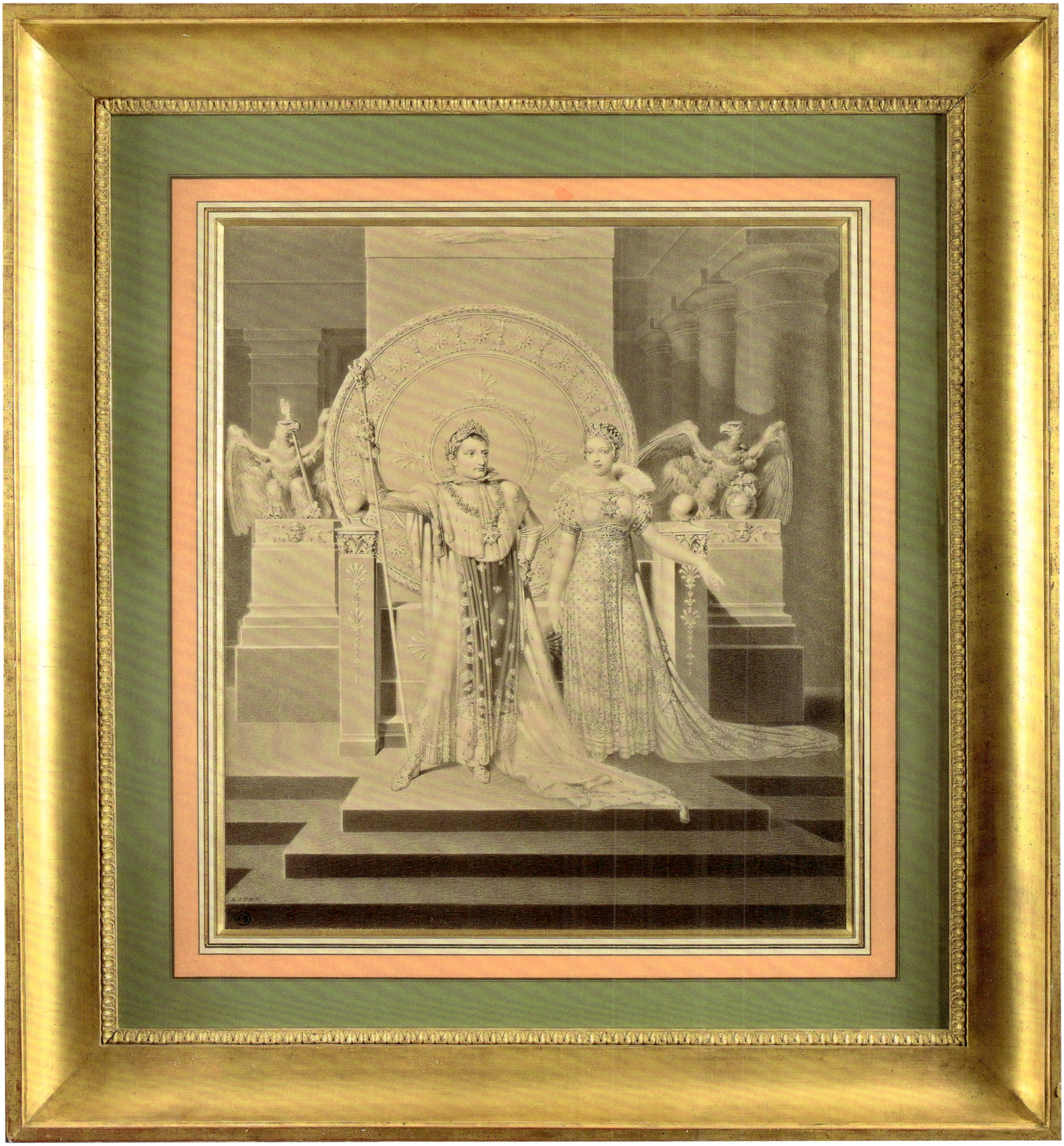

MATTHÄUS LODER (1781-1828), *THE EMPEROR AND EMPRESS IN CORONATION REGALIA*

This ink drawing with white highlights signed by Loder places Napoleon and Marie-Louise in front of a monumental throne flanked by two eagles holding the emblems of power. The addition of Doric columns in the background gives this representation a strong stamp of majesty. After the fall of the Empire, Loder, the Empress's drawing teacher, accompanied her to Vienna and from there to Parma.

HORTENSE AND EUGÈNE

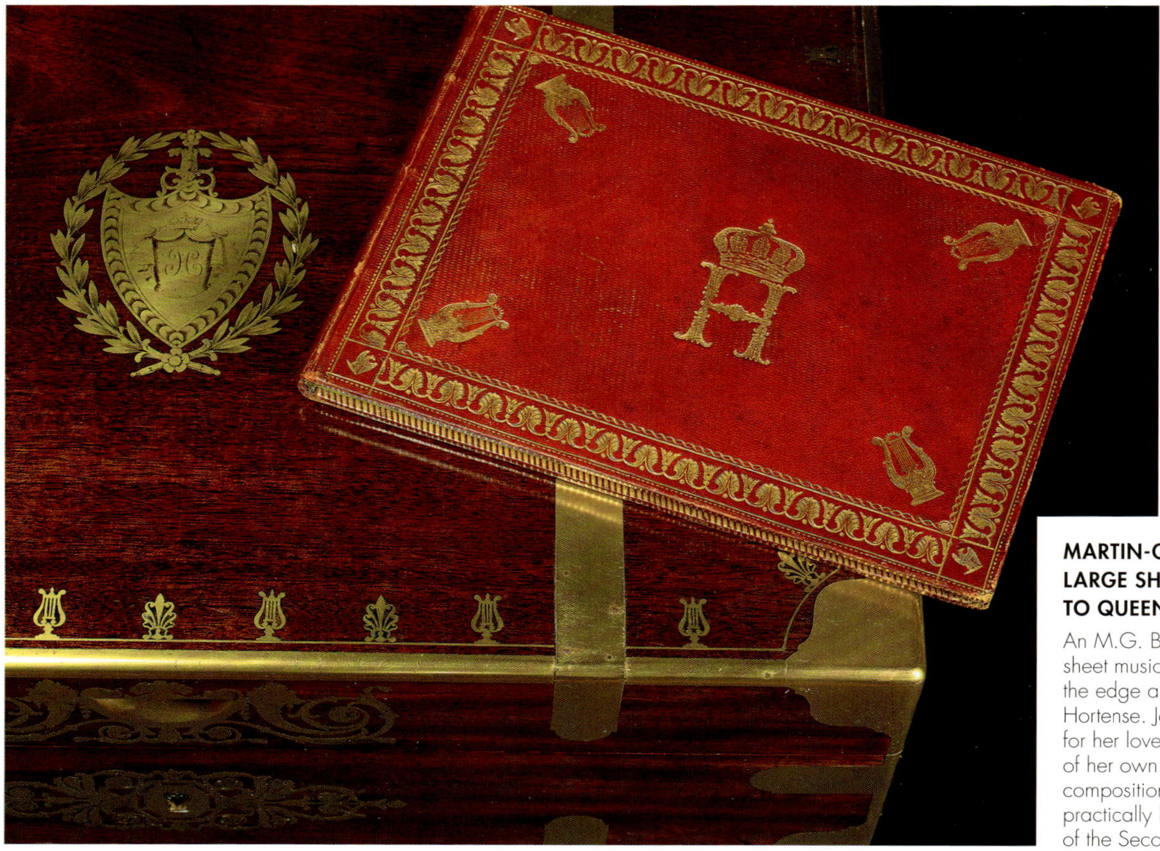

MARTIN-GUILLAUME BIENNAIS (1764-1843), LARGE SHEET MUSIC CABINET BELONGING TO QUEEN HORTENSE

An M.G. Biennais mahogany and gilded brass sheet music cabinet, with lyre motif around the edge and lid bearing the monogram of Queen Hortense. Josephine's daughter was well known for her love of music and composed several of her own romances, including her most famous composition *En partant pour la Syrie*, which practically became the national anthem in the time of the Second French Empire.

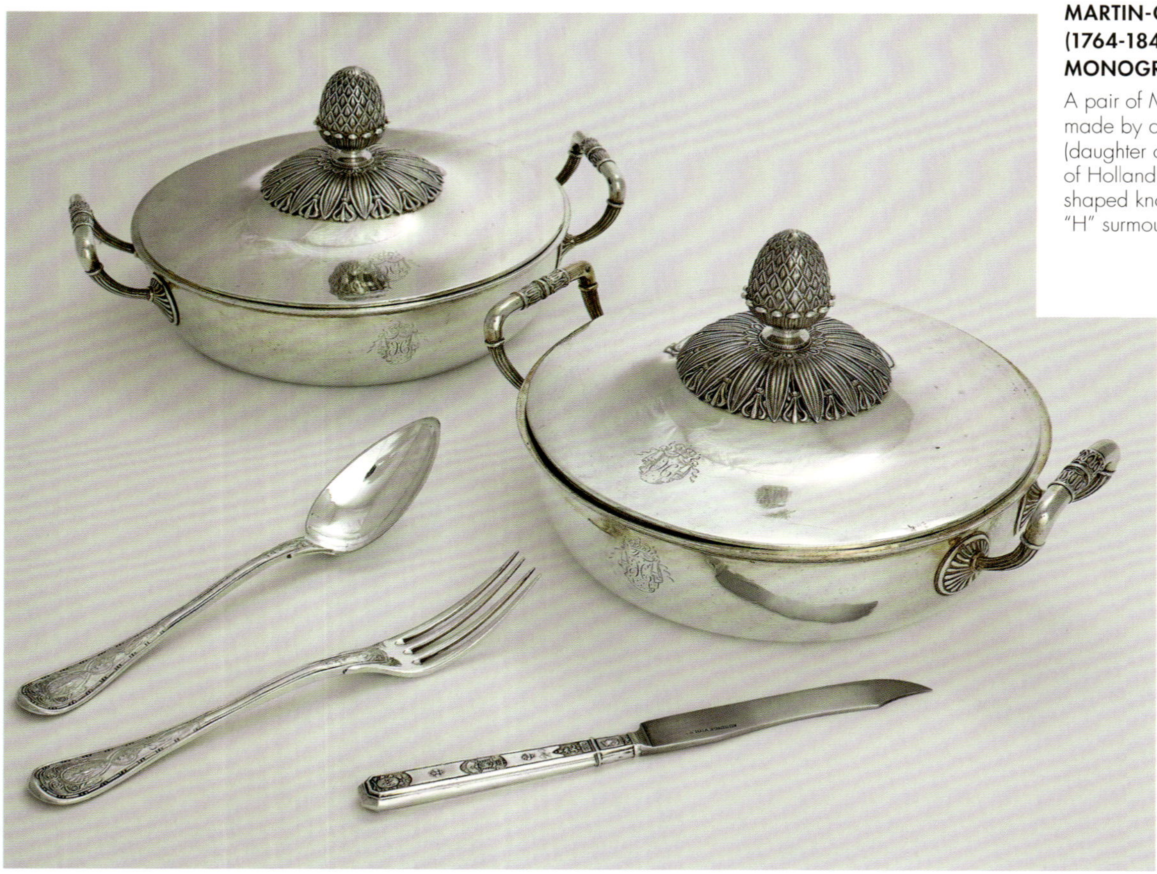

MARTIN-GUILLAUME BIENNAIS (1764-1843), VEGETABLE DISHES WITH MONOGRAM OF QUEEN HORTENSE

A pair of M.G. Biennais silver vegetable dishes made by appointment to Queen Hortense (daughter of the Empress Josephine and Queen of Holland), with lid featuring a pineapple-shaped knob and an embossed monogram "H" surmounted by the imperial crown.

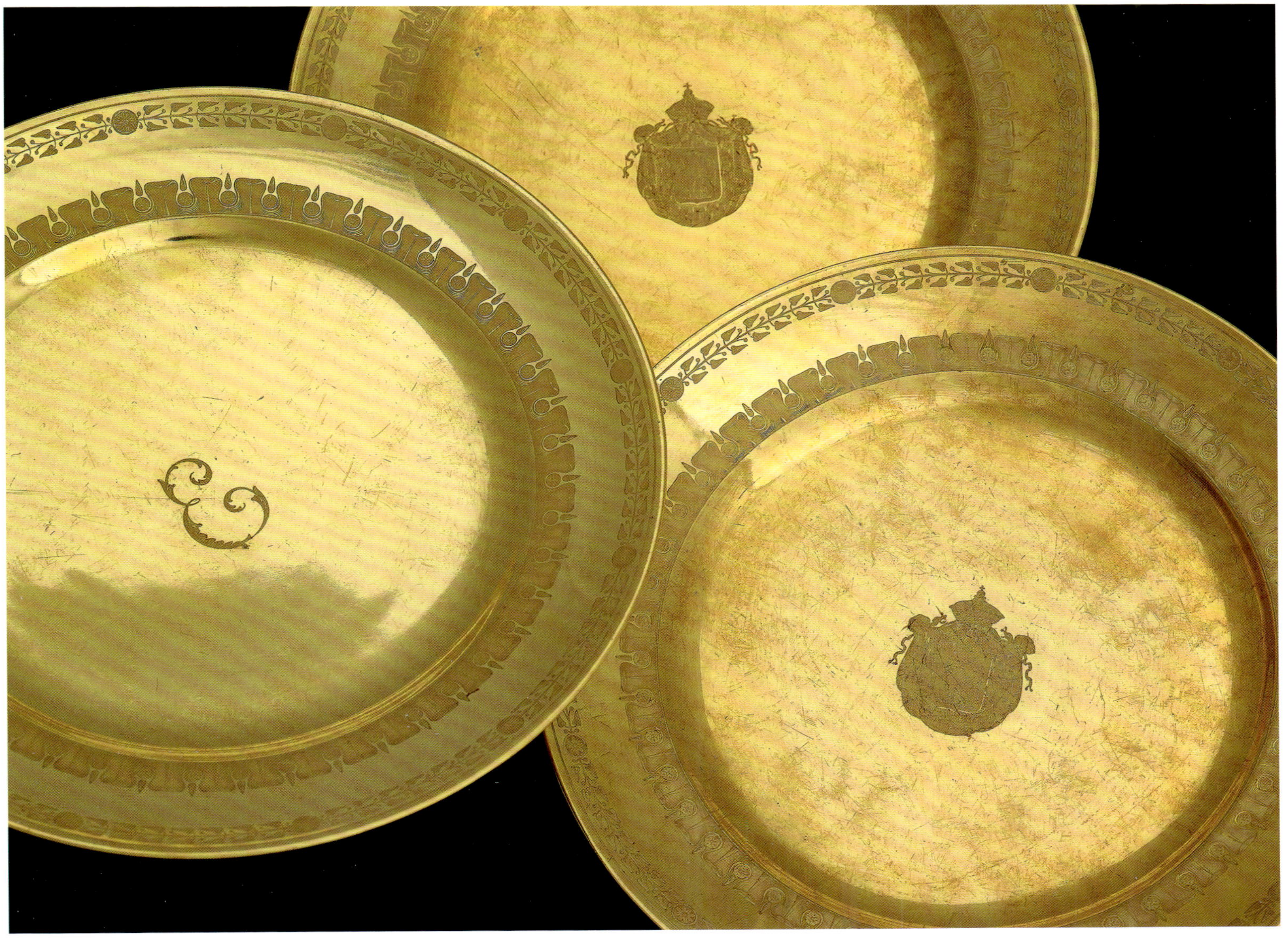

DIHL ET GUÉRHARD PORCELAIN FACTORY, PLATES FROM PRINCE EUGÈNE'S AND EMPRESS JOSEPHINE'S SERVICE

Prince Eugène commissioned a porcelain dessert service from the Dihl et Guérhard manufactory, which matched the service belonging to his mother, Empress Josephine. Of two plates with the Empress's coat-of-arms, this fully gilded piece – made to resemble vermeil – bears the Prince's monogram and was intended for fruit.

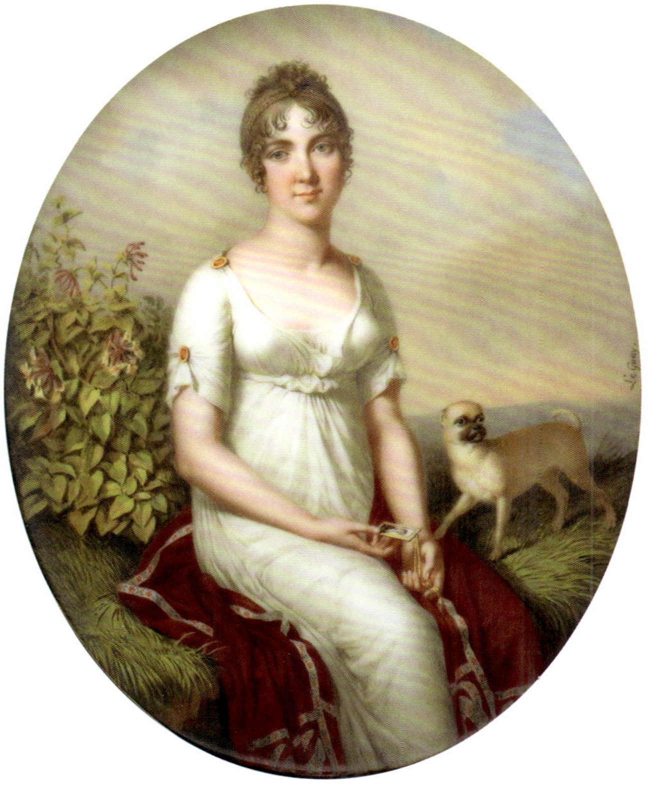

DIHL ET GUÉRHARD PORCELAIN FACTORY, ÉTIENNE-CHARLES LE GUAY (1762-1846), *PORTRAIT OF QUEEN HORTENSE*

Étienne-Charles Le Guay (1762-1846) was a foremost porcelain painter of his day who worked for Sèvres and also for the Dihl et Guérhard porcelain factory in Paris. Shown here is his portrait of Hortense de Beauharnais, then aged 19, painted in 1802 in the year of her marriage to Louis Bonaparte and bearing maker's plaque marked "Dihl et Guérhard."

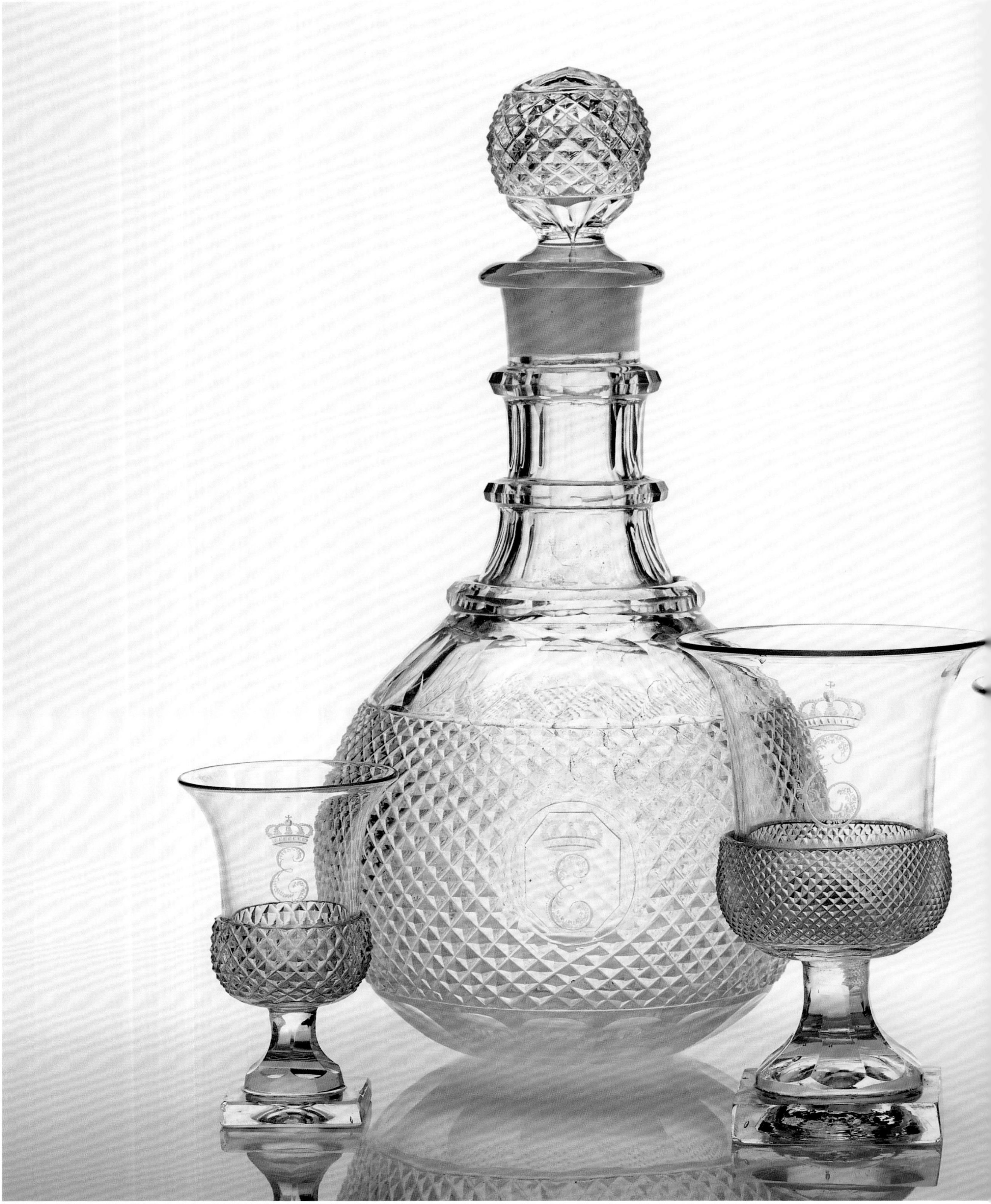

GLASSWARE WITH MONOGRAM OF PRINCE EUGÈNE

An unusual collection of glassware, apparently made by the Mont Cenis crystal works near Creusot and marked with the crowned "E" monogram of Prince Eugène. It comprises a carafe, water glass, two wine glasses, one for red wine and one for white, one liqueur glass and one trumpet-shaped champagne flute, all decorated by means of diamond-point engraving.

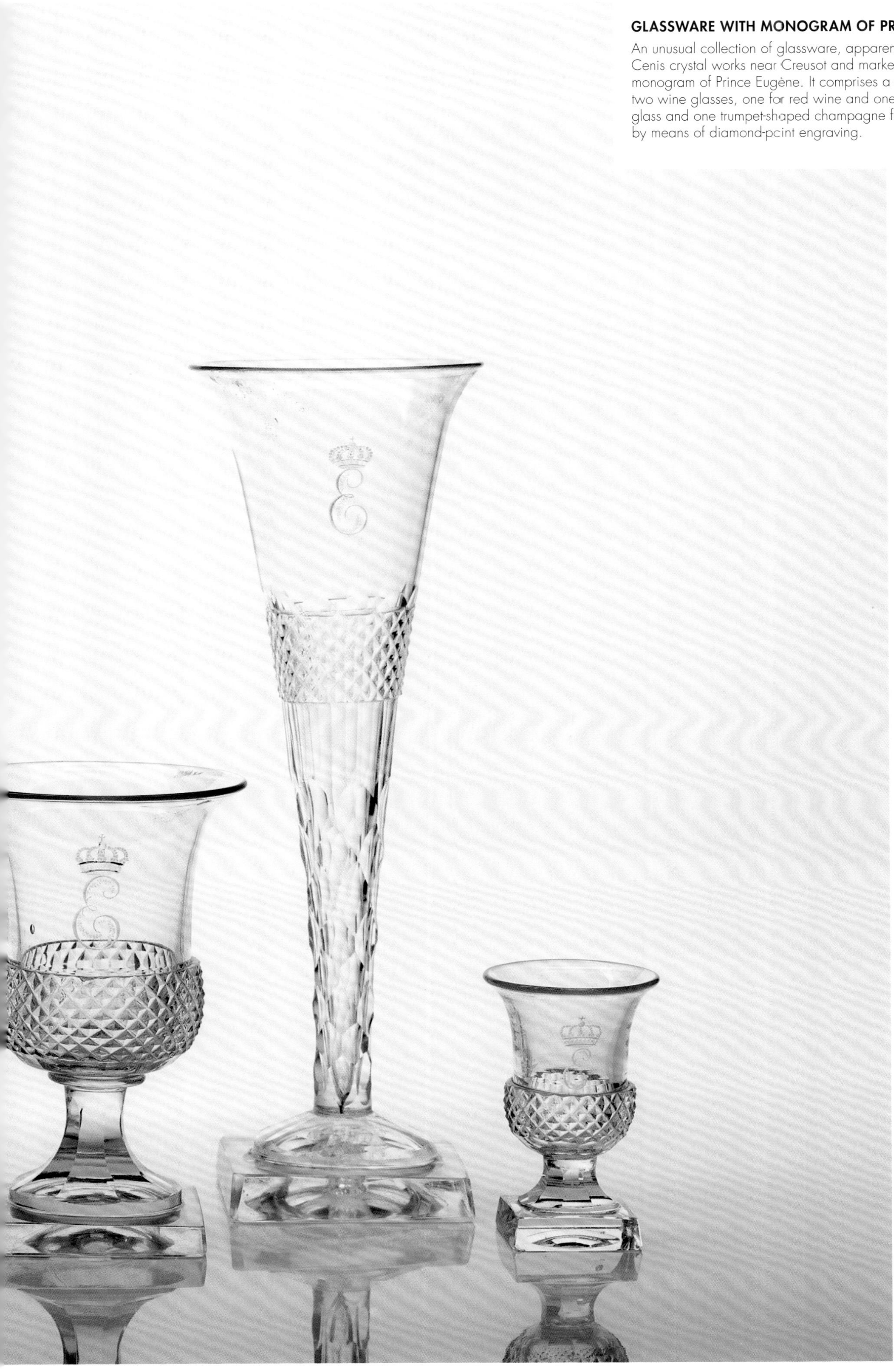

MADAME MÈRE

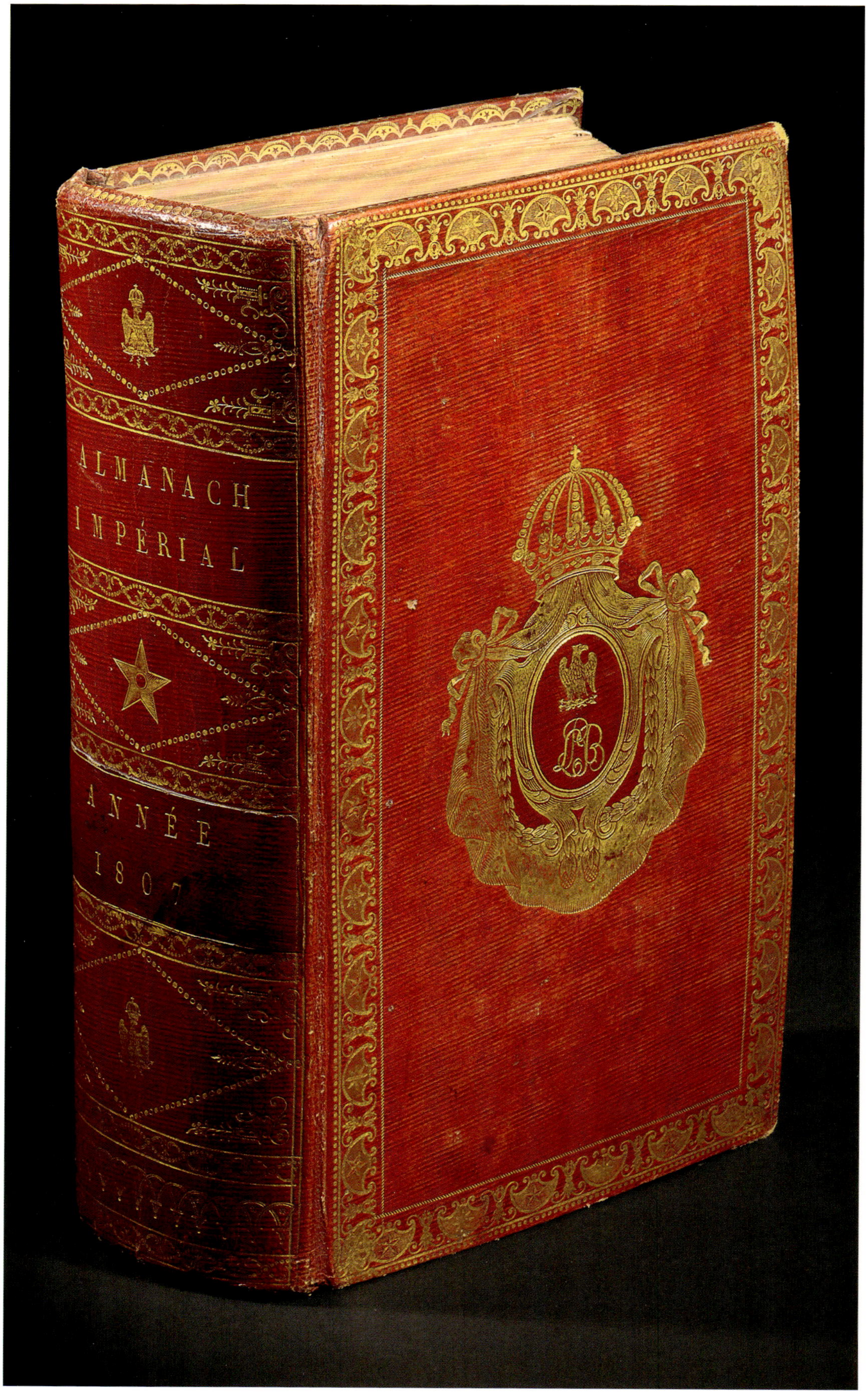

***ALMANACH IMPÉRIAL* FOR 1807, WITH COAT-OF-ARMS OF MADAME MÈRE**

Almanach Impérial for the year 1807, with a very unusual red Morocco leather binding emblazoned with the coat-of-arms of Madame Mère. The "M" for Madame featured on her vermeil dinner service is replaced by the monogram "L.R.B" (for Letizia Ramolino-Bonaparte) topped by an eagle, which stands out from the cover beneath the imperial crown.

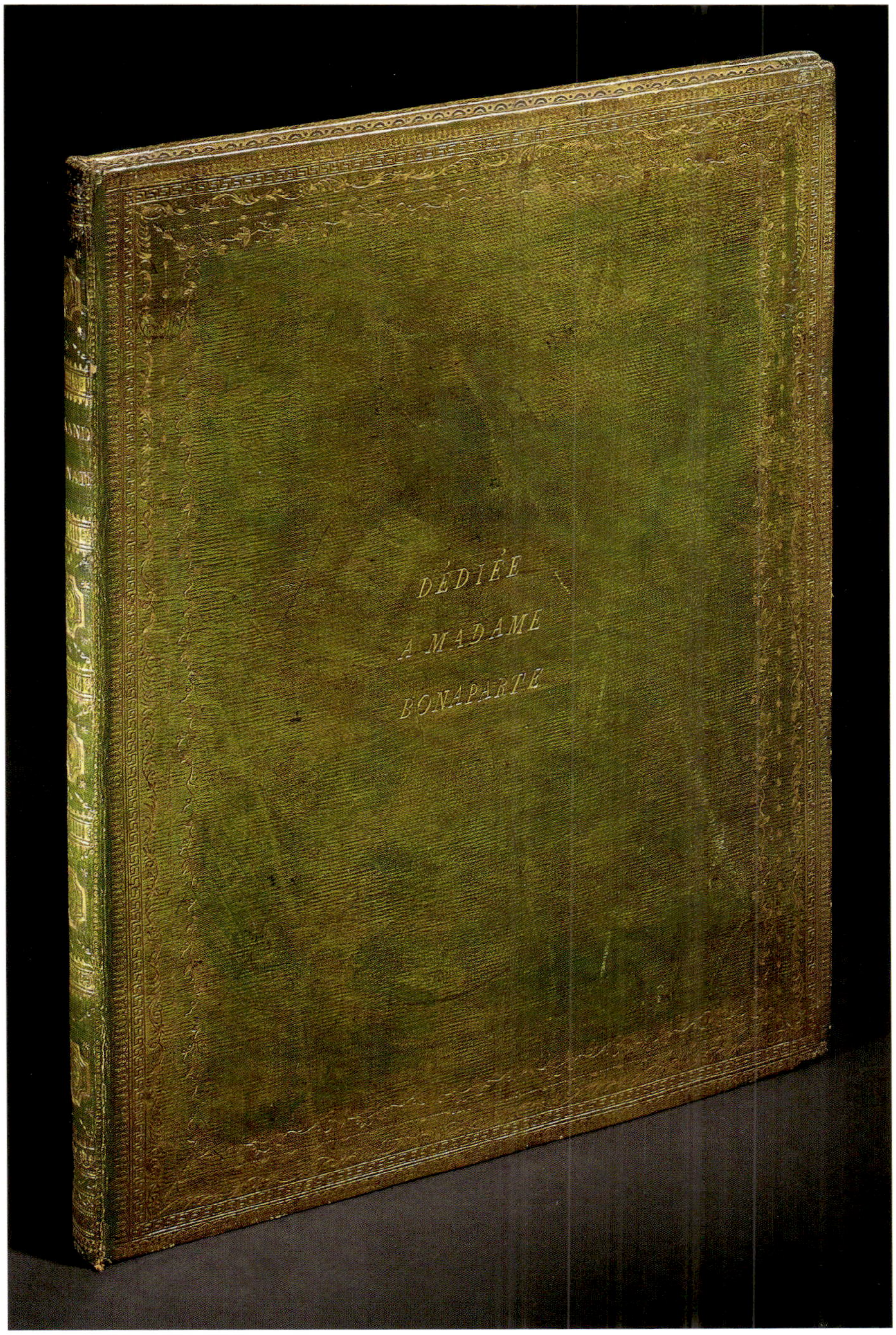

"SONATAS" BY DANIEL STEIBELT, DEDICATED TO MADAME BONAPARTE

This leather volume bound by Pierre-Joseph Bisiaux encloses the sonatas by acclaimed composer Steibelt. He was music master to Hortense de Beauharnais, who herself went on to compose one of the best-known hymns of the Second Empire, "Partant pour la Syrie". The gold-tooled dedication to Madame Mère as "Madame Bonaparte" on its front cover makes this volume unusual.

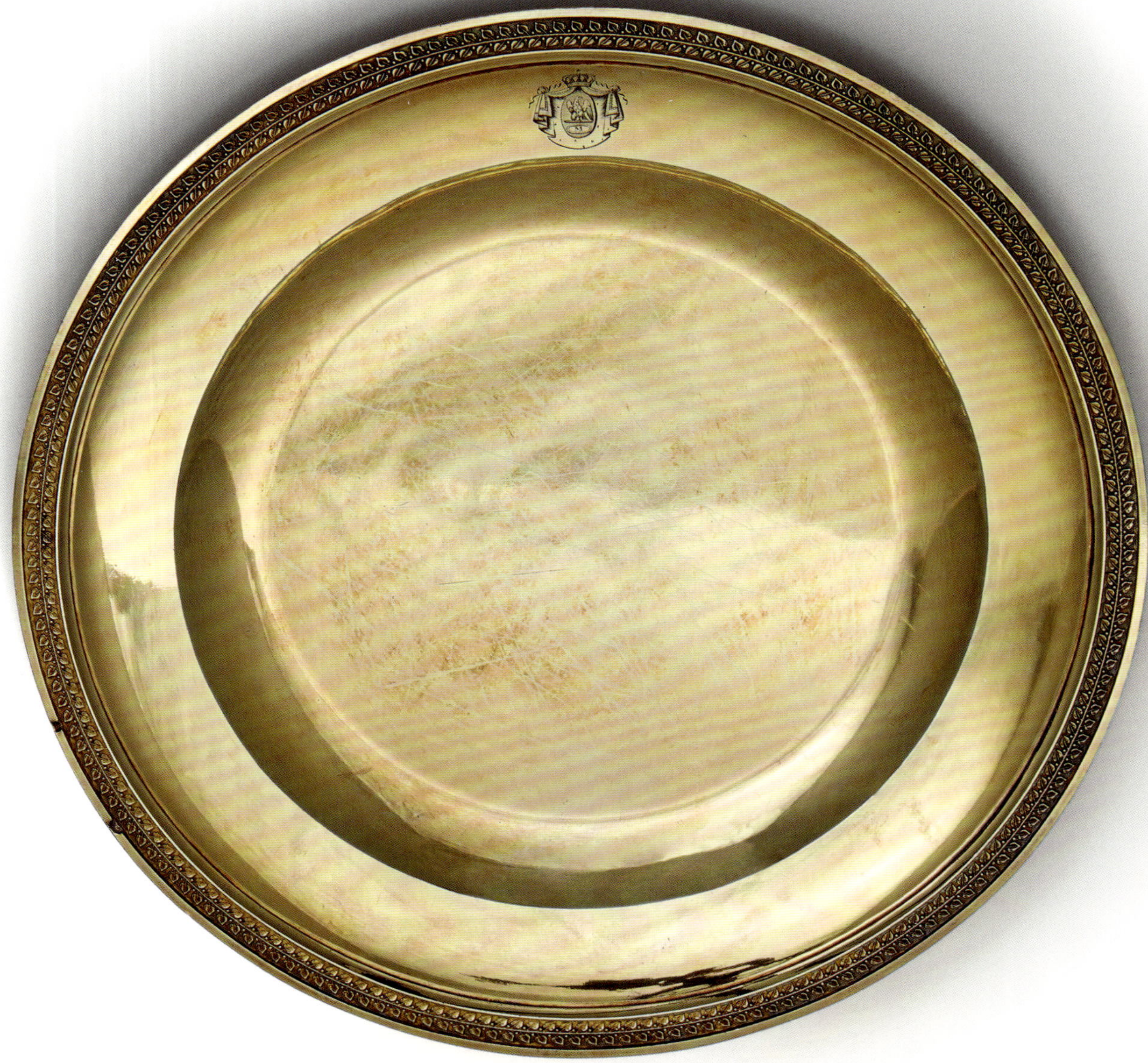

JEAN-BAPTISTE-CLAUDE ODIOT (1763-1850), PLATES FROM MADAME MÈRE'S DINNER SERVICE

Rare plate bearing the imperial coat-of-arms. One of 72 identical plates made by the goldsmith Odiot as part of a vermeil dinner service for Madame Mère, 18 pieces now preserved at the Napoleon Museum at Fontainebleau.

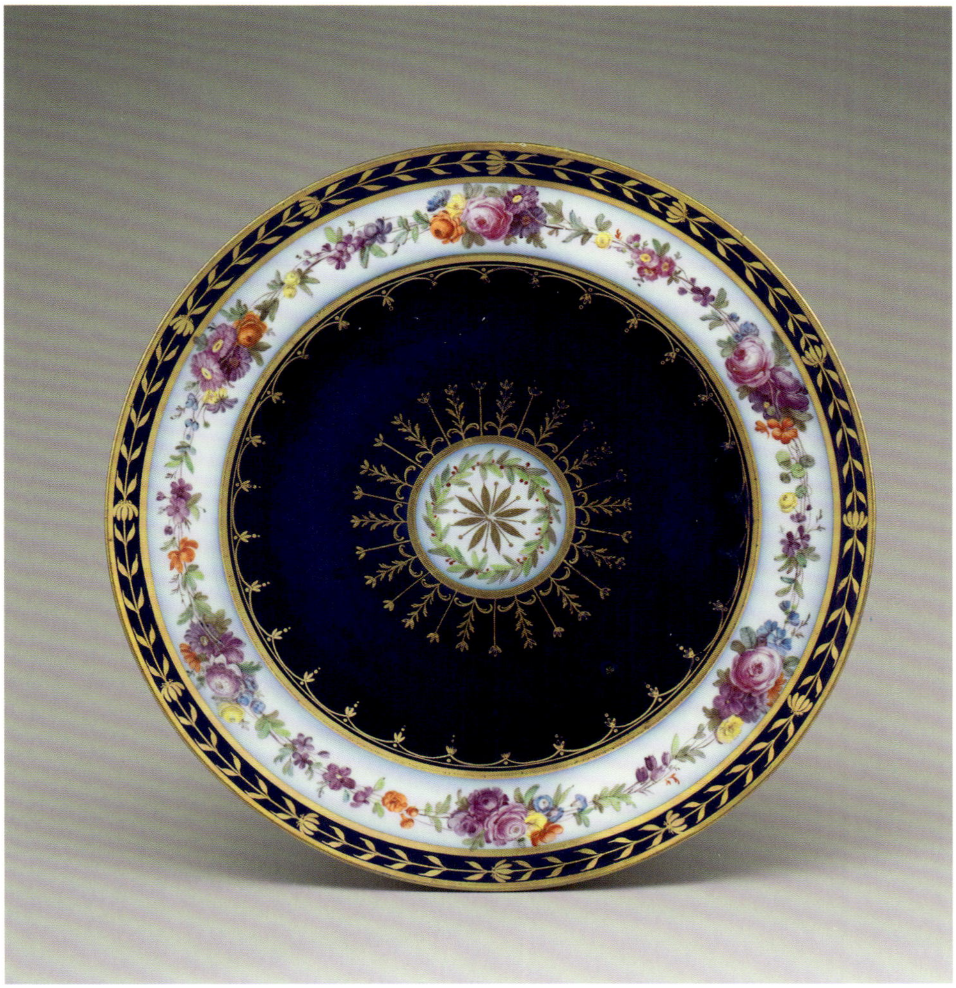

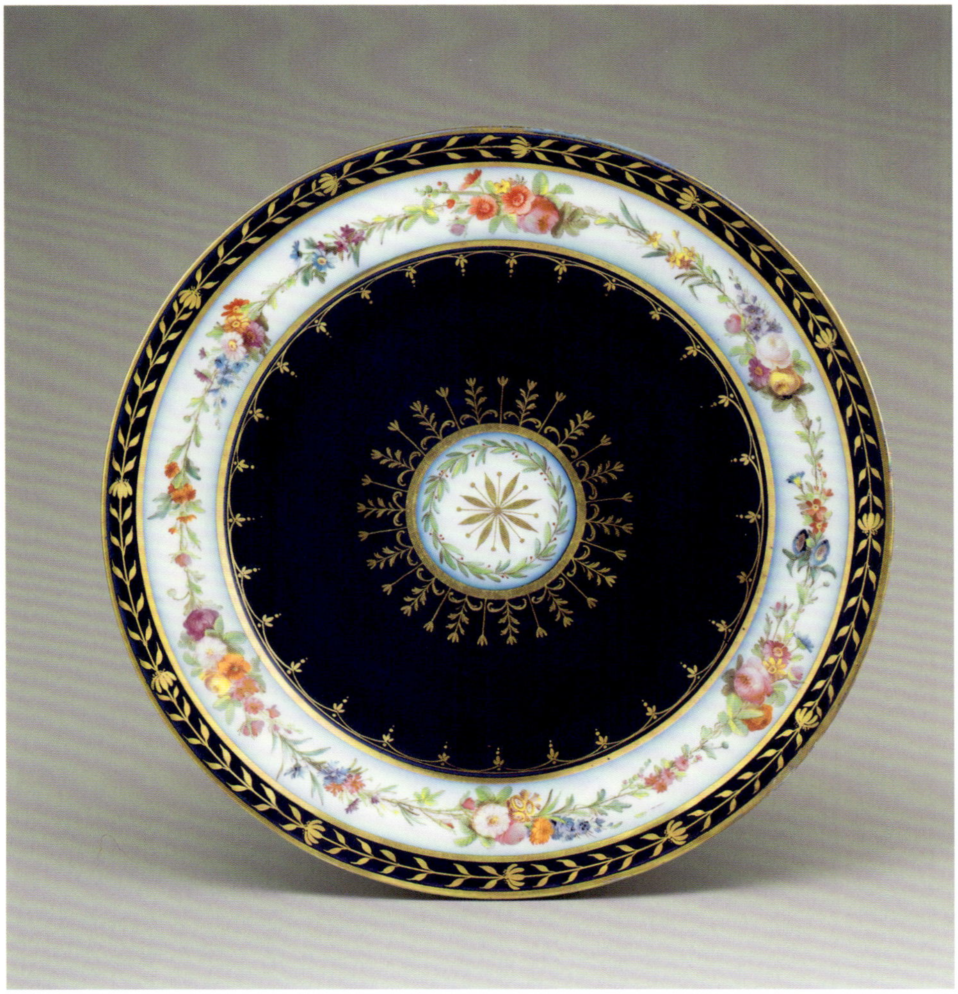

SÈVRES IMPERIAL MANUFACTORY, PLATES FROM MADAME MÈRE'S DINNER SERVICE

These plates from the service with a "beau bleu" ground color are bordered with a garland of colored flowers. It was bought from the manufactory by Napoleon's mother Letizia Bonaparte in March 1802.

THE BROTHERS AND SISTERS

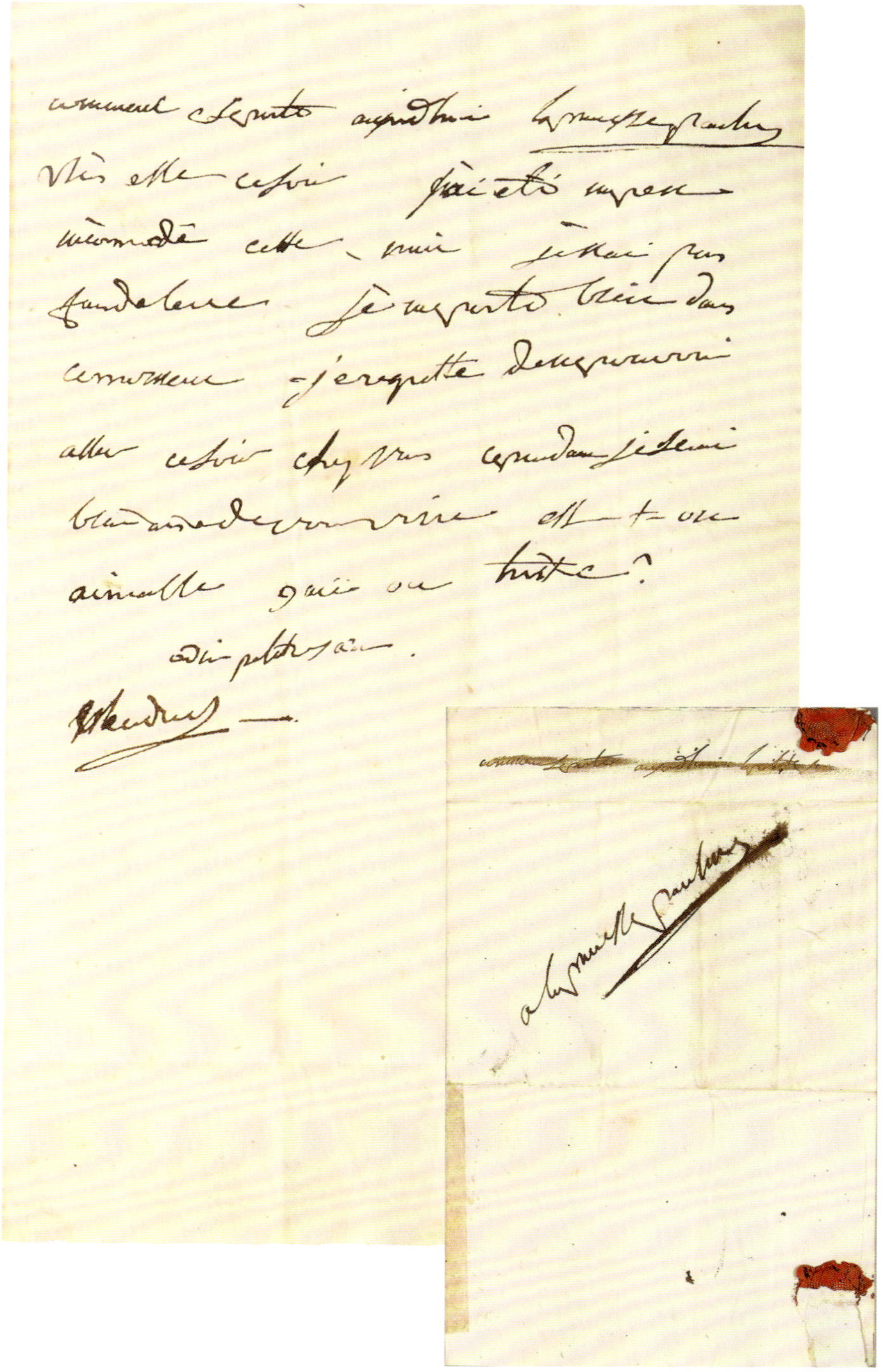

HANDWRITTEN LETTER FROM NAPOLEON TO PAULINE

When Napoleon divorced Josephine, his sister Pauline Borghèse pushed one of her ladies-in-waiting into his arms. Her name was Christine de Mathis and she remained Napoleon's mistress from December 1809 to January 1810. Their affair prompted an intimate exchange of handwritten notes between the Emperor and his matchmaking sister, such as this one that reads: "To Pauline. How is the Princess Pauline today[?] Will she come tonight[?] I was slightly unwell last night. I was not for leaving my bed. I am quite well at present. I regret not being able to visit you tonight but would be very pleased to see you. Are we feeling amiable, gay or sad? Adieu little sister… Napoleon."

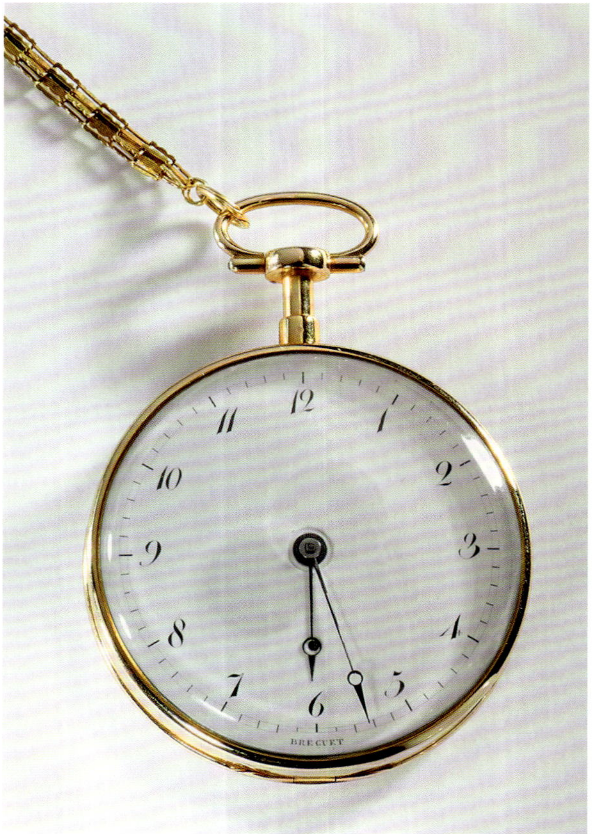

ABRAHAM BREGUET GOLD WATCH BELONGING TO JOSEPH BONAPARTE

The House of Breguet was founded in 1775 by watchmaker Abraham-Louis Breguet (1747-1823) and by 1798 was making watches for most of Napoleon's family. Records show that in 1802 the House sold this gold repeating watch to Joseph Bonaparte. It features a highly sophisticated mechanism that indicates the hours and fractions of hours and has retained its original key and chain. The Breguet Museum aims to collect and preserve the watches made for members of the imperial family so there are very few in private hands.

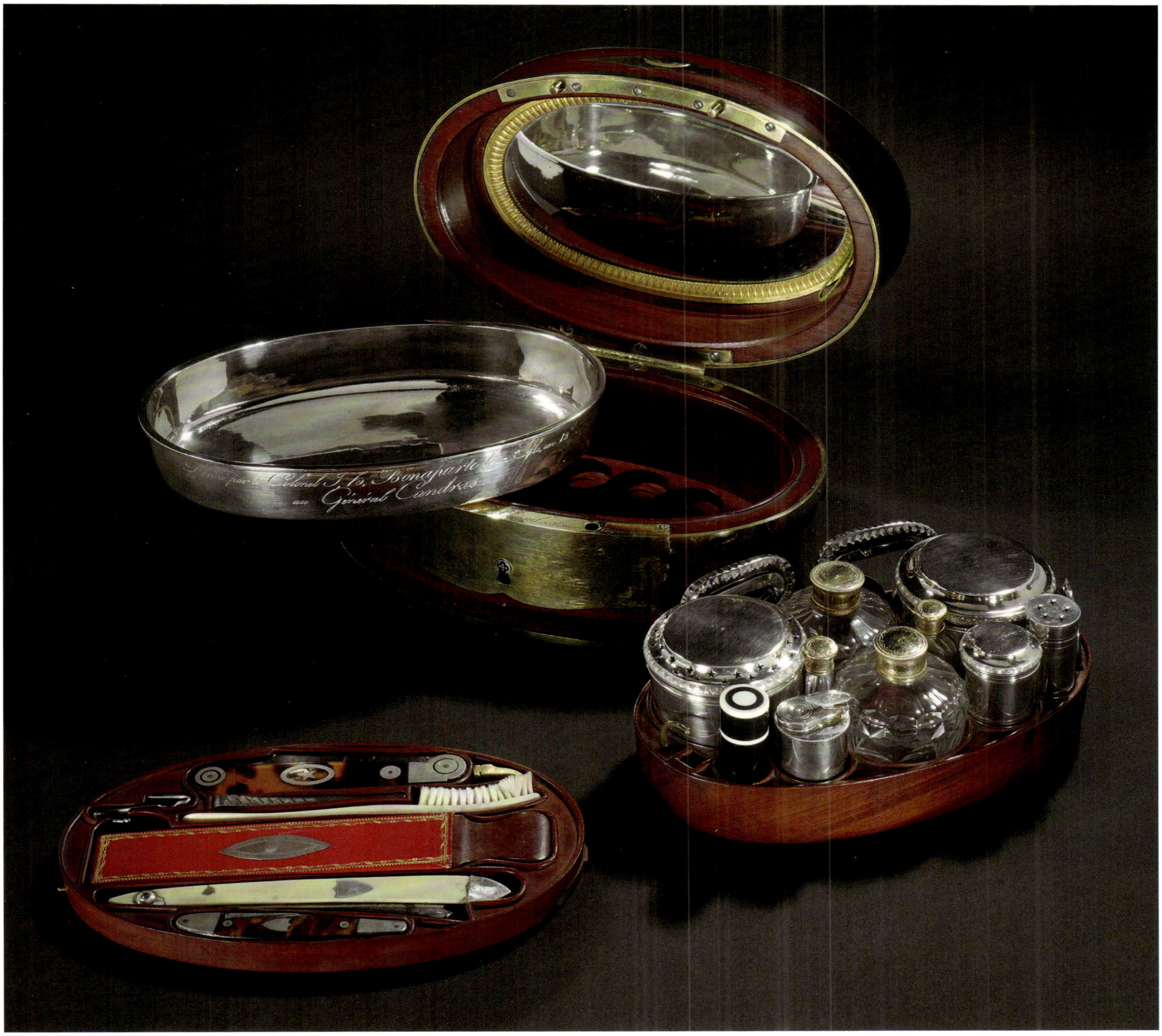

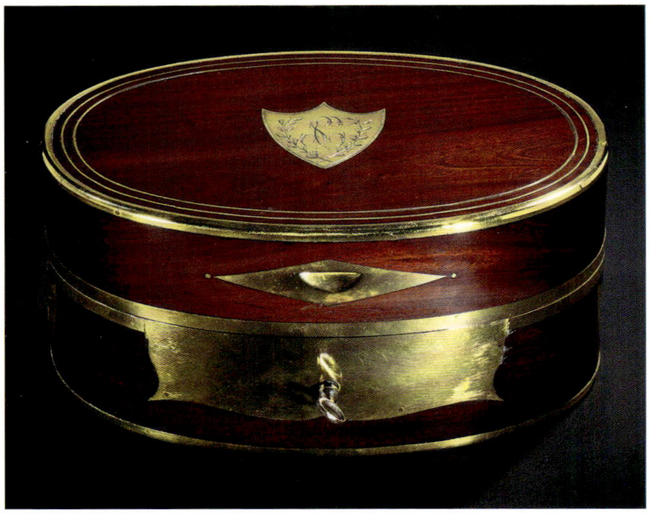

MARTIN-GUILLAUME BIENNAIS (1764-1843), *NÉCESSAIRE* OFFERED BY JOSEPH BONAPARTE TO GENERAL CANDRAS

Pictured here is one of very few oval-shaped *nécessaires* that were made by Biennais. This one bears the initials "S.C," for Jacques-Lazare de Savettier Candras, together with the dedication, engraved cn the silver oval-shaped shaving bowl: *Donné par le colonel Bonaparte le 17 floréal an 12 [7 mai 1804] au génércl Candras* (presented by Colonel Bonaparte on 17 Floréal Year 12 [17 May 1804] to General Candras). Joseph Bcnaparte is thought to have offered this *nécessaire* to Candras, when they assumed joint command of the fourth regiment of the line. After seeing combat at the battles of Austerlitz, Jena and Eylau, Candras was killed on 28 November 1812 in an attack by 10,000 Russian troops as he and his 1,500-strong brigade of Swiss soldiers were crossing the Berezina River.

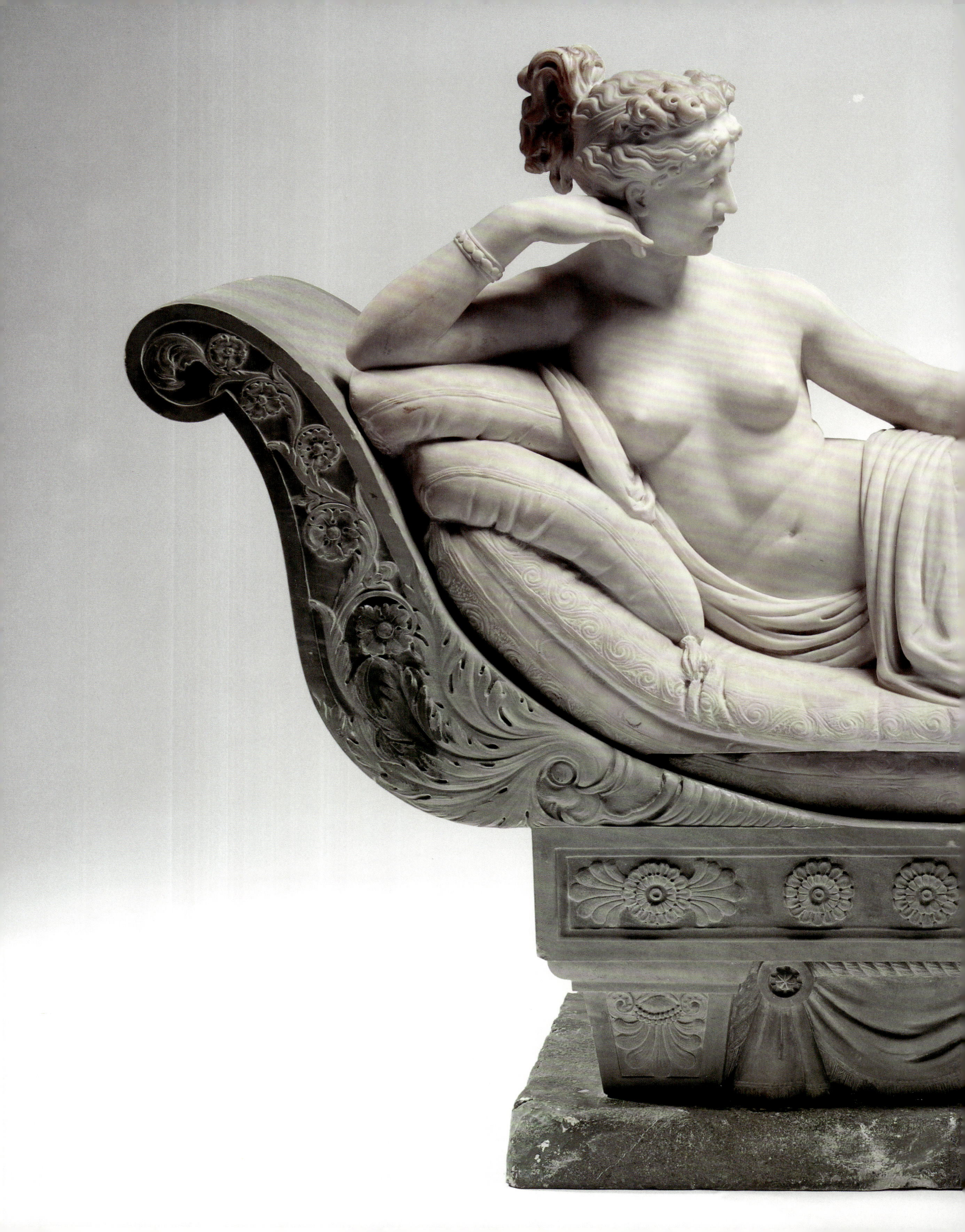

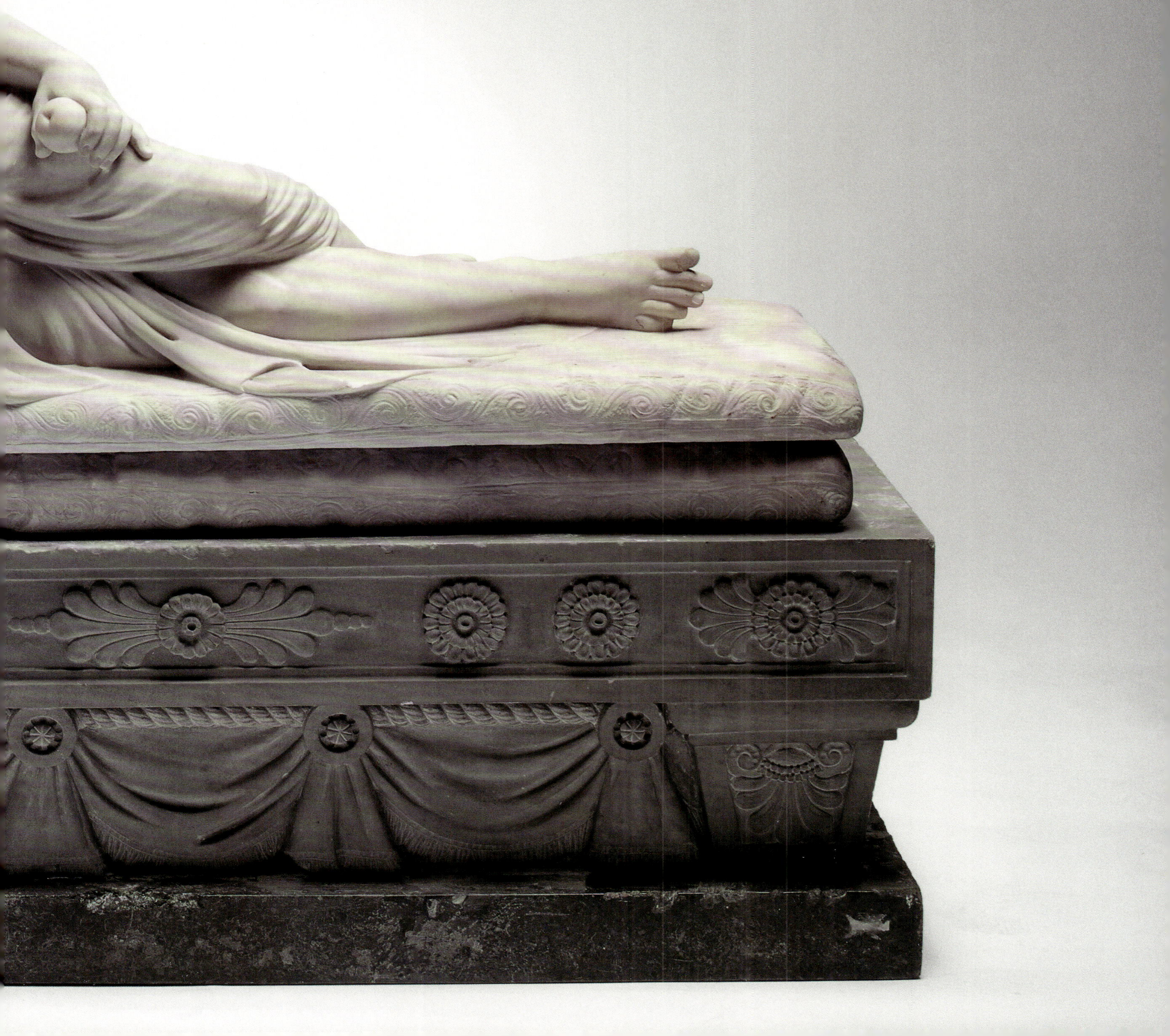

ANTONIO CANOVA (1757-1822), AFTER HIS ORIGINAL, *PAULINE BORGHÈSE AS VENUS*

This representation of Pauline Bonaparte (1780-1825) by one of the greatest sculptors of his time is a cornerstone of Napoleonic iconography, attesting to the beauty of the Emperor's capricious favorite sister. A patron and friend of artists, she posed naked as Venus Victrix or Venus Victorious, heedless to fears of scandal. The original in white Carrara marble was commissioned by Pauline's second husband, Camille Borghèse, and executed between 1805 and 1808. It is kept in the Villa Borghèse in Rome. Several replicas were produced subsequently. This superb unsigned example features the figure of Pauline sculpted in white Carrara marble, reclining on a base of Turquin blue marble decorated with draperies. The curved backrest is carved with stylized flowers and acanthus leaves. The size and quality of this marble dating from the first half of the 19th century make it particularly rare.

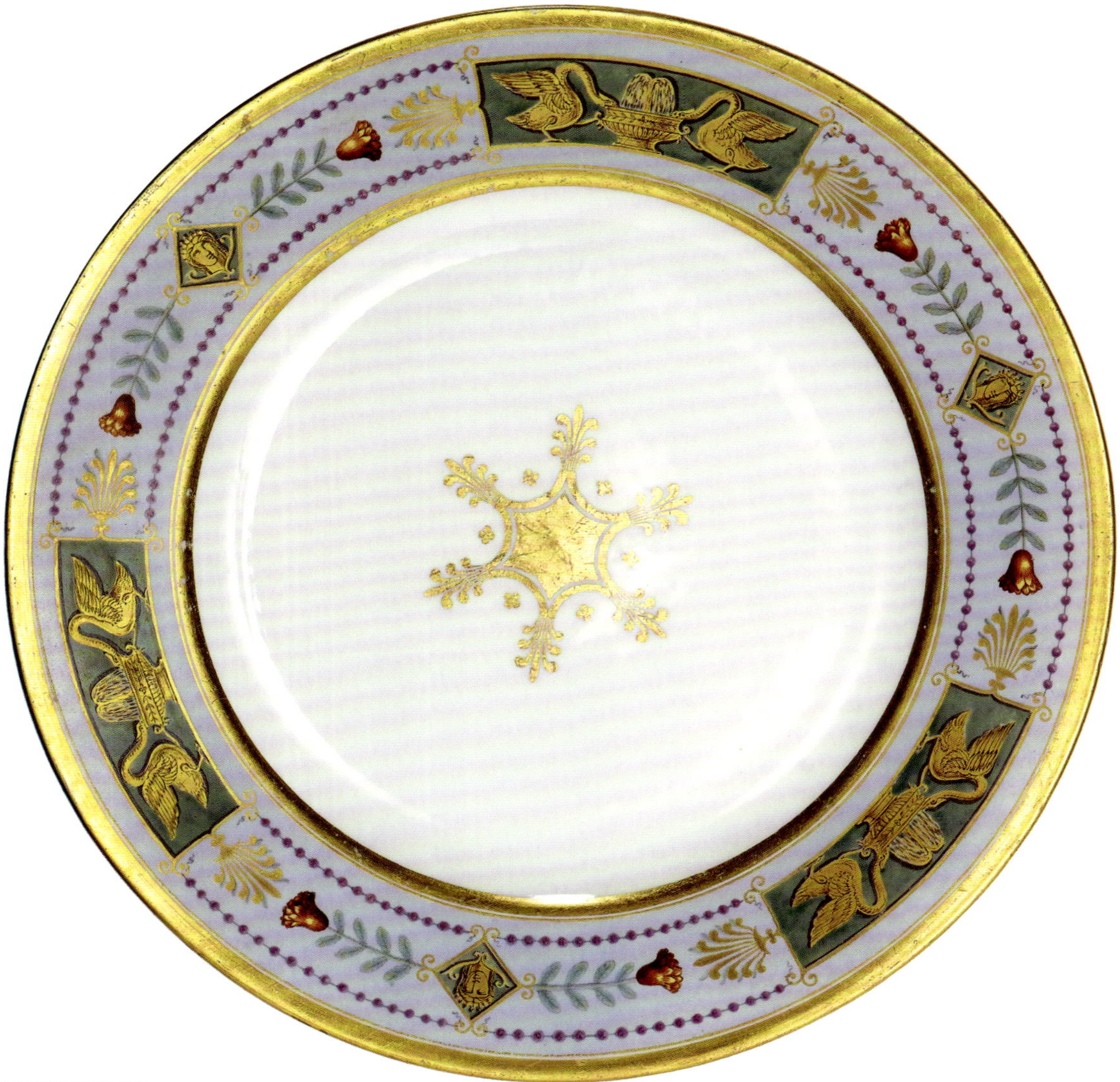

**SÈVRES IMPERIAL MANUFACTORY,
PLATE FROM PAULINE'S DINNER SERVICE**

This hard porcelain plate comes from the gold swan dinner service with pale blue ground and gold decorative motif commissioned by Empress Josephine for Princess Pauline Bonaparte and supplied on 15 Brumaire Year XIV (6 November 1805). The service was divided into a 132-piece dinner service comprising 72 flat plates costing 55 francs each, and a 108-piece dessert service also made up of 72 flat plates, which cost 70 francs each. Their higher cost was justified by the presence of an imitation cameo-style portrait in their center. Two of them are preserved in the collection. Their decoration is described as pale blue ground, swans and heads in gold accentuated in brown on a bronze ground, with a central rose edged with six palm leaves and on the rim two swans in gold, accentuated with brown, around a fountain.

**MARTIN-GUILLAUME BIENNAIS (1764-1843),
SOUP TUREEN FROM PAULINE BONAPARTE'S
GRAND DINNER SERVICE**

This sumptuous piece of goldsmithery demonstrates the virtuoso skills of Biennais. It belonged to the Emperor's sister Pauline Bonaparte, who took for her second husband the very rich Prince Camille Borghèse, scion of one of Rome's oldest families. The superb vermeil service was a gift from Napoleon and comprised over one thousand six hundred pieces, after the designs of Prud'hon, Percier and Fontaine. A substantial part of this service featured in the Rockefeller collection.

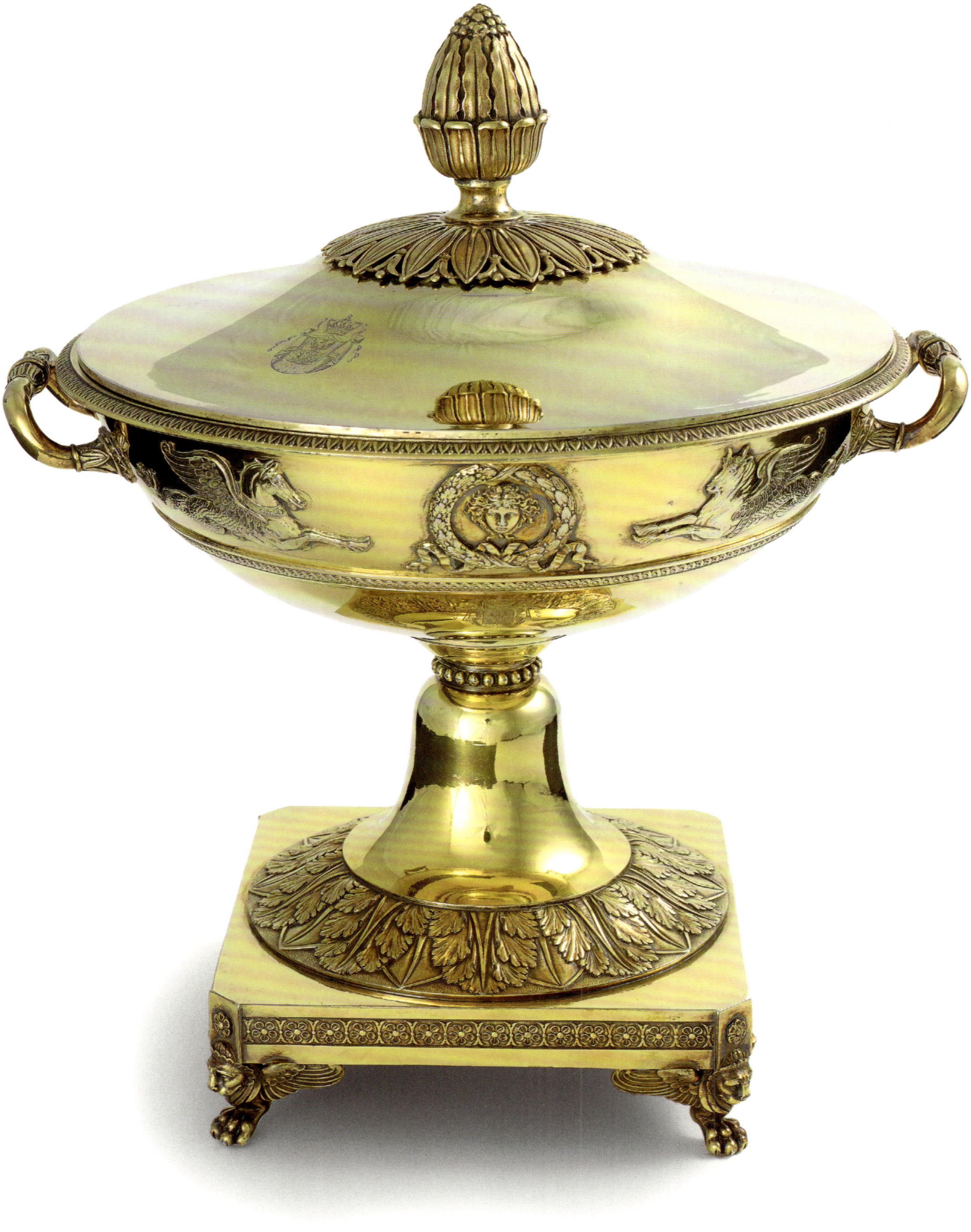

MARTIN-GUILLAUME BIENNAIS (1764-1843), LITTLE BUSTS KNOWN AS THE "NAPOLÉONIDES"

These small busts belong to the series known as the *Napoléonides*. Totaling 28 pieces (including the wax models) and mostly in gilded bronze, they were intended to be given as official gifts to members of the imperial family. They were executed by Biennais as portraits of members of the imperial family including the Emperor himself, Pauline, Caroline, Louis, Jérôme, Hortense, Murat, Catherine de Wurtemberg, Marie-Louise, and Elisa. The collection still holds the last three of these busts.
No mention is made of them in any invoice, correspondence, or inventory. However, the Louvre Museum's graphic arts department possesses sketches by Biennais including those for the busts of Napoleon, Elisa and Marie-Louise.

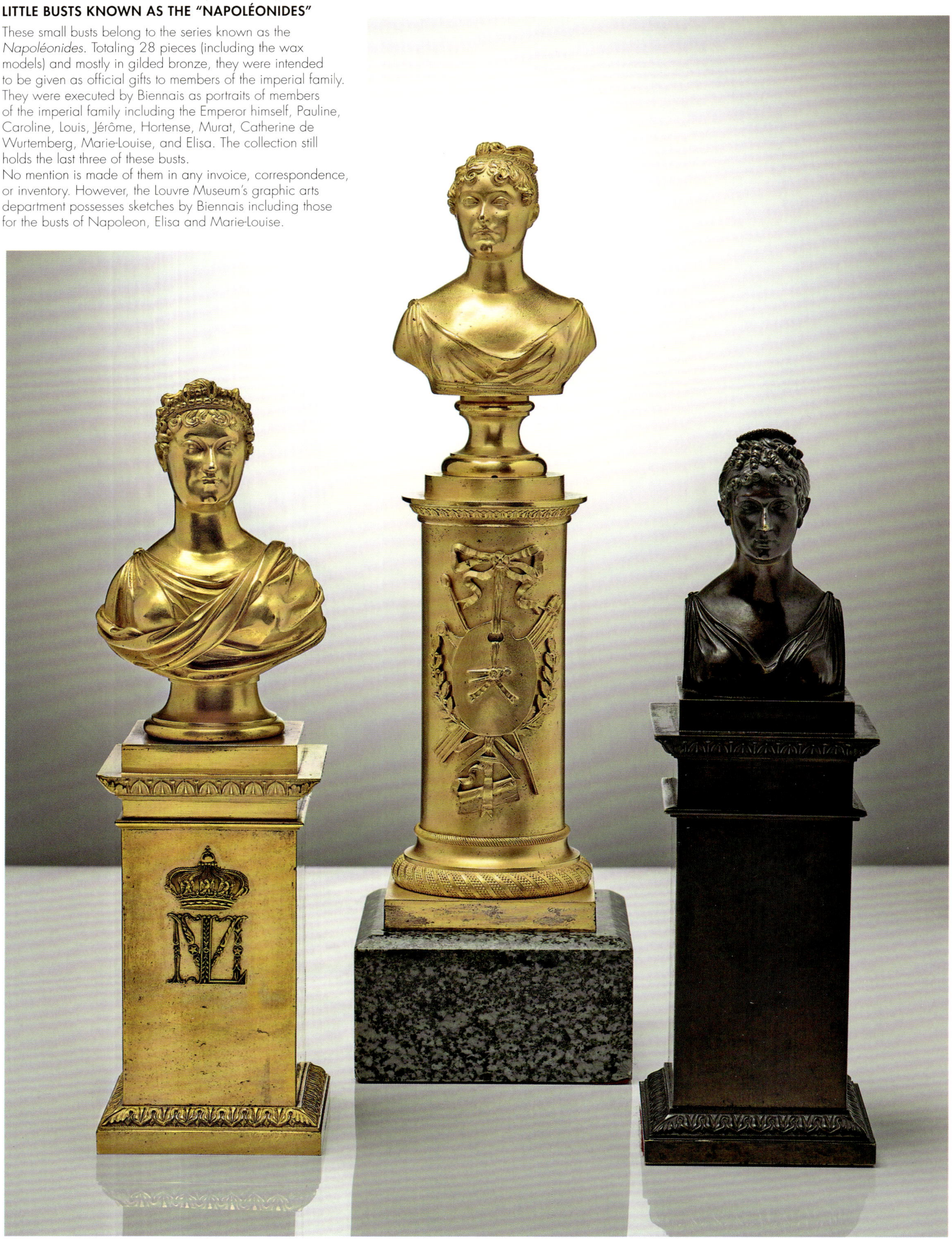

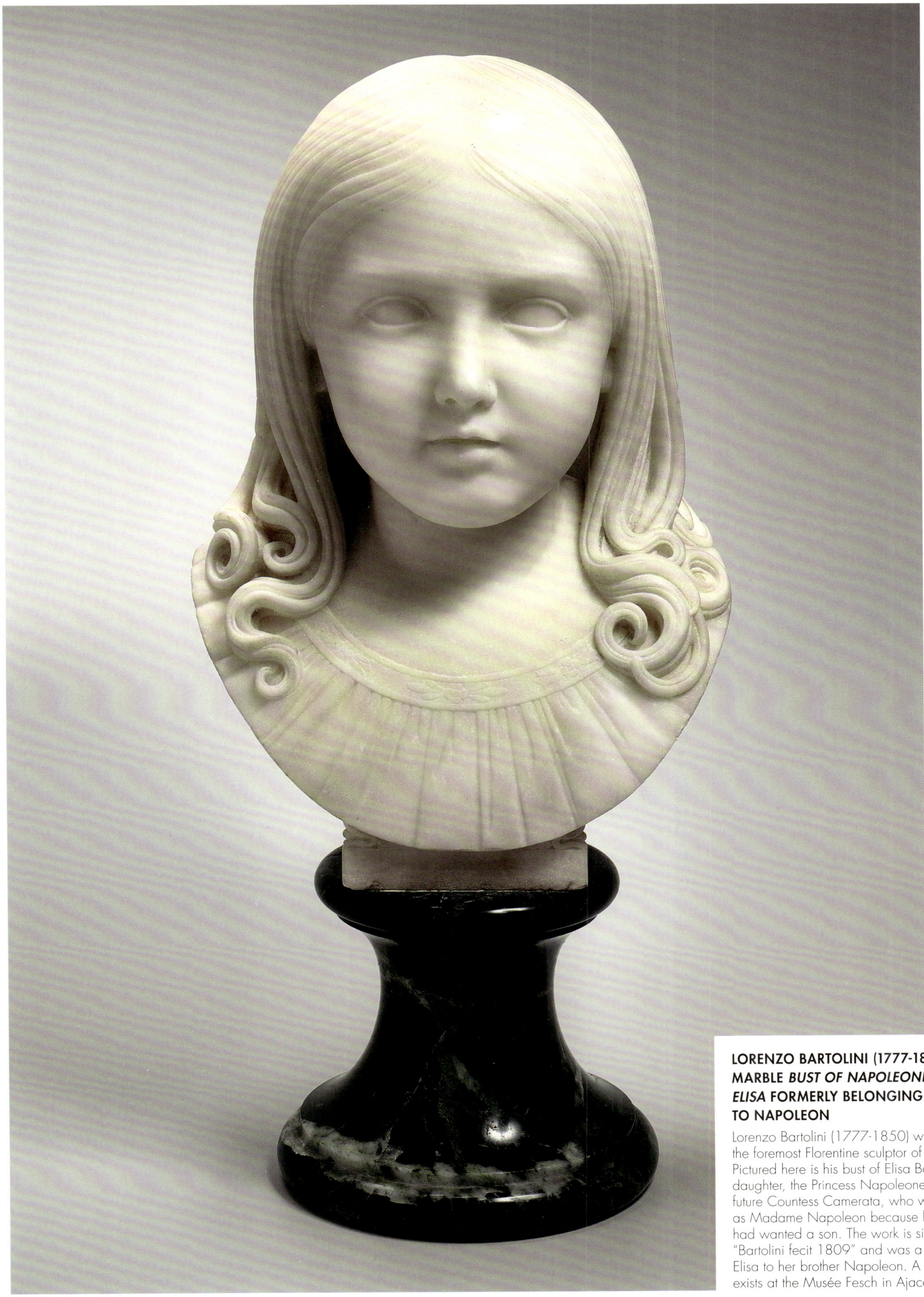

LORENZO BARTOLINI (1777-1850), MARBLE *BUST OF NAPOLEONE ELISA* FORMERLY BELONGING TO NAPOLEON

Lorenzo Bartolini (1777-1850) was the foremost Florentine sculptor of his time. Pictured here is his bust of Elisa Bonaparte's daughter, the Princess Napoleone Elisa, future Countess Camerata, who was known as Madame Napoleon because her mother had wanted a son. The work is signed "Bartolini fecit 1809" and was a gift from Elisa to her brother Napoleon. A replica exists at the Musée Fesch in Ajaccio.

SÈVRES IMPERIAL MANUFACTORY, PAIR OF PLATES WITH GOLD RIMS, PROBABLY FROM MURAT'S DINNER SERVICE

The Sèvres manufactory's archives feature a plate with gold rim listed under 24 September 1817, with a "burnished decorative effect, View of the Milan Courthouse". No doubt this is a reference to the plate shown here. It is accompanied by a second plate, decorated with a view of the Milan Theater. Their choice of Italian views suggests they may have belonged to Joachim Murat's service. What is certain is that the service known as "A marly d'or" can be correlated to a continuous order, with an unlimited amount of plates. It was begun in 1805 and completed under the Restoration. Twenty-four of these plates were given to King Frederick Augustus III of Saxony in 1809, and the Austrian Ambassador received forty-eight of them in 1811.

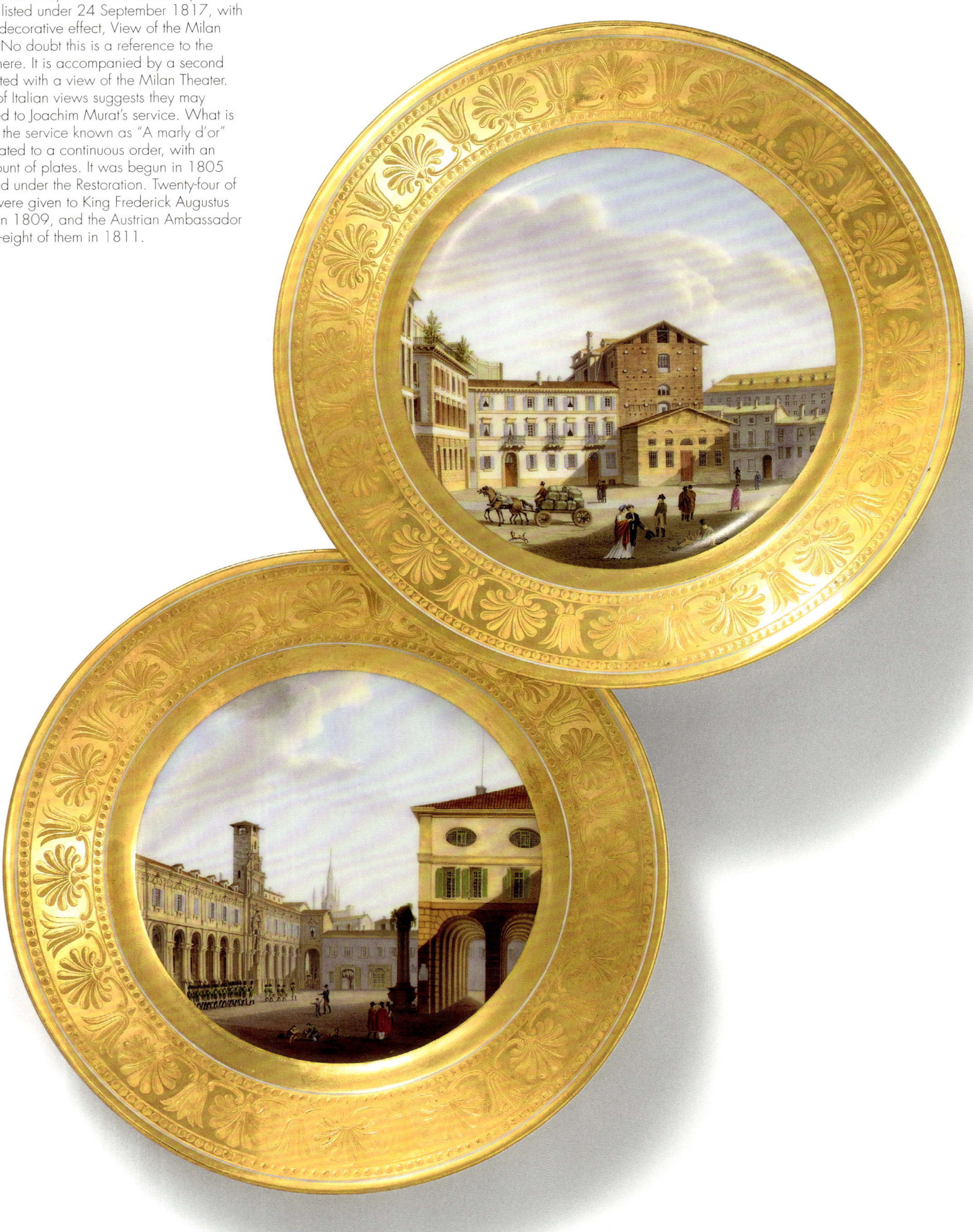

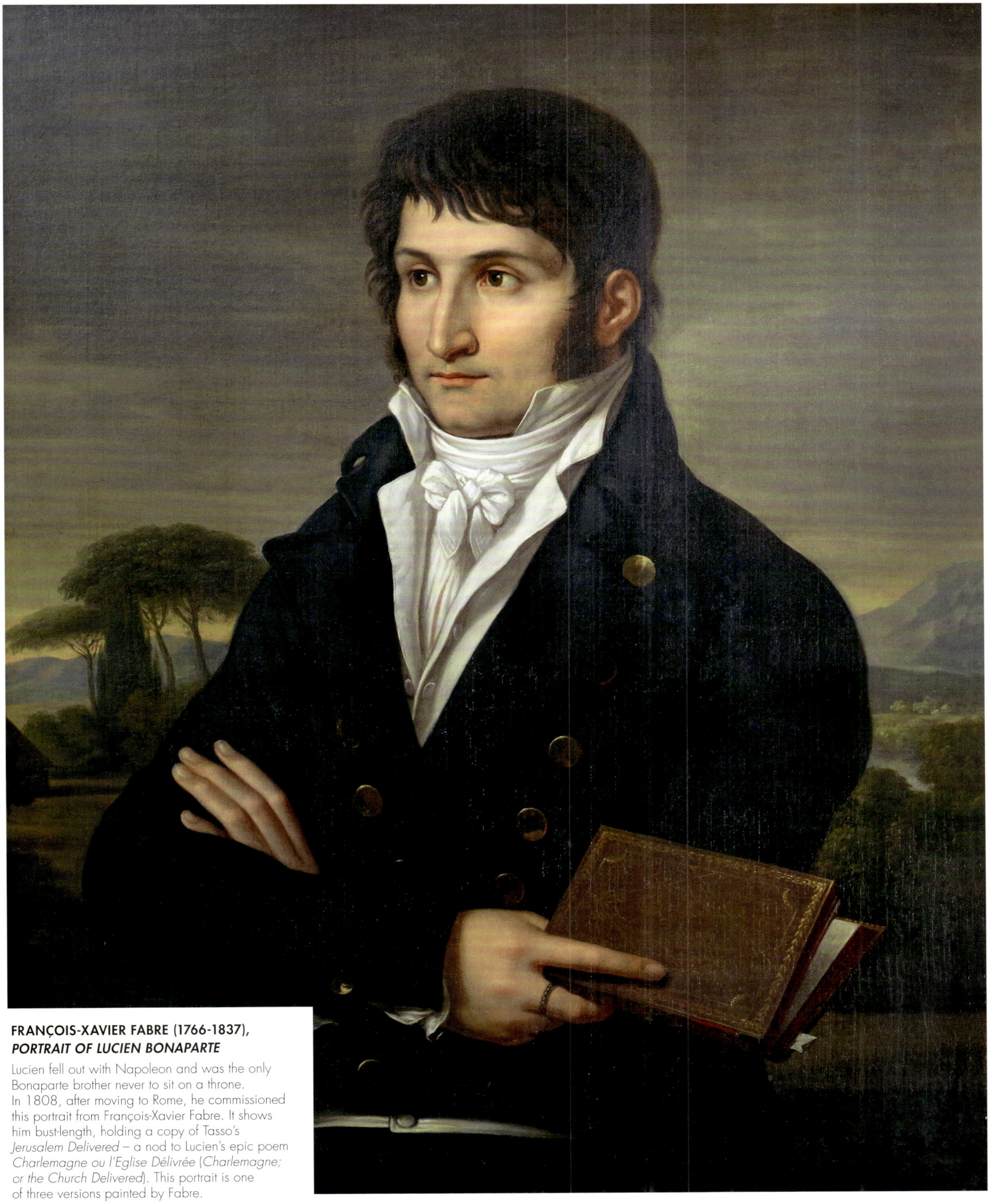

FRANÇOIS-XAVIER FABRE (1766-1837), *PORTRAIT OF LUCIEN BONAPARTE*

Lucien fell out with Napoleon and was the only Bonaparte brother never to sit on a throne. In 1808, after moving to Rome, he commissioned this portrait from François-Xavier Fabre. It shows him bust-length, holding a copy of Tasso's *Jerusalem Delivered* – a nod to Lucien's epic poem *Charlemagne ou l'Eglise Délivrée* (*Charlemagne; or the Church Delivered*). This portrait is one of three versions painted by Fabre.

CEREMONIAL SEAT: A MASTERPIECE OF NEOCLASSICISM

JACOB-DESMALTER (1770-1841), ATTRIBUTED, CEREMONIAL SEAT

The exact provenance of this exceptional chair has not yet been established. In the absence of any mark or stamp, we are unable to assign it to any artist or patron. Nevertheless, this commanding seat seems to be unique both in its shape and style, and all evidence points to it being a masterpiece of the early 19th-century French decorative arts. The opulence of its striking decoration marks it out as a prestigious piece, inevitably associated with a figure of very high status. The seat and backrest are upholstered in green silk velvet with a border of embroidered silver foliage. On the seat back, a sculpted design of laurel leaves frames a medallion bearing the portrait of a woman in profile, in the Classical style. Either side of it are two large cornucopias. A pattern of roses, arabesques and tulips is sculpted in relief on the lower section. Two legs support the seat, sculpted with the heads of eagles and the bodies of lions. Underneath the piece stands a mahogany base decorated with a lyre. The incorporation of flowers – much loved by Josephine – in the form of a bouquet, and a lyre recalling her daughter Hortense's passion for music, probably indicates the seat belonged to the imperial family. The highly "Davidian" style could also suggest a ceremonial seat ordered as a one-off for a very important occasion, perhaps even by the painter Jacques-Louis David himself for a decorative scheme he was put in charge of.

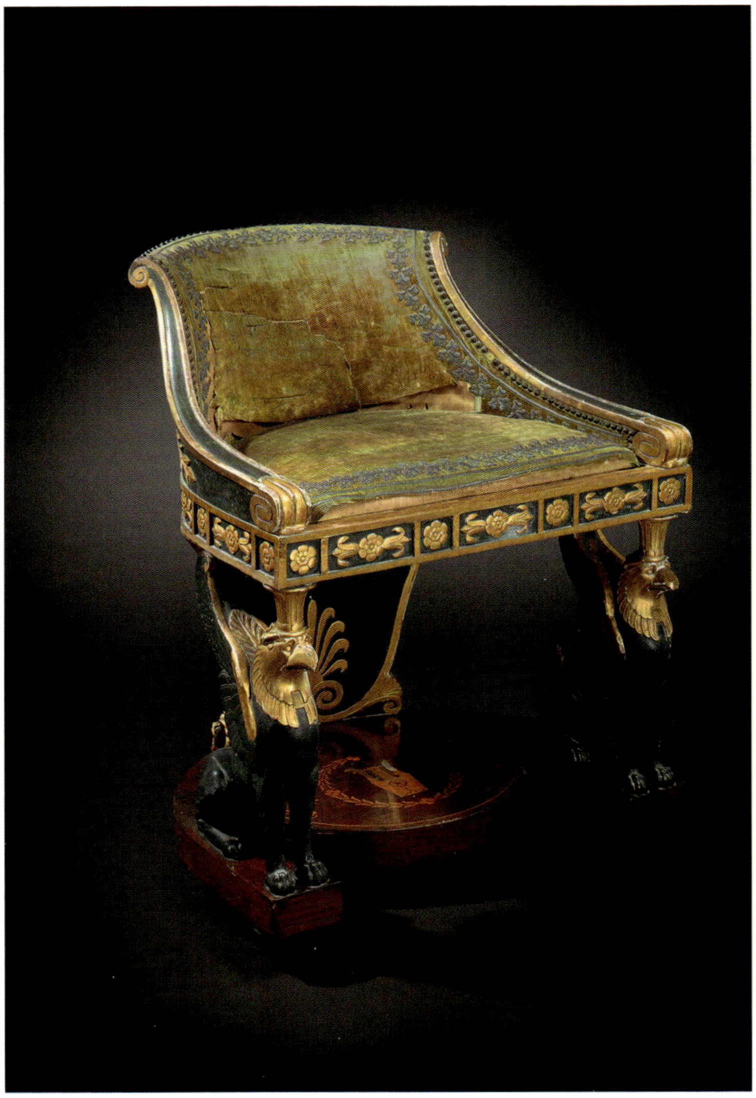

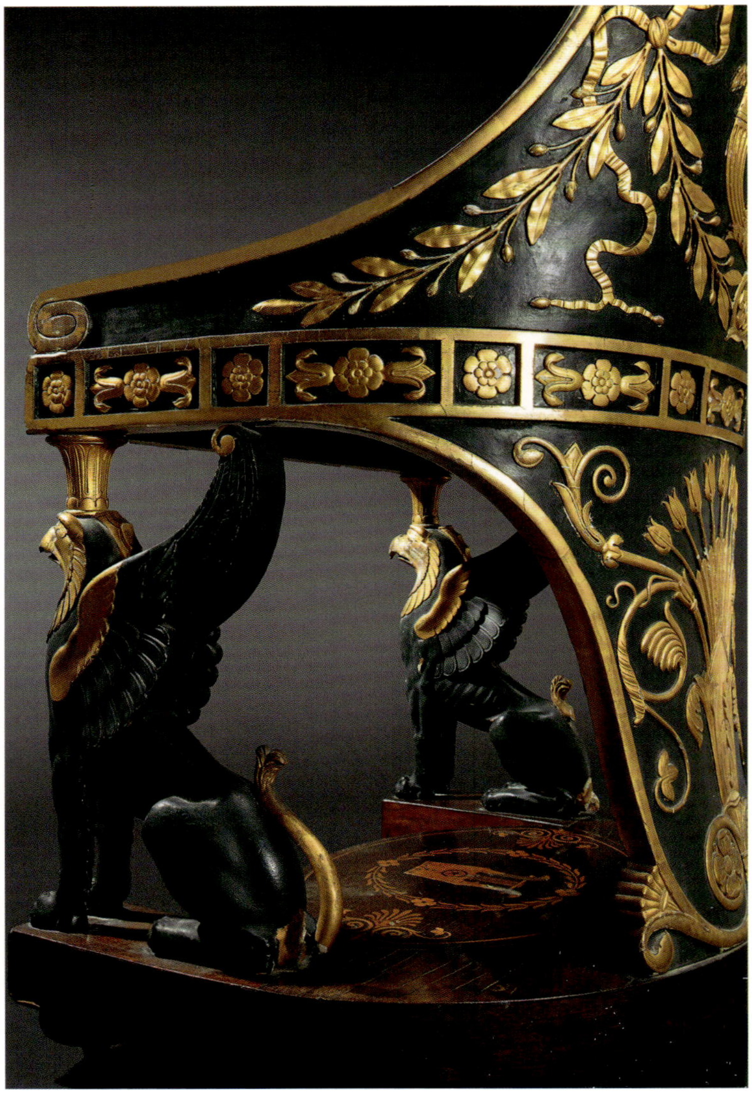

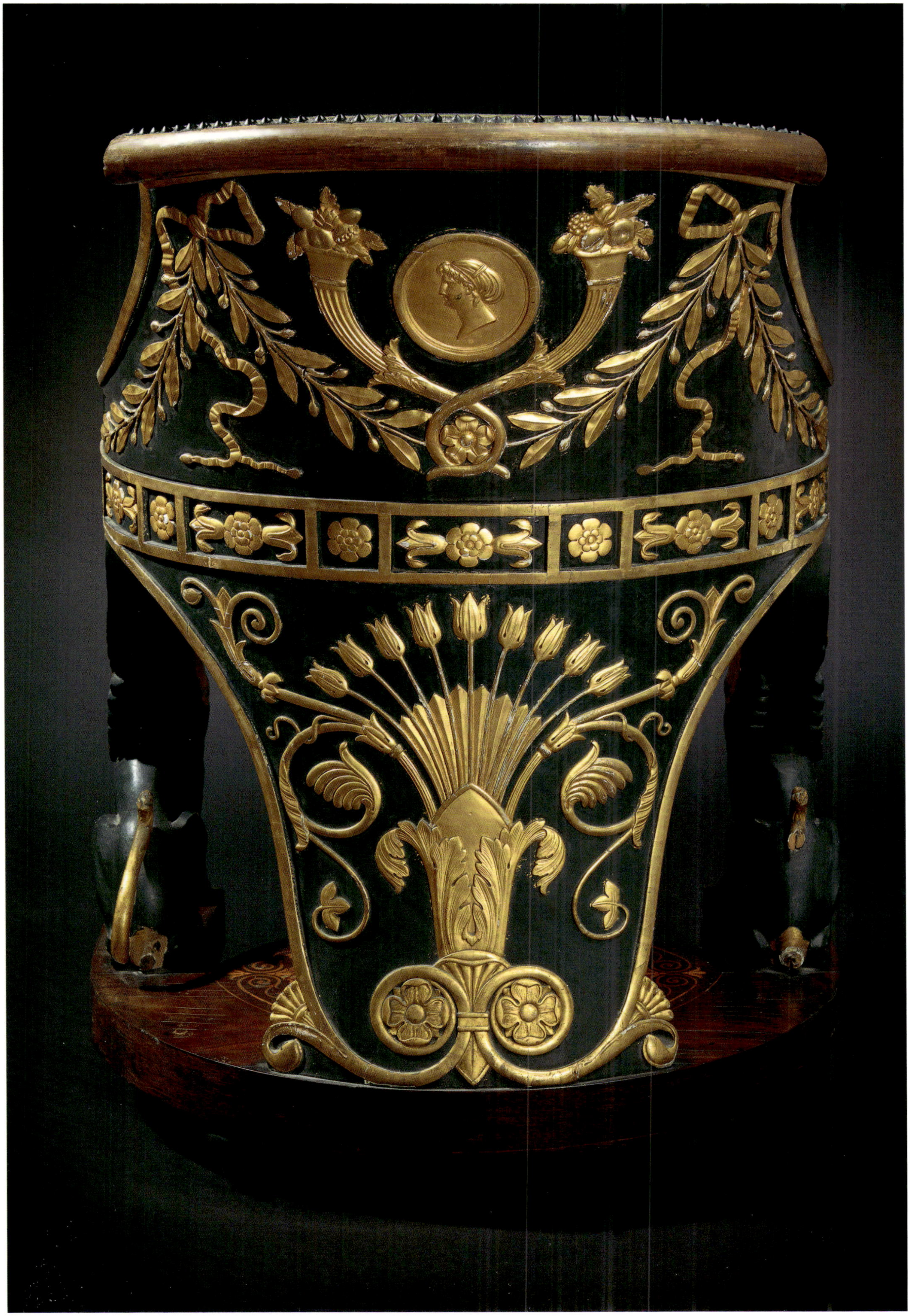

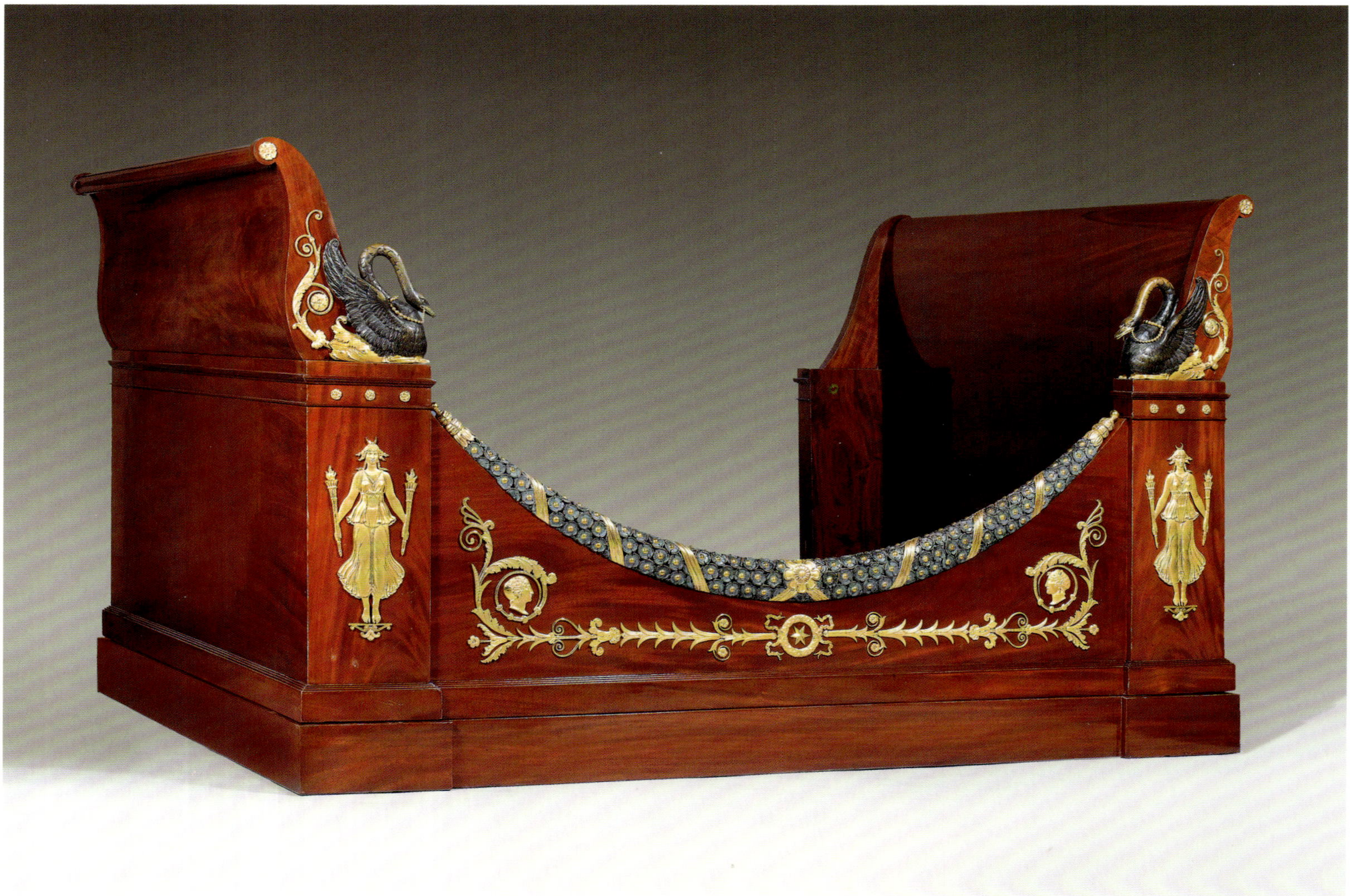

JACOB-DESMALTER (1770-1841), ATTRIBUTED, CEREMONIAL BED FROM THE DIRECTORY PERIOD, MODELED ON THE ONE BELONGING TO MADAME RÉCAMIER

This bed is the product of a likely collaboration between Louis-Martin Berthault (1770-1823) and Charles Percier (1764-1838). It is one of three nearly identical pieces known of, including one that belonged to Madame Récamier (1777-1849), now on exhibit at the Louvre and considered a masterpiece of Directory furniture. Of the three, the Louvre piece – from the Ledoux-Lebard collection – features bronzes whose motif differs from the design Berthault produced for the room where Madame Récamier held her salon in her hôtel particulier on Rue du Mont-Blanc (formerly Rue de la Chaussée d'Antin). None of them is stamped. They were probably made by Jacob Frères, a major supplier of the Empire under the name "Jacob-Desmalter".

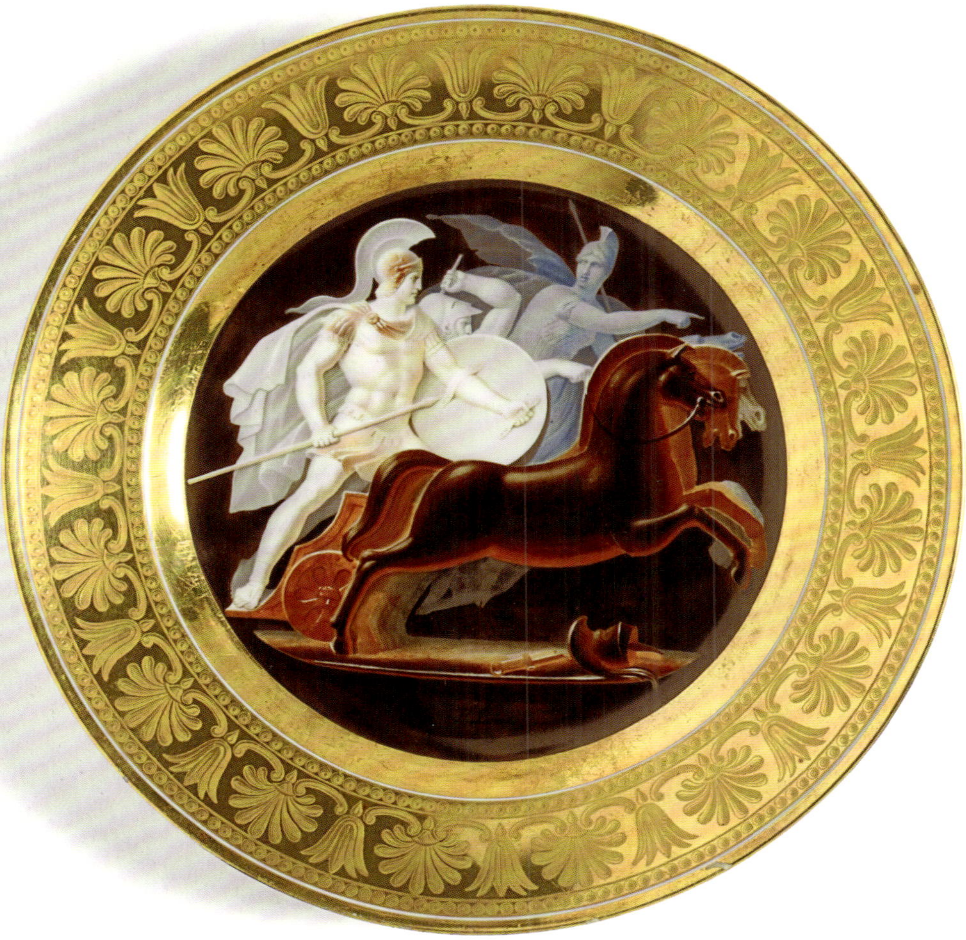

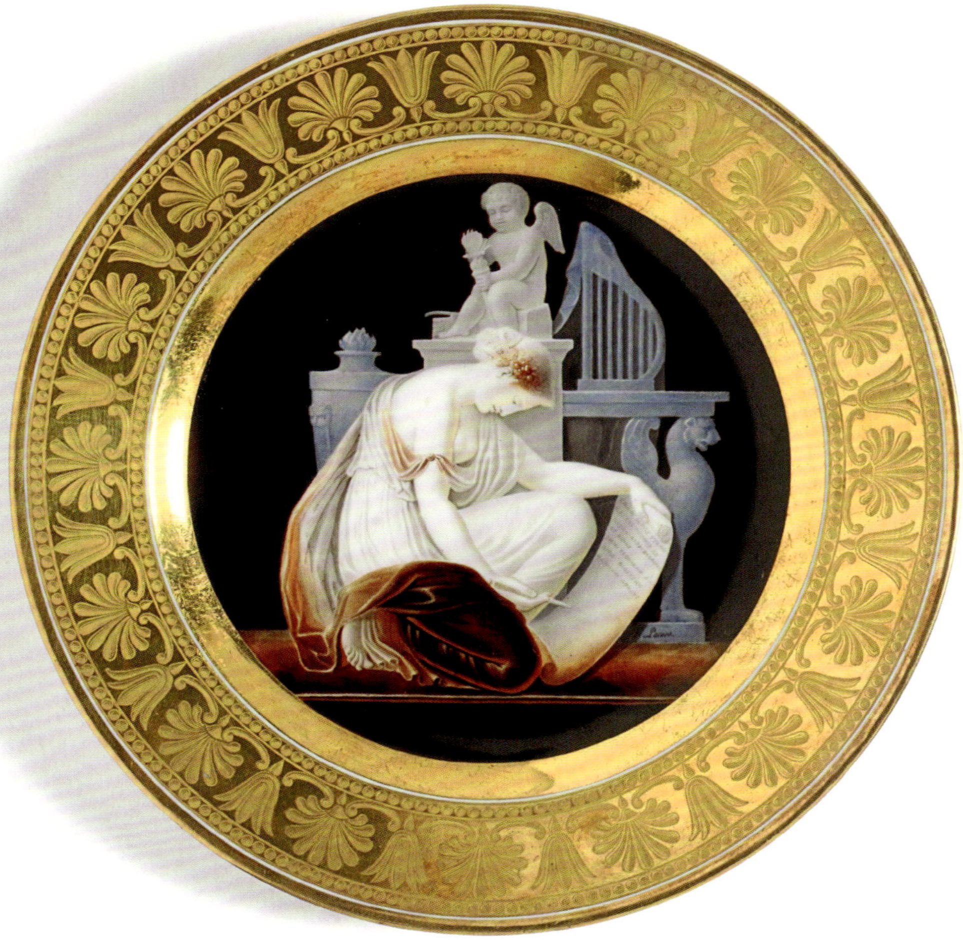

**SÈVRES IMPERIAL MANUFACTORY,
PAIR OF PLATES FROM THE MARLY D'OR SERVICE
KNOWN AS "AUX CAMÉES", 1812**

This superb pair of plates draw the eye with their exquisitely skilful decorations, painted in the manner of classical cameos. Signed by Louis-Bertin Parant (1768-1851) and dated 1812, they confirm the painter's mastery in the art of trompe l'oeil, imitating agate and sard. The illusion produced by the paintings is deepened by excellent taste in their composition. One depicts Sappho writing an Ode to Phao, the other shows Achilles returning to combat to avenge the death of his friend Patroclus.

MARTIN-GUILLAUME BIENNAIS (1764-1843), CUTLERY BELONGING TO JÉRÔME BONAPARTE (1784-1860), KING OF WESTPHALIA

This exceptional set comprising 21 pieces of silver cutlery was made by one of the Empire's most illustrious smiths, Martin-Guillaume Biennais. The cutlery forms part of the first of two sets of silverware ordered by Napoleon's youngest brother, Jérôme, for his new kingdom, and is engraved with his coat-of-arms. Jérôme sold this silverware at auction in Stuttgart on 4 March 1819. Part of it went to the King of Bavaria and is still kept in Munich. Other pieces are at the Hessisches Landesmuseum, the regional museum of Hessen.

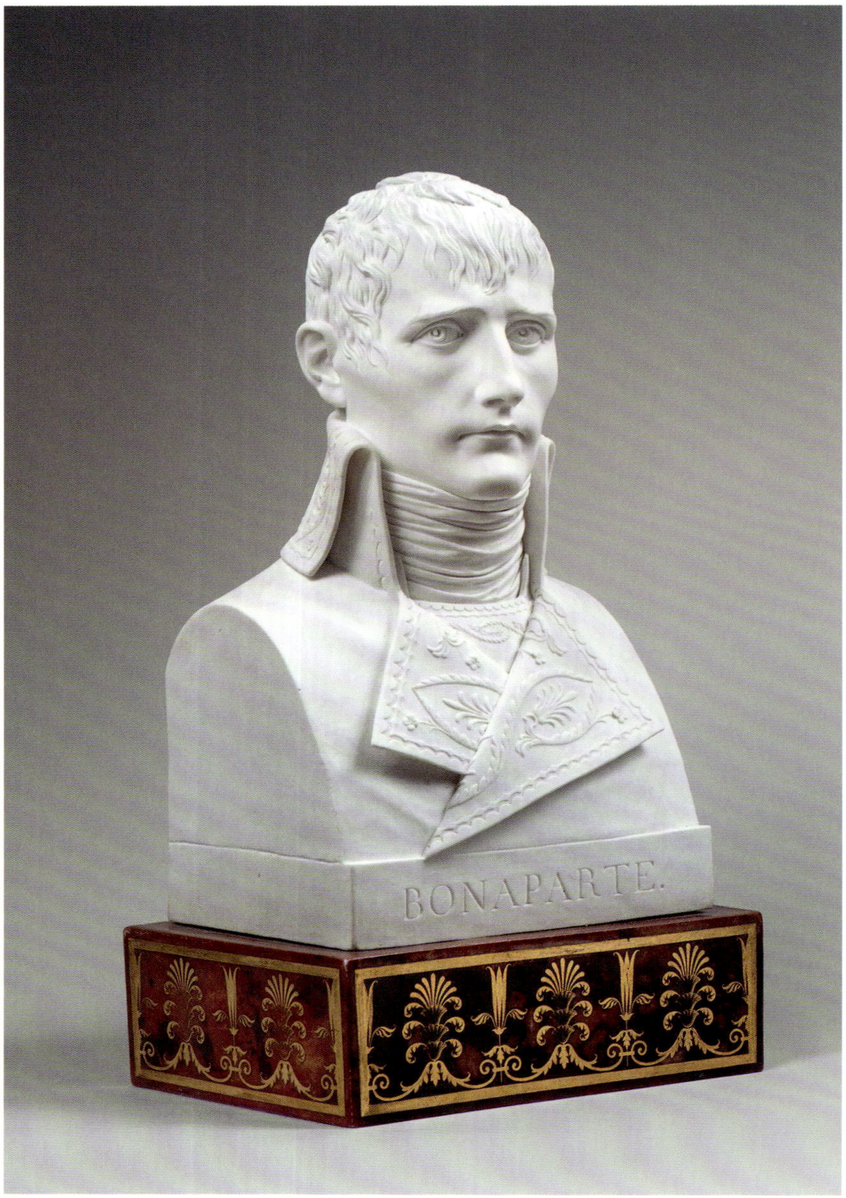

DIHL ET GUERHARD PORCELAIN FACTORY, *BUST OF BONAPARTE, FIRST CONSUL*, ABOUT 1800

This extremely rare biscuit, with its original base, is probably the only representation of Bonaparte by the Dihl et Guerhard manufactory to have been rendered in the form of a bust. Dihl et Guerhard was without a doubt the most prestigious of all the Parisian porcelain manufactories. Founded in 1781 under the Ancien Régime, the company reached its zenith under the Consulate and the Empire, before falling into decline and shutting down under the Restoration, in 1823. It was renowned for its sophisticated decoration and the virtuosity of its craftsmen. From 1811 to 1813, they crafted a porcelain dinner service for the Empress Josephine that ranks among the most lavish ever made – and probably one of the most expensive, at the colossal price of 46,976 francs in total. The service is an absolute masterpiece of the Empire period, and several of its plates are in the collection. The bust of Bonaparte was undoubtedly an imperial order, particularly since the only other copy that we know of is on display at New York's Metropolitan Museum of Art (incomplete, without its base).

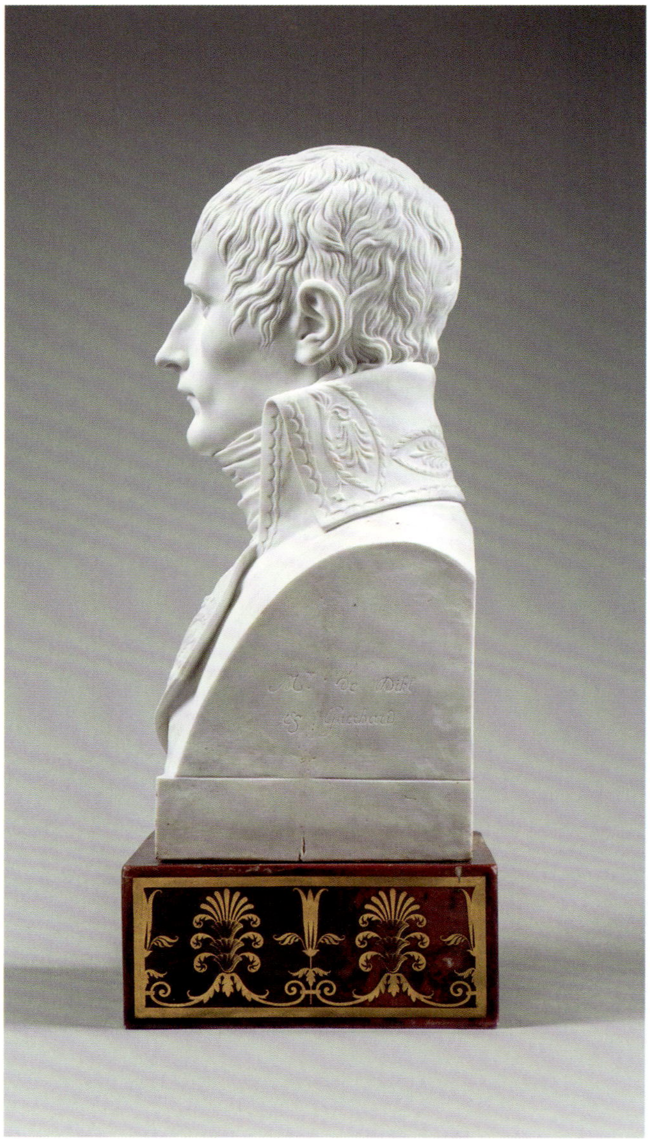

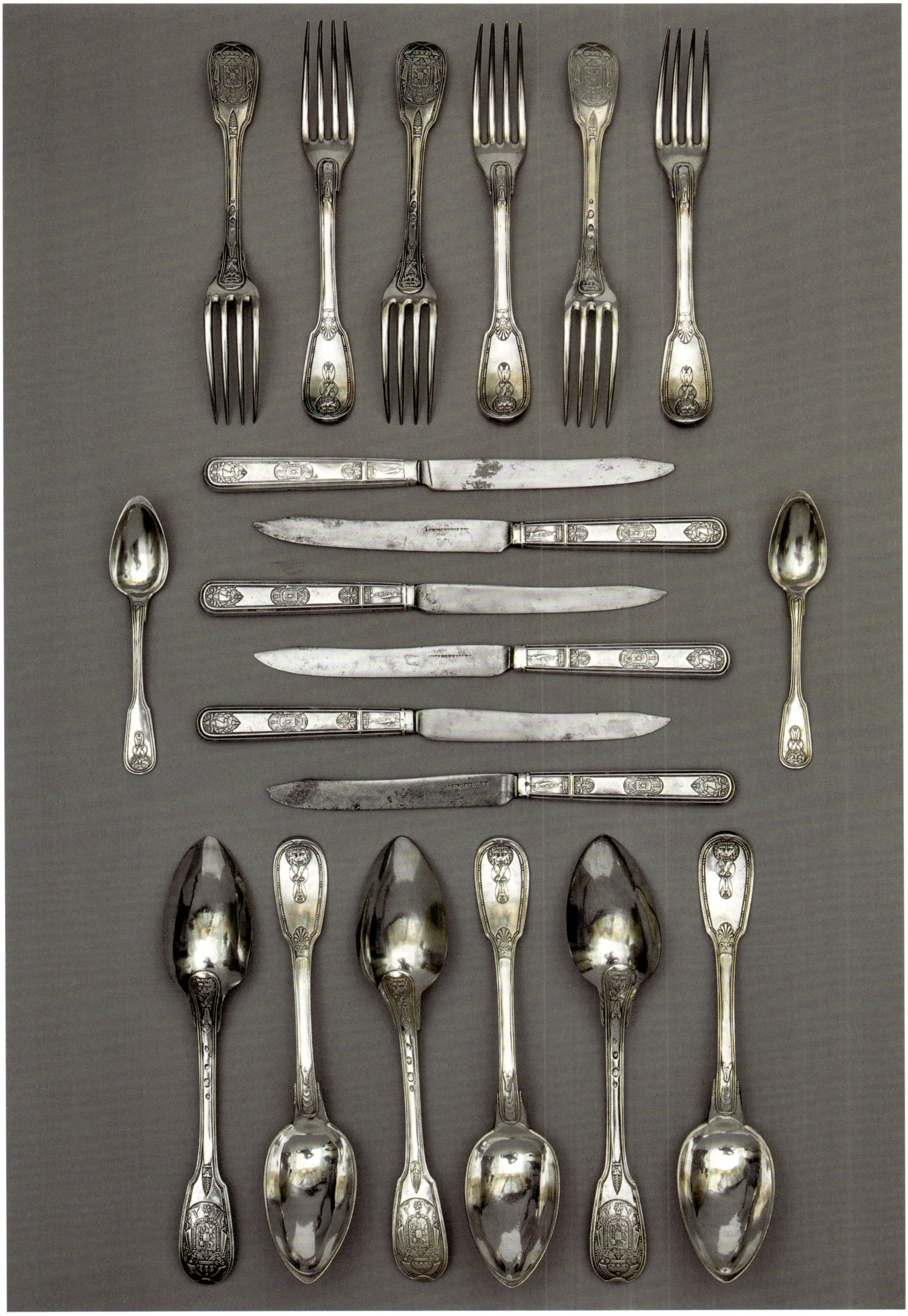

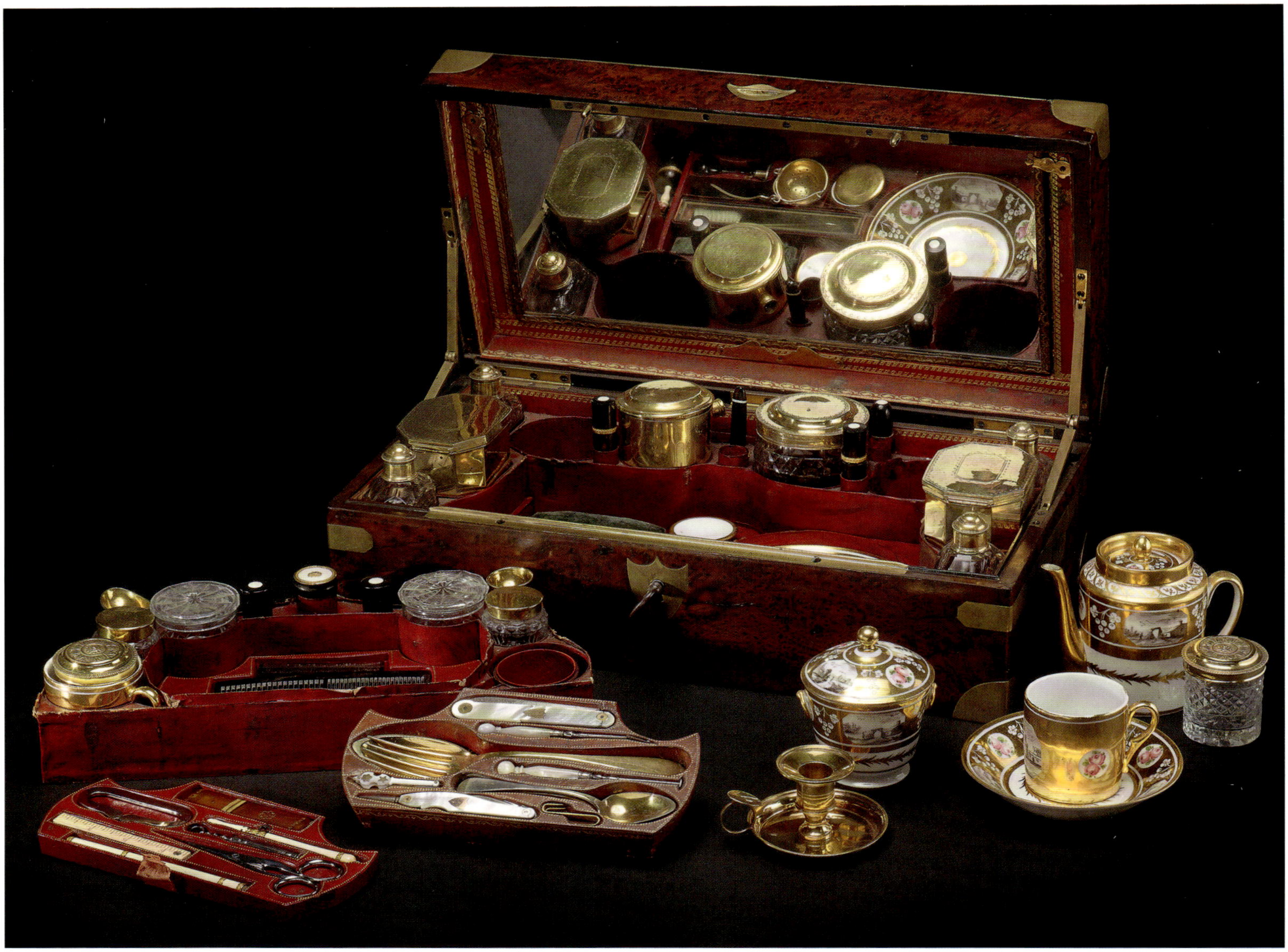

PIERRE-DOMINIQUE MAIRE (1763-1827), LARGE TRAVELING SET PROBABLY GIVEN TO AGLAÉ AUGUIER-NEY

This impressive traveling set bearing the initials "LB" was probably a gift from Louis Bonaparte to Aglaé Auguier, a close friend of Hortense's. The women met at Madame Campan's boarding school for girls, and Auguier went on to marry Marshal Ney. This provenance is suggested by the seal bearing her first name, discreetly placed in one of the little compartments in the box. The set is signed by Maire, the famous Parisian manufacturer based in Rue Saint-Honoré who received several orders from Hortense. Exquisitely made and very comprehensive, the set comprises a gilded two-person tea set, two vermeil tea caddies, a crystal and vermeil mixing pot, a tea strainer, one complete set of cutlery, two small vermeil spoons, and one high-sided pot with vermeil lid, along with travel sets holding essentials for writing, personal toiletries, and sewing.

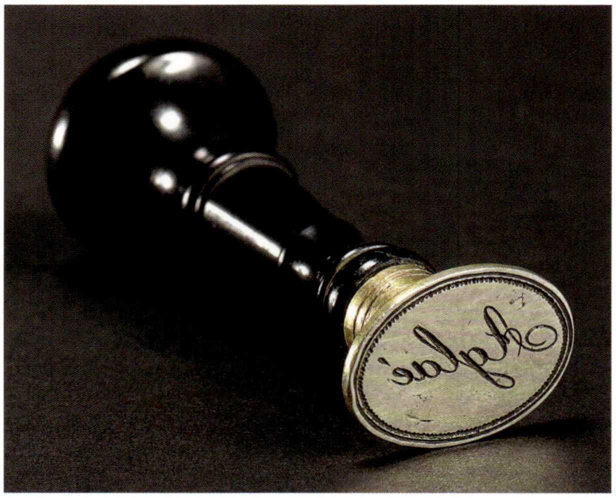

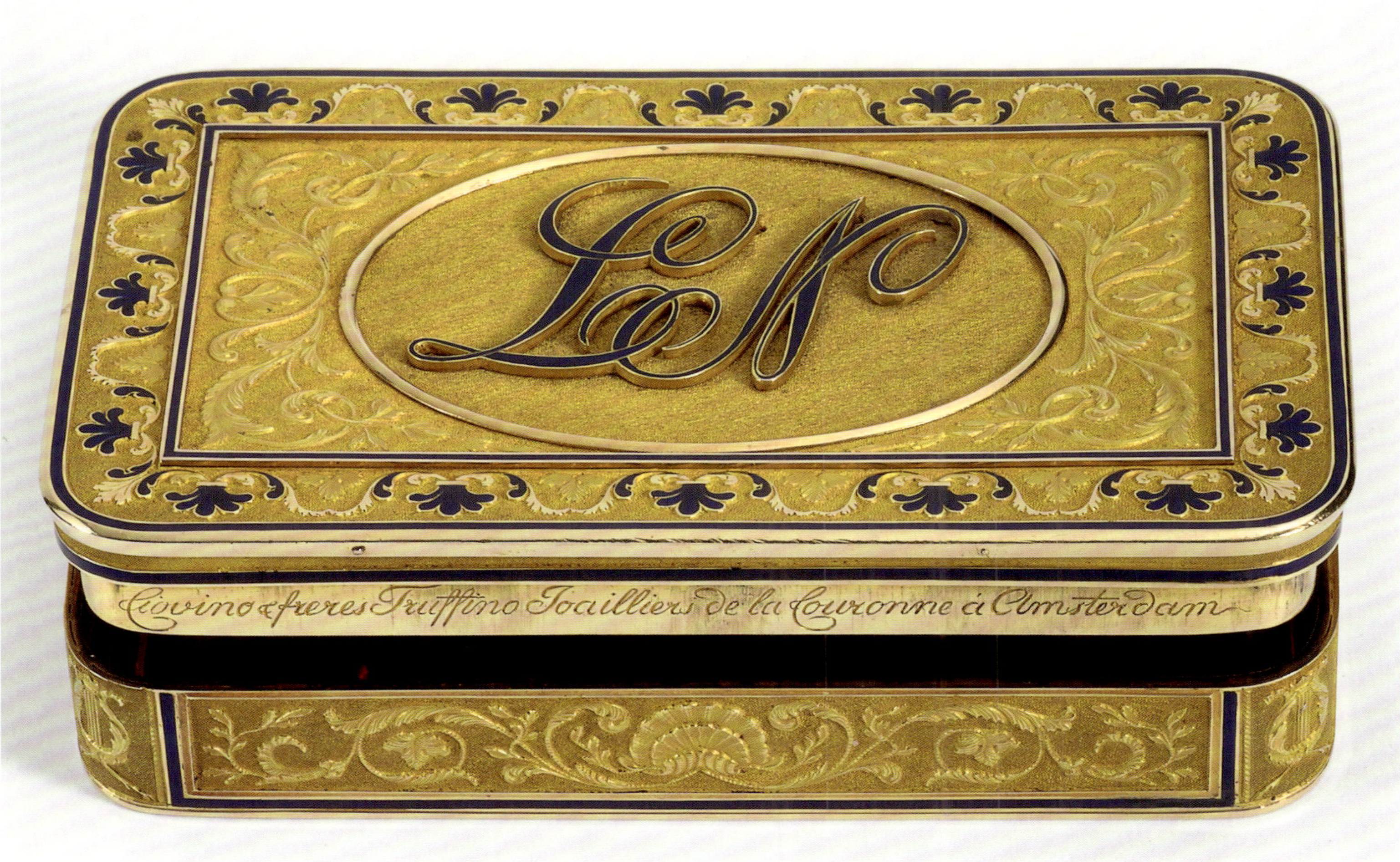

CIOVINO & FRÈRES TRUFFINO, SNUFFBOX GIVEN BY LOUIS BONAPARTE, KING OF HOLLAND

A sensational present, this gold and blue enamel box bears the monogram of Louis Napoleon, King of Holland. Napoleon's brother gave it to the Mayor of Breda, Gisbertus Bernardus Buijsen (1747-1812), during his visit to the town in April 1809. It was made by "Ciovino et frères Truffino Joailliers de la Couronne à Amsterdam", suppliers to the imperial court.

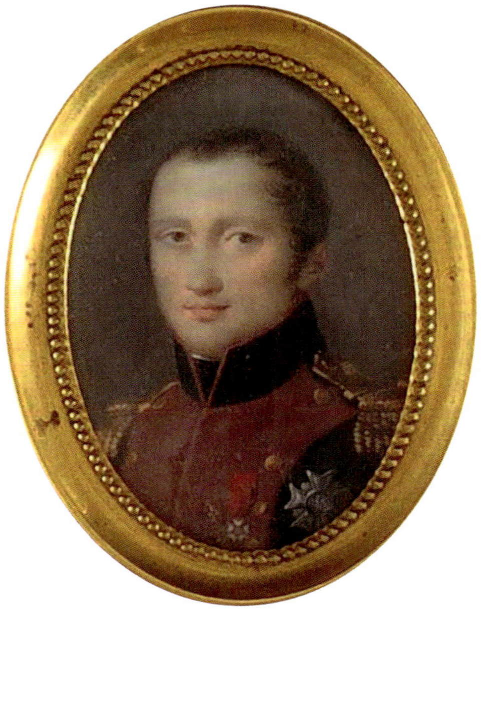

JEAN-BAPTISTE ISABEY (1767-1855), *PORTRAIT OF LOUIS BONAPARTE*

In this miniature by Jean-Baptiste Isabey we can see what Prince Louis Bonaparte, King of Holland (1778-1846), looked like. The head-and-shoulders portrait shows him turned to the left, wearing uniform and decorations.

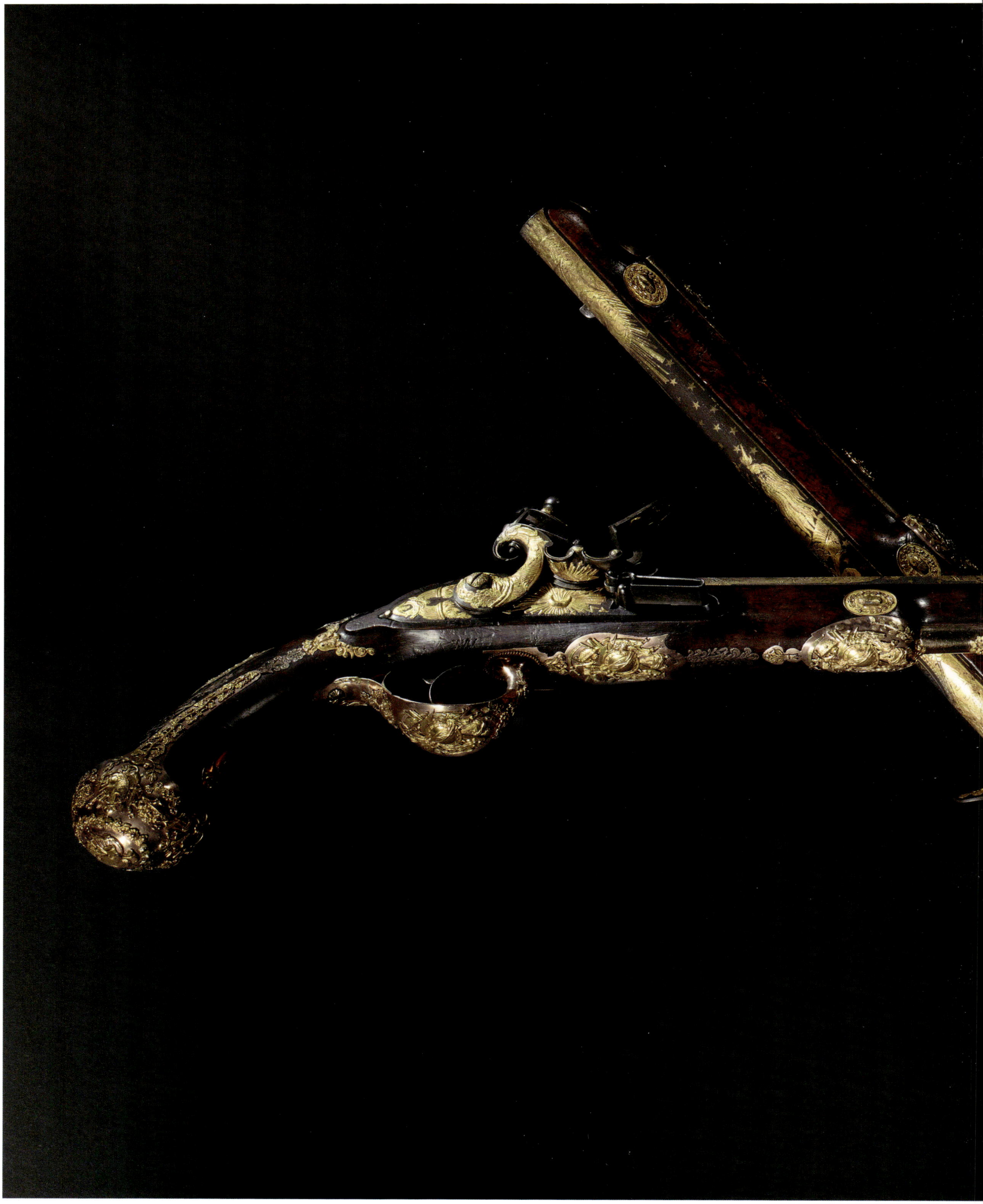

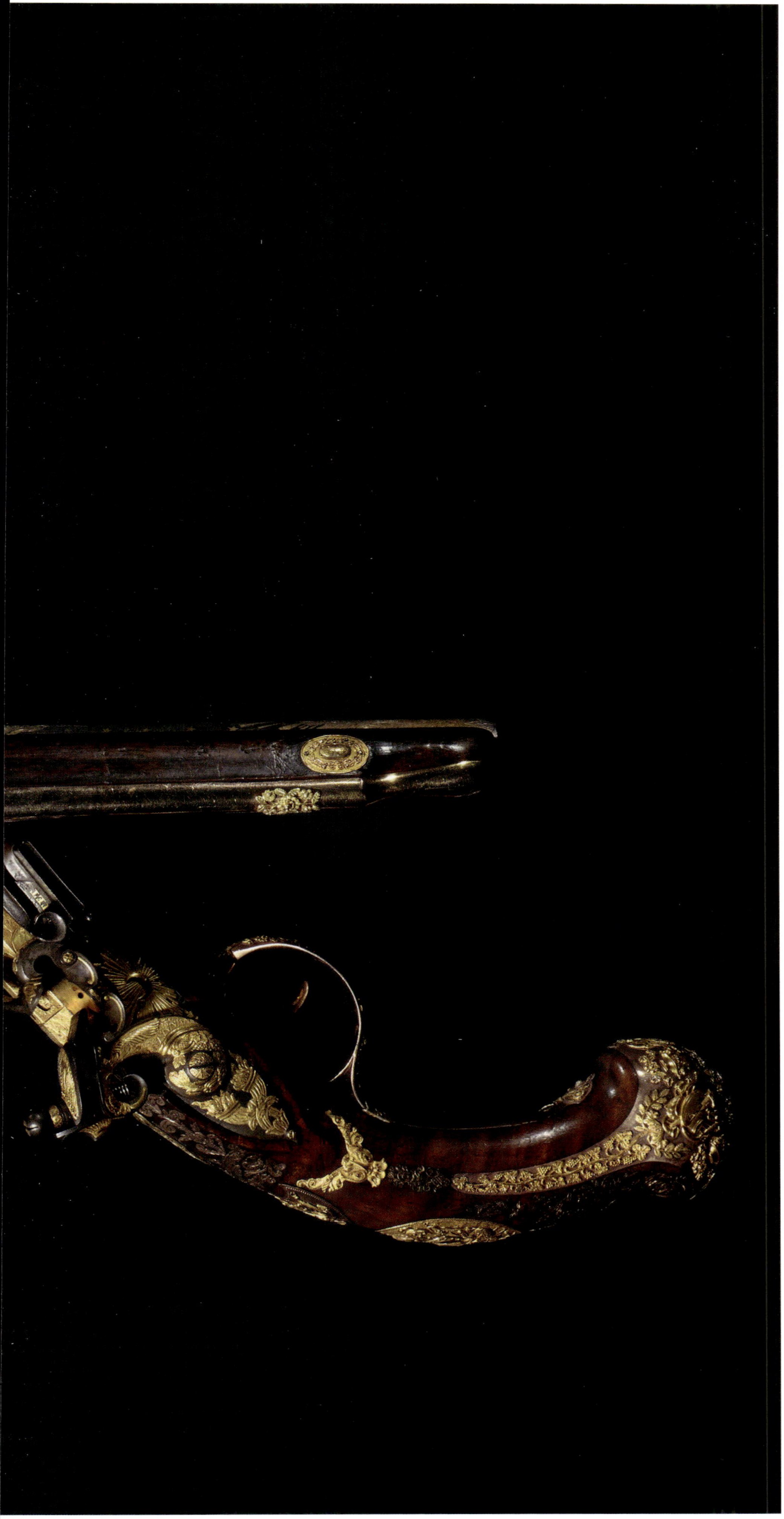

NICOLAS-NOËL BOUTET (1761-1833), PAIR OF GOLD-ENCRUSTED PISTOLS TO BE GIVEN AS AN OFFICIAL GIFT

This pair of presentation pistols in finely chiseled walnut encrusted with gold exemplifies the most splendid work to come out of the Versailles Arms Manufactory at the time of the second Restoration, around 1820. Intended as an official gift from King Louis XVIII to high dignitaries from the Orient, they are a manifest declaration of prestige. For a long time they belonged to the famous English newspaper magnate Baron Astor of Hever, and were on exhibit at the Victoria and Albert Museum in London from 1958 to 1973. A similar pair is on display in the Musée de l'Armée in Paris.

LOUIS BONAPARTE'S VERMEIL SWORD

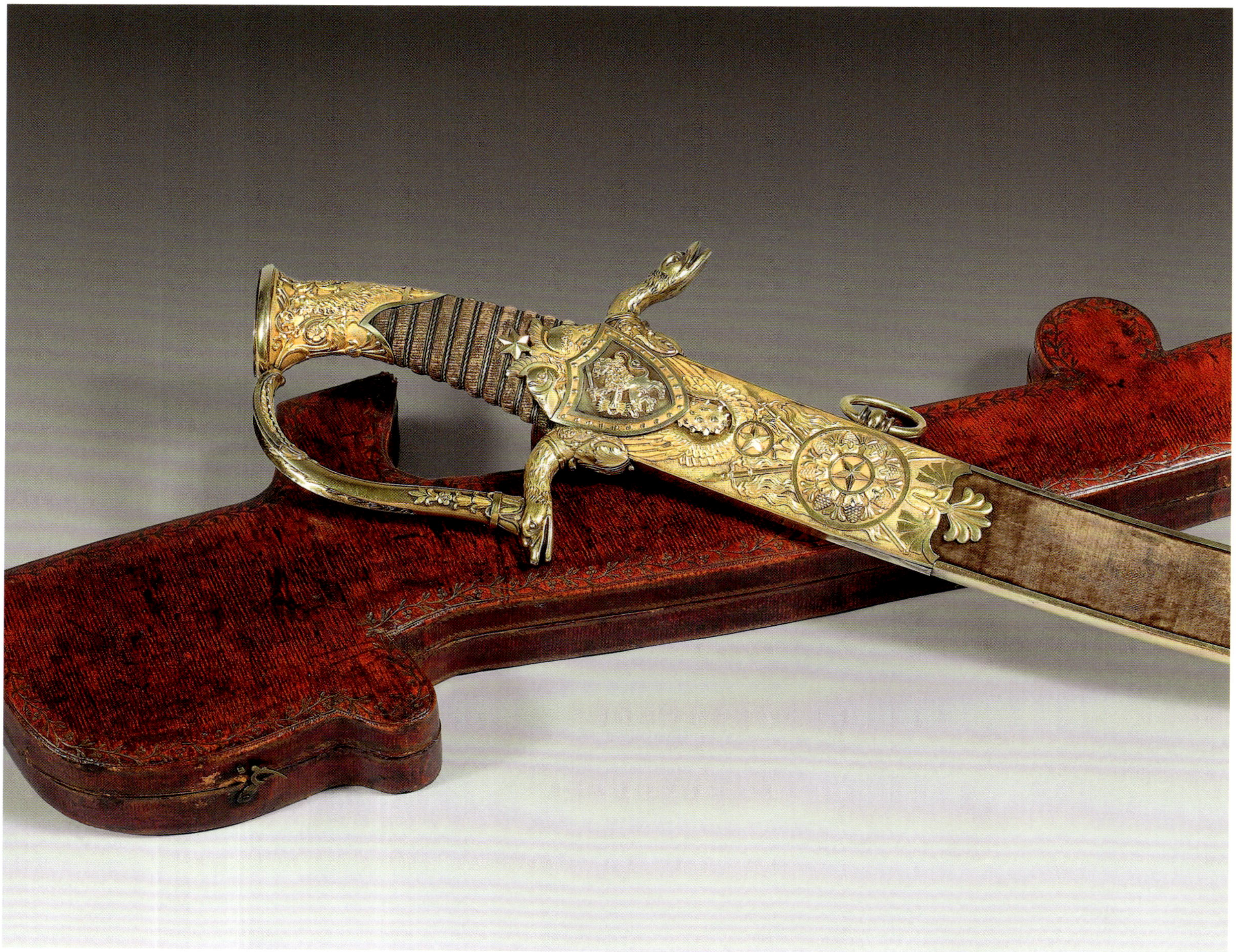

NICOLAS-NOËL BOUTET (1761-1833), VERMEIL CEREMONIAL SWORD BELONGING TO LOUIS NAPOLEON, KING OF HOLLAND

This masterpiece of craftsmanship by Nicolas-Noël Boutet is one of the finest weapons ever made at the Versailles Arms Manufactory, no doubt unequaled in private hands. The vermeil guard bears the coat-of-arms of Holland and the red Morocco leather scabbard has miraculously remained intact. The sword was probably a gift from King Louis to General Jean-Antoine de Collaert (1761-1816) on his being made Colonel-General of the Holland Royal Guard in 1807.

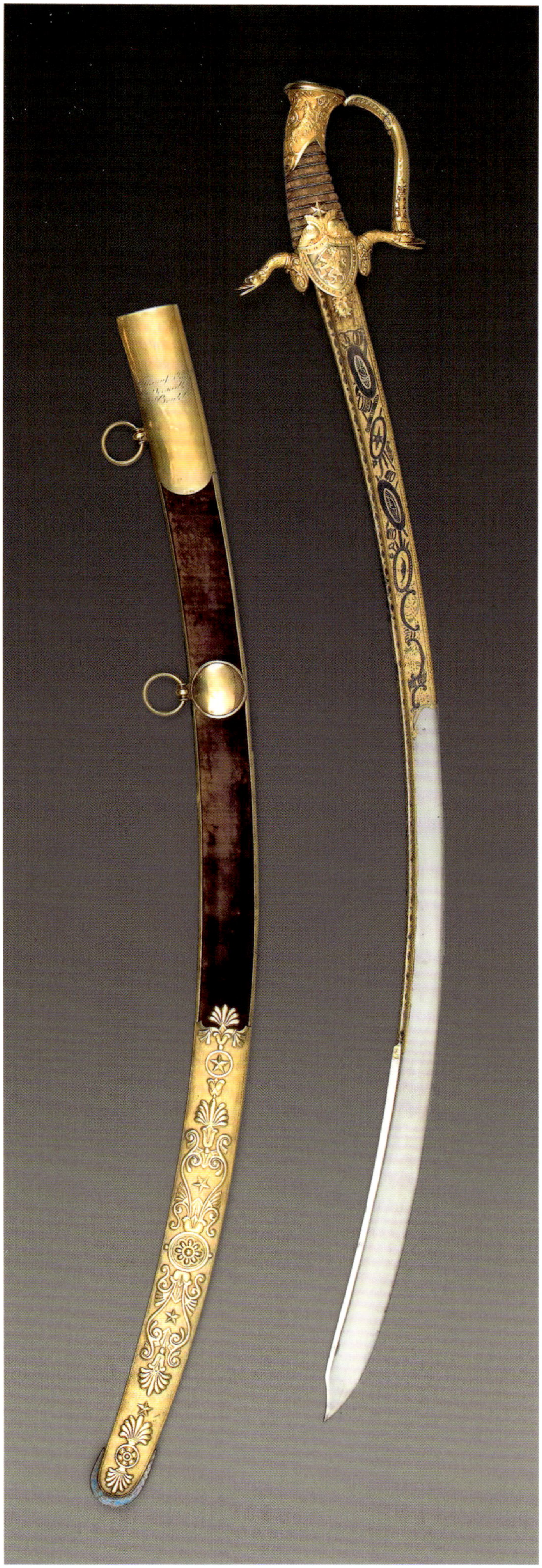

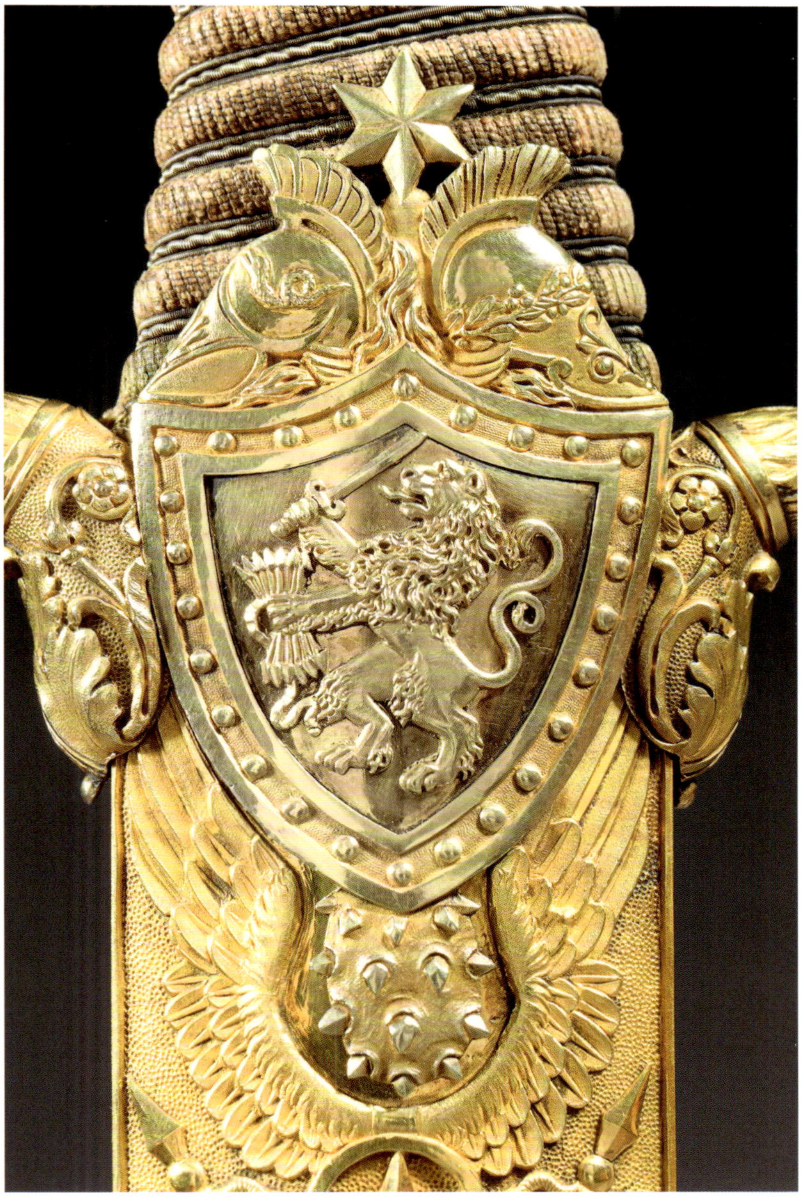

The King of Rome: a Shattered Dream

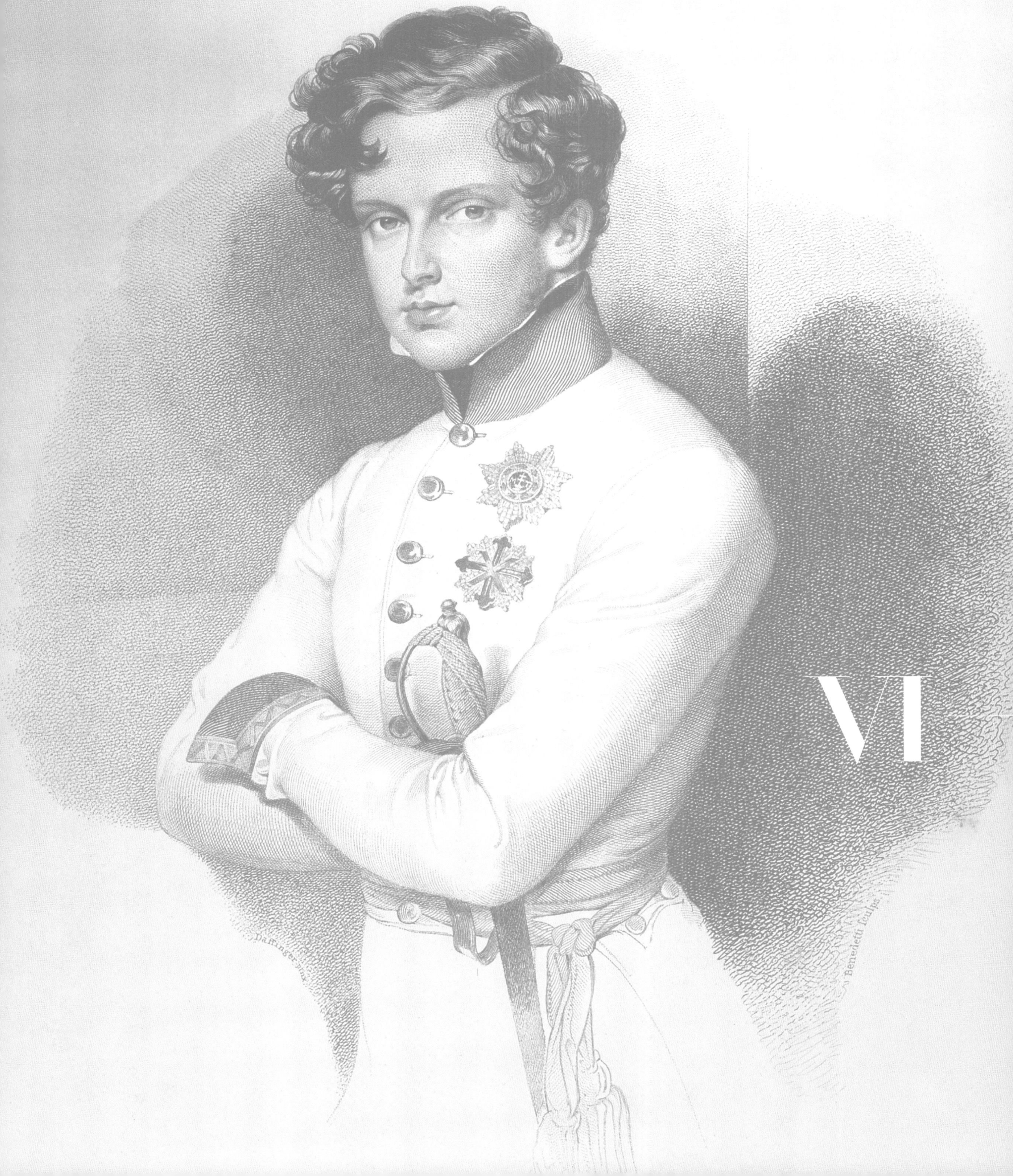

VI

"My birth and my death, that is all there is to say about me[1]." The King of Rome, born amid splendor at the Tuileries Palace, was just three years old when he left France for Austria. So began a lifetime of separations. Even his name would be taken from him. He became an Austrian prince, accorded the title Duke of Reichstadt and raised under the constant surveillance of his retinue. The Habsburgs kept him a virtual prisoner — a slave to a faceless future, romantically known as "L'Aiglon" (the eaglet).

Laetitia de Witt
Doctor of History

A CELESTIAL GIFT

At 10am on 20 March 1811, Paris held its breath as the first cannon boomed. A 101-gun salute would herald a boy. A 21-gun salute would herald a girl. On the twenty-second boom, the entire city erupted in celebration. The wishes of the Emperor had been fulfilled. Marie-Louise had given him the long-desired heir. But the birth had cost Napoleon dear. Coming so soon after his anguished repudiation of Josephine, Marie-Louise's delivery had been a harrowing experience. At 5am that morning he was visibly shaken by the news that things were not going well. Asked by the *accoucheur* (obstetrician) Dubois whether they should save the mother or the infant, Napoleon advised: "Act as if you were delivering the wife of a merchant on the rue Saint-Denis [...] but remember that the mother's health must prevail over every other consideration."[2] Marie-Louise was meanwhile howling, terrified at the prospect of being sacrificed for her child. Four hours later, she was finally delivered following a painful labor that left her unconscious. Napoleon rushed to her bedside. The extraordinary thing was that everybody forgot about the baby, who meanwhile lay on the floor inert and apparently stillborn. It was only Corvisart, the Emperor's physician, who thought to pick him up and make him swallow a few drops of eau-de-vie, triggering his first cries. Napoleon span around and stared stupefied at his son. The miracle had happened. The baby was named Napoleon, François, Charles, Joseph, and given the highly symbolic title "King of Rome" — a nod to his father's supremacy over Europe and the pomp and circumstance of Antiquity, foundation of imperial rule.

Napoleon had made elaborate preparation for the birth, as shown by the collection of bills and invoices presented below (page 354). One of his chief preoccupations was to provide his heir with his own personal entourage: a Maison des Enfants de France, after the manner of the kings of France. The House was run by a governess and included a full complement of staff: wet-nurses, nursemaids, chambermaids, plus squires, a secretary and a doctor. The imperial governess was responsible for the health and well-being of her young charge and for awakening his intellectual faculties. The person appointed to the post, by imperial decree issued on 24 October 1810, was Madame de Montesquiou, a woman of great sensitivity who took her duties as governess very seriously.

The Emperor was also passionate about the christening ceremony. The christening was intended as a high point of the Empire that would enhance imperial propaganda, as shown below by the little preparatory drawing for an engraving by Philippoteaux (page 353). Napoleon's newborn son, part Bonaparte, part Habsburg, alone embodied the future of the dynasty and the prospect of peace. The christening was accordingly celebrated on 9 June at the Cathedral de Notre-Dame de Paris, modeled on the baptism of the eldest son of Louis XVI. At the end of the ceremony, Napoleon kissed the newly baptized child three times then held him up at arm's length above the crowd. Cries of "Long Live the Emperor, long live the King of Rome" resounded on all sides. The moment left a lasting impression — though some said Napoleon looked more worried than exultant. Was he perhaps deceiving himself about his heir? One thing is certain: within less than 12 months, when the child had barely begun to talk, the war with Russia would already have distanced Napoleon from his much-cherished son.

The King of Rome enjoyed a happy, cosseted childhood. Madame de Montesquiou commenced his education very early, constantly looking to stimulate the curiosity of her young pupil. Almost as soon as he could read, she took out subscriptions on his behalf to journals such *Le Moniteur* and *Le Journal de l'Empire* and introduced him to the world of books. Religious instruction was part of his education, along with drawing and music. He was taught to play the main waltzes of the time together with military marches, on a small barrel organ called the *serinette*, which is preserved today in the Ledoux collection (page 358).

Deep bonds of affection were formed between the governess and her young charge, whose first words were "Maman Quiou". The other important figure in his life was his father. Napoleon loved to spend time with his son, saying that he felt "all the tenderness of a mother". As a source of joy to everyone, the King of Rome had great propaganda value for Napoleon. The image of the loving family man was after all very useful to him at a time when the burden of conscription weighed heavily on his subjects. Hence the large number of artists who were commissioned to produce representations of the heir to the Empire, among them busts after models by Henri-Joseph Rutxhiel (page 349) who was given the honor of modeling the first portrait bust of the King of Rome. But alas, in just three short years the child's gilded existence would begin to crumble. On 24 January 1814, Napoleon embarked on his French Campaign. That night, before leaving the Tuileries, he placed one last kiss on the forehead of his infant son. He would never see him again.

AN HEIR WITHOUT A KINGDOM

On 4 April 1814, having failed to prevent the allies from taking Paris, Napoleon abdicated in favor of his son, Napoleon II, who became Emperor of the French for just two days. On 6 April the Senate approved a motion to depose the Emperor and restore the Bourbon monarchy. Napoleon now had no choice but to abdicate unconditionally, renouncing all claims to the throne for himself and his descendants. Under the terms of the Treaty of Fontainebleau of 11 April 1814, Napoleon agreed to go into exile on the island of Elba on the understanding that suitable provision would be made for his family. The former Empress Marie-Louise was given the duchies of Parma, Piacenza and Guastalla while her son took the title of Prince of Parma. Henceforth his destiny lay in the hands of Austria's envoy, the Chancellor of State Prince Klemens von Metternich. Vienna was his destiny. On 21 May 1814, the new Prince of Parma and his mother took up residence in Schönbrunn Palace. For the young Napoleon, the relocation was a terrible wrench that left him totally bewildered. Why was he no longer the King of Rome? Where was his father? Why wasn't he on his way to Italy? All that remained of his French entourage were his governess and a few of her assistants who comforted him by keeping the memory of his father alive. His mother had meanwhile left to take the waters, escorted by General von Neipperg — a deliberate move by Metternich to bring the two together.

Then came the news that Napoleon had escaped from the island of Elba. The whole of Europe held its breath. In theory at least, the "Hundred Days" reinstated the child as the *Prince Impérial*. But in practice, the campaign placed him and his mother at the mercy of Metternich who fully understood that he had a valuable political asset in his possession — not just vis-à-vis Napoleon but also vis-à-vis the Bourbons. Why else, if not to secure France for Austria, would he let it be known that he favored a Regency on behalf of the King of Rome? On 22 June 1815, following the defeat at Waterloo, Napoleon was forced to abdicate for a second time in favor of his son. The provisional government under Fouché carried on regardless and the two chambers refused to issue a proclamation. But legally speaking, Napoleon II ruled as Emperor of the French for two weeks. The Congress of Vienna had meanwhile ratified his mother's accession to Parma but stripped her son of his title and rights as Prince of Parma. For the next two years, the question of how to address the former King of Rome would remain unresolved. As a result of Napoleon's return to power (famously known as the *Vol de L'Aigle* or flight of the eagle), the member's of his son's entourage came under suspicion and were eventually sacked. Among them was the Comtesse de Montesquiou, who was dismissed on 20 March 1815, the young prince's fourth birthday. The separation affected him deeply and there were more to follow. Marie Marchand, one of his nursemaids, would be forced to go in February of the following year. Left without a single French companion, the young Napoleon was distraught. The final blow was the departure of his mother, who left him early in 1816 to take possession of her dominions. Though he rarely saw her after that, he never lost his love for her. The Duchess of Parma, on the other hand, soon forgot about her firstborn, too busy managing her kingdom and making a new life for herself with Neipperg (to whom she would bear two children). This estrangement from his mother marked a watershed in the life of the young prince. Seeing that the world he had known no longer existed, he retreated into himself. Henceforth his only recourse was to bury his feelings and conceal his thoughts.

His French household was now replaced by an all-male, Austrian entourage. Three men were in charge of his education. At their head was Count Maurice Dietrichstein, a high-ranking Viennese nobleman who had made a name for himself, amongst other things, as musical director of the imperial court. He had been appointed on the basis of his loyalty and sensitivity, but he was totally unprepared for his new role as the prince's mentor. Though dutiful to a fault, with rigid standards, he was in no way a teacher and his pupil's complex personality soon left him quite disconcerted. Dietrichstein was assisted in his role by Jean-Baptiste Foresti and Mathieu de Collin — two men whose undeniable qualities said a lot about the genuine interest that Francis I devoted to his grandson's education.

Dietrichstein's mission was quite simple: to transform "Marie-Louise's son" (as he was known to the Austrian cabinet) into an authentic Austrian prince. Step one had been the removal of all of the French women in the child's entourage, together with anything likely to remind him of France. Changes were made to every aspect of his daily life, from the food he ate to the hours he kept. It was only then that the child's education could start in earnest, focusing on the study of the German language. But contrary to what has been said, the intention was not to make him forget his mother tongue. As shown by the translation exercises in the Ledoux Collection (page 369) the French language retained its place in the curriculum throughout his years of schooling. One thing is certain, however: "Marie-Louise's son" was an unwilling student who showed no enthusiasm whatsoever for German. Having already lost so much in his young life, his mother tongue was no doubt especially precious to him. None of this cut any ice with Dietrichstein who viewed the prince's refusal to learn German as no more than laziness and perversity. Unable to grasp just how distressed his pupil really was, Dietrichstein responded with a severity that was often excessive, eroding the child's self-confidence and making an enemy of him in the process. For all of that, the prince had a lot to offer. Bright and extremely sensitive, he was unusually knowledgeable for his age and well able to converse with adults — an ability much appreciated by his Austrian family. There was a special bond of affection between the prince and his grandfather, Francis I. The Austrian Emperor had a real fondness for the child, quite taken by his charms and natural elegance, not to mention a gift for witty repartee that put many an archduke in the shade. The prince regularly ate with his grandfather and would accompany him and his Austrian uncles when they went hunting or took up their summer residence (in Austria, of course). He participated in all of the entertainment at court — ball, plays — bringing joy wherever he went. He danced divinely and was widely admired for his grace and beauty. Dietrichstein frowned on such idle distractions but still made sure that his young protégé received the treatment (and the invitations) commensurate with his status. Because the prince did inevitably remain something of an outsider at court until the issue of his status was resolved. His destiny hung in the balance for two years, from the end of the Congress of Vienna in 1815 to the signing of the Treaty of Paris in December 1817. It was only then that Francis I vaguely agreed to grant him lands in Bohemia, which were then promoted to a duchy by letters patent dated 22 July, with the prince as the newly appointed Duke of Reichstadt. Henceforth he would be addressed as His Serene Highness, without the predicate "royal". Having being formally made a Prince of Austria, he could now take his rightful place at court and, more important still, go by a name that did not reflect his lineage.

Was his Austrian-style education ultimately worth it? By 1817 Napoleon's son was so fluent in German that he had started to forget his French. Dietrichstein was convinced that he was only doing it to annoy his tutors, just as he was deliberately careless about his writing. A calligraphy tutor was accordingly appointed but did little to improve things. The prince would always find writing difficult, always struggle with spelling and style. Perhaps he guessed that others used his writing as a way to spy on him. He was no fool. He knew his letters were being read and corrected... As to whether his teachers succeeded in making him forget France, it is hard to say due to the child's secretive nature. He probably soon learned to stop asking questions about his father and his former life as King of Rome. But that doesn't mean he had forgotten. Far from it. The efforts of his French entourage to keep his childhood memories alive had borne fruit and his head was full of images that would never fade. A dog called Vizir, for instance, was an instant reminder of his father's horse. But his transformation into an Austrian prince was no less complete because of it. The landscapes he contemplated and the castles he lived in were Austrian. He hunted like an Austrian and went riding like an Austrian. His friends were Austrian and on the rare occasions when he was reunited with his mother, it was always in Austria. Dietrichstein must have noticed this change because he obtained permission from Marie-Louise to break the silence surrounding the boy's father, arguing that not to do so would be detrimental to the child's development. So began the young Napoleon's gradual introduction to the story of his father as told through the prism of his tutors. According to their highly simplified version of events, the unbridled ambition of the Emperor of the French was alone to blame for throwing Europe into disorder and ultimately precipitating his downfall.

AN ORPHAN WITHOUT SUPPORT

In early July 1821, Vienna heard of Napoleon's death. Dietrichstein being absent at the time, it fell to Foresti to break the news to his pupil. "He shed more tears than I expected,"[3] said the tutor afterwards. But then no one could have known just how large Napoleon featured in his son's mind. The young Duke withdrew into silence, unable to share his grief with others. Better to say nothing than to suffer the frustration of childish explanations. He was after all the new head of the Bonaparte family — a fact apparently overlooked by his entourage. Though aged only ten at the time, he wanted to know about the political issues at stake. But there was no one he trusted enough to ask. Not his tutors, not his grandfather and even less his mother, whose expressions of sorrow rang false. "I feel sure," she wrote in her letter, "that the pain you felt was as deep as mine."[4] The feeling of utter isolation that came over him then would remain with him forever.

He carried on with his life just the same and, having passed his first exams, he set his sights firmly on a military career. Nothing else mattered to him. His few surviving drawings are always about the art of war and horses, as shown by the two preliminary sketches in the Ledoux collection (page 368). A career in the armed forces was of prime importance to him. It gave him a future while also honoring the memory of his father. With it went his passion for riding, plus a political curiosity that was whetted even further by the arrival of a new tutor in January 1825. After Collin died in late 1824, his replacement was Baron Joseph d'Obenaus, a former teacher of political science and a conspicuous admirer of Napoleon. His appointment as Collin's successor must have been approved by Francis I and Metternich, which would suggest that they were preparing the child for the future. Or maybe it was just a calculated propaganda effort by Metternich intended to convince people that the now-adolescent Duke of Reichstadt was receiving a liberal education. In the months that followed, the young Napoleon learned about recent political history in general, and his father's history in particular. He pored lovingly over the eyewitness accounts written by Napoleon's companions on St Helena. Military history remained his field of predilection. His imagination was haunted by the exploits of iconic military figures — Napoleon of course, but also Hannibal and Eugene of Savoy. Their achievements made his thirst for independence all the more acute. He longed to be free at last. As his eighteenth birthday approached, he wanted more than ever to make a name for himself and prove his bravery.

On 22 February 1829, Count von Neipperg died, the long-term lover that Marie-Louise had secretly married after Napoleon's death in 1821. Dietrichstein now felt the time had come to reveal the truth about their relationship to the duke. The young man received the news with perfect equanimity. But though he had learned to suppress his thoughts, he sensed that there would be more deceptions to follow. What rankled was the lie, not the fact that his mother had remarried. He had been betrayed, not only by his mother but by everyone around him. They had all conspired against him. Feeling increasingly ill at ease at court, soon all he could think of was escape and emancipation. Never forget that he was born a French prince — that was the recommendation that emerged from the will left by his father in the *Mémorial de Sainte-Hélène,* and it now made perfect sense. But how to proceed?

The quest for freedom in nineteenth century Europe inevitably raised questions about the young duke's political future. As predicted by Napoleon after he was banished to St Helena, the Bourbon dynasty ended when Charles X was overthrown in July 1830. The way was now open to the duke as the heir apparent to the imperial throne. The Bonapartists rallied to his cause, championing the beginnings of an insurrection that could have worked but for their own mismanagement. In the event, they proved incapable of securing the throne for an unknown and absentee pretender — a weakness that the Orleanist faction was quick to exploit, seizing power on 7 August in the name of Louis Philippe. The situation in France was now settled, but other opportunities soon presented themselves. Within just a few months of each other, Belgium, Poland and Italy all moved toward independence, with clear factions emerging in each country that favored the Duke of Reichstadt. But the young man never really stood a chance. Considered a threat to the monarchies of Europe, he was more than ever under the thumb of Metternich. There were people watching his every move, spying on his contacts and combing his correspondence. Even his friendship with Anton von Prokesch-Osten was perhaps not all it seemed to be. This young Austrian officer was the duke's sole confidant, the only person he trusted enough to speak freely about his father. But we surely cannot be expected to believe that this intimacy could have developed without attracting suspicion. Even less that the duke would have confided in Osten under the very noses of the Austrian cabinet (which monitored all of their meetings).

As early as 1826 a Parisian decorator called Doudeuil had been denied a meeting with Napoleon's son and sent back to France. A rumor began to circulate about a certain prince who had been turned into an Austrian and compelled to forget his past. This was the myth promulgated by the French satirical poet Auguste Barthélemy following his visit to Vienna in 1828 to present his book *Napoléon en Égypte*. Permission to see the duke was again denied, prompting Barthélemy to write *Le Fils de l'homme*, a poem where he develops the theme of the uprooted prince suffocating by degrees in his gilded cage. Barthélemy was the first to mention the duke's physical deterioration — a deliberate nod to his legendary father's agonizing ordeal at the hands of his victorious captors. So began the myth of the *Aiglon* (the eaglet), a story that probably did nothing to improve his chances of ascending the throne. The only person who still believed in his imperial destiny by then was Napoléone, countess Camerata, daughter of Élisa Bonaparte. In the fall of 1830 she went to Vienna to urge her cousin to fulfill his duty as pretender to the throne. The whole of France awaited him, she said. The prince was too distraught to respond, torn between the fear of disappointing those who believed in him and the fear of reprisals by Metternich. So he turned to his friend Prokesch. Within moments the countess had been told to cease her entreaties, on the grounds that they jeopardized the freedom of the duke. His own attitude at the time says a lot about the conflicting influences that controlled him. His glorious destiny did of course beckon, but he could consider no action against Austria, particularly in this year 1830 when the issue of his emancipation was so close to resolution.

On 7 July that year he was appointed *chef de bataillon* (battalion commander) then on 6 November promoted to Lieutenant-Colonel. Following lengthy negotiations, he was finally able to replace his tutors with his own military Household: General Count Hartmann, Captain Baron Moll and Captain Standeisky. The duke formed strong attachments to his men, who each received a personal memento as a token of his appreciation for their devotion in the last months of his life. The cavalry officer's sword that he bestowed on Standeisky is pictured below (page 367). Entering on his military career marked a high point in the duke's life. On 9 June 1831 he transferred to the infantry, given command of his own battalion in a regiment under the orders of Count Ignác Gyulay. His physician, Malfatti, deplored the move: "From that time he rejected all my advice; I was only the spectator of an unmeasured zeal and unlimited eagerness for his new pursuits."[5] Fear that he might be deprived of his newfound freedom had led his patient to conceal the disease that gripped him. First they treated him for bowel problems. It was only much later that it became clear that the infection lay in the lungs. Day by day he grew thinner and paler but he continued to push his body to its limits. He slept little and ate even less. Then his voice began to give way. "I resent this miserable body of mine," he said, "that cannot follow the will of my soul."[6] Following repeated enforced periods of leave, he resumed his military activities on

2 January 1832. His health deteriorated almost immediately. On 23 January he developed a high fever, and would never see active service again. He had only a few months to live.
In May he was taken to Schönbrunn for its pure air. But it was already too late. On 12 June his doctors knew he was dying. His last days were racked with pain and he suffered to the bitter end. On 22 July at 5am in the morning he breathed his last. His tragic death, in the full flower of youth, would fuel the myth of the romantic hero. In 1900, when the desire for revenge against Germany ran high, the legend of the *Aiglon* reached its apogee in the writings of French poet and dramatist Edmond Rostand, as illustrated in the portrait of the Duke of Reichstadt by Desvarreux (page 366).

1 de Montbel, G.I. *Le Duc de Reichstadt, notice sur la vie et la mort de ce prince, rédigée à Vienne d'après des documents authentiques.* Paris: 1932, p 375.

2 *Mémoires inédits de Cambacérès*, presented and annotated by Laurence Chatel de Brancion. Paris: Perrin, 1999, p 366.

3 Letter from Collin to Dietrichstein, 17 July 1821, cited by de Bourgoing, J, in *Le Fils de Napoléon.* Paris: Payot, 1932, p 125.

4 Letter from Marie-Louise to her son, 24 July 1821, cited by de Bourgoing, J, op. cit. p 126.

5 *Confidences of Malfatti*, compiled by G.I. de Montbel, *op. cit.*, p 409.

6 *Ibid.*

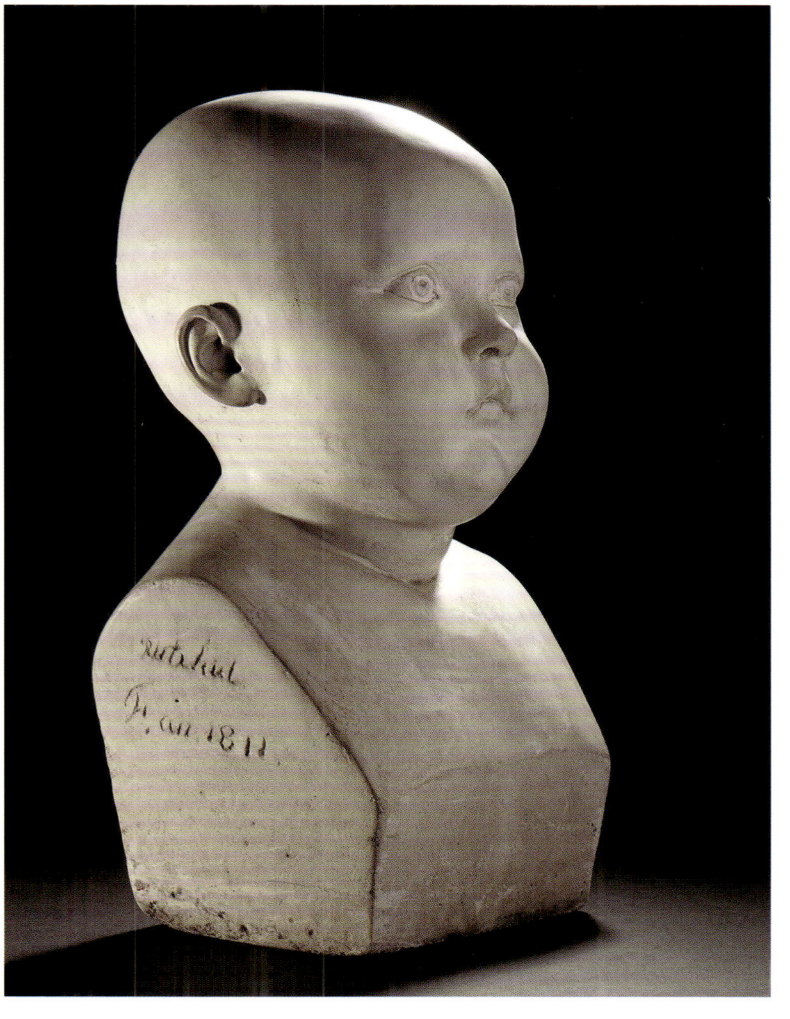

HENRI JOSEPH RUTXHIEL (1775-1837), *BUST OF THE KING OF ROME*

This plaster bust of the King of Rome, aged ten months, made by the sculptor Rutxhiel from Liège, was an undeniable success with the imperial family. The Countess of Montesquiou found the likeness remarkable and ordered several plaster versions to give as gifts to members of her household.
The only marble version, reportedly kept by the Emperor at St Helena, is now on show at the Malmaison et Bois-Préau museum.

BIRTH AND CHRISTENING

THE KING OF ROME'S LINEN

According to a custom dating from the Ancien Régime, when a child's linen was no longer used, it was handed to the members of his household. These items were thus kept by his governess, the Countess of Montesquiou.

THE KING OF ROME'S ROBE AND LACE

A full layette was ordered for the King of Rome. Lesueur, a lace merchant, produced some of the items.

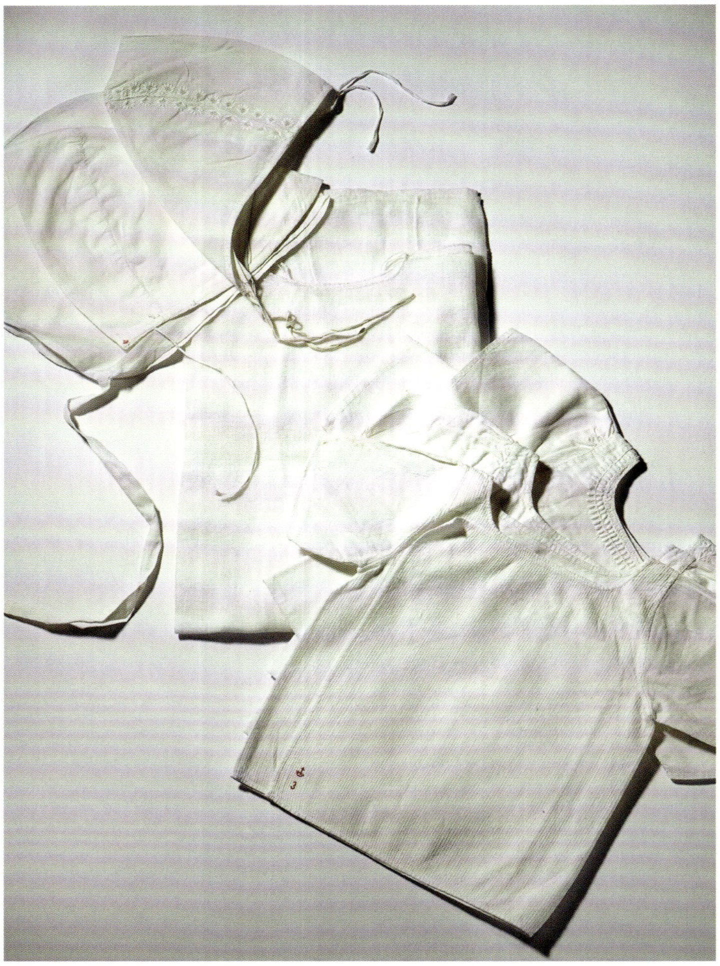

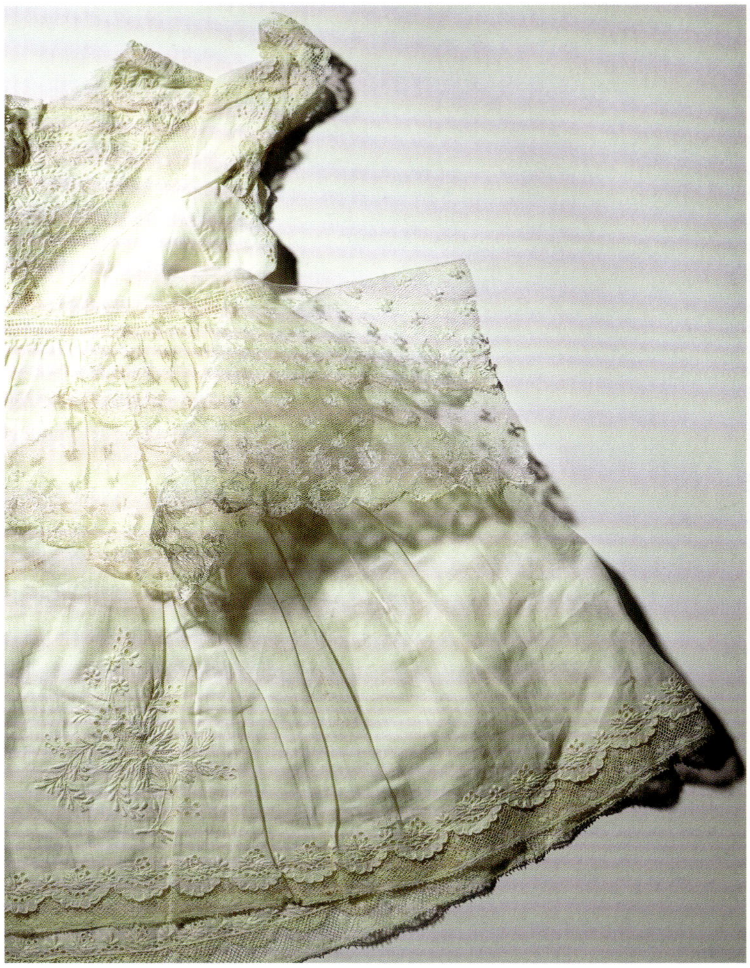

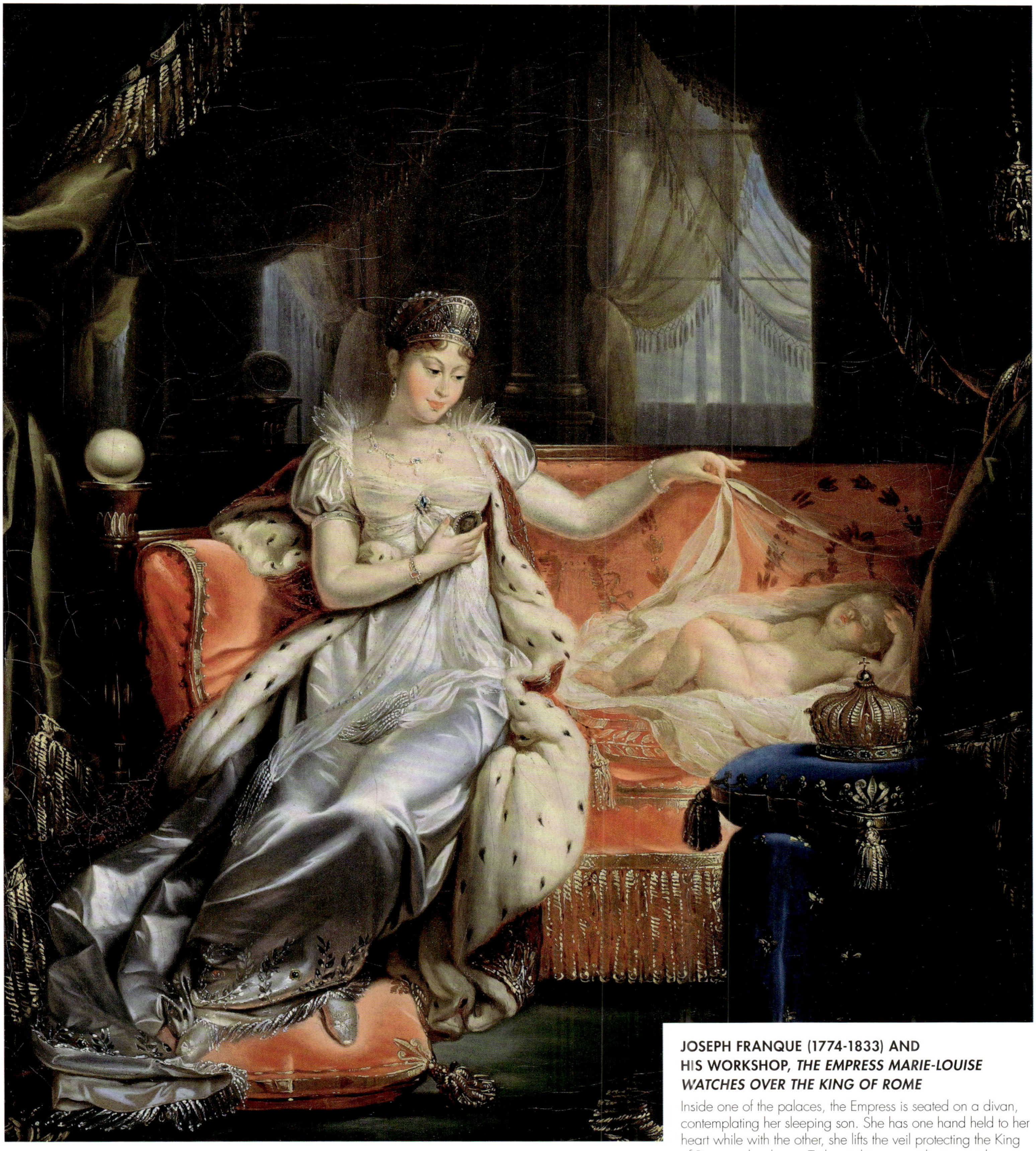

JOSEPH FRANQUE (1774-1833) AND HIS WORKSHOP, *THE EMPRESS MARIE-LOUISE WATCHES OVER THE KING OF ROME*

Inside one of the palaces, the Empress is seated on a divan, contemplating her sleeping son. She has one hand held to her heart while with the other, she lifts the veil protecting the King of Rome as he sleeps. To her right, we see the imperial crown placed on a cushion, on a blue velvet mantle adorned with gold bees. Despite the somewhat intimate subject, the painter has captured the nobility of the people shown and evokes the hoped-for dynasty that would follow this birth. Commissioned by Napoleon, Joseph Franque painted this scene, which went on show at the 1812 Salon de Paris and is now part of the collections of the Château de Versailles and the Trianon. The painter also produced a replica for the Court of Vienna, maybe our oil on canvas, in the Mallet collection.

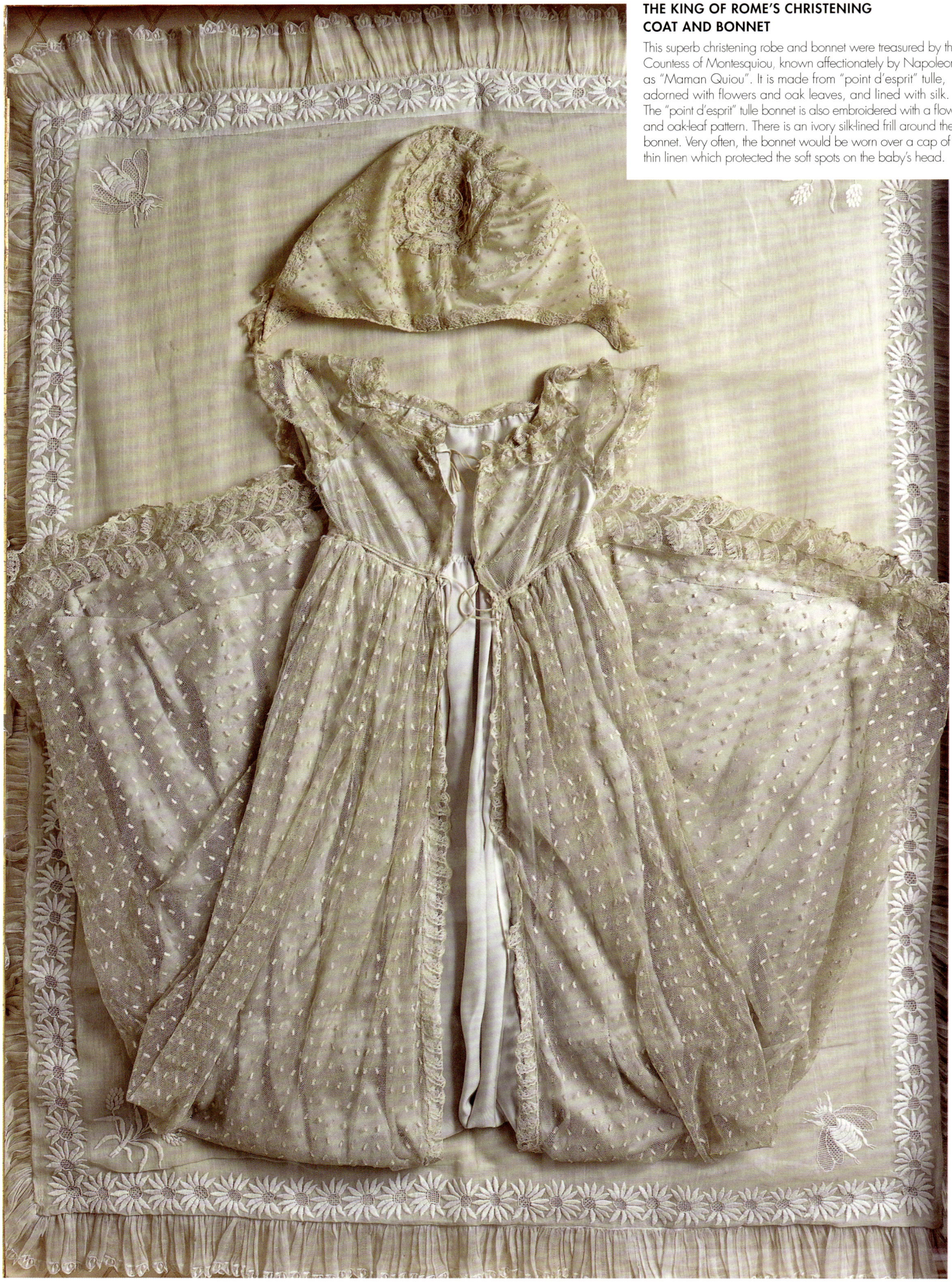

THE KING OF ROME'S CHRISTENING COAT AND BONNET

This superb christening robe and bonnet were treasured by the Countess of Montesquiou, known affectionately by Napoleon as "Maman Quiou". It is made from "point d'esprit" tulle, adorned with flowers and oak leaves, and lined with silk. The "point d'esprit" tulle bonnet is also embroidered with a flower and oak-leaf pattern. There is an ivory silk-lined frill around the bonnet. Very often, the bonnet would be worn over a cap of thin linen which protected the soft spots on the baby's head.

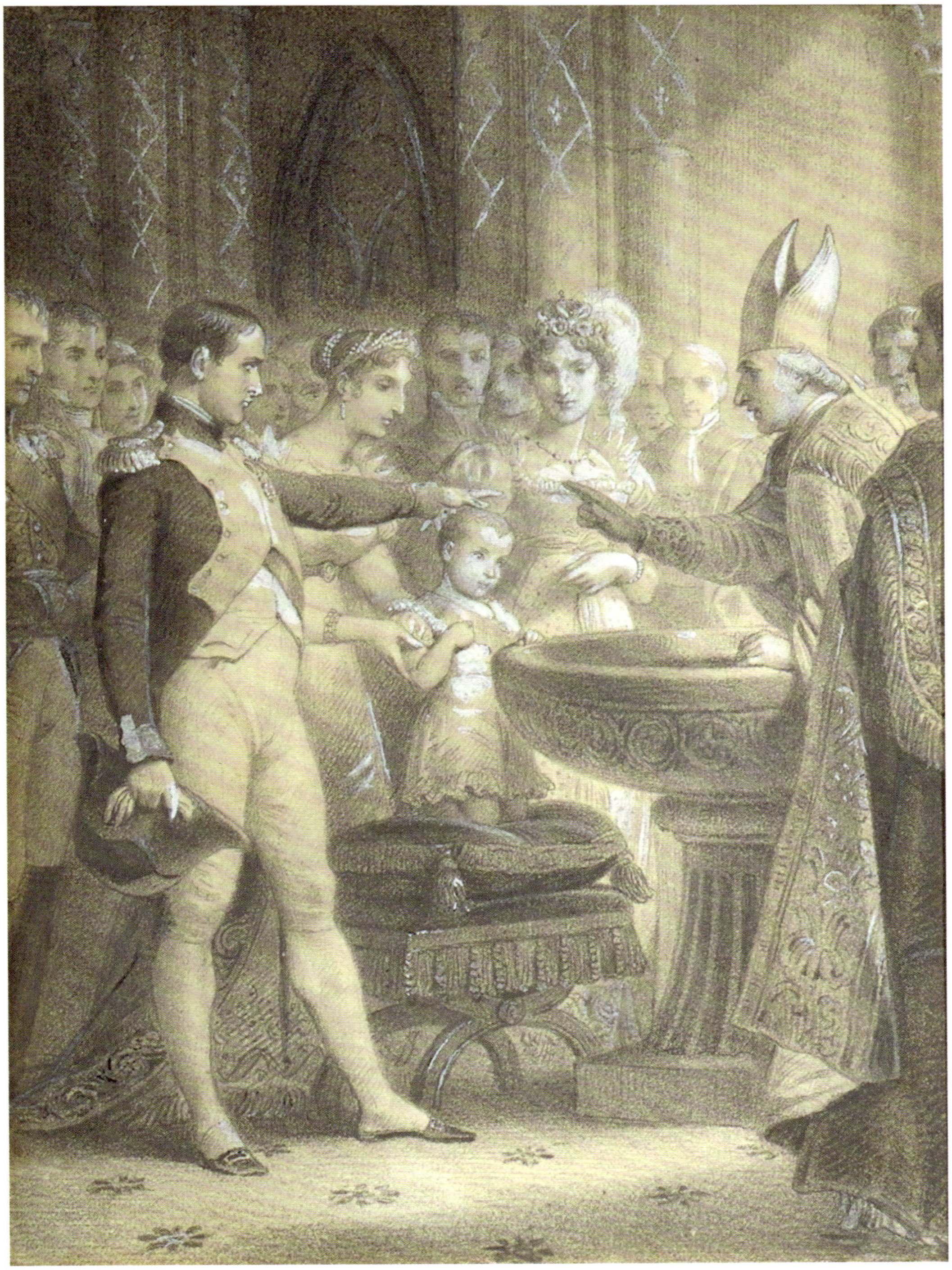

FÉLIX EMMANUEL PHILIPPOTEAUX (1815-1884),
CHRISTENING OF THE KING OF ROME

Napoleon wanted his son's baptism to be a highlight in the imperial story. Henri Félix Emmanuel Philippoteaux, a painter who chronicled the rise of Napoleon, thus depicted it as such. On this image, he places the key players—Napoleon, the King of Rome and Cardinal Fesch—at the center.

NOTES AND INVOICES FOR THE FESTIVITIES MARKING THE BIRTH OF THE KING OF ROME IN 1811

Echoing the expected public joy on the King of Rome's birth, ephemeral decorations were produced and installed by craftsmen, painters, lighting designers and gardeners. This book collects their notes, which served as invoices.

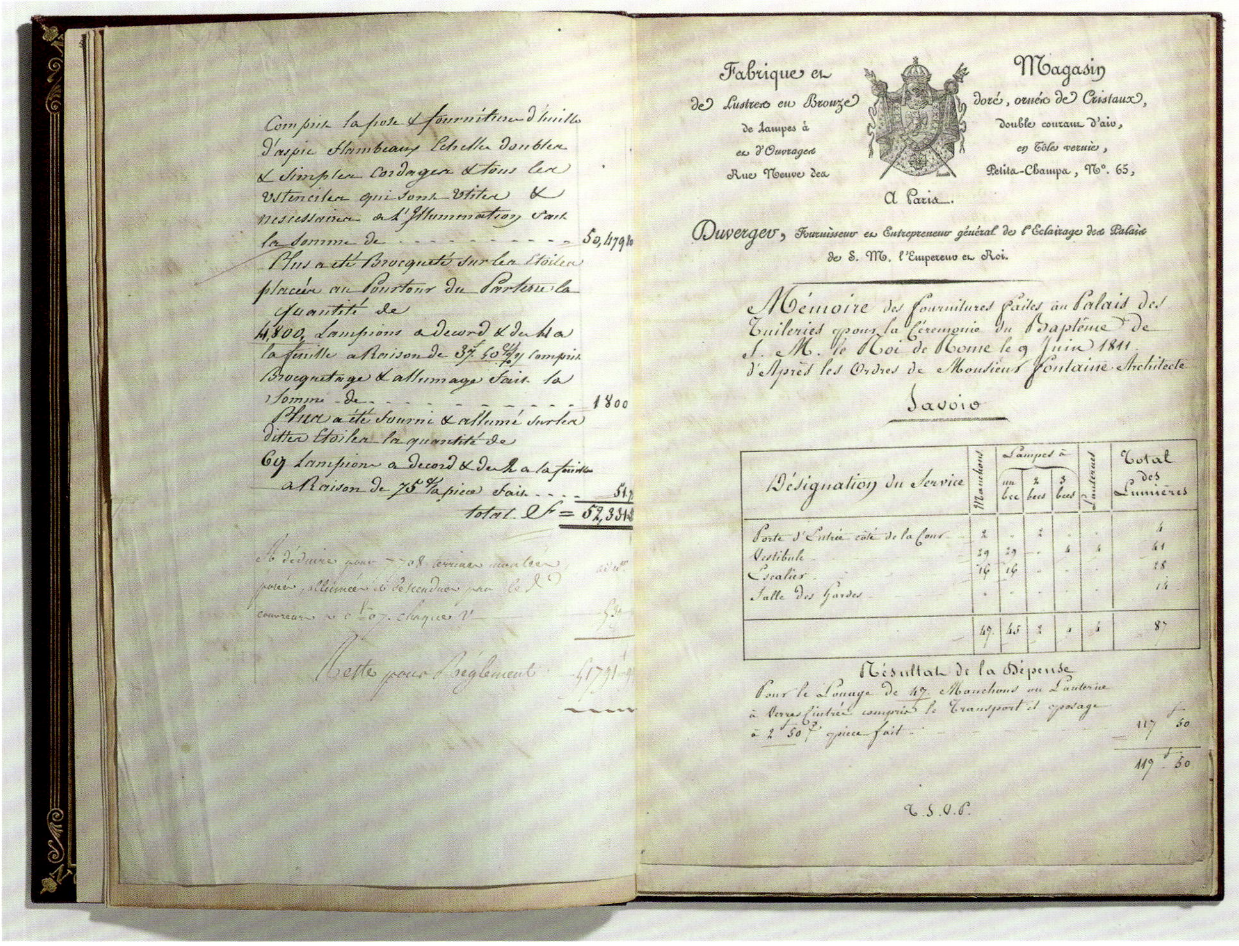

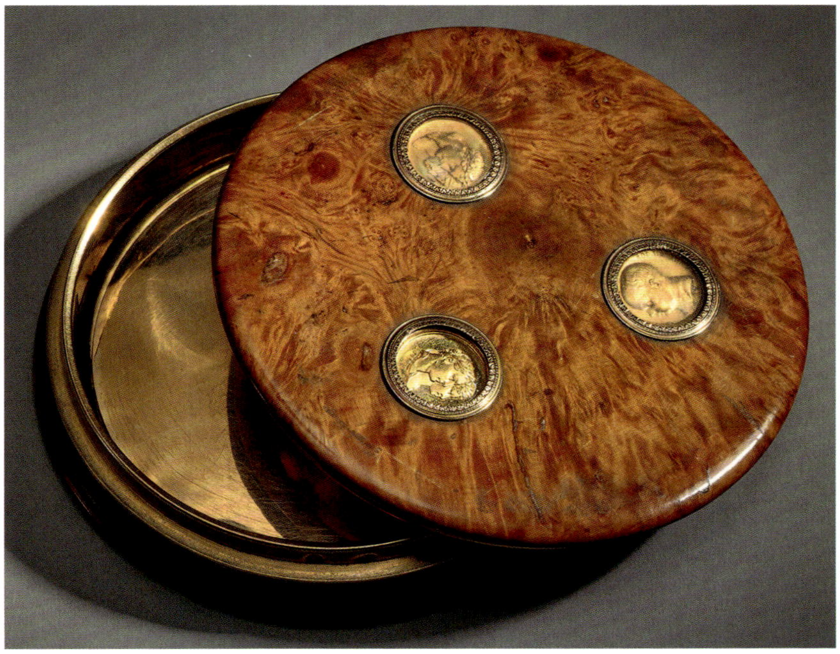

BOX FEATURING MEDALS OF NAPOLEON, MARIE-LOUISE AND THE KING OF ROME

This burl wood box is lined with gold and its lid is adorned with three gold medals made by Andrieu. Two, dated 1810 and featuring the profiles of Napoleon and Marie-Louise, are commemorative wedding medals. The third, showing the profile of the King of Rome, commemorates his birth. The box was no doubt a gift given at the christening.

THE KING OF ROME'S BOOTEES AND BONNET

This pair of fine beige-colored bootees has a bouquet of flowers depicted in tiny beads on their upper, the same color as those on the bonnet. The ribbons are green silk, a color frequently used to decorate the newborn's rooms. This wonderful souvenir comes to us from Countess Jeanne-Charlotte de Luçay, lady-in-waiting to the Empress Josephine. She was particularly appreciated by the Emperor, as shown in this letter, received on 24 February 1810 and which she treasured: "I have been very happy with your services […]. Circumstances having required me to dissolve the current Household of the Empress, I wanted to offer you this token of my feelings and my wish to maintain pleasant relations with you at all times…". In April 1810, she became lady-in-waiting to the new Empress, Marie-Louise, and was in her service at the time of the King of Rome's birth on 20 March 1811. The Empress let her go in Rambouillet in April 1814 when she left for Austria.

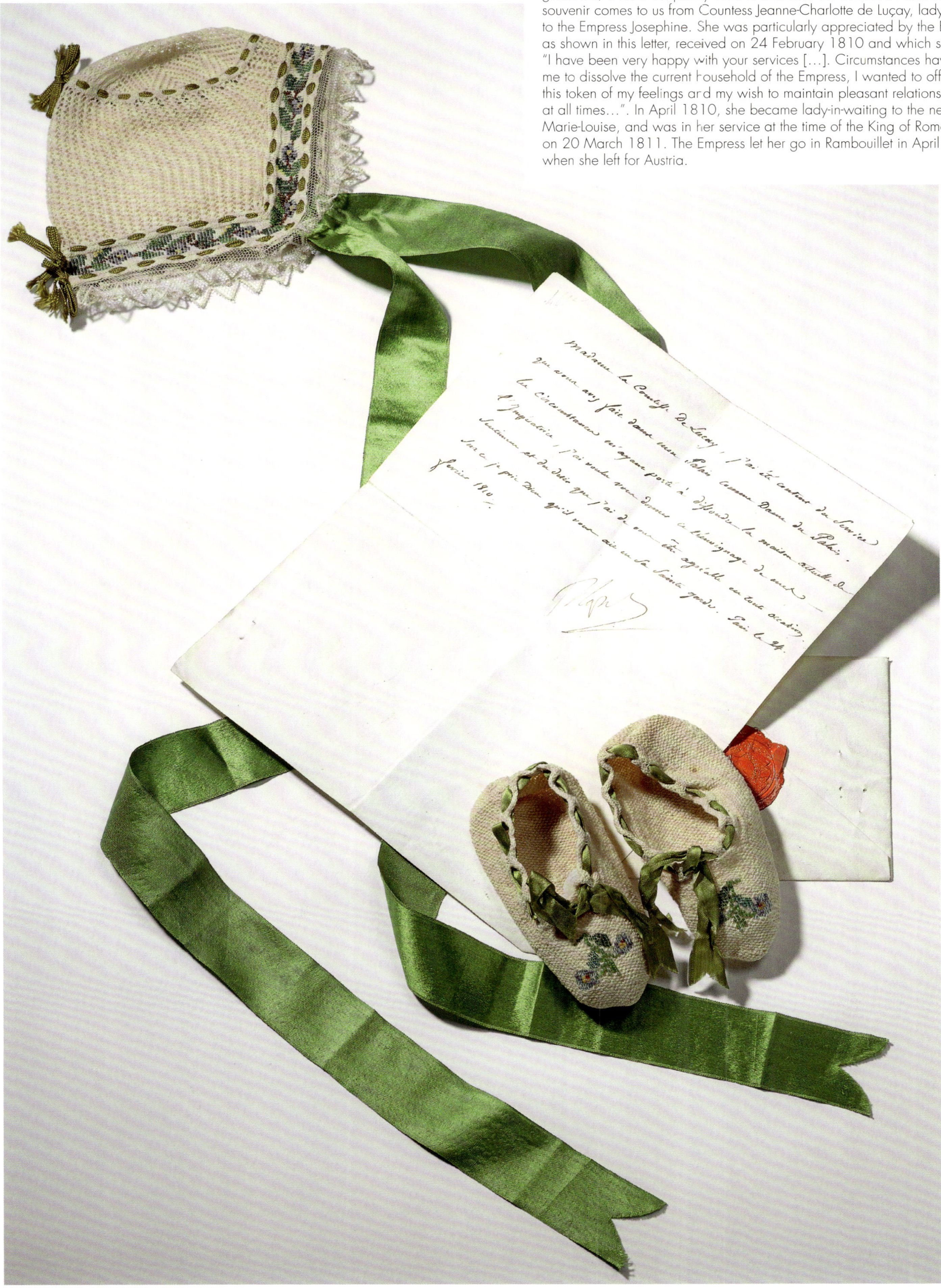

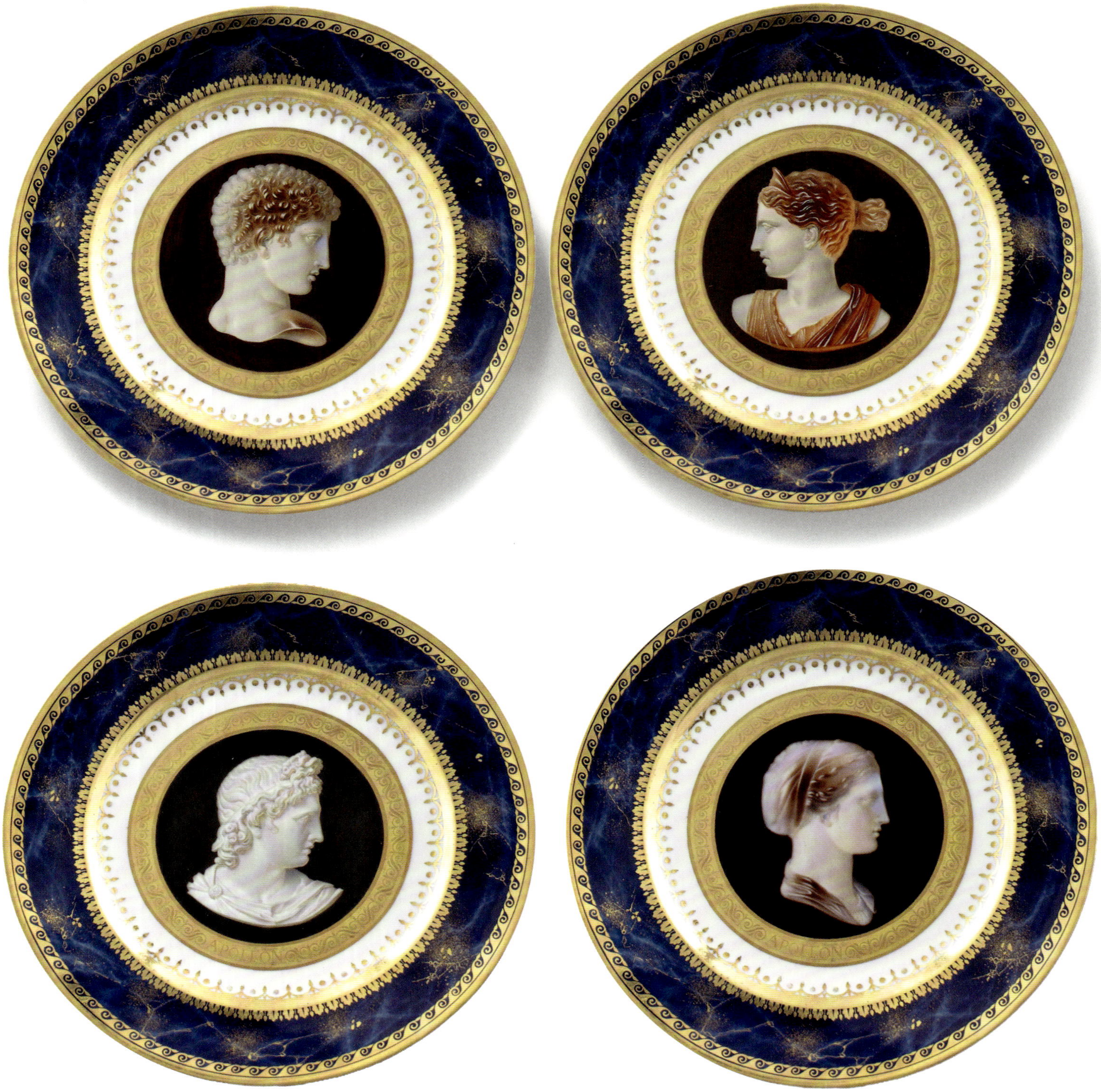

SÈVRES IMPERIAL MANUFACTORY, PLATES FROM THE ANTIQUE ICONOGRAPHIC SERVICE BELONGING TO CARDINAL FESCH

At the King of Rome's christening, Napoleon gave his uncle, Cardinal Fesch, a superb Sèvres porcelain service known as the "Antique iconographic service". These plates belonged to the second series, produced between 1812 and 1817 for "the court of Rome" although the recipient has not been identified. The edge of the plates imitates lapis lazuli while the center is adorned with cameo-style medallions featuring the profiles of Antique characters.

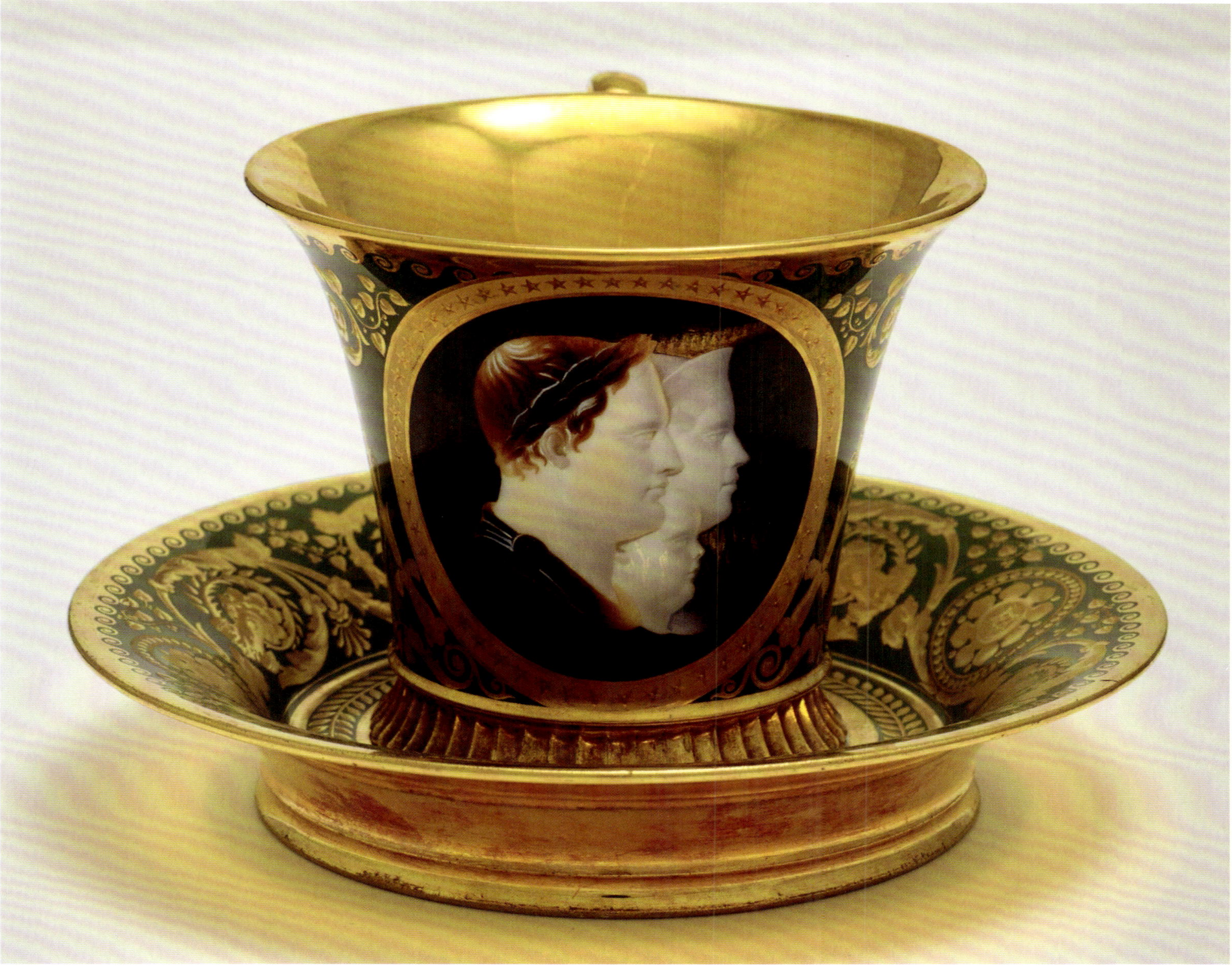

SÈVRES IMPERIAL MANUFACTORY, CUP WITH PORTRAITS OF NAPOLEON, MARIE-LOUISE AND THE KING OF ROME

This very rare "jasmine"-shaped porcelain cup was made at the Sèvres manufactory and features a very rich gold and chrome green design. It was ordered by Napoleon and delivered in 1812. The cameo-style portraits of the imperial family were painted by Louis Bertin Parant (1768-1851). Profile busts of Napoleon and Marie-Louise surround that of the King of Rome.

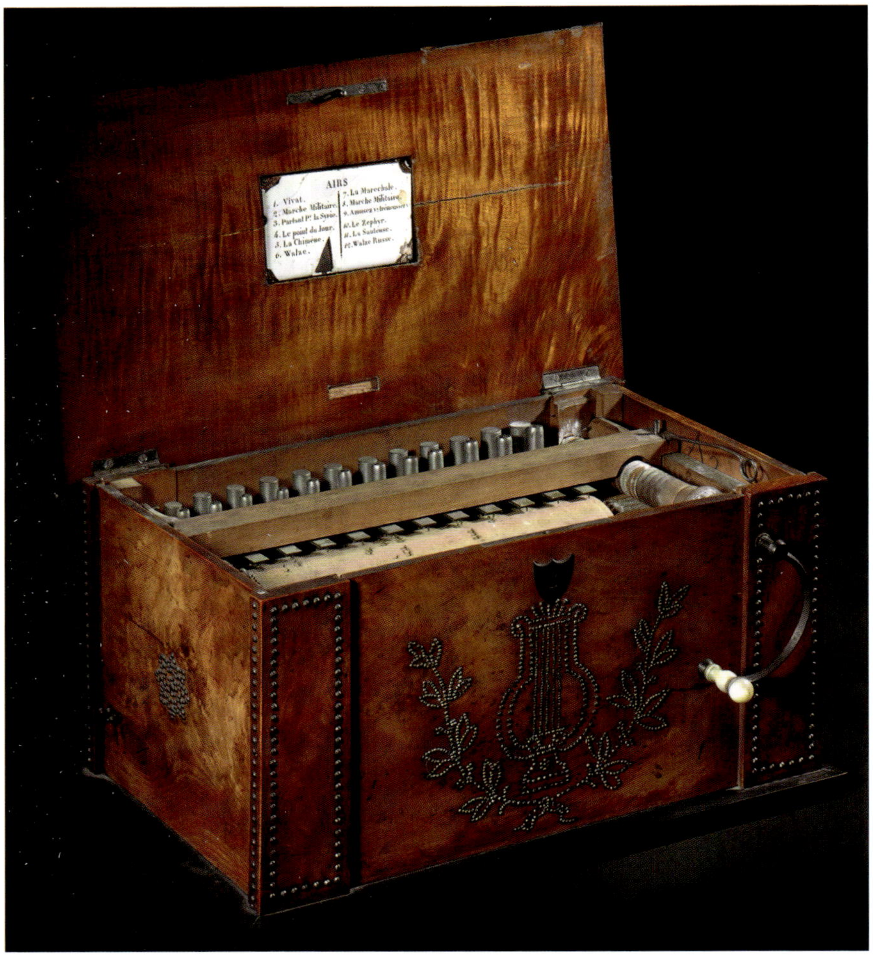

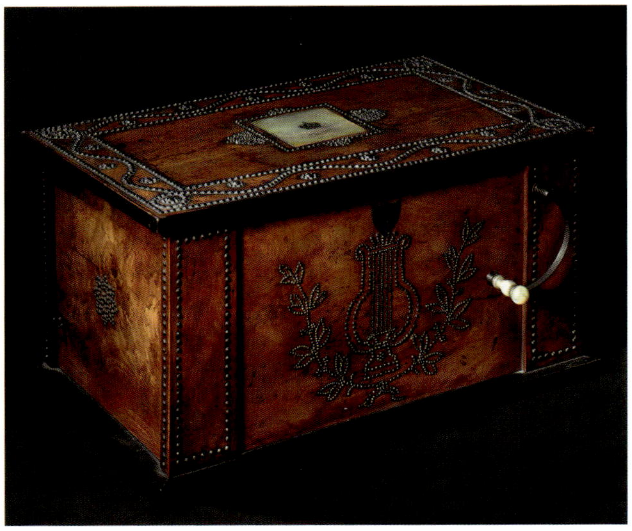

THE KING OF ROME'S SERINETTE

This delightful instrument plays twelve different tunes. It is made from natural wood and adorned with faceted studs forming a lyre on the front and stars on the sides, and has a mother-of-pearl plate engraved with the imperial crown on the lid. It was used by Marie Marguerite Marchand, the King of Rome's first rocking nurse and mother of Louis Marchand, the Emperor's valet who followed him to St Helena, to rock the child and introduce him to waltzes and military marches. Accompanied by Mme de Montesquiou, the King of Rome's governess, she left for Vienna in 1814 to continue to serve Napoleon's son. The child was very fond of her and called her "Chanchan". The serinette became part of the Marchand family's inheritance.

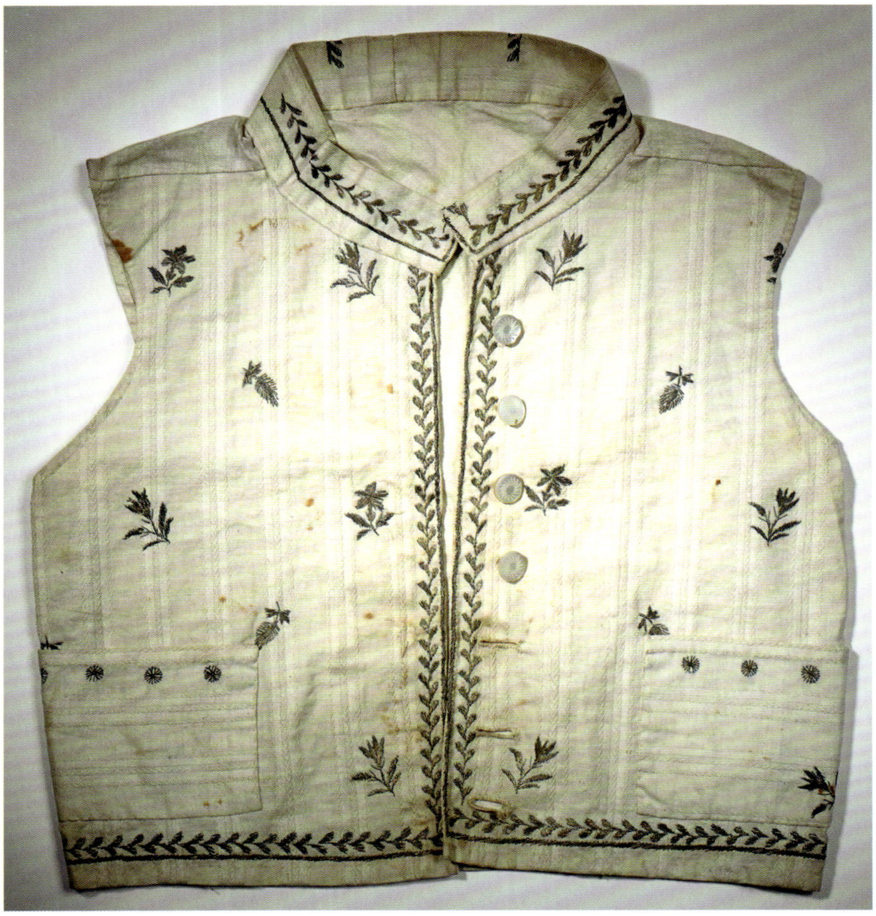

CHILD'S WAISTCOAT THOUGHT TO HAVE BELONGED TO THE DUKE OF REICHSTADT

This cream-colored waistcoat was very likely part of the Duke of Reichstadt's attire. It is made from linen and silk and is embroidered with flowers and a leaf-motif edge in gold thread. A handwritten note in the front, right-hand pocket says "Waistcoat belonging to the Herzogs von Reichstadt".

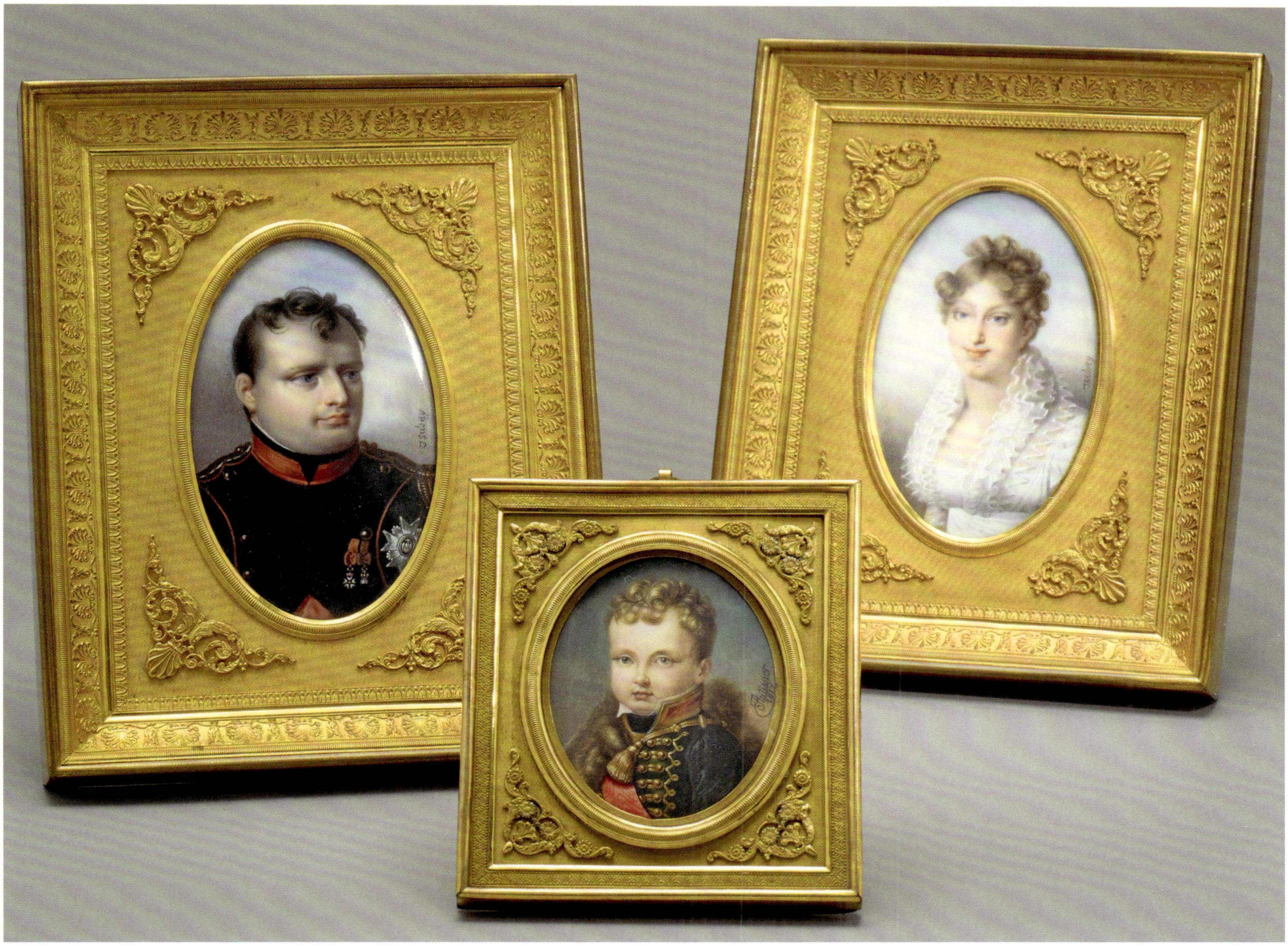

JEAN-BAPTISTE ISABEY (1767-1855), LOUIS-MARIE AUTISSIER (1772-1830), PORTRAITS OF THE IMPERIAL FAMILY

Renowned painter Isabey produced these portraits of Napoleon and Marie-Louise. Between them, there is a miniature on ivory, revealing the face of the King of Rome. Signed Louis-Marie Autissier, it was painted in 1817 based on a portrait by Baron Gérard (not located), an engraving of which is kept at the Château de Fontainebleau. The child is wearing the ribbon of the Legion of Honor and a hussar's costume. Images of the King of Rome aged over two years old are rare.

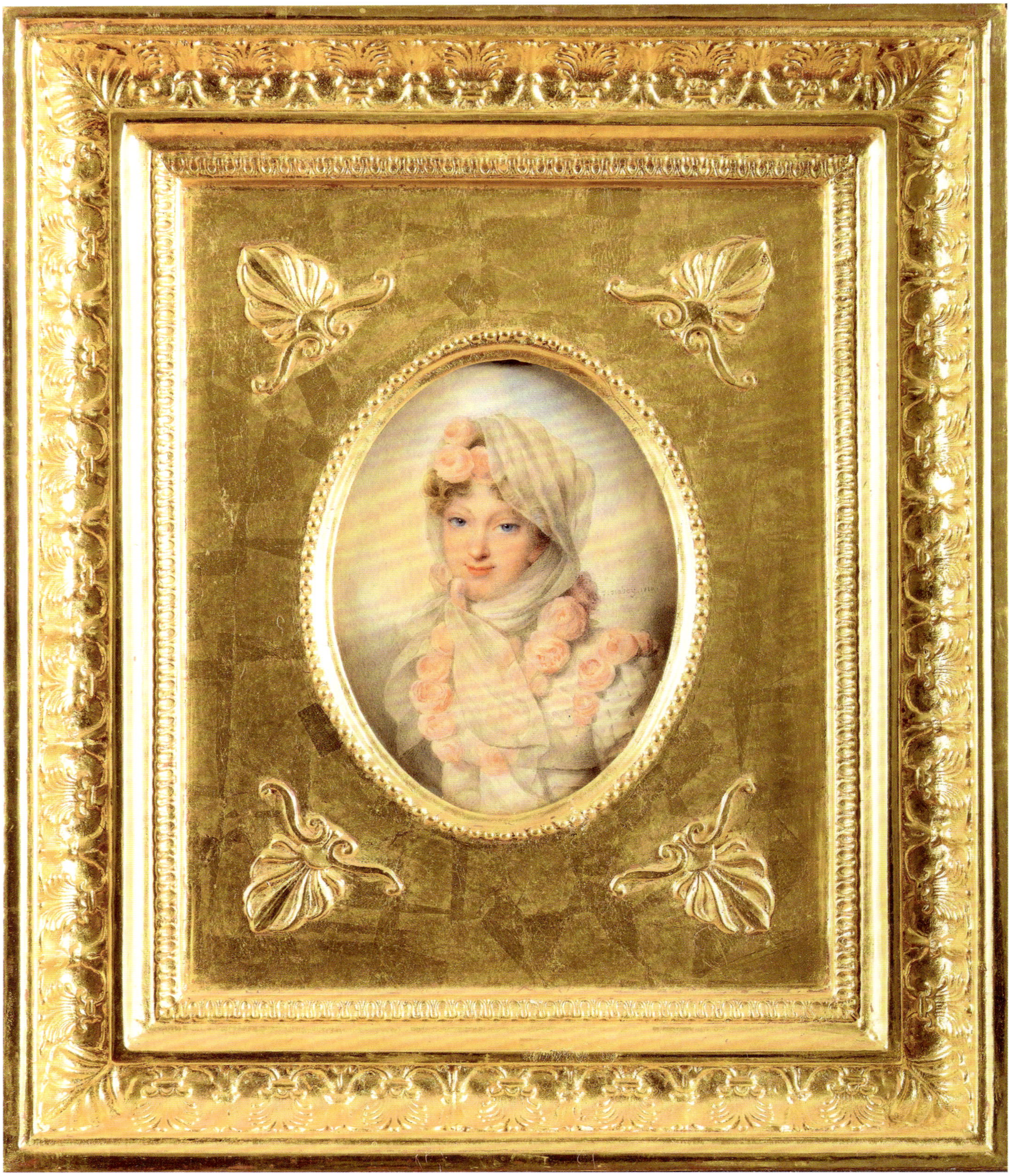

JEAN-BAPTISTE ISABEY (1767-1855), MINIATURES OF THE KING OF ROME AND MARIE-LOUISE

Isabey's hand is clearly felt in these two portraits which appear to have been composed as pendants. The softness of the faces and the rose garlands surrounding them are in perfect harmony with the pastel-colored clothing. The Empress and the King of Rome appear simply as mother and son, far removed from official representations.

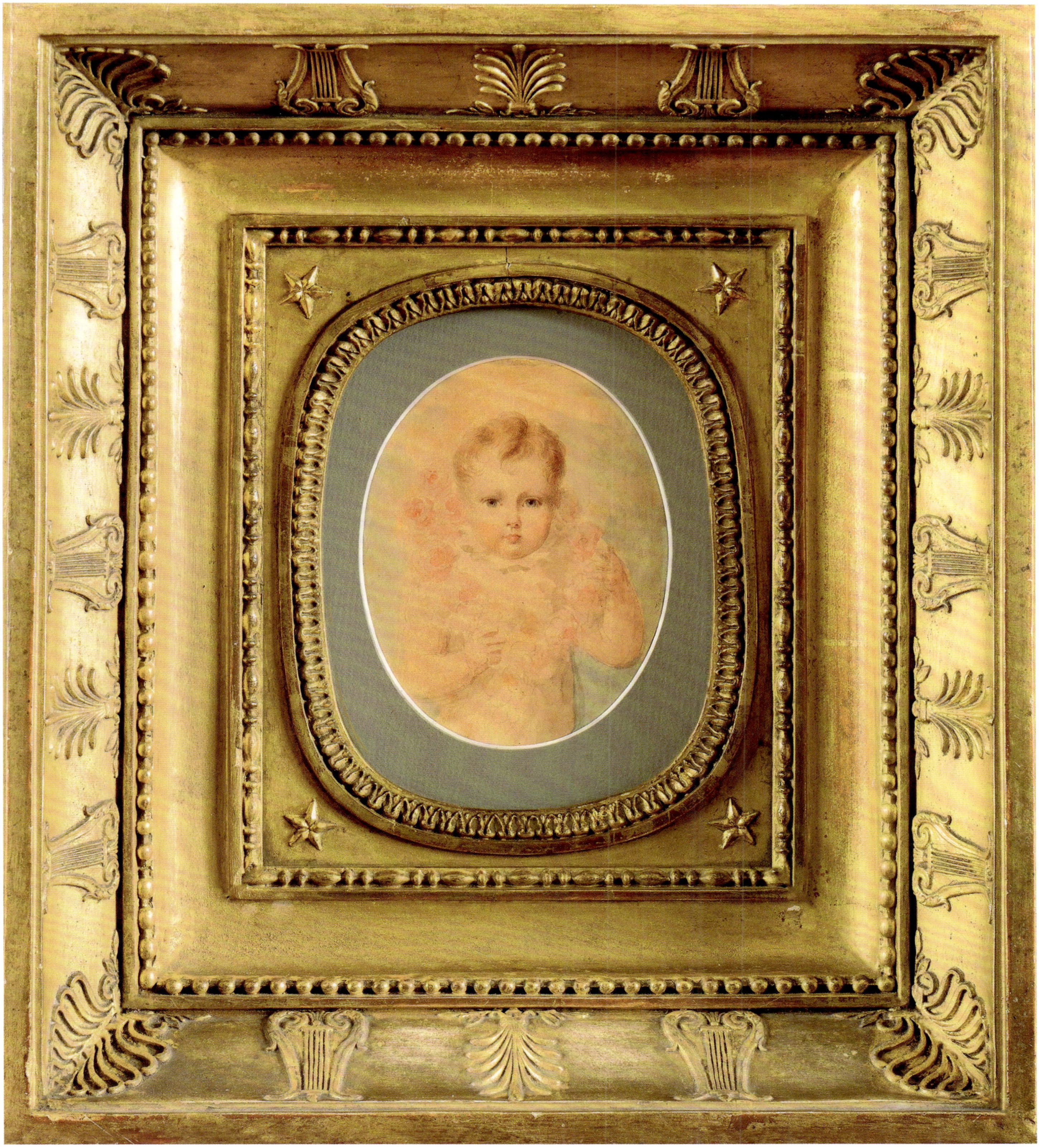

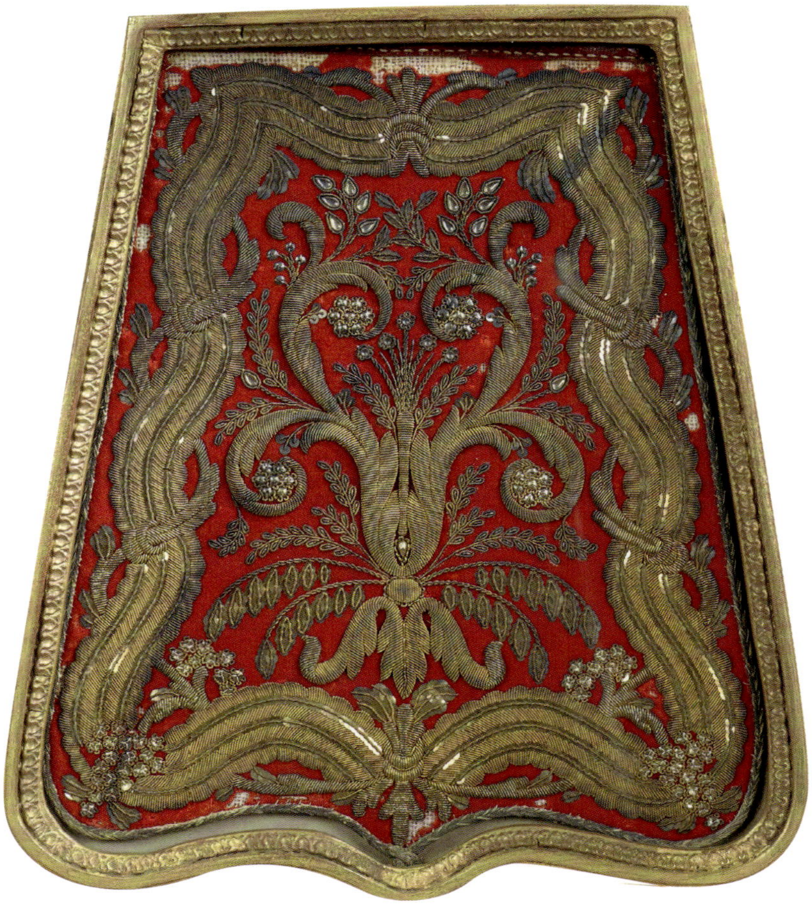

CHILD'S SABRETACHE THAT BELONGED TO THE KING OF ROME

This gold-embroidered red Morocco leather sabretache was no doubt part of one of the solider kits that Napoleon's son loved. A miniature produced by Isabey in 1818, kept at the Victoria and Albert Museum, shows the Duke of Reichstadt in a hussar's costume with a red sabretache on his belt. For many years, it was on show at the Musée des Souverains in Paris, the museum founded by Napoleon III in 1852 within the Louvre to exhibit souvenirs of the dynasties that had reigned over France.

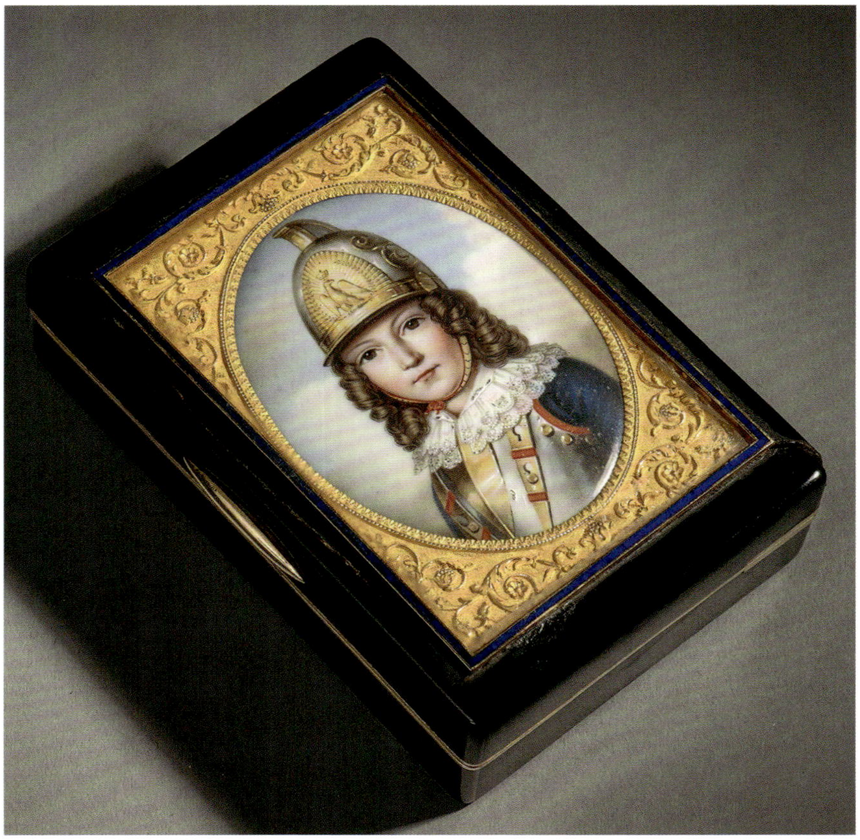

GABRIEL-RAOUL MOREL (1764-1832), SNUFFBOX BEARING THE PORTRAIT OF THE KING OF ROME

This rectangular tortoiseshell box, signed by goldsmith Morel, is adorned with the portrait of a child wearing a breastplate, surrounded by a carved gold rinceaux frame and a border of blue enamel. The child's helmet is bedecked with the imperial eagle, telling us that it is the King of Rome. An identical portrait, unsigned but attributed to Salomon-Guillaume Counis, a Swiss painter close to Elisa Bonaparte, can be found at the Bonaparte House museum in Ajaccio (Corsica).

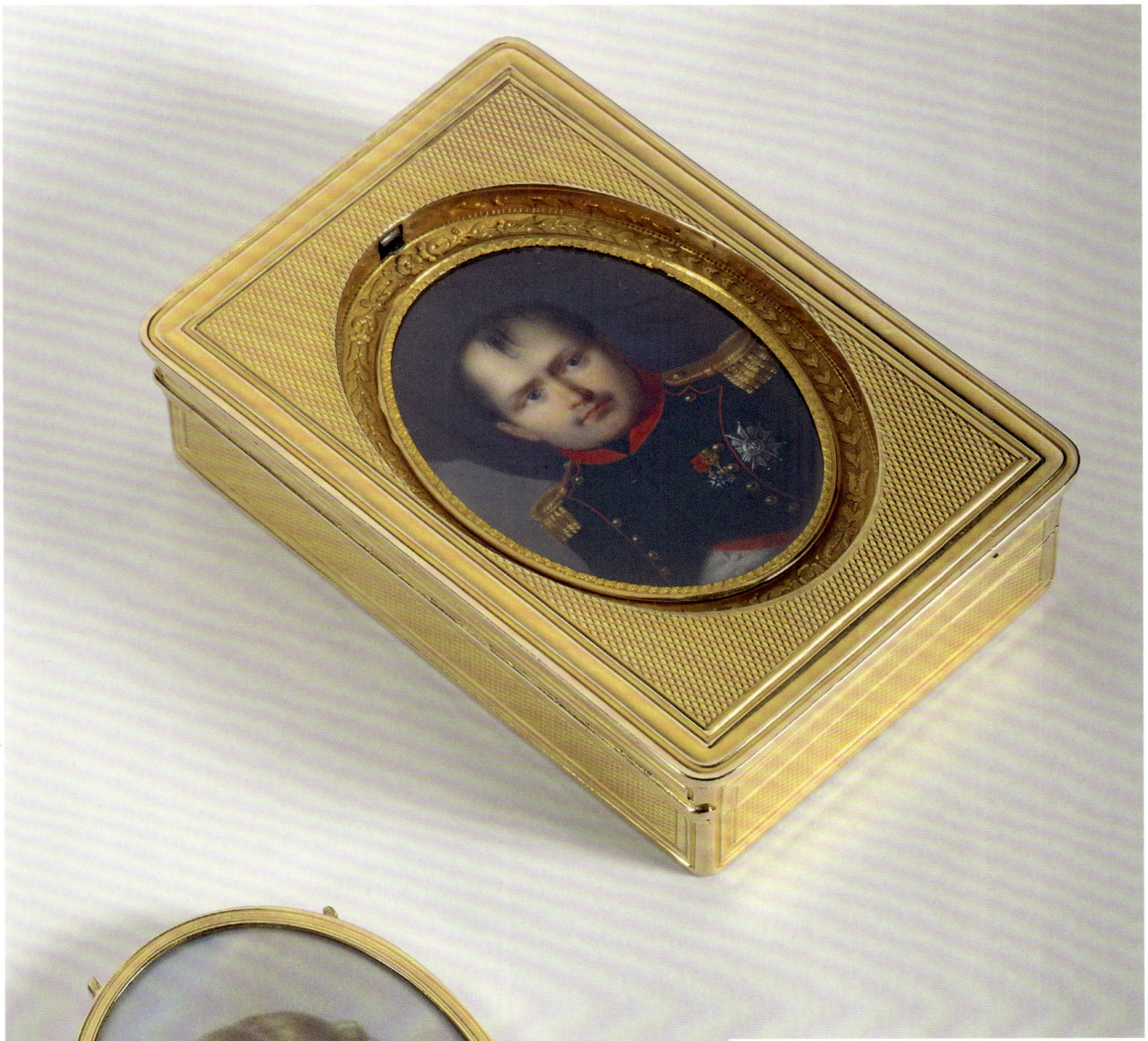

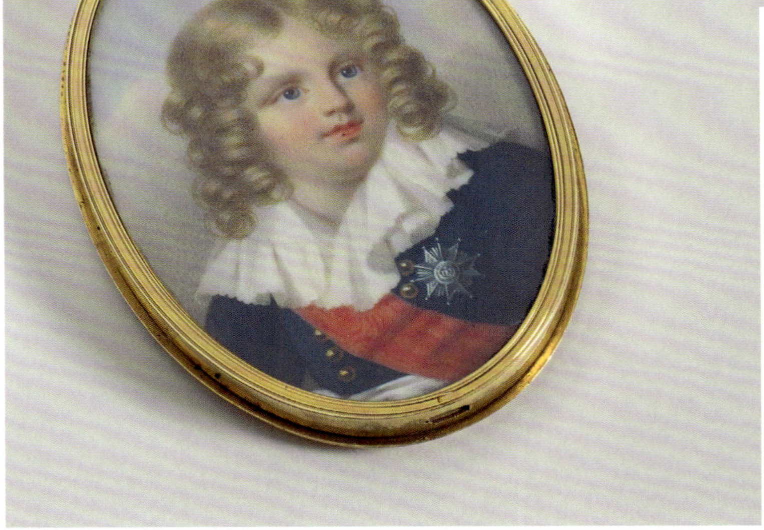

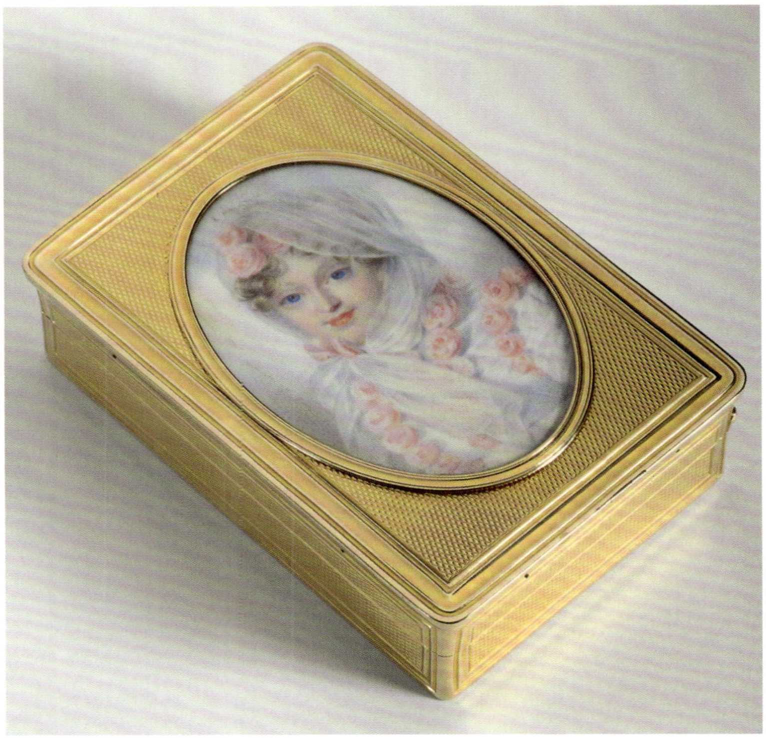

"SECRET" SNUFFBOX CONTAINING PORTRAITS OF MARIE-LOUISE, NAPOLEON AND THE KING OF ROME

This extremely rare "secret" box is made from yellow gold and has rounded corners and a guilloché pattern. Its lid features an oval miniature of Marie-Louise, inspired by one of Isabey's well-known portraits. The Empress's portrait can be lifted out to reveal an image of Napoleon. The reverse side of her portrait features that of the King of Rome, aged four. These miniatures are unsigned but have been attributed to Nicolas Jacques (1780-1844), a miniature painter.

THE KING OF ROME'S TIN SOLDIERS

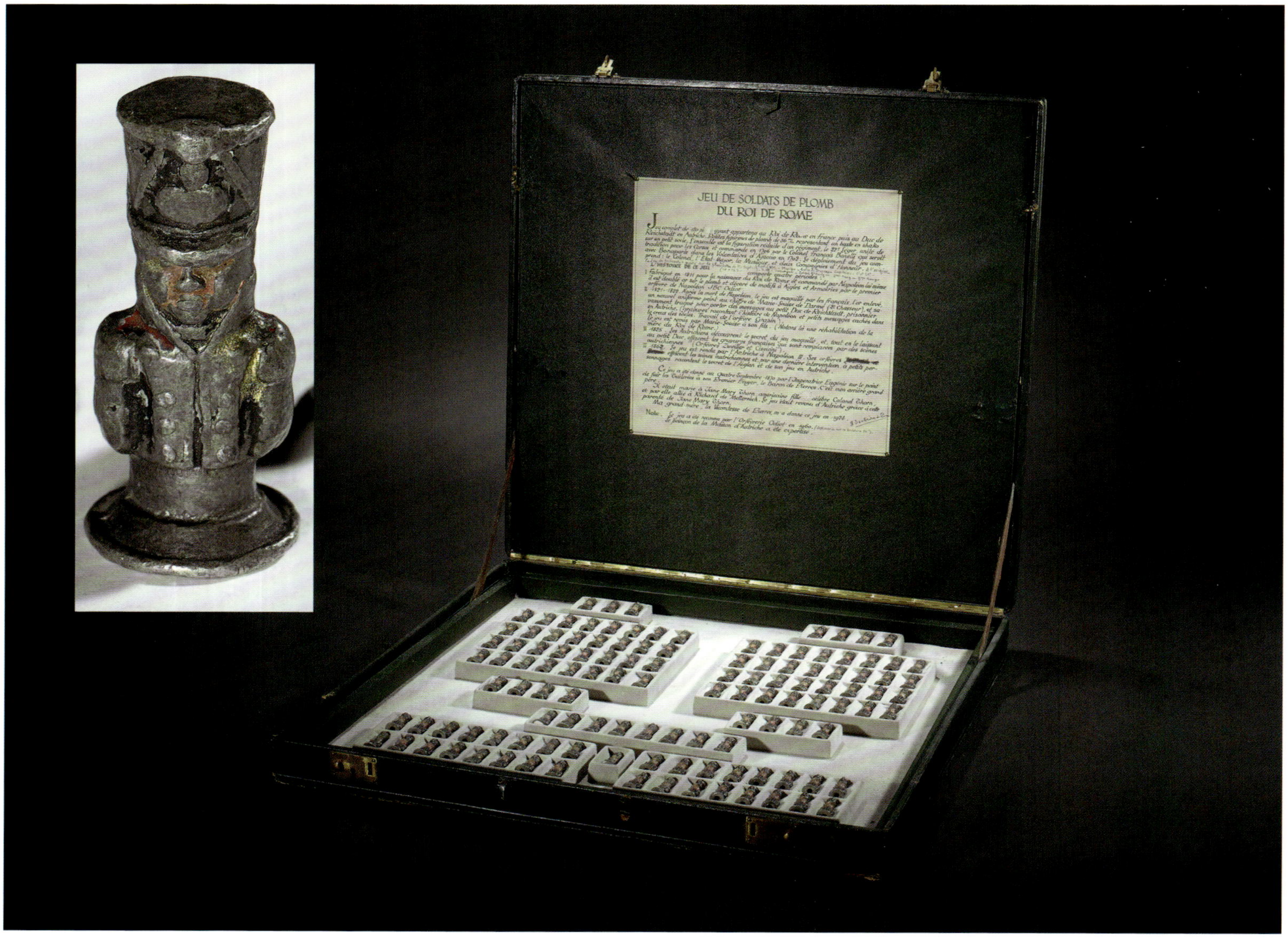

Contrary to a very popular idea, the King of Rome received very few commissioned or luxury toys. The Empress bought items from Parisian toy sellers such as Cacheleux, 116 rue St Denis, or Mittou, 81 rue Neuve-des-Petits-Champs, entitled to bear the much-envied title of "toy supplier to the Children of the Imperial and Royal Family". These tin soldiers, which belonged to the "Aiglon" (or "Eaglet", the nickname given to the King of Rome), split into several light infantry regiments comprising 120 figurines each, were no exception. A note left by Mittou, dated 15 January 1814, says "Sold to Her Highness the Empress [...] a large box of tin soldiers comprising five cavalry regiments and five infantry regiments, all in order and complete". To set the collection apart, the Emperor wanted the soldiers gold plated, which is where the legend of the *King of Rome's gold soldiers* comes from. This work was done by Odiot. And this is what makes them so uniquely recognizable.

A certain mythology has surrounded them since the 19th century. Rumor had it that the figurines were used to transport secret messages on tiny pieces of paper slipped into the hollow underneath, or that they were engraved with messages indiscernible to the naked eye.

What is sure is that these soldiers went to Austria in April 1814, following the child during his exile. The gold plating was removed for greater discretion. When the Duke of Reichstadt died, these regiments, the exact number of which we are unsure, went to different heirs. Some of the regiments remained complete and went to Napoleon III and Empress Eugénie, who gave them to their son, the Imperial Prince. When the Second Empire fell, one of the regiments was given by Eugénie to the Baron de Pierres, her First Ecuyer and a relation of Klemens Wenzel von Metternich. It was exhibited at the Navy Museum in 1961 and at the Museum of Education in 1962. Today it is part of the collection. When studied under a magnifying glass, tiny traces of gold, barely visible to the naked eye, can be seen in the folds of some of the soldiers' uniforms (including the above example).

Three figurines from another regiment were brought back from Austria by Mme Soufflot, sub-governess of the King of Rome. They are now kept by the Fondation Napoléon (inv. 905). Other soldiers have resurfaced over the years, such as those in the Napoleon collection belonging to Prefect Milliat, or those of André Maurois, whose great-grandmother was very close to Empress Eugénie.

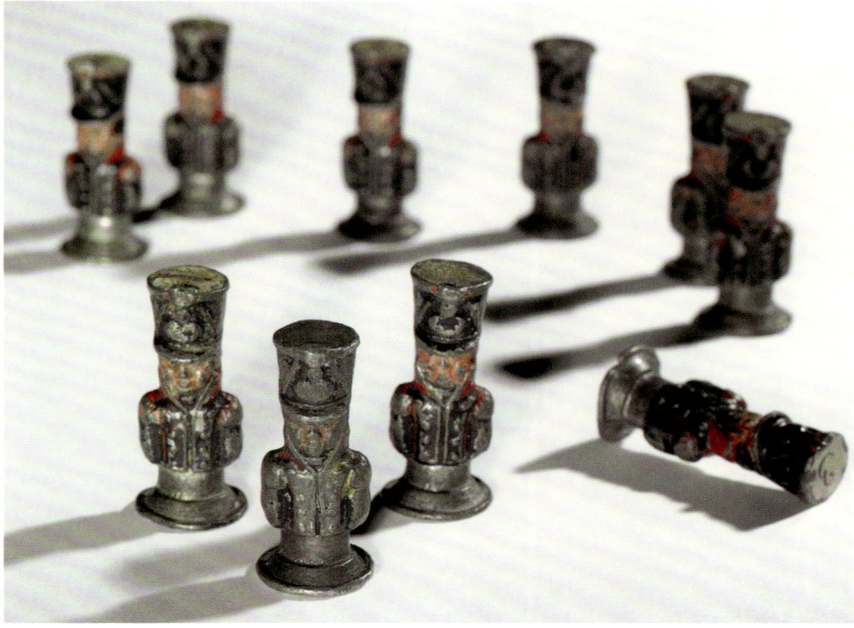

JOHANN FRIEDRICH LEYBOLD (1755-1838), *PORTRAIT OF THE EMPEROR AND HIS SON AT THE TUILERIES PALACE* (DETAIL)

In this composition by Ange-Louis Janet (1811-1872), otherwise known as Janet-Lange, showing Napoleon playing with his son, the artist includes a number of toys that were part of the King of Rome's childhood games but also of his education. On the floor is a small bronze cannon, identical to the one taken by Napoleon to St Helena, and we can see the instantly recognizable tin soldiers placed on a military map.

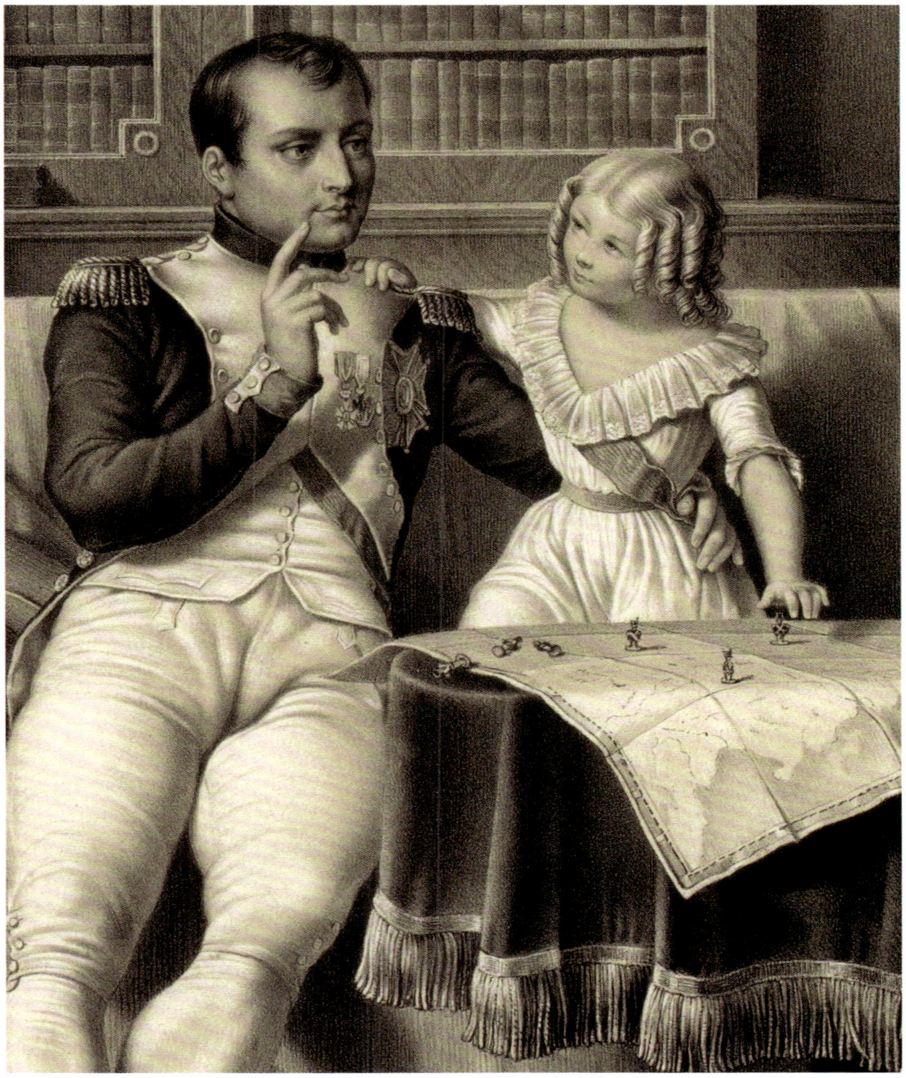

RAYMOND DESVARREUX (1876-1961),
PORTRAIT OF THE DUKE OF REICHSTADT

A pupil of Gérôme and Detaille, Desvarreux is best known for his landscapes. Nevertheless, he did produce a few military and Napoleonic subjects, including *The Defenders of the Eagle*, exhibited at the 1905 Salon. This portrait of Napoleon's son, Duke of Reichstadt since 1818, is another example. The young man is depicted on horseback in the Austrian senior officer uniform. Painted shortly after the first performances of Edmond Rostand's play, it points to the influence of the legend of the "Aiglon" when there was real thirst for revenge on Germany.

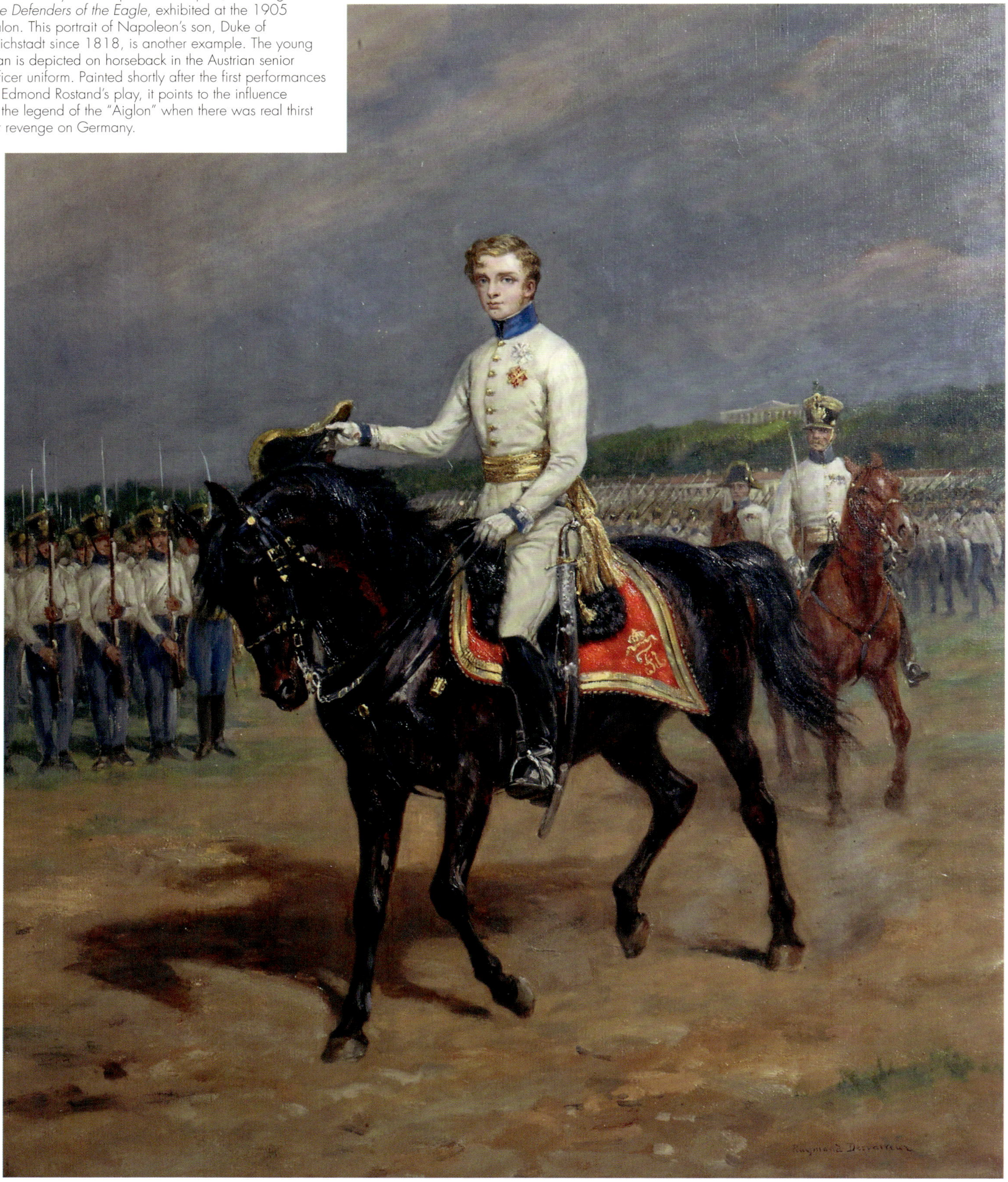

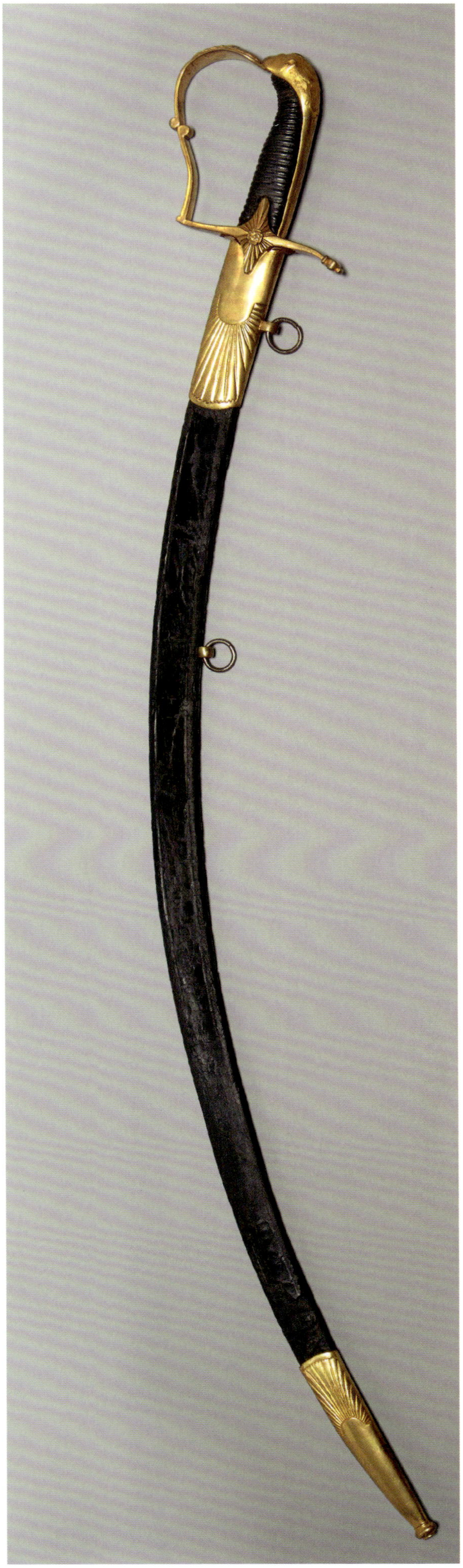

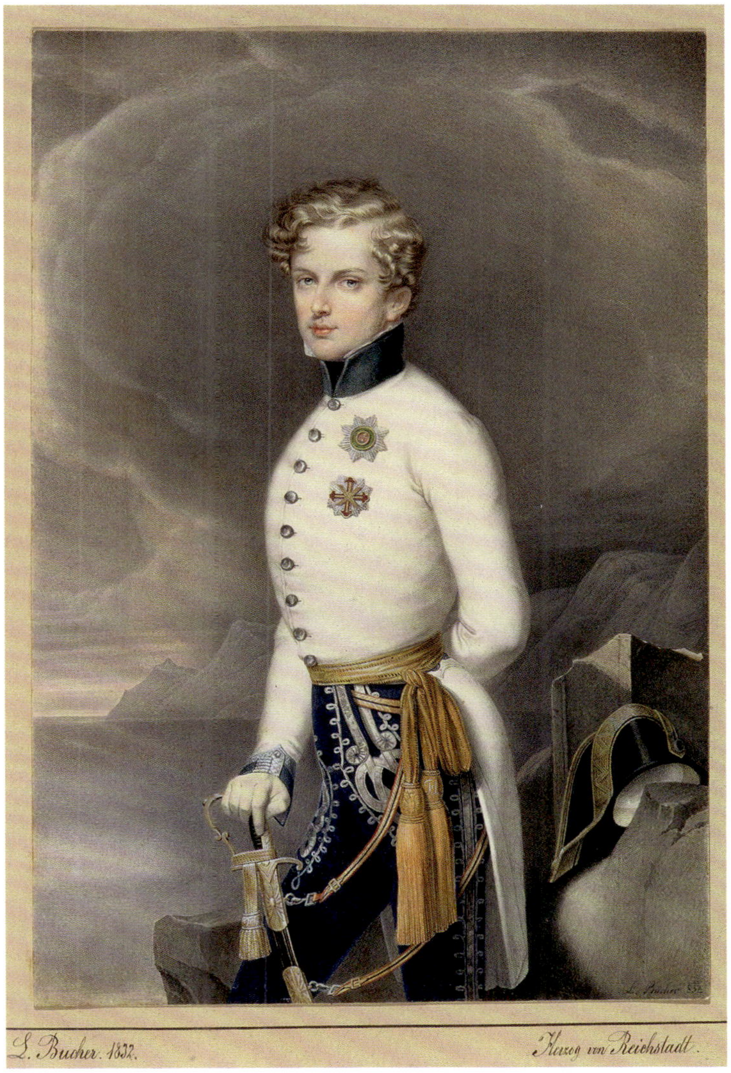

LÉOPOLD BUCHER (1797-1858),
FULL-LENGTH PORTRAIT OF THE DUKE OF REICHSTADT

There are few representations of Napoleon's son once he had become Duke of Reichstadt. The three-quarter pose paints him with a piercing gaze and a determined attitude, clearly presented as the heir to the imperial crown. It is one of the best-known portraits and was widely circulated thanks to engraving.

THE DUKE OF REICHSTADT'S CAVALRY OFFICER SABER

In the summer of 1822, Emperor Francis I of Austria made his grandson a corporal, which amused the court greatly. A few years later, having chosen a career as an officer, he underwent military training and, on 17 August 1828, was named captain in his grandfather's Tyrolean Hunter regiment. In July 1830, he joined the Lamezan-Salins regiment as battalion commander and, on 14 June 1831, the Hungarian infantry regiment, a career abruptly brought to an end by his early death in 1832, aged just 21. Shortly after his death, Marie-Louise handed some of her son's personal items to family and friends. This simply yet classically designed Austrian-made saber, with its curved blade, flat back and hollow sides, evocative of the first military ranks held by the young prince, was given to Captain Joseph Standeisky, a member of the Duke's military household who entered his service on 14 June 1831, the last day on which the Duke served the Hungarian infantry regiment. It can be compared to the saber of the same model given to his friend Prokesch and kept in the Napoleonico Museum in Rome. The above engraving depicts the Duke of Reichstadt holding a very similar saber.

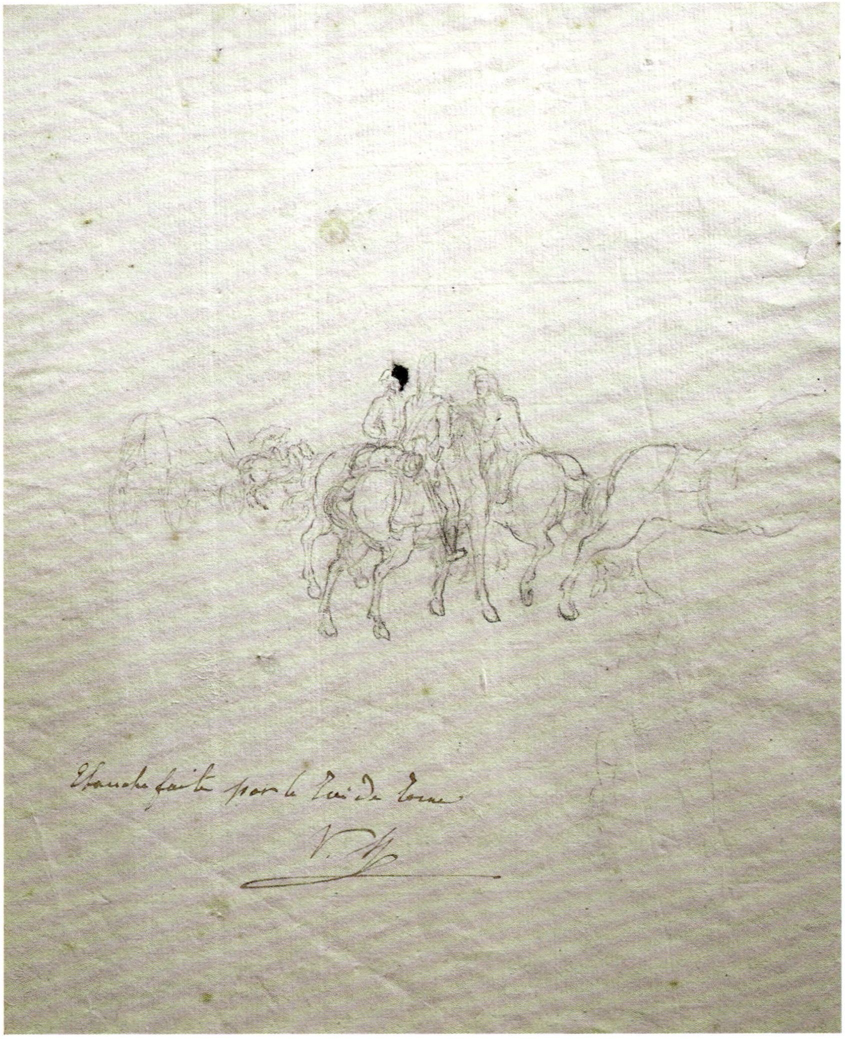

SKETCHES DRAWN BY THE DUKE OF REICHSTADT, CIRCA 1825

Several drawings by the Duke of Reichstadt are known. This is a pencil sketch of three revolutionary soldiers on horseback, including a dragon, a hussar and a carriage. His talent was awakened at an early age by the King of Rome's mother, who chose Goubaud to teach drawing to the children of France. His Austrian teachers, however, deplored his lack of enthusiasm for the art, other than for military subjects and horses. The other pencil drawing depicts a trumpeter on horseback, a dismounted rider and a pikeman.

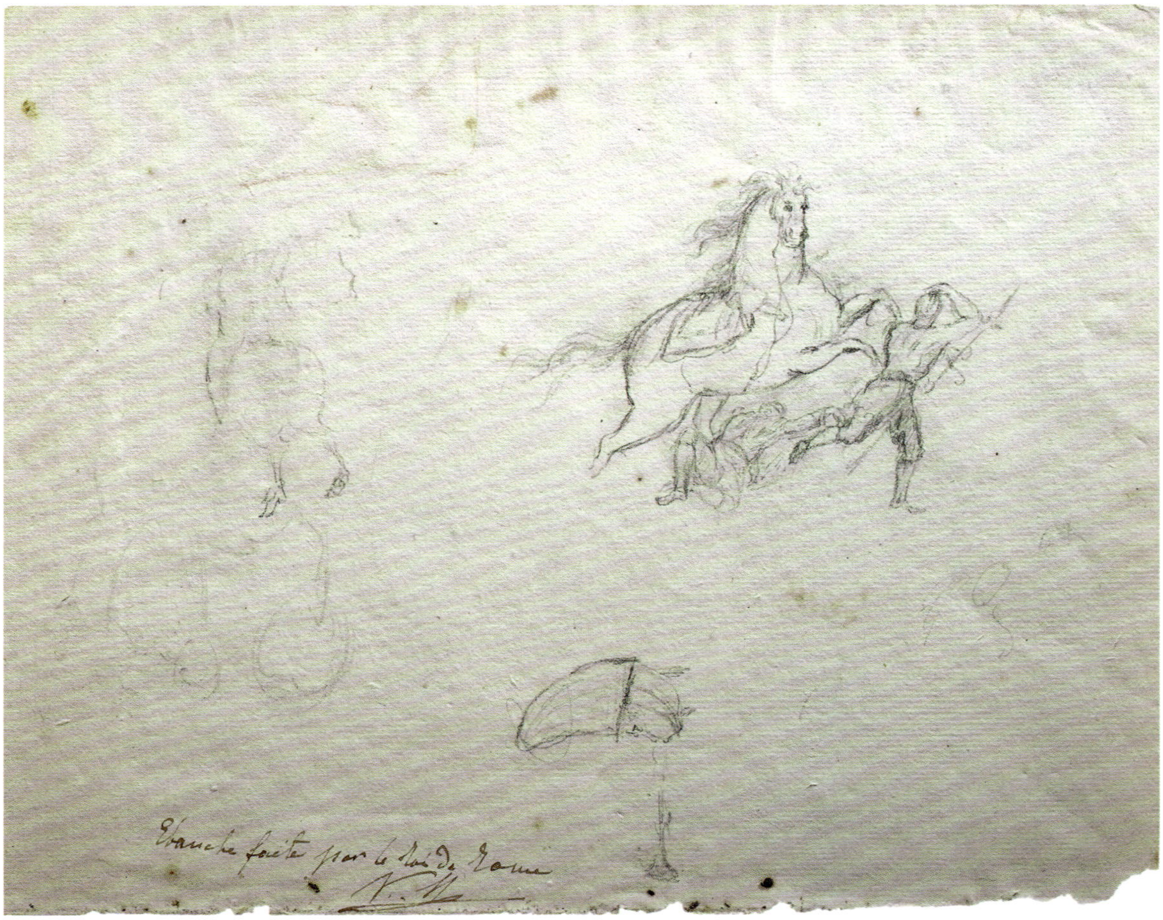

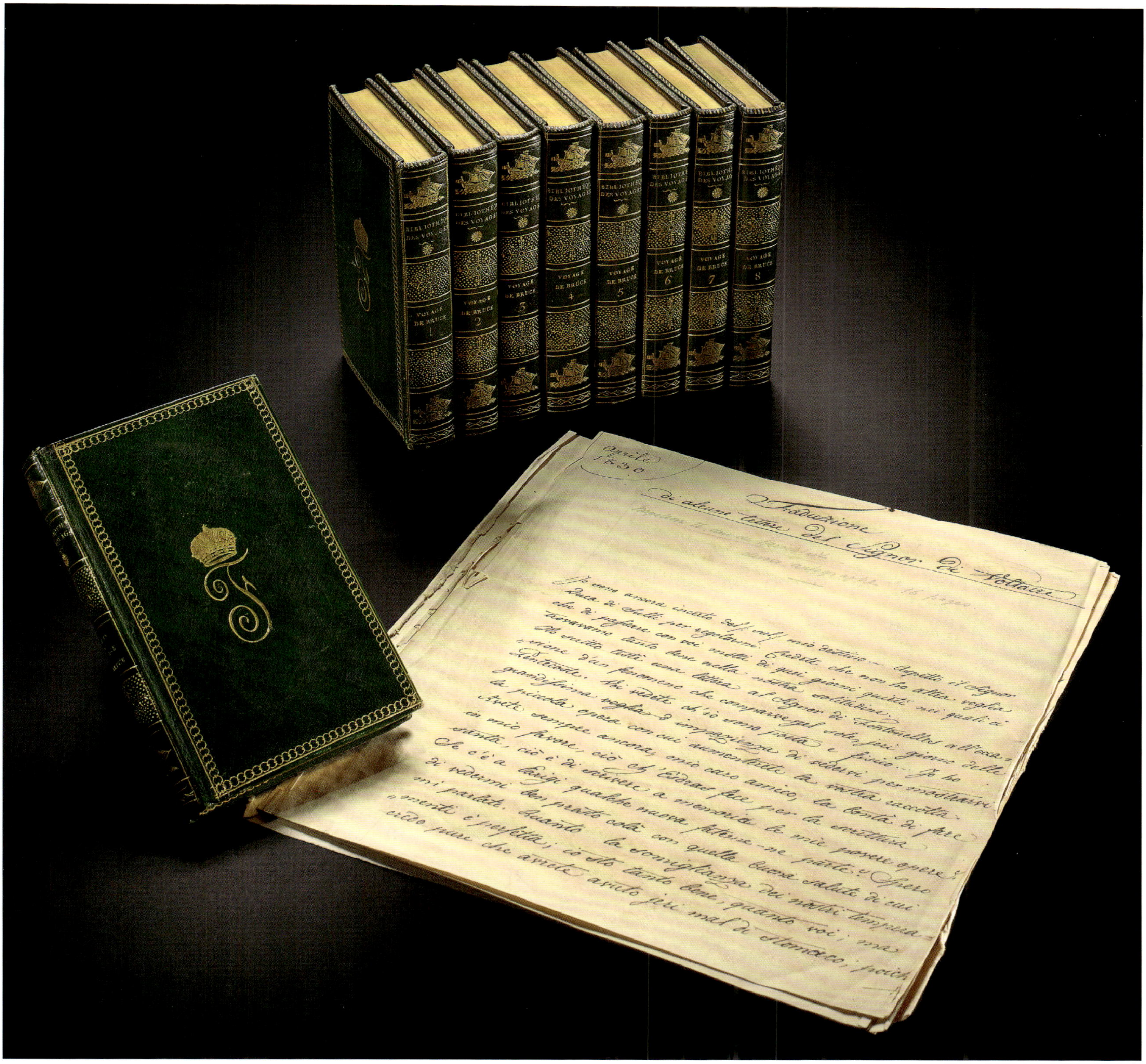

MANUSCRIPT AND BOOKS FROM THE DUKE OF REICHSTADT'S LIBRARY

When he died at the age of 21, the King of Rome, by then the Duke of Reichstadt, left few traces of his existence. Mementoes of his education, such as this assignment, are therefore very rare. Here, the Aiglon has copied several letters from Voltaire and Rousseau in Italian. This document goes against the argument that he was forcibly Germanized and cut off from his French origins.
The books from his library bear an extremely rare insignia. None of the bookbinding iron directories list a branding iron featuring a crowned F initial (for François-Charles-Joseph Napoleon). These books come from the small portable or "travel" library that traces the major 18th-century exploratory voyages (James Bruce, Frédéric Louis Norden, James Cook, John Barrow, Jean-Baptiste Tavernier and so on). The Emperor envisaged the creation of such a library for the Children of France in 1810 and commissioned Count Daru to contact the printer Didot to this end.

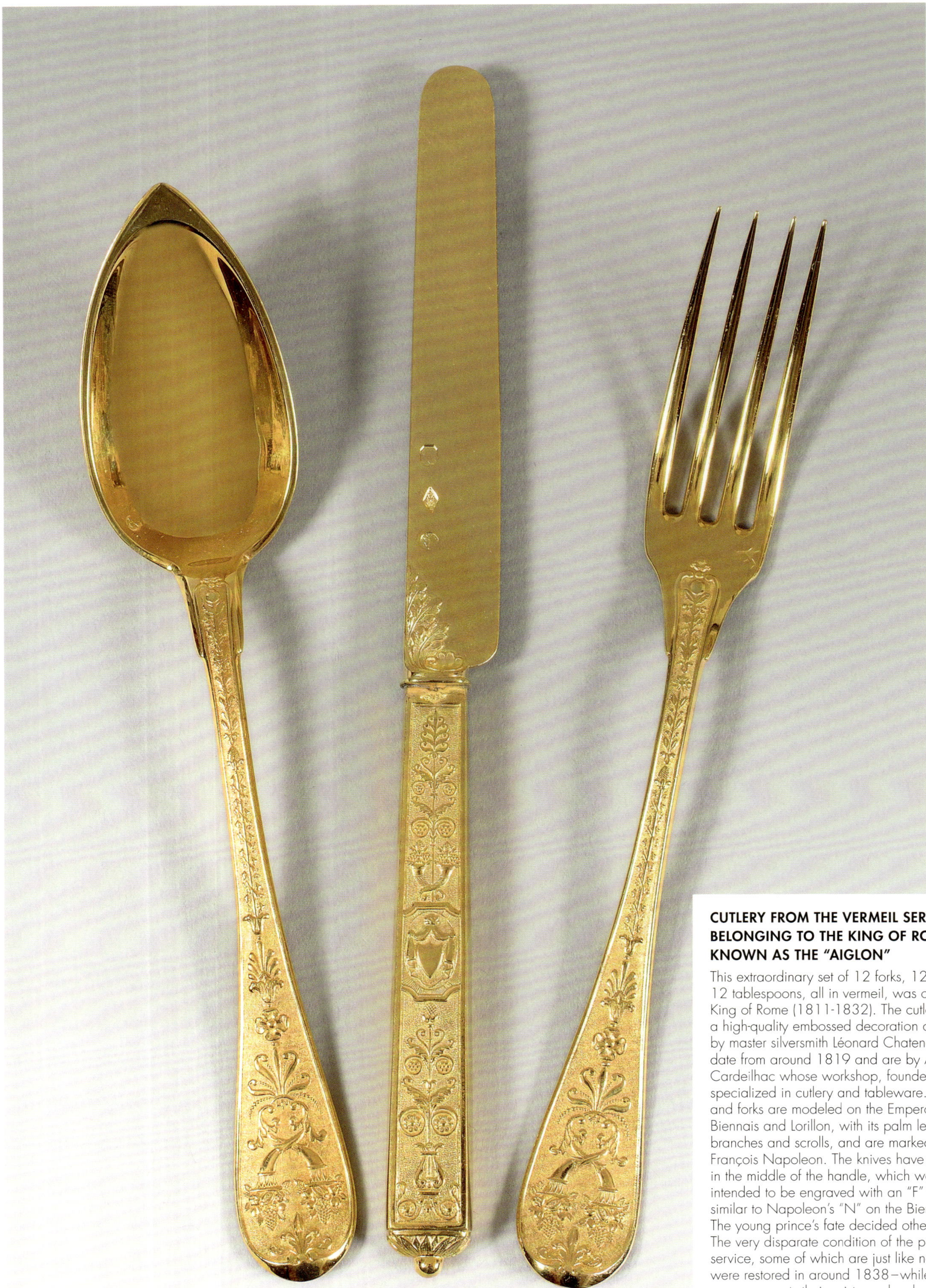

CUTLERY FROM THE VERMEIL SERVICE BELONGING TO THE KING OF ROME, KNOWN AS THE "AIGLON"

This extraordinary set of 12 forks, 12 knives and 12 tablespoons, all in vermeil, was ordered for the King of Rome (1811-1832). The cutlery features a high-quality embossed decoration and was made by master silversmith Léonard Chatenet. The knives date from around 1819 and are by Antoine Vital-Cardeilhac whose workshop, founded in 1804, was specialized in cutlery and tableware. The spoons and forks are modeled on the Emperor's cutlery by Biennais and Lorillon, with its palm leaves, laurel branches and scrolls, and are marked "FN" for François Napoleon. The knives have a blank shield in the middle of the handle, which was probably intended to be engraved with an "F" for François, similar to Napoleon's "N" on the Biennais knives. The young prince's fate decided otherwise.
The very disparate condition of the pieces in the service, some of which are just like new–six knives were restored in around 1838–while others are very worn, suggests their existence has been very chaotic, as was the life of the King of Rome, later Duke of Reichstadt, remembered by history as the "Aiglon".

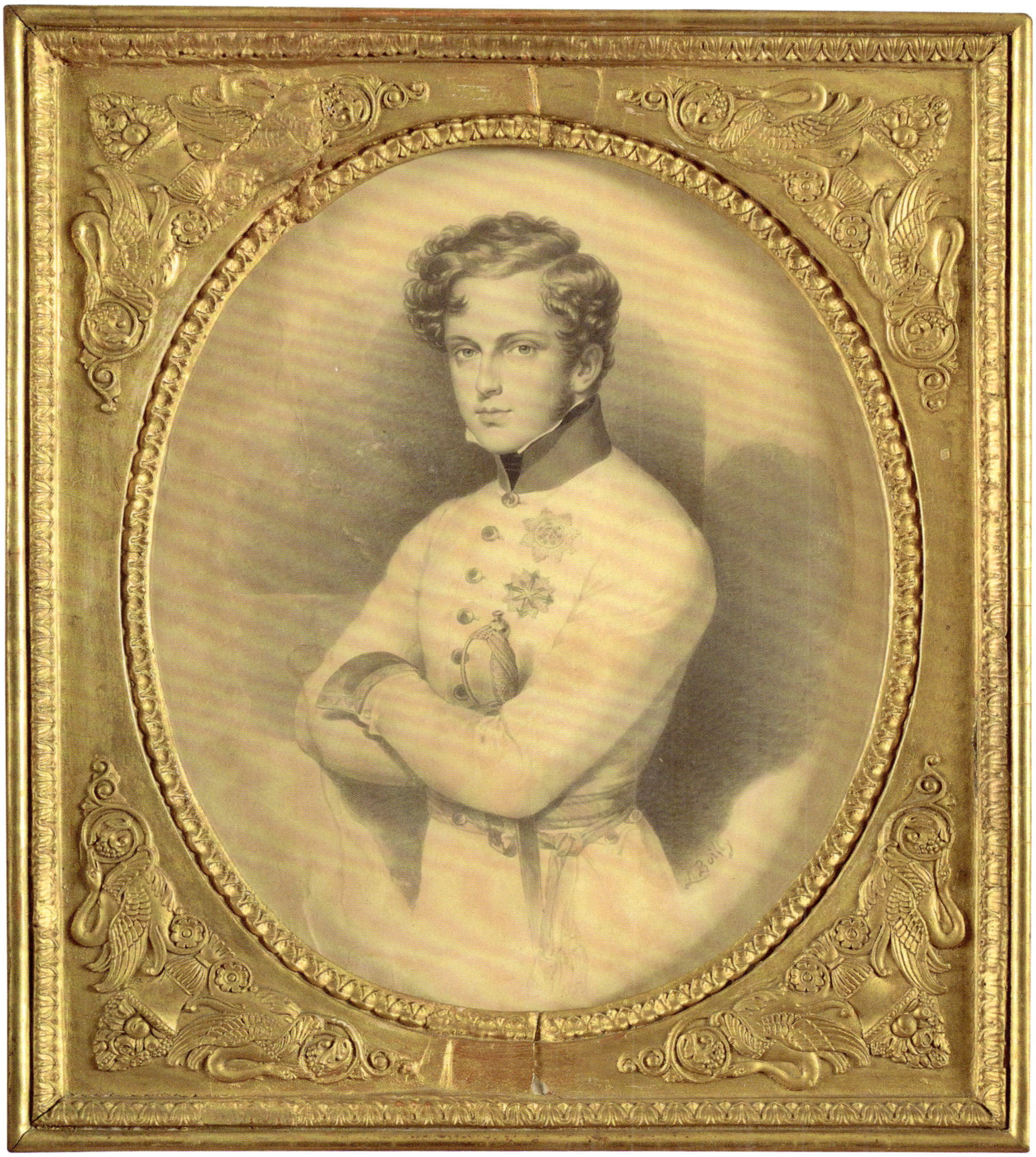

JULIEN LÉOPOLD BOILLY (1796-1874),
PORTRAIT OF THE DUKE OF REICHSTADT,
AFTER DAFFINGER

This very rare gray-wash drawing is signed by the painter and lithographer Julien Boilly, son and pupil of Louis-Léopold Boilly, and is his interpretation of Daffinger's famous portrait of the Duke of Reichstadt. Boilly made many reproductions. The drawing was exhibited in several American museums between 2006 and 2009.

Exile and the Construction of a Myth

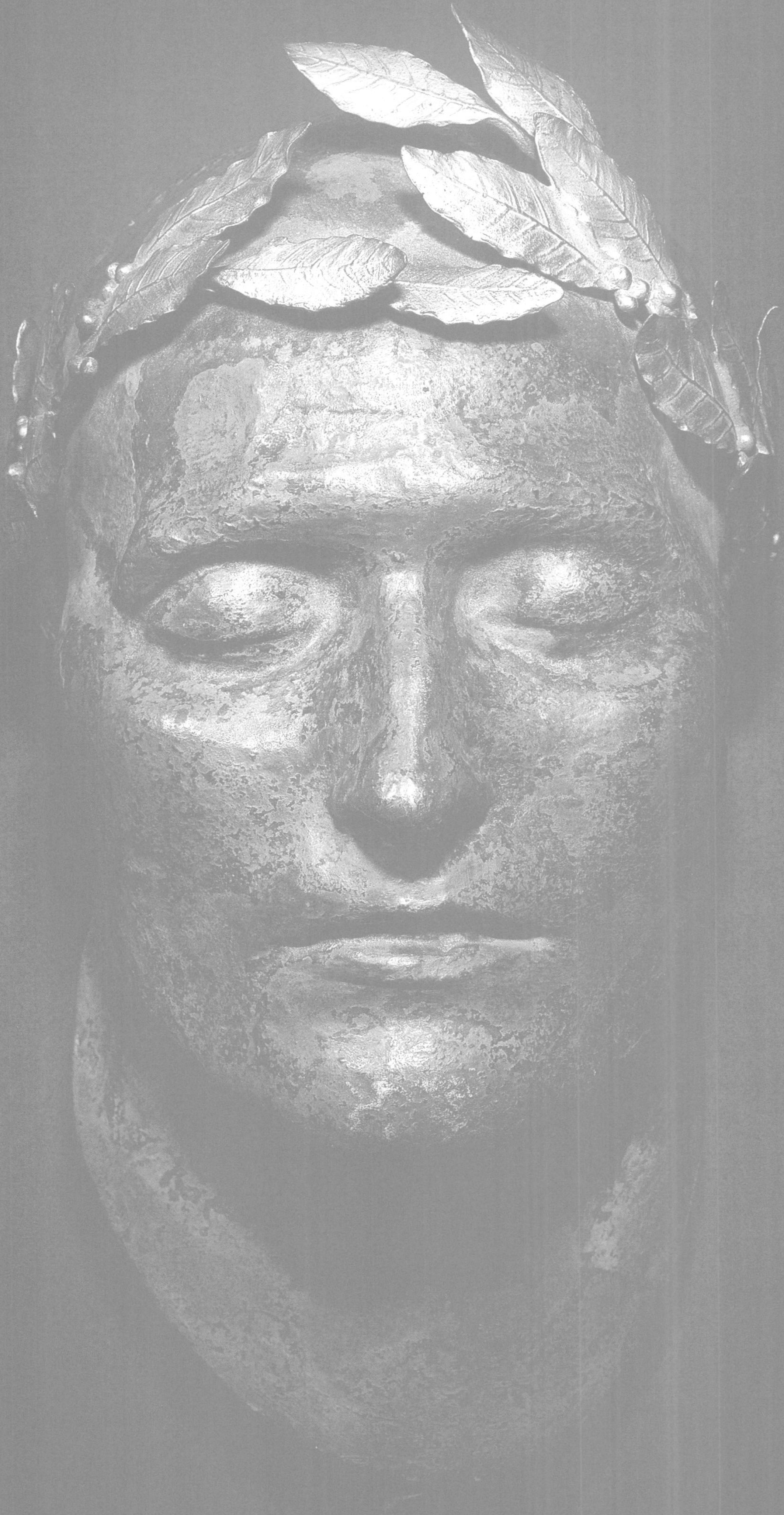

VII

Had Napoleon not been exiled twice, to the island of Elba and particularly to St Helena, the outcome would have been very different. The drama of those final years, captured and fuelled by talented chroniclers, has ensured that for historians and collectors alike the Napoleonic legend will forever be remembered in the annals of history.

David Chanteranne
Historian and editor-in-chief
of the magazines *Napoléon 1er*
and the *Revue du Souvenir Napoléonien*

EXILE

Napoleon's heroic campaign in France in the first three months of 1814 was ultimately not enough to reverse a trend that saw him forced to abdicate in April. First there had been the retreat from Russia, beginning with the conflagration of Moscow and ending with the disastrous crossing of the Berezina. Then had come his defeat at Leipzig, where hundreds of thousands of soldiers of different nationalities had come together on one battlefield. Napoleon's only choice after that had been to fight the enemy on home ground. The coalition forces under the command of Schwarzenberg and Blücher had initially pulled back pending the arrival of reinforcements with which to surround him.

On 6 April 1814, in a historical setting normally associated with happier times, Napoleon signed his unconditional abdication at the Chateau of Fontainebleau. He acted out of desperation, under pressure from his entourage who refused to continue the fight. The final blow was the announcement that Paris had fallen despite the resistance offered by Marshal Moncey and the Parisians themselves. His renunciation of the crown was formally acknowledged by the then minister of war, Pierre Dupont de l'Étang, in a letter dated 9 April 1814 that is preserved today in the Ledoux Collection (page 377).

The allies enforced their wishes and picked the place of exile. A victorious allied coalition of British, Prussian, Austrian and Russian commissioners accordingly consigned Napoleon to Elba, an island that had been a French possession since 1802 despite having very few natural resources. As sole compensation, the Emperor was granted an annual income of two million francs, enough to maintain a small army and support a lifestyle befitting his rank. It was a dramatic downfall with devastating effect. It is possible that he attempted suicide in those dark days at Fontainebleau (Napoleon had, after all, already knowingly courted death when he placed himself in the line of fire at Montereau).

His adieux to his Old Guard were loaded with emotion. On 20 April he descended the grand double staircase above the Cour du Cheval Blanc at Fontainebleau and addressed the men drawn up in ranks before him. His words, as recorded by Baron Fain, bear repetition — the words of a man who had once dominated Europe and marched triumphant into Milan, Vienna, Berlin and Moscow: "Soldiers of my Old Guard, I bid you farewell! For twenty years you have been my constant companions on the road to honor and glory [...] I [...] have sacrificed all of our interests to those of *la patrie*; I shall depart. But you, my friends, continue to serve France. Her happiness was my only thought; it shall continue to be the object of my desire. Do not lament my fate; the only reason I have allowed myself to survive was so that I could further serve our glory. [...] Adieu, my children! Would that I could press you all to my heart. Let me at least embrace your standard!"[1] He then kissed the flag as General Petit relieved him of his sword. The sadness in the ranks was palpable.

Napoleon's route to the coast went by way of the traditionalist pro-royalist Midi, where his carriage narrowly missed being seized by hostile crowds. The British commissioner Campbell, who was to accompany the now defunct Emperor into exile and had set off in advance, meanwhile arranged for Napoleon to be picked up at Fréjus by the frigate HMS Undaunted. On 29 April, Napoleon took ship for Elba. He disembarked on 4 May in Portoferraio to the cheers of a delighted crowd. The town was decked out in the colors of the new kingdom: argent, on a bend Gules three bees Or (a reminder of Napoleon's imperial reign and Corsican heritage). A Te Deum was sung in the modest church, which was far too small to contain the throng of curious locals eager to catch a glimpse of their newly exiled arrival.

The early days were spent renovating the Palazzina dei Mulini – then a palace in name only — and setting up residence in the villa San Martino, which looked out over the bay toward Napoleon's beloved Corsica. He then busied himself improving living conditions for the residents. He laid roads, brought iron mines into operation, promoted commerce and planted potatoes. By September, his sister Pauline and Madame Mère had joined him on Elba. In the same month, he also received a visit from his mistress Marie Walewska and their infant son, Alexandre. But their short stay was not enough to bring him happiness, for he longed to be reunited with Marie-Louise and the King of Rome.

His situation was anyway far from idyllic. The stipend of two million francs granted him under the Treaty of Fontainebleau had never materialized and the plenipotentiaries at the Congress of Vienna, convened to decide the fate of Europe, were already talking of deporting him to the Azores or some other island offering greater security. In Paris meanwhile, King Louis XVIII was struggling to win the support of the masses, unable to redress France's economy or erase the impression that he had returned to power "in the baggage train of the enemy". Napoleon made up his mind to return to France.

Several personal objects from his time on Elba have survived to this day, such as a small, round tortoiseshell box (page 194).

Napoleon left Elba on 26 February 1815 aboard the brig *L'Inconstant*. So began the extraordinary saga of his return to power. Three days later, having successfully avoided all obstacles in its path, *L'Inconstant* sailed into Golfe-Juan on the south coast of France. It was here that Napoleon uttered these now famous words: "Victory shall march in double quick time; the eagle bearing the colors of the nation will fly from steeple to steeple until it reaches the spires of Notre Dame."[2] The mission entrusted to his escort of some 500 men was to reach Paris "without spilling a single drop of blood". The first leg of his now-famous march on Paris took him from Cannes to Grenoble, passing through Grasse, Castellane, Digne, Sisteron, Gap, Corps, La Mure and eventually Laffrey. It was here, just outside the town of Laffrey, that he encountered a battalion of troops formerly under his orders but now in the service of the King. In a confrontation that has since become iconic, Napoleon threw open his gray overcoat and offered his breast to their muskets. "Soldiers of the 5th Line," he exclaimed, "I am your Emperor. Recognize me! If there is a soldier among you who would kill his Emperor, here I am." At which a chorus of "Vive L'Empereur" resounded from the ranks, testifying to the men's continuing attachment to their sovereign. From Grenoble, Napoleon marched up through France passing by way of Lyon and Auxerre (where he met Ney, the man who had famously sworn to "bring him back in an iron cage") and arriving in Paris on 20 March. He resumed residence at the Tuileries immediately on arrival, putting the final touch to what was by any standard a fantastic journey. King Louis XVIII was forced to make a hasty departure from the throne and fled to the Gard region. Yet for all that, the "Hundred Days" was not an unmitigated success. The proclamation of the so-called Additional Act to the constitutions of the Empire received a guarded response from his subjects, Napoleon having after all been banished by the plenipotentiaries at Vienna. A new war seemed inevitable.

After the battles of Ligny and Quatre-Bras, Napoleon's defeat at Waterloo on 18 June by the combined forces of Wellington and Blücher put paid to his aspirations once and for all. Four days later, in the Salon d'Argent (silver room) of the Élysée Palace he abdicated for the second time in favor of his son, even though *L'Aiglon* was by then detained in Vienna with his mother Marie-Louise. But the two chambers and especially the provisional government were in no mood to compromise and Napoleon's last attempts to achieve the transmission of power were rejected. He retreated to Malmaison with Hortense de Beauharnais, his mind filled with the memory of Josephine who had died there in the previous year, reminding him of the happy years of the Consulate. Then on 29 June he suddenly left the house, escorted by his few faithful companions and under the supervision of one of Fouche's agents. The party made its way to Rambouillet and from there to Chartres, Tours, Niort and eventually the Ile d'Aix.

THE BESSON AFFAIR AND PLANS FOR ESCAPE TO AMERICA (1815)

Napoleon then spent several days reviewing his options. Only three possibilities presented themselves. He could once again resort to arms and repel the coalition forces that occupied the north of France. He could surrender to the English in the hope of departing for London. Or he could cross the Atlantic and go into exile in the United States with his brother Joseph. In the end he rejected the third option, unwilling to stake his now legendary reputation on an ignominious escape that would require him to sail incognito to America.

Realizing that he was trapped, he chose to surrender to Admiral Maitland, who welcomed him aboard HMS Bellerophon on 15 July. He meanwhile wrote a letter to the Prince Regent: "Exposed to the factions which divide my country and the enmity of the European Powers, I have ended my political career. I come, like Themistocles, to seat myself at the hearth of the British people; I put myself under the protection of its laws, which I claim from your Royal Highness as the most powerful, the most constant and most generous of my enemies."[3] In the days that followed, as he waited for the British to make up their minds, he was famously given a tour of HMS Superb, the flagship of Admiral Hotham whose vessels were patrolling off the coast of France. Napoleon's visit would later be described by Las Cases in his *Mémorial* and also by a British Royal Navy officer called John Hood Wolseley.

On 31 July, while the Bellerophon lay at anchor in Plymouth Sound, Napoleon and his small group of followers learned of the British Government's decision to deport them to St Helena. As the island was then a possession of the East India Company, exempt from the laws governing other Crown Dependencies, Napoleon's lawyers could not serve a writ for *habeas corpus*.

It took HMS Northumberland two and a half months to ferry Napoleon to his final place of exile. The days aboard ship seemed interminable, serving only as a dreary reminder that this was a voyage of no return. On 15 October St Helena's black cliffs finally came into view. "It is not an attractive place," said Napoleon as he reported on what he saw to Las Cases (newly appointed to take down the Emperor's memoirs). "I should have done better to have stayed in Egypt. By now I would be Emperor of the entire Orient."[4]

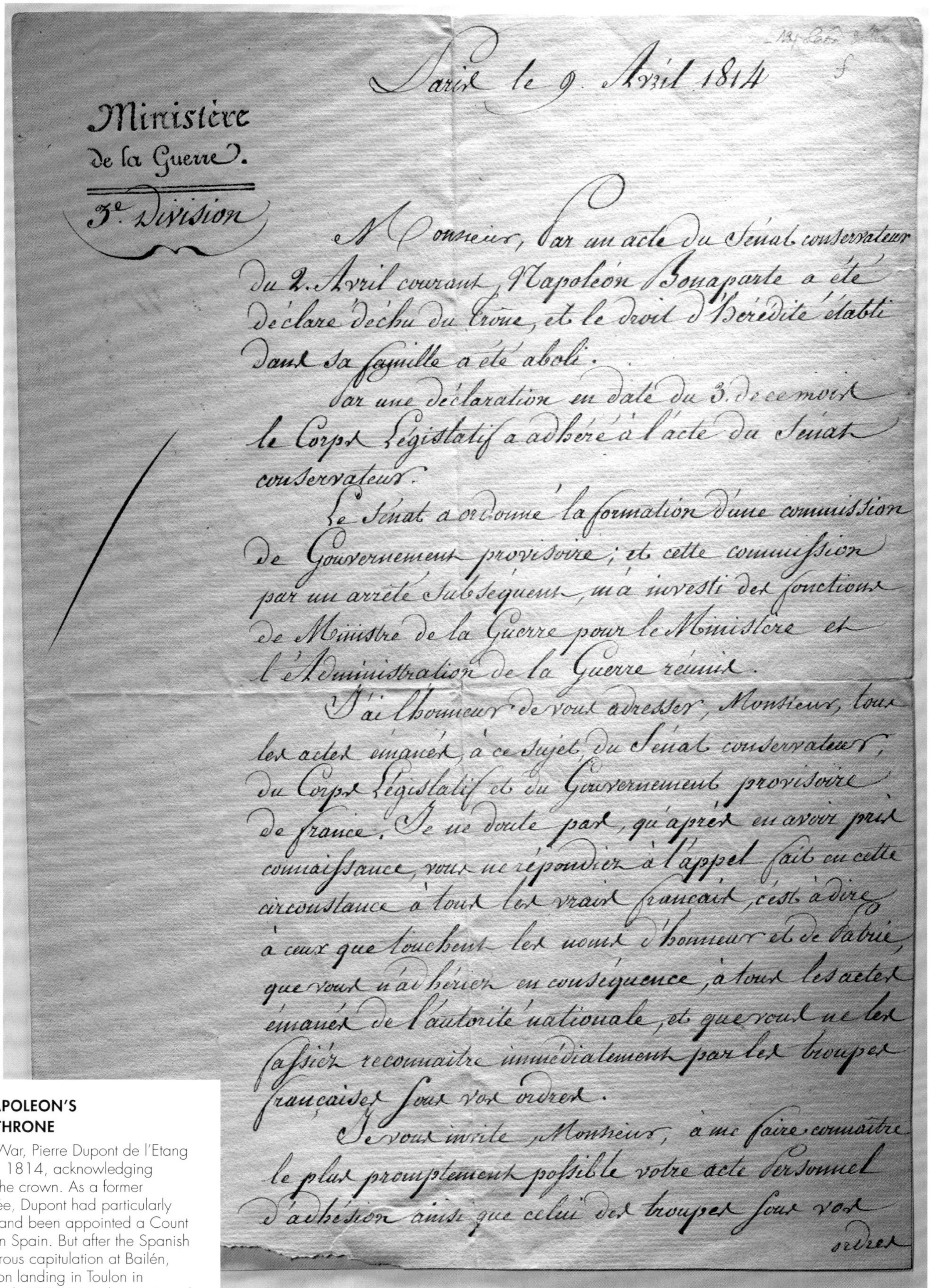

Ministère de la Guerre.

3e. Division

Paris le 9. Avril 1814

Monsieur, par un acte du Sénat conservateur du 2. Avril courant, Napoléon Bonaparte a été déclaré déchu du trône, et le droit d'hérédité établi dans sa famille a été aboli.

Par une déclaration en date du 3. de ce mois le Corps Législatif a adhéré à l'acte du Sénat conservateur.

Le Sénat a ordonné la formation d'une commission de Gouvernement provisoire; et cette commission par un arrêté subséquent, m'a investi des fonctions de Ministre de la Guerre pour le Ministère et l'Administration de la Guerre réunis.

J'ai l'honneur de vous adresser, Monsieur, tous les actes émanés, à ce sujet, du Sénat conservateur, du Corps Législatif et du Gouvernement provisoire de France. Je ne doute pas, qu'après en avoir pris connaissance, vous ne répondiez à l'appel fait en cette circonstance à tous les vrais français, c'est à dire à ceux que touchent les noms d'honneur et de Patrie, que vous n'adhériez en conséquence, à tous les actes émanés de l'autorité nationale, et que vous ne les fassiez reconnaître immédiatement par les troupes françaises sous vos ordres.

Je vous invite, Monsieur, à me faire connaître le plus promptement possible votre acte personnel d'adhésion ainsi que celui des troupes sous vos ordres

LETTER CONCERNING NAPOLEON'S RENUNCIATION OF THE THRONE

A letter from the Minister of War, Pierre Dupont de l'Etang (1765-1840), dated 9 April 1814, acknowledging Napoleon's renunciation of the crown. As a former General of the Grande Armée, Dupont had particularly distinguished himself in Italy and been appointed a Count of the Empire while serving in Spain. But after the Spanish debacle and Dupont's disastrous capitulation at Bailén, he was arrested for treason on landing in Toulon in September 1808. On 1 March 1812 Napoleon stripped Dupont of his titles, rank and decorations and imprisoned him in a state penitentiary for two years.
So in 1814 it was entirely natural, not to say symbolic, that the provisional government that held office until Louis XVIII's restoration to the throne on 13 May should appoint Dupont as Minister of War on 3 April – in which capacity he had the pleasure of announcing Napoleon's downfall.

DAILY LIFE ON ST HELENA

His first days on the island were remarkably carefree. After residing temporarily at Porteus House, Napoleon's stay with the Balcombes from 17 October onwards almost made him feel like a child again. He enjoyed the lush gardens and being surrounded by children, particularly the young Betsy. Despite his reputation as the "Corsican ogre", the Balcombes soon came to adore him. He meanwhile continued to dictate his *Mémorial de Sainte-Hélène* to Las Cases (father and son alike). From 28 October onward, the other officers in his entourage also saw themselves entrusted with the task of taking down the political and military memoirs of the great man. Montholon, Gourgaud and Bertrand, former grand marshal of the palace, were each required to research particular periods of his career then listen for hours to the speaker's reflections, remarks and regrets. On 9 October, just before he was forced to move into Longwood, Napoleon meanwhile met Mrs Stuart and the slave Toby and learned about the problems facing the residents of St Helena. He and his entire suite of courtiers and servants took up new residence the very next day — in the house that Napoleon knew would be his final prison.

The building had traditionally served as the official home of the governors of St Helena and was originally much too small to accommodate Napoleon's entire household. Though newly refurbished and enlarged, Longwood House was a far cry from the comforts of the Tuileries. The interior that greeted the fallen Emperor was mainly furnished with small, typically English pieces, scavenged from various places with varying degrees of success. Examples include the worktable (page 396) and card table (page 398) placed at Napoleon's disposal by cabinetmaker George Bullock and now preserved in the Ledoux Collection.

Napoleon devoted his days to study (the Classics and works by the philosophers of the Enlightenment), to walking and discussions with his entourage. He also returned to some of his favorite childhood pursuits to take his mind off his nostalgia. He was for instance quite prepared to take English lessons so as to understand his British jailers and the people of St Helena. As at the Tuileries, meals were always served at a fixed time and presented by liveried staff. Tableware from the Imperial Palaces continued to grace the otherwise rather ordinary table. Keeping up appearances was Napoleon's only way to relieve the tedium of his surroundings. He received Governor Wilks, read the news that seeped through from Europe and went horseback riding alone along the few paths that were open to him — a freedom that would soon be heavily curtailed. In the evening, the ladies would play music and make polite conversation while the assembled Frenchmen entertained themselves with cards, dice, chess, Lotto — anything to pass the time. But the atmosphere was no less oppressive and no one knew better than Napoleon that it was all just a charade.

He stopped wearing the traditional uniform of a colonel of the Grenadiers and instead opted for more conventional dress. Being sensitive to humidity, he also exchanged his famous bicorn hat for a Madras headpiece, including one example that survives today in the Ledoux collection (page 387). He suffered bouts of pain but continued to dictate regardless, confident that his writings would one day be published to wide acclaim. His Household was meanwhile run by Bertrand and his wife who were quartered in a house outside the estate.

In early 1816, Napoleon learned that his brother Joseph had settled in the United States and secretly envied him his easy lifestyle. Murat's death was another sad blow but Napoleon had no time to grieve, the news being followed by the announcement that the island now had a new governor: Sir Hudson Lowe. For Napoleon, his appointment was the coup de grace.

Hudson Lowe's arrival on the island seemed like the ultimate provocation. As a former French officer who had striven to liberate his native island from the British, Napoleon recoiled at the prospect of being placed under the supervision of the former commander of the Royal Corsican Rangers — an anti-French Corsican force that Napoleon despised as traitors. Hudson Lowe meanwhile refused to acknowledge the former First Consul as a sovereign in exile. He addressed him only as "General Bonaparte" (not "Your Highness") and ostentatiously positioned regiments around Longwood House. To prevent any possibility of Napoleon's escape, the seas around the island were heavily patrolled and 600 cannons were placed along its coasts.

Napoleon responded to these humiliations by maintaining a profound and contemptuous silence. His daily routine at Longwood was always the same. He would wash, shave, eat breakfast and very occasionally take a walk in the gardens. His so-called "evangelists" (the men who took down his memoirs) were meanwhile kept busier than ever. His afternoons were spent reading, casting his critical eye over the few books that came his way.

In June 1816, following allegations of mistreatment and a conspiracy to remove Napoleon to a place of safety (South America, Louisiana...) three allied commissioners arrived on the island. Their mission was to supervise the proper execution of the resolutions passed at the Congress of Vienna — which certainly did nothing to alleviate the tedium of daily life at Longwood. Napoleon began by complaining then retreated into boredom. He would spend hours in the bath, which he had specially installed in a small, dark room away from prying eyes.

One day he quarreled violently with Hudson Lowe, a mistake that was to cost him dear. By way of reprisal Hudson Lowe inflicted a series of punishments on his prisoner, which included confiscating the passports of his entourage and restricting Napoleon's freedom away from the house. General de Montholon protested, but to no avail. Hudson Lowe remained unmoved and personally ensured that the measures put in place to monitor Napoleon's movements were applied down to the smallest detail. The two men would never again meet face to face.

The closing months of 1816 marked the beginning of a string of departures. Santini, Rousseau, Piontkowski and Archambault left in October, followed by Las Cases in November, Gourgaud in March 1817, then other domestic staff and friends. The last to leave for Europe was Napoleon's physician O'Meara. The atmosphere at Longwood deteriorated noticeably. Jealousy was rife and promiscuity was rampant. Napoleon meanwhile made demands on his entourage that made their stay even more unbearable, not to say downright depressing. The place itself — a bleak plateau swept by the Trade Winds and drenched in humidity — did nothing to improve relations. As arguments degenerated into quarrels, the tensions approached breaking point. The women who came into Napoleon's orbit at Longwood, particularly Albine de Montholon and Fanny Bertrand, only fuelled the animosity, stoking rumors of affairs and pregnancies — the granting of sexual favors in other words.

After the final rejection of the allies, Napoleon knew that his fate was sealed. On the recommendation of Madame Mère and Cardinal Fesch (both resident in Italy) several people were then sent to look after him, arriving in St Helena in September 1819. They included a new butler (Cipriani having met a gruesome death), a cook, the surgeon Antommarchi and two churchmen Vignali and Buonavita. A Catholic mass kit used by the Abbé Vignali on the island is preserved today in the Ledoux Collection (page 400). But after embarking on an energetic project to redesign the gardens and some of the outbuildings, Napoleon soon slipped back into his former melancholy state. The absence of his loved ones weighed heavy on his heart — his brothers and sisters, his wife and especially his son, since renamed the Duke of Reichstadt. His health declined rapidly. The fits of vomiting and nausea became more frequent. He seemed to have no more than a few months to live.

THE DEATH OF NAPOLEON

The time had come for Napoleon to draw up his last will and testament. At the start, he was reluctant to include people whose loyalty had sometimes faltered, but he relented shortly before his death and added them in a number of codicils. By January 1821 his condition had worsened and his doctors could do nothing to alleviate his suffering. Though he showed signs of improvement in February, from mid-March the pain became increasingly intense and by the end of April Napoleon was essentially confined to bed.

On 5 May after a protracted agony, the former Emperor uttered his last audible words: "My son... head of the army... France." He died at 5.49pm that afternoon, surrounded by his now much-reduced entourage: Bertrand and Fanny and their children; Montholon, who had stayed behind after Albine's departure; Marchand and Antommarchi; and the Mamluk Ali and his English wife. The scene would later become the subject of numerous paintings and prints. In tribute to their selfless commitment over the past six years, Napoleon's friends were given mementoes of his final hours — relics taken from his deathbed and eventually divided up after bitter wrangling. Plaster molds were made of Napoleon's face before and after the traditional autopsy conducted by Antommarchi. The bloodstained pillowcase used in the course of this examination was set aside by his entourage and is preserved today in the Ledoux Collection (page 412).

Napoleon's obsequies were to end with one final argument between the British and the French. The funeral cortege, as represented in the print below (page 400), bore the coffin to a shady valley surrounded by weeping willow trees. It was the spot chosen by the deceased himself in his lifetime. But the gravestone was left unmarked because while the French wanted to inscribe the tomb "Emperor Napoleon" the Brits would only agree to "General Bonaparte". The site did at least respect the wishes of the dead. The man who had originally wanted to be laid to rest "by the banks of the Seine in the midst of the French nation I have loved so dearly" had been reduced to asking Bertrand "to bury my remains in this spot if ever my body should fall into the hands of my enemies".[5]

RETURN OF THE ASHES

The announcement of Napoleon's death sent shock waves across the Old Continent. On hearing of Napoleon's demise, Talleyrand reportedly observed: "It is not an event. It is an item of news." A storm of indignation swept through Europe, fanned by successive editions of the *Mémorial de Sainte-Hélène* that received wide critical acclaim. By 1825, Napoleon had become a cult figure for the artists and writers of the Romantic era, who seized their chance to denounce inequalities or who simply took inspiration from his destiny and injected it into their works. Stendhal, Chateaubriand, Hugo, Vigny, Balzac, Lamartine along with the painters Ingres, Vernet, Meissonier, Toulouse-Lautrec all sang the glory of the imperial saga, immortalizing the notorious figure of the former Emperor in his black bicorn hat and signature gray overcoat.

After the *Aiglon* died in 1832, Louis-Napoleon (the future Napoleon III) became heir to the Bonaparte dynasty. But after two abortive attempts to seize power (first in Strasbourg in 1836 then in Boulogne in 1840) Louis and Hortense's youngest son was sent into exile. That same year, King Louis-Philippe and the President of the Council of Ministers, Adolphe Thiers, obtained

Queen Victoria's permission to bring Napoleon's body back to Les Invalides. A French delegation, led by the King's son the Prince de Joinville and including several of Napoleon's former companions in exile, accordingly set sail for St Helena aboard a succession of ships. Napoleon's remains were then returned to France by the French frigate, *Belle-Poule,* which arrived in France in late 1840.
The coffin was borne up the River Seine to Courbevoie (a suburb of Paris) and placed on a richly ornate, monumental catafalque. On 15 December a funeral cortege carried the Emperor's remains down the Champs-Élysées (appropriately decorated for the occasion) to a new sarcophagus under the Dome of Les Invalides, where France's highest dignitaries were assembled. The Ledoux collection includes a fragment of the original, bee-studded pall that covered Napoleon's casket (following page). At the end of the ceremony, the elderly First Empire Marshal Moncey, who had insisted on attending despite his poor health, remarked to his physician: "And now let us go home: we can die in peace." Napoleon's remains would ultimately be interred in a specially built mausoleum, watched over by bas-reliefs and white marble caryatides. It would be another century before the body of his son was also transferred to Les Invalides — *L'Aiglon,* whose thwarted destiny was to inspire the eponymous play by Edmond Rostand with Sarah Bernhardt in the title role.

MEMORIES AND IMPERIAL CULT

Napoleon's memory would live on throughout the 19th century and for many years thereafter. In 1921 ceremonies were held all over France to commemorate the centenary of his death. On the anniversary day itself, Marshal of France Ferdinand Foch stood by Napoleon's tomb and delivered a eulogy. As a hero of World War I, he well understood the part played by strategy in some of the battles won by the Emperor in his time. Napoleon's final resting place, the tomb designed by Visconti in the previous century, has since become a major pilgrimage destination.
At the end of his life, Napoleon himself had wanted to be remembered as a pioneer and a misunderstood visionary. He expected that history would represent him as a martyr. So while ready to acknowledge his errors, he was eager to vindicate his social and political achievements and present himself as a defender of nationalities. He not only identified the emergence of a new balance of power dominated by the United States and Russia, but also predicted the rise to power of China at a time when it scarcely registered on the European radar. He is at any rate quoted as saying: "When China wakes, the whole world will tremble."
On the eve of his death, he would rank two achievements before all others: the creation of the Code Civil; and the symbolic importance of the Légion d'Honneur. Both institutions remain unquestionably relevant today.
Among the "Napoleonic" memorabilia that have been lovingly preserved for posterity are locks of his hair (page 413) and fragments of his coffin and the weeping willows that surrounded his tomb on St Helena. Fueled by growing demand, such objects now have huge commercial value — like holy relics. Major collectors are too many to mention and auction prices can be astronomical.
As the German poet Heinrich Heine so rightly remarked, the fact that Napoleon has passed into legend is largely because he died in the middle of the South Atlantic, abandoned by most of his loved ones. "The Emperor is dead. On a waste island in the Atlantic Ocean is his lonely grave, and he for whom the world was too narrow lies quietly under a little hillock. [...] And St Helena is the Holy Grave, whither the races of the East and West will make their pilgrimage in ships with flags of many a color, and their hearts will grow strong with great memories of the deeds of the Worldly Savior, who suffered and died under Hudson Lowe."

1 Baron Fain. *Manuscrit de 1814, trouvé dans les voitures impériales prises à Waterloo.* Paris: Hector Bossange, 1830, pp. 251-252.

2 Duverger, Jean-Baptiste. *Collection complète des lois, décrets, ordonnances, règlements, avis du conseil d'État.* Paris: A. Guyot et Scribe, 1836, p. 374.

3 Goldsmith, Lewis. *Cours politique et diplomatique de Napoléon Bonaparte...,* London: J. Booth, 1816, p. 353.

4 Lord Rosebery, *Napoléon, la dernière phase.* Paris: Hachette, 1901, p. 248. Translated from the original: *Napoleon, the Last Phase.* London: A.L Humphreys, 1900.

5 *Mémoires de Marchand, premier valet de chambre et exécuteur testamentaire de l'Empereur:* St Helena, Paris: Tallandier, 1985, p. 334.6, cited by David Chanteranne in *L'Insulaire. Les neuf vies de Napoléon.* Paris: Le Cerf, 2015, p. 248.

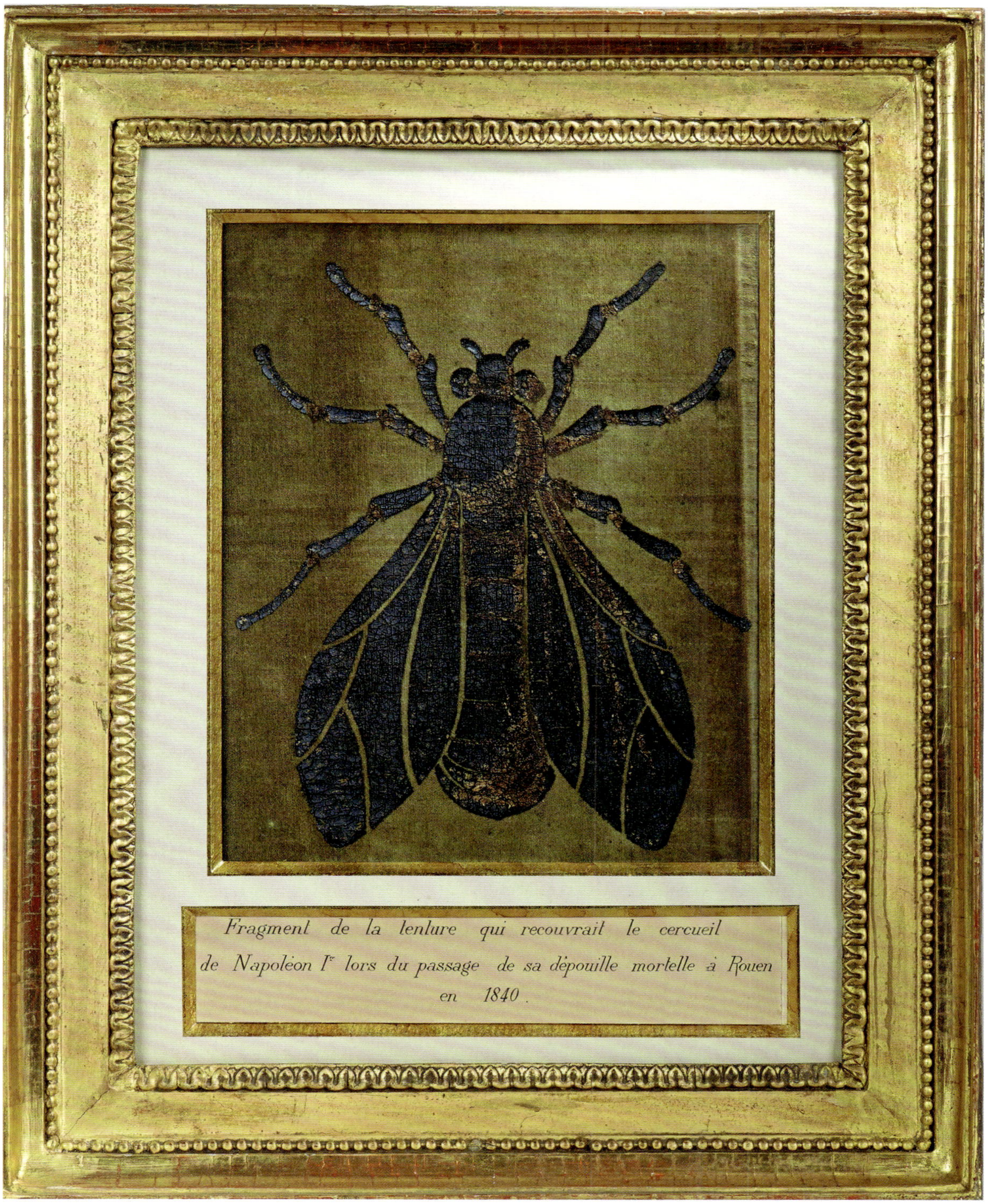

FRAGMENT OF THE PALL THAT COVERED THE EMPEROR'S CASKET FOR THE RETURN OF THE ASHES

This rare rectangular fragment of gold velvet, stenciled with a decorative bee motif, comes from the funeral pall that covered Napoleon's casket when it passed through Rouen in 1840. On 12 May 1840, at the instigation of then President Adolphe Thiers, King Louis-Philippe decided to repatriate the Emperor's mortal remains. A delegation led by his son, the Prince de Joinville, was dispatched to St Helena after some bitter wrangling with the British Crown. The frigate *Belle Poule* brought the Emperor's remains to Cherbourg on 30 November 1840. The coffin was then transported down the Seine to Rouen, where Archbishop Monsignor de Croÿ received the body and blessed it. This is when the coffin was draped in the pall that this fragment was taken from. When it reached Paris, the casket was set on a catafalque to process across the capital on its way to Les Invalides.

EXILE

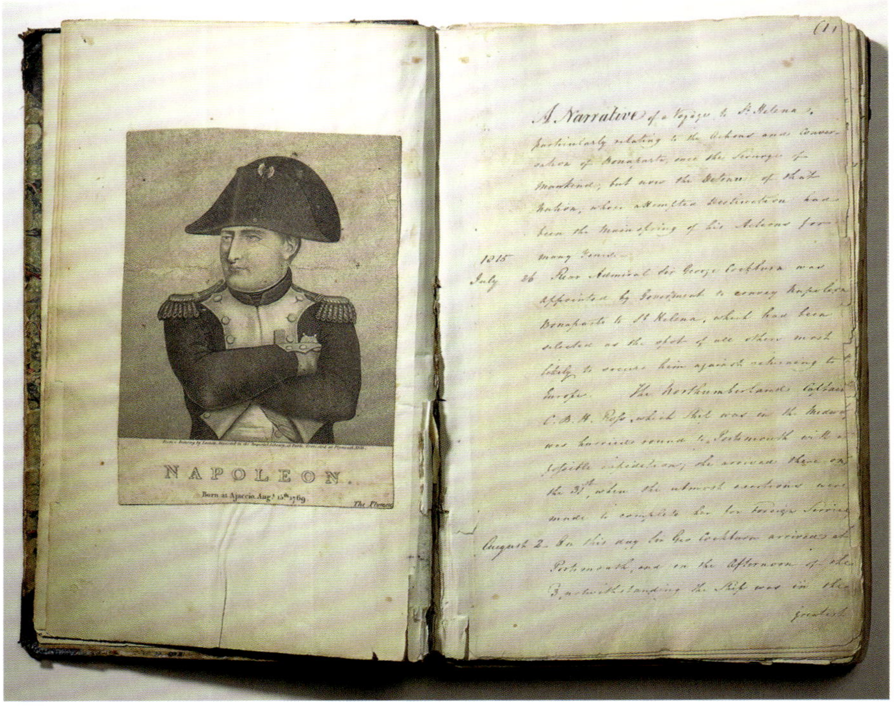

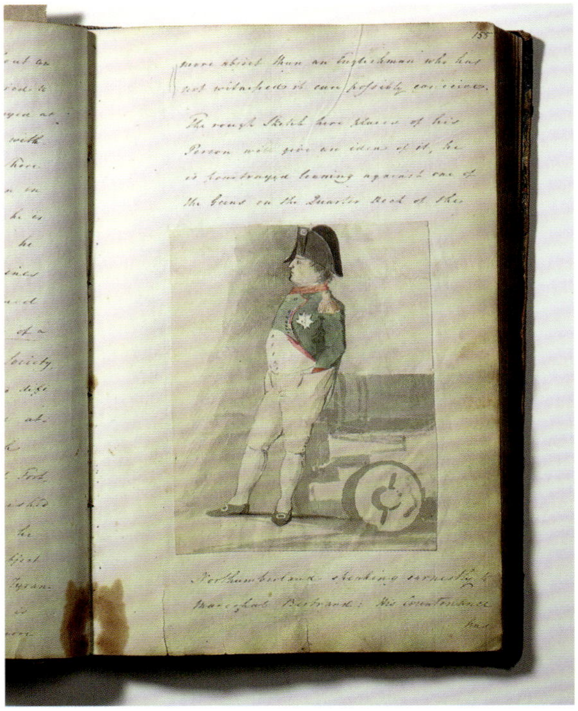

JOHN RICHARD GLOVER, ORIGINAL MANUSCRIPT OF LOGBOOK OF HMS NORTHUMBERLAND

This 170-page manuscript volume, illustrated with cuttings of printed material, was published almost simultaneously in French and English in 1893. The writer was John Richard Glover, secretary to the British Admiral, George Cockburn, who was entrusted with Napoleon's safe conduct to St Helena. It gives a detailed account of the voyage on board the Northumberland up to and including its landing on the island. It also includes a famous watercolor of Napoleon on deck leaning against a cannon by Denzil Ibbetson, himself on board the ship, plus a previously unpublished plan of Longwood House, also executed in watercolor. According to Joseph de Mougins-Roquefort, author of the only review of the British accounts of Napoleon's exile on St Helena, Glover's journal was very likely dictated by Cockburn, who published a very similar journal of his own in 1833. Glover meanwhile confined himself to the odd personal remark. It is astonishing that this manuscript has survived to this day.

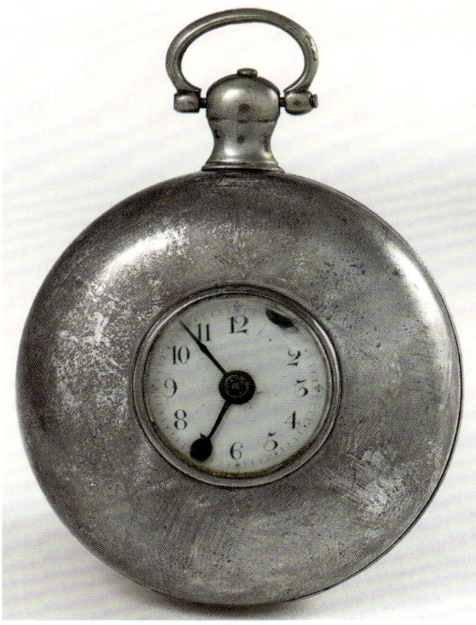

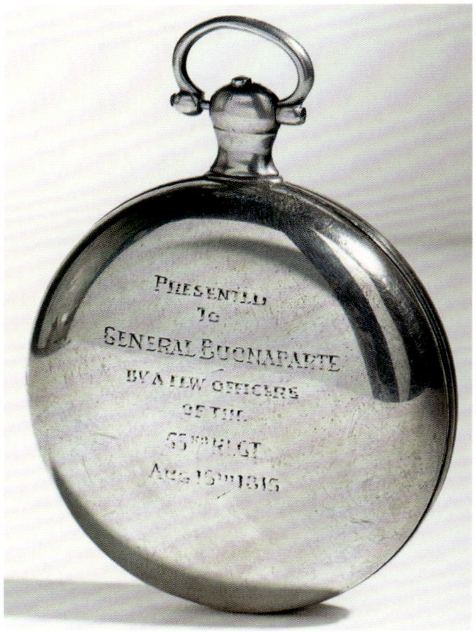

WATCH USED BY NAPOLEON AT ST HELENA

This silver pocket watch bearing the inscription "hallmarked Birmingham 1814" was presented to Napoleon for his birthday, 15 August 1815, by the officers of the 53rd Regiment on board the Northumberland during the voyage to St Helena. Napoleon used it until 19 September 1816, when he had it sold along with some of his silverware in the hope that this gesture would alert Europe to his inadequate means and the humiliations he was suffering. It was bought by Mr Saul Salomon, a trader from Jamestown, who sold it to Sergeant James Bull of the 66th Regiment.

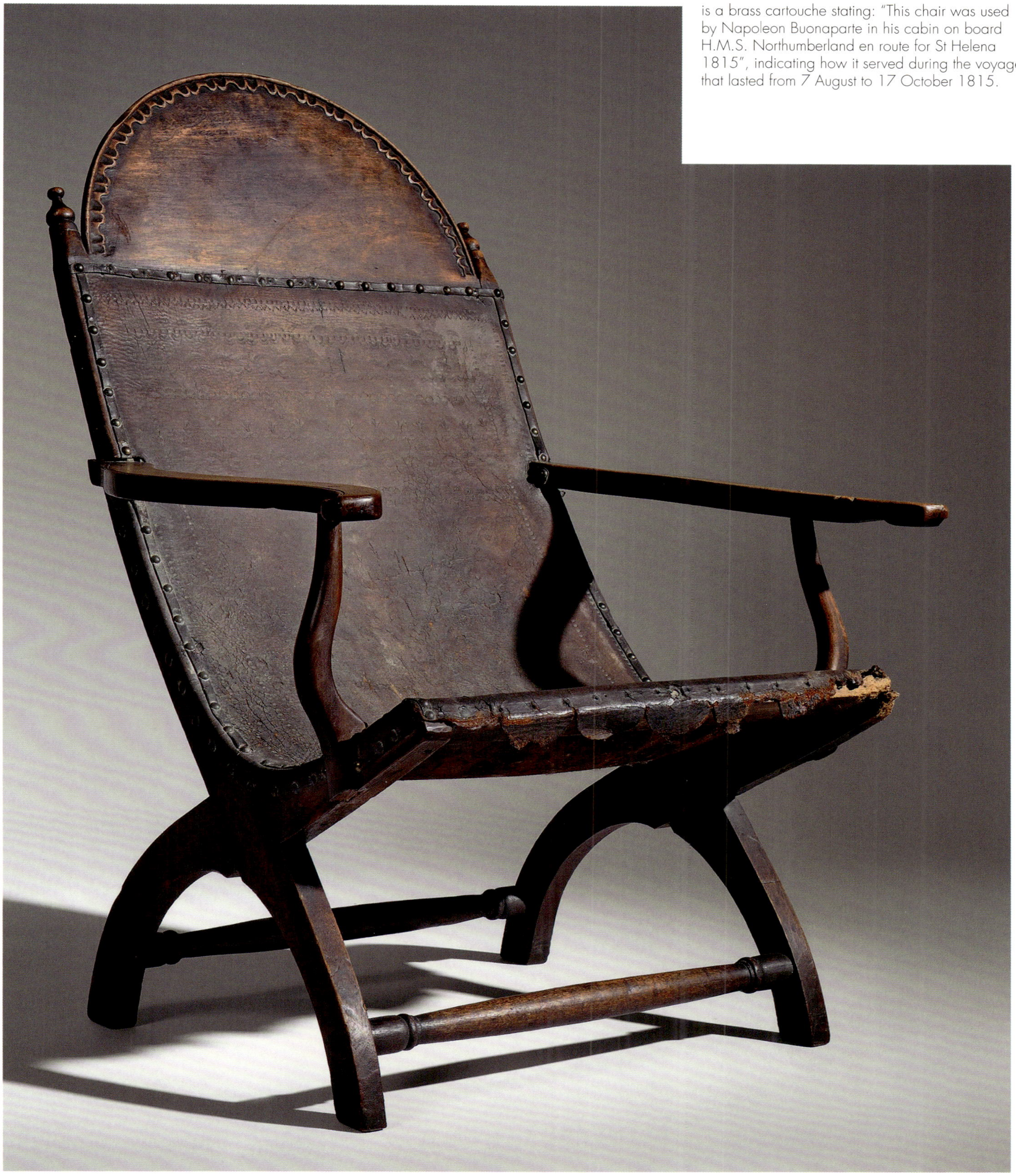

ARMCHAIR USED BY NAPOLEON IN HIS CABIN ON THE NORTHUMBERLAND

A frieze of acanthus leaves decorates the upper part of the backrest on this wooden folding chair, which has a crossed base and leather seat. On the back is a brass cartouche stating: "This chair was used by Napoleon Buonaparte in his cabin on board H.M.S. Northumberland en route for St Helena 1815", indicating how it served during the voyage that lasted from 7 August to 17 October 1815.

LONGWOOD

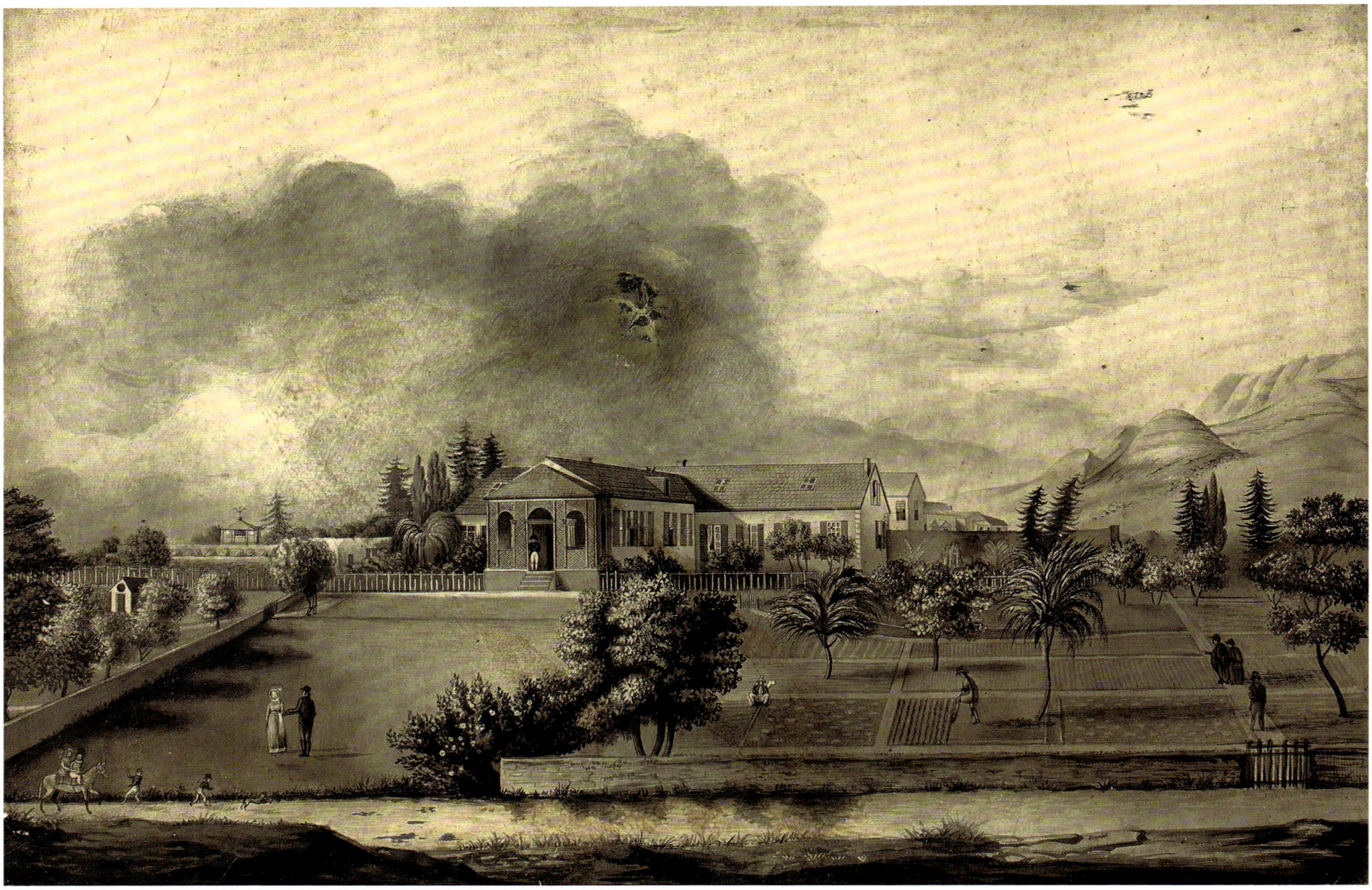

LOUIS-JOSEPH-NARCISSE MARCHAND (1791-1876), ATTRIBUTED, *VIEW OF LONGWOOD HOUSE*

Marchand was a loyal companion to Napoleon, replacing Constant at the Emperor's side. He accompanied him from Elba to Waterloo, and then to Longwood House. He remained Napoleon's valet, in charge of his meals and personal care, and the Emperor considered him a "friend". Napoleon even made him an executor of his will, along with the Counts Bertrand and Montholon. Marchand would accompany the Return of the Ashes procession. According to Lieutenant Oakley's journal, he was "very good at drawing", and this view of Longwood House and the gardens in the foreground bears that out. The scene is brought alive with several figures, some of them strolling, others gardening. Napoleon appears on the steps of the house, wearing his bicorne hat and the military uniform of a General. This drawing can be compared with another view of Longwood House, given to Napoleon by Marchand on 1 January 1820.

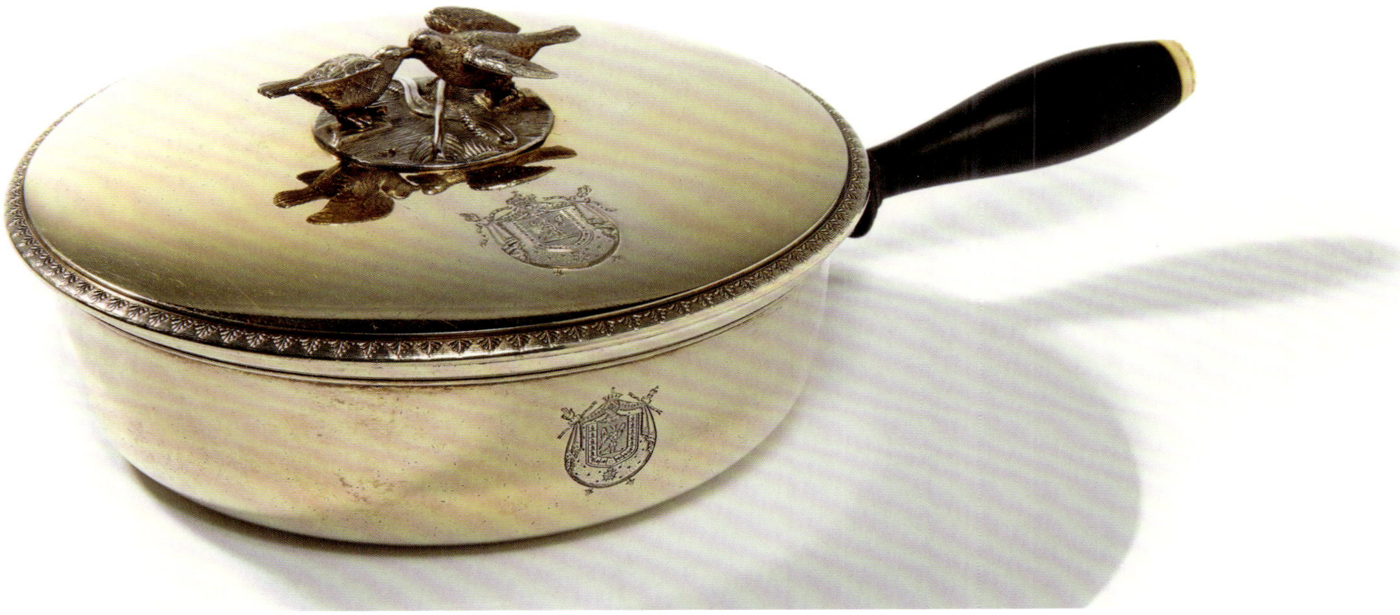

MARTIN-GUILLAUME BIENNAIS (1764-1843), SMALL PAN WITH LID FROM A *NÉCESSAIRE DE CAMPAGNE* OF NAPOLEON'S

This little pan is hallmarked with the stamp of metalsmith Biennais and engraved with the imperial coat-of-arms. It has one feature in common with the *nécessaire* (kit) that Napoleon took with him to St Helena, which was donated to the City of Paris by General Bertrand in 1840 and is now preserved in the Musée Carnavalet. Both are decorated with lid handles sculpted in the round into the form of two doves. The *nécessaires de campagne* used regularly by the Emperor frequently needed pieces to be re-ordered. One of Biennais' invoices displayed in the collection gives evidence of this.

SILVER TRAY GIVEN TO MARK WILKS, GOVERNOR OF ST HELENA, IN 1816

The tray is engraved on the upper part of its rim with the words: "Presented by the inhabitants of St Helena to Colonel Mark Wilks late Governor of that Island as a Memorial of their Esteem, Respect, & Gratitude, 1816" and stamped with the Governor's coat-of-arms with his family motto "Pro Rege", and was given as a souvenir when Wilks left the island in 1816. Colonel Mark Wilks (1760-1831) had been appointed Governor of St Helena in April 1813 on behalf of the East India Company. When he greeted Napoleon and Admiral Cockburn on their arrival to the island on 15 October 1815, he was told not only of St Helena's new status, but also that the Admiral would replace him. Nevertheless, he remained in charge of civil affairs on the island until Hudson Lowe arrived in April 1816. Napoleon received Wilks for long visits on 12 December 1815 and 20 January 1816, and again on 20 April 1816, the day before the latter's departure. Emmanuel de Las Cases reported their worldly and cultured conversations in his *Memorial of Saint Helena.*

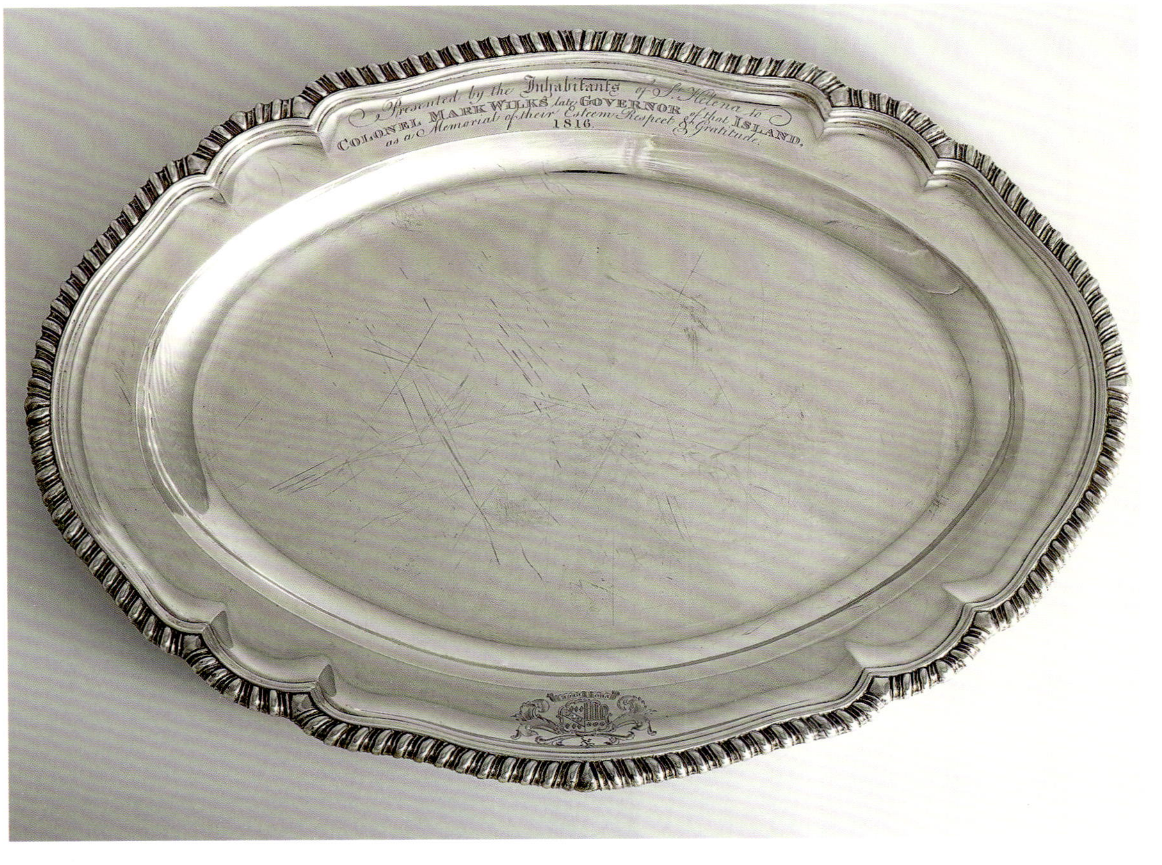

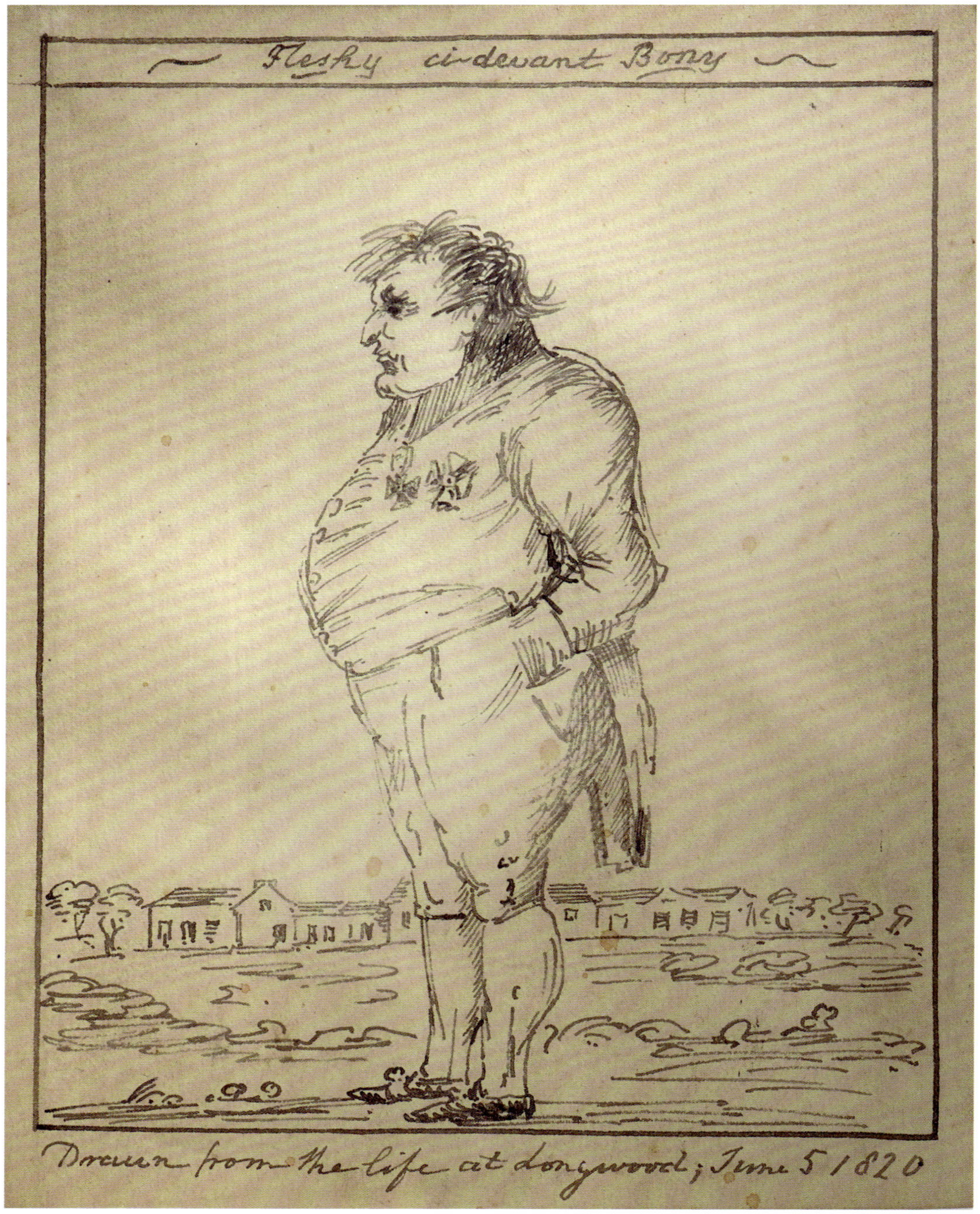

CARICATURE OF NAPOLEON DRAWN FROM LIFE ON ST HELENA

This famous drawing dated 5 June 1820 depicts the exiled Emperor in a rather unflattering way. He is shown disheveled and paunchy, under the title "Fleshy ci-devant Bony" ("Fleshy, formerly known as Boney"). "Boney" was a disparaging nickname for Bonaparte, which had suited him to perfection when he was still a thin young general. He had grown heavier on St Helena, earning the newer sobriquet "Fleshy". Engravings of this caricature drawn from life were circulated, and colors were added.

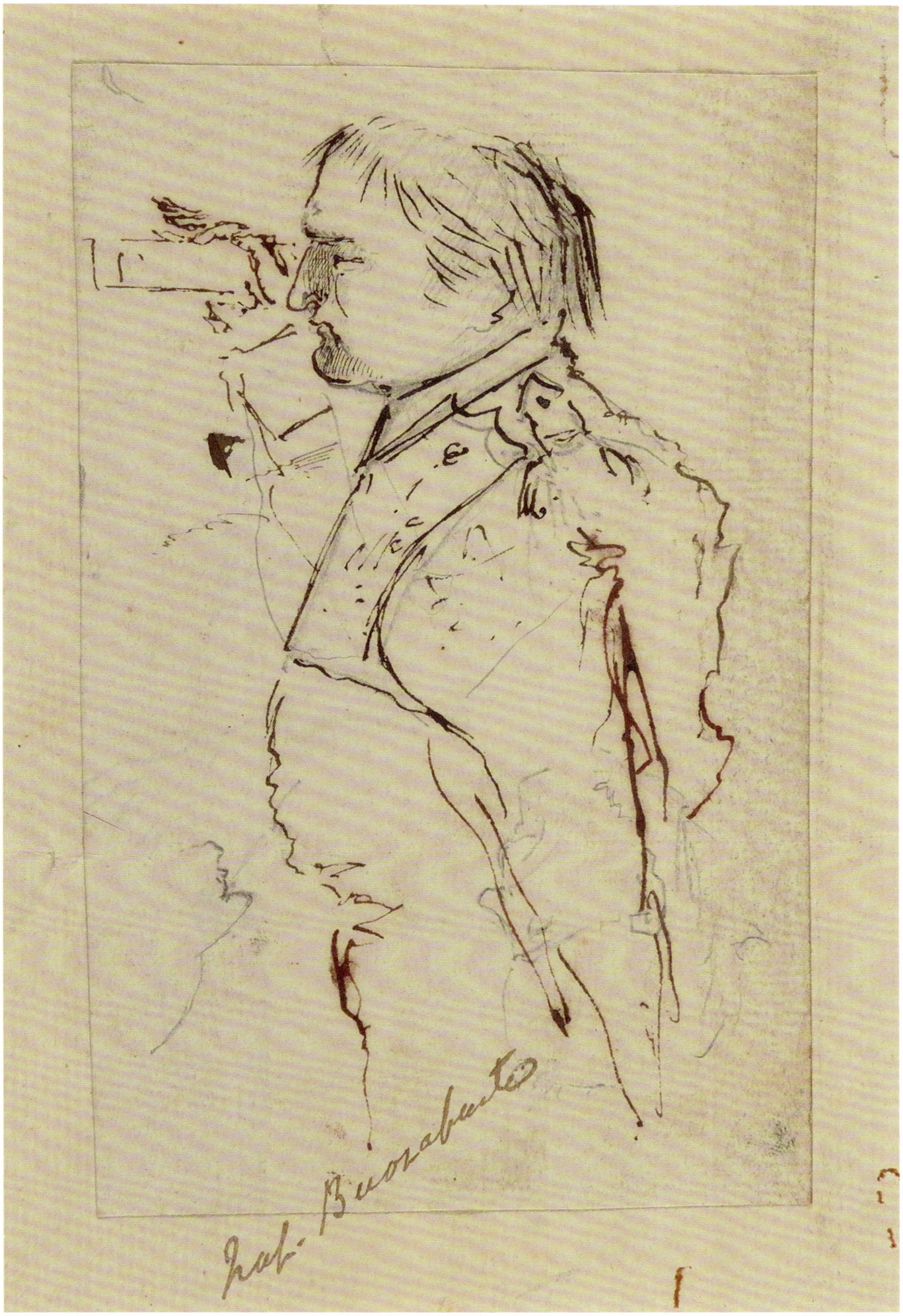

DENZIL IBBETSON (1788-1857), *NAPOLEON SCANNING THE HORIZON*

This pen and ink sketch captures Napoleon going about his everyday activities. Officer Denzil Ibbetson, an amateur artist, was among Napoleon's traveling companions aboard the Northumberland. He was also present at the Emperor's death in 1821. He sketched Napoleon during the crossing, and later on the island. Several other drawings have been attributed to him, including the one in Glover's journal (preserved in the collection) that shows Napoleon on the bridge of the boat, leaning on a cannon barrel.

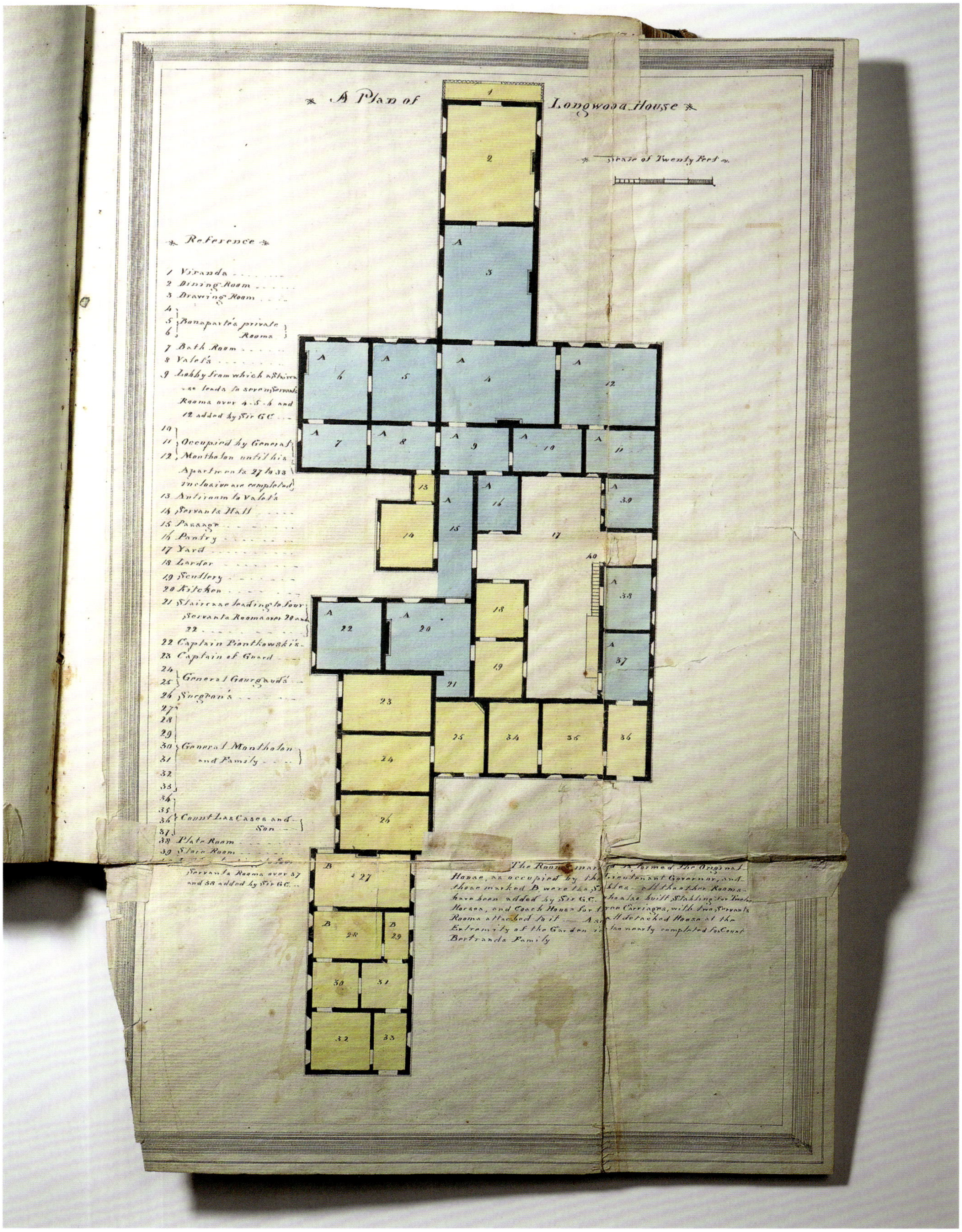

PLAN OF LONGWOOD HOUSE

This very rare hand-drawn plan of Longwood with watercolor fill is affixed to Glover's logbook, which belongs to the collection. It shows the exact layout of the house Napoleon lived in. His bedroom was in the corner of the right wing. Guests entered by the billiards room and walked through to the drawing room. Those who were invited to further intercourse had to go through the dining room to reach the door to the Emperor's office, which was permanently guarded by Louis-Etienne Saint-Denis known as "Mamluk Ali". The office adjoined Napoleon's bedroom.

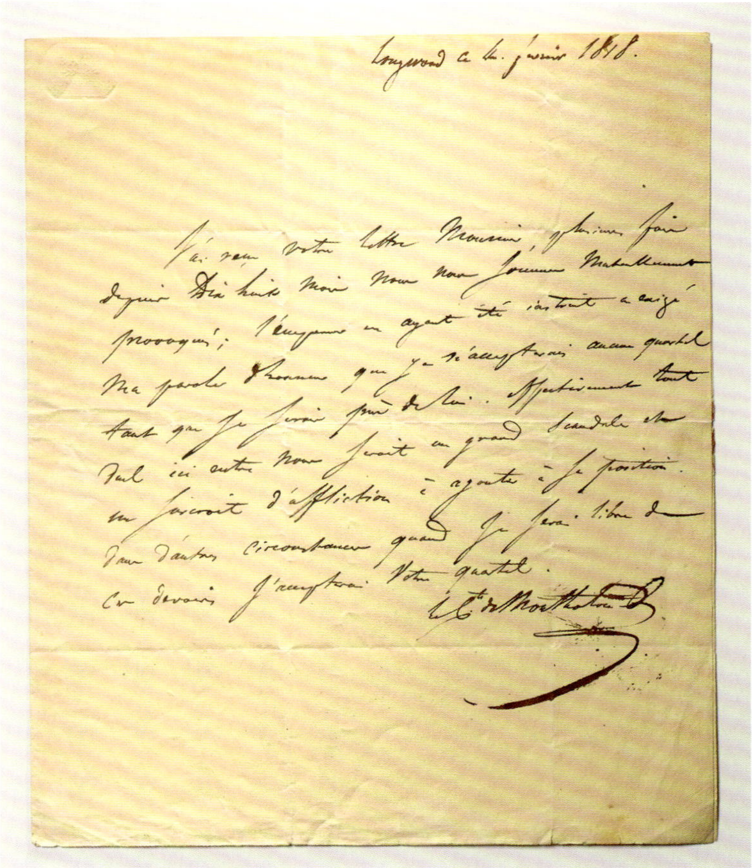

Longwood le 4 février 1818.

J'ai reçu votre lettre Monsieur, depuis Dix huit mois nous nous sommes mutuellement provoqués; l'Empereur en ayant été instruit a exigé ma parole d'honneur que je n'accepterai aucun cartel tant que je serai près de lui. Effectivement tout duel ici entre nous serait un grand scandale et un surcroît d'affliction ajouté à sa position. Dans d'autres circonstances quand je serai libre de ces devoirs j'accepterai votre cartel.

Cte de Montholon

HANDWRITTEN LETTER FROM COUNT MONTHOLON TO GENERAL GOURGAUD

General Gourgaud spent several months with the Emperor on St Helena but then left for France, unable to tolerate Montholon any longer and having challenged him to a duel. This letter, dated Longwood, 4 February 1818, was Montholon's response (English translation): "I have received your letter Sir. For 18 months now we have been provoking each other; the Emperor, having been informed, has made me give my word that I will accept no such cartel while I am by his side. In truth, any duel between us here would be a major scandal and an added affliction for a man in his position. In other circumstances, when released from my duties, I will accept your cartel." His letter provides a unique and vivid insight into the tensions felt by the handful of faithful who were imprisoned with the Emperor on the island.

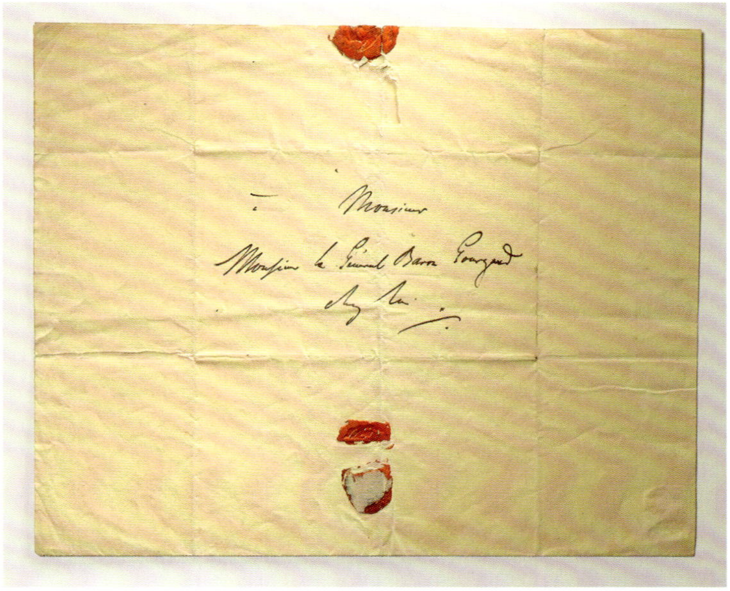

Monsieur

Monsieur le Général Baron Gourgaud

chez lui.

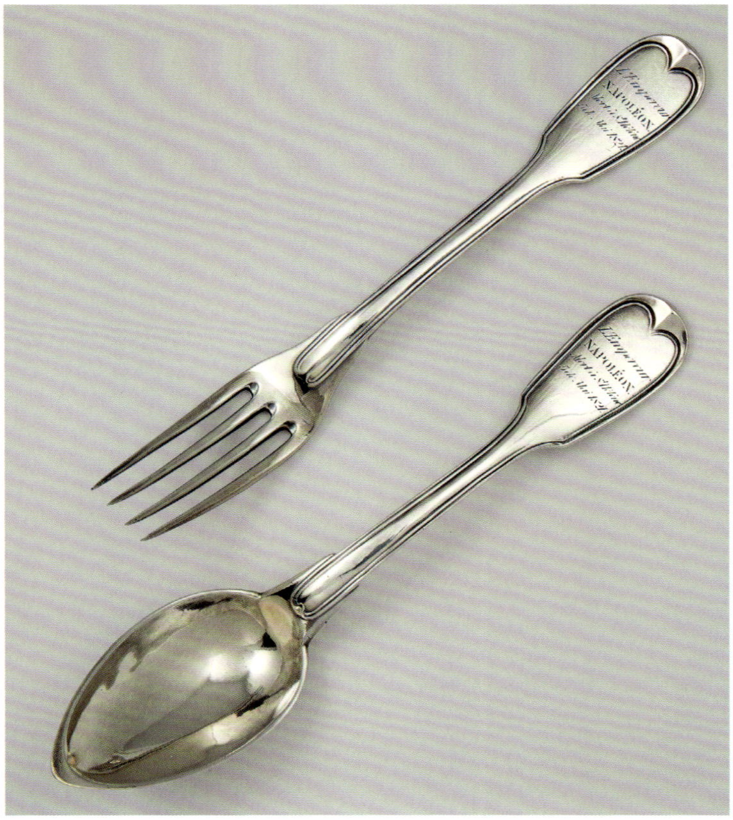

PIERRE-BENOIT LORILLON (1757-1816), CUTLERY USED BY NAPOLEON ON ST HELENA

This very rare cutlery used by the Emperor during his exile on St Helena was made by the silversmith Lorillon, a sub-contractor who produced some of the tableware put into travel nécessaires by the fine cabinetmaker Biennais. The spoon and fork that make up this set are distinguished by their engravings, with the imperial coat-of-arms on one side and on the other, the words: "Emperor NAPOLEON Died on St Helena 5 May 1821".

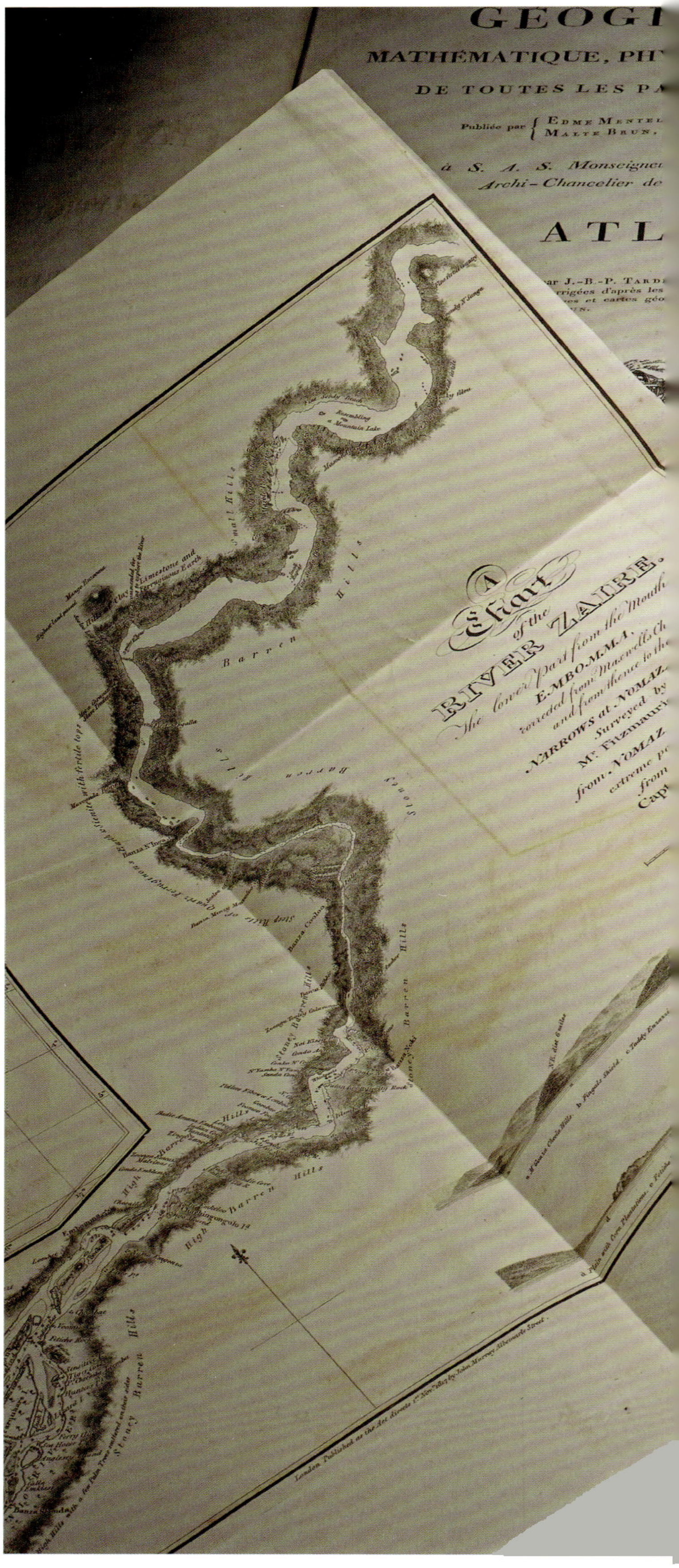

NAPOLEON'S LIBRARY AT LONGWOOD

Years of exile did nothing to diminish Napoleon's appetite for reading, which remained one of his principal occupations at Longwood. So he was particularly thankful for the support of people like Englishwoman Lady Holland, whose book gifts added to the few editions from the imperial palaces that accompanied Napoleon into exile. Most were on geography and history, but there were also a few novels. The Mamluk Ali did duty as Napoleon's librarian, entrusted with stamping the works with a seal of his making that featured the grand imperial coat-of-arms in the center.

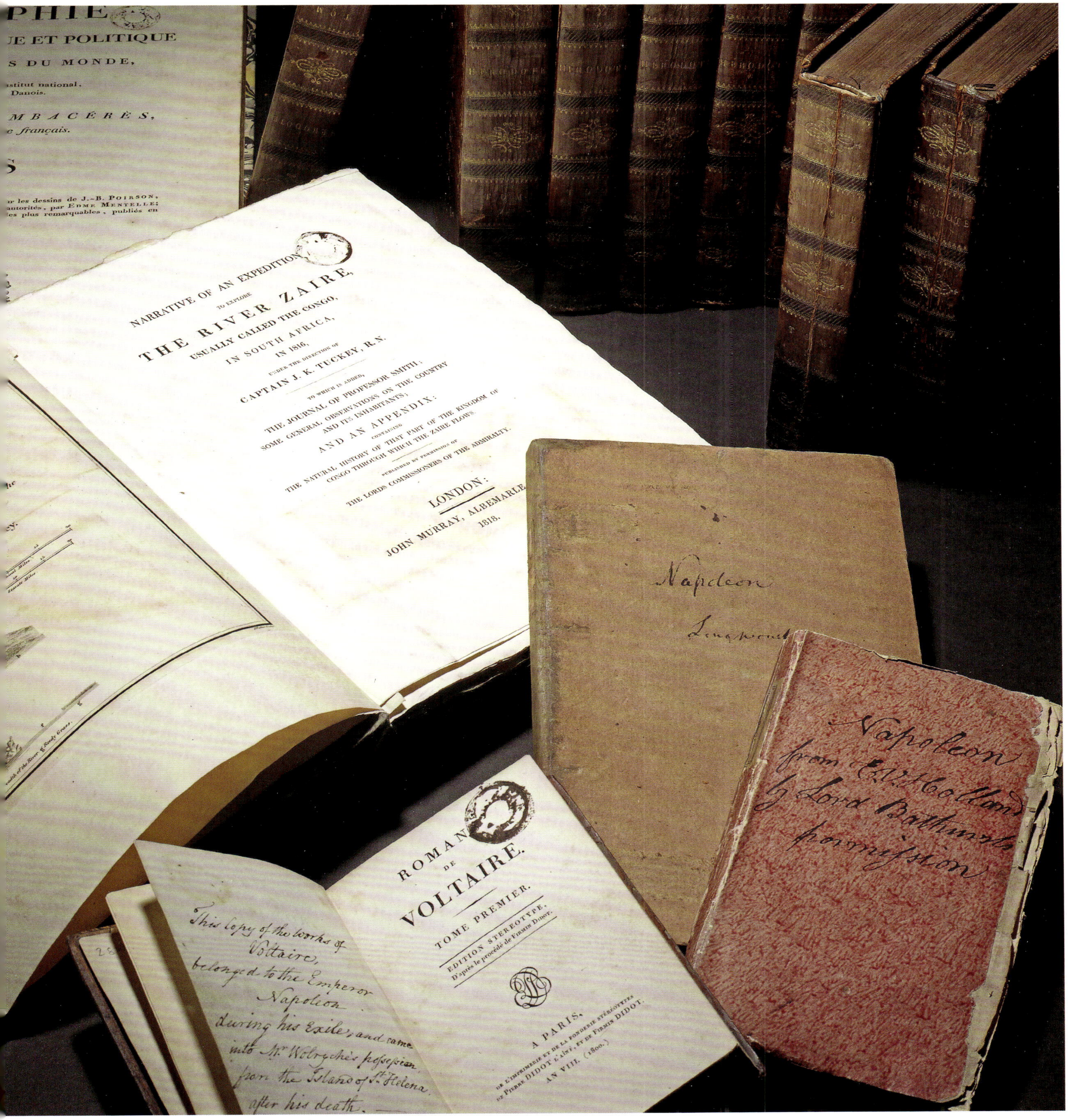
NARRATIVE OF AN EXPEDITION
TO EXPLORE
THE RIVER ZAIRE,
USUALLY CALLED THE CONGO,
IN SOUTH AFRICA,
IN 1816,
UNDER THE DIRECTION OF
CAPTAIN J. K. TUCKEY, R.N.
TO WHICH IS ADDED,
THE JOURNAL OF PROFESSOR SMITH;
SOME GENERAL OBSERVATIONS ON THE COUNTRY
AND ITS INHABITANTS;
AND AN APPENDIX:
CONTAINING
THE NATURAL HISTORY OF THAT PART OF THE KINGDOM OF
CONGO THROUGH WHICH THE ZAIRE FLOWS.
PUBLISHED BY PERMISSION OF
THE LORDS COMMISSIONERS OF THE ADMIRALTY.
LONDON:
JOHN MURRAY, ALBEMARLE
1818.
Napoleon
Longwood
Napoleon
ROMAN
DE
VOLTAIRE.
TOME PREMIER.
EDITION STÉRÉOTYPE,
D'après le procédé de Firmin Didot.
A PARIS,
DE L'IMPRIMERIE ET DE LA FONDERIE STÉRÉOTYPES
DE PIERRE DIDOT L'AÎNÉ, ET DE FIRMIN DIDOT.
AN VIII. (1800.)
This copy of the works of
Voltaire,
belonged to the Emperor
Napoleon
during his Exile, and came
into Mr Wolrych's possession
from the Island of St. Helena
after his death.

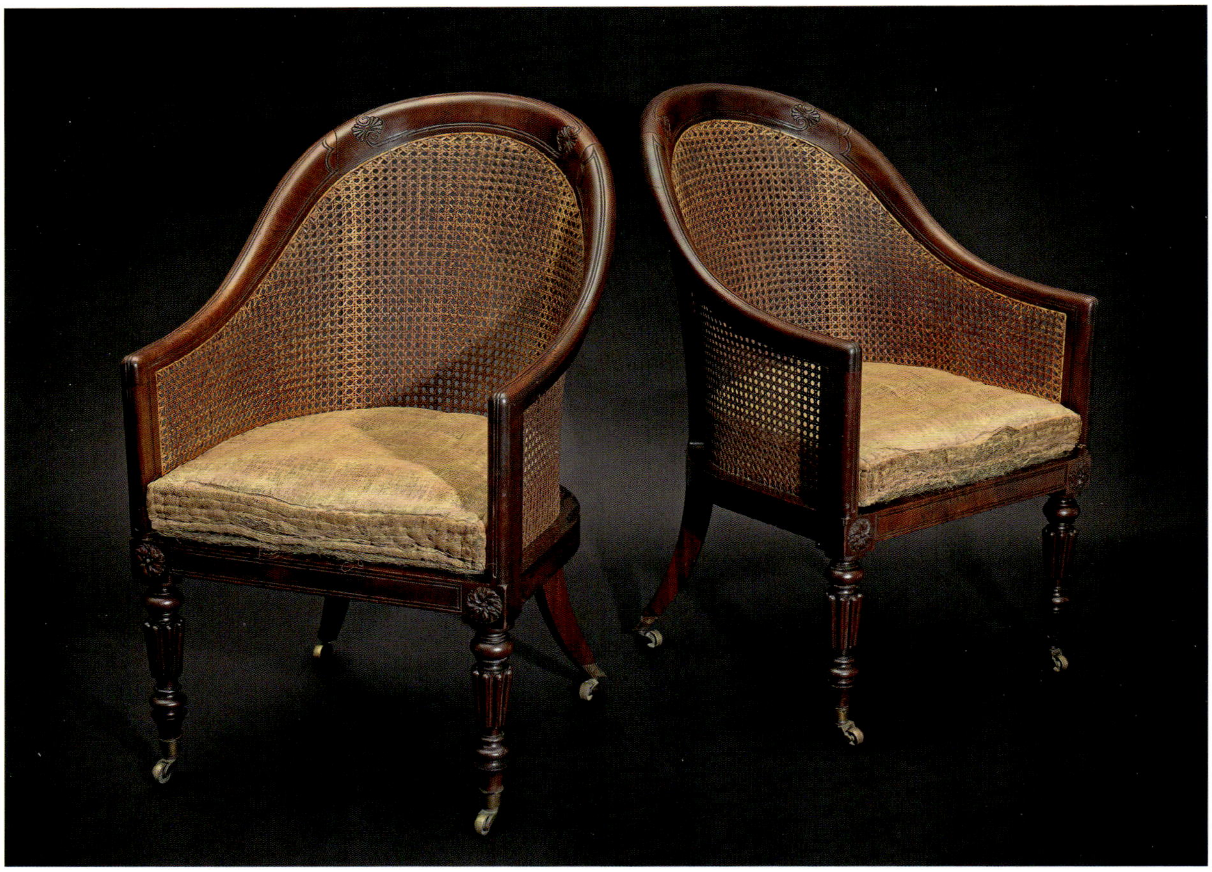

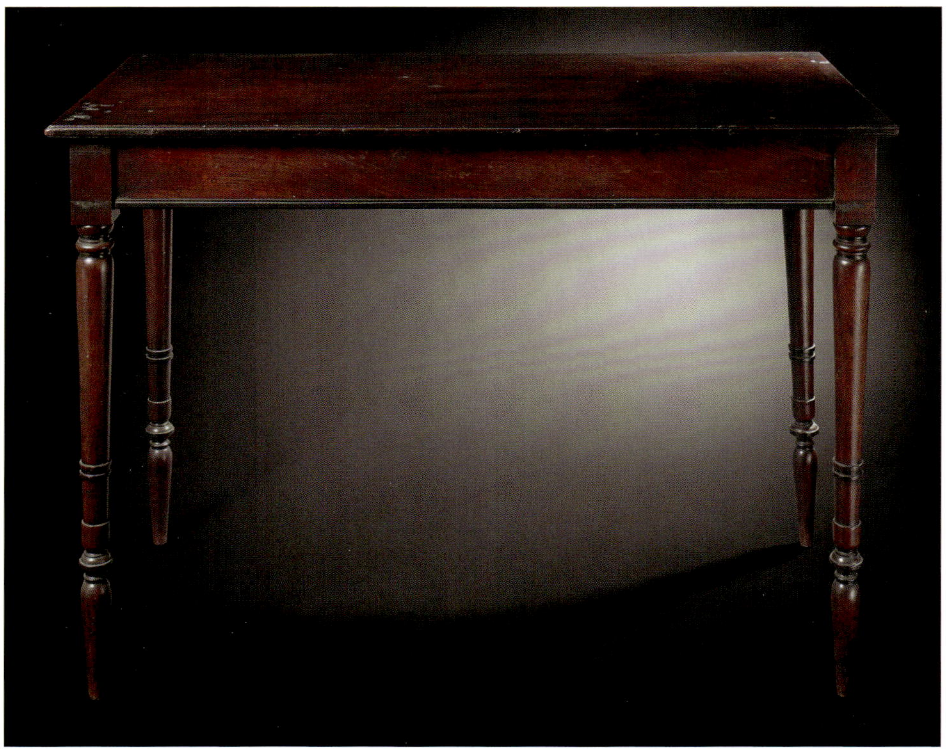

GEORGE BULLOCK, TABLE FROM NAPOLEON'S BEDROOM AT LONGWOOD HOUSE

This ebony and mahogany table of simple design, dating from 1816, is one of the pieces made by English cabinetmaker George Bullock to furnish Napoleon's bedroom at Longwood House. There are few relics whose history can be so certainly traced, from 1822 when Christie's auctioned off the Emperor's effects on the island between 1 April and 12 August, to the table's reappearance in London on 24 April 2008, also at Christie's. Such rarity gives this piece tremendous symbolic and historical importance. It featured in the inventory of pieces cited by G. Bullock in his Account of furniture supplied for St Helena, 1816, under: "Room 10 - Bedroom of General contd" priced at £3.10, and subsequently appears in the inventory of furniture at Longwood House (or Old Longwood House), drawn up by upholsterer Andrew Darling on 12, 15, and 25 May 1821, as one of "2 small Mehogany Tables". When it was bought in 1822 (lot 27), Darling was no doubt aware of its unique and historic nature. The table shows traces of indentations from burns at one corner, which are mentioned in an old handwritten note added at the time of the Christie's sale: "This table was formerly in the possession of Napoleon Bonaparte, the hole burns by Bonaparte burning pastilles, and purchased at the sale of his effects at Longwood by Andrew Darling, St Helena, 1821".

GEORGE BULLOCK (1777-1818), PAIR OF WING CHAIRS FROM LONGWOOD HOUSE

Four mahogany wing chairs with caned backs and cushions have come down to us. Drawn on the elevation plans for New House (or New Longwood House), they were delivered to St Helena by Bullock under the heading "arm chairs with cushions", initially to furnish what were to be the Officers' bedrooms in the Emperor's new home; one pair for "Sitting room for Officer A" at a cost of £32; another pair, at the same price, for "Sitting room for Officer B". The inventory of furniture at Longwood House drawn up by upholsterer Andrew Darling following Napoleon's death in May 1821 was not detailed enough to differentiate the chairs, all of which were listed simply as "armchair". We can be certain that the Reverend Richard Boys, Chaplain of St Helena from 1811 to 1830, acquired two of the four wing chairs at the sale of Napoleon's effects held on the island in 1822, as the purchase was recorded in the sale register (lots 188 and 434). Boys maintained that Napoleon had given him one of the Longwood wing chairs as thanks for his conduct. In 1926, his granddaughter Lilian Boys-Behrens related this information in her volume *Under Thirty-Seven Kings;* "As a token of appreciation of their conduct Napoleon desired to give the two chaplains a present; a snuffbox was offered to Boys... Napoleon also left Boys an armchair", which was confirmed by Martin Levy in his work *Napoleon in Exile.* A chair bearing the inscription "belonged to Napoleon Bonaparte and came into possession of Rear Admiral Robert Lambert in charge of naval forces at St Helena at the time of his death 5 May 1821", was also at one stage owned by the descendants of Rear Admiral Lambert, who arrived in Jamestown on 14 July 1820. One wing chair is now in Britain in the Maidstone Museum & Art Gallery.

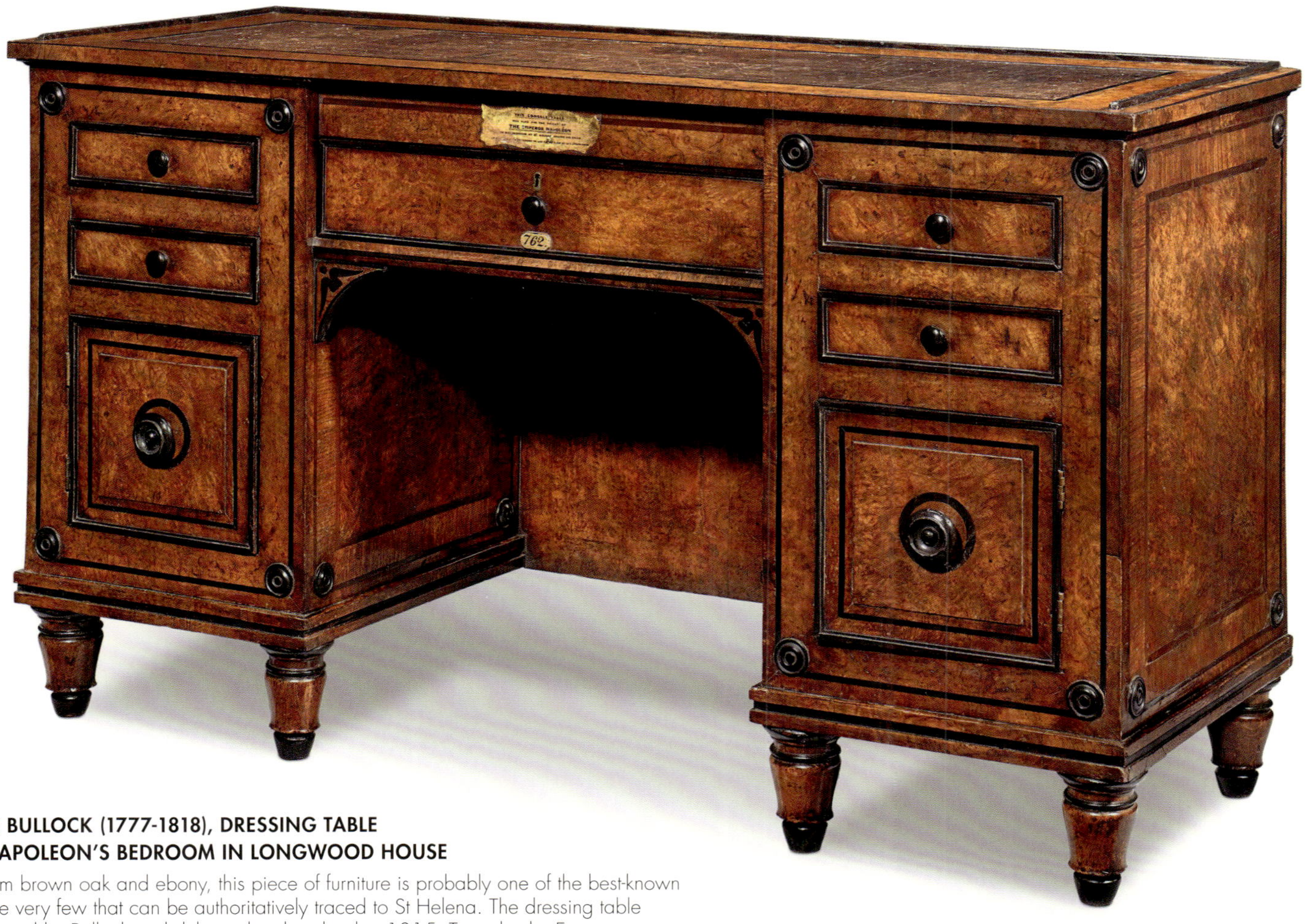

GEORGE BULLOCK (1777-1818), DRESSING TABLE FROM NAPOLEON'S BEDROOM IN LONGWOOD HOUSE

Made from brown oak and ebony, this piece of furniture is probably one of the best-known among the very few that can be authoritatively traced to St Helena. The dressing table was designed by Bullock and delivered to the island in 1815. To make the Emperor more comfortable while awaiting his new home, this table was eventually brought into use at Longwood House (or Old Longwood House) in Napoleon's bedroom. On his return to England, Hudson Lowe had a copper plate affixed stating: "THIS CONSOLE TABLE / WAS USED FOR THE TOILET OF / THE EMPEROR NAPOLEON / IN HIS BEDROOM AT ST. HELENA DURING HIS EXILE / IT ... (F) ... COUNT DE LAS CASAS' PLAN OF LONGWOOD HOUSE", followed by the number 762 underneath. This plate can be found on the very few items of furniture that Hudson Lowe shipped back to England after Napoleon's death, showing what great pains he took to select those he considered genuine relics because he knew they had been in regular use by his illustrious prisoner. The piece has lost its tabletop mirror, and was subsequently moved to Count Montholon's bedroom at Longwood House, where it stood at the time of Napoleon's death. Described in the inventory of upholsterer Andrew Darling as "Oak dressing table", it was one of the very first items Lowe took, which attests to its importance. The table went with him on his return to England aboard the Dunira on 12 July 1821. He kept it in his possession until his death in 1844, when his heirs entrusted it to Phillips Auctioneers. It was acquired by a John Copling, and sold again on his death in 1867 by Puttick & Simpson. On two subsequent occasions it was auctioned by Christie's, in 1989 and again in 2003.

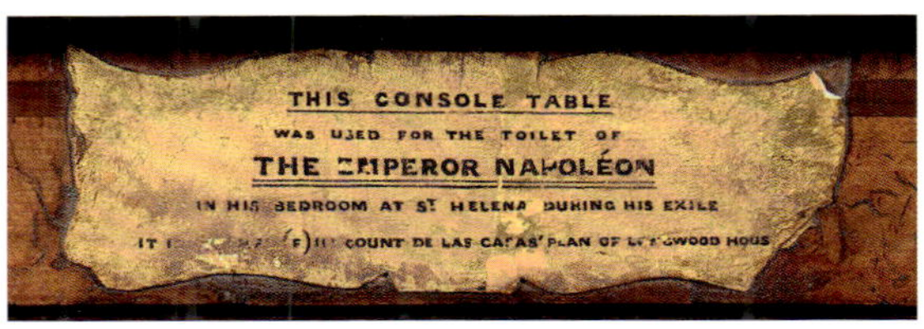

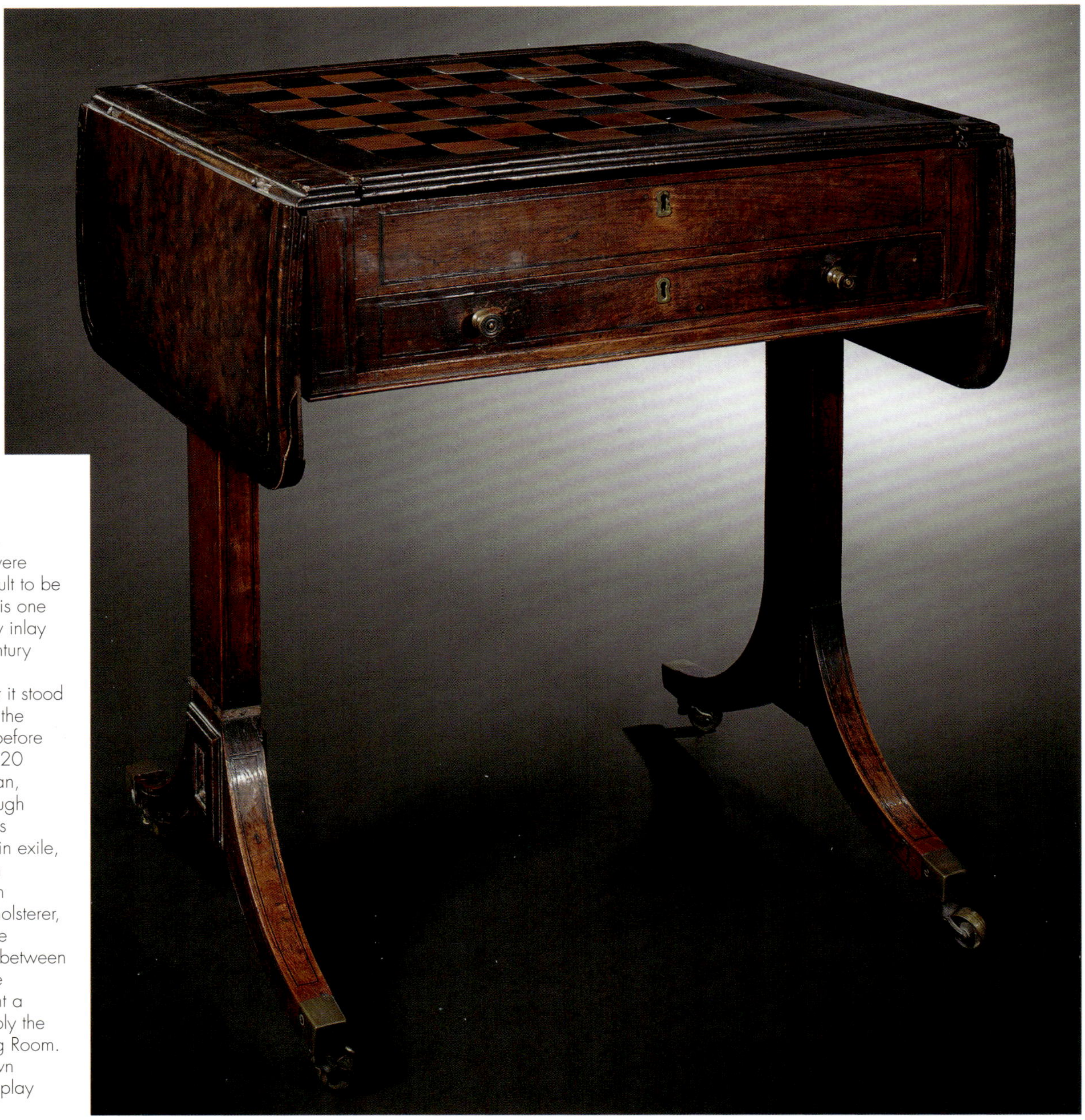

GAMES TABLE PROBABLY USED IN LONGWOOD HOUSE

Several games tables were in use as part of the island's social life. They were regularly moved around so it is difficult to be certain of their exact provenance. This one made of lemonwood with mahogany inlay is accompanied by an early 19th century map of St Helena. There is also a handwritten document indicating that it stood first in Longwood House and then in the Governor of St Helena's residence, before being given as a wedding gift in 1920 to Harold Godfrey St George Morgan, who held the post at that time. Although there is no formal evidence to link this piece to Napoleon's final residence in exile, Longwood House was furnished with this type of table. We know that both Governor Lowe and Darling, the upholsterer, bought many lots at the auction of the Emperor's effects, held on the island between 1 April and 12 August 1822. As the sales register states, "'Darling' bought a backgammon table (lot 29)", probably the one that stood in the Servants' Dining Room. The French Domains of St Helena own a games table that is currently on display in Longwood House.

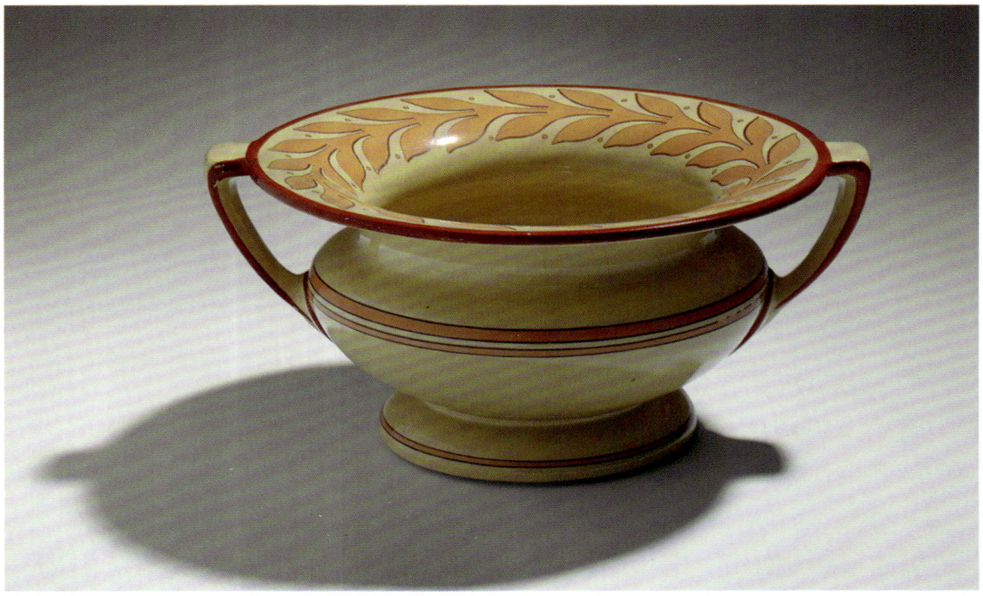

GEORGE BULLOCK (1777-1818), ENGLISH EARTHENWARE BASIN FROM THE SET ORDERED FOR NAPOLEON ON ST HELENA

This basin belonged to the earthenware washing set that the British government ordered from Bullock for the Emperor's new residence on St Helena, New House (or New Longwood House). The set is decorated with a frieze of laurel leaves – the traditional emblem of a victorious general – and before it was shipped, the Secretary of State for the Colonies, Lord Bathurst, decreed that it should not be delivered. It was acquired in its entirety by Matthew Robinson Boulton for his manor at Great Tew in Oxfordshire, before being dispersed. Boulton's father was the famous English artist and industrialist, Matthew Boulton, who pioneered gilded bronze and steam engines. Part of the set is now held in the Museum of Liverpool's collections.

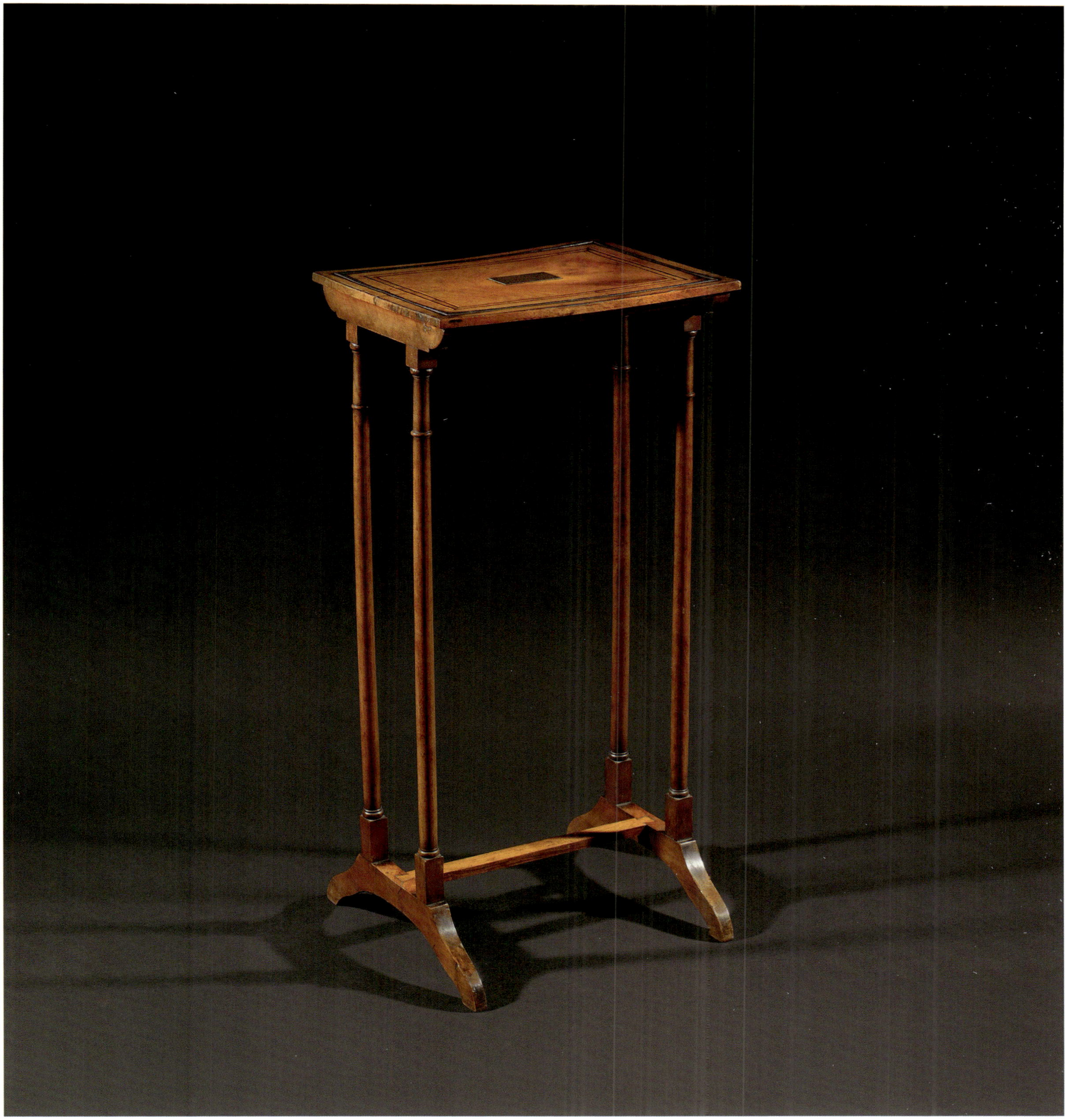

GEORGE BULLOCK (1777-1818), PEDESTAL TABLE USED BY NAPOLEON ON ST HELENA

This small mahogany table from England belongs to a nest of tables, one of which was probably placed at the bedside of the dying Emperor at Longwood House. It may be the one described by Mamluk Ali. It complements the other table from the same nest, described as such at the big exhibition held in Paris in 2016 at the Musée de l'Armée: "Napoleon in Saint Helena. The Conquest of Memory". In its center sits an old silver plate engraved: "This table was among Emperor Napoleon's furniture and was carried onto the terrace where HM had coffee every day on St Helena". The third table in the nest is still unaccounted for.

DEATH OF NAPOLEON

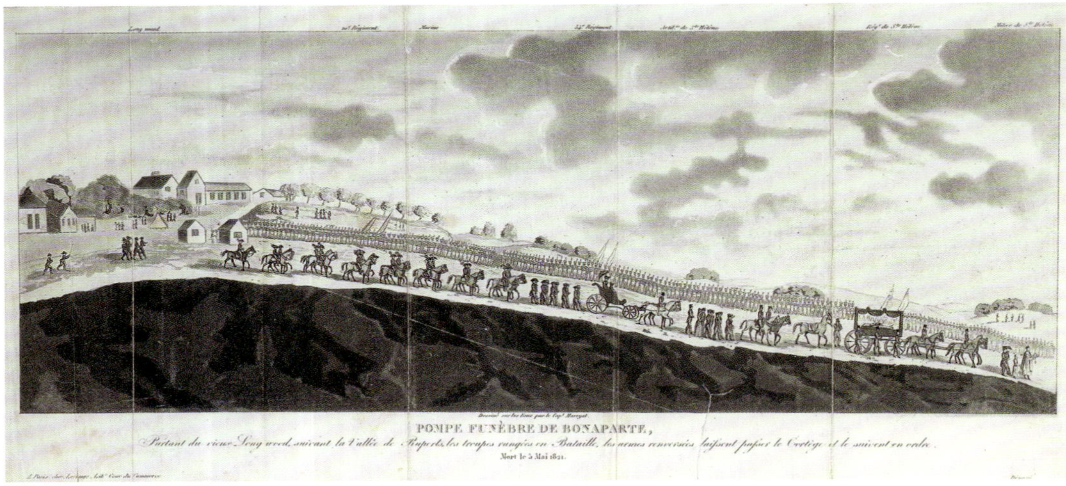

BONAPARTE'S FUNERAL AS DEPICTED BY FREDERICK MARRYAT (1792-1848)

Frederick Marryat (1792-1848) was a captain in the Royal Navy who became a pioneer of maritime fiction. Stationed on St Helena at the time of Napoleon's death, he is the hand behind two drawings that capture a landmark moment in history: Napoleon on his deathbed and Napoleon's funeral procession.

NAPOLEON ON HIS DEATHBED, WEARING HIS UNIFORM OF A COLONEL OF THE GRENADIERS OF HIS IMPERIAL GUARD, HIS HEAD RESTING ON A PILLOW

A very rare and moving wax effigy of Napoleon on his deathbed, with handwritten label indicating that it was modeled from life on St Helena, but most probably dating from the time of the *retour des cendres* (return of the ashes), intended as a wax model for a bronze sculpture that to our knowledge was never executed.

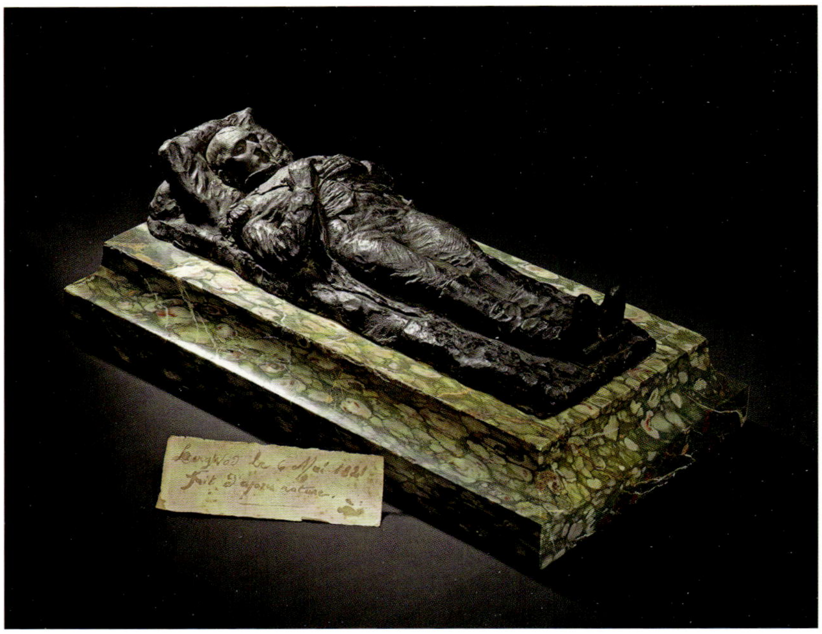

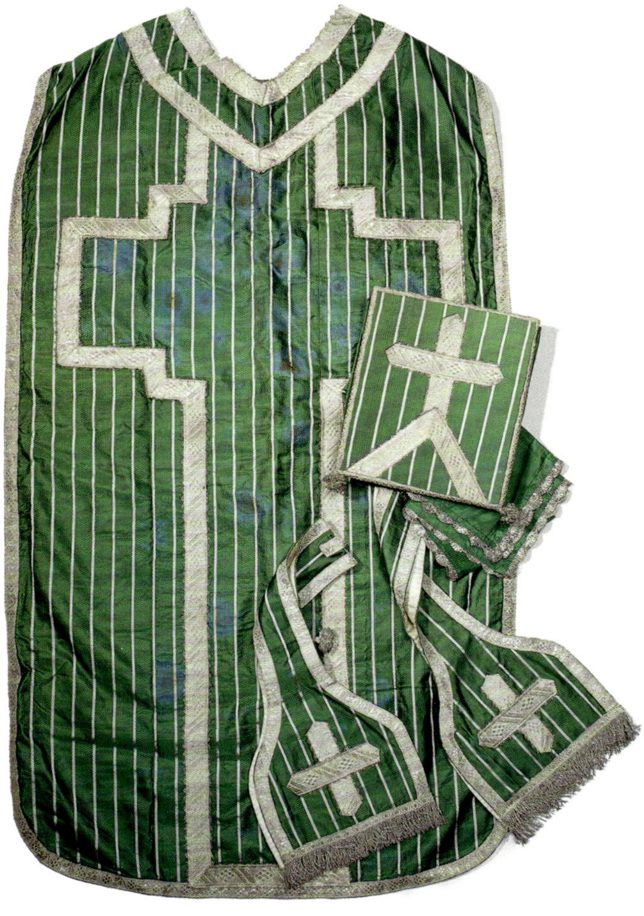

SACERDOTAL ROBES WORN BY ABBOT VIGNALI WHILE GIVING NAPOLEON THE LAST RITES

This green silk chasuble with thin white stripes, embroidered with silver braiding and featuring a cross design, was worn by Abbot Angelo Paulo Vignali (1784-1836) when he administered the last rites to Napoleon and officiated at his funeral. After going to Rome in 1814 to obtain a doctorate in medicine and theology, he offered to go to St Helena for Madame Mère and Cardinal Fesch, accompanying Abbot Buonavita who had been chosen as the Emperor's spiritual adviser. They set off from Rome on 25 February 1819, and disembarked on St Helena on 20 September with "la petite caravane". Abbot Vignali was to serve as chaplain, and replaced Abbot Buonavita as Napoleon's spiritual adviser on 18 March 1821. He administered extreme unction to Napoleon on 1 May 1821, and was by his side as he breathed his last on 5 May. Four days later, Vignali conducted the funeral service. He left St Helena for Rome on 25 May 1821, before heading for Corsica in April 1823 – the native land that he and the Emperor had in common. He was assassinated on 13 June 1836. These memorial artifacts are taken from Abbot Vignali's collection, which was dispersed on 26 October 1977.

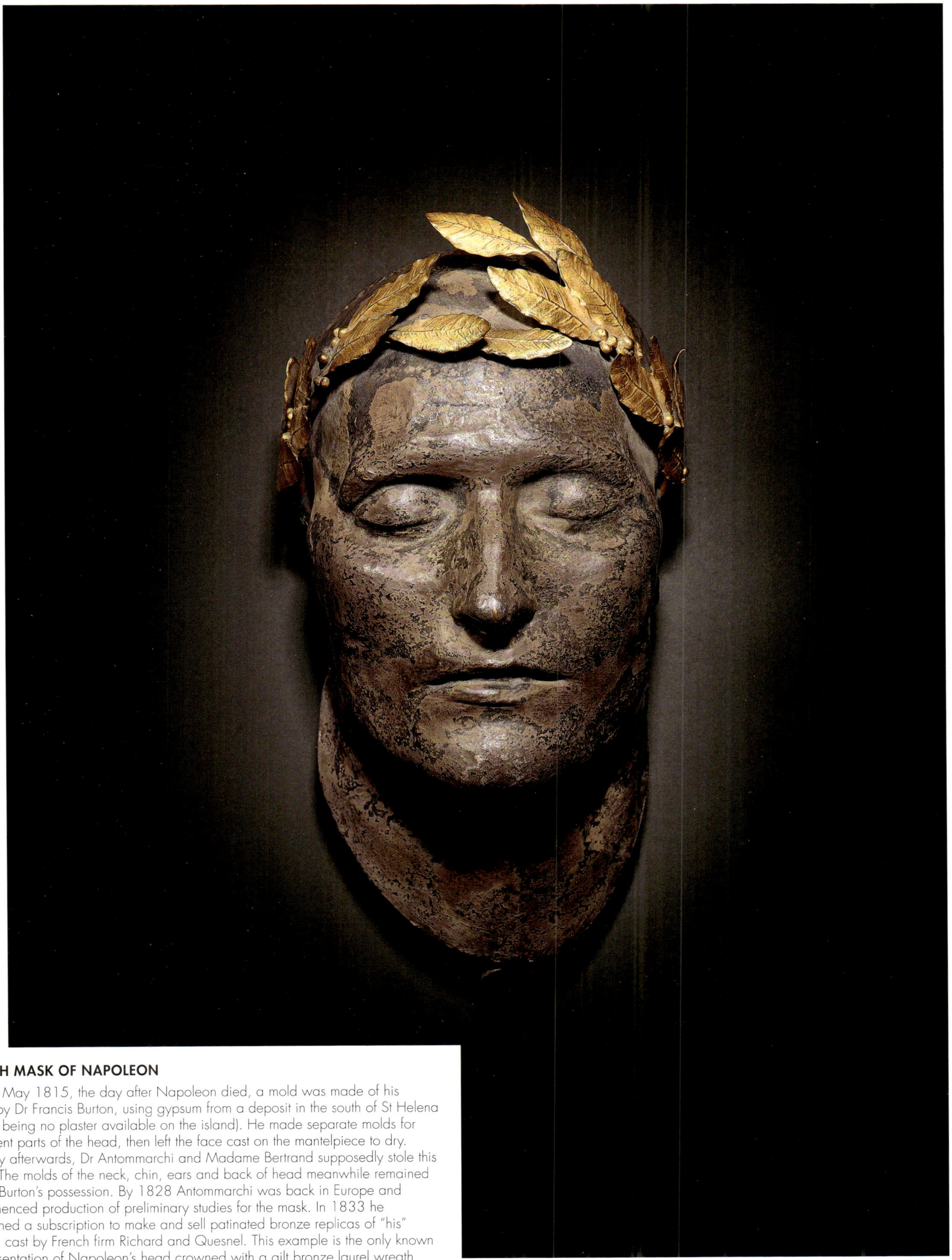

DEATH MASK OF NAPOLEON

On 6 May 1815, the day after Napoleon died, a mold was made of his face by Dr Francis Burton, using gypsum from a deposit in the south of St Helena (there being no plaster available on the island). He made separate molds for different parts of the head, then left the face cast on the mantelpiece to dry. Shortly afterwards, Dr Antommarchi and Madame Bertrand supposedly stole this cast. The molds of the neck, chin, ears and back of head meanwhile remained in Dr Burton's possession. By 1828 Antommarchi was back in Europe and commenced production of preliminary studies for the mask. In 1833 he launched a subscription to make and sell patinated bronze replicas of "his" mask, cast by French firm Richard and Quesnel. This example is the only known representation of Napoleon's head crowned with a gilt bronze laurel wreath – probably a test piece made by Antommarchi to judge from the number "2" engraved on the back.

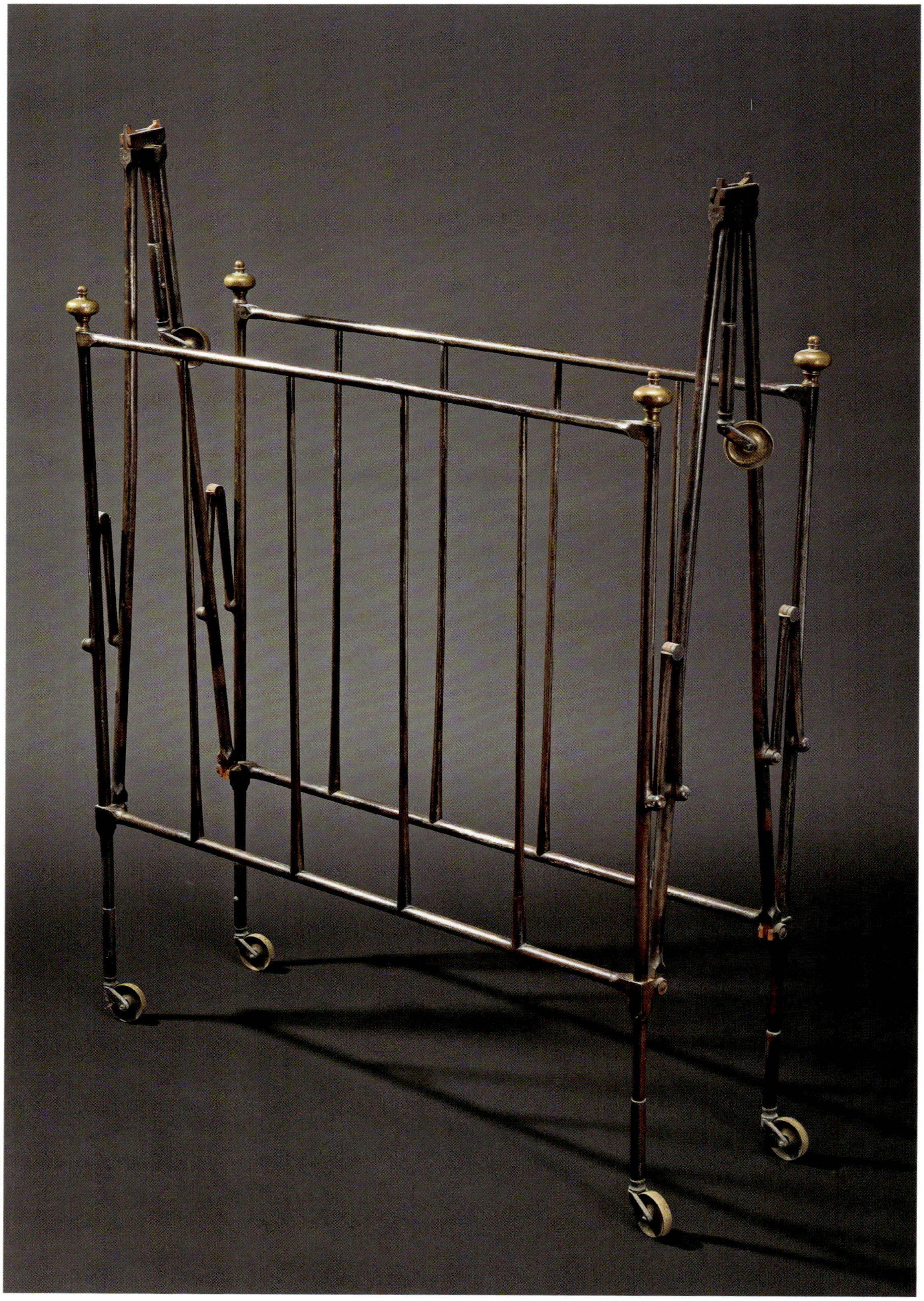

MARIE-JEAN DESOUCHES (1764-1828), NAPOLEON'S IRON BEDSTEAD

This iron bedstead is modeled on the Emperor's (described earlier in Chapter 3 (page 184) and bears the stamp of its ingenious supplier "Desouches" beneath an imperial crown. It takes up very little space when folded, and this is what appealed to Napoleon who immediately started using it. From then on, this bed would be forever associated with the image of the "little Corporal" camping out among his soldiers, or the fallen Emperor dying alone among his faithful followers on St Helena, an isolated rocky island in the middle of the ocean.

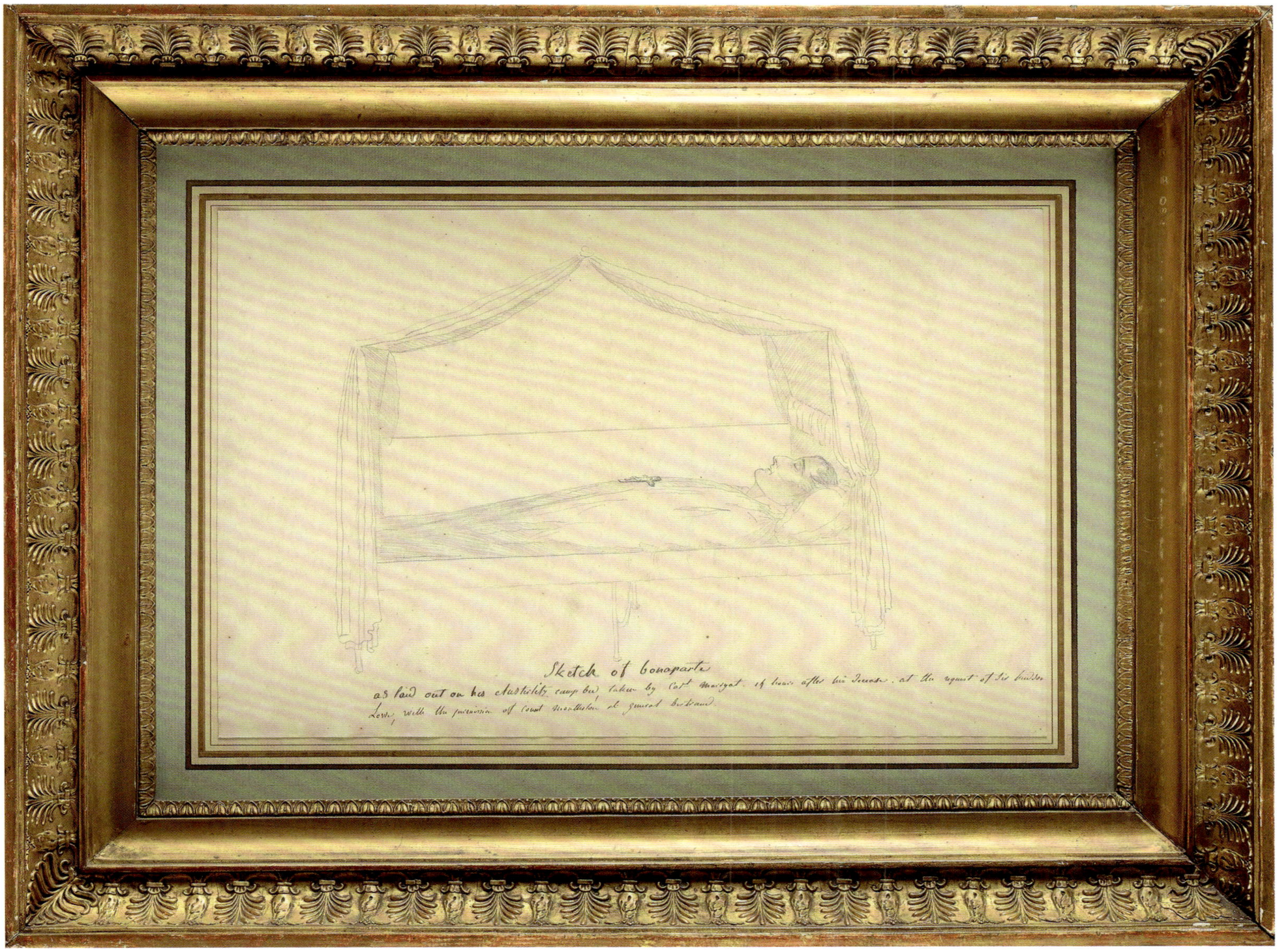

FREDERICK MARRYAT (1792-1848), *NAPOLEON ON HIS DEATHBED*

This moving drawing shows the still form of the Emperor in death, covered in a sheet. The surroundings of the bedroom and friendly entourage on St Helena have been obliterated to focus attention on the chill of the moment. Fleuriot de Langle's *Cahiers de Sainte-Hélène* give an account of how this view came to be drawn on 6 May 1821: "At 10 o'clock, Mr Ibbetson and the Frigate Captain Mariette [Marryat] came to draw the Emperor on his deathbed: Mr Mariette seemed to have produced a sketch in profile that was quite alike".

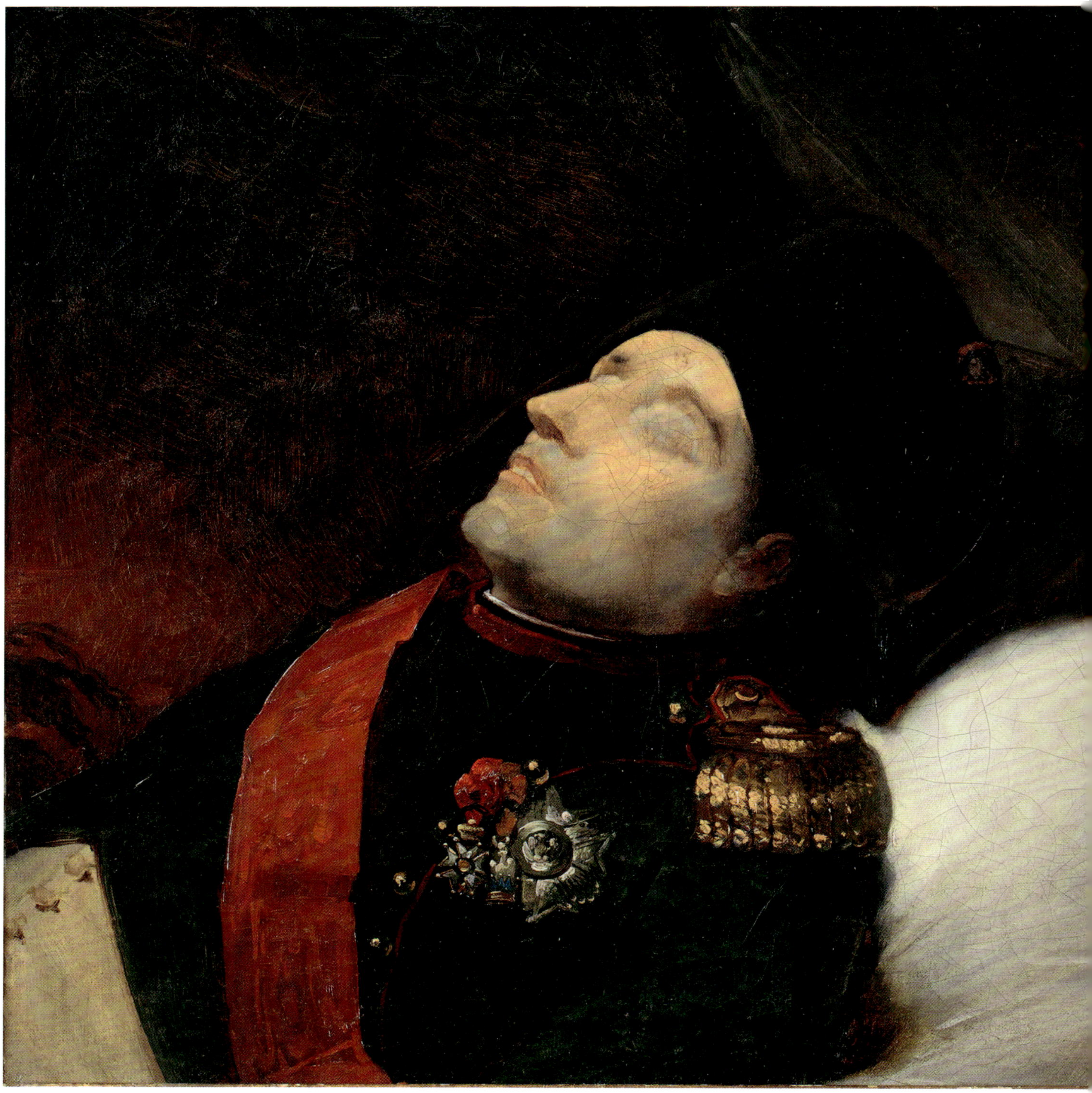

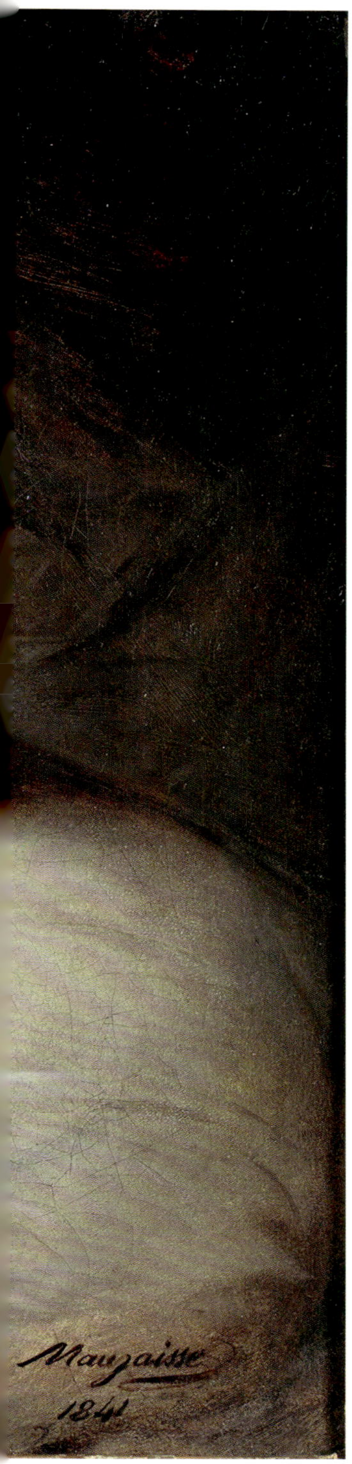

JEAN-BAPTISTE MAUZAISSE (1784-1844),
NAPOLEON ON HIS DEATHBED

Napoleon is laid out on his bed wearing the uniform of the Chasseurs de la Garde, the red ribbon of the Legion of Honor, and his famous hat. His head resting on a pillow, his face is in the light but the background remains in shadow. This painting from 1841 is directly copied from a larger canvas by the same painter, entitled: "Napoleon on his deathbed, an hour before being buried", preserved in the Château de Malmaison et Bois-Préau. It can also be likened to a composition by the painter Joseph William Rubidge (1802-1827) produced on St Helena in the presence of Counts Bertrand and Montholon, and circulated as an etching in Britain. Joseph William Rubidge was staying on the island at the time of Napoleon's death.

LOUIS LE BRETON (1818-1866),
NAPOLEON'S ASHES BEING BROUGHT ABOARD

There is no certainty as to whether Louis Le Breton was present when the Emperor's ashes were removed from St Helena for his last voyage to Paris. His view of Jamestown Bay is nonetheless rich in emotion and realistic detail. The artist has captured the moment when the boat transporting the Emperor's casket, shown in the center of the composition, approaches *Belle Poule*, the ship commanded by the Prince de Joinville. The bay seems to have fallen under a pall of silence, with the watercraft floating in a near-mystical atmosphere.

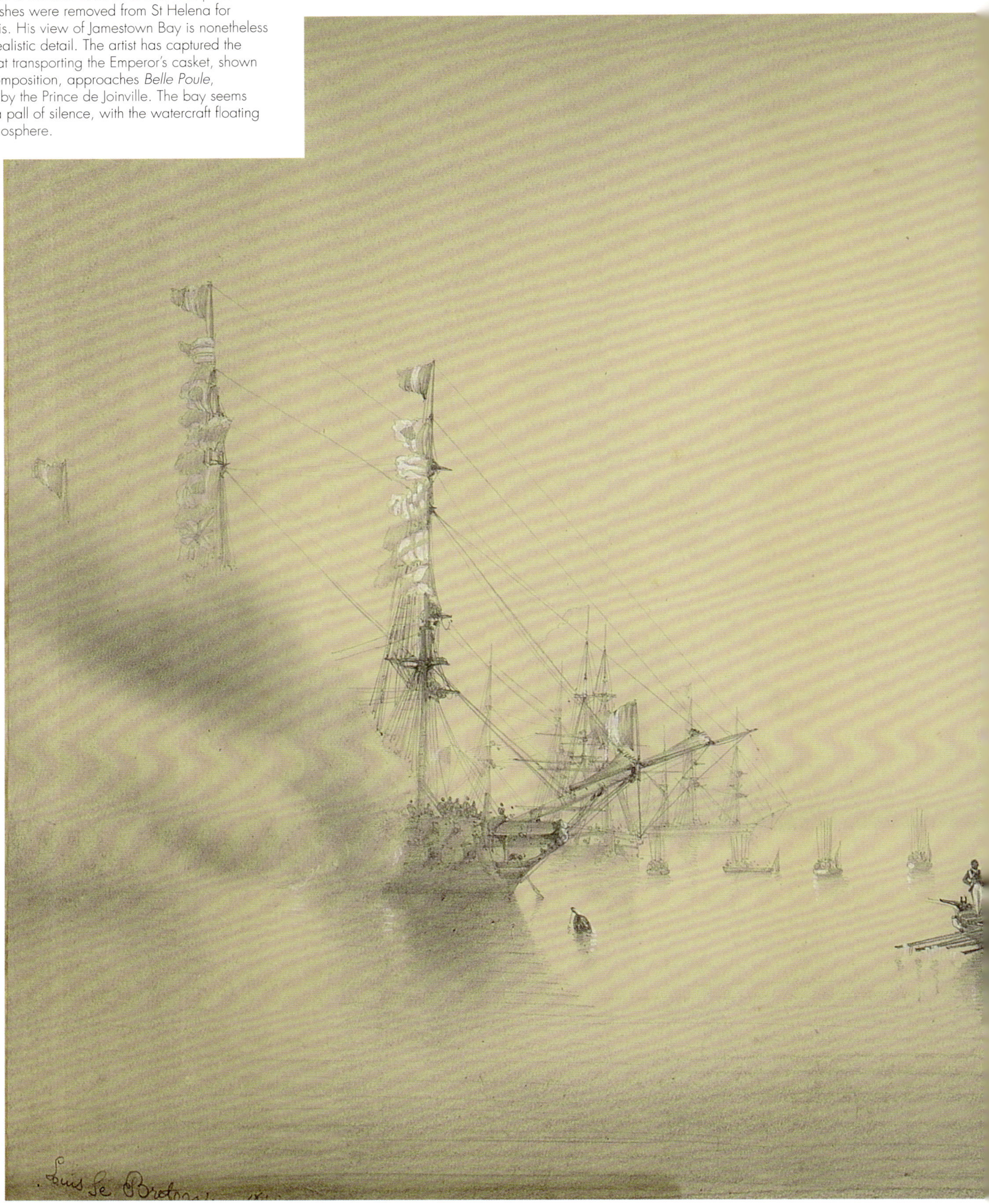

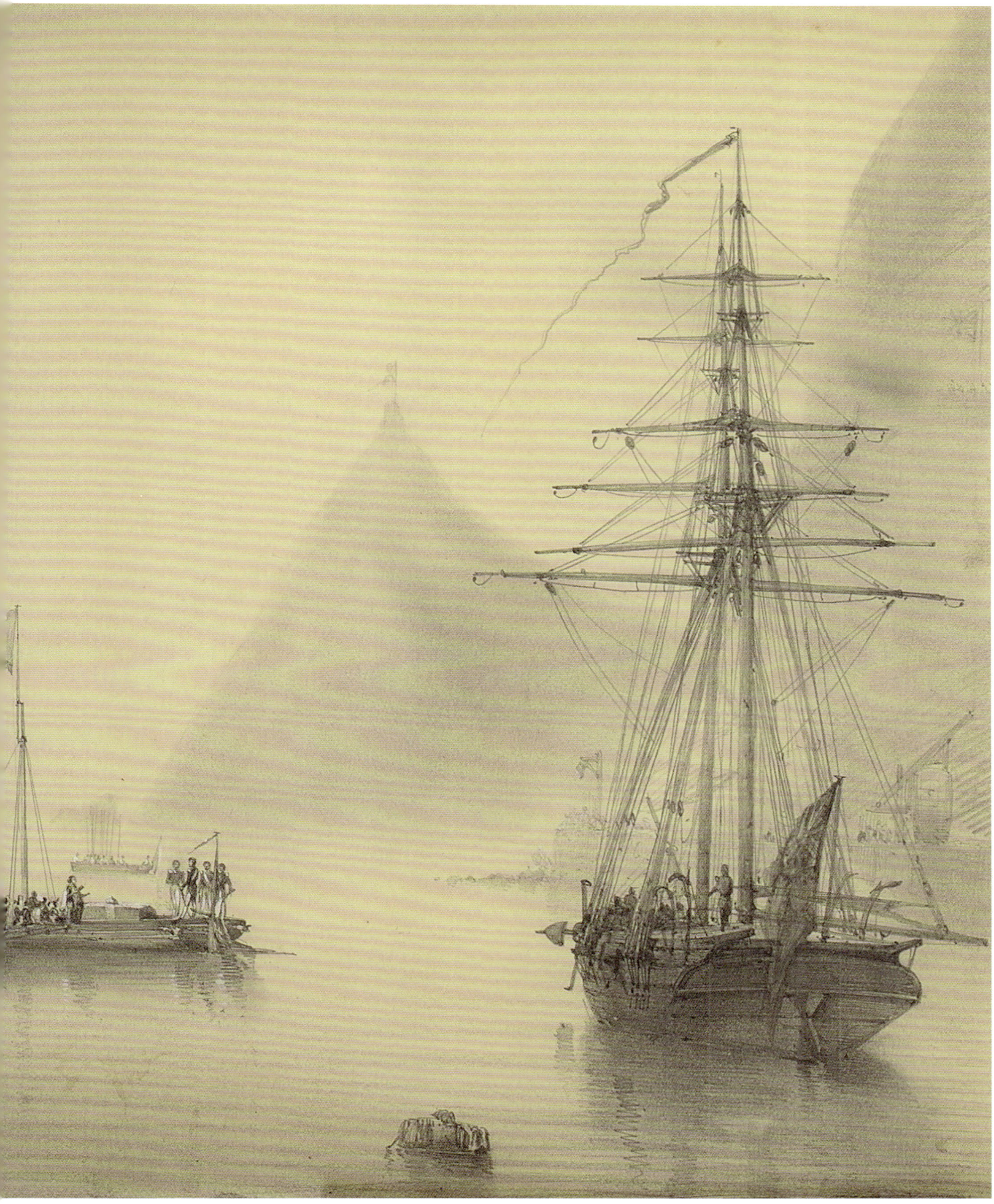

RETURN OF THE ASHES

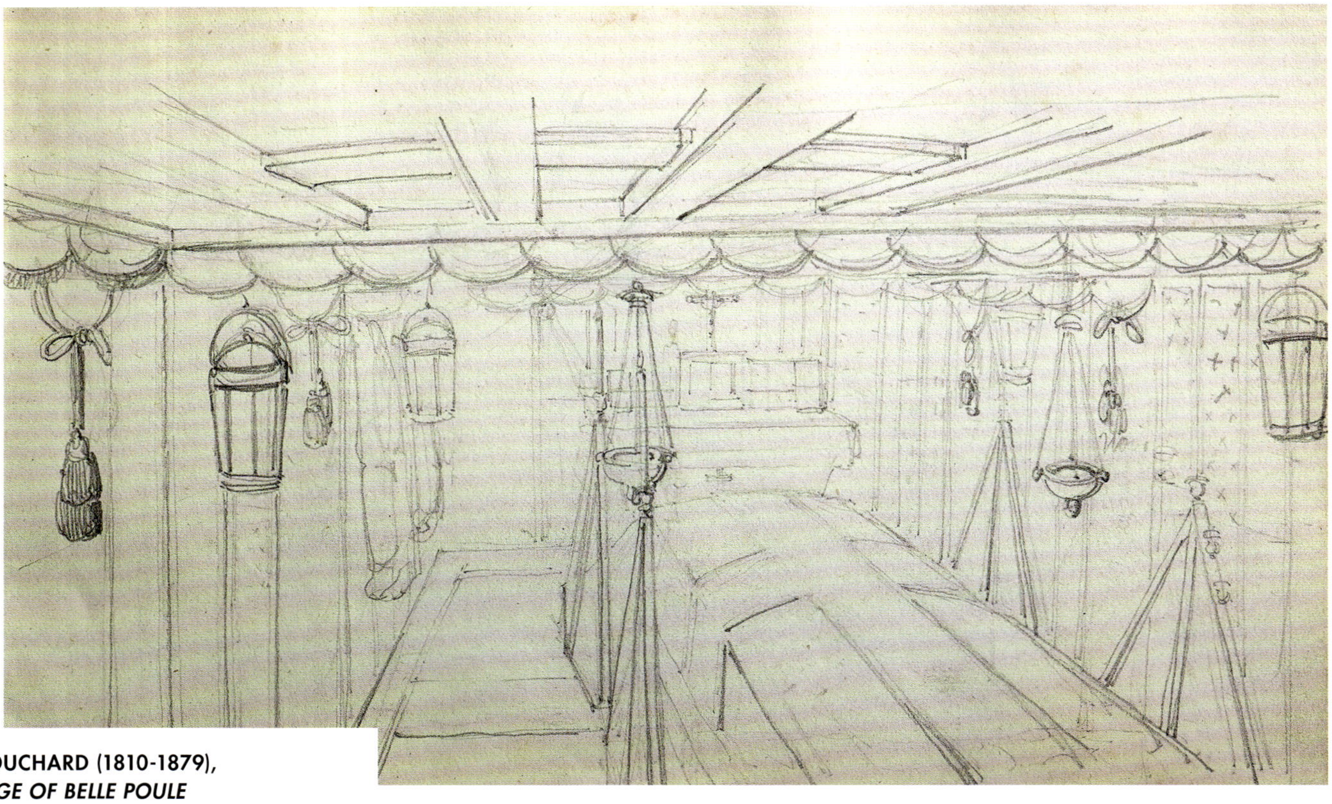

VICTOR TOUCHARD (1810-1879),
THE VOYAGE OF BELLE POULE

These two pen and ink drawings were taken from notebooks recounting the travels of Lieutenant Victor Touchard, orderly to Louis-Philippe's son the Prince de Joinville, who was in charge of the voyage to St Helena and the return of Napoleon's ashes to Paris in 1840. The 2nd and 3rd notebooks are devoted to the voyage from St Helena to Cherbourg. There is also an associated sketchbook with 13 pencil drawings, including the coast of St Helena, the casket sitting in the mortuary on the bridge of *Belle Poule*, and the casket in the ship's chapel.

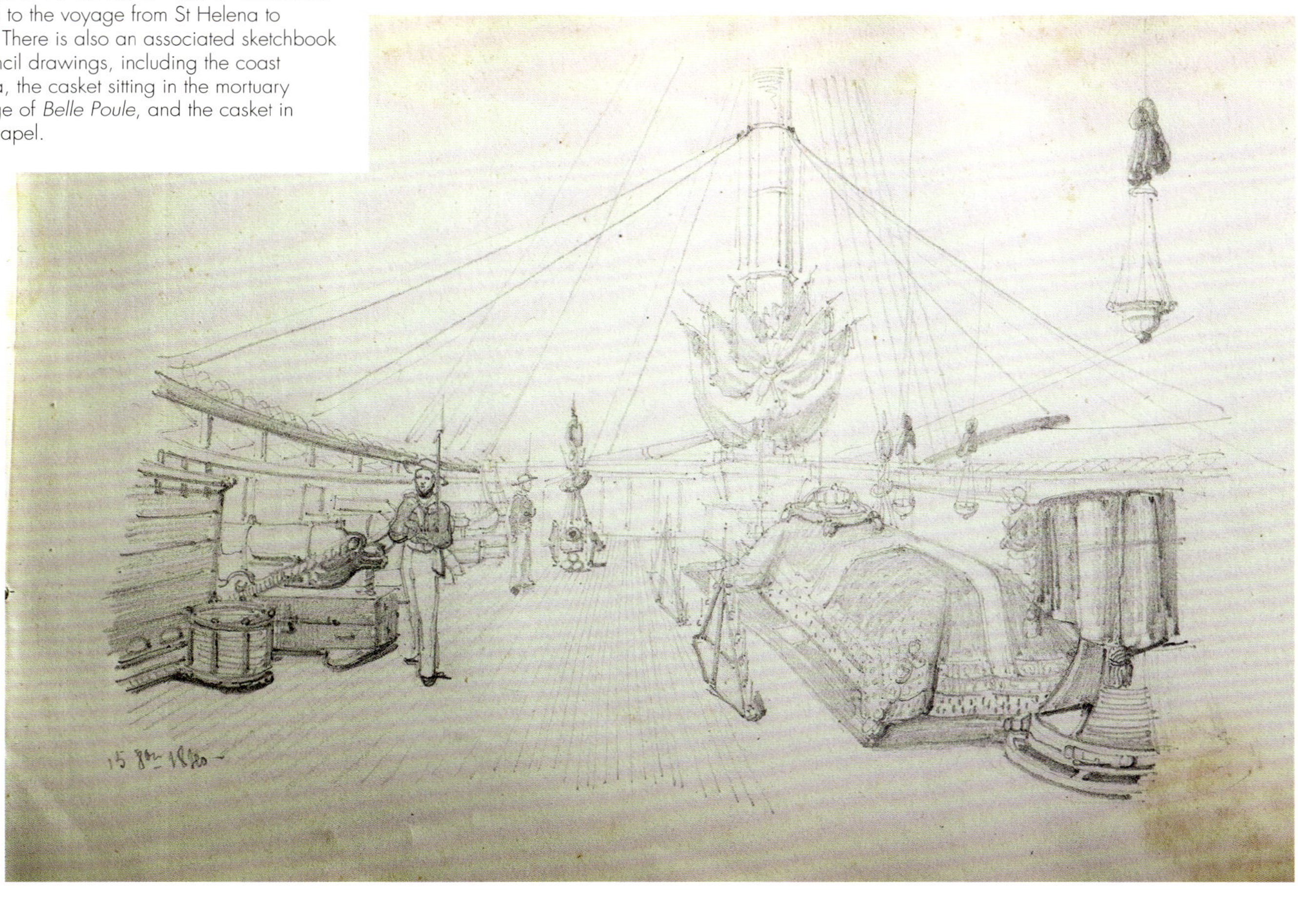

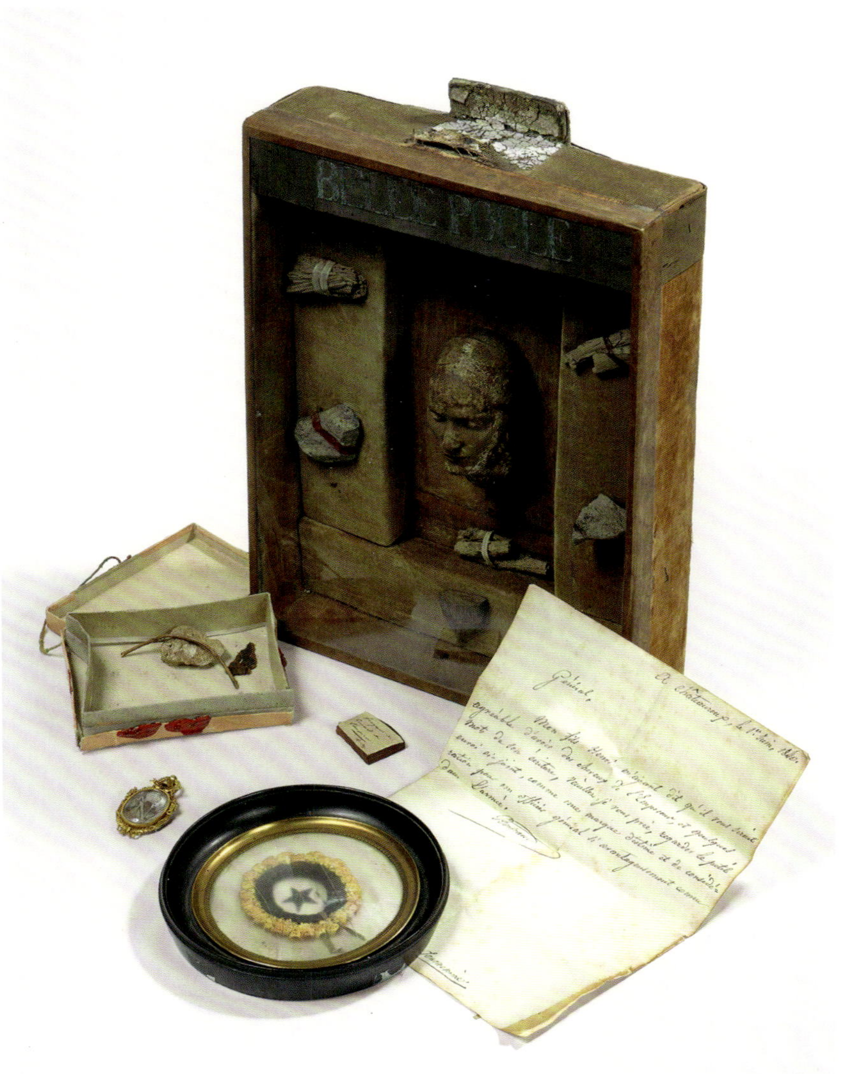

SOUVENIRS FROM ST HELENA

Napoleon's final companions were convinced that what they had witnessed was no ordinary captivity, so after his death they collected an array of souvenirs from the Emperor's surroundings to take away with them. Examples shown here include a reliquary frame lined in bronze velvet and containing a miniature plaster replica of Antommarchi's funerary mask, two fragments of Napoleon's coffin, two sprigs of the weeping willow that shaded his grave, a leaf from the oak tree the Emperor liked (?) to read under, a plant from the Longwood House gardens, various pieces of plants from the garden, and stones. Shown alongside are another fragment of the mahogany coffin and a round frame holding the "Imperial relics / The hair of Emperor / Napoleon cut at / St Helena and given / by General Bertrand". It is accompanied by a letter from General Bertrand addressed to the General d'Artillerie de Tournemine and dated 1 June 1840.

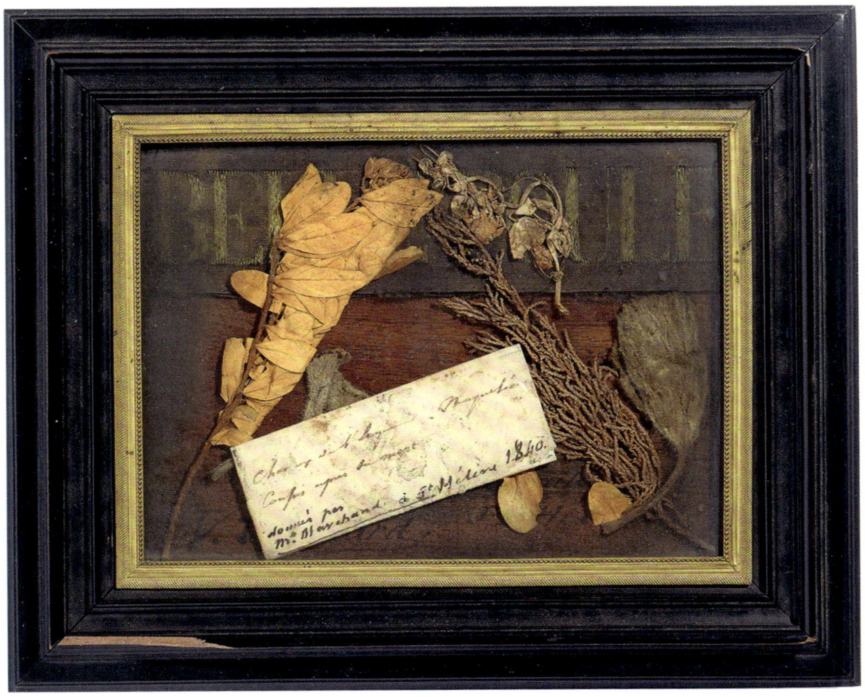

SOUVENIRS FROM *BELLE POULE*

This frame holds an assortment of relics from St Helena collected by Lieutenant Victor Touchard at the time of the return of ashes. They include a small envelope bearing the handwritten inscription "Emperor Napoleon's hair cut off after his death, given by Mr Marchand on St Helena 1840", two sprigs of cypress and willow, some flowers gathered near Napoleon's grave, and a silk ribbon bearing the name *Belle Poule*.

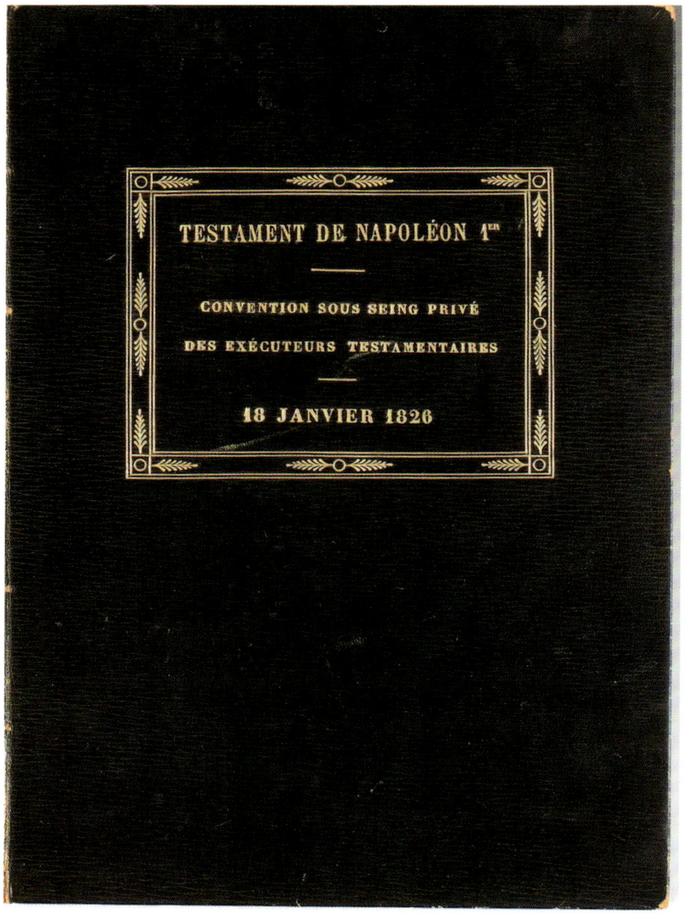

NAPOLEON'S LAST TESTAMENT, AGREEMENT BETWEEN THE EXECUTORS OF THE WILL

Agreement written on stamped paper, initialed by the legatees on all odd-numbered pages and bearing their signatures at the end. Napoleon had handed over the sum of six million to the banker Laffitte following the battle of Waterloo. After his will had been written on 15 April 1821, he chose Montholon, Bertrand and Marchand as executors and legatees.
In this document of the highest historical importance, the legatees and executors declare themselves ready to carry out Napoleon's wishes, with the money held by the banker Laffitte as their bond.

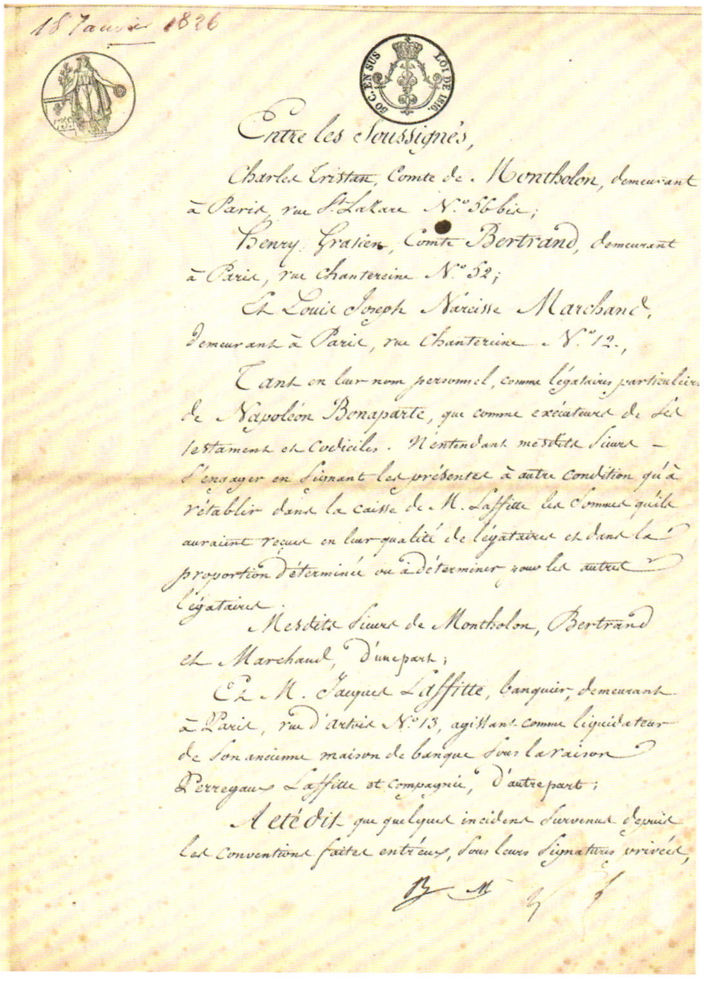

18 Janvier 1826

50 C. EN SUS LOI DE 1816.

Entre les Soussignés,

Charles Tristan, Comte de Montholon, demeurant à Paris, rue S.t Lazare N.o 56 bis;

Henry Gratien, Comte Bertrand, demeurant à Paris, rue Chantereine N.o 52;

Et Louis Joseph Narcisse Marchand, demeurant à Paris, rue Chantereine N.o 12,

Tant en leur nom personnel, comme légataires particuliers de Napoléon Bonaparte, que comme exécuteurs de ses testament et codiciles. N'entendant mesdits sieurs s'engager en signant les présentes à autre condition qu'à rétablir dans la caisse de M. Laffitte les sommes qu'ils auraient reçues en leur qualité de légataires et dans la proportion déterminée ou à déterminer pour les autres légataires.

Mesdits sieurs de Montholon, Bertrand et Marchand, d'une part;

Et M. Jacques Laffitte, banquier, demeurant à Paris, rue d'Artois N.o 13, agissant comme liquidateur de son ancienne maison de banque sous la raison Perregaux Laffitte et Compagnie, d'autre part;

A été dit que quelques incidens survenus depuis les conventions faites entr'eux, sous leurs signatures privées,

B M L

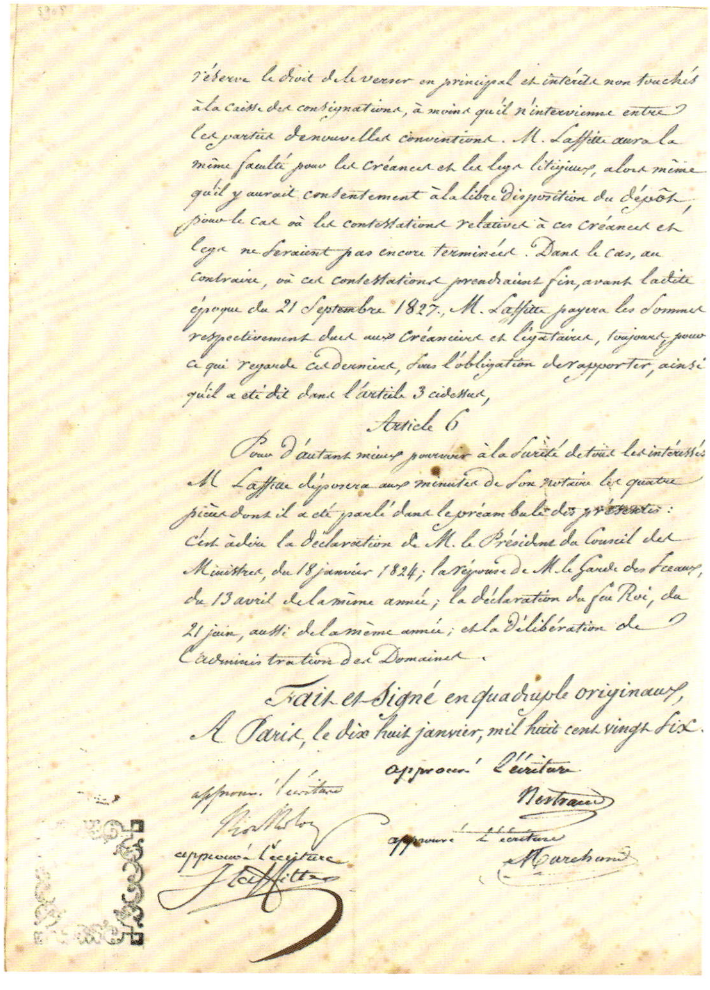

réserve le droit de le verser en principal et intérêts non touchés à la caisse des consignations, à moins qu'il n'intervienne entre les parties de nouvelles conventions. M. Laffitte aura la même faculté pour les créances et les legs litigieux, alors même qu'il y aurait consentement à la libre disposition du dépôt, pour le cas où les contestations relatives à ces créances et legs ne seraient pas encore terminées. Dans le cas, au contraire, où ces contestations prendraient fin, avant ladite époque du 21 Septembre 1827, M. Laffitte payera les sommes respectivement dues aux créanciers et légataires, toujours pour ce qui regarde ces derniers, sous l'obligation de rapporter, ainsi qu'il a été dit dans l'article 3 ci-dessus,

Article 6

Pour d'autant mieux pourvoir à la sûreté de tous les intéressés M. Laffitte déposera aux minutes de son notaire les quatre pièces dont il a été parlé dans le préambule des présentes: c'est à dire la déclaration de M. le Président du Conseil des Ministres, du 18 janvier 1824; la réponse de M. le Garde des Sceaux, du 13 avril de la même année; la déclaration du feu Roi, du 21 juin, aussi de la même année; et la délibération de l'administration des Domaines.

Fait et signé en quadruple originaux, A Paris, le dix huit janvier, mil huit cent vingt six.

approuvé l'écriture
Montholon

approuvé l'écriture
Bertrand

approuvé l'écriture
J. Laffitte

approuvé l'écriture
Marchand

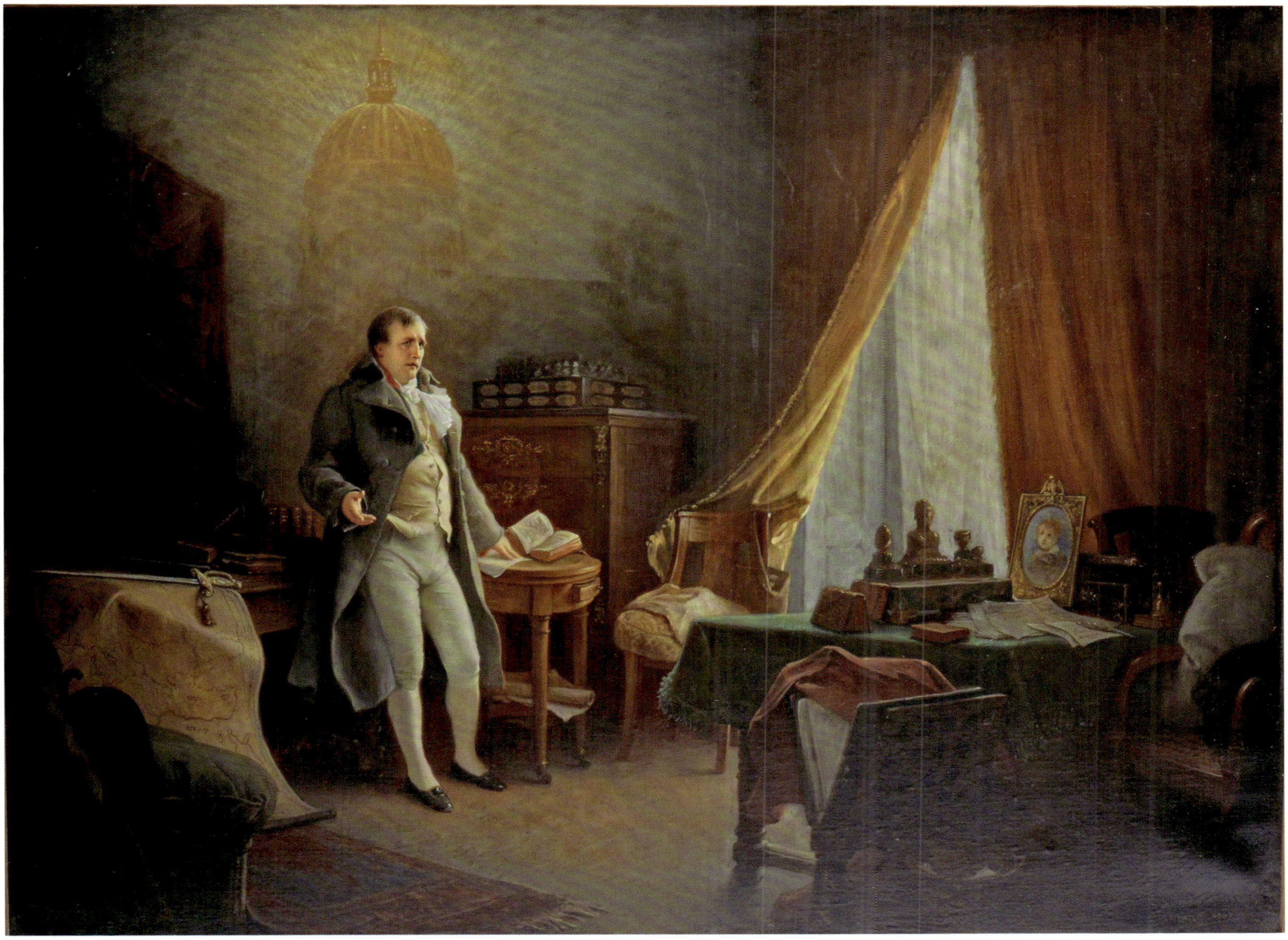

JEAN-JULES ANTOINE LECOMTE DU NOUŸ (1842-1923),
***THE IMPERIAL DESTINY*, 1891**

After making his debut at the Salon in 1863, Lecomte du Nouÿ showed there every year. From 1872 on, he regularly received state commissions for the Musée du Luxembourg. This painting shows Napoleon standing in a room, absorbed in his thoughts, with the Dôme des Invalides visible above his head like an evocation of his destiny. It was exhibited at the Salon in 1923. Another canvas Lecomte du Nouÿ painted in 1867, *Bonaparte à Beaucaire* (sometimes known as *Le souper de Beaucaire*) ranks among scenes of Napoleonic iconography that were widely circulated.

RELICS

PILLOWCASE FROM NAPOLEON'S AUTOPSY

This pillowcase is the one that was used at the autopsy carried out by Dr Antommarchi on St Helena. Mamluk Ali wrote in his *Memoirs*: "The sheet on which the operation [the autopsy] had just been carried out, being stained with blood in many places, was cut up by most of the assistants, and each got a piece; the English took the greater part." The equally blood-spattered pillowcase appears to have been preserved intact. It was sold with the estate following the death of Fernand de Girardin, private secretary to Prince Victor Napoleon. Girardin was the grandson of Madame de Monstequiou, Governess to the King of Rome.

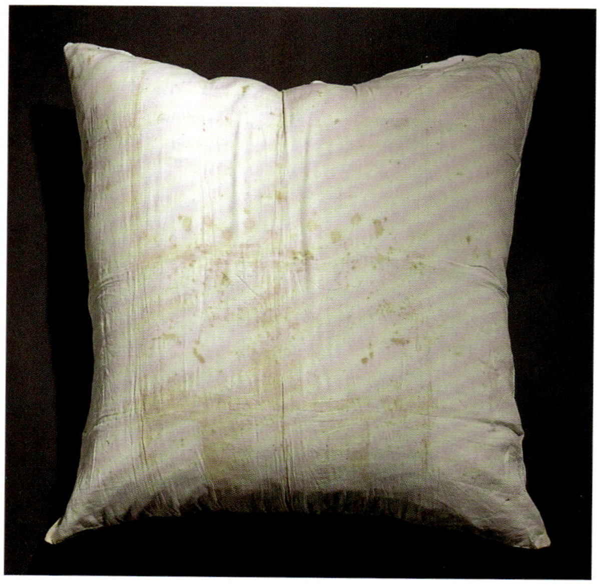

MEMENTOES OF THE EMPEROR NAPOLEON

The sheet of paper to which these fragments are attached tells us their provenance; there is a piece of "Emperor Napoleon's grand cordon [Legion of Honor decoration]", a piece of scarlet velvet from a "coat of the Emperor's", and a piece of red velvet (slightly lighter) taken from a "piece of a coat of Marie-Louise's".

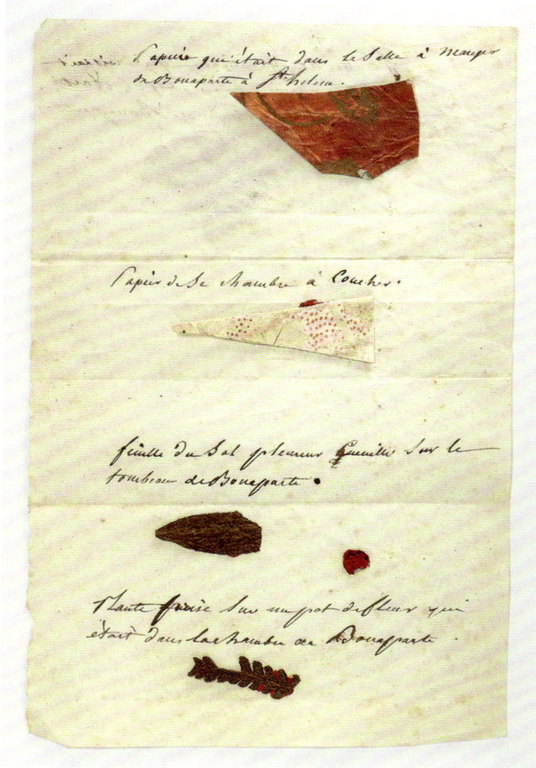

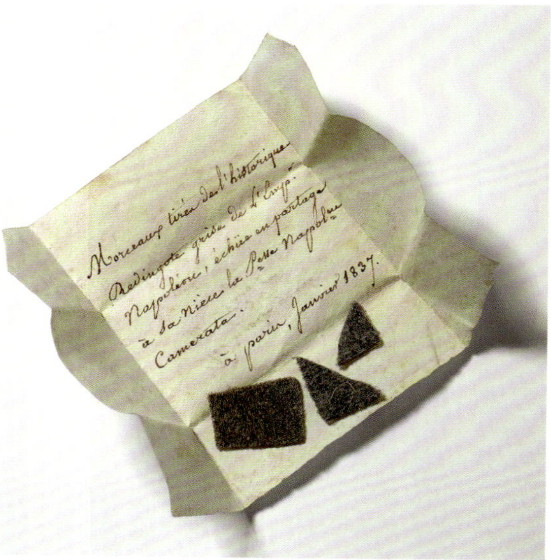

THREE FRAGMENTS FROM ONE OF THE EMPEROR'S GRAY REDINGOTE GREATCOATS

These three fragments of gray woolen cloth are preserved in an old piece of paper, with these words handwritten on the front: "Redingote de Napo[on]". Inside it says: "Pieces taken from the historic/gray redingote of Empr/Napoleon, shared bequest to his niece P[ess] Napolne/Camerata./Paris, January 1837". Napoléone Camerata (1806-1869) was the daughter of Félix Baciocchi and Elisa Bonaparte, the Emperor's sister. We know that Napoleon wore his greatcoat in cold or wet weather, slipping it on over his uniform. His image was strongly associated with the gray greatcoat and the bicorne hat, so it is not surprising that his admirers should have kept fragments. The few pieces that have survived are all in national museums.

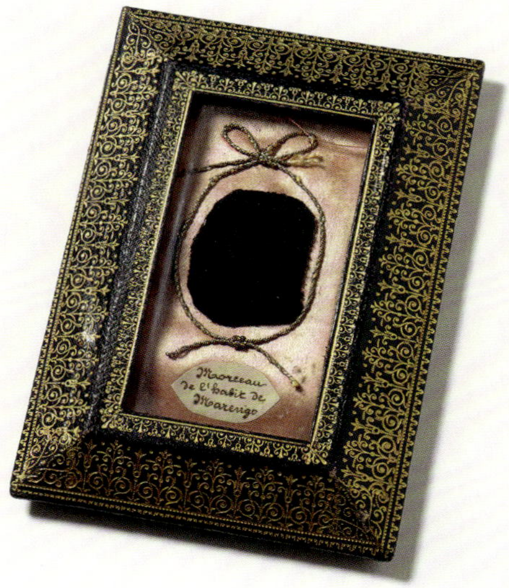

FRAGMENT OF THE COAT BONAPARTE WORE IN MARENGO ON 14 JUNE 1800

This extremely rare fragment was taken from a blue serge coat preserved in the Musée de l'Armée, which shows clear traces of having been cut in its lower part. This design was specified for general officers on 17 August 1798, and Bonaparte was wearing one on the day of the memorable Marengo victory, 14 June 1800. He took it with him to St Helena. The official report written on his burial day mentions the coat: "On this day, seventh May, eighteen hundred and twenty-one, at Longwood House, on the island of St Helena, the body of Emperor Napoleon, dressed in the uniform of his Chasseurs de la Garde, was placed by us the undersigned [Bertrand, Marchand and Montholon] in a tin coffin lined with white satin, its pillow and mattress of the same cloth. [...]. The coffin was placed on the camp bed in the mortuary and draped in a pall of purple velvet, on which we spread the coat that the Emperor had worn in every campaign since the battle of Marengo." Some fragments of it were snipped off by his entourage, no doubt before this ceremony, to be kept as prized relics.

LOCK OF HAIR AND PIECE OF SHEETING STAINED WITH THE BLOOD OF EMPEROR NAPOLEON

They are kept with a little piece of folded paper, with these words handwritten on it: "hair and piece of the sheet stained with Emperor Napoleon's blood, given to Madame la Duchesse de Gaëte by her devoted Dr Antommarchi this 25 June 1825, at Jennevilliers". These items are presented in a large easel-back frame of openworked and engraved silvered metal, composing the letter "N" surrounded by foliage and crowned by the imperial coat-of-arms (mounted at a later date, in a frame produced during the Second Empire). Napoleon's body was washed after his death, and Dr Antommarchi carried out an autopsy. Once the examination was over, the sheet and pillowcase that the body had been lying on were cut into pieces and given as relics.

LOCKS OF HAIR FROM EMPEROR NAPOLEON

This circlet combines two locks of Napoleon's hair, and was placed in its frame of black Morocco leather decorated with the imperial crown at the end of the 19th century. The first lock was cut off in 1815 on the island of Elba by Jean-Pierre Charvet, custodian of the Emperor's wardrobe. Charvet subsequently gave it to Madame Berthel, Colonel Marnier's wife. The second lock used to create this circlet was cut off on St Helena by Count Marchand, who brought it back and made a gift of it. Later on, the Marnier and Marchand families were joined, and all the locks of hair were given to one of their descendants who piously encased them in this reliquary frame. The locks of Napoleon's hair provided by Marchand are the most indisputably authentic, since it was his responsibility to snip off the precious mementoes and fulfill the wishes of the illustrious deceased by conveying them to various members of the Emperor's family.

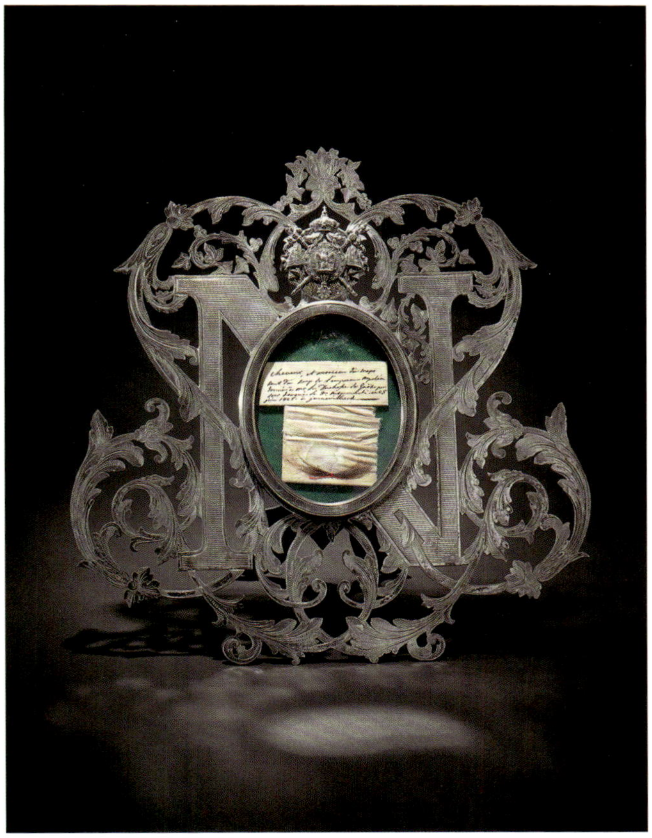

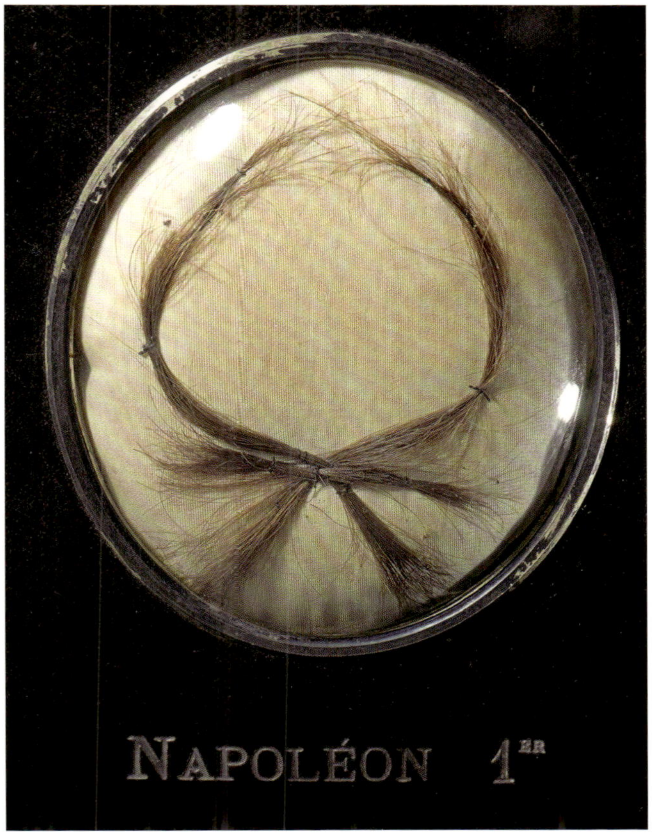

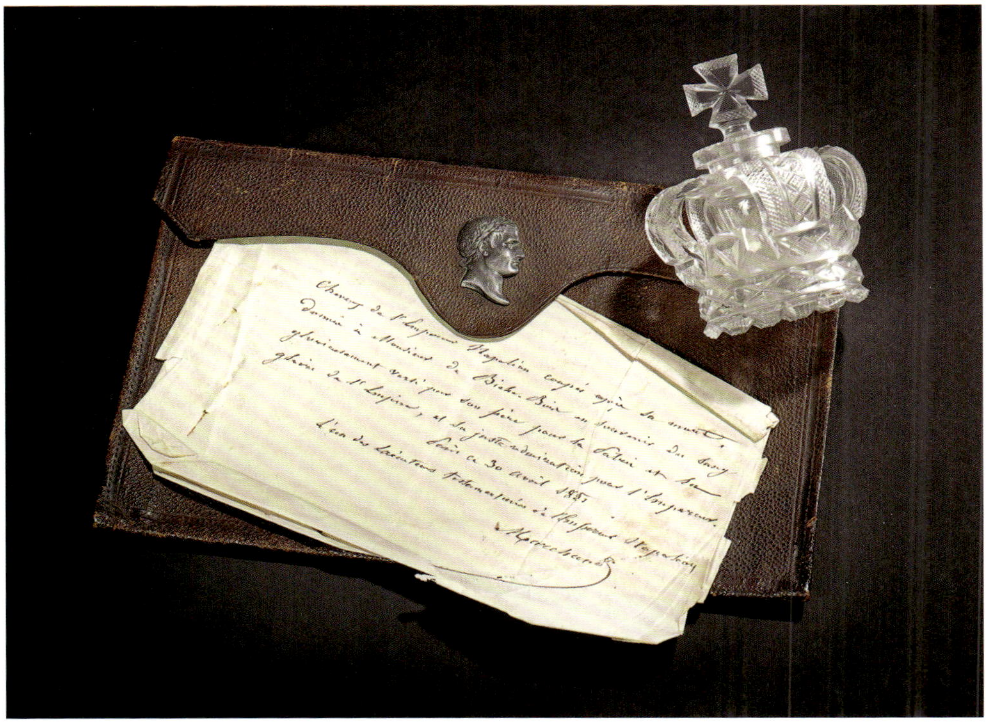

LOCK OF HAIR

A lock of Napoleon's hair was placed in this crystal crown, and paired with a Havana leather wallet with his profile in silvered metal on its flap. The set came from Marchand, an executor of Napoleon's will, as the personally signed letter to Mr de Biche Bois in memory of the Emperor and dated "Paris, 30 April 1851" attests.

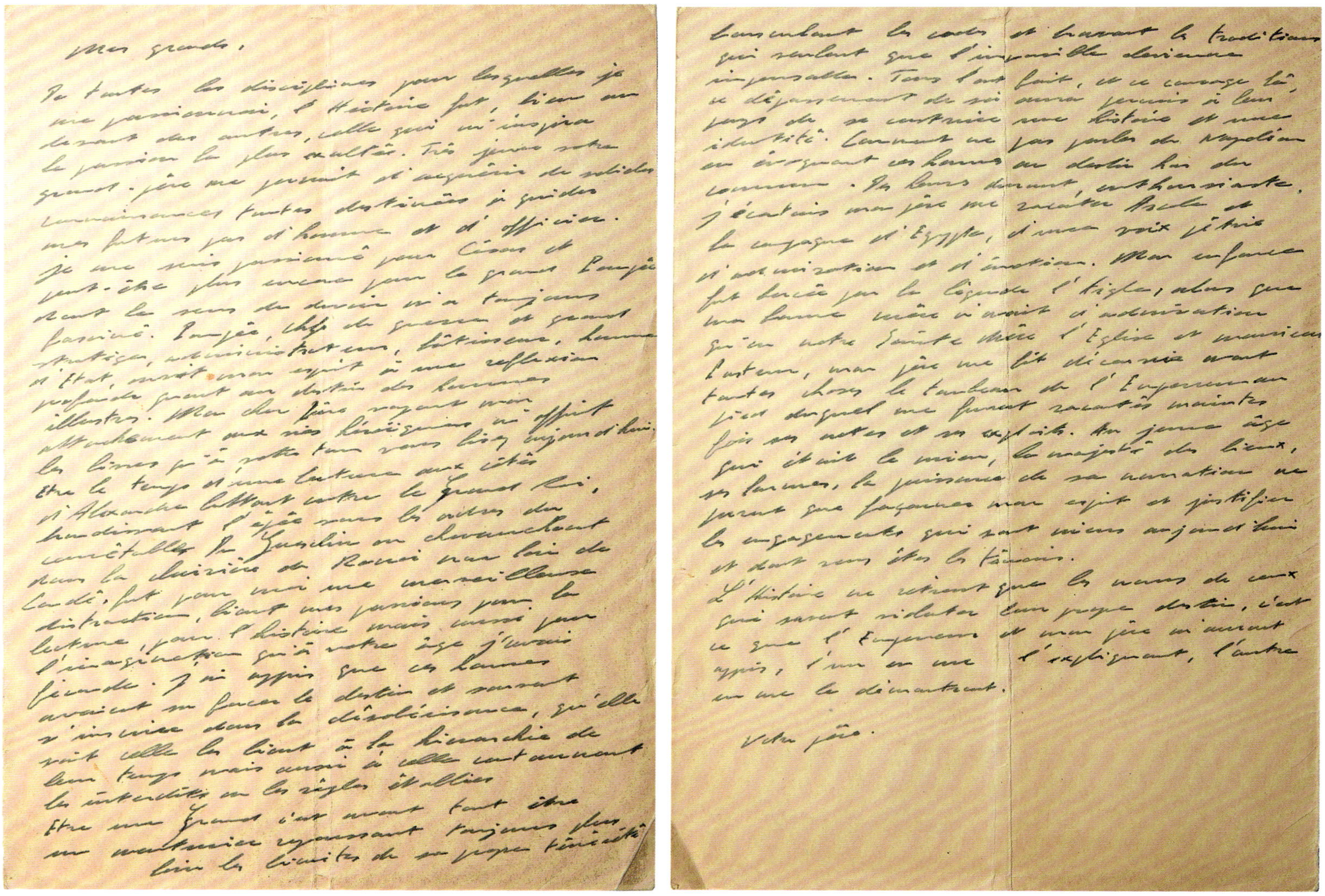

HANDWRITTEN LETTER FROM CHARLES DE GAULLE (1890-1970) TO HIS CHILDREN, CIRCA 1936 (EXCERPT OPPOSITE)

"My children,

[...]

Of all the disciplines I loved, History was, far and away, the one that inspired and exhilarated me the most [...].

The Great are first and foremost adventurers, always taking their recklessness to the very limit, breaking conventions and flouting the traditions that would make the impossible become unthinkable [...].

In speaking of men with remarkable destinies, how could I not mention Napoleon? I'd listen eagerly for hours to my father telling me in admiring tones about Arcole, and the campaign of Egypt, his voice laden with emotion. My childhood was steeped in Napoleonic mythologizing; while my good mother's admiration extended only to our Holy Mother Church and Monsieur Pasteur, my father lost no time introducing me to the Emperor's tomb, where I was to hear his deeds and exploits recounted time and time again [...].

History retains only the names of those who know how to violate their own destiny; that's what the Emperor and my father taught me – one by explaining it, the other by showing me.

Your father,

Charles de Gaulle"

I would like to wholeheartedly thank all those who assisted me in enriching this collection, often at great effort.

Loyal friends of the Emperor, Richard Baron Cohen, Alain Baudot-Visser, Pierre-Jean Chalençon, Maxime Charron, Jean-Christophe Châtaignier, Roch de Coligny, Bernard Croissy, Jean-Claude Dey, Arnaud de Gouvion Saint-Cyr, Camille Leprince, Bertrand Malvaux, Jean-Pierre Osenat, Patrice Reboul, Didier Segon.

The Chief Curator of the Napoleon Museum at the Château de Fontainebleau, Christophe Beyeler.

The Heritage Curator of the Museum of the Legion of Honor, Anne de Chefdebien.

The Heritage Curator of the Musée Carnavalet, Valérie Guillaume.

The Heritage Curator of the Musée de l'Armée, General Christian Baptiste.

The Consul and Curator of the French Domains of St Helena, Michel Dancoisne-Martineau.

The Fondation Napoléon and its Director, Thierry Lentz.

The specialists, booksellers, auctioneers and auction houses, Alde, Artcurial, Patrick de Bayser, Beaussant-Lefèvre, Pierre Bergé and associates, Binoche & Giquello and Alexandre Giquello, Thierry Bodin, Bonham's, Christie's and Anne Qaimmaquami, Bruno Borean, Serge Davoudian, Delorme & Collin du Bocage, Coutau-Bégarie & associates, Olivier Coutau-Bégarie and Cyril Boulay, Andrew Fields, Nathalie Lemoine-Bouchard, Thierry de Maigret, Philippe Missillier, Alain Nicolas, Osenat, Emmanuel Raux, Michel Renonciat, Gabriel Rossignol, Sotheby's and Thierry de Lachaise, Sofia Gorse-Poniatowski, Patrick and Elisabeth Sourget, Fabrice Teissedre, and Michel Vandermeersch.

I also want to mention those who helped assemble the collection or enabled the production of this book: BESV et Philippe Quillet, Élisabeth Bureau, Mark Chester, Gaëlle Demouth, Philippe Garcia, Estelle Gaudry, Wouter et Bastiaan Guis, Juste Ciel, Tatiana Luginbuhl, Virginie Mahieux, Frédéric Mauget, NJG, Laetitia Réal-Moretto, Cyril de Romance, Agathe Rosnet, Carine Ruault, Corinne Schmidt, Vincent Tucci, Sophie Virrion, and Élisabeth Welter.

I would like to express my sincere gratitude to the authors: Xavier Aiolfi, Jacques-Olivier Boudon, Pierre Branda, David Chanteranne, Alain Chevallier, Emmanuelle Papot, Laetitia de Witt, and Bernard-Henri Lévy who was kind enough to write the preface to this book.

I would like to thank Georgina Letourmy-Bordier in particular, who is responsible for conservation of the collection, and who contributed to the documentation of this book.

And finally thank you to all those I may have omitted to mention.

Bruno Ledoux

IMAGE CREDITS

All photographs are by Philippe Garcia, with the exception of:

Artcurial: p. 225; Camille Leprince-Jérémie Beylard/Agence Phar: p. 108-109, 110-111, 112-113, 255, 319, 333, 334, 356 bas; Christie's : p. 169 bas, 208 right, 209 top; ECPAD Arnaud Roiné/ Johann Peschel: p. 149 left; Studio Sébert: p. 167, 332; Olivier Coutau-Bégarie et Associés: p. 16-17, 33, 61, 71, 78 below; Osenat: p. 56-57, 100, 101, 119, 162-163, 165, 298-299, 311, 360, 361, 366 top, 370, 371, 384, 386, 387 top left gauche, 392, 399, 403, 404-405, 406-407; Étude Thierry de Maigret: p. 18 below, p. 233; Galerie de Bayser: p. 268 ; Sotheby's: p. 35; Rau Antiques: p. 397.
Réunion des Musées Nationaux: p. 70 ©RMN-Grand Palais / Agence Bulloz; p. 77 bcs ©RMN-Grand Palais (musée du Louvre) / Michel Urtado; p. 127 bas ©RMN-Grand Palais / image RMN-GP; p. 166 bas ©RMN-Grand Palais / Gérard Blot; p. 180 top ©Château de Versailles, Dist. RMN-Grand Palais / Jean-Marc Manaï; p. 180 below ©RMN-Grand Palais (Château de Versailles) / Franck Raux; p. 232 top: ©RMN-Grand Palais (Château de Fontainebleau) / Gérard Blot; p. 258 ©RMN-Grand Palais / Agence Bulloz; p. 351 ©RMN-Grand Palais (Château de Versailles) / Daniel Arnaudet; p. 365 below ©RMN-Grand Palais (musée des châteaux de Malmaison et de Bois-Préau) / Gérard Blot; p. 367 top ©RMN-Grand Palais (musée des châteaux de Malmaison et de Bois-Préau) / André Martin; p. 394 ©RMN-Grand Palais (musée des châteaux de Malmaison et de Bois-Préau) / Mathéus.

Printed in December 2017 by Graphicom
Photoengraving: Quadrilaser
ISBN: 978-1-4197-2145-8
Legal deposit: January 2018
Printed in Italy